ECONOMICS

Glencoe – The Nation's Leading Economics Publisher

Glencoe Introduces A New Success-Oriented Textbook

Inside:

- **Highly Visual and Readable Text**
  (See pages 2-5)
- **NEW Teacher's Wraparound Edition**
  (See pages 6-7)
- **A Wealth of Classroom Resources**
  (See pages 8-9)
- **Multimedia Support**
  (See pages 10-11)

An Exciting New Approach Makes Teaching and Learning Economics Easy, Effective, and Enjoyable for Today's Media-Oriented Students.

SECTION **1** *Starting a Business*

SECTION 1 FOCUS

Terms to Know entrepreneur, inventory
Objectives *After reading this section, you should be able to:*
① List the steps in starting a business.
② Explain the four elements involved in every business.

Starting a Business Involves Risks and Expectations

Suppose that you have been tinkering with electronic equipment since you were a child. By now you can take apart and reassemble cassette and CD players, VCRs, and televisions without difficulty. You are so good at repairing this kind of equipment that you have been doing it for your friends and relatives for some time. Then an idea occurs to you: Why not charge people for your services? Why not go into business for yourself? By starting your own business, you will become an entrepreneur.

The Steps in Starting a Business

Nearly every person who makes the decision to start a business is an **entrepreneur** because he or she is willing to take a risk. Usually people decide to start a business to gain profits and to "do something on their own" or to be their own boss.

Entrepreneurs then gather the factors of production and decide on the form of business organization that best suits their purposes. Anyone hoping to become an entrepreneur must also learn as much as possible about the business he or she plans to start. This process includes learning about the laws, regulations, and tax codes that will apply to the business.

Elements of Business Operation

Figure 9.1 shows the four elements every business must consider.

To start a business, you must make potential customers aware that your services are available for a price. You could have one-page fliers printed to advertise your business and pass them out. You could also buy advertising space in the local newspaper.

208 *Unit 3 Microeconomics: Markets, Prices, and Business Competition*

Figure 9.1
Four Elements of Business
Every business, regardless of size, involves four elements: expenses, advertising, receipts and record keeping, and risk.

C Receipts and Record Keeping
No matter how small your business is, having a system to track your expenses and income is key to your success. All receipts should be safely filed and saved.

B Advertising ▲
You will quickly find out that letting potential customers know that you are in business is costly. Once you have customers, however, information about your business will spread by word of mouth.

◄ **A Expenses**
If you own a painting business, you will need to purchase brushes and paint. As your business grows, you might invest in paint sprayers or electric sanders so that you can complete jobs faster. This new equipment would add to your income, but will probably take more money capital than you have on hand.

D Risk
Every business involves risks. You must balance the risks against the advantages of being in business for yourself—including profit versus loss.
◄

209

Striking Presentation.
The all new design makes it easy for students to see theory in action — and to understand the exacting subject matter.

Dynamic Visuals.
The captions, charts, graphs, and photographs are more than illustrations. They are important teaching tools.

Timely.
The text is completely updated for today's students.

Life-Like.
A strong applications approach shows students how economic concepts apply to their daily lives.

News-Worthy.
A dynamic presentation includes articles, graphs, charts, and colorful visuals.

Real-Life Applications Make Economics Relevant and Understandable.

Case Study: Focus on Free Enterprise.

Each unit features a study that traces the history of successful corporations, such as Harley Davidson, Blue Bell Creameries, and Motown Records, and demonstrates the free enterprise system in action. ▶

CASE STUDY

Focus on Free Enterprise

Harley-Davidson

The Early Years When you think about motorcycles, there is a very good chance you will think of Harley-Davidsons. In 1901, William S. Harley and Arthur Davidson of Milwaukee strapped a gasoline engine to a bicycle, and started production shortly thereafter. Harley-Davidson has been building motorcycles since 1903. For years motorcycles were a small but profitable segment of the motor vehicle industry. Harley-Davidson motorcycles became a symbol of defiance and the "age-old hobo-rebel."

Bad Times In 1969 Harley-Davidson was bought by sporting goods manufacturer AMF. AMF immediately modernized production facilities and increased production from 15,000 units annually to more than 50,000 units. Most business analysts agreed that the heavy investment in equipment was necessary for the firm, but it was also accompanied by a decline in quality. The quick rise in production led to lower-quality motorcycles. Harley-Davidsons slowly lost their image.

In the 1970s the public perception of motorcycles changed. The oil crisis and resulting high gasoline prices left the average driver searching for alternatives. Experts predicted that gasoline prices would continue to rise to astronomical levels. Motorcycles suddenly seemed to be a fuel-saving alternative to traditional automobiles. People started buying more motorcycles, and forecasters predicted that demand would continue to increase. What happened, instead, was that the experts significantly overestimated demand. Japanese manufacturers flooded the American market with motorcycles and then were left with large inventories. Motorcycle prices collapsed.

Emphasis on Quality Against this backdrop, a group of AMF executives led a management buyout and took Harley-Davidson private. Since that time, this group has worked to upgrade its motorcycles. The owners revived the company by completely changing the way it did business. They changed the production process, management philosophy, and marketing strategy.

Harley-Davidson started to use some Japanese production techniques, reducing inventory and freeing up capital and labor. By reducing inventory, any defects and quality problems became easier to spot, while at the same time inventory costs were reduced. Workers were encouraged to make suggestions and were given more authority to make quality checks.

Harley-Davidson devised a new marketing technique, encouraging the formation of the Harley Owners Group (HOG), a social club for Harley owners operating out of local dealerships. These clubs became a means of getting Harley owners together. This made Harley-Davidsons more visible to the general public.

Since the buyout in 1981, Harley-Davidson's success has been steady and impressive. Harley is now a major exporter of motorcycles, shipping 25 percent of its production abroad—much of it to Germany. Harley-Davidson once again is a symbol for quality.

Free Enterprise in Action

1. Who bought Harley-Davidson in 1969?
2. Why did the oil crisis of the 1970s stimulate demand for Harley-Davidsons?
3. How did the new management and production techniques employed by Harley-Davidson after its buyout in 1981 lead to a higher-quality product?

News Clip

Readings in Economics

THE NEW YORK TIMES   JUNE 6, 1993

BEHIND THE 'CLEAR' TREND
by Barnaby J. Feder

From drinks to deodorants to dishwashing liquid, not to mention gasoline and mouthwash, the hot color for new products is no color at all.

Marketers like to have something novel to sell, but the driving force in the trend is an effort to tap into consumers' associations of clarity with health, purity, freshness and no-frills functionality. And if consumers see a transparent antiperspirant as more "natural" than colored competitors, so much the better.

But clear products are usually as thoroughly processed as any tinted cousins, if not more so. In creating Crystal Pepsi, for example, Pepsi needed 14 months to iron out the formula and production process. Pepsi takes longer and spends more to produce the clear cola, which requires greater quality controls than the brown stuff....

"This isn't rocket science," said Thomas Pirko, president of Bevmark, food and beverage consultants based in Los Angeles. "The technology is clearly subservient to the marketing consideration."

...Perhaps the clearest case of technology being subservient to marketing in the trend toward clear products is that of Crystal Clear Amoco Ultimate gasoline. The colorless premium gasoline has been on the market since 1915 in the eastern United States, originally under the White Crown name.

Only in the last five years, though, has the petroleum industry had the tools to analyze auto emissions in great detail. One result was that the Amoco Oil Company discovered that its clear gas—renamed as Crystal Clear last year—has an environmental advantage over its competitors.... [it] cut emissions of hydrocarbons by 13 percent.

● THINK ABOUT IT

1. Why are "clear" products gaining popularity?
2. What is the environmental advantage of Crystal Clear Amoco?

72 Unit 2 Practical Economics: How Theory Works for You

Newsclip.

Articles from news magazines such as *Time, Newsweek,* and *Forbes* generate lively discussions about current economic issues.

◀

Plus:

Spanish Handbook.

The *Spanish Handbook* in the student edition and the *Spanish Resource Binder* help you meet the needs of Spanish-speaking students.

Your Economics Journal.

Inspires students to write and record how economic concepts relate to their own life experiences. This two-phase writing strand is a powerful tool that builds student portfolios and provides a method of alternative assessment. ◄

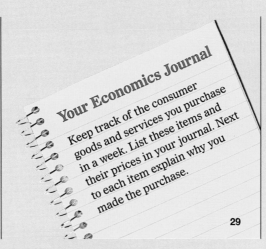

Your Economics Journal

Keep track of the consumer goods and services you purchase in a week. List these items and their prices in your journal. Next to each item explain why you made the purchase.

29

Economics Lab.

Hands-on activities developed by experienced classroom teachers provide opportunities for alternative assessment. The required lab report can be included in students' portfolios. ◄

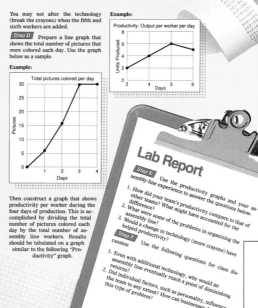

ECONOMICS LAB

Measuring Productivity

From the classroom of Jamie G. Daily, Holmes High School, San Antonio, Texas

In Unit 4 you read about financing and producing goods. In this experiment, you will learn about productivity and the law of diminishing returns. (You may want to reread the material on pages 271–275 of the text.)

Productivity is the ability to produce better goods and services faster. In part, it is a measure of the amount of output per worker. An assembly line improves worker productivity up to the point where the law of diminishing returns sets in. In this lab, you will develop an assembly-line process and add workers to the team to determine at what point the law of diminishing returns affects productivity.

Tools

1. Supply of simple pictures to be colored
2. 6-8 boxes of eight crayons
3. Several prototypes of finished product (picture colored with four different colors)
4. A pocket calculator

Procedures

Step A Organize into production teams, with seven students per team. One student on each team will serve as the quality control manager for the team, and the others will be production workers. Arrange desks so that each team is an assembly line. Begin with three production workers on Day

1, expanding as instructed later. Each team needs a box of crayons, a supply of uncolored pictures, and a prototype. Each group must color as many pictures to match the prototype as possible within four minutes. Pictures that do not meet quality standards should be discarded. Record these results for Day 1 on a chart like the following:

Example

Group Name	Total Pictures Colored			
	Day 1	Day 2	Day 3	Day 4

Step B From the students on your team who are not yet working, add one member to the assembly line for Day 2. Work for another four minutes. Record the amount of work produced with teams of four students under Day 2 on your chart.

Step C Repeat this process, adding one student to the assembly line each day, coloring and recording the results until you have six members working on the assembly line (Day 4).

You may not alter the technology (break the crayons) when the fifth and sixth workers are added.

Step D Prepare a line graph that shows the total number of pictures that were colored each day. Use the graph below as a sample.

Example:

Total pictures colored per day

(graph: Pictures vs. Days)

Then construct a graph that shows productivity per worker during the four days of production. This is accomplished by dividing the total number of pictures colored each day by the total number of assembly line workers. Results should be tabulated on a graph similar to the following "Productivity" graph.

Example:

Productivity: Output per worker per day

(graph: Units Produced vs. Days)

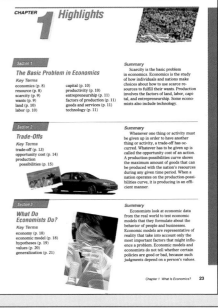

Lab Report

Step E Use the productivity graphs and your assembly-line experience to answer the questions below.
1. How did your team's productivity compare to that of other teams? What might have accounted for the difference?
2. What were some of the problems in organizing the assembly line?
3. Would a change in technology (more crayons) have helped productivity?

Step F Use the following questions for class discussion.
1. Even with additional technology, why would an assembly line eventually reach a point of diminishing returns?
2. Did individual factors, such as personality, influence the team to any extent? How can businesses deal with this type of problem?

CHAPTER 1 Highlights

Section 1
The Basic Problem in Economics
Key Terms
economics (p. 8)
resource (p. 8)
scarcity (p. 9)
wants (p. 9)
land (p. 10)
labor (p. 10)
capital (p. 10)
productivity (p. 10)
entrepreneurship (p. 11)
factors of production (p. 11)
goods and services (p. 11)
technology (p. 11)

Summary
Scarcity is the basic problem in economics. Economics is the study of how individuals and nations make choices about how to use scarce resources to fulfill their wants. Production involves the factors of land, labor, capital, and entrepreneurship. Some economists also include technology.

Section 2
Trade-Offs
Key Terms
trade-off (p. 13)
opportunity cost (p. 14)
production possibilities (p. 15)

Summary
Whenever one thing or activity must be given up in order to have another thing or activity, a trade-off has occurred. Whatever has to be given up is called the opportunity cost of an action. A production-possibilities curve shows the maximum amount of goods that can be produced with the nation's resources during any given time period. When a nation operates on the production-possibilities curve, it is producing in an efficient manner.

Section 3
What Do Economists Do?
Key Terms
economy (p. 18)
economic model (p. 18)
hypotheses (p. 19)
values (p. 20)
generalization (p. 21)

Summary
Economists look at economic data from the real world to test economic models that they formulate about the behavior of people and businesses. Economic models are representative of reality that take into account only the most important factors that might influence a problem. Economic models and economists do not tell whether certain policies are good or bad, because such judgments depend on a person's values.

Chapter 1 What Is Economics? 23

Chapter Highlights.

These concise chapter overviews are effective for review, reteaching, and covering ideas within a chapter quickly. This useful feature helps you easily structure the content to meet a one-semester course. ►

NEW Teacher's Wraparound Edition Puts all the Support You'll Need at Your Fingertips.

Performance Assessment Activities.

Suggestions in every chapter give students an opportunity to demonstrate their understanding of a concept in a non-traditional assessment method.

Economic Simulations.

Whether recreating the stock market or developing a consumer price index, these activities simulate real-life situations and bring economic concepts to life for students.

Economics Portfolio.

Strategies that help you build student portfolios. They include economic writings, simulations, and other activities. Allows you to customize your assessment strategies.

Free Enterprise Activities.

Numerous entrepreneurship activities help students understand the opportunities and challenges of the free enterprise system.

INTRODUCING
CHAPTER 1

Chapter Overview
Economics is the study of how individuals and nations make choices about how to use scarce resources to fulfill their wants. Chapter 1 explains or describes: scarcity; the four factors of production; the relationship between trade-offs and opportunity costs; and how economists use economic data to test the economic models they formulate about people and businesses.

⊙ **VIDEODISC**

Nightly Business Report
Economics in Action
To introduce the videodiscs, use Disc 1, Side A, Video 1.

Search 307, Play to 2334

CHAPTER
1 WHAT IS ECONOMICS?

What benefit are these students receiving from this activity?

What would be the benefit of studying instead of watching television?

6   Unit 1 An Introduction to Economics

Answering Economic Questions

The questions in the above illustration are designed to lead into the main concepts in Chapter 1. Students might not understand the importance of choices in the study of economics. The questions will help them focus on the frequency of making economic choices in their own lives and the ramifications of the choices they make. Have students discuss the questions and explain the process they go through in making choices.

6

What are the long-term effects of watching too much television?

How do students make the choice between studying and watching television?

What are these students doing?

Your Economics Journal

During a one-week period, keep track of how you spend your time. At the end of the week, list the most frequent activities in which you engage and how many hours you spent on each.

Economic Portfolio

Have students start an **Economic Portfolio** in which they include **Your Economics Journal** writing activities for this and every chapter. Have students list activities they participate in, such as shopping, physical fitness, and studying. List these activities on the chalkboard. Then, in their portfolios,

have students develop a table showing the time spent on various activities. Have them write a paragraph explaining why they spent so much time on the top three activities and so little time on the bottom three. They should also indicate what other activities they did not choose.

INTRODUCING
CHAPTER 1

Connecting to Past Learning

Ask students what they think economics is. Ask students to describe how, in their opinion, economics affects them. Tell students that in Chapter 1 they will learn that economics is the study of the ways individuals as well as nations make choices about how to fulfill their economic wants. After completing the chapter, compare students' initial ideas with the chapter information.

Applying Economics

Tell students to imagine that they have $100 to spend. Have them make a list of items they would like to buy and the approximate price of each. Have them add up the prices, and, if they exceed $100, remove the items they would like the least. Discuss students' choices and the thought process that went into making these choices. Tell students they will learn why choices are an important aspect of economics.

🎗 EXTRA CREDIT PROJECT

Read a book about one of America's major entrepreneurs. Write a summary explaining the key decisions this person made and which skills were responsible for his or her success.

7

✔ PERFORMANCE ASSESSMENT

Refer to page 6B for "Conducting an Interview," a Performance Assessment Activity for this chapter.

7

Plus:

Videodisc Barcodes.

Economics Today and Tomorrow is correlated to Glencoe's new videodisc program **Economics In Action** produced in conjunction with the highly acclaimed PBS news program, *The Nightly Business Report*. Now you can access video presentations that highlight chapter concepts at the touch of a button.

Extra Credit Activities.

The perfect activities for students who need extra reinforcement of chapter concepts allow you to extend classroom lessons without preparing project ideas on your own.

Additional Activities.

A wealth of additional activities help you create interesting lessons in a limited time:
* **Meeting Special Needs**
* **Global Economics**
* **Cooperative Learning**
* **Did You Know**
* **Cultural Diversity in Economics**

A Wealth of Resources Meets Every Ability Level.

All Classroom Resources are Cross-Referenced in the *Reproducible Lesson Plans* To Make Planning a Snap.

- Reproducible Lesson Plans
- Guided Reading Activities

- **Reinforcing Economic Skills**
- **Reteaching Activities**
- **Economic Vocabulary Activities**
- **Enrichment Activities**
- **Primary and Secondary Source Readings**

A Variety of Assessment Resources Meet All Your Needs.

- **Performance Assessment Activities** strengthen student understanding and provide you an alternative method of assessment.
- **Chapter and Unit Tests: Forms A and B** provide you with flexibility to meet a variety of needs.
- **Section Quizzes** allow you to easily monitor daily comprehension.
- **Testmaker Software: IBM, Apple, and Macintosh Versions** generate tests and allow you to easily edit, add and delete questions where desired.

Interesting and Innovative Hands-On Resources.

- **Consumer Application Activities** demonstrate economics in action and teach students to be wise consumers.
- **Free Enterprise Activities** help students understand the opportunities and challenges of the free enterprise system and participate in entrepreneurship activities.

- **Cooperative Learning Activities** teach economic concepts through the collaborative group process.
- **Economic Simulations** use real-life situations to demonstrate economic theory in action.
- **Economic Laboratories** help students understand major concepts by using economic models. Hands-on activities require your students to complete a lab report.
- **Math Practice for Economics** gives students additional prac-

tice in the math skills they need to succeed in economics.
- **New SAT Test Practice** provides questions and test-taking strategies that help your students excel on the new version of the SAT exam.
- **Writer's Guidebook** reinforces writing skills essential to communicating effectively.

Outstanding Resources Meet the Needs of Spanish-Speaking Students.

Spanish Resource Binder Includes:
- Spanish Vocabulary Activities
- Spanish Reteaching Activities
- Spanish Section Quizzes
- Spanish Transparencies

Reinforce Your Teaching with the Dynamics of Light, Sound, and Motion.

Economics in Action Videodisc.

Learning becomes interactive with chapter video segments that highlight key points. Based on the esteemed PBS news program, *The Nightly Business Report.* Includes Teacher's Guide and reproducible student activities. (Available in VHS.)

The Nightly Business Report Videotape Library.

Gives students practical insights into the workings of Wall Street and the insurance industry.

- **How Wall Street Works 1**
- **How Wall Street Works 2**
- **How To Buy Insurance**

Plus:

Economic Survival: A Financial Simulation.

Hands-on simulation helps students make day-to-day economic decisions and shows theory in action. Teaching strategies and lesson plans are included.

- **Economic Concepts Transparencies.** Visually reinforces the twenty-two basic economic concepts outlined in the National Council on Economic Education Framework.

- **Section Focus Transparencies.** A motivational tool for each textbook section. Cartoons and graphics capture the essence of economic principles and issues.

- **Economics Forms Transparencies.** You can customize your own lessons with these high quality charts and graphs.

English Chapter Digest Audiocassettes.

An outstanding resource for students with reading deficiencies or who need to review or catch-up because of missed classes. Includes student activities and tests.

Spanish Chapter Digest Audiocassettes.

Meets the needs of Spanish-speaking students by providing Spanish versions of all the materials in the English package.

Vocabulary Puzzlemaker Software.

You can create word searches and crossword puzzles that reinforce chapter vocabulary. (IBM and Macintosh versions available.)

Stocktracker: A Software Simulation.

Interactive software package allows your students to make investment decisions and chart the course of their investments. (IBM and Macintosh versions available.)

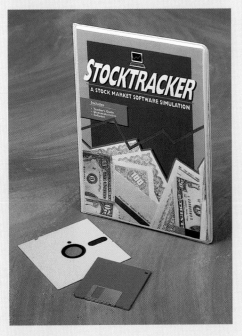

Economics Today and Tomorrow
From Glencoe, the Nation's Leading Economics Publisher

For more information contact your nearest regional office or call: 1-800-334-7344.

Glencoe Social Studies
Making a World of Difference

ECONOMICS
TODAY & TOMORROW

Roger LeRoy Miller
The University of Texas at Arlington

GLENCOE
Macmillan/McGraw-Hill

New York, New York   Columbus, Ohio   Mission Hills, California   Peoria, Illinois

ABOUT THE AUTHOR

Roger LeRoy Miller graduated Phi Beta Kappa from the University of California at Berkeley, where he also won the Department Prize in Economics. He was a Woodrow Wilson Honor Fellow, National Science Foundation Fellow, and Lilly Honor Fellow at the University of Chicago, where he received his Ph.D. in economics in 1968. Now at the University of Texas, Arlington, Dr. Miller has taught at the University of Washington, the University of Miami, and Clemson University. He has also taught methodology to teachers of high school economics for the National Council on Economic Education. Among the more than 100 books he has written or co-authored are works on economics, statistics, law, consumer finance, and government. Dr. Miller also has operated several businesses and served as a consultant to government agencies, private corporations, and law firms.

Send all inquiries to:
Glencoe Division, Macmillan/McGraw-Hill, 936 Eastwind Drive, Westerville, Ohio 43081

ISBN 0-02-823102-3 (Student Edition) ISBN 0-02-823104-X (Teacher's Wraparound Edition)
Printed in the United States of America

1 2 3 4 5 6 7 8 9 A-KP/LH-P 99 98 97 96 95 94

Contents

Contents

SCOPE AND SEQUENCE

Economics Today and Tomorrow incorporates the 22 Basic Concepts published by the National Council on Economic Education.

NCEE Economic Concepts	Full Chapter Coverage	Additional Chapter Coverage	Special Features
1 Scarcity		CHAPTER 1, SECTION 1 The Basic Problem in Economics CHAPTER 2, SECTION 3 The Goals of the Nation CHAPTER 13, SECTION 1 Americans at Work CHAPTER 18, SECTION 1 Unemployment and Inflation	PERSONAL PERSPECTIVE H. Ross Perot on Saving and Investing
2 Opportunity Cost and Trade-Offs	CHAPTER 3 Your Role As a Consumer CHAPTER 6 Buying the Necessities: Housing and Transporation	CHAPTER 1, SECTION 2 Trade-Offs CHAPTER 4, SECTION 1 Americans and Credit CHAPTER 7, SECTION 1 Why Save?	PERSONAL PERSPECTIVE Thomas Sowell on Discrimination
3 Productivity		CHAPTER 1, SECTION 2 Trade-Offs CHAPTER 8, SECTION 3 The Law of Supply and the Supply Curve CHAPTER 10, SECTION 1 Perfect Competition CHAPTER 11, SECTION 3 The Production Process	ECONOMICS LAB Measuring Productivity
4 Economic Systems	CHAPTER 20 Converging Economic Systems	CHAPTER 2, SECTION 1 Economic Systems CHAPTER 21, SECTION 4 Industrialization and the Future	PERSONAL PERSPECTIVE Adam Smith on Free Enterprise; Karl Marx on Communism

NCEE Economic Concepts	Full Chapter Coverage	Additional Chapter Coverage	Special Features
5 Economic Institutions and Incentives	CHAPTER 4 Going Into Debt	CHAPTER 2, SECTION 2 Characteristics of the American Economy	
		CHAPTER 7, SECTION 3 Special Savings Plans and Goals	
		CHAPTER 9, SECTION 3 The Corporate World and Franchises	
		CHAPTER 13, SECTION 2 Organized Labor	
6 Exchange, Money, and Interdependence	CHAPTER 4 Going Into Debt	CHAPTER 8, SECTION 4 Putting Supply and Demand Together	
	CHAPTER 7 Saving and Investing		
	CHAPTER 15 Money and Banking		
	CHAPTER 18 Controlling Unemployment and Inflation		
	CHAPTER 22 The Global Economy		
7 Markets and Prices	CHAPTER 2 Economic Systems and the American Economy	CHAPTER 12, SECTION 2 The Marketing Mix	LEARNING ECONOMIC SKILLS Using Index Numbers: Price Indexes; Using the Consumer Price Index
	CHAPTER 5 Buying the Necessities: Food and Clothing	CHAPTER 14, SECTION 1 National Income Accounting	
	CHAPTER 6 Buying the Necessities: Housing and Transportation	CHAPTER 20, SECTION 1 Comparing Capitalism and Socialism	
	CHAPTER 8 Supply and Demand		

NCEE Economic Concepts	Full Chapter Coverage	Additional Chapter Coverage	Special Features
8 Supply and Demand	CHAPTER 8 Supply and Demand CHAPTER 10 Competition and Monopolies	CHAPTER 13, SECTION 1 Americans at Work	PERSONAL PERSPECTIVE Alfred Marshall on Supply and Demand CRITICAL THINKING SKILL Determining Cause and Effect
9 Competition and Market Structure	CHAPTER 9 Business Organizations	CHAPTER 2, SECTION 2 Characteristics of the American Economy CHAPTER 10, SECTION 3 Government Policies Toward Competition CHAPTER 19, SECTION 3 Restrictions on World Trade CHAPTER 22, SECTION 3 Multinationals and Economic Competition	FOCUS ON FREE ENTERPRISE Blue Bell Creameries, Inc.; The Body Shop; Harley-Davidson; Adams National Bank; The Chicago Pizza Pie Factory PERSONAL PERSPECTIVE Susan Bowen on Running a Business in Tough Times; Ronald Homer on Running a Bank; William Gates on Running a Business; Joan Robinson on Imperfect Competition; Charles Wang on Challenges in the Computer Industry
10 Income Distribution	CHAPTER 2 Economic Systems and the American Economy	CHAPTER 3, SECTION 1 Consumption, Income, and Decision Making	
11 Market Failures	CHAPTER 10 Competition and Monopolies	CHAPTER 14, SECTION 5 Causes and Indicators of Business Fluctuations	
12 The Role of Government	CHAPTER 16 The Federal Reserve System and Monetary Policy CHAPTER 17 Government Spends, Collects, and Owes	CHAPTER 1, SECTION 1 The Basic Problem in Economics CHAPTER 2, SECTION 3 The Goals of the Nation CHAPTER 4, SECTION 4 Government Regulation of Credit CHAPTER 10, SECTION 3 Government Policies Toward Competition	POINT/COUNTERPOINT Should the Government Require Domestic National Service?; Should "Pollution Taxes" Be Used to Help the Environment and Lower the Deficit?; Role of the Government in the Economy: Should Industry Be Deregulated?; Is Affirmative Action Necessary to End Discriminatory Hiring Practices? PERSONAL PERSPECTIVE Robert Reich on Government
13 Gross Domestic Product*	CHAPTER 14 Measuring the Economy's Performance	CHAPTER 17, SECTION 1 Growth in the Size of Government	

* In the fall of 1991, the United States Department of Commerce replaced Gross National Product with Gross Domestic Product as the nation's most inclusive measure of output.

NCEE Economic Concepts	Full Chapter Coverage	Additional Chapter Coverage	Special Features
14 Aggregate Supply		CHAPTER 14, SECTION 3 Aggregate Supply and Demand	
15 Aggregate Demand	CHAPTER 18 Controlling Unemployment and Inflation	CHAPTER 14, SECTION 3 Aggregate Supply and Demand	
16 Unemployment	CHAPTER 18 Controlling Unemployment and Inflation	CHAPTER 13, SECTION 1 Americans at Work	PERSONAL PERSPECTIVE John Maynard Keynes on Equilibrium Employment; Paul Samuelson on Unemployment and Inflation
17 Inflation and Deflation	CHAPTER 18 Controlling Unemployment and Inflation	CHAPTER 16, SECTION 1 Money Supply and the Economy	
18 Monetary Policy	CHAPTER 16 The Federal Reserve System and Monetary Policy	CHAPTER 18, SECTION 3 Monetarism and the Economy	PERSONAL PERSPECTIVE Milton Friedman on the Federal Reserve
19 Fiscal Policy	CHAPTER 18 Controlling Unemployment and Inflation	CHAPTER 17, SECTION 2 The Federal Budget and the National Debt	PERSPONAL PERSPECTIVE John W. Rogers on Money Management
20 Absolute and Comparative Advantage and Barriers to Trade	CHAPTER 19 Trading With Other Nations	CHAPTER 21, SECTION 3 Obstacles to Growth in Developing Nations	PERSONAL PERSPECTIVE David Ricardo on Trading With Other Nations
21 Exchange Rates and the Balance of Payments		CHAPTER 19, SECTION 2 Financing World Trade	LEARNING ECONOMIC SKILLS Exchanging Foreign Currency
22 International Aspects of Growth and Stability	CHAPTER 19 Trading With Other Nations CHAPTER 20 Converging Economic Systems CHAPTER 21 Economic Growth in Developing Nations CHAPTER 22 The Global Economy		POINT/COUNTERPOINT Does Free Trade Help or Hurt Americans? PERSONAL PERSPECTIVE Laura Tyson on the Global Economy; Barbara Ward on Saving Our Resources for the Future

ALTERNATIVE COURSE OUTLINES

Economics Today and Tomorrow is a comprehensive text that is suitable for a full-year course. Because some economics courses are taught for only one semester or are part of a government course, the following outlines suggest several alternative syllabi.

Outline 1

Emphasizes microeconomics concepts.

Unit 1	An Introduction to Economics Chapters 1, 2
Unit 3	Microeconomics: Markets, Prices, and Business Competition Chapters 8, 9, 10
Unit 4	Microeconomics: American Business in Action Chapters 11, 12, 13
Unit 6	The International Scene Chapters 19, 20

Outline 2

Emphasizes consumer and market economics concepts.

Unit 1	An Introduction to Economics Chapters 1, 2
Unit 2	Practical Economics: How Theory Works for You Chapters 3, 4, 5, 6, 7
Unit 3	Microeconomics: Markets, Prices, and Business Competition Chapters 8, 9, 10
Unit 4	Microeconomics: American Business in Action Chapters 11, 12, 13
Unit 6	The International Scene Chapter 19

Outline 3

Emphasizes macroeconomics and comparative economics concepts.

Unit 1	An Introduction to Economics Chapters 1, 2
Unit 5	Macroeconomics: Managing the Nation's Economy Chapters 14, 15, 16, 17
Unit 6	The International Scene Chapters 19, 20, 21, 22

Outline 4

Emphasizes economic theory.

Unit 1	An Introduction to Economics Chapters 1, 2
Unit 3	Microeconomics: Markets, Prices, and Business Competition Chapter 8
Unit 5	Macroeconomics: Managing the Nation's Economy Chapters 16, 17, 18
Unit 6	The International Scene Chapter 20

At-Risk Students

Most educators today agree that the nation's schools are facing an epidemic of students who are at risk of failure. It is difficult to define exactly what constitutes an at-risk student because being at risk is often linked to several environmental causes such as limited English proficiency, poverty, low self-esteem, homelessness, substance abuse, or pregnancy. Whatever the causes, at-risk students have extreme difficulty with learning and are almost always low achievers.

Current educational research has shown that certain teaching methods can make a difference with at-risk students. One method is to maximize time-on-task. By doing so, teachers can help students overcome the outside stimuli that distract them from academic work.

Another method is to establish high expectations. Expecting students to succeed will help them believe that they are capable of succeeding. Many schools actively involve parents in this process so that the expectations for success are not left inside the classroom after school is out.

Because at-risk students have often failed in school, it is important to give them as much positive feedback as possible. Many teachers try to give this feedback at the end of each successfully completed assignment and regularly include awards ceremonies for those students who are meeting expectations. This feedback familiarizes students with success and also helps build their self-esteem.

Many educators believe that at-risk students need to learn at a *faster* rate than other students in order to catch up to normal achievers. Rather than emphasizing remedial techniques, these educators believe that instruction for at-risk students *must* include numerous opportunities for enrichment and accelerated learning. This instruction must build on the strengths of individual students rather than on their weaknesses. Appropriate methods to incorporate such a curriculum emphasize the assets that at-risk students often bring to the classroom. These assets include interest and curiosity in oral and artistic expression and kinesthetic learning abilities. For example, at-risk students often excel at presenting dramatizations in which they also construct the sets.

Cooperative Learning

Although cooperative learning is a useful teaching strategy in many subject classrooms, it occupies a special place in the social studies curriculum. This is because of its success in imparting the abilities needed to work effectively in a group. Such social skills are beneficial for all citizens who live in a participatory democracy.

Characteristics of Cooperative Learning Cooperative learning requires careful structuring and monitoring by the teacher if it is to be something more than a group activity. Characteristics of cooperative learning include the following:

- Students work face to face in heterogeneous groups.
- The activity promotes a sense of positive interdependence.
- Each member of a group has individual accountability.
- The group has a common product or goal.

The Role of the Teacher Although successful cooperative learning groups may appear to work independently, this is no doubt due to the astute coaching of a good teacher. Students will need the teacher's help at key moments during a group project: in agreeing upon goals, in establishing a structure of accountability, and in evaluating their success.

Program Components The program provides many opportunities for cooperative learning. Each **Chapter Review** includes one cooperative learning assignment related to the content of the chapter. The Teacher's Wraparound Edition provides other suggestions at point of use. The **Cooperative Learning Activities** ancillary includes an activity for each chapter. Activities are outlined in sufficient detail that student groups can carry them out independently.

PROFESSIONAL NOTES

Performance Assessment

Performance assessment requires students to use prior knowledge and relevant skills to solve significant real or authentic problems. For example, performance tests require the application of problem-solving skills rather than mere recall. Instead of using a multiple-choice test to assess knowledge of corporate stock, a performance-based test asks students to place themselves in the role of an investor and to write a first-person account of recent stock trading. Such assessment is pertinent to measurable objectives associated with each fragment or division of a course of study. Performance tasks have more than one correct answer or outcome and require more than one step to complete. A key element in scoring such activities is to analyze the *process* the students use to clarify and solve the problem.

The Teacher's Wraparound Edition introduces a **Performance Assessment Activity** in the planning guide for each chapter. Each individual or group project is related to key chapter concepts, and each entails several days (the life of the chapter) to complete.

In addition, each unit of the student edition includes an **Economics Lab** that may be used in performance assessment. The labs require students to apply economic concepts learned in the unit. Each experiment measures objectives associated with a main division of the curriculum and deals with real economic activities or simulations of such economic activities.

Portfolios

The portfolio approach to assessment is often used with performance-based assessment as part of an overall approach to authentic assessment. Portfolios contain samples of students' work collected over a period of time—often an entire grading period or even a semester. Students may work with their teachers to choose which items will be included in their portfolios.

Portfolios provide authentic assessment by measuring a broader range of skills than traditional tests evaluate. One of the strengths of portfolio assessment is that it involves students in their own assessment because they help choose the work that will be included in their portfolios. Another strength is that this type of assessment allows students to see how much progress they are making by comparing the work they have completed throughout the course.

Your Economics Journal is a writing activity found on chapter opening pages of the student edition. This journal and the follow-up writing assignment in every Chapter Review may be used in a portfolio approach along with other activities the teacher and students choose.

Outcome-Based Education

As an assessment based on performance, Outcome-Based Education provides an alternative measurement of student achievement that perhaps reflects real skills most tangibly. If a teacher wants to determine whether learned concepts can be applied in real conditions, the assessment should incorporate real conditions.

Economics Today and Tomorrow provides a comprehensive series of **Outcome-Based Education Projects** that develop step-by-step through each unit. Carried to its conclusion, this project, called Understanding the Job Market, will result in students gaining an understanding of the variety of careers available in local and national markets, developing skills needed to target specific job opportunities, and perhaps finding a job or choosing a career. While this assessment reflects only a small portion of the economic skills and concepts presented in this course of study, it is a significant assessment that relates to a representative selection of economics concepts.

Multiculturalism

Shortly after the United States enters the twenty-first century, demographers predict that more than one-third of Americans will trace their roots to Africa, Latin America, or Asia. Issues of multiculturalism are the core of a national debate concerning materials and approaches in education. Many panels, commissions, and individuals have attempted to define the issue and address the need for change that reflects a multicultural approach. The Association of Teacher Educators said schools should develop programs "whose major theme is fostering an ethnically and culturally diverse perspective in all students."

While the limitations of traditional and command economic systems are pointed out, the peoples living under those systems are treated as being capable of economic decisions equal to those of market-oriented societies. Students are asked to identify with diverse cultures by making economic choices within the framework of the economic systems that govern those cultures.

Economics Today and Tomorrow seeks to widen students' understanding of the richness and complexity of American society and to deal objectively with the world's peoples and systems. **Personal Perspective** and **Focus on Free Enterprise** features represent the views and achievements of a culturally diverse group of economists and entrepreneurs. In the chapter on developing nations economic issues are presented from the perspectives of both industrialized nations and developing nations.

John W. Rogers, founder
of Ariel Capital Management

TEACHER'S CLASSROOM RESOURCES

The Teacher's Classroom Resources provide you with a wide variety of supplemental materials to enhance the classroom experience. These resources meet your teaching needs and your students' abilities. Included are reading comprehension activities, reteaching activities, extension and enrichment activities, evaluation materials, visual instruction materials, Spanish resources, multimedia materials, and other kinds of teaching support.

Reading Comprehension

Reading Comprehension activities help students organize their study and enhance their understanding.

Guided Reading Activities help students master chapter information as they read the text. These activities are particularly useful for students who have difficulty with reading comprehension.

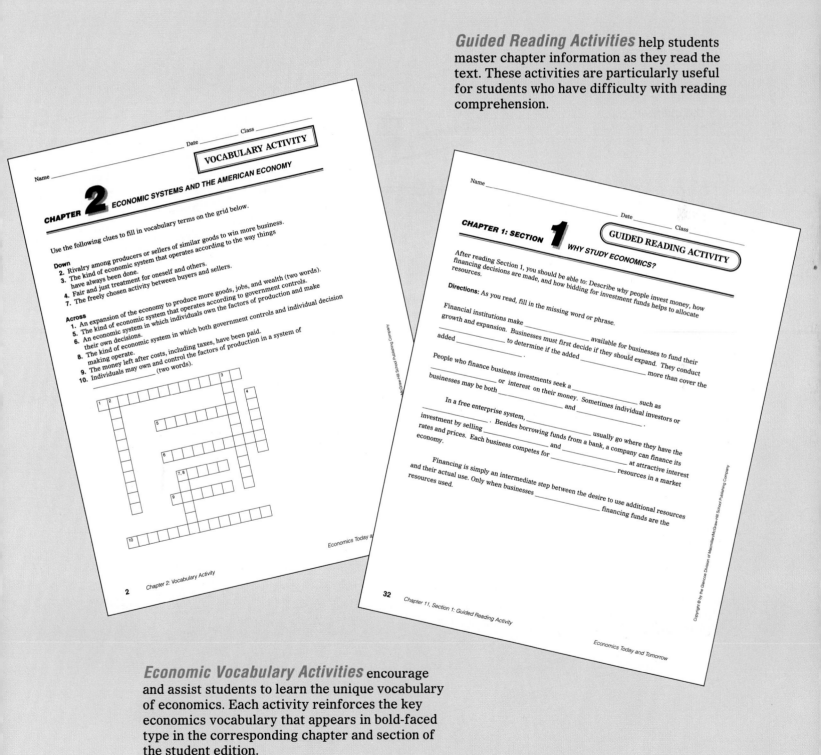

Economic Vocabulary Activities encourage and assist students to learn the unique vocabulary of economics. Each activity reinforces the key economics vocabulary that appears in bold-faced type in the corresponding chapter and section of the student edition.

TEACHER'S CLASSROOM RESOURCES

Reteaching

Reteaching activities provide a comprehensive reinforcement of chapter information and study skills.

Reteaching Activities help students focus on the main ideas and themes in each chapter. The activities are particularly useful for students who have not yet mastered the basic concepts of the chapter.

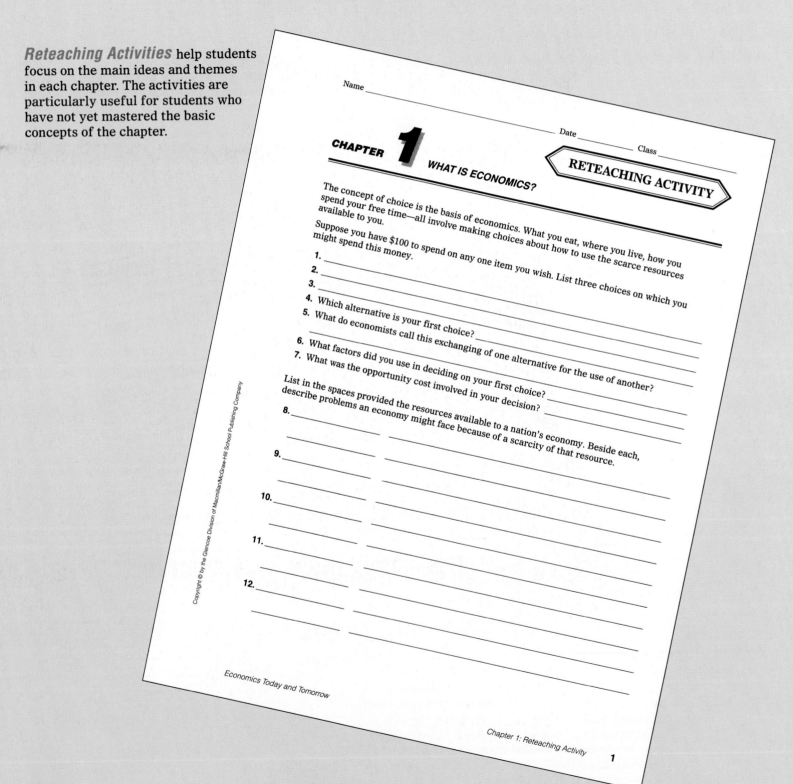

Name _____

Date _____

Class _____

CHAPTER 1

WHAT IS ECONOMICS?

RETEACHING ACTIVITY

The concept of choice is the basis of economics. What you eat, where you live, how you spend your free time—all involve making choices about how to use the scarce resources available to you.

Suppose you have $100 to spend on any one item you wish. List three choices on which you might spend this money.

1. _____
2. _____
3. _____

4. Which alternative is your first choice? _____
5. What do economists call this exchanging of one alternative for the use of another? _____

6. What factors did you use in deciding on your first choice? _____
7. What was the opportunity cost involved in your decision? _____

List in the spaces provided the resources available to a nation's economy. Beside each, describe problems an economy might face because of a scarcity of that resource.

8. _____   _____

9. _____   _____

10. _____   _____

11. _____   _____

12. _____   _____

Economics Today and Tomorrow

Chapter 1: Reteaching Activity   1

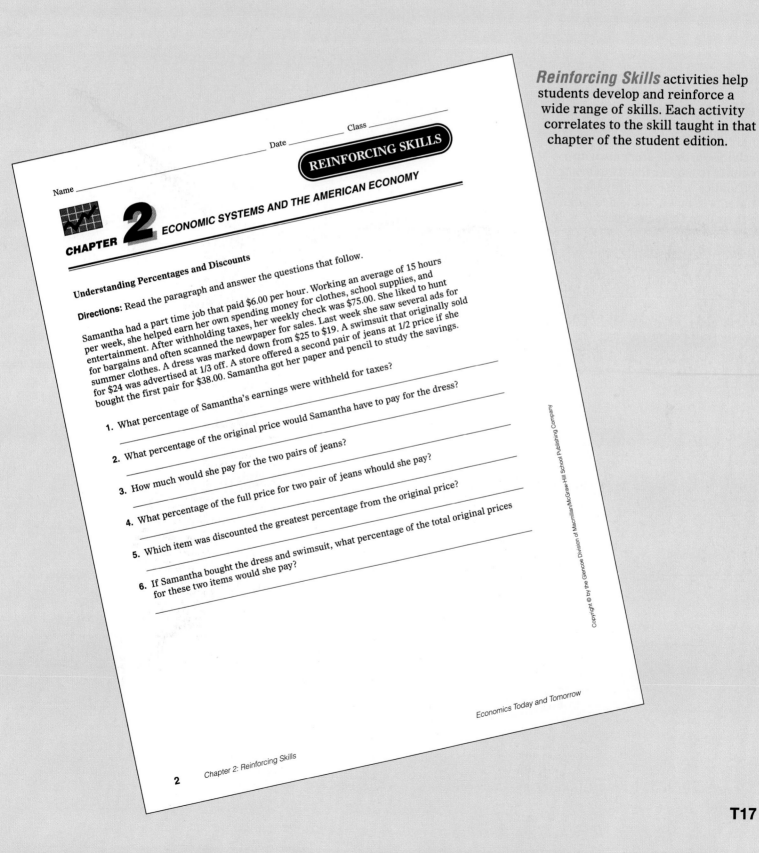

Reinforcing Skills activities help students develop and reinforce a wide range of skills. Each activity correlates to the skill taught in that chapter of the student edition.

Name _____

Date _____ Class _____

REINFORCING SKILLS

CHAPTER 2 ECONOMIC SYSTEMS AND THE AMERICAN ECONOMY

Understanding Percentages and Discounts

Directions: Read the paragraph and answer the questions that follow.

Samantha had a part time job that paid $6.00 per hour. Working an average of 15 hours per week, she helped earn her own spending money for clothes, school supplies, and entertainment. After withholding taxes, her weekly check was $75.00. She liked to hunt for bargains and often scanned the newpaper for sales. Last week she saw several ads for summer clothes. A dress was marked down from $25 to $19. A swimsuit that originally sold for $24 was advertised at 1/3 off. A store offered a second pair of jeans at 1/2 price if she bought the first pair for $38.00. Samantha got her paper and pencil to study the savings.

1. What percentage of Samantha's earnings were withheld for taxes?

_____

2. What percentage of the original price would Samantha have to pay for the dress?

_____

3. How much would she pay for the two pairs of jeans?

_____

4. What percentage of the full price for two pair of jeans whould she pay?

_____

5. Which item was discounted the greatest percentage from the original price?

_____

6. If Samantha bought the dress and swimsuit, what percentage of the total original prices for these two items would she pay?

_____

Economics Today and Tomorrow

2 Chapter 2: Reinforcing Skills

TEACHER'S CLASSROOM RESOURCES

Extension and Enrichment

Extension and Enrichment activities motivate and challenge students while building skills and expanding understanding.

Mathematics Practice for Economics provides activities that help students learn the math most commonly used in building and studying economic models. The activities provide students with real-life examples that help bring economics to life and prepare students to make viable decisions in their own financial lives.

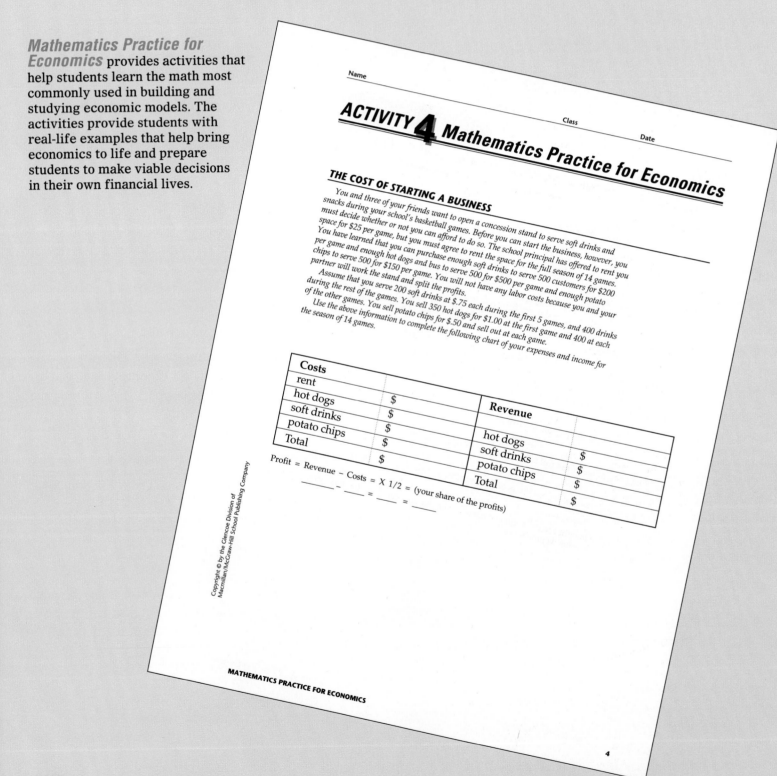

Name _____

ACTIVITY **4** Mathematics Practice for Economics

Class _____   Date _____

THE COST OF STARTING A BUSINESS

You and three of your friends want to open a concession stand to serve soft drinks and snacks during your school's basketball games. Before you can start the business, however, you must decide whether or not you can afford to do so. The school principal has offered to rent you space for $25 per game, but you must agree to rent the space for the full season of 14 games. You have learned that you can purchase enough soft drinks to serve 500 customers for $500 per game and enough hot dogs and bus to serve 500 for $150 per game and enough potato chips to serve 500 for $150 per game. You will not have any labor costs because you and your partner will work the stand and split the profits.

Assume that you serve 200 soft drinks at $.75 each during the first 5 games, and 400 drinks during the rest of the games. You sell 350 hot dogs for $1.00 at the first game and 400 at each of the other games. You sell potato chips for $.50 and sell out at each game.

Use the above information to complete the following chart of your expenses and income for the season of 14 games.

Costs			Revenue	
rent				
hot dogs	$			
soft drinks	$		**Revenue**	
potato chips	$			
Total	$		hot dogs	
	$		soft drinks	$
			potato chips	$
			Total	$

Profit = Revenue – Costs = X 1/2 = (your share of the profits)

_____ – _____ = _____ = _____ = (your share of the profits)

	$

1. What gave the new competition of the late 1700s and the early 1800s a dynamic quality? _____

_____

_____

_____

2. What does the author mean by saying Adam Smith gave "classic expression" to the philosophy of the late eighteenth and early nineteenth centuries? _____

_____

_____

_____

3. Explain the analogy between a purely competitive market and a thermostat. _____

PRIMARY AND SECONDARY SOURCES

Name _____

Class _____

Date _____

READING 10 Primary & Secondary Sources

PRICE-MAKING IN A DEMOCRACY

The theory of perfect competition and automatic price-making by the laws of supply and demand was a product of the era in which it first appeared, as economist Edwin G. Nourse makes clear in this reading from "Price-Making in a Democracy." Read the excerpt and answer the questions that follow.

The essence of automatic price-making is to be found in the process of individual bargaining. Economics got its start as a branch of formal learning at a time when the tide of individual freedom of productive effort and bargaining activity was just beginning to rise or to reassert itself....

Money exchange was highly developed, but financial controls had not grown much beyond individual or family limits....From top to bottom of society, the individual was released from old obligations and endowed with new rights and resources....The new competition which emerged in the late eighteenth and early nineteenth centuries took on a more dynamic quality as increases in productive efficiency, derived from new exploration and techniques, became more and more available.

The times begot their relevant philosophy. Adam Smith gave it classic expression. The heart of his doctrine was that if the individual was left free to exert himself in the midst of opportunities and was given responsibility for his own well-being, self-interest would produce results better than could be achieved under any program of official direction. Prices, reflecting the actions of economically free men, could not be quarreled with any more than one could quarrel with the thermometer for registering the temperature. Moreover, this free price system would, like a thermostat, be not merely a recording device but

also one of control. If prices went up sharply, production would be stimulated to reduce the shortage; if down, it would be checked until the glut was relieved....

In this remote and somewhat idealized situation, prices will be registered automatically as the expression of the balance which spontaneous supplies and demands strike in the market. The "economic man," using only common sense in the pursuit of the individual interest or advantage...may be relied upon to keep supplies constantly adjusting themselves to demands....

While it was the professional economist who elaborated this theory of automatic price-making, the businessman has been quick to admire the picture and accept it for himself. He has indeed been prone to put it forward as an explanation of price movements even today, although conditions are quite different from those to which the original theory was applied. The major point of difference is that economic life is no longer dominated by the business operations of individual producers and traders. Great blocks of capital, management, and labor having crystallized in modern business, the flow of automatic price-making and its accompanying economic adjustments gives place to consciously previewed and purposely directed group operations.

Edwin G. Nourse.
Price-Making in a Democracy.
Brookings Institution, pp. 9-17.

10

PRIMARY AND SECONDARY SOURCES

Primary and Secondary Source Readings provide interesting supplemental readings that help students learn practical applications of economics in their nation and the world. Each activity includes a reading and questions that allow students to use the critical thinking skills taught throughout the course.

Enrichment Activities extend and expand each lesson through motivating activities that engage students in meaningful analyses and interpretations of economics.

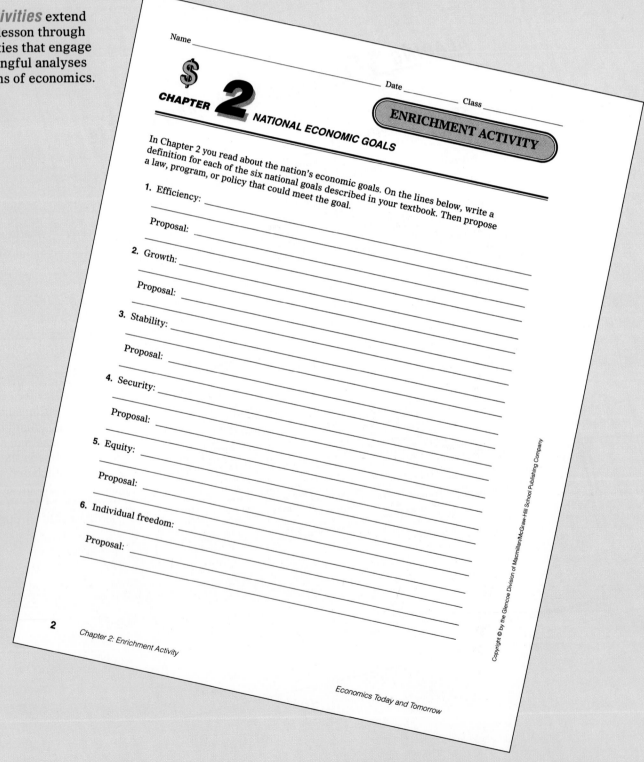

Name _____

$

CHAPTER 2

Date _____

Class _____

ENRICHMENT ACTIVITY

NATIONAL ECONOMIC GOALS

In Chapter 2 you read about the nation's economic goals. On the lines below, write a definition for each of the six national goals described in your textbook. Then propose a law, program, or policy that could meet the goal.

1. Efficiency: _____

Proposal: _____

2. Growth: _____

Proposal: _____

3. Stability: _____

Proposal: _____

4. Security: _____

Proposal: _____

5. Equity: _____

Proposal: _____

6. Individual freedom: _____

Proposal: _____

2   Chapter 2: Enrichment Activity

Copyright © by the Glencoe Division of Macmillan/McGraw-Hill School Publishing Company

Economics Today and Tomorrow

Consumer Application Activities show students how the basic economic concepts they have learned can be applied to real-life financial situations.

Name _____

Class _____   Date _____

ACTIVITY 2 Consumer Application

FINDING A JOB

In a market economy, people are free to sell their labor to earn money. However, in order to find buyers for this labor—that is, employers who will hire them—job seekers must possess the qualifications required for the jobs offered. To help them find the right jobs, therefore, applicants should take the following steps:

- List their qualifications: skills, achievements, education, training, previous work experience, access to a car, a personal computer, and any special knowledge that may be required.
- Determine what they want in a job: hours, conditions, pay, distance from home.
- Check available positions: help-wanted ads, signs in stores, employment agencies, friends in the business.
- Match available positions to qualifications and criteria.
- Apply for several jobs.

1. On the following lines, list your qualifications and what you want in a job. Be as specific as possible, because you need to know yourself well to get the most out of job interviews.

Qualifications: _____

_____

Job Requirements: _____

2. Read the following help-wanted ads. Below each one, list the qualifications the job requires. Also, state whether or not you qualify for the job and if it meets your job requirements.

a. **WANTED:** Teenager willing to do difficult labor for gardening company. Summer employment only. $150 a week. Must have own car. 6 months work experience needed.

_____

_____

_____

b. **WANTED:** Sales clerk for Antons' Department Store. Evenings and weekends year round. Positions open in all departments. Will train. $5 an hour.

_____

_____

_____

c. **COUNSELOR** needed for community youth group. Must be good in sports and be able to work with 7-10-year-olds. $50 a week; opportunity to learn field.

_____

_____

d. **MECHANIC** trainee wanted for busy shop. Must have basic tools and good knowledge of car engines. $125 a week, with possibility of permanent position.

_____

_____

CONSUMER APPLICATION

2

Extension and Enrichment

Free Enterprise Activities contain a variety of activities to help students understand how economic concepts and principles contribute to the free enterprise system.

Name _____

ACTIVITY **2** Free Enterprise

Class _____

Date _____

BUSINESS AND GOVERNMENT

You have learned that government plays an important role in regulating business and industry. However, businesses also influence government. For example, national business associations often use lobbyists to impress their ideas on our elected representatives. Businesses also contribute money to the election campaigns of people who agree with their ideas. And government is usually very sensitive to the needs of business, for if businesses are hurt, their employees are also hurt.

Assume that you own a factory that makes children's clothes for both the U.S. market and for export. State whether you would want your elected representative to support the following proposals, and explain your reasons.

1. Stricter pollution controls on electric generating stations

_____

2. Higher standards of quality for clothing

_____

3. A tax on imported clothing that will raise its price by 15 percent

_____

4. Government support for daycare for single parents with children

_____

5. An import tax on inexpensive foreign fabrics raising the price by 20 percent

_____

6. Deregulation of the trucking industry designed to increase competition among firms that transport manufactured goods

_____

7. An increase in the business tax to help reduce the federal budget deficit

_____

FREE ENTERPRISE

2

Cooperative Learning Activities reinforce learning and build management and interpersonal skills by requiring students to work together to acquire, organize, and present information.

Name _____

Class _____   Date _____

ACTIVITY 1 Cooperative Learning

THE FACTORS OF PRODUCTION

Group Project

You have learned about the four factors of production. Land refers to natural resources, not just to surface land. Labor refers to the work that people do, while capital is the property that people use to make other goods and services. Finally entrepreneurship refers to individuals' ability to start new businesses and to take risks with their financial capital. Work with the members of your group to complete the following chart by classifying each factor listed as an example of land, labor, capital, or entrepreneurship. The items in the chart refer to a nearby restaurant specializing in pan pizza. Use the questions that follow the chart to analyze the information on your chart.

Castroglovanni's Pizza

Items	Factors
Location on a buysy intersection	
Delivery vans	
Waiters	
Plentiful water supply	
Extra profits used to finance expansion	

Cooperative Group Process

1. **Decision-Making** Determine how the group will decide how to classify each item in the chart. Select a group member to record the decisions.

2. **Individual Work** Choose one of the factors of production and give other group members a detailed explanation about the factor.

3. **Group Sharing** Make a list of other items that represent different factors of production. Ask our group members to classify the items on your list.

4. **Analysis** Using data on the chart, have group members select one factor they consider to be most important to the business and explain why it is so important.

Group Process Questions

Did the group agree on the assignment tasks?

Did members respect each other's point of view and give helpful criticism?

Did each member share information?

Did each member contribute ideas at group meetings?

Economic Simulations bring economic concepts to life by furnishing students simulations of real economic ventures or events. Students are provided with step-by-step instructions to organize these in-class games that help bring economics to life and show how economic concepts apply to real-life situations.

Name _____

Class _____

Date _____

ACTIVITY 2 Economic Simulation

BUYING AND SELLING USED CARS

To the Teacher

Buying a used car involves some risk, but it can be an exciting experience. The buyer should be careful to investigate as many aspects of the purchase as possible, such as who the previous owner(s) of the vehicle were, where and how often the vehicle was serviced, and what parts have been repaired or replaced lately. The seller should be able to answer these kinds of questions, represent the vehicle accurately to potential buyers, and establish a fair price for the vehicle.

This simulation allows students to experience some of the bargaining that accompanies the sale of used cars by individuals. It teaches something of the effect of supply and demand on the market and the meaning of the market, where buyers meet sellers.

A. Prepare for the simulation by making enough copies of the loan application form for half of the students in your class and clipping out the Financial Statements and Vehicle Descriptions.

B. Organize the class into two equal groups. The first group will become buyers. Choose one of every four from the second group to become loan officers. The rest are the sellers. Pass out to each student the simulated Ad Section that describes the cars for sale.

C. Give each seller a copy of the **Used Cars for Sale** page and assign each a phone number from that page. This identifies the vehicle that each is going to try to sell. Make sure that all advertised vehicle price ranges are scattered across each seller the more detailed **Vehicle Description** that matches the car each person will try to sell. Meanwhile, sellers should make large phone number ID tags by writing their number on a paper, folding the paper so that the number is easily visible, and placing it on the front of their desks. Tell sellers that they must give potential buyers who ask for it information that is on their **Vehicle Description** and that they may offer additional information or answer other questions as they wish.

D. Give each buyer a **Financial Statement** that describes their needs or wants and enables buyers to determine what they may be able to afford in monthly payments on the car they would like to buy. Tell buyers that they need to take their **Financial Statement** to the loan officer in order to apply for a loan.

E. Give the loan officers copies of **Loan Applications** and the table that lists monthly payment schedules and values/rules for car

lending. Show the loan officers how to determine whether the buyer qualifies for a loan: (a.) has identified the car he or she wants to buy; (b.) has the necessary down payment; (c.) can afford the monthly payments. If the buyer qualifies, the loan officer completes the loan application. The total interest and principle equals 36 X the monthly payment. This completes the loan. Both parties then sign.

F. Announce a specific period of time, such as 15 or 20 minutes, for buyers and sellers to negotiate. All buying and selling will end at the designated time, however, loan approvals may extend for an additional 2-3 minutes. Then instruct buyers to approach sellers and make offers to purchase vehicles. When an offer is accepted, the buyer should go to the lender to obtain financing. Or a buyer may save time by approaching a lender for pre-approval of a loan before negotiating for a vehicle. In cases when the amount that can be loaned is less than the buyer needs, the buyer may want to go back to the seller and make a lower offer or approach another seller with an offer.

G. Wrap Up Discuss with students the kinds of decisions that they had to make during the sale or purchase of their car. What concerns about the transaction were important to each person? Point out that in this simulation there were more sellers than buyers in the market and that this worked in favor of the buyers. Some sellers were not able to sell their cars. What would have happened to price negotiations if there had been more buyers than sellers? How did loan officers feel about having to turn down a person for a loan? How did applicants feel?

ECONOMIC SIMULATION

Economics Laboratories provide hands-on applications of economic concepts. Closely tied to chapter content, the labs help students analyze information presented in the text.

Name _____

Class _____ Date _____

ACTIVITY 2 Economics Lab

USING A HYPOTHESIS

Economists use certain steps in testing a hypothesis. In this lab activity, you will apply steps often used in testing a hypothesis to an economic problem. Step one identifies and defines a problem. Follow the additional steps to form a generalization that can be applies in similar cases.

1. **Define the problem:** Colleges and other post-secondary institutions that are experiencing increasing costs pass these on to students. The high costs of college and other post-secondary education prohibit many students from entering the fields of their choice, and force others to borrow large sums that they must pay back over several years.

2. **State a hypothesis that offers a solution to this problem:**

   _____

   _____

3. **What data supports this hypothesis? What principles are involved?**

   _____

   _____

   _____

   _____

   _____

4. **Evaluate the data:**

   _____

   _____

5. **Are there enough data to test the hypothesis?**

   _____

   _____

6. **Based on this data, what conclusion have you reached?**

   _____

   _____

7. **Do other data support this hypothesis?**

   _____

   _____

8. **What generalization that would affect economic policy can be applied to this case?**

   _____

   _____

12

ECONOMICS LAB

TEACHER'S CLASSROOM RESOURCES

Evaluation

Evaluation materials help you measure students' progress through a large selection of testing resources.

Section Quizzes provide a quick, effective way to monitor the daily progress of your students.

Performance Assessment Activities provide opportunities to implement alternative assessment strategies in your classroom. The booklet also contains rubrics and classroom assessment lists that give teachers the flexibility of monitoring student progress or allowing students to check themselves.

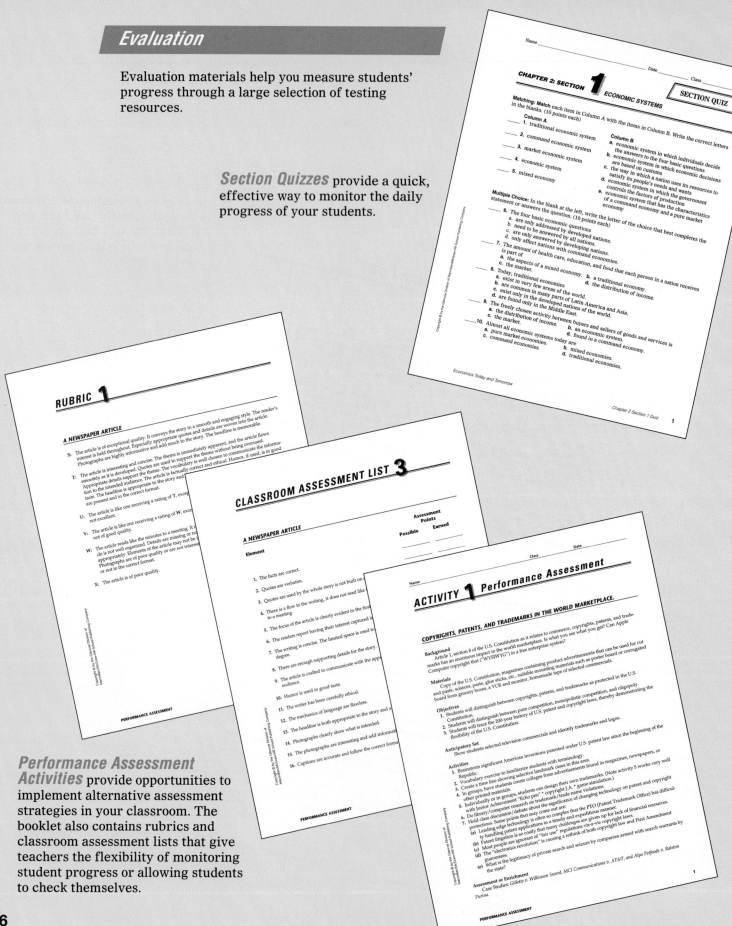

TEACHER'S CLASSROOM RESOURCES

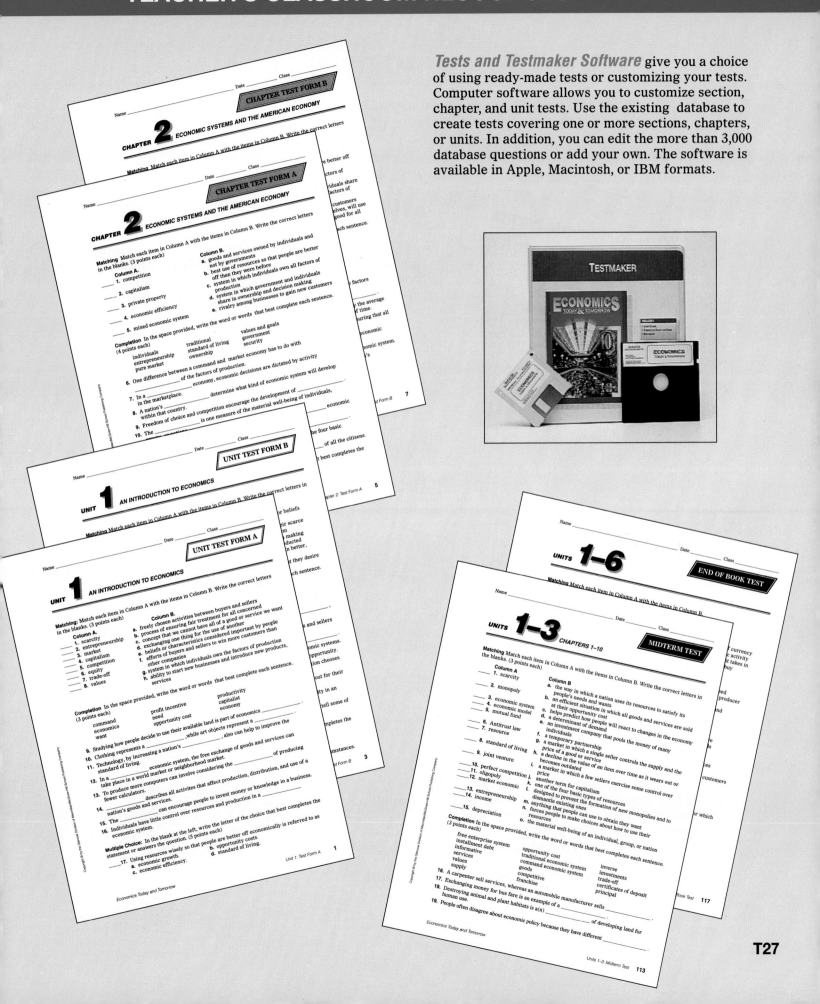

Tests and Testmaker Software give you a choice of using ready-made tests or customizing your tests. Computer software allows you to customize section, chapter, and unit tests. Use the existing database to create tests covering one or more sections, chapters, or units. In addition, you can edit the more than 3,000 database questions or add your own. The software is available in Apple, Macintosh, or IBM formats.

TEACHER'S CLASSROOM RESOURCES

Visual Aids

Visual Aids provide a variety of alternatives to introduce, teach, or reinforce lessons.

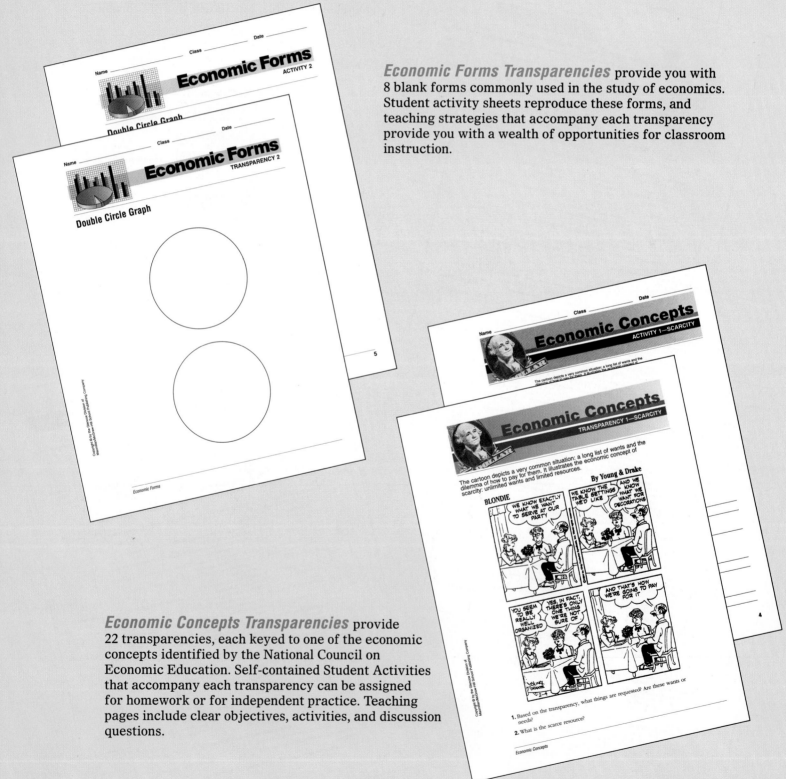

Economic Forms Transparencies provide you with 8 blank forms commonly used in the study of economics. Student activity sheets reproduce these forms, and teaching strategies that accompany each transparency provide you with a wealth of opportunities for classroom instruction.

Economic Concepts Transparencies provide 22 transparencies, each keyed to one of the economic concepts identified by the National Council on Economic Education. Self-contained Student Activities that accompany each transparency can be assigned for homework or for independent practice. Teaching pages include clear objectives, activities, and discussion questions.

Focus Activity Transparencies provide 100 high-interest, visually motivating transparencies that allow you to introduce each text section with an arresting visual in order to pique student interest in the major concepts of the section. An accompanying **Focus Activity Sheet** as well as a **Teaching Strategy** page is provided for each transparency.

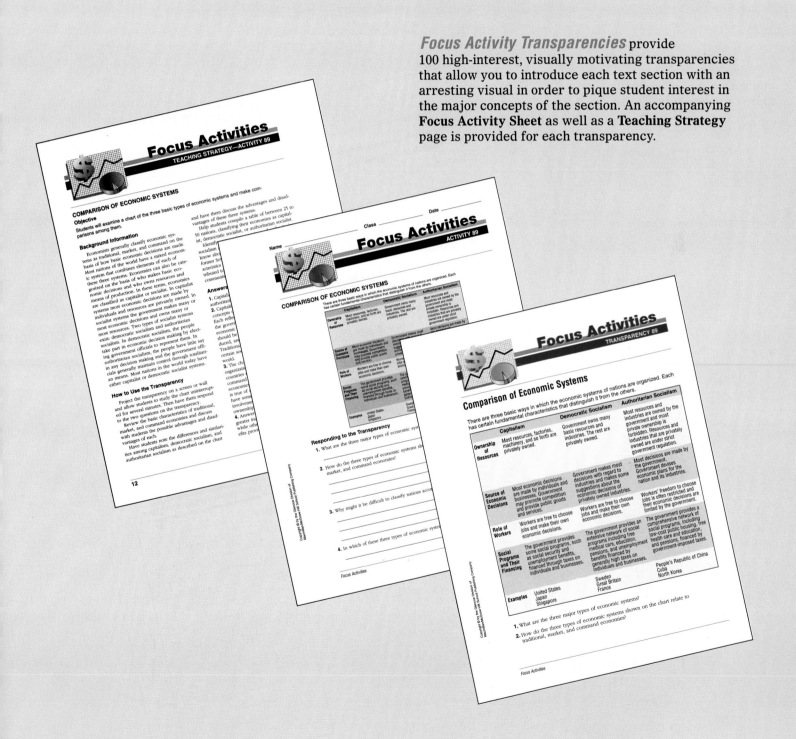

Reproducible Lesson Plans let you spend less time planning and more time teaching.

SECTION 1.1 *The Basic Problem in Economics*

LESSON PLAN

Teacher's Name _____

Grade _____

_____ Class(es) _____

SE/TWE pp. 8–12

Date _____

Dates _____

M Tu W Th F

FOCUS

■ **Objectives**
- To explain why scarcity faces all people at all times.
- To distinguish between wants and needs.
- To list and summarize the four types of resources.

■ **Prepare**

_____ Nightly Business Report Video 1
_____ Bellringer, TWE p. 8
_____ Focus Activity Transparency 1, TCR
_____ Focus Activity Sheet 1, TCR
_____ Motivational Activity, TWE p. 8
_____ Preteaching Vocabulary, TWE p. 8

TEACH

_____ Economics—The Study of Choices, p. 8
_____ The Problem of Scarcity, pp. 8–9
_____ Wants Versus Needs, pp. 9–10
_____ Types of Resources, pp. 10–11
_____ Reading Tables and Graphs, p. 12
_____ Reinforcing Economic Skills 1, TCR
_____ Meeting Special Needs, TWE p. 9
_____ Guided Practice, TWE p. 9
_____ Independent Practice, TWE p. 10
_____ Guided Reading Activity 1.1, TCR
_____ Cooperative Learning, TWE p. 10

ASSESS

_____ Meeting Lesson Objectives, TWE p. 11
_____ Section 1 Review, p. 11
_____ Evaluate, TWE p. 11
_____ Section 1 Quiz, TCR
_____ Reteach, TWE p. 11
_____ Enrich, TWE p. 11

CLOSE

_____ TWE p. 11

TCR = Teacher's Classroom Resources

Economics Today and Tomorrow

• Homework Assignments •

Date _____

_____
_____
_____
_____
_____
_____
_____
_____
_____
_____
_____
_____
_____
_____
_____
_____
_____

Lesson Plan: Section 1.1 The Basic Problem in Economics

1

Economics Update and *Current Events Update* booklets provide supplemental activities and define significant current political, social, and economic events.

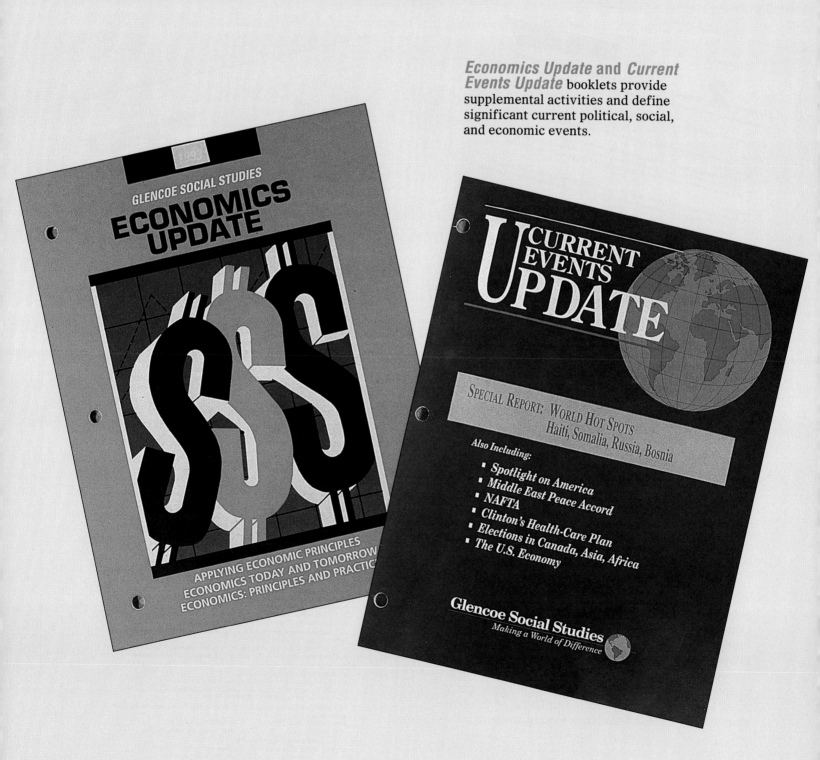

GLENCOE SOCIAL STUDIES

ECONOMICS UPDATE

APPLYING ECONOMIC PRINCIPLES
ECONOMICS TODAY AND TOMORROW
ECONOMICS: PRINCIPLES AND PRACTICE

CURRENT EVENTS UPDATE

SPECIAL REPORT: WORLD HOT SPOTS
Haiti, Somalia, Russia, Bosnia

Also Including:

- Spotlight on America
- Middle East Peace Accord
- NAFTA
- Clinton's Health-Care Plan
- Elections in Canada, Asia, Africa
- The U.S. Economy

Glencoe Social Studies
Making a World of Difference

TEACHER'S CLASSROOM RESOURCES

Spanish Resources

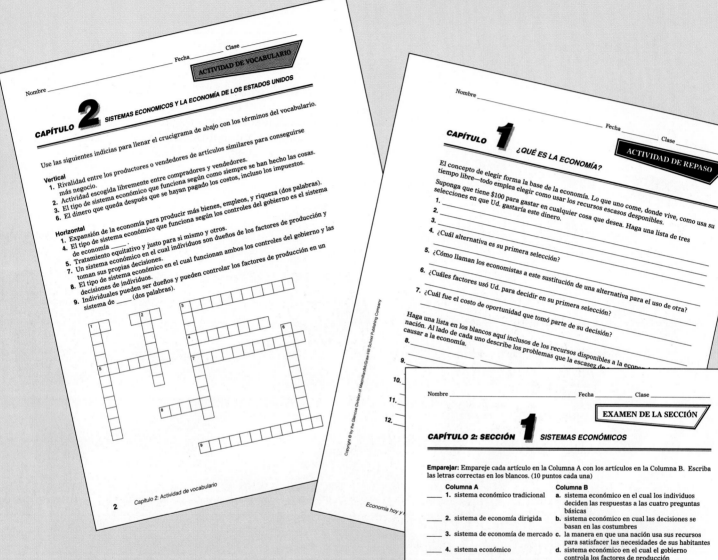

Spanish Resources include vocabulary activities, reteaching activities, section quizzes, and 22 Economic Concepts transparencies packaged in an easy-to-use binder. The Spanish Chapter Digest Audiocassettes provide Spanish summaries of chapter content and include a 1-page activity and a 1-page test for each chapter on the audiocassette. This vital resource allows you to review, reteach, reinforce, or condense chapter content for Spanish-speaking students.

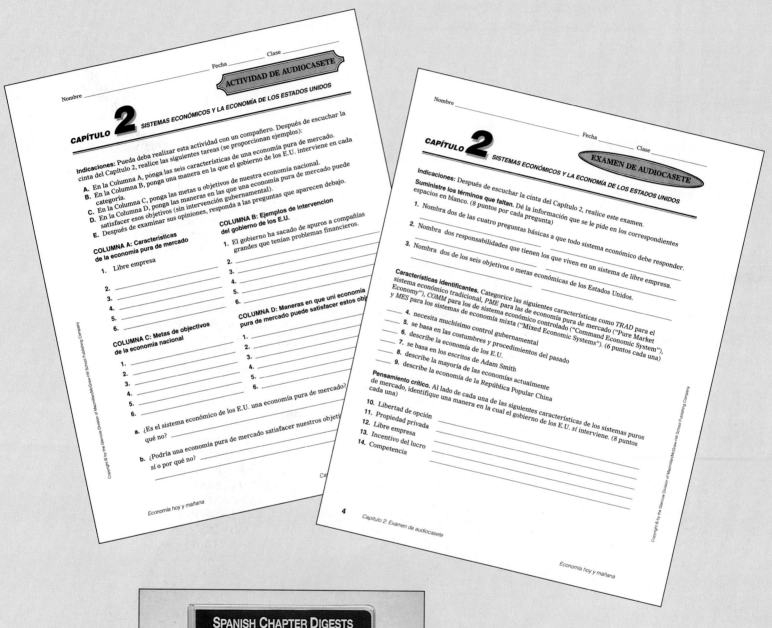

Fecha _____ Clase _____

Nombre _____

ACTIVIDAD DE AUDIOCASETE

CAPÍTULO 2 SISTEMAS ECONÓMICOS Y LA ECONOMÍA DE LOS ESTADOS UNIDOS

Indicaciones: Pueda deba realizar esta actividad con un compañero. Después de escuchar la cinta del Capítulo 2, realice las siguientes tareas (se proporcionan ejemplos):

A. En la Columna A, pónga las seis características de una economía pura de mercado.
B. En la Columna B, ponga una manera en la que el gobierno de los E.U. interviene en cada categoría.
C. En la Columna C, ponga las metas u objetivos de nuestra economía nacional.
D. En la Columna D, ponga las maneras en las que una economía pura de mercado puede satisfacer esos objetivos (sin intervención gubernamental).
E. Después de examinar sus opiniones, responda a las preguntas que aparecen debajo.

COLUMNA A: Características de la economía pura de mercado

1. Libre empresa
2. _____
3. _____
4. _____
5. _____
6. _____

COLUMNA B: Ejemplos de intervencion del gobierno de los E.U.

1. El gobierno ha sacado de apuros a compañías grandes que tenían problemas financieros.
2. _____
3. _____
4. _____
5. _____
6. _____

COLUMNA C: Metas de objetivos de la economía nacional

1. _____
2. _____
3. _____
4. _____
5. _____
6. _____

COLUMNA D: Maneras en que uni economía pura de mercado puede satisfacer estos obj

1. _____
2. _____
3. _____
4. _____
5. _____
6. _____

a. ¿Es el sistema económico de los E.U. una economía pura de mercado? qué no?

b. ¿Podría una economía pura de mercado satisfacer nuestros objeti sí o por qué no? _____

Economía hoy y mañana

Nombre _____

Fecha _____ Clase _____

EXAMEN DE AUDIOCASETE

CAPÍTULO 2 SISTEMAS ECONÓMICOS Y LA ECONOMÍA DE LOS ESTADOS UNIDOS

Indicaciones: Después de escuchar la cinta del Capítulo 2, realice este examen.

Suministre los términos que faltan. Dé la información que se le pide en los correspondientes espacios en blanco. (8 puntos por cada pregunta)

1. Nombra dos de las cuatro preguntas básicas a que todo sistema económico debe responder.
2. Nombra dos de las responsabilidades que tienen los que viven en un sistema económico.
3. Nombra dos de los seis objetivos o metas económicas de los Estados Unidos.
_____

Características identificantes. Categorice las siguientes características como *TRAD* para el sistema económico tradicional, *PME* para las de economía pura de mercado ("Pure Market Economy"), *COMM* para los de sistema económico controlado ("Command Economic System"), y *MES* para los sistemas de economía mixta ("Mixed Economic Systems"). (6 puntos cada una)

___ 4. necesita muchísimo control gubernamental
___ 5. se basa en las costumbres y procedimientos del pasado
___ 6. describe la economía de los E.U.
___ 7. se basa en los escritos de Adam Smith
___ 8. describe la mayoría de las economías actualmente
___ 9. describe la economía de la República Popular China

Pensamiento crítico. Al lado de cada una de las siguientes características de los sistemas puros de mercado, identifique una manera en la cual el gobierno de los E.U. sí interviene. (8 puntos cada una)

10. Libertad de opción _____
11. Propiedad privada _____
12. Libre empresa _____
13. Incentivo del lucro _____
14. Competencia _____

4 *Capítulo 2: Examen de audiocasete*

Economía hoy y mañana

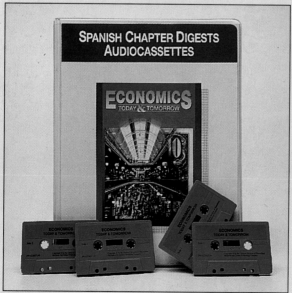

SPANISH CHAPTER DIGESTS AUDIOCASSETTES

ECONOMICS
TODAY & TOMORROW

TEACHER'S CLASSROOM RESOURCES

Nightly Business Report, Economics in Action Videos teach students economic concepts through stimulating television features. Available on laser discs or videotape, these 30 high-interest video segments were produced in conjunction with the award-winning staff and crew of *Nightly Business Report*. A student activity sheet and teaching strategies accompany each video segment.

Also Available

- *Stocktracker Software* is a simulation of stock trading that teaches students the effects of news events on stock prices.

- *Economic Survival: A Financial Simulation* provides all the tools for a week-long game in which students chart their professional and financial lives after high school.

- *Student Self-Test Software* reinforces the economic terms used in each chapter. A complete bank of multiple choice questions allows students to test their understanding of basic economic concepts at the unit, chapter, or section levels. A tutorial explains why incorrect answers to the questions are wrong. A glossary locator allows the students to instantly retrieve all of the vocabulary terms listed at the end of the textbook.

Vocabulary Software allows you to create crossword puzzles and word searches to reinforce economic terms used in the chapter.

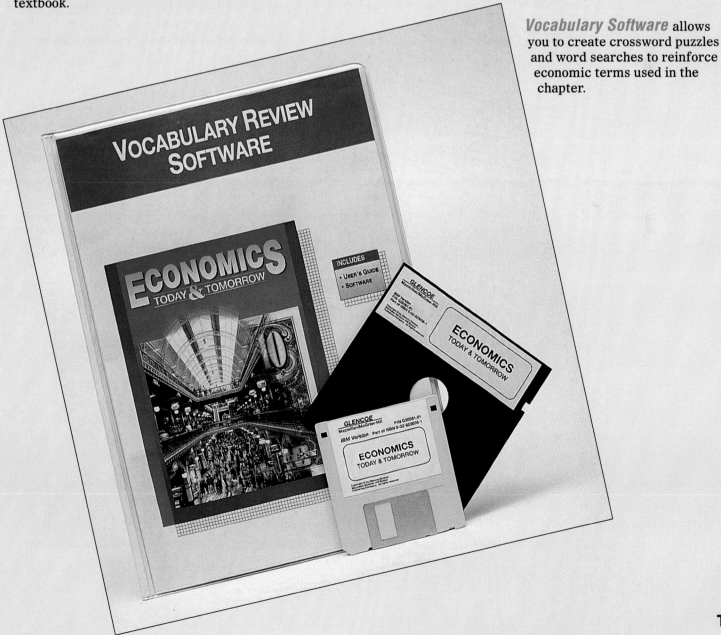

Multimedia Materials

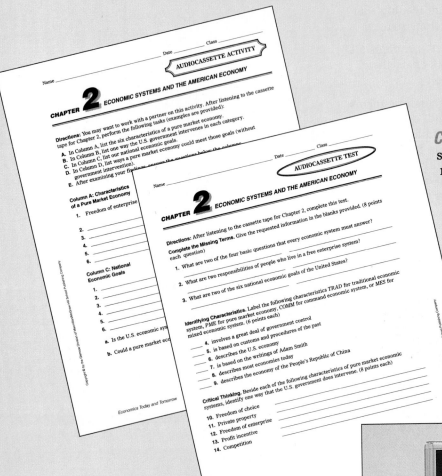

Chapter Digest Audiocassettes provide summaries of chapter content for review, reteaching, or for use when you do not have time to teach a particular chapter. Each summary is accompanied by a chapter activity and test based on the content of the audiocassettes. Spanish Chapter Digest Audiocassettes are also available.

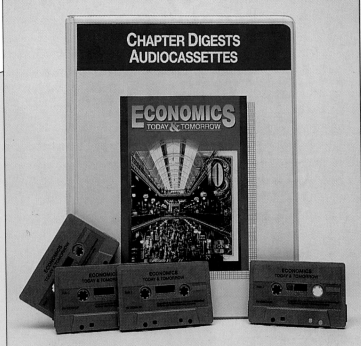

ECONOMICS
TODAY & TOMORROW

Roger LeRoy Miller
The University of Texas at Arlington

GLENCOE
Macmillan/McGraw-Hill

New York, New York   Columbus, Ohio   Mission Hills, California   Peoria, Illinois

ABOUT THE AUTHOR

Roger LeRoy Miller graduated Phi Beta Kappa from the University of California at Berkeley, where he also won the Department Prize in Economics. He was a Woodrow Wilson Honor Fellow, National Science Foundation Fellow, and Lilly Honor Fellow at the University of Chicago, where he received his Ph.D. in economics in 1968. Now at the University of Texas, Arlington, Dr. Miller has taught at the University of Washington, the University of Miami, and Clemson University. He has also taught methodology to teachers of high school economics for the National Council on Economic Education. Among the more than 100 books he has written or co-authored are works on economics, statistics, law, consumer finance, and government. Dr. Miller also has operated several businesses and served as a consultant to government agencies, private corporations, and law firms.

Send all inquiries to:
Glencoe Division, Macmillan/McGraw-Hill, 936 Eastwind Drive, Westerville, Ohio 43081

ISBN 0-02-823102-3 (Student Edition) ISBN 0-02-823104-X (Teacher's Wraparound Edition)
Printed in the United States of America

1 2 3 4 5 6 7 8 9 A-KP/LH-P 99 98 97 96 95 94

CONTENTS

UNIT

3 MICROECONOMICS: MARKETS, PRICES, AND BUSINESS COMPETITION

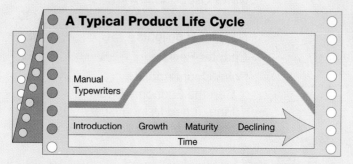

A Typical Product Life Cycle

Manual Typewriters

Introduction   Growth   Maturity   Declining

Time

Before Devaluation
Japanese VCR
costs 20,000 yen

Exchange Rate:
100 yen = $1 U.S.

$VCR = \dfrac{20,000 \text{ yen}}{100 \text{ yen per \$}} = \$200.00$

An American would have to pay
$200 for the Japanese VCR

After Devaluation
Japanese VCR
costs 20,000 yen

Exchange Rate:
200 yen = $1 U.S.

$VCR = \dfrac{20,000 \text{ yen}}{200 \text{ yen per \$}} = \$100.00$

An American would have to pay
$100 for the Japanese VCR

UNIT

6 THE INTERNATIONAL SCENE

SKILLS

Personal Perspective

News Clip

Point ◀ Counterpoint

CASE STUDY Focus on Free Enterprise

ECONOMICS LAB

xi

Checklist

CHECKLISTS

TABLES AND CHARTS

Home Equity Loan
40% Interest

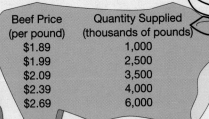

Beef Price (per pound)	Quantity Supplied (thousands of pounds)
$1.89	1,000
$1.99	2,500
$2.09	3,500
$2.39	4,000
$2.69	6,000

GRAPHS

MAPS

Basic Economic Concepts

Economics: Today and Tomorrow incorporates the 22 Basic Concepts established in "A Framework for Teaching the Basic Concepts," published by the National Council on Economic Education.

FUNDAMENTAL ECONOMIC CONCEPTS

1 Scarcity

Scarcity is the condition that results from the imbalance between relatively unlimited wants and the relatively limited resources available for satisfying those wants.

2 Opportunity Costs and Trade-Offs

Opportunity cost is the foregone benefit of the next best alternative when scarce resources are used for one purpose rather than another. **Trade-offs** involve accepting or choosing less of one thing to get more of something else.

3 Productivity

Productivity is the amount of output (goods and services) produced per unit of input (productive resources) used.

4 Economic Systems

Economic Systems are the ways in which people organize economic life to deal with the basic economics problems of scarcity and opportunity cost.

5 Economic Institutions and Incentives

Economic institutions include households and families and formal organizations such as corporations, government agencies, banks, labor unions, and cooperatives. **Incentives** are factors that motivate and influence human behavior.

6 Exchange, Money, and Interdependence

Exchange indicates the transactions in which producers trade their surpluses. **Money** serves as a medium of exchange. **Interdependence** means that decisions or events in one part of the world or in one sector of the economy affect decisions and events in other parts of the world or sector of the economy.

MICROECONOMIC CONCEPTS

7 Markets and Prices

Markets are institutional arrangements that enable buyers and sellers to exchange goods and services. **Prices** are the amounts of money that people pay in exchange for a unit of a particular good or service.

8 Supply and Demand

Supply is defined as the different quantities of a resource, good, or service that will be offered for sale at various possible prices during a specific time period. **Demand** is defined as the different quantities of a resource, good, or service that will be purchased at various possible prices during a specific time period.

9 Competition and Market Structure

Competition is determined by the number of buyers and sellers in particular markets. **Market structures** refer to the extent to which competition prevails in particular markets.

10 Income Distribution

Income distribution may be classified into functional distribution— the division of an economy's total income into wages and salaries, rent, interest, and profit; or income distribution may be classified into personal distribution of income, classifying the different population groups by the number of them receiving different amounts of income.

MACROECONOMIC CONCEPTS

INTERNATIONAL ECONOMIC CONCEPTS

*In the fall of 1991, the United States Department of Commerce replaced GNP with GDP as the nation's most inclusive measure of output.

UNIT

AN INTRODUCTION TO ECONOMICS

....

CHAPTER 1
WHAT IS ECONOMICS?

....

CHAPTER 2
ECONOMIC SYSTEMS AND THE AMERICAN ECONOMY

....

Economic Simulation

Trade-offs Have the class assume the role of a government committee charged with hearing arguments for and against increasing the amount of timber that can be cut in Tongass National Forest, Alaska. Choose six students to research the issue; three to speak for a timber company and three to speak as environmentalists. After arguments are presented, have the class discuss the issue to reach a consensus or to vote.

Beginning the Unit

Refer students to the "Did You Know" questions on page 5. Ask them how knowing the facts presented in the questions could influence them and their decisions. (*For example, the kinds of careers they decide to pursue might be influenced by potential job availability; knowing that travel will double in the next 25 years might make getting a job in a travel-related business a possibility.*)

Outcome-Based Project

Using an Economic Model
The following unit project is the first step in a six-part activity that can be used during the entire economics course. In Unit 1 students collect information to build a model that will reveal job opportunities and trends.

Have students compile job information, using the newspaper want ads from the nearest city. This should be done each week for at least three weeks. Compile statistics on:
1. The total number of ads each week for a broad range of job categories such as sales, skilled trades, data processing, clerical, medical, professional (categories will vary depending on economics of local areas and newspaper want ad headings)
2. Descriptions of job requirements for each job
3. Salaries, whenever listed

Did You Know

- Your choice of jeans as a consumer determines how many will be produced.
- Most new jobs in the 1990s are in the services and professional specialties.
- Taxes account for about 60 percent of the price of fuel in the United States.
- Experts predict that the amount of travel will double in the next 25 years.
- Russia plans to turn over most state factories to private individuals.

In this unit you will learn what economics is, and how different societies have chosen what goods and services should be produced and how they should be distributed.

5

Did You Know

Most new jobs in the 1990s are in services and professional specialties. Predictions for the best employment opportunities include jobs such as:
- **Accountants/Auditors:** Due to an increase in the size and complexity of the business world.

- **Chefs/Cooks:** Due to increasing population, higher incomes, and more leisure time.
- **Home Health Care Providers:** Due to an increase in the elderly population, the trend to provide home health care, and new technology.

- **School Teachers:** Due to increasing population, decreasing class size, and large number of current teachers nearing retirement.
- **Travel Agents:** Due to an expected increase in leisure and business travel.

CHAPTER 1 **WHAT IS ECONOMICS?**

CHAPTER ORGANIZER

Daily Objectives	Special Features	Classroom Resources
Section 1 The Basic Problem in Economics • **Explain** why scarcity faces all people at all times. • **Distinguish** between wants and needs. • **List** and summarize the four types of resources.	**Learning Economics Skills:** Reading Tables and Graphs, p. 12	Reproducible Lesson Plan 1.1 *NBR* Video 1 Focus Activity Transparency 1 Focus Activity Sheet 1 Economic Concepts Transparency 1 Guided Reading Activity 1.1 Cooperative Learning Activity 1 Primary and Secondary Source Readings 1 Section Quiz 1.1 Spanish Section Quiz 1.1 Testmaker Reinforcing Skills 1
Section 2 Trade-Offs • **Explain** the relationship between trade-offs and opportunity cost. • **Describe** how society's trade-offs can be shown on a production possibilities curve.	**Personal Perspective:** Robert L. Heilbroner on The Great Economists, p. 17	Reproducible Lesson Plan 1.2 *NBR* Video 2 and Video Still 1 Focus Activity Transparency 2 Focus Activity Sheet 2 Economic Concepts Transparency 2 Guided Reading Activity 1.2 Section Quiz 1.2 Spanish Section Quiz 1.2 Testmaker
Section 3 What Do Economists Do? • **Describe** and give examples of economic models. • **Explain** the purpose of economic models. • **Explain** why there are different schools of economic thought. • **Tell** why economists do not normally work with values.	**News Clip:** "Runner's High," *The Boston Globe*, p. 22	Reproducible Lesson Plan 1.3 Focus Activity Transparency 3 Focus Activity Sheet 3 Guided Reading Activity 1.3 Consumer Application Activity 1 Mathematics Practice for Economics 1 Performance Assessment Activity 1 Section Quiz 1.3 Spanish Section Quiz 1.3 Testmaker Enrichment Activity 1

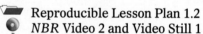 **OUT OF TIME?** If time does not permit teaching this chapter, you may use the Chapter 1 Highlights and the Audiocassettes that include a 1-page activity and a 1-page test.

Chapter 1 Review and Evaluation

Special Features

Chapter 1 Highlights, p. 23
Chapter 1 Review, pp. 24–25
Point/Counterpoint, pp. 26–27

Classroom Resources

- Chapter 1 Test Forms A and B
- Economics Vocabulary Activity 1
- Spanish Economics Vocabulary Activity 1

- Audiocassette 1
- Spanish Audiocassette 1
- Reteaching Activity 1
- Spanish Reteaching Activity 1

Key to Ability Levels

Teaching strategies have been coded for varying learning styles and abilities.

L1 Level 1 activities are **basic** activities and should be within the ability range of all students.

L2 Level 2 activities are **average** activities designed for the ability range of average to above-average students.

L3 Level 3 activities are **challenging** activities designed for the ability range of above-average students.

LEP activities should be within the ability range of **Limited English Proficiency** students.

Performance Assessment

The following chapter project may be assigned at the beginning of the chapter and used for performance assessment. See page T12 for additional Performance Assessment information.

Conducting an Interview Have students work in pairs to develop interview questions to determine what other classmates perceive as their economic needs and wants. The question should also ask what trade-offs their classmates have made recently and the opportunity costs of these trade-offs. Students should conduct interviews of their classmates and record classmate responses during the time they study Chapter 1. After they complete their interviews, have the interviewers report on the types of things their classmates consider economic needs and those they consider economic wants and on the trade-offs their classmates have made recently. Students might report their findings in the form of a chart, table, or bar graph.

Additional Resources

Readings for the Student

Heilbroner, Robert L., and Thurow, Lester C. *Economics Explained.* Englewood Cliffs, N.J.: Prentice-Hall, 1985.

Swartz, Thomas R., and Bonello, Frank J., eds. *Taking Sides: Clashing Views on Controversial Economic Issues.* Guilford, Conn.: Dushkin, 1990.

Readings for the Teacher

Boulding, Kenneth E. *Economics as a Science.* Lanham, Md.: University Press of America, 1988.

Fusfeld, Daniel R. *The Age of the Economist.* 6th ed. Glenview, Ill.: Scott Foresman and Co., 1990.

Multimedia Materials

Introduction to Economics. Filmstrip set. Social Studies School Service. P.O. Box 802, Culver City, CA 90232-0802

People on Market Street. Film. Walt Disney Educational Media Corporation. 500 S. Buena Vista, Burbank, CA 91521

The World of Economics. Videotape. 15 min. Federal Reserve Bank of San Francisco. Public Information Department. P.O. Box 7702, San Francisco, CA 94120

Hard Choices. Tutorial. With Teacher's Guide. Apple. Diversified Educational Enterprises. 725 Main Street, Lafayette, IN 47901. Effects of making economic decisions.

Chapter Overview

Economics is the study of how individuals and nations make choices about how to use scarce resources to fulfill their wants. Chapter 1 explains or describes: scarcity; the four factors of production; the relationship between trade-offs and opportunity costs; and how economists use economic data to test the economic models they formulate about people and businesses.

 VIDEODISC

Nightly Business Report

Economics in Action
To introduce the videodiscs, use Disc 1, Side A, Video 1.

Search 307, Play to 2334

CHAPTER

1 WHAT IS ECONOMICS?

What benefit are these students receiving from this activity?

What would be the benefit of studying instead of watching television?

Answering Economic Questions

The questions in the above illustration are designed to lead into the main concepts in Chapter 1. Students might not understand the importance of choices in the study of economics. The questions will help them focus on the frequency of making economic choices in their own lives and the ramifications of the choices they make. Have students discuss the questions and explain the process they go through in making choices.

What are the long-term effects of watching too much television?

How do students make the choice between studying and watching television?

What are these students doing?

Your Economics Journal

During a one-week period, keep track of how you spend your time. At the end of the week, list the most frequent activities in which you engage and how many hours you spent on each.

Connecting to Past Learning

Ask students what they think economics is. Ask students to describe how, in their opinion, economics affects them. Tell students that in Chapter 1 they will learn that economics is the study of the ways individuals as well as nations make choices about how to fulfill their economic wants. After completing the chapter, compare students' initial ideas with the chapter information.

Applying Economics

Tell students to imagine that they have $100 to spend. Have them make a list of items they would like to buy and the approximate price of each. Have them add up the prices, and, if they exceed $100, remove the items they would like the least. Discuss students' choices and the thought process that went into making these choices. Tell students they will learn why choices are an important aspect of economics.

 EXTRA CREDIT PROJECT

Read a book about one of America's major entrepreneurs. Write a summary explaining the key decisions this person made and which skills were responsible for his or her success.

 PERFORMANCE ASSESSMENT

Refer to page 6B for "Conducting an Interview," a Performance Assessment Activity for this chapter.

 **Economic Portfolio**

Have students start an **Economic Portfolio** in which they include **Your Economics Journal** writing activities for this and every chapter. Have students list activities they participate in, such as shopping, physical fitness, and studying. List these activities on the chalkboard. Then, in their portfolios, have students develop a table showing the time spent on various activities. Have them write a paragraph explaining why they spent so much time on the top three activities and so little time on the bottom three. They should also indicate what other activities they did not choose.

7

Overview

See the student page for section objectives.

Section 1 explains or describes: the importance of economics; the relationship of scarcity to unlimited wants; and the four factors of production.

Bellringer

Before presenting the lesson, display Focus Activity Transparency 1 on the overhead projector or copy the material on the chalkboard. Assign the accompanying Focus Activity Sheet.

Motivational Activity

Write the following statements on the chalkboard for students to complete:
Things I need to live include _____.

Things I want to have include _____..
Call on volunteers to read their statements. Ask students how they distinguished between what they need and what they want.

Preteaching Vocabulary

Ask students to arrange six of the vocabulary words on graph paper in crossword puzzle form. Then have them find the definitions of the words in the Glossary and use the definitions as clues for the puzzle.

SECTION **1**
The Basic Problem in Economics

S E C T I O N   1   F O C U S

Terms to Know economics, resource, scarcity, wants, land, labor, capital, productivity, entrepreneurship, factors of production, goods and services, technology

Objectives *After reading this section, you should be able to:*
① Explain why scarcity faces all people at all times.
② Distinguish between wants and needs.
③ List and summarize the four types of resources.

Economics—The Study of Choices

Economics is the study of how individuals and nations make choices about how to use scarce resources to fulfill their wants. A **resource** is anything that people can use to make or obtain what they want.

As a student, you probably have a small amount of money—from an allowance or a part-time job—to spend. As a result, you have to make choices about its use. Whenever you make such a spending decision, each available choice competes with every other available choice. Suppose you have $20 to spend. You could use it to buy lunch for four days or two budget compact discs or a sweatshirt and so on as shown in Figure 1.1.

The Problem of Scarcity

The need to make choices arises because everything that exists is limited, even though some items may appear to be in overabundant supply. At any one moment in the United States, or anywhere, a fixed, or set, amount of resources is available. At the same time, people may have competing uses

◄ **Figure 1.1 Economic Choices** When you decide whether to spend your money on clothes or a new CD, you are making an economic choice. The basic economic problem of scarcity makes the choice necessary.

Classroom Resources for Section 1

- Reproducible Lesson Plan 1.1
- *NBR* Video 1
- Focus Activity Transparency 1
- Focus Activity Sheet 1
- Economic Concepts Transparency 1
- Guided Reading Activity 1.1
- Cooperative Learning Activity 1

- Primary and Secondary Source Readings 1
- Section Quiz 1.1
- Spanish Section Quiz 1.1
- Testmaker
- Reinforcing Skills 1

for these resources. This situation results in the problem of scarcity—the basic problem of economics.

Scarcity means that people do not and cannot have enough income, time, or other resources to satisfy their every desire. What you can buy with your income as a student is limited by the amount of income you have. In this case, your income is the scarce resource. Scarcity is not the same as *shortage*, as Figure 1.2 shows.

Choices The problem of scarcity faces businesses as well as individuals. Businesspeople make decisions daily about what to produce now, what to produce later, and what to stop producing. These decisions in turn affect people's income and their ability to buy. Nations, too, face the problem of choosing how to spend their scarce resources. The United States, for example, must decide how much to spend on Social Security benefits and aid to higher education. How people make these choices is the subject of economics.

Wants versus Needs

How many times have you said that you "need" something? How often do you think about what you "want"? When you say, "I need some new clothes," are you stating a want, or a real need? Typically the term *need* is used very casually. When most people use the word *need*, they really mean that they want something they do not have.

The difference between wants and needs is not a clear one. Everyone needs certain basic things—enough food, clothing, and shelter to survive. Americans also consider a good education and adequate health care as needs.

Economists call everything other than these basic needs **wants.** People want such items as new cars and personal computers. Although more and more people have these items, this does not mean that anyone actually needs them.

▲

B Temporary shortages of products such as gasoline may be caused when imports are dramatically decreased for any reason.

Figure 1.2
Shortage vs Scarcity
It is important not to confuse shortage and scarcity. Scarcity always exists, whereas shortages are always temporary.

A Shortages often exist after major hurricanes or floods that destroy goods and property.

Chapter 1 What Is Economics? **9**

Teach

Guided Practice

L1 Classifying Write the following headings on the chalkboard: Land, Labor, Capital, Entrepreneurship. Then read, one at a time, the following list of items: soil (*Land*), welding tools (*Capital*), starting a new business (*Entrepreneurship*), machine operators (*Labor*), river (*Land*), offices (*Capital*). Ask students to decide which factor of production each item is, and have a volunteer write the item under the appropriate heading. LEP

L2 Hypothesizing Ask students to hypothesize and discuss what life would be like without economic scarcities.

Visual Instruction

Refer students to Figure 1.2, its caption, and the text discussion of the problem of scarcity. Ask them to draw political cartoons illustrating how the problem of scarcity and the unlimited wants of humans are related. Display completed cartoons in the classroom.

◆◆◯ **Meeting Special Needs**

Reading Disability Students with various reading and organizational difficulties may have problems relating pictures, captions, and the main text. Before reading the text in Section 1, ask students to look at the pictures. Have them tell what the pictures illustrate. Then have them read Section 1, explain again what the pictures illustrate, and explain why they were included in the section.

Independent Practice

L1 Creating Posters Have students create posters that illustrate the differences between economic needs and economic wants. Display posters in the classroom.

 Have students complete Guided Reading Activity 1.1 in the TCR. LEP

🌐 GLOBAL ECONOMICS

Economic development in developing countries, as in developed countries, is linked to the factors of production. Many economists believe that the biggest impediment to economic growth in developing countries is the quality of labor. With poor health conditions and low literacy rates, the labor force does not have the skills needed to keep up with modern technology.

For example, people entertained themselves and informed themselves of news long before the invention of the radio. As the wonders of radio were advertised, more people began to believe they needed one. What began as a luxury, or want, became to many people a necessity. This cycle of wants and perceived needs is repeated over and over. In economics, however, only a few true needs, such as minimal food and shelter, exist.

Types of Resources

Besides the question of whether you need or want a VCR, there is the issue of whether there will be enough VCRs to allow every person to own one. Also, not everyone would have enough money to buy one. Only a certain amount of resources exist, regardless of wants and needs. Traditionally, economists have classified resources as land, labor, capital, or entrepreneurship.

Land As an economic term, **land** refers to natural resources, as shown in

Figure 1.3 Natural Resources
Natural resources are all the things found in nature—on or in water and the earth—such as fish, animals, forests, and minerals as well as land and water.

▼

Figure 1.3, not just to surface land. Among the most important natural resources in economic terms are land and mineral deposits such as iron ore. In economics, the location of land is also important in establishing its value as a resource.

Labor The work people do is **labor**—often called a human resource. The labor resource includes anyone who works.

Capital All the property people use to make other goods and services is **capital**. For example, the machines used to make automobiles are capital. The cars are not considered capital unless they are used, for example, as taxicabs, to produce services. Combining capital with land and labor increases the value of all resources by increasing their productivity. **Productivity** is the ability to produce greater quantities of goods and services in better and faster ways.

When you read references to "capital" in newspapers, they generally mean *financial capital*, such as the funds made available in the stock market for starting a new business. In this book, if we mean such funds, we will always say *financial* or *money* capital.

Cooperative Learning

Have the class list on the chalkboard a number of activities they can do for at least half-hour time periods, such as watch television or listen to the radio, or do homework. Have them assign values to these activities, such as study 2 hours equals an A grade and study 1.5 hours equals a B grade. Have

groups of three or four each choose a future profession for an imaginary student. Each group should plan six hours of activities for the "student" to do after a school day. Groups should make a five-day schedule. Have a student from each group present and explain the schedule to the class.

Entrepreneurship The fourth type of resource is **entrepreneurship** (AHN-truh-pruh-NUHR-ship), which refers to the ability of individuals to start new businesses, to introduce new products and techniques, and to improve management techniques.

All changes in business organization are part of entrepreneurship. It involves initiative and individual willingness to take risks to make profit. Entrepreneurs succeed when they produce new products, improve an existing product or produce it more efficiently, or reorganize a business to run more smoothly.

Together, the resources of land, labor, capital, and entrepreneurship are called the **factors of production.** They are used to produce **goods and services.** Goods are the items that people buy. Services are the activities done for others for a fee.

Technology Some economists add technology to the list of resources. Any use of land, labor, and capital that produces goods and services more efficiently is technology. For example, a computer keyboard is a technological advance over the typewriter.

Today, however, **technology** usually describes the use of science to develop new products and new methods for producing and distributing goods and services. **Figure 1.4** illustrates a modern application of technology.

Figure 1.4 ▲
Technology in Action
Advanced machinery and new production and distribution methods increase the productivity of the other resources. For example, without modern drilling machinery, it would be impossible to tap the oil resources of the ocean.

Assess

Meeting Lesson Objectives

Assign Section 1 Review as homework or an in-class activity. Each question in the Review addresses the corresponding numbered objective in the Section Focus.

Evaluate

Assign the Section 1 Quiz in the TCR or use the Testmaker to develop a customized quiz.

Reteach

Ask students to copy the headings in Section 1 as the main headings of an outline. Have students complete the outline by using the section information.

Enrich

Have students research information and write a short biography about an American entrepreneur.

Close

Have students write a paragraph, using the following as the topic sentence: Everyone makes economic choices.

SECTION 1 REVIEW

Understanding Vocabulary

Define economics, resource, scarcity, wants, land, labor, capital, productivity, entrepreneurship, factors of production, goods and services, technology.

Reviewing Objectives

1. Why does scarcity always exist?
2. What is the difference between wants and needs?
3. What are the four types of resources? Give an example of each.

Section 1 Review Answers

Understanding Vocabulary
economics (p. 8), **resource** (p. 8), **scarcity** (p. 9), **wants** (p. 9), **land** (p. 10), **labor** (p. 10), **capital** (p. 10), **productivity** (p. 10), **entrepreneurship** (p. 11), **factors of production** (p. 11), **goods and services** (p. 11), **technology** (p. 11)

Reviewing Objectives
1. Scarcity always exists because there are not enough resources to satisfy everyone's wants.
2. Needs—food, clothing, shelter—are basic to survival; wants are things other than these basic needs.
3. Land, labor, capital, entrepreneurship. Examples will vary. Land—oil, trees; labor—plumber, bus driver; capital—tools, factories; entrepreneurship—manager, owner who organizes factors of production.

Teach

Use the following activity to guide students through the use of tables and bar, line, and circle graphs. Use the following statistics to make a table and draw each type of graph on the chalkboard: In a recent year, $79.8 billion was given by donors to help support the following areas: religion, $37.7 billion (47 percent); education, $11.1 billion (14 percent); health and hospitals, $11.3 billion (14 percent); social welfare, $8.6 billion (11 percent); arts and humanities, $5.1 billion (6 percent); civic and public, $2.2 billion (3 percent); and other, $3.9 billion (5 percent). Then point out to students that graphs may present data more clearly than a table.

Additional Practice

Have students complete Reinforcing Skills 1 in the TCR.

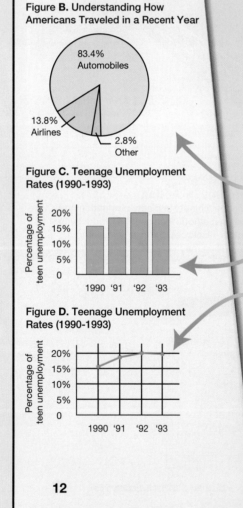

Figure **B.** Understanding How Americans Traveled in a Recent Year

- 83.4% Automobiles
- 13.8% Airlines
- 2.8% Other

Figure **C.** Teenage Unemployment Rates (1990-1993)

Percentage of teen unemployment
20%
15%
10%
5%
0
1990 '91 '92 '93

Figure **D.** Teenage Unemployment Rates (1990-1993)

Percentage of teen unemployment
20%
15%
10%
5%
0
1990 '91 '92 '93

12

LEARNING ECONOMIC SKILLS
Reading Tables and Graphs

Tables and graphs are easy to read and show much information in a small space. Do you know how to interpret them?

Tables

Tables, such as Figure A below, represent data in rows and columns according to topics.

Figure A. Understanding How Americans Traveled in a Recent Year

Forms of Transportation	Miles in Billions	Percent Distribution
Automobiles	1,287	83.4
Airlines	213	13.8
Other	43	2.8

Graphs

Graphs are a visual representation of statistical data and are often easier to read than tables. The three types of graphs include circle ("pie") graphs, bar graphs, and line graphs.

Circle Graph Circle graphs show the proportions of the elements of a whole. Figure B shows the percentage distribution of forms of transportation from Figure A in a circle graph.

Bar Graph The bar graph in Figure C shows teenage unemployment over four years.

Line Graph Line graphs are often used to show the same information as a bar graph. Figure D, for example, is a line graph representation of the information in Figure C.

Practicing the Skill

❶ What information does Figure A provide that Figure B does not?

❷ According to Figure C, when was teenage unemployment highest?

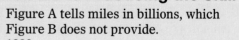
Answers to Practicing the Skill

1. Figure A tells miles in billions, which Figure B does not provide.
2. 1992

SECTION **2** *Trade-Offs*

SECTION 2 FOCUS

Terms to Know trade-off, opportunity cost, production
possibilities

Objectives *After reading this section, you should be able to:*
1 Explain the relationship between trade-offs and
opportunity cost.
2 Describe how society's trade-offs can be shown on a
production possibilities curve.

Choices Involve Opportunity Costs

Scarcity forces people to make choices about how they will use their resources. Those choices affect not only how people live today, but how people will live in the future. It is important to realize that the economic choices people make involve exchanging one good or service for another. If you choose to buy a video for your VCR, you are exchanging your money for the right to own the video. Exchanging one thing for the use of another is called a **trade-off.**

Opportunity Costs

As Figure 1.5 shows, individuals, businesses, and nations are forced to make trade-offs every time they use their resources in one way and not

**Figure 1.5
Trade-Offs**
Trade-offs involve
making choices that
are unavoidable be-
cause of the problem
of scarcity. Having
high levels of automo-
bile pollution or higher
car manufacturing
costs (to reduce pollu-
tion) is an example.

▼

Chapter 1 What Is Economics? **13**

13

Teach

Guided Practice

L1 Recording Ask students to keep a record of the recreational choices and purchases they make in a given day and to identify the opportunity cost for each.

Visual Instruction

Refer students to Figure 1.6. Ask them to summarize how the two dollar figures for each point on the graph illustrate trade-offs.

VIDEODISC

Nightly Business Report

Economics in Action
Use Video Still 1,
"Federal Spending," on
Disc 1, Side A, Video 2.

Search Frame 7604

another. For example, as a student you may be faced with a decision about going to college or vocational school to increase future earnings, or going to work right after high school.

The Cost of Choices Another way to describe a trade-off is in terms of the cost of something a person gives up in order to get something else. When you decide to study economics for one hour, you are making a choice. You are giving up any other activities you could choose to do. Because time is a scarce resource—there are only so many hours in a day—you must decide how to use it.

In other words, there is a cost involved in time spent studying this book. Economists call it an **opportunity cost**—the value of the next best alternative that had to be given up for the alternative that was chosen. Whatever you consider as the value of the next best alternative to studying—watch-

ing television, for example—is the opportunity cost of your studying for one hour.

The opportunity cost of any action is the value of what is given up because the choice was made. What is important is the choice that you would have made if you had not studied one hour. Your opportunity cost is generated from the next-highest-ranked alternative, not all alternatives. Therefore, in economics, cost is always a foregone opportunity.

A good way to think about opportunity cost is to realize that when you choose to do something, you lose. What do you lose? You lose the ability to engage in your next-highest-valued alternative.

A Practical Example Consider an example at the national level. Suppose Congress votes $2 billion for projects to clean up polluted rivers. The opportunity cost of its vote is the next best alternative use of those same tax dollars. For example, Congress could have voted for increased spending on space research. Then the opportunity cost of clean rivers would be fewer space flights.

Meeting Special Needs

Visual Learning Disability Students with visual-spatial processing problems may have difficulty interpreting graphs. Because information is often presented in graph form, it is important that students become proficient in reading and interpreting graphs. Refer students to the production-

possibilities curve in Figure 1.6. Have them identify the vertical and horizontal axes and the units of measurement, or scales, used on these two axes. Then have them write a sentence summarizing the information shown on the graph.

Considering Opportunity Costs

Being aware of opportunity costs and trade-offs is important in making economic decisions of all kinds. For example, you will be able to make wiser use of your own resources if you know the opportunity costs and trade-offs involved. You will be able to vote more intelligently if you are aware of the choices your elected officials face. Businesspeople, too, must consider opportunity costs and trade-offs.

Production Possibilities

The term *mix* brings up another fact about resources. How do people determine how much of each item to produce? What are the trade-offs and opportunity costs involved in each decision? The concept of production possibilities is useful in examining this problem.

Production possibilities are all the combinations of goods and services that can be produced from a fixed amount of resources in a given period of time. For each situation, only a limited number of factors are considered. A fixed amount of resources and a given period of time exist.

The Classic Example The classic example for explaining production possibilities in economics is the trade-off between military defense and civilian goods, sometimes referred to as *guns* versus *butter*. The extremes for a nation would be using all its resources to produce only one or the other. Figure 1.6 shows the two extremes.

The federal government determines where on the production-possibilities curve the nation will be. The government takes income from citizens through taxes. It uses this revenue, which could have been used for butter, to produce guns. "The nation" on the curve is Congress and the

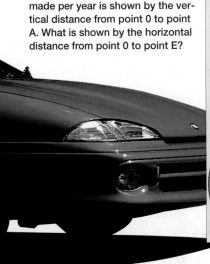

▼ Figure 1.6
Guns or Butter?

Point A on the graph represents all resources being used to produce only guns (military defense). Point E represents the other extreme—all resources being used to produce only butter (civilian goods).

Countries produce combinations, or mixes, of goods. That is shown by the curve between points A and E. The curve represents the production possibilities between guns and butter in a nation during one year.

The maximum quantity of guns made per year is shown by the vertical distance from point 0 to point A. What is shown by the horizontal distance from point 0 to point E?

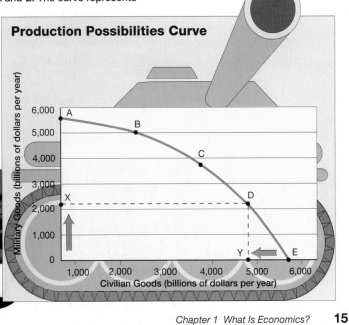

Production Possibilities Curve

(Military Goods (billions of dollars per year) vs. Civilian Goods (billions of dollars per year))

Chapter 1 What Is Economics? **15**

Independent Practice

L2 Writing an Editorial Have students write a newspaper editorial indicating their opinion about the guns-and-butter issue. Have volunteers share their editorials.

L3 Graphing Tell students that they have five hours to either listen to music or do their homework. Ask students to draw a production-possibilities curve illustrating the different ways they could spend their time.

Have students complete Guided Reading Activity 1.2 in the TCR. LEP

GLOBAL ECONOMICS

An example of the production-possibilities curve is evident in Uganda, which has strict tariffs on exported finished-wood products. The tariffs make the finished-wood products more valuable than raw timber. However, if the government reduces the tariffs on finished-wood products, but still restricts the number of trees that can be cut, furniture manufacturers can make more money while using fewer trees.

Cooperative Learning

Have the class decide on an amount of money to be budgeted for school improvements, such as $5000. Have them list on the chalkboard suggested "improvements" that could be purchased and have them assign these improvements a price, such as buying new textbooks for one class ($1000) or resurfacing the school track ($5000). Then organize the class into groups of three to five students. Have each group decide how they would spend the money and have them prepare a presentation of their budget for the class including the trade-offs involved.

Assess

Meeting Lesson Objectives

Assign Section 2 Review as homework or an in-class activity. Each question in the Review addresses the corresponding numbered objective in the Section Focus.

Evaluate

📁 Assign the Section 2 Quiz in the TCR or use the Testmaker to develop a customized quiz.

Reteach

Have students work in small groups to create posters illustrating a variety of choices in terms of opportunity costs. Students' posters might illustrate personal choices or choices made by businesses or governments.

Enrich

Invite a manager of a local factory to point out the company's production possibilities—choices of what it may produce.

Close

Discuss with students how using a production-possibilities curve enables a nation or business to use its resources in an economically efficient manner.

Figure 1.7 ▲ From Military to Civilian Goods

A small defense contractor, Harris, was able to outbid AT&T to obtain a $1.66 billion contract to manufacture a new civilian air-traffic control system such as the one shown.

President, who make decisions for the American public.

Production-possibilities curves are a good way to show trade-offs and opportunity costs visually. As you can see from Figure 1.6 (page 15), a nation or a business cannot produce more of one thing without giving up something. For example, if a nation starts with all civilian goods production and no military production—point E— it can only get to point D—some weapons production—by giving up some butter production. In other words, the price of having some weapons production (represented by the vertical distance from 0 to point X) is giving up some butter

production (represented by the horizontal distance from point E to point Y). The amount of civilian goods production given up in the year is the opportunity cost for increasing military production.

By using a production-possibilities curve, a nation or a business can decide how best to use its resources. By "best" is meant using resources most efficiently for economic growth. Such a curve is useful in locating the opportunity costs if a particular course of action is followed.

A Real-World Example: Military Downsizing in the 1990s From the 1950s until the early 1990s, the United States was engaged in a so-called cold war with the Soviet Union, and we produced more and more military goods. When that country split up into 15 separate republics, our major military adversary disappeared. Consequently, we needed to move from, say, point C to point D in Figure 1.6.

The real world and our graphs are not always quite the same, however. In the real world, it takes time to move from point C to point D. For example, our military had been purchasing guns, bombs, and planes from such major contractors as McDonnell-Douglas and Rockwell. In the 1990s, much of their military business evaporated. Some former military-hardware companies started making civilian goods as Figure 1.7 shows.

SECTION 2 REVIEW

Understanding Vocabulary

Define trade-off, opportunity cost, production possibilities.

Reviewing Objectives

❶ How are trade-offs and opportunity cost related?

❷ Explain how a production possibilities curve can show society's trade-offs.

Section 2 Review Answers

Understanding Vocabulary
trade-off (p. 13), **opportunity cost** (p. 14), **production possibilities** (p. 15)

Reviewing Objectives
1. Every trade-off involves an opportunity cost.

2. It shows a society's trade-offs as one moves from point to point on the curve. A quantity of one product is given up when a greater quantity of the other product is produced.

Personal Perspective

Robert L. Heilbroner on the Great Economists

Profile

- 1919–
- attended Harvard University and the New School for Social Research in New York City
- has taught at the New School for Social Research since 1972
- published works include *The Worldly Philosophers* (1953), *The Future as History* (1960), *The Great Ascent* (1963), *Between Capitalism and Socialism* (1970), and *The Nature and Logic of Capitalism* (1985)

Robert L. Heilbroner's book *The Worldly Philosophers* gives a unique and insightful look into the lives and works of the great economists of the past. In his introduction, Heilbroner explains the importance of these great economists to history.

By all the rules of schoolboy history books, they were nonentities: they commanded no armies, sent no men to their deaths, ruled no empires, took little part in history-making decisions. . . . Yet what they did was more decisive for history than many acts of statesmen who basked in brighter glory, often more profoundly disturbing than the shuttling of armies back and forth across frontiers, more powerful for good and bad than the edicts of kings and legislatures. It was this: they shaped and swayed men's minds.

Heilbroner expresses his belief that economists have a major impact on the world:

And because he who enlists a man's mind wields a power even greater than the sword or the scepter, these men shaped and swayed the world. Few of them ever lifted a finger in action; . . . But they left in their train shattered empires and exploded continents, they buttressed and undermined regimes, they set class against class and even nation against nation— not because they plotted mischief, but because of the extraordinary power of their ideas.

He disagrees with the perception that the work of economists is dull and boring:

. . . A man who thinks that economics is only a matter for professors forgets that this is the science that has sent men to the barricades. . . . No, the great economists pursued an inquiry as exciting—and as dangerous—as any the world has ever known. . . . The notions of the great economists were world-shaking, and their mistakes nothing short of calamitous.

Checking for Understanding

1. Why is it important to study the great economists of the past?
2. Have economists made a real difference in the world?
3. What does Heilbroner believe about the power of economists' ideas?

Answers to Checking for Understanding

1. Answers will vary but should indicate that it is important to study the great economists because their ideas had historical implications.
2. Answers will vary but should indicate that economists made a difference in that their ideas, when incorporated, shaped economic policies and practices.
3. Answers will vary but should indicate that economists' ideas have affected ideas about politics and government and how societies should be ruled.

TEACHING
Personal Perspective

Background

Robert Heilbroner is a well-known economist whose works reflect the belief that economics is a dynamic, exciting science. In the 1930s, during his studies at Harvard University, he became fascinated with the economic theories of Adam Smith, Karl Marx, and John Stuart Mill. Heilbroner received his doctoral degree from the New School for Social Research in New York City.

Teach

Have volunteers read aloud the quoted excerpts from Heilbroner's *The Worldly Philosophers*. Then have students paraphrase each excerpt to gain a better understanding of Heilbroner's ideas. Finally, have students answer the questions in Checking for Understanding.

You might have interested students choose chapters from *The Worldly Philosophers* to read and write a report on the particular philosopher's or economist's theories. Have them summarize the person's theory and comment on its relevance today.

Focus

Overview

See the student page for section objectives.

Section 3 explains or describes the use of economic models by economists.

Bellringer

Before presenting the lesson, display Focus Activity Transparency 3 on the overhead projector or copy the material on the chalkboard. Assign the accompanying Focus Activity Sheet.

Motivational Activity

Write the following on the chalkboard for students to answer: What do weather forecasters use to predict the weather? Discuss students' responses. Tell students that weather forecasters use models to predict the weather.

Preteaching Vocabulary

Write the terms *values*, *hypothesis*, and *generalization* on the chalkboard. Have students find definitions. Ask which terms deal with scientific procedures. (*hypothesis, generalization*)

SECTION 3 What Do Economists Do?

SECTION 3 FOCUS

Terms to Know economy, economic model, hypotheses, values, generalization

Objectives *After reading this section, you should be able to:*
1. Describe and give examples of economic models.
2. Explain the purpose of economic models.
3. Explain why there are different schools of economic thought.
4. Tell why economists do not normally work with values.

Economists Use Models to Study the Real World

Economics is concerned with the ways individuals and nations choose to use their scarce resources. For example, economists might analyze teenagers' spending and its effect on the economy. See **Figure 1.8**. To economists, **economy** means all the activity in a nation that together affects the production, distribution, and use of goods and services.

To carry out their investigations, economists often gather information from the real world. These data then become the basis for testing theories that explain an event, such as rising unemployment. The theories or solutions then become the basis for actual decisions by private business or government agencies.

Figure 1.8
Teen Buying Power
United States teenagers spend billions of dollars each year on clothing and other items. Their buying patterns definitely affect the types of goods that are produced.

Economic Models

In their work, economists use economic models, or theories. An **economic model** is a simplified representation of the real world. Physicists, chemists, biologists, and other scientists also use models to explain in simple terms the complex workings of the world.

What Models Show Economic models show the way people react to changes in the economy. The most frequently used model explains how people react to changes in the prices of goods and services they want to purchase. An economist has three ways of presenting such a model: through an

---

Classroom Resources for Section 3

- Reproducible Lesson Plan 1.3
- Focus Activity Transparency 3
- Focus Activity Sheet 3
- Guided Reading Activity 1.3
- Consumer Application Activity 1
- Mathematics Practice for Economics 1

- Performance Assessment Activity 1
- Section Quiz 1.3
- Spanish Section Quiz 1.3
- Chapter 1 Test Forms A and B
- Testmaker
- Enrichment Activity 1

- Economics Vocabulary Activity 1
- Spanish Economics Vocabulary Activity 1
- Audiocassette 1
- Spanish Audiocassette 1
- Reteaching Activity 1
- Spanish Reteaching Activity 1

explanation in words, in a graph, or with a mathematical equation. Whichever method is chosen, the information in the model is the same, as shown in Figure 1.9.

Limits of Models No economic model records every detail and relationship that exists about a problem to be studied. A model will show only the basic factors needed to analyze the problem. For example, economists have found that they need to analyze only three basic factors to determine buyer reaction to price changes. These factors are the price of the item, the income of the average buyer, and the price of alternative items.

The Purpose of Models

As you study economics, it is important to keep in mind the purpose of economic models. They are not supposed to account for all the possible factors that might influence a problem. They take into account only the most important ones.

Creating An economist considers a model *good* if it provides useful material for analyzing the way the real world works. As in forming a hypothesis, an economist begins with some idea about the way things work, then collects facts and discards those that are not relevant. Once a conclusion is reached, the only way an economist can find out whether a model works is to test it.

Testing Suppose an economist has developed the model shown in Figure 1.10 (page 20). The economist tests the model in the same way that other scientists test **hypotheses,** educated guesses, or predictions, used as the starting points for investigations, as shown in Figure 1.11 (page 21).

For the model in Figure 1.10 (page 20), an economist would collect data on the amount of teenage unemployment every year for the last 30 years.

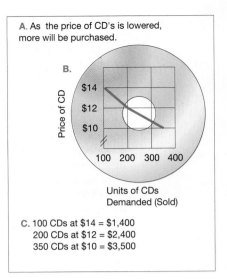

A. As the price of CD's is lowered, more will be purchased.

B.

C. 100 CDs at $14 = $1,400
200 CDs at $12 = $2,400
350 CDs at $10 = $3,500

**Figure 1.9
Economic Models of CD Prices**
In the case of prices, these three ways of presenting the model all show that consumers respond to lower prices by purchasing more of less expensive items.

He or she also would gather information on the frequency of federal legislation increasing the legal minimum wage paid to teenagers.

Suppose the economist finds that every time the minimum wage rate increased, teenage unemployment increased. The economist can be fairly satisfied with the model. See Figure 1.10, graph A.

Suppose that the data does not seem to show a relationship between teenage unemployment and increases in the legal minimum wage. See Figure 1.10, graph B. The economist then will have to develop another model to explain changes in teenage unemployment.

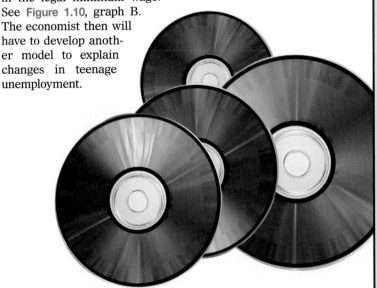

Chapter 1 What Is Economics? **19**

Teach

Guided Practice

L3 Synthesizing Have students use the information in Figure 1.11 (page 21) and the example on pages 19–20 regarding minimum wage and teenage unemployment to develop and test a hypothesis.

Visual Instruction

Refer students to Figure 1.9 and Figure 1.10 (page 20) along with the text discussion of economic models. Then organize the class into small groups to develop a model for some familiar situation such as plans for football plays, or a diagram for putting an item together.

Group members should discuss ideas for their model, decide on ways to represent and create it, and choose someone to present it.

? DID YOU KNOW

Economic models do not always predict accurately. For example, economists in the 1970s were surprised when the traditional method of tightening monetary and fiscal policy failed to slow the rate of inflation but did increase the unemployment rate, creating a situation known as *stagflation.*

◆ ▷ ◯ Meeting Special Needs

Language Disability Practice is an important part of learning. Those with weaker reading skills need guided practice, which is phased out as mastery of the skill occurs. Have students restate sentences in Section 3, using

common language. Listen to students' sentences to be sure that they understand that you are not asking simply for a rearrangement of words, but for them to state the idea of the sentence in their own words.

Independent Practice

L1 Creating a Mural Have students review the definition of *economy*. Then have them work in small groups to create a mural depicting the factors that contribute to a nation's economy (*production, distribution, and use of goods and services*). `LEP`

L3 Debating To provide an example of economic issues about which opinions differ, have volunteers debate the following: More money should be spent on education, even if it means raising taxes. Have the class analyze the differences in values that the debate illustrates.

Have students complete Guided Reading Activity 1.3 in the TCR. `LEP`

Assess

Meeting Lesson Objectives

Assign Section 3 Review as homework or an in-class activity.

Evaluate

Assign the Section 3 Quiz in the TCR or use the Testmaker to develop a customized quiz.

Assign the Chapter 1 Test Form A or Form B or use the Testmaker to develop a customized test.

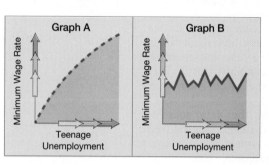

Applying Much of the work of economists involves predicting how people will react in a particular situation. Individual human behavior is not always predictable, however. As a result, an economist's answer to a specific problem may turn out not to work for everyone.

For example, to stimulate the economy, some economists believe that taxes should be cut and government spending increased. These economists believe that cutting taxes will raise personal spending, which, in turn, will increase total production.

However, some people's fears concerning possible higher taxes in the future might cause them to save the extra money rather than spend it. As this illustrates, economists cannot predict all the factors that may influence people's behavior.

Schools of Economic Thought

Economists deal with facts. Their personal opinions and beliefs may nonetheless influence how they view those facts and fit them to theories. The government under which an economist lives also shapes how he or she views the world. As a result, all economists will not agree that a partic-

Figure 1.10 ▲ **Testing an Economic Model** Economists, like scientists, must collect data to prove or disprove their theories. Graph A supports the direct relationship between increases in the legal minimum wage rate and increases in teenage unemployment. Graph B does not support that relationship.

ular theory offers the best solution to a problem. Often, economists from competing schools of thought claim that their theories alone will predict a certain result.

At a particular time, a nation's political leaders may agree with one school of economic thought and develop policies based on it. Later, leaders may agree with another group of economists. For example, during the 1980s, many economists stressed the role of businesses and consumers rather than of the government in preventing increased unemployment and inflation. In the 1990s, however, many influential national leaders proposed that the federal government should intervene in the economy to reduce unemployment.

Values and Economics

Economics will help you to predict what may happen if certain events occur or certain policies are followed. Economics will not, however, tell you whether the result will be good or bad. That judgment will depend on your values.

Values are the beliefs or characteristics that a person or group considers important, such as religious freedom,

Cooperative Learning

Organize the class into groups of three or four. Have each group try to find economic models in issues of newspapers or magazines. Groups should record whether the method of presentation was in words, in a graph, or as a mathematical equation. Have the class create a graph to show which method was used most often.

Figure 1.11 Using a Hypothesis

The list below reviews the steps involved in making and testing hypotheses. In working with models, economists use these same steps.

1. Define the problem.

2. From the possible alternatives, state a hypothesis that appears to offer the best solution to a problem or explanation of an event.

3. Gather data to test the hypothesis. Besides using facts from the real world, an economist must identify economic principles involved.

4. Evaluate the data and discard any that are not relevant, or related to the immediate situation, or that are not objective (those that are based on fact).

5. Make sure there are enough data to test the hypothesis thoroughly.

6. Develop a conclusion based on the data. To do this, an economist evaluates whether the alternative is the best, in view of its consequences and trade-offs.

7. If the hypothesis appears to be proved, retest it with new data to see if the same results can be obtained again.

8. If the hypothesis appears to be proved, form a generalization that can be applied to other cases. A **generalization** pulls together common ideas among facts and is true in most cases. For an economist, this step involves developing an economic policy based on the best alternative.

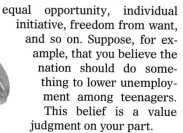

equal opportunity, individual initiative, freedom from want, and so on. Suppose, for example, that you believe the nation should do something to lower unemployment among teenagers. This belief is a value judgment on your part.

If you were a legislator, you might show your commitment to this value by introducing a bill to decrease teenage unemployment. The economists who help you research the causes of teenage unemployment may not tell you whether your bill is good or bad. They will tell you whether the proposed solution may be workable or not.

Having the same values does not mean that people will agree about solutions, strategies, or interpretation of data. For example, those in favor of decreasing teenage unemployment may disagree about the best way to solve this problem.

SECTION 3 REVIEW

Understanding Vocabulary

Define economy, economic model, hypotheses, values, generalization.

Reviewing Objectives

1 What are three ways of presenting an economic model?

2 What is the purpose of economic models?

3 Why do not all economists agree on the same solutions to problems?

4 Briefly explain why economists do not deal with values.

News Clip

Readings in Economics

THE BOSTON GLOBE   JUNE 8, 1993

RUNNER'S HIGH
by Aaron Zitner

A few well chosen complimentary words in a consumer magazine have meant more than a few dollars to Hyde Athletic Industries Inc. Sales of Hyde's Saucony running shoes soared after both men's and women's models received "No. 1" performance ratings from *Consumer Reports* in May 1992. Shares in the Peabody footwear company raced ahead 275 percent for the 12 months ended on May 14, the biggest gain by a Massachusetts stock.

Saucony shoes were selling well before the rating appeared, said Lisa Costa, a company spokeswoman. But they were little known outside the small world of high-performance athletes.

"The article got our name out there to the masses," Costa said.

"We had some momentum going, and when the article hit, it took the momentum and really carried it."

Hyde also makes roller skates, ice skates and skateboards under the Brookfield name and shoes for coaches and officials under the Spotbilt name.

Saucony produces walking, tennis, and hiking shoes.

But the Saucony running shoes are Hyde's chief product. The company employs about 120 people at its corporate office in Peabody and about 300 at its running shoe factory in Bangor, Maine.

In 1992, Hyde's earnings rose 230 percent to $3.4 million. Revenue rose 40 percent to $81.3 million. Hyde shares went for 22½ in mid-May, up from 6 a year earlier.

The company is redoubling its efforts to make its name known overseas. It recently opened an office in Britain and enhanced its relationships with distributors in the Netherlands and Canada.

• THINK ABOUT IT •

1. *How did* Consumer Reports' *rating of Saucony shoes affect sales?*

2. *How is Hyde Athletic Industries trying to broaden its markets?*

Highlights

Use the Chapter 1 Highlights to preview, review, condense, or reteach the chapter. A Spanish Chapter Highlights is available in the Spanish Handbook.

Preview/Review

After students read the Chapter 1 Highlights, have them complete Economics Vocabulary Activity 1 in the TCR. Spanish Vocabulary Activities are also available in the Spanish Resource Binder.

Vocabulary Software reinforces the economic terms used in Chapter 1.

Condense

Have students listen to Chapter 1 on the Audiocassettes in the TCR. A 1-page written activity and 1-page test accompany this material. These materials are also available in Spanish.

Reteach

Have students complete Reteaching Activity 1 in the TCR. Spanish Reteaching Activities are also available.

 VIDEODISC

Nightly Business Report
Economics in Action
Use "Introduction" on Disc 1, Side A, Video 1.

Search 307, Play to 2334

Section 1

The Basic Problem in Economics

Key Terms

economics (p. 8)
resource (p. 8)
scarcity (p. 9)
wants (p. 9)
land (p. 10)
labor (p. 10)

capital (p. 10)
productivity (p. 10)
entrepreneurship (p. 11)
factors of production (p. 11)
goods and services (p. 11)
technology (p. 11)

Summary
Scarcity is the basic problem in economics. Economics is the study of how individuals and nations make choices about how to use scarce resources to fulfill their wants. Production involves the factors of land, labor, capital, and entrepreneurship. Some economists also include technology.

Section 2

Trade-Offs

Key Terms

trade-off (p. 13)
opportunity cost (p. 14)
production
   possibilities (p. 15)

Summary
Whenever one thing or activity must be given up in order to have another thing or activity, a trade-off has occurred. Whatever has to be given up is called the opportunity cost of an action. A production-possibilities curve shows the maximum amount of goods that can be produced with the nation's resources during any given time period. When a nation operates on the production-possibilities curve, it is producing in an efficient manner.

Section 3

What Do Economists Do?

Key Terms

economy (p. 18)
economic model (p. 18)
hypotheses (p. 19)
values (p. 20)
generalization (p. 21)

Summary
Economists look at economic data from the real world to test economic models that they formulate about the behavior of people and businesses. Economic models are representative of reality that take into account only the most important factors that might influence a problem. Economic models and economists do not tell whether certain policies are good or bad, because such judgments depend on a person's values.

Chapter 1 What Is Economics? **23**

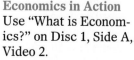 **VIDEODISC**

Nightly Business Report
Economics in Action
Use "What is Economics?" on Disc 1, Side A, Video 2.

Search 2438, Play to 8412

ANSWERS

Identifying Key Terms

1. scarcity
2. wants
3. factors of production
4. goods and services
5. technology
6. trade-off
7. opportunity cost
8. production possibilities

9. economic models
10. hypothesis
11. values
12. generalization

Student paragraphs should reflect understanding of the terms.

Recalling Facts and Ideas

Section 1
1. scarcity
2. Scarcity refers to the fixed, or set, amount of resources available and the limitations imposed by individuals' time and income. Shortages are temporary deprivations.

3. Answers will vary. It would be a need if the clothes were an absolute necessity; it would be a want if the friend was just expressing a desire.

4. land, labor, capital, entrepreneurship

Section 2
5. to exchange one thing for the use of another
6. opportunity cost
7. a foregone opportunity

8. production possibilities curve

Section 3
9. as the basis for testing theories that explain an event or offer a solution to a problem
10. an economic model
11. if it provides useful material for analyzing the way the real world works

---

Identifying Key Terms

Use the correct terms to fill in the blanks in the paragraph below:

scarcity (p. 9)
wants (p. 9)
factors of pro-
duction (p. 11)
goods and
services (p. 11)
technology (p. 11)
trade-off (p. 13)

opportunity cost (p. 14)
production
possibilities (p. 15)
economic models (p. 18)
hypotheses (p. 19)
values (p. 20)
generalization (p. 21)

Human __(1)__ are unlimited. Consequently, the problem of __(2)__ faces even the richest person on earth, particularly because that person has a limited amount of time on earth. When __(3)__ are used together to produce __(4)__, human wants can be satisfied. The use of __(5)__ can help us increase the amount of production we get from the resources in our economy. No matter how many resources we have, though, we always face a __(6)__. The production of one good always involves giving up the production of some other good or goods. This is called a __(7)__. The graphic representation of this trade-off is called a __(8)__ curve. Economists use __(9)__ to represent how the economy works. They set up a __(10)__ that they test with real-world information. If their tests work well, they come up with a __(11)__, but economists never can tell us about __(12)__.

Write a short paragraph about the factors of production in the United States using the following terms:

land (p. 10)
labor (p. 10)
capital (p. 10)
entrepreneurship (p. 11)

Recalling Facts and Ideas

Section 1
1. What is the condition that results because wants are unlimited, yet people cannot satisfy every desire?
2. What is the difference between scarcity and shortages?
3. Your friend says, "I need some new clothes." Under what conditions would this be expressing a need? A want?
4. List the four factors of production.

Section 2
5. What does making a trade-off require you to do?
6. What do economists call the next best alternative that had to be given up for the one chosen?
7. In economics, what is cost?
8. What do economists call a graph showing the combination of goods and services that can be produced from a fixed amount of resources in a given time period?

Section 3
9. For what purposes do economists use real-world data in building models?
10. An economic theory is another name for what?
11. When will an economist consider an economic model useful?

Critical Thinking

Section 1
Identifying Central Issues Tell why entrepreneurship is considered a factor of production.

Critical Thinking

Section 1
Entreprenership is considered a factor of production because it combines land, labor, and capital to form a business. It also involves a willingness to take the risks involved in forming and managing a business.

Section 2
The balance between military and civilian production at point C is about equal.

Section 3
Economists describe or predict behavior—the way people react. They are not concerned with value judgments and do not attempt to describe what people ought to think about a decision.

Section 2

Synthesizing Information Look again at the Production Possibilities Curve in Figure 1.6 (page 15). What is the balance between military and civilian production that is represented by point C on the graph?

Section 3

Analyzing Information What is the reason that economists will not tell you whether a possible solution to a problem will be good or bad?

Applying Economic Concepts

Trade-Offs and Opportunity Costs Because your time is scarce, you are constantly facing trade-offs. Make a list of the trade-offs you have made in choosing how you used your time during a one-week period. What activities did you choose to do? What were the opportunity costs involved in your choices?

Chapter Projects

1. **Individual Project** Watch the TV news and read newspapers for one week. Make a list of proposed actions on the part of federal, state, or local governments that may involve opportunity costs.
2. **Cooperative Learning Project** Working in groups of four, choose a consumer product such as a VCR, pencil, or automobile. Try to determine the elements of each of the four factors of production that went into making that consumer product. Consider, for example, that in making a VCR, there has to be land on which to put a factory. Consider also that in making a VCR, somebody has to take the risk of putting together the other three factors of production to form a company that will produce the VCR, and so on.

Reviewing Skills

Reading Tables and Graphs

1. The following graph shows the number of men and women in the U.S. labor force from 1980 to 2005. Approximately how many men were in the labor force in 1990? How many women? What is the estimated total number of people in the labor force in 2000?

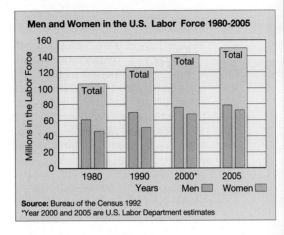

Men and Women in the U.S. Labor Force 1980-2005

Source: Bureau of the Census 1992
*Year 2000 and 2005 are U.S. Labor Department estimates

2. Make a bar graph of the following information.

Age of School Teachers in a Recent Year

Under 30 years old	66,000
30 to 39 years old	104,000
40 to 49 years old	83,000
over 50 years old	49,000

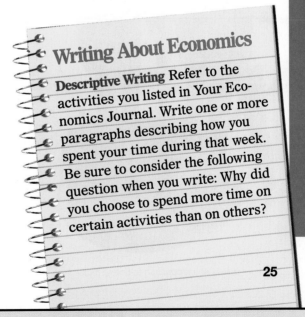

Writing About Economics

Descriptive Writing Refer to the activities you listed in Your Economics Journal. Write one or more paragraphs describing how you spent your time during that week. Be sure to consider the following question when you write: Why did you choose to spend more time on certain activities than on others?

25

Applying Economic Concepts

Answers will vary. Students should make sure that the opportunity cost includes only the next-highest-ranked alternative.

Chapter Projects

1. Review with students the definition of opportunity costs.
2. Students might present their information in the form of a diagram.

Reviewing Skills

1. 69 million; 57 million; 151 million
2. Encourage students to use the proper increments on the vertical or horizontal axes.

Writing About Economics

Encourage students to give specific reasons for spending time on certain activities.

? BONUS QUESTION

The following bonus question may be written on the chalkboard when students take the chapter test.
Q: When is an automobile considered to be capital?
A: when it is used to produce a service, such as pizza delivery, or in some cases to produce a good

ISSUE: Should the Government Require Domestic National Service?

During times of war, many Americans have been required to join the military. Until 1973, males over the age of 18 could be drafted into the military for a two-year period, even in peacetime. Never, however, has this nation required its young people to perform any other type of public service. Nonetheless, the idea of national service has been around for at least 100 years.

PRO One proposal by the Democratic Leadership Council in the late 1980s suggested that the government should form a "citizens' corps" of up to a million "volunteers" who would be paid $100 per week plus room and board. They would then be rewarded with government vouchers worth about $10,000 for each year of service. These vouchers could be used only for education or for buying a home.

Sociologist Charles C. Moskos claims that we need more national service programs because of the nation's unmet needs. Moskos contends that 3.5 million tasks that should be done are presently left undone in our society. These include many environmental and health-related tasks.

Nicola Clark, an editorial writer for the *Wall Street Journal*, believes strongly in the use of a national service corps. She argues that many countries use such a method:

The Danes, for example, dispatch their national servants as civilian public works laborers and foresters. French and Portuguese [national servants] are funneled to various humanitarian organizations or are sent to do development work in their former colonies. And in 1992 ... doctors in Switzerland actually proposed supplementing the newly introduced Swiss national service with a corps devoted to providing low-cost ambulatory care for the elderly. [President] Clinton has inundated Americans with proposals for expanded government programs in public works, environmental conservation, child care, health care, community policing—many of which are the kinds of things that are done by extremely low-paid conscripted national servants in other advanced industrialized countries. Why? Because it's the only way these governments can afford to make good on the generous welfare promises they have made to voters without burying their nations in debt. . . .

Counterpoint

CON Opponents of domestic national service stress that except in times of war, no one should be required to participate in any work that that person does not wish to do. They also contend that there is no way to define or quantify a nation's "unmet" needs because they are in fact infinite—there is no limit.

Opponents of domestic national service also use the opportunity cost concept. If a skilled individual holds a job for which he or she has no particular expertise, the opportunity cost is the lost production for the nation. We would be operating inside the production possibilities curve in Figure 1.6 (page 15) and would, therefore, be using resources inefficiently. Critics contend that requiring people to work in jobs that pay less than the market wage rate they could obtain elsewhere involves tremendous opportunity costs.

Another issue is the impact on private charities that would not receive funds. Bruce Chapman, president of Discovery Institution (a public policy center in Seattle, Washington), says: *Congressional hearings on President Clinton's national service plan and the public relations campaign advancing it almost always bring forward as spokesmen young, ingenuous participants in private charities. . . . But these admirable youngsters are not the organizers of the scheme, and they are not likely to understand its long-term implications for the voluntary sector as a whole. Nei-*

ther, apparently, does much of the disorganized opposition.

One sees this especially in respect to religious organizations, now the source of roughly half of all charitable activities. Because of understandable concerns over separation of church and state, national service will not support any programs that provide "religious instruction, conduct worship services or proselytize." But, effectively, that means that a church or synagogue running a youth leadership program or day-care center will be at a disadvantage against comparable national service programs.

Exploring the Issue

Reviewing Facts

1. What types of jobs would be done by people in a domestic national service program?
2. Explain the opportunity cost argument against having a domestic national service.

Critical Thinking

3. Who would most benefit from a mandatory domestic national service program? Who would lose the most?

L3 Research and Writing
Have students compare a national domestic service program with the Peace Corps. Have students research the organization and the effectiveness of the Peace Corps in its early years under Presidents Kennedy and Johnson. Students' written reports should compare the costs and benefits of the Peace Corps to potential costs and benefits of domestic national service. After presenting the similarities and differences of the two programs, students should conclude with a paragraph supporting or opposing domestic national service.

Assess

Have students answer the Exploring the Issue questions.

Close

Survey the class, asking how many students would work full-time in domestic national service for one year after college in exchange for the minimum wage and a $10,000 reduction of their student loan. Ask students to give reasons for their views.

Answers to Exploring the Issue

Reviewing Facts

1. tutoring students, restoring and protecting the environment, and providing health care
2. Any domestic national service requiring people to work in jobs paying less than market wages obtainable elsewhere involves tremendous opportunity cost.

Critical Thinking

3. Private charities that receive government funds would benefit most; religious-sponsored charities would lose most.

CHAPTER 2 *ECONOMIC SYSTEMS AND THE AMERICAN ECONOMY*

CHAPTER ORGANIZER

Daily Objectives	Special Features	Classroom Resources
Section 1 Economic Systems • **List** the four questions that all economic systems must answer. • **List and summarize** the major types of economic systems and their differences.	**Learning Economic Skills:** Understanding Percentages and Discounts, p. 36	Reproducible Lesson Plan 2.1 *NBR* Video 3 Focus Activity Transparency 5 Focus Activity Sheet 5 Economic Concepts Transparency 4 Guided Reading Activity 2.1 Cooperative Learning Activity 2 Primary and Secondary Source Readings 2 Free Enterprise Activity 1 Section Quiz 2.1 Spanish Section Quiz 2.1 Testmaker Reinforcing Skills 2
Section 2 Characteristics of the American Economy • **Describe** the role of government in the free enterprise system. • **Explain** the importance of freedom of enterprise in the American economy. • **Define** freedom of choice as it applies to the American free enterprise system. • **List** the advantages of private property. • **Identify** the role of the profit incentive. • **Evaluate** competition in the American free enterprise system.	**Personal Perspective:** Adam Smith on Free Enterprise, p. 41 **Focus on Free Enterprise:** Case Study, Blue Bell Creameries, pp. 42–43	Reproducible Lesson Plan 2.2 Focus Activity Transparency 6 Focus Activity Sheet 6 Economic Concepts Transparencies 3 and 5 Guided Reading Activity 2.2 Free Enterprise Activity 2 Consumer Application Activity 2 Section Quiz 2.2 Spanish Section Quiz 2.2
Section 3 The Goals of the Nation • **Describe** the major aims of a market economy. • **List** ways in which people can balance economic rights with economic responsibilities.	**News Clip:** "Prince of Midair," *Time,* p. 48	Reproducible Lesson Plan 2.3 Focus Activity Transparency 7 Focus Activity Sheet 7 Guided Reading Activity 2.3 Economics Laboratory 1 Economics Simulation 1 Mathematics Practice for Economics 2 Performance Assessment Activity 2 Section Quiz 2.3 Spanish Section Quiz 2.3 Enrichment Activity 2

 OUT OF TIME? If time does not permit teaching this chapter, you may use Chapter 2 Highlights and the Audiocassettes that include a 1-page activity and a 1-page test.

Chapter 2 Review and Evaluation

Special Features

Chapter 2 Highlights, p. 49
Chapter 2 Review, pp. 50–51
Economics Lab, pp. 52–53

Classroom Resources

Chapter 2 Test Forms A and B
Economics Vocabulary Activity 2
Spanish Economics Vocabulary
Activity 2

Audiocassette 2
Spanish Audiocassette 2
Reteaching Activity 2
Spanish Reteaching Activity 2

Key to Ability Levels

Teaching strategies have been coded for varying learning styles and abilities.

L1 Level 1 activities are **basic** activities and should be within the ability range of all students.

L2 Level 2 activities are **average** activities designed for the ability of the average to above-average students.

L3 Level 3 activities are **challenging** activities designed for the ability range of above-average students.

LEP activities are within the ability range of **Limited English Proficiency** students.

Performance Assessment

The following chapter project may be assigned at the beginning of the chapter and be used for performance assessment. See page T12 for additional Performance Assessment information.

Producing a Commercial Organize the class into four groups. Assign each group one of the four main economic systems: traditional, command, market, or mixed. Tell students in each group that they are to devise a commercial that will convince the rest of the class that their economic system is preferable. Commercials must answer the four basic questions about how their economy uses resources.

Allow some class time for brainstorming ideas and writing the script. Students can practice their commercials out of class. Have each group present their persuasive commercial. If equipment is available, videotape the commercials. Then let the class vote on the economic system they prefer, based on information given in the commercials.

Additional Resources

Readings for the Student

Friedman, Milton, and Friedman, Rose. *Free to Choose: A Personal Statement.* New York: Harcourt Brace Jovanovich, 1980.

Readings for the Teacher

Carson, Robert B. *What Economists Know: An Economic Policy for the 1990s and Beyond.* New York: St Martin's Press, 1989.

Eatwell, John et al. *New Palgrave Series: The World of Economics: Essays in the Worldly Philosophy.* New York: W. W. Norton, 1991.

Multimedia Materials

Economic Simulations. Computer Software. 127 East MacArthur Ave., Eau Claire, WI 54701

Mr. Both. Videotape. 28 min. American Economic Foundation, 50 Public Square, Suite 1215, Cleveland, OH 44113

The Mixed Economy System. Videotape. 12 min. Zenger Video, A Division of Social Studies School Service, 10200 Jefferson Boulevard, Room D, Culver City, CA 90232-0802

Chapter Overview

An economic system is the means by which society produces and distributes goods and services. Chapter 2 explains or describes: how principles taught in Chapter 1 affect the way businesses, individuals, and governments make economic decisions; how economic systems answer basic questions about production and distribution of goods and services; how economic systems differ; and what constitutes the major characteristics of the United States market system.

VIDEODISC

Nightly Business Report

Economics in Action
Use "Economic Systems and the American Economy" on Disc 1, Side A, Video 3.

Search 8492, Play to 14994

CHAPTER

2 ECONOMIC SYSTEMS AND THE AMERICAN ECONOMY

Who produced these jeans?

How were they produced?

How did they know how many to make?

Answering Economic Questions

Questions from the above illustration are designed to lead into the main concepts in Chapter 2. Production and distribution of goods and services are areas most students take for granted. The questions ask them to think about related economic decisions. For example, the answer to "Who produced these jeans?" involves more than the name of a manufacturer. It includes all the capital and labor for each step of production. "How were they produced?" introduces the many factors of production: land, labor, capital, and entrepreneurship. Have students explore the economic decisions behind each question.

Does the producer or the government guarantee the quality of these jeans?

What factors determined the price of these jeans?

How much do these jeans cost?

Who will buy this product?

Your Economics Journal

Keep track of the consumer goods and services you purchase in a week. List these items and their prices in your journal. Next to each item explain why you made the purchase.

29

Connecting to Past Learning

Review with students the concepts of scarcity, trade-offs, and opportunity costs presented in Chapter 1.

Applying Economics

Organize the class into groups representing traditional, command, and market systems. Instruct members of the traditional group to arrange themselves in rows from front to back according to height, shortest to tallest. Assign seats for the command group alphabetically. Tell market group members they have 30 seconds to choose their own seats. Anyone who is not seated after 30 seconds will be assigned a seat. Discuss their reactions to each of the three systems. Relate the activity to economic systems.

EXTRA CREDIT PROJECT

Suggest writing a research paper on the history of economics in the nineteenth century and make an oral report to the class.

PERFORMANCE ASSESSMENT

Refer to page 28B for "Producing a Commercial," a performance assessment for this chapter.

Economic Portfolio

Have students add to their **Economic Portfolio,** begun in Chapter 1, by including **Your Economics Journal** writing activities. Tell students to complete their lists of items and explanations for each purchase in the journal. Direct them to write a paragraph titled "Influences on the Consumer in a Free Enterprise System" that explains the major factors influencing their buying habits.

Focus

Overview

See the student page for section objectives.

Section 1 explains or describes the four basic questions that define the major economic systems, and the concepts of traditional, command, market, and mixed economies.

Bellringer

Before presenting the lesson, display Focus Activity Transparency 5 on the overhead projector or copy the material on the chalkboard. Assign the accompanying Focus Activity Sheet.

Motivational Activity

Have the class brainstorm words that come to mind when they think of the economy. Choose a student to write these expressions on the chalkboard. After several suggestions are made, discuss the reasons for some of the responses.

Preteaching Vocabulary

Write the vocabulary terms on the chalkboard and ask volunteers to tell what they think they mean. Have a student list responses next to the terms. Then compare students' ideas with definitions in the Glossary.

SECTION 1 Economic Systems

SECTION 1 FOCUS

Terms to Know economic system, distribution of income, traditional economic system, command economic system, market economic system, market, mixed economy

Objectives *After reading this section, you should be able to:*

① List the **four questions** that all economic systems must answer.

② List and summarize the **major types of economic systems** and their differences.

Economic Systems Determine Use of Resources

As a young adult, you probably have set some goals for your life, even if they are short-term. They might be no more distant than finishing this year in school or getting a part-time job. You may have long-term goals such as going to vocational school or to college, learning a trade or profession, or opening a business.

If you were to make a list of your personal goals and compare it with a list a person of your age made in another part of the world, the lists would be very different. One of the reasons the lists would be very different is that each nation has a different **economic system,** or way in which it uses its resources to satisfy its people's needs and wants.

Four Basic Questions

Every nation's economic system is faced with answering the same four basic questions: What goods and services and how much of each should be produced? Who should produce them? How should they be produced? Who should share in their use? Figure 2.1 examines these questions.

Businesses must determine the most efficient mix of the factors of production. Prices affect decisions about what and how much to produce. The type of economic system determines who should produce what.

Classroom Resources for Section 1

Reproducible Lesson Plan 2.1
NBR Video 3
Focus Activity Transparency 5
Focus Activity Sheet 5
Economic Concepts Transparency 4
Guided Reading Activity 2.1
Cooperative Learning Activity 2

Primary and Secondary Source Readings 2
Free Enterprise Activity 1
Section Quiz 2.1
Spanish Section Quiz 2.1
Testmaker
Reinforcing Skills 2

Figure 2.1 The Four Basic Economic Questions

The way each economic system answers these questions affects how every person within that system uses goods and services.

A How Should Goods and Services ▶
Be Produced?
For each good and service produced, there is always a trade-off possible among the available factors of production. For example, a farmer could use 10 laborers with horse-drawn plows to plow a field or 1 tractor and driver. Owners and/or managers of businesses must decide what combination of available resources will get the job done for the least cost.

B What and How Much Should Be Produced?
We live in a world of scarcity and
◀ trade-offs. If more of one item is
produced, then less of something else will be produced. For example, an automobile manufacturer must decide how to use its limited supply of labor, steel, rubber, and so on. Should it produce pickup trucks or full-sized automobiles? How much of each?

C Who Should Produce What?
Within each economic system, different people do different jobs. Who decides which people will produce which goods and services? This question relates directly to choice of career—auto mechanic, teacher, musician, and so forth. ▼

D Who Should Share
in What is Produced?
Money payment for work, the amount of health care, education, food, and so on, that each person receives are all part of the **distribution of income.** This last question relates to how goods and services are distributed among all members of
◀ an economic system.

Chapter 2 *Economic Systems and the American Economy* **31**

Teach

Guided Practice

L2 Research and Analysis
Organize the class into small groups to prepare a report on the basic question of who should produce goods and services. Suggest that students locate employment statistics for the United States at five-year intervals from 1951 through 1990, specifically for size of work force, principal industries, and numbers of men and women in each. Recommend incorporating data in a written report illustrated with graphs and tables as needed. Have a volunteer make an oral presentation and encourage students to make inferences about our economy over the four decades surveyed.

 DID YOU KNOW

The total number of people enrolled in college rose by 1.8 million in the 1980s despite a decline of 2.7 million people in the "traditional" college-age population. College attendance by students more than 25 years old increased dramatically.

 Meeting Special Needs

Reading Disability To increase text comprehension, tell students to read the Section Focus before reading the entire section. Students with visual disabilities may want to read the section orally. Knowing what to look for before reading helps students who have difficulty focusing attention to gain direction.

Types of Economic Systems

Each society answers the four basic questions according to its view of how best to satisfy the needs and wants of its people. The values and goals that a society sets for itself determine the kind of economic system it will have. Economists have identified four types of economic systems: traditional; command, or controlled; market, or capitalist; and mixed. Remember as you read this section that the economic systems described are pure, or ideal, types. They are economic models, not examples of the real world.

**Figure 2.2
Traditional Economy**
The San people of the Kalahari (kal-uh-HAHR-ee) Desert of South Africa continue to live in a traditional economy. They are nomadic, or roving, hunters and plant gatherers. When the food in an area is used up, the group moves on in search of new food supplies. ▶

Traditional System A pure **traditional economic system** answers the four basic questions according to tradition. **Figure 2.2** illustrates one such system in which tradition dictates the role each individual plays. In such a system, things are done "the way they have always been done." Economic decisions are based on customs, beliefs—often religious—and ways of doing things that have been handed down from generation to generation. Traditional economic systems exist today in very limited parts of Asia, the Middle East, Africa, and Latin America.

Cooperative Learning

Review the four basic questions and organize the class into groups of 4 to 6 students. Tell groups they each represent a governing body that must solve a problem by considering the economic questions. Write the problem on the chalkboard: "The people of your nation are experiencing health problems because of a vitamin C deficiency in their diets. You know that citrus fruit could solve this problem, but your climate prohibits growth of these fruit trees." Tell students they have 10 minutes to solve this problem. Have groups share their solutions with the class, and ask how each group used the basic economic questions to address this issue.

Command, or Controlled, System

The traditional economic system is in some ways similar to a pure command economic system. In a pure **command economic system,** the individual has little, if any, influence over how the basic economic questions are answered. See **Figure 2.3**. Government controls the factors of production and, therefore, makes all decisions about their use. This is why this form of economic system is also called a controlled economy.

The government may be one person, a small group of leaders, or a group of central planners in a government agency. These people choose how resources are to be used at each stage in production and decide the distribution of goods and services. They even decide who will do what. The government, through a series of regulations about the kinds and amount of education available to different groups, guides people into certain jobs.

Market, or Capitalist, System

The opposite of a pure command economic system is a pure **market economic system**—or capitalism. In a pure market economic system, government does not intervene. Individuals own the factors of production, and they decide for themselves the answers to the four basic economic questions.

Economic decisions are made through the free interaction of individuals looking out for their own best interests in the market. **Market** in this sense is not a place. Rather, it is the freely chosen activity between buyers and sellers of goods and services.

Buyers and sellers freely choose to do business with those

who best satisfy their needs and wants. The exchange of goods and services may take place in a worldwide market for a good such as crude oil. It may also take place in a neighborhood market for the services of someone to mow lawns, deliver papers, or shovel the snow.

In a pure market economic system, producers of goods and services decide how to use their resources based solely on signals from the market. Government planning has no part in the decisions. Whether people buy a certain good or service or not indicates to producers the various ways to use or not use their resources, as shown in **Figure 2.4** (page 34).

People are also free in a pure market economic system to sell their

Figure 2.3 ▲
Command Economy
Only a couple of countries in the entire world still have much of a command economy—North Korea and parts of the People's Republic of China are the two main examples because so much economic activity there is government-planned.

Independent Practice

L2 Comparing and Contrasting Ask students to prepare a table profiling the economies of North and South Korea during the period 1971 to 1980. Suggest that they concentrate on agriculture, natural resource development or mining, manufacturing, and foreign trade.

L3 Writing Tell students they each represent an imaginary country that has a command economy. Direct them to write a paragraph identifying the officials in their country who plan economic functions. Suggest that they indicate what these individuals or groups control and the effect on citizens. Let volunteers read their description to the class.

 GLOBAL ECONOMICS

Geographic disadvantage does not necessarily preclude a developed economy. Although Switzerland is land-locked, mountainous, small in area, and lacking in many natural resources needed for modern industry, it has one of the world's most highly developed and technologically advanced manufacturing economies. It also exerts influence on market economies worldwide through its role in international banking.

 Free Enterprise Activity

Organize the class into four groups. Have each group plan starting up a business. The first group should choose a business in manufacturing, the second group one from transportation, the third group one from communications, and the fourth group one from the service industry. Explain that they must consider how they will obtain start-up capital. Groups must also research whether government regulation will affect manufacture of the products or delivery of services. Finally, groups should plan how they will operate the business. Have each group give an oral report on its business.

Independent Practice

L2 Compiling Data Have students research and locate places in Central and South America that have traditional economies. Recommend presenting these findings in a chart that names traditional economic features in the headings and lists below them the nations or places where they apply.

 Have students complete Guided Reading Activity 2.1 in the TCR. **LEP**

Visual Instruction

Have students study the Figure 2.5 flow chart. Ask them to draw a similar flow chart that shows how income and products flow to businesses and individuals in a command economy. Ask what components need to be added or subtracted.

? DID YOU KNOW

An element of traditional economy persists in the United States. This is barter, or the exchange of goods and services of approximately equal value. Loss of tax revenues in the 1980s resulted from unreported barter through private agreements.

---

labor as they wish. They may take, refuse, or change jobs whenever they choose. This assumes, of course, that there is a demand for their labor. **Figure 2.5** illustrates the flow of economic activity through the market in the capitalist system.

Mixed Economic System With the exception of the traditional economic system, it is doubtful whether these pure or ideal systems ever existed. They are useful models for analyzing existing systems, however. Today, almost all economic systems are what economists call mixed

economies. A **mixed economy** contains characteristics of a command economy and a pure market economy. **Figure 2.6** shows the two most prominent examples of mixed economies—one leans heavily toward the market model, the other toward the command model.

Figure 2.4 Demand Affects Production

Suppose that in a specific market economy more people begin buying the compact discs (CDs) of a particular rap group. This increase in demand signals the record company to invest more resources—time, money, effort—into producing CDs by that group. If, however, few people are buying CDs by another rap group, the CD company will not sign that group again. Buyers have signaled that they do not want more CDs by that group. ▼

Figure 2.5 ▲ Circular Flow of Economic Activity in a Market Economy

The inside arrows on the graph show individuals selling the factors of production to businesses, who use them to produce goods and services. The flow of money from businesses to individuals in the form of rent, wages, interest, and profits and its return to business as consumer spending, is illustrated on the outside of the graph.

Consumer Spending for Goods and Services

Production of Goods and Services

Business

Individuals

Sale or Rent of Resources (Land, Labor, Capital, Entrepreneurship)

Payments for Use of Resources (Wages, Interest, Rents, Profits)

👥 Cultural Diversity and Economics

Ask students to research and write a report on the effect of religious beliefs and value systems on economies in different parts of the world. Suggest study of all continents and major regions, such as the Middle East, Southeast Asia, India, and Oceania, as well as Europe, Africa, and the Americas.

Approve individual choices to avoid duplication. You may wish to combine the reports in a handbook to use as a class resource. Have students choose a handbook title and encourage volunteers to illustrate the reports and bind them together.

Figure 2.6
Two Mixed Economies
In mixed economies, the mix will vary so that any one economic system leans more toward one pure type than another.

A The United States tends much more toward the market system than toward the command system. Not all decisions, however, are made by individuals reacting to the market. Federal, state, and local governments make laws regulating some areas of business. Among these, for instance, are the rates that electric companies may charge.

▶

B Although the People's Republic of China still tends much more toward the command than toward the pure market system, the economy is changing. Many factories in China are owned by the government. Government officials tell the managers of those factories what to produce and how much. They also tell the factory managers at what price they should sell their output. There is a growing unrestricted market sector within that country, however. In some "special economic zones," citizens in the People's Republic of China make economic decisions without any interference by the government.

SECTION 1 REVIEW

Understanding Vocabulary
Define economic system, distribution of income, traditional economic system, command economic system, market economic system, market, mixed economy.

Reviewing Objectives
1. What four questions must all economic systems answer?
2. What are the major types of economic systems, and what are their differences?

Assess

Meeting Lesson Objectives
Assign Section 1 Review as homework or an in-class activity. Each question in the Review addresses the corresponding numbered objective in the Section Focus.

Evaluate
Assign the Section 1 Quiz in the TCR or use the Testmaker to develop a customized quiz.

Reteach
Have students imagine that they are castaways on a desert island. What do they need to survive? Write the four basic economic questions on the chalkboard as the focus for student responses. Record responses under the appropriate questions.

Enrich
Have students use newspaper or magazine articles that relate to each of the four basic economic questions to create a bulletin board display.

Close

Have students prepare a two-minute oral report about one of the major economic systems that explains why they would like to live under this system.

Section 1 Review Answers
Understanding Vocabulary
economic system (p. 30), **distribution of income** (p. 31), **traditional economic system** (p. 32), **command economic system** (p. 33), **market economic system** (p. 33), **market** (p. 33), **mixed economy** (p. 34)
Reviewing Objectives
1. What and how much should be produced? Who should produce what? How should goods and services be produced? Who should share in what is produced?
2. traditional—past practice dictates decisions; command—government controls factors of production; market—individuals guide, control factors of production; mixed—combines command, market approaches

Teach

Many students have difficulty understanding percentages. The purpose of this lesson is to define *percent*, solve percentage problems, and apply the skill to understanding discounts.

Empty two rolls of pennies (100 coins) into a container. Remove five pennies and ask students what percentage of the total number of pennies the five represent. Write the decimal .05 on the board. Tell students that *percent* means parts per hundred, just as cents are a portion or percentage of a dollar.

Call on a student who can determine the sales tax on an item that sells for $10.00 if the tax rate is 4 percent. Have the student write the calculation on the chalkboard (.04 × $10.00 = $.40).

Have students discuss the importance of percentages in everyday life. Read and compute the sample problems on the Learning Economic Skills page together. Then have students complete Practicing the Skill independently. Watch for students who place the decimal points incorrectly. Remind them that *percent* means parts per hundred.

Additional Practice

Have students complete Reinforcing Skills 2 in the TCR.

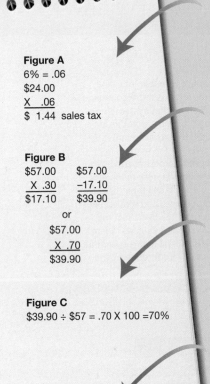

Figure A
6% = .06
$24.00
X .06
$ 1.44 sales tax

Figure B
$57.00 $57.00
X .30   −17.10
$17.10 $39.90
    or
  $57.00
  X .70
  $39.90

Figure C
$39.90 ÷ $57 = .70 X 100 =70%

Figure D
100% + 50% = 150%
150% ÷ 2 = 75%
100% − 75% = 25%

LEARNING ECONOMIC SKILLS
Understanding Percentages and Discounts

Economists use statistics to describe different population characteristics—occupations, income, and so on. Percentages are a useful form of statistics. Do you know how to use them?

Percentages

Percent means "parts per hundred." Sales taxes are figured in percents. Suppose a skirt costs $24 and the sales tax is 6 percent. As **Figure A** shows, the tax adds $.06 for every dollar of the price.

Figuring Percentages

Suppose a pair of shoes is 30 percent off the regular price. If the regular price was $57, what will the new price be? You can find the price by multiplying percent off by the original price and subtracting the discount. Or, as **Figure B** shows, you can multiply the original price by the percent you will pay (70 percent).

If the $57 shoes are on sale for $39.90, you can find the percent you are paying by dividing the amount you pay by the original price. See **Figure C**.

Percent and Actual Number

Is it a better discount if the store says you can buy the first pair for $57 and get the second pair for half price? You would pay 100 percent for the first pair of shoes and 50 percent (half) of the second. Total these percentages and divide by the number of pairs of shoes. You would pay 75 percent. **Figure D** shows that the discount is only 25 percent.

Practicing the Skill

❶ A store advertises jeans at 33 percent off the original price of $37. What is the new price?

Answers to Practicing the Skill
1. $24.79

SECTION 2 FOCUS

Terms to Know invisible hand, capitalism, free enterprise system, private property, profit, profit incentive, competition

Objectives *After reading this section, you should be able to:*

❶ Describe the role of government in the free enterprise system.

❷ Explain the importance of freedom of enterprise in the American economy.

❸ Define freedom of choice as it applies to the American free enterprise system.

❹ List the advantages of private property.

❺ Identify the role of the profit incentive.

❻ Evaluate competition in the American free enterprise system.

Free Enterprise with Some Regulations

A pure market economic system has six major characteristics: (1) little or no government control, (2) freedom of enterprise, (3) freedom of choice, (4) private property, (5) profit incentive, and (6) competition. These characteristics are interrelated, and to varying degrees all are present in the American economy.

In his book, *The Wealth of Nations*, Adam Smith in 1776 described a system in which government has little to do with a nation's economic activity. He said that individuals left on their own would work for their own self-interests. In doing this, they would be guided as if by an **invisible hand** of competition to achieve the maximum good for society.

The Role of Government

Smith's idea of the ideal economic system is called capitalism, another name for the market system. Economists argue whether capitalism in its pure form, as Smith described it, has ever existed. **Capitalism** as practiced in the United States today would be best defined as an economic system in which private individuals own the factors of production and decide how to use them within the limits of the law.

Smith's ideas influenced the Founders of the United States, who limited the role of government mainly to

Classroom Resources for Section 2

- 📂 Reproducible Lesson Plan 2.2
- 🔲 Focus Activity Transparency 6
- 📂 Focus Activity Sheet 6
- 🔲 Economic Concepts Transparencies 3 and 5
- 📂 Guided Reading Activity 2.2

- 📂 Free Enterprise Activity 2
- 📂 Consumer Application Activity 2
- 📂 Section Quiz 2.2
- 📂 Spanish Section Quiz 2.2
- 💽 Testmaker

Teach

Guided Practice

L2 Research Ask students to name a business they would like to start. Have them research and report on possible government regulations that might affect starting or running the business.

Visual Instruction

Refer students to Figure 2.7 and its caption and review individual rights under pure capitalism and discuss government responsibilities mentioned in the caption. Tell students to write a persuasive paragraph explaining why they prefer more or less government intervention in the economy.

Figure 2.7 U.S. Government Regulation Today the work of federal agencies includes regulating the quality of various foods and drugs, watching over the nation's money and banking system, inspecting workplaces for hazardous conditions, and guarding against damage to the environment. The federal government also uses tax money to provide social programs such as Medicare. State and local governments have also expanded their role in recent years in such areas as education, job training, recreation, support for the arts, and care for the elderly. ▶

38

national defense and keeping peace. Also, the Constitution as originally written and interpreted, limits the national government's control over economic activities.

Since the 1880s, the role of government—federal, state, and local—has increased significantly in the United States. This is especially true in the areas of regulating business and providing public services, as shown in **Figure 2.7**.

Freedom of Enterprise

The American economy is also called the **free enterprise system.** This term emphasizes that individuals are free to own and control the factors of production. For example, if you decide to go into business for yourself, your abilities and resources will help you decide the good or service to produce, the quantity, and the methods of production. Of course, you may lose your money. You, or any entrepreneur, have no guarantee of success. In addition, as **Figure 2.8** shows, certain legal limits restrict freedom of enterprise.

Freedom of Choice

Freedom of choice is the other side of freedom of enterprise. Freedom of choice means that buyers make the decisions about what should be produced. The success or failure of a good or service in the marketplace depends on individuals freely choosing what they want. The earlier example of people buying or not buying a particular group's CDs and the effects on the CD company illustrates this idea. The music company, in reality, may choose to continue making CDs with the group anyway, even though it knows it will not make much profit.

Although buyers are free to exercise their choice, the marketplace has become increasingly complex in this century. As a result, the government has intervened in various areas of the economy to protect buyers. Laws set safety standards for such things as toys, appliances, and automobiles. In industries in which only a few companies provide services, government regulates the price they may charge. This has happened with public utilities.

Private Property

Private property is simply what is owned by individuals or groups rather than by the federal, state, or local government. The Constitution guarantees an owner's rights to private property and its use. You as an individual are free to buy whatever you can afford whether it is land, a business, a home, an automobile, and so on. You can also control how, when, and by whom your property is used. If you own a business, you can keep any profit you make.

Meeting Special Needs

Attention Disorders To help students grasp the main idea, have them create a web as they read the section. Students should write the section title in the center of the web surrounded by a bubble for each important fact.

Bubbles with supporting details can extend from each fact. By taking small bits of information at a time and analyzing their importance, students with attention problems are better able to stay focused.

Profit is the money left after all the costs of production have been paid. These costs include wages, rent, interest, and taxes.

Within the United States, government at all levels owns some property. Parks, fire-fighting and police equipment, military bases, municipal buildings, and post offices are some examples of government-owned property. Under no circumstances, though, can any level of government in the United States expand its economic role by simply taking private property. This provision is one of the underlying principles of the Bill of Rights. Part of the Fifth Amendment reads:

Nor shall private property be taken for public use, without just compensation.

That clause simply means that if the federal, state, or local government believes it has to use private property, it must pay the private owners. Also, the government cannot make citizens use their private property to house soldiers.

Figure 2.8 ▲
Limits on Free Enterprise
In most states, teenagers must be 16 before they can work, and then laws set limits on how many hours they can work.

Profit Incentive

Whenever a person invests time, know-how, money, and other capital resources in a business, that investment is made with the idea of making a profit. The desire to make a profit is called the **profit incentive** (in-SENT-iv), and it is mainly this hope that moves people to produce things that others want to buy. After all, if no one buys what a seller produces, there will be no profit, only losses. See Figure 2.9.

The risk of failing is part of the free enterprise system. Some industries, however, are so large that their failure would seriously damage the economy and throw thousands of people out of work. In the past several decades, the federal government has passed laws providing special private loan guarantees to big corporations such as Lockheed and Chrysler, and even to the city of New York. The federal government has also aided farmers by providing them with loans.

Competition

Competition is the rivalry among producers or sellers of similar goods to win more business by offering the lowest prices or better quality.

Number of Competitors In many industries, effective competition requires a large number of independent buyers and sellers. This large number of competitors means that no one company can noticeably affect the price of a particular product.

Figure 2.9 ▲
Making a Profit
If you went into business decorating and selling T-shirts, you would expect to make enough money to cover your expenses and make some profit. What would some of this seller's expenses be?

Independent Practice

L1 Understanding Our Economy Because the United States has a mixed economy, there are often controls on the way Americans use their resources. Have students list the six characteristics of a pure market economic system. Next to each characteristic have them write different ways government limits these options.

L2 Mapmaking Have students research the type of economic systems that exist in each country on a given continent. Have students draw a map of their continent that identifies the countries and their economic systems. Display the maps on a bulletin board.

 Have students complete Guided Reading Activity 2.2 in the TCR. **LEP**

GLOBAL ECONOMICS

Belgium, where the major natural resource was coal, abandoned mining in the late 1950s as deposits became exhausted and production costs eroded profitability. Nearly self-sufficient in food production, Belgium today bases its economy on manufacture of chemicals, textiles, and steel products, mainly for export. Belgium is also a center for European trade organization.

Cooperative Learning

Have students review the six major components of a market economy. Then organize the class into small groups. Give each group a card with the name of a type of business, such as oil, computers, or fruit farming. Tell students their business is in trouble, and they must improve profits by evaluating alternatives offered within our free enterprise economy. Allow about 20 minutes for discussion before one member of each group reports on a business and how the group employed freedom of choice, free enterprise, profits, property, competition, and weak barriers to entry and exit to expand business.

Assess

Meeting Lesson Objectives

Assign Section 2 Review as homework or an in-class activity.

Evaluate

Assign the Section 2 Quiz in the TCR or use the Testmaker to develop a customized quiz.

Reteach

Direct students to write a letter to an imaginary person in The People's Republic of China explaining the six major characteristics of the American economy.

Enrich

Have students research a health-related profession and report on any related restrictions including government laws and licensing.

Close

Ask students to write a paragraph about how the free enterprise system affects their daily lives.

Figure 2.10 Competition and Price
Suppose that only one business makes a particular product such as a personal computer. It could charge as much as people who really want a personal computer are willing to pay. They have no alternative seller to turn to. Suppose a second company enters the market with a similar computer at a lower price. Then competition for buyers between the two businesses would force the price down. ▼

If one company attempts to raise its prices, potential customers can simply go to one of the many other sellers. In the ideal world, this is how competition would work. In practice, however, the federal government over the past 100 years has regulated some business practices in an attempt to make sure that competition exists. The opportunity to make a profit encourages competition, as Figure 2.10 shows.

Businesses have to keep prices low enough to attract buyers yet high enough to make a profit. This forces businesses to keep the costs of production as low as possible. Competitors who succeed do so because they are able to produce those goods that people want most at a price that makes people want to buy.

Easy Entry and Exit Competition also requires that companies can enter or exit any industry they choose. Those who feel that they could make more profit in another industry are free to get out of the industry they are in. Some companies expand into new industries while staying in their old one. A company currently producing and selling VCRs may determine that people prefer the added convenience and higher quality of videodiscs. The company may decide to move out of its old business and begin making videodisc players.

Economists say that such an economy has weak barriers to entry and exit from industries. For the most part, the United States has such weak barriers. Some industries, however, have tougher barriers to entry. For example, a person cannot become a doctor until he or she has passed through an approved medical school and received a license from a state government to practice medicine in that state. Government approval is needed to start a public utility or set up a television or radio station.

LOWEST PRICE $1099!

NOW $629

HURRY! LIMITED STOCK

NEW LOWER PRICE

SECTION 2 REVIEW

Understanding Vocabulary

Define invisible hand, capitalism, free enterprise system, private property, profit, profit incentive, competition.

Reviewing Objectives

1. What role does government play in the free enterprise system?
2. Why is freedom of enterprise one of the cornerstones of the American economy?
3. How does freedom of choice apply to the American free enterprise system?
4. What are the advantages of private property?
5. How does the profit incentive encourage business in the American economy?
6. Why is competition important in the American free enterprise system?

Section 2 Review Answers

Understanding Vocabulary
invisible hand (p. 37), **capitalism** (p. 37), **free enterprise system** (p. 38), **private property** (p. 38), **profit** (p. 39), **profit incentive** (p. 39), **competition** (p. 39)

Reviewing Objectives
1. a limited role
2. Americans may establish businesses, decide methods and quantities of production, and take risks in making or losing money.
3. Freedom of choice means buyers make decisions about what is produced.
4. Individuals can buy property, control how property is used, and keep profits from that property.
5. Profit incentive moves people to produce what others want to buy.
6. Competition ensures that prices reflect supply and demand, and it encourages sellers to create incentives to buy.

Personal Perspective

Adam Smith on Free Enterprise

Profile

- 1723-1790
- born Kirkaldy, County Fife, Scotland
- teacher at University of Glasgow
- lectured and wrote on moral philosophy
- published *An Inquiry into the Nature and Causes of the Wealth of Nations*, 1776
- called by many the founder of modern economics

In Adam Smith's *An Inquiry into the Nature and Causes of the Wealth of Nations*, he explains why government should not regulate business. He believed that individuals, seeking profit, direct their resources more efficiently than governments.

... No regulation of commerce can increase the quantity of industry in any society beyond what its capital [resources] can maintain. It can only divert a part of it into a direction into which it might not otherwise have gone. ... It is only for the sake of profit that any man employs a capital in support of industry; and he will always, therefore, endeavor to employ it in the support of that industry of which the produce is likely to be of the greatest value.

Smith then describes how the sum of all individual decisions will benefit society as a whole.

... As every individual, therefore, endeavors ... to employ his capital in the support of domestic industry, and so to direct that industry that its produce may be of the greatest value, every individual necessarily labours to render [direct] that annual revenue of the society as great as he can. He ... neither intends to promote the public interest, nor knows how much he is promoting it. By preferring the support of domestic to that of foreign industry, he intends only his own security; ... he intends only his own gain. ...

Smith concludes that government officials who would try to regulate business are overstepping their authority or lack good sense.

The statesman, who would attempt to direct private people in what manner they ought to employ their capitals, would ... assume an authority which could safely be trusted, not only to no single person, but to no council or senate whatever, and which would nowhere be so dangerous as in the hands of a man who had folly and presumption [reckless disregard] enough to fancy himself fit to exercise it.

Checking for Understanding

1. Why do individuals invest their capital?
2. How will the economic choices of the individual benefit society as a whole?
3. According to Smith, which government officials are presumptuous?

Chapter 2 *Economic Systems and the American Economy* **41**

Background

Adam Smith is often considered the founder of modern-day economics. His book about moral philosophy attracted the attention of Charles Townshend, a high government official who chose Smith to tutor his stepson and financed their travel to France. There Smith met Voltaire, and Montesquieu. Later, after meeting Benjamin Franklin, Smith wrote that the American Colonies seemed a nation "very likely to become one of the most formidable that ever was in the world." Smith had already made a name for himself as a teacher and writer of philosophy before producing *An Inquiry into the Nature and Causes of the Wealth of Nations*.

Teach

Discuss Smith's observations of government regulation, profit incentives, resource utilization, and the invisible hand. Point out that his observations still raise relevant questions: Can government create jobs? Can federal spending stimulate the economy?

Answers to Checking for Understanding

1. Individuals invest their capital for their own security and gain.
2. Individual economic choices benefit society by supporting domestic industry.
3. Government officials who attempt to authorize how individuals spend their capital are presumptuous.

Focus

Tell students that this feature focuses on a producer's ability to respond to market needs and wants. Suggest thinking about what makes a business successful while they read this feature.

Teach

After students finish reading, ask what key decisions the creamery made after 1958. List each answer on the chalkboard. (*Answers may include expanding to other towns; creating its own advertising agency; building a visitor center; adding light and diet ice cream to its product line; marketing Nonfat Frozen Yogurt; offering ice cream and yogurt in many shapes and sizes; keeping quality as a priority*)

Refer to the list and discuss which decisions were most directly related to supplying a consumer need and why they were important to the needs of the market.

CASE STUDY

Focus on Free Enterprise

Blue Bell Creameries, Inc.

 The Main Ingredient In 1907 the Brenham Creamery Company of Texas found a good use for the excess cream in the milk from area farms. They started making butter. Four years later the creamery found another, more delightful use for the cream. They made their first ice cream in a wooden tub filled with ice. Maximum production was two gallons per day. By 1919 Brenham Creamery was still small and struggling. E. F. Kruse, the new plant manager, knew that it was close to going out of business. He kept the company from going under by not cashing his paychecks until the creamery became profitable several months later.

Rising to the Top In 1930 the Brenham Creamery Company changed its name to Blue Bell Creameries, after a Texas wildflower. Like cream, Blue Bell began to rise to the top of the frozen dessert business. One factor that helped the company was the invention of home freezers.

Having freezers in the home created demand for a packaged take-home product. During World War II, E. F. Kruse's sons Ed and Howard, at ages 13 and 11, came to work, hand-wrapping ice cream sandwiches. Today they are respectively chairman of the board and chief executive officer of Blue Bell. One key move in Blue Bell's history was its decision to replace butter with ice cream as the featured product in 1958. Blue Bell began to branch out, opening facilities in Houston, Austin, Beaumont, and Dallas in the next 20 years.

 Advertising and Growth Opening new branches in major Texas cities nearly every year, Blue Bell decided to build its own advertising agency. Blue Bell Advertising Associates was launched in 1987. A new corporate headquarters and visitor center in Brenham opened the following year.

Diversifying Like other businesses, Blue Bell learned to pay attention to its customers' wants. As a result, the company added many new products. In 1989 Diet Blue Bell, the nation's first frozen dairy dessert made with NutraSweet and marketed in a half-gallon container, was introduced. Blue Bell Nonfat Frozen Yogurt and Blue Bell Free, a no-fat, no-sugar frozen dietary dessert, followed in 1991. In addition, the dairy now offers ice cream and yogurt in containers of many shapes and sizes: mini sandwiches, creme pops, fudge bars, drumsticks, cups, and tubs.

Crossing the State Line Distribution of Blue Bell products to Louisiana, Kansas, and Mexico began in the 1990s. Strict quality control measures and fresh ingredients have enhanced the company's reputation. *TIME*, *Sports Illustrated*, and *Forbes* have each touted Blue Bell's products. Perhaps that's because one key ingredient has not changed over the years—care.

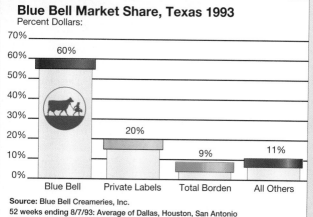

Blue Bell Market Share, Texas 1993
Percent Dollars:

Blue Bell	60%
Private Labels	20%
Total Borden	9%
All Others	11%

Source: Blue Bell Creameries, Inc.
52 weeks ending 8/7/93: Average of Dallas, Houston, San Antonio

Serving the Community Today Blue Bell Creameries, Inc., employs more than 600 Brenham-area workers. In addition, the company has about 900 workers distributing its ice cream in its distribution areas. In a recent year more than 100,000 people toured the facilities in Brenham.

Free Enterprise in Action

1. What was Brenham Creamery's first product?
2. What invention in the 1930s allowed the creamery to expand its take-home business?
3. Why do you think Blue Bell diversified its product line?

Focus

Overview

See the student page for section objectives.

Section 3 explains or describes the major goals of the U.S. market economy, and the benefits and responsibilities of individuals within a free enterprise economy.

Bellringer

Before presenting the lesson, display Focus Activity Transparency 7 on the overhead projector or copy the material on the chalkboard. Assign the accompanying Focus Activity Sheet.

Motivational Activity

Ask students to think of the benefits they experience in a free enterprise economy and write them in a column. In a second column have them write rules they follow in this economy. Discuss what students have written.

Preteaching Vocabulary

Ask students how their daily jobs and tasks relate to this section's vocabulary terms.

SECTION **3** The Goals of the Nation

SECTION 3 FOCUS

Terms to Know economic efficiency, economic growth, equity, standard of living

Objectives *After reading this section, you should be able to:*
❶ Describe the major **aims of a market economy.**
❷ List ways in which people can **balance economic rights with economic responsibilities.**

Policies and Goals in a Free Market Economy

Nations—and the United States is no exception—have national values and set goals for themselves based on these values. These goals are evident in government policies and in the actions of people like yourself and those around you. The values and goals of a nation determine which of the several kinds of economic systems that nation will have.

Aims of a Market Economy

The United States tends toward a market, or capitalist, system. Therefore, the major characteristics of a market economy should be evident in its goals. Among the national goals of Americans are efficiency, growth, security, equity, stability, and individual freedom. Figure 2.11 describes these goals in economic terms because this is an economics text. These goals however, have ethical, social, and religious elements as well.

Turning National Goals into Reality
A plan of action must be developed in order to accomplish the nation's goals. Such a plan often involves economic policy-making by elected or appointed officials who must also deal with the reality of scarcity. Because all resources are scarce, when one person gets something, that something will not be available for anyone else.

Consider the goal of economic (income) security. Many individuals can afford to buy private insurance policies and retirement plans. The government, however, has public policies such as Social Security, Medicare, and Medicaid that offer income security and health care.

Classroom Resources for Section 3

- Reproducible Lesson Plan 2.3
- Focus Activity Transparency 7
- Focus Activity Sheet 7
- Guided Reading Activity 2.3
- Economics Laboratory 1
- Economic Simulation 1
- Mathematics Practice for Economics 2

- Performance Assessment Activity 2
- Section Quiz 2.3
- Spanish Section Quiz 2.3
- Chapter 2 Test Forms A and B
- Testmaker
- Enrichment Activity 2
- Economics Vocabulary Activity 2

- Spanish Economics Vocabulary Activity 2
- Audiocassette 2
- Spanish Audiocassette 2
- Reteaching Activity 2
- Spanish Reteaching Activity 2

Figure 2.11 Our National Goals

There are many national goals. Differences on how these goals should be accomplished are reasons for the existence of political parties.

A Economic Efficiency ▶
Economic efficiency means using resources wisely so that people will be as well off as possible given our available resources.

B Economic Growth ▲
Economic growth means an expansion of the economy to produce more goods, jobs, and wealth. Some disagreement exists about whether or not economic growth too often causes problems such as environmental pollution.

C Security and Equity ▶
Security means protecting people against poverty and supplying them with the means to provide for a medical emergency through an increasing number of government social programs directed, among others, to the elderly. The related goal of **equity** means that which is fair and just.

D Individual Freedom
The goal of individual freedom allows each member of society to enjoy the freedoms of enterprise, choice, and private property and to make his or her own decisions ◀ in the marketplace.

E Stability
The goal of stability seeks to reduce extreme ups and downs in the standard of living. **Standard of living** is the material well-being of an individual, group, or nation measured by the average value of goods and services used by the average citizen during a given period of time, usually a year.

Chapter 2 Economic Systems and the American Economy **45**

Teach

Guided Practice

L1 Understanding Information Write the key national goals from the captions of Figure 2.11 on the chalkboard. Ask students how each goal applies to economics practiced within their family.

L2 Evaluating Ideas Discuss how each benefit of free enterprise can produce disadvantages for some people. Tell students to make two columns on a sheet of paper, one headed Advantages and one headed Disadvantages. Review listings and reasons why as a class.

Meeting Special Needs

Reading Disabilities Some students have difficulty differentiating between important and trivial facts. Direct these students to write one important fact or detail for each paragraph they read. Review facts with the students to make sure they grasp essential elements of the section.

Independent Practice

L2 Comparing and Contrasting Have students choose a country to study its economic system and write a short report about how this economy compares with the United States market economy.

 Have students complete Guided Reading Activity 2.3 in the TCR. LEP

Visual Instruction

Refer students to Figure 2.12. Have them select the views expressed in one of the captions and write a critique of them, supporting their own remarks with facts or solidly reasoned judgments.

? DID YOU KNOW

Differences of economic view can sometimes lead to disaster. Consider an example from 1876. The United States government and settlers in the area of present-day Montana (like other white Americans) believed that land could be held as private property. Native Americans of the region did not agree, and attempts to force them to relocate so that white men could mine gold ended in the battle of the Little Bighorn River Valley and the death of General George Custer and his army.

Figure 2.12
Advantages of Free Enterprise
The American economic system offers many benefits.

▲ **A A High Level of Economic and Personal Freedom**
Proponents of the free enterprise system point out that of all nationalities, Americans enjoy perhaps the highest degree of freedom in the world to start their own businesses and to pursue their own economic choices. This freedom extends to all aspects of life. With this extreme amount of economic and personal freedom, though, come certain costs. In particular, in our free enterprise system individuals must normally accept the consequences of their decisions.

▲ **B A High Standard of Living**
Supporters of the American economy explain that the nation has more individuals enjoying a high standard of living than almost anywhere else in the world. They believe that the ability of Americans to enjoy such high standards of living is directly tied to the ability of individuals to work where they want, how they want, and with whom, and to invest in whichever businesses they think will make profits.

C Diverse Lifestyles ▶
The great variety of economic opportunities in the United States allows for a wide range of lifestyles. People may choose to work nights, part-time, at two jobs in different parts of the country for different seasons of the year, and so on. In contrast, command economies result in much less diversity in styles of living.

46 *Unit 1 An Introduction to Economics*

 Cooperative Learning

Have students review economic rights and responsibilities. Then organize the class into two groups. Tell each group they are commissioners who must vote for or against a Federal Communications Commission regulation that requires every radio and television station to "afford reasonable opportunity for discussion of conflicting views on issues of public importance." Direct one group to support the economic rights of broadcast stations to plan more profitable and interesting programming. The other group is to champion rights of individuals to receive unbiased programming. Have two representatives of each group present their arguments.

When the government provides for plans such as Medicare, some people must agree to give up some of their income in order to transfer it to people in need. These people may be in need because they are too poor, too disabled, or too ill to care for themselves, or because they have not saved enough for emergencies or retirement.

In a world of scarcity, achieving national goals requires sacrifices by certain members of society. Any program to provide more economic security, more justice, or more equitable treatment of people involves a trade-off. Once you understand this, you will be well on your way to understanding not only the nation's economic system but also its political system. It is this economic and political system that makes many of the decisions about how resources are used in the nation. Such an understanding will help you realize that not all political desires can be turned into economic reality.

Benefits of the Free Enterprise System Those who support the American free enterprise system emphasize the many benefits that it provides for its citizens. **Figure 2.12** illustrates some of these benefits.

Balancing Economic Rights and Responsibilities

The American free enterprise system bestows numerous economic rights and protections on individuals like you, your teachers, your relatives, and your friends. You have the right to enter into just about any profession or business you want. You have the right to work very little or to become a "workaholic." You have the right to buy those products and brands that you like and to reject all others. In short, you have the right to do just about anything that is legal.

A well-functioning free enterprise system will not continue if individuals do not take on certain economic responsibilities. The first, of course, is to be able to support yourself. Additionally, just because education may be offered to you free of charge, it is not free to society. An opportunity cost goes along with it. Consequently, you have a responsibility to use that education in a reasonable manner that helps you become a productive member of the free enterprise system.

Finally, because government has become such an important part of our economy, individuals in our system have the responsibility of electing responsible government officials. This responsibility requires both the knowledge of possible government policies and the ability to analyze the consequences of different government policies.

SECTION 3 REVIEW

Understanding Vocabulary
Define economic efficiency, economic growth, equity, standard of living.

Reviewing Objectives
1. What are the major aims of a market economy?
2. How can you balance your economic rights with your economic responsibilities?

Chapter 2 Economic Systems and the American Economy **47**

Chapter 2, Section 3

Assess

Meeting Lesson Objectives
Assign Section 3 Review as homework or an in-class activity.

Evaluate
Assign the Section 3 Quiz in the TCR or use the Testmaker to develop a customized quiz.
Assign the Chapter 2 Test Form A or Form B or use the Testmaker to develop a customized test.

Reteach
Have students research and write an economic plan to solve a need such as affordable housing, basing their plan on the aims of our economy.
Have students complete Reteaching Activity 2 in the TCR.

Enrich
Tell students to collect editorial articles that support or oppose a single economic issue or topic for a week. Have them write an analysis of both positions.

Have students complete Enrichment Activity 2 in the TCR.

Close
Have students write a paragraph supporting or opposing the statement: National goals are more important than individual economic freedoms.

Section 3 Review Answers
Understanding Vocabulary
economic efficiency (p. 45), **economic growth** (p. 45), **equity** (p. 45), **standard of living** (p. 45)

Reviewing Objectives
1. Market economy aims for efficiency, growth, security, equity, stability, and individual freedom.
2. Citizens balance economic rights and responsibilities by knowing and staying within the law, taking advantage of opportunities, and electing responsible government officials.

Readings in Economics

Teach

Explain that government deregulation of airlines led to fierce competition during the 1980s and 1990s. Losses among major airlines in the United States between 1989 and 1993 reached $10 billion. Some major airlines, like USAir, cut leisure fares up to 70%. Others, like Southwest, focused on finding a niche that would separate them from the competition.

Discuss the unusual measures Herb Kelleher took to help Southwest stand apart from the competition. Organize the class into groups of five to seven students to be the board of directors for an imaginary airline that is losing money. Have them brainstorm ideas to attract passengers and boost sales. Tell them to base plans on the most workable and creative alternatives. Have a representative of each group tell the name of its airline and plan for economic recovery. List all suggestions on the chalkboard and have the class decide which plan seems most promising.

PRINCE OF MIDAIR

by Richard Woodbury

Imagine a major airline that seems to go out of its way to put its passengers in a blind rage: it routinely denies them assigned seats, refuses to transfer their baggage or arrange connections, and crams them three abreast into planes with only crackers and cookies to nibble. It sells no tickets through the industry's computerized reservations system and avoids flying to many large-city airports. As though to compensate for all this, its chief executive dresses in clown suits and Elvis costumes and paints his planes to resemble whales.

Yet Southwest Airlines has used just such perverse tactics to accomplish what no other big carrier has during the current aviation

downturn, the industry's worst: make consistent operating profits. . . .

When it was a Texas puddle jumper, Southwest and its fun-loving chairman were dismissed as an oddity. But now that the Dallas-based airline has made money for 20 straight years and spread to 34 cities in 15 states, the industry is paying it sober respect. . . .

None of this would have happened without [Chief Executive Officer Herb] Kelleher, 61, a folksy ex-San Antonio, Texas, lawyer who runs the company like a carnival sideshow. He schmoozes with employees, who know him as "Uncle Herb"; stages weekly parties at corporate headquarters; and encourages such zany antics by his flight attendants as organizing trivia contests, delivering instructions in rap and awarding prizes for the passengers with the largest holes in their socks. The wackiness has a calculated purpose—to generate a gung-ho spirit that will boost productivity, the key to Southwest's goal of carefully scripted growth.

• THINK ABOUT IT •

1. How does Southwest's service differ from that of other airlines?

2. Why does Kelleher try to instill a "gung-ho" spirit among his employees?

Answers to Think About It

1. Southwest tries to make flying fun. It does not pay attention to the usual conveniences that airlines offer. Instead, it uses wackiness to attract and keep customers.

2. Kelleher believes that a gung-ho spirit boosts productivity.

2 Highlights

Section 1

Economic Systems

Key Terms

economic system (p. 30)
distribution of income (p. 31)
traditional economic system (p. 32)
command economic system (p. 33)

market economic system (p. 33)
market (p. 33)
mixed economy (p. 34)

Summary

Every economic system answers four basic questions that determine the use of resources. In a traditional system economic decisions are dictated by what was done in the past. The government controls the factors of production in a command system. In a market system individuals serving their own interests decide the answers to the four basic questions. A mixed system contains elements of command and market systems.

Preview/Review

After students read the Chapter 2 Highlights, have them complete Economics Vocabulary Activity 2 in the TCR. Spanish Vocabulary Activities are also available in the Spanish Resource Binder.

Vocabulary Software reinforces the economic terms used in Chapter 2.

Section 2

Characteristics of the American Economy

Key Terms

invisible hand (p. 37)
capitalism (p. 37)
free enterprise system (p. 38)

private property (p. 38)
profit (p. 39)
profit incentive (p. 39)
competition (p. 39)

Summary

Consumer choice is the key to the use of resources in a free enterprise system. Free enterprise means that private individuals own property, compete in free markets, and earn profits. The government's role in a market economy is a subject of public debate.

Condense

Have students listen to Chapter 2 on the Audiocassettes in the TCR. A 1-page written activity and 1-page test accompany this material. These materials are also available in Spanish.

Section 3

The Goals of the Nation

Key Terms

economic efficiency (p. 45)
economic growth (p. 45)
equity (p. 45)
standard of living (p. 45)

Summary

A nation sets economic goals based on its values. Some goals of the American economic system are efficiency, growth, security, equity, stability, and individual freedom. Personal freedom, lifestyle diversity, and a high standard of living are benefits of the free enterprise system.

Reteach

Have students complete Reteaching Activity 2 in the TCR. Spanish Reteaching Activities are also available.

 VIDEODISC

Nightly Business Report
Economics in Action
Use "Economic Systems and the American Economy" on Disc 1, Side A, Video 3.

Search 8492, Play to 14994

ANSWERS

Identifying Key Terms

1. free enterprise system
2. capitalism
3. standard of living
4. private property
5. profit
6. competition
7. mixed
8. command economic system
9. economic growth
10. equity

Paragraphs will vary, but the writing should indicate understanding of economic system, market, mixed economy, invisible hand, profit incentive, and competition.

Recalling Facts and Ideas

Section 1

1. trade-off
2. Who should produce what?
3. How should goods and services be produced?
4. because their views of how to satisfy the needs and wants of people differ
5. according to tradition, or how things were done in the past
6. the government
7. individuals
8. because it is a market system with government regulations

Section 2

9. limited government intervention, freedom of enterprise, freedom of choice, private property, profit incentive, competition
10. Adam Smith
11. Government's role under capitalism is to provide for national defense and eliminate business practices that limit trade.
12. Private property rights protect ownership, use, and profit.

Section 3

13. a high standard of living, diverse lifestyles, and a high level of economic and personal freedom
14. provides public programs, such as in income distribution, health care, and job training

---

Identifying Key Terms

Use terms from the following list to fill in the blanks in the paragraph below.

traditional economic system (p. 32)
command economic system (p. 33)
mixed economy (p. 34)
capitalism (p. 37)
free enterprise system (p. 38)
private property (p. 38)

profit (p. 39)
competition (p. 39)
economic growth (p. 45)
equity (p. 45)
standard of living (p. 45)

Another term for the market economic system is the ___(1)___, or ___(2)___. Many Americans believe that this system helps to account for the high ___(3)___ in the United States. This system is based on concepts such as ___(4)___ that allows people to buy and own land, a home, or their own business. A person may keep the ___(5)___ earned from selling in ___(6)___ with other businesses. Most people, including Americans, actually live in a ___(7)___ economic system that contains some characteristics of a ___(8)___. The government promotes both ___(9)___ and ___(10)___, or fair and just policies.

Write a short paragraph about the American economy using all of the following terms.

economic system (p. 30)
market (p. 33)
mixed economy (p. 34)
invisible hand (p. 37)
profit incentive (p. 39)
competition (p. 39)

Recalling Facts and Ideas

Section 1

1. "The more of one item that is produced, the less of something else will be produced." What term describes this economic condition?
2. What basic economic question helps determine the career path of individuals?
3. What economic question is being answered if an industry decides to replace some workers with machines?
4. Why do economic systems differ in the way they answer the question "Who should share in what is produced?"
5. How does a traditional economic system answer the question "Who should produce what?"
6. Who answers the basic economic questions in a command system?
7. Who owns the factors of production in a market economic system?
8. Why should the United States economic system be called a mixed system?

Section 2

9. What are six important characteristics of free enterprise?
10. Who wrote *The Wealth of Nations*?
11. What is government's limited role in pure capitalism?
12. Why is private property important in the American economic system?

Section 3

13. What are three benefits of the free enterprise system?
14. What does the United States do to promote economic security for individuals?

Critical Thinking

Section 1

Answers to the four basic economic questions determine the amount of personal economic freedom an individual has.

Section 2

Answers will vary but students should indicate that there is a movement in Russia that favors a market economy, although a

Critical Thinking

Section 1
Determining Cause and Effect How might the answers to each of the four basic economic questions affect your personal decisions?

Section 2
Making Comparisons Are recent economic trends in Russia and the United States similar or different? Explain your answer.

Section 3
Identifying Alternatives What are two ways that each of the following services may be provided: health care, mass transit, energy?

Applying Economic Concepts

Economic Systems An economic system within your school determines the answer to the basic question *who should share in what is produced.* Make a list of the goods and services available to students within the school. After each, write whether the distribution of this good or service is determined according to market, command, or traditional economic system principles.

Chapter Projects

1. **Individual Project** Review economic news from national magazines. List the economic decisions of several nations and make a table that classifies them as supporting free markets or command systems.
2. **Cooperative Learning Project** In small groups that will serve as committees, submit proposals for planning a national education system in a command economy. The system should provide answers to such questions as:
   - What level of education should be available without cost to everyone?
   - Should academic achievement or testing be used to qualify students for higher levels of education or specialized fields?

Compare the different answers to each of the issues. What other issues have surfaced during student discussions within each group? What are the major hurdles to building a national education system?

Reviewing Skills

Understanding Percentages and Discounts
1. **Figuring Percentages** A local insurance company increased the number of its employees from 550 to 667 over a five-year period. What was the percentage increase in employees?
2. **Using Percentages** Study the table below, then apply your skills to determine the numbers that fit the four blank spaces.

original price	percent off	discount	new price
$100.00	30%	$30.00	$70.00
$80.00	15%		
$56.00		$3.92	$52.08
	20%	$12.00	$48.00

Writing About Economics

Descriptive Writing Imagine you are a young person writing to a group of students who live in a society that has a traditional economic system. Social customs determine the economic decisions they make. Write a letter describing how the economic decisions you make are a part of your daily life. Refer to the list of goods and services in Your Economics Journal as you write.

51

segment of the population and leadership is opposed to this. In the United States, market economy continues in the midst of conflicting calls for increased and decreased government regulation.

Section 3
Two ways of providing services are through free enterprise of individuals or businesses and through government programs.

Applying Economic Concepts

Make sure students list at least five goods or services and demonstrate understanding of the different economic systems.

Chapter Projects

1. Prepare a bulletin board with continent names and have students place their table under the appropriate name.
2. Allot time for each committee to explain its plan. Make sure presentations answer both questions. Discuss any other issues that surfaced during students' discussions.

? BONUS QUESTION

The following bonus question may be written on the chalkboard when students take the chapter test.
Q: Japanese private industry determines production goals in conjunction with government economic forecasting. What kind of economic system does this interaction suggest?
A: mixed

Reviewing Skills
1. 21.5 percent
2. $12.00—discount; $68—new price; 7%—percent off; $60—original price

Writing About Economics
Encourage students to include examples of specific reasons for their economic decisions and any examples of social customs that determine these decisions.

Focus

In free enterprise, businesses strive for advantage through price competition and nonprice competition. Review with students business use of nonprice competition. Emphasize factors such as product quality, services, location, reputation, and expertise of firm personnel.

The purpose of this lab is to compare the ways businesses use price and nonprice competition.

Teach

Using Economic Models can be extended over several weeks or condensed by giving dated advertisements to students. Begin the lab by completing Step A and preparing the tables in Steps B, C, and D. If the lab extends over many weeks, allot time at the end of each week to check student's progress.

When customers become aware that there is little difference among competing

Using Economic Models
From the classroom of Michelle Farthing, Alvin High School, Alvin, Texas

In Unit 1 you read about using models, a basic tool of the economist. In this experiment, you will use models to study competition. (You may want to reread the material on pages 18–21 of the text.)

Competition among producers forces businesses to keep prices low enough to attract customers. Some businesses emphasize price when marketing their products. This is called **price competition.** Some businesses choose to emphasize service, product quality, packaging, or factors other than price to distinguish their products. In this lab study, you will try to determine whether certain businesses are using price competition and, if so, how they are using it.

Tools

1. Copies of a local newspaper over a 4-week period
2. Pencils, writing paper, graph paper

Procedures

Step A Depending on the size of your class, choose 5 to 10 products or services from the following list:

1. gasoline
2. hair cuts
3. jeans
4. face soap
5. hamburgers
6. dishwashers
7. motorcycles
8. pizza
9. tennis shoes
10. oranges
11. golf fees
12. motel rooms

Step B Write the names of the brands, stores, distributors, etc., for one product or service that you plan to study in the left column of a table such as the one below.

Example
Gasoline
(87 octane)

Sunoco (Oak St.)				
Ray's Texaco				
Shell (downtown)				
Certified				

Step C Keep a record of the price changes by the supplier of the service or product you are studying over time.

Example
Gasoline (87 octane)

	March 5	12	19	26
Sunoco (Oak St.)	$1.09	$1.14	$1.19	$1.13
Ray's Texaco	1.09	1.12	1.15	1.12
Shell (downtown)	1.04	1.10	1.13	1.15
Certified	.99	1.05	1.06	1.04

products, they often make buying decisions based on price. In some cases, sellers price their products slightly higher than the competition's because they believe the quality of product or service is higher. To compete, they choose methods of nonprice competition. The list of products and services in Step A includes some that are similar in

quality and others that differ substantially. Have each student choose a product or service to study. Be sure that some students choose products that are similar in quality (gasolines, soft drinks, oranges) and other students choose products or services that can differ considerably in quality (tennis shoes, jeans, motorcycles).

Step D Make a list of the different kinds of advertising messages used for the competing products or services during this period.

Example

Sunoco	better mileage	more selection	quality
Ray's Texaco	lower price	friendly	contest, prizes

Step E Build a graph similar to the one below that shows the price changes of the products or services you studied.

Example

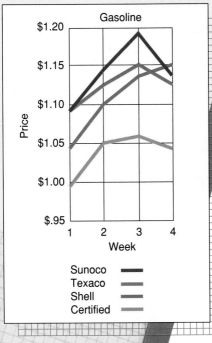

Gasoline

Price ($1.20, $1.15, $1.10, $1.05, $1.00, $.95)

Week (1, 2, 3, 4)

Sunoco ▬▬▬
Texaco ▬▬▬
Shell ▬▬▬
Certified ▬▬▬

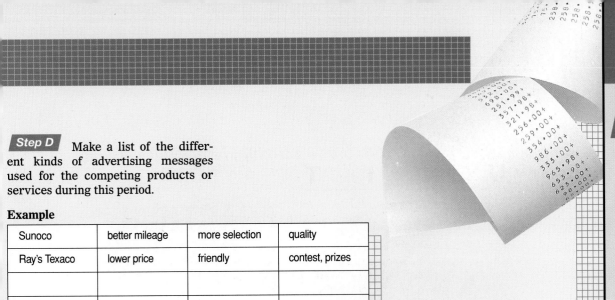

Lab Report

Step F Study the table and graph that you created in Steps D and E and answer the questions below.

1. How frequently did the price of the product or service change?
2. How wide was the price difference among competing brands?
3. What other kinds of competition were evidenced by advertising for this product or service?
4. Is price competition the main kind of competition for this product or service?

Step G Compare the tables and graphs for different products or services that were completed by each member of the class and answer the questions below.

1. What products or services use price competition as their main form of competition? Why?
2. What products use packaging and product quality to distinguish them from their competition? How?

53

Answers to Lab Report

Lab Report F
Student tables and graphs should include four or five products or services studied over a four-week period. Students should cite sources for the advertisements they collected.

Lab Report G
Review student paragraph summaries in their journals. Look for an understanding of price competition and nonprice competition and the role they play for buyers and sellers in resource distribution.

Unit Goals

After studying this unit, students will be able to:

Evaluate the individual role of the consumer;

Analyze buying decisions;

Understand how to balance a household budget;

Learn the value of saving and investing money.

Unit Overview

The five chapters in Unit 2 address how economic theory applies to everyday buying and budgeting.

Chapter 3 explains: discretionary income; the role of advertising; and consumers' rights.

Chapter 4 explains what forces families into debt.

Chapters 5 and 6 explain or describe responsible budget planning, including for food, clothing, housing, and transportation.

Chapter 7 describes options for saving and investing.

Connecting to Past Learning

Have students discuss one week's television or radio stories that have an economic impact on the people involved.

`0:00` OUT OF TIME?

If time does not permit teaching each chapter in this unit, you may use the Chapter Highlights and the Audiocassettes that include a 1-page activity and a 1-page test for each chapter.

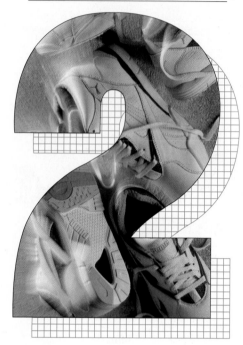

UNIT 2

PRACTICAL ECONOMICS: HOW THEORY WORKS FOR YOU

Economic Simulation

Consumer Cooperatives Ask students to imagine they are citizens of a town with only one mediocre grocery supermarket. As an alternative, have students research consumer cooperative food markets and develop a plan for one that reflects community's wants.

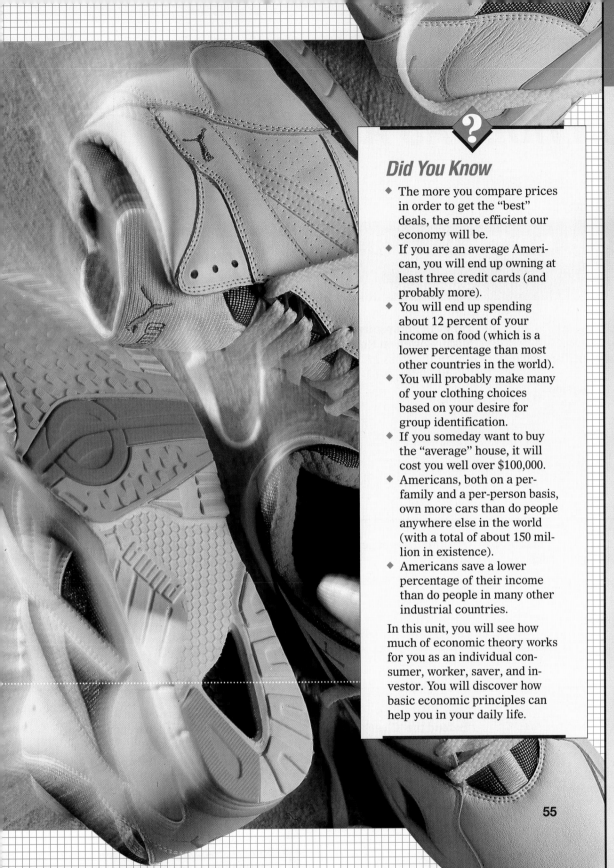

Did You Know

- The more you compare prices in order to get the "best" deals, the more efficient our economy will be.
- If you are an average American, you will end up owning at least three credit cards (and probably more).
- You will end up spending about 12 percent of your income on food (which is a lower percentage than most other countries in the world).
- You will probably make many of your clothing choices based on your desire for group identification.
- If you someday want to buy the "average" house, it will cost you well over $100,000.
- Americans, both on a per-family and a per-person basis, own more cars than do people anywhere else in the world (with a total of about 150 million in existence).
- Americans save a lower percentage of their income than do people in many other industrial countries.

In this unit, you will see how much of economic theory works for you as an individual consumer, worker, saver, and investor. You will discover how basic economic principles can help you in your daily life.

Beginning the Unit

Refer students to the "Did You Know" questions on page 55. Ask them to react to the facts they read. (For example, do these facts reflect how their family or neighbors spend money? Do these figures make sound economic sense? How does their economic situation compare with the rest of the nation?)

Outcome-Based Project

Building Economic Models
The following unit project is the second step in a six-part activity that can be used during the entire economics course. In Unit 2 students build charts and graphs to visualize job opportunities and trends.

Using information collected in Unit 1, have students build graphs that compare the relative availability of jobs in the local market and that compare salaries in the categories they selected to study. Students should also develop charts to compare advertised job requirements in selected categories. (See Careers feature in the appendix of this book for additional comparative salaries and requirements.)

55

Did You Know

It is important for consumers who use credit cards to be aware of hidden fees and practices. These include:
- Interest charges can begin immediately on cash advances and from the date of purchases.
- Some interest rates are compounded monthly or even daily, thus charging a larger percent than what is advertised.
- Many finance charges are based on the average daily balance instead of the balance owed.
- Many credit cards now charge late-payment and over-limit fees.

CHAPTER 3 *YOUR ROLE AS A CONSUMER*

CHAPTER ORGANIZER

Daily Objectives	Special Features	Classroom Resources
Section 1 Consumption, Income, and Decision Making • **Explain** the difference between disposable and discretionary income. • **List** three considerations in decision making as a consumer.	**Personal Perspective:** Susan Bowen on Running a Business in Tough Times, p. 62	📂 Reproducible Lesson Plan 3.1 💿 *NBR* Video 4 and Video Stills 2 and 3 🖐 Focus Activity Transparency 8 📂 Focus Activity Sheet 8 📂 Guided Reading Activity 3.1 📂 Cooperative Learning Activity 3 📂 Primary and Secondary Source Readings 3 📂 Section Quiz 3.1 📂 Spanish Section Quiz 3.1 💾 Testmaker
Section 2 Buying Principles, or Strategies • **Evaluate** the trade-offs when gathering information. • **Analyze** various forms of advertising wisely. • **Practice** comparison shopping.	**Learning Economic Skills:** Handling a Consumer Problem, p. 67	📂 Reproducible Lesson Plan 3.2 🖐 Focus Activity Transparency 9 📂 Focus Activity Sheet 9 📂 Guided Reading Activity 3.2 📂 Section Quiz 3.2 📂 Spanish Section Quiz 3.2 💾 Testmaker 📂 Reinforcing Skills 3
Section 3 Consumerism • **List** five consumer rights. • **List** sources of private and federal help for consumers. • **Define** consumer responsibilities. • **Describe** ethical consumer behavior.	**News Clip:** "Behind the 'Clear' Trend," *The New York Times,* p. 72	📂 Reproducible Lesson Plan 3.3 🖐 Focus Activity Transparency 10 📂 Focus Activity Sheet 10 📂 Guided Reading Activity 3.3 📂 Free Enterprise Activity 3 📂 Consumer Application Activity 3 📂 Mathematics Practice for Economics 3 📂 Performance Assessment Activity 3 📂 Section Quiz 3.3 📂 Spanish Section Quiz 3.3 💾 Testmaker 📂 Enrichment Activity 3

 OUT OF TIME? If time does not permit teaching this chapter, you may use the Chapter 3 Highlights and the Audiocassettes that include a 1-page activity and a 1-page test.

Chapter 3 Review and Evaluation

Special Features

Chapter 3 Highlights, p. 73
Chapter 3 Review, pp. 74–75
Point/Counterpoint, pp. 76–77

Classroom Resources

- Chapter 3 Test Forms A and B
- Economics Vocabulary Activity 3
- Spanish Economics Vocabulary Activity 3
- Audiocassette 3
- Spanish Audiocassette 3
- Reteaching Activity 3
- Spanish Reteaching Activity 3

Key to Ability Levels

Teaching strategies have been coded for varying learning styles and abilities.

L1 Level 1 activities are **basic** activities and should be within the ability range of all students.

L2 Level 2 activities are **average** activities designed for the ability range of average to above-average students.

L3 Level 3 activities are **challenging** activities designed for the ability range of above-average students.

LEP activities should be within the ability range of **Limited English Proficiency** students.

Performance Assessment

The following chapter project may be assigned at the beginning of the chapter and used for performance assessment. See page T12 for additional Performance Assessment information.

Planning an Event To have students explore their role as consumers, ask them to plan their ideal wedding over the course of studying Chapter 3. They should list all the products and services they would like for their wedding and ways to go about making rational choices in purchasing them, including following the consumer decision-making checklist. Tell students to include information about advertisements they consulted, comparison shopping they conducted, and whether they opted for generic or brand name products for their final choices and why. Have students tell about the consumer rights and responsibilities involved in planning such an important event, even if they would choose to elope.

Additional Resources

Readings for the Student

Clark, Eric. *The Want Makers.* New York: Viking/Peguin, 1990.

Buying America Back. Edited by Jonathon Greenburg. Tulsa, Okla.: Council Oaks Books, 1992.

Readings for the Teacher

Warsh, David. *Economic Principals: Masters and Mavericks of Modern Economics.* New York: Free Press, 1993.

Goodrun, Charles. *Advertising in America: The First Two Hundred Years.* New York: Harry N. Abrams, 1990.

Multimedia Materials

Consumer Economics and You. 16mm film. 18 min. Encyclopedia Britannica, 310 South Michigan Avenue, Chicago, IL 60601

Consumer Fraud. 16mm film. 15 min. Aims Media, 626 Justin Avenue, Glendale, CA 91201

Consumer Power. Series of three 16mm films. Each 20 min. BFA Educational Media, 211 Michigan Avenue, P.O. Box 1795, Santa Monica, CA 90406

Shopping Strategies. Two-disk set for practicing buying decisions in a mall. Apple/IBM. Educational Resources, 1550 Executive Drive, Elgin, IL 60123

Chapter Overview

Practical economics relates economic principles taught in Unit 1 to everyday situations. Chapter 3 explains the difference between disposable and discretionary income and examines how each is spent. The emphasis is on consumer awareness for making responsible buying decisions. Chapter 3 explores the role of advertising on buying choices and the rights and responsibilities of consumers.

VIDEODISC

Nightly Business Report
Economics in Action
Use "Your Role as a Consumer" on Disc 1, Side A, Video 4.

Search 15084, Play to 21480

CHAPTER

3

YOUR ROLE AS A CONSUMER

Do you know what is required to make rational decisions when you shop for a computer?

Do you think that when you are shopping for a computer you should visit every store carrying that product in your community?

Economic Portfolio

Have students add to their **Economic Portfolio** (suggested in Chapter 1 opener) by including **Your Economics Journal** writing activities for this chapter. Ask them to identify the steps they, or someone they know, took to buy a small appliance or electronic item. Tell them to list alternative items and alternative stores to the final purchase, and identify why these choices were not selected. Have them write a paragraph that explains what first attracted them to these stores and items.

Do you have alternative sources from which you can buy a computer in addition to stores in your community?

If you and a friend visit the same stores and hear the same sales pitch in each one, will you necessarily decide on the same brand and model computer?

Your Economics Journal

Keep track of the steps used by you, a friend, or one of your parents in buying a small appliance or electronic item. List the number of alternative sources that were considered. Next to each source, write why that store or catalog was or was not chosen.

57

Connecting to Past Learning

Ask students to consider how the free enterprise system embraced by the economy of the United States affects their role as a consumer. List the options they suggest on the chalkboard. Ask what freedoms the system gives others, such as sellers and advertisers, to influence their individual rights and choices as a consumer.

Applying Economics

Ask students to list any money they received during the past month and where it came from, such as allowance and wages. In another column have them list their purchases for the last month. Discuss whether more money is going out or coming in and the types of expenditures students are responsible for, such as food, clothing, health care, or recreation. Ask whether any students follow a plan, or budget, for how they spend their money. Tell students they will learn considerations that will help them become wiser consumers.

EXTRA CREDIT PROJECT

Ask students to do a research paper on consumer protection against fraudulent advertising in another country and give an oral report to the class.

PERFORMANCE ASSESSMENT

Refer to page 56B for "Planning an Event," a Performance Assessment Activity for this chapter.

Answering Economic Questions

The questions in the above illustration guide students into the main concepts of Chapter 3. Students may be unaware that they follow certain patterns when making buying decisions. The questions ask them to think about how they shop and what helps them as consumers to make the choices they do. Have students describe some recent shopping excursions. Ask whether their purchase choices are influenced by outside forces, such as persuasive salespeople, their friends' choices, or advertising, and whether they could think of ways to make better buying decisions.

Focus

Overview

See the student page for section objectives.

Section 1 explains or describes the difference between disposable and discretionary income and five considerations in decision making as a consumer.

Bellringer

Before presenting the lesson, display Focus Activity Transparency 8 on the overhead projector or copy the material on the chalkboard. Assign the accompanying Focus Activity Sheet.

Motivational Activity

Ask students to name goods and services their parents buy. List the items on the chalkboard and discuss which are necessities. Encourage students to think about taxes, transportation, savings, and health care as well as familiar spending for recreation and clothing.

Preteaching Vocabulary

Write *consumer, discretionary income,* and *disposable income* on the chalkboard. Instruct students to find definitions for these words in the Glossary and to write a short paragraph that indicates the different types of goods and services consumers buy, depending upon their income.

SECTION 1 Consumption, Income, and Decision Making

> ### SECTION 1 FOCUS
>
> **Terms to Know** consumer, disposable income, discretionary income, warranty, rational choice
>
> **Objectives** *After reading this section, you should be able to:*
> 1. Explain the difference between **disposable and discretionary income.**
> 2. List three considerations in **decision making as a consumer.**

Consumers Can Learn to Make Rational Choices

You and everyone around you are consumers and, as such, play important roles in the economic system. A **consumer** is any person or group that buys or uses goods and services to satisfy personal wants. As consumers, people buy a wide variety of things—food, clothing, dental and medical care, automobiles, computers, and so on. To see how typical American consumers spend their money, study the circle graph in Figure 3.1.

Figure 3.1 Consumer Spending
The circle graph shows how Americans spend their income. What are the top three categories of consumer spending?

Disposable and Discretionary Income

A person's role as a consumer depends on his or her ability to consume. This ability to consume, in turn, depends on the income available and how much of it a person chooses to spend now or save for the future.

Income can be both disposable and discretionary (dis-KRESH-uh-ner-ee). **Disposable income** is the money income a person has left after all taxes have been paid. People spend their disposable income on many kinds of goods and services. First, they buy the necessities: food, clothing, and housing. Once these needs have been met, there may be some income left. This income, which can be spent on extras such as entertainment and luxury items, is called **discretionary income.** See Figure 3.2.

Education, occupation, age, gender, and health can all make differences in a person's earning power and

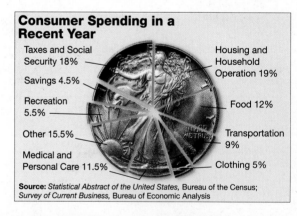

Consumer Spending in a Recent Year

- Taxes and Social Security 18%
- Savings 4.5%
- Recreation 5.5%
- Other 15.5%
- Medical and Personal Care 11.5%
- Housing and Household Operation 19%
- Food 12%
- Transportation 9%
- Clothing 5%

Source: *Statistical Abstract of the United States,* Bureau of the Census; *Survey of Current Business,* Bureau of Economic Analysis

58 *Unit 2 Practical Economics: How Theory Works for You*

Classroom Resources for Section 1

- Reproducible Lesson Plan 3.1
- *NBR* Video 4 and Video Stills 2 and 3
- Focus Activity Transparency 8
- Focus Activity Sheet 8
- Guided Reading Activity 3.1
- Cooperative Learning Activity 3
- Primary and Secondary Source Readings 3
- Section Quiz 3.1
- Spanish Section Quiz 3.1
- Testmaker

thus in his or her ability to consume. Where a person lives can also influence how much he or she earns. City dwellers tend to earn more than those who live in rural areas. Wages in some regions of the country tend to be higher than those in other regions. How much a person has to spend can also be influenced by inheriting money or property.

Regardless of the size of a person's income, spending that income requires constant decision making. As a consumer, each person has a series of choices to make.

Decision Making as a Consumer

The first decision a consumer must make is whether to buy an item or not. This may sound so basic as to be unnecessary to mention, but how many times do you actually think about the reasons for the purchase you are about to make? Do you think about whether you really need the item? Do you consider the trade-offs involved? Part I of Figure 3.3—Checklist for Consumer Decision Making—on page 60 will help you analyze this first consumer decision.

Scarce Resources Once you have decided to make a purchase, at least two scarce resources are involved— income and time. Once you have decided to spend your money income, you need to invest time in obtaining information about the product you wish to buy. The time you spend making a decision to buy something cannot be used for anything else. Suppose you decide to buy a mountain bike. The time spent visiting stores checking models and prices is a cost to you.

Making consumer decisions involves three parts, each including several steps. The Checklist for

Consumer Decision Making in Figure 3.3 can help to guide you through the entire process.

Opportunity Cost Virtually all of the steps in consumer decision making shown in Figure 3.3 involve an opportunity cost. Opportunity cost is the value of your highest alternative choice that you did not make. In step 1 of Part II of the checklist, for example, your choice between a low-, medium-, or high-quality product involves an opportunity cost.

In general, a high-quality product costs more than a low-quality product. Here is an example: You are trying to decide between new cross-training shoes. One model has a pump system that allows you to get a closer fit on your foot. The other model does not. The pump system model costs $80 more than the other model. If you choose the superior-quality, higher-priced pump system shoe, you will

Figure 3.2 ▲ Using Discretionary Income
The consumer's wants are his or her guide in spending income. Some people have more disposable and discretionary income and can therefore spend more than others on entertainment.

Teach

Guided Practice

L2 Analyzing Ask students to consider a cotton farmer in the High Plains region of northern Texas and a reporter for the *Austin Business Journal* in the state capital, and to write a comparison of their disposable and discretionary incomes based on ability to consume, income, where they live, and job-related factors.

Visual Instruction

Review Figure 3.1 on page 58 with students. Explain that consumer spending figures in other countries differ. Tell students to research a country and to draw a circle graph of consumer spending there. If exact figures are unavailable, suggest estimating percentages.

VIDEODISC

Nightly Business Report
Economics in Action
Use Video Stills 2 and 3, "Disposable Income" and "Discretionary Income," on Disc 1, Side A, Video 4.

Search Frame 16422

Search Frame 16626

◆▶◯ **Meeting Special Needs**

Reading Disability Allow students who have difficulty with reading comprehension to read aloud with a partner. Have readers stop at the end of each page and discuss what they read, highlighting important facts and definitions. The auditory cues of reading aloud and discussing the material should increase comprehension.

Independent Practice

L1 Decision Making Tell students they were each invited to the senior prom. Have them list the steps they would follow to buy or rent their complete outfit. Remind them to apply the considerations listed in their book to buying the goods or services they may want. Discuss their lists as a class.

L2 Consumer Cartoon Ask students to draw a cartoon that illustrates their spending and buying habits. Display the completed cartoons on a classroom bulletin board.

Have students complete Guided Reading Activity 3.1 in the TCR. **LEP**

Checklist

**Figure 3.3
Consumer Decision Making**

Part I. Deciding to Spend Your Money

Before you buy anything, you should ask yourself:

1. Do I really need this item? Why? Remember the discussion about wants and needs in Chapter 1. Real needs are few, but wants are unlimited. Unless you answer this question honestly, you may find your wants are always greater than your ability to satisfy them.

2. Is this good or service worth the time I spent earning the income to pay for it?

3. Is there any better use for my income now? Should I save instead for future needs?

Part II. Deciding on the Right Purchase

Once you have made up your mind to buy a certain good or service, you are faced with more questions:

1. Do I want high, medium, or low quality? Quality refers to appearance, materials used, and the length of time a product will last. Most goods are of medium or average quality. For a higher price, you can usually get higher quality. For a lower price, you can usually expect a product that may not be as attractive or as long lasting. At times such a purchase may suit your needs very well, however.

2. If I am buying an appliance or car, do I want one that will be the most efficient—least costly—to operate each year? The answer will probably involve a trade-off. A small automobile, for example, may use less gasoline than a larger one, but it provides less protection in an accident.

3. Does this particular item—a Brand Y stereo, for example—require more service than Brands A, B, and C? If so, do I want this additional problem and expense?

4. Should I wait until there is a sale on the item I want? Sales of certain items are seasonal. For example, winter clothes are on sale after Christmas and summer clothes in August.

5. If I am looking for an expensive item, such as an entertainment center, should I buy it new or used? What things are better to buy new than used? How can I protect myself if I buy a used item?

6. Should I choose a product with a well-known brand name even though it costs more than a similar product without a brand name? Are there any benefits to buying a brand-name product? What are they?

7. Does anyone I know own this product so that I can get a firsthand opinion?

8. Is the warranty on this particular product comparable to warranties on similar items? A **warranty** is a promise made by a manufacturer or a seller to repair or replace a product if it is found to be faulty within a certain period of time.

9. Is the return or exchange policy where I am thinking of buying a product comparable to the policies of other stores selling similar items?

10. What do consumer magazines say about it?

Part III. Deciding How to Use Your Purchase

Decision making for you, the consumer, does not stop after you have bought an item. It continues for as long as you have a choice about using it. Once you own something—whether it is clothing, a VCR, or an automobile—you must decide:

1. How much time and effort should I spend on repairs and maintenance?

2. How much money should I spend on repairs and maintenance?

3. At what point should I replace this item? Why? (This brings you back to number 1 under Deciding to Spend Your Money.)

Cooperative Learning

Organize the class into small groups to conduct a consumer poll to find out how citizens in their community decide on making purchases. Have one group develop a questionnaire based on the checklist in Figure 3.3. Have another group survey the consumers. Have a third group prepare a report of the findings and present the data in a class discussion.

Figure 3.4 Buying Decisions

If you choose the higher-priced product, you must believe that the opportunity cost for the higher quality is worth $80—nothing else at that instant will give you as much value. ▼

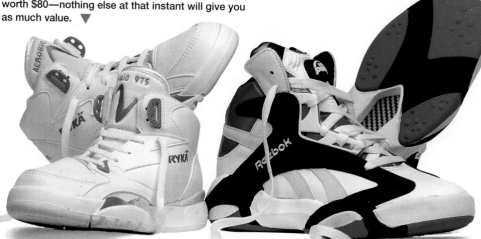

sacrifice $80. The opportunity cost of the pump model over the lesser-quality model shoe is therefore $80, or what you could have bought with that $80. See Figure 3.4.

Rational Choice When you make consumer decisions based on opportunity cost, you are engaging in **rational choice.** Economists define rational choice as the alternative that has the greatest value.

Rational choice involves choosing the item that is the least expensive from among comparable quality products. As a consumer, you will make rational choices when you purchase the goods and services you believe can best satisfy your wants.

Do not get the impression that rational consumers will all make the same choices. Remember the definition: A rational choice is one that generates the greatest value for any given expenditure. Rational choices that are based on careful consumer decision making will still lead to billions of different consumer choices yearly.

Value is very subjective. You may choose to buy the higher-priced, superior-quality pump cross-training shoes, and your best friend may think you are crazy. If he or she tells you, "That's a rip-off; you shouldn't pay that kind of money for those shoes," your friend is expressing a value judgment about how you are choosing to spend your limited income.

SECTION 1 REVIEW

Understanding Vocabulary
Define consumer, disposable income, discretionary income, warranty, rational choice.

Reviewing Objectives
❶ What kinds of products are purchased with discretionary income?
❷ What three things should a consumer consider when making a purchase?

Assess

Meeting Lesson Objectives
Assign Section 1 Review as homework or an in-class activity. Each question in the Review addresses the corresponding numbered objective in the Section Focus.

Evaluate
Assign the Section 1 Quiz in the TCR or use the Testmaker to develop a customized quiz.

Reteach
Have students create a flow chart starting with *consumer* and ending with *product choice* that illustrates the main points covered in the section.

Enrich
Tell students to write a short report that describes how they would apply decision-making considerations to purchasing goods in a country where individuals barter in open markets.

Close
Have students prepare a consumer checklist for hiring (purchasing) a disc jockey to entertain at a school dance.

Section 1 Review Answers
Understanding Vocabulary
consumer (p. 58), **disposable income** (p. 58), **discretionary income** (p.58), **warranty** (p. 60), **rational choice** (p. 61)
Reviewing Objectives
1. Products that are extras, such as entertainment, are purchased with discretionary income.
2. When making a purchase, consumers should consider whether to invest time in obtaining information about it, or spend the money; what type (quality, brand) to buy; and how the purchase will be used.

Background

Susan Bowen is a savvy businessperson who examined every aspect of her retail business to cut expenses. Throughout this process customers and sales staff remained her main concern. Bowen realized that a happy, well-paid staff was her best defense against competition, because satisfied employees project a positive image that attracts customers.

Teach

Organize students into small groups and have each group represent a business from a different industry. Tell them that their industry is going through some hard times and that they need to develop a plan to attract business and cut costs. Refer to the considerations consumers use when making buying decisions.

Following this activity have students answer the questions in Checking for Understanding.

Susan Bowen on Running a Business in Tough Times

Profile

- 1941–
- founder and president of Memphis-based Champion Awards, Inc.
- started Champion Awards in a friend's barn in 1970
- originally sold trophies to saddle clubs and expanded into T-shirt printing
- over $10 million in sales by early 1990s

Susan Bowen runs a retail business that sells trophies and T-shirts and is very sensitive to economic downturns. In 1990 her company, Champion Awards, Inc., had to cut a number of employees in order to survive during the worst financial situation in its history. By the end of 1991, however, it was well on the road to recovery and had hired back most of its employees. In the *Memphis Business Journal*, January 28, 1991, Bowen shares some insights on how her company coped in a tough retail environment.

… In good times, our sales people are more like order-takers. In harder times, they've got to be more aggressive.
… We're taking some orders we wouldn't have taken before. We haven't lowered prices, but we've lowered the volume we do. We have a distribution business where we sell blank goods to other printers—that business has really slowed.

Bowen explains how hard times forced her company to make wise economic choices.

… When you see your equipment just sitting there, that's really going to cost you.
… It's probably the best thing that we have had happen to us. It's made us more aware of the

expense side of the business, instead of sales. … When you're growing and the money's coming in, you don't pay attention to that. We still want to grow—you're going to have to grow in our industry to stay even. But we're not going to grow at the expense of the bottom line.

I don't want any inventory in this building until the day we need it. We should cut inventory. We're just going to get lean and mean, and get aggressive with our sales.

In *Commercial Appeal*, October 30, 1991, Bowen explains why Champion raised salaries in spite of tough times.

It's these people out here that work their rears off that need the money, not somebody sitting up there at a computer. These are the people we want to keep…. We're getting the best employees we've ever had.

Checking for Understanding

❶ What kind of adjustments did Champion Awards have to make?

❷ How did hard times make Champion Awards more efficient?

❸ Why did Champion raise salaries at the same time they cut costs in other areas?

Answers to Checking for Understanding

1. Champion Awards reduced inventory, cut staff until they were solvent enough to rehire them, paid harder-working employees a higher salary, and evaluated how to use equipment more cost-effectively.
2. Hard times made Bowen more aware of the expense side of business and forced her to make economic changes.
3. Champion saw the need to keep good people who were better workers to make the company grow, so Bowen raised salaries while cutting costs.

2 Buying Principles, or Strategies

SECTION 2 FOCUS

Terms to Know competitive advertising, informative advertising, bait and switch, generic brands, brand name, comparison shopping

Objectives After reading this section, you should be able to:
1. Evaluate the trade-offs when gathering information.
2. Analyze various forms of advertising wisely.
3. Practice comparison shopping.

The Three Basic Buying Principles

Assume that you have decided to make a purchase. Because of the problems of scarce income and time, your goal should be to obtain the most satisfaction from your limited income and time. Three basic buying principles can help you and all consumers achieve this goal. They are: (1) gathering information; (2) using advertising wisely; and (3) comparison shopping.

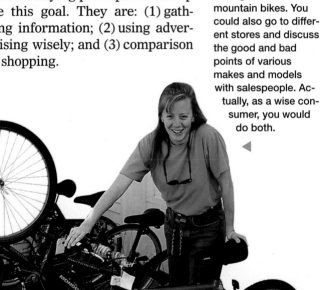

**Figure 3.5
How Much Time and Effort?**
You can spend time testing out friends' mountain bikes. You could also go to different stores and discuss the good and bad points of various makes and models with salespeople. Actually, as a wise consumer, you would do both.

Gathering Information

Suppose that you are going to buy a mountain bike. Once you have decided that, you have to decide on a brand and a model. How? You first have to obtain information about mountain bikes. See Figure 3.5.

Information is costly because obtaining it involves your time. You are

Chapter 3 Your Role as a Consumer **63**

Classroom Resources for Section 2

- Reproducible Lesson Plan 3.2
- Focus Activity Transparency 9
- Focus Activity Sheet 9
- Guided Reading Activity 3.2

- Section Quiz 3.2
- Spanish Section Quiz 3.2
- Testmaker 2
- Reinforcing Skills 3

LESSON PLAN
Chapter 3, Section 2

Focus

Overview

See the student page for section objectives.

Section 2 explains or describes: the trade-offs required in gathering buying information; various forms of advertising; and how consumers practice comparison shopping.

Bellringer

Before presenting the lesson, display Focus Activity Transparency 9 on the overhead projector or copy the material on the chalkboard. Assign the accompanying Focus Activity Sheet.

Motivational Activity

Ask students to list the number of advertisements they see and hear from the time they leave school until they go to bed that evening. The next day, ask students to compare the number of advertisements they encountered.

Preteaching Vocabulary

Have students brainstorm definitions for the Terms to Know. Call on volunteers for responses and write them on the chalkboard. After discussion, have students write the definitions from the Glossary and compare them with those on the board.

Teach

Guided Practice

L1 Preparing a Table Have students design a two-column table headed Pro and Con that lists arguments for and against the use of advertising in their school. Ask whether advertising is to their advantage as a consumer.

Visual Instruction

Refer students to Figure 3.7 and its captions. Tell them to consider the steps they followed in a purchase they have made, and how much time they spent on this process. Have them report orally.

DID YOU KNOW

Studies reveal that Americans are bombarded with about 3,000 to 5,000 advertising messages each day. The assault is so overwhelming that people scarcely notice they are getting these messages.

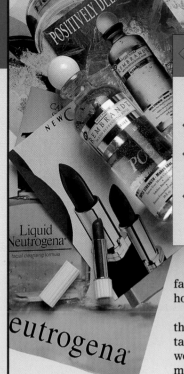

Checklist

Figure 3.6 Analyzing Advertisements

Ask yourself these questions as you read advertisements:

1. Does the ad only appeal to my emotions or does it provide facts?

2. What are the special features of the product? Do these special features make any sense in terms of my needs?

3. If I am interested in an automobile or appliance, does the ad tell me anything about operating costs?

4. Does the ad tell me anything about a product's durability, or ability to last?

5. Does the advertised price compare favorably with the price of similar products?

6. Is the advertised price the entire price, or are there extra costs in small print for installation or for separate parts, such as batteries?

---

faced with the problem of deciding how much information to obtain.

In the case of the mountain bike, the buying principle to follow is: Obtain only as much information as is worthwhile. What does *worthwhile* mean? The value of your time and effort spent gathering information should not be greater than the value you receive from making the best choice of product for yourself.

You would not, for example, want to go to every bike store in your town or city and spend two hours with every salesperson discussing every model. In contrast, you would probably want to spend more than two minutes reading one advertisement about one model. The less valuable a person considers his or her time, the more comparison shopping he or she should do. A nonworking college student generally should spend more time in comparison shopping than a business executive.

As you shop for different products, you will begin to develop a consumer-knowledge base. Information you obtain looking for a mountain bike might help you someday to make decisions about choosing a car or a computer.

Simply getting salespeople to give you accurate information is a skill that you can acquire and hone, or sharpen, over time while you shop for other products.

Using Advertising Wisely

Advertising is all around you. Whenever you turn on the radio or television, you will more than likely hear or see a commercial. Wherever you go, you read advertising on billboards, on posters on buses, and so on. The Checklist for Analyzing Advertisements in **Figure 3.6** gives you some tips for reading these ads, which can generally be classified as competitive or informative.

Competitive Advertising Advertising that attempts to persuade consumers that a product is different from and superior to any other is **competitive advertising.** Its purpose may be to take customers away from competitors or to keep competitors from taking away customers. Ads for well-established brand names and products, such as Apple computers and L.A. Gear, are often of this type. The ads are meant to keep the public aware of a company's name and its specific products.

Informative Advertising Informative advertising benefits consumers by giving information about a product. From such ads, you can learn about the existence, price, quality, and special features of products without spending much time or effort.

Meeting Special Needs

Auditory Learning Disability Some students are unable to recall words they have heard. To develop a facility with the chapter terms, create sentence completion exercises on a tape recorder. Record the definition for each word in a partial sentence. Leave a pause where the student is to complete the sentence. The student can either record the answer on the tape recorder for independent practice, review responses with the teacher or a partner, or write the answers.

Informative advertising may also be competitive in nature.

Bait and Switch Unfortunately, advertising can be misleading. Although most advertisers try to present their products accurately, some use deceptive, or false, advertising. Sellers may misrepresent the quality, features, or the true (full) price of goods.

One of the most widely used methods of deceptive advertising is **bait and switch.** The bait is an advertised item at an unrealistically low price. When the consumer gets to the store, the item is no longer available, or the salesperson points out all the bad features of the advertised item and how dissatisfied the customer will be with it.

The salesperson then shows higher-priced models and points out all their good features. This is the switch. Instead of being able to buy a $249

videodisc player, for example, the customer finds all the available ones are $400 or more. This practice is both deceptive and illegal.

Comparison Shopping

Once you have gathered the information and made a decision about a product you want, you must decide where to buy it. The price you will have to pay will affect your decision. Because you have limited income, a lower price will mean that you will have more income to spend on other purchases. You will be best off as a consumer when you are able to pay the lowest price for what you want. See Figure 3.7.

**Figure 3.7
Efficient Comparison
Shopping**
To efficiently comparison shop for bikes, read newspaper advertisements, make telephone calls, and visit different stores. Remember, however, that finding out price information requires time. ▶

Independent Practice

L3 Analyzing Advertisements Direct students to cut out three advertisements from magazines or newspapers and write a brief analysis of each ad, telling whether its main appeal is to the reader's intelligence or emotions. Pair students to discuss their ads and analyses.

L1 Comparison Shopping Have students list 10 household items they use. Tell them to visit 2 stores that have these items and to price the items by store and brand. Suggest including both brand and generic product prices if applicable. Have them organize their data into a table and post it on a bulletin board.
Have students complete Guided Reading Activity 3.2 in the TCR. LEP

? DID YOU KNOW

Although written advertising existed about 3,000 years ago in Egypt, newspaper advertising first appeared in London in the 1600s. The first products advertised were coffee, chocolate, and tea. Ads for books and medicine followed. Today, general interest magazines worldwide, such as *Asahi* (Japan), *Paris-Match* (France), *Der Spiegel* (Germany), and *Ms.* (United States), offer advertisers a chance to reach a wide cross section of consumers.

Cooperative Learning

Organize students into small groups and tell members they work for an advertising agency that needs to create an advertisement they think fits client needs. Assign groups a variety of informative and competitive topics: for example, a pet service for people with AIDS; glow-in-the-dark socks; a weight-loss program; a guide to making career choices; a video that helps teenagers overcome alcoholism; a book about women inventors. Display ads and discuss reasons for each approach.

65

Assess

Meeting Lesson Objectives

Assign Section 2 Review as homework or an in-class activity.

Evaluate

Assign the Section 2 Quiz in the TCR or use the Testmaker to develop a customized quiz.

Reteach

Organize the class into thirds for a debate. Have one third argue that advertising contributes positively to decision-making in buying. Have another third oppose advertising as interfering with a buyer's decision making. Have the third group vote.

Enrich

Have an advertising manager from a retailer or manufacturer talk about developing for ad campaigns.

Close

Have students outline how they would buy a television. Have them make a heading for each of the three basic buying principles.

A Some companies produce and sell **generic brands.** The word *generic* means "pertaining to a general class." A generic brand of cereal means there is no brand name at all. It is difficult to know who produced the product. ▼

B A **brand name** is a word, picture, or logo on a product that helps consumers distinguish it from similar products. Brand names are usually sold nationwide and are backed by major companies. ▼

Figure 3.8 Generic versus Brand Name
Your selection of generic or brand–name products makes a difference in price and sometimes in quality. Wise shoppers can often find non-brand names of equally high quality and reliability.

Shopping around suggests a third buying principle. Whenever you decide to make a purchase, it is generally worthwhile to get information on the types and prices of products available from different stores or companies. This process is known as **comparison shopping.**

Even when you apply rational buying principles to consumer decision making, you may still find that being a wise consumer is not always easy. The marketplace is a complex world with many sellers. Some sellers do not always include complete or reliable information about their products. Others may not readily repair or replace faulty products.

Brand-Name or Generic Products
Another consumer choice is between buying generic and brand-name products. Some consumers find that national brand-name products are worth the higher prices they often command. **Figure 3.8** explains more about choosing between brand-name and other products.

SECTION 2 REVIEW

Understanding Vocabulary
Define competitive advertising, informative advertising, bait and switch, generic brands, brand name, comparison shopping.

Reviewing Objectives
1. What trade-offs should a consumer consider when gathering information?
2. How does informative advertising differ from competitive advertising?
3. What is comparison shopping?

66 Unit 2 *Practical Economics: How Theory Works for You*

Section 2 Review Answers

Understanding Vocabulary
competitive advertising (p. 64), **informative advertising** (p. 64), **bait and switch** (p. 65), **generic brands** (p. 66), **brand name** (p. 66), **comparison shopping** (p. 66)

Reviewing Objectives
1. Consumers trade time and effort when gathering information. Time can also be money for some consumers.
2. It gives information, whereas competitive advertising tries to persuade.
3. It is the gathering of information about types and prices of products from different outlets.

LEARNING ECONOMIC SKILLS

Handling a Consumer Problem

Dealing with a faulty product or with a repair that was done incorrectly are two common consumer problems. Getting the results you want requires special communications skills.

Problem-Solving Steps

The Office of Consumer Affairs suggests that you:

❶ Report the problem immediately. Do not try to fix a product yourself, because doing so may cancel the warranty.

❷ State the problem and suggest a fair and just solution—replacement, refund, etc.

❸ Include important details and copies of receipts, guarantees, and contracts to support your case.

❹ Describe any action you have taken to try to correct the problem.

❺ Keep an accurate record of your efforts to get the problem solved. Include names of people you speak or write to and dates.

❻ Allow each person reasonable time, such as three weeks, to solve the problem before contacting another source.

❼ Keep cool. The person who will help you solve your problem is probably not responsible for the problem.

If you need to write to the manufacturer, be sure your writing is neat and easy to read. Type your letter, if possible. Keep a copy of the letter for your records and future reference.

Your Address
City, State, Zip Code
Date

Customer Service Department
Company Name
Street Address
City, State, Zip Code

Dear Customer Service Representative:

I bought a (product name, serial no., model no.) at (location and date of purchase). Unfortunately, (state problem, history of problem, and efforts to solve it).

I would appreciate your (state specific actions to be taken). Enclosed are copies of the following records: (list and enclose all documents connected with the problem).

I am looking forward to your reply and resolution of my problem and will wait (state reasonable time period) before seeking third party assistance. Please contact me at the above address or by phone (work and home numbers).

Sincerely,

Your Name

Practicing the Skill

❶ Using the sample, write a letter to the company that shipped you a computer game diskette that will not operate in your home computer.

❷ If you do not receive satisfaction on a complaint in a reasonable time, what might you do next?

67

Answers to Practicing the Skill

1. Answers will vary, but the letter should have the same components as the sample letter.
2. Answers will vary, but students may suggest filing a complaint with a private agency such as the Better Business Bureau or the consumer affairs department of their city, county, or state.

Focus

Overview

See the student page for section objectives.

Section 3 explains or describes: five consumer rights; private and government agencies that can take action to enforce them; and the relation between consumer responsibilities and ethical behavior.

Bellringer

Before presenting the lesson, display Focus Activity Transparency 10 on the overhead projector or copy the material on the chalkboard. Assign the accompanying Focus Activity Sheet.

Motivational Activity

Ask students if they have ever bought items that were faulty. Ask if they think it is their consumer responsibility to return these items. Why or why not?

Preteaching Vocabulary

Refer students to the Glossary definitions, but remind them that people may interpret differently what kind of behavior is ethical.

SECTION **3** *Consumerism*

SECTION 3 FOCUS

Terms to Know consumerism, ethical behavior

Objectives *After reading this section, you should be able to:*

1. List five **consumer rights.**
2. List sources of **private and federal help for consumers.**
3. Define **consumer responsibilities.**
4. Describe **ethical consumer behavior.**

Consumers Have Rights and Responsibilities

Today the decisions Americans face as consumers are increasingly complex. Many Americans are greatly concerned with the safety and reliability of the products and services they use. **Consumerism** is a movement to educate buyers about the purchases they make and to demand better and safer products from manufacturers. Many government agencies and private groups work to ensure the well-being of consumers. Since the early 1960s, consumerism has grown steadily. Business can no longer assume it is the buyer's responsibility to know whether a product is safe, food is healthful, or advertising is accurate. See **Figure 3.9.**

Figure 3.9 Consumer Protection Government inspection of many products protects consumers' health and safety and raises quality standards. ▼

Consumer Rights

In 1962 President John F. Kennedy sent the first consumer protection message to Congress. In that message, Kennedy stated four consumer rights:

- the right to safety—protection against goods that are dangerous to life or health;
- the right to be informed—information for use not only as protection against fraud but also as the basis for reasoned choices;
- the right to choose—the need for markets to be competitive (have many firms) and for protection by government in those other markets, such as electric service, where competition does not exist;
- the right to be heard—the guarantee that consumer interests will be listened to when laws are being written.

Classroom Resources for Section 3

- Reproducible Lesson Plan 3.3
- Focus Activity Transparency 10
- Focus Activity Sheet 10
- Guided Reading Activity 3.3
- Free Enterprise Activity 3
- Consumer Application Activity 3

- Mathematics Practice for Economics 3
- Performance Assessment Actitvity 3
- Section Quiz 3.3
- Spanish Section Quiz 3.3
- Chapter 3 Test Forms A and B

- Testmaker
- Enrichment Activity 3
- Economics Vocabulary Activity 3
- Audiocassette 3
- Spanish Audiocassette 3
- Reteaching Activity 3

Figure 3.10
Informing Yourself

A good consumer reads all contracts and warranties and asks about return and refund policies. After the purchase, he or she reads any instruction booklet and follows the directions for proper use of the product. ▶

To the four listed by President Kennedy, most consumer advocates would add a fifth:

- the right to redress—the ability to obtain from the manufacturers adequate payment in money or goods for financial or physical damages caused by their products.

Following the concepts that President Kennedy listed, Congress passed consumer-protection legislation. Today, consumers dissatisfied with a specific product can complain to the store manager or write to the manufacturer. They can also hire a lawyer or take the case to small claims court. Many private and public agencies can also help consumers.

Consumer Help: Private and Federal

Among the private groups that aid consumers are local citizens' action groups and local chapters of the Better Business Bureau. Many major cities and some smaller ones have better business bureaus. The bureaus provide information on products as well as selling practices to consumers and help settle disagreements between consumers and sellers. Before using these agencies, however, consumers need to learn about the products they wish to purchase as **Figure 3.10** shows.

A trade association is a group of companies in the same business that work together to promote that specific industry. Trade associations in some industries also provide consumers with information.

Two national organizations provide excellent sources of consumer information. The Consumers Union of the United States, Inc., publishes a monthly magazine called *Consumer Reports*. An informational magazine, *Consumer Reports* accepts no advertising. A competing publication is *Consumers' Research Magazine*, published by Consumers' Research, Inc.

Numerous federal agencies also have programs to aid consumers. **Figure 3.11** (pages 70–71) lists these agencies and what they do. Much of the information that now appears on product labels and in warranties is a result of federal regulations to protect consumers. States also have consumer affairs councils or agencies.

Consumer Responsibilities

Consumers have responsibilities as well as rights. Learning as much as possible about the product or service he or she wishes to buy will enable the consumer to purchase the best product at the best price.

Chapter 3 Your Role as a Consumer **69**

Guided Practice

L2 Understanding Have students prepare a table that lists each of the five consumer rights in one column. In another column tell students to list at least two specific instances when they might need to assert each of these rights.

Visual Instruction

Review with students the material in Figure 3.10 and its caption about a buyer's responsibility to be an informed consumer. Ask students to bring in any brochures, flyers, warranties, or policies they received from the last major purchase they or their family made. Have them read the information and write a paragraph about their product and the rights and responsibilities they accepted by purchasing it.

? DID YOU KNOW

The total number of consumer inquiries handled by the 166 Better Business Bureaus in 1992 was 9,606,176—up nearly 7 percent from the previous year. The top three industries receiving the most inquiries were retail businesses, home improvement companies, and service firms (excluding auto, which was fourth).

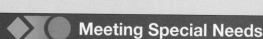

Meeting Special Needs

Reading Disability A good way to help students understand what they read is known by the acronym KWL. With KWL, students brainstorm what they **know (K)** about the topic covered in the section and think about what they **want (W)** to learn about the topic before reading. After reading, ask students to discuss what they **learned (L)**. By focusing on the topics before reading and reviewing what they read, students gain improved comprehension.

Independent Practice

L2 Cartoon Faulty products may not be a laughing matter, but how people deal with them can be. Have students draw a cartoon about a product or service that fell short of their expectations, showing their discontent with the product or their problems with rectifying the situation.

L3 Interview Have students interview at least five people who purchased a product or service they found unsatisfactory. Students should ask them how they identified which product or service to purchase and how they dealt with the problem. Tell students to write a short evaluation of each situation and, if appropriate, suggest how the purchase or complaint could have been handled differently.

Have students complete Guided Reading Activity 3.3 in the TCR. LEP

Assess

Meeting Lesson Objectives

Assign Section 3 Review as homework or an in-class activity.

Figure 3.11 Federal Agencies and Consumerism

Agency	How It Helps the Consumer	For More Information
Consumer Information Center Program	Provides free catalog of government publications on consumer topics	*Consumer's Resource Handbook* Consumer Information Center Pueblo, Colorado 81009
Federal Trade Commission	Promotes free and fair competition by enforcing laws against monopolies, price fixing, false advertising, and other illegal business practices; regulates packaging and labeling of products and protects the public against violations of consumer credit laws	Federal Trade Commission 6th St. and Pennsylvania Avenue, N.W. Office of Public Information Washington, D.C. 20580
Consumer Product Safety Commission	Protects the public against unreasonable risk of injury from consumer products; sets product safety requirements, forbids the production and sale of dangerous consumer products, and conducts research and education programs on safety concerns for industry and the public	Office of the Secretary, Consumer Product Safety Commission 5401 Westbard Avenue Bethesda, MD 20207
Government Printing Office	Sells more than 15,000 government publications on a wide variety of topics; lists those of interest to consumers in free booklet: *Consumer Information Subject Bibliography*	Superintendent of Documents Government Printing Office Washington, D.C. 20402
U.S. Postal Service	Through its Inspection Services protects public from mail fraud and other violations of postal laws; through Consumer Advocate's office acts on complaints and suggestions from individual consumers and provides information on past and present schemes used to cheat the public	Consumer Advocate U.S. Postal Service Washington, D.C. 20260
U.S. Department of Agriculture	Inspects and grades meat, fish, poultry, dairy products, and fruits and vegetables through the department's Food Safety and Quality Service; ensures that food production is sanitary and that products are labeled truthfully	Office of the Consumer Adviser Administration Building U.S. Department of Agriculture Washington, D.C. 20250

Cooperative Learning

Organize the class into small groups and tell each group to choose one of these products to purchase: CD player, expensive business suit, microwave oven, puppy, motorcycle, computer printer, or high school equivalency correspondence course. Have students discuss what their group has a right to know before purchasing their product and what recourse they have if they find their product is defective. One student from each group should record main points and present them to the class. Evaluate as a class the actions each group followed.

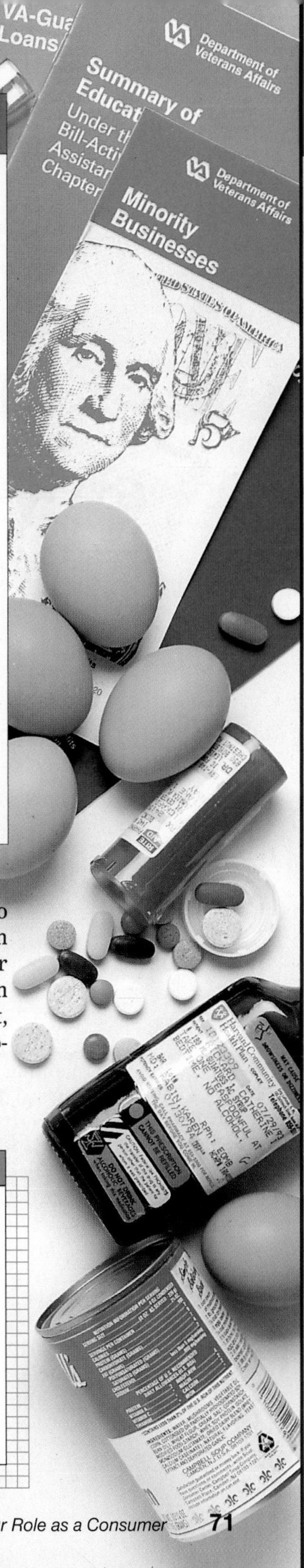

Figure 3.11 Federal Agencies and Consumerism

Agency	How It Helps the Consumer	For More Information
U.S. Office of Consumer Affairs (Department of Health and Human Services)	Coordinates all federal activities on behalf of consumers, advises President on consumer affairs, and works for and testifies on behalf of consumer legislation; the Complaint Coordination Center helps solve consumer problems	U.S. Office of Consumer Affairs Humphrey Building 200 Independence Avenue Washington, D.C. 20201
Food and Drug Administration (Department of Health and Human Services)	Protects the public against impure and unsafe foods, drugs, and cosmetics; researches and tests new products in these areas and ensures accurate labeling; publishes *FDA Consumer* magazine and maintains regional consumer affairs offices	Food and Drug Administration 5600 Fishers Lane Rockville, Maryland 20857
National Highway Traffic Safety Administration (Department of Transportation)	Sets requirements for automobile safety, maintenance, and fuel economy and tests products for compliance; researches ways to save fuel and make highways safer and investigates complaints from consumers about vehicle safety	National Highway Traffic Safety Administration Department of Transportation Washington, D.C. 20590

Ethical Behavior

Consumers should respect the rights of producers and sellers of goods and services. **Ethical behavior** involves acting in accordance with one's moral and ethical convictions about right and wrong. For example, a responsible consumer will not try to return a used item because it has been advertised elsewhere for a lower price. Nor will a consumer misuse an item and then attempt to return it, saying it was defective—faulty or broken—when bought.

SECTION 3 REVIEW

Understanding Vocabulary

Define consumerism, ethical behavior.

Reviewing Objectives

1. What are the five important rights that consumers have?
2. What private and federal groups aid consumers?
3. Why should consumers learn about products they wish to buy?
4. What role does ethical behavior play in consumers' actions?

Chapter 3, Section 3

Evaluate

Assign the Section 3 Quiz in the TCR or use the Testmaker to develop a customized quiz.

Assign the Chapter 3 Test Form A or Form B or use the Testmaker to develop a customized test.

Reteach

Have students prepare a web that shows the main points and details in the section.

Have students complete Reteaching Activity 3 in the TCR.

Enrich

Tell students to prepare a report proposing a consumer program to aid access to more medicines. Have them list private and government agencies they would contact for help.

Have students complete Enrichment Activity 3 in the TCR.

Close

Have students write a paragraph about how knowing their consumer responsibilities makes them better citizens.

Section 3 Review Answers

Understanding Vocabulary

consumerism (p. 68), **ethical behavior** (p. 71)

Reviewing Objectives

1. the right to safety; the right to be informed; the right to choose; the right to be heard; the right to redress
2. the Better Business Bureau, trade associations, Consumer Action Panels, the Consumers Union of the United States, Inc., and Consumers' Research, Inc.
3. Answers may vary but should suggest having enough information to make a wise decision about buying.
4. It is a consumer responsibility.

Teach

Inform students that consumerism has had a major impact on directions that companies took in recent years. Consumers are becoming more aware of business advertising gimmicks and better able to resist being pressured. Many products fail each year because companies misjudge the power of consumerism. Ask students which new products they have seen on television that interest them and why. Ask whether color is enough to make them alter their buying decisions. Refer students to the products mentioned in this feature, and discuss how sometimes consumerism produces positive results and sometimes spurs misguided attempts at profits.

Have students choose a product from the article and survey at least 10 people to determine whether they would choose the original over the newer colorless version and why. Tell students to ask respondents whether they believe the transparent version is more "natural" and therefore healthier. Ask students to tally their results in a bar graph that will be displayed on a bulletin board. Compare the results with those from other classmates.

News Clip

Readings in Economics

THE NEW YORK TIMES   JUNE 6, 1993

BEHIND THE 'CLEAR' TREND
by Barnaby J. Feder

From drinks to deodorants to dishwashing liquid, not to mention gasoline and mouthwash, the hot color for new products is no color at all.

Marketers like to have something novel to sell, but the driving force in the trend is an effort to tap into consumers' associations of clarity with health, purity, freshness and no-frills functionality. And if consumers see... transparent antiperspirant as more "natural" than colored competitors, so much the better.

But clear products are usually as thoroughly processed as any tinted cousins, if not more so. In creating Crystal Pepsi, for example, Pepsi needed 14 months to iron out the formula and production process. Pepsi takes longer and spends more to produce the clear cola, which requires greater quality controls than the brown stuff....

"This isn't rocket science," said Thomas Pirko, president of Bevmark, food and beverage consultants based in Los Angeles. "The technology is clearly subservient to the marketing consideration."

... Perhaps the clearest case of technology being subservient to marketing in the trend toward clear products is that of Crystal Clear Amoco Ultimate gasoline. The colorless premium gasoline has been on the market since 1915 in the eastern United States, originally under the White Crown name.

Only in the last five years, though, has the petroleum industry had the tools to analyze auto emissions in great detail. One result was that the Amoco Oil Company discovered that its clear gas—renamed as Crystal Clear last year—has an environmental advantage over its competitors.... [it] cut emissions of hydrocarbons by 13 percent.

• THINK ABOUT IT •

1. Why are "clear" products gaining popularity?
2. What is the environmental advantage of Crystal Clear Amoco?

Answers to Think About It

1. They are perceived as being more natural.
2. It cuts emission of hydrocarbons by 13 percent.

3 *Highlights*

Consumption, Income, and Decision Making

Key Terms
consumer (p. 58)
disposable income (p. 58)
discretionary income (p. 58)
warranty (p. 60)
rational choice (p. 61)

Summary
Some disposable income is discretionary and does not have to be spent on necessities. A wise consumer considers many factors before making a purchase.

Buying Principles, or Strategies

Key Terms
competitive advertising (p. 64)
informative advertising (p. 64)
bait and switch (p. 65)
generic brands (p. 66)
brand name (p. 66)
comparison shopping (p. 66)

Summary
The value of a consumer's time and effort in obtaining information should not be greater than the value received from making the best choice of a product. Some advertising is informative, other advertising is mainly competitive. Before buying, consumers should practice comparison shopping.

Consumerism

Key Terms
consumerism (p. 68)
ethical behavior (p. 71)

Summary
Consumers have important rights as well as sources of help. Private agencies and government agencies offer consumer information and assistance. Consumers also have several responsibilities, including the responsibility to behave ethically.

Chapter 3 Your Role as a Consumer **73**

Use the Chapter 3 Highlights to preview, review, condense, or reteach the chapter. A Spanish Chapter Highlights is available in the Spanish Handbook.

Preview/Review

After students read the Chapter 3 Highlights, have them complete Economics Vocabulary Activity 3 in the TCR. Spanish Vocabulary Activities are also available in the Spanish Resource Binder.

Vocabulary Software reinforces the economic terms used in Chapter 3.

Condense

Have students listen to Chapter 3 on the Audiocassettes in the TCR. A 1-page written activity and 1-page test accompany this material. These materials are also available in Spanish.

Reteach

Have students complete Reteaching Activity 3 in the TCR. Spanish Reteaching Activities are also available.

 VIDEODISC

Nightly Business Report
Economics in Action
Use "Your Role as a Consumer" on Disc 1, Side A, Video 4.

Search 15084, Play to 21480

ANSWERS

Identifying Key Terms
1. c
2. e
3. a
4. b
5. d
6. consumer
7. discretionary income
8. informative advertising

9. brand name
10. generic brand
11. ethical behavior

Recalling Facts and Ideas
Section 1
1. discretionary income
2. time
3. Do I really need this? Is it worth the time? Is there any better use for my money?
4. No. People disagree about what generates the greatest value for any expenditure.

Section 2
5. gathering information, using advertising wisely, comparison shopping
6. competitive and informative
7. enough to make an informed choice
8. comparison shopping

Section 3
9. Consumerism educates buyers about their purchases and about demanding better, safer products from manufacturers.
10. Federal agencies set health and safety requirements, inspect products, and promote free and fair competition.
11. the rights to safety, to be informed, to choose, and to be heard
12. Answers will vary but may include: to learn as much as they can about

Identifying Key Terms

Write the letter of the definition in Column B that correctly defines each term in Column A.

Column A
1. disposable income (p. 58)
2. warranty (p. 60)
3. bait and switch (p. 65)
4. comparison shopping (p. 66)
5. competitive advertising (p. 64)

Column B
a. deceptive advertising intended to defraud the consumer
b. getting information about similar types of products and prices
c. money income left after taxes have been paid
d. attempts to persuade consumers that certain products are different and superior to others
e. written guarantee of a product for a certain period of time

Use terms from the following list to fill in the blanks in the paragraph below.

ethical behavior (p. 71) consumer (p. 58)
informative discretionary
  advertising (p. 64)   income (p. 58)
generic brand (p. 66) brand name (p. 66)

Every one of us is at one time or another a (6) . Sometimes we have (7) to spend on "fun" things. In order to make our purchases, we may use (8) , which tells us about the product. We often have the choice between a (9) and a (10), which is usually cheaper. In any event, as a consumer, you should always be responsible and be concerned about your (11) .

Recalling Facts and Ideas

Section 1
1. After people have bought necessities, they are left with what type of income?
2. Income is one scarce resource that you use when you are a consumer. What is the other scarce resource?
3. Before you buy anything, what three questions should you ask yourself?
4. Do all rational consumers think alike? Why or why not?

Section 2
5. What are three important buying principles?
6. What are the two major types of commercial advertising?
7. How much information should you obtain before you make a purchase?
8. What type of shopping allows you to be a rational consumer?

Section 3
9. What are the major purposes of consumerism today?
10. What three types of help do federal agencies give to consumers?
11. What are the four consumer rights that President John F. Kennedy stated?
12. What are two consumer responsibilities?

Critical Thinking

Section 1
Determining Cause and Effect How might education, occupation, and health make a difference in a person's earning power (income) and therefore in his or her ability to consume?

a product before buying, respect the rights of producers and sellers, and practice ethical behavior.

Critical Thinking
Section 1
Answers may vary but could include: more education can lead to higher paying jobs; occupations with more earning power increase disposable income; healthy individuals have greater capacity for work and earnings.

Section 2
Brand-name products ensure more consistent quality and reliability; generic products offer cost savings.

Section 3
Consumer rights protect the buyer, and consumer responsibilities protect the buyer, manufacturer, and seller.

Section 2

Analyzing Information Why do some people buy brand–name products and other people buy generic products? What are the trade-offs involved in this decision?

Section 3

Making Comparisons How do consumer rights compare with consumer responsibilities?

Applying Economic Concepts

Competition and Market Structure Choose an advertisement from a newspaper or a magazine, and use the checklist on page 64 to analyze it. Write a sentence to answer each of the questions on the checklist. Do you think it is a competitive ad, an informative ad, or both? Explain the reasons for your choice.

Reviewing Skills

Handling a Consumer Problem
1. List 10 items of information that a person should include in a letter of complaint to a product manufacturer.
2. What should consumers keep in their records when dealing with the problem of a faulty product?
3. What impact do you think your consumer complaint will have on the product manufacturer? Do you think your complaint will result in an improved product?

Chapter Projects

1. Individual Project Imagine that you have decided to buy a car, but you still have to decide on the size (not the make and model, but only the size). Go through the steps you would use to research your decision. Keep a record of the information you find.
2. Cooperative Learning Project Working in groups of four, take the Checklist for Consumer Decision Making on page 60 and the

three buying principles listed in the text and shop for one of the following: VCR, portable compact disc player, or personal computer. Each of you should keep a record of the steps you take and the information you gather using a table like the one shown. Compare your information with what others in the class found.

Checklist Number	Step	Information
1.		
2.		
3.		
4.		
5.		
6.		
7.		
8.		
9.		
10.		

Writing About Economics

Persuasive Writing Choose one of the items you purchased and recorded in Your Economics Journal. Write a persuasive letter trying to convince a friend to purchase a similar item from the same store.

75

Applying Economic Concepts

Answers will vary. Make sure students analyze an advertisement according to the points listed on the checklist.

Reviewing Skills

1. A letter of complaint should include the problem; a fair and just solution; details and copies of receipts, guarantees, or contracts; description of actions you have already taken; record of efforts taken to correct the problem; names of people you spoke with; dates of contacts; the amount of time you are willing to wait for resolution of the problem; your name, address, and telephone number(s).
2. Consumers should keep all receipts, guarantees, or contracts concerning the product and records concerning any transactions about the product.

BONUS QUESTION

The following bonus question may be written on the chalkboard when students take the chapter test.
Q: What manufacturer's agreement lets you return a wristwatch for free repair during a stated period?
A: warranty

Chapter Projects

1. Student records should reflect some understanding of the concepts covered on the consumer decision-making checklist.
2. Students should have a detailed account of shopping for one of the items listed that includes points covered on the consumer checklist and the buying principles.

3. Answers may vary, ranging from expectations of no response to full compliance.

Writing About Economics

Students should cover at least three reasons to convince a friend to buy an item similar to the one they want from the same store.

Point

Focus

Give students time to read Point/Counterpoint in class. Then have them create a table that lists the pros and cons detailed in the article about the issue of using pollution taxes to help the environment. Tell students to begin by drawing a vertical line down the center of a paper and label one section Pros and the other section Cons.

Teach

L3 Research and Writing
How do pollution taxes compare with other taxes? Have students research the effectiveness of different taxes to help lessen the federal budget deficit. Describe their overall benefits, if any, to the American people. Have students write a report that compares the costs and benefits of pollution taxes with other taxes. Students should conclude with a paragraph supporting or opposing pollution taxes.

ISSUE: Should "Pollution Taxes" Be Used to Help the Environment and Lower the Deficit?

In 1970 the Environmental Protection Agency (EPA) was set up to combat the growing problem of pollution. After President Clinton took office in 1993, the idea of pollution taxes to help the environment and reduce the federal budget deficit gained popularity and became the subject of debate.

PRO Some of the groups in favor of pollution taxes seem to think that these taxes will not only help the environment, but will increase productivity and raise individual welfare as well.

According to the World Resources Institute, shifting 10 to 15 percent of the nation's tax burden from "goods" to "bads" could yield an annual economic "dividend" that is greater than 1 percent of annual national output. The National Commission of the Environment argues that such a tax would send the "right economic signals." The Progressive Policy Institute asserts that government regulations to help the environment end up hampering innovation in pollution control methods, while pollution taxes can promote energy efficiency and put the U.S. "on an energy path consistent with sustainable development."

Jonathan Marshall, the economics editor of the *San Francisco Chronicle*, writes in *Reason* that pollution taxes have too much potential *not* to give them a try. He feels that the benefits of such taxes are too great to ignore:

And yet, for all these objections, pollution taxes deserve a hearing among free-market advocates as a viable "second-best" strategy in the absence of some libertarians' utopia. You don't have to be a green zealot to concede that heavy smog impairs lungs and toxic compounds can kill people.

Barring an intellectual or institutional breakthrough, some form of collective action is needed to control pollution. Once that premise is accepted, pollution taxes in principle are cheaper and more effective in most instances than command-and-control regulations.

Like any social policy, pollution taxes must be done right. Given the political system's overwhelming predisposition toward "government failure," that may be wishful thinking. But killing the idea is hardly a superior alternative if it just means accepting the status quo by default.

Answers to Exploring the Issue

Reviewing Facts
1. Pollution taxes increase productivity, reduce the deficit, and raise individual welfare. The costs involve administration of pollution controls.
2. Environmental groups support pollution taxes. Large corporations that must make pollution adjustments and workers who must pay a large portion of their income for gas and heating oil tend to oppose pollution taxes.

Critical Thinking
3. Answers will vary but should include logically supported governmental alternatives to pollution taxes that can be used to encourage the use of natural resources.

Counterpoint

CON Those against pollution taxes tend to be political conservatives, who are worried that the costs of such taxes will outweigh their benefits. Unfortunately, both costs and benefits are hard to measure; the benefits even more so than the costs. Fred Smith, president of the Competitive Enterprise Institute, expresses the concern that pollution tax schemes "look a lot better than they may turn out to be in practice."

With one particular type of pollution tax, the carbon tax (a tax based on the carbon content of fossil fuels such as gasoline), Lawrence Goulder of Stanford University questions whether the uncertain benefits will really be greater than the costs. He had been a supporter of carbon taxes, but in his study of the potential effects of the tax, he came up with higher costs and greater economic distortions than expected.

Critics also argue that carbon or energy taxes will hurt U.S. competitiveness in foreign markets, and lead to higher prices for consumers. Economist Anthony Riccardi asserts that taxes on energy are essentially regressive taxes. The working poor would be the group most severely hurt by this type of tax, as a large percentage of their income goes to costs such as gasoline and heating oil.

Writing for the *Asbury Park* (New Jersey) *Press*, Larry McDonnell points out some local criticisms of a carbon tax:

> *Who could argue with a tax on pollutants threaten-ing the planet? Especially a tax that would take a big bite out of the deficit. As it turns out, many people will argue, particularly the chemical and petroleum industries, two of New Jersey's larger employers.*

"Attempting to impose yesterday's costs on today's U.S.-based production undermines our international competitiveness," said Sean T. Crimmins, vice president and general tax counsel for Ashland Oil Inc., testifying before Congress this spring. "To do so at this time—in the face of already large U.S. trade deficits—is the economic equivalent of shooting oneself in the foot."

Exploring the Issue

Reviewing Facts

1. What would be the benefits of pollution taxes? What would be the costs?
2. What individuals and groups support pollution taxes? What individuals and groups oppose pollution taxes?

Critical Thinking

3. **Identifying Alternatives** What methods, other than pollution taxes, might the government use to encourage the wise use of natural resources?

Assess

Have students answer the Exploring the Issue questions.

Close

Organize students into small groups to read their reports. Then vote to see how many support President Clinton's pollution taxes and how many oppose them.

CHAPTER 4 **GOING INTO DEBT**

CHAPTER ORGANIZER

Daily Objectives	Special Features	Classroom Resources
Section 1 Americans and Credit • **List** the advantages of repaying installment debt over a long period. • **Explain** why people use credit. • **Describe** how consumers decide to use credit.	**Personal Perspective:** "Ronald Homer on Running a Bank," p. 84	Reproducible Lesson Plan 4.1 *NBR* Video 5 and Video Still 4 Focus Activity Transparency 11 Focus Activity Sheet 11 Guided Reading Activity 4.1 Cooperative Learning Activity 4 Primary and Secondary Source Readings 4 Consumer Application Activity 4 Section Quiz 4.1 Spanish Section Quiz 4.1 Testmaker
Section 2 Sources of Loans and Credit • **List** the six types of lending institutions. • **Explain** the three types of charge accounts. • **Describe** how **credit** and **debit cards** are used. • **Contrast** a finance charge and the annual percentage rate.		Reproducible Lesson Plan 4.2 Focus Activity Transparency 12 Focus Activity Sheet 12 Guided Reading Activity 4.2 Free Enterprise Activity 4 Section Quiz 4.2 Spanish Section Quiz 4.2
Section 3 Applying for Credit • **Explain** the four factors that determine a person's credit rating. • **List** your responsibilities as a borrower.	**Learning Economic Skills:** Determining a Safe Debt Load, p. 97	Reproducible Lesson Plan 4.3 Focus Activity Transparency 13 Focus Activity Sheet 13 Guided Reading Activity 4.3 Section Quiz 4.3 Spanish Section Quiz 4.3 Reinforcing Skills 4
Section 4 Government Regulation of Credit • **State** how the Equal Credit Opportunity Act affected consumer credit. • **Describe** state usury laws. • **Explain** why a person might declare personal bankruptcy.	**News Clip:** "Digging Out of the Debt Trap," *Changing Times*, p. 102	Reproducible Lesson Plan 4.4 Focus Activity Transparency 14 Focus Activity Sheet 14 Guided Reading Activity 4.4 Mathematics Practice for Economics 4 Performance Assessment Activity 4 Section Quiz 4.4

`0:00` **OUT OF TIME?** If time does not permit teaching this chapter, you may use the Chapter 4 Highlights and the Audiocassettes that include a 1-page activity and a 1-page test.

Chapter 4 Review and Evaluation

Special Features

Chapter 4 Highlights, p. 103
Chapter 4 Review, pp. 104–105

Classroom Resources

- Chapter 4 Test Forms A and B
- Economics Vocabulary Activity 4
- Spanish Economics Vocabulary
  Activity 4

- Audiocassette 4
- Spanish Audiocassette 4
- Reteaching Activity 4
- Spanish Reteaching Activity 4

Key to Ability Levels

Teaching strategies have been coded for varying learning styles and abilities.

L1 Level 1 activities are **basic** activities and should be within the ability range of all students.

L2 Level 2 activities are **average** activities designed for the ability range of average to above-average students.

L3 Level 3 activities are **challenging** activities designed for the ability range of above-average students.

LEP activities should be within the ability range of **Limited English Proficiency** students.

Performance Assessment

The following chapter project may be assigned at the beginning of the chapter and used for performance assessment. See page T12 for additional Performance Assessment information.

Finding the Best Credit Bargain Organize the class into four groups. Tell them they will need to borrow $5,000 to furnish an apartment with a refrigerator, dishwasher, stove, and furniture. Assign each group to research how much it will cost to borrow the money from one of the following: commercial bank, savings and loan association, credit union, and consumer finance company. Students should conduct their research throughout their study about the costs and benefits of credit in Chapter 4. At the end of the chapter, have each group report their findings. Compare the four institutions' payment periods, amount of monthly payments, interest rates, finance charges, and total costs of the loans.

Additional Resources

Readings for the Student

Cook, John A., and Wool, Robert. *All You Need to Know About Banks.* New York: Bantam Books, 1984.
Credit Card Secrets. Edited by Howard Strong. Beverly Hills, CA: Boswell Corporation, 1989.

Readings for the Teacher

Berman, Daniel K. *Credit Power Handbook for American Consumers.* San Francisco: Creditpower Publishing, 1989.

Multimedia Materials

Banking and Money Management Series. Two disks and two guides. Apple. Marshware. Social Studies School Service, 10200 Jefferson Blvd., Culver City, CA 90232-0802

Consumers and the Law. Three-disk interactive video, 8 booklets, and a guide. Apple. Social Studies School Service, 10200 Jefferson Blvd., Culver City, CA 90232-0802. Case studies of consumer problems.

Credit Cards: Living with Plastic. Learning Seed. Social Studies School Service, 10200 Jefferson Blvd., Culver City, CA 90232-0802

Survival Finances: Personal Money Management. One disk with photocopy masters and guide. Apple. J. Weston Walsh. Social Studies School Service, 10200 Jefferson Blvd., Culver City, CA 90232-0802

78B

Chapter Overview

Individuals often use installment loans and credit cards to buy goods and services when they do not have enough cash to purchase a particular item. Chapter 4 explains or describes: the advantages of buying items on credit and why people decide to use credit; six types of lending institutions; different credit cards and charge accounts; the costs of credit; how credit ratings are determined; borrowers' responsibilities; state and federal laws regulating consumer credit; and reasons for declaring bankruptcy.

VIDEODISC

Nightly Business Report
Economics in Action
Use "Going Into Debt" on Disc 1, Side A, Video 5.

Search 21560, Play to 26885

CHAPTER

4 GOING INTO DEBT

What are the costs of using credit cards?

What is this card?

Answering Economic Questions

The questions in the above illustration are designed to lead into the main concepts in Chapter 4. Some students may have used their parents' credit cards or may have credit cards of their own. Others have seen them used on TV or in stores. Few students, however, know how credit really works and the costs and fees associated with the use of credit cards. The questions should help them focus on the differences among credit cards and other types of loans and how much going into debt really costs.

How does having this kind of card make shopping more convenient?

When do you think you might be offered a credit card?

What types of companies issue this kind of card?

Your Economics Journal

Keep track of the ads that you see or hear about that relate to credit and debt. List the different types of companies that advertise to offer you credit. Next to each name, indicate which companies offer credit for large purchases and which offer credit for small purchases.

79

Connecting to Past Learning

Ask students to list the reasons they would borrow money to purchase an item right away rather than to wait and save for it. Tell students that in Chapter 4 they will learn the benefits and costs of going into debt and how to make wise decisions about credit buying. After finishing the chapter, have students review their reasons for borrowing and ask if they would now revise their opinions.

Applying Economics

Tell students to imagine that someone is offering to loan them $1,000 to buy whatever they want, and they do not have to return the money for one year. Ask how many would accept the money. Now tell students that, with interest, monthly payments on this loan will be $100 for 12 months. Ask how many would take the money now. Tell students they will learn the opportunity and financial costs of credit that many borrowers do not understand.

EXTRA CREDIT PROJECT

Do a research paper on consumer lending and borrowing laws in an African, Asian, European, or Central or South American country. Try to include a table summarizing your findings.

Economic Portfolio

Have students look over the ads they collected for **Your Economics Journal.** Ask them to write a paragraph responding to the following question: Should credit be made easily available to many people? Have students give reasons for their opinions and cite examples that either support easy credit availability or argue against it.

PERFORMANCE ASSESSMENT

Refer to page 78B for "Finding the Best Credit Bargain," a Performance Assessment Activity for this chapter.

Focus

Overview

See the student page for section objectives.

Section 1 explains or describes: the importance and uses of consumer credit and loans in the economy; the advantages of repaying loans over the long term; and why and how consumers decide to use credit.

Bellringer

Before presenting the lesson, display Focus Activity Transparency 11 on the overhead projector or copy the material on the chalkboard. Assign the accompanying Focus Activity Sheet.

Motivational Activity

Ask students whether they ever bought an item and then found they did not really want it. Discuss how advertisements encourage people to "buy now—pay later." Have students discuss how easy credit might encourage poor buying choices for consumers.

Preteaching Vocabulary

Ask students to list terms on a sheet of paper and number them 1 to 6. Next, write the definitions on separate slips of paper and turn them over. Mix up the slips. Have students pull one slip out of the pile and match the definitions to the vocabulary words.

SECTION **1** Americans and Credit

SECTION 1 FOCUS

Terms to Know credit, principal, interest, installment debt, consumer durables, mortgage

Objectives *After reading this section, you should be able to:*

1. List the advantages of repaying **installment debt** over a long period.
2. Explain **why people use credit.**
3. Describe how consumers **decide to use credit.**

Americans Use Credit to Make Many Purchases

For the nation as a whole, the total amount of money borrowed and lent each year is enormous. Federal, state, and local governments all borrow each year. The nation's economy depends on individuals and groups being able to buy and borrow on credit. **Credit** is the receiving of money either directly or indirectly to buy goods and services today with the promise to pay for them in the future. The amount owed—the debt—is equal to the principal plus interest. The **principal** is the amount originally borrowed. The **interest** is the amount the borrower must pay for the use of someone else's money. That someone else may be a bank, a credit card company, or a store. Figure 4.1 shows the total amount of consumer debt owed each year in the United States from 1982 to 1992.

Any time you receive credit, you are borrowing money and going into debt. Taking out a loan is the same as buying an item on credit. In both cases, you must pay interest for the use of someone else's purchasing power.

**Figure 4.1
How Much Debt?**
By how much did consumer debt increase between 1982 and 1992?
▼

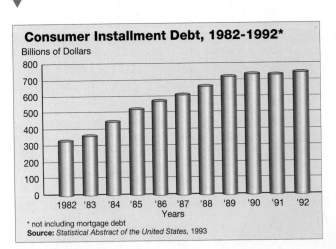

Consumer Installment Debt, 1982-1992*
Billions of Dollars

* not including mortgage debt
Source: *Statistical Abstract of the United States, 1993*

Installment Debt

One of the most common types of debt is **installment debt.** Consumers repay this type of loan with equal payments, or installments, over a period of time, for example, 36 months. Many people buy such consumer durables as automobiles, refrigerators, washers, and other appliances on an installment plan. **Consumer durables** are manufactured items that people use for long periods of time before

80   *Unit 2 Practical Economics: How Theory Works for You*

Classroom Resources for Section 1

Reproducible Lesson Plan 4.1
NBR Video 5 and Video Still 4
Focus Activity Transparency 11
Focus Activity Sheet 11
Guided Reading Activity 4.1
Cooperative Learning Activity 4

Primary and Secondary Source Readings 4
Consumer Application Activity 4
Section Quiz 4.1
Spanish Section Quiz 4.1
Testmaker

replacing them. People can also borrow cash and pay it back in installments.

The length of the installment period is important in determining the size of the borrower's monthly payments and the total amount of interest he or she must pay. A longer repayment period results in a smaller monthly payment. For example, Figure 4.2 shows that if the repayment of a loan is spread over three years, the monthly payments will be smaller than if the loan were repaid in two years. There is a trade-off, however. The longer it takes to repay an installment loan, the greater the total interest the lender charges.

The largest form of installment debt in this country is the money people owe on mortgages. A **mortgage** is an installment debt owed on real property—houses, buildings, or land. See Figure 4.3.

Figure 4.2
Loan Payments
How much more interest will a borrower pay who spreads loan payments over 36 rather than 24 months? ▼

$1,000 Installment Loan at 9% Interest		
Term of Loan	24 months	36 months
Monthly Payments	$45.69	$31.80
Total Interest	$96.56	$114.80
Total Payments	$1,096.56	$1,144.80

▼ **Figure 4.3 Mortgages as Debts**
Most people who owe only a mortgage on their home or farm do not consider themselves deeply in debt. They do not think of a mortgage as being similar to other kinds of debt. A mortgage is a debt, however, because somebody has provided the owner with money to purchase property. In return, the owner must repay the loan with interest in installments over a number of years.

Teach

Guided Practice

L2 Speculating Help students see the positive uses of credit. Ask students to imagine our economy without credit. Have them think about how people would make major purchases such as houses, durable goods, and cars without the cash. Write students' ideas on the chalkboard.

Visual Instruction

Refer students to Figure 4.1 to use as a model for constructing their own bar graph that shows a major category of consumer debt—credit card debt, bank loans for home improvements such as remodeling or landscaping, installment purchases for durable goods, medical or health care debts, and so on. Approve their choices to avoid duplicating graphs. Ask volunteers to show their graphs. Discuss trends in consumer debt.

 VIDEODISC

Nightly Business Report
Economics in Action
Use Video Still 4, "Consumer Loan/Saving Rate," on Disc 1, Side A, Video 5.

Search Frame 23339

◆▶◯ **Meeting Special Needs**

Reading Disability Students with reading or organizational difficulties may not be able to understand readily the idea that installment debt can be both an asset and a liability in terms of opportunity costs. Go over the material in this section to show them how installment debt can be a liability if the value of the item goes down over the term of the loan. Reinforce that, on the other hand, an installment debt can be an asset if the monthly payments match more closely the value of the consumer's *use* of an item.

Independent Practice

L1 Recording Ask students to keep a list for one week of all the goods and services they find that can be paid for by credit card either through the mail, over the telephone, or at a place of business. Display the lists at the end of the week.

L3 Analyzing Have students analyze their own purchases for a week and construct a circle graph showing what percentage of the items are necessities and what percentage are wants (CDs, paperbacks, snacks, video games). Students should note what percentage of items in each category can be charged.

 Have students complete Guided Reading Activity 4.1 in the TCR. LEP

DID YOU KNOW

The Federal National Mortgage Association (known as Fannie Mae) is the largest single investor in home mortgages. Fannie Mae does not lend money directly to consumers; rather, it purchases mortgages from a nationwide network of 4,000 financial institutions. The money is then used by lenders to offer a wide variety of mortgages to consumers.

Why People Use Credit

Most Americans are accustomed to borrowing and buying on credit. At times, especially when buying such expensive consumer durables as automobiles and fine furniture, they consider borrowing to be necessary.

Immediate Need In a sense, people feel forced to buy items on credit because they believe they need them immediately. They do not want to wait. Of course, consumers are not really "forced" to buy most goods and services on credit. They could decide instead to save the money needed to make their purchases.

Figure 4.4
If a person saved for 36 months to buy a $15,000 truck, the truck would cost only $13,500. The remaining $1,500 would be made up by the interest paid on the savings over the three years. According to the ad, however, if the person bought the $15,000 truck immediately on a 36-month installment plan, the actual cost would be $18,500. The $3,500 difference would be the interest the person would have to pay on the borrowed money. In addition, the person would not receive any interest on savings.

▼

To illustrate this point, a savings bank once ran a clever advertisement on buying a truck. See Figure 4.4. Obviously, there is a big difference between $13,500 and $18,500. As these figures show, it is better to save now and buy later than to buy now and go into debt. The ad, however, omitted an important point. During the three-year saving period, the person would not be able to enjoy the use of the truck. Many people would not wait that long for an important durable good they want. They would rather buy on credit and enjoy the use of the item now rather than later.

Spread Payments Another reason for going into debt is to spread the payments over the life of the item being purchased. For example, people do not buy a truck or car to have it sit in the garage. What they buy is the availability of the vehicle each day, week, month, and year that they own it.

Suppose you buy a car that costs $15,000 and plan to keep it for five years. At the end of that time, it will be worth only $5,000. Over that five-year period, you will get approximately $2,000 worth of use per year, or $166 per month. By buying on the installment plan, a person makes monthly payments that more or less correspond to the value of the use he or she receives.

Cooperative Learning

Remind students that just as all savings institutions do not necessarily pay savers the same rate of interest, not all credit card companies charge card holders the same rate of interest. Organize the class into two groups to research nationally the savings institutions and credit card companies that offer the most favorable rates to consumers. Have a member of each group present its findings to the entire class. Then suggest a class discussion of ways to improve bringing useful financial information to consumers.

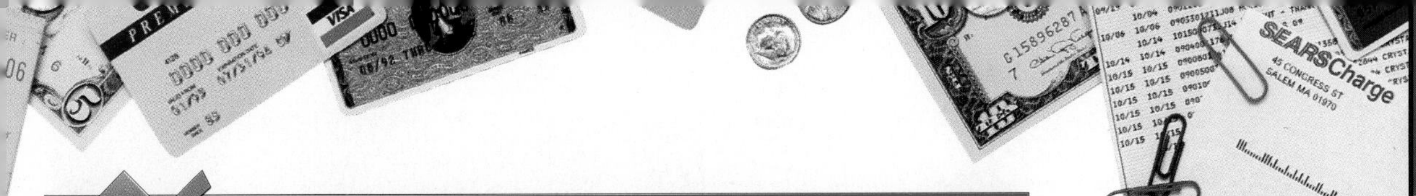

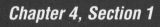

Checklist — Figure 4.5 Buying on Credit

No hard and fast rules can tell you whether or not to buy on credit. The following list of questions, however, can help you determine if you are making a good decision.

1. Do I really need this item? Can I postpone purchasing the item until later?
2. If I pay cash, what will I be giving up that I could buy with this money? This is an opportunity cost.
3. If I borrow or use credit, will the satisfaction I get from the item I buy be greater than the interest I must pay? This is also an opportunity cost.
4. Have I done comparison shopping for credit? In other words, once you have determined that you are not going to pay cash for something, you should look for the best loan or credit deal—lowest interest rate and other conditions of repayment.
5. Can I afford to borrow or use credit now? Will I be over my safe limit of debt?

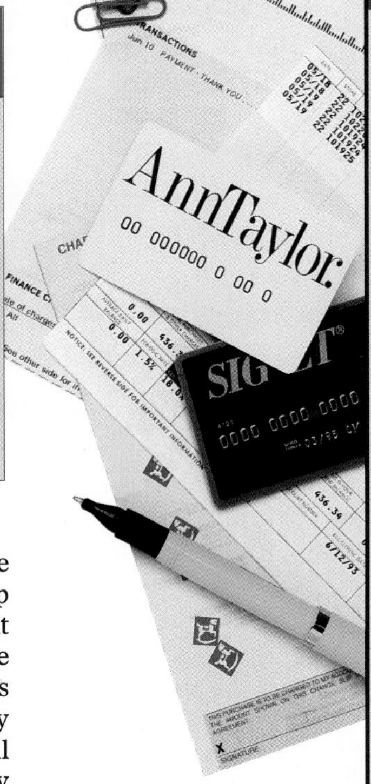

Deciding To Use Credit

Borrowing or using credit is a question of whether the satisfaction the borrower gets from the purchases is greater than the interest payments. It is basically a question of comparing costs and benefits. The benefit of borrowing is being able to buy and enjoy the good or service now rather than later. The cost is whatever the borrower must pay in interest or lost opportunities to buy other items. The benefit of borrowing is something only you can decide for yourself. You and every other borrower, however, should be aware of the costs involved.

The Checklist for Buying on Credit, **Figure 4.5** above, can help you decide when to use credit. It can also help you avoid the improper use of credit by overspending. Every day in the United States, thousands of families get into financial trouble because they have ignored the total costs of all their borrowing. They have too many credit cards and too many charge accounts and own a home that is too expensive with too large a mortgage. Just because someone offers you credit or allows you to borrow does not mean that you must accept. Buying on credit is a serious consumer activity. You should keep the information in the checklist in mind before you take the credit plunge.

SECTION 1 REVIEW

Understanding Vocabulary

Define credit, principal, interest, installment debt, consumer durables, mortgage.

Reviewing Objectives

1. What are the advantages of repaying installment debt over a long period?
2. Why do people use credit?
3. What factors should you consider when deciding whether or not to use credit?

Assess

Meeting Lesson Objectives

Assign Section 1 Review as homework or an in-class activity.

Evaluate

Assign the Section 1 Quiz in the TCR or use the Testmaker to develop a customized quiz.

Reteach

Have students organize in groups of three or four and discuss the main points of the chapter. Ask volunteers to report the main points to the class.

Enrich

Ask students to write a report on how banks affect the local economy.

Close

Have students write a paragraph on the following topic: How I make wise credit choices. Students might refer to the information in Section 1 to write their paragraph.

Section 1 Review Answers

Understanding Vocabulary

credit (p. 80), **principal** (p. 80), **interest** (p. 80), **installment debt** (p. 80), **consumer durables** (p. 80), **mortgage** (p. 81)

Reviewing Objectives

1. Monthly payments are smaller, so people can afford to purchase consumer durables over time; people can borrow cash for immediate needs and pay it back in installments.
2. People use credit because they want to purchase items right away rather than wait, and they can pay monthly installments that match the value of the use they obtain from an item.
3. Considerations as to using credit include whether the item is really needed, costs of credit, opportunity costs of paying cash, satisfaction derived from the item, and current debt load.

Ronald A. Homer was born and raised in the working-class Brooklyn neighborhood of Bedford-Stuyvesant. A psychology major, he intended to go on to medical school after college. After Homer worked for the War on Poverty Program in South Bend, Indiana, he became convinced that deteriorating neighborhoods needed more than social programs. He became a banker primarily to open avenues to providing more housing and business loans in black communities.

Teach

Help students understand how a bank can be a major asset to a community and how small banks can serve the community in ways larger banks may not be able to.

Use the information in the article to discuss what issues banks must consider to be successful in their community. Have students discuss what banks must know about their customers, what services they need to offer, and what services or types of loans banks should *not* make. Finally, have students answer the Checking for Understanding questions.

Personal Perspective

Ronald Homer on Running a Bank

Profile

- 1947–
- born and raised in Brooklyn, New York
- graduated from Notre Dame with a degree in psychology
- MBA (Masters in Business Administration) from University of Rochester
- Chair and CEO of Boston Bank of Commerce, a minority-owned-and-operated bank

Ronald Homer described his efforts to make the Boston Bank of Commerce successful in *New England Business*, April 1, 1989.

The bank was an embarrassment to the community. It really wasn't serving much of a purpose, other than as a place that didn't charge you if you bounced checks. It was a bank of last resort for people who had difficulty getting checking accounts other places....

At the start, we had to figure out quickly how we would stop the bleeding and make money. But more important, we had to make ourselves relevant to the community. There was an innate sense that there should be a minority-owned bank in town, and everybody wanted it. But for what purpose? Was it there to cash welfare checks, so that the large banks won't have to deal with those people? Or was it supposed to be doing something more?

Homer decided to serve the needs of the local community.

We approached all the major businesses and institutions in Roxbury and said, "We want to be your bank: what will it take?"... Gradually, we showed them we could help in a way the other banks weren't equipped or able to do.

... We've grown the maximum we can grow with our capital, without raising additional capital....

On the other hand, [the capital situation] has turned out to be a blessing in disguise, because had we raised capital two years ago—a public offering, for example, to raise $5 million—we would probably have been tempted like a lot of these other banks to start doing condo loans and other things. But because we were growing in a controlled area, we found enough business among our core constituency to satisfy us.... If we had gotten capital outside of that, we would probably have been lending money outside of our community rather than inside.

Checking for Understanding

❶ What problems did the Boston Bank of Commerce face?

❷ What important questions did Ronald Homer believe his bank had to answer?

❸ How did the bank's financial (capital) situation help it to respond to local needs?

Answers to Checking for Understanding

1. Most of the accounts had small balances, businesses did not use the bank, and it was losing money and needed to find a way to serve the community better.

2. Answers will vary but may include the following questions: How could the bank become relevant to the community? How could it become profitable? What was its purpose or mission?

3. Answers will vary but should include the following points. The bank had a two-year delay in raising capital, which prevented it from investing in condos and other items outside the community. It therefore had money to lend to businesses and individuals within the community.

SECTION 2 Sources of Loans and Credit

SECTION 2 FOCUS

Terms to Know commercial bank, savings and loan association, savings banks, credit union, finance company, consumer finance company, charge account, regular charge account, credit limit, revolving charge account, installment charge account, credit card, debit card, finance charge, annual percentage rate

Objectives *After reading this section, you should be able to:*

❶ List the six **types of financial institutions**.
❷ Explain the three types of **charge accounts**.
❸ Describe how **credit and debit cards** are used.
❹ Contrast a **finance charge and the annual percentage rate**.

Lending Institutions Differ

Borrowing money directly by taking out a loan is one of the two major types of credit. Many financial institutions, including commercial banks, savings and loan associations, savings banks, credit unions, and finance and consumer finance companies grant loans. Each of these sources, however, works in the same way, by charging interest on the money it lends. The amount of interest charged can vary widely as Figure 4.6 shows.

Types of Financial Institutions

As with other items you buy, you should comparison shop when you have decided to apply for a loan. You should check various lending agencies by visiting or phoning them to gather information, because financial institutions differ in several ways as Figure 4.7 (pages 86–87) shows.

Figure 4.6 Interest Rates Vary
On a typical day interest rates may be higher or lower at any given lending institution.
▼

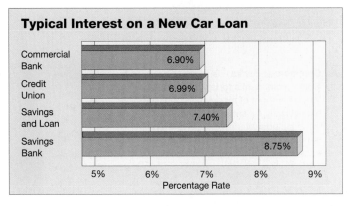

Typical Interest on a New Car Loan

Commercial Bank 6.90%
Credit Union 6.99%
Savings and Loan 7.40%
Savings Bank 8.75%

Percentage Rate (5%–9%)

Chapter 4 Going Into Debt **85**

LESSON PLAN
Chapter 4, Section 2

Focus

Overview
See the student page for section objectives.

Section 2 explains or describes: the credit choices available to consumers through different lending institutions and charge accounts; and how to calculate finance charges and annual percentage rates when choosing among different credit options.

Bellringer
Before presenting the lesson, display Focus Activity Transparency 12 on the overhead projector or copy the material on the chalkboard. Assign the accompanying Focus Activity Sheet.

Motivational Activity
Tell students to imagine they need to borrow a large sum of money. Ask them how they would try to get the lowest interest rate and how they would plan to repay the debt. Discuss students' responses.

Preteaching Vocabulary
Have students write out the definition of each term on one side of an index card. On the other side write the word itself. Students can use these cards as they study the chapter material.

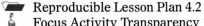

Classroom Resources for Section 2

- Reproducible Lesson Plan 4.2
- Focus Activity Transparency 12
- Focus Activity Sheet 12
- Guided Reading Activity 4.2
- Free Enterprise Activity 4
- Section Quiz 4.2
- Spanish Section Quiz 4.2
- Testmaker

Teach

Guided Practice

L1 Comparing and Contrasting Refer students to the first two sections and have them create a matrix that compares and contrasts the six types of lending institutions in terms of services, resources, and ownership. Have them create a second matrix that compares and contrasts the three types of charge accounts.

Visual Instruction

Refer students to Figure 4.7. Ask which institutions primarily offer each of the following: checking *(comercial banks, credit unions, and savings and loan associations)*; home mortgages *(savings banks, savings and loan associations)*; installment cash loans for nondurables *(consumer finance companies)*.

DID YOU KNOW

Banks formerly charged interest on credit card purchases from the date a charge was posted at the bank. Now many charge interest from the date the purchase was made. This costs consumers several dollars more every month in interest charges and nets banks some $2 billion profit each year.

Commercial Banks The first place you might think to go for a loan is a **commercial bank.** Their main functions are to accept deposits; to lend money; and to transfer funds among banks, individuals, and businesses.

Savings and Loan Associations A **savings and loan association** (S&L), like a commercial bank, accepts deposits and lends money. When S&Ls were first established in the United States in the mid-nineteenth century, they were called "building societies." Members of a society would combine their money over a period of time and take turns borrowing until each member was able to build a home. Today, most savings deposits still come from individuals and families.

Savings Banks **Savings banks** are similar to S&Ls in that most of their business comes from savings accounts and home loans. Since 1980, savings banks, like commercial banks, have been able to offer services similar to checking accounts. Savings banks were first set up in the United States in the early nineteenth century. They were meant to serve the small savers who were overlooked by the large commercial banks.

Figure 4.7 Comparing Financial Institutions
The financial institution you choose will depend on several factors, including differences in interest rates and loan repayment terms.

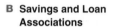

A Commercial Banks ▲
Commercial banks today control the largest amount of money and offer the widest range of services. These services include offering checking, savings, and loan services to individual consumers.

B Savings and Loan Associations
Savings and loan associations make many single-family and multi-family mortgage loans. They also finance commercial mortgages and auto loans. In the 1980s federal laws permitted savings and loans to provide some of the same services as banks. ▼

◆▶▣ Meeting Special Needs

Students With Poor Math Skills Calculating interest and finance charges can be confusing to students whose math skills are below average. Make sure they know how to use the formulas for determining the cost of credit. Have them go through an exercise where they make an imaginary credit purchase and must calculate and compare the costs under different charge accounts. Explain that knowing how to find the best credit bargain can save them hundreds or even thousands of dollars.

Credit Unions Union members and employees of many companies often have a credit union. A **credit union** is owned and operated by its members to provide savings accounts and low-interest loans only to its members. In general, credit unions offer higher interest rates on savings and charge lower interest rates on loans than other financial institutions.

Finance Companies and Consumer Finance Companies A **finance company** takes over contracts for installment debts from stores and adds a fee for collecting the debt. The consumer pays the fee in the form of slightly higher interest than he or she would pay to the retailer. Retailers use this method to avoid the risks involved in lending money to consumers. Finance companies also make loans directly to consumers.

Guided Practice

L1 Evaluating Tell students to write a list of all the advantages and disadvantages they can think of in connection with buying with cash. Have them present their points in a two-column table headed Advantages and Disadvantages. Ask them to add a paragraph explaining when they think it might be preferable or advantageous to buy with a credit card or by obtaining a loan. Encourage volunteers to read their lists and paragraphs as part of a class discussion.

D Credit Unions
Credit unions primarily make personal, auto, and home improvement loans, though some larger credit unions offer home mortgages as well. They also offer share drafts, which are similar to checking accounts at commercial banks.

▲
C Consumer Finance Companies
People who use consumer finance companies are usually unable to borrow from commercial banks or other sources with lower rates because of nonpayment of loans in the past or an uneven employment record. Consumer finance companies are the largest supplier of installment cash loans for purposes other than buying consumer durables.

▼ E Savings Banks
Names of savings banks often include such words as *farmers'* or *seamen's* to indicate the group for whom the bank was originally intended. The majority of savings banks are located in New England and the Mid-Atlantic states. Most of their loans are for home mortgages, although they do make personal and auto loans. Because of their small number, savings banks account for only a small percentage of the country's home mortgages and other consumer installment debt. Their interest rates for loans, like those of S&Ls, are often slightly less than those for commercial banks.

Chapter 4 Going Into Debt **87**

Cooperative Learning

Ask students to develop an advertising campaign to promote consumer saving. Let class members organize themselves into teams to do research, write copy, and develop visual materials for print and broadcast media, as well as posters, billboards, bumper stickers, and novelty items such as buttons and T-shirts (so-called advertising specialty items). Reserve school display space to exhibit the saving campaign.

Ask students to study Figure 4.8 and write a paragraph explaining the main point that they think the cartoonist intends to make. Tell them to then restudy the cartoon and write a second interpretation that they think is justifiable. Ask volunteers to read their first interpretation and discuss. Do likewise for students' second interpretation. Conclude with a discussion of why people may interpret a cartoon differently.

GLOBAL ECONOMICS

In the 1970s and early 1980s, banks in Western nations loaned billions of dollars to developing countries in Latin America, Africa, and Asia. As the developing countries' economies worsened, many nations became unable to repay the loans. To reduce the debt, some nations, such as Brazil, negotiated with Western banks to trade off conservation for dollars. Brazil agreed to stop cutting down parts of its rain forest in exchange for a reduction in the debt.

A **consumer finance company** makes loans directly to consumers at high rates of interest. These rates are often more than 20 percent a year. Some states allow consumer finance companies to charge as much as 36 percent a year on small amounts of money.

Crisis and Changes In the 1980s changes in federal laws expanded the activities of S&Ls, permitting them to offer checking-type accounts and business and consumer loans. While most loans were still used to buy homes, many S&Ls made risky commercial investments. By 1988 many S&Ls were in financial trouble. Congress set up the Resolution Trust Corporation to manage the crisis and save the S&L industry. Experts predicted that the bailout would cost the federal government and taxpayers hundreds of billions of dollars. See **Figure 4.8**.

The Resolution Trust Corporation sold off assets of failed savings and loans, bailed out other S&Ls with federal money, and stabilized the weaker institutions. The so-called bailout was the way the government began to meet its obligation to insure depositors' accounts.

When it became evident that the Federal Deposit Insurance Corporation had nearly depleted its funds, the agency voted to increase its insurance premiums. This meant that lending institutions would have to pay more for FDIC coverage.

▼ **Figure 4.8**
The Bailout
The Resolution Trust Corporation continued to ask Congress for more and more money to bail out S&Ls. Taxpayers began to wonder whether the bailout would ever end.

Free Enterprise Activity

Have the class do the brainstorming and committee organizing to present a school fair or workshop on consumer credit and debt. Remind students that they will need sufficient time for planning and implementation if they want a real event to take place.

Encourage them to consider support from and participation by local representatives of business, banking, and government. Suggest that they consider charging an admission fee to pay for honorariums to outside experts.

Charge Accounts

A major type of credit is extended directly to an individual, without that person's having to borrow money first. This credit may be in the form of a charge account or a credit card. A **charge account** allows a customer to buy goods or services from a particular company and pay for them later. Department stores, for example, offer their customers three basic types of charge accounts: regular, revolving, or installment.

Regular Charge Accounts A **regular charge account,** also known as a 30-day charge, has a credit limit such as $500 or $1,000. A **credit limit** is the maximum amount of goods or services a person or business can buy on the promise to pay in the future. The cardholder and usually any member of his or her family can charge items up to this limit. At the end of every 30-day period, the store sends a bill for the entire amount. No interest is charged, but the entire bill must be paid at that time. If it is not, interest is charged on that part of the account.

Revolving Charge Accounts A **revolving charge account** allows you to make additional purchases from the same store even if you have not paid the previous month's bill in full. See Figure 4.9. Usually you must pay a certain portion of your balance each month, for instance one-fifth of the amount due. Interest is charged on the

◀ **Figure 4.9
Store Charge Cards**
Stores allow their customers to choose regular, revolving, or installment accounts. They all allow consumers to purchase more now, but with the latter two customers must normally pay interest.

Independent Practice

L2 Journalism Have students research the savings and loan debacle and report on why so many bad loans were made. Ask them to report on the present status of the bailout and to find out what steps have been taken to prevent such a disaster from recurring. Encourage volunteers to give an oral report and discuss.

 GLOBAL ECONOMICS

The International Bank for Reconstruction and Development (World Bank) provides loans and technical assistance to economically developing member nations. An affiliate of World Bank, International Development Association, specializes in low-cost loans to poorer nations. Another affiliate, International Finance Corporation, stimulates the growth of private capital within developing nations. Since the 1970s, these organizations have loaned several billion dollars to member countries.

Chapter 4 Going Into Debt **89**

 Cultural Diversity and Economics

Ask students to conduct a public opinion survey on attitudes about consumer credit and debt. Suggest that they develop a short questionnaire that asks respondents to also state their age, sex, and ethnic identification or nationality. Encourage students to conduct the survey at various locations to obtain as varied a sampling as possible. Suggest that they organize their data in tables and/or charts, along with any necessary explanatory notes. Discuss results of the survey with the class.

Independent Practice

L3 Interviewing Tell students to interview an officer or manager in a credit union or savings and loan institution about the services offered. The interview should touch upon the advantages and disadvantages there are in using the services of a credit union or savings and loan institution compared with using those of commercial banks. Have students report on their findings to the class.

amount you do not pay. Of course, if you pay everything you owe each month, no interest is charged. This type of account also has a credit limit.

Installment Charge Accounts Major items such as couches, televisions, and refrigerators are often purchased through an **installment charge account.** The items are purchased and paid for through equal payments spread over a period of time. Part of the amount paid each month is applied to the interest, and part is applied to the principal. At the end of the payment period, the borrower owns whatever he or she has made payments on.

Figure 4.10
The Credit Card Trade-Off
Individual stores, such as Pier I and Home Depot, issue their own charge cards, which consumers may use to purchase goods. Consumers may also use credit cards, such as MasterCard and Optima. Although using credit cards is convenient, it is also costly. Stores must pay a certain percentage of credit purchases to the credit card company or bank that issued the card. The stores include this cost in the price they charge customers, making prices higher for everyone.

Credit and Debit Cards

A **credit card**, like a charge account, allows a person to make purchases without paying cash. The difference is that credit cards can be used at many kinds of stores, restaurants, hotels, and other businesses throughout the United States and even foreign countries. Visa, MasterCard, and others issue cards through banks. These cards can be used to purchase items in stores that accept them, or they may be used to borrow money, up to a certain limit. This gives consumers access to loans at all times without having to apply for them. So many cards have been marketed that it is not unusual for a person to have several different kinds. Figure 4.10 illustrates sample credit and charge cards.

Credit cards usually charge high interest. In the early 1990s, banks

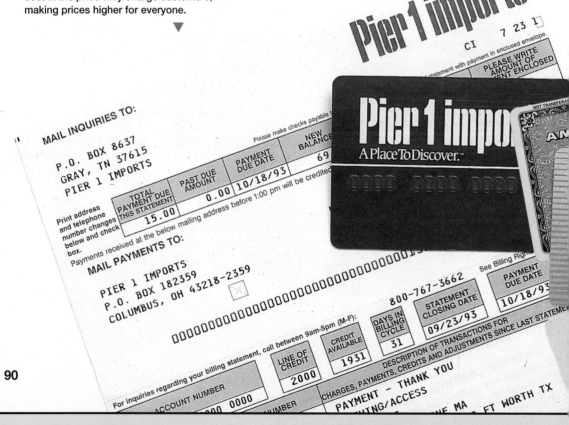

90

charged an average of 18 percent on MasterCard and Visa. The high interest rates eventually brought additional issuers into the market. Sears, Roebuck & Co. issued its Discover Card. General Electric Co. and General Motors joined American Telephone & Telegraph in issuing cards with more attractive interest rates and other benefits.

Gradually the competition brought credit card interest rates down, but one factor kept rates from dropping very low—bad loans. Visa and MasterCard issuers charge off almost 25 percent of the revenues collected in bad loans. Because of this some issuers began to offer lower rates to special categories of customers who they believed were more reliable.

A **debit card** does not provide a loan. Instead it makes cashless purchases easier by enabling the customer to transfer funds electronically. Debit cards were first available in the 1970s, but they did not catch on with the public. Popular use of automated teller machines (ATMs) has paved the way for acceptance of debit cards. In 1992 Visa and MasterCard launched a campaign to sign up banks combining their credit cards with debit cards.

Finance Charges and Annual Percentage Rates

The terms *finance charge* and *annual percentage rate* tell the consumer the same thing—the cost of credit—but each is expressed in a different way.

Finance Charges The **finance charge** is the cost of credit expressed in dollars and cents. It must take into account interest costs plus any other charges connected with credit. For example, yearly membership fees for the use of a credit card are included in the finance charge.

Computing Finance Charges The way finance charges are computed is an important factor in determining the cost of credit. The method can vary from creditor to creditor. Store charge accounts and credit cards use one of four methods to determine how much people will pay for credit: previous balance, average daily balance,

91

Independent Practice

L2 Investigate Ask students to research and write a report on how people can learn their own credit rating. Have them try to determine what standards credit card companies use for extending their most favorable terms. Suggest that their reports also mention the most frequent reason for denial of credit. Encourage volunteers to report orally in a class discussion.

 DID YOU KNOW

Although agricultural products are a mainstay among our nation's exports, many farmers carry a large burden of debt. Outstanding farm real estate debt rose from about $30.4 billion in 1980 to about $114 in 1983. This high diminished to about $79.1 billion in 1991.

Free Enterprise Activity

Ask the class to create a board game that they might call Credit Crunch. Indicate that the object of the game would be for players to take on debt and have to pay it off. Lucky breaks (for example, a pay raise, a contest cash prize, a bequest, and so forth) and bad breaks (for example, loss of job, large tax increase, unexpected repair bill, and so forth) could advance or stall a player's progress. The first player to pay off his or her debt would win. Suggest that students research various board games to help them create their own.

Independent Practice

L2 Calculation Refer students to Figure 4.11 and have them use the three methods of calculation to determine the interest and finance charges on a $2,000 loan, using the same annual and monthly percentage and a midmonth payment of $200. Have students write a paragraph summarizing the results.

 Have students complete Guided Reading Activity 4.2 in the TCR. LEP

? DID YOU KNOW

Persons who are too poor or otherwise unable to get credit or a loan from a bank or other mainstream lender may pawn their possessions to get money. A pawnbroker, sometimes called the poor person's banker, may make a small loan on such personal items as watches, jewelry, cameras, musical instruments, and clothes. If the debt is not repaid by a specified date, the pawnbroker may sell the pawned item.

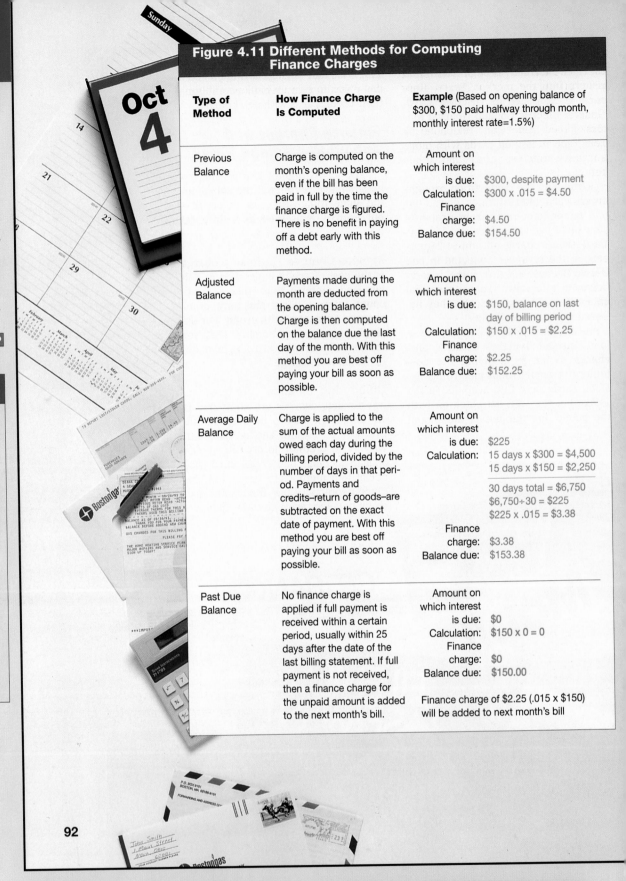

Figure 4.11 Different Methods for Computing Finance Charges

Type of Method	How Finance Charge Is Computed	Example (Based on opening balance of $300, $150 paid halfway through month, monthly interest rate=1.5%)	
Previous Balance	Charge is computed on the month's opening balance, even if the bill has been paid in full by the time the finance charge is figured. There is no benefit in paying off a debt early with this method.	Amount on which interest is due: Calculation: Finance charge: Balance due:	$300, despite payment $300 x .015 = $4.50 $4.50 $154.50
Adjusted Balance	Payments made during the month are deducted from the opening balance. Charge is then computed on the balance due the last day of the month. With this method you are best off paying your bill as soon as possible.	Amount on which interest is due: Calculation: Finance charge: Balance due:	$150, balance on last day of billing period $150 x .015 = $2.25 $2.25 $152.25
Average Daily Balance	Charge is applied to the sum of the actual amounts owed each day during the billing period, divided by the number of days in that period. Payments and credits–return of goods–are subtracted on the exact date of payment. With this method you are best off paying your bill as soon as possible.	Amount on which interest is due: Calculation: Finance charge: Balance due:	$225 15 days x $300 = $4,500 15 days x $150 = $2,250 30 days total = $6,750 $6,750÷30 = $225 $225 x .015 = $3.38 $3.38 $153.38
Past Due Balance	No finance charge is applied if full payment is received within a certain period, usually within 25 days after the date of the last billing statement. If full payment is not received, then a finance charge for the unpaid amount is added to the next month's bill.	Amount on which interest is due: Calculation: Finance charge: Balance due:	$0 $150 x 0 = 0 $0 $150.00

Finance charge of $2.25 (.015 x $150) will be added to next month's bill

---

👥 Cultural Diversity and Economics

Organize students into groups of three or four to research the kinds and extent of consumer credit used in other countries in both the Eastern and Western hemispheres. Each group should pick a different country to study. Suggest including information on restrictions on the use of credit, if available, and also on the effect of credit use on saving. After each group presents its information, have the class discuss whether Americans could learn some credit lessons from other nations.

adjusted balance, or past due balance. Each method applies the interest rate to an account's balance at a different point during the month. The different methods can result in widely varying finance charges. Figure 4.11 describes these four methods for computing and shows the difference in finance charges that can result. Creditors must inform their customers in writing of which method they use for computing finance charges.

Annual Percentage Rates The **annual percentage rate** (APR) is the cost of credit expressed as a yearly percentage. Like the finance charge, the APR must take into account any non-interest costs of credit such as a membership fee. Figure 4.12 shows how a sample APR affects the cost of credit.

Understanding and using APRs makes it easier to shop around for the best deal on credit. For example, if you are looking for a car, creditor A might ask for a large down payment and offer in return small monthly payments. Creditor B might not require a down payment at all, but charge large monthly payments instead. Creditor C might ask for small payments over a much longer period of time.

Knowing which creditor is charging the most for credit would be very difficult without some guide for comparison. The APR provides that guide by allowing consumers to compare costs regardless of the dollar amount of those costs or the length of the credit agreement. Suppose creditor A is charging an APR of 16 percent, while creditor B is charging 17 percent, and creditor C is charging 18½ percent. On a yearly basis, creditor C is charging the most for credit and creditor A the least.

Meeting Lesson Objectives

Assign Section 2 Review as homework or an in-class activity. Each question in the Review addresses the corresponding numbered objective in the Section Focus.

Evaluate

Assign the Section 2 Quiz in the TCR or use the Testmaker to develop a customized quiz.

Reteach

Ask students to use the main headings of Section 2 as the main headings of an outline. Have them fill in the outline with the information presented under each section heading.

Enrich

Invite a banker to the class to discuss bank services.

Close

Discuss the importance of having a choice of lending institutions and knowing the cost of credit.

Figure 4.12 ▶
Annual Percentage Rates
Say you charge $200 worth of clothes. The interest rate charged to you, let's say, is 10 percent, but the annual fee for the credit card is $5. Your APR will be $20 of interest plus the $5 fee, or 12½ percent. The APR is normally larger than the interest because it includes the noninterest cost of extending credit.

Credit Card Charge of $200 at 10% Interest		
Amount Charged	$200.00	$200.00
Interest at 10%	$20.00	$20.00
Annual Membership Fee	none	$5.00
APR	10%	12.5%

SECTION 2 REVIEW

Understanding Vocabulary
Define commercial bank, savings and loan association, savings banks, credit union, finance company, consumer finance company, charge account, regular charge account, credit limit, revolving charge account, installment charge account, credit card, debit card, finance charge, annual percentage rate.

Reviewing Objectives
1. What are the six types of financial institutions?
2. How do regular, revolving, and installment charge accounts differ?
3. How are credit and debit cards used?
4. How is a finance charge different from an annual percentage rate?

Section 2 Review Answers
Understanding Vocabulary
commercial bank (p. 86), **savings and loan association** (p. 86), **savings banks** (p. 86), **credit union** (p. 87), **finance company** (p. 87), **consumer finance company** (p. 88), **charge account** (p. 89), **regular charge account** (p. 89), **credit limit** (p. 89), **revolving charge account** (p. 89), **installment charge** account (p. 90), **credit card** (p. 90), **finance charge** (p. 91), **annual percentage rate** (p. 93).

Reviewing Objectives
1. commercial banks, S&L associations, savings banks, credit unions, finance companies, and consumer finance companies
2. regular: 30-day payment period; revolving: charged on the unpaid amount; installment: equal payments.
3. Credit cards allow instant access to loans; debit cards allow electronic transfer of funds.
4. finance charge: interest plus other fees; annual percentage rate: the cost of credit plus other fees expressed as a yearly percentage

Focus

Overview

See the student page for section objectives.

Section 3 explains or describes: the factors that establish a person's credit rating; the differences between a secured and unsecured loan; and the responsibilities a borrower assumes when taking out a loan.

Bellringer

 Before presenting the lesson, display Focus Activity Transparency 13 on the overhead projector or copy the material on the chalkboard. Assign the accompanying Focus Activity Sheet.

Motivational Activity

Ask students to write their responses to the following: When someone asks you for a loan, what factors make you decide to say yes or no? How and when would you want the person to repay the loan?

Tell students that lending institutions use specific criteria to determine who should be given a loan. Section 3 explains these criteria and the responsibilities of a borrower.

Preteaching Vocabulary

Have students read the definitions of the terms. Then ask them to write a note explaining the words to someone else.

SECTION **3** *Applying for Credit*

SECTION 3 FOCUS

Terms to Know credit bureau, credit check, credit rating, collateral, secured loan, unsecured loan, cosigner, past-due notices

Objectives *After reading this section, you should be able to:*

① Explain the four factors that determine a person's **credit rating**.

② List your **responsibilities as a borrower**.

Several Factors Determine a Person's Credit Worthiness

When you apply for credit, you usually will be asked to fill out a credit application. Once you have filled out the application, the store, bank, or other lending agency will hire a **credit bureau**, a private business, to do a **credit check**. This investigation will reveal your income, any current debts, details about your personal life, and how well you have repaid debts in the past.

The Credit Rating

The information supplied by the credit bureau provides the creditor with a **credit rating** for you. This is a rating of the risk—good, average, or poor—involved in lending money to a specific person or business. If a person has a history of poor credit

Figure 4.13
Three Credit Check Factors

A Capacity to Pay
Capacity to pay is related to income and debt. If your employment has been spotty, your capacity to pay will be considered questionable. The amount of debt that you are already carrying is also a factor. If your debts are large, creditors will be reluctant to loan you ◀ more.

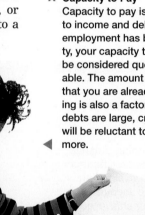

94

Classroom Resources for Section 3

 Reproducible Lesson Plan 4.3
 Focus Activity Transparency 13
Focus Activity Sheet 13
Guided Reading Activity 4.3

 Section Quiz 4.3
Spanish Section Quiz 4.3
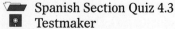 Testmaker
Reinforcing Skills 4

use—usually late in paying debts—he or she will receive a poor credit rating. As a result, the creditor reviewing the credit check will be less willing to lend that person money.

Though past history of credit use is important in deciding a person's creditworthiness, the creditor also looks at three other factors that a credit check reveals. These are: capacity to pay, character, and collateral (kuh-LAT-uh-ruhl). **Figure 4.13** examines these three factors.

Secured Loans Usually when a bank, S&L, or other financial institution makes a loan, it will ask for collateral from the borrower. The **collateral** may be the item purchased with the loan money, such as a house or car. It may be something of value the borrower already owns. For example, a borrower might offer his or her car as collateral to obtain cash for home im-provements. The borrower then signs a legal agreement allowing the lender to claim the collateral if the loan is not repaid. A loan that is backed up with collateral in this way is called a **secured loan.**

Unsecured Loans Usually a young person will have little to offer as collateral. When dealing with a trusted customer, financial institutions will sometimes lend money on the person's reputation alone. Such a loan is called an **unsecured loan.** It is not guaranteed by anything other than a promise to repay it. Most young people have not had enough experience

B Character ▶
Character refers to a person's reputation as a reliable and trustworthy person—educational background, whether or not he or she has had any problems with the law, and any other factors that might indicate something questionable.

◀ **C Collateral**
Lenders also consider collateral. The size of your capital, or personal wealth, is important because it indicates your past ability to save and accumulate. It also indicates your present ability to pay off a loan, even if you lose your job, because you could sell some of your belongings in order to make the payments.

Chapter 4 Going Into Debt **95**

Teach

Guided Practice

L1 Evaluating Have students evaluate their own credit worthiness and write four headings: Credit History, Capacity, Character, Collateral. Have them list loans they repaid, current pay or allowance, their determination to repay a loan, and what property/assets they own. Suggest assigning one point to each item in each category and add up the score. Higher scores mean better risk. Ask for suggestions to improve their creditworthiness.

Independent Practice

L1 Literature and Economics Refer students to Bartlett's *Familiar Quotations* or a similar source to collect literary references and/or aphorisms about borrowing and lending. Ask volunteers to read their choices.

🗀 Have students complete Guided Reading Activity 4.3 in the TCR. LEP

Visual Instruction

Tell students to imagine someone has asked them to cosign a loan. Have them list reasons why they would or would not be willing to cosign. Discuss cosigning from the standpoint of the borrower and the cosigner.

◆▷◯ **Meeting Special Needs**

Analyzing Cause and Effect In many cases, students may not fully appreciate how actions a person takes today can have a long-range impact on his or her credit worthiness.

For example, if borrowers are chronically late with payments, default on a credit card account, or fail to fulfill their obligations, such facts will be reported on their credit history. Two or three years later, potential lenders may read these histories and turn down their request for a loan or credit card. Discuss with them ideas they may have for keeping their credit history sound.

Assess

Meeting Lesson Objectives

Assign Section 3 Review as homework or an in-class activity. Each question in the Review addresses the corresponding numbered objective in the Section Focus.

Evaluate

Assign the Section 3 Quiz in the TCR or use the Testmaker to develop a customized quiz.

Reteach

Refer students to Section 3. Ask them to list examples of the following: capacity to pay, character, collateral, secured loan, unsecured loan.

Enrich

Have students interview a loan officer at a bank to determine how banks deal with people who cannot repay their loans or who fall behind in their payments.

Close

Tell students to use the information from Sections 1–3 to write a paragraph explaining how knowing the basic facts about debt and credit can help people make better choices regarding how they pay for items.

◀ **Figure 4.14**
Cosigning a Loan
A bank will sometimes lend money to a person without a financial reputation if he or she has a cosigner. A **cosigner** is a person who signs a loan contract along with the borrower and promises to repay the loan if the borrower does not.

with borrowing and repaying money to have established this type of trust. See Figure 4.14.

Your Responsibilities as a Borrower

Once you have applied for credit and obtained it, you have also taken on responsibilities. After all, the businesses that gave you credit expect to earn a profit, although in earning that profit they are helping you satisfy your consumer needs by allowing you to buy goods and services on credit.

Paying on Time If you do not pay your debts on time, the costs to businesses are higher. At the very least, there will be extra mailing costs to send **past-due notices.** The business that lends you money may have to hire a collection agency to help get back the money loaned to you. If you never pay off your debt, the lending institution has to write it off and take a loss.

When lending institutions end up paying higher costs, they have to pass these costs on to all consumers in the form of higher prices—higher interest rates charged. Ethical consumers pay their debts on time except under extraordinary circumstances.

Another thing happens when you do not pay your debts. You get a bad credit history. You may then have a difficult or impossible time when you really need credit for something else, say, to purchase a house. Consumers who cannot obtain credit sometimes find it difficult to achieve their personal goals.

Keeping Records If you applied for a credit card and got one, you have additional responsibilities. You need to keep a complete record of all the charges you made. This way you will not go over your credit limit in any one month. You also have the responsibility of notifying the credit-card issuer immediately if your card is lost or stolen.

SECTION 3 REVIEW

Understanding Vocabulary

Define credit bureau, credit check, credit rating, collateral, secured loan, unsecured loan, cosigner, past-due notices.

Reviewing Objectives

1. What four factors determine a person's credit rating?
2. What are your responsibilities as a borrower?

Section 3 Review Answers

Understanding Vocabulary
credit bureau (p. 94), **credit check**
(p. 94), **credit rating** (p. 94), **collateral** (p 95),
secured loan (p. 95), **unsecured loan** (p. 95),
cosigner (p. 96), **past-due notices** (p. 96)

Reviewing Objectives
1. Factors that determine a person's credit

rating are credit history, capacity to pay, character, and collateral.
2. Responsibilities of a borrower include paying debts on time, keeping complete records of all credit charges made, and notifying card issuers immediately if credit cards are lost or stolen.

LEARNING ECONOMIC SKILLS

Determining a Safe Debt Load

At some time in your life, you will most likely use credit. Everyone does. Do you know how to determine your *safe debt load*--the amount of debt you can safely afford after paying for necessities?

Determining Your Safe Debt Load

To figure out the amount of credit debt that is safe for you to carry, follow these steps, as shown in **Figure A**, Smith Family Safe Debt Load:

❶ List your total annual income after taxes. Include any gifts from parents and friends.

❷ Estimate your total annual expenses for the necessities of housing, food, clothing, and transportation.

❸ Subtract the total from your after-tax income.

❹ Divide the difference by three. This is your "safe debt load." (By dividing by three, this calculation takes unforeseen expenses into consideration.

This safe debt load is the amount of credit debt you can safely afford. Look at **Figure B**. It shows the amount of credit carried by the Smith family. Note that their present credit debt is more than their safe debt load. It would not be wise for the Smiths to assume additional credit at this time.

Practicing the Skill

❶ Charlene's after-tax income is $24,250. Her annual expenses for necessities are $6,500 for housing, $4,250 for food, $1,100 for clothing, and $750 for transportation. What is her safe debt load?

❷ She currently has no credit debt. Can she safely afford to buy a new car with monthly loan payments of $250? Why or why not?

Figure A

Smith Family Safe Debt Load

Total annual after-tax income	$ 21,750
Annual expenses for:	
housing	$ 5,000
food	$ 3,750
clothing	$ 1,250
transportation	$ 500
TOTAL ANNUAL EXPENSES	$ 10,500
Subtract expenses from income	$ 11,250
Divide difference by 3 to determine safe debt load	$ 3,750

Figure B

Smith Family Credit Debt (per month)

Car payments	$ 225
Payment on store revolving charge account	$ 46
Payment on credit cards	$ 52
Payment on loan for last year's vacation	$ 41
MONTHLY TOTAL	$ 364

Total for year $364 x 12 = $4,368

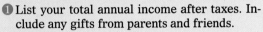
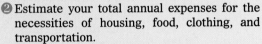

Focus

Overview

See the student page for section objectives.

Section 4 explains or describes state usury laws and federal laws that regulate the credit industry and why a person who cannot repay debts might file for bankruptcy.

Bellringer

 Before presenting the lesson, display Focus Activity Transparency 14 on the projector or copy the material on the chalkboard. Assign the accompanying Focus Activity Sheet.

Motivational Activity

Ask students to imagine there are no laws regulating lenders and card issuers. How could lenders abuse their power? Discuss students' responses. Explain that Section 4 describes how state and federal laws protect consumers from unethical practices.

Preteaching Vocabulary

Have students look up the origins of the words *usury* and *bankruptcy* in a dictionary of etymology.

SECTION **4 Government Regulation of Credit**

SECTION 4 FOCUS

Terms to Know usury law, bankruptcy

Objectives *After reading this section, you should be able to:*
1. State how the **Equal Credit Opportunity Act** affected consumer credit.
2. Describe **state usury laws**.
3. Explain why a person might declare **personal bankruptcy**.

The Government Regulates Credit to Protect Consumers

Both the federal and state governments regulate the credit industry. Most states, for example, have set a maximum on the interest rates charged for certain types of credit. The federal government has also passed laws designed to increase the flow of credit information to consumers and to protect consumers from unfair credit practices.

The Truth in Lending Act of 1968 was the first of a series of major federal laws that greatly expanded the government's role in protecting users of consumer credit. An important aspect of the government regulation of credit is to make sure that everyone has equal access.

The Equal Credit Opportunity Act

In 1974 Congress enacted the Equal Credit Opportunity Act (ECOA) as an addition to the Truth in Lending Act of 1968. Among other things, those who provide credit cannot deny you such credit solely on the basis of your race, religion, national origin, gender, marital status, or age. In addition, no one is allowed to discriminate against you in offering you credit simply because your income might come from public assistance benefits.

Classroom Resources for Section 4

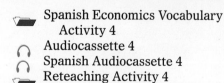

- Reproducible Lesson Plan 4.4
- Focus Activity Transparency 14
- Focus Activity Sheet 14
- Guided Reading Activity 4.4
- Mathematics Practice for Economics 4
- Performance Assessment Activity 4

- Section Quiz 4.4
- Spanish Section Quiz 4.4
- Chapter 4 Test Forms A and B
- Testmaker
- Enrichment Activity 4
- Economics Vocabulary Activity 4

- Spanish Economics Vocabulary Activity 4
- Audiocassette 4
- Spanish Audiocassette 4
- Reteaching Activity 4
- Spanish Reteaching Activity 4

Because there had been so much credit discrimination against married women, the 1974 Credit Act made it illegal for a creditor to require an applicant's spouse to sign unless an application for credit was made jointly by husband and wife. See Figure 4.15. If a woman on her own qualifies for the amount and terms of credit requested, she does not have to get her husband to sign the credit application. Figure 4.16 (pages 100–101) presents the important points about five major federal government laws that regulate credit.

State Usury Laws

A law restricting the amount of interest that can be charged for credit is called a **usury** (YOOZH-uh-ree) **law.** Often states set up different maximum rates for different types of consumer credit. Maximum rates on charge accounts and credit cards, for example, are often about 18 percent a year, or 1½ percent per month. Consumer finance agencies, in contrast, are often allowed to charge higher rates because their loans involve higher risks.

Interest Ceilings The ceilings for usury laws were controversial in past years when interest ceilings in many states were as low as 6 or 10 percent. When interest rates in general began to rise in the early 1970s, many lenders complained that they could not keep within such ceilings and still make a profit. In states that were slow to raise interest ceilings, some lenders cut back on the amount of credit they offered. Others stopped lending money completely. Many consumers, particularly those who were poor credit risks, found it hard to obtain credit. People opposed to raising interest ceilings claimed people with lower incomes would not be able to afford credit. Supporters of higher ceilings claimed that low rates made credit less available because it was less profitable for lenders. Low rates actually hurt those they were supposed to help.

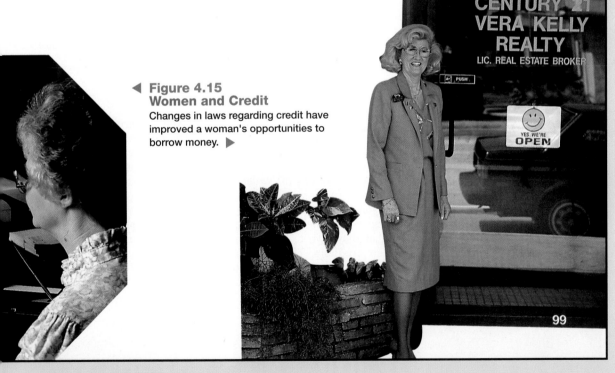

◀ **Figure 4.15**
Women and Credit
Changes in laws regarding credit have improved a woman's opportunities to borrow money. ▶

Teach

Guided Practice

L2 Synthesizing Have students read through the section on state and federal laws regulating credit. Ask them what law offers protection in the following situations and what steps you as a consumer can take:
- A debt collector is calling you several times a day.
- You discover a mistake on your credit card bill that has not been corrected.
- You have been refused a loan but given no reason.
- You find out the interest on your loan is not what you were told.
- You want to know who has been requesting a copy of your credit report.

Ask students to look at Figure 4.15 and the part of Figure 4.16 (page 100) that discusses the Equal Credit Opportunity Act of 1974. Have them research the origins of the act and why it was deemed necessary. Have them report their findings to the class.

◆ ◯ **Meeting Special Needs**

Limited Proficiency in English Students with limited proficiency in English may have trouble distinguishing among the different federal acts. Have them copy the main points of each act onto different colored paper, in effect color-coding the information. They will then be able to associate the different colors with the information for different acts.

DID YOU KNOW

To get the protection of the Fair Credit Card Billing Act, *you must notify the card company in writing within 60 days of receiving the bill that there is a billing error on your account.* A telephone call will not give you protection under the law. Always keep a copy of your letter. Once the company receives your letter, it must correct the problem or write back to you within 30 days explaining what action it is taking.

GLOBAL ECONOMICS

In many countries, lenders may charge any interest rates and need not reveal the annual percentage rate (APR). Some nations are now instituting truth-in-lending or consumer-protection laws.

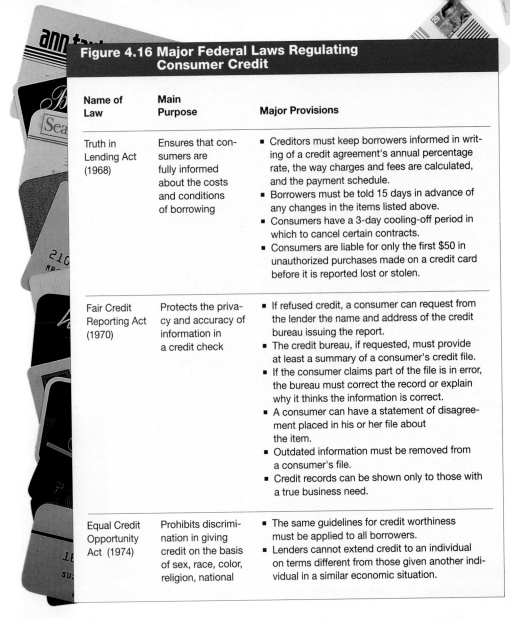

Figure 4.16 Major Federal Laws Regulating Consumer Credit

Name of Law	Main Purpose	Major Provisions
Truth in Lending Act (1968)	Ensures that consumers are fully informed about the costs and conditions of borrowing	• Creditors must keep borrowers informed in writing of a credit agreement's annual percentage rate, the way charges and fees are calculated, and the payment schedule. • Borrowers must be told 15 days in advance of any changes in the items listed above. • Consumers have a 3-day cooling-off period in which to cancel certain contracts. • Consumers are liable for only the first $50 in unauthorized purchases made on a credit card before it is reported lost or stolen.
Fair Credit Reporting Act (1970)	Protects the privacy and accuracy of information in a credit check	• If refused credit, a consumer can request from the lender the name and address of the credit bureau issuing the report. • The credit bureau, if requested, must provide at least a summary of a consumer's credit file. • If the consumer claims part of the file is in error, the bureau must correct the record or explain why it thinks the information is correct. • A consumer can have a statement of disagreement placed in his or her file about the item. • Outdated information must be removed from a consumer's file. • Credit records can be shown only to those with a true business need.
Equal Credit Opportunity Act (1974)	Prohibits discrimination in giving credit on the basis of sex, race, color, religion, national	• The same guidelines for credit worthiness must be applied to all borrowers. • Lenders cannot extend credit to an individual on terms different from those given another individual in a similar economic situation.

Personal Bankruptcy

If you take out too many loans, use too many credit cards, and pile up debts that you cannot pay off, federal legislation gives you a way out. It is called personal **bankruptcy.** Bankruptcy occurs when debtors give up most of what they own to be distributed to their creditors. Thousands of Americans file for personal bankruptcy every week.

If you declare personal bankruptcy, you may have a fresh start. Be aware, however, that it is very difficult to reestablish credit as long as the bankruptcy proceedings remain on your credit record. That is why choosing bankruptcy to get out of your credit "mess" should be a last resort. Also, when you declare bankruptcy, you are making sure that your creditors will never be paid off (at least not in full) for what they loaned you.

Figure 4.16 Major Federal Laws Regulating Consumer Credit

Name of Law	Main Purpose	Major Provisions
Equal Credit Opportunity Act (1974) (cont.)	origin, marital status, age, or receipt of public assistance	• Questions about age, sex, and marital status can be asked only if those questions relate directly to a person's ability to repay a loan. • Loan applicants must receive notice of a decision within 30 days. If the loan is denied, the lender must give the reasons or inform the applicant of the right to request the information.
Fair Credit Billing Act (1974)	Sets up a procedure for the quick correction of mistakes that appear on consumer credit accounts	• Consumers may challenge a billing statement for errors. • Consumers have 60 days to notify a creditor of a disputed item. The creditor must investigate and either correct the mistake or explain why the charge is not an error. • While the mistake is checked, the consumer can withhold payment of the disputed sum but must pay for other items on the account. • Under certain circumstances, a consumer can withhold payment for merchandise that has been purchased and found defective. • Creditors must supply consumers with a statement of their rights under the act.
Fair Debt Collection Practices Act (1977)	Prevents abuse by professional debt collectors; applies to anyone employed to collect debts owed to others; does not apply to banks or other businesses that collect their own accounts	• Collectors can contact a person other than the debtor only to discover the debtor's location. • The debtor cannot be contacted at an inconvenient time or place. • All harassing behavior is prohibited. This includes the use or threat of violence, the use of annoying or repetitive phone calls, etc.

Assess

Meeting Lesson Objectives
Assign Section 4 Review.

Evaluate
Assign the Section 4 Quiz in the TCR or use the Testmaker to develop a customized quiz.

Assign the Chapter 4 Test Form A or Form B or use the Testmaker to develop a customized test.

Reteach
Have small groups each research a federal or state consumer protection law. Ask them to summarize the provisions of the law.

Have students complete Reteaching Activity 4 in the TCR.

Enrich
Ask students to bring in articles about credit fraud or debt collection harassment.

Have students complete Enrichment Activity 4 in the TCR.

Close
Discuss why consumer protection is important.

SECTION 4 REVIEW

Understanding Vocabulary
Define usury law, bankruptcy.

Reviewing Objectives
1. What are the major provisions of the Equal Credit Opportunity Act?

2. Why do many states have usury laws?

3. Why might a person declare personal bankruptcy?

Section 4 Review Answers

Understanding Vocabulary
usury law (p. 99), bankruptcy (p. 100)
Reviewing Objectives
1. The same guidelines for credit worthiness must be applied to all borrowers; lenders cannot create different terms of credit for individuals in similar economic situations; and if a loan is denied, the reasons must be given or the applicant informed of the right to request the reasons.
2. Usury laws set limits on the amount of interest lenders can charge.
3. A person who has piled up debts that he or she cannot pay may decide to declare personal bankruptcy to get a fresh start.

Teach

Inform students that when people find themselves overwhelmed by debts, they can take action to deal with the situation rather than wait for creditors to contact them. They should know what rights they have under the law, what pitfalls to avoid, and what organizations can help debtors negotiate with their creditors. Tell students that in this feature article they will learn four important steps toward getting out of debt and avoiding bankruptcy court.

Have students do research on consumer credit counselors in their area. Have students find out how they help debtors restructure their debt so that they can repay creditors.

News Clip

Readings in Economics

DATELINE: CHANGING TIMES   MARCH 1991

DIGGING OUT OF THE DEBT TRAP
by Kristin Davis and Rebecca Little

It's no surprise that consumer credit counselors say they're getting busier. Here's what they advise for consumers overwhelmed with debt.

Don't avoid creditors. Instead of skipping a payment, contact creditors to explain why you can't pay. "Creditors will fall off their chairs if you contact them first," says Tom Hufford, executive director of the Consumer Credit Counseling Service (CCCS) of Northeastern Indiana. They have a lot of latitude early on, he says, to temporarily waive or reduce payments.

Beware of consolidation loans. Many people hope to stretch out payments over a

Home Equity Loan 40% Interest

longer period with a consolidation loan. But the finance companies that offer those loans typically charge high interest rates. Using a home-equity loan for this purpose may seem an ideal solution—interest rates are relatively low and inter-

est on up to $100,000 is tax-deductible. But your home is collateral and you risk losing it if you fall behind. Warns Hufford: "You start again with zero balances on your credit cards, and old habits die hard."

Work out your own plan. Although secured creditors may not be as flexible, unsecured creditors may be receptive to a revised payment plan. William Kent Brunette, author of *Conquer Your Debt*, suggests figuring out how much you can afford to pay toward all debts monthly and prorating payments based on how much you owe each creditor. Assure creditors that they're all being treated equally and that you won't take on new debt until the accounts are paid, he advises. . . .

Seek credit counseling. If bill collectors' calls get unpleasant, contact a CCCS. These nonprofit agencies can serve as a buffer between you and anxious creditors.

• THINK ABOUT IT •

1. What four major things do the authors urge indebted consumers to do?

2. What is the drawback of a consolidation loan?

Answers to Think About It

1. Do not avoid creditors, beware consolidation loans, work out your own plan, and seek credit counseling.

2. high interest rates, potential loss of collateral items, temptation to charge up credit cards again or acquire more debt

CHAPTER 4 *Highlights*

Section 1

Americans and Credit

Key Terms

credit (p. 80)
principal (p. 80)
interest (p. 80)
installment debt (p. 80)
consumer durables (p. 80)
mortgage (p. 81)

Summary
  Repaying an installment debt over a long period provides some advantages to the borrower. People use credit for a variety of reasons. In all cases, however, consumers must carefully decide whether to use credit as well as how much to use.

Section 2

Sources of Loans and Credit

Key Terms

commercial bank (p. 86)
savings and loan association (p. 86)
savings banks (p. 86)
credit union (p. 87)
finance company (p. 87)
consumer finance company (p. 88)
charge account (p. 89)
regular charge account (p. 89)
credit limit (p. 89)
revolving charge account (p. 89)
installment charge account (p. 90)
credit card (p. 90)
debit card (p. 91)
finance charge (p. 91)
annual percentage rate (p. 93)

Summary
  Consumers who wish to borrow money may choose from among six types of financial institutions. Consumers who wish to open a charge account may choose between a regular, a revolving, or an installment account. In all cases, consumers should realize that the annual percentage rate is not the same as the stated finance charge.

Section 3

Applying for Credit

Key Terms

credit bureau (p. 94)
credit check (p. 94)
credit rating (p. 94)
collateral (p. 95)
secured loan (p. 95)
unsecured loan (p. 95)
cosigner (p. 96)
past-due notices (p. 96)

Summary
  Several factors are considered when financial institutions determine a person's credit rating. Once a person is granted credit, he or she has a responsibility to use it wisely.

Section 4

Government Regulation of Credit

Key Terms

usury law (p. 99)
bankruptcy (p. 100)

Summary
  The Equal Credit Opportunity Act prohibits discrimination in lending based upon several factors. Many states have usury laws that also protect borrowers. Borrowers who overextend their credit may choose to declare personal bankruptcy.

Chapter 4 Going Into Debt **103**

Using Chapter 4 HIGHLIGHTS

Use the Chapter 4 Highlights to preview, review, condense, or reteach the chapter. A Spanish Chapter Highlights is available in the Spanish Handbook.

Preview/Review

 After students read the Chapter 4 Highlights, have them complete Economics Vocabulary Activity 4 in the TCR. Spanish Vocabulary Activities are also available in the Spanish Resource Binder.

Vocabulary Software reinforces the economic terms used in Chapter 4.

Condense

Have students listen to Chapter 4 on the Audiocassettes in the TCR. A 1-page written activity and 1-page test accompany this material. These materials are also available in Spanish.

Reteach

Have students complete Reteaching Activity 4 in the TCR. Spanish Reteaching Activities are also available.

VIDEODISC

Nightly Business Report
Economics in Action
Use "Going Into Debt" on Disc 1, Side A, Video 5.

Search 21560, Play to 26885

103

Identifying Key Terms

Answers will vary, but students should be able to distinguish the different services offered and types of customers each lending institution serves.

1. c
2. a
3. d
4. e
5. b

Recalling Facts and Ideas

Section 1

1. principal plus any interest and fees
2. In both cases, you must pay interest for the use of someone else's purchasing power.
3. Consumer durables and real property
4. People want or need items immediately and wish to spread the payments over time. The payments correspond to the actual value of the item's use.

Section 2

5. commercial bank, savings and loan association, savings bank, credit union, finance company, consumer finance company
6. bank cards such as Visa and cards issued by companies such as Discover
7. finance charges

Section 3

8. credit history, capacity, character, collateral

9. Secured loans are backed by collateral; unsecured loans are made on the reputation of the borrower.
10. Borrowers must repay the loan on time, keep records of charges made, and notify issuers promptly if credit cards

---

Write a short paragraph about the different types of lending institutions and their differences using all of the following terms.

commercial bank (p. 86)   credit union (p. 87)
savings banks (p. 86)   consumer finance
                          company (p. 88)

Write the letter of the definition in Column B below that correctly defines each term in Column A.

Column A
1. principal (p. 80)
2. usury law (p. 99)
3. collateral (p. 95)
4. annual percentage rate (p. 93)
5. unsecured loan (p. 95)

Column B
a. restricts the amount of interest that can be charged for credit
b. requires only a promise to repay
c. amount of money borrowed in a loan
d. something of value that a borrower uses as a promise of loan repayment
e. cost of credit expressed as a yearly percentage

Recalling Facts and Ideas

Section 1
1. What do you have to pay when you borrow?
2. How is taking out a loan similar to buying an item on credit?
3. People typically use installment debt to buy what type of goods?
4. Why do people use credit?

Section 2
5. What are the six types of basic lending insti-

---

tutions in our economy?
6. What are some of the most common types of credit cards used today?
7. When you take out a loan, what do you call the total cost of credit expressed in dollars and cents?

Section 3
8. When you make an application for a loan, what are four factors that a creditor looks at to determine whether you are creditworthy?
9. What is the difference between a secured and unsecured loan?
10. What are your responsibilities as a borrower?

Section 4
11. What does the Equal Credit Opportunity Act of 1974 prohibit?
12. States often restrict the maximum amount of interest that can be charged on loans. What are such laws called?
13. What are the three important federal laws regulating consumer credit?

Critical Thinking

Section 1
Evaluating Information In deciding whether to pay cash or use credit for a personal purchase, what are the costs involved and the benefits of each choice?

Section 2
Identifying Alternatives How would you decide which of the six types of lending institutions discussed in this section would be most appropriate for a particular loan?

---

are lost or stolen.

Section 4

11. It prohibits discrimination in lending based on factors such as race, national origin, or sex that have no bearing on an applicant's ability to repay the loan.
12. usury laws
13. Truth in Lending Act, Fair Credit Reporting Act, and Equal Credit Opportunity Act (oth-

ers are Fair Credit Billing Act, Fair Debt Collection Practices Act)

Critical Thinking
Section 1
Students should weigh opportunity costs of paying cash against the finance and APR costs of credit. Benefits of credit are immediate use of the item, payments spread over time, and pay-

Section 3

Making Comparisons What are the differences between a secured and an unsecured loan?

Section 4

Demonstrating Reasoned Judgment If you declare personal bankruptcy, your creditors clearly lose. What ethical concerns should you have before ever taking this action?

Applying Economic Concepts

The Role of Government Sometimes credit cards are lost or stolen. The owner must take steps to keep his or her card from being used by an unauthorized person. Find out by researching the Truth in Lending Act what a credit card holder must do when his or her card is lost or stolen.

Chapter Projects

1. **Individual Project** Call various retail stores in your area as well as some gas stations and ask them to send you a credit card application. Write a list of the questions asked that are virtually the same on each application.
2. **Cooperative Learning Project** Work in small groups to create a loan application that is appropriate for high school students and circulate it in class. Based on the application, discuss why it is or is not difficult to decide who should receive loans. Is it difficult to decide who should *not* receive loans?

Reviewing Skills

Determining a Safe Debt Load

1. Look at the table below. What is this family's safe debt load?
2. How much more can this family safely take on in debt?

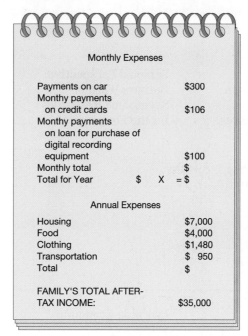

Monthly Expenses	
Payments on car	$300
Monthy payments on credit cards	$106
Monthy payments on loan for purchase of digital recording equipment	$100
Monthly total	$
Total for Year	$ X = $

Annual Expenses	
Housing	$7,000
Food	$4,000
Clothing	$1,480
Transportation	$ 950
Total	$
FAMILY'S TOTAL AFTER-TAX INCOME:	$35,000

Writing About Economics

Persuasive Writing Write a letter to the editor about the positive or negative effects of credit on the American economy and on consumers. Refer to Your Economics Journal to mention the kinds of advertising on TV and radio that relate to credit and debt.

ment correspondence to value of item's use. Benefits of paying cash are use of the item and no additional costs or payments to burden future income.

Section 2
Students must first decide on the item they wish to purchase and its price. They must then decide which of the six institutions have the resources to finance best terms in interest and fees.

Section 3
Collateral backs secured loans. Unsecured loans are made solely on the borrower's promise to repay.

Section 4
By taking out a loan or charging items on credit, you assume an ethical responsibility to repay the debt. If you fail, you violate this ethical concern by ensuring that creditors are never repaid the full amount they loaned you.

Applying Economic Concepts

Students should mention that credit card holders must notify issuers of lost or stolen credit cards immediately either by telephone or in writing. Card holders are responsible for the first $50 of new charges on a lost or stolen card.

? BONUS QUESTION

The following bonus question may be written on the chalkboard when students take the chapter test.
Q: How can a bank credit card help if you run out of cash?
A: You can use it to get a cash advance.

Chapter Projects

1. Review the questions that are the same on each application and discuss what information these questions are designed to elicit. Have students determine what they tell the lender about the applicant.
2. Discuss what a lender would look for in terms of creditworthiness in a high school student. Have students consider factors that would determine whether a student is a good, fair,

or poor risk for a loan.

Reviewing Skills

1. $7,157 (rounded from $7,156.6)
2. $1,084 per year

Writing About Economics

Conduct a class discussion on the positive or negative effects of credit on the economy and on consumers.

CHAPTER 5 *BUYING THE NECESSITIES: FOOD AND CLOTHING*

CHAPTER ORGANIZER

Section 1 Shopping for Food
- **Describe** the advantages of comparison food shopping.
- **List** the three major types of food stores.

Personal Perspective:
Barbara Ward on Saving Our Resources for the Future, p. 112

- 📁 Reproducible Lesson Plan 5.1
- 💿 *NBR* Video 7
- 🔖 Focus Activity Transparency 15
- 📁 Focus Activity Sheet 15
- 📁 Guided Reading Activity 5.1
- 📁 Cooperative Learning Activity 5
- 📁 Primary and Secondary Source Readings 5
- 📁 Section Quiz 5.1
- 📁 Spanish Section Quiz 5.1
- 💾 Testmaker

Section 2 Clothing Choices
- **Explain** how personal values affect clothing choices.
- **List** three factors that determine clothing value.
- **Decide** when to take advantage of clothing sales.

Learning Economic Skills:
Learning About Percentage Changes, p. 117

News Clip:
Vanessa O'Connell, "Don't Get Cheated by Supermarket Scanners," *Money*, April 1993, p. 118

- 📁 Reproducible Lesson Plan 5.2
- 🔖 Focus Activity Transparency 16
- 📁 Focus Activity Sheet 16
- 📁 Guided Reading Activity 5.2
- 📁 Free Enterprise Activity 5
- 📁 Mathematics Practice for Economics 5
- 📁 Performance Assessment Activity 5
- 📁 Section Quiz 5.2
- 📁 Spanish Section Quiz 5.2
- 💾 Testmaker
- 📁 Enrichment Activity 5
- 📁 Reinforcing Economics Skills 5

0:00 **OUT OF TIME?** If time does not permit teaching this chapter, you may use the Chapter 5 Highlights and the Audiocassettes that include a 1-page activity and a 1-page test.

Chapter 5 Review and Evaluation

Special Features

Chapter 5 Highlights, p. 119
Chapter 5 Review, pp. 120–121

Classroom Resources

- Chapter 5 Test Forms A and B
- Economics Vocabulary Activity 5
- Spanish Economics Vocabulary Activity 5
- Audiocassette 5
- Spanish Audiocassette 5
- Reteaching Activity 5
- Spanish Reteaching Activity 5

Key to Ability Levels

Teaching strategies have been coded for varying learning styles and abilities.

L1 Level 1 activities are **basic** activities and should be within the ability range of all students.

L2 Level 2 activities are **average** activities designed for the ability range of average to above-average students.

L3 Level 3 activities are **challenging** activities designed for the ability range of above-average students.

LEP activities should be within the ability range of **Limited English Proficiency** students.

Performance Assessment

The following chapter project may be assigned at the beginning of the chapter and used for performance assessment. See page T12 for additional Performance Assessment information.

Buying for the Family Tell students to imagine that they are responsible for buying the groceries for a family of four for two weeks and winter clothing for two high school students. Give them a list of items they must buy. Have students work in small groups to determine the best places to shop, how to use sales and coupons, and what items might be cheaper bought in bulk. Students should use what they learn in the chapter to help them with this project. Have them write a brief report on the results, describing what factors influenced their decisions about the brands they bought and the places they purchased the items on their lists.

Additional Resources

Readings for the Student

Consumer Reports Buying Guide. Updated yearly. Consumer Reports, Boulder, CO 80322-3029. Guide on how to shop, how to get the most value for your money, and what products are the best on the market.

The Wholesale by Mail Catalog. Updated yearly. New York: Harper Perennial, 1993. Buying food and clothing (and other items) through mail order catalogs.

Readings for the Teacher

Clothing Selection Charts. Agriculture Research Administration, Department of Agriculture, Alexandria, Va.

Mlyniec, Richard A. "Integrating life-skills into a consumer education course," *Business Education Forum,* Vol. 41, No. 2, pp. 12–14, Nov. 1986. Features a discussion on teaching students budgeting, consumer purchases, and lifestyle choices.

Multimedia Materials

Buyer Be Aware. LSC192V. Social Studies School Service

Shopping Strategies. Two-disk set. Apple/IBM. Educational Resources, 1550 Executive Drive, Elgin, IL 60123. Making good decisions about buying groceries, clothing, and other consumer goods.

Chapter Overview

Food and clothing purchases make up two of the largest items in a family's budget. Chapter 5 explains or describes: the value of comparison shopping among different stores and brands; how to take advantage of sales and discounts in food buying; how to obtain the best value in clothing for the price; and how to save money on clothes purchases through sales and discounts.

 VIDEODISC

Nightly Business Report
Economics in Action
Use "Buying the Necessities: Food and Clothing" on Disc 1, Side A, Video 7.

Search 32078, Play to 38780

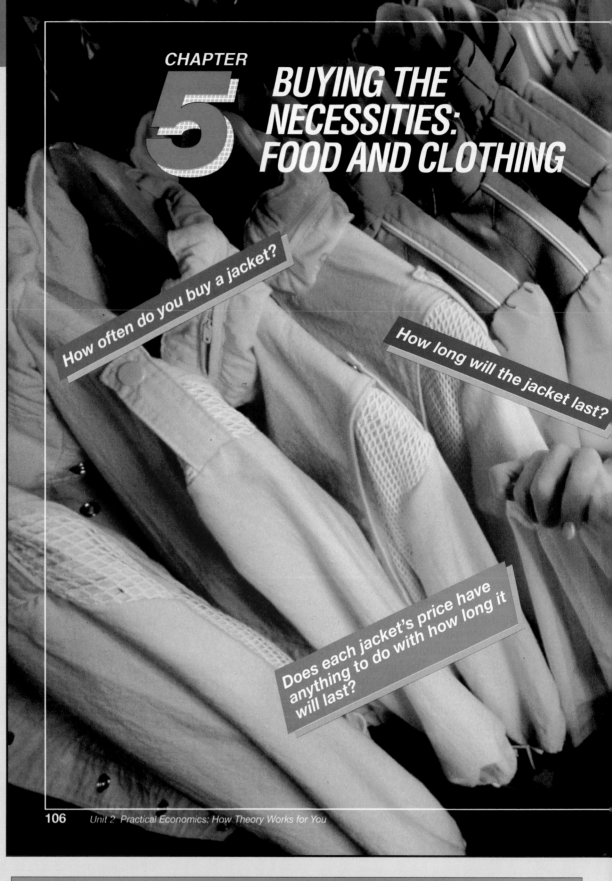

CHAPTER

BUYING THE NECESSITIES: FOOD AND CLOTHING

How often do you buy a jacket?

How long will the jacket last?

Does each jacket's price have anything to do with how long it will last?

106 *Unit 2 Practical Economics: How Theory Works for You*

Answering Economic Questions

The questions in the above illustration are designed to lead into the main concepts in Chapter 5. Students may not always think about durability or value when buying clothes, particularly fad items. Ask students to describe a time when they bought an item of clothing on impulse or because other students were wearing similar items, only to discover the item did not last or they did not like it after a short time.

Why does the style of jackets change?

What happens to the value of a jacket when it is out of style?

Your Economics Journal

Keep track of where your parents purchase food over a period of one week. List the types of food stores and the items purchased for each type. Next to each type of food store indicate why your parents went there.

107

Connecting to Past Learning

Ask students to write down the stores where they commonly buy clothing and the reasons why they shop there (convenience, price, discounts, quality, brand names). Discuss their answers in class. Tell them that in Chapter 5 they will learn how to evaluate the best buys in food and clothing by analyzing opportunity costs and the ways stores use sales, discounts, and other methods to sell merchandise.

Applying Economics

Tell students to suppose that a friend asks their help to buy a new school outfit that has to last for two or three years. The friend has $120 to spend. Discuss with students how they would help their friend buy the clothes. Have students list questions they would ask the friend about style, quality, type of clothing desired, durability, and comfort. Students should then make suggestions as to where they would go to purchase the clothes.

EXTRA CREDIT PROJECT

Develop a simple questionnaire to poll shoppers about a choice they make pertaining to buying food or clothing. Explain the purpose of the survey to the class and present your findings.

Economic Portfolio

Refer students to the information in **Your Economics Journal** and have them analyze their parents' grocery list to see where the family can save money. Ask them to list which items represent the largest dollar purchases, which are purchased most often, which are purchased least often, which can be deleted, and which generally are purchased with coupons or on sale. Have students write a paragraph of suggestions for reducing the weekly grocery bill. Ask students to discuss the opportunity costs of this effort to save money on food.

PERFORMANCE ASSESSMENT

Refer to page 106B for "Buying for the Family," a Performance Assessment Activity for this chapter.

Focus

Overview

See the student page for section objectives.

Section 1 explains or describes: the basic principles of comparison shopping for food items and the different types of food stores; the differences among brand-name, generic, and private-labeled products; and the trade-off among price, quality, and quantity in shopping for food.

Bellringer

Before presenting the lesson, display Focus Activity Transparency 15 on the overhead projector or copy the material on the chalkboard. Assign the accompanying Focus Activity Sheet.

Motivational Activity

Ask students to list the types of food they buy most often and where they buy these items. Discuss why they select those particular foods and why they shop at a particular store (convenience, price, choice of items, brand).

Preteaching Vocabulary

Instruct students to create a matrix in which they list the words, their definitions, and then examples of each type of store or product.

SECTION **1** *Shopping for Food*

SECTION 1 FOCUS

Terms to Know warehouse food store, convenience stores, private-labeled products

Objectives *After reading this section, you should be able to:*
1. Describe the advantages of comparison food shopping.
2. List the three major types of food stores.

Grocery Shopping Is a Skill You Can Learn

Americans consume more than 30 percent of the agricultural output of the world. They can choose from thousands of different food products and buy them at thousands of stores. Hundreds of brands offer numerous choices: sliced carrots, whole carrots, carrots with peas—canned or frozen. In all, American consumers spend hundreds of billions of dollars a year on food.

Comparison Shopping

Because American families spend so much for food, comparison shopping is important. A consumer should, however, do only as much comparison shopping as is worthwhile to that person. It does not pay a shopper to go far out of his or her way to shop at a store that has only a few needed items at low prices. Such savings would be outweighed by the additional costs of time and transportation.

Reading advertisements is a good, inexpensive way to comparison shop. Food store ads describe sales and often contain cents-off coupons.

Comparison shopping involves making comparisons among brands and sizes as well as stores. You need to decide not only where to shop but what to shop for. Figure 5.1 will also be a useful guide.

Food Stores

Figure 5.2 shows the three major types of stores. Each has its own characteristics.

Classroom Resources for Section 1

- Reproducible Lesson Plan 5.1
- *NBR* Video 7
- Focus Activity Transparency 15
- Focus Activity Sheet 15
- Guided Reading Activity 5.1
- Cooperative Learning Activity 5

- Primary and Secondary Source Readings 5
- Section Quiz 5.1
- Spanish Section Quiz 5.1
- Testmaker

✓ Checklist

**Figure 5.1
Food Shopping**

The following are some helpful tips for getting the most from your money when you food shop.

1 Read the newspapers ahead of time for sales and cents-off coupons.

2 Go with a shopping list and your coupons. If possible, plan your week's meals before you shop so that you will buy only what you need. A list will also help you avoid additional trips to the store for items that you forgot.

3 Avoid impulsive buying, or buying without thinking about the purchase beforehand. Be especially careful in the check-out line because stores often place special offers for nonessential items such as cookies and gum by the cash register.

4 Check labels on canned and frozen goods for nutritional value.

5 Check freshness dates on dairy and bakery items.

6 Compare prices on private, generic, and national brands.

7 Check unit prices. Buy large sizes only if you will be able to use the items immediately or can store them.

8 Do not shop when you are hungry. You will be tempted to buy snack foods.

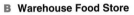

**Figure 5.2
Major Types of Food Stores**
Where you choose to shop for food regularly can have a major impact on your budget.

B Warehouse Food Store
The **warehouse food store** has only a *limited number of brands and items*. They are less expensive than in supermarkets, however. In many warehouse stores, goods are *sold only by the case*. Therefore, warehouse food stores are best for consumers who can buy in large quantities. ▼

C Convenience Stores
Convenience stores seem to be everywhere. They are usually open 16 to 24 hours a day and carry a limited selection of items. The price per unit of almost anything is higher than in a supermarket or warehouse store because consumers are paying for the cost of convenience. ▼

A Supermarkets
Just about anything in the way of meats, fresh vegetables, paper products, canned goods, and so on, can be bought in a supermarket. Prices may be relatively high, however, so it is important to be aware of supermarket sales.

Chapter 5 Buying the Necessities: Food and Clothing **109**

Teach

Guided Practice

L1 Comparing and Contrasting On the chalkboard, draw a map showing a house, then a warehouse food store some distance away, a convenience store close by, and a supermarket about midway between the two. Ask students to write a paragraph explaining which store they might use to buy which items and why. **LEP**

L2 Evaluating Refer students to the section on comparing brands. Discuss a time when they bought a generic or private-labeled product rather than the brand-name item. Ask whether they were satisfied with the quality and quantity of the product and whether it justified the savings in price.

🌐 GLOBAL ECONOMICS

In many famine-ridden areas of the world, the soil has become too poor to grow enough food to support the population. Current international relief efforts include agricultural research as well as food. If poorer nations can find ways to feed themselves, they will have more resources to develop other industries, enabling them to participate in world trading markets on a more equal footing with other nations.

◆▷◑ Meeting Special Needs

Minority Students The parents of Asian, Hispanic, or other ethnic or minority students may shop primarily at ethnic stores rather than supermarkets, convenience stores, or warehouse food stores. Have minority students write a brief report or explain in class how their parents select and purchase foods.

Ask them to describe ways that their parents get the best value for their money and how they make comparison-shopping decisions. Explain to students that, in some cases, the types of foods people eat may affect their selection of stores, brands, and options of quality, quantity, and price.

Independent Practice

L3 Reporting Encourage students to investigate how prices for fresh items such as apples are set at a large supermarket, a convenience store, and a warehouse food store. Have students report back to class.

 Have students complete Guided Reading Activity 5.1 in the TCR. LEP

Visual Instruction

Refer students to Figure 5.3. Ask them to do a price comparison of unit cost for brand-name, store-label, generic, and (if appropriate) bulk forms of orange juice, spaghetti, canned peas, and oatmeal. Have them report on their findings to the class regarding differences in quantity, quality, and price.

? DID YOU KNOW

The federal government is cracking down on manufacturers to prove the nutritional claims on packaging to protect consumers from nutritional fraud.

Brand-Name Products Versus Private-Labeled Products When you go shopping in virtually any food store, many of the food items have well-known brand names. Some food stores also carry regional brands that are found only in certain areas of the country.

As an alternative to expensive national brands, some big supermarket chains as well as club wholesale chains carry their own store-brand products. These are also called **private-labeled products.** According to some consumer surveys, it is possible to save as much as 40 percent by buying store-brand (private-labeled) products. As Figure 5.3 shows, you can save even more when you buy generic or bulk items.

The Trade-Off Between Price, Quantity, and Quality There is often a trade-off between quality and price in the products you buy. A lower-priced generic dishwasher soap might leave a slight film on your drinking glasses compared to a more expensive national-brand alternative.

Often you will find that the larger the quantity of any item you buy in a supermarket, the lower the per-unit price. Most states require stores to provide unit pricing for food and other products. That makes it easy to compare prices not only for different brands, but for different sizes of the same brand. For example, the price of milk might be expressed in terms of cents per ounce. You can then tell how much you save per ounce if you buy milk in larger containers.

Cents-Off Coupons Many manufacturers give cents-off coupons as shown in Figure 5.4. To take advantage of them, a consumer has to buy the brand, size, and quantity named on the coupon. The store then reduces the price paid by the amount printed on the coupon. The manufacturer, in turn, pays the store.

Convenience Foods In most food stores, you can buy either foods that require preparation, such as fresh meat and vegetables, or foods that require little or no preparation, such as complete frozen dinners. The latter are called convenience foods and usually require no work other than heating. Some nutritionists (noo-TRISH-uh-nists)—experts on food and health—believe that convenience foods are

Figure 5.3
Generic and Bulk Foods
Some food products are available in brand-name, store-label, generic, or bulk form. Generally, price decreases in that order. ▼

BRAND NAME
Rice
$2.59
32 OZ.

STORE BRAND
Rice
$1.29
32 OZ.

GENERIC
Rice
$1.09
32 OZ.

BULK
Rice
$ .89
32 OZ.

 Cooperative Learning

Organize students into small groups to brainstorm and develop a checklist of shopping reminders aimed at getting maximum value for every dollar spent on food purchases. Ask a member of each group to present its checklist for review and discussion by the class. Suggest that students use the best elements from all the checklists to develop a single checklist that every student's family could use. Later, survey the class to learn how many families have used the checklist and whether it has helped save money or been useful in some other way.

unhealthful. They believe they contain too many added chemicals, too much sugar, and too many preservatives. The economic issue involved is time.

The purchase of a convenience food involves a trade-off. Convenience foods are more expensive than foods that you must prepare. Because of the higher price you pay when you buy convenience foods, you sacrifice the purchase of other goods and services. You are gaining more time for leisure or making extra money, however, because convenience foods require less work. Convenience foods illustrate one of the situations in which the consumer must choose between having more free time or having more money to spend on other items.

◄ **Figure 5.4**
Coupon Trade-Off
If you make a habit of using coupons, you can reduce your food bill by as much as 5 percent over a one-year period. The use of such coupons, however, requires time—the time to collect and match them to items when shopping. Because time is a scarce resource, you have to decide if the money you save using coupons is worth the time you spend.

SECTION 1 REVIEW

Understanding Vocabulary
Define warehouse food store, convenience stores, private-labeled products.

Reviewing Objectives
1. What are the advantages of comparison food shopping?
2. How do the three kinds of food stores differ?

Assess

Meeting Lesson Objectives

Assign Section 1 Review as homework or an in-class activity. Each question in the Review addresses the corresponding numbered objective in the Section Focus.

Evaluate

Assign the Section 1 Quiz in the TCR or use the Testmaker to develop a customized quiz.

Reteach

Tell students to write out the main headings of the section and then write out in their own words the main points under each heading.

Enrich

Invite the manager of a supermarket to explain sale items and pricing and to offer shopping tips.

Close

Have students write a paragraph explaining the importance of making wise decisions when they are purchasing food.

Section 1 Review Answers
Understanding Vocabulary
warehouse food store (p. 109), **convenience stores** (p. 109), **private-labeled products** (p. 110)
Reviewing Objectives
1. Comparison shopping will give consumers more groceries or better quality for their money.
2. Supermarkets—large selection of foods, but higher prices than warehouse food stores; warehouse food stores—more limited selection of items and brands than supermarkets, but lower prices for large quantities; convenience stores—most limited selection and the highest prices, but open 16 to 24 hours a day.

Background

Barbara Ward was a British journalist and economist who wrote for about 40 years on equalizing distribution of the world's food and other resources and campaigned for conservation of natural resources. Over that time, the gap between economically developing nations of the southern half of the globe and wealthy nations of the northern half grew. She knew this posed a threat to the security of both and proposed cooperation between nations to meet this challenge. Ward's writings have appeared in the *Economist*, an influential British newspaper.

Teach

Ask students to write a brief paragraph summarizing the reasons Barbara Ward gives for the growing gap between rich and poor nations. Have them list their own ideas on how nations can cooperate to share the wealth and conserve the earth's resources. Finally, have them answer the Checking for Understanding questions.

Personal Perspective

Barbara Ward on Saving Our Resources for the Future

Profile

- 1914-1981
- born in England
- educated in France, Germany, and England
- lectured on the growing gap between the rich nations and the poor nations
- authored many books, including *The West at Bay* (1948), *Nationalism and Ideology* (1966), *The Rich Nations and the Poor Nations* (1962), *Spaceship Earth* (1966), and *Only One Earth* (1972) with René Dubos

Ward's earlier works, such as *The Rich Nations and the Poor Nations*, emphasized the growing gap between the wealth of different countries. Her later works, including *Only One Earth* excerpted below, extended her ideas to look at the availability of resources such as energy for the future.

... *But the really new risk, foreseen in the past by only a few of the world's economists, is that such a pressure of rising demand may begin to put intolerable strains on what had appeared to be the planet's limitless resources. This risk had been masked in the thrusting nineteenth century by the opening up of all the planet's temperate lands to European settlement and later by the extraordinary productivity of new forms of energy and chemical transformations.*

Ward offers ideas for planning for the future.

... *The first step toward devising a strategy for planet Earth is for the nations to accept a collective responsibility for discovering more— much more—about the natural system and how it is affected by man's activities and vice versa. This implies cooperative monitoring, research, and study on an unprecedented scale. It implies an intensive world-wide network for the systematic exchange of knowledge and experience.*

... *Here again, no one nation, not even groups of nations, can, acting separately, avoid the tragedy of increasing divisions between wealthy north and poverty-stricken south in our planet. No nations, on their own, can offset the risk of deepening disorder.... Either they will move on to a community based upon a more systematic sharing of wealth—through progressive income tax, through general policies for education, shelter, health, and housing—or they will break down in revolt and anarchy.*

Checking for Understanding

1. Why are resources once regarded as unlimited proving to be limited?
2. What should we do now to prepare for the future?
3. According to Ward's view of the world, what should happen to the availability of such necessary items as food and clothing in the future?

Answers to Checking for Understanding

1. The pressure of rising demand puts intolerable strains on what once appeared to be the earth's unlimited resources.
2. To prepare for the future, we need to know much more about the earth's natural systems, how they are affected by human activity and, in turn, how they influence human activity. Such knowledge must be made available to all nations via a worldwide network of communication.
3. They must be shared more equally between nations of the north and south. There must be a cooperative effort among nations to help developing nations, or there may be revolt and anarchy within many poorer nations.

SECTION 2 FOCUS

Terms to Know durability, service flow

Objectives *After reading this section, you should be able to:*
❶ Explain how **personal values affect clothing choices.**
❷ List three factors that determine **clothing value.**
❸ Decide when to take advantage of **clothing sales.**

Focus

Overview

See the student page for section objectives.

Section 2 explains or describes how personal values influence our clothing choices, and factors to consider in comparing clothing values.

Factors to Consider When Buying Clothing

Americans spend about $300 billion annually on clothing and other personal products, as Figure 5.5 shows. Most people could buy a few very durable, sturdy, and even good-looking pieces of clothing that would last much longer than their owners might want to keep them. By purchasing such clothing, consumers could reduce their clothing budget considerably. These clothes would protect them from the cold, sun, wind, and so on. The clothes, however, would not serve another purpose—variety. Variety is just one factor involved in clothing choice. Custom, attitude about one's self, and values are other factors that cannot be judged statistically.

**Figure 5.5
Sales of Clothing and Personal Products**
Personal care and clothing are huge industries. How many dollars does each category on this graph represent? ▼

Clothing and Personal Values

Historically, people's dress reflected their social position, or status. When the American colonies were founded, the influence of social class on clothing began to break down. In this country today, clothing is more a reflection of personal values than of position. In this sense, the clothing that a person buys makes a statement about his or her values. For example, it may not be important to you to have special clothes to wear for a date, while it may be important to someone else. An individual's values are linked to the larger value system—family, friends, and culture. See Figure 5.6 (pages 114–115).

Bellringer

🗐 Before presenting the lesson, display Focus Activity Transparency 16 on the overhead projector or copy the material on the chalkboard. Assign the accompanying Focus Activity Sheet.

Motivational Activity

Ask students to list three factors that determine what type and style of clothing they buy, naming the most important factor first. Discuss their responses.

Preteaching Vocabulary

Have students read over the definitions of the vocabulary words and then list the items in their own wardrobe that illustrate the concepts.

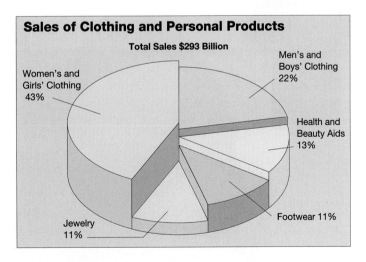

Sales of Clothing and Personal Products

Total Sales $293 Billion

Women's and Girls' Clothing 43%

Men's and Boys' Clothing 22%

Health and Beauty Aids 13%

Footwear 11%

Jewelry 11%

Classroom Resources for Section 2

- 📁 Reproducible Lesson Plan 5.2
- 🗐 Focus Activity Transparency 16
- 📁 Focus Activity Sheet 16
- 📁 Guided Reading Activity 5.2
- 📁 Free Enterprise Activity 5
- 📁 Mathematics Practice for Economics 5

- 📁 Performance Assessment Activity 5
- 📁 Section Quiz 5.2
- 📁 Spanish Section Quiz 5.2
- 💿 Chapter 5 Test Forms A and B Testmaker
- 📁 Enrichment Activity 5

- 📁 Reinforcing Economics Skills 5
- 📁 Economics Vocabulary Activity 5
- 📁 Spanish Economics Vocabulary Activity 5
- 🎧 Audiocassette 5
- 🎧 Spanish Audiocassette 5
- 📁 Reteaching Activity 5
- 📁 Spanish Reteaching Activity 5

Teach

Guided Practice

L2 Evaluating and Comparing Ask students to bring in clothing sale advertisements in local newspapers. Tell students to use the information in this section to evaluate what is a real bargain. Direct students to write a paragraph describing what they believe is the best bargain among the newspaper ads.

Visual Instruction

Refer students to Figure 5.6 and its captions. Organize the class into small groups and have them discuss how values, self-esteem, customs, and variety influence their choices regarding the types and styles of clothing they wear.

GLOBAL ECONOMICS

Most of the casual and sports clothing sold in the United States is made in Korea, Taiwan, China, Mexico, the Philippines, and India. These countries produce the items for far less than it would cost in the United States. They then sell the clothing to United States retail companies to feature in their ready-to-wear departments. The wealth flows from United States markets to developing nations, each country using its resources efficiently.

Comparing Clothing Value

Comparison shopping is an important part of buying wisely. Comparing value in clothing means more than simply purchasing an item from the store that offers the best price. Clothing value depends on at least three other factors: style, durability, and cost of care.

Figure 5.6
Why So Many Clothes?
Several major factors combine to influence the types and styles of clothing we choose to wear.

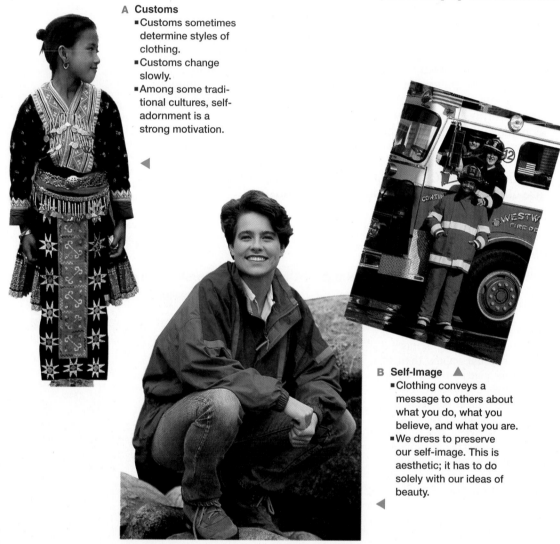

A **Customs**
- Customs sometimes determine styles of clothing.
- Customs change slowly.
- Among some traditional cultures, self-adornment is a strong motivation.

B **Self-Image** ▲
- Clothing conveys a message to others about what you do, what you believe, and what you are.
- We dress to preserve our self-image. This is aesthetic; it has to do solely with our ideas of beauty.

Style You may be able to buy the minimum amount of clothing you need at a very low cost. You will, however, generally give up style to do it. Wearing clothes that are stylish—up-to-date—is usually expensive because you need to buy new clothes each year.

Wearing current styles costs more than wearing what are called classic styles, which are the more basic clothing designs and colors that do not change much through the years. Again, you are faced with a trade-off. Should you buy stylish clothes each year to keep up with fashion and have

---

◆▶⬤ Meeting Special Needs

Students With Poor Math Skills Some students may have trouble calculating how much they can save on clothing sales. They can use an equation to find the amount of money off the original price.

r(% rate) × p(original price) = s(savings)

Point out that the percent should be written as a decimal or a fraction. For example, if a store advertises 25 percent off a $40 blouse, what is the savings?

$0.25 \times \$40 = \$10$

or

$\frac{1}{4} \times \$40 = \$10$

less money to spend on other items? Or should you buy less stylish clothes that you can wear from year to year and have more money?

Durability The ability of an item to last is known as **durability.** The longer a piece of clothing—or any item— lasts, the more durable it is. When you purchase an item of clothing, you are purchasing it for the service flow that it yields per time period. This **service flow** is how much you get to use it over time and the value you place on this use. If you buy a jacket that will last three years and costs $300, the cost per service flow per year is $100.

A consumer would not really be comparing similar value if he or she automatically bought the less expensive coat, dress, or shirt. In the long run, it might be more expensive. An inexpensive but poorly made pair of pants, for example, might have to be replaced after one season. A slightly more expensive but more durable pair might last for several seasons.

In comparison shopping for clothing, you should try to determine how long an item will last and how long you will need it. Then you should compare prices. Suppose you think Coat A will last twice as long as Coat B, and Coat A costs only 20 percent more. Then Coat A is a better buy. You should also try to decide, however, if the coat will still be in style in a year.

C **Values**
- Values determine choice of clothes because such choice is a statement of what we consider important.
- Clothing reflects values instilled in us by society as well as our own individual attitudes and values.
- Values inherent in clothes are self-expression, esteem, and comfort.
- Unconventional dress often identifies a person as part of a small group. ▼

D **Variety**
- Many people want to have different "looks" for different occasions.
- People in different climates need different wardrobes for summer and winter. ▶

Chapter 5 Buying the Necessities: Food and Clothing **115**

Chapter 5, Section 2

Independent Practice

L1 Analyzing Refer students to the Checklist in Figure 5.7 (page 116). Have them analyze their wardrobe by answering the five questions.
L3 Reporting Encourage interested students to survey the local clothing shops and rate the clothing in each shop in terms of style, durability, and cost of care. Have them write a report on the shop that offers the best value for the price. If the stores are having sales, have the students report on which sale offers the best value and why this is true.

Have students complete Guided Reading Activity 5.2 in the TCR. **LEP**

Cooperative Learning

Have small groups research and analyze advertising of clothing sales by various kinds of stores. The object of the activity is to determine whether the advertising gives consumers clear and sufficient information about the merchandise on sale, original and sale prices, percentage of saving, and exchange and refund policy. Encourage students to include broadcast advertising, circulars, and catalogs, if available, as well as newspaper ads, in their analyses.

Have a member of each group report the group's findings for class evaluation and discussion.

Assess

Meeting Lesson Objectives

Assign Section 2 Review as homework or an in-class activity. Each question in the Review addresses the corresponding numbered objective in the Section Focus.

Evaluate

Assign the Section 2 Quiz in the TCR or use the Testmaker to develop a customized quiz.

Assign the Chapter 5 Test Form A or Form B or use the Testmaker to develop a customized test.

Reteach

Have students outline the chapter and explain in a paragraph how its information applies to their lives.

Have students complete Reteaching Activity 5 in the TCR.

Enrich

Have students research and write a brief report on clothing fads over the past 30 years.

Have students complete Enrichment Activity 5 in the TCR.

Close

Have students discuss how the chapter information can help them become wiser consumers of food and clothing.

Checklist
Figure 5.7
Determining Clothing Needs

In deciding on clothing purchases, ask yourself the following questions:

1. What do I already have? Check the condition of the clothes you have, and see what you need to replace.
2. What clothes do I need for:
   - school?
   - job?
   - social life?
   - recreational activities?
3. How many changes of clothes do I need to meet my minimum requirements for:
   - cleanliness?
   - variety?
   - social status, or standing in society?
4. How do my answers to questions 1 through 3 compare with the amount of money I have to spend?
5. Should I pay cash or charge my purchases? Consider the trade-offs involved in paying cash or using credit.

Cost of Care Finally, the cost of care is another important factor in deciding value. Two shirts or blouses may cost the same, but one may need dry cleaning, an expensive alternative to hand or machine washing. When deciding on the best choice in a clothing purchase you must consider maintenance costs.

Figure 5.8 ▶
Seasonal Sales
In many cases when you buy clothes on sale, you will not be able to wear them until the following year. For example, you might be buying winter clothes at the end of the winter or summer clothes in late August.

Clothing Sales

Clothing sales are numerous throughout the year, and it is easy to become a bargain fanatic, buying sale items just because they are on sale. Before going shopping, wise consumers make a list of the clothing they have and decide what they need. **Figure 5.7** can help you evaluate your needs. Take your list with you when you go shopping. It will help you keep your spending within limits. Remember, too, that finding the best deal involves using time.

You should be aware of the timing factor in clothing sales. Generally, a clothing sale occurs when a store owner is trying to get rid of goods that he or she could not sell during the regular selling season. See **Figure 5.8**.

SECTION 2 REVIEW

Understanding Vocabulary
Define durability, service flow.

Reviewing Objectives
1. How do personal values affect clothing choices?
2. What three factors determine clothing value?
3. When should you buy clothing that is on sale?

Section 2 Review Answers
Understanding Vocabulary
durability (p. 115), service flow (p. 115)
Reviewing Objectives
1. Answers may vary but should include the following points: Values determine choice of clothes because such choices are a statement of what people consider important. Clothing reflects both those values instilled in us by society and our own attitudes and values. The values inherent in clothing choices are self-expression, self-esteem, and comfort.

2. style, durability, and cost of care
3. after the regular selling season is over

LEARNING ECONOMIC SKILLS

Learning About Percentage Changes

Many important economic statistics change every year. Economists use *percentages* to describe such changes. Can you express a change in percentage terms?

Calculating Arithmetic Changes

The calculation of an arithmetic change is a simple task of subtraction. This year Americans consumed 1.6 billion pounds of butter. Last year they consumed 1.5 billion pounds. As **Figure A** shows, the difference is 0.1 billion pounds. This seems large. Is it?

Computing Percentage Change

It is often more meaningful to compare the arithmetic change in a statistic with what that statistic was before it changed. In this example, how does the arithmetic change in pounds of butter consumed from last year to this year (0.1 billion) compare to the total amount consumed last year (1.5 billion pounds)? After all, 0.1 billion pounds of butter sounds like a tremendous amount. Expressed as a percentage of last year, however, it is not so much.

Figure B shows how to determine the percentage change in the amount of butter consumed. First calculate the arithmetic difference, which in this case is 0.1 billion pounds of butter. Then divide the difference by the original quantity (1.5) and multiply by 100.

Figure A

1.6 billion pounds
− 1.5 billion pounds
0.1 billion pounds

Figure B

Increase in butter =
0.1 billion pounds
Original quantity =
1.5 billion pounds
Percentage change =

$\frac{0.1}{1.5} = .067 \times 100 = 6.7$ percent

Figure C
(expressed in thousands)

Year	Men's Suits	Men's Shirts
1991	9,559	90,439
1992	10,062	106,855

Practicing the Skill

1. Last month 3,300,000 women's coats were sold. This month 3,450,000 women's coats were sold. What was the percentage increase in coat sales?
2. Look at **Figure C.** It shows annual sales of men's suits and shirts in 1991 and 1992. Which had a greater percentage increase?

117

TEACHING Economic Skills

Teach

Use the information in the table to make sure students understand the difference between a simple arithmetic change and a percentage change. Show them that although changes can sound significant in arithmetic terms (millions or billions of units increasing or decreasing), the actual percentage of increase or decrease may be small. That is why calculating percentage changes to determine the rate of increase or decrease in any item is such a useful skill, especially in tracking statistical trends or movements in an economy.

Use economic statistics from an almanac to have students practice calculating percentage changes in such items as per capita food consumption, clothing purchases, and so on.

Additional Practice

Have students complete Reinforcing Economics Skills 5 in the TCR.

Answers to Practicing the Skill

1. 4.5 percent (3,450,000 - 3,300,000 = 150,000; 150,000 ÷ 3,300,000 = 4.5 percent).
2. Men's shirts had the greater percentage increase (18.1 percent versus only 5.2 percent for men's suits).

Technology increases efficiency at the checkout counter, but it may come at a price to consumers. Point out to students that automated inventory systems are still subject to human error and that consumers need protection from possible abuses of computerized systems.

Ask students to write a paragraph on ways consumers can double-check the prices of food items to make sure they are not being overcharged. Have them include steps that consumers can take if they believe the computerized checkout system is not accurately recording prices.

Readings in Economics

MONEY   APRIL 1993

DON'T GET CHEATED BY SUPERMARKET SCANNERS

by Vanessa O'Connell

Like most smart shoppers, you probably scout supermarket specials and compare prices. Yet you have a one-in-10 chance of losing some savings when you hit the checkout counter. Consumer rights attorney Eugene DeSantis, 39, noticed mistakes in his grocery bills so often he decided to fight back. Last December, a small-claims court judge ruled DeSantis had been overcharged five times in three months. . . . "I'm incensed," says DeSantis. "The same errors happen over and over. It's worth my time to take a stand." . . .

Money's reporting, plus an exclusive, two-month survey, has discovered:
- Scanners may overcharge at 30% of stores. . . .
- While scanner abuse may represent only nickels and dimes for any one customer, those errors add up. Based on *Money*'s sample, we estimate annual losses to consumers of $1 billion owing to scanner overcharges. *Information Week*, a trade publication for computer system managers, estimates those losses at $2.5 billion.
- Scanner errors

account for more than half of supermarket profits.

How do scanners cheat? When a cashier whisks your groceries over the glass-enclosed electronic eye, the scanner reads the bar code, called the Universal Product Code (UPC), on each item and calls up the price from the store's computer. Many supermarket chains, especially the larger ones, have a central data base that electronically sends as many as 1,000 to 3,000 weekly price changes to each store. But store personnel may neglect to correctly or immediately update either the shelf tags or the store's own computer listings.

• THINK ABOUT IT •

1. How much of a supermarket's profits come from scanner errors?
2. How do scanners cheat?

Answers to Think About It

1. Scanner errors account for more than half of supermarket profits.
2. Scanners "cheat" by reading the bar code, called the Universal Product Code, on each item and calling up the price from the store's computer. If store personnel neglect to change or update the price, the scanner will report the wrong price to the cash register. The customer may be charged extra money for the item.

5 *Highlights*

Use the Chapter 5 Highlights to preview, review, condense, or reteach the chapter. A Spanish Chapter Highlights is available in the Spanish Handbook.

Preview/Review

After students read the Chapter 5 Highlights, have them complete Economics Vocabulary Activity 5 in the TCR. Spanish Vocabulary Activities are also available in the Spanish Resource Binder.

Vocabulary Software reinforces the economic terms used in Chapter 5.

Condense

Have students listen to Chapter 5 on the Audiocassettes in the TCR. A 1-page written activity and 1-page test accompany this material. These materials are also available in Spanish.

Reteach

Have students complete Reteaching Activity 5 in the TCR. Spanish Reteaching Activities are also available.

Section 1

Shopping for Food

Key Terms
warehouse food store
(p. 109)
convenience stores (p. 109)
private-labeled products
(p. 110)

Summary
Consumers should be aware of many helpful suggestions in comparison shopping for food. There are three major types of food stores, each offering certain advantages.

Section 2

Clothing Choices

Key Terms
durability (p. 115)
service flow (p. 115)

Summary
Each person's own values affect his or her choices of clothing. Clothing value is determined by style, durability, and cost of care. Timing is an important factor in clothing sales.

 VIDEODISC

Nightly Business Report
Economics in Action
Use "Buying the Necessities: Food and Clothing" on Disc 1, Side A, Video 7.

Search 32078, Play to 38780

ANSWERS

Identifying Key Terms

1. convenience stores
2. warehouse food store
3. private-labeled products

4. durability
5. service flow

Recalling Facts and Ideas
Section 1

1. Answers will vary but may include the following: doing only the amount of comparison shopping that time and transportation costs justify; reading store and manufacturer ads; comparing stores; comparing brands.
2. most expensive: convenience store; least expensive: warehouse food store.
3. The trade-off in buying a generic brand is that price may be cheaper and quantity larger, but quality may be less.
4. The trade-off in buying convenience food involves higher price and more leisure time; less preparation time versus loss of purchasing power for other items; and perhaps poorer quality food.

Section 2

5. Self-image, values, variety, and custom influence the clothing choices people make.
6. Generally, the more expensive the item, the more durable it is expected to be. Thus, the longer the time of use, the more economical the price.
7. Make a list to keep within your spending limits and be aware of the sale's timing. You may be buying clothes now for use in another season.

Identifying Key Terms

Use terms from the following list to fill in the blanks in the sentences below.

service flow (p. 115)   durability (p. 115)
private-labeled   warehouse food
  products (p. 110)   store (p. 109)
convenience stores (p. 109)

When you are shopping for food, the most expensive place to buy is in __(1)__. The cheapest place to buy is usually in a __(2)__. When you are in a store, you will see national brands, generic brands, and __(3)__. This last kind of food products usually carries the name of the store.

You can buy clothes that are attractive, but fall apart after a while. They lack the quality of __(4)__. If you buy a coat that you think will last five years, it will give you a __(5)__ per year.

Recalling Facts and Ideas

Section 1

1. What is one of the best ways to engage in comparison shopping for food products?
2. What are the most expensive and the least expensive places to buy food?
3. What is the trade-off involved when you buy a generic brand rather than a brand-name product?
4. What trade-off does buying convenience food involve?

Section 2

5. What four factors influence the kind of clothing choices people make?
6. What is the normal relationship between how long an article of clothing will last and its price?

7. State two things consumers should remember about clothing sales.

Critical Thinking

Section 1
Identifying Alternatives Warehouse food stores almost always sell food at a lower price than any other place from which you can buy food. Why do some consumers, nonetheless, shop at supermarkets instead of at warehouse stores?

Section 2
Recognizing Bias "I went clothes shopping with Ingrid last weekend. You won't believe what she bought. She went to one of the most expensive stores in the neighborhood and paid way too much for the blouses that she got. I don't know what's wrong with her." Could the opinion this person is expressing ever be valid? Why or why not?

Applying Economic Concepts

Competition and Market Structure Examine the food ads in your local newspaper for one week. Write down those food items that are common to each ad. For example, milk is usually advertised by all supermarkets on a specific day of the week. Compare the prices from the different food stores for the common items advertised. What is the largest percentage difference between the highest and lowest price for an advertised common food item? Are any of the food items advertised at exactly the same price for the same brand and the same size?

Critical Thinking
Section 1
Warehouse food stores stock fewer products at lower prices, so consumers shop at supermarkets because they offer greater variety and regular sales on selected items.

Section 2
Answers will vary but should include the following points: The person's opinion is valid because it reflects personal values. These may include preferring to spend less money on clothes, coming from a less affluent family or a family or society that believes in spending less money on clothes, and shopping for the best buy in less expensive stores.

Chapter Projects

1. **Individual Project** Go to your favorite clothing store or department store. Look at all of the suits, coats, or dresses. Write down the prices for one type of clothing item, such as a raincoat. With your list in hand, ask a salesperson to show you the most durable and least durable brand. Is there a relationship between the price and what the salesperson believes is the most durable brand? What is that relationship?

2. **Cooperative Learning Project** You now know that the type of clothes that we choose to buy and wear depends on many things such as customs, aesthetic considerations, values, and group identification. Work in small groups to analyze what is most important in determining the clothes that you buy and wear.

   Write down the list of determinants in order of importance. In a class discussion, see if there is a consensus—a meeting of the minds—about which determinant is most important for the class. During the discussion, make sure that you distinguish between what is truly an aesthetic consideration that you, as an individual, and your classmates, as individuals, really believe and what is the result of "peer pressure."

   At the end of this exercise, you might want to discuss the importance of clothing you have seen on television in terms of what you and your friends think is "in style." Are you influenced by clothing styles seen on television? If so, why?

Reviewing Skills

Learning About Percentage Changes

1. **Figuring Percentage Changes** Last year stores in your city sold 26,450 T-shirts. This year those same stores sold 23,160. Describe what happened in terms of percentage of T-shirts sold.

2. **Using Percentages** Study the table below and then apply your skills to determine the numbers that fit in the blank spaces and complete the table.

Price Last Year	Price This Year	Percentage Change in Price
$1.00		53.7%
	$2,000	100%
$5,721.00	$6,821.00	
$2.00	$1.00	

Writing About Economics

Persuasive Writing Use the entries in Your Economics Journal about your parents' food purchases as the basis for a persuasive essay. Your essay should persuade consumers to shop at a specific kind of food store.

121

Answers will vary, but check to be sure students have done the percentage calculations correctly. Ask them to write a brief paragraph summarizing their findings.

Chapter Projects

1. Generally, there should be a relationship between higher price and greater durability. However, in some cases, the more durable brand may be on sale or the manufacturer may be able to produce the item more cheaply than its competitors and offer the item at a lower price. The least durable brand should be the least expensive.

2. Students should be clear about what they consider the most important determinants in choosing clothes. They may, however, think the determinant is a personal value even when their choice may actually be influenced by group identification. Help students see what really determines their choices and have them ask questions about the choices they make.

? BONUS QUESTION

The following bonus question may be written on the chalkboard when students take the chapter test.
Q: Do you save actual cash if a two-dollar item is marked 50 percent off or if it is marked 2 for the price of 1?
A: if it is marked 50 percent off

Reviewing Skills

1. 12.4 percent decrease
2. $1.537; $1,000; 19.2%; –50%

Writing About Economics

Students' essays persuading people to shop at a particular store should include points about the price, value, and quality offered at that store, compared with the price, value, and quality offered at other stores.

CHAPTER 6 BUYING THE NECESSITIES: HOUSING AND TRANSPORTATION

CHAPTER ORGANIZER

Daily Objectives	Special Features	Classroom Resources
Section 1 Housing Needs and Wants • **List** five types of housing available. • **Explain** the pros and cons of sharing an apartment or house.	**Personal Perspective:** Thorstein Veblen on Conspicuous Consumption, p. 128	Reproducible Lesson Plan 6.1 *NBR* Video 9 and Video Still 6 Focus Activity Transparency 17 Focus Activity Sheet 17 Guided Reading Activity 6.1 Cooperative Learning Activity 6 Primary and Secondary Source Readings 6 Free Enterprise Activity 6 Section Quiz 6.1 Spanish Section Quiz 6.1 Testmaker
Section 2 To Rent or to Buy • **List** three rules that determine how much you should spend for a house. • **Explain** the rights and responsibilities of renters.	**Learning Economic Skills:** Comparing Insurance, p. 134	Reproducible Lesson Plan 6.2 Focus Activity Transparency 18 Focus Activity Sheet 18 Guided Reading Activity 6.2 Section Quiz 6.2 Spanish Section Quiz 6.2 Testmaker Reinforcing Economics Skills 6
Section 3 Buying and Operating an Automobile • **List** the costs of buying an automobile. • **Identify** four costs of operating an automobile.	**News Clip:** "Fighting Racial Discrimination in Home Lending," *Kiplinger's Personal Finance Magazine,* p. 140	Reproducible Lesson Plan 6.3 Focus Activity Transparency 19 Focus Activity Sheet 19 Guided Reading Activity 6.3 Spanish Guided Reading Activity 6.3 Consumer Application Activity 6 Mathematics Practice for Economics 6 Performance Assessment Activity 6 Section Quiz 6.3 Spanish Section Quiz 6.3 Testmaker Enrichment Activity 6

`0:00` **OUT OF TIME?** If time does not permit teaching this chapter, you may use the Chapter 6 Highlights and the Audiocassettes that include a 1-page activity and a 1-page test.

Chapter 6 Review and Evaluation

Special Features

Chapter 6 Highlights, p. 141
Chapter 6 Review, pp. 142–143

Classroom Resources

- Chapter 6 Test Forms A and B
- Economics Vocabulary Activity 6
- Spanish Economics Vocabulary Activity 6

- Audiocassette 6
- Spanish Audiocassette 6
- Reteaching Activity 6
- Spanish Reteaching Activity 6

Key to Ability Levels

Teaching strategies have been coded for varying learning styles and abilities.

L1 Level 1 activities are **basic** activities and should be within the ability range of all students.

L2 Level 2 activities are **average** activities designed for the ability range of average to above-average students.

L3 Level 3 activities are **challenging** activities designed for the ability range of above-average students.

LEP activities should be within the ability range of **Limited English Proficiency** students.

Performance Assessment

The following chapter project may be assigned at the beginning of the chapter and used for performance assessment. See page T12 for additional Performance Assessment information.

Conducting a Survey Have students work in pairs to conduct a survey of housing arrangements or transportation arrangements used by their classmates. The survey should list the type of housing or transportation used by classmates and the advantages and disadvantages the students perceive. After they complete the surveys, have student teams report on the most popular types of housing and transportation among the families of their classmates. Students might report their findings in an illustrated table.

Additional Resources

Readings for the Student

Catalano, Joe. *J.K. Lasser's Guide to Buying Your First Home*. New York: Prentice Hall, 1991.

Ross, James R. *How to Buy a Car: A Former Car Salesman Tells All*. New York: St. Martin's Press, 1992.

Readings for the Teacher

Berg, Ivan. *The Guiness Current Car Index*. Osceola, Wis.: Motorbooks International, 1992.

Lewis, Evelyn L. *Housing Decisions*. South Holland, Ill.: Goodheart-Willcox Company, 1990. Teacher's Resource Guide, Activity Guide, and Answer Key available.

Multimedia Materials

Auto Insurance Tutorial. From the Consumer Education Program. Apple. (Post-Test Disk, also available.) BLS, Inc., 2503 Fairlee Road, Wilmington, MD 19810

Loan Amortization. TRS-80. Single disk. Big G Software, Route 2, Box 111, Alleyton, TX 78935. Calculates and prints loan amortization schedules.

Surviving in the Real World: Housing and Transportation. Videotape. Reelizations/Human Relations Media, 175 Tompkins Avenue, Pleasantville, NY 10570. Teacher's guide available.

Chapter Overview

For most Americans, necessities extend beyond food and clothing and include housing and transportation. Chapter 6 explains or describes: housing and transportation and discusses the various ways in which people satisfy their need for each; the advantages and disadvantages of buying or renting a home and living in various forms of housing; the costs and responsibilities of buying and operating an automobile; and an overview of auto insurance options and costs.

 VIDEODISC

Nightly Business Report
Economics in Action
Use "Buying the Necessities: Housing and Transportation" on Disc 1, Side A, Video 9.

Search 43886, Play to 51864

CHAPTER

6 BUYING THE NECESSITIES: HOUSING AND TRANSPORTATION

Why are Americans so fascinated with cars?

What are the costs of owning a car?

Do you automatically think that you "need" a car?

How much insurance does a car owner need?

Answering Economic Questions

The questions in the above illustration are designed to lead into the main concepts in Chapter 6. Students might not be aware of the many different kinds of values associated with automobiles. They also might take for granted their need for a car. These questions will help them become more aware of the responsibilities associated with owning a car and the alternative choices they might decide to make.

Have students discuss the questions and explain their reasons for thinking as they do.

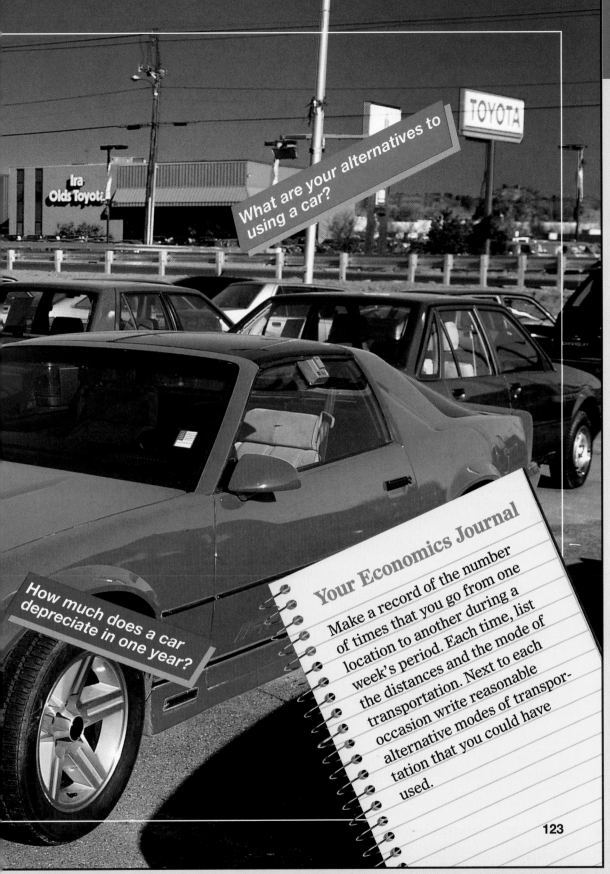

What are your alternatives to using a car?

How much does a car depreciate in one year?

Your Economics Journal

Make a record of the number of times that you go from one location to another during a week's period. Each time, list the distances and the mode of transportation. Next to each occasion write reasonable alternative modes of transportation that you could have used.

123

Connecting to Past Learning

Ask students what criteria they will use to help them decide where to live and how to get around when they are self-supporting. Record these responses for later use. Tell students that in Chapter 6 they will gain the basis for wise decision making about housing and transportation, including costs. After completing the chapter, compare and contrast students' early ideas about housing and transportation with their ideas after reading the chapter.

Applying Economics

Tell students to imagine they take home a monthly paycheck of $1,500. They have a car with payments of $200 a month, car insurance of $60 a month, and a food budget of $200 a month. Have them add up the expenses and consider other expenses including housing, clothing, and entertainment. Discuss with students the amounts they listed and tell them that this chapter will examine housing and transportation considerations.

 PERFORMANCE ASSESSMENT

Refer to page 122B for "Conducting a Survey," a Performance Assessment Activity for this chapter.

 EXTRA CREDIT PROJECT

Give an oral report on the economic impact of rehabilitating houses in decaying neighborhoods of American cities.

 Economic Portfolio

Have students think about and list the places they go over the course of a week and then estimate the miles they travel in each trip. Have students record the total number of routes and the total miles traveled. Then have them develop a transportation map of their most frequently traveled routes. Encourage students to write a paragraph about the most efficient way for them to get where they need to go.

123

Focus

Overview

See the student page for section objectives.

Section 1 explains or describes the types of housing people use and the advantages and disadvantages of each; the pros and cons of sharing an apartment with a roommate; and the relationship between housing starts and the health of the economy.

Bellringer

 Before presenting the lesson, display Focus Activity Transparency 17 on the overhead projector or copy the material on the chalkboard. Assign the accompanying Focus Activity Sheet.

Motivational Activity

Write the following statement for students to complete: I want to live in a(n) _____ .

Call on volunteers to read their statements. Ask students how they decided on the kind of place they want for a home.

Preteaching Vocabulary

Ask students to write a short scenario using the five vocabulary terms. Next, have them delete the terms from the paragraph and insert blanks. Encourage students to trade papers and complete one another's scenarios.

SECTION **1** Housing Needs and Wants

SECTION 1 FOCUS

Terms to Know real estate taxes, condominium, cooperative, lease, depreciate

Objectives *After reading this section, you should be able to:*
1 List five **types of housing** available.
2 Explain **the pros and cons of sharing an apartment or house.**

American Consumers Have Many Housing Alternatives

Besides food and clothing, housing and transportation are the two important necessities in virtually everybody's budget. If you are living at home with your parents, you are probably not too concerned with housing. Some day, however, you are going to have to make the decision about renting an apartment or a house. At some time you may have to make the decision about buying a house. As Figure 6.1 shows, construction begins on an average of 1 to 2 million new houses each year. Americans also spend billions of dollars remodeling existing houses.

**Figure 6.1
Housing
Construction**
New housing starts peaked in the early 1970s. Although they have decreased since then, Americans still demand more than 1 million new homes each year.

▼

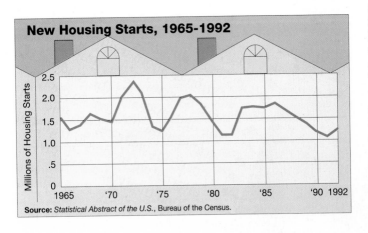

New Housing Starts, 1965–1992

Millions of Housing Starts

2.5
2.0
1.5
1.0
.5
0
1965   '70   '75   '80   '85   '90 1992

Source: *Statistical Abstract of the U.S.*, Bureau of the Census.

Types of Housing

The average American family spends about one-fourth of its annual income on housing. The United States has more than 100 million housing units, of which about 60 percent are owned by the people living in them. The rest are rented. Families or individuals are not just buying or renting a place to live. They are also paying for the satisfaction gained by living in a place called "home." The amount of satisfaction depends on many things. Among them are the size of the dwelling, the neighborhood, the quality of construction and furnishings, and how well the house suits the family's or individual's needs. Figure 6.2 explains some types of housing.

124 *Unit 2 Practical Economics: How Theory Works for You*

Classroom Resources for Section 1

Figure 6.2 Housing Choices
Several types of housing are available in the United States for single people, families, and different age groups. Besides renting apartments, Americans may choose to buy, rent, or lease housing. This housing includes single-family homes, town houses, condominiums, cooperatives, and mobile homes.

A Single-Family Houses
The single-family house is one that is separate from neighboring homes and has some land around it. This type of housing usually is the most expensive type to buy and maintain. Owners are responsible for insurance and real estate taxes. **Real estate taxes** are taxes paid on land and buildings. The single-family house perhaps is also the type of housing that most Americans hope to own. It is part of the American dream and here, more than in any other country, it is a symbol of success and happiness.

B Town Houses
A town house is a house of two or more floors with a front yard and backyard but with common sidewalls. The advantage of a town house is its economy of construction. Its style saves on the amount of land, insulation, windows, foundation, roof, and walls needed, which makes it less expensive to buy and maintain. Unfortunately, noise often carries through the common walls.

125

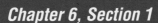

Teach

Guided Practice

L2 Expressing Problems Clearly Ask students to think about the conflicts and concerns that might come up if they were to share an apartment or house with friends. Encourage students to draw up a sample list of house rules that they would propose to a roommate. Have volunteers read their lists to the class.

Visual Instruction

Ask students to review Figure 6.2, noting the captions. Write the following headings on the chalkboard: Single Family House, Townhouse, Condominium, Cooperative, Mobile Home. Encourage volunteers to write at least one advantage and disadvantage for each. Then have students discuss the type of housing they would prefer and tell why.

 **VIDEODISC**

Nightly Business Report
Economics in Action
Use Video Still 6, "Loan vs. Cash," on Disc 1, Side A, Video 9.

Search Frame 45294

Meeting Special Needs

Reading Disability Students with various reading and organizational difficulties may have problems relating pictures, captions, and the main text. Before reading the text in Section 1, ask students to look at the tables and pictures. Have them tell what the pictures illustrate. Then have them read Section 1, explain again what the pictures illustrate, and tell why they were included in the section.

L3 Ranking Have students list the five types of housing and rank them by most to least expensive and most to least convenient. Have students explain the reasons for their rankings.

L1 Calendar Ask students to develop a calendar of household chores to be shared by three or more roommates. Encourage students to color code the calendars for different roommates and to create symbols and a key for different tasks.

 Have students complete Guided Reading Activity 6.1 in the TCR. LEP

GLOBAL ECONOMICS

North America has experienced an explosive growth in housing starts. Since 1949, at least one million housing units have been built in the United States each year. Canada's housing boom, from the mid-1940s to the mid-1960s resulted in a total of 3 million new housing units.

Figure 6.2 Housing Choices (cont.)

C Condominiums ▶
Some town houses are condominiums. A **condominium** (KAHN-duh-MIN-ee-uhm) is a single unit in an apartment building or in a series of town houses that is owned separately. Common areas such as hallways and the land on which the building is built are owned in common by the owners of the single units. Owners pay a monthly maintenance fee for upkeep of these common areas. Ownership rights in a condominium are similar to those in a single-family house, with some exceptions. Owners are free to make any changes they wish within their own units. However, the need for repairs to common areas is usually determined by a majority vote of the owners of all the units.

D Cooperatives ▶
Owners of **cooperative** apartments, in contrast, own equal shares in the company that owns the apartment building and the land on which the building stands. They do not own their apartments but rather hold leases on them. A **lease** is a long-term agreement describing the terms under which the property is being rented. All operating costs such as real estate taxes and maintenance are divided among the owners according to the number of shares each owns. A major problem with cooperative apartments is that individual members usually must obtain approval from the co-op before remodeling, renting, or selling their units.

126

E Mobile Homes
Mobile homes are a popular form of low-cost housing in the United States. One reason is that mobile homes are often taxed as motor vehicles rather than as real estate. Another reason is that they often are the least expensive form of housing to buy and maintain. However, owners of mobile homes face unique problems. The purchase of a mobile home does not always guarantee a space in a mobile home park. Mobile homes are also more likely to suffer damage during storms than are other types of housing. Third, mobile homes, like automobiles and boats, **depreciate** (di-PREE-shee-AYT)—decline in value over time—as the mobile homes or the fixtures that are part of them wear out or become outdated in style. ◀

Cooperative Learning

Organize students into groups, half of which will develop a how-to guide to locating and renting housing while the other half develops a similar guide for buying housing. A member of each group should present its guide for class review. Afterward, the class should choose the best elements from the guides presented and prepare a "master" guide to renting and another for buying.

The Pros and Cons of Sharing an Apartment or House

If you go on to college or start working right out of high school, you may find that sharing a rented house or apartment with one or more friends makes sense. Sharing involves a number of human problems and a number of economic problems as shown in Figure 6.3.

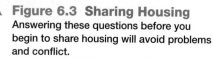

▲ **Figure 6.3 Sharing Housing**
Answering these questions before you begin to share housing will avoid problems and conflict.

- How will responsibilities be shared? Are you splitting the rent in exactly the same amounts? If something needs to be repaired, will you share in the expenses?
- Will one person be responsible to the landlord, or will each of you put money in a special bank account from which the rent can be paid?
- How will you share the payment of telephone and utility bills?
- Who is going to be responsible for household expenses such as cleaning supplies and light bulbs?
- What about furniture? What if a nice sofa that your parents gave you gets stained by someone else? Who is responsible?
- Who is responsible for cleaning up what and when?

SECTION 1 REVIEW

Understanding Vocabulary
Define real estate taxes, condominium, cooperative, lease, depreciate.

Reviewing Objectives
1. What are the five types of housing available to consumers?
2. What pros and cons should persons consider if they plan to share an apartment or house?

Chapter 6 Buying the Necessities: Housing and Transportation **127**

Background

Thorstein Veblen was an original and creative critic of the American capitalist system of economics. Veblen considered how scientists and engineers would be very important in building a successful planned economy.

Teach

Have volunteers read aloud the quoted excerpts from Veblen's *The Theory of the Leisure Class*. Then have students paraphrase each excerpt to gain a better understanding of Veblen's ideas. Finally, have students answer the questions in Checking for Understanding.

You might have interested students read chapters from *The Theory of the Leisure Class*, report on the ideas expressed, and comment on their relevance today.

Personal Perspective

Thorstein Veblen on Conspicuous Consumption

Profile

- 1857-1929
- lectured at University of Chicago
- harsh critic of American capitalism
- major published work: *The Theory of the Leisure Class*, 1899

In *The Theory of the Leisure Class*, Veblen criticized the rich, or leisure, class and its spending habits. He talked about conspicuous consumption, which is buying goods and services to impress others.

The quasi-peaceable gentleman of leisure, then, not only consumes of the staff of life beyond the minimum required for subsistence and physical efficiency, but his consumption also undergoes a specialization as regards the quality of good consumed. . . . Since the consumption of these more excellent goods is an evidence of wealth, it becomes honorific [conferring honor]; and conversely, the failure to consume in due quantity and quality becomes a mark of inferiority and demerit.

Veblen adds that conspicuous consumption is more common in an urban population than in a rural one.

. . . Conspicuous consumption claims a relatively larger portion of the income of the urban than of the rural population, and the claim is also more imperative. . . . In the struggle to outdo one another the city population push their normal standard of conspicuous consumption to a higher point.

Veblen calls conspicuous consumption waste because it does not serve human life well. He concludes that it does not have the approval of the conscience—it is not ethical.

In the view of economic theory the expenditure . . . is here called "waste" because this expenditure does not serve human life or human well-being on the whole.

. . . The popular reprobation [disapproval] of waste goes to say that in order to be at peace with himself the common man must be able to see in any and all human effort and human enjoyment an enhancement of life and well-being on the whole. . . . Relative or competitive advantage of one individual in comparison with another does not satisfy the economic conscience, and therefore competitive expenditure has not the approval of this conscience.

Checking for Understanding
1. What is conspicuous consumption?
2. What groups tend to engage more in conspicuous consumption?
3. According to Veblen, what is wrong with conspicuous consumption or with competitive expenditures?

128 *Unit 2 Practical Economics: How Theory Works for You*

Answers to Checking for Understanding

1. Answers will vary but should indicate that conspicuous consumption is consumption beyond the minimum required for subsistence and physical efficiency. It includes acquiring more excellent goods as a sign of wealth.

2. Answers will vary but should identify urban populations more so than rural populations. Students may also indicate that the rich engage in it more than the poor.

3. Answers will vary but should include an understanding that Veblen disapproved of conspicuous consumption because it is competitive and because neither competition nor waste enhances life and well-being on the whole.

S E C T I O N 2 F O C U S

Terms to Know closing costs, points, equity, security deposit

Objectives *After reading this section, you should be able to:*

1. List three rules that determine **how much you should spend** for a house.
2. Explain the **rights and responsibilities** of renters.

Deciding to Buy Housing Is a Big Step, But Renters Also Have Responsibilities

Some people will save for years and scrimp on food and clothing their whole lives in order to buy a nice house. Others simply rent most of their lives.

No matter what type of housing you decide to live in, you have to make the decision whether to rent or buy. Figure 6.5 (page 130) compares the advantages and disadvantages—both economic and psychological—of owning and renting. Wise consumers should consider both when deciding whether to buy or to rent housing.

If You Buy, How Much Should You Spend?

When you decide to buy housing, it is important that you do not take on financial obligations that are beyond your budget. As Figure 6.4 shows, lenders use certain rules to help buyers determine how much housing they can afford.

In addition to the cash down payment, you will need money for **closing costs.** These are costs involved in arranging for a mortgage or in transferring ownership of the property. Closing costs can include fees for such items as the title search, legal costs, loan application, credit report,

house inspections, and taxes. Although the person buying the house usually pays these fees, the seller may agree to pay part or all of them if this will make it easier to sell the house.

In arranging for a mortgage, it is important to know about **points,** which are included in closing costs. Points are the fee paid to the lender and computed as percentage points of the

**Figure 6.4
What Can You Borrow?**
Why would it be unwise for both you and the lender if you spent more than a third of your income on the mortgage?

▼

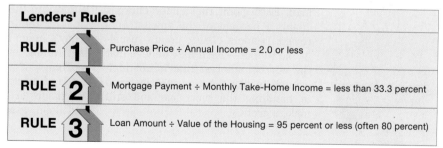

Lenders' Rules

RULE 1	Purchase Price ÷ Annual Income = 2.0 or less
RULE 2	Mortgage Payment ÷ Monthly Take-Home Income = less than 33.3 percent
RULE 3	Loan Amount ÷ Value of the Housing = 95 percent or less (often 80 percent)

Chapter 6 Buying the Necessities: Housing and Transportation **129**

Focus

Overview

See the student page for section objectives.

Section 2 explains or describes: the pros and cons of renting or buying a home; mortgage costs and the responsibilities of renters; and the types of mortgages available to home buyers.

Bellringer

Before presenting the lesson, display Focus Activity Transparency 18 on the overhead projector or copy the material on the chalkboard. Assign the accompanying Focus Activity Sheet.

Motivational Activity

Have students list on a sheet of paper the things that would help them attain their preferred lifestyle. Call on volunteers to read their lists. Tell students that Section 2 will discuss the pros and cons of renting and buying housing.

Preteaching Vocabulary

Ask students to form groups of four and write each term and its definition on a separate slip of paper. Have the students in each group pick one of the slips from a hat or box and take a turn building a story by contributing a sentence that correctly uses the vocabulary word they picked.

Teach

Guided Practice

L1 Evaluating Options
Direct students to write the advantages and disadvantages of renting on slips of paper and attach one, two, or three cents to each slip to express whether they consider the advantage or disadvantage minor, average, or major. Have them sort the advantages and disadvantages and place them on sides of a scale (or in separate boxes). Then ask them to weigh (or count) and record their results. Do the same for advantages and disadvantages of buying.

L2 Calculating Ask students to calculate the minimum and maximum amount of money needed to buy homes priced at $50,000, $100,000, $150,000, and $200,000. Remind students to include down payment, closing costs, and points.

GLOBAL ECONOMICS

Since the 1940s, when many European homes were destroyed by war, most of the newer housing in Europe is apartment housing. Many European apartments are owned by the government and leased inexpensively to citizens of every income level.

Figure 6.5 Advantages and Disadvantages of Owning and Renting

Advantages	Disadvantages
Ownership provides the following for a family or individual: ■ freedom of use; owners can remodel whenever or however they choose ■ the pride of ownership; people tend to take better care of things they own ■ greater privacy ■ a good investment that in the past has risen in value as much as, or more than, the general rise in prices ■ significant income tax benefits ■ creation of **equity** (EK-wuht-ee), the amount of money invested in the property minus the debt—mortgage payments—still owed ■ a good credit rating if mortgage payments are made on time ■ property to use as collateral for other loans	**Ownership has the following drawbacks:** ■ less mobility, especially in years when interest rates on mortgages are high and housing is difficult to sell ■ less feeling of being able to move to another property because the present one is too small, too big, and so on ■ necessity of a large outlay of money for a down payment ■ maintenance costs, real estate taxes, and possible depreciation ■ less money for other purchases because of high monthly mortgage payments ■ possibility of overextending a family's debt load to make home improvements or repairs
Renting provides an individual or family: ■ greater mobility; a renter does not have to worry about trying to sell property quickly if he or she must move ■ a feeling of freedom to choose another place to live if dissatisfied with current rental unit ■ having to pay only a small security deposit rather than a large outlay of money for a down payment. A **security deposit** is money the renter gives to the owner to hold in case the rent is not paid or the apartment is damaged. ■ no maintenance costs, real estate taxes, or depreciation ■ a good credit rating if rent is paid on time ■ more money for other purchases because monthly rental payments are often less than monthly mortgage payments ■ no temptation to overspend on home improvements	**Renting has the following drawbacks:** ■ no freedom of use; renters may not remodel or even paint without the owner's permission ■ no return on rental money; a renter will never own the property regardless of how much rent he or she pays, regardless of the length of this period of time ■ little or no tax benefits ■ often less privacy ■ little feeling of responsibility for seeing that the property is well taken care of ■ no property for use as collateral ■ need to wait for maintenance work at the convenience of the owner

loan. Each point the lender charges equals 1 percent of the amount borrowed. Lenders charge points—usually one to four—when they believe that the current interest rate is not high enough to pay the expenses involved in handling the mortgage and still make a profit.

Financing a Housing Purchase

One of the major problems facing today's home buyer is that of financing. Almost every home buyer has a mortgage. **Figure 6.6** shows several kinds of mortgages that are available. Mortgages are available from savings and loan associations, savings and

Meeting Special Needs

Hearing Disability Students with hearing difficulties may have problems following role-playing exercises. Before assigning Independent Practice, ask students to let their hearing-impaired classmates read the lists of lease clauses.

Figure 6.6 Types of Mortgages

Type of Mortgage	Interest Rate Changes	Monthly Payment Changes	Term Changes	Description
Standard Fixed-Rate Mortgage	No	No	No	Interest rate and monthly payments remain the same over the term of the mortgage. Term is fixed, usually at 15 to 30 years.
Flexible Rate Mortgage	Yes	Yes	Yes	The interest rate and monthly payments float up or down along with interest rates in general. Rates can increase by no more than a few percentage points over the life of a mortgage, while there is often no limit on the amount of decrease. Three such plans are variable rate mortgage (VRM), adjustable rate mortgage (ARM), and renegotiable rate mortgage (RRM).
Federal Housing Administration (FHA) Mortgage	No	No	No	The FHA will insure the entire amount of its mortgages. This added security makes it possible for borrowers to obtain a larger loan than they could with an uninsured mortgage.
Graduated Payment Mortgage (GPM)	No	Yes	No	Interest rate and term are usually fixed for the life of the mortgage. Monthly payments are small at the beginning and increase gradually over the years. GPMs are used by people who expect their incomes to increase steadily from year to year.
Veteran's Administration (VA) Mortgage	No	No	No	These loans can be obtained only by qualified veterans or their widows. The interest rate is generally lower than for other mortgages. The VA guarantees a large percentage of the loan. Loans with no down payment are possible under the VA program.

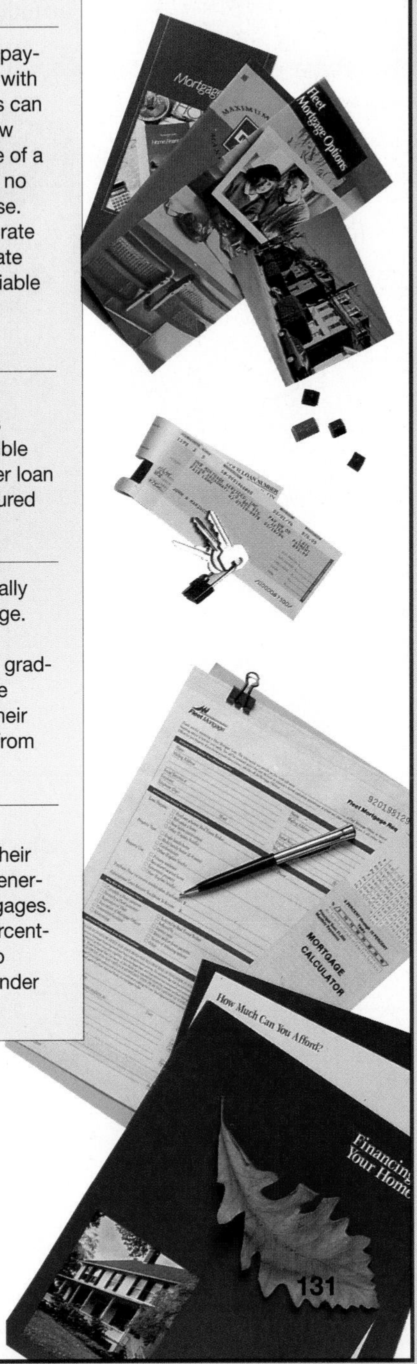

Independent Practice

L3 Researching Encourage students to find out the average starting wage for several occupations using information from the Careers Handbook beginning on page 560. Have students calculate the amount they could spend on a house if they followed each occupation.

Visual Instruction

Ask students to study Figure 6.8 (page 133) and read the caption. Then have them work in pairs to role-play the parts of a landlord and prospective tenant. Encourage each student pair to write a list of tenant and landlord agreements to be included as clauses in the lease. Ask volunteers to present their lists to the class.

? DID YOU KNOW

When economists consider the profit made on selling a home, they take into account cumulative tax breaks as well as appreciation value.

Cooperative Learning

Organize students into groups and have each group create a model of the ideal situation for renting and the ideal situation for buying a home. Encourage students to use a combination of writing, charts, and visuals such as illustrations of renters and buyers in the situations they describe. You might also ask students to create a presentation in which the group as a whole creates a script and individual members of the group play the roles of buyer and seller, renter and landlord.

Independent Practice

L2 Interviewing and Reporting Ask students to interview real estate and/or rental agents about their occupation. Suggest asking about specialized training, responsibilities, work schedules, and their "typical day." Have students write a short report for oral presentation.

 Have students complete Guided Reading Activity 6.2 in the TCR. **LEP**

? DID YOU KNOW

State laws establish local organizations, called authorities, to provide public housing for low-income families through federally aided programs. Authority members, called commissioners, receive their appointments from local governments.

The authorities plan, develop, and operate the housing, for which renters pay no more than 30 percent of their income for rent. In the middle 1980s, demand for public housing exceeded supply.

132

---

commercial banks, and sometimes from the seller of the house, co-op, or condominium.

A mortgage usually involves a down payment and interest. If you buy a house for $100,000 and make a $20,000 down payment, you will need to obtain a mortgage for the remaining $80,000. The mortgage will then be repaid in monthly installments that include interest on the loan.

If You Rent: Rights and Responsibilities

Most renters sign a lease that contains several clauses. A prospective tenant should read the lease carefully. See **Figure 6.7**. Most leases are for one to three years.

✓ Checklist

**Figure 6.7
Clauses in Housing Leases**

You should be aware of several types of clauses to avoid in leases.

1 According to a confession-of-judgment clause, the lawyer for the owner of the rental unit has the right to plead guilty for you in court in the event the owner thinks his or her rights have been violated. If you sign a lease with a confession-of-judgment clause, you are admitting guilt before committing any act. Such a clause is, in fact, illegal in some states.

2 According to the inability-to-sue clause, you give up your right to sue the owner if you suffer injury or damage through some fault of the owner, such as neglected repair work.

3 Leases may include arbitrary clauses, or those based on one's wishes rather than a rule or law. These give the owner the right to cancel the lease because he or she is dissatisfied with your behavior. Some leases include clauses that:

- forbid hanging pictures.
- forbid overnight guests. This is usually done to make sure the apartment is occupied only by the renter and members of the renter's immediate family.
- forbid subleasing, or the leasing of the apartment by the tenant to someone else.
- allow the owner to cancel the lease if you are only one day late in paying the rent but hold you legally responsible to pay the rent for the rest of the lease.
- allow the owner or a representative, such as a plumber, to enter your apartment when you are not home.
- make you legally responsible for all repairs.
- make you obey rules that have not yet been written.

If you have the opportunity, these are some clauses that you should have added to your lease.

1 If the person renting the unit to you says that it comes with dishwasher, garbage disposal, and air conditioner, make sure the lease lists them.

2 If you have been promised the use of a recreation room, a parking lot, or a swimming pool, make sure that the lease states this. Also have it indicate whether or not you must pay extra for their use.

3 If the owner has promised to have the apartment painted, have this stated in the lease. If you wish to be able to choose the color, also have this stated in the lease.

4 In certain cases, you may be able to cancel your lease if you are transferred to a job in another city or state. Usually, however, you must agree to pay a certain amount to do this. The amount should be stated in the lease.

5 If you plan to put in lighting fixtures, shelves, and so on, and wish them to remain your property when you move, have this stated in the lease. Otherwise they become part of the apartment and you may not take them with you.

🇺🇸 Free Enterprise Activity

Have students work cooperatively to research and develop a written plan for starting up a real estate development company that intends to specialize in building public housing. Suggest including information on obtaining capitalization and guidelines for hiring employees and subcontractors. Follow an oral presentation with a class discussion.

Tenant Rights Among the rights of tenants is the use of the property for the purpose stated in the lease. Tenants also have the right to a certain amount of privacy. A landlord usually cannot enter an apartment any time he or she chooses. A landlord may enter only to make necessary repairs or to show the apartment to a potential renter.

Tenant Responsibilities In turn, the tenant must pay the rent on time and take reasonable care of the property. If major repairs such as replacing a leaky roof are needed, the tenant is responsible for notifying the landlord. Often a lease will limit how an apartment can be used. The lease may forbid pets, for example, or forbid anyone other than the person named on the lease from living there. In signing a lease, the tenant is usually required to give a security deposit equal to one month's rent. The deposit is returned after the tenant has moved. The purpose of the security deposit is to pay for repairing any damages that the tenant caused, such as cracked plaster from hanging pictures. The amount returned depends on the condition of the apartment, as determined by the landlord. Figure 6.8 offers tips on ensuring that your deposit is returned.

The tenant is also required to give notice, or a formal warning, if he or she plans to move before the term of

the lease is up. In this event, the landlord may ask for several month's rent to pay for any time the apartment is empty before a new tenant moves in.

Landlord Responsibilities In many states, landlords must make sure apartments have certain minimum services, such as heat, and that their apartments are fit to live in. Landlords may also have to obey building safety laws. For example, fire escapes and smoke detectors may be required. Leases usually call for the landlord to make repairs within a reasonable amount of time. In many states, a tenant has the right to pay for the repairs and withhold that amount of rent if the landlord does not make the repairs.

Figure 6.8 ▲ Making Sure You Get Your Security Deposit Returned

1. Do a "walk through" with the manager or owner to record any damage that already exists.
2. Take photos of the apartment when you move in and when you leave.
3. Keep copies of all the bills that you paid for repairs, improvements, or cleaning.
4. Find out what the local regulations are. They might require that an apartment be "broom cleaned" before you move out.

SECTION 2 REVIEW

Understanding Vocabulary
Define closing costs, points, equity, security deposit.

Reviewing Objectives
1. How much should a consumer spend on a house?
2. What are the rights and responsibilities of renters?

Chapter 6 Buying the Necessities: Housing and Transportation **133**

Assess

Meeting Lesson Objectives
Assign Section 2 Review as homework or an in-class activity. Each question in the Review addresses the corresponding numbered objective in the Section Focus.

Evaluate
Assign the Section 2 Quiz in the TCR or use the Testmaker to develop a customized quiz.

Reteach
Ask students to review the lending rules regarding mortgages. Encourage them to calculate the down payment, points, and income they would need to buy a house in their community.

Enrich
Ask students to consult with a real estate broker or mortgage lender to learn how to calculate the monthly payment on a loan with various interest rates. Have students apply their knowledge using hypothetical home prices, down payments and interest rates.

Close
Discuss with students how to create a mutually acceptable tenant-landlord relationship in advance of signing a lease.

Teach

Use the following activity to guide students through the mathematics for calculating auto insurance costs and benefits. Have students imagine a driver has purchased liability insurance with 50/200/50 coverage; medical, collision, and comprehensive insurance; and a $200 deductible. The driver hit a municipal light post while traveling at 40 miles per hour. The driver's hospitalization costs $20,500. The passengers' hospitalization costs $40,000. The city is charging $55,000 for replacing the light post. The car is totally wrecked, and replacing it will cost $15,000. Lead students through calculations to conclude that the insurance company will pay $125,300. The driver will pay the $200 deductible and the $5,000 not covered for damages to public property for a total of $5,200.

Additional Practice

Have students complete Reinforcing Skills 6 in the TCR.

LEARNING ECONOMIC SKILLS
Comparing Insurance

When you are purchasing automobile insurance there are many options available to you. Do you know how to compare auto insurance coverages?

The Basic Policy

Insurance companies sell individual insurance agreements—called policies—to cover almost any type of risk. In general, the higher the risk, the more the insurance premium will cost.

Liability Insurance

This type of insurance covers you, or anyone you allow to drive your car, against financial obligation for injury or death to others and for property damage caused by your car. Liability insurance is usually described by the amount of coverage. Look at the set of numbers in **Figure A**. **Figure B** lists other types of coverage that you can and usually should buy.

The Deductible

The deductible is the portion of the cost of repairs that you must pay before the insurance company pays anything. For example, if your policy has a $500 deductible and repairs cost $1,000, you would pay $500 and the insurance company would pay the remaining $500.

Practicing the Skill

❶ Look at **Figure C**. Describe the limits of the liability coverage shown.

❷ You have an insurance policy that provides for collision coverage. To make it cheap, you took out a $750 deductible. You are involved in an auto accident in which the total repairs cost $2,167.47. How much does your insurance company have to pay?

Figure A

10/50/10
This set of numbers means that the insurance company would pay up to $10,000 for any one person injured in an accident, up to a total of $50,000 for all personal injuries, and up to $10,000 for damages to private or public property.

Figure B

Medical	Covers the cost of health care and hospitalization resulting from an accident for you, your family, and any passengers.
Collision	Covers the cost of repairs to your car resulting from an accident.
Comprehensive physical damage	Protects against damage to, or loss of, your car due to fire, flood, theft, vandalism, and so on.

Figure C

100/300/50

134

Answers to Practicing the Skill

1. The insurance company would pay up to $100,000 for any one person injured in an accident, up to a total of $300,000 for all personal injuries suffered in the accident, and up to $50,000 for damages to private or public property.

2. The insurance company pays $1,417.47.

3 Buying and Operating an Automobile

LESSON PLAN
Chapter 6, Section 3

SECTION 3 FOCUS

Terms to Know excise tax, registration fee, liability insurance

Objectives *After reading this section, you should be able to:*
1. List the costs of buying an automobile.
2. Identify four costs of operating an automobile.

Automobiles Cost More Than a Monthly Loan Payment

In many places in the United States, an automobile is a necessity. Some Americans rent or lease cars because they do not have the down payment or because they wish to gain a tax advantage by leasing or renting for business purposes. Nevertheless, most people prefer to own their own automobiles. Therefore, it is probable that at some point in your life you will buy a car. You should be aware of certain factors as you shop for a car. Your choice of an automobile, like all other decisions, involves trade-offs. See Figure 6.9 for some of the major trade-offs you should consider.

The Costs of Buying an Automobile

Buying a car involves opportunity costs. One is the amount of money and time spent shopping for the car. Another is the amount of money and time spent in actually purchasing the car. Because people have limited resources, most people have to borrow to buy a car. The costs of the loan are the interest, the down payment, and the monthly payments on the principal. Interest is an important cost of buying an automobile on credit, but buying a car with cash has a cost, too. By paying cash, a person loses the ability to purchase other goods and services. See Figure 6.10 (page 136) for tips on choosing a new or used car.

**Figure 6.9
Car Buying
Trade-Offs**

- Usually, the smaller the engine, the less gas an automobile burns. This makes a car with a smaller engine less costly to operate, but the car will accelerate less quickly.
- Newer automobiles cost more, but they require fewer repairs than older ones.
- The smaller the automobile, the more energy efficient it is and the easier it is to park and turn. In an accident, however, larger automobiles usually protect passengers better than smaller automobiles.

Chapter 6 Buying the Necessities: Housing and Transportation **135**

Focus

Overview

See the student page for section objectives.

Section 3 explains or describes: the costs of owning an automobile; a checklist for buyers; and a guide to factors affecting auto insurance rates.

Bellringer

Before presenting the lesson, display Focus Activity Transparency 19 and assign the accompanying Focus Activity Sheet.

Motivational Activity

Have students write the estimated price and features of their favorite automobile models. Encourage students to brainstorm about hidden costs connected with each type of car. Tell students that Section 3 will describe the principal costs of owning and operating a car.

Preteaching Vocabulary

Have students use the vocabulary terms in a paragraph about buying a car.

Classroom Resources for Section 3

- Reproducible Lesson Plan 6.3
- Focus Activity Transparency 19
- Focus Activity Sheet 19
- Guided Reading Activity 6.3
- Consumer Application Activity 6
- Mathematics Practice for Economics 6

- Performance Assessment Activity 6
- Section Quiz 6.3
- Spanish Section Quiz 6.3
- Chapter 6 Test Forms A and B
- Testmaker
- Enrichment Activity 6

- Economics Vocabulary Activity 6
- Spanish Economics Vocabulary Activity 6
- Audiocassette 6
- Spanish Audiocassette 6
- Reteaching Activity 6
- Spanish Reteaching Activity 6

Teach

Guided Practice

L3 Evaluate Have students list in order, from most to least, the costs of operating a new car and a used car. Then have students discuss which kind of purchase they feel is more economical.

Visual Instruction

Refer students to Figure 6.9 for restudy. Ask them to prepare a table for a side-by-side evaluation of transportation choices they may have, such as public transportation, bicycle, motor scooter, and car. Suggest that their aim be to find a balance of convenience and economy for their present lifestyle. Discuss students' choices.

GLOBAL ECONOMICS

The cost of automobiles extends further than immediate cost to consumers. Over its lifetime, an average gasoline-powered automobile creates 26 tons of hazardous waste for every ton it weighs. This waste creates costs in health care and environmental cleanup.

Checklist

**Figure 6.10
Buying an Automobile**

These tips will help you in making a good choice of a new car or used car:

1. Ask friends and relatives about their satisfaction or dissatisfaction with their cars.
2. Read articles about different makes and models in car magazines such as *Car and Driver* and *Road and Track*.
3. Read *Consumer Reports* and *Consumers' Research Magazine* for reviews of new automobiles. Read their reports on repair records of different models carefully.
4. Visit various dealers and read the material they hand out about their automobiles. Remember that these pamphlets are advertisements that promote the best features.
5. Personally inspect various makes and models. Automobile showrooms are open to provide you the chance to complete your inspection.
6. Check what is covered by the service warranty for each make and model as you compare automobiles. Warranties may vary from manufacturer to manufacturer. If you are buying a used car that is only a year or two old, check to see if it is still covered under the original manufacturer's warranty. Also, some dealers offer their own limited warranties for used cars.
7. Once you decide on the particular make and model that you want, compare the prices offered by several dealers.
8. If you are buying an automobile off the lot rather than ordering one, check the options on the car and their prices. Options are the extra features and equipment on a car—such as air conditioning, a compact disc player, special paint, and so on—that you must pay for in addition to the basic price. If you do not want any of the options, such as white sidewall tires, you may be able to get the dealer to take some additional money off the price.
9. If you are buying a used car, have an automobile diagnostic (DY-ig-NAHS-tik) center or a mechanic not connected with the dealer check it. Add to the dealer's price the cost of any repairs the mechanic thinks the car will need. This is the real cost of the automobile to you.
10. Make sure the price given includes federal excise tax and dealer preparation charges. An **excise** (EK-syz) **tax** is a tax on the manufacture, sale, or use within the country of specific products, such as liquor, gasoline, and automobiles. Dealer preparation charges cover the costs of taking a car as it arrives from the factory and preparing it to be driven away. This can include the costs of cleaning, installing certain options, and checking the car's engine. The price given by the dealer will not include state and local sales taxes. These will be added later.
11. Check various dealers for the reputation of their service departments. Your warranty usually allows you to take your car to any dealer selling that make of car. However, it may be most convenient to return to the service department of the dealer who sold you the car for maintenance and repair work.
12. Do not put a deposit on a car unless you are sure you are going to buy it. You may have a problem getting your deposit back if you change your mind.

Meeting Special Needs

Language Disability Have students read statements in Section 3 and then restate them by giving an example of how they would apply the information to an actual experience. Listen carefully to make sure that students are not restating phrases directly from the book.

The Costs of Operating an Automobile

As with other purchases, a consumer's responsibilities do not end with the purchase of the automobile; nor do the costs. Ongoing costs include a registration fee, normal maintenance, major repairs, depreciation, and insurance.

Registration Fee The owner of an automobile must pay a state licensing fee, or a **registration fee,** to use the car. Usually the fee must be paid annually. In many states, the amount of the fee varies depending on the car's age, weight, type, and value.

Normal Maintenance and Major Repairs The amount of normal maintenance—oil and filter changes and minor tune-ups—that an owner gives a car depends on the amount the car is driven and how carefully the owner maintains the car. The more maintenance an owner gives a car, the better service it will give and the longer it will last. The trade-off is that the owner will have less money available for other things.

Major repairs are those that are normally unexpected and expensive. They include rebuilding the transmission and replacing the exhaust system. No one can guarantee that an automobile will not require major repairs while you own it, but you can follow certain steps to reduce the probability.

As you read in Figure 6.10, you should check the repair records of different cars before deciding on a particular make and model. If you are considering a used car, you should also take it to a diagnostic center, or have a mechanic check it. Sometimes dealers offer warranties for used cars for a limited time period, such as 30 days, or you can purchase a warranty covering a longer period for a used car. See Figure 6.11.

Extended Warranty One way to guard against having to pay for major repairs is to buy extended warranty coverage. New-car warranties generally protect owners for all major repairs except tune-ups and damage resulting from improper use of the automobile. New-car warranties usually last only a few years, or up to a certain limit of miles or kilometers. These warranties, however, can often

Figure 6.11 Used Car Warranties Used car dealers' warranties often provide for the buyer and the dealer to share the cost of repairs. The warranty coverage may be an indication of the used car's quality.

137

Chapter 6, Section 3

Independent Practice

L2 Buyer's Guide Encourage students to use the checklist on page 136 to create a buyer's guide to automobiles. Suggest that students list each step a buyer might take to investigate an automobile and create a column for each of several automobiles. Encourage students to create a set of notations, such as fuel efficiency, in order to rate automobiles in each stage of the investigation.

DID YOU KNOW

Once a luxury, automobiles have quickly become standard equipment for modern life in developed countries. There are close to 400 million passenger cars on roads around the world. Each of those cars requires maintenance, parts, and services. The need for these goods and services creates jobs in local economies throughout the world.

Cooperative Learning

Organize the class into small groups to research and develop a fact book on the direct and indirect contribution of the automobile to the U.S. economy. Ask students to survey information on manufacturing and sales, energy production (gasoline, other fuel) maintenance products and services, insurance, and public works (highways, parking). Have students combine written reports, with charts and graphs as needed, and choose a title for this book. Ask a volunteer from each group to give an oral summary of its findings and discuss.

Independent Practice

L1 Making a Graph Ask students to use the information in Figure 6.13 (p. 139) to create a graph comparing car insurance rates for different drivers.

 Have students complete Guided Reading Activity 6.3 in the TCR. **LEP**

Visual Instruction

Ask students to reexamine Figure 6.12. Have them research the owner's manual of two or three models of automobiles and develop a car maintenance schedule comparing manufacturer recommendations. Ask volunteers to give a class report on their schedule. Discuss possible reasons for differences among recommendations.

🌐 GLOBAL ECONOMICS

A major factor in world trade, automobile production weighs heavily in measuring the economic development of nations such as Germany, Japan, Sweden, and the United States. State subsidies of automotive industries in some nations, together with tariffs and quotas enacted to protect domestic industry from competition by imports, may penalize consumers who must pay higher prices.

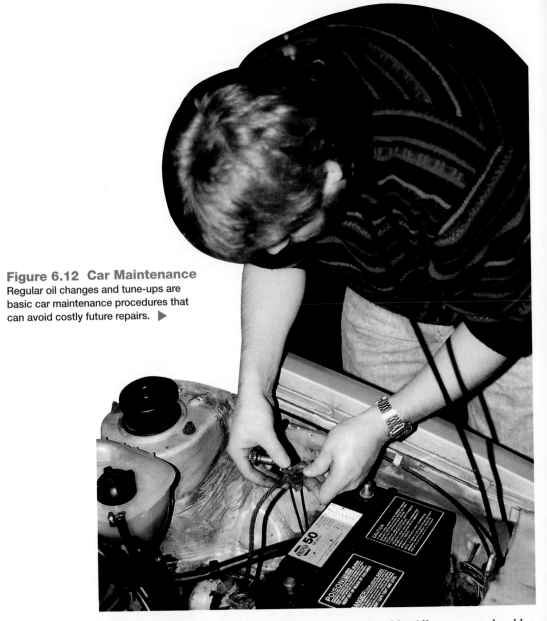

Figure 6.12 Car Maintenance
Regular oil changes and tune-ups are basic car maintenance procedures that can avoid costly future repairs. ▶

be extended for another one, two, or three years by paying additional money when the car is purchased.

Depreciation Depreciation—a decline in value over time—takes place as an item wears out or becomes outdated. Age, obsolescence, and wear and tear cause a car to depreciate. Age is the major factor. A car loses value every year even if it is not driven because an automobile is a con-sumer durable. All consumer durables deteriorate, or become worse. Second, new makes and models include current technology and new features. These changes make older models obsolete—out of date and out of style.

Physical wear and tear depends on how hard a car is driven, how many miles or kilometers it is driven, and how well it is maintained. See **Figure 6.12**. Generally, cars depreciate about 20 percent each year.

 Free Enterprise Activity

Encourage students to develop a transportation plan in which students who have cars earn money by providing cost-effective rides to those who do not. Direct students to create models of their plans and explain to the class how the plan benefits car owners, riders, and the environment.

Figure 6.13 Factors Affecting Automobile Insurance Rates

When you buy automobile insurance, the rate you are charged is determined, in addition to your age and sex, by the following:

1. **The type of car you drive.** Insurance companies consider the safety record of a car and the costs to repair it if it is involved in an accident.
2. **Where you drive.** If the rate of thefts and accidents is high in an area, the risk to the insurance company is greater. A city, for example, would have more thefts and accidents than would a rural area. Therefore, the rate the insurance company charges in a city will be higher.
3. **What you use the car for.** If you drive your car for business on a daily basis, the rate will be higher than if you use it only for errands and occasional trips.
4. **Marital status.** In general, married men and women have lower accident rates than single men and women and, therefore, pay lower insurance rates.
5. **Safety record.** If you have a history of accidents and traffic tickets, then you will be charged a high rate. Whether a new driver has had driver education is often considered in determining a rate.
6. **Number of drivers.** The number of drivers using a car increases the insurance rate.

Insurance A major cost of owning an automobile, especially for someone under age 25, is insurance. Many states require that **liability insurance** be purchased before an automobile can be licensed. Insurance companies classify drivers in various ways, usually according to age, gender, and marital status. Rates depend on the category into which a person fits. These amounts are based on statistics that show that different types of drivers have different accident rates.

Young people almost always have to pay higher insurance rates. For example, single males in the 16–25 age group have the highest accident rate of all drivers. Not surprisingly, most insurance companies charge these drivers the highest insurance rates. Married women 25–45 have the fewest accidents and the lowest rates. **Figure 6.13** shows factors in addition to age and sex that affect insurance rates. Rates cannot vary widely because states set limits on the rates companies can charge within their borders.

SECTION 3 REVIEW

Understanding Vocabulary
   Define excise tax, registration fee, liability insurance.

Reviewing Objectives
   ❶ What are the costs of buying an automobile?
   ❷ What are the costs of operating an automobile?

Chapter 6 Buying the Necessities: Housing and Transportation **139**

Assess

Meeting Lesson Objectives
   Assign Section 3 Review as homework or an in-class activity.

Evaluate
   Assign the Section 3 Quiz in the TCR or use the Testmaker to develop a customized quiz.

   Assign the Chapter 6 Test Form A or Form B or use the Testmaker to develop a customized test.

Reteach
   Have small groups of students list the section headings and write a summarizing sentence under each one. Let each group read its summary to the class.

   Have students complete Reteaching Activity 6 in the TCR.

Enrich
   Have students research and rate the types of warranties currently available on new and used cars including the costs and stated value of each type of warranty.

   Have students complete Enrichment Activity 6 in the TCR.

Close

   Have students write a paragraph about the main concerns in choosing housing and transportation.

Point out to students that this article about protecting rights comes from *Kiplinger's Personal Finance Magazine*. Explain that *Kiplinger's* offers in-depth coverage of issues related to finance. This article examines laws against discrimination, which represent an attempt by government to ensure fairness. When businesses fail to follow the laws, citizens can take action to make sure their rights are protected.

Have students use the information in the feature to write an advice column suggesting warning signals that indicate unfair lending practices. As they continue the course, students might collect additional clips about people who obtained financing in unusual ways.

News Clip

Readings in Economics

KIPLINGER'S PERSONAL FINANCE MAGAZINE   **FEBRUARY, 1993**

FIGHTING RACIAL DISCRIMINATION IN HOME LENDING

by Elizabeth Razzi

Despite years of open-housing laws, African-American and Hispanic mortgage applicants are still much more likely to be turned down than whites, regardless of income, reports the Federal Reserve Board. Nationwide last year, the mortgage applications of 38% of African Americans, 27% of Hispanics, 17% of whites and 15% of Asians were rejected by lenders.

Two years ago, Orlando and Gail Walton applied for a low-interest loan through an Ohio program for first-time buyers.... Gail's calls to the lender went unreturned.

Finally Gail arranged a meeting. She was told by the loan officer that there was "no way" she could get the loan because of her credit record.... Embarrassed and upset, she assumed that she and her husband didn't have a chance of getting the home they wanted.

"My husband got so discouraged," she says, "but I was determined that something was not right here."... The Waltons applied to another lender for the same loan in the same program. They got it, based on the same underwriting standards. Then, Gail's mother pointed her toward a Toledo fair-housing group.

The Waltons and the Toledo Fair Housing Center filed suit, charging that the first mortgage company had handled the Waltons' loan application differently from other borrowers' because of race. They settled with the mortgage company last fall for $20,000.

If you are a member of a minority group and are turned down for a mortgage, describe your experience to a local fair-housing group. They can help confirm whether a denial was legitimate. Know your rights; if a lender denies you credit, the institution has 30 days from the day you applied to tell you why.

If you believe you've been treated unfairly,... call the HUD Housing Discrimination Hotline... to file a complaint.

• THINK ABOUT IT •

1. *How do the figures for African Americans turned down for mortgages compare to the number of whites that are turned down?*

2. *What should you do if you suspect that a lender has discriminated against you?*

Answers to Think About It

1. More than twice as many African Americans as whites are turned down.
2. Describe your experience to a fair-housing group and ask the lending institution to explain its refusal to give you a loan. You may also call the HUD Housing Discrimination Hotline to file a complaint.

CHAPTER 6 Highlights

Section 1

Housing Needs and Wants

Key Terms
real estate taxes
(p. 125)
condominium (p. 126)
cooperative (p. 126)
lease (p. 126)
depreciate (p. 126)

Summary
There are five different types of housing available to consumers. Renters should consider the pros and cons of sharing an apartment or house before signing a lease.

Section 2

To Rent or to Buy

Key Terms
closing costs (p. 129)
points (p. 129)
equity (p. 130)
security deposit
(p. 130)

Summary
Several advantages and disadvantages of renting and buying should be considered when deciding about housing. There are rules that determine how much you should spend on a house. Both renters and landlords have rights and responsibilities.

Section 3

Buying and Operating an Automobile

Key Terms
excise tax (p. 136)
registration fee
(p. 137)
liability insurance
(p. 139)

Summary
There are several costs of buying an automobile. The auto owner also must pay for operating and maintaining an automobile.

141

Identifying Key Terms

1. f
2. c
3. b
4. a
5. e
6. d
7. cooperative
8. lease
9. real estate taxes
10. condominium
11. depreciate

Recalling Facts and Ideas

Section 1

1. condominium ownership

2. The single family home has land around it, but it is expensive. Townhouses are less expensive, but noise sometimes carries through common walls. Condominiums afford an investment in real estate with few of the responsibilities, but they require a maintenance fee. Cooperatives divide the cost of real estate taxes and maintenance, but they require consent from other owners for changes, sale, or leasing the apartments. Mobile homes are inexpensive, but they depreciate.

3. financial and personal conflict

Section 2

4. less mobility; less choice; large outlay of money; maintenance costs, real estate taxes, and possible depreciation; high mortgage payments; possibility of overextending debt load

5. no freedom of use, no return on rental money, few tax benefits, little sense of responsibility, no collateral, need to

Identifying Key Terms

Write the letter of the definition in Column B below that correctly defines each term in Column A.

Column A

1. equity (p. 130)
2. depreciate (p. 126)
3. excise tax (p. 136)
4. liability insurance (p. 139)
5. closing costs (p. 129)
6. security deposit (p. 130)

Column B

a. pays for bodily injury or property damage
b. a tax on the manufacture, sale, or use within a country of specific products
c. to decline in value over time
d. usually one month's rent left on deposit with the landlord
e. fee charged by lender for paperwork, taxes, and other activities
f. market value of property minus debt owed on it

Use terms from the following list to fill in the blanks in the paragraph below.

lease (p. 126)
cooperative (p. 126)
depreciate (p. 126)
real estate taxes (p. 125)
condominium (p. 126)

Owners of __(7)__ apartments do not own their apartments, but rather hold a __(8)__ on their apartments so that they have a long-term agreement describing the terms under which the property is being rented. One of the things that such owners have to pay are __(9)__, which are paid on the value of the land and buildings. The owner of a __(10)__, in contrast, owns his or her unit separately. All types of housing tend to __(11)__ and therefore must be maintained.

Recalling Facts and Ideas

Section 1

1. What is the type of ownership called if a person owns part of an apartment building and also owns in common the lobbies, recreational facilities, and so on?
2. What is one advantage and one disadvantage of living in each of the five types of housing?
3. What potential human and economic problems should friends seriously consider before sharing a rented house or apartment?

Section 2

4. What are some of the disadvantages of owning a house?
5. What are some of the disadvantages of renting a house or apartment?
6. What are some responsibilities of landlords?
7. How can you help make sure that you get your security deposit back if you rent?

Section 3

8. If you do not pay cash for a car, what expense must be included in the cost of buying the car?
9. What is included in the cost of operating an automobile?
10. A car's value tends to decrease over time. What do we call this process?
11. Virtually every state requires what type of insurance for owners of automobiles?

Critical Thinking

Section 1

Making Inferences Why do you think that in recent years condominiums have become increasingly popular among Americans?

wait for maintenance

6. providing minimum serv-ices such as heat and safe conditions, providing reasonable maintenance, maintaining the tenant's right to privacy in the apartment

7. Do a walk-through before moving in, keep copies of bills for maintenance, take photos when moving in and leaving, and find out and follow local regulations.

Section 3

8. loan expenses, including interest, down payment, and monthly payments
9. registration fee, normal maintenance and major repairs, depreciation, insurance
10. depreciation
11. liability

Section 2

Making Comparisons The two basic types of mortgages used today are flexible rate and fixed rate. What are the advantages and disadvantages of each?

Section 3

Demonstrating Reasoned Judgment Why do you think that automobile insurance companies charge more for unmarried males between the ages of 16 and 25 than they do for married males between the ages of 16 and 25?

Applying Economic Concepts

Competition and Market Structure Examine your local newspaper carefully for at least one week. Cut out all of the ads that banks and mortgage companies present for mortgages. Write out a comparison table that shows the different mortgage rates.

Chapter Projects

1. **Individual Project** In the library, look up the section of the most recent Census of Housing entitled *Selected Housing Characteristics by States and Counties*. Make a table listing the following statistics for your county: (1) number of total housing units; (2) number of year-round housing units (those used throughout the year); (3) number of units occupied by owners; and (4) number occupied by renters.
2. **Cooperative Learning Project** Working in six groups, call separate automobile insurance agents and ask for a rate quote by giving the following facts:
   - Age: 21
   - Gender: Male or female (depending on who is calling)
   - Automobile type: 1994 Chevy Caprice
   - Use: Drive to college and part-time job—80 miles a week
   - Coverage desired: 100/300/50, which means up to $100,000 for one person injured in an accident, up to a total of

$300,000 for all personal injuries suffered in the accident, and up to $50,000 for damages to private or public property
   - Collision and comprehensive deductible: $500; no medical or towing

After you receive the quotes, compare them.
   a. Which agent/insurance company gave the highest quote? The lowest?
   b. Was there a substantial difference between the rates for females and males?
   c. What was the average percentage difference between the rates quoted for females and males?

Reviewing Skills

Comparing Insurance

1. **Figuring Liability** The following policies are presented to you:
   a. 10/500/200 policy
   b. 100/300/1,000 policy
   Which policy pays the most to any one person injured? Which policy pays the most for damage to private or public property?
2. **Understanding Deductibles** You have an insurance policy with an $800 deductible. If you have an accident that causes $6,123.43 in damages, how much will the insurance company pay?

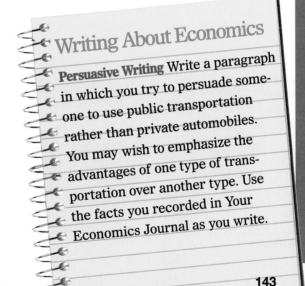

Writing About Economics

Persuasive Writing Write a paragraph in which you try to persuade someone to use public transportation rather than private automobiles. You may wish to emphasize the advantages of one type of transportation over another type. Use the facts you recorded in Your Economics Journal as you write.

143

Critical Thinking

Section 1

They offer privacy, ownership advantages, and a good chance for appreciation without the responsibility of outside maintenance .

Section 2

Flexible mortgages often offer low mortgage payments for at least part of the life of a loan. Fixed rate mortgages offer the security of a rate that will not change.

Section 3

Answers may vary but should note that unmarried males between ages 16 and 25 suffer the most accidents.

Applying Economic Concepts

Answers will vary, but students should make sure they are comparing the same type of mortgage among different lending institutions.

> **? BONUS QUESTION**
>
> The following bonus question may be written on the chalkboard when students take the chapter test.
> **Q: Why do many states require car owners to carry liability insurance?**
> A: Car owners are required to carry liability insurance to assure compensation to others for harm to them and their property.

Chapter Projects

1. Review with students the information in their tables.
2. Students might present their information in a chart or table.

Writing About Economics

In their essays about which form of transportation to use, students should address issues of direct costs, opportunity costs, costs in convenience, and environmental costs.

Reviewing Skills

1. The 100/300/1,000 policy pays more for one person injured and for property damage.
2. $5,323.43

CHAPTER 7 *SAVING AND INVESTING*

CHAPTER ORGANIZER

Daily Objectives	Special Features	Classroom Resources
Section 1 Why Save? • **Decide** when to save and invest. • **Compare** passbook, statement, and money market savings accounts. • **Explain** the advantages of time deposits.	**Personal Perspective:** H. Ross Perot on Saving and Investing, p. 151 **Focus on Free Enterprise:** Case Study, Motown Records, pp. 152–153	Reproducible Lesson Plan 7.1 *NBR* Video 10 and Video Stills 1, 2, 3, 4, and 5 Focus Activity Transparency 20 Focus Activity Sheet 20 Guided Reading Activity 7.1 Cooperative Learning Activity 7 Primary and Secondary Source Readings 7 Consumer Application Activity 7 Section Quiz 7.1 Spanish Section Quiz 7.1 Testmaker
Section 2 Investing: Taking Risks With Your Savings • **Summarize** the differences between stocks and bonds. • **Describe** two types of investment funds available in stock and bond markets. • **Explain** why "hot" tips will not help an investor to get rich quick in the stock market.		Reproducible Lesson Plan 7.2 Focus Activity Transparency 21 Focus Activity Sheet 21 Guided Reading Activity 7.2 Free Enterprise Activity 7 Section Quiz 7.2 Spanish Section Quiz 7.2 Testmaker
Section 3 Special Savings Plans and Goals • **Describe** three kinds of retirement investments. • **Decide** how much to save and invest.	**Learning Economic Skills:** Understanding Interest, p. 165 **News Clip:** "The Case for U.S. Savings Bonds," *Money*, p. 166	Reproducible Lesson Plan 7.3 Focus Activity Transparency 22 Focus Activity Sheet 22 Guided Reading Activity 7.3 Economics Laboratory 2 Economic Simulation 2 Mathematics Practice for Economics 7 Performance Assessment Activity 7 Section Quiz 7.3 Spanish Section Quiz 7.3 Testmaker Reinforcing Skills Enrichment Activity 7

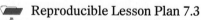

0:00 **OUT OF TIME?** If time does not permit teaching this chapter, you may use the Chapter 7 Highlights and the Audiocassettes that include a 1-page activity and a 1-page test.

Chapter 7 Review and Evaluation

Special Features

Chapter 7 Highlights, p. 167
Chapter 7 Review, pp. 168–169
Economics Lab, pp. 170–171

Classroom Resources

- Chapter 7 Test Forms A and B
- Economics Vocabulary Activity 7
- Spanish Economics Vocabulary Activity 7
- Audiocassette 7
- Spanish Audiocassette 7
- Reteaching Activity 7
- Spanish Reteaching Activity 7

Key to Ability Levels

Teaching strategies have been coded for varying learning styles and abilities.

L1 Level 1 activities are **basic** activities and should be within the ability range of all students.

L2 Level 2 activities are **average** activities designed for the ability range of average to above-average students.

L3 Level 3 activities are **challenging** activities designed for the ability range of above-average students.

LEP activities should be within the ability range of **Limited English Proficiency** students.

Performance Assessment

The following chapter project may be assigned at the beginning of the chapter and used for performance assessment. See page T12 for additional Performance Assessment information.

Tracking Market Performance Have students work in pairs to follow the performance of selected stocks and bonds. Direct the pairs to graph the performance of the individual stocks and bonds they chose and their "holdings" as a whole. After they complete the graphs, have the student teams report on the strongest and weakest performers among their chosen stocks and bonds. Students might want to include in their reports some background information about the strongest and weakest performers.

Additional Resources

Readings for the Student

Dutile, Patty, ed. *Mutual Fund Sourcebook, 1991.* Chicago: Morningstar, 1991. Annual directory of more than 1,700 mutual funds, with statistical tables.

Lowry, R. P. *Good Money.* New York: W. W. Norton Company, 1991. Guide to profitable investing.

Readings for the Teacher

Hayes, S. L. *Investment Banking.* Boston: Harvard Business School Press, 1990. An overview of the history of investment banking.

White, Lawrence J. *The S & L Debacle.* Oxford, England: Oxford University Press, 1991. A complete, unbiased analysis of the S&L collapse in the 1980s.

Multimedia Materials

Banking Tutorial/Banking Simulation. Two-disk series. Apple. EMC Publishing, Div. of EMC Corp., 300 York Ave., St. Paul, MN 55101

Investments and Risk Capital. From the Running Your Own Business Series. Videotape, 24 min. Public Television Library, 475 L'Enfant Plaza, SW, Washington, DC 20024

Stock Market. From the Personal Finance Series. Videotape, 30 min. Coast District Telecourses. 11460 Warner Avenue, Fountain Valley, CA 92708

Wall Street On Line: An Investment Simulation for the Classroom. Apple, IBM. J. Weston Walch Publishing Co., P.O. Box 658, Portland, ME 04104-0658

144B

Chapter Overview

Most Americans make more money at their jobs than they need for immediate necessities. On the other hand, many large purchases cost more than a worker earns in a single pay period. Thus, most wage earners must decide whether to save their extra earnings for large purchases or invest them for future use. Chapter 7 explains or describes various types of savings accounts and investment opportunities and the advantages and disadvantages of each.

VIDEODISC

Nightly Business Report
Economics in Action
Use "Saving and Investing" on Disc 1, Side B, Video 10.

Search 10, Play to 6869

DID YOU KNOW

Many people use life insurance as a form of long-term investment. The cash value of a life insurance policy increases over time and carries interest, so, in addition to insurance, a policy provides savings.

CHAPTER

7

SAVING AND INVESTING

Where can a person save besides banks and savings and loan associations?

Why are some investments risky?

How much should a person save?

Answering Economic Questions

The questions in the above illustration are designed to lead into the main concepts in Chapter 7. Students might not be aware of the many different types of savings accounts available or the kinds of investments people make and the levels of risk associated with each. These questions will help them become more aware of the options available to them as savers and investors.

Have students discuss the questions and give reasons for their answers.

What is the difference between savings and investments?

What are some reasons you might want to save?

What are some of the reasons people save money?

Who insures bank savings deposits?

Your Economics Journal

Keep a record of the names and types of the various institutions that offer to pay you interest for your savings. Next to each entry list the interest rate offered for different kinds of accounts.

145

Economic Portfolio

Have students think about and list the things they want to save for. Suggest dividing their lists into long-term and short-term goals and including the price of each item they wish to buy. Write on the chalkboard a sample of long-term and short-term objectives. Ask volunteers to tell how they plan their savings to make purchases over the short term and the long term. Have students develop a calendar with target dates for long-term and short-term goals and a savings plan to reach their goals.

Connecting to Past Learning

Ask students to identify items they have saved for in the past. Encourage students to discuss the amount of time and money they invested in order to earn extra money. Tell students that in Chapter 7 they will learn about savings plans and investments. After completing the chapter, ask if their ideas about saving and investing have changed.

Applying Economics

Tell students to imagine they have $5,000 to save or invest as they please. Ask if they would deposit all the money in a 1-year certificate of deposit (CD) savings account with a guaranteed interest rate of 5 percent, paid quarterly, or invest in stock (the value of which has doubled in 18 months). Discuss the differences in risk and return.

EXTRA CREDIT PROJECT

Encourage students to interview and write a report on an employee in the financial field, such as a stockbroker or personal banker. Reports should include the day-to-day activities and responsibilities of the employee.

PERFORMANCE ASSESSMENT

Refer to page 144B for "Tracking Market Performance," a Performance Assessment Activity for this chapter.

145

Focus

Overview

See the student page for section objectives.

Section 1 explains or describes: the types of savings accounts available through savings institutions; the advantages and disadvantages of time deposits, as compared with other types of savings accounts; and saving patterns of Americans in the 1980s and early 1990s.

Bellringer

Before presenting the lesson, display Focus Activity Transparency 20 on the overhead projector or copy the material on the chalkboard. Assign the accompanying Focus Activity Sheet.

Motivational Activity

Write the following statement for students to complete: The most important part of savings for me is ___. Discuss responses.

Preteaching Vocabulary

Have students write the definitions of the terms on one side of an index card. On the other side, ask them to write the term. They can use these cards as they study the chapter.

SECTION **1** Why Save?

SECTION 1 FOCUS

Terms to Know saving, interest, passbook savings account, statement savings account, money market deposit account, time deposits, maturity, certificates of deposit

Objectives *After reading this section, you should be able to:*
1. Decide when to save and invest.
2. Compare passbook, statement, and money market savings accounts.
3. Explain the advantages of time deposits.

When You Save, You Have Several Investment Choices

Suppose you have a part-time job that pays $60 a week and you want to buy a stereo that costs $240. Because your monthly income equals the price of the stereo, you cannot collect enough money to buy the stereo and pay your other monthly expenses. An adult could charge the stereo, but as a dependent you probably have no credit rating. You will have to save the money. Economists define **saving** as the nonuse of income for a period of time so that it can be used later. You may already be setting aside some of your income for some future use such as continuing your education.

Deciding to Save and Invest

Any saving that you do now may be only for purchases that require more money than you usually have at one time. When you are self-supporting and have more responsibilities, you will probably save for other reasons. For example, you may save to have money in case of emergencies, such as losing your job, and for your retirement. Most Americans who save do so for these reasons. Saving evens out a person's ability to spend throughout his or her lifetime. Figure 7.1 shows the rate of personal saving of Americans in recent years.

The saving of any individual benefits the economy as a whole. Saving provides money for others to invest or spend. Additional savings also allow businesses to expand, which provides increased income for consumers and raises the standard of living.

Generally, when people think of saving, they think of putting their money in a savings bank or a similar institution where it will earn interest. **Interest** is the payment people receive when they lend money—allow someone else to use their money. A person receives interest on his or her savings account or similar savings plan for as long as money is in the account.

Classroom Resources for Section 1

- Reproducible Lesson Plan 7.1
- *NBR* Video 10 and Video Stills 1, 2, 3, 4, and 5
- Focus Activity Transparency 20
- Focus Activity Sheet 20
- Guided Reading Activity 7.1
- Cooperative Learning Activity 7

- Primary and Secondary Source Readings 7
- Consumer Application Activity 7
- Section Quiz 7.1
- Spanish Section Quiz 7.1
- Testmaker

You have many options of places and ways to invest your savings. The most common places are commercial banks, savings and loan associations, savings banks, and credit unions. Before depositing money, investigate the different types of financial institutions in your area and the services they offer. Each institution usually has several types of savings plans, each paying a different interest rate. In comparison shopping for the best savings plan for you, you need to consider the trade-offs. Some savings plans allow immediate access to your money but pay a low rate of interest. Others pay higher interest and allow immediate use of your money, but require a large minimum balance.

Savings Accounts

Passbook savings accounts are also called regular savings accounts. With a **passbook savings account,** the depositor receives a booklet in which deposits, withdrawals, and interest are recorded. A customer must present the passbook each time one of these transactions, or business operations, takes place. A **statement savings account** is basically the same type of account. Instead of a passbook that must be presented for each transaction, however, the depositor receives a monthly statement showing all transactions. The chief appeal of these accounts is that they offer easy availability of funds. The depositor can usually withdraw money at any

**Figure 7.1
Personal Saving**
Compare the percentage of personal saving in 1992 with that in 1982. ▼

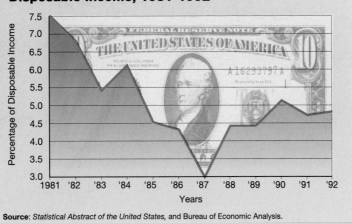

Personal Saving Expressed as a Percentage of Disposable Income, 1981-1992

Percentage of Disposable Income (y-axis: 3.0 to 7.5)
Years (x-axis: 1981 '82 '83 '84 '85 '86 '87 '88 '89 '90 '91 '92)

Source: *Statistical Abstract of the United States,* and Bureau of Economic Analysis.

Chapter 7 Saving and Investing **147**

Teach

Guided Practice

L2 Considering Have students select the best savings account for each goal: coat, car, unemployment security, retirement.

Visual Instruction

Have students speculate on and discuss reasons for changes in Figure 7.1.

🔘 VIDEODISC

Nightly Business Report
Economics in Action
Use Video Stills 1–5, "Corporate Bonds," "Stock Certificates," "College Costs—Today," "College Costs—Projected," and "$1 Invested 1971–1991," Disc 1, Side B, Video 10.

Search Frame 1430

Search Frame 1938

Search Frame 3852

Search Frame 3940

Search Frame 5001

◆▶⬤ Meeting Special Needs

Language Disability Students with language difficulties may have problems understanding the main text. Before reading the text in Section 1, ask students to look at the headlines, tables, and captions. Have them tell what they think the section will explain. Then have volunteers read paragraphs aloud and paraphrase them as they read.

Independent Practice

L3 Creating an Ad Have students work in groups to create an advertisement or brochure for a particular savings institution. Suggest that they include in their ad the benefits of their kind of savings institution, the types of savings accounts they offer, and their recommendations for using each account. Ask students to use graphics to illustrate their concepts.

L1 Graphing Have students create a graph showing the difference between earnings on $1,000 when interest is compounded monthly, quarterly, and annually. Remind students to use a different color or pattern representing each method of computing interest and to provide a key at the bottom of the page.

time without paying a penalty—forfeiting any money—but there is a trade-off, as **Figure 7.2** shows.

A **money market deposit account** (MMDA) is another type of account that pays relatively high rates of interest and allows immediate access to money. The trade-off is that these accounts also have a $1,000 to $2,500 minimum balance requirement. Customers can usually make withdrawals from a money market account in person at any time, but they are allowed to write only a few checks a month against the account.

Time Deposits

The term *time deposits* refers to a wide variety of savings plans that require a saver to leave his or her money on deposit for a certain period of time. The period of time is called the **maturity**, and may vary from seven days to eight years or more. Time deposits are often called **certificates of deposit** (CDs), or savings certificates as shown in **Figure 7.3**. They state the amount of the deposit, the maturity, and the rate of interest being paid. The amount of deposit and interest rates vary widely. Some CDs, particularly those paying higher interest, require a minimum deposit. The minimum may be as small as $250 or as large as $100,000. CDs at credit unions are called share certificates.

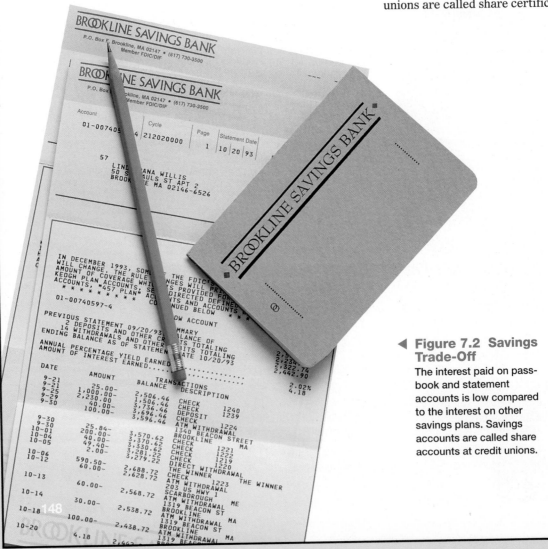

◄ **Figure 7.2 Savings Trade-Off**
The interest paid on passbook and statement accounts is low compared to the interest on other savings plans. Savings accounts are called share accounts at credit unions.

Cooperative Learning

Have small groups investigate the connection, if any, between the amount of savings by citizens of a country and the gross domestic product (GDP) of the country. Explain that GDP expresses the total value of goods and services produced by a nation in a given period, such as a year. Suggest that each group compare savings and GDP for the United States and another nation, such as Australia, Brazil, Germany, Japan, or Saudi Arabia. Have groups graph their findings and decide whether they think they can draw any valid conclusions.

Insuring Deposits Before the 1930s, people who deposited money in banks risked losing their entire deposits if the bank failed. When the stock market collapsed in 1929, it caused a panic in the banking industry. The resulting crisis wiped out people's entire savings and destroyed investors' confidence in banks. Congress passed, and President Franklin Roosevelt signed, legislation to restore confidence in banks and to protect deposits. This legislation created the Federal Deposit Insurance Corporation (FDIC).

Today there are several federal agencies that insure most savings institutions in the United States. Each depositor's money is insured up to $100,000. If an insured institution fails, each depositor will be paid the full amount of his or her savings up to $100,000. Figure 7.4 (page 150) lists the federal agencies that insure each type of institution and shows comparisons of the various places where you

◀ **Figure 7.3**
Time Deposits

Time deposits offer higher interest rates than passbook or statement savings accounts. The longer it is to the maturity date, the higher the interest rate that is paid. For example, a certificate of deposit (CD) with a short-term maturity of 90 days pays less interest than a CD with a two-year maturity. Savers who decide to cash a time deposit before maturity pay a penalty.

Financial institutions also offer a number of special CDs. One example is the small saver's certificates. Their rates are tied to the current interest rates the federal government pays on certain types of borrowing that it does.

Independent Practice

L2 Comparing and Contrasting Tell students that savings institutions may offer a variety of banking services. Ask them to prepare a chart or table naming several institutions and listing the customer services offered and fees charged for them. Have students use their data to discuss which institutions they think offer the best value to customers.

 Have students complete Guided Reading Activity 7.1 in the TCR. LEP

GLOBAL ECONOMICS

During the Great Depression years of 1930 to 1933, about 9,000 banks failed in the United States. None, however, failed in Canada, Great Britain, and many other countries. In an effort to reduce bank failures, our government began requiring banks to follow rules and undergo periodic examinations by the Federal Reserve systems.

? DID YOU KNOW

Deregulation of banking in the United States has enabled banks to broaden their range of consumer services. It has also been a factor in bank failures in the 1980s, which raised debate about the role of government in banking.

 Free Enterprise Activity

Ask students to work cooperatively to develop a plan to start up and manage a student credit union. Suggest that the main purpose of the credit union might be to make loans to members "in a pinch" and to show a profit at the end of the year. Discuss the feasibility of the plan in class.

Assess

Meeting Lesson Objectives

Assign Section 1 Review as homework or an in-class activity. Each question in the Review addresses the corresponding numbered objective in the Section Focus.

Evaluate

Assign the Section 1 Quiz in the TCR or use the Testmaker to develop a customized quiz.

Reteach

Ask students to create a section outline using each major and minor headline and the topic sentences.

Enrich

Have students research the savings and loan (S&L) crisis that began in the late 1970s.

Close

Direct students to write a five-year savings plan for their own earnings.

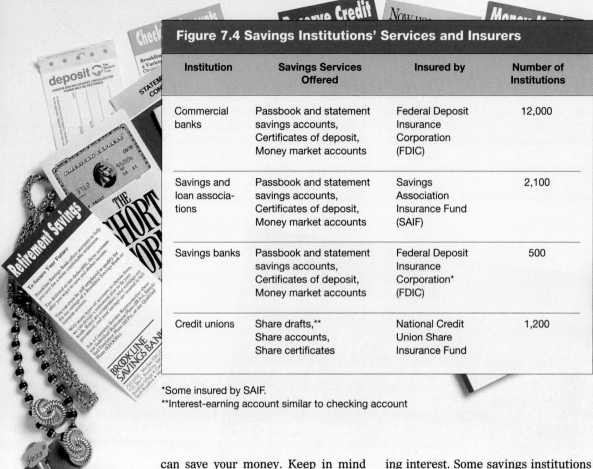

Figure 7.4 Savings Institutions' Services and Insurers

Institution	Savings Services Offered	Insured by	Number of Institutions
Commercial banks	Passbook and statement savings accounts, Certificates of deposit, Money market accounts	Federal Deposit Insurance Corporation (FDIC)	12,000
Savings and loan associations	Passbook and statement savings accounts, Certificates of deposit, Money market accounts	Savings Association Insurance Fund (SAIF)	2,100
Savings banks	Passbook and statement savings accounts, Certificates of deposit, Money market accounts	Federal Deposit Insurance Corporation* (FDIC)	500
Credit unions	Share drafts,** Share accounts, Share certificates	National Credit Union Share Insurance Fund	1,200

*Some insured by SAIF.
**Interest-earning account similar to checking account

can save your money. Keep in mind that different institutions may offer different rates on the same type of accounts. Different institutions may also use different methods for figur-ing interest. Some savings institutions are not insured, or they carry private insurance. Those who put their money in these institutions run a higher risk of losing funds if the institution fails.

SECTION 1 REVIEW

Understanding Vocabulary

Define saving, interest, passbook savings account, statement savings account, money market deposit account, time deposits, maturity, certificates of deposit.

Reviewing Objectives

① What are three reasons that people save and invest?

② Why is it more difficult for the beginning saver to open a money market deposit account than a passbook savings account?

③ What determines the rate of interest on a time deposit?

Section 1 Review Answers

Understanding Vocabulary
saving (p. 146), interest (p. 146), passbook savings account (p. 147), statement savings account (p. 147), money market deposit account (p. 148), time deposits (p. 148), maturity (p. 148), certificates of deposit (p. 148)

Reviewing Objectives
1. Many people save for purchases and retirement and to meet emergencies.
2. Money market accounts often require a $1,000 to $2,500 initial deposit.
3. The interest rate depends on the maturity and the amount of deposit.

Personal Perspective

H. Ross Perot on Saving and Investing

Profile

- born June 27, 1930, in Texarkana, Texas
- graduate of the U.S. Naval Academy at Annapolis, Maryland
- started out as a sales representative for IBM
- incorporated EDS (Electronic Data Systems) in 1962
- unsuccessful bid for President as an independent candidate in 1992
- authored *United We Stand* in 1992

H. Ross Perot has many ideas on how to improve this country and the American standard of living. These ideas were well publicized during his 1992 presidential bid. Among other things, he believes that Americans must increase their levels of saving and investment. Many of his ideas are stated in some detail in his book *United We Stand*.

*N*obody believes any longer that their home equity values will rise indefinitely, giving them a tidy nest egg for retirement. In fact, in this recession many home values have declined.... Nobody believes that their paychecks will increase ahead of inflation every year. Most feel fortunate to have a paycheck at all. Everyone knows someone who is unemployed. Nobody in the baby boom generation that I've met believes any longer that he or she will be able to count on Social Security being solvent twenty-five or thirty years from now when it's time for their retirement. Many believe they will have to provide for themselves.

... Our economic engine needs capital, and it needs it now.

We need it for two good reasons.

First, our companies now pay a higher cost for money than companies in Japan and Germany. It's tough to compete when your interest payments are higher than your competitors'.

Second, we are borrowing foreign money. Foreign money kept us afloat during the 1980s. That money can leave just as easily as it came.

... We need to take steps to reinstill the ethic of saving among the American people.

... We need to press immediately for pro-savings incentives on all fronts.

... Our children today need to know how important savings are. Our goal should be to ingrain in the next generation the lesson that was temporarily lost in the present one.

... We're not investing in our future. From 1980 to 1989 Japan had an investment rate of 16 percent of gross domestic product. Ours was 4.5 percent. Who is going to win the race?

Checking for Understanding

1. What are two reasons Americans who do not save may face difficult retirement years?
2. What goal that was temporarily lost does Perot believe America should teach their children?
3. What was the savings rate in the United States from 1980 to 1989?

Answers to Checking for Understanding

1. Answers will vary but should indicate that home equity values may not rise in the future, paychecks may not outpace inflation, and Social Security may not be solvent in 25 or 30 years.

2. Answers will vary but should discuss the ethic of saving—the idea that savings are important.

3. 4.5 percent

Background

In addition to having amassed one of the nation's largest personal fortunes, H. Ross Perot emerged as an outspoken and colorful figure in American politics during his presidential candidacy in 1992. According to Perot, government should be run like a business and creating jobs is one of the most important responsibilities of government.

Teach

Ask volunteers to read aloud the excerpts from interviews with H. Ross Perot. Then have students paraphrase each excerpt to gain a better understanding of Perot's ideas. Finally, have students answer the questions in Checking for Understanding.

You might have interested students read campaign speeches from Perot's presidential candidacy and report on the ideas he emphasized then.

Focus

The focus of this feature points out the importance of having a sound marketing plan to help make a product succeed.

Also point out to students that Berry Gordy combined personal enthusiasm for music, willingness to take a chance, and determination to start his own business—and succeeded in creating a legendary record company.

Teach

L1 Creating a Time Line
Have students make a time line of Berry Gordy's life from 1953 to 1988, including failures, achievements, and milestones in his remarkable career. Ask students to shade the most active period of Gordy's life and to name the reasons they think these years were his most active.

Focus on Free Enterprise

CASE STUDY

Motown Records

From Failure to Success  In Detroit during the 1950s, Berry Gordy was a lover of music (especially jazz) and an aspiring songwriter. When he came out of the Army in 1953, he purchased the 3-D Record Mart, a store specializing in jazz records. In 1955, 3-D went under and Gordy went to work for Ford Motor Company. Working for Ford, however, did not satisfy Gordy. In 1957 he quit to concentrate on songwriting. He and Tyran Carlo co-wrote "Reet Petite," the song that launched pop singer Jackie Wilson's career. Gordy's own career, though, did not take off until 1959, when he borrowed $800 to found his first record label, Tamla Records. The first release on Tamla records was Marvin Gaye's "Come to Me."

From Tamla to Motown Gordy expanded his fledgling empire by establishing a second record label, Motown Records, in 1960. The first release under the Motown label was the Satintones' "My Beloved." Gordy established two separate record labels for a variety of reasons. At that time, his record labels were actually released by different record distributors. Gordy felt he could market the different labels to different distributors, thus getting more individual attention. The second label would also allow for more airplay, because many program directors would agree to play only one record per label at any given time. Finally, Gordy felt that having his employees compete against each other for competing labels would lead to greater productivity and creativity.

The Tamla and Motown record labels became successful very quickly. Tamla Records had its first million seller in 1961 (the Miracles' "Shop Around"). In 1962, yet a third record label, Gordy Records (originally Miracle Records) was established. Motown expanded still further when it went into the record pressing and distribution business. By the early 1960s, Gordy was running out of record companies to distribute his records, so he decided to press "Way Over There" by the Miracles himself, and ended up selling 60,000 copies.

Hitsville, U.S.A. From this beginning, Motown Records went on to be one of the most successful record labels of the 1960s and 1970s. Between 1960 and 1970, Motown released 535 singles, of which 357 were chart hits. In 1966 alone, 75 percent of the company's releases made the charts, in an industry where the average is about 10 percent. Part of the reason for this success came from Gordy's philosophy in choosing

which songs to release. Unlike other record labels, Gordy did not release songs he did not believe were hit material. Overall, Gordy released less than 10 percent of the material that Motown recorded.

The $61 Million Sale By 1972 Gordy moved his company to Los Angeles and turned to film, producing such movies as "Lady Sings the Blues" and "The Wiz." During the 1980s, Motown's popularity declined. In 1984 Motown lost its ranking as the largest African American-owned company. In 1988 Gordy sold Motown Records to MCA and a private investment firm (Boston Ventures) for $61 million, but retained Motown's publishing division and film and television production company. It continues to publish sheet music and produce television shows today.

Free Enterprise in Action

1. What was Gordy's first record label called?
2. Why did Gordy choose to establish more than one record label?
3. Why do you think Motown was so successful in the 1960s and 1970s?

TEACHING: Focus on Free Enterprise

L2 Interpreting Content
After students read the feature, ask: What did Gordy do to try to assure the commercial success of the songs he released? (*He released only those songs that he thought could become chart hits—less than 10 percent of the songs recorded.*)

Between 1960 and 1970, what percentage of Gordy's singles records appeared on the charts? (*66.7 percent*)

L3 Research and Writing
Have students research the movie-making career of Spike Lee and write a short report. Suggest that they include information on the financing of his films.

Assess

Have students discuss the personal qualities they think are necessary in an individual who wants to develop a large successful business. Encourage sharing anecdotes they may have heard or read concerning successful entrepreneurs.

Close

Ask volunteers to name a business they would like to start and to identify who they think their customers would be.

Answers to Free Enterprise in Action

1. Tamla Records
2. He wanted to market his recordings to more than one distributor. He also wanted to market more than one record at a time to radio stations. He thought competing labels would encourage employee productivity and creativity.
3. Answers will vary but should include an understanding of Gordy's marketing philosophy and tactics. Students also might discuss the unique quality of the music he brought to the public.

Focus

Overview

See the student page for section objectives.

Section 2 explains or describes: stock and bond investment funds and the differences between them; "hot tips" and why they do not help stock market investors get rich.

Bellringer

Before presenting the lesson, display Focus Activity Transparency 21 on the overhead projector or copy the material on the chalkboard. Assign the accompanying Focus Activity Sheet.

Motivational Activity

Write the column headings and three stock listings from the daily stock market quotations on the chalkboard and ask students to copy them on a sheet of paper. Ask students to imagine that these stocks reflect their investments. Help students (see skill on reading stock quotations in Ch. 9) identify whether these stocks gained or lost value.

Preteaching Vocabulary

Using cards with terms on one side and definitions on the other, have pairs of students test each other on their understanding of the terms.

SECTION **2** *Investing: Taking Risks With Your Savings*

SECTION 2 FOCUS

Terms to Know stock, stockholders, dividends, bond, tax-exempt bonds, savings bonds, Treasury bills, Treasury notes, Treasury bonds, over-the-counter market, capital gain, broker, capital loss, mutual fund, money market fund, inside information

Objectives *After reading this section, you should be able to:*

① Summarize the differences between stocks and bonds.
② Describe two types of investment funds available in stock and bond markets.
③ Explain why "hot" tips will not help an investor to get rich quick in the stock market.

Stocks and Bonds Offer Investors Better Returns, But With More Risk

People usually distinguish between saving and investing. People have savings plans because they want a sure, fixed rate of interest. If people are willing to take a chance on earning a higher rate of return, however, they can invest their money in other ways, such as stocks and bonds. Nevertheless, it is usually impossible to get a higher rate of return without taking some risk. Of course, the very nature of risk implies that such investment may yield a lower rate of interest, too.

Stocks and Bonds

Stock, or shares of stock, entitles the buyer to a certain part of the future profits and assets of the corporation selling the stock. The person buying stock, therefore, becomes a part owner of a corporation. As proof of ownership, the corporation issues stock

---

Classroom Resources for Section 2

Reproducible Lesson Plan 7.2
Focus Activity Transparency 21
Focus Activity Sheet 21
Guided Reading Activity 7.2

Free Enterprise Activity 7
Section Quiz 7.2
Spanish Section Quiz 7.2
Testmaker

certificates similar to the ones in **Figure 7.5**. By issuing stock for sale, a company obtains funds for use in expanding its business and, it hopes, in making a large profit.

Stockholders—owners of stock—make money from stock in two ways. One is through **dividends,** the money return a stockholder receives on the amount he or she originally invested in the company.

The corporation may declare a dividend at one or more times during a year. Dividends, however, are paid only when the company makes a profit. The other way people make money on stock is by selling it for more than they paid for it. Some people buy stock just to speculate. They buy stock hoping that the price will increase greatly so they can sell at a profit. They do not buy it for the dividends.

Instead of buying stock, people with money to invest can buy bonds. A **bond** is a certificate a company or the government issues in exchange for borrowed money. It promises to pay a stated rate of interest over a stated period of time, and then to repay the borrowed amount in full at the end of that time. A bondholder lends money for a period of time to a company or government and is paid interest on that money. At the end of the period, the full amount of borrowed money is repaid. The period of time is called the bond's maturity.

Unlike buying stock, buying a bond does not make a bondholder part owner of the company or government that issued the bond. The bond becomes part of the debt of the corporation or government, and the bondholder becomes a creditor. **Figure 7.6** (page 156) lists some of the other differences between stocks and bonds.

Tax-Exempt Bonds Local and state governments also sell **tax-exempt bonds.** The interest on this type of bond, unlike bonds issued by companies, is not taxed by the federal government. Interest that you earn on bonds your own city or state issues is also exempt from city and state income taxes. Tax-exempt bonds are good investments for wealthier people who would otherwise pay high taxes on interest earned from investments.

Savings Bonds The United States government issues **savings bonds** as one of its ways of borrowing money. They range in face value from $50 up to $10,000. The purchase of a U.S. savings bond is similar to buying a bank's certificate of deposit. A very safe form of investment, savings bonds are attractive to people with limited money to invest. A person buying a savings bond pays half the bond's face value. Then the bond increases in

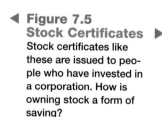

◀ **Figure 7.5**
Stock Certificates ▶
Stock certificates like these are issued to people who have invested in a corporation. How is owning stock a form of saving?

Teach

Guided Practice

L1 Hypothesizing Ask students to hypothesize ways in which corporations would have to raise money if they could not create and sell stock. Call on volunteers for their ideas and record them on the chalkboard.

L2 Rating Have students identify the six kinds of government bonds. Write each kind on the chalkboard. Ask students to rate the bonds by size of investment they require. Then ask them to rate the bonds by the amount of tax advantage they offer.

🌐 GLOBAL ECONOMICS

Although stock markets have national, regional, or even local bases, stock market trading transcends national boundaries. Events in one nation or its market can affect values and prices in others. Thus international brokers must be aware of trends throughout the world. American stock brokers sometimes buy and sell stock in the middle of the night in order to do business as soon as Japanese markets open each day.

◆ ◗ ◯ Meeting Special Needs

Hearing Disability Students with hearing difficulties may be especially interested to learn about the hand signals and gestures that are an integral part of trading on the floors of some stock exchanges and commodities and futures markets. Encourage students to research and learn these signals and demonstrate them to the class.

Independent Practice

L2 Creating a Checklist
Have students create a checklist chart of the characteristics of stocks and bonds. Direct students to list in a column all the characteristics of stocks and bonds they read about in Section 2 and Figure 7.6. Then have them create a second column called Stocks and a third column called Bonds. Ask students to place a check in the proper column to show each characteristic of stocks and each characteristic of bonds. Ask them to shade or color the characteristics stocks and bonds have in common.

Figure 7.6 Difference Between Stocks and Bonds

Stocks	Bonds
1. All corporations issue or offer to sell stock. That act is what makes them corporations.	1. Corporations are not required to issue bonds.
2. Stocks represent ownership.	2. Bonds represent debt.
3. Stocks do not have a fixed dividend rate (except preferred stocks).	3. Bonds pay a fixed rate of interest.
4. Dividends on stock are paid only if the corporation makes a profit.	4. Interest on bonds normally must always be paid, whether or not the corporation earns a profit.
5. Stocks do not have a maturity date. The corporation issuing the stock does not repay the stockholder.	5. Bonds have a maturity date. The bondholder is to be repaid the value of the bond, although if the corporation goes out of business it does not normally repay the bondholders.
6. Stockholders (except those with preferred stock) can elect a board of directors who control the corporation.	6. Bondholders usually have no voice in or control over how the corporation is run.
7. Stockholders have a claim against the property and income of a corporation only after the claims of all creditors (including bondholders and holders of preferred stock) have been met.	7. Bondholders have a claim against the property and income of a corporation that must be met before the claims of any stockholders, including those holding preferred stock.

value every six months until its full face value is reached—usually within 10 years. If you choose to turn in a U.S. savings bond before it matures, you are guaranteed a certain rate of interest, which changes depending on rates of interest in the economy. Many savers purchase these bonds because of the tax advantages they offer. The interest on U.S. savings bonds is not taxed by the federal government until the bond is turned in for cash. These bonds are also exempt from state and local taxes.

The Treasury Department also sells several types of larger investments. **Treasury bills** mature in anywhere from 3 months to 1 year. The minimum amount of investment for Treasury bills is $10,000. **Treasury notes** have maturity dates of 2 to 10 years, and **Treasury bonds** mature in 10 or more years. Notes and bonds are

sold in minimums of $1,000 or $5,000. The interest on all three of these government securities is exempt from state and local income taxes, but not from federal income tax.

Stock and Bond Markets

Stocks are bought and sold through brokers. See **Figure 7.7**. The largest stock market is the New York Stock Exchange (NYSE) in New York City. The second largest is the American Stock Exchange (AMEX), also in New York. The stocks listed on these 2 exchanges account for more than 70 percent of the market value of all stocks listed on all of the exchanges in the United States.

In addition to the New York and American exchanges, there are supplemental stock exchanges and regional exchanges. One is the Midwest

Cooperative Learning

Organize students into small investment planning services that need to advise two clients, each with $100,000 to invest. One client wants a large growth in capital during the next 10 years. The other wants to preserve capital, receive a dependable income, and reduce tax liability. Both would consider

mutual fund investment. Ask each "service" to research investment options for both clients and develop an investment portfolio. Have each service present its investment plans for class review and discussion. Ask the class to choose the plans that best meet the clients' needs.

Stock Exchange in Chicago. Stocks must be listed to be sold on all of these exchanges. A corporation offering stocks for sale must prove to the exchange that it is in good financial condition and engages in legal business. Most of the companies traded on stock exchanges are among the larger corporations.

Over-the-Counter Markets Stocks can also be sold on the **over-the-counter market.** Most of them are quoted on the National Association of Securities Dealers Automated Quotations (NASDAQ) national market system. Unlike stock exchanges, over-the-counter stocks are not traded in any specific place. Brokerage firms hold quantities of shares of stock that they buy and sell for investors. The stocks of smaller, lesser-known companies are often traded in this way. For example, assume that XYZ Corporation is a small company that sells computers. If an investor wanted to buy stock in it, he or she would check the stock market listings in the local newspaper. The table of over-the-counter stocks would list XYZ Corporation, the number of shares of stock sold the day before, and the price at which shares were bought and sold that

day. The investor would then call a broker and tell him or her to buy a certain number of shares. Usually stocks are sold in amounts of 100 shares, but some brokers will handle smaller amounts. The largest volume of over-the-counter transactions occurs through the NASDAQ.

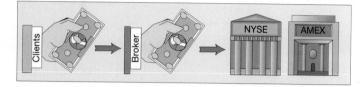

Bond Markets The New York Stock Exchange Bond Market and the American Exchange Bond Market are the two largest bond exchanges. Bonds, including U.S. government bonds, are also sold over-the-counter.

Capital Gains and Losses Suppose a person buys stock at $20 a share and sells it for $30. The profit of $10 per share is called a **capital gain.** The person has had an increase in his or her capital, or wealth, of $10 a share. Of course, the value of stock may also

Figure 7.7 ▲
Buying Stocks or Bonds
If you decide to buy stocks or bonds, you will have to use a broker. A **broker** is a person who acts as a go-between for buyers and sellers. Thousands of brokerage firms throughout the country buy and sell daily for ordinary investors. Brokerage houses communicate directly with the busy floors of the stock exchanges.
▼

Independent Practice

L2 Comparing and Contrasting Ask students to develop a table comparing how the buying and selling of stock are carried out by NASDAQ in the United States and by the London and Tokyo stock exchanges. Ask volunteers to give an oral report.

 DID YOU KNOW

Stock tickers were once used by brokerage firms to show the latest trades in the stock market. These machines displayed the data on narrow paper ribbon, or ticker tape. Today quotations are displayed electronically.

 Free Enterprise Activity

Ask volunteers to brainstorm starting a student-run business that would require investment to pay for start-up costs such as renting space, buying equipment, paying for advertising, and so forth. Have them prepare an outline of the business and how they would obtain start-up capital. Ask for a volunteer to present the proposal to the class for review and discussion.

Independent Practice

L2 Researching and Reporting Ask students to find out what financial information and advice are available to investors on radio and television, in magazines and newspapers, and in financial newsletters. Have students write a brief report and critique on one example each of three kinds of resources. Ask volunteers to make an oral report to the class.

Visual Instruction

Figure 7.9 displays a variety of mutual funds. Ask students to find out how load and no-load mutual funds differ. Have them also locate annual figures on the number of both kinds of funds registered in the United States from 1971 through 1990. Suggest charting their data on a line graph and including a caption explaining both kinds of funds. Discuss whether load or no-load should be the main reason for investing in a fund.

Figure 7.8 ▶
Capital Gains and Losses
Potential gains or losses may be calculated "on paper" before a person makes a decision to sell securities. No taxable gain or loss takes place, however, until the sale is completed.

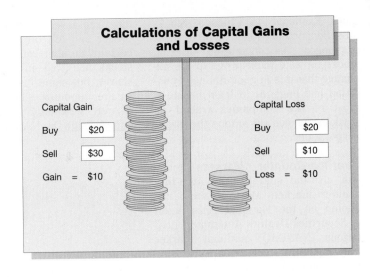

Calculations of Capital Gains and Losses

Capital Gain

Buy $20
Sell $30
Gain = $10

Capital Loss

Buy $20
Sell $10
Loss = $10

fall. If a person decides to sell stock at a lower price than he or she paid for it, that person suffers a **capital loss.** Money may be made or lost on bonds in much the same way. See Figure 7.8.

Mutual Funds: An Easy Way to Invest One of the easiest ways to invest in stocks and bonds is to participate in a mutual fund. A **mutual fund** is an investment company that pools the money of many individuals to buy stocks, bonds, or other investments. By putting savings into a mutual fund, an individual usually is able to purchase a little bit of a large number of stocks or bonds.

Mutual funds have several other important advantages for small investors. One is that the risk of losing money from a poor investment is decreased. Professionals with experience in the stock or bond market make decisions about how to invest the fund's money. Most mutual funds hold a variety of stocks or bonds. Losses in one area are likely to be made up by gains in another. Some funds invest in stocks that are likely to increase rapidly in value, some in stocks and bonds that pay high dividends and interest, and some in tax-exempt bonds. As Figure 7.9 shows, a

bewildering array of mutual funds is available to investors.

One type of mutual fund, called a **money market fund,** normally uses investors' money to buy the short-term debt of businesses and banks. Most money market funds allow investors to write checks against their money in the fund. Any check, however, must be above some minimum amount, usually $500. The investor then earns money only on the amount left in the account. Banks, savings and loan associations, and savings banks now offer a similar service, called money market deposit accounts (MMDA). A major advantage of MMDA accounts is that the federal government insures them against loss. Mutual funds and money market funds are not insured by the federal government.

Regulating Securities and Exchanges The securities market is heavily regulated today, both at the state and federal levels. The Securities and Exchange Commission (SEC), created by the Securities Exchange Act of 1934, is responsible for administering all federal securities laws. It has regulatory authority over brokerage firms, stock exchanges, and most businesses that issue stock. It

Cultural Diversity and Economics

Organize students into small groups to report on minority (African American, Asian American, Hispanic, Native American, and so forth) ownership or management of financial institutions and investment funds and services in the United States. Advise students to consult a reference librarian about directories of minority business and other resources for data. Suggest including charts and graphs as needed. After a representative from each group reports its findings, lead a discussion.

also investigates any dealings between or among corporations, such as mergers, that affect the value of stocks.

Congress passed the Securities Act of 1933 to avoid another stock market crash like that of 1929. The act requires that all essential information concerning the issuing of stocks or bonds be made available to investors. This requirement is fulfilled with a registration statement filed with the federal government. A briefer description, called a prospectus, must be given to each potential buyer. It lists the amount offered, the price, and the use that the company plans to make of the money raised by the stock or bonds. Mutual funds must also distribute a prospectus describing the fund and the way in which the money will be invested.

Today states also have securities laws. These are designed mostly to prevent schemes that would take advantage of small investors.

Can You Get Rich Quick in the Stock Market?

You may have heard about some persons becoming millionaires overnight by making smart investments in the stock market. A stockbroker may give you advice about which stocks to buy; he or she may even have a "hot" tip. If that broker truly has information that no one else has, he or she is in possession of **inside information.** It is illegal for a broker to give out this information and also illegal for a client to profit from it.

Figure 7.9
Many Mutual Funds
The small investor should find out how the mutual fund he or she may choose has performed compared to other funds over a period of several years. Investors' magazines track the performance of well-known funds.

▼

Independent Practice
L3 Creating a Flow Chart
Have students create flow charts showing the path of money invested in stocks. Have them begin with money earned by an employee of a company and ask them to take it as far as they can. Ask volunteers to design meaningful drawings or graphic symbols to illustrate the flow charts.

📁 Have students complete Guided Reading Activity 7.2 in the TCR. LEP

 DID YOU KNOW

To many people the term *mutual fund* means an open-end investment company that pools investors' resources and has no fixed number of shares. There are, however, investment companies traded like stocks and having a limited number of shares. Although they are sometimes called closed-end mutual funds, a more accurate designation might be closed-end investment company, or publicly traded investment fund.

Cooperative Learning

Ask the class to organize and present an American mutual funds seminar. Suggest that students form teams to research and write a short description of each category of fund, such as growth fund, balanced fund, tax-free municipal bond fund, and so forth. Recommend giving the present total number of funds in each category. Encourage developing posters showing the most recent five-year performance of the five most successful and five least successful funds in each category. A member of each team should present its report to the class.

Assess

Meeting Lesson Objectives

Assign Section 2 Review as homework or an in-class activity.

Evaluate

Assign the Section 2 Quiz in the TCR or use the Testmaker to develop a customized quiz.

Reteach

Ask students to plan, track, and report on a $4,000 mutual fund investment for their own portfolio. Ask them to choose actual funds and follow their performance for a month.

Enrich

Have students research and report on investment professionals charged with and convicted of insider trading.

Close

Discuss with students the kinds of investments they believe would further their financial goals.

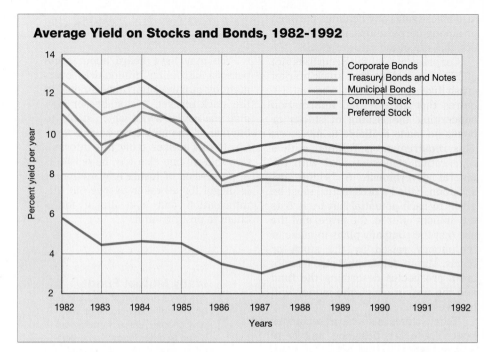

Average Yield on Stocks and Bonds, 1982-1992

Figure 7.10 ▲
Yield on Stocks and Bonds
The term *yield* means actual return on investment. Which type of investment has had the highest average yield from 1982 to 1992? Which type of investment has the lowest percentage yield?

If the broker's information came from his or her company's research department, then that information is available to a large number of people. The value of public investment research information to you as an investor is essentially zero.

You will do no better by following the advice of researchers from a stock brokerage company than you would by randomly selecting stocks. **Figure 7.10** gives a more realistic reflection of what an investor in stocks and bonds should expect to earn.

Public Information Information flows rapidly in the stock market. The value of public information for an investor is basically what that investor paid for it—zero. According to Nobel prize-winning economist Paul Samuelson:

Even the best investors seem to find it hard to do better than comprehensive common stock averages, or better on the average than random selection among stocks of comparable variability.

SECTION 2 REVIEW

Understanding Vocabulary

Define stock, stockholders, dividends, bond, tax-exempt bonds, savings bonds, Treasury bills, Treasury notes, Treasury bonds, over-the-counter market, capital gain, broker, capital loss, mutual fund, money market fund, inside information.

Reviewing Objectives

① How do stocks differ from bonds?

② What are the benefits of mutual funds and money market funds?

③ Why are "hot" tips of no value to investors?

Section 2 Review Answers

Understanding Vocabulary
stock (p. 154), **stockholders** (p. 155), **dividends** (p. 155), **bond** (p. 155), **tax-exempt bonds** (p. 155), **savings bonds** (p. 155), **Treasury bills** (p. 156), **Treasury notes** (p. 156), **Treasury bonds** (p. 156), **over-the-counter market** (p. 157), **capital gain** (p. 157),

broker (p. 157), **capital loss** (p. 158), **mutual fund** (p. 158), **money market fund** (p. 158), **inside information** (p. 159)

Reviewing Objectives
1. Stocks confer ownership, may rise or fall in value, have no fixed dividend. Bonds are debt, pay interest

at a fixed rate, and must have face value repaid at maturity.
2. mutual funds: purchase of a variety of stocks, bonds with relatively little money, but a degree of security; money market: check writing against investments
3. They are public knowledge.

Focus

Overview

See the student page for section objectives.

Section 3 explains or describes: the three types of retirement plans—pension plans, Keogh Plans, and Individual Retirement Accounts; and deciding how much to save and invest.

Bellringer

Before presenting the lesson, display Focus Activity Transparency 22 and assign the accompanying Focus Activity Sheet.

Motivational Activity

Have students write a short paragraph describing the level of income they hope to have during retirement and ask how they plan to accrue that income.

Preteaching Vocabulary

Have students read the Glossary definitions of the terms and use them to write a scenario about retirement.

SECTION 3 FOCUS

Terms to Know pension plans, Keogh Plan, Individual Retirement Account, diversification

Objectives *After reading this section, you should be able to:*
① Describe three kinds of **retirement investments**.
② Decide **how much to save and invest**.

Special Savings Plans Protect Your Future

One of the reasons that people save is to have income to spend when they retire. In addition to their savings, most Americans have additional sources of income for the years after they stop work.

Investing for Retirement

Many individuals have company retirement plans called **pension plans** that provide retirement income. Also, most people are eligible for, or able to receive, Social Security payments when they reach retirement. Nevertheless, many people choose to save and invest in private retirement plans. See **Figure 7.11**.

A major benefit of a private or personal pension plan is the tax savings. You do not have to pay federal income tax *immediately* on the earned income that you invest in one of these retirement plans, or on the interest that the plan earns if it does not exceed a certain amount. Should you need to take money out of the plan early, however, you have to pay a tax penalty. Otherwise, you pay income tax only as you withdraw money from the plan at retirement. Because your yearly income will in all probability be less then, your tax rate will be lower.

Individual Pension Plans The Keogh (KEE-oh) Act of 1972 was passed to help self-employed people set up their own pension plans. The **Keogh Plan** allows those people who are

Figure 7.11 Comfortable Retirement
Americans are living longer so there are more years of retirement for many. How do their earlier investing and saving decisions affect their lives?

▼

Chapter 7 Saving and Investing **161**

Classroom Resources for Section 3

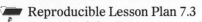

- Reproducible Lesson Plan 7.3
- Focus Activity Transparency 22
- Focus Activity Sheet 22
- Guided Reading Activity 7.3
- Economics Laboratory 2
- Economic Simulation 2

- Mathematics Practice for Economics 7
- Performance Assessment Activity 7
- Section Quiz 7.3
- Spanish Section Quiz 7.3
- Chapter 7 Test Forms A and B

- Testmaker
- Reinforcing Skills 7
- Enrichment Activity 7
- Economics Vocabulary Activity 7
- Audiocassette 7
- Spanish Audiocassette
- Reteaching Activity 7

Teach

Guided Practice

L2 Evaluating Ask students to discuss how their choice of occupation might influence the savings and investment plans they choose for themselves.

Visual Instruction

Have students study Figure 7.2 and ask if a house purchased in the West for $40,000 would sell for $140,000 in 1990? (It may depend on its maintenance, its location, etc.) Point out that the chart shows the changes in the median price of all existing homes in a region; not that a particular house would increase a certain amount.

DID YOU KNOW

The Social Security Act of 1935 was passed partly in response to the popularity of the Townsend Plan, proposed by a Dr. Francis E. Townsend of Long Beach, California. Townsend had proposed that all citizens over age 60, regardless of their employment status, would receive $200 per month, which they would be obligated to spend during that month. The money was expected to come from a 2 percent national sales tax. A version of the Townsend plan was voted down in 1939.

self-employed to set aside a maximum of 15 percent of their income up to a specified amount each year and deduct that amount from their yearly taxable income.

Another form of retirement plan is the **Individual Retirement Account** (IRA). As of 1986, a person who earns less than $25,000 can contribute up to $2,000 per year and deduct it from taxable income. For married couples who both work outside the home and have a combined income of less than $40,000, the allowable deduction is $4,000. If only one spouse works, the amount allowed is $2,250. For people covered by an employer pension plan, only a partial deduction is allowed for single people who earn between $25,000 and $35,000 and married couples who earn between $40,000 and $50,000. For people whose incomes exceed those limits, the law allows yearly nondeductible contributions of up to $2,000 or $2,250, with tax deferred on the interest.

Real Estate as an Investment Buying real estate, such as land and buildings, is another form of investing. For the past 50 years or so, an investment in one's own home, condominium, or co-op has often proven to be wise in many parts of the country. Resale values have soared at times, especially during the late 1970s. See Figure 7.12. In the early 1980s and again in the early 1990s, however, the growth in the price of housing slowed in some areas. In some places real estate values fell for a few years. Buying raw, or undeveloped, land is a much riskier investment. No one can guarantee that there will be a demand in the future for a particular piece of land. The same is true for housing, too, but most people do not buy housing for the purpose of selling it.

Figure 7.12 ▶
Home Prices
Variations in supply and demand produce different prices in different parts of the country. Which two regions of the country have had the highest housing price increases since 1975?

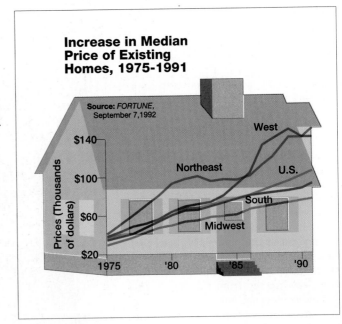

 Meeting Special Needs

Visual Disability Students who have visual disabilities may have trouble following calculations on the chalkboard. Call on these students to do calculations of interest on the chalkboard for the rest of the class.

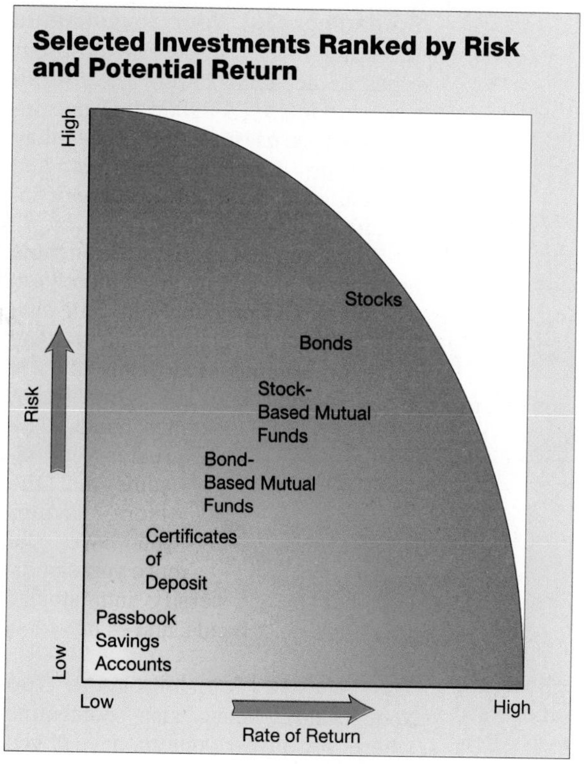

Selected Investments Ranked by Risk and Potential Return

◀ **Figure 7.13 Risk and Returns**

Figure 7.13 Risk and Returns

Perhaps the most risk-free investment is an insured pass-book savings account. Certainly, a CD is relatively risk-free. A slightly riskier investment is a mutual fund that invests in bonds issued by businesses. Why is this riskier? The market value of those bonds could fall. Some of the companies might go out of business and not be able to repay the bonds at maturity. In both cases, the value of your shares in the mutual fund would fall. You could also invest your savings in the stock or bond market directly. Here, you are taking the most risk. The market value of stocks can rise and fall dramatically and so, too, can the value of your investment.

L2 Planning Have students imagine they are investment consultants who want to diversify the holdings of a client. Have them create a personal profile of the client based on his or her job, values, and plans. Then have students write a proposal stating how the client should save or invest his or her income.

L3 Making a Concept Map Ask students to brainstorm about the companies, goods, and services they think are most valuable to individuals, the environment, and the economy. They might list existing investment possibilities or potential investments for the future. Ask students to note whether they think the businesses, goods, and services are secure or risky. Have students organize their ideas in a concept map of their personal investment values.

Have students complete Guided Reading Activity 7.3 in the TCR. **LEP**

Assess

Meeting Lesson Objectives

Assign Section 3 Review as homework or an in-class activity.

Real estate, either as raw land or developed land, is not very easy to turn into cash on short notice. Sometimes real property stays on the market for long periods of time. This difficulty in getting cash for your investment is one of the trade-offs involved in investing in real estate. You cannot get your money as quickly as you could if you had invested in stocks, bonds, a CD, or some other savings plan.

Deciding How Much to Save and Invest

Saving involves a trade-off like every other activity. The more you save today, the more you can buy and consume a year from now, 10 years from now, or 30 years from now. You will, however, have less to spend today. Deciding what percentage of income to save depends on the following factors:

- How much do you spend on your fixed expenses?
- What are your reasons for saving?
- How much interest can you earn on your savings and, therefore, how fast will they grow?
- How much income do you think you will be earning in the future?

If you expect to make a much higher income tomorrow, you have less reason to save a large percentage of today's income. In this case, it would be better to wait to start a large savings plan. It is a good idea, however, to have some sort of savings plan. There are several questions to answer before you decide on this plan:

- What degree of risk are you willing to take? Figure 7.13 ranks various investments according to risk.
- How important is it that your savings be readily available in case you need immediate cash?
- Will your standard of living at retirement depend largely on your accumulated savings?

Cooperative Learning

Organize students into small groups and ask each group to research and develop a plan for an investment club. Plans should consider conditions for membership, amount and frequency of contribution, delegation of responsibilities, types of investments to be made, distribution to members (or reinvest-

ment) of dividends or capital gains, and so forth.

Ask a representative from each club to present its plan to the class for review and discussion. Then suggest that the class select elements from the plans presented to form a club for the entire class membership.

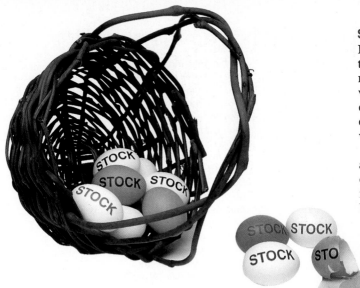

▲
**Figure 7.14
Lowering Risk**
"Don't put all your eggs in one basket" is a phrase you have certainly heard before. The theory behind it can be applied to how a person chooses to invest.

Spreading Out Your Investments
Investing money in several different types of accounts lowers the overall risk, as Figure 7.14 shows. If one investment turns sour, the others may do better. Financial planners and economists call spreading out your investments **diversification.**

When you have very little income and cannot afford any investment losses, you should probably put your savings in insured accounts in a local bank or savings and loan, or you should buy U.S. government savings bonds. The greater your income and the more savings you have, the more you can diversify into stocks, bonds, and so on.

Amount of Risk Such questions are difficult to answer because there are so many ways to save and invest. Perhaps the most important factor to consider is the amount of risk that you are willing to take with your savings.

If you put a lesser amount in the more risky types of investments, you would have some security with your savings and have some money available should you need cash in a hurry. You would also have a chance of making high returns.

Your Values Are Important, Too
Your values may also determine where you invest your money. If you believe that your community needs more development, you might choose to put your savings in a savings and loan there that guarantees that a large percentage of its investments are made in community loans. You may also choose to invest in stocks issued by environmentally responsible companies or companies that have aggressive equal opportunity programs.

SECTION 3 REVIEW

Understanding Vocabulary
Define pension plans, Keogh Plan, Individual Retirement Account, diversification.

Reviewing Objectives
1. What are three ways of investing for retirement?
2. How should a person determine the amount to save and invest?

Section 3 Review Answers
Understanding Vocabulary
pension plan (p. 161), **Keogh Plan** (p. 161), **Individual Retirement Account** (p. 162), diversification (p. 164)

Reviewing Objectives
1. Keogh Plans, IRAs, and real estate investments

2. Consider present fixed expenses; reasons for saving; savings growth rate; future income needs; cash availability need; risk; and standard of living at retirement.

LEARNING ECONOMIC SKILLS

Understanding Interest

Two types of interest exist: simple and compound. Do you know what the difference is?

Simple Interest

Simple interest is figured only on the original amount deposited, not on any interest earned. Figuring interest is similar to figuring percents. **Figure A** shows that a $100 savings account that pays 6 percent simple interest will earn $6 the first year. Therefore the account balance at the end of the year will be $106—the original amount plus the first year's interest. The second year the interest will also be $6, even though the account has grown, and the balance will be $112.

Compound Interest

Compound interest is paid on the original amount deposited plus any interest that has been earned. As **Figure B** shows, if you deposit $100 in an account earning 6 percent interest compounded annually, it will earn $6 the first year and $6.36 the second year. With compound interest, your savings the second year will amount to $112.36.

Figure A

6% = .06

```
$ 100
x  .06
$ 6.00  interest earned each year

$ 100   Original amount saved
    6   First year's interest
+   6   Second year's interest
$ 112   Total after two years
```

Figure B

```
$ 100
x  .06
$ 6.00  interest earned first year

$ 106
x  .06
$ 6.36  interest earned second year
```

Total after two years
$100 + $6 + $6.36 = $112.36

Practicing the Skill

❶ Assume that your bank pays 5.5 percent on savings deposits. What is the simple interest paid in the third year on an initial $50 deposit? How much is the total savings at the end of the third year?

❷ Assume that on $100 the interest paid is 5.5 percent compounded annually. How much interest is earned in the first, second, and third year? What is the total amount in the savings account after three years?

165

Answers to Practicing the Skill

1. $2.75, $58.25
2. $5.50/$5.80/$6.12; $117.42

Readings in Economics

MONEY   SEPTEMBER 1992

THE CASE FOR U.S. SAVINGS BONDS

by Michael Sivy

How can you beat the pitiful yields on today's CDs [certificates of deposit] without taking crazy risks? . . .

If you think you might need your money [soon], go with U.S. Savings Bonds. That's right: Series EE savings bonds. . . .

■ Fully backed by the U.S. Government, the bonds can be bought at most banks and may be available through payroll-deduction plans.

■ You can invest as much as $15,000 each year.

■ The bonds come in denominations as small as . . . a $50 face value. (The face value, which is double the purchase price, shows the minimum that a bond would grow to in 12 years.)

■ EE bonds don't pay cash interest; instead, the interest accrues and the bonds rise in value until you cash them in.

■ You can redeem the bonds after six months or hold them for as long as 30 years.

■ If you cash them in after six months, you collect an annualized rate that starts at 4.16% and rises to a minimum of 6% for bonds held five years or longer. . . .

■ In addition to being exempt from state and local taxes, your interest is not subject to federal income tax until you redeem the EEs.

■ After six months, you have the option of swapping $500 or more of Series EE bonds for Series HH issues, which pay 6% cash interest. If you swap, you don't have to pay taxes on the accumulated EE interest until you redeem the HHs. . . .

If all those terms sound complicated, just keep your eye on the bottom line: You get more than the average 3.2% a money fund pays if you cash in after six months. . . . So don't buy savings bonds only for patriotic reasons—buy them for profit, too.

7 Highlights

Use the Chapter 7 High-lights to preview, review, condense, or reteach the chapter. A Spanish Chapter Highlights is available in the Spanish Handbook.

Section 1

Why Save?

Key Terms

saving (p. 146)
interest (p. 146)
passbook savings account
  (p. 147)
statement savings
  account (p. 147)

money market deposit
  account (p. 148)
time deposits (p. 148)
maturity (p. 148)
certificates of deposit
  (p. 148)

Summary

Every person must decide when it is best to save and invest. Beginning investors should compare passbook, statement, and money market savings accounts. There are also advantages to saving in time deposit accounts.

Preview/Review

After students read the Chapter 7 Highlights, have them complete Economics Vocabulary Activity 7 in the TCR. Spanish Vocabulary Activities are also available in the Spanish Resource Binder.

Vocabulary Software reinforces the economic terms used in Chapter 7.

Section 2

Investing: Taking Risks With Your Savings

Key Terms

stock (p. 154)
stockholders (p. 155)
dividends (p. 155)
bond (p. 155)
tax-exempt bonds (p. 155)
savings bonds (p. 155)
Treasury bills (p. 156)
Treasury notes (p. 156)
Treasury bonds (p. 156)

over-the-counter market
  (p. 157)
capital gain (p. 157)
broker (p. 157)
capital loss (p. 158)
mutual fund (p. 158)
money market fund
  (p. 158)
inside information
  (p. 159)

Summary

Stocks and bonds offer an investor choices with distinct advantages. There are investment funds available in stock and bond markets that have less risk than individual stocks and bonds. "Hot" tips will not help an investor get rich quick in the stock market.

Condense

Have students listen to Chapter 7 on the Audiocassettes in the TCR. A 1-page written activity and 1-page test accompany this material. These materi-als are also available in Spanish.

Reteach

Have students com-plete Reteaching Activity 7 in the TCR. Spanish Reteaching Activities are also available.

Section 3

Special Savings Plans and Goals

Key Terms

pension plans (p. 161)
Keogh Plan (p. 161)
Individual Retirement
  Account, or IRA (p. 162)
diversification (p. 164)

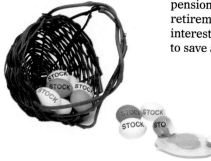

Summary

Individual and company-sponsored pensions plans help people save for retirement. A person should consider interest and risk in deciding how much to save and invest.

 VIDEODISC

Nightly Business Report
Economics in Action
Use "Saving and Invest-ing" on Disc 1, Side B, Video 10.

Search 10, Play to 6869

ANSWERS

Identifying Key Terms

1. d
2. e
3. a
4. c
5. b

Paragraphs will vary but should include terms specified.

Recalling Facts and Ideas

Section 1

1. easy availability of funds, usually without penalty or forfeit
2. because it requires the saver to leave money on deposit for a certain period of time
3. because they are insured by the federal government

Section 2

4. Stocks are ownership in a corporation; bonds are debt by governments and corporations; bondholders must be repaid both interest and principal.
5. They are an extremely safe investment, and the interest earned is exempt from federal taxes until the bond is redeemed.
6. capital gain or capital loss
7. a mutual fund
8. the Securities and Exchange Commission (SEC)

Section 3

9. company retirement plans and Social Security
10. You can calculate fixed expenses, analyze your reasons for saving, calculate the amount you can earn on savings, and think about probable future earnings.
11. diversification

Identifying Key Terms

Write the letter of the definition in Column B below that correctly defines each term in Column A.

Column A
1. mutual fund (p. 158)
2. savings bond (p. 155)
3. stock (p. 154)
4. dividend (p. 155)
5. capital gain (p. 157)

Column B
a. represents part ownership in a corporation
b. an increase in wealth realized when a person sells an asset
c. the money return a stockholder receives from a corporation on an investment
d. a less risky way to invest in stocks and bonds
e. a government security attractive to small investors

Write a paragraph describing the different types of accounts that are available in banks, savings and loan associations, and credit unions. Make sure you include the following:

passbook savings account (p. 147)
statement savings account (p. 147)
money market deposit account (p. 148)

time deposit (p. 148)
certificate of deposit (CD) (p. 148)

Recalling Facts and Ideas

Section 1

1. What is the main advantage of passbook and statement savings accounts?
2. Why is a certificate of deposit (CD) called a time deposit?

3. Why are deposits of up to $100,000 in savings institutions often considered very safe?

Section 2

4. What is the basic difference between a stock and a bond?
5. What are two advantages of United States savings bonds?
6. What term describes the difference between the purchase price of a stock and the sale price of a stock?
7. What kind of investment company hires professionals to manage the investments of a pool of investors?
8. What government agency regulates stock and bond markets?

Section 3

9. What are the two most common types of pension plans for individuals?
10. What are some of the ways you can decide how much you should save?
11. "Don't put all your eggs in one basket." This quotation is an example of what principle of investing?

Critical Thinking

Section 1

Understanding Cause and Effect How does buying a U.S. savings bond increase the United States government's debt?

Section 2

Drawing Conclusions Bonds yield a more certain return than stocks. Why do individuals, nonetheless, invest in stocks?

Critical Thinking

Section 1

When an investor purchases a bond, he or she is loaning money. U.S. savings bonds are loans to the United States. Therefore, they increase the debt of the United States.

Section 2

because they may offer a greater opportunity to increase their capital and/or obtain a return on their money from dividends

Section 3

Answers will vary but may include combinations of the following: money market and other mutual funds; time deposits; individual stocks, bonds, and treasury securities; and savings bonds. Some may be included in retirement plans such as a Keogh Plan or an Individual Retirement Account.

Section 3

Identifying Alternatives Assume that you have $100,000 in savings. Write a list of the potential investments you might make and what percentage of the $100,000 you would invest in each. Would your plan be diversified?

Applying Economic Concepts

Scarcity Write down a list of short-term saving goals, such as saving to buy a new portable CD player. Make a list of the typical ways in which you can save for such a purchase. Then make a list of long-term saving goals, such as saving for a house or retirement. Make a separate list of the ways you could achieve your goals. What is the major difference between the two ways of saving?

Chapter Projects

1. **Individual Project** Choose two stocks on the New York or American stock exchange, and follow their prices for two weeks in the financial pages of a newspaper. You will need to read only the last column of figures. Note the daily closing prices for each stock, and then make a line graph showing the stocks' performance over the two-week period.
2. **Cooperative Learning Project** Work in groups of four. Each group will study the results of an investment of $100,000 in one of the following (choose from the list depending on the number of groups you have):

   ■ One particular stock
   ■ One particular bond
   ■ A mutual fund
   ■ U.S. Treasury bonds
   ■ Residential real estate

   ■ Commercial real estate (office buildings, for example)
   ■ Old masters paintings (such as those by Renoir and Rembrandt)
   ■ Gold
   ■ Diamonds

Each group should research either in the library or through a securities brokerage firm in your area to determine what $100,000 placed in each one of those investments 10 years ago would be worth today. Rank and compare those rates of return.

Reviewing Skills

Understanding Interest

1. **Figuring Simple Interest** A local bank is offering simple interest on savings accounts at 6.6 percent per year. If you deposit $1,000, how much will you have in the account at the end of four years?
2. **Understanding Compound Interest** Another bank in the same area is offering the same interest rate but indicates that it is compounding interest annually. If you deposit your $1,000 there, how much more will you have in your savings account at the end of three years in the second bank than in the first bank?

Writing About Economics

Descriptive Writing Reexamine the list of interest rates paid by various institutions that you compiled for Your Economics Journal. Write a descriptive paragraph explaining in which institution you will deposit your savings. Explain why.

169

A Word From the Teacher

This project may be adjusted to fit the time period you have available. Encourage your students and their families to take the trips the students have planned. Students will amaze you with their grasp of economics and geography.

Art Benfield

Focus

An educated consumer is one who has determined his or her needs and wants, considered trade-offs and opportunity costs, and then found the best choice to balance wants and costs. Review with students the effects of opportunity costs and time and money costs in deciding upon purchases and courses of action.

The purpose of this lab is to apply consumer decisions in a real-life situation.

Teach

Planning a Trip can be done in class, but it works better if students have time to visit a library, do outside research, and ask questions at home. If the lab extends over many days or weeks, allow time to occasionally check students' progress.

Steps A and C may be completed in class if students and/or the teacher brings travel guides and road maps. Step B may be completed in class, if the

Planning a Trip
From the classroom of Art Benfield, South High School, Pueblo, Colorado

In Unit 2 you studied practical economics for the consumer. In this experiment, you will apply consumer decisions in planning a vacation trip. (You may want to reread the material on pages 58–61 of the text.)

One important means of making wise consumer choices is planning those choices. For example, planning a vacation trip is a challenge because of the many trade-offs and opportunity costs involved in your decisions. Also, you should determine before taking a vacation what the total costs in time and money are going to be.

Libraries and media centers contain many materials that will help you plan the trip. Many have newspapers from several cities that carry local advertising for food, lodging, and entertainment. In addition, travel agents, family, and friends may suggest places to visit and may be able to estimate costs for lodging or entertainment in these locations.

Tools

1. A travel atlas
2. Motel guidebooks
3. Chamber of Commerce guide books
4. Government guides

Procedures

Step A Using a travel atlas and other guidebooks and resources, plan a trip from your home to anywhere in North America that can be reached by car. The round-trip must be at least 2,000 miles in length, but not more than 350 miles in one day. You should include the names or number of people who will be going along. At some point along the way, you must do all of the following at least once:
1. Visit a geographic point of interest: high mountain, body of water, desert, national forest, etc.
2. Visit a scientific point of interest: aquarium, natural history museum, museum of science and industry, NASA, etc.
3. Stay overnight in one large city and eat in a fancy restaurant.
4. Attend one cultural event such as a play, symphony, or ethnic festival.
5. Attend one sports event or entertainment point of interest such as a theme park or dude ranch.

170

teacher provides a table of average costs for food, fuel, lodging, and entertainment.

When consumers become aware that planning can help them find alternatives with the lowest opportunity costs and total costs in time and money, they can execute plans in an efficient way, without stopping to rethink or abort

their plans. The list of activities in Step A provides a variety of circumstances requiring different expenditures of time and money. Have each student choose a route to follow. Some students may choose solo trips and others group trips.

Step B Research the costs and complete a daily journal, like the one on this page, for each day of the trip. Include the following:
1. route and miles traveled
2. fuel and food costs
3. lodging (name of motel or other lodging and location) and cost
4. itemized list of entertainment and costs

Step C Complete a map highlighting the route of your trip.

Example

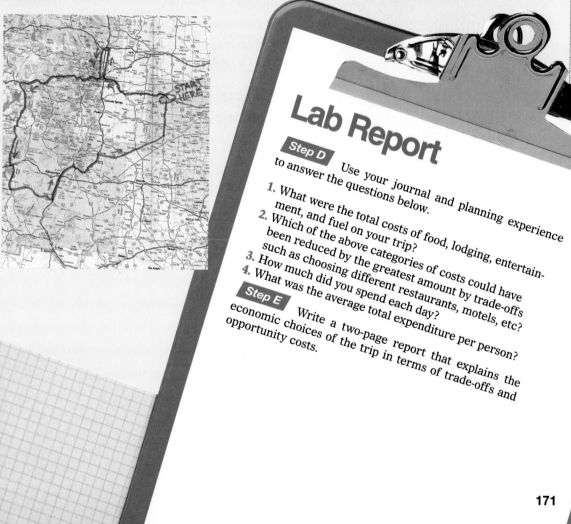

Sample Daily Journal
DAY 1
Route and miles traveled: _____
Places of interest visited: _____

Item	Cost		
Entertainment			
Fuel			
Food	breakfast	lunch	dinner
Shopping/other costs			
Lodging	room	phone	other

Lab Report

Step D Use your journal and planning experience to answer the questions below.
1. What were the total costs of food, lodging, entertainment, and fuel on your trip?
2. Which of the above categories of costs could have been reduced by the greatest amount by trade-offs such as choosing different restaurants, motels, etc?
3. How much did you spend each day?
4. What was the average total expenditure per person?

Step E Write a two-page report that explains the economic choices of the trip in terms of trade-offs and opportunity costs.

Have each student complete Step D (the journal) and Step E (the report). Assign the class to small groups that mix individual and group plans. Have students in each group share their reports and comment on ways their classmates might save opportunity costs. Encourage students to revise their plans in response to group comments.

Close

Discuss with students the trade-offs they made to minimize costs for their trips. After discussion, have students write evaluations of the trade-offs they made.

❓ DID YOU KNOW

State tourist bureaus and local chambers of commerce can provide information about historic sites, tourist attractions, and food and lodging. Many areas of the United States also are served by American Youth Hostels, an association that provides inexpensive lodging to young people and, sometimes, families.

Answers to Lab Report

Lab Report D
Students' journal entries should be organized into tables that show food, lodging, entertainment, and fuel costs of each day of the trip. Students should be able to cite sources for their estimates about costs in various locations.

Lab Report E
Review students' two-page reports written in their journals. Look for revisions and amendments based on information and advice given in the small groups.

Unit Goals

After studying this unit, students will be able to:

Explain the laws of supply and demand as they apply to voluntary markets.

Characterize the types of business organizations.

Discuss how competition and monopolies affect prices.

Unit Overview

Unit 3 introduces the laws of supply and demand, business organization, and the effect of competition and monopolies on prices.

Chapter 8 explains: the law of demand; the demand curve; elasticity of demand; the law of supply; and the supply curve in a voluntary market.

Chapter 9 describes: starting a business; operating a business; full partnerships, limited partnerships, and joint ventures; corporations; and franchises.

Chapter 10 explains or describes: perfect competition, its desirability, and agriculture as a model of it; pure monopoly, oligopoly and monopolistic competition; interlocking directorates; federal regulation; and reregulation.

`0:00` OUT OF TIME?

If time does not permit teaching each chapter in this unit, you may use the Chapter Highlights and the Audiocassettes that include a 1-page activity and a 1-page test for each chapter.

U N I T

MICROECONOMICS: MARKETS, PRICES, AND BUSINESS COMPETITION

172

Economic Simulation

Price Setting and Competition Choose three small groups to represent companies A, B, and C, which make videotapes of the same quality. The remainder of the class will simulate the buying public. In scenario I, allow three rounds of price setting and three rounds of voting to buy by the class.

Observe whether demand is affected. In scenario II, company A can always underprice the competition. Allow another three rounds of price setting and voting to buy. Encourage discussion of possible strategies by companies B and C to overcome company A's competitive edge.

Did You Know

- More than 10 million individuals own their own businesses.
- Corporations account for about 90 percent of all business revenues each year.
- About two out of three new businesses fail within the first few years after being started.
- Franchises like McDonald's and Hilton Hotels account for hundreds of billions of dollars of retail sales each year.
- The federal government often helps small businesses get started.

In this unit you will learn how supply and demand interact in our economy, and the different types of business organizations and how they affect the prices of the products you buy.

 Did You Know

The following were leading franchises in 1992.

McDonald's, Subway (fast food), Dunkin' Donuts, Jani-King (commercial cleaning), Baskin-Robbins USA (ice cream), ServiceMaster (home and office cleaning), Chem-Dry (cleaning services), Hardee's (fast food), Arby's (fast food), Domino's Pizza, Dairy Queen (ice cream), Choice Hotels, Coverall North America (commercial cleaning), Jazzercise (fitness center), Midas (auto repair), Mail Boxes Etc. (shipping services), 7-Eleven Stores, H&R Block (income-tax services), Coldwell Banker Residential (real estate), Blockbuster Video, Budget Rent A Car, KFC (fast food), Merle Norman Cosmetics, Re/Max International (real estate), Electronic Realty Associates

CHAPTER 8 SUPPLY AND DEMAND

CHAPTER ORGANIZER

Daily Objectives	Special Features	Classroom Resources
Section 1 Demand • **Describe** how the principle of voluntary exchange operates in a market economy. • **Explain** how diminishing marginal utility, the real income effect, and the substitution effect relate to the law of demand.	**Focus on Free Enterprise:** Case Study, The Body Shop, pp. 180–181	Reproducible Lesson Plan 8.1 *NBR* Video 6 and Video Stills 6 and 7 Focus Activity Transparency 26 Focus Activity Sheet 26 Economic Concepts Transparency 6 Guided Reading Activity 8.1 Primary and Secondary Source Readings 8 Section Quiz 8.1
Section 2 The Demand Curve and the Elasticity of Demand • **Explain** what you can learn by graphing the demand curve. • **Describe** how the price elasticity of demand affects how much the price for a given product can vary. • **Discuss** the determinants of demand.	**Personal Perspective:** Alfred Marshall on Supply and Demand, p. 190	Reproducible Lesson Plan 8.2 Focus Activity Transparency 27 Focus Activity Sheet 27 Guided Reading Activity 8.2 Section Quiz 8.2 Spanish Section Quiz 8.2 Testmaker
Section 3 The Law of Supply and the Supply Curve • **Explain** how the incentive of greater profit affects supply. • **Describe** the relationships that the supply curve shows.	**Critical Thinking Skills:** Determining Cause and Effect, p. 195	Reproducible Lesson Plan 8.3 *NBR* Video 8 and Video Still 5 Focus Activity Transparency 29 Focus Activity Sheet 29 Guided Reading Activity 8.3 Section Quiz 8.3 Testmaker Reinforcing Skills 8
Section 4 Putting Supply and Demand Together • **List** the four determinants of supply and describe how they change supply. • **Explain** how the equilibrium price is determined. • **Explain** how shortages and surpluses affect price. • **Describe** how shifts in equilibrium price occur. • **Discuss** how the forces underlying supply and demand affect prices.	**News Clip:** "Blue Jeans As Tuna Fish," *Forbes*, p. 202	Reproducible Lesson Plan 8.4 *NBR* Video 11 Focus Activity Transparency 35 Focus Activity Sheet 35 Economic Concepts Transparencies 7 and 8 Guided Reading Activity 8.4 Free Enterprise Activity 8 Consumer Application Activity 8 Section Quiz 8.4 Enrichment Activity 8

0:00 **OUT OF TIME?** If time does not permit teaching this chapter, you may use the Chapter 8 Highlights and the Audiocassettes that include a 1-page activity and a 1-page test.

Chapter 8 Review and Evaluation

Special Features	Classroom Resources	

Chapter 8 Highlights, p. 203
Chapter 8 Review, pp. 204–205

- Chapter 8 Test Forms A and B
- Economics Vocabulary Activity 8
- Spanish Economics Vocabulary Activity 8

- Audiocassette 8
- Spanish Audiocassette 8
- Reteaching Activity 8
- Spanish Reteaching Activity 8

Key to Ability Levels

Teaching strategies have been coded for varying learning styles and abilities.

L1 Level 1 activities are **basic** activities and should be within the ability range of all students.

L2 Level 2 activities are **average** activities designed for the ability of average to above-average students.

L3 Level 3 activities are **challenging** activities designed for the ability range of above-average students.

LEP activities are within the ability range of **Limited English Proficiency** students.

Performance Assessment

The following chapter project may be assigned at the beginning of the chapter and be used for performance assessment. See page T12 for additional Performance Assessment information.

Analyzing Sales Have students work in small groups to investigate local demand for given products. Students should work with a local merchant to obtain weekly sales figures over a three- or four- week period. Have students use the information to predict the level of demand that can be expected and to give reasons for their predictions.

Additional Resources

Readings for the Student

Ambry, Margaret K., and Cheryl Russell. *The Official Guide to the American Marketplace.* Ithaca, N.Y.: New Strategist Publications, 1992.

Prus, Robert C. *Pursuing Customers.* Newbury Park, Calif.: Sage Publications, 1989.

Readings for the Teacher

Conroy, Thomas F,. editor. *Markets for U.S. Business Planners.* Detroit: Omnigraphics, 1992.

Rugman, Alan M. *Multinationals and Canada-U.S. Free Trade.* Columbia, S.C.: University of South Carolina Press, 1990.

Multimedia Materials

Gadgetronics: A Retail Decision-Making Simulation. Apple, IBM. South-Western Publishing Co., Subsidiary of International Thomson, Inc. 5101 Madison Road, Cincinnati, OH 45227

Market Prices: Supply and Demand. Part 9 of the Give and Take Series. Videotape. 15 min. Agency for Instructional Technology. Box A, Bloomington, IN 47402.

Supply. From the People on Market Street Series. 16 mm film or videotape. 19 min. Walt Disney Educational Media Corp. 500 S. Buena Vista St., Burbank, CA 91521.

Chapter Overview

Consumers base their decision to buy goods and services on anticipated satisfaction, price, and affordability. Businesses set prices according to the profit needed, the demand anticipated, and the competition expected. Chapter 8 discusses the laws of supply and demand and the ways in which a voluntary market alters them.

 VIDEODISC

Nightly Business Report
Economics in Action
Use "What Is Demand?"
on Disc 1, Side A,
Video 6.

Search 26984, Play to 31984

CHAPTER

8 SUPPLY AND DEMAND

What are these people doing?

Does anyone tell them how many CDs to purchase?

What determines how many CDs they want to purchase?

174   Unit 3   Microeconomics: Markets, Prices, and Business Competition

Answering Economic Questions

The questions in the above illustration are designed to lead into the main concepts in Chapter 8. Students may not have thought about the value of compact discs, because the price of them seems set by the time the CDs reach a store. These questions will help students become more aware of the decision making that goes into pricing the goods and services they buy.

Have students discuss the questions and explain their reasons for thinking as they do.

Will the price of CDs go up or down in the future?

Why are there sales for specific CDs at certain stores?

Does the government ever regulate the price of CDs?

Your Economics Journal

Keep a record of the things that you thought about buying, but did not buy during one week. After you list these items, indicate next to each one why you decided *not* to buy that item.

175

Connecting to Past Learning

Ask students how they decide where to shop and what to buy. List their responses on the chalkboard as a volunteer records them for discussion after finishing the chapter. Tell students that in Chapter 8 they will learn how prices are set by the laws of supply and demand and the effects of competition and of monopolies. After students read the chapter, compare and contrast their ideas about purchases with their ideas before reading the chapter.

Applying Economics

Tell students to imagine they have $500 to spend as they please. However, they will not be able to obtain large amounts of spending money for another six months. Have them make a list of the purchases they would consider and then highlight those they would probably make. Discuss with students the factors that went into the decisions they made.

 EXTRA CREDIT PROJECT

Do a research paper on the history of business trusts and their effects on competition in the United States. Be sure to include some discussion of government responses to trusts.

 PERFORMANCE ASSESSMENT

Refer to page 174B for "Analyzing Sales," a Performance Assessment Activity for this chapter.

Economic Portfolio

Ask students to examine their contribution to the local retail economy and record their data in their portfolios. First, have students record an estimate of their personal spending per month in four categories: food, clothing, entertainment, and other items. Have students copy these amounts on an unsigned slip of paper. Let volunteers collect the papers and tally the amounts on the chalkboard. Students should use the totals to create a circle graph showing the percentage of spending by the class in each category. Elicit student reactions about their total contribution to the economy.

Focus

Overview

See the student page for section objectives.

Section 1 explains or describes the principle of voluntary exchange as it applies to a market economy and how diminishing marginal utility, the real income effect, and the substitution effect each alter demand and affect prices.

Bellringer

Before presenting the lesson, display Focus Activity Transparency 26 on the overhead projector or copy the material on the chalkboard. Assign the accompanying Focus Activity Sheet.

Motivational Activity

Write the following statement on the chalkboard for students to complete: When I buy something, I usually expect ____. Discuss responses.

Preteaching Vocabulary

Ask students to work in small groups to create improvisational scenes about buying goods from a small business. Have the rest of the class call out vocabulary terms at intervals and have the student actors show how the concept behind the term would affect the scene.

SECTION **1** Demand

SECTION 1 FOCUS

Terms to Know voluntary exchange, law of demand, utility, law of diminishing marginal utility, real income effect, substitution effect

Objectives *After reading this section, you should be able to:*
1. Describe how the principle of voluntary exchange operates in a market economy.
2. Explain how diminishing marginal utility, the real income effect, and the substitution effect relate to the law of demand.

Demand Plays a Major Role in a Market Economy

When you buy something, do you ever wonder why it sells at that particular price? Few individual consumers feel they have any influence over the price of an item. In a market economy, however, all consumers collectively, or as a group, have a great influence on the price of all goods and services. Perhaps the best way to understand this is to look first at how people in the marketplace decide what to buy and at what price. This is demand. Then examine how the people who want to sell those things decide how much to sell and at what price. This is supply.

What is the marketplace? A market represents the freely chosen action between buyers and sellers of goods and services. A market for a particular item can be local, national, and international. In a market economy, individuals looking out for their own best interests decide for themselves the answers to the four basic economic questions you studied in Chapter 2.

Figure 8.1 Voluntary Exchange
By definition, the two parties to a voluntary exchange are freely choosing to engage in that transaction, or business deal. In order to make the exchange, both must believe they will be better off—happier and richer.

The Market and Voluntary Exchange

The basis of activity in a market economy is the principle of **voluntary exchange.** A buyer and a seller exercise their economic freedoms by working out on their own the terms of an exchange. For example in **Figure 8.1**, the seller of an automobile sets a price based on the market, and the buyer,

176

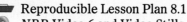

Classroom Resources for Section 1

- Reproducible Lesson Plan 8.1
- *NBR* Video 6 and Video Stills 6 and 7
- Focus Activity Transparency 26
- Focus Activity Sheet 26
- Economic Concepts Transparency 6
- Guiding Reading Activity 8.1

- Section Quiz 8.1
- Cooperative Learning Activity 8
- Primary and Secondary Source Readings 8
- Spanish Section Quiz 8.1
- Testmaker

through the act of buying, agrees to the product and the price.

Through the principle of voluntary exchange, supply and demand enter into the activity of a market economy. Remember, supply and demand analysis is a model of how buyers and sellers operate in the marketplace. Such analysis is a way of explaining cause and effect in relation to price.

The Law of Demand

The **law of demand** explains how people react to changing prices in terms of the quantities of a good or service that they purchase. Look at **Figure 8.2** to see this relationship. The word *demand* has a special meaning in economics. It represents all of the different quantities of a good or service that consumers will purchase at various prices. It includes both the willingness and the ability to pay. A person may say he or she wants a new compact disc. Until that person is both willing and able to buy it, no demand for compact discs has been created by that individual.

Several factors affect how much people will buy of any item at a particular price. These factors include diminishing marginal utility, real income, and possible substitutes.

Diminishing Marginal Utility Almost everything that people like, desire, use, think they would like to use, and so on, gives satisfaction. The term economists use for satisfaction is *utility*. **Utility** is defined as the power that a good or service has to satisfy a want. People decide what to buy and how much they are willing and able to pay based on utility. In deciding to make a purchase, they decide the amount of satisfaction, or use, they think they will get from a good or service. Consider the utility that can be derived from a compact disc.

At $8.00 per compact disc, how many will you buy? Assuming that you have money, you will buy at least one. Will you buy a second? A third? A

fourth? That decision depends on the additional utility, or satisfaction, you expect to receive from buying and listening to another compact disc. You will have a higher level of total, or overall, satisfaction from owning more compact discs. Most likely, the satisfaction you receive from each additional one, however, will be less than for each previous one. This example explains the **law of diminishing marginal utility.** See **Figure 8.3**.

Your *total* satisfaction will rise with each unit bought. But the amount of *additional* satisfaction, or marginal

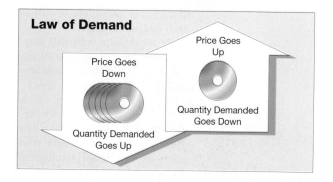

Law of Demand

Price Goes Down

Price Goes Up

Quantity Demanded Goes Up

Quantity Demanded Goes Down

▲ **Figure 8.2 The Law of Demand**
According to the law of demand, quantity demanded and price move in opposite directions.

As price goes up, quantity demanded goes down. As price goes down, quantity demanded goes up. There is an inverse, or opposite, relationship between demand and price.

Figure 8.3 Diminishing Satisfaction ▼
Regardless of how satisfying the first taste of an item is, satisfaction declines with additional consumption. Even at a zero price, eventually the consumer receives no additional satisfaction and stops eating.

177

Meeting Special Needs

Conceptual Disability Students with conceptual difficulties might benefit by using the concepts of the law of diminishing marginal utility, the real income effect, and the substitution effect in a concrete way. With the students, develop a simulation in which they alter the level of their demand for an item according to different conditions.

L3 Business Planning Have students develop plans to increase demand for a given item or service. Have them include in their plans the pitfalls, risks, and trade-offs they foresee and the measures they suggest to deal with them.

L1 Cartooning Have students create a cartoon (the cartoons may use stick figures) showing how people in different occupations or lifestyles might affect demand for goods and services in different ways. Encourage students to display their cartoons in the classroom.

Have students complete Guided Reading Activity 8.1 in the TCR. **LEP**

Visual Instruction

Ask students to restudy Figure 8.4 and to reread the captions. Encourage volunteers to discuss how their buying habits changed because of a rise in prices and/or a reduction in income.

---

utility, will diminish, or lessen, with each additional unit.

At some point, you will stop buying additional compact discs. At that point, the satisfaction that you receive from owning more compact discs is less than the value you place on the $8.00 that you must pay for the item. People stop buying an item when one event occurs—when the value that they place on additional satisfaction from the next unit of the same item becomes less than the price they must pay for it. Assume that at a price of $8.00 per disc, you have enough after buying three. Thus, the value you place on additional satisfaction from a fourth one would be less than $8.00. According to what will give you the most satisfaction, you will save or spend the $8.00 on something else.

What if the price drops? Suppose the owner of the music store decided to have a special and sell compact discs at $7.00 each. You might buy at least one additional one.

If you look at the law of diminishing marginal utility again, the reason becomes clear. People will buy an item to the point at which the value they place on the satisfaction from the last unit bought is equal to the price. At that point, people will stop buying. If the price falls again, the lower price will attract people to buy more. This principle is true even though the satisfaction from each additional unit is less. People will continue to buy to the point again at which the satisfaction they receive falls below the price they must pay. This concept explains part of the law of demand. As the price of an item that people want decreases, they will generally buy more.

Real Income Effect The basis for the law of demand, however, does not rest only on diminishing marginal utility. No one—not even the wealthiest person in the world—will ever be able to buy everything he or she wants to buy. People's incomes limit the amount of

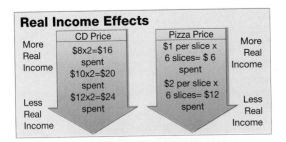

Real Income Effects

	CD Price	Pizza Price	
More Real Income	$8x2=$16 spent $10x2=$20 spent $12x2=$24 spent	$1 per slice x 6 slices= $ 6 spent $2 per slice x 6 slices= $12 spent	More Real Income
Less Real Income			Less Real Income

▲ **Figure 8.4**
Income Limits Spending

A Suppose that you normally buy two new compact discs (CDs) per month at $8 per disc. That means that you spend $16. If the price goes up to $10 per CD, you would have to spend $20 per month to buy two. If the price of CDs continues to rise while your income does not, eventually you would not be able to buy two CDs per month because your real income, or purchasing power, has been reduced.

Cooperative Learning

Organize students into small groups to research consumer demand and its effect, if any, on the prices of goods and services during the U.S. recession period of 1991 and 1992. Have students explore such purchases as housing, shoes, soft drinks, food, and movies. Ask a member of each group to report its finding. Compare results to rate the effect of consumer demand from most to least.

money they are able to spend as shown in **Figure 8.4**.

Individuals cannot keep buying the same quantity of a good if its price rises while their income stays the same. This concept is known as the **real income effect** on demand. In order to keep buying the same number of compact discs per month, you would need to cut back on buying other things. The real income effect forces you to make a trade-off. The same is true for every item you buy, particularly those you buy on a regular basis.

The real income effect works in the opposite direction, too. If you are already buying two compact discs a month and the price drops in half, your real income increases. You will have more purchasing power and will probably increase the number of compact discs that you buy each month.

Substitution Effect Suppose two items that are not exactly the same satisfy basically the same need. Their cost is about the same. If the price of one falls, people will most likely substitute it in favor of the now higher-priced good. If the price of one of the items rises in relation to the price of the other, people will substitute the now lower-priced good. This principle is called the **substitution effect.** Suppose, for example, that you listen to both compact discs and audiocassettes. If the price of audiocassettes drops dramatically, you will probably buy more cassettes and fewer compact discs. In effect, you are substituting the lower-priced cassettes for the now relatively higher-priced compact discs. Alternatively, if the price of audiocassettes doubles, you probably will increase the number of compact discs you buy.

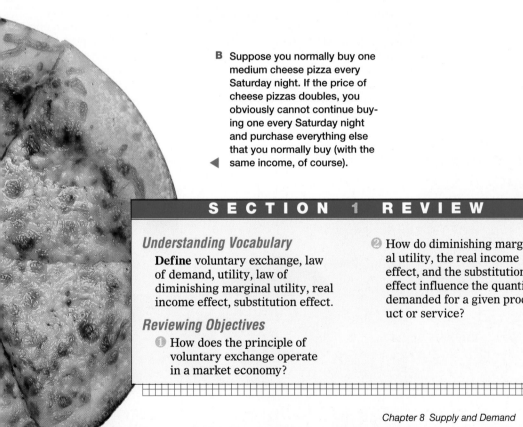

B Suppose you normally buy one medium cheese pizza every Saturday night. If the price of cheese pizzas doubles, you obviously cannot continue buying one every Saturday night and purchase everything else that you normally buy (with the same income, of course).

SECTION 1 REVIEW

Understanding Vocabulary

Define voluntary exchange, law of demand, utility, law of diminishing marginal utility, real income effect, substitution effect.

Reviewing Objectives

① How does the principle of voluntary exchange operate in a market economy?

② How do diminishing marginal utility, the real income effect, and the substitution effect influence the quantity demanded for a given product or service?

Assess

Meeting Lesson Objectives

Assign Section 1 Review as homework or an in-class activity. Each question in the Review addresses the corresponding numbered objective in the Section Focus.

Evaluate

Assign the Section 1 Quiz in the TCR or use the Testmaker to develop a customized quiz.

Reteach

Have students create a flow chart showing the decisions a consumer considering two or more items at two or more stores must make.

Enrich

Encourage students to research gasoline price wars in relation to changes in demand.

Close

Have students write about examples from personal experience to describe how individual and group buying patterns affect the market economy.

Section 1 Review Answers

Understanding Vocabulary

voluntary exchange (p.176), **law of demand** (p.177), **utility** (p.177), **law of diminishing marginal utility** (p.177), **real income effect** (p.179), **substitution effect** (p.179)

Reviewing Objectives

1. The buyer and seller work out the terms of an exchange. The seller sets a price based on the market; the buyer agrees to the product and price by purchasing the product.

2. Diminishing marginal utility is the lower level of satisfaction that results from additional purchases of a good or service. The real income effect recognizes that people are able to buy less of an item if the price goes up more than their income rises. The substitution effect states that if two items satisfy the same want, the lower-priced object will be more in demand.

CASE STUDY

The Body Shop

Starting Out The Body Shop was founded by Anita Roddick, a 33-year-old English woman with two young daughters and a husband—Gordon. The original idea was to open a store that would feature lotions and cosmetics made from all-natural ingredients. Shortly after the first store was established, Gordon left on an extended trip to South America (a lifelong dream to ride from Buenos Aires to New York on horseback). Anita proceeded and opened her second store (in Chichester, U.K.) using a small loan from a local gas station owner. By the time Gordon returned, the second store was successful. The Roddicks were ready to expand The Body Shop throughout England.

The company grew quickly, raising capital by a public stock offering in 1984. On the first day of its trading, the price of a share of The Body Shop stock rose dramatically. By 1988, Anita Roddick decided to expand to the United States. Originally, she planned to start slowly and forego franchising, but the slow expansion left The Body Shop lagging in the United States natural cosmetics market. Vigorous expansion in the United States began when Roddick started franchising The Body Shop in 1990.

Anita's Causes The success of The Body Shop is driven not only by its products, but by its "causes." Anita Roddick may be as well known for her environmentalism as for her business sense. From the beginning, The Body Shop has been environmentally conscious, using, for example, biodegradable products and refillable containers. Roddick also uses her stores to promote such causes as saving the whales and saving rain forests. In 1992 she used her United States shops as voter registration centers, signing up 50,000 new voters. In late 1993, she planned to open a store in Harlem, and invest the store's profits in the surrounding community.

Information Please Part of The Body Shop's success stems from its unique marketing plan. The Body Shop has no official marketing department and does not advertise, but instead makes plenty of information available to clients inside the stores. Store shelves are packed with all sorts of information (labels, pamphlets, etc.) about its products. While most of the cosmetics industry promotes fantasy and glamour, The Body Shop promotes well-being. To reach the more socially conscious customer of the '90s, The Body Shop presents information that shows it really cares about its clients, as well as about environmental and social issues.

Free Enterprise in Action

1. What type of products does The Body Shop sell?
2. How does The Body Shop show concern for environmental and social issues?
3. Why would information replace advertising as a marketing tool?

Answers to Free Enterprise In Action

1. lotions and cosmetics made from all natural ingredients
2. The Body Shop uses biodegradable products and reusable containers; it promotes causes such as saving whales and rain forests, voter registration, and investing in minority communities.
3. Answers will vary but should indicate that information attracts customers to the store and shows that The Body Shop really cares about its customers, environmental issues, and social problems.

TEACHING: Focus on Free Enterprise

L2 Interpreting Information
Have students discuss the differences between The Body Shop and many other cosmetics stores or lines. Ask: How did investors react when stock in The Body Shop was first offered? Explain your answer. (*They showed strong interest, because the price rose dramatically.*) How does the market plan of The Body Shop differ from that of most of the cosmetics industry? (*The Body Shop promotes well-being rather than fantasy or glamour.*)

L2 Analyzing and Inferring
Ask students to keep track of broadcast and print advertisements for cosmetics and personal care products such as hair shampoos and deodorants for a week. Suggest creating a chart naming each product under the suitable heading, Glamour or Well-being, together with the advertised reason it belongs there. Have students critique the advertised claims.

Assess

Have students write an editorial about whether laws should require cosmetics advertisers to prove all claims about products. Discuss the editorials.

Close

Ask students to think of ways that cosmetics makers could better satisfy consumers' wants.

Focus

Overview

See the student page for section objectives.

Section 2 explains or describes: graphing the demand curve; elastic and inelastic demand; and what factors determine demand.

Bellringer

Before presenting the lesson, display Focus Activity Transparency 27 on the overhead projector or copy the material on the chalkboard. Assign the accompanying Focus Activity Sheet.

Motivational Activity

Write on the chalkboard several traffic symbols and other international signs such as stop, no trucks, no left turn, and exit.

Ask students to explain the benefit of using visuals instead of words. Tell students that Section 2 will describe the advantages of graphs in providing visual information about demand.

Preteaching Vocabulary

Have students play a game of "Clues on Demand." Ask eight volunteers (one for each term plus one foil) to develop several clues for each one of the vocabulary terms. Play proceeds with volunteers one by one giving clues to a term until someone guesses correctly.

SECTION **2** The Demand Curve and the Elasticity of Demand

SECTION 2 FOCUS

Terms to Know demand curve, elasticity, price elasticity of demand, elastic demand, inelastic demand, complementary good

Objectives *After reading this section, you should be able to:*
1. Explain what you can learn by **graphing the demand curve**.
2. Describe how the **price elasticity of demand** affects how much the price for a given product can vary.
3. Discuss the **determinants of demand**.

Price and Quantity Demanded Are Directly Related

They say that a picture is worth a thousand words. For much of economic analysis the "picture" is a graph. The graph shows a picture of the relationship between two statistics or concepts that are related. Think about the relationship between height and weight. On average, people who are six feet tall weigh more than people who are five and one-half feet tall. If we wanted to graph this relationship it would look something like Figure 8.5.

Figure 8.5
Height and Weight
The graph shows a composite of heights and weights of men and women in the United States.

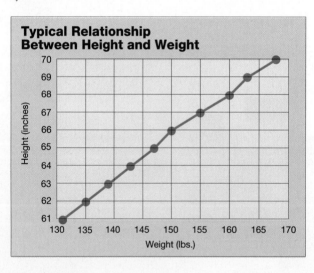

Typical Relationship Between Height and Weight

Graphing the Demand Curve

The law of demand can also be graphed. The relationship between the quantity demanded and price is one in which as the price goes up, the quantity demanded goes down. As the price goes down, the quantity demanded goes up. We should therefore be able to graph this relationship the same way we did the relationship between height and weight. We do so in Figure 8.6.

Let us use compact discs as an example. Figure 8.6A shows various prices and the quantity of compact discs demanded in a table. Figure 8.6B

Classroom Resources for Section 2

 Reproducible Lesson Plan 8.2
Focus Activity Transparency 27
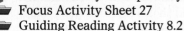 Focus Activity Sheet 27
Guiding Reading Activity 8.2

 Section Quiz 8.2
 Spanish Section Quiz 8.2
 Testmaker

and Figure 8.6C show this same information as graphs.

Time and Quality Are Important Notice that on the bottom of the graphs in Figures 8.6B and 8.6C we refer to the quantity of compact discs demanded per year. The time period is one year. We could have said one day, one week, one month, or two years. Typically, economists talk about quantity demanded per year. It is important to know the

Various Prices and Quantity Demanded of Compact Discs

Price per compact disc	Quantity demanded (in millions)	Points in Figure 8.6B
$20	100	A
$19	200	B
$18	300	C
$17	400	D
$16	500	E
$15	600	F
$14	700	G
$13	800	H
$12	900	I
$11	1,000	J
$10	1,100	K

**Figure 8.6
Relationship of
Demand to Price**
The series of three graphs shows how the price of goods and services affects the quantity demanded.

A Table of Prices and Quantity Demanded ▲
The numbers in Figure 8.6A show that as the prices per CD decrease, the quantity of CDs demanded increases.

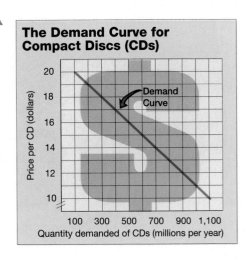

The Demand Curve for Compact Discs (CDs)

▲ **B Plotting the Price-Quantity Pairs**
The bottom axis shows the quantity demanded. The side axis shows the price per compact disc.
Each pair of price and quantity demanded represents a point on the graph. We label these points A, B, C, D, E, F, G, H, I, J, K.

C **Demand Curve**
When we connect the points from Figure 8.6B with a line, we end up with the **demand curve.**
A demand curve shows the quantity demanded of a good or service at each possible price. It slopes downward (falls from left to right). You can see the *inverse* relationship between price and quantity demanded here.

◀

Chapter 8 Supply and Demand   **183**

Teach

Guided Practice

L1 Hypothesizing Have students work in small groups to hypothesize how shortages might affect demand.

Visual Instruction

Ask students to review Figure 8.6. Have them then prepare a table showing the price-demand relation for local sales of a brand of videotapes. In 1989, 10,000 sold at $2.99. From 1990 through 1993, the price dropped 25 cents annually as volume rose by 1,000 each year. Ask students to use their table to graph the price-demand relation from 1989 through 1993.

GLOBAL ECONOMICS

In 1959 and 1960, crude oil production was greater than demand. As a response to the resulting drop in oil prices, five petroleum-producing nations formed OPEC, the Organization of Petroleum Exporting Countries, which now has 13 members. OPEC had little effect on petroleum prices until demand for oil increased greatly in the 1970s. OPEC then raised oil prices significantly.

◆ ◉ Meeting Special Needs

Visual Disability Students with visual difficulties may find the graphing techniques presented in this section helpful. Encourage students to use graphing as a way of taking notes and summarizing information through-

out the course. You might suggest that students use rulers or index cards to help them keep track of columns and rows when they interpret tables and charts.

Independent Practice

L3 Planning a Trip Ask students to plan for a trip they would like to take, such as a boating or camping trip. In their preparation for the trip, they should list all the goods they will need and the quantities in which they will need them. Have students make notations on their lists to indicate the elasticity of each need or want for the trip.

Visual Instruction

Ask students to look at Figure 8.7 and reread the caption. Have them research a significant fad of the 1950s, 1960s, 1970s, or 1980s and write a short report about its economic impact.

DID YOU KNOW

In the United States, the Agricultural Stabilization and Conservation Service guarantees that farmers will not undergo extreme shifts in supply and demand. The ASCS encourages conservation and environmental protection, grants loans to farmers, and even buys excess crops in order to support the prices farmers need to survive.

time period during which you are measuring the quantity demanded. The longer the time period, the more the quantity demanded will be for any given price. Therefore, do not forget to indicate the time period in any discussion of the quantity demanded of anything.

Compact discs are not all of the same quality. Often in the "budget-lines" of CDs the sound quality is sort of tinny. When you talk about the demand curve for different items, you have to assume a *constant-quality unit.* You do not have to actually figure out what that standard quality unit is. Just be aware that when you draw a demand curve such as in Figure 8.6C (page 183) you are holding quality constant.

What if Demand Increases? Sometimes something happens that causes demand to increase for certain items. As Figure 8.7 shows, demand increases can occur for many varied reasons. Using CDs as an example, Figure 8.8

shows what happens when demand increases.

Actually, the shift in the demand curve in Figure 8.8 happens all the time to many goods and services simply because population increases. Even at the same price, more compact discs will be demanded 5 years from now because there will be more consumers.

The Price Elasticity of Demand

The law of demand is straightforward: The higher the price charged, the lower the quantity demanded, and vice versa. If you were the owner of a music store selling compact discs, how could you use this information? You know that if you lower prices, consumers will buy more compact discs. Imagine you have extra inventory, and you want to sell it quickly because you are expecting a new shipment of compact discs. You know that if you have a big sale and lower the price of compact discs, you are

**Figure 8.7
Increases in
Demand**
If suddenly fashion trends make everybody want to wear high-top tennis shoes, we say that the demand for high-top tennis shoes has increased. If latest medical research proves that taking vitamin E pills reduces the chance of heart attacks, the demand for vitamin E pills will increase. If scientists were to prove that listening to more music increases life span, then the demand for compact discs would increase.

 Cooperative Learning

Organize the class into small groups to determine the point when diminishing marginal utility and the real income effect become significant deterrents to buying new items. Encourage students to discuss how they use the substitution effect in their own purchases. Then have the groups create a handbook to teen-aged buyers for the manufacturers of the items they discussed. Suggest that students use graphs, charts, and illustrations, where applicable, to illustrate their booklets.

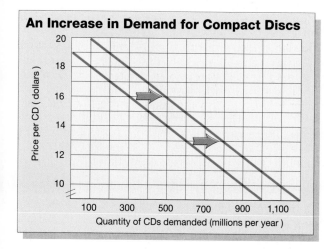

An Increase in Demand for Compact Discs

Quantity of CDs demanded (millions per year)

Price per CD (dollars)

Figure 8.8
An Increase in Demand for Compact Discs

An increase in demand for compact discs means that people will want, and be willing to buy, more compact discs per year at all prices. How do we show this with our demand curve? Here you see two demand curves. The first one is exactly the same as the one in Figure 8.6C. The second one has moved to the right. It has moved because of the increase in the demand for compact discs. Just take one price, for example, $13. Before the scientists proved that listening to more music increases life span, the quantity demanded was 600 million compact discs per year. Now that number has increased to 800 million compact discs per year. The quantity demanded at any price has gone up.

Independent Practice
L3 Research and Evaluate
Explain that airline deregulation in the 1980s widened the opportunity for free-market competition. Ask students to research the effect of deregulation on fares and, in turn, whether the demand response was elastic or inelastic, and why. Have them write a short report on their findings and conclusions for oral presentation in a class discussion.

 DID YOU KNOW

With the increase in discretionary income worldwide, travel to the United States has grown substantially since the 1970s. In fact, spending by foreign tourists adds significantly to the economies of places such as Florida, California, and many national parks. Domestic airlines and other carriers also benefit from foreign visitors.

going to sell more. That is the law of demand. Should you lower your prices by 1 percent, 2 percent, or 30 percent in order to sell your excess stock? You cannot really answer this question unless you know how *responsive* consumers will be to a decrease in the price of compact discs. Economists call this price responsiveness **elasticity**. The measure of the **price elasticity of demand** is how much consumers respond to a given change in price.

A good way to think about elasticity is to use the example of two rubber dollar bills: one you can stretch very easily and the other you can hardly stretch at all, as Figure 8.9 (page 186) shows.

Elastic Demand For some goods a rise or fall in price greatly affects the amount people are willing to buy. The demand for these goods is considered elastic, as is the demand for the highly specific food products on the left side of Figure 8.10 (page 186). For example, one particular brand of coffee probably has a very **elastic demand.** Consumers consider the many competing brands to be almost the same. A small rise in the price of one brand will probably cause many consumers to purchase the cheaper substitute brands.

Inelastic Demand If a price change does not result in a substantial change in the quantity demanded, that demand is considered inelastic, as the general food categories on the right side of Figure 8.10 show. Electricity, salt, pepper, sugar, and certain types

Chapter 8 Supply and Demand **185**

 Free Enterprise Activity

Ask students to imagine they will take a class trip to be financed by proceeds from a business they will start and operate. Have students brainstorm the kind of business, time, and place of operation, management and delegation of responsibilities, and fees or prices to be charged.

Independent Practice

L2 Analyzing Data Have students research consumer demand for a high-tech product over a recent five-year period. Items may include lap-top computers, camcorders, cordless telephones, facsimile (fax) machines, exercise machines, or some product of their own choosing. Ask students to graph annual sales volume against average price. Have them explain in the caption for the graph the reason for the price-volume relationship. Ask volunteers to present their findings in a class discussion.

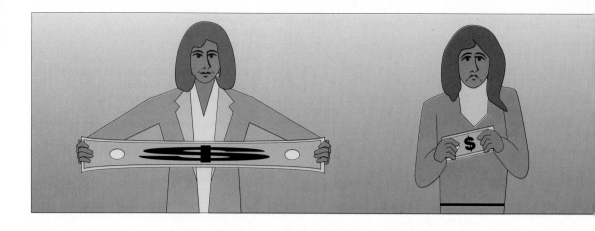

Figure 8.9 ▲
Elasticity
The economic concept of price elasticity deals with how much quantity demanded changes in reaction to a change in price.

of medicine normally have **inelastic demand.** We can compare a relatively inelastic demand with a relatively elastic demand at a particular price using two demand curves in one diagram. See Figure 8.11.

What Determines Price Elasticity of Demand? Why do some goods have elastic demand and others have inelastic demand? At least three factors determine the price elasticity of demand of a particular item: (1) the existence and similarity of substitutes, (2) the percentage of a person's total budget devoted to the purchases

of that good, and (3) how much time we allow for the consumer to adjust to the change in price.

Clearly, the more substitutes that exist for a good, the more responsive consumers will be to a change in the price of that good. A diabetic needs insulin, which has virtually no substitutes. The price elasticity of demand

Figure 8.10
Elastic versus Inelastic Demand
If the prices of certain goods rise, consumers will buy more of other goods—an example of elastic demand. Inelastic demand means that price changes have little impact on quantity demanded.

▼

elastic demand

inelastic demand

 Cultural Diversity and Economics

Have students organize themselves into small groups and assign tasks to prepare written reports on the economy of Canada, comparing and contrasting it with the economy of the United States. Encourage developing visual aids to summarize findings. Have a member of each group make an oral report of its findings and lead a class discussion.

for insulin, therefore, is very low—it is inelastic. The opposite is true for Diet Coke. If the price of Diet Coke goes up by very much, many consumers may switch to Diet Pepsi. Because of the many substitutes available, its demand is relatively elastic.

If you do not spend much of your total budget on a particular good, you probably will not often notice increases in the price of that good. The percentage of a family's budget devoted to pepper is very small. If the price of pepper goes up, most people will keep buying about the same amount. Their demand for pepper is relatively inelastic. People spend much of their budget, however, on housing. If the price of new housing increases rapidly, fewer new homes will be sold. Housing demand is relatively elastic because it represents such a large proportion of a household's total yearly budget.

Finally, people take time to adjust and adapt to all changes, even changes in prices. If the price of electricity goes up by 100 percent tomorrow, you will have a hard time adjusting your behavior immediately in the face of this higher price. The longer the time allowed for adjustment, however, the more you can figure out ways to reduce the amount of electricity you use—by putting in lower wattage light bulbs, learning to live with a warmer house in the summer and a colder house in the winter, adding insulation to your attic, and so on. Therefore, the longer the time allowed for adjustment to the changes, the greater the price elasticity of demand.

Determinants of Demand

Many factors help determine demand for a specific product. Among these factors are changes in population and income, and in people's tastes

Figure 8.11
Graphing Elasticity of Demand
The green line shows that with a very slight decrease in price, the quantity demanded increases dramatically (elastic demand). The purple line shows that the quantity demanded is not as responsive to price (inelastic demand).

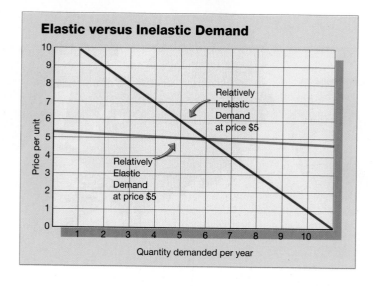

Elastic versus Inelastic Demand

Relatively Inelastic Demand at price $5

Relatively Elastic Demand at price $5

Price per unit

Quantity demanded per year

Independent Practice
L2 Developing Visual Materials Ask students to explore the effect of recycling on the demand for raw materials. Have them concentrate on recyclable products of major raw materials, such as crude oil, metals, and wood pulp. Suggest presenting their data in graphs and charts for use as examples in a class discussion.

DID YOU KNOW

Demand for raw materials has sometimes been met at least in part through recycling. For example, during World War II, Americans saved, collected, and submitted for reuse various consumer products. Items such as old newspapers, fat drippings from cooked meat, and iron and other metal items were used to make munitions and other defense-related products.

Cooperative Learning

Remind students that economics distinguishes between needs and wants, with needs being few and wants being nearly limitless. Organize students into small groups. Each group should choose a good or service and explore and write a report on how marketing and advertising create demand for their product or service by clouding the distinction between needs and wants. Ask a volunteer from each group to make an oral report on its product or service and discuss findings and observations.

and preferences. **Figure 8.13** shows some of the determinants of demand and the reasons for demand changes.

Substitutes The existence of substitutes also affects demand. People often think of butter and margarine as substitutes. Suppose that the price of butter remains the same and the price of margarine falls. People will buy more margarine and less butter at all prices. The demand curve for butter will shift to the left. As the price of the substitute (margarine) decreases, the demand for the item under study (butter) also decreases. If the price of margarine rises, however, people will buy less margarine and more butter at all prices. The demand curve for butter will shift to the right. As the price of the substitute (margarine) increases, the demand for the item under study (butter) also increases. **Figure**

8.12 shows that not all substitutes are equal, however.

Complementary Goods Although bread and butter can be used separately, they are often used together. Suppose the price of butter remains the same. If the price of bread drops, people will probably buy more bread. They will also probably buy more butter to use on the bread. Therefore, a decrease in the price of bread leads to an increase in the demand for its **complementary good,** butter. As a result, the demand curve for butter will shift to the right. If the price of bread increases, however, consumers will buy less bread and, as a result, will need less butter. An increase in the price of bread leads to a decrease in the demand for butter. Consequently, the demand curve for butter will shift to the left.

Figure 8.12
Substitutes
Margarine is an obvious substitute for butter. The price of one directly affects the price of the other. If, in contrast, the price of carrots increased, it would not affect the price of broccoli as directly. People might substitute one of several other vegetables.

 Free Enterprise Activity

Ask the class to brainstorm starting and running a student business to raise funds for the school: for example, a refreshments concession at home games, science fairs, plays, or concerts. After students decide on the kind of business, they should plan the management, staffing, and pricing or fees, and consider any operating expenses.

What Determines Demand?

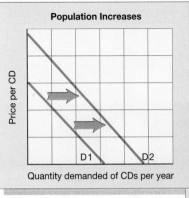

Population Increases

Price per CD

Quantity demanded of CDs per year

D1   D2

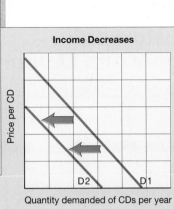

Income Decreases

Price per CD

Quantity demanded of CDs per year

D2   D1

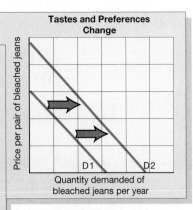

Tastes and Preferences Change

Price per pair of bleached jeans

Quantity demanded of bleached jeans per year

D1   D2

**Figure 8.13
What Determines Demand?**

A Population ▲
When population increases, the market increases. Naturally, the demand for most products increases. This means that the demand curve for, say, CDs, shifts to the right. At each price, more CDs will be demanded as population increases. D1 represents CD demand before the population increased. D2 represents demand after the population increased.

B Income ▲
The demand for most goods and services depends on income. Your demand for compact discs would certainly decrease if your income dropped in half and you expected it to stay there. The demand curve for CDs for you would shift to the left as shown above. D1 represents CD demand before income decreased. D2 represents CD demand after income decreased.

C Tastes and Preferences ▲
One of the key factors that determines demand is people's tastes and preferences. If there were a sudden new fad at schools around the country in which everyone wants to wear bleached jeans, then the demand curve for bleached jeans will shift to the right as shown here. D1 represents demand for bleached jeans before they became a fad. D2 represents demand after they became a fad.

SECTION 2 REVIEW

Understanding Vocabulary
Define demand curve, elasticity, price elasticity of demand, elastic demand, inelastic demand, complementary good.

Reviewing Objectives
① What does graphing the demand curve show you about the relationship between price and quantity demanded?

② What is the difference between a good that has elastic demand and one that has inelastic demand?

③ What are the determinants of demand?

Chapter 8 Supply and Demand **189**

Assess

Meeting Lesson Objectives
Assign Section 2 Review as homework or an in-class activity. Each question in the Review addresses the corresponding numbered objective in the Section Focus.

Evaluate
📁 Assign the Section 2 Quiz in the TCR or use the Testmaker to develop a customized quiz.

Reteach
Have students list the elastic, moderately elastic, and inelastic demands of their household. Have them create a chart, noting whether the demand for each item responds to changes in price, income, quality, need, available substitutes, time adjustments, and taste.

Enrich
Have students consult with a local merchant to graph the demand of a particular item. Encourage students to complement their graphs with a paragraph telling what factors most affect demand.

Close

Discuss with students how demand for a good or service can shape an entire local economy.

Teach

Have volunteers read aloud paragraphs of the quoted excerpts from Marshall's *Elements of Economics.* Then have students paraphrase each paragraph by writing a topic sentence on the chalkboard. Finally, have students answer the questions in Checking for Understanding.

You might have interested students read additional chapters from *Elements of Economics* and report Marshall's theory of welfare economics.

Personal Perspective

Alfred Marshall on Supply and Demand

Profile

- 1842–1921
- started career as a mathematician
- chair of political economy at Cambridge University, England
- developed supply and demand analysis as centerpiece of his work
- published his *Principles of Economics* in 1890 and *Elements of Economics* in 1892

Alfred Marshall is known for introducing the concept of supply and demand analysis to economics. The following excerpt from *Elements of Economics* explains the equilibrium of supply and demand.

The simplest case of balance, or equilibrium, between desire and effort is found when a person satisfies one of his wants by his own direct work. When a boy picks blackberries for his own eating, the action of picking may itself be pleasurable for a while. . . .

Equilibrium is reached, when at last his eagerness to play and his disinclination for the work of picking counterbalance the desire for eating. The satisfaction which he can get from picking fruit has arrived at its maximum. . . .

Marshall explains how equilibrium is established in a local market. Buyers and sellers, having perfect knowledge of the market, freely negotiate for their own best interest. In so doing they arrive at a price that exactly equates supply and demand.

. . . [A price may be] called the true equilibrium price: because if it were fixed on at the beginning, and adhered to throughout, it would exactly equate demand and supply. (i.e. the amount which buyers were willing to purchase at that price would be just equal to that for which sellers were willing to take that price). . . .

*I*n our typical market then we assume that the forces of demand and supply have free play; that there is no combination among dealers on either side; but each acts for himself, and there is much free competition; that is, buyers generally compete freely with buyers, and sellers compete freely with sellers. But though everyone acts for himself, his knowledge of what others are doing is supposed to be generally sufficient to prevent him from taking a lower or paying a higher price than others are doing.

Checking for Understanding
❶ What does Marshall mean by "equilibrium between desire and effort"?
❷ What is an equilibrium price?
❸ What market conditions are necessary to establish an equilibrium price?

190 *Unit 3 Microeconomics: Markets, Prices, and Business Competition*

Answers to Checking for Understanding

1. Answers will vary but should indicate the point at which satisfaction created by effort has arrived at its maximum. Students should note that at this point, additional effort takes away from the pleasure of attaining the desire.
2. An equilibrium price is a price that is fixed at the beginning and adhered to throughout marketing. It equates supply and demand.
3. Answers will vary but should indicate that an equilibrium price requires knowledge on the part of the buyers and sellers of what others are doing.

3 The Law of Supply and the Supply Curve

SECTION 3 FOCUS

Terms to Know law of supply, law of diminishing returns, supply curve

Objectives *After reading this section, you should be able to:*

1. Explain how the incentive of greater profit affects supply.
2. Describe the relationships that the supply curve shows.

In Addition to Demand, Supply is a Factor in Determining Price

The law of demand alone is not enough to explain what determines price. To understand how prices are set, you also have to look at supply—the willingness and ability of producers to provide goods and services at different prices in the marketplace. The **law of supply** states:

As the price rises for a good, the quantity supplied rises. As the price falls, the quantity supplied also falls.

Figure 8.14 shows this law. Unlike demand, a direct relationship between the price and quantity supplied exists. With demand, price and quantity demanded move in opposite directions.

Although producers may be willing, they may not be able. Increased costs and possibly a time lag affect a company's ability to respond to changes in price.

The Incentive of Greater Profit

The higher the price of a good, the greater the incentive is for a producer to produce more. The producer will expect to make a higher profit because of the higher price. The profit incentive is one of the factors that motivates people in a market economy. Suppose you own a music company that produces and sells compact discs. Figure 8.15 (page 192) shows some of the costs involved in producing compact discs.

**Figure 8.14
The Law of Supply**

A larger quantity will generally be supplied at higher prices than at lower prices. A smaller quantity will generally be supplied at lower prices than at higher prices.

▼

Chapter 8 Supply and Demand **191**

Focus

Overview

See the student page for section objectives.

Section 3 explains or describes how the incentive of greater profit, including the law of diminishing returns, affects supply, and the relationships the supply curve shows.

VIDEODISC

Nightly Business Report
Economics in Action
Use "What Is Supply?" on Disc 1, Side A, Video 8.

Search 38882, Play to 43807

Bellringer

Before presenting the lesson, display Focus Activity Transparency 29 and assign the accompanying Focus Activity Sheet.

Motivational Activity

Have students compare their estimates of the price they would set for mowing someone's lawn.

Tell students that Section 3 will explain how incentive affects supply, and describe the relationships shown in a supply curve.

Preteaching Vocabulary

Have students tell a progressive story using the vocabulary terms.

Classroom Resources for Section 3

- Reproducible Lesson Plan 8.3
- *NBR* Video 8 and Video Still 5
- Focus Activity Transparency 29
- Focus Activity Sheet 29
- Guided Reading Activity 8.3

- Section Quiz 8.3
- Spanish Section Quiz 8.3
- Testmaker
- Reinforcing Skills 8

Teach

Guided Practice

L1 Giving Examples Ask students to think of examples of how the incentive of greater profit might affect a community. Students might discuss a sudden increase in fancy stores and restaurants, a sale of overstocked merchandise, or a fad related to certain goods.

Visual Instruction

Ask students to study Figure 8.17 (p.194) and then to prepare first a table and then a graph based on the following data: An area manufacturer produced 10,000 videotapes that sold for $2.95. During the next 4 years, production grew by 1,000 annually, and the price rose by 25 cents each year.

VIDEODISC

Nightly Business Report
Economics in Action
Use Video Still 5, "Closing IBM Stock Prices," on Disc 1, Side A, Video 8.

Search Frame 43176

▲
Figure 8.15
Some Costs of Producing CDs
The costs of producing CDs include: the price of the machines to make them; the price of the materials used in the compact disc itself; the price of the plastic "jewel box" in which they are sold; and even the price of paper and printing used to make the cover and booklet insert. You also have buildings in which to produce the compact discs, and you may have mortgage payments on those buildings and the land. You have employees to whom you must pay wages. You have taxes and insurance. These are all considered costs of

Suppose, for the moment, that the price you charge for your compact discs covers all of your costs and gives you a small profit. Under what circumstances would you be willing to produce more compact discs? Remember that increasing output means expanding production. Expanding production usually means higher costs because of the law of diminishing returns.

The Law of Diminishing Returns
Normally after some point, if you are expanding production, the additional workers that you hire do not add as much to total output as the previous workers that you hired. Assume you

employ 10 workers. You hire an eleventh worker. Compact disc production increases by 1,000 per week. When you hire the twelfth worker, compact disc production might increase by only 900 per week. This example illustrates the **law of diminishing returns.** According to this law, after some point, adding units of a factor of production—such as labor—to all the other factors of production—such as equipment—increases total output for a time. After a certain point, however, the extra output for each additional unit hired will begin to decrease.

You Must Charge a Higher Price To take on the expense of expanding production, you would have to be able to charge a higher price for your compact discs. If the price at which you could sell compact discs went up enough, you would probably be willing to hire more workers, buy more machines, and even build more factories.

At a higher price per compact disc, you would be willing to supply—

 Meeting Special Needs

Visual Disability It is important to be accurate when entering amounts into graphs and charts. Encourage students with visual disabilities to read numbers aloud to themselves for sense and to read them to a class-

mate or friend to check for accuracy. Have students use rulers or index cards to help them keep track of columns and rows when they interpret tables and charts.

Figure 8.16 ▲
Higher Prices Attract New Suppliers
For many years, McDonald's restaurants had little competition because their prices were so low. When McDonald's prices reached the level at which competitors could make a profit, other fast-food restaurants such as Wendy's entered the market.

produce and sell—more than you would at the current lower price. Even though each compact disc might cost more to produce—because of overtime payments to workers, more repairs on machines, and so on—you could afford to pay the additional cost of increasing the quantity sold. This fact is the basis of the law of supply.

Many businesses produce compact discs in the United States. The law of supply works not only for each individual producer, but also for the industry as a whole. At a higher selling price of compact discs, it is even possible that new producers will enter the industry. They could be computer businesses that decide to branch out into the compact disc business because the profits seem so high. At a higher price, these potential compact disc producers see a possibility for a larger profit in that business than before the price of compact discs went up. This example, of course, assumes that no other prices in the economy increase.

An interesting question arises when new producers enter the industry simply because the price of the product went up. Why were they not producing before? The answer is that they were not as efficient as the other producers already in the industry. Their costs were too high. They had to wait until the price of the product went up in order to cover their higher costs. See Figure 8.16.

In any event, at higher prices, present suppliers will increase what they make or sell. And at higher prices *potential* suppliers will become *actual* suppliers because of the attraction of profits. Both add to the total output.

The Supply Curve

As with the law of demand, special tables and graphs can show the law of supply. Using the example of compact disc producers, how could we show a visual relationship between the price and the quantity supplied? Figure 8.17 (page 194) shows this process.

Independent Practice
L3 Consulting Have students imagine that younger children are consulting them about planning a lemonade stand. Suggest that students determine production costs and set the price according to estimated sales of 10, 20, and 30 cups of lemonade. Tell students to imagine that cups and lemonade mix come in 10-cup packages.

Have students complete Guided Reading Activity 8.3 in the TCR. **LEP**

Visual Instruction
Ask students to reexamine the demand curve in Figure 8.6 (p.183) and the supply curve in Figure 8.17 (p.194). Have them explain in a paragraph whether one set of data offers a more compelling argument than the other. Also ask them to discuss whether one curve might tend to predominate at certain times in a nation's economy.

Cooperative Learning

Encourage students to bring to class books, CDs, audiotapes, or other items to be traded. (If students do not wish to trade actual items, they can be returned after the activity.) Have them "set up shop" with one or more partners to offer their goods and buy other goods. Have students set initial prices on their goods and try to "sell" them.

Have students regroup and adjust their prices to reflect demand. Hold a second market. Have partners discuss how they came to their pricing decisions.

Assess

Meeting Lesson Objectives

Assign Section 3 Review as homework or an in-class activity. Each question in the Review addresses the corresponding numbered objective in the Section Focus.

Evaluate

Assign the Section 3 Quiz in the TCR or use the Testmaker to develop a customized quiz.

Reteach

Organize the class into two groups and ask each group to make a list of pros and cons for increasing production of an item. Then have students debate one another about whether to increase production of the item.

Enrich

Have students research the law of supply as it applies to the merchandise choices of a local business. Ask students to interview a local business professional to find out how the law of supply influences what stock is purchased and what the business sells.

Close

Discuss with students how supply shapes profit and employment in a market economy.

Figure 8.17
Relationship of Supply to Price

The series of three graphs shows how the price of goods and services affects the quantity supplied.

A Table of Prices and Quantity Supplied ▶
The numbers here show that as the price per CD increases, the quantity supplied increases.

Various Prices and Quantities Supplied Of Compact Discs

Price per compact disc	Quantity supplied (in millions)	Points in Figure 8.17B
$10	100	L
$11	200	M
$12	300	N
$13	400	O
$14	500	P
$15	600	Q
$16	700	R
$17	800	S
$18	900	T
$19	1,000	U
$20	1,100	V

Supply Curve for Compact Discs

◀ **B Plotting the Price-Quantity Pairs**
The bottom axis shows the quantity supplied. The side axis shows the price per compact disc.

Each pair of price and quantity supplied represents a point on the graph. We label these points L, M, N, O, P, Q, R, S, T, U, V.

C Supply Curve ▶
When we connect the points from Figure 8.17B with a line, we end up with the **supply curve**.

A supply curve shows the quantities supplied at each possible price. It slopes upward from left to right. You can see that the relationship between price and quantity supplied is direct.

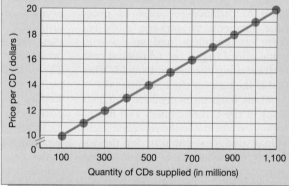

Supply Curve for Compact Discs

SECTION 3 REVIEW

Understanding Vocabulary

Define law of supply, law of diminishing returns, supply curve.

Reviewing Objectives

① How does the incentive of greater profit affect the supply of a given good or service?

② What does the supply curve show?

Section 3 Review Answers

Understanding Vocabulary
law of supply (p.191), **law of diminishing returns** (p.192), **supply curve** (p.194)

Reviewing Objectives
1. The supply of the good or service grows because the producer has the incentive to produce more.
2. The supply curve shows the quantities supplied at each possible price.

Critical Thinking Skills

Determining Cause and Effect

In order to understand economics, you have to know about cause and effect. Can you determine what is a cause and what is an effect?

Defining Cause and Effect

A cause is the action or situation that produces an event. An effect is the result or consequence of an action or situation. Often, the effect of one action or event causes yet another action or event. See **Figure A**.

Price and Quantity Demanded

The classic cause-and-effect relationship in economics is between price and quantity demanded. The law of demand is simply that: at higher prices, consumers purchase lower quantities. Look at the demand curve for home interactive entertainment systems in **Figure B**. If the price of interactive entertainment systems is $5,000, only 1 million will be demanded per year. If the price drops to $1,000, 5 million will be demanded per year. This cause-effect relationship is valid if other determinants of demand, such as population and income, do not change.

Figure A

```
┌──────────┐
│  CAUSE   │
└──────────┘
     ▼
┌──────────┐
│  EFFECT  │
│ (CAUSE)  │
└──────────┘
     ▼
┌──────────┐
│  EFFECT  │
└──────────┘
```

Figure B

Price (in $1,000) vs *Quantity demanded (in millions)*

Practicing the Skill

❶ Every time the moon is full, the price of a particular stock seems to go up. Can you therefore infer that the moon causes stock prices to change? Why or why not?

❷ Every President from William Henry Harrison to John F. Kennedy who was elected on the first year of a new decade died in office. What cause-and-effect conclusion, if any, can you draw from these data?

195

TEACHING Critical Thinking Skills

Teach

Use the following activity to guide students in determining whether a cause-effect relationship is present. Have students imagine that a man sits on a certain park bench each day for an hour and that a squirrel approaches him. Ask students to explain why the relationship they picture is a coincidental relationship rather than a cause-effect relationship. Have students discuss the additional information or event required to establish a cause-effect relationship. *(Students might suggest seeing the man feed the squirrel or seeing crumbs drop from his lunch bag.)*

Additional Practice

Have students complete Reinforcing Skills 8 in the TCR.

Answers to Practicing the Skill

1. No, there is no evidence to show cause and effect.

2. none

195

Focus

Overview

See the student page for section objectives.

Section 4 explains or describes: how shortages affect price; shifts in price equilibrium and forces underlying supply and demand.

VIDEODISC

Nightly Business Report

Economics in Action
Use "Supply and Demand" on Disc 1, Side B, Video 11.

Search 6964, Play to 13441

Bellringer

Before presenting the lesson, display Focus Activity Transparency 35 and assign the accompanying Focus Activity Sheet.

Motivational Activity

Have students complete the following sentence: Sometimes the store is all out of ___. Tell students that Section 4 will identify the determinants of supply.

SECTION **4** Putting Supply and Demand Together

S E C T I O N   4   F O C U S

Terms to Know equilibrium price, technology, shortages, surplus

Objectives *After reading this section, you should be able to:*
1. List the four determinants of supply and describe how they change supply.
2. Explain how the equilibrium price is determined.
3. Explain how shortages and surpluses affect price.
4. Describe how shifts in equilibrium price occur.
5. Discuss how the forces underlying supply and demand affect prices.

The Interaction of Supply and Demand Determines Price

As with demand, several factors help determine supply. We know that when the price changes, the quantity supplied changes. What if factors other than price change? What would happen to the supply of compact discs if the cost of the machines used to produce them decreased? Producers would be able to supply more CDs at the same market price. See Figure 8.18. The price of inputs used to produce the product is, therefore, another factor that determines its supply.

◄ **Figure 8.18 Technology**
As the cost of technology decreases, the supply of CDs increases.

The Determinants of Supply

Look at Figure 8.19 and you will see an explanation of the price of inputs and some of the other determinants of supply. You see in Figure 8.19 that we show supply curves that shift in each of the explanations. A change in supply causes the entire supply curve to shift. See Figure 8.20 on page 198.

Equilibrium Price

In the real world, demand and supply operate together. As the price of a

196

Classroom Resources for Section 4

good goes down, the quantity demanded rises, and the quantity supplied falls. As the price goes up, the quantity demanded falls, and the quantity supplied rises.

Is there a price at which the quantity demanded and the quantity supplied meet? Yes. This level is called the **equilibrium price.** It means that the price of any good or service will find the level at which the quantity demanded and the quantity supplied are balanced. At this point, there is

Figure 8.19 The Determinants of Supply
Four of the major determinants of supply are explained here. These include the price of inputs, taxes, and the number of firms in the industry. They also include **technology—** the use of science to develop new products and new methods for producing and distributing goods and services.

The Determinants of Supply

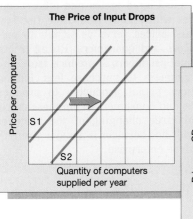

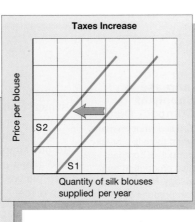

A The Price of Inputs ▲
If the price of inputs drops dramatically, the supply curve will shift to the right. This occurred, for example, when the price of computer processing and memory chips fell during the 1980s and 1990s. More computers were supplied at any given price than before. On the graph S1 equals the supply of computers before the price of memory chips fell. S2 equals the supply of computers after the price of memory chips fell.

B Technology ▲
Any improvement in technology will increase the supply curve to the right. The technology for making compact discs improved during the 1980s. The supply curve shifted to the right so that at each price a larger quantity was supplied. On the graph S1 equals the supply of CDs before the improvement in technology. S2 equals supply after the improvement.

C Number of Firms in the Industry
When more firms enter the industry, the supply curve shifts outward ▲ to the right. For example, if more firms entered the videodisc player industry, the supply curve would shift to the right as in **A** and **B** above.

D Taxes ▲
If the government imposes more taxes on businesses, they will not be willing to supply as much as before. The supply curve for products will shift to the left. For example, if taxes increased on businesses supplying silk blouses, the supply curve would shift to the left. On the graph S1 equals the supply of silk blouses before the government raised taxes on this business. S2 equals the supply after the government raised taxes.

Chapter 8 Supply and Demand **197**

Teach

Guided Practice

L1 Itemizing Have students work in small groups to brainstorm reasons why a particular item might experience upward or downward shifts in price equilibrium.

Visual Instruction

Have students examine Figure 8.19 and read the captions. Ask them to research any changes in corporate income tax between 1981 and 1990 and to write a short report on the effects, if any, on American manufacturing or service industries. Ask volunteers to give an oral report.

GLOBAL ECONOMICS

The market value of all of a country's retail goods and services bought during a year is known as its gross domestic product (GDP). The per capita GDP is the gross domestic product divided by the population of a country. The United States has the highest GDP in the world, but Switzerland has the highest per capita GDP.

◆ ●● Meeting Special Needs

Speech Disability Students with speech disabilities may want to develop their speeches as a written assignment or have a classmate deliver the speeches they write. Encourage speech writers to direct their presenters so that their speeches are delivered in the way they wish them to be heard.

Independent Practice

L1 Designing a Game Have students work in small groups to create a board game called Supply and Demand. Have students earmark a group of four to six items players hope to sell in the marketplace. Students should direct players to choose one or two items and try to achieve the highest sales possible of these items. Point out to students that spaces on the board can signal determinants of supply and demand. Students might also want to use stacks of cards for variables such as population.

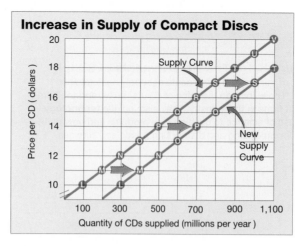

Increase in Supply of Compact Discs

Figure 8.20 ▲
Increase in Supply of Compact Discs
You see what happens when there is a breakthrough in compact disc production technology. Now producers can produce compact discs at one-half the cost they used to pay. The supply curve shifts outward to the right. That means that at all prices, producers will be willing to produce and sell more compact discs. Before the new technology, at a price of $15, suppliers would be willing to supply 600 million compact discs per year. After the breakthrough in technology they would be willing to supply 800 million compact discs per year.

enough of the good to satisfy consumers. Suppliers provide the amount that is demanded by consumers. One way to visualize equilibrium price is to put supply and demand curves on one graph as in Figure 8.21. Where the two curves intersect is the equilibrium price.

Shortages and Surpluses

Shortages occur when, at the going price, the quantity demanded is greater than the quantity supplied. If the market is unrestricted, without government regulations or other restrictions, shortages put pressure on prices to rise. Consumers reduce their purchases while suppliers increase the quantity they supply.

At prices above the equilibrium price, suppliers produce more than consumers want to purchase in the marketplace. Suppliers end up with large inventories of goods, and this and other forces put pressure on the price to drop to the equilibrium price. When the price drops, suppliers have less incentive to supply as much as before, while consumers begin to purchase a greater quantity. The drop in

price toward the equilibrium price, therefore, eliminates the **surplus**.

One of the benefits of the market economy is that when it operates without restriction, it eliminates shortages and surpluses. See Figure 8.22. Whenever shortages occur, the market ends up taking care of itself—the price goes up to eliminate the shortage. Whenever surpluses occur, the market again ends up taking care of itself—the price falls to eliminate the surplus. In command, or controlled, economies, such automatic market forces usually are not allowed to operate. In the United States and other countries with mainly free enterprise systems, prices serve as signals to producers and consumers. Rising prices signal producers to produce more and consumers to purchase less. Falling prices signal producers to produce less and consumers to purchase more. This free changing of the price of goods and services is a major strength of free enterprise.

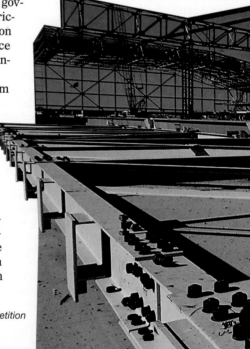

 Cooperative Learning

Have students organize themselves into small groups to research and debate the question "Resolved, the benefits of the trickle-down principle should be considered an unqualified success (or failure)." Explain that the so-called trickle-down principle was

advanced in the 1980s as a benefit of implementing the theory of supply-side economics, then highly favored. Encourage those not participating in the debate to prepare questions based on their own research to challenge the pro and con positions.

Shifts in Equilibrium Price

Now we can show what happens when there is an increase in the demand for compact discs. Assume that scientists prove that listening to more

**Figure 8.21
Reaching Equilibrium Price** ▶
We have taken the demand curve for compact discs from Figure 8.6C and the supply curve for compact discs from Figure 8.17C and put them into one diagram. The demand and the supply curves for compact discs intersect at a special place. It is called the equilibrium price. In our particular example it is $15 per compact disc. At that price, the quantity of compact discs that consumers are willing and able to purchase is 600 million per year. At the same time, suppliers are willing to supply exactly that same amount. If the price were to go above $15, the quantity demanded would be less than the quantity supplied. There would be a surplus as is indicated in the diagram. If the price fell below $15 per compact disc, the quantity demanded would exceed the quantity supplied. There would be a shortage.

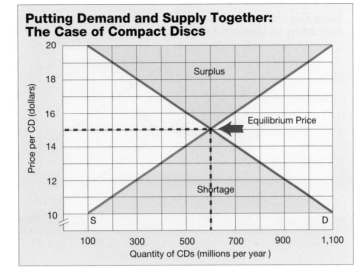

**Putting Demand and Supply Together:
The Case of Compact Discs**

**Figure 8.22
Construction**
Changing prices effectively help to eliminate shortages and surpluses in the construction industry.

◀

Independent Practice

L1 Comparing and Evaluating Have students choose a specific name-brand consumer item that is available in supermarkets. Ask them to compare the selling price over two weeks in two or three different socioeconomic communities to try to tell whether the equilibrium price has been reached. If the prices vary, tell them to try to explain why and to estimate what they think the equilibrium price should be. Ask volunteers to report orally

 DID YOU KNOW

From 1991 to 1992, the average change in consumer prices was 3.1 percent for Canada, France, Germany, Italy, Japan, Spain, Sweden, Switzerland, the United Kingdom, and the United States. The lowest change was in Canada (1.5 percent) and the highest was in Spain (5.8 percent). The change in the United States was closest to average (3.0 percent).

Free Enterprise Activity

Have students brainstorm producing a booklet of retail discount coupons for students and teachers. Suggest organizing into committees for general planning, contact and liaison with local merchants and businesses, budget and materials, writing and design, advertising and promotion, distribution, and so forth. Have each committee make an oral report and evaluate the possibility of implementing plans and producing the booklet.

Independent Practice

Independent Practice

L2 Writing a Speech Have students organize their ideas, then write a speech about whether the prices of any items or services should be fixed in a market economy. You might want to have students record their speeches on audio or video-tape before turning them in.

📁 Have students complete Guided Reading Activity 8.4 in the TCR. LEP

Visual Instruction

Answer to Figure 8.23: the price would decrease.

Refer students to Figure 8.24. Ask them to obtain figures on the per capita cost of health care in Australia, Canada, France, Germany, Italy, Japan, Sweden, the United Kingdom, and the United States. In addition, have them research the ranking of these nations in quality of health care. Suggest organizing their data graphically. Encourage volunteers to report their findings, and have the class speculate on the implications of the data for Americans.

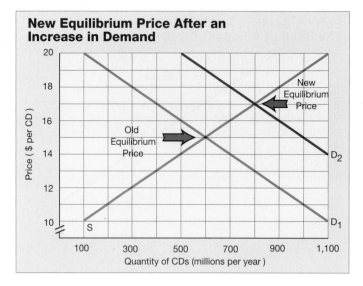

New Equilibrium Price After an Increase in Demand

Figure 8.23 ▲ Change in Equilibrium Price The old equilibrium price was $15. But now the new demand curve intersects the supply curve at a higher price—$17. Price will go up at the same time that quantity supplied and demanded will increase. Can you show what would happen if, instead, scientists proved that listening to music decreases life span?

music increases life span. This discovery will cause the demand curve to shift outward to the right, as shown in Figure 8.23.

What about changes in supply? You can show these in a similar fashion. Assume that there is a major break-through in the technology of producing compact discs. The supply curve shifts outward to the right. The new equilibrium price will fall, and the quantity both supplied and demanded will increase.

Forces Underlying Supply and Demand

Do supply and demand determine all prices? Yes and no. Supply and demand are important aspects of the economy, and they do affect prices. The *forces* that determine supply and demand, however, really determine prices. Many such forces operate in the economy. On the demand side are people's income and their tastes and preferences. On the supply side, among determining factors are the ability of suppliers to produce, the profit incentive, and costs of production. The forces underlying supply and demand really determine price. *Underlying* is the important word.

Difficult to Measure The forces underlying demand and supply are sometimes obscure and often hard to measure. This makes the task of determining the effect of demand and supply on price a difficult one. For example, in the 1950s and early 1960s, the supply of doctors in the United States grew at an annual rate of less than 2%. Medical costs meanwhile increased at about 8% per year. At this point it seemed easy to show that the forces of demand and supply were affecting health-care costs (prices). Demand for medical services was rising faster than the supply of doctors and accounted for much of the increase in prices. Doctors' incomes rose rapidly, attracting more people into the med-

---

Cultural Diversity and Economics

Point out to students that consumable goods are not the only source of economic activity available to entrepeneurs. Services are also subject to the laws of supply and demand. Native Americans aware of the demand for recreational facilities and the

current popularity of casinos have responded by constructing and operating casinos on reservation lands. Have students research Native American casinos and report on how they affect the quality of life for the nations who own and operate them.

ical profession. By the 1980s there were many more doctors per capita than there were in the 1960s. One would have expected rising medical costs to slow down. They did not. Other underlying factors affected price. Increasing per capita use of medical services, rising costs of technology, the growth of the medical insurance industry, and aging of the population, among other things, affected medical care costs. See Figure 8.24.

Then, too, even these forces do not always determine price. Legislation or government regulations, for example, fix many prices in the United States. Many states set the rates public utilities may charge for natural gas and electricity. The forces of supply and demand set prices only in a market system. In a command economy, such as that of North Korea or parts of the People's Republic of China, government planners set most prices.

Figure 8.24 Rising Medical Costs
The difficulty in determining the causes of rising medical costs was reflected in the great debate that followed President Clinton's announced plan to create a national health-care program.

SECTION 4 REVIEW

Understanding Vocabulary
Define equilibrium price, technology, shortages, surplus.

Reviewing Objectives
1. What are some of the determinants of supply?
2. When one of these determinants changes, what happens to the supply curve?
3. How do shortages and surpluses affect price?
4. In what ways do shifts in equilibrium price occur?
5. How do the forces underlying supply and demand affect prices?

Section 4 Review Answers

Understanding Vocabulary
equilibrium price (p.197), **technology** (p.197), **shortages** (p.198), **surplus** (p.198)

Reviewing Objectives
1. ability of suppliers to produce, profit incentive, and costs of production
2. It shifts to the left (lowering production)

or to the right (raising production).
3. Shortages cause prices to rise; surpluses cause prices to fall.
4. through shifts in the demand curve or the supply curve
5. by creating the surpluses and shortages that affect prices

Assess

Meeting Lesson Objectives
Assign Section 4 Review as homework or an in-class activity.

Evaluate
Assign the Section 4 Quiz in the TCR or use the Testmaker to develop a customized quiz.

Assign the Chapter 8 Test Form A or Form B or use the Testmaker to develop a customized test.

Reteach
Assign students to work in small groups to develop and perform simulations of supply and demand scenarios using a narrator.

Have students complete Reteaching Activity 8 in the TCR.

Enrich
Have students interview a local businessperson to discuss the most common underlying forces that affect supply and demand in his or her particular business.

Have students complete Enrichment Activity 8 in the TCR.

Close

Have students write a paragraph describing how changes in supply and demand would affect housing prices.

Teach

Point out to students that this article from *Forbes* magazine shows how careful use of pricing and supply can create demand for an item. A low price on one item in a store can create demand for all items in stock by bringing in customers who respond to taste and preference once they are in the store.

Have students use the information in the feature to create a plan for increasing business in a local book, music, or auto parts store. Ask students to include pricing strategies designed to increase traffic into the store. Remind students to consider their need for an overall profit.

News Clip

Readings in Economics

FORBES   **APRIL 26, 1993**

BLUE JEANS AS TUNA FISH

by Amy Feldman

"**D**enim works for us like tuna fish works for a grocery store," says Harry Call, executive vice president of Goody's Family Clothing, of Knoxville, Tenn. He means that Goody's customers come in for discounted blue jeans, and leave with armloads of higher-margin Alfred Dunner dresses, Bugle Boy kiddie clothes, and other name-brand apparel goods. There's nothing accidental about this. The jeans shelves are in the back of Goody's stores, meaning customers must walk as much as 35 yards past racks of merchandise on which Goody's makes its real money.

Jeans are great bait. In the past five years Goody's sales and earnings have tripled, and the number of stores it leases and operates in small towns throughout the Southeast has almost doubled to 127. In its latest fiscal year (ended last Jan. 30) sales were up 26% to $455 million; profits climbed 49% to $16 million ($1.50 per share). Goody's comparable store sales rose 9% last year.... Bobby Goodfriend [the founder's son] joined the company in 1972, after graduating from Babson College. When his father turned the company over to him in 1977, the young man changed the company name to Goody's, his college nickname, and began focusing his buying on brand-name merchandise. If bought right, Goodfriend understood, brand-name merchandise could yield big markups from Goody's cost, yet still be sold at big markdowns relative to department store prices.

The business evolved.... By taking a $5 markup on a pair of jeans that cost Goody's $15, the company gave up over half its percentage markup. But it was able to undercut the going price of $30 and sell out quickly—and send the customers home with other items that more than made up for the margins given up on the jeans....

• THINK ABOUT IT •

1. What product do most Goody's customers come to buy?
2. How does Goody's make up for the low profit margins on blue jeans?

Answers to Think About It

1. jeans
2. by selling higher-margin apparel along with the blue jeans

8 Highlights

Use the Chapter 8 Highlights to preview, review, condense, or reteach the chapter. A Spanish Chapter Highlights is available in the Spanish Handbook.

Preview/Review

 After students read the Chapter 8 Highlights, have them complete Economics Vocabulary Activity 8 in the TCR. Spanish Vocabulary Activities are also available in the Spanish Resource Binder.

Vocabulary Software reinforces the economic terms used in Chapter 8.

Condense

Have students listen to Chapter 8 on the Audiocassettes in the TCR. A 1-page written activity and 1-page test accompany this material. These materials are also available in Spanish.

Reteach

Have students complete Reteaching Activity 8 in the TCR. Spanish Reteaching Activities are also available.

Section 1

Demand

Key Terms

voluntary exchange (p. 176)
law of demand (p. 177)
utility (p. 177)
law of diminishing marginal utility (p. 177)
real income effect (p. 179)
substitution effect (p. 179)

Summary

In a market economy, the principle of voluntary exchange helps determine the price that people are willing to pay for a given good or service. The law of demand, as generated by diminishing marginal utility, the real income effect, and the substitution effect, explains how people react to changing prices.

Section 2

The Demand Curve and the Elasticity of Demand

Key Terms

demand curve (p. 183)
elasticity (p. 185)
price elasticity of demand (p. 185)
elastic demand (p. 185)
inelastic demand (p. 186)
complementary good (p. 188)

Summary

Economists often graph the demand curve in order to understand more about price determination. The price elasticity of demand has an impact on how much the price for a given product can vary. In addition to this elasticity, several factors determine demand in a market economy.

Section 3

The Law of Supply and the Supply Curve

Key Terms

law of supply (p. 191)
law of diminishing returns (p. 192)
supply curve (p. 194)

Summary

In the free enterprise system, the incentive of greater profit affects the quantity of goods that producers are willing and able to supply. As with the demand curve, the supply curve shows the relationship between quantity supplied and price.

Section 4

Putting Supply and Demand Together

Key Terms

equilibrium price (p. 197)
technology (p. 197)
shortages (p. 198)
surplus (p. 198)

Summary

Four factors determine supply in a market economy. A change in supply can often result in tremendous changes in price. Both shortages and surpluses also affect price in a market economy. Sometimes this change takes the form of a change in equilibrium price. Although supply and demand interact to determine price, the forces underlying supply and demand also can actually alter the price of a good or service.

VIDEODISC

Nightly Business Report
Economics in Action
Use "Supply and Demand" on Disc 1, Side B, Video 11.

Search 6964, Play to 13441

VIDEODISC

Nightly Business Report
Economics in Action
Use "What Is Demand?" on Disc 1, Side A, Video 6.

Search 26984, Play to 31984

Use "What Is Supply?" on Disc 1, Side A, Video 8.

Search 38882, Play to 43807

ANSWERS

Identifying Key Terms

Student paragraphs should show an understanding of the terms .
1. law of supply
2. supply curve
3. law of diminishing returns
4. equilibrium price
5. surplus
6. shortage

Recalling Facts and Ideas

Section 1
1. the principle of voluntary exchange
2. demand decreases
3. diminishing marginal utility
4. real income effect and substitution effect

Section 2
5. the demand curve
6. moving the demand curve to the right
7. Inelastic demand remains nearly the same; elastic demand varies.
8. Existence of similar substitutes makes the price of a good more elastic.
9. They shift to the right.

Section 3
10. They supply more because there is greater incentive for profit.
11. the supply curve

Section 4
12. move it to the left
13. by finding the place where the demand curve and the supply curve intersect
14. a surplus
15. a shortage

Identifying Key Terms

Write a short paragraph about demand using all of the following terms.

law of demand (p. 177)
law of diminishing marginal utility (p. 177)
real income effect (p. 179)

substitution effect (p. 179)
demand curve (p. 183)
price elasticity of demand (p. 185)

Use terms from the following list to fill in the blanks in the paragraph below.

law of supply (p. 191)
law of diminishing returns (p. 192)
supply curve (p. 194)

shortage (p. 198)
equilibrium price (p. 197)
surplus (p. 198)

The (1) indicates that at higher prices a larger quantity will generally be supplied than at lower prices. Therefore, the (2) slopes upward (rises from left to right). Suppliers face the (3) ; therefore when they add more workers, each worker contributes less and less to the increase in total output. When we put a supply curve and demand curve on the same graph, we come up with the (4) . Any price that is above the equilibrium price will create a (5) . Any price that is below the equilibrium price will create a (6) .

Recalling Facts and Ideas

Section 1
1. What is the basis of most activity in a market economy?

2. What generally happens to quantity demanded when the price of a good goes up (and other prices stay the same)?
3. Generally, the more you have of something, the less satisfaction you get from an additional unit. This principle is called what?
4. When the price of a good changes, what two effects tend to create the law of demand?

Section 2
5. What term identifies the graphic representation of the law of demand?
6. How do we show in a graph an increase in the demand for a good?
7. What is the distinction between elastic and inelastic demand?
8. How do the existence and similarity of substitutes affect the price elasticity of demand for a good?
9. If income and population increase, what tends to happen to demand curves?

Section 3
10. Do suppliers tend to produce more or less when the price goes up? Why?
11. What term identifies the graphic representation of the law of supply?

Section 4
12. What would an increase in taxes do to the position of the supply curve?
13. How do you find the equilibrium price on a graph of demand and supply?
14. If the price of a product is above its equilibrium price, what is the result?
15. If the price of a product is below its equilibrium price, what is the result?

Critical Thinking

Section 1
Answers will vary but should include students' reasons for their answers.

Section 2
Demand for insulin, a necessity, is inelastic. Demand for CDs, a luxury, is elastic.

Section 3
Answers will vary but should recognize that as computers become more necessary, the demand for them may become inelastic.

Section 4
Answers will vary but should indicate that international telecommunications will increase as computer prices, following the law of demand, fall.

Critical Thinking

Section 1

Making Generalizations To what extent do you think the law of demand is applicable in the world around you? Are there any goods or services that you think do not follow the law of demand?

Section 2

Making Comparisons If you had to guess the relative price elasticities of demand for compact discs compared to that of insulin needed by diabetics, what would you say?

Section 3

Making Predictions The price of computing power continues to fall, but some scientists believe that it cannot continue to fall as rapidly as it has in the last decade. What do you predict will happen to the change in the price of computers over the next 20 years?

Section 4

Drawing Conclusions You have been told that telecommunications depends on computers. Computers are getting cheaper. What conclusion can you draw about how much interchange will occur between nations in the future?

Applying Economic Concepts

The Interaction of Supply and Demand Some prices change in our economy very seldom and others change all the time, even daily. Make a list of products whose prices change slowly, if at all. Make another list of products whose prices you think change quickly. For example, the price of houses changes slowly. In contrast, the prices of other countries' currencies change every day and, in fact, change every second.

Chapter Projects

1. **Individual Project** Clip articles from newspapers or magazines that show the laws of supply and/or demand operating in the real-world. Possibilities would be weather damages to crops and economic conditions affecting housing starts, and so on.

2. **Cooperative Learning Project** Working in groups of four, each group will interview a local merchant. During the interview, ask the merchant at least the following questions:

   - What determines the prices that you charge?
   - What determines when you change prices?
   - Are there any costs to you of changing prices (such as reprinting price lists)?

   One person in each group should write a summary of the interview. Now compare these summaries.

Reviewing Skills

Determining Cause and Effect
The Supply of Beef Look at the table below. What do you infer as the cause-and-effect relationship here?

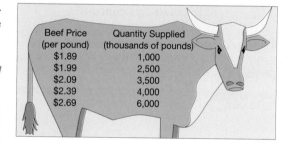

Beef Price (per pound)	Quantity Supplied (thousands of pounds)
$1.89	1,000
$1.99	2,500
$2.09	3,500
$2.39	4,000
$2.69	6,000

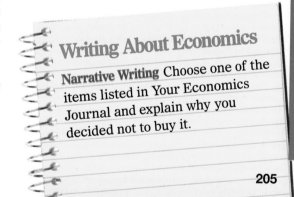

Writing About Economics

Narrative Writing Choose one of the items listed in Your Economics Journal and explain why you decided not to buy it.

Applying Economic Concepts

Answers will vary, but students should make sure they define what they consider a quick change and a slow change.

Chapter Projects

1. Review with students the way in which their clippings reflect the laws of supply and demand.

2. Students might present their information in a feature article about the merchant they interviewed and the business the merchant practices.

Reviewing Skills

The rising price is causing production to increase.

Writing About Economics

Encourage students to draw on elements of the laws of supply and demand in giving their explanation.

? BONUS QUESTION

The following bonus question may be written on the chalkboard when students take the chapter test.
Q: What is a sure sign that the law of supply is prevailing?
A: Prices are going up.

205

CHAPTER 9 *BUSINESS ORGANIZATIONS*

CHAPTER ORGANIZER

Daily Objectives	Special Features	Classroom Resources

Section 1 Starting a Business
- **List** the steps in starting a business.
- **Explain** the four elements involved in every business.

Personal Perspective:
William Gates on Running a Business, p. 212

- Reproducible Lesson Plan 9.1
- *NBR* Video 12
- Focus Activity Transparency 36
- Focus Activity Sheet 36
- Guided Reading Activity 9.1
- Cooperative Learning Activity 9
- Primary and Secondary Source Readings 9
- Section Quiz 9.1
- Spanish Section Quiz 9.1
- Testmaker

Section 2 Sole Proprietorships and Partnerships
- **Describe** the advantages and disadvantages of a sole proprietorship.
- **Explain** how people can get help starting a small business.
- **List** the advantages and disadvantages of a partnership.

Learning Economic Skills:
Reading the Financial Page, p. 218

- Reproducible Lesson Plan 9.2
- Focus Activity Transparency 37
- Focus Activity Sheet 37
- Guided Reading Activity 9.2
- Section Quiz 9.2
- Spanish Section Quiz 9.2
- Testmaker
- Reinforcing Skills 9

Section 3 The Corporate World and Franchises
- **Summarize** the advantages and disadvantages of corporations.
- **Explain** what types of businesses are involved in franchises.

News Clip:
"The Nordic Way," *The Boston Globe*, p. 224

- Reproducible Lesson Plan 9.3
- Focus Activity Transparency 38
- Focus Activity Sheet 38
- Guided Reading Activity 9.3
- Free Enterprise Activity 9
- Consumer Application Activity 9
- Mathematics Practice for Economics 8
- Performance Assessment Activity 8
- Section Quiz 9.3
- Spanish Section Quiz 9.3
- Testmaker
- Enrichment Activity 9

 0:00 OUT OF TIME? If time does not permit teaching this chapter, you may use the Chapter 9 Highlights and the Audiocassettes that include a 1-page activity and a 1-page test.

Chapter 9 Review and Evaluation

Special Features

Chapter 9 Highlights, p. 225
Chapter 9 Review, pp. 226–227
Point/Counterpoint, pp. 228–229

Classroom Resources

- Chapter 9 Test Forms A and B
- Economics Vocabulary Activity 9
- Spanish Economics Vocabulary Activity 9

- Audiocassette 9
- Spanish Audiocassette 9
- Reteaching Activity 9
- Spanish Reteaching Activity 9

Key to Ability Levels

Teaching strategies have been coded for varying learning styles and abilities.

L1 Level 1 activities are **basic** activities and should be within the ability range of all students.

L2 Level 2 activities are **average** activities designed for the ability range of average to above-average students.

L3 Level 3 activities are **challenging** activities designed for the ability range of above-average students.

LEP activities should be within the ability range of **Limited English Proficiency** students.

Performance Assessment

The following chapter project may be assigned at the beginning of the chapter and used for performance assessment. See page T12 for additional Performance Assessment information.

Presenting a Report Have students work in small groups to find information about the different types of businesses found in their community. The report should include the major businesses found there; the number of businesses that are single proprietorships, partnerships, and corporations; the products or services the businesses offer; and the number of people employed in each business. Each group should present its information in an oral report and include visuals with its report.

Additional Resources

Readings for the Student

Mauser, Ferdinand F., and Schwartz, David J. *American Business: An Introduction.* 6th ed. New York: Harcourt Brace Jovanovich, 1986.

Sharp, Ansel M. *Economics of Social Issues.* 8th ed. Plano, Texas: Business Publications, Inc., 1988.

Readings for the Teacher

Armstrong, Fred C. *The Business of Economics.* St. Paul, Minnesota: West, 1986.

Sobel, Robert, and Sicilia, David B. *The Entrepreneurs: An American Adventure.* Boston: Houghton Mifflin, 1986.

Multimedia Materials

American Business. Filmstrip set. Social Studies School Service. P.O. Box 802, Culver City, CA 90232-0802

Corporations. Filmstrip. Social Studies School Service. P.O. Box 802, Culver City, CA 90232-0802

Analyzing an Ad. Computer software. Graphics and sound. MCE, Inc., 157 South Kalamazoo Mall, Kalamazoo, MI 49007. Students analyze an ad and create their own.

Manage (Business Volume I). Simulation. MECC, 3490 Lexington Avenue, North, St. Paul, MN 55126. Simulates three competing companies; each team or player manages a company.

Chapter Overview

There are three major types of business organizations: sole proprietorships, partnerships, and corporations. Chapter 9 explains or describes: how a business gets started; the advantages and disadvantages of sole proprietorships and partnerships; and the advantages and disadvantages of corporations as business organizations.

VIDEODISC

Nightly Business Report
Economics in Action
Use "Business Organizations" on Disc 1, Side B, Video 12.

Search 13526, Play to 22278

CHAPTER
9
BUSINESS ORGANIZATIONS

BONANZA
Steak • Chicken • Seafood • Salad

Who owns these businesses?

What are the costs of operating this kind of business?

FIVE LUNCH SPECIALS
WITH DRINK FOR 2.99
MON THRU FRI 11 TILL 4

TACO MAYO

THRU

Why have they been successful?

Answering Economic Questions

The questions in the above illustration are designed to lead into the main concepts in Chapter 9. Students might not be aware of the different types of businesses that exist. The questions will help students focus on the many kinds of businesses that they encounter and support daily. The questions will also help students think of the elements involved in running a business. Have students discuss the questions and explain what they think are the advantages and disadvantages of owning a business.

Could you ever own a business such as this yourself?

What kinds of businesses are these?

Your Economics Journal

Keep track of all the goods that you and your family buy and the services that you purchase during one week. List these items with the name of the business that provided them. Indicate whether you think each business is small, medium, or large and whether it has one owner or several owners.

207

Connecting to Past Learning

Ask students to recall the four factors of production. (*land, labor, capital, entrepreneurship*) Have a volunteer write them on the chalkboard. Refer students to the pictures on page 209 and ask them to explain how the four factors of production relate to that business. List their responses on the chalkboard. Tell students that Chapter 9 introduces the three basic types of business organizations.

Applying Economics

Organize the class into small groups and ask them to imagine they each plan to start a business. Have the groups identify the kind of business and list the items they think would be needed to run it. Also, have them decide whether they would like to own the business, individually or in partnership.

 EXTRA CREDIT PROJECT

Ask students to conduct an in-depth interview of a franchise owner in regard to becoming an owner and operator. Have students tape record their interviews, if this is possible, for replay in class, or have them take notes for a written report to be presented in class.

 **PERFORMANCE ASSESSMENT**

Refer to page 206B for "Presenting a Report," a Performance Assessment Activity for this chapter.

Economic Portfolio

Refer students to the information in **Your Economics Journal** and suggest that they compile their information in a chart with the following headings: Goods and Services, Place of Purchase, Size of Business, Kind of Ownership. Then ask students to choose three of the goods and services listed and to write a paragraph explaining how they or their families decide from which business they should buy the particular goods or services. Call on volunteers to read their paragraphs to the class and discuss the factors that led to their decisions.

Focus

Overview

See the student page for section objectives.

Section 1 explains or describes steps involved in starting a business and the four elements of a business operation that entrepreneurs need to consider.

Bellringer

Before presenting the lesson, display Focus Activity Transparency 36 on the overhead projector or copy the material on the chalkboard. Assign the accompanying Focus Activity Sheet.

Motivational Activity

Write the following statement on the chalkboard for students to complete: I think that having a business of my own would be _____
_____.

Call on volunteers to read their completed statements, and ask students to explain why they completed the statement the way they did.

Then tell students that Section 1 will clarify the steps in starting a business and the elements involved in every business.

Preteaching Vocabulary

Have students find the definition of *inventory*. Ask them what inventory they need to have for doing their school assignments.

SECTION 1 FOCUS

Terms to Know entrepreneur, inventory

Objectives *After reading this section, you should be able to:*
1 List the **steps in starting a business**.
2 Explain the **four elements involved in every business**.

Starting a Business Involves Risks and Expectations

Suppose that you have been tinkering with electronic equipment since you were a child. By now you can take apart and reassemble cassette and CD players, VCRs, and televisions without difficulty. You are so good at repairing this kind of equipment that you have been doing it for your friends and relatives for some time. Then an idea occurs to you: Why not charge people for your services? Why not go into business for yourself? By starting your own business, you will become an entrepreneur.

The Steps in Starting a Business

Nearly every person who makes the decision to start a business is an **entrepreneur** because he or she is willing to take a risk. Usually people decide to start a business to gain profits and to "do something on their own" or to be their own boss.

Entrepreneurs then gather the factors of production and decide on the form of business organization that best suits their purposes. Anyone hoping to become an entrepreneur must also learn as much as possible about the business he or she plans to start. This process includes learning about the laws, regulations, and tax codes that will apply to the business.

Elements of Business Operation

Figure 9.1 shows the four elements every business must consider.

To start a business, you must make potential customers aware that your services are available for a price. You could have one-page fliers printed to advertise your business and pass them out. You could also buy advertising space in the local newspaper.

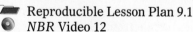

Classroom Resources for Section 1

- Reproducible Lesson Plan 9.1
- *NBR* Video 12
- Focus Activity Transparency 36
- Focus Activity Sheet 36
- Guided Reading Activity 9.1
- Cooperative Learning Activity 9

- Primary and Secondary Source Readings 9
- Section Quiz 9.1
- Spanish Section Quiz 9.1
- Testmaker

Figure 9.1
Four Elements of Business

Every business, regardless of size, involves four elements: expenses, advertising, receipts and record keeping, and risk.

B Advertising ▲

You will quickly find out that letting potential customers know that you are in business is costly. Once you have customers, however, information about your business will spread by word of mouth.

C Receipts and Record Keeping

No matter how small your business is, having a system to track your expenses and income is key to your success. All receipts should be safely filed and saved.

▼

A Expenses ◀

If you own a painting business, you will need to purchase brushes and paint. As your business grows, you might invest in paint sprayers or electric sanders so that you can complete jobs faster. This new equipment would add to your income, but will probably take more money capital than you have on hand.

D Risk

Every business involves risks. You must balance the risks against the advantages of being in business for yourself—including profit versus loss.

◀

209

Teach

Guided Practice

L1 Classifying Write the following headings on the chalkboard: Advertising, Expenses, Receipts, Record Keeping, Risk. As you read the following list of items, have a volunteer write each item under the appropriate heading: flier announcing the start of a new business (*advertising*), electricity to run a business (*expenses*), employees' salaries (*expenses*), paid invoices (*receipts*), customer who refuses to pay a bill (*risk*), computer program that keeps track of receipts and expenses (*record keeping*), competitor opens business nearby (*risk*). **LEP**

L2 Analyzing Ask students to work in pairs to analyze the kinds of rewards entrepreneurs might get from running a business. Call on volunteers to list the rewards on the chalkboard. (*Students might indicate profits, providing services to others, and personal satisfaction.*)

? DID YOU KNOW

In the United States about $125 billion is spent annually on advertising. The major advertising media include newspapers, magazines, television, radio, outdoor advertising, and direct mail.

◆●◯ Meeting Special Needs

Memory Disability Taking notes is an important skill for all students, but especially for students with organization or memory problems. Tell students that they will practice taking notes. Point out that good notes will help them to focus on the important information in the text, organize the information in understandable formats, and aid memory by helping them review for tests. Ask students to take notes of Section 1 in the ways they did in the past. Talk about note-taking procedures and discuss with students what works best for them.

210

Independent Practice

L2 Advertising Have students identify an interest they have that they could channel into a business. Then have the students create a flier or a newspaper ad that advertises their business.

L3 Writing Ask students to write a want ad seeking a person to start his or her own business. Tell students that the ad should name personality traits that they think are necessary for such an entrepreneur.

Have students complete Guided Reading Activity 9.1 in the TCR. LEP

Visual Instruction

Ask small groups of students to review Figure 9.3 and develop a list of answers to the questions posed in the caption. Ask volunteers from each group to share and discuss their lists.

Calculating Your Profit

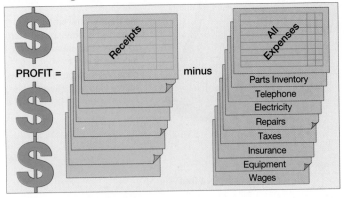

◀ **Figure 9.2 Calculating Your Profit** By adding your wages to your other expenses, including taxes, and then subtracting the total from your receipts, you will have your profit. Keep records of how much you owe and to whom, and of how much your business is taking in. You will need this information to do your taxes.

Depending on the kinds of jobs you do, you will need equipment and replacement parts. At first, you might buy parts as you need them for a particular job. In time, you will find it easier to have an **inventory**. An inventory is a supply of whatever items are used in a business.

Will your business make a profit? Figure 9.2 shows how to determine your profit. Because you could be working for someone else and earning an income, you should pay yourself a wage equal to what you could earn elsewhere. It's important not to forget this opportunity cost when you figure out the profits and losses your new business is making.

Computers Probably one of the first things you want to do, if you have not already done so, is buy a computer. With the computer, you also should purchase the programs that will allow you to keep track of all your expenses and all your receipts. Many such programs exist and are relatively inexpensive. Programs write checks for you, calculate your monthly profit and loss, tell you the difference between

what you own and what you owe (called net worth), and so on. As an entrepreneur, you are taking many risks, but the profit you expect to make is your incentive for taking those risks. For example, if you spend part of your savings to pay for advertising and equipment, you are taking a risk. You may not get enough business to cover these costs. Whenever you buy a special part for a job, you are taking a risk. Suppose you do the work and your customer never pays you. The owner who started the small business shown in Figure 9.3 had to consider the risks.

The Time Factor You are even taking a risk with the time you spend. You are using time to think about what you will do, to write ads, to set up the bookkeeping, and so on. This time is an opportunity cost. You could have used it to do something else, including work for someone for a wage. If you work for someone else, you take only the risk of not being paid, which is usually small. As an entrepreneur your risks are great, but so are the potential rewards.

 Cooperative Learning

Tell students that a new business has an increased chance for success if it provides a product or service for which there is growing demand or potential demand. Then organize students into small groups to brainstorm and research such a product or service. After at least a week of research, invite a representative from each group to describe its product or service and its prospects for a successful business. Cost and availability of materials, economy of production, and cost to consumers or other businesses are factors groups may also want to consider.

**Figure 9.3
Owning a Business**
What factors do you think the owner considered before he started his own business? What rewards do you think he might expect? ▼

Assess

Meeting Lesson Objectives
Assign Section 1 Review as homework or an in-class activity. Each question in the Review addresses the corresponding numbered objective in the Section Focus.

Evaluate
Assign the Section 1 Quiz in the TCR or use the Testmaker to develop a customized quiz.

Reteach
Tell students to rewrite the subheads in Section 1 as questions. Then have them reread the paragraphs to find the answers to their questions.

Enrich
Have students visit the local Chamber of Commerce to interview a representative about the elements of running a successful business. Ask students to present their findings in an oral report.

Close

Write the following statement on the chalkboard: Owning a business means freedom and profits. Have students write a paragraph explaining why the statement is only partially true.

SECTION 1 REVIEW

Understanding Vocabulary
Define entrepreneur, inventory.

Reviewing Objectives
❶ What are two steps you must take to start a business?

❷ What are the four elements common to all businesses?

Chapter 9 Business Organizations **211**

Section 1 Review Answers

Understanding Vocabulary
enterpeneur (p. 208), **inventory** (p. 210)

Reviewing Objectives
1. The two steps you need to take in deciding to start a business are gathering the factors of production and deciding on the best form of business organization.
2. The four elements are expenses, advertising, receipts and record keeping, and risk.

Background

Background

William Gates left Harvard University in 1975, when he co-founded Microsoft. Gates's big chance came in 1980, when IBM asked him to establish the operating system for the personal computer that it was developing. (The operating system is the program that manages the inner workings of a computer.) Today, William Gates owns several billion dollars of Microsoft stock. A workaholic and an avid reader, Gates has built Microsoft into the world's largest and most profitable software company for personal computers.

Teach

Call on volunteers to read the interview with William Gates. Ask students to write questions that they would have asked Gates about his company and about starting a business. Call on volunteers to write their questions on the chalkboard. Finally, have students answer the questions in Checking for Understanding.

You might have interested students find more information about Microsoft—the company location, its organization, and its most recent profit figures. Students might report their findings in a written report.

Personal Perspective

William Gates on Running a Business

Profile

- 1955–
- founder and chief executive officer of Microsoft, probably the most successful corporation of the 1980s
- "the richest man in America," according to *Forbes* annual survey

The following excerpts are taken from an interview with William Gates by *Forbes* (December 7, 1992). Gates answers questions about Microsoft's success and the company's future.

Somebody reports down profits and they say, This industry is in trouble! No, this industry has become more competitive.... Is the structure of the industry changing? Units of PCs [computer sales] have gone up very healthily, more than the industry followers suggest that they have. We've been very open about that.

... I never think we are unassailable. We are in a bizarre position where there is this wild mixture of people who overestimate us and people who underestimate us. They cook up wild scenarios. They certainly tend to overestimate us when they go back and look at why we did various things and come up with how certain events are all part of some master plan. They wildly overestimate us in terms of thinking that we couldn't be in a lot of trouble very quickly if we didn't keep in touch with customers....

Gates talked about the intense competition in the computer software industry. He said his focus is not on short-term profits, but rather on long-term leadership.

... We try to get expectations to be realistic, both about growth and about profitability, because we aren't a company that's really thinking of this in short-term ways. You know, you're dealing with a company where, despite all of its profitability, all the decisions have been based toward being a force and doing good things in five years. I may be making mistakes, but ... I think I have smarter guys just in my research group alone than any other software company has in their entire company. Can I translate that into good products that people care about? That's up to me. It's a bet. It's a risk. I think we'll be around for quite some time doing good things.

Checking for Understanding

❶ How does Gates respond to people who think the computer business is in trouble?

❷ Why does Microsoft try to develop realistic expectations?

❸ What is the risk that Gates talks about?

Answers to Checking for Understanding

1. His response is that the industry has become more competitive.
2. because its concerns are for the long term.
3. Answers will vary but might include risk in producing a product people will not be interested in buying, thus decreasing the company's profitability.

2 Sole Proprietorships and Partnerships

SECTION 2 FOCUS

Terms to Know sole proprietorship, proprietor, unlimited liability, assets, startups, small business incubator, partnership, limited partnership, joint venture

Objectives *After reading this section, you should be able to:*

1. Describe the advantages and disadvantages of a **sole proprietorship**.
2. Explain how people can get **help starting a small business**.
3. List the advantages and disadvantages of a **partnership**.

Sole Proprietorships and Partnerships Are Common in the United States Today

Business can be organized in the United States in a number of ways. The two most common are a sole proprietorship and a partnership.

Sole Proprietorship

The most basic type of business organization is the **sole proprietorship,** a business owned by one person. It is the oldest form of business organization and also the most common. The colonies of Maryland and Pennsylvania were founded as sole proprietorships. When we speak of a **proprietor,** we are always referring to the owner of a business as Figure 9.4 shows. The word *proprietor* comes from the Latin word *proprietas,* meaning "property." A business is a kind of property.

Today, the United States has about 14 million such businesses, and many of them are small. For that reason,

**Figure 9.4
One Owner**
This business has one owner as a sole proprietor who enjoys all the profits, but also must bear all the risks and losses.

▼

Focus

Overview

See the student page for section objectives.

Section 2 explains or describes: two kinds of business organizations: the sole proprietorship and the partnership; and the advantages and disadvantages of both kinds of organizations.

Bellringer

Before presenting the lesson, display Focus Activity Transparency 37 on the overhead projector or copy the material on the chalkboard. Assign the accompanying Focus Activity Sheet.

Motivational Activity

Ask students to develop a list of the businesses in their neighborhood that they frequent and write it on the chalkboard. Ask students to indicate the businesses for which they know the owner or owners.

Preteaching Vocabulary

Give students graph paper and ask them to arrange and number the items from Terms to Know in the form of a crossword puzzle. Then have them find the definitions of the words in Section 2 and write them in numbered sequence as "clues" for their puzzles.

Classroom Resources for Section 2

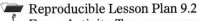 Reproducible Lesson Plan 9.2
Focus Activity Transparency 37
Focus Activity Sheet 37
Guided Reading Activity 9.2

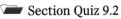 Section Quiz 9.2
Spanish Section Quiz 9.2
Testmaker
Reinforcing Skills 9

Teach

Guided Practice

L2 Writing Have students imagine that they have decided to start a grocery store organized as a sole proprietorship. Have them write a letter to a friend, explaining why they decided to start a grocery store and chose that type of business organization. Call on volunteers to read their letters to the class and discuss their reasons for starting a sole proprietorship.

LEP

L1 Using Tables Have students study Figure 9.5 and discuss the advantages and disadvantages of sole proprietorships. Ask which advantage would be most important to them in deciding to start a sole proprietorship and why.

GLOBAL CONNECTION

Many joint ventures amounting to billions of dollars were established between Mexican and foreign companies between 1991 and 1993, with an estimated investment in these projects amounting to around $5.6 billion. Most of the ventures were in the manufacturing and processing industries.

Figure 9.5 Advantages and Disadvantages of Sole Proprietorships

	Advantages	Disadvantages
Profits and losses	As sole owner, the proprietor receives all the profits because he or she takes all the risks.	Losses are not shared.
Liability		The proprietor has complete legal responsibility for all debts and damages brought upon oneself in doing business. This is known as **unlimited liability**. If the firm is unable to pay its bills or if someone is injured as a result of the business, the proprietor can be forced to sell his or her personal assets as well as the business to pay these debts. **Assets** are items of value such as houses, cars, jewelry, and so on.
Management	Decisions on starting and running the business can be made quickly because the owner does not have to consult with other people. Because a proprietorship is usually small, the operation of the business is less complicated than other types of business. There are generally fewer government regulations than with corporations.	A proprietor must handle all decision making, even for unfamiliar areas of the business. For example, the owner of a manufacturing firm may know a great deal about product design, but very little about selling. This is a severe problem for many sole proprietorships.

they usually are easier and less expensive to start and run. You probably have contact with many sole proprietorships every day without realizing it—owners of corner grocery stores, repair shops, dry cleaners, and so on. Many doctors, dentists, lawyers, and accountants are sole proprietors. In farming, construction, and contracting, sole proprietorships are the most numerous types of business organization. **Figure 9.5** lists the advantages and disadvantages of operating a sole proprietorship.

Help in Starting a Small Business

For a person who wants to start a sole proprietorship, help is available. The federal government's Small Business Administration often helps finance **startups**, which are new small businesses. State departments of commerce and community affairs also offer assistance. Many community college and university campuses have federally funded small business development centers that will help a small business get started.

 Meeting Special Needs

Visual Learning Disability Students with visual-spatial processing problems may have difficulty reading tables. Because information is often presented in tabular form, it is important that students become proficient in reading and interpreting tables. Refer students to Figures 9.5 and 9.6 and guide them to get a broad understanding of the information presented by helping them to identify the headings by column and row.

Figure 9.5 Advantages and Disadvantages of Sole Proprietorships

	Advantages	Disadvantages
Taxes	A proprietor must pay personal income taxes on profits, but these taxes may be lower than taxes for a corporation.	
Personal satisfaction	The proprietor has full pride in owning the business. The person is his or her own boss and makes the business whatever it is.	Running a sole proprietorship is demanding and time-consuming. If the proprietor does not enjoy such responsibility, he or she will find ownership a burden.
Financing growth	Because the proprietor has liability for all debts, it is occasionally easier for a proprietorship to obtain credit than for a corporation of the same size. Lenders are more willing to extend credit knowing that they can take over not only the assets of the business, but also the assets of the proprietor if the loan is not paid back.	A sole proprietor must rely on his or her own funds plus money that can be borrowed from others. Borrowing small amounts may be easier for a sole proprietorship than for a corporation of similar size, but borrowing large amounts can be difficult.
Life of the business		A sole proprietorship depends on one individual. If that person dies, goes bankrupt, or is unwilling or unable to work, the business will probably close. This uncertainty about the future increases the risk to both employees and creditors.

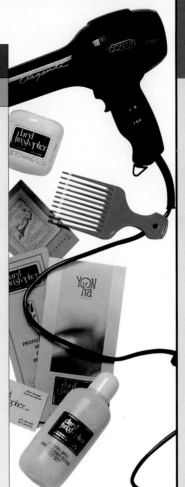

A **small business incubator** might also aid businesses. Just as incubators help hatch chickens, there are business incubators that help "hatch" small businesses. They are often operated with state and federal funds. A small business incubator might provide a low-rent building, management advice, and computers. The incubator's goal is to generate job creation and economic growth, particularly in depressed states.

Partnerships

To take the example of your repair business a little further, suppose that your business is doing so well that your workload has increased to the point at which you have little time for anything else. You could expand your business by hiring an employee. You also need financial capital, but would rather not take out a loan. You may look into taking on a partner.

Chapter 9 Business Organizations **215**

Independent Practice

L1 Comparing Ask students to create a chart comparing sole proprietorships and partnerships in terms of profits and losses, management, liability, and taxes. Discuss completed charts and ask students which business organization they would prefer to own. LEP

L2 Developing Graphics Organize the class into small groups. Ask them to create posters advertising a business of their choice. Display completed posters in the classroom and ask students to decide which business is most effectively presented.

 DID YOU KNOW

In 1991 the Small Business Administration gave out 19,400 loans, with a value of $4.6 billion. Loans from the Small Business Administration accounted for 15 percent of all business loans that year.

 Cooperative Learning

Organize the class into groups of three or four. Refer students to figure 9.6 on page 216. Tell each group to imagine that they are going to form a partnership. Each group should determine what goods or services the partnership will provide. Then have each group draw up an agreement between the partners. The agreement should consider the role of each partner in providing capital and work, how each partner will share in the profits and benefits, and what will happen to organization assets if one partner leaves the organization. Call on volunteers to read their group's agreement to the class.

Independent Practice

L2 Interviewing Have students work in pairs. Ask them to create an imaginary interview between a prospective small business owner seeking assistance and a federal government employee. Call on volunteers to act out their interviews.

L1 Comparing Have students study Figure 9.6 and discuss the advantages and disadvantages of partnerships. Then ask students which disadvantage would be most important in discouraging them from forming a partnership.

Have students complete Guided Reading Activity 9.2 in the TCR. LEP

Visual Instruction

Have students look at Figure 9.7 (p. 217) and review the caption. Form small groups to brainstorm possibilities for joint business ventures (exclude real estate) they might wish to enter. Suggest that they write two profiles of expectations for participation, one for themselves, the other for partners. Ask volunteers to read their lists, and follow this with discussion.

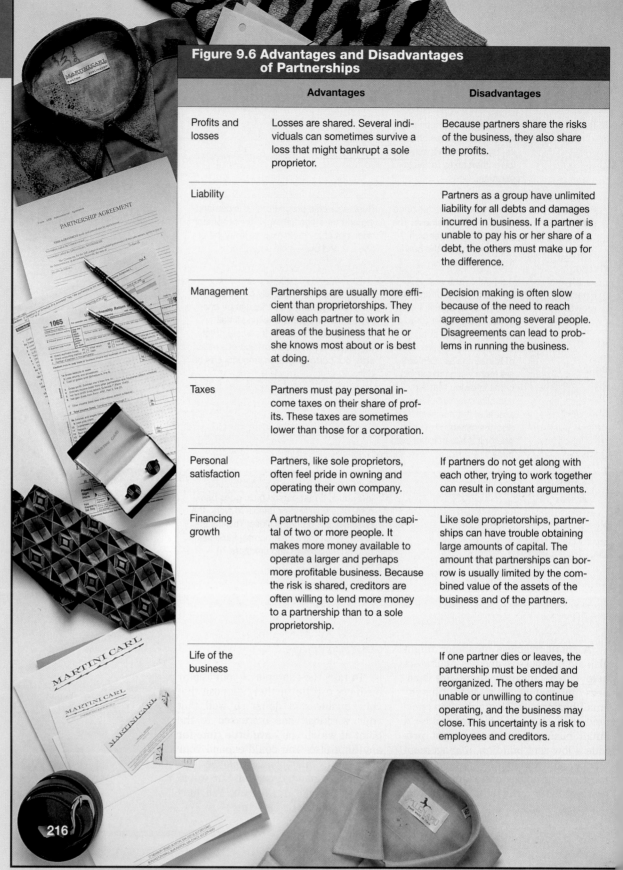

Figure 9.6 Advantages and Disadvantages of Partnerships

	Advantages	Disadvantages
Profits and losses	Losses are shared. Several individuals can sometimes survive a loss that might bankrupt a sole proprietor.	Because partners share the risks of the business, they also share the profits.
Liability		Partners as a group have unlimited liability for all debts and damages incurred in business. If a partner is unable to pay his or her share of a debt, the others must make up for the difference.
Management	Partnerships are usually more efficient than proprietorships. They allow each partner to work in areas of the business that he or she knows most about or is best at doing.	Decision making is often slow because of the need to reach agreement among several people. Disagreements can lead to problems in running the business.
Taxes	Partners must pay personal income taxes on their share of profits. These taxes are sometimes lower than those for a corporation.	
Personal satisfaction	Partners, like sole proprietors, often feel pride in owning and operating their own company.	If partners do not get along with each other, trying to work together can result in constant arguments.
Financing growth	A partnership combines the capital of two or more people. It makes more money available to operate a larger and perhaps more profitable business. Because the risk is shared, creditors are often willing to lend more money to a partnership than to a sole proprietorship.	Like sole proprietorships, partnerships can have trouble obtaining large amounts of capital. The amount that partnerships can borrow is usually limited by the combined value of the assets of the business and of the partners.
Life of the business		If one partner dies or leaves, the partnership must be ended and reorganized. The others may be unable or unwilling to continue operating, and the business may close. This uncertainty is a risk to employees and creditors.

Free Enterprise Activity

Ask small groups to plan starting a small business that requires little or no capitalization and could be run successfully by teenagers.

Have each group decide on a place of business, days and hours of operation, and delegation of responsibilities, in addition to addressing the basic concerns of risk, receipts, record keeping, expenses, and advertising.

Ask each group to develop its plan in a list or outline that a group member can present to the class. Follow with a student-led discussion of the pros and cons of each enterprise plan.

You decide that the best solution is to look for someone who can keep books, handle customers, and invest in the business. You offer to form a partnership. A **partnership** is a business that two or more individuals own and operate. You may sign a partnership agreement that is legally binding. It describes the duties of each partner, the division of profits, and the distribution of assets should the partners end the agreement.

Many doctors, dentists, architects, and lawyers work in partnerships. Two or more people often own small stores. Figure 9.6 lists some of the major advantages and disadvantages of partnerships.

Limited Partnerships A **limited partnership** is a special form of partnership in which the partners are not equal. One partner is called the general partner. This person (or persons) assumes all of the management duties and has full responsibilities for the debts of the limited partnership. The other partners are "limited" because all they do is contribute money or property. They have no voice in the partnership's management.

The advantage to the limited partners is that they have no liability for the losses beyond what they initially invest. The disadvantage, of course, is that they have no say in how the business is run. Limited partnerships must follow specific guidelines when they are formed. Two or more partners must sign a certificate of limited partnership in which they present, at a minimum, the following information:

- The company name
- The nature of the business
- The principal place of business
- The name and place of residence of each partner
- How long the partnership will last
- The amount of cash or other property contributed by each partner

Joint Ventures Sometimes individuals or companies want to do a special project together. They do not have any desire to work together after the project is done. What they might do is form a **joint venture.** A joint venture is a temporary partnership set up for a specific purpose and for a short period of time. Figure 9.7 shows one example.

**Figure 9.7
A Typical Joint Venture**
Suppose investors want to purchase real estate as a short-term investment. They may later plan to resell the property for profit. At that point, the joint venture ends—unlike a general partnership that is set up to be a continuing business.

▼

Assess

Meeting Lesson Objectives

Assign Section 2 Review as homework or an in-class activity.

Evaluate

Assign the Section 2 Quiz in the TCR or use the Testmaker to develop a customized quiz.

Reteach

Have students write five questions about Section 2. Have students take turns answering them.

Enrich

Have some students research the Pennsylvania colony and others research the Maryland colony to find out why they were established as proprietorships.

Close

Have students complete the sentence : In my opinion the _____ is the more efficient type of business organization. Ask them to give reasons for their choice.

SECTION 2 REVIEW

Understanding Vocabulary
Define sole proprietorship, proprietor, unlimited liability, assets, startups, small business incubator, partnership, limited partnership, joint venture.

Reviewing Objectives
1. What are two advantages and two disadvantages of a sole proprietorship?
2. How can people starting a small business get help?
3. What are two advantages and two disadvantages of a partnership?

Section 2 Review Answers
Understanding Vocabulary
sole proprietorship (p. 213), **proprietor** (p. 213), **unlimited liability** (p. 214), **assets** (p. 214), **startups** (p. 214), **small business incubator** (p. 215), **partnership** (p. 217), **limited partnership** (p. 217), **joint venture** (p. 217)
Reviewing Objectives
1. advantages: profits, decision making, taxes lower than corporate, ownership pride, ease in getting credit; disadvantages: responsibility for debt, decisions; time demands; no one to depend on
2. Contact Small Business Administration; state commerce, community affairs department; small business development centers
3. advantages: shared losses, taxes lower than corporate, combined capital; disadvantages: sharing profits, slower decision making, problems in raising capital, dependence on partners

Teach

Use the following activity to help students read and understand the financial information contained in the stock market quotations published in newspapers and financial publications. Ask students to bring the financial pages of their local newspaper to compare the types of information given with the quotations appearing on page 218. Then have students complete the Practicing the Skill section of the feature.

Additional Practice

Have students complete Reinforcing Skills 9 in the TCR.

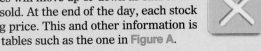

LEARNING ECONOMIC SKILLS

Reading the Financial Page

You can buy and sell shares of stock in corporations. The financial pages of newspapers provide information about the stocks.

Reading Stock Market Quotations

At the beginning of each trading day, stocks open at the same prices they closed at the day before. Prices will move up or down as shares are bought and sold. At the end of the day, each stock has a closing price. This and other information is provided in tables such as the one in Figure A.

Figure A Sample Stock Quotations

52-Week High	52-Week Low	Stock	Sales 100s	High	Low	Last	Change
$25^{1}/_4$	$20^{3}/_4$	TxEt pf	13	$24^{3}/_4$	$24^{1}/_4$	$24^{1}/_4$	$-^{3}/_4$
$37^{1}/_4$	$22^{1}/_4$	TexGT	77	$31^{5}/_8$	31	$31^{5}/_8$	$+^{5}/_8$
$32^{1}/_8$	18	TexInd	180	$31^{5}/_8$	$30^{5}/_8$	$31^{1}/_2$	$+ 1$
$111^{1}/_2$	$70^{1}/_2$	TexInst	1738	110	$105^{5}/_8$	110	$+ 4^{1}/_8$

Prices are listed in dollars and fractions of a dollar. $24^{1}/_4$, for example, means $24.25.

The name of each company is printed in an abbreviated form. In this listing, TexInst refers to Texas Instruments. The 52-Week High/Low columns show the highest and lowest price of the stock during the previous 52 weeks.

The number of shares bought and sold (in hundreds) is reported in the Sales column. The High column reports the highest price for that day, and the Low column reports the lowest. The closing price is shown in the Last column. The Change column shows the change in closing price from the previous day.

Figure B Stock Quotations

Stock	Sales 100s	High	Low	Last	Change
GlbPrt	347	$14^{7}/_8$	$14^{3}/_4$	$14^{3}/_4$	---
GlobYld	2175	$7^{7}/_8$	$7^{3}/_4$	$7^{3}/_4$	$-^{1}/_8$
GldWF	1278	$39^{5}/_8$	$39^{1}/_4$	$39^{1}/_2$	$+1$
Gdrich	621	$41^{7}/_8$	$41^{1}/_2$	$41^{5}/_8$	$-^{1}/_2$
Goodyr	4361	$44^{7}/_8$	44	44	$+^{5}/_8$
Grace	1513	$40^{3}/_8$	40	$40^{1}/_8$	$-^{1}/_4$
Graco	244	$34^{1}/_2$	33	$34^{1}/_2$	$+2$
GrhmFl	1242	$4^{7}/_8$	$4^{1}/_4$	$4^{1}/_4$	$+^{1}/_2$
Graingr	551	$58^{3}/_8$	$57^{1}/_4$	$57^{5}/_8$	---
Grndmet	2424	$27^{1}/_4$	$26^{3}/_4$	$27^{1}/_4$	$+^{3}/_4$

Practicing the Skill

❶ Find the listing for Goodyear Tire and Rubber Company (Goodyr) in Figure B. What was the closing price for this stock?

❷ How much of a change was this from the previous day?

Answers to Practicing the Skill

1. 44
2. +5/8

SECTION 3 The Corporate World and Franchises

SECTION 3 FOCUS

Terms to Know corporation, limited liability, articles of incorporation, corporate charter, franchise

Objectives *After reading this section, you should be able to:*

1. Summarize the advantages and disadvantages of corporations.
2. Explain what types of businesses are involved in franchises.

Many People Share in the Ownership of a Corporation

Suppose your electronic repair business has grown. You now have several partners and have turned your garage into a shop. You would like to expand and rent a store so that your business would be more visible. See Figure 9.8. You would like to buy the latest equipment, charge a little less than your competitors, and capture a larger share of the market for electronic repair work. You need money capital, however.

You have decided that you do not want any more partners. You would have to consult with them about every detail of the business as you do now with your present partners. What you want is financial backers who will let you use their money while letting you run the business. What you are proposing is a corporation. Figure 9.9 (page 220) shows the advantages and disadvantages of corporations.

Corporations

A **corporation** is an organization owned by many people but treated by the law as though it were a person. It can own property, pay taxes, make contracts, sue and be sued, and so on. It has a separate and distinct existence from the stockholders who own

Figure 9.8 Business Location
When you select a location for your business, you must consider many factors including cost and parking areas for your customers.

Focus

Overview
See the student page for section objectives.

Section 3 explains or describes: corporations; the advantages and disadvantages of this type of business organization; and franchises.

Bellringer
Before presenting the lesson, display Focus Activity Transparency 38 and assign the accompanying Focus Activity Sheet.

Motivational Activity
Write the word *corporation* on the chalkboard. Ask students what images come to mind and why.

Preteaching Vocabulary
Write the terms *articles of incorporation, corporate charter,* and *franchise* on the chalkboard. Have students find the definitions of these words in Section 3. Then ask students what all three terms have in common. *(They are all legal arrangements of some aspect of a corporation.)*

Classroom Resources for Section 3

Teach

Guided Practice

L2 Debating Call on volunteers to debate the following: Buying stock in a corporation is a good way to invest money. *(Students taking the pro position might indicate that it is a good way to help businesses grow and to make money for oneself. Those taking the con position might indicate that it is too risky; that corporations are too powerful, when compared with small businesses.)*

L1 Comparing Have students study Figure 9.9 and discuss the advantages and disadvantages of corporations. Then discuss with students how the personality characteristics needed to work for a large corporation might differ from those needed to begin a sole proprietorship.

GLOBAL ECONOMICS

Of the 500 largest foreign companies in 1993, four were based in Brazil, two in Mexico, and one in India. To make this list, companies must have revenues of at least $3.7 billion, be based outside the United States, and be publicly traded.

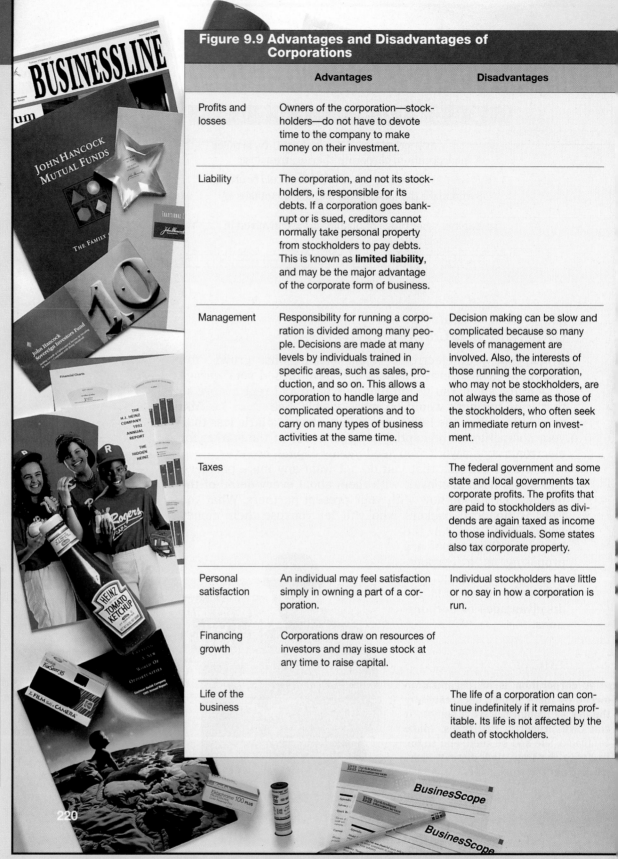

Figure 9.9 Advantages and Disadvantages of Corporations

	Advantages	Disadvantages
Profits and losses	Owners of the corporation—stockholders—do not have to devote time to the company to make money on their investment.	
Liability	The corporation, and not its stockholders, is responsible for its debts. If a corporation goes bankrupt or is sued, creditors cannot normally take personal property from stockholders to pay debts. This is known as **limited liability**, and may be the major advantage of the corporate form of business.	
Management	Responsibility for running a corporation is divided among many people. Decisions are made at many levels by individuals trained in specific areas, such as sales, production, and so on. This allows a corporation to handle large and complicated operations and to carry on many types of business activities at the same time.	Decision making can be slow and complicated because so many levels of management are involved. Also, the interests of those running the corporation, who may not be stockholders, are not always the same as those of the stockholders, who often seek an immediate return on investment.
Taxes		The federal government and some state and local governments tax corporate profits. The profits that are paid to stockholders as dividends are again taxed as income to those individuals. Some states also tax corporate property.
Personal satisfaction	An individual may feel satisfaction simply in owning a part of a corporation.	Individual stockholders have little or no say in how a corporation is run.
Financing growth	Corporations draw on resources of investors and may issue stock at any time to raise capital.	
Life of the business		The life of a corporation can continue indefinitely if it remains profitable. Its life is not affected by the death of stockholders.

220

◆▷◗ Meeting Special Needs

Physical Disability Students who have difficulties with fine motor skills are often inefficient and slow writers. Because many assignments require some type of writing, these students are at a disadvantage. Teach these students to read short segments of the text and to use an abridged form of note taking, in which they write only single words and associated facts.

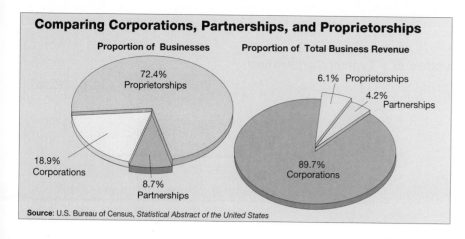

Comparing Corporations, Partnerships, and Proprietorships

Proportion of Businesses

72.4% Proprietorships

18.9% Corporations

8.7% Partnerships

Proportion of Total Business Revenue

6.1% Proprietorships

4.2% Partnerships

89.7% Corporations

Source: U.S. Bureau of Census, *Statistical Abstract of the United States*

Figure 9.10 Comparing Types of Business
Although only about 19 percent of American businesses are organized as corporations, they generate almost 90 percent of total business revenue.

Visual Instruction

Refer students to Figure 9.10. Have them study the graphs and help them generalize about proprietorships, partnerships, and corporations. *(Proprietorships make up the largest percentage of businesses but bring in a small percentage of total revenues. Corporations are a small percentage of businesses but bring in the most revenue. Partnerships form a small percentage of businesses and revenues.)*

 DID YOU KNOW

Point out to students that the concept of corporations dates back to ancient Rome. As a part of Roman law, this concept spread throughout Europe. Corporations in America after the Revolutionary War were chartered to build roads, canals, and bridges, as well as the new nation's industries.

---

the corporation's stock. Stock represents ownership rights to a certain portion of the profits and assets of the company that issues the stock.

In terms of the amount of business done (measured in dollars), the corporation is the most important type of business organization in the United States today. Figure 9.10 compares corporations to other forms of business in terms of numbers and revenue.

In order to form a corporation, its founders must do three things. First, they must register their company with the government of the state in which it will be headquartered. Second, they must sell stock. Third, along with the other shareholders, they must elect a board of directors.

Registering the Corporation Every state has laws governing the formation of corporations, but most state laws are similar. Suppose that you and your partners decide to form a corporation. You will have to file an **articles of incorporation** application with the state in which you will run your corporation. In general, these articles include four items:

1. Name, address, and purpose of the corporation;
2. Names and addresses of the initial board of directors (these men and women will serve until the first stockholders' meeting, when a new board may be elected);
3. Number of shares of stock to be issued;
4. Amount of money capital to be raised through issuing stock.

If the articles are in agreement with state law, the state will grant you a **corporate charter**—a license to operate from that state.

Selling Stock To continue the example of your electronic repair business, you could sell shares of either common or preferred stock in your new corporation. Common stock gives the holder part ownership in the corporation and voting rights at the annual stockholders' meeting. It does not guarantee a dividend—money return on the money invested in a company's stock. Preferred stock does guarantee a certain amount of dividend each year. Preferred stock also guarantees to the stockholder first claim, after creditors have been paid, on whatever value is left in the corporation if it goes out of business. Holders of preferred stock usually do not have voting rights in the corporation, although they are part owners.

If your corporation were to become large, you might find its stock

Chapter 9 Business Organizations **221**

Cooperative Learning

Organize the class into small groups and ask them to decide on a franchise they would like to own. Have each group divide up the following tasks: listing the group's reasons for wanting to buy the particular franchise, finding out the procedure for buying the franchise, interviewing a franchise owner about the pros and cons of owning a franchise, and developing a plan for getting capital needed to buy the franchise. Have each group compile its information in an oral report accompanied by visuals. Call on a member from each group to present the group's findings to the class.

Independent Practice

L2 Analyzing Review with students the duties of a corporation's board of directors and those of a company's officers. Have students write a short paragraph explaining which group is more responsible for the success or failure of a corporation. Discuss students' paragraphs.

L3 Researching Have students review and report on the contents of a bulletin or annual stockholder's report from a local company.

 Have students complete Guided Reading Activity 9.3 in the TCR. LEP

? DID YOU KNOW

NASDAQ is now one of the largest over-the-counter exchanges and lists more companies than the New York or American stock exchanges.

Structure of a Typical Corporation

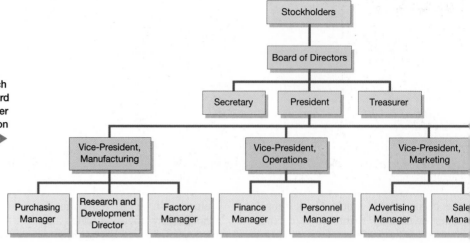

Figure 9.11 Typical Structure of a Corporation
Based on what you have read, how much power does the board of directors have over the way a corporation is run? ▶

traded in the local stock market as over-the-counter stock. *Over-the-counter* means that individual brokerage firms hold quantities of shares of stocks that they buy and sell for investors. Should your corporation continue to grow, it would be traded on a regional stock exchange. It might be listed as an over-the-counter stock with the National Association of Securities Dealers Automated Quotation (NASDAQ) in one of their three lists. The largest corporations are usually listed on the New York Stock Exchange (NYSE).

Selling stock is not the only way a corporation can raise capital to develop or expand. It can also sell debt by issuing bonds. A bond promises to pay a stated rate of interest over a stated period of time; it also promises to repay the full amount borrowed at the end of that time.

Naming a Board of Directors To become incorporated, a company must have a board of directors. You and your partners, as founders of the corporation, would select the first board

for your corporation. After that, stockholders at their annual stockholders' meetings would elect the board. The bylaws of the corporation govern this election. Bylaws are a set of rules describing how stock will be sold and dividends paid, with a list of the duties of the company's officers. They are written after the corporate charter has been granted.

The board is responsible for supervising and controlling the corporation. It does not run business operations on a day-to-day basis, however. Rather, it hires officers for the company—president, vice-president(s), secretary, and treasurer—to run the business and hire other employees. Figure 9.11 shows the typical structure of a corporation.

Franchises

Many hotel, motel, gas station, and fast-food chains are franchises. A **franchise** is a contract in which a franchisor (fran-chy-ZOR) sells to another business the right to use its name and sell its products. The person or business buying these rights,

 Free Enterprise Activity

Allocate $25,000 to each student to start a personal investment portfolio of common stocks purchased in round lots of 100 shares. Purchase prices should be based on today's closing price. Remind students to add a 12-percent broker's commission for each stock purchased, to be paid out of their allocation.

Any differences between $25,000 and the total they pay to their brokerage goes into a savings account.

For the next 10 trading days they should check the daily stock quotations and graph closing prices on a line graph. After 10 days, have students compare their portfolios.

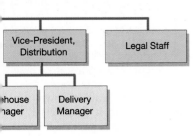

Figure 9.12 ▲
A Motel Franchise
One advantage of owning a motel franchise is that most people will decide to stay in a well-known motel chain in an unfamiliar city rather than spending the time looking for other lodging. They also want to be able to count on a certain quality of service.

called the franchisee (fran-chy-ZEE), pays a fee that may include a percentage of all money taken in. If a person buys a motel franchise like the one shown in Figure 9.12, that person agrees to pay the motel chain a certain fee plus a portion of the profits for as long as his or her motel stays in business. In return, the chain will help the franchisee set up the motel. Often, the chain will have a training program to teach the franchisee about the business and set the standards of business operations.

The chain will help in choosing a location for the building and in ar-

ranging credit. If necessary, it will train the new owner and his or her staff. Because the motel is part of the chain, the new owner benefits from the advertising campaigns that the chain runs. Travelers will identify his or her motel with the national chain.

SECTION 3 REVIEW

Understanding Vocabulary
Define corporation, limited liability, articles of incorporation, corporate charter, franchise.

Reviewing Objectives
1. What are the advantages and disadvantages of corporations?
2. What types of businesses are involved in franchises?

Assess

Meeting Lesson Objectives
Assign Section 3 Review as homework or an in-class activity.

Evaluate
📁 Assign the Section 3 Quiz in the TCR or use the Testmaker.
📁 Assign the Chapter 9 Test Form A or Form B or use the Testmaker.

Reteach
Have students outline the section and write a paragraph related to each major headline.
📁 Have students complete Reteaching Activity 9 in the TCR.

Enrich
Have students research the history of a leading Fortune 500 corporation.
📁 Have students complete Enrichment Activity 9 in the TCR.

Close

Ask students to indicate whether they agree or disagree with this statement: The economy is better off if there are more corporations than other kinds of businesses.

Section 3 Review Answers

Understanding Vocabulary
corporation (p. 219), **limited liability** (p. 220), **articles of incorporation** (p. 221), **corporate charter** (p. 221), **franchise** (p. 222)

Reviewing Objectives
1. Advantages: owners need not devote time to receive profit; the corporate responsibility for debts; shared management responsibility; individual satisfaction in being a stockholder; corporate use of resources of many investors; corporate life. Disadvantages: slow decision making; higher taxes; individual stockholders have little say-so.
2. hotels, motels, gas stations, and fast-food chains

Teach

Survey students to find out the ways they and their families keep fit. Take a count of how many use fitness machines. Discuss with students the importance of fitness to American society today. Then ask students whether they think a corporation that addresses the idea of fitness would be successful today. Tell students that this feature discusses such a corporation.

Have students use the information in the feature to create a poster advertising the CML group. Display completed ad posters in the classroom.

Readings in Economics

THE BOSTON GLOBE   JUNE 8, 1993

THE NORDIC WAY
by Frederic M. Biddle

From the NordicTrack store, it's a brisk mall lap to Scientific Revolution. Then, around the corner to another store, NordicSport by NordicTrack. Finally, down the corridor to The Nature Co. and Britches Great Outdoors.

Schlepping around the Mall of America with Charles M. Leighton, chairman of CML Group Inc., doesn't match the aerobic benefits of the company's Nordic-Track fitness machines. But there's probably no better place to see what CML has become—and how the company has tapped a 1990s consumer philosophy as few other retailers have—than here in the country's biggest shopping mall, where most of CML's retail businesses can be found under one roof....

Leighton, 58, can feel good about his Acton [Massachusetts]-based holding company. CML pumped up sales 45 per-cent to a record $582 million in the four quarters ended Jan. 30, while profits rose 38 percent to $47.4 million. Those results, plus a 35 percent return on equity, won it the title of The Globe 100 Company of the Year....

Just four years ago, however, CML was targeted by corporate raider Irwin Jacobs after it loaded up on debt to make several acquisitions. Leighton fought off Jacobs but was forced to restructure. When the dust settled three main units were left; NordicTrack; The Nature Co., a retailer of products considered environmentally responsible; and Britches of Georgetowne, a men's apparel retailer....

But ... NordicTrack is the star of Leighton's miniconglomerate. It generates just over half of CML's sales and more than 80 percent of earnings.

• THINK ABOUT IT •

1. How did CML win the title of The Globe 100 Company of the Year?

2. What are the three divisions of CML?

Answers to Think About It

1. by increasing sales 45 percent to $582 million, by raising profits 38 percent to $47.4 million, and by getting a 35 percent return on equity
2. NordicTrack, The Nature Co., and Britches of Georgetowne

CHAPTER

9 *Highlights*

Section 1

Starting a Business

Key Terms
entrepreneur (p. 208)
inventory (p. 210)

Summary
Two steps are involved in starting a business. Once these steps have been taken, entrepreneurs must carefully consider the four key elements that every business involves.

Section 2

Sole Proprietorships and Partnerships

Key Terms
sole proprietorship (p. 213)
proprietor (p. 213)
unlimited liability (p. 214)
assets (p. 214)
startups (p. 214)
small business incubator (p. 215)
partnership (p. 217)
limited partnership (p. 217)
joint venture (p. 217)

Summary
The most common form of business organization in the United States is a sole proprietorship, which has advantages and disadvantages. Partnerships, owned by two or more people, involve their own set of advantages and disadvantages. Limited partnerships must follow specific guidelines.

Section 3

The Corporate World and Franchises

Key Terms
corporation (p. 219)
limited liability (p. 220)
articles of incorporation (p. 221)
corporate charter (p. 221)
franchise (p. 222)

Summary
Many people share in the ownership of corporations, which have advantages and disadvantages different from those of other forms of business organization. Franchises, in which a franchisor sells to another business the right to use its name and sell its products, are common in some industries.

Chapter 9 Business Organizations **225**

Using Chapter 9
HIGHLIGHTS

Use the Chapter 9 Highlights to preview, review, condense, or reteach the chapter. A Spanish Chapter Highlights is available in the Spanish Handbook.

Preview/Review
After students read the Chapter 9 Highlights, have them complete Economics Vocabulary Activity 9 in the TCR. Spanish Vocabulary Activities are also available in the Spanish Resource Binder.

Vocabulary Software reinforces the economic terms used in Chapter 9.

Condense
Have students listen to Chapter 9 on the Audiocassettes in the TCR. A 1-page written activity and 1-page test accompany this material. These materials are also available in Spanish.

Reteach
Have students complete Reteaching Activity 9 in the TCR. Spanish Reteaching Activities are also available.

 VIDEODISC

Nightly Business Report
Economics in Action
Use "Business Organizations" on Disc 1, Side B, Video 12.

Search 13526, Play to 22278

225

Identifying Key Terms

1. b
2. d
3. a
4. c
5. e

Paragraphs will vary but should include all the terms.

Recalling Facts and Ideas

Section 1

1. advertising and risk
2. an opportunity cost

Section 2

3. sole proprietorship
4. Advantages include receiving all profits, quick decision making, paying lower taxes than corporations, pride in sole ownership, greater ease in obtaining credit. Disadvantages include not sharing losses, complete responsibility for debts, all decision making, demand on time, complete reliance on one's own funds, complete dependence on one individual for the life of the business.
5. the Small Business Administration, state departments of commerce and community affairs, community college and university small business centers, National Business Incubation Association
6. a partnership
7. in a limited partnership, responsibilities for debt and management are not shared equally among the partners. A joint venture is a temporary partnership set up for a specific purpose and a brief period.

Section 3

8. It must be registered with the state in which it will be headquartered, it must sell stock, and it

must elect a board of directors.
9. the state from which the corporation will operate
10. stockholders
11. The franchisor sells the right to use its name and sells its product or service to the franchisee. The franchisor may help the franchisee to operate profitably. The franchisee pays a fee that may include a percentage of sales.

Identifying Key Terms

Write the letter of the definition in Column B below that correctly defines each term in Column A.

Column A
1. inventory (p. 210)
2. corporate charter (p. 221)
3. assets (p. 213)
4. franchise (p. 222)
5. unlimited liability (p. 214)

Column B
a. items of value
b. supply of items that are used in a business
c. sale by a business of the right to use its name to another business or individual
d. right to operate
e. legal responsibility for all debts and damages incurred when doing business

Write a paragraph about the advantages and disadvantages of different types of business organizations using the following terms.

sole proprietorship (p. 213)
partnership (p. 217)
limited partnership (p. 217)
joint venture (p. 217)
corporation (p. 219)
franchise (p. 222)

Recalling Facts and Ideas

Section 1

1. Every business involves expenses and receipts and record keeping. What are two other elements?
2. When you calculate your profits, it is especially important for you to include the value of your time. What is this called?

Section 2

3. What is the most common form of business organization?
4. What are the advantages and disadvantages of a sole proprietorship?
5. If you need help in starting a small business, where can you look?
6. Often two or more individuals want to start a business. What is one form of business organization they can use?
7. What is the difference between a limited partnership and a joint venture?

Section 3

8. What are the elements of every corporation?
9. Who grants corporate charters?
10. Which group within a corporation chooses the board of directors?
11. How does a franchise operate?

Critical Thinking

Section 1

Demonstrating Reasoned Judgment Why do you have to include the opportunity cost of your time when you calculate your profits in your own business?

Section 2

Drawing Conclusions Why would a person decide in favor of a partnership rather than a sole proprietorship?

Section 3

Analyzing Information What kind of problems in a corporation might be due to its complex organizational structure?

Critical Thinking

Section 1

because the time used in running your business could have been used to do something else, including working for a wage

Section 2

to expand the business, or to share the work, profits, and losses

Applying Economic Concepts

Comparing Business Organizations In this chapter you have seen numerous advantages and disadvantages of different types of business organizations. Make a list of the following: sole proprietorship, partnership, limited partnership, joint venture, corporation, and franchise. After each type, indicate the single most important advantage that you believe this form of business organization has.

Chapter Projects

1. **Individual Project** Three major business news magazines report the top several hundred corporations in America every year, usually in May or June. They are *Forbes, Fortune,* and *Business Week*. Find one or more of these magazines in a library. Make a list of the latest information on the top five industrial corporations, such as General Motors and Microsoft. Indicate for each the following information: (1) number of employees, (2) total sales in billions of dollars, (3) total market value as given by the stock market (if available), and (4) change in ranking from the previous year.

2. **Cooperative Learning Project** Work in groups of four. Each group should select a corporation listed in the financial pages of a newspaper. Then use business magazines and financial and annual reports, if possible, to determine the annual earnings, dividends, and stock prices of that corporation over the last year. Compare the corporation with those selected by other groups and discuss which stocks would have been the best investments during the past year.

Reviewing Skills

Reading the Financial Page

1. How many shares of Apple Computer (AppleCptr) were traded?
2. What was the net change in the price of the stock of Apple Computer on this day?
3. Compare this day's closing price for Apple Computer with its 52-week high. How much less is this day's closing price?

52 Weeks High	Low	Stock	Sales 100s	High	Low	Last	Change
$19\frac{1}{4}$	$14\frac{1}{2}$	AMTROL	45	$19\frac{1}{2}$	$18\frac{1}{2}$	$18\frac{1}{2}$	$-\frac{3}{4}$
$16\frac{7}{8}$	$5\frac{15}{16}$	AmvstrFnl	314	$10\frac{3}{8}$	10	$10\frac{1}{8}$	$-\frac{1}{4}$
$15\frac{1}{2}$	$5\frac{3}{4}$	AmylinPharm	96	9	$8\frac{3}{4}$	$8\frac{3}{4}$	$-\frac{1}{4}$
$16\frac{3}{4}$	$10\frac{1}{4}$	Analogic	489	$15\frac{1}{2}$	15	$15\frac{1}{8}$	$-\frac{3}{8}$
$14\frac{1}{2}$	$9\frac{3}{4}$	Anly&Tech	532	$14\frac{1}{2}$	$13\frac{5}{8}$	$13\frac{5}{8}$	$-\frac{3}{8}$
$35\frac{3}{4}$	$16\frac{1}{4}$	Anlyint	72	29	28	29	...
18	$10\frac{7}{8}$	Anangel	2	$17\frac{1}{8}$	$17\frac{1}{8}$	$17\frac{1}{8}$	...
15	$5\frac{5}{8}$	AnchrBcp	560	$14\frac{1}{4}$	14	$14\frac{1}{4}$	...
$24\frac{3}{4}$	$11\frac{7}{8}$	AnchrBcpWis	117	$22\frac{1}{2}$	22	$22\frac{1}{2}$	$+\frac{1}{4}$
$14\frac{3}{4}$	$5\frac{3}{4}$	AndovrBcp	193	$14\frac{1}{4}$	$13\frac{7}{8}$	$14\frac{1}{8}$	...
$4\frac{3}{4}$	$2\frac{1}{4}$	AndovrTog	67	$2\frac{1}{2}$	$2\frac{1}{4}$	$2\frac{1}{2}$	...
$30\frac{1}{4}$	16	AndrewCp	1055	$28\frac{1}{4}$	$27\frac{3}{4}$	28	$+\frac{1}{4}$
$19\frac{1}{4}$	$10\frac{7}{8}$	Andros	44	$14\frac{1}{2}$	14	$14\frac{3}{8}$	$-\frac{1}{8}$
$13\frac{1}{2}$	$5\frac{1}{2}$	Anergen	8	7	$6\frac{1}{2}$	$6\frac{1}{2}$	$-\frac{1}{2}$
$5\frac{5}{8}$	$1\frac{7}{16}$	ApertusTech	341	$3\frac{1}{4}$	3	3	$-\frac{1}{8}$
$12\frac{1}{2}$	$8\frac{5}{8}$	ApogeeEnt	82	12	$11\frac{3}{4}$	12	$+\frac{1}{4}$
$65\frac{1}{4}$	$26\frac{1}{2}$	AppleCptr	72258	$28\frac{3}{4}$	$25\frac{1}{2}$	$25\frac{5}{8}$	$-1\frac{7}{8}$
$24\frac{3}{4}$	$5\frac{5}{8}$	AppleSouth	402	23	$22\frac{1}{4}$	23	...
$22\frac{1}{4}$	$8\frac{1}{4}$	Applebee	323	$20\frac{1}{4}$	$19\frac{3}{4}$	$19\frac{3}{4}$	$-\frac{1}{4}$
20	$8\frac{3}{4}$	ApplncRecyc	136	$9\frac{3}{4}$	9	$9\frac{1}{4}$	$-\frac{1}{4}$
$15\frac{1}{4}$	$4\frac{1}{2}$	AppldBiosci	254	6	$5\frac{7}{8}$	$5\frac{7}{8}$	...
$2\frac{1}{4}$	$\frac{7}{8}$	AppliedCrbn	39	$1\frac{1}{2}$	$1\frac{3}{8}$	$1\frac{3}{8}$	$-\frac{1}{8}$
$25\frac{1}{4}$	11	AppldImuSci	393	$20\frac{1}{4}$	$19\frac{1}{2}$	$19\frac{1}{2}$	...
$62\frac{1}{2}$	18	AppldMati	2338	$59\frac{1}{4}$	$56\frac{1}{2}$	$58\frac{1}{4}$	$+1$

Writing About Economics

Persuasive Writing Review the information that you recorded in Your Economics Journal for this chapter. Then write a persuasive paragraph explaining why someone should patronize locally owned businesses.

227

Chapter 9
REVIEW

Section 3
Decision making can be slow because of all the levels of management involved.

Applying Economic Concepts

Answers will vary, but students should indicate the most important advantage for each type of business organization.

Chapter Projects

1. Students might present their information in the form of a chart.
2. Review with students the ways to read the financial pages of a newspaper.

Reviewing Skills

1. 7,225,800
2. $-1\frac{7}{8}$
3. $39\frac{5}{8}$

Writing About Economics

Encourage students to provide specific reasons for patronizing locally owned businesses.

? BONUS QUESTION

The following bonus question may be written on the chalkboard when students take the chapter test.
Q: Which investment generally poses less risk to investors, common stock or preferred stock? Why?
A: preferred stock, because it guarantees a dividend and first claim to the value that remains after creditors are paid if the corporation goes out of business.

Point

For many years the government regulated a number of important industries to protect the interests of consumers. The Reagan administration thought there was too much government interference in some industries and that deregulation would better serve the interests of consumers. With deregulation, the government exercises less control over an industry, thereby allowing the market forces to determine how the industry will function. Have students read the arguments for and against deregulation.

Teach

L1 Classifying Have students create a chart indicating the reasons for and the reasons against deregulation of the airline industry as presented in the feature. *(for: lower fares, higher productivity, increase in safety; against: price cutting designed to drive weaker airlines out of business, thereby leading to less competition and higher fares in the long run)*

ISSUE: Role of the Government in the Economy: Should Industry be Deregulated?

Deregulation of industries gained popularity in the 1980s, especially during the Reagan years (1981-89). Airlines, banking, and trucking were three of the most important industries deregulated. Cable TV had also been deregulated, so consumers blamed rising cable charges on this action. In 1992 Congress reregulated the cable TV industry in the hope of promoting competition and lowering prices. Many now believe that the government should reregulate other industries.

PRO Deregulation brought many changes to the airline industry. Economist Alfred E. Kahn, a former chairman of the Civil Aeronautics Board (disbanded with deregulation), writes that the two most important consequences of airline deregulation have been lower fares and higher productivity. He also asserts that safety has increased since deregulation. Accident rates dropped 20-45 percent from the regulated years.

Economist Thomas Gale Moore also argues that deregulation works. He writes that previous regulation of the trucking industry increased costs and rates significantly, as well as lowered quality of service. Rates for the industry fell after deregulation, and competition increased as well. Moore writes on this success of deregulation in stimulating competition:

The number of new firms has increased dramatically. By 1990 the total number of licensed carriers exceeded forty thousand, considerably more than double the number authorized in 1980. The ICC [Interstate Commerce Commission] had also awarded nationwide authority to about five thousand freight carriers. The value of operating rights granted by the ICC, once worth hundreds of thousands of dollars when such authority was almost impossible to secure from the commission, has plummeted to close to zero now that operating rights are easy to obtain.

Finally, Alfred Kahn warns against the recent reregulation trend:

Airline deregulation has worked. It would be ironic if, by misdiagnosing our present discontents, we were to return to policies of protectionism and centralized planning at the very time when countries as dissimilar as China, the Soviet Union, Chile, Australia, France, Spain, and Poland are all discovering the superiority of the free market.

Counterpoint

CON Those who oppose deregulation argue that it has a tendency to make markets less competitive. Since deregulation in 1986, monthly basic cable rates have increased sharply. Gene Kimmelman, legislative director of the Consumer Federation of America, states that the reregulating of the cable TV industry is "a first step in the right direction. It's the first real cost savings to consumers that's come out of the (FCC) in a decade."

Others worry that deregulating the airlines also may not have been such a good idea. Airline fares are lower, but those against deregulation see the price cutting as fare wars designed to drive weaker competitors out of business, thus leading to less competition and higher fares in the long run. John Greenwald explains this position in *TIME* :

> But there is a darker side to the fare war: many experts see it as a thinly veiled declaration of war against low-cost rivals like TWA and Continental, which currently fly under the protective wing of the bankruptcy courts and thus pay no interest on part of their debt. Life will get rougher for them once they emerge from Chapter 11 protection and are forced to survive on their own resources—something many analysts fear these weaker carriers may be unable to do for long. Once rid of such pesky competitors and their cutthroat tactics, the major airlines could regain full control of airfares—and might then be free to raise them.

Exploring the Issue

Reviewing Facts
1. What kind of changes did deregulation bring to the airline industry?
2. What is one argument for deregulation? One against?

Critical Thinking
3. Why do you think deregulation brought higher cable rates but lower airline fares?

TEACHING
Point/Counterpoint

L2 Holding a Panel Discussion Ask volunteers to participate in a panel discussion about the positive and negative aspects of deregulation on the airline and cable TV industries. Considering the issues, students on the panel should indicate what they think about the deregulation of these industries.

L3 Researching Have students research other industries that have been deregulated in recent years, such as savings and loans and telecommunications. Have students report on what happened in these industries and whether deregulation benefited the industry and the public. Students might present their information in a written report.

Assess

Have students answer the Exploring the Issue questions.

Close

Ask students if they think there are industries that should be regulated more or that should be deregulated. Have students explain their views.

Answers to Exploring the Issue

1. lower fares, higher productivity, driving weaker competitors out of business
2. Answers will vary but may include lower fares because of competition (for) and price fixing after eliminating competition (against).
3. Answers will vary, but students may speculate that cable television began without regulation and charged whatever the market would appear to tolerate. On the other hand, airlines emerged from regulation and needed to face competition, so prices tended to go down.

CHAPTER 10 COMPETITION AND MONOPOLIES

CHAPTER ORGANIZER

Daily Objectives	Special Features	Classroom Resources
Section 1 Perfect Competition • **List** the five conditions of perfect competition. • **Explain** why agriculture is sometimes considered an example of perfect competition. • **Assess** the desirability of perfect competition.	**Critical Thinking Skills:** Analyzing Economic Cartoons, p. 236	Reproducible Lesson Plan 10.1 *NBR* Video 14 Focus Activity Transparency 39 Focus Activity Sheet 39 Guided Reading Activity 10.1 Cooperative Learning Activity 10 Primary and Secondary Source Readings 10 Section Quiz 10.1 Spanish Section Quiz 10.1 Testmaker Reinforcing Skills 10
Section 2 Monopoly, Oligopoly, and Monopolistic Competition • **List** the four characteristics of a pure monopoly. • **Describe** the five characteristics of an oligopoly. • **Explain** the five characteristics of monopolistic competition.	**Personal Perspective:** Joan Robinson on Imperfect Competition, p. 243	Reproducible Lesson Plan 10.2 Focus Activity Transparency 40 Focus Activity Sheet 40 Economic Concepts Transparencies 9 and 11 Guided Reading Activity 10.2 Section Quiz 10.2 Spanish Section Quiz 10.2 Testmaker Enrichment Activity 10
Section 3 Government Policies Toward Competition • **Explain** the difference between interlocking directorates and mergers. • **List** at least four major federal regulatory agencies. • **Explain** the movement toward reregulation	**News Clip:** "Is Nike Getting Too Big?" *Time,* p. 248	Reproducible Lesson Plan 10.3 Focus Activity Transparency 41 Focus Activity Sheet 41 Economic Concepts Transparency 12 Guided Reading Activity 10.3 Free Enterprise Activity 10 Consumer Application Activity 10 Economics Laboratory 3 Economic Simulation 3 Mathematics Practice for Economics 33 Performance Assessment Activity 33 Section Quiz 10.3 Spanish Section Quiz 10.3 Testmaker Enrichment Activity 10

0:00 OUT OF TIME? If time does not permit teaching this chapter, you may use the Chapter 10 Highlights and the Audiocassettes that include a 1-page activity and a 1-page test.

Chapter 10 Review and Evaluation

Special Features

Chapter 10 Highlights, p. 249
Chapter 10 Review, pp. 250–251
Economics Lab, pp. 252–253

Classroom Resources

- Chapter 10 Test Forms A and B
- Economics Vocabulary Activity 10
- Spanish Economics Vocabulary Activity 10
- Audiocassette 10
- Spanish Audiocassette 10
- Reteaching Activity 10
- Spanish Reteaching Activity 10

Key to Ability Levels

Teaching strategies have been coded for varying learning styles and abilities.

L1 Level 1 activities are **basic** activities and should be within the ability range of all students.

L2 Level 2 activities are **average** activities designed for the ability range of average to above-average students.

L3 Level 3 activities are **challenging** activities designed for the ability range of above-average students.

LEP activities should be within the ability range of **Limited English Proficiency** students.

Performance Assessment

The following chapter project may be assigned at the beginning of the chapter and used for performance assessment. See page T12 for additional Performance Assessment information.

Classifying Information Have students work in small groups to examine the organization of businesses they frequent or are familiar with. Students should make a list of these businesses during the time they study Chapter 10. Then they should develop a chart that classifies these businesses by their organization type— monopoly, oligopoly, monopolistic competition. Students might report their findings orally.

Additional Resources

Readings for the Student

Brue, Stanley L., and Wentworth, Donald R. *Economic Scenes: Theory in Today's World*, 4th ed. Englewood Cliffs, N.J.: Prentice-Hall, 1988.

Mauser, Ferdinand F., and Schwartz, David J. *American Business: An Introduction*, 6th ed. New York: Harcourt Brace Jovanovich, 1986.

Readings for the Teacher

Carson, Robert B. *Economic Issues: Alternative Approaches*, 5th ed. New York: St. Martin's Press, 1990.

Edgmand, Michael R. et al. *Economics and Contemporary Issues*. Hinsdale, Ill.: Dryden Press, 1991.

Multimedia Materials

Free Choices and Enterprise. Filmstrip. National Schools Committee on Economic Education, P.O. Box 326, Old Greenwich, CT 06870

Is There Competition in the System? Film. Modern Talking Picture Service, 5000 Park Street, North, St. Petersburg, FL 33709

The System. Film series. Exxon Company, P.O. Box 2180, Houston, TX 77001

Milky Way Merchant. Simulation. Includes Teacher's manual. Apple. Blythe Valley Software, 40879 Highway 41, Silver Creek Center, P.O. Box 1, Oakhurst, CA 93644.

230B

Chapter Overview

Chapter 10 explains or describes: the influence of competition on supply and demand and price; perfect competition and pure monopoly; oligopoly and monopolistic competition; and government regulation of business.

VIDEODISC

Nightly Business Report

Economics in Action
Use "Competition and Monopolies" on Disc 1, Side B, Video 14.

Search 35044, Play to 40416

CHAPTER

10 COMPETITION AND MONOPOLIES

Where can you obtain information on air fares?

How do airlines determine air fares?

How many airline companies can you name?

How do these companies compete for business?

230 Unit 3 Microeconomics: Markets, Prices, and Business Competition

Answering Economic Questions

The questions in the above illustration are designed to lead into the main concepts of Chapter 10. Encourage students to list the ways airline companies compete for business. Stress to them that the desire for profit is an important aspect of most businesses. Have students discuss the questions and have them explain why they think airlines do or do not make profits.

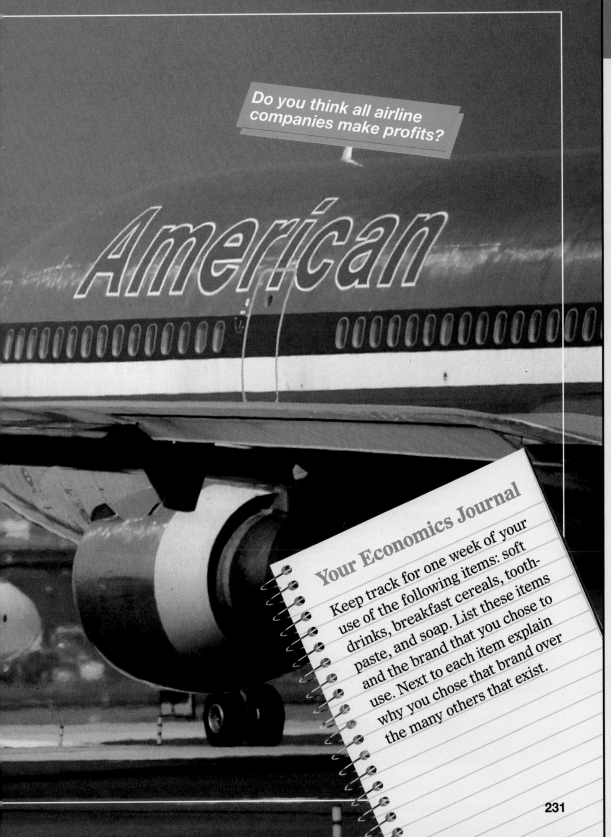

Do you think all airline companies make profits?

Economic Portfolio

Have students think about the brands of items they use, such as soft drinks, breakfast cereals, toothpaste, and soap. Then have students create a three-column table for **Your Economics Journal** that lists the item, the brand, and the reasons why they chose that particular brand. When determining the reasons for choosing a particular brand, students should focus on specific things that influenced their buying the brand. *(print advertisements, television commercials, and so forth)*

Your Economics Journal

Keep track for one week of your use of the following items: soft drinks, breakfast cereals, toothpaste, and soap. List these items and the brand that you chose to use. Next to each item explain why you chose that brand over the many others that exist.

231

INTRODUCING **CHAPTER 10**

Connecting to Past Learning

Ask students to recall the characteristics of a market economy. *(little or no government control, freedom of enterprise, freedom of choice, private property, profit incentive, and competition)* List students' responses on the chalkboard. Then ask students to recall what competition is. *(the rivalry among producers or sellers of similar goods to win more business by offering the lowest prices or better quality)* Ask students how local industries compete for their business.

Applying Economics

Ask students what factors play a part in their decision to buy headphones. Then ask students to imagine what buying headphones would be like if there were no choice of stores. *(Students might mention that the store owners could charge any price and sell inferior quality products because they would know that people had no choice.)*

EXTRA CREDIT PROJECT

Research and write a 1-page report on one former United States monopoly and the steps that were taken to break it up.

PERFORMANCE ASSESSMENT

Refer to page 230B for "Classifying Information," a Performance Assessment Activity for this chapter.

231

Focus

Overview

See the student page for section objectives.

Section 1 explains or describes perfect competition and the factors that are needed for perfect competition to exist.

Bellringer

Before presenting the lesson, display Focus Activity Transparency 39 on the overhead projector or copy the material on the chalkboard. Assign the accompanying Focus Activity Sheet.

Motivational Activity

Write the following on the chalkboard: List the ways that you are involved in competition.

Call on volunteers to read their lists. *(Students might indicate things such as sports, grades, and contests.)* Discuss with students how they feel about competitive situations. Then tell students that in Section 1 they will learn about competition in business and what constitutes perfect competition.

Preteaching Vocabulary

Have students speculate on the meaning of *perfect competition*. Write students' ideas on the chalkboard. Then have students compare their definitions with the one in the Glossary.

SECTION **1** *Perfect Competition*

SECTION 1 FOCUS

Terms to Know perfect competition

Objectives After reading this section, you should be able to:
1. List the five conditions of perfect competition.
2. Explain why agriculture is sometimes considered an example of perfect competition.
3. Assess the desirability of perfect competition.

Perfect Competition—An Ideal Rarely Realized

Competition is one of the basic characteristics of our market economic system. Regardless of its legal form of organization, each business attempts to capture as large a share of its market as possible. Figure 10.1 shows the four basic market structures in the American economy.

Conditions of Perfect Competition

All businesses must engage in some form of competition as long as other businesses produce similar goods or services. When a market includes so many sellers of a particular good or service that each seller accounts for a small part of the total market, a special situation exists. Economists term it **perfect competition.** Perfect competition has five conditions as shown in Figure 10.2.

On the supply side, perfect competition requires a large number of suppliers of a similar product. On the demand side, perfect competition requires a large number of informed buyers who know exactly what the market price is for the good or service. The market price is the equilibrium price. In a perfectly competitive market, total supply and total demand are allowed to interact to reach the equilibrium price. That is the only

Comparing Four Market Structures

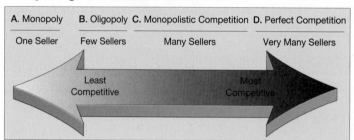

A. Monopoly — One Seller
B. Oligopoly — Few Sellers
C. Monopolistic Competition — Many Sellers
D. Perfect Competition — Very Many Sellers

Least Competitive — Most Competitive

**Figure 10.1
Comparing Market Structures**
Markets that are either perfectly competitive or pure monopolies are rare. Most industries in the United States fit one of the two other forms.

◀

Classroom Resources for Section 1

Reproducible Lesson Plan 10.1
NBR Video 14
Focus Activity Transparency 39
Focus Activity Sheet 39
Guided Reading Activity 10.1
Cooperative Learning Activity 10

Primary and Secondary Source Readings 10
Section Quiz 10.1
Spanish Section Quiz 10.1
Testmaker
Reinforcing Skills 10

price at which quantity demanded equals quantity supplied. In a world of perfect competition, each individual seller would accept that price. Because so many buyers and sellers exist, one person charging a higher or lower price would not affect the market price.

Perfect competition is rarely seen in the real world. For one thing, information is not often easily obtainable. In order for the price of a good or service to be the same for all sellers at every moment, all buyers and sellers would have to know what is happening to prices for that good or service everywhere at every moment. Obviously, business information is never that complete.

Agriculture as an Example

Few perfectly competitive industries exist in the United States. The one that perhaps comes closest is agriculture before the 1930s, when the federal government started to protect and regulate it. Since that time the government has sought to protect farmers by keeping the prices of some

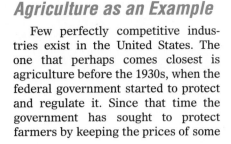

▼ **Figure 10.2**
The Five Conditions of Perfect Competition
Perfect competition is rare, as these five conditions are difficult to attain.

1 **A Large Market** Numerous sellers and buyers.
2 **Similar Product** A nearly identical good or service is sold.
3 **Easy Entry and Exit** Sellers already in the market cannot prevent competition, or entrance into the market. In addition, the initial costs of investment are small, and the good or service is easy to learn to produce.
4 **Easily Obtainable Information** Information about prices, quality, and sources of supply is easy for both buyers and sellers to obtain.

As a result, there is:

5 **No Control Over Price** The workings of supply and demand control the market, not a single seller or buyer.

Teach

Guided Practice

L1 Classifying Ask students to name the conditions of perfect competition. Construct a table titled Perfect Competition on the chalkboard. Use the following conditions as heads on the left side of the table: Number of Sellers, Product, Entry Into the Industry, Information, and Control Over Price. As students read Section 1, have them classify the way the five conditions are reflected in perfect competition. **LEP**

Visual Instruction

Refer students to Figure 10.1. Ask them which market structure is the most competitive and which is the least competitive. *(most competitive: perfect competition; least competitive: pure monopoly)* Then ask students to list the advantages and disadvantages of having a most competitive market structure.

◆◯ **Meeting Special Needs**

Difficulties With Studying Learning-disabled students often have a difficult time generalizing the use of a strategy, such as Survey, Question, Read, Recite, and Review, in different situations. They need to review both the steps of the strategy they are using and the procedures that are used in each of the steps. Tell students that in this section they will use the study strategy independently. Have each student make a chart with grids to self-evaluate each one of the following when studying this section: Did I skim for the title, headings, main ideas? Did I ask questions? Did I answer my questions?

Independent Practice

L2 Synthesizing Provide students with the headings for the table in "Classifying" in Guided Practice. Have students complete the chart using the agriculture industry as an example of perfect competition.

L3 Developing Graphics

Organize students in small groups. Have each group review the desirability of perfect competition. Then ask students to create posters illustrating the positive aspects of perfect competition. Display completed posters in the classroom.

 Have students complete Guided Reading Activity 10.1 in the TCR. **LEP**

? DID YOU KNOW

In 1933 Congress passed the Agricultural Adjustment Act (AAA). This legislation was an attempt by the United States government to control the problem of agricultural overproduction. Under the AAA, the government paid farmers who reduced production of basic crops, such as wheat, cotton, corn, and hogs.

Figure 10.3 ▶
Five Factors that Make Wheat Farming Competitive
Consider the wheat market.

1. Thousands of wheat farmers and thousands of wholesalers buy wheat.
2. All wheat is fairly similar.
3. The costs of buying or renting farmland are low compared to starting a corporation, and farming methods can be learned.
4. Because wheat is sold to wholesalers, information about prices is fairly easy to obtain.
5. No one farmer has any great influence on price.

agricultural products high and by restricting the production of some products. Nonetheless, the agricultural market is often used as an example of perfect competition, because individual farmers have almost no control over the market price of their goods. The wheat farm illustrated in **Figure 10.3** provides one example.

The interaction of supply and demand determines the price of wheat. The supply is the total supply all wheat farmers produce. The demand is the total demand for all uses of wheat. The equilibrium price is the price where supply and demand meet.

Individual wheat farmers have to accept the market price. If the price is $5 per bushel, that is the price every farmer must accept. Farmers who attempt to raise their price above $5 will find that no one will buy their wheat. Neither will a farmer sell his or her crop for less than $5 per bushel. The market price is the only price that both buyers and sellers will accept.

The demand for wheat—and food in general—is somewhat different from the demand for many other products. People's demand for food is, for the most part, inelastic. People can use wheat in only so many ways, and people can eat only so many wheat products. The supply side of most agricultural markets is also unique. It is highly dependent on conditions over which farmers have little control such as those shown in **Figure 10.4**

The Desirability of Perfect Competition

While we know that perfect competition is possible only in theory, any industry that tends toward it does have special characteristics. The intense competition in a perfectly competitive industry forces the price down to one that just covers the costs of production plus a normal profit. This price is beneficial to society because it means that consumers of products from perfectly competitive industries are paying only what society has to put in to make those products—the opportunity cost of the use

 Cooperative Learning

Have students work in groups to choose and research a local company or a company whose goods or services they use. Have them find out as much as they can about that company, including its way of competing in the market—both in the past and at present.

Have each group present an oral report. Groups might divide the research among their members, with each member providing a particular part of the information in the oral report.

Meeting Lesson Objectives

Assign Section 1 Review as homework or an in-class activity.

Evaluate

Assign the Section 1 Quiz in the TCR or use the Testmaker to develop a customized quiz.

Reteach

Have students prepare a web showing the main points of the section.

Enrich

Ask students to research and report on the Farmers' Holiday Association of the early 1930s in Iowa.

Close

Ask students to write a paragraph using the following as a topic sentence: It is almost impossible to meet all the conditions for perfect competition.

of land, labor, capital, and entrepreneurship. The price that consumers pay for such products is a correct signal about the value of that product in society. Perfectly competitive industries yield economic efficiency. No rearrangement of the land, labor, capital, and entrepreneurship would generate a higher valued output. In an efficient situation such as this, it is impossible to make one person better off without making some other individual worse off. All inputs are used in the most advantageous way possible, and society therefore enjoys an efficient allocation of productive resources. All goods and services are sold at their opportunity cost.

**Figure 10.4 ▲
Disasters for Farmers**
Variations in weather, a crop disease, or a crop-destroying insect can wipe out entire harvests. This means that farmers may have a good harvest one year and a poor one the next. As a result, there are widely fluctuating, or changing, supplies of goods in the agricultural market.

SECTION 1 REVIEW

Understanding Vocabulary
Define perfect competition.

Reviewing Objectives
❶ What five requirements are needed to have perfect competition?

❷ What elements of agriculture make it almost perfectly competitive?

❸ Why is perfect competition good for consumers?

Section 1 Review Answers

Understanding Vocabulary
perfect competition (p. 232)

Reviewing Objectives
1. a large market, a similar product, easy entry and exit, easily obtainable information, and no control over price

2. thousands of farmers and wholesalers buy food; costs of buying or renting farmland are relatively low; farming methods can be learned and price data is fairly easy to obtain; and with so many farmers, no one farmer can set prices, which the market determines

3. because it means that consumers of products from perfectly competitive industries are paying only what society has to put in to make those products

Teach

Bring some editorial cartoons to class and explain that such cartoons usually express an opinion. Discuss with students the opinions presented in the cartoons on page 236. Then call on volunteers to read the feature. Help students apply the steps in analyzing economic cartoons to the cartoons in their book and to those you brought to class. Then have students complete Practicing the Skill.

Additional Practice

Have students complete Reinforcing Skills 10 in the TCR.

Critical Thinking Skills

Analyzing Economic Cartoons

Editorial cartoonists often make economic news the subject of their cartoons. Being able to analyze these cartoons helps you understand the news.

Steps to Analyze Economic Cartoons

Editorial/economic cartoons are usually based on current economic events. To understand the cartoon it is important to know about the events or the economic issue behind the cartoon. Follow these steps:

❶ Read the economic news in a newspaper or magazine.
❷ Check the opinion page for related editorials.
❸ Study the labels and symbols in the cartoon to identify people or issues.
❹ Ask what the cartoonist is trying to say about the economic event or issue.

Example

Look at **Figure A**. To interpret the cartoon, apply the last two directions under "Steps to Analyze Economic Cartoons." The automobile labeled "Total Deficit" has crashed; the vehicle is totaled. At the wheel is President Ronald Reagan with a Democrat sitting in the back seat. Looking to deflect the blame for the mishap, Reagan immediately remarks that the car—the deficit—was not in perfect shape when he inherited it from the Democrats. The cartoonist thinks Reagan's explanation is unsatisfactory.

Practicing the Skill

Look at **Figure B**. Apply the last two directions under "Steps to Analyze Economic Cartoons." How does this cartoonist feel about the economic recovery?

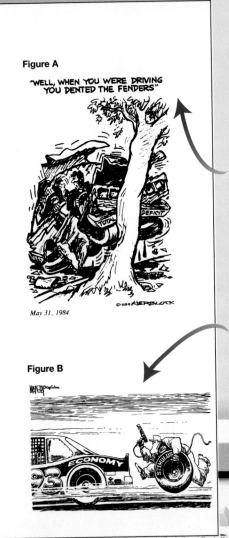

Figure A

"WELL, WHEN YOU WERE DRIVING YOU DENTED THE FENDERS"

May 31, 1984   ©1984 HERBLOCK

Figure B

Answers to Practicing the Skill

The cartoonist feels that the economy is accelerating (speeding car) and does not require government stimulus (President Clinton with spare tire).

2 Monopoly, Oligopoly, and Monopolistic Competition

Focus

SECTION 2 FOCUS

Terms to Know imperfect competition, pure monopoly, barriers to entry, cartel, natural monopolies, geographic monopolies, technological monopoly, patent, government monopolies, product differentiation, oligopoly, monopolistic competition

Objectives *After reading this section, you should be able to:*
1. List the four characteristics of a pure monopoly.
2. Describe the five characteristics of an oligopoly.
3. Explain the five characteristics of monopolistic competition.

Overview

See the student page for section objectives.

Section 2 explains and describes the concepts and characteristics of pure monopoly, oligopoly, and monopolistic competition.

Bellringer

Before presenting the lesson, display Focus Activity Transparency 40 on the overhead projector or copy the material on the chalkboard. Assign the accompanying Focus Activity Sheet.

Motivational Activity

Write the following on the chalkboard: How do you play the game *Monopoly*? Ask students to explain the basic elements of the game. Ask students to explain what they think a monopoly is, based on the game. Tell students that in this section they will learn about actual business monopolies as well as about other types of business organizations and their characteristics.

Preteaching Vocabulary

List the section's terms on the chalkboard. Have volunteers skim the section to find each term and concept and read it in context. LEP

From One Seller to Many Sellers— Different Market Structures

Most industries in the American economy are not perfectly competitive. Most represent some form of imperfect competition. **Imperfect competition** exists when any individual or group buys or sells a good or service in amounts large enough to affect price. Many market structures are imperfectly competitive, including monopoly, oligopoly, and monopolistic competition.

Monopoly

The most extreme form of imperfect competition is a **pure monopoly** whereby a single seller controls the supply of the good or service and thus determines the price. A few such markets do exist in the real world. Local electric utilities like the one in Figure 10.5 are monopolies. The United States Postal Service's delivery of first-class mail is another example of a pure monopoly. Figure 10.6 (page 238) shows four characteristics of a pure monopoly.

Figure 10.5 Local Electric Companies
Because local electric utilities are the sole providers and the consumer has no other option, they are monopolies. ▼

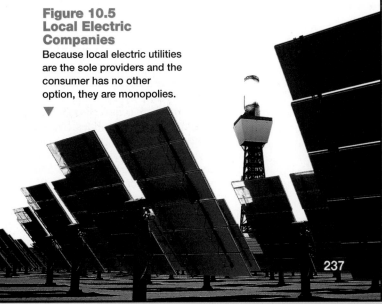

237

Classroom Resources for Section 2

- Reproducible Lesson Plan 10.2
- Economic Concepts Transparencies 9 and 11
- Focus Activity Transparency 40
- Focus Activity Sheet 40
- Guided Reading Activity 10.2
- Section Quiz 10.2
- Spanish Section Quiz 10.2
- Testmaker

Teach

Guided Practice

L2 Comparing As students read Section 2, have them compare pure monopoly, oligopoly, and monopolistic competition. Construct a chart on the chalkboard. Column heads should be titled Number of Sellers, Product, Entry Into the Industry, and Control Over Price. Row heads should be titled Pure Monopoly, Oligopoly, and Monopolistic Competition. As students read Section 2, have them compare the characteristics of each type of industry. Call on volunteers to fill in the information in the chart. Discuss the similarities and differences among these types of industry.

GLOBAL ECONOMICS

The European shipping companies that operated under royal charters during the Renaissance were some of the earliest monopolies. Rulers gave these companies exclusive rights to trade with Asia and other regions.

**Figure 10.6 ▶
What Makes a
Pure Monopoly?**
Four specific characteristics must exist:
1 A Single Seller
2 No Substitutes
3 No Entry
4 Almost Complete Control of Market Price

Four Characteristics of a Pure Monopoly

1. A Single Seller There is only one seller of the good or service.

2. No Substitutes There is no adequate substitute for the good or service that the monopolist is selling.

3. No Entry The market is protected by **barriers to entry**. These are obstacles to competition that prevent others from entering the market. The major barriers are goverment regulations, large initial investment, and ownership of raw materials.

4. Almost Complete Control of Market Price The monopolist can control the market price by controlling the supply available.

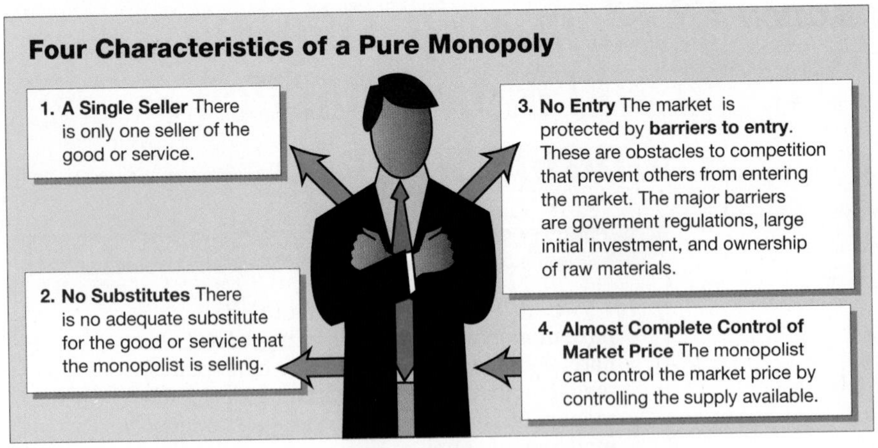

In a pure monopoly, the supplier can raise prices without fear of losing business to competitors. Unless buyers choose to pay the new price, they have nowhere else to buy the good or service. A monopolist, however, cannot charge outrageous prices. In a monopoly market, the law of demand is still operating. As the price of a good or service rises, consumers buy less. Profits, as a result, may decrease. In other cases buyers may turn to an alternative good or service.

For example, some people believe that for years the United States Postal Service has provided poor service for the delivery of first-class mail, at steadily rising prices. Customers have increasingly turned to alternatives, such as telephone calls, fax transmissions, and overnight delivery service provided by such competitors as Federal Express, Airborne, United Parcel Service, and DHL. Also, it is now possible to easily send documents around the world through computers via modems and phone lines. Hence, the United States Postal Service's monopoly on first-class mail has not meant that it can charge any price and provide any level of service and still keep customers using it at the same level as before.

Barriers to Entry The most obvious barriers to entry into a monopolistic market are legal ones. For example, state laws prevent a competing electric, gas, or water company from operating in an area where there already is a public utility company. The reasoning against competition in public utility industries is that too much competition may lead to wasteful duplication. For example, if your town had two electric companies, they might both have electric lines strung around the city. They might be duplicating efforts, which might result in a wasteful use of resources. It might also result in higher rates to customers because of the lack of efficiency in operation.

Another barrier to entry is the cost of getting started. This barrier to entry is called excessive money capital costs. It is found in industries, such as cars and steel, in which initial investment is high because of the amount and cost of the equipment. The first company to make the investment will clearly have an advantage over later companies that want to enter the market.

Ownership of essential raw materials can also provide a barrier to entry. A good example is the diamond industry. The DeBeers Company of the Republic of South Africa controls the marketing of nearly all the world's

◆ ▶ ● Meeting Special Needs

Inefficient Readers Students often benefit by using a form of rapid reading, called *scanning*, to locate specific information. Tell students you are going to demonstrate scanning to investigate barriers to entry into a monopolistic market, discussed on pages 238–239. Take your finger and model the scanning procedure by sliding your finger rapidly down the middle of each column. Then help students scan pages 240 and 241 to find the characteristics of an oligopoly and of monopolistic competition.

diamonds. An example from American history is the Aluminum Company of America (ALCOA). At the turn of the twentieth century, it controlled almost all sources of bauxite (BAHK-syt), the major ore used in aluminum. For many years, ALCOA was able to keep its near-monopoly in aluminum because it would not sell bauxite to potential competitors.

Types of Monopolies Pure monopolies can be separated into four categories depending on why the mono-poly exists. Figure 10.7 explains these categories.

An international form of monopoly is the cartel. A **cartel** is an arrangement among groups of industrial businesses, often in different countries, to reduce international competition by controlling price, production, and the distribution of goods. Among the best-known cartels is the Organization of Petroleum Exporting Countries (OPEC), which was formed in 1960. Today OPEC includes several nations in the Middle East and North Africa,

Independent Practice

L2 Charting Organize the class into small groups. Work with students to develop a chart that illustrates how supply, demand, and price operate in a perfectly competitive market. Refer to student page 199. Discuss how these forces operate in a pure monopoly. Ask students to write brief statements explaining the reasons for the differences.

**Figure 10.7
Types of
Monopolies**

Monopolies can be separated into four categories:

A Natural Monopolies
- Produce products for lowest cost and force competitors out of business
- Need large investment
- More efficient to have one company

Example: An electric company
▼

B Geographic Monopolies
- Best location
- But less important now; customers can buy from catalogs, etc.

Example: A small-town auto repair shop
▼

C Technological Monopoly
- Seller has a government **patent,** the right to exclusively manufacture an invention for a specified number of years

Example: Polaroid film
▼

D Government ▶ **Monopolies**
- Created by legal barriers to entry

Example: Tennessee Valley Authority (TVA)

Cooperative Learning

Have students work in small groups to interview an owner or manager in an industry found in their area that can be considered as an example of monopolistic competition. Have students find out how the firm uses price and nonprice competition in retailing the product. Groups might divide the following tasks among their members: deciding on the industry to study, writing questions for the interview, conducting the interview, and summarizing the interview for the class.

Independent Practice

L1 Developing Graphics
Have students work in small groups to create posters that illustrate examples of the four types of monopolies. Display completed posters in the classroom.

Visual Instruction

Refer students to Figure 10.9. Point out that, for these industries, the four largest firms account for more than 80 percent of total domestic shipments. Then have students give examples of how product differentiation by advertising may affect their own choice of a car—one of the oligopolies in Figure 10.9.

DID YOU KNOW

Wal-Mart stores, which supply a variety of well-known brands, created a geographic monopoly. The company went into small towns, especially those that were served by a few small retailers, and sold their products for up to 15 percent less than those available in "mom and pop" operations. Once established, Wal-Mart was seldom threatened by local competition.

**Figure 10.8
Characteristics of an Oligopoly**

The domestic airline industry illustrates the characteristics of an oligopoly.

1. **Domination by a Few Sellers**
   Several large firms dominate the entire industry.
2. **Barriers to Entry**
   Capital costs of airlines are high, and it is difficult for new companies to enter major markets.
3. **Identical or Slightly Different Products**
   Most airlines offer essentially the same service.
4. **Nonprice Competition**
   While most airline services are about the same, some competition takes the form of **product differentiation.** Advertising emphasizes minor differences and attempts to build customer loyalty.
5. **Limited Control Over Price**
   The airline industry has frequent price wars. If one airline lowers its fares, other airlines lower theirs even more.

▼

as well as Nigeria, Gabon, Venezuela, Ecuador, and Indonesia.

How Important Are Monopolies?
Monopolies today are far less important than they once were. Geographic monopolies probably have little effect because of potential competition from mail-order businesses. You can also be fairly certain that a technological monopoly will not last much longer than the life of a patent. Because of modern technology, competitors can make and patent slight variations in new products quickly. The microcomputer revolution in the early 1980s followed such a pattern. One company copied another's product, making changes and adding features to obtain a patent of its own.

International Business Machines (IBM) had at one time controlled a "lock" on the computer business. It sold mainframes—the biggest kind of computer—and made huge profits. In the 1990s, IBM faced decline because of the technological revolution in microcomputers. IBM failed to adapt quickly enough to the changing market and lost its near monopoly.

Oligopoly

An **oligopoly** (AHL-uh-GAHP-uh-lee) is an industry in which a few suppliers that exercise some control over price dominate. Some economists argue that the airline industry, as **Figure 10.8** suggests, is an example of an

oligopoly. They point out that until very recently, it was almost impossible for foreign airlines to compete in domestic markets.

Figure 10.9 shows a number of industries in which the four largest firms produce more than 80 percent of the total industry output. All these industries are oligopolies. Saying that an industry is an oligopoly does not necessarily mean that the situation should be changed.

Stable Prices A surprising feature of the general criticism of oligopolies is that little proof exists that they are harmful. It is true that consumers may be paying more than if they were buying in a perfectly competitive market in which supply and demand would set the price. Oligopolistic markets, however, tend to have generally stable prices. They also offer consumers a wider variety of different products than would a perfectly competitive industry.

Monopolistic Competition

In **monopolistic competition,** a large number of sellers offer similar but slightly different products. Obvious examples are such brand-name items as toothpaste, cosmetics, and designer clothes.

Free Enterprise Activity

Call on volunteers to list elements of a free enterprise system on the chalkboard. (*Individuals own the factors of production and decide the answers to basic economic questions for themselves through the interaction of individuals looking out for their own best interests.*) Stress to students that in a free enterprise economy, efforts are always being made to protect competition. Then ask students to write a paragraph in which they explain how monopolies fit into the free enterprise system. The paragraphs should focus on whether monopolies support the characteristics of a free enterprise system.

Monopolistic competition characterizes many industries in the United States. Qualities of this type of industry are shown in Figure 10.10 (page 242).

Comparisons of Oligopolies and Pure Monopolies

Many of the characteristics of monopolistic competition are the same as those of an oligopoly. The major differences, however, are in the number of sellers of a product and in the product. In an oligopoly, a few companies dominate an industry, and control over price is interdependent. The products may or may not be similar. Monopolistic competition has many firms, no real interdependence, and some slight difference among products.

Perfect competition has so many buyers and sellers that no one has any control over price. Everyone must take the price the interaction of total demand and total supply determines. In monopolistic competition each competitor has some control over the price of its product. A monopolistic competitor, however, does not have as much control over price as a pure

Selected Oligopolies

Industry	Percentage of value of total domestic shipments accounted for by the top four firms
Domestic motor vehicles	
Household refrigerators and freezers	
Electric bulbs	
Cigarettes	
Flat glass	
Greeting cards	

50 55 60 65 70 75 80 85 90 95 100

Source: U.S. Bureau of the Census. *Concentration Ratio in Manufacturing*

▲
Figure 10.9 Oligopolies
Oligopolies exist in a number of industries throughout the United States. Here, a wide range of industries are highlighted.

Independent Practice

L2 Debating Ask volunteers to debate the following: The federal government should play a role in regulating monopolies. Encourage students on each side to provide reasons for their position.

L3 Creating Cartoons Ask students to draw an economics cartoon that shows the relationship between consumers and a monopoly. Display completed cartoons and discuss the cartoons with the class. (*Cartoons should illustrate how a consumer is at a disadvantage when dealing with a monopoly.*)

Have students complete Guided Reading Activity 10.2 in the TCR. **LEP**

🌐 GLOBAL ECONOMICS

In Japan, cartels are a part of business life. The Japan Fair Trade Commission has estimated that about 90 percent of domestic business transactions are part of some type of cartel activity. Many cartels established to set prices and to respond to depressed markets have been permitted by law.

241

Cultural Diversity and Economics

Recently, Kentucky Fried Chicken's operations in China have faced serious competition from Ronghua Chicken, a Chinese fast-food restaurant that combines Western-style service with Chinese-style food preparation. Ronghua's management has declared that its branches will open wherever Kentucky Fried Chicken opens. Ask students what kind of business organization the two restaurants comprise. (*oligopolies or a monopolistic competition*) Then ask them why businesses should take into account an area's culture. (*to be popular and, therefore, profitable*)

Assess

Meeting Lesson Objectives

Assign Section 2 Review as homework or an in-class activity.

Evaluate

Assign the Section 2 Quiz in the TCR or use the Testmaker.

Reteach

Have students write three questions about the section, exchange papers, and write answers.

Enrich

Have students choose a type of product, such as toothpaste or bicycles. Ask them to research the type of competition that exists in that industry, including the major companies and market share. Have students report orally.

Close

Have students write a paragraph explaining which of the following they think is best for consumers: monopoly, oligopoly, or monopolistic competition.

Figure 10.10
Characteristics of Monopolistic Competition
The characteristics of monopolistic competition within an industry are:

1 **Numerous Sellers**
No one seller or small group dominates the market.

2 **Relatively Easy Entry**
Entry is easier than in other types of imperfectly competitive markets. One drawback is the high cost of advertising.

3 **Differentiated Products**
Each seller sells a slightly different product to attract customers.

4 **Nonprice Competition**
Businesses compete by product differentiation and by advertising.
These result in:

5 **Some Control Over Price**
Each firm has some control over the price it charges due to customer loyalty and product differentiation.

monopolist because other monopolistic competitors are selling almost, but not quite, the same product. The quantity demanded of a good or service will drop if the price is raised and cheaper substitutes are available. If one monopolistic competitor raises the price too much, most customers will buy another brand, or substitute, of the same good.

Neighborhood Businesses Neighborhood businesses such as cleaners and drugstores are involved in monopolistic competition. Each business within the neighborhood has an identity of its own even though the differences between its good or service and those of its competitors may be small.

Competitive Advertising Competitive advertising is especially important in monopolistic competition. Competitive advertising attempts to persuade consumers that the product being advertised is different from, and superior to, any other. Businesses also compete for shelf space—space on store shelves for displaying their products and attracting buyers. A cosmetics company, for example, may produce several lines of cosmetics. Each is aimed at a different market segment, or section. By having three lines, the company competes in three areas with competitors. The differences in products attract different customers and add to the profits of the company.

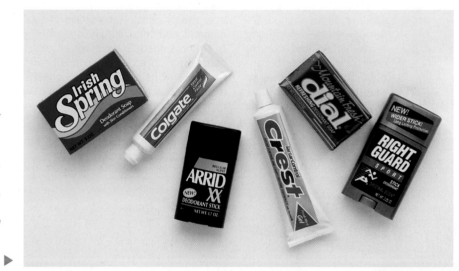

SECTION 2 REVIEW

Understanding Vocabulary

Define imperfect competition, pure monopoly, barriers to entry, cartel, natural monopolies, geographic monopolies, technological monopoly, patent, government monopolies, product differentiation, oligopoly, monopolistic competition.

Reviewing Objectives

❶ What are the four characteristics of a pure monopoly?
❷ What characteristics of an oligopoly allow it to have a limited control over price?
❸ What are the five characteristics of monopolistic competition?

Section 2 Review Answers

Understanding Vocabulary
imperfect competition (p. 237), **pure monopoly** (p. 237), **barriers to entry** (p. 238), **cartel** (p. 239), **natural monopolies** (p. 239), **geographic monopolies** (p. 239), **technological monopoly** (p. 239), **patent** (p. 239), **government monopolies** (p. 239),

product differentiation (p. 240), **oligopoly** (p. 240), **monopolistic competition** (p. 240)

Reviewing Objectives
1. a single seller, no substitutes, no entry into the market, and control of market price
2. domination by a few sellers, sub-

stantial barriers to entry into the market, similar products, and nonprice competition
3. numerous sellers, relatively easy entry into the market, differentiated products, nonprice competition, and some control over price

Personal Perspective

Joan Robinson on Imperfect Competition

Profile

- 1903–1986
- was Professor of Economics at Cambridge University in England
- best known for developing theory of monopolistic competition
- authored many books, including *The Economics of Imperfect Competition* (1933) and *Economic Heresies: Some Old-Fashioned Questions in Economic Theory* (1971)

Joan Robinson, who produced her first major work in economics during the Great Depression, believed that there was something wrong with the theory of competition. Adam Smith had said competition would benefit society as individuals maximized their own best interests. Robinson disagreed. She criticized economists who ignored social and moral issues. In *The Economics of Imperfect Competition*, Robinson said the model of competition Smith used does not exist in the real world.

The traditional assumption of perfect competition is an exceedingly convenient one for simplifying the analysis of price but there is no reason to expect it to be fulfilled in the real world. It depends, in the first place, upon the existence of such a large number of producers that a change in the output of any one of them has a negligible effect upon the output of the commodity as a whole, and it depends, in the second place, upon the existence of a perfect market. The first condition may often be approximately fulfilled, but the existence of a perfect market is likely to be extremely rare in the real world.

Robinson believed that price is only one of the factors that consumers consider. Convenience, quality, speed of service, or even the manners of salespeople influence consumers.

. . . Rival producers compete against each other in quality, in facilities, and in advertisement, as well as in price, and the very intensity of competition, by forcing them to attract customers in every possible way, itself breaks up the market and ensures that not all the customers, who are attached in varying degrees to a particular firm by the advantages which it offers them, will immediately forsake it for a rival who offers similar goods at an infinitesimally smaller price.

Checking for Understanding

1. What two conditions are necessary to have perfect competition?
2. Which condition of perfect competition is extremely rare?
3. Besides price, what do producers use to attract customers?

Background

Joan Robinson is considered one of the most important twentieth-century economists. She taught for more than 40 years and was a professor of economics at Cambridge University. Robinson wrote and lectured widely on economic theory. She disagreed with Adam Smith that morality will take care of itself, citing as her proof the worldwide Great Depression of the 1930s. Robinson believed that it showed that self-interest does not necessarily make everyone better off.

Teach

Have volunteers read aloud the quoted excerpts from Robinson's *The Economics of Imperfect Competition*. Ask students to paraphrase each excerpt to gain a better understanding of her ideas. Then have students answer the questions in Checking for Understanding.

Answers to Checking for Understanding

1. The two conditions necessary to have perfect competition are the existence of a large number of producers and the existence of a perfect market.

2. a perfect market
3. Besides price, producers use quality, facilities, and advertisement to attract customers.

LESSON PLAN
Chapter 10, Section 3

Focus

Overview

See the student page for section objectives.

Section 3 explains the laws and agencies that the federal government established to prevent monopolies and the government's move toward reregulation.

Bellringer

🔲 Before presenting the lesson, display Focus Activity Transparency 41 and assign the accompanying Focus Activity Sheet.

Motivational Activity

Ask students why government has passed laws to encourage competition and to regulate pricing and product quality. *(to protect consumers from high prices and poor quality goods.)*

Preteaching Vocabulary

Have students find the definitions for each term in the Glossary. Then have them explain how a horizontal, a vertical, and a conglomerate merger differ, and also explain the difference between deregulation and reregulation.

SECTION **3** Government Policies Toward Competition

S E C T I O N 3 F O C U S

Terms to Know antitrust legislation, interlocking directorate, merger, horizontal merger, vertical merger, conglomerates, conglomerate merger, deregulation, reregulation

Objectives *After reading this section, you should be able to:*

❶ Explain the difference between **interlocking directorates and mergers.**

❷ List at least four major federal **regulatory agencies.**

❸ Explain the movement toward **reregulation.**

The Government Regulates Business in an Attempt to Protect Consumers

Historically, one of the goals of government in the United States has been to encourage competition in the economy. Through the years, federal and state governments have passed laws and established regulatory agencies in an attempt to force monopolies to act more competitively. Known as **antitrust legislation,** these laws act to prevent new monopolies, or trusts, from forming and to break up those that already exist. See Figures 10.11 and 10.12.

Interlocking Directorates and Mergers

You should be familiar with two terms from the table: *interlocking directorate* and *merger*. An **interlocking directorate** occurs when some members of the boards of directors of competing corporations are the same. In effect, only one group of people manages both companies. Because the same people control both companies, it is easy for them to make sure that the two companies do not compete with one another.

The last point in the table under the Clayton Act refers to corporate mergers. A **merger** occurs when one

**Figure 10.11
Antitrust History**
President Theodore Roosevelt, portrayed here breaking up trusts in the early 1900s, believed monopolies were "the tyranny of mere wealth."

244

NO MOLLY-CODDLING HERE

Classroom Resources for Section 3

Figure 10.12 Antitrust Legislation

Federal Law	Function
Sherman Act (1890)	Outlawed agreements and conspiracies that restrain interstate trade. Made it illegal to monopolize or even attempt to monopolize any part of interstate commerce.
Clayton Act (1914)	Restricted the practice of selling the same good to different buyers at different prices. Prohibited seller from requiring that a buyer not deal with a competitor. Outlawed interlocking directorates between competitors. Outlawed mergers that substantially lessen competition.
Federal Trade Commission Act (1914)	Established the Federal Trade Commission (FTC) as an independent antitrust agency. Gave the FTC power to bring court cases against private businesses engaging in unfair trade practices.
Robinson-Patman Act (1936)	Strengthened the law against charging different prices for the same product to different buyers. An amendment to the Clayton Act of 1914.
Celler-Kefauver Antimerger Act (1950)	Strengthened the law against firms joining together to control too large a part of the market. An amendment to the Clayton Act of 1914.
Hart-Scott-Rodino Antitrust Improvement Act (1980)	Restricted mergers that would lessen competition. It required big corporations planning to merge to notify the Federal Trade Commission (FTC) and the Department of Justice. They would then decide whether to challenge the merger under the terms of the Clayton Act of 1914.

Teach

Guided Practice

L1 Listing Have students use the information in Section 3 and Figure 10.12 to list the ways in which antitrust legislation protects consumers.

Visual Instruction

Have the class examine the cartoon in Figure 10.11. Ask students to research financial debacles and malfeasance of the last decade and a half, such as the banking crisis, the savings and loan failures, insider securities trading, and crash of the "junk" bond market. Encourage students to create a cartoon (stick figures okay) based on their research. Display cartoons and lead a class discussion.

corporation joins with another corporation.

Three kinds of mergers exist. When the two corporations are in the same business, it is called a **horizontal merger.** When a business that is buying from or selling to another business merges with that business, a **vertical merger** takes place. Some corporations have become big by buying out other corporations dealing in totally unrelated activities. These expanded corporations are called **conglomerates.** The buying out of an unrelated business is termed **conglomerate merger.**

The Clayton Act forbids mergers when they tend to lessen competition substantially. The Clayton Act, however, does not state what the term *substantially* means. As a result, it is up to the federal government to make a subjective decision as to whether the merging of two corporations would substantially lessen competition.

Regulatory Agencies

Besides using antitrust laws to foster a competitive atmosphere, the government uses direct regulation of business pricing and product quality

Chapter 10 Competition and Monopolies **245**

Meeting Special Needs

Language Deficiencies Students with language problems often have trouble seeing distinctions among words with related meanings. Learning objectives may require students to identify, explain, or discuss. Tell students that identifying usually involves listing by category, explaining requires giving reasons in a complete form, and discussing requires giving pros and cons. Provide students with opportunities for identification, explanation, and discussion during normal lesson time.

Independent Practice

L2 Writing Editorials Discuss with students how government regulation affects competition and consumers. Then have students write newspaper editorials in which they explain why they believe that government regulation either helps or hinders economic activity and the public welfare. Students might consider events in the airline industries and in the banking industry.

L3 Researching Have students research and write about the impact of the Sherman Act on the Standard Oil Trust. Have them find out why John D. Rockefeller established the trust and how it eliminated competition.

L3 Reviewing Information Refer students to Figure 10.14. Ask them to review the functions of the agencies listed. Then ask students how any of the agencies listed affect them or their families.

 Have students complete Guided Reading Activity 10.3 in the TCR. **LEP**

? DID YOU KNOW

Today, the Antitrust Division of the Department of Justice and the Federal Trade Commission (FTC) enforce antitrust laws in the United States.

Government regulatory agencies oversee these regulations. See **Figure 10.14.** These agencies exist not only at the federal level, but at the state level and even at local levels.

Although the aim of most government regulations is to promote efficiency and competition, recent evidence indicates something quite different. Many regulations, as a by-product of their goals to protect consumers and companies within industries from unfair practices, have actually decreased the amount of competition in the economy.

The Interstate Commerce Commission (ICC) raised the prices that consumers paid to ship goods by preventing entry into the trucking industry and restricting price competition.

For many years the Federal Communications Commission (FCC), in an effort to help UHF stations, in effect prevented the entry of competitive pay-TV, cable, and satellite systems into the television market.

While the Civil Aeronautics Board (CAB) regulated air fares, these fares were 20 to 30 percent higher than they were after deregulation when competition was allowed to set prices.

Because of findings such as these, the 1980s were called the years of **deregulation** as government gradually reduced regulations and control over business activity. For example, the

CAB no longer controlled air fares or route selection by the nation's airlines. The cable television industry provides another example, as **Figure 10.13** shows. The many regulations in the banking industry were slowly decreased, allowing consumers to obtain competitive interest rates on savings for the first time in years.

Should There Be Reregulation?

Congress has considered **reregulation** of a number of formerly heavily regulated industries. Many heads of airlines have asked for reregulation of the airline industry. Many people criticized the deregulation of the cable TV industry. Consequently, Congress began reregulation with the 1992 Cable Reregulation Act. Since then, rates that cable operators can charge per month have been regulated.

Figure 10.13 ▶
Cable Deregulation
The Federal Communications Commission (FCC), which had prevented the entry of pay-TV, cable, and satellite systems into the TV market, now allows almost open competition in the direct-satellite television transmission fields.

 Cooperative Learning

Organize the class into three groups. Have each group investigate the impact of deregulation on the American economy. Ask one group to focus on the transportation industry, one on the banking industry, and one on the telecommunications industry. Have each group write a report showing whether the impact of deregulation on its assigned area of the economy was positive or negative. Students might divide the following tasks among themselves: researching the information, preparing graphics to accompany the report, writing the report, and presenting the information to the class.

Figure 10.14 Federal Regulatory Agencies

Agency	Function
Interstate Commerce Commision (ICC) (1887)	Regulates interstate commerce, primarily railroads and trucking.
Federal Trade Commission (FTC) (1914)	Regulates product warranties, unfair methods of competition in interstate commerce, and fraud in advertising.
Food and Drug Administration (FDA) (1927)	Regulates purity and safety of foods, drugs, and cosmetics.
Federal Communications Commission (FCC) (1933)	Regulates television, radio, telegraph, and telephone; grants licenses, creates and enforces rules of behavior for broadcasting; most recently, regulates satellite transmissions and cable TV.
Securities and Exchange Commission (SEC) (1934)	Regulates the sale of stocks, bonds, and other investments.
Equal Employment Opportunity Commission (EEOC) (1964)	Responsible for working to reduce discrimination based on religion, gender, race, national origin, or age.
Occupational Safety and Health Administration (OSHA) (1970)	Regulates the workplace environment; makes sure that businesses provide workers with safe and healthful working conditions.
Nuclear Regulatory Commission (NRC) (1975)	Regulates the nuclear power industry; licenses and oversees the design, construction, and operation of nuclear power plants.

SECTION 3 REVIEW

Understanding Vocabulary

Define antitrust legislation, interlocking directorate, merger, horizontal merger, vertical merger, conglomerates, conglomerate merger, deregulation, reregulation.

Reviewing Objectives

① How do interlocking directorates differ from mergers?

② What are some major federal regulatory agencies in the United States?

③ Why do some Americans favor reregulation?

Chapter 10 Competition and Monop...

Assess

Meeting Lesson Objectives

Assign Section 3 Review as homework or an in-class activity.

Evaluate

Assign the Section 3 Quiz in the TCR or use the Testmaker.

Assign the Chapter 10 Test Form A or Form B or use the Testmaker.

Reteach

Have students reread selected paragraphs, close the book, and write three facts from memory.

Have students complete Reteaching Activity 10 in the TCR.

Enrich

Have students write news articles on antitrust legislation.

Have students complete Enrichment Activity 10 in the TCR.

Close

Have students write a paragraph explaining why the American system is a mixed economy.

Section 3 Review Answers

Understanding Vocabulary
antitrust legislation (p. 244), **interlocking directorate** (p. 244), **merger** (p. 244), **horizontal merger** (p. 245), **vertical merger** (p. 245), **conglomerates** (p. 245), **conglomerate merger** (p. 245), **deregulation** (p. 246) **reregulation** (p. 246)

Reviewing Objectives
1. Interlocking directorates—some members of the boards of directors of competing corporations are the same; mergers—one corporation joins with another

2. the ICC, FTC, FDA, FCC, SEC, EEOC, OSHA, and NRC
3. because they are critical of the effects that deregulation has had on some industries

Teach

Ask students to recall television commercials featuring a famous athlete or other public figure. Ask students to recall what products these figures endorsed. Ask students how effective such commercials are in the sale of the product. Ask whether these types of commercials have influenced their choice of a product and, if so, why.

Tell students that this feature focuses on a company—Nike—that has grown very powerful by using famous athletes to endorse their products. Have students read the feature and answer the questions in Think About It.

Readings in Economics

| TIME | APRIL 26, 1993 |

IS NIKE GETTING TOO BIG?

by David E. Thigpen

Every sports fan has seen the flashy TV commercials: Michael Jordan, leaping for the basket, seems to break free of gravity as he goes up, up, and still higher up. The trajectory has been the same for the company whose shoes the commercial touts. Since its founding 21 years ago, Nike, the Beaverton, Oregon, sportswear conglomerate, has soared to greater and greater heights, becoming the $3.7 billion-a-year titan of the industry. The key has been Nike's endorsement contracts with such top professional athletes as Jordan, baseball's Bo Jackson ("Bo knows . . . "), football's Jerry Rice and, to a lesser extent, several hundred others. But as it has lavished ever more millions of dollars on such tie-ins, Nike has seen something else rise along with its profile and its profits: concern in the sports world about whether it exerts too much control over its player-pitchmen and wields too much influence over the sports in which they compete.

Nike's increasing clout has long troubled the National Football League, and even the mighty National Basketball Association. Two years ago, Nike ordered 90 of the athletes it has under contract to withdraw from part of the rich apparel-licensing deal by which the N.B.A. sells the players' likenesses on shirts and hats—depriving the league of $1.5 million a year in revenue. In February Nike, along with Michael Jordan, wrestled from the N.B.A. the rights to the multimillion-dollar market for T shirts bearing Jordan's image. "In marketing, Nike is far more powerful than the league," says N.B.A. deputy commissioner Russ Granik. . . .

• THINK ABOUT IT •

1. **What about the Nike contracts concerns many in the sports world?**

2. **Why does Nike wield so much power in professional sports?**

Answers to Think About It

1. whether Nike exerts too much control over its player-pitchmen and wields too much influence over the sports in which they compete

2. Nike wields so much power because of its endorsement contracts with top professional athletes, thereby making it a marketing force more powerful than individual sports leagues.

10 *Highlights*

Section 1

Perfect Competition

Key Terms

perfect competition (p. 232)

Summary

Perfect competition has five conditions that include businesses having no control over price. In the United States, agriculture comes closest to meeting these conditions. Although ideal, perfect competition almost never exists in the real world.

Section 2

Monopoly, Oligopoly, and Monopolistic Competition

Key Terms

imperfect competition (p. 237)

pure monopoly (p. 237)

barriers to entry (p. 238)

cartel (p. 239)

natural monopolies (p. 239)

geographic monopolies (p. 239)

technological monopoly (p. 239)

patent (p. 239)

government monopolies (p. 239)

product differentiation (p. 240)

oligopoly (p. 240)

monopolistic competition (p. 240)

Summary

Pure monopoly has four conditions that include one business having almost complete control over the market price. The five characteristics of an oligopoly include limited control over price. Monopolistic competition is the most common type of market structure in the United States.

Section 3

Government Policies Toward Competition

Key Terms

antitrust legislation (p. 244)

interlocking directorate (p. 244)

merger (p. 245)

horizontal merger (p. 245)

vertical merger (p. 245)

conglomerates (p. 245)

conglomerate merger (p. 245)

deregulation (p. 246)

reregulation (p. 246)

Summary

Federal laws prohibit interlocking directorates, yet allow mergers as long as they do not create monopolies. To foster competition and protect consumers, the government has created numerous federal regulatory agencies. Some of this regulation has been eliminated, though certain people favor reregulation.

Using Chapter 10 HIGHLIGHTS

Use the Chapter 10 Highlights to preview, review, condense, or reteach the chapter. A Spanish Chapter Highlights is available in the Spanish Handbook.

Preview/Review

After students read the Chapter 10 Highlights, have them complete Economics Vocabulary Activity 10 in the TCR. Spanish Vocabulary Activities are also available in the Spanish Resource Binder.

Vocabulary Software reinforces the economic terms used in Chapter 10.

Condense

Have students listen to Chapter 10 on the Audiocassettes in the TCR. A 1-page written activity and 1-page test accompany this material. These materials are also available in Spanish.

Reteach

Have students complete Reteaching Activity 10 in the TCR. Spanish Reteaching Activities are also available.

 VIDEODISC

Nightly Business Report
Economics in Action
Use "Competition and Monopolies" on Disc 1, Side B, Video 14.

Search 35044, Play to 40416

249

CHAPTER

10 Review

ANSWERS

Identifying Key Terms

1. c
2. d
3. a
4. f
5. e
6. b
7. oligopoly
8. monopolistic competition
9. geographic monopoly

10. government monopoly

11. antitrust legislation

Recalling Facts and Ideas

Section 1
1. no control
2. The products are almost the same.
3. agriculture

Section 2
4. monopoly, oligopoly, monopolistic competition

5. geographic monopoly: an individual seller has control over the market because of location; technological monopoly: a seller develops a product or production process for which it obtains a patent

6. limited control
7. numerous sellers

Section 3
8. A horizontal merger is a buy-out of a company by one in the same business; a vertical merger is the joining of one business with another from which it buys or to which it sells.
9. through antitrust legislation and regulatory agencies

Critical Thinking

Section 1
Answers will vary but might include the following:

Identifying Key Terms

Write the letter of the definition in Column B below that correctly defines each term in Column A.

Column A
1. barriers to entry (p. 238
2. deregulation (p. 246)
3. conglomerate (p. 245)
4. interlocking directorate (p. 244)
5. natural monopoly (p. 239)
6. merger (p. 245)

Column B
a. large corporation made up of smaller companies dealing in unrelated activities
b. the joining together of two corporations two corporations
c. obstacles to competition that prevent new companies from being formed
d. process of removing goverment restrictions of business
e. production by one company rather than several, due to efficient operation
f. situation in which some of the board of directors for competing companies are the same

Use terms from the list below to fill in the blanks in the paragraph that follows.

monopolistic competition (p. 240)
oligopoly (p. 240)
government monopoly (p. 239)
geographic monopoly (p. 239)
antitrust legislation (p. 244)

One form of imperfect competition in which a few firms compete is __(7)__. Another form of imperfect competition in which many firms compete, but each has a differentiated product is __(8)__. Monopolies have great control over price. Even a small mom and pop store in an isolated town has a __(9)__. Many times the federal government creates legal barriers to entry and thereby forms a __(10)__, such as the United States Postal Service. In order to prevent monopolies, there are federal laws called __(11)__.

Recalling Facts and Ideas

Section 1
1. In a perfectly competitive market structure, how much control does a single seller have over market price?
2. What is the relationship between the types of products that sellers sell in a perfectly competitive market?
3. What is one example of an almost perfectly competitive market?

Section 2
4. What are the three types of imperfectly competitive market structures?
5. What is the difference between a geographic monopoly and a technological monopoly?
6. How much control does an oligopoly have over price?
7. In monopolistic competition, how many sellers are there?

Section 3
8. What is the difference between a horizontal merger and a vertical merger?
9. What two methods does the federal government use to keep business competitive?

When there are no government controls at work, the agricultural market is almost perfectly competitive. In an agricultural market, there are thousands of farmers and thousands of wholesalers. With so many farmers, no one farmer has any great influence on price. Therefore, price is determined by the interaction of supply—total produced by all farmers of a commodity—and demand—all demand for the commodity. The equilibrium price is the price at which supply and demand meet. In addition, price information is easily obtained and individual farmers must accept the market price or no one will buy their goods.

Critical Thinking

Section 1
Identifying Central Issues Explain in a paragraph how supply and demand work in the agricultural market when government controls are not operating.

Section 2
Making Generalizations Explain how the free enterprise system works to break the power of monopolies.

Section 3
Making Comparisons What are the fundamental differences between the goals of antitrust legislation and the goals of federal government regulations enforced through regulatory agencies?

Applying Economic Concepts

Competition and Market Structure Make a list of the different types of monopolies that can exist. Under each type, make a list of examples. Under government monopolies, for example, you have already learned about the United States Postal Service and the Tennessee Valley Authority. Others exist at the state and local levels.

Chapter Projects

1. **Individual Project** Choose one of the regulatory agencies mentioned in this chapter and write to the agency for information about its functions. Use the information you receive to write a report summarizing the main functions of that agency.
2. **Cooperative Learning Project** Numerous firms operate in imperfectly competitive market structures. Work in three groups—one representing monopolies, one oligopolies, and one monopolistic competition. Each member of each group should clip out ads and articles that give examples of firms that have the characteristics of the type of mar-

ket structure her or his group represents.

Compare the sets of ads for each of the three groups. There undoubtedly will be some overlap. One group might claim that a particular company is an oligopoly, whereas another group might claim that it is a monopoly. Your group should be able to defend the reason it places a particular company in its particular grouping.

Reviewing Skills

Analyzing Economic Cartoons
Defense Spending After the cold war ended in the early 1990s, the United States began to scale back its defense spending. What is this cartoonist's opinion of this cut in spending? What hidden costs does this cartoonist think the cuts have had?

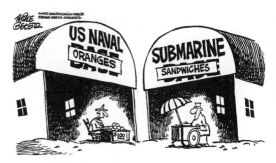

NOT SO GOOD....HOW'S *YOUR* DEFENSE CONVERSION ?

Writing About Economics

Persuasive Writing Write copy for an advertisement for the toothpaste, soft drink, soap, or breakfast cereal that you chose in Your Economics Journal.

251

Section 2
Answers will vary but should explain that free enterprise works to break the power of monopolies through competition.
Section 3
The goals of antitrust legislation are to prevent new monopolies from forming and to break up those that already exist; the goal of regulatory agencies is to direct regulation of business pricing and product quality in order to protect consumers and companies within industries from unfair practices.

Applying Economic Concepts

Examples will vary but should include the following types of monopolies: natural, geographic, technological, and government.

Chapter Projects

1. Review with students the regulatory agencies that are listed in Figure 10.14.

2. Ads, articles, and notes might be posted on a bulletin board. Students should be able to justify placing a company in a particular grouping.

? BONUS QUESTION

The following bonus question may be written on the chalkboard when students take the chapter test.
Q: When advertising air time in a few existing television networks is nearly the same cost, how are the networks acting?
A: as an oligopoly

Reviewing Skills
Answers will vary, but students might indicate that the cartoonist thinks that the conversions from existing facilities have not been economically productive.

Writing About Economics
Encourage students to include in their advertisements reasons why people should choose that particular brand.

Focus

In a free market, businesses succeed and fail as a result of decisions the proprietors make when they respond to supply and demand, choose marketing plans, and determine their distribution methods. Point out to students that businesspeople who can make clear decisions based on fact have a greater chance of succeeding than those who rely upon instinct and enthusiasm alone.

The purpose of this lab is to create an opportunity to practice the decisions and calculations that business owners face.

Teach

Developing a Business Plan can be extended over several weeks or condensed into one session. Begin the lab by having students complete Step A and use their work to draw up the financial plan in Step B. Have students consider information from steps A and B when they complete steps C, D, E, and F. If the lab extends over many weeks, allot time at the end of each week to check students' progress.

Business owners who base their pricing and profit on a clear knowledge of expenses and demand for the product often are able to respond profitably to changes in demand or expenses. The list of expenses in Step A provides a clear itemization of production costs.

ECONOMICS LAB

Running a Business
From the classroom of Judy B. Smitherman, Thompson High School, Alabaster, Alabama

In Unit 3 you read about markets, prices, and business competition. In this lab, you will make decisions as the sole proprietor of a business called Sidewalk Tees that sells screen printed T-shirts. (You may want to reread the material on pages 208–211 of the text.)

Tools

1. Ruler, pencils, writing paper, graph paper
2. Calculator

Procedures

Step A Read the following description of your production requirements and costs:

The screen printing equipment and display hangers cost $4,800. For this you need a bank loan. The monthly payment on this loan is $220. One month's supply of ink and screens costs $240. The best wholesale price for good T-shirts is $3.25. You should order an equal number of large and extra-large shirts in assorted colors. Gas for your car for business purposes costs $15 each week. Utilities and miscellaneous costs will be an additional $40 per month. Bank checking charges total $8 monthly. A yearly business license costs $52, and you can rent a booth from the Beachfront Flea Market for $26 per day. You plan to rent a booth Friday, Saturday, and Sunday each week. Operating alone, you can produce 80 shirts in a 20-hour week (4 per hour). By adding a part-time worker for 20 hours, you can produce 200 shirts (10 per hour). Expenses for a part-time worker total $7 per hour.

Step B Using a table like the one below, draw up a weekly financial plan for Sidewalk Tees.

Example

TOTAL WEEKLY COSTS

Item	Cost per week
Booth rental	
Utilities, gasoline, and miscellaneous costs	
Bank loan	
Bank checking	
Ink and screens	
T-shirts	
License	
Wages	
Total weekly costs	

Have students use the table to help them draw up a reasonable weekly financial plan. Be sure that student plans take into account each of the expenses listed in the table. Direct students to use their analyses when they develop their product pricing and profit plans. Encourage interested students to try more than two alternative plans.

252

Step C Pricing your product is important because your prices will help determine how well the product sells and how much profit you make. After studying the market for T-shirts, you project the effect of price changes on quantities demanded in a table like this one:

Price per shirt	Quantity demanded per week
$ 8.00	200
$ 9.00	170
$10.00	140
$11.00	110
$12.00	90

Determine your costs for each shirt, and find your profits. Remember that labor and other variable costs will change depending on the quantity of goods you produce. Copy the following table and complete different pricing plans:

Example

PRODUCT PRICING AND PROFIT

Item	Amount	
	Plan A	Plan B
Price per unit		
Estimated units sold per weekend		
Net revenues per weekend		
Less expenses per week		
Weekly gross profits		
Less 8% taxes		
Weekly net profits		

Step D Review your decisions. What are your variable costs? Could you have earned more profit by increasing or reducing your part-time worker's hours? What would result if you increased or reduced prices for the T-shirts?

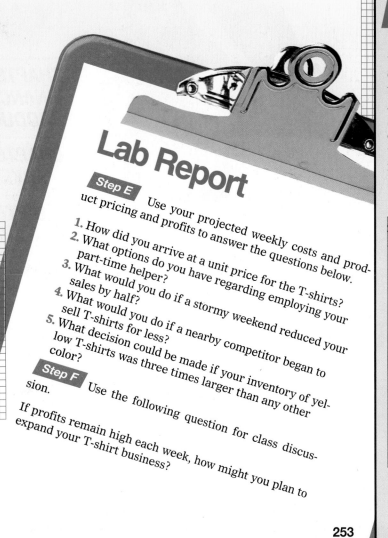

Lab Report

Step E Use your projected weekly costs and product pricing and profits to answer the questions below.

1. How did you arrive at a unit price for the T-shirts?
2. What options do you have regarding employing your part-time helper?
3. What would you do if a stormy weekend reduced your sales by half?
4. What would you do if a nearby competitor began to sell T-shirts for less?
5. What decision could be made if your inventory of yellow T-shirts was three times larger than any other color?

Step F Use the following question for class discussion.

If profits remain high each week, how might you plan to expand your T-shirt business?

253

Assess

Have each student complete Step D and Step E (the report). Encourage students to share their reports and discuss which plan is most immediately profitable, which plan is most flexible, and which plan employs the most people.

Close

Discuss with students ways in which they might expand their businesses they planned in their labs. After the discussion, have students write evaluations of their original plan and ways in which they would revise it to allow for future growth.

 DID YOU KNOW

In some planned economies, government may control prices. In such economies, businesspeople must manipulate demand and expenses to increase profit. In free-market economies, price is an additional variable, allowing for greater savings to consumers or profits to businesses.

Answers to Lab Report

Lab Report E

Students should be able to defend their opinion about ways in which pricing, employment options, weather, and competition might affect profits.

Unit Goals

After studying this unit, students will be able to:

Specify sources and types of financing and methods of production available to companies;

Explain basic marketing principles and distribution of goods and services;

Describe the makeup of the American labor force and types of jobs.

Unit Overview

The three chapters in Unit 4 discuss finance and production, marketing and distribution, and the role of labor in producing goods.

Chapter 11 explains or describes: investment financing; types of financing for businesses; and the production process.

Chapter 12 explains and describes how goods are marketed and distributed from producer to consumer.

Chapter 13 describes the labor force and management/labor relations.

Connecting to Past Learning

Tell students to collect recent articles that describe business expansion because of changes in technology or changes in production methods.

`0:00` OUT OF TIME?

Use the Chapter Highlights and the Audiocassettes that include a 1-page activity and 1-page test for each chapter.

U N I T

MICROECONOMICS: AMERICAN BUSINESS IN ACTION

254   *Unit 4 Microeconomics: American Business in Action*

Economic Simulation

Business Borrowing and Lending Organize the class into four groups. Each of the first three groups should imagine that it is a business that plans to expand. Have each group decide what its business is and what its assets are. Then each group should plan its expansion, including reasons for expansion, estimated cost of expansion (up to $100,000), and projected profits after expansion. The fourth group will play the role of a financial institution with only $200,000 currently available to lend. It should determine a lending rate, which could be flexible depending on the term and amount of the loan.

Beginning the Unit

Refer students to the "Did You Know?" questions on page 255. Tell them that these questions reveal facts about the productivity and wealth of the United States. Ask students to think of themselves as consumers and discuss the types of goods and services they purchase or use. Then ask them to think of themselves as producers and discuss the types of goods or services they would like to provide. Ask students to describe the ways they take part in producing or providing goods or services now.

Outcome-Based Project

Conducting Research Interviews The following unit project is the fourth step in a six-part activity that can be used during the entire economics course. In Unit 4 students collect more specific information about the skills and experience necessary for selected jobs.

Have each student select a job title from the categories that the class researched in Units 1 through 3. Each student should locate and interview a person in the local community who does that job or a similar job. Include questions about education and training, personal reasons for choosing the job, opportunities for advancement, and other benefits.

Did You Know

♦ Home shopping through your television is estimated to be a $2.5 billion industry, growing at 20 percent a year.

♦ Retailing in general in the United States is close to a $1-trillion-a-year business.

♦ During any one trading day on the New York Stock Exchange more than 200 million shares of stocks in American companies are bought and sold.

♦ The U.S. produces more than 20 percent of the world's entire output of goods.

♦ Every year, more than 5 million teenagers between the ages of 16 and 19 work full time.

In this unit you will learn how businesses finance and produce the goods that are marketed and distributed to you as a consumer. You will also learn about the makeup of the American labor force

255

Did You Know

Here are some tips to use when shopping via television, telephone, or mail.
• Compare the price of an item at other shopping sources.
• Ask about the company's return policy and its shipping policy.
• If you are concerned that the company is disreputable, check with the Better Business Bureau, the U.S. Postal Service, or your state or local consumer protection agency.
• Never give a caller your credit card number or social security number as a means of personal identification.
• Keep a complete written record of any order.

CHAPTER 11 *FINANCING AND PRODUCING GOODS*

CHAPTER ORGANIZER

Daily Objectives	Special Features	Classroom Resources

Section 1 Investing in the Free Enterprise System
- **List** the different institutions through which people can turn savings into investments.
- **Explain** why people are willing to finance investment.
- **Describe** how bidding for investment financing allocates resources in a market economy.

Learning Economic Skills:
Building Graphs, p. 264

- 📁 Reproducible Lesson Plan 11.1
- 💿 *NBR* Video 16
- 🔧 Focus Activity Transparency 42
- 📁 Focus Activity Sheet 42
- 📁 Guided Reading Activity 11.1
- 📁 Cooperative Learning Activity 11
- 📁 Primary and Secondary Source Readings 11
- 📁 Section Quiz 11.1
- 📁 Spanish Section Quiz 11.1
- 💻 Testmaker
- 📁 Reinforcing Skills 11

Section 2 Types of Financing for Business Operations
- **List** three kinds of debt financing according to the length of repayment.
- **List** four factors companies consider in choosing the right financing.

Personal Perspective:
Judith Resnick on Starting Up a Financial Business, p. 270

- 📁 Reproducible Lesson Plan 11.2
- 🔧 Focus Activity Transparency 43
- 📁 Focus Activity Sheet 43
- 📁 Guided Reading Activity 11.2
- 📁 Free Enterprise Activity 11
- 📁 Section Quiz 11.2
- 📁 Spanish Section Quiz 11.2
- 💻 Testmaker

Section 3 The Production Process
- **List** the four major steps in production operations.
- **Describe** five advances in technology and methods of production.

News Clip:
"Whistle Blower," *Forbes*, p. 276

- 📁 Reproducible Lesson Plan 11.3
- 🔧 Focus Activity Transparency 44
- 📁 Focus Activity Sheet 44
- 📁 Guided Reading Activity 11.3
- 📁 Consumer Application Activity 11
- 📁 Mathematics Practice for Economics 34
- 📁 Performance Assessment Activity 34
- 📁 Section Quiz 11.3
- 📁 Spanish Section Quiz 11.3
- 💻 Testmaker
- 📁 Enrichment Activity 11

 0:00 OUT OF TIME? If time does not permit teaching this chapter, you may use the Chapter 11 Highlights and the Audiocassettes that include a 1-page activity and a 1-page test.

Chapter 11 Review and Evaluation

Special Features	Classroom Resources

Chapter 11 Highlights, p. 277
Chapter 11 Review, pp. 278–279

📁 Chapter 11 Test Forms A and B
📁 Economics Vocabulary
    Activity 11
📁 Spanish Economics Vocabulary
    Activity 11

🎧 Audiocassette 11
🎧 Spanish Audiocassette 11
📁 Reteaching Activity 11
📁 Spanish Reteaching Activity 11

Key to Ability Levels

Teaching strategies have been coded for varying learning styles and abilities.

L1 Level 1 activities are **basic** activities and should be within the ability range of all students.

L2 Level 2 activities are **average** activities designed for the ability range of average to above-average students.

L3 Level 3 activities are **challenging** activities designed for the ability range of above-average students.

LEP activities should be within the ability range of **Limited English Proficiency** students.

Performance Assessment

The following chapter project may be assigned at the beginning of the chapter and used for performance assessment. See page T12 for additional Performance Assessment information.

Creating a Business Have students form a mock company to make school stationery or decorated T-shirts. As they study Chapter 11, they will learn how to do a cost-benefit analysis, how to choose the right type of financing for their company, and how to select the best method of production to make their product.

Organize the class into three groups. Each group will perform a different task: Group 1 will do a cost-benefit analysis of the chosen item, Group 2 will investigate the best types and sources of financing, and Group 3 will determine the best method of production.

Students can complete this process as a hypothetical exercise or actually make some of the items. By going through this process, they will learn to make basic business decisions and to understand some of the steps involved in starting and running a business of their own. Students might convey their experiences through oral or written reports.

Additional Resources

Readings for the Student

Kidder, Tracey. *Soul of a New Machine.* Boston: Little Brown, 1981. Describes financial and production decisions in developing a new computer.

Dunnan, Nancy. *Entrepreneurship.* New York: Silver Burdett, 1990. Discusses how a young person can turn a hobby or interest into a profitable business.

Readings for the Teacher

Miller, S. *Impacts of Industrial Robotics.* Madison, Wis.: University of Wisconsin Press, 1988.

National Research Council. *Toward a New Era in Manufacturing.* Washington, D.C.: National Academy Press, 1986.

Multimedia Materials

Division of Labor by Process. VHS videocassette, guide. Describes how productivity is increased by division of labor and in turn increases wealth. Social Studies School Service, 10200 Jefferson Blvd., P.O. Box 802, Culver City, CA 90232-0802

Wall Street On-Line: An Investment Simulation for the Classroom. Apple or IBM, 24 photocopy masters, guide. Uses real stocks and bonds to show the workings of the stock market and how to invest money. Social Studies School Service, 10200 Jefferson Blvd., P.O. Box 802, Culver City, CA 90232-0802

Chapter Overview

Decisions about financing and production are the first steps in making goods and services available to consumers and industry. Chapter 11 explains or describes: sources and allocations of funds for business investment; how businesses make financing decisions; different production methods; and the impact of technology on these methods.

VIDEODISC

Nightly Business Report
Economics in Action
Use "Financing and Producing Goods" on Disc 1, Side B, Video 16.

Search 40500, Play to 46948

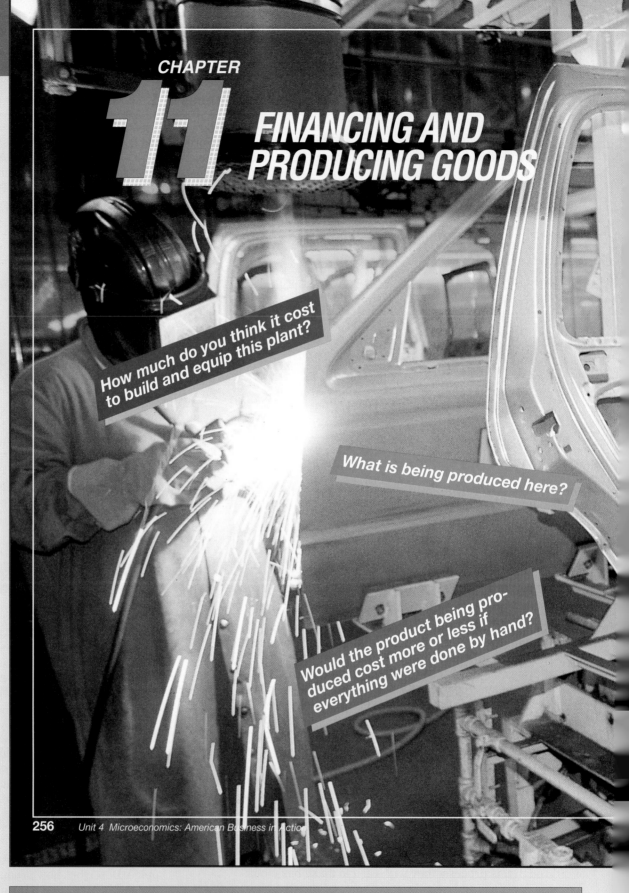

CHAPTER

11

FINANCING AND PRODUCING GOODS

How much do you think it cost to build and equip this plant?

What is being produced here?

Would the product being produced cost more or less if everything were done by hand?

Answering Economic Questions

The questions in the above illustration are designed to lead into the main concepts in Chapter 11. Students might take for granted the diversity of products and the production methods that enable firms to produce these goods. The questions will help them consider how products are made and the integration of humans and machines in the workplace. Have students discuss the questions and consider alternative ways the work could be done. Have them consider the impact those alternative ways would have on productivity, type of work performed, variety of goods produced, and costs.

Do you think this physical work would be interesting or boring?

Why is the production process set up in this way?

Your Economics Journal

Keep track of the consumer products that you use in your house during a one-week period, excluding food, cosmetics, and the like. List these items as simple or complex and explain whether you think the production process used for each was highly automated.

257

Connecting to Past Learning

Refer students to Chapter 4: Going Into Debt. Tell them that many of the principles they learned in Chapter 4 apply to Chapter 11 as well. Then have them list products for which they may have purchased replacement parts. After completing Chapter 11, have students look at their lists. Then have students write a brief paragraph explaining how companies finance their business operations and why many products have interchangeable parts.

Applying Economics

Tell students to imagine they make advertising posters and that a retailer has ordered 100 posters. The order must be delivered in one week. Ask students how they would set up a production line to get the work done. Have them consider what could be done by hand and what could be done by machine. Tell students that these questions and decisions are the same ones facing all companies that produce goods and services.

EXTRA CREDIT PROJECT

Using facts from a business's annual report, students should write a report on whether they think this is a good business to invest money in.

Economic Portfolio

Ask students to select one of the products they listed in **Your Economics Journal** and investigate how it is manufactured. Have them investigate how the manufacturer obtains raw materials and other resources, where and how the product is produced, and if the product cannot be mass produced, what the reason is for this. Have students write a brief report on their findings and present it to the class.

✓ **PERFORMANCE ASSESSMENT**

Refer to page 256B for "Creating a Business," a Performance Assessment Activity for this chapter.

Focus

Overview

See the student page for section objectives.

Section 1 explains or describes: how savings are used as investment funds to finance business startup and growth; how companies use cost-benefit analyses; and how bidding for funds affects the allocation of resources in a free market economy.

Bellringer

Before presenting the lesson, display Focus Activity Transparency 42 on the overhead projector or copy the material on the chalkboard. Assign the accompanying Focus Activity Sheet.

Motivational Activity

Ask students to recall a time when they had to raise money for a school event or other activity, or for a personal project.

Discuss their responses by posing the following questions: Were their fundraising efforts successful? What did investors gain (raffle prize or items purchased)?

Preteaching Vocabulary

Ask students to read the Glossary definition of *cost-benefit analysis* and to complete a rough one related to buying a car.

Investing in the Free Enterprise System

SECTION 1 FOCUS

Terms to Know cost-benefit analysis

Objectives *After reading this section, you should be able to:*
1. List the different institutions through which people can turn savings into investments.
2. Explain why people are willing to finance investment.
3. Describe how bidding for investment financing allocates resources in a market economy.

Investment is the Backbone of the Free Enterprise System

If you were an entrepreneur who started a small electronics repair company, you would face many hurdles on your road to success. One hurdle would be finding sufficient financing to pay for your company's current needs—parts and so on—and its long-term needs—growth. Both the short-term and long-term needs of business can be financed in a variety of ways. Financing business operations and growth is an integral part of our free enterprise system.

Turning Savings into Investments

People who save money often deposit their funds in one of several types of financial institutions in exchange for interest on their accounts. The financial institutions, in turn, make these deposits available to businesses to finance growth and expansion as Figure 11.1 shows.

Making Financing Decisions Let's assume that you own an electronics repair company that you have incorporated. You now have the opportunity to open additional repair shops in other locations, but you do not have enough extra cash to invest in the expansion. Fortunately, you can obtain this financing in one of many ways, including borrowing from a financial institution, digging into your own personal savings, asking your friends and parents to loan the company money, or selling more shares of stock. Even if you are able to finance the expansion, one important question remains. Should you expand?

Businesses usually answer this question by making a standard **cost-benefit analysis.** This analysis requires that you estimate the cost of an action and compare it with the benefits of that action.

Classroom Resources for Section 1

- Reproducible Lesson Plan 11.1
- *NBR* Video 16
- Focus Activity Transparency 42
- Focus Activity Sheet 42
- Guided Reading Activity 11.1
- Cooperative Learning Activity 11

- Primary and Secondary Source Readings 11
- Section Quiz 11.1
- Spanish Section Quiz 11.1
- Testmaker
- Reinforcing Skills 11

Financing Business Expansion

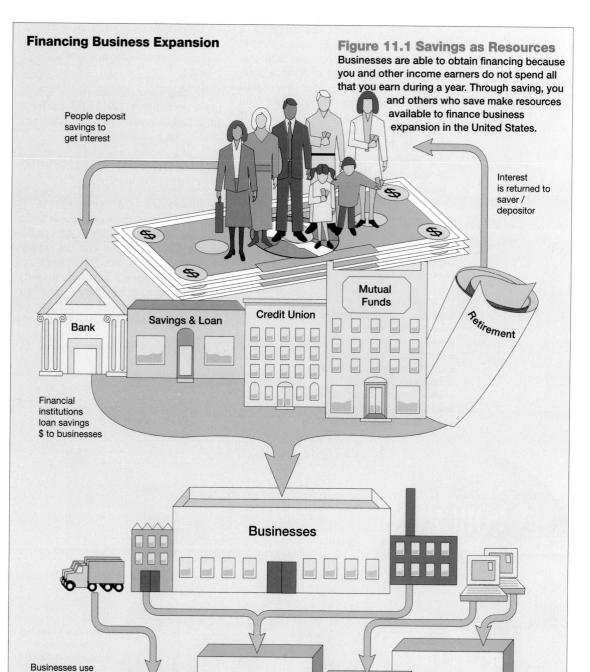

Figure 11.1 Savings as Resources
Businesses are able to obtain financing because you and other income earners do not spend all that you earn during a year. Through saving, you and others who save make resources available to finance business expansion in the United States.

People deposit savings to get interest

Interest is returned to saver / depositor

Bank

Savings & Loan

Credit Union

Mutual Funds

Retirement

Financial institutions loan savings $ to businesses

Businesses

Businesses use savings $ to expand and improve

Trucks

Equipment

Plant

Computers

Teach

Guided Practice

L1 Flow Charting Ask students to draw a flow chart that traces the flow of money from an individual investor to a financial institution to a business. Have them chart what happens at each stage. Also have them show how money returns to the investor.

GLOBAL ECONOMICS

Many people in economically developing nations get their start as business owners with help from private investment companies in the United States and Europe. These companies, often run by retired business people, work directly with people in towns, villages, and urban neighborhoods in Latin America, Asia, and Africa to help them start small businesses. Such enterprises range from craft shops to small power companies. These new businesses help boost the local economy.
7B

Meeting Special Needs

Limited English Proficiency Students with limited English proficiency may have trouble understanding how bidding for funds in a free market affects the allocation of resources. Tell them to imagine they have $10,000 to invest and that five people have asked for the money to expand their businesses. Ask them how they would decide who should receive the money. Based on the information in Chapter 4 and in this chapter, students should decide that the most creditworthy candidate whose company has the best performance record should receive the bulk of any limited resources.

259

Ask students to study Figure 11.2. Have them decide on an independent business, such as child-sitting or lawn care, that they could begin. Ask them to do a cost-benefit analysis to determine the likely profit of the company. Ask them to investigate and include the costs of supplies, any type of labor needed, any work space required, and the likelihood of profits on sales. Have students present their analysis to the class in a brief report.

DID YOU KNOW

Both the federal Small Business Administration (SBA) and many state small business agencies offer special assistance to companies headed by women or minorities. Often such companies are eligible for low-interest loans and free services such as tax preparation and advice on how to run a successful business. These SBA agencies help thousands of women and minorities start their own businesses each year.

Figure 11.2 shows the steps of a cost-benefit analysis. Here is a simple numerical example. Assume that you can borrow $1 million to finance your business expansion. Your bank will charge 10 percent per year for the loan. That equals $100,000 per year. If you could generate additional profits because of the expansion of $200,000 per year, then borrowing $1 million would certainly be worthwhile. Remember the rule that always applies:

Undertake an activity up to the point at which the additional benefit equals the additional cost.

In this case the activity is financing an expansion. The additional benefit is higher profits, and the additional cost is the cost of borrowing.

Why People Are Willing to Finance Investment

Businesses are interested in financing so that they can invest in expansion, hoping to make higher profits in the future. People who are willing to finance such an investment are seeking a reward from their activity. The reward may be interest on a savings account or a certificate of deposit. The reward, however, may be

Figure 11.2
A Cost-Benefit Analysis
Developing a cost-benefit analysis involves five steps.

Step 1:
Estimate the following costs:
- renting new stores
- training new workers
- additional bookkeeping
- opportunity cost of your time to check on new shops
- electricity and other utilities
- additional insurance
- any other expenses that apply

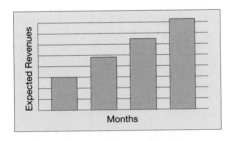

Step 2: Calculate expected revenues. ▼

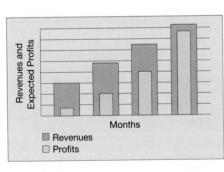

Step 3:
Calculate expected profits: revenues minus costs listed in Step 1.
◄

Cooperative Learning

As a class, have students plan and conduct an in-class interview of a small-business owner who started her or his business. The interview should focus on how the business was started, including ways finances were obtained and how they were used to help build or expand the business.

Both short-term and long-term growth should be discussed.

Before the interview, students should work together to investigate local lending institutions and organizations that help people start small businesses and should write and refine interview questions.

interest on a corporate bond that they purchase, or dividends (or an increase in value) from the stock that they buy in an expanding company.

Sometimes the same individual is both a lender and a borrower. As the owner of an electronics repair corporation, you could be going to a bank to ask for a loan to finance expansion, while personally having money on deposit in the same bank in the form of savings accounts or certificates of deposit. Even corporations themselves may be financing the expansion of an unrelated company while asking their bank for financing for their own expansion. Most of us are both creditors and debtors. The same is true for businesses and governments. Some day you may be paying interest on a mortgage while earning interest on a savings account.

Bidding for Investment Financing

In a free enterprise system, resources normally go where they generate the highest value. Financing investment often directs the allocation of these resources. If you are certain that expanding your business into other locations will yield high profits, then you will be aggressive in finding financing for that expansion. If one bank turns down your loan, you may decide to borrow elsewhere, even at a higher interest rate. Another way to finance expansion would be to sell corporate bonds at relatively high interest rates. You might also offer stock to new and old shareholders at an attractive price per share. The point is that the more convinced you are that you will make high profits by expanding, the more you will be willing to finance this investment.

Step 4: Now calculate how much it will cost you to borrow the money to finance your proposed business expansion. ◀

Step 5: If expected profits more than cover the cost of financing the expansion, then the expansion is probably warranted. ▼

Independent Practice

L1 Graphing Tell the class that investors in commercial theatrical productions are sometimes called angels. Ask students to research the cost of financing Broadway theater productions from 1971 to 1990. Suggest reporting findings in separate graphs for musical and nonmusical productions and to include captions detailing the financial return to angels on their investments. Ask students to share interesting facts about angels that they may learn in their research.

 DID YOU KNOW

Entertainment is a major industry in the United States and a major export product. Large corporations sometimes engage in stock bidding wars as they compete to control entertainment businesses they hope will add to their profitability.

 Free Enterprise Activity

Ask the class to put on a show. Suggest that the production can be funny or sober and take the form of a play, skit, pantomine, or song and dance acts—as long as it accurately deals with finance and investing. Recommend dividing tasks into writing, staging, and performing. Encourage presenting the show during a school assembly or before other classes. Complete the activity with a discussion of what students learned about finance.

Independent Practice

L2 Hypothesizing Ask students to hypothesize what it would be like if funds were allocated to businesses by lottery instead of by bidding. Ask them also to hypothesize what would happen to resources. Call on volunteers and write their ideas on the chalkboard.

 Have students complete Guided Reading Activity 11.1 in the TCR. LEP

When one business succeeds at obtaining financing, it uses funds that might have helped another business. In a market economy each business competes for scarce financial resources. If the cost to finance business expansion is relatively high, only those businesses that believe they have the most profitable expansion projects will be willing to pay the high cost of financing. Figure 11.3 shows one example of such a business expansion. If the cost of financing is relatively low, more companies will decide that they, too, can profitably engage in additional business investment.

**Figure 11.3
Typical Business
Expansion**
Many American hotels have expanded by building in other countries after calculating that their profits will outweigh the costs of financing the expansion. ▼

Cultural Diversity and Economics

Remind students that, in the past 20 years, immigration to the United States has accelerated from a number of regions, including western and southern Asia, China, Southeast Asia, Latin America, Eastern Europe and Russia, and the Caribbean. Ask students to research and write a report on the integration of these arrivals into the American labor force and, in general, their influence on our economy. Have volunteers give oral reports in the context of a class discussion.

Financing is simply an intermediate step between the desire to use additional resources and the actual use of those resources. The financing of investment itself does not create the investment and use the resources. It is when the financing funds are spent that the resources become used. Financing is, in effect, the "grease" that makes America's free enterprise system work.

Remember, there are several methods of financing business expansion, including borrowing, selling bonds, and offering stock. You can borrow money from banks or other institutions. Figure 11.4 discusses alternative financing.

Figure 11.4
Alternate Financing
You must be sure to recalculate the total cost of your loan if it is offered at a higher interest rate than a bank would charge you. Many loan shops and "money stores" offer financing that may not be worth the price.

Meeting Lesson Objectives

Assign Section 1 Review as homework or an in-class activity. Each question in the Review addresses the corresponding numbered objective in the Section Focus.

Evaluate

Assign the Section 1 Quiz in the TCR or use the Testmaker.

Reteach

Organize students into three groups. Assign each group a main section heading and have them outline the main points discussed.

Enrich

Have students investigate and write a brief report about how famous entrepreneurs, such as Steven Jobs (Apple Computer), started their businesses.

Close

Have student write a brief paragraph on the importance of investment funds.

SECTION 1 REVIEW

Understanding Vocabulary
Define cost-benefit analysis.

Reviewing Objectives
1. Where can people deposit their savings so that businesses can obtain investment funds for expansion?
2. What do people who finance investments hope to gain?
3. How does bidding for investment financing affect resources in a market economy?

Section 1 Review Answers
Understanding Vocabulary
cost-benefit analysis (p. 258)
Reviewing Objectives
1. People can deposit their savings in commercial banks, savings and loans, mutual savings banks, credit unions, and other financial institutions that lend money to businesses.
2. People are willing to finance investments because they seek a reward from the activity.
3. In a market economy, financial resources are allocated to those bidders with the best creditworthiness and performance record. This means resources go to those businesses most likely to succeed in their expansion plans. Other bidders must pay a higher price for the remaining funds.

Teach

Tell students that graphs are a good way to present data in a form that readers can grasp easily and quickly. Inform them that each type of graph has a different way to display information. Bar graphs show data in relation to a fixed scale, which is good for comparing items to each other. Line graphs show data moving through a fixed period in time, which is good for showing trends and predictions. Circle graphs show a given item as a percentage of a whole. Students can use these graphs to illustrate reports and presentations. Discuss with them which type of graph might be best for showing certain types of data. Have students explain why the graph is the best one to be used for showing the data.

Additional Practice

Have students complete Reinforcing Skills 11 in the TCR.

LEARNING ECONOMIC SKILLS
Building Graphs

It is important that you know how to present statistical material graphically in your presentations, reports, and research projects.

Developing a Bar Graph

To create a bar graph, put the correct measurements on the two axes of your graph and enter the data in the form of horizontal or vertical bars. The following 1992 changes in selected consumer price index categories are shown in the bar graph in Figure A: food, 1.5%; shelter, 2.9%; medical care, 6.6%.

Data Over Time—the Line Graph

The following actual and predicted percentages of total population 75 years or older are plotted on Figure B: 1950 = 2.5%, 1970 = 3.7%, 1980 = 4.4%, 1990 = 5.2%, 2000 = 6.2%, 2010 = 6.5%.

Developing Circle Graphs

If your information totals 100 percent, you can present it in a circle graph. The following imaginary data for a family are used to create Figure C: Total income, $200; amount spent on food, $32; on housing, $48; on transportation, $36; all other expenditures, $84. To build the graph, convert the figures to percentages, then enter them in the circle.

Practicing the Skill

❶ Convert the information in Figure C to a bar graph.

❷ Make a line graph using these statistics about crude oil production: 1988, 693 million barrels; 1989, 646 million; 1990, 640 million; 1991, 638 million; 1992, 605 million.

Figure A

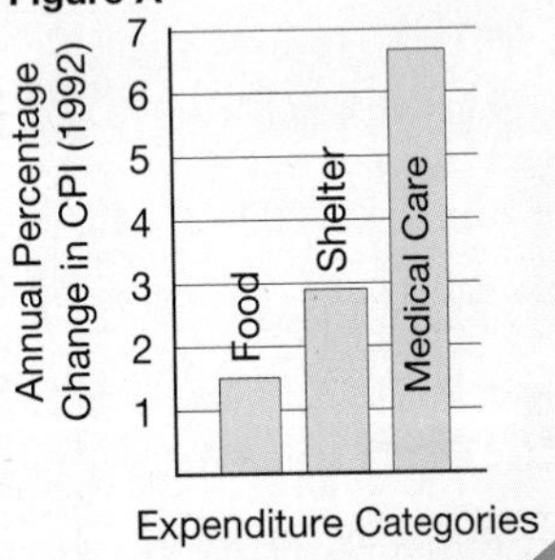

Annual Percentage Change in CPI (1992)

Food · Shelter · Medical Care

Expenditure Categories

Figure B

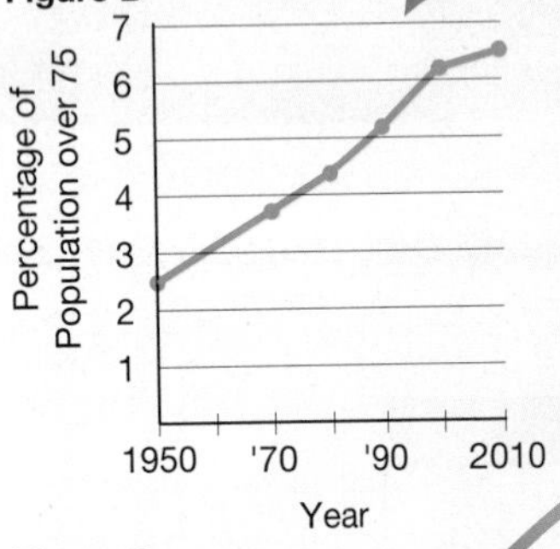

Percentage of Population over 75

1950 · '70 · '90 · 2010

Year

Figure C

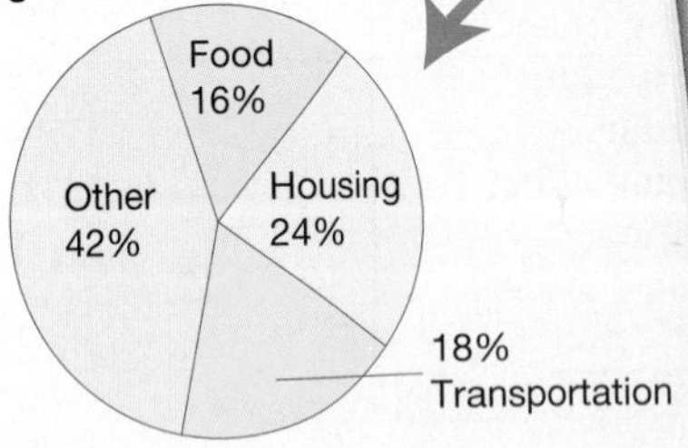

Food 16%
Other 42%
Housing 24%
18% Transportation

264

Answers to Practicing the Skill

1. Graphs should show "Expenditure Categories" on one axis (probably the *x*-axis) and "Percent of Total Income" on the other. The percent axis should range from 0 percent to 100 percent and be marked off at regular intervals.

2. Graphs should show "Years" on one axis and "Barrels of Crude Oil Produced" on the other. The axis showing the number of barrels should start at zero and may be multiplied by a factor of one million. The graph should begin with 1988 and slope downward on each equal increment to 1992.

2 Types of Financing for Business Operations

SECTION 2 FOCUS

Terms to Know debt financing, short-term financing, intermediate-term financing, long-term financing, trade credit, promissory note, accounts receivable, line of credit, leasing, equity financing

Objectives *After reading this section, you should be able to:*

❶ List **three kinds of debt financing** according to the length of repayment.

❷ List four factors companies consider in **choosing the right financing**.

Businesses Choose from Among Several Financing Options

Business borrowing is similar in many ways to borrowing by individuals. A business that wants to borrow must show credit worthiness by undergoing a credit check. A credit rating of good, average, or poor is then assigned to the business. Like an individual who borrows money, a business must pay interest on its loan. It must also repay the loan within a stated period of time.

Three Kinds of Financing

Raising money for a business through borrowing, or **debt financing,** can be divided into three categories—short-term, intermediate-term, and long-term financing. **Short-term financing** involves borrowing money for any period of time less than a year. Borrowing money for 1 to 10 years is considered **intermediate-term financing.** Borrowing for any longer period is called **long-term financing.** As **Figure 11.5** (pages 266–267) shows, the types and sources of financing differ depending upon the types of debt.

Short-Term Financing A business may seek short-term financing for many reasons. Because most billing is done monthly, a company may have excellent business during the month but not be paid until the beginning of the following month. In the meantime, the company needs money to pay salaries and its bills. During a growing season, a farmer may have to borrow to buy seed, repair equipment, and pay workers. In both cases, it would be unwise for the business to take out a long-term loan for a short-term need.

Focus

Overview

See the student page for section objectives.

Section 2 explains or describes: the types of short-term, intermediate-term, and long-term financing available to businesses; and four factors businesses consider before borrowing funds.

Bellringer

Before presenting this lesson, display Focus Activity Transparency 43 on the overhead projector or copy the material on the chalkboard. Assign the accompanying Focus Activity Sheet.

Motivational Activity

Ask students to list their ideas on how a company can obtain money to buy inventory, supplies, or equipment. Refer them to some of the loan choices discussed in Chapter 4. Have volunteers read aloud their ideas.

Preteaching Vocabulary

On separate index cards, have students write the definition of each term. On the back of the card, have them write the matching Glossary definition. Have them refer to these cards as they study the section.

Classroom Resources for Section 2

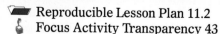 Reproducible Lesson Plan 11.2
Focus Activity Transparency 43
Focus Activity Sheet 43
Guided Reading Activity 11.2

Free Enterprise Activity 11
Section Quiz 11.2
Spanish Section Quiz 11.2
Testmaker

Teach

Guided Practice

L1 Evaluating Have students list the different types of financing available to businesses. Ask them to answer these questions for each type of financing: What advantage does a company gain by using this type of financing? What is the risk to the company?

L2 Trade-offs Refer students to the information in Figures 11.5 and 11.6 on page 268. Have students imagine that they own a company. Ask them to write a brief paragraph explaining whether they would sell stock to raise money if it meant sharing control of their company. If they would not sell stock, ask them what their alternative would be.

GLOBAL ECONOMICS

At one time, the United States and Europe dominated the stock market arena. Today, however, stock markets in Japan and Australia are competing for the world's investment capital. New computer networks linking these stock markets to one another let investors know what is happening in any market the moment it occurs. Now even small investors can take part in the worldwide trading of stocks and bonds.

Figure 11.5 Types of Financing

Short-Term Financing

Trade credit	**Trade credit** is extended by a seller to a business buying goods. It allows a buyer to take possession of goods immediately and pay for them at some future date–usually 30 to 90 days later. Trade credit	accounts for more than 85 percent of all transactions involving goods. By using trade credit, a business does not have to tie up its money capital in inventory. At the same time, trade credit benefits the seller by increasing its sales. Trade credit involves a	cost to the user. Often a buyer receives a discount, for example 2 percent, if a bill is paid within 10 days. If the buyer does not receive the discount, he or she is, in effect, paying 2 percent interest for the use of the trade credit.
Unsecured loans	Most short-term bank credit for businesses is in the form of unsecured bank loans. These are loans not guar-	anteed by anything other than the promise to repay them. The borrower must sign a **promissory** (PRAHM-uh-SOHR-ee) **note** to repay the money in full	by a specified time and with a specified rate of interest. The usual repayment period is one year.
Secured loans	Secured loans are backed by collateral—something of	value that a borrower uses as a promise to repay a loan. Businesses offer as collateral property such as	machinery, inventories, or **accounts receivable**— money owed to a business by its customers.
Line of credit	A **line of credit** is the maximum amount of money a company can borrow from a bank during a period of	time, usually one year. Rather than apply each time for a loan, a company may automatically borrow up to the amount of the line of credit, for example,	$100,000. Banks establish lines of credit for larger businesses with good credit ratings.

Intermediate-Term Financing

Loans	Intermediate-term loans have repayment periods of from 1 to 10 years and generally require collateral such as	stocks, bonds, equipment, or machinery. The loan is considered a mortgage if it is secured by property, such as the building in which the business is	located. Sometimes large, financially sound companies may be able to get unsecured intermediate-term loans.
Leasing	**Leasing** means renting rather than buying equipment. One advantage of leasing is that the leasing company will often service the	equipment at low cost. Another advantage is that the company may deduct a part of the money spent on a lease before figuring its income taxes. One disadvantage is that taking out a	long-term lease often costs more than borrowing the money to buy the same equipment.

Meeting Special Needs

Reading Disability Students with reading and organizational problems may have trouble classifying the different types of financing. Have students draw cartoons or other drawings to illustrate each type of financing. Tell them to use different colored paper for short-term, intermediate-term, and long-term types of financing. For example, for lines of credit, students might draw borrowers standing in line taking their money out of an automated teller machine. The combination of colors, symbols, and words will help students distinguish and group each type of financing.

Figure 11.5 Types of Financing

Long-Term Financing

Bonds	Bonds promise to pay a stated	rate of interest over a stated period of time and to repay the full amount bor-	rowed at the end of that time.
Stock	Selling stock is called **equity** (EK-wuht-ee) **financing**	because part of the ownership, or equity, of the company is being sold. Corporations may sell	either preferred or common stock. The differences are described below.

Common Stock	Preferred Stock
1. Common stock is issued by all corporations; it is the stock most often bought and sold. A corporation is an organization owned by many people but treated by the law as though it were a person; it can own property, pay taxes, make contracts, sue and be sued, and so on.	1. Many corporations do not issue preferred stock.
2. Holders of common stock have voting rights in a corporation. As a group, they elect the board of directors.	2. Holders of preferred stock have no voting rights.
3. Common stock pays dividends based on a corporation's performance. If the company does well, dividends may be high; if it does poorly, the dividends may be low or zero.	3. Preferred stock pays a fixed dividend. This amount must be paid before holders of common stock receive any dividends. If a company is unable to pay a fixed dividend on time, it must usually make up the missed payment at a later date.
4. Value of common stock rises and falls in relation to the corporation's performance and what investors expect it to do in the future.	4. The value of preferred stock changes in relation to how well the company is doing.
5. If a corporation fails, holders of common stock are the last to be paid with whatever money is left after paying all creditors.	5. If a corporation fails, holders of preferred stock must be paid before any holders of common stock are paid.

Independent Practice

L3 Reporting Encourage interested students to investigate the "junk-bond" scandals of the late 1980s and early 1990s. Have students write a brief report on their findings. The reports should include explanations of why companies sold these bonds, why investors bought them, and what caused the scandal.

L1 Analyzing Ask students to imagine they own a company that decorates items of clothing with fabric paints, buttons, beads, decorative pins, and so forth. Have students determine which type of financing is best for the company's needs. Students should decide if they should borrow or sell shares in the firm and for what length of time money should be borrowed. Students should consider such factors as the inventory the company may need, supplies, labor costs, equipment, and cost of borrowing. Have students present their findings to the class.

 Have students complete Guided Reading Activity 11.2 in the TCR. **LEP**

Cooperative Learning

Organize the class into groups of three to five students and have each group investigate major business news stories from the past two months. Each group should choose a major national company that was in the news during that time period. Have each group investigate its company's stock market prices for that time period. Each group should compare stock market prices and fluctuations in stock market prices with the occurrence of any newsworthy events. Have each group report its findings to the class. The class should discuss any trends that are shown by more than one company.

Have students turn to Figure 11.7 and review the information. Ask them to research and write a report on the trends in corporate financing from 1975 to the present. Suggest including consideration of how the general state of the economy affects the trends. Encourage volunteers to give oral reports and discuss their findings.

Intermediate-Term Financing When a company wants to expand its business by buying more land, buildings, or equipment, short-term financing generally is not adequate. For example, if you decided to expand your electronics repair business by opening another shop, you would not apply for a 90-day loan. In 90 days, you would not be able to do enough repair jobs to earn the additional revenue to repay the loan. Instead, you would look for intermediate-term financing.

Long-Term Financing For financing debts lasting 10 to 15 years or more, corporations either sell bonds or issue stock. Long-term financing is used for major expansion, such as building a new plant or buying new machines to replace outdated ones. See Figure 11.6. Usually only large corporations finance long-term debt by selling bonds. Unlike smaller companies, large corporations with huge assets appear to be better risks to investors who are interested in buying bonds.

**Figure 11.6
Major Equipment
Purchases**
Long-term financing is used to match the length of the borrowing with the useful life of the building or the equipment being purchased.
▼

Free Enterprise Activity

Ask small groups of students to brainstorm starting a joint venture business and then to plan a strategy for financing it. Suggest formulating their strategy in an outline.

Have groups give oral reports of their strategies and have the class speculate on their potential effectiveness.

Meeting Lesson Objectives

Assign Section 2 Review as homework or an in-class activity.

Evaluate

Assign the Section 2 Quiz in the TCR or use the Testmaker.

Reteach

Have students write a brief paragraph summarizing the advantages and disadvantages of each type of financing, and another paragraph explaining why the four factors used to make financial decisions are so important.

Enrich

Invite a Small Business Administration officer to the class to discuss starting up a new company and keeping it going.

Close

Have students create posters explaining companies' need for financing.

Choosing the Right Financing

Financial managers try to obtain capital at a minimum cost to the company. To do so, they try to choose the best mix of financing. The length of a loan that a company takes out or a corporation's decision regarding whether to sell bonds or issue stock depends on several factors as shown in Figure 11.7. These factors include interest costs, market climate, control of the company, and the financial condition of the company itself.

Figure 11.7 ▲
Four Factors Affecting Loan Choices

1 Interest Costs
When interest rates in general are high, a business may be reluctant to take out a loan. For example, a company may delay its expansion until it can borrow at better interest rates or take out a series of short-term loans at high rates, hoping that interest rates will drop. When that happens, the company will then take out a long-term loan. Interest rates also affect the decision to issue bonds. When rates are high, corporations must offer high rates of interest on their bonds to attract investors. When interest rates in general drop, corporations can offer lower rates of return on their bonds.

2 Market Climate
If economic growth appears to be slow, investors may prefer the fixed rate of return of bonds or preferred stock to the unknown return on common stock.

3 Control of the Company
Bonds do not have voting rights attached to them. Most preferred stocks do not give voting rights to shareholders either. The owners of common stocks, however, do have the right to vote in company elections.

4 Financial Condition of the Company
If a company's or corporation's sales and profits are stable or are expected to increase, taking on more debt would probably be safe—if its current debt load is not too large.

SECTION 2 REVIEW

Understanding Vocabulary

Define debt financing, short-term financing, intermediate-term financing, long-term financing, trade credit, promissory note, accounts receivable, line of credit, leasing, equity financing.

Reviewing Objectives

1. What three kinds of debt financing are available according to the repayment period?
2. What four factors affect a company's financing plans?

Chapter 11 *Financing and Producing Goods* **269**

Section 2 Review Answers

debt financing (p. 265), **short-term financing** (p. 265), **intermediate-term financing** (p. 265), **long-term financing** (p. 265), **trade credit** (p. 266), **promissory note** (p. 266), **accounts receivable** (p. 266), **line of credit** (p. 266), **leasing** (p. 266), **equity financing** (p. 267)

Reviewing Objectives
1. short-term (borrowing money for any period of time less than a year), intermediate-term (borrowing money for 1–10 years), and long-term (borrowing money for more than 10 years)
2. interest costs, market climate, control of the company, and the financial condition of the company

Personal Perspective

Judith Resnick on Starting Up a Financial Business

Profile

- 1941–
- chair and CEO of Dabney/Resnick & Wagner, Inc., a California investment banking, brokerage, and money management firm
- entered brokerage business at age 41 in 1983 with no professional experience
- started as a broker with Drexel Burnham Lambert
- founded Dabney/Resnick in 1989

Judith Resnick, a divorced, single mother, had been supported by her father until he died in 1977. Without job skills, without an income, she says, "All of a sudden, I had nowhere to turn." She looked to the stock market because it interested her, even though her broker had lost what little investment she had.

... Although I was losing money, I noticed that he [the broker] was making it. I said to myself, "Even I could do that."

When the larger firms would not hire her, a friend introduced Resnick to a broker at Drexel Burnham Lambert in downtown Los Angeles, and the broker's office manager hired her as a trainee. How did she get started selling?

I made a list of everyone I knew on the earth and called them. I just didn't have time to make excuses for myself. I guess I didn't know that I was oppressed.

By her third year, Resnick was one of the top producers at the brokerage house. A colleague urged her to sell some Eastern Air Lines bonds to her clients. They were trading at 75 cents on the dollar, but Resnick refused. The bonds fell to only 4 cents on the dollar by 1993.

I didn't think they were appropriate for my customers, so I said 'no.' That was the day I figured it was time to go out on my own.

In 1989 Judith Resnick and another salesperson at Drexel, Neil Dabney, launched out to start their own firm. At first they faced an uphill battle because Drexel's reputation for selling junk [high risk] bonds preceded them.

We went to the NASD [National Association of Securities Dealers] and told them we were from Drexel and wanted to start our own firm. They looked at us like we had three heads.

The firm of Dabney/Resnick secured a local bank loan and opened for business in July 1989. After only four months in business, the firm paid off its bank debt.

Checking for Understanding

1. How did Judith Resnick get her first job in the brokerage business?
2. What obstacle did Dabney/Resnick have to overcome to obtain financing?
3. What was the new firm's early evidence of successful management?

Answers to Checking for Understanding

1. Judith Resnick got her first job in the brokerage business when a friend introduced her to a broker at Drexel Burnham Lambert. She was hired as a trainee by the broker's office manager.
2. Dabney/Resnick had to overcome Drexel's negative reputation for selling junk bonds. This reputation made people reluctant to loan them money. They finally secured a loan from a local bank.
3. The firm showed early evidence of successful management when it repaid the bank loan after only four months in business.

> ### SECTION 3 FOCUS
>
> *Terms to Know* production, consumer goods, producer goods, mechanization, assembly line, division of labor, automation, robotics
>
> *Objectives After reading this section, you should be able to:*
> ❶ List the four major steps in production operations.
> ❷ Describe five advances in technology and methods of production.

Perfecting the Production Process is Key to a Business's Success

O nce businesses have the necessary financing, they can begin production. **Production** is the process of changing resources into goods that satisfy the needs and wants of individuals and other businesses. Businesses may produce one of two kinds of goods. Goods that are produced for individuals are called **consumer goods.** They are sold directly to the public to be used as they are. Goods produced for businesses to use in making other goods are called **producer goods.** The machines used in an auto assembly line are examples of producer goods.

Steps in Production Operations

Besides the actual manufacturing of a good, the production process for both types of goods involves several operations. Figure 11.8 provides an example of one of these operations, which include planning, purchasing, quality control, and inventory control. Each becomes a cost of production. You will read more about product design in Chapter 12.

Planning Planning includes choosing a location for the business and scheduling production. Where a business is located is directly related to how successful the business will be. This fact is as true for a company that is opening its first factory or store as it is for

Figure 11.8 Production Costs
Designing, engineering, and planning all add substantially to the total cost of producing goods such as automobiles.
▼

Chapter 11 Financing and Producing Goods **271**

Focus

Overview
   See the student page for section objectives.
   Section 3 explains or describes four steps in production operations and the role of technology in developing production methods.

Bellringer
   Before presenting the lesson, display Focus Activity Transparency 44 on the overhead projector and assign the accompanying Focus Activity Sheet.

Motivational Activity
   Ask students to list items they have made or assembled, such as scale models. Ask students to describe their production process: their planning steps, necessary purchases, quality checks, and any spare parts or materials they needed.

Preteaching Vocabulary
   Have students create a crossword puzzle using the vocabulary words.

Classroom Resources for Section 3

- Reproducible Lesson Plan 11.3
- Focus Activity Transparency 44
- Focus Activity Sheet 44
- Guided Reading Activity 11.3
- Consumer Application Activity 11
- Mathematics Practice for Economics 34

- Performance Assessment Activity 34
- Section Quiz 11.3
- Spanish Section Quiz 11.3
- Chapter 11 Test Forms A and B
- Testmaker
- Enrichment Activity 11

- Economics Vocabulary Activity 11
- Spanish Economics Vocabulary Activity 11
- Audiocassette 11
- Spanish Audiocassette 11
- Reteaching Activity 11
- Spanish Reteaching Activity 11

Teach

Guided Practice

L3 Debate Have students debate the pros and cons of automating jobs when such action puts human laborers out of work. Have students debate whether more technology is always the answer or whether automation is unavoidable in today's global economy.

Visual Instruction

Refer students to Figure 11.9 and have them review the information to develop a format for interviewing purchasing agents about their decision making. After discussing formats that volunteers present, have the class devise a single format. Encourage students to use the format for real life interviews and to tell what they learned.

an older business that is expanding into a new area. Among the factors to consider are nearness to markets, raw materials, labor supply, and transportation facilities. In the past, most cities grew up near waterways. Today, with railroads, airlines, and pipelines, it is not so important to be located near waterways.

Scheduling production operations involves setting beginning and ending times for each step in the production process. It includes planning and checking the use of labor, machinery, and materials so that production moves smoothly. Scheduling ensures that work will be finished on time whether it is manufacturing automobiles or books or dry cleaning a blouse or shirt.

Purchasing In order to do business, a company needs the raw materials to produce its goods or offer its services. It also must have machinery, office supplies, and any other supplies it uses. Obtaining raw materials, machines, and supplies is the purchasing function of the production process and involves getting the best deal for the company. The people who buy goods for a business have to decide what to buy, from whom, and at what price. Figure 11.9 outlines the major factors to consider in making purchasing decisions.

A Price
Is this the best price?

B Quality
Are these goods made well? Will they last?

C Number of Suppliers
Should the company buy from several suppliers to encourage competition?

D Services
Does this supplier offer such services as equipment repair?

**Figure 11.9
Purchasing Decisions**
A company must include all of these factors before purchasing.

Meeting Special Needs

Math Skills Deficiencies Creating circle graphs can be intimidating to students with math skills deficiencies. Tell these students that the secret is to wait to round their figures until the very end to obtain the final percentage and degree numbers. Refer students to Chapter 1 for instructions on creating these graphs. Have them practice making simple graphs until they understand the steps involved.

Quality Control Quality control is checking the quality of the goods produced. It involves overseeing the grade or freshness of goods, their strength or workability, the workmanship or design, harmlessness, adherence to federal or industry standards, and many other factors. Quality control systems can be as simple as testing the thousandth item produced or testing each product as it is finished. As Figure 11.10 (page 274) shows, every production manager faces a trade-off in quality control.

Inventory Control Almost all manufacturers and many service businesses, such as dry cleaners, need inventories, or stockpiles, of the materials they use in making their products or offering their services.

Manufacturers and businesses, such as supermarkets, also keep inventories of finished goods on hand for sale, but inventories are costly. The more inventory a business has, the less capital it has for other activities. For example, it costs money to warehouse and insure goods against fire and theft. Some goods such as film and medicines spoil if kept beyond a certain period of time. Other goods such as cars and stylish clothes become obsolete, or out of date, in time.

Independent Practice

L2 Interviewing Encourage students to interview the manager of a local fast-food restaurant to see how food items are produced. Have them find out what jobs people have and what jobs machines have in mass-producing hamburgers, salads, french fries, and so forth. Have students write a brief report that outlines the production steps in the fast-food restaurant.

GLOBAL ECONOMICS

Although automation may make production methods more efficient, it does not address the most pressing problem in many economically developing countries: high unemployment. Some experts believe the solution is to automate only part of a process and use human workers for the rest. Such projects are already underway in India and Africa and may be used in other economically developing nations as well.

E Shipping
Who pays shipping costs and how will goods be shipped?

F Delivery
How much time is there between ordering and receiving goods?

273

Cooperative Learning

Have the class work together to decide on an item to be made, possibly as a fund-raising project. Projects could include Homecoming corsages, pizzas, or household items. Have the class bring materials to school to make a prototype of the item. Students should plan a rough production method before constructing the item. After the prototype is completed, have the class write out a final production process for the project, including statements of which jobs will be handled by people, which jobs will be handled by machines, and how assembly will be managed.

273

Independent Practice

L1 Analyzing Have students imagine they are in charge of producing stuffed figures of their school mascot. Have students choose the best production method to make stuffed figures. Encourage them to focus their discussion on the four production steps: planning, purchasing, quality control, and inventory control. Have students consider what tasks need to be done, how the labor can be divided among the class, what jobs people will do, and what jobs machines will do. Have students prepare reports to present in class.

Have students complete Guided Reading Activity 11.3 in the TCR. **LEP**

Figure 11.10 ▲ The Quality Control Trade-Off The more time spent on quality control, the higher the production costs. This extra cost raises the price to consumers. Less quality control, however, may result in items of poor quality and unhappy customers.

Figure 11.11 Technology and Production From the time of the Industrial Revolution, methods of production have been changing. Five major advances in technology have most affected this process. These are mechanization, the assembly line, division of labor, automation, and robotics.

In deciding how much inventory to keep on hand, those in charge of inventory control also have other costs to consider. If the price of a raw material is expected to rise, a business may stockpile it to keep future costs down. Often a supplier will discount large orders. Some businesses may decide that the discounts outweigh the other costs of maintaining a large inventory.

Technology and Methods of Production

Technology is the use of science to develop new products and new methods for producing and distributing goods and services. Technology influences businesses in many ways.

The use of technology on a large scale began in the textile industry in England in the late 1700s. From there the machine-powered textile industry spread to the United States. Figure 11.11 shows five advances that have since changed the way goods are produced.

A Mechanization The Industrial Revolution, as the beginning of the factory system is called, came about through **mechanization,** which combines the labor of people and large power-driven machines. For example, with the introduction of spinning and weaving machines in factories, entrepreneurs replaced skilled handwork with machines run by unskilled workers. The rate of output per labor hour increased greatly as a result. ▼

 Free Enterprise Activity

Ask students to brainstorm starting an after-school delivery service. Encourage them to outline an organizational structure and a plan for recruitment of staff and purchase of needed equipment. Recommend preparing a list of every competitive advantage they think their service can offer to prospective clients. Have students evaluate the feasibility of starting up the business.

B The Assembly Line
An outgrowth of mechanization is the assembly line. An **assembly line** is a production system in which the good being produced moves on a conveyor belt past workers who perform individual tasks in assembling it. The Ford Motor Company developed the modern assembly-line process at the beginning of the twentieth century. Because the assembly line results in more efficient use of machines and labor, the costs of production drop. ▼

C Division of Labor ▲
Assembly-line production is only possible with interchangeable parts made in standard sizes and with **division of labor,** the breaking down of a job into small tasks. A different worker performs each task.

D Automation ▲
Mechanization combines the labor of people and machines. In **automation,** machines do the work and people oversee them.

E Robotics
Robotics refers to sophisticated computer-controlled machinery that operates the assembly line. ▼

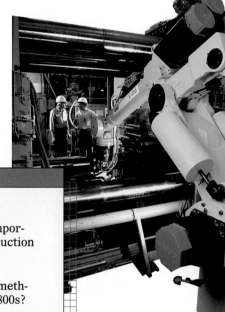

SECTION 3 REVIEW

Understanding Vocabulary
Define production, consumer goods, producer goods, mechanization, assembly line, division of labor, automation, robotics.

Reviewing Objectives
❶ What are the most important steps in the production process?
❷ How has technology changed production methods since the early 1800s?

Chapter 11 Financing and Producing Goods **275**

Assess

Meeting Lesson Objectives
Assign Section 3 Review as homework or an in-class activity.

Evaluate
🗀 Assign the Section 3 Quiz in the TCR or use the Testmaker.
🗀 Assign the Chapter 11 Test Form A or Form B or use the Testmaker.

Reteach
Have students summarize the major point of the section orally.
🗀 Have students complete Reteaching Activity 11 in the TCR.

Enrich
Have students research the production process of one locally made product.

🗀 Have students complete Enrichment Activity 11 in the TCR.

Close
Have students list some of the main financing and production decisions of businesses.

Section 3 Review Answers

Understanding Vocabulary
production (p. 271), **consumer goods** (p. 271), **producer goods** (p. 271), **mechanization** (p. 274), **assembly line** (p. 275), **division of labor** (p. 275), **automation** (p. 275), **robotics** (p. 275)

Reviewing Objectives
1. The most important steps in the production process are product design, planning, purchasing, quality control, and inventory control.

2. Technology has radically changed production methods since the early 1800s through the introduction of mechanization, the assembly line, division of labor, and automation.

275

News Clip

Readings in Economics

FORBES   **APRIL 12, 1993**

WHISTLE BLOWER
by Fleming Meeks

Teach

Ask students if they or someone they know has ever invented something or thought of something that should be invented. Ask volunteers to explain what happened to these inventions or ideas, including whether or not the inventors followed up on them. Tell students that the article shows some of the difficulties that an inventor faces in bringing a product into existence. The article also shows how persistence as well as ingenuity is necessary to succeed.

Have students investigate inventors, such as Thomas Edison or Charles Goodyear, who experienced many setbacks or failures before succeeding. Have students consider what prompted the inventors to keep going and what benefits and problems their success brought about. Students might also collect news articles about other entrepreneurs who have invented a product after many tries.

When Howard Wright was a teenager ... his two preoccupations were skin diving and inventing. After reading a *Scientific American* story about the physics of whistles, young Wright set out to design a whistle he and his buddies could use while diving.

After six months of trial and error, ... he attached two hollowed-out flash-cubes to a plastic whistle. It worked. But after making up three or four for his friends, he lost interest. ...

So the idea sat on the shelf through college [and dental school] ... Finally, in January 1989, it was time for a break. He took his wife, Victoria ... and their three kids on a Caribbean cruise.

When the passengers lined up for the mandatory life vest drill, Vicki turned to her husband with an excited grin and said, "Look Howard, we even have whistles." Wright shook his head. "If that whistle gets wet, it's not gonna work," he said. "But don't worry." Then he told her about his old invention. ...

Once back home, Wright began spending every night in his basement, often past midnight, experimenting with different whistles. ...

Thus in early 1992 was born the All-Weath-er Safety Whistle Co. In their first 12 months of selling, ... the Wrights sold 40,000 whistles for $107,000. Ranked loudest by *Boating* magazine, their $5.95 (retail price) Storm Safety whistle is today used by the Army Special Forces as well as by the Los Angeles County Department of Beaches and Harbors. ...

Which leaves Wright with a problem. "I love dentistry," he says, ... But with cash flow increasing and with capacity up to 10,000 whistles a day, he and his spouse are trying to talk their way into Wal-Mart. Howard Wright concedes he may soon have to cut his dentistry back to three days a week.

• THINK ABOUT IT •

1. What prompted Wright to start working on a new whistle design?

2. What problem has Wright's success caused?

Answers to Think About It

1. Wright was prompted to work on a new whistle design because he wanted a whistle that could be used underwater while he and his friends were diving. His interest was reawakened when he saw that the whistles being used in a life vest drill wouldn't work if they got wet.

2. Wright is so busy that he might have to cut back on his dental practice.

CHAPTER

11 Highlights

Use the Chapter 11 Highlights to preview, review, condense, or reteach the chapter. A Spanish Chapter Highlights is available in the Spanish Handbook.

Preview/Review

 After students read the Chapter 11 Highlights, have them complete Economics Vocabulary Activity 11 in the TCR. Spanish Vocabulary Activities are also available in the Spanish Resource Binder. Vocabulary Software reinforces the economic terms used in Chapter 11.

Condense

Have students listen to Chapter 11 on the Audiocassettes in the TCR. A 1-page written activity and 1-page test accompany this material. These materials are also available in Spanish.

Reteach

Have students complete Reteaching Activity 11 in the TCR. Spanish Reteaching Activities are also available.

Section 1

Investing in the Free Enterprise System

Key Terms
cost-benefit analysis
  (p. 258)

Summary
People and businesses invest their savings in many places including various banks, mutual funds, and pension plans. By financing investment, people hope to earn interest. Businesses draw upon these investments in order to finance expansion. This financing of expansion is one way that the allocation of resources is eventually determined in a free market system.

Section 2

Types of Financing for Business Operations

Key Terms
debt financing (p. 265)
short-term financing
  (p. 265)
intermediate-term
  financing (p. 265)
long-term financing
  (p. 265)

trade credit (p. 266)
promissory note (p. 266)
accounts receivable
  (p. 266)
line of credit (p. 266)
leasing (p. 266)
equity financing (p. 267)

Summary
When businesses borrow, the length of the repayment term is an important consideration. Businesses that borrow also consider the rate of interest, the climate of the market, and their ability to handle the debt load. Sometimes businesses raise financial capital by selling stocks or bonds.

Section 3

The Production Process

Key Terms
production (p. 271)
consumer goods (p. 271)
producer goods (p. 271)
mechanization (p. 274)

assembly line (p. 275)
division of labor (p. 275)
automation (p. 275)
robotics (p. 275)

Summary
The production process involves product design, planning, purchasing, quality control, and inventory control. Technology has increased productivity. Mechanization, the assembly line, division of labor, automation, and robotics have combined to make production more efficient.

VIDEODISC

Nightly Business Report

Economics in Action
Use "Financing and Producing Goods" on Disc 1, Side B, Video 16.

Search 40500, Play to 46948

CHAPTER 11 Review

Chapter 11
REVIEW

ANSWERS

Identifying Key Terms

Answers will vary but should include the following: Businesses can obtain financing for short-term needs through **trade credit** offered by a seller, unsecured loans for which they sign a **promissory note,** secured loans for which they offer their **accounts receivable** as collateral, or a **line of credit** provided by a financial institution. Intermediate-term needs can be met through **leasing** rather than buying equipment.

1. cost-benefit analysis
2. long-term financing
3. trade credit
4. consumer goods (producer goods)
5. producer goods (consumer goods)
6. assembly line
7. division of labor

Recalling Facts and Ideas

Section 1

1. by depositing savings into a financial institution (in exchange for interest), which then loans the money to businesses (to finance growth and expansion)
2. Do a cost-benefit analysis: estimate all expected operating costs, calculate expected revenues, calculate expected profits, calculate the cost of financing, and determine if expected profits are greater than the cost of financing the operation.

3. businesses that are expanding

Section 2

4. to fill in during periods of time when cash is low and to finance the business while the product is being made (such as dur-

ing a farmer's growing season)
5. Leasing is intermediate-term financing.
6. Holders of common stock have voting rights in the corporations whose stock they own. As a group, they elect the board of directors.

Identifying Key Terms

Write a short paragraph about alternative types of short-term and intermediate-term financing using all of the following terms.

trade credit (p. 266)   line of credit (p. 266)
promissory note (p. 266)   leasing (p. 266)
accounts receivable (p. 266)

Use terms from the following list to fill in the blanks in the paragraph below.

trade credit (p. 266)   producer goods
consumer goods (p. 271)   (p. 271)
long-term   cost-benefit analysis
   financing (p. 265)   (p. 258)
assembly line (p. 275)   division of labor
                                  (p. 275)

As with any activity, the decision to obtain financing for an investment expansion requires using a __(1)__. Besides short-term and intermediate-term financing, there is __(2)__. Sometimes businesses finance purchases by taking possession now but paying for them in the future. This is called __(3)__. The goods that businesses make are either __(4)__ or __(5)__. Sometimes they are produced on a highly automated __(6)__. This leads to an extreme form of __(7)__.

Recalling Facts and Ideas

Section 1
1. How do individuals turn savings into investments?
2. Outline the steps you would use in reaching a necessary financial decision.
3. Which types of businesses will most often pursue financing?

Section 2
4. What are two reasons a business may need short-term financing?
5. Leasing is a form of what type of financing?
6. Do holders of common stock have any rights in a corporation? Explain.

Section 3
7. Besides quality and inventory control, what other steps are involved in the production process?
8. When did assembly-line production first develop in the United States?
9. What does assembly-line production require?

Critical Thinking

Section 1
Understanding Cause and Effect How does the free enterprise system cause financing to be used for projects that have the most profit potential?

Section 2
Identifying Alternatives Assume that you have to buy new inventory that you sell off completely by the end of each month. Determine the most appropriate type of financing to use when you buy this inventory.

Section 3
Evaluating Information "Because full automation eliminates workers from the assembly line, soon there will be no need for any workers." What is wrong with the line of reasoning in this statement?

Section 3
7. product design, planning, and purchasing
8. at the begining of the twentieth century
9. movement of a product along a conveyor belt and past workers who perform individual assembly tasks

Applying Economic Concepts

Making Financing Decisions In your lifetime, you will make a large number of financing decisions to purchase things that will last, such as expensive stereos, major appliances, cars, and houses. Imagine you are a businessperson who has to make decisions about financing. Make a list of the kind of business expansions that might require financing. Note after each type of business expansion, such as buying a low-powered desk computer, what the appropriate type of business financing might be.

Chapter Projects

1. **Individual Project** The federal government's Small Business Administration (SBA) was designed to help small businesses with short-term financing. You can obtain information about this federal government agency by calling or writing the SBA in Washington, D.C. You can also obtain information about the SBA from your local library. Research and write a three-paragraph report describing the functions of the SBA.
2. **Cooperative Learning Project** Work in three groups. As a group, work on one of the following topics:

   A. Division of Labor The most famous example of the division of labor focuses on a pin factory. Adam Smith discussed it in his book *The Wealth of Nations*. The group studying this example should do the following:
   - find the passage in the book about the pin factory
   - develop a chart showing the elements of Adam Smith's arithmetic example
   - calculate the percentage increase in productivity due to the division of labor

   B. Assembly-Line Techniques This group can divide into two smaller groups. One will develop a short report on how Henry Ford first developed the assembly-line process. The second group will look at what Eli Whitney

developed with the use of interchangeable parts. This second group will write a short report explaining the importance of interchangeable parts in the manufacturing process.

C. Robotics This group will research how robotics developed and how much of American manufacturing is controlled by robotics. One part of this group can look at the future of robotics.

Reviewing Skills

Building Graphs

Making a Circle Graph Here is some sample information about the ownership of Texas farms. Make a circle graph showing this information.

> sole proprietorships = 167,602
> partnerships = 15,947
> family held corporations = 3,414

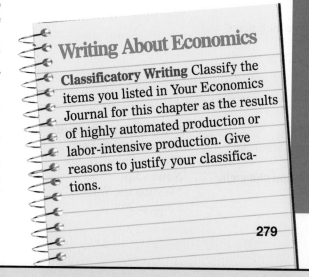

Writing About Economics

Classificatory Writing Classify the items you listed in Your Economics Journal for this chapter as the results of highly automated production or labor-intensive production. Give reasons to justify your classifications.

279

Reviewing Skills

1. Refer students to Chapter 1 **Learning Economic Skills** for instructions on how to create a circle graph. The percentages and degrees of the graph should be: sole proprietorships, 167,602 = 89 percent and 320 degrees; partnerships, 15,947 = 8 percent and 30 degrees; family held corporations, 3,414 =

2 percent and 7 degrees; and other, 1,826 = 1 percent and 3 degrees (total = 188,789 farms)

Writing About Economics

Review students' reasons for classifying the items.

Critical Thinking

Section 1
Answers will vary but should note that firms which can earn high profits will compete for available funds and will be willing to pay the finance, interest, and opportunity costs involved.

Section 2
Answers will vary but should note that, in this case, trade credit is best.

Section 3
Answers will vary but should mention that workers must still operate, monitor, and maintain machines.

Applying Economic Concepts

Answers will vary. Suggest to students that, for each expansion, they do a quick cost-benefit analysis.

Chapter Projects

1. Students should list their sources and cover the main functions of the SBA.
2. Have students document their research on division of labor, assembly-line techniques, or robotics and present their results to the class.

? BONUS QUESTION

The following bonus question may be written on the chalkboard when students take the chapter test.
Q: Design an item to be mass produced using only the students and the materials in the room. Plan to make at least 100. Describe the item, the materials used, and the assembly process.
A: Answers will vary but students should describe a reasonable production process.

CHAPTER 12 *MARKETING AND DISTRIBUTION*

CHAPTER ORGANIZER

Daily Objectives	Special Features	Classroom Resources
Section 1 The Changing Role of Marketing • **List** the four stages of the development of marketing in the United States. • **Describe** the elements of market research.	**Focus on Free Enterprise:** Case Study, Harley-Davidson, pp. 286–287	Reproducible Lesson Plan 12.1 *NBR* Video 17 Focus Activity Transparency 45 Focus Activity Sheet 45 Guided Reading Activity 12.1 Cooperative Learning Activity 12 Primary and Secondary Source Reading 12 Free Enterprise Activity 12 Section Quiz 12.1 Spanish Section Quiz 12.1 Testmaker
Section 2 The Marketing Mix • **Explain** the importance of product identification. • **Identify** marketing strategies that depend on price. • **Explain** how a firm decides in which place to sell its products. • **List** four types of promotion a firm may use.	**Personal Perspective:** Charles Wang on Challenges in the Computer Industry, p. 292	Reproducible Lesson Plan 12.2 Focus Activity Transparency 46 Focus Activity Sheet 46 Guided Reading Activity 12.2 Section Quiz 12.2 Spanish Section Quiz 12.2 Testmaker
Section 3 Distribution Channels • **Explain** the difference between wholesale and retail distribution. • **List** two new types of distribution channels.	**Critical Thinking Skills:** Distinguishing Fact From Opinion, p. 297 **News Clip:** "Testing the Waters" *Time,* p. 298	Reproducible Lesson Plan 12.3 Focus Activity Transparency 47 Focus Activity Sheet 47 Guided Reading Activity 12.3 Consumer Application Activity 12 Mathematics Practice for Economics 35 Performance Assessment Activity 35 Section Quiz 12.3 Spanish Section Quiz 12.3 Testmaker Reinforcing Skills 12 Enrichment Activity 12

0:00 **OUT OF TIME?** If time does not permit teaching this chapter, you may use the Chapter 12 Highlights and the Audiocassettes that include a 1-page activity and a 1-page test.

Chapter 12 Review and Evaluation

Special Features	Classroom Resources	
Chapter 12 Highlights, p. 299	Chapter 12 Test Forms A and B	Audiocassette 12
Chapter 12 Review, pp. 300–301	Economics Vocabulary Activity 12	Spanish Audiocassette 12
Point/Counterpoint, pp. 302–303	Spanish Economics Vocabulary Activity 12	Reteaching Activity 12
		Spanish Reteaching Activity 12

Key to Ability Levels

Teaching strategies have been coded for varying learning styles and abilities.

L1 Level 1 activities are **basic** activities and should be within the ability range of all students.

L2 Level 2 activities are **average** activities designed for the ability range of average to above-average students.

L3 Level 3 activities are **challenging** activities designed for the ability range of above-average students.

LEP activities should be within the ability range of **Limited English Proficiency** students.

Performance Assessment

The following chapter project may be assigned at the beginning of the chapter and used for performance assessment. See page T12 for additional Performance Assessment information.

Conducting a Survey Have pairs of students conduct a survey of brands that people trust and are loyal to and find out the reasons for their loyalty. Have the team surveys include information about qualities the consumers expect from their brands and the advertising they have responded to. After the teams complete the surveys, have members report on the most popular brand names among the consumers they polled. Students might report their findings in an illustrated table.

Additional Resources

Readings for the Student

Clemente, Mark N. *The Marketing Glossary.* New York: AMACOM, 1992.

Gay, Kathryn. *Caution: This May Be an Advertisement.* New York: Franklin Watts, Inc., 1992.

Readings for the Teacher

Mayer, Martin. *Whatever Happened to Madison Avenue?* Boston: Little, Brown, and Company, 1991.

Norris, J. T. *Advertising and the Transformation of American Society, 1865–1920.* Westport, Conn.: Greenwood Press, 1990.

Multimedia Materials

Marketing Peanut Butter: A Simulation. Apple, IBM, TRS-80. Gregg McGraw-Hill, 1221 Sixth Ave., New York, NY 10020

Marketing Perspectives—A Series. Twenty-nine videotapes. 30 min. Wisconsin Foundation for Vocational, Technical, and Adult Education, 5402 Mineral Point Rd., Madison, WI 53705

Marketing the Myths. 16mm film or videotape. 25 min. Phoenix/BFA Films and Video, Inc., 470 Park Avenue South, New York, NY 10016

Service With a Smile. Part of the Business Basics Series. Apple. Media Materials, Inc. 2936 Remington Ave., Baltimore, MD 21211. (800-638-1010) Explores concepts behind wholesale, retail, price, and profit.

Chapter Overview

Over the past hundred years, marketing has changed from a part of production to a way of creating demand and even predicting demand for a given item. Marketing research has therefore become extremely important, and marketers have become more sophisticated in responding to that research. Many companies test consumer interest by having special promotions of their goods, and most companies choose wholesale and retail distribution patterns carefully.

VIDEODISC

Nightly Business Report
Economics in Action
Use "Marketing and Distribution" on Disc 1, Side B, Video 17.

Search 47032, Play to 52309

CHAPTER

12 MARKETING AND DISTRIBUTION

Is listening to music a need or a want?

What influenced the type of portable cassette player each person decided to buy?

Where can you buy these products?

Answering Economic Questions

The questions in the above illustration are designed to lead into the main concepts in Chapter 12. Students might not be aware of the many choices they make automatically as consumers. They might also be unaware of the far-reaching impact of those choices.

These questions will help them become more aware of the marketplace from which they choose their own consumer goods.

Have students discuss the questions and explain their reasons for thinking as they do.

Could these students have bought such small cassette players 20 years ago?

Are there alternatives to portable cassette players today?

Your Economics Journal

During a one-week period, keep track of the products that you see offered for sale directly to consumers, either through the mail or over the phone, whether they are advertised on TV, in magazines, or in the newspaper. Make a list, noting after each item how it was advertised and why you think it was advertised for sale directly to you.

281

Connecting to Past Learning

Ask students what criteria they use when they decide which brand or model of an item to buy. Ask students how much they think marketing forces influence their decisions. Tell them that in Chapter 12 they will learn about the marketing strategies and distribution processes that companies use to make their goods more prominent in the marketplace. After completing the chapter, compare and contrast students' early ideas about their purchases.

Applying Economics

Tell students to imagine they have designed a new fashion belt made from discarded industrial strapping. Have them describe the people they think would be their main customers and then list the ways they would create demand for their product. Remind them to consider both the need for adequate production and distribution and the use of marketing tools.

 EXTRA CREDIT PROJECT

Do a book report on an entrepreneur or other influential figure in the field of advertising or marketing. Include a discussion of the achievements that brought the person to prominence.

 PERFORMANCE ASSESSMENT

Refer to page 280B for "Conducting a Survey," a Performance Assessment Activity for this chapter.

🗂 **Economic Portfolio**

Have students think about and list the inconveniences they experience over the course of a day. Collect the lists and write on the chalkboard a sample of the most common inconveniences. Then ask students to invent goods or services to help eliminate or lessen the inconveniences. Have students write a marketing plan for their product.

Focus

Overview

See the student page for section objectives.

Section 1 explains or describes: the four stages of marketing as they have developed in the United States; the elements of market research; and the different types of utility a product can have.

Bellringer

Before presenting the lesson, display Focus Activity Transparency 45 on the overhead projector or copy the material on the chalkboard. Assign the accompanying Focus Activity Sheet.

Motivational Activity

Write the following statement for students to complete: The customer is _____. Ask students to write down as many sayings and slogans as they can regarding the role of the customer. Encourage students to discuss the status that customers have in the marketplace.

Preteaching Vocabulary

Lead students in a game of "Marketing Lingo." Assign to students one term each and have them give short clues to the term they have been given. Have the rest of the class guess the terms.

The Changing Role of Marketing

SECTION 1 FOCUS

Terms to Know marketing, utility, form utility, place utility, time utility, ownership utility, market research, market survey, test marketing

Objectives *After reading this section, you should be able to:*

1. List the four stages of the **development of marketing** in the United States.
2. Describe the elements of **market research**.

Marketing Helps Determine the Economic Value of Goods and Services

In addition to financing and producing a product, businesses must promote and eventually sell the products and services they produce. **Marketing** involves all of the activities needed to move goods and services from the producer to the consumer. These activities include market research, advertising and promotion, and the actual distribution of goods and services from the producer to the consumer. Some economists estimate that about 50 percent of the price people pay for an item is for the cost of marketing.

The Development of Marketing

The idea and importance of marketing in the United States has changed considerably since 1900. Historically, marketing has developed through four stages: production, sales, marketing, and consumer sovereignty. **Figure 12.1** shows this development.

The 1950s saw the rise of marketing as a combining of the production and sales functions. At the same time, a greater variety of goods became available to satisfy consumer needs.

By the late 1950s and early 1960s, marketing had changed. Instead of just creating demand, businesses found they could take a larger share of the consumer dollar by designing products that matched what consumers wanted.

Today, marketing involves many activities, all of which add to the utility that marketing creates. **Utility** is the ability of any good or service to satisfy consumer wants. Utility can be divided into four major types: form utility, place utility, time utility, and ownership utility. **Figure 12.2** (page 284) illustrates the differences among these types of utility.

Classroom Resources for Section 1

- Reproducible Lesson Plan 12.1
- *NBR* Video 17
- Focus Activity Transparency 45
- Focus Activity Sheet 45
- Guided Reading Activity 12.1
- Cooperative Learning Activity 12

- Primary and Secondary Source Readings 12
- Free Enterprise Acitvity 12
- Section Quiz 12.1
- Spanish Section Quiz 12.1
- Testmaker

Figure 12.1 Four Stages of Marketing

A The Early 1900s
Marketing at this time dealt with getting goods to the consumers who wanted them. Supply was often unable to satisfy demand. Companies emphasized the production of goods.

B The 1920s and 1930s
Many consumers had most of the necessities and some of the luxuries of American life by this time. Technology was increasing productivity. Companies found that to increase sales they had to stimulate demand by actively selling their products. They began to use advertising to promote their goods.

C The 1950s
Businesses were able to produce more than consumers normally would use, actively created demand for the goods and services that they sold, and faced increased competition.

D The Late 1950s and Early 1960s
Producers began researching and meeting consumer tastes and preferences. The consumer became the most important element in product development. Consumer sovereignty had arrived.

Teach

Guided Practice

L3 Analyzing and Synthesizing Encourage pairs of students to choose a business in their community and write a proposal detailing ways to improve sales by increasing one or more forms of utility. Suggest that they illustrate their proposals with advertising layouts and sample copy.

Visual Instruction

Ask students to study Figure 12.1. Have them write a brief essay on how a company would sell a refrigerator in each of the four marketing stages. Have them base their answer on the information provided in the figure. They should include how and when companies would use advertising, product differentiation, and so on.

GLOBAL ECONOMICS

Marketing plans are more essential to businesses in free markets than in tightly controlled markets. To succeed, however, all businesses must use some form of market research, product development, production, and promotion.

283

Meeting Special Needs

Reading Disability Students with various reading and organizational difficulties may have problems relating pictures, captions, and the main text. Before reading the text in Section 1, ask students to look at the pictures. Have them tell what the pictures illustrate. After students read Section 1, ask them to again tell what the pictures illustrate and discuss why they were included in the section.

Independent Practice

L2 Market Research
Encourage students to develop their own market surveys to find out what their neighbors or peers want from a particular type of item. Students might focus on such items as bath soap, movies, magazines, jeans, and fast food.

L3 Developing a Product
Have students use information from their own or other market surveys to develop a product they think will sell. Encourage students to develop plans for manufacturing and test marketing.

 Have students complete Guided Reading Activity 12.1 in the TCR. LEP

? DID YOU KNOW

Market research is not the preserve of businesses only. Governments and watchdog groups conduct market research to develop appropriate regulations for marketing, sales, and product safety.

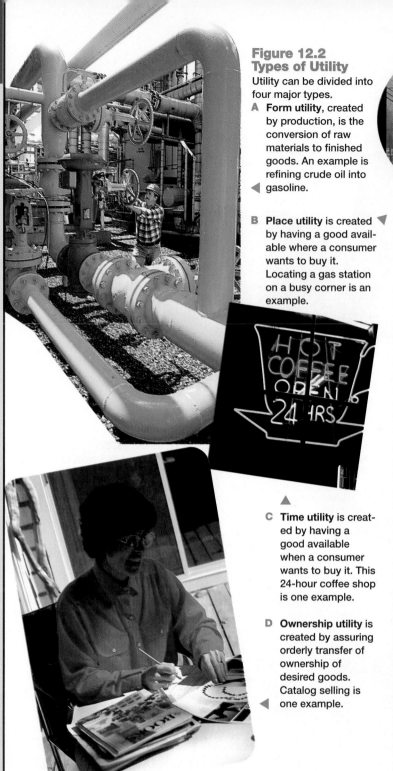

Figure 12.2
Types of Utility
Utility can be divided into four major types.

A **Form utility**, created by production, is the conversion of raw materials to finished goods. An example is refining crude oil into gasoline.

B **Place utility** is created by having a good available where a consumer wants to buy it. Locating a gas station on a busy corner is an example.

C **Time utility** is created by having a good available when a consumer wants to buy it. This 24-hour coffee shop is one example.

D **Ownership utility** is created by assuring orderly transfer of ownership of desired goods. Catalog selling is one example.

Market Research

Finding out what consumers want can be difficult. It is crucial, however, because so many markets are nationwide. An increase in sales of a few percentage points can result in millions of dollars in profits. Therefore, before a product is produced or a service is offered, businesses research their market. Market in this sense means the people who are potential buyers of the good or service. Through **market research** a company gathers, records, and analyzes data about the types of goods and services that people want. From cosmetics companies to automakers to frozen food processors, all major companies and many smaller ones do market research.

During the **market survey,** researchers gather information about who might be possible users of the product. Such characteristics as age, sex, income, education, and location—urban, suburban, rural—are important to a producer in deciding the market at which to aim a product. For example, in the 1980s and 1990s the concern of Americans with physical fitness and good health led many cereal companies to test and then market bran, oat, and granola cereals. Though there had been some "adult" cereals before this, most cereals had been presweetened and aimed at children.

Cooperative Learning

Have the class conduct a community survey about an actual public facility (such as a library, park, playground, or swimming pool), or one that is needed, with a possible goal of public funding for improvement or construction. Suggest that one group research facilities and make recommendations, another develop a questionnaire, a third conduct the survey and report results, and a fourth develop a plan to promote funding and implementation. Discuss whether to petition the local government about implementing the improvement.

A market survey typically involves a series of carefully worded questions. The questions may be administered in the form of a written questionnaire, which is mailed to consumers. Market researchers might also conduct personal interviews. Manufacturers of such small appliances as hair dryers and microwave ovens often put a questionnaire on the back of the warranty card that purchasers are to return.

When Should Market Research Be Done? Market research may be done at several stages of product development. It can be done at the very beginning when the first ideas about a new product are being developed. It can be conducted again to test sample products and alternative packaging designs.

Early market research has several purposes. It helps producers determine whether there is a market for their good or service and what that market is. It can also indicate any changes in quality, features, or design that should be made before a product is offered for sale.

To investigate initial consumer response, market research is often done immediately after a product is released for sale. Some companies even test their advertising to make sure it is attracting the market for which the product was designed. Information can also be gathered about a product that has been on the market for a while. Market researchers then attempt to discover what should be done to maintain or increase sales.

Testing New Products As a final step before offering a product for national distribution, market researchers will often test market a product such as a detergent or a toothpaste. **Test marketing** means offering a product for sale in a small area, perhaps several cities, for two months to two years to see how well it sells before offering it nationally. For example, before attempting to market a new granola cereal, a company might sell it in several selected areas where the product is most likely to attract the market that the company is seeking.

Researchers keep track of the units sold and test different prices and ad campaigns within the test markets. If the cereal is successful, the company will offer it nationally. If sales are disappointing, the company has two choices. It can make changes based on the data collected in the test market. Or, rather than spend more money redesigning the product, the company can abandon the idea.

Most new products introduced every year in the United States are not profitable and do not survive in the marketplace. It is the constant lure of developing a high-profit item, however, that motivates companies to continue developing new products.

SECTION 1 REVIEW

Understanding Vocabulary
Define marketing, utility, form utility, place utility, time utility, ownership utility, market research, market survey, test marketing.

Reviewing Objectives
1. What are the four stages of the development of marketing in the United States?
2. If you want to do market research, what do you have to do?

Assess

Meeting Lesson Objectives
Assign Section 1 Review as homework or an in-class activity. Each question in the Review addresses the corresponding numbered objective in the Section Focus.

Evaluate
Assign the Section 1 Quiz in the TCR or use the Testmaker to develop a customized quiz.

Reteach
Ask students to create a flow chart showing the major steps of product development.

Enrich
Have students interview their parents or grandparents to discover how certain products have changed over their lifetime.

Close

Have students write a paragraph beginning with the following: Market research is helpful in every stage of product development.

Section 1 Review Answers

Understanding Vocabulary
marketing (p. 282), **utility** (p. 282), **form utility** (p. 284), **place utility** (p. 284), **time utility** (p. 284), **ownership utility** (p. 284), **market research** (p. 284), **market survey** (p. 284), **test marketing** (p. 285)

Reviewing Objectives
1. The four stages of marketing are production, sales, marketing (production and sales), and consumer sovereignty.

2. You must gather data from questionnaires or interviews and analyze responses to find out what consumers want.

CASE STUDY Focus on Free Enterprise

Harley-Davidson

The Early Years When you think about motorcycles, there is a very good chance you will think of Harley-Davidsons. In 1901, William S. Harley and Arthur Davidson of Milwaukee strapped a gasoline engine to a bicycle, and started production shortly thereafter. Harley-Davidson has been building motorcycles since 1903. For years motorcycles were a small but profitable segment of the motor vehicle industry. Harley-Davidson motorcycles became a symbol of defiance and the "age-old hobo-rebel."

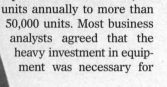

Bad Times In 1969 Harley-Davidson was bought by sporting goods manufacturer AMF. AMF immediately modernized production facilities and increased production from 15,000 units annually to more than 50,000 units. Most business analysts agreed that the heavy investment in equipment was necessary for the firm, but it was also accompanied by a decline in quality. The quick rise in production led to lower-quality motorcycles. Harley-Davidsons slowly lost their image.

In the 1970s the public perception of motorcycles changed. The oil crisis and resulting high gasoline prices left the average driver searching for alternatives. Experts predicted that gasoline prices would continue to rise to astronomical levels. Motorcycles suddenly seemed to be a fuel-saving alternative to traditional automobiles. People started buying more motorcycles, and forecasters predicted that demand would continue to increase. What happened, instead, was that the experts significantly overestimated demand. Japanese manufacturers flooded the American market with motorcycles and then were left with large inventories. Motorcycle prices collapsed.

286

Emphasis on Quality Against this backdrop, a group of AMF executives led a management buyout and took Harley-Davidson private. Since that time, this group has worked to upgrade its motorcycles. The owners revived the company by completely changing the way it did business. They changed the production process, management philosophy, and marketing strategy.

Harley-Davidson started to use some Japanese production techniques, reducing inventory and freeing up capital and labor. By reducing inventory, any defects and quality problems became easier to spot, while at the same time inventory costs were reduced. Workers were encouraged to make suggestions and were given more authority to make quality checks.

Harley-Davidson devised a new marketing technique, encouraging the formation of the Harley Owners Group (HOG), a social club for Harley owners operating out of local dealerships. These clubs became a means of getting Harley owners together. This made Harley-Davidsons more visible to the general public.

Since the buyout in 1981, Harley-Davidson's success has been steady and impressive. Harley is now a major exporter of motorcycles, shipping 25 percent of its production abroad—much of it to Germany. Harley-Davidson once again is a symbol for quality.

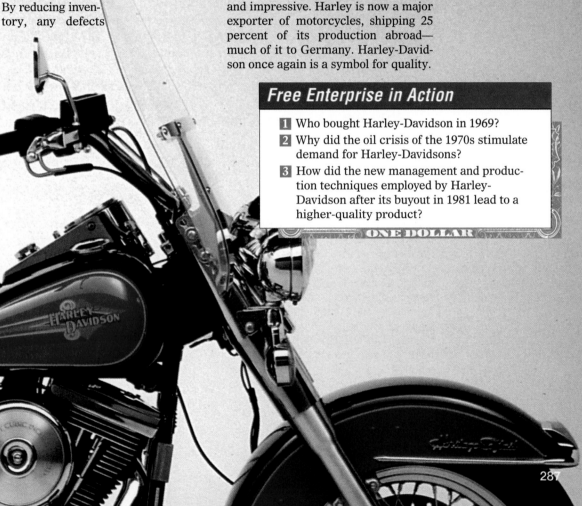

Free Enterprise in Action

1. Who bought Harley-Davidson in 1969?
2. Why did the oil crisis of the 1970s stimulate demand for Harley-Davidsons?
3. How did the new management and production techniques employed by Harley-Davidson after its buyout in 1981 lead to a higher-quality product?

287

TEACHING: Free Enterprise

L2 Analyzing Information
After students read the feature, ask: What combination of factors under AFM tarnished Harley-Davidson's reputation? (*a rise in production with a decline in quality*) What mistake led to the collapse of the motorcycle market in the United States during the 1970s? (*Forecasters overestimated demand.*)

Assess

Ask volunteers to develop a scenario for a get-together of a Harley Owners Group and to perform it for the class, which may interact by asking questions. Suggest basing the scenario on information presented in the feature.

Close

Have students discuss what they know about production techniques in Japan and their applicability to manufacturing in the United States.

Answers to Free Enterprise in Action

1. AMF
2. Motorcycles are more fuel efficient than automobiles, and during the oil crisis, drivers were looking for ways to cut gasoline costs.
3. Lowering production allowed workers to monitor the product and to emphasize quality rather than quantity. An emphasis on teamwork and quality control allowed workers to take responsibility for and pride in the quality of individual motorcycles.

Focus

Overview

See the student page for section objectives.

Section 2 explains or describes: the "four *P*'s" of marketing: product, price, place, and promotion; the importance of product identification; how a firm decides on positioning for its product; and the four types of promotion a firm may use.

Bellringer

Before presenting the lesson, display Focus Activity Transparency 46 on the overhead projector or copy the material on the chalkboard. Assign the accompanying Focus Activity Sheet.

Motivational Activity

Write on the chalkboard the following sentence: I know it's time for a new one when _____. Call on volunteers to write their responses on the chalkboard. Encourage students to discuss the ways that a product becomes obsolete.

Preteaching Vocabulary

Ask students to work in groups of five to improvise a business meeting. Have each student choose one term as his or her guiding principle. Tell students that every remark or suggestion they make in the meeting should reflect their concern with their concept.

S E C T I O N 2 F O C U S

Terms to Know price leadership, penetration pricing, promotion, direct-mail advertising, product life cycle

Objectives *After reading this section, you should be able to:*
1. Explain the importance of product identification.
2. Identify marketing strategies that depend on price.
3. Explain how a firm decides in which place to sell its products.
4. List four types of promotion a firm may use.

The Four "Ps" of Marketing

In today's highly competitive world, simply producing a product and offering it for sale is not enough. Companies, through their marketing departments, plan a marketing strategy, which details how the company will sell the product effectively. The marketing strategy, or plan, combines the "four *Ps*" of marketing: product, price, place, and promotion. Decisions about each topic are based on the data collected through the company's market research.

Product

Besides deciding on the actual product, market research helps a company determine what services to offer with the product, how to package it, and what kind of product identification to use.

Warranties are customary with many manufactured products, but some manufacturers offer special services free or for a small charge. For example, if you buy a camera, you may be able to purchase from the manufacturer a 2-year extended warranty in addition to the 1-year warranty given by the company. Automakers used to offer 1-year or 12,000-mile warranties on new cars. Today a 5-year or 50,000-mile warranty is a common offer.

Classroom Resources for Section 2

Reproducible Lesson Plan 12.2
Focus Activity Transparency 46
Focus Activity Sheet 46
Guiding Reading Activity 12.2

Section Quiz 12.2
Spanish Section Quiz 12.2
Testmaker

Packaging is also an important factor in selling a product. The "right" packaging combines size, design, and color to attract potential consumers. Compact discs, books, and food are especially dependent on packaging. Such words as *New and Improved* or *Economy Size* are used to attract customers. For economy-minded shoppers, manufacturers add cents-off coupons and rebate offers to their packages. Cents-off coupons are used to persuade consumers to make a repeat purchase and develop the habit of buying the product.

Once a product is offered for sale, product identification becomes important. Product identification can involve the use of a logo or of certain colors on a package. It can also involve a certain type of packaging, a particular slogan, or anything that can be associated with and identify a product.

As Figure 12.3 shows, product identification is meant to attract consumers to look at, buy, and remember a particular product.

Price

Supply and demand help determine the price of a good or service. According to the law of supply, at higher prices, a larger quantity of a product will generally be supplied than at lower prices. The law of demand states that as the price of a good or service falls, a larger quantity will be bought. Conversely, as the price rises, a smaller quantity will be bought.

Because of the laws of supply and demand, the price at which a product

sells may help determine whether it is successful in attracting buyers, while being profitable to its maker. In setting a price, a company has to consider the costs of producing, advertising, selling, and distributing the product, and the amount of profit it hopes to make. Often companies sell similar goods at similar prices. This practice is especially true in oligopolies and is known as **price leadership.** For example, one major airline may lower its price and then all of the other major airlines will follow.

Figure 12.3
Product Identification
From the Pillsbury Dough Boy to the colorful Pepsi logo, all of these items are good examples of packaging to achieve product identification.

Teach

Guided Practice

L2 Analyzing Meaning Have students write on the chalkboard some of the product slogans and jingles they know. Encourage students to discuss what makes those slogans memorable. Also discuss with students what the slogans and jingles imply about the products.

Visual Instruction

Have students review the items in Figure 12.3. Assign students to research how national brand logos and packaging have changed in the past 30 to 50 years. In some instances, brands may go back to the turn of the century. Ask students to note how companies appeal to consumers through changes in their packaging and logos.

GLOBAL ECONOMICS

Philip Morris, one of the top advertisers in the United States, spends more than $2,000,000,000 a year on advertisements worldwide. Philip Morris is a tobacco company that also owns Kraft Foods, General Foods, and several other large companies.

Meeting Special Needs

Visual Disability Students with visual difficulties may find it helpful to use charts and graphs whenever they compile information. Encourage students to present their data in tabular or graphic form.

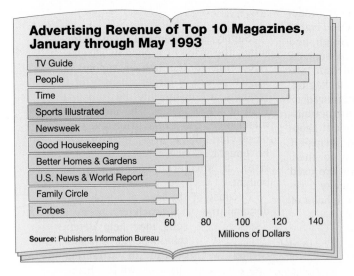

Advertising Revenue of Top 10 Magazines, January through May 1993

TV Guide
People
Time
Sports Illustrated
Newsweek
Good Housekeeping
Better Homes & Gardens
U.S. News & World Report
Family Circle
Forbes

60 80 100 120 140
Millions of Dollars

Source: Publishers Information Bureau

Figure 12.4 Advertising Revenues
Together the top 10 magazines grossed about $1 billion in the first half of 1993. Advertisers spent more than $3 billion in all magazine advertising during that period.

Selling a new product at a low price is another marketing strategy. This strategy is called **penetration pricing.** The low price is meant to attract customers away from an established product.

Place to Sell

Where the product should be sold is another decision of the marketing department. Should it be sold through the mail, by telephone, in department stores, in specialty shops, in supermarkets, in discount stores, or door-to-door? Usually, the answer is obvious because of past experience with similar products. A cereal company, for example, would most likely market a new cereal in supermarkets. Another company might decide that its goods would appeal to only a limited market and therefore choose to sell its goods in specialty shops.

Promotion

Promotion is the use of advertising and other methods to inform consumers that a new or improved product or service is available and to convince them to purchase it. As Figure 12.4 indicates, businesses spend billions of dollars each year to advertise through direct-mail pieces and in newspapers, magazines, radio, and television. Other promotional efforts include free samples, cents-off coupons, gifts, and rebates. Where and how a product is displayed are important as well. For example, paperbacks and magazines are often placed on racks next to checkout lines where people wait.

Figure 12.5 A Typical Product Life Cycle
A product life cycle has no fixed number of months or years. A fad item has a much shorter product life cycle than established items such as typewriters.

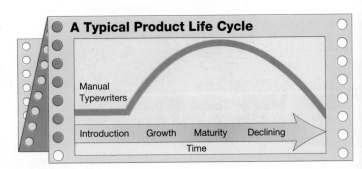

A Typical Product Life Cycle

Manual Typewriters

Introduction Growth Maturity Declining
Time

Cooperative Learning

Have students work together to develop a list of words and phrases advertisers like to use. Encourage the students to brainstorm freely at first, writing down words, phrases, and sentences as they remember them. Then have students list the words and phrases under the following column headings: Informational, Emotional Appeal, Humorous, Memorable, and Miscellaneous. You might want to have the class use the categorized list in a collage or other display showing how advertisers sell their products.

Types of Promotion The particular types of promotion that a producer uses depend on three factors: (1) the product, (2) the type of consumer that the company wants to attract, and (3) the amount of money it plans to spend. Magazines, credit card companies, and insurance companies often use **direct-mail advertising.** The mailer usually includes a letter describing the product or service and an order blank or application form.

Product Life Cycle If you were to look in a Sears & Roebuck catalog from the early 1900s, it would seem strange. Many of the products adver-

tised no longer exist. The cruel fact of marketing is that most products go through what is known as a **product life cycle.** This cycle is a series of stages from first introduction to complete withdrawal from the market. Figure 12.5 shows the four stages of a typical product life cycle.

People involved in marketing products need to understand the stages of each product's life cycle because marketing programs are different for each stage. A product in its introductory stage has to be explained and promoted much differently from one in its maturity stage. Also, pricing can be different depending on the stage. Prices of products tend to be relatively high during the growth stage.

Many marketers attempt to extend the life of old products by using a number of techniques. Figure 12.6 illustrates how this can be accomplished.

◀ **Figure 12.6**
Three Ways to Extend the Life of an Old Product

1 **Find New Uses for the Product**
Arm & Hammer Baking Soda is now advertised as a cleaning agent, toothpaste, first aid remedy, and refrigerator deodorizer.

2 **Change How the Product Looks**
Packaging, labeling, and size can all be changed.

3 **Change Advertising Focus**
Persuade consumers they need the product and its new uses.

SECTION 2 REVIEW

Understanding Vocabulary
Define price leadership, penetration pricing, promotion, direct-mail advertising, product life cycle.

Reviewing Objectives
❶ How does packaging contribute to product identification?

❷ What two marketing strategies depend on price?

❸ How does a firm decide where to sell its products?

❹ What are four ways a firm may promote a product?

Assess

Meeting Lesson Objectives

Assign Section 2 Review as homework or an in-class activity. Each question in the Review addresses the corresponding numbered objective in the Section Focus.

Evaluate

Assign the Section 2 Quiz in the TCR or use the Testmaker to develop a customized quiz.

Reteach

Help students create a marketing plan for one product. Have students suggest packaging ideas, slogans, direct marketing tools, and pricing strategies.

Enrich

Have students create advertising for the product they designed in Section 1. Ask students to create a radio script with a jingle, a TV story board (cartoon strip), a magazine or newspaper ad, or direct mail piece.

Close

Discuss with students how computers will be marketed differently as they reach maturity in the product life cycle.

Section 2 Review Answers
Understanding Vocabulary
price leadership (p. 289), **penetration pricing:** (p. 290), **promotion** (p. 290), **direct-mail advertising** (p. 291), **product life cycle** (p. 291)
Reviewing Objectives
1. attracts new buyers and creates brand identification

2. price leadership; penetration pricing
3. location of consumers and most efficient use of advertising dollars
4. direct mail; newspaper, magazine, radio, and television ads; free samples, coupons, gifts, rebates; displays

General interest magazines such as *TIME* and *Newsweek* include a section devoted to business and economic news. Several magazines have charted the career of Charles Wang, who built an enormously successful firm by thoughtful technological innovation and careful acquisition.

Teach

Have volunteers read aloud paragraphs of the quoted excerpts from Wang's interviews. Ask students to summarize Wang's ideas by writing on the chalkboard a sentence or two to summarize each excerpt. Finally, have students answer the questions in Checking for Understanding.

You might have interested students read the complete interviews in the *New York Post*, *Newsday*, or *Mass High Tech* and report on the development of Wang's software company.

Personal Perspective

Charles Wang on Challenges in the Computer Industry

Profile

- 1944–
- born in Shanghai, China
- immigrated to the United States at age 8
- graduated from Queen's College in New York
- started Computer Associates International, Inc., a computer software company, in 1976
- Computer Associates became the first computer software company to bring in $1 billion in revenue

Charles Wang built a successful software firm through technological innovation and acquisition. Wang, a college math and physics major, is not a typical business manager. His unconventional style is evident in the following excerpts from interviews in the *New York Post*, February 17, 1992; *Newsday*, April 16, 1989; and *Mass High Tech*, July 13, 1992.

... We developed more products than we acquired. People don't realize this.... You've got to make sure what comes in exceeds what goes out. If you can count, you can do that. It's not that complicated. That's it! And the difference is called profit.

Charles Wang trains his own executives, moves managers often, and reorganizes the entire company every April based on what he calls zero-based thinking.

You ever hear of the government saying we need less people anywhere? No. That's incremental thinking. So what I try to do is force my people to look at it fresh. Justify it to me again. [For example, suppose] we went and bought a new computer. It's supposed to save something, so why are you asking for more people again?

Another unique approach Wang takes is that he does not adopt every new system that comes along, just because it is new.

... The common characteristic of the mythmakers is that they must destroy the old in order for the new to succeed. Old technologies must be proven to be useless to create a market for the new....

Wang explains his evolutionary approach.

... One, you do not throw your legacy systems away. Imagine leveling a building every time you wanted to add a new door or central air-conditioning. It's the same thing with implementing new technology.

Checking for Understanding
1. What is Wang's definition of "profit"?
2. What does Wang mean by zero-based thinking?
3. According to Wang, how should old technology be treated when new technology is developed?

Answers to Checking for Understanding
1. Answers will vary, but should indicate that what comes in should exceed what goes out of a business, and that the difference, according to Wang, is profit.
2. Zero-based thinking means taking a fresh look at things.
3. Answers will vary, but should indicate that Wang thinks old technologies should be treated as the structure upon which new technologies are built.

SECTION **3** *Distribution Channels*

SECTION 3 FOCUS

Terms to Know channels of distribution, wholesalers, retailers

Objectives *After reading this section, you should be able to:*

1 Explain the difference between wholesale and retail distribution.

2 List two new types of distribution channels.

Moving Goods to Market

Distribution, moving goods from where they are produced to the people who will buy them, is another function of marketing. The routes by which goods are moved are called **channels of distribution.** Figure 12.8 (page 294) Shows the various distribution channels for different kinds of goods.

Wholesalers and Retailers

Some consumer goods, such as clothing and farm products, are usually sold by a producer to a wholesaler and then to a retailer, who sells them to consumers. See Figure 12.7. Other consumer goods, such as automobiles, are normally sold by the producer directly to a retailer and then to consumers. With each transaction, or business deal, the price increases. Some goods, such as vegetables sold at a farmer's roadside stand, go directly from producer to consumer.

Wholesalers **Wholesalers** are businesses that purchase large quantities of goods from producers for resale to other businesses. They may buy goods from manufacturers and sell them to retail stores that then deal directly with consumers. They may also buy and sell raw materials or producer goods to manufacturers. Various types of wholesalers exist.

Full-service wholesalers warehouse goods and deliver them once retailers buy them. They may also extend trade

**Figure 12.7
Distributing
Goods**
Orchard owners have sold these limes to wholesalers who will package them and transport them to grocery stores to be sold to consumers.

293

Focus

Overview
See the student page for section objectives.

Section 3 explains: the role of producers, wholesalers, and retailers in distribution; the difference between wholesale and retail; two growing distribution channels: wholesale clubs and direct mail; and typical channels of distribution.

Bellringer
Before presenting the lesson, display Focus Activity Transparency 47 and assign the accompanying Focus Activity Sheet.

Motivational Activity
Write the following statement for the students to complete: My favorite way to shop is ____. Have students compare and contrast the types of outlets.

Preteaching Vocabulary
Organize into two teams for a game of "Distribution Feud." Call out a definition or example about each term and have representatives from each team compete to identify it most quickly.

Classroom Resources for Section 3

Reproducible Lesson Plan 12.3
Focus Activity Transparency 47
Focus Activity Sheet 47
Guided Reading Activity 12.3
Consumer Application Activity 12
Mathematics Practice for Economics 35

Performance Assessment Activity 35
Section Quiz 12.3
Spanish Section Quiz 12.3
Chapter 12 Test Forms A and B
Testmaker
Reinforcing Skills 12
Enrichment Activity 12

Economics Vocabulary Activity 12
Spanish Economics Vocabulary Activity 12
Audiocassette 12
Spanish Audiocassette 12
Reteaching Activity 12
Spanish Reteaching Activity 12

293

Teach

Guided Practice

L1 Researching and Comparing Ask half of the students to count for a week the advertisements they see that invite consumers to request a catalog. Ask the other half to do the same for advertisements inviting consumers to telephone for information. Have each group combine lists to avoid duplication and then compare findings. Encourage discussion of which marketing approach seems more efficient for the consumer.

Visual Instruction

Have students study Figure 12.8 outlining the channels of distribution. Ask them to provide examples of products or materials that would illustrate each type of distribution channel. Have students describe how each channel might affect the final cost of the product to consumers.

GLOBAL ECONOMICS

As the economies of different nations have become increasingly interdependent, protectionist trade laws have been losing their usefulness. Countries of western Europe have developed the European Union and the Free Trade Association to eliminate trade barriers among members.

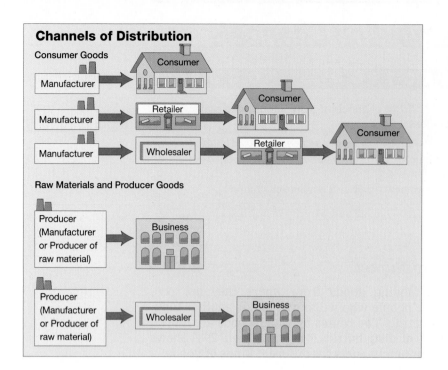

Channels of Distribution

Consumer Goods

Manufacturer → Consumer

Manufacturer → Retailer → Consumer

Manufacturer → Wholesaler → Retailer → Consumer

Raw Materials and Producer Goods

Producer (Manufacturer or Producer of raw material) → Business

Producer (Manufacturer or Producer of raw material) → Wholesaler → Business

Figure 12.8 Channels of Distribution
The routes by which goods are moved depend upon the type of good being sold.

credit. Wholesalers known as drop shippers, in contrast, never take possession of goods. They buy merchandise with the agreement that the producer will store it. After the drop shipper sells the goods, the producer must deliver them. A cash-and-carry wholesaler has inventory and sells merchandise, but the buyer must ship it. A truck wholesaler sells and delivers at the same time.

Retailers Retailers sell consumer goods directly to the public. Hundreds of thousands of retailers sell all types of goods. You are probably familiar with many of them: department stores, specialty stores such as bookshops, discount stores, supermarkets, mail-order houses, and so on.

Storage and Transportation Part of the distribution process is warehousing goods for future sales. The producer, wholesaler, or retailer may perform this function. Most retailers keep some inventory on hand for immediate sale. Many have a two- to three-month supply, depending on the type of merchandise.

Transportation involves the physical movement of goods from producers and/or sellers to buyers. Various means of transportation, such as airlines, railroads, trucks, and automobiles, can be used. Pipelines transport some goods such as petroleum and natural gas. In deciding the method of transportation, businesspeople must consider the type of good, such as perishable food. The size and weight of the good are also important. Airfreighting tons of wheat is impractical, but airfreighting small machine parts is not. Speed may be necessary to fulfill a sale or to get fresh fruit to a

 Meeting Special Needs

Hearing Disability Students with hearing disabilities may have trouble keeping pace in games requiring spoken replies to auditory clues. You may want to alter activities and games so that clues are written rather than spoken.

food plant. The cost of the different types of transportation is a factor.

Expanding Types of Distribution Channels

In the last 10 to 15 years, distribution channels have expanded rapidly due to the growth of club warehouses and direct marketing. Some of the biggest club warehouses are Price/Costco and Sam's (a division of Wal-Mart). Figure 12.9 shows some of the characteristics of warehouse club shopping.

Direct marketing is done mainly through catalogs as illustrated in Figure 12.10 (page 296). Advertising called space ads in newspapers and magazines is also direct marketing.

One reason that catalog shopping has become a popular distribution channel is to avoid state sales taxes. As state sales taxes have increased in most states, consumers have purchased more goods through catalogs from out-of-state companies. The purchaser of catalog goods normally does not pay sales tax if the catalog company is located in another state.

Figure 12.9
Differences in Warehouse Club Shopping

A typical club warehouse requires membership. Memberships usually cost $25 a year for individuals and more for businesses. Individual club members usually have to be part of a larger group such as a teacher's union or a credit union. A typical club warehouse, unlike other stores, is an extremely large building, where the choices of merchandise and food are often limited, but the prices are usually lower than most others available in the immediate geographical area. The club warehouse formula is to buy a limited number of models and brands of each product in such huge quantities that the club warehouse gets very favorable prices from the manufacturers. Typically, the listed price in the club warehouse is what the individual member pays. Businesses get a 5 percent discount off that price.

Independent Practice

L3 Analyzing Distribution Have students list the items they use every day and those they use on special occasions. Ask them to name the best channel of distribution for each item and tell why it is best. Ask students to include whether the channel they identified as best is the one used.

L2 Comparing and Contrasting Have students write a short essay comparing and contrasting the pros and cons of warehouse shopping and buying wholesale. Students should illustrate their essays with a chart or table summarizing their main points.

Have students complete Guided Reading Activity 12.3 in the TCR. LEP

 DID YOU KNOW

More than 19.6 million people in the United States are employed in retail jobs. Knowledge of marketing and distribution increases their chances of success on the job.

Cooperative Learning

Ask students to cooperate in developing a marketing and distribution plan for a new product of their choosing. Have them organize themselves into committees for production, marketing, promotion, and distribution. Each committee should create a detailed plan for performing its function. Ask committees to meet together or through representatives to work out an overall plan. The plan should use some of each committee's detailed plans. Have students publish their overall plan, with the appropriate details from the committees, in a plan document for the new product.

Assess

Meeting Lesson Objectives

Assign Section 3 Review as homework or an in-class activity. Each question in the Review addresses the corresponding numbered objective in the Section Focus.

Evaluate

Assign the Section 3 Quiz in the TCR or use the Testmaker to develop a customized quiz.

Assign the Chapter 12 Test Form A or Form B or use the Testmaker to develop a customized test.

Reteach

Ask students to discuss the specific channels of distribution.of goods that they can see in the classroom.

Have students complete Reteaching Activity 12 in the TCR.

Enrich

Have students predict the future of shopping by computer.

Have students complete Enrichment Activity 12 in the TCR.

Close

Have students discuss the impact it would have on the economy if wholesaling were to disappear.

**Figure 12.10
Catalog Boom**
Catalog shopping has increased dramatically in the United States in the last 20 years. Virtually everything is available by catalog overnight. As an expanding distribution channel, this form of direct marketing has yet to reach its full potential. ▼

SECTION 3 REVIEW

Understanding Vocabulary

Define channels of distribution, wholesalers, retailers.

Reviewing Objectives

① How would you describe the difference between a wholesaler and a retailer?

② What are two relatively new distribution channels for goods?

296   Unit 4 Microeconomics: American Business in Action

Section 3 Review Answers
Understanding Vocabulary
channels of distribution (p. 293), **wholesalers** (p. 293), **retailers** (p. 294)
Reviewing Objectives
1. Wholesalers purchase large quantities of goods to sell to other businesses. Retailers sell goods directly to the public.
2. Warehouse clubs and direct mail are expanding channels for the distribution of goods.

Critical Thinking Skills

Distinguishing Fact From Opinion

Whenever you are listening to someone talk, reading a newspaper, or watching a news program on TV, you are bombarded with facts. Many times, however, you are being given personal opinions. Do you know how to distinguish between fact and opinion?

What is a Fact?

A *fact* is a statement that can be proven by such evidence as records, documents, government statistics, and unbiased historical sources. Figure A lists some facts that few people would dispute.

Discovering Opinions

An *opinion* is a statement that may contain some truth, but it also contains a personal view or judgment, sometimes called a value-based statement. Consider the following statement: "The state fund for the arts does not have enough money." Whether this agency has enough money is a matter of opinion, based on personal values. Consider the statements of opinion in Figure B.

Use the following guidelines when distinguishing between fact and opinion.

1 For each statement ask yourself what idea the writer or speaker wants you to accept.
2 Ask yourself if and how these statements can be verified or proven.

Practicing the Skill

Read several paragraphs of a politician's speech from a newspaper or magazine. Make a list of statements of fact and statements of opinion. Tell why you classify each statement as you do.

Figure A
Facts

- The population of the United States exceeds 250 million people.
- There is normally less sun on rainy days than on other days.
- President Bill Clinton took office in 1993.
- During the majority of years since World War II, average prices have increased in the United States.

Figure B
Opinions

- The crime rate is too high.
- We should eliminate poverty in the United States.
- We are not spending enough money on public education.
- Young people today do not take school seriously enough.

297

Teach

Point out to students that labels can be misleading because of accidents or carelessness in wording or a desire to deceive consumers. Labeling laws seek to create uniform standards to reduce the chances for careless mistakes in language. They also set penalties for advertisers who intentionally mislead consumers.

Encourage students to use the information in the feature to develop a flattering, but factual, description for Crystal Geyser, Naya, or Poland Spring bottled water. If possible, have students rate bottled waters on the local market for adherence to truth in advertising.

Readings in Economics

TIME	APRIL 26, 1993

TESTING THE WATERS

by Thomas McCarroll

The label on Crystal Geyser Natural Alpine spring water boasts that it is nothing less than "nature's perfect beverage." The drink, reads the label, "begins as the pure snow and rain that falls on 12,000-ft. Olancha peak in the towering Sierra. This pristine water is naturally filtered through the mountain's bedrock."

The language is evocative and the imagery idyllic. Unfortunately Crystal Geyser's claims are something of an exaggeration. Or so says the North Carolina agriculture department, which recently ordered Crystal Geyser and seven other bottled waters, including the popular Naya and Poland Spring brands, removed from store shelves in that state because of "false and deceptive labeling."

That is bad news for producers of the nation's 700 brands of bottled water, many of which convey the impression in their advertising that they have tapped an unspoiled river.... Regulators an consumer groups are starting to question whether bottled waters are worth the $2.7 billion a year that customers spend on them....

In an effort to clean up the industry, the FDA is proposing the most sweeping new regulations in two decades. The most controversial would set uniform definitions for types of bottled waters, such as "artesian," "mineral," "distilled," and "natural spring." These terms are now generally ill-defined. Some names, such as Grayson's "mountain water" and Music's "glacier water," defy definition since no such categories exist.

• THINK ABOUT IT •

1. Why did the North Carolina agriculture department pull certain brands of water from store shelves?

2. What is the FDA currently proposing?

Answers to Think About It

1. North Carolina found that some bottled water producers either purposely misled the consumer or actually lied about the source of their water.

2. To set uniform definitions for types of bottled waters, such as artesian, mineral, distilled, and natural spring waters.

Use the Chapter 12 Highlights to preview, review, condense, or reteach the chapter. A Spanish Chapter Highlights is available in the Spanish Handbook.

Section 1

The Changing Role of Marketing

Key Terms

marketing (p. 282)
utility (p. 282)
form utility (p. 284)
place utility (p. 284)
time utility (p. 284)

ownership utility (p. 284)
market research (p. 284)
market survey (p. 284)
test marketing (p. 285)

Summary

Marketing in the United States has developed through four stages ending with consumer sovereignty. Through a series of predesigned questions, market research attempts to discover the quality, features, and style that consumers find desirable in a product, the type of packaging that will attract consumers, and the price that will get them to buy.

Preview/Review

After students read the Chapter 12 Highlights, have them complete Economics Vocabulary Activity 12 in the TCR. Spanish Vocabulary Activities are also available in the Spanish Resource Binder.

Vocabulary Software reinforces the economic terms used in Chapter 12.

Condense

Have students listen to Chapter 12 on the Audiocassettes in the TCR. A 1-page written activity and 1-page test accompany this material. These materials are also available in Spanish.

Section 2

The Marketing Mix

Key Terms

price leadership (p. 289)
penetration pricing
  (p. 290)
promotion (p. 290)

direct-mail advertising
  (p. 291)
product life cycle (p. 291)

Summary

The "four *P*s" of the marketing mix are product, price, place, and promotion. In setting price, a company has to consider the costs of producing, advertising, selling, and distributing the product, as well as the profit it wishes to make and the price its competitors are charging for the same product. Price is also used in marketing strategies. The place to sell a product and the kinds of promotion used help to determine the success of a product.

Reteach

Have students complete Reteaching Activity 12 in the TCR. Spanish Reteaching Activities are also available.

 VIDEODISC

Nightly Business Report
Economics in Action
Use "Marketing and Distribution" on Disc 1, Side B, Video 17.

Section 3

Distribution Channels

Key Terms

channels of distribution
  (p. 293)
wholesalers (p. 293)
retailers (p. 294)

Summary

Wholesalers purchase large quantities of goods from producers for resale to other businesses. Retailers sell consumer goods directly to the public. As part of the distribution process, goods may be warehoused by the producer, wholesaler, or retailer for future sales. The largest growth in distribution of goods is through club warehouses and direct-mail marketing.

Search 47032, Play to 52309

Identifying Key Terms

1. d
2. c
3. e
4. b
5. a

Recalling Facts and Ideas

Section 1

1. Marketing involves activities that add to the utility of a product.
2. Researchers find out what customers want through surveys of their needs and desires. They conduct surveys at the planning stage, upon customer purchase of goods, and when a product has been on the market for some time.
3. production, sales, marketing, and consumer sovereignty

Section 2

4. product, price, place, and promotion
5. through direct mail; magazines, newspapers, radio, and television; free samples, gifts, coupons, and rebates; and prominent display
6. Place refers to where the product is sold: mail or phone order, department stores, specialty shops, supermarkets, discount stores, or door-to-door.
7. maturity and decline

Section 3

8. routes by which goods are moved from place of production to place of selling
9. Club warehouses offer less variety, bigger containers, and more savings than standard retail outlets. They also offer discounts for businesses.
10. producer, wholesaler, or retailer

Identifying Key Terms

Write the letter of the definition in Column B below that correctly defines each term in Column A.

Column A
1. test marketing (p. 285)
2. penetration pricing (p. 290)
3. price leadership (p. 289)
4. retailer (p. 294)
5. promotion (p. 290)

Column B
a. use of advertising to inform consumers about a product and to persuade them to purchase it
b. business that sells goods directly to the consumer
c. selling a new product at a low price to attract new customers away from an established product
d. offering a product in a small area for a limited time to see how well it sells
e. setting prices close to those of competing companies

Recalling Facts and Ideas

Section 1
1. What is the relationship between marketing and utility?
2. How is market research conducted?
3. What are the historic stages of development of marketing in the United States?

Section 2
4. What are the "four Ps" of planning a marketing strategy?

5. How are goods and services promoted?
6. In the marketing mix, to what does *place* refer?
7. What are the last two stages of a typical product life cycle?

Section 3
8. What are distribution channels?
9. How does a club warehouse differ from a standard retail outlet?
10. Who may perform the storage function of distribution?
11. What are the factors that a business must consider in choosing a method of transporting goods?

Critical Thinking

Section 1
Formulating Questions Suppose you were put in charge of doing a market survey for a new type of running shoe. What questions should you ask? Where would you conduct the survey?

Section 2
Identifying Alternatives What are alternative ways to extend the life of an old product that is in its declining stage?

Section 3
Making Generalizations Write a summary of the information on channels of distribution found in **Figure 12.8**.

Applying Economic Concepts

The Rising Opportunity Cost of Time When individuals earn higher incomes, by definition the opportunity cost of their time increases. Eco-

---

11. size, weight, type of good, cost of each type of transport

Critical Thinking

Section 1

Answers will vary, but should include questions about the customers, their needs, and their past purchases, and name where the survey would be conducted.

Section 2

Answers will vary, but should include finding new uses for the product, changing the labeling, packaging, and sizes, and persuading consumers that they need additional items.

Section 3

Answers will vary, but should indicate that consumer goods go from manufacturer to consumer, often with wholesale or retail sales in between. Raw material and producer goods go nomic theory says that they will react in a predictable way—reducing the amount of time they spend shopping. Make a list of the various methods that people can use to reduce the time they spend when they shop for (1) presents for various holidays, Mother's Day, birthdays, etc., (2) food, and (3) photographic and stereo equipment.

Chapter Projects

1. **Individual Project** Suppose you are about to try a new product on the market such as cereal or soap. **(a)** In making your decision to try the new product, how important is each of the "four *Ps*"? **(b)** Rank them in their order of importance to you, and write a paragraph explaining why you chose this ranking related to trying the new product.

2. **Cooperative Learning Project** Work in three or more groups. Each group will choose a particular product from the following categories of consumer goods:
   - Home electronics
   - Food
   - Clothing
   - Electric steam generators
   - Automobiles
   - Computers

   After each group has chosen one product or brand within one of the above categories, re search, as a team or alone, depending on the number in your group, the following:
   - Product packaging
   - Pricing strategies
   - The place where the product is sold
   - How the product is promoted
   - The product life cycle

   Each person or team within each group should write a summary of the research results, preferably in graphic form. When the results of each group are finished, contrast and compare the differences in the five categories across the various products.

Reviewing Skills

Distinguishing Fact From Opinion

1. **When the Distinction is Clear** Which of the following statements are fact and which are opinion?
   a. Unemployment in the early 1990s exceeded 6 percent.
   b. Millions of Americans did not have jobs.
   c. During the early 1990s, the inflation rate was less than 6 percent per year.
   d. This was a good rate of inflation.

2. **When the Distinction is Not Clear** Try to pick out the statements in the following paragraph that are not necessarily facts or at least that you would want to confirm.

   The club warehouse phenomenon has been around the United States since the 1970s. The people who shop at club warehouses swear by them. They know that they are a good deal for everybody because prices are so low. Because club warehouses price their products so low, though, they force many small retailers out of business. This is bad. Nonetheless, club warehouses are here to stay because they offer such a great deal.

Writing About Economics

Descriptive Writing Choose one advertisement from Your Economics Journal. Write a description of the ad including its visual appeal, placement, target market (consumer), and effectiveness.

from producer/manufacturer to businesses, sometimes with business wholesalers in between.

Applying Economic Concepts

Answers will vary, but students should identify gifts, groceries, and other items that can be purchased through the mail, over the phone, or by computer.

Chapter Projects

1. Answers will vary, but should include an understanding of the four *P*'s.

2. Students should present their information in both written and graphic form.

? BONUS QUESTION

The following bonus question may be written on the chalkboard when students take the chapter test.
Q: What marketing tool could a hospital use to improve care given to patients?
A: market survey of patients

Reviewing Skills

1. a. fact
   b. fact
   c. fact
   d. opinion
2. Answers will vary, but students should indicate an inclination to check sentences 2–6.

Writing About Economics

Remind students that descriptive writing is more evocative when it includes sense words, adjectives, and adverbs.

Point

Point out to the students that the issue of affirmative action seeks to create greater equality in employment by shifting the balance of opportunity to include increased numbers of women and minorities.

L1 Organizing Information Have students organize their information about affirmative action by creating a table of pros and cons noted by various experts. Encourage them to add to the table by contributing their own ideas about the pros and cons of affirmative action.

ISSUE: Is Affirmative Action Necessary to End Discriminatory Hiring Practices?

Affirmative action means that employers and other institutions must take steps to remedy the effects of past discrimination against women and minorities. Does it work? Or does it harm the economy by giving special status to certain groups? Affirmative action began in 1965 with the monitoring of the hiring and promotion practices of federal contractors. In the 1970s, a series of executive orders required businesses and universities that received federal moneys to set affirmative action goals.

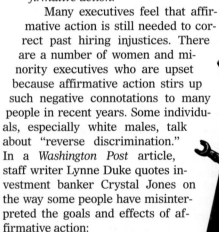

PRO Those who favor government-sponsored affirmative action programs feel that, even though affirmative action has not worked perfectly, things are better today than they would have been without it. David J. Shaffer, staff writer for the *Indianapolis Star*, tells about some of the positive aspects of affirmative action. He presents the following view:

"While it has helped, it hasn't been completely successful," said Suzanne Steinmetz, sociology department chairwoman of the IU School of Liberal Arts at Indiana University-Purdue University at Indianapolis.

"It's going to take many generations until our visions of what kinds of people are appropriate for certain jobs are no longer tied to race and gender," Steinmetz said. "However," she added, "as bad as things are, we don't know what things would have been like without affirmative action."

Many executives feel that affirmative action is still needed to correct past hiring injustices. There are a number of women and minority executives who are upset because affirmative action stirs up such negative connotations to many people in recent years. Some individuals, especially white males, talk about "reverse discrimination." In a *Washington Post* article, staff writer Lynne Duke quotes investment banker Crystal Jones on the way some people have misinterpreted the goals and effects of affirmative action:

While I believe that the concept of affirmative action needs to stay in place in order to preserve access, people twist it around to make us feel we don't deserve to be where we are.

302

Counterpoint

CON Those who argue against affirmative action say that it is nothing but a system of quotas that has devastating effects on the American economy. According to Peter Brimelaw and Leslie Spencer, writing for *Forbes* magazine, the two major arguments— that quotas are necessary to force companies to tap new labor pools and that companies need a diverse work force to service a diverse population— are simply wrong. The markets should take care of these things.

Economist and Nobel Laureate Gary Becker also argues that free markets and competition should eventually tend to eliminate discrimination. The process is hampered by government intervention and monopoly; in competitive situations, discrimination should decline itself with no need for quotas.

Finally, those against affirmative action claim it is very expensive. Economist Peter Griffin estimates that affirmative action programs have increased federal contractors' labor and capital costs by about 6.5 percent. Brimelaw and Spencer write in *Forbes* about these costs:

What does the replacement of merit with quotas cost the American people? The answer is: plenty. The impact may easily have already depressed GNP [now GDP] by a staggering four percentage points—about as much as we spend on the entire public school system. . . .

Corporate America seems to have resigned it-self to quotas as yet another tax. But they are a peculiarly debilitating sort of tax, levied not on the bottom line but on every phase of the corporation's activities, increasing inefficiency throughout.

That affirmative action quotas lead to lowered standards is all but guaranteed by the fact that all standards are suspect to Equal Employment enforcers. "Many of these people believe there really is no such thing as job performance or productivity objectively defined . . . ," says Frank Schmidt, a University of Iowa industrial psychologist.

Exploring the Issue

Reviewing Facts

1. What is affirmative action?
2. Who benefits from affirmative action? Who loses?

Critical Thinking

3. Do you think the benefits of affirmative action outweigh the costs? Why or why not?

Answers to Exploring the Issue

Fact Review

1. Affirmative action is a set of steps taken by employers and other institutions to remedy the effects of past discrimination against women and minorities.
2. Women and minorities benefit from increased job opportunity. The market-place may benefit from greater diversity. White males lose out, as a group, on the preferred status they once enjoyed.

Critical Thinking

3. Answers may vary, but should take into account the pros and cons listed in answer to Question 2.

303

CHAPTER 13 *THE AMERICAN LABOR FORCE*

CHAPTER ORGANIZER

Daily Objectives	Special Features	Classroom Resources

Section 1 Americans at Work
- **List** four categories of workers depending on skill level and training.
- **Explain** how skill, type of job, and location affect supply and demand in the labor market.

Learning Economic Skills:
Determining Averages:
Mean and Median,
p. 310

- Reproducible Lesson Plan 13.1
- *NBR* Video 18 and Video Still 1
- Focus Activity Transparency 48
- Focus Activity Sheet 48
- Guided Reading Activity 13.1
- Cooperative Learning Activity 13
- Primary and Secondary Source Readings 13
- Consumer Application Activities 13 and 19
- Section Quiz 13.1
- Spanish Section Quiz 13.1
- Testmaker
- Reinforcing Skills 13

Section 2 Organized Labor
- **Describe** the difficulties that labor unions faced when they began to organize in the 1800s.
- **Explain** the difference between closed, union, and agency shops as forms of labor organization.

Personal Perspective:
Thomas Sowell on
Discrimination, p. 317

- Reproducible Lesson Plan 13.2
- Focus Activity Transparency 49
- Focus Activity Sheet 49
- Guided Reading Activity 13.2
- Section Quiz 13.2
- Spanish Section Quiz 13.2
- Testmaker

Section 3 Collective Bargaining
- **List** the six major issues that are involved in labor-management negotiations.
- **Describe** two workers' actions that can accompany a strike and two management responses to a strike.
- **Explain** the modern trend in collective bargaining in the United States.

News Clip:
"The Plague of Downward Job Mobility,"
Congressional Quarterly, p. 322

- Reproducible Lesson Plan 13.3
- Focus Activity Transparency 50
- Focus Activity Sheet 50
- Guided Reading Activity 13.3
- Free Enterprise Activity 13
- Economics Laboratory 4
- Economic Simulation 4
- Mathematics Practice for Economics 18
- Performance Assessment Activity 18
- Section Quiz 13.3
- Spanish Section Quiz 13.3
- Testmaker
- Enrichment Activity 13

0:00 OUT OF TIME? If time does not permit teaching this chapter, you may use the Chapter 13 Highlights and the Audiocassettes that include a 1-page activity and a 1-page test.

Chapter 13 Review and Evaluation

Special Features

Chapter 13 Highlights, p. 323
Chapter 13 Review, pp. 324–325
Economics Lab, pp. 326–327

Classroom Resources

📁 Chapter 13 Test Forms A and B
📁 Economics Vocabulary Activity 13
📁 Spanish Economics Vocabulary
    Activity 13

🎧 Audiocassette 13
🎧 Spanish Audiocassette 13
📁 Reteaching Activity 13
📁 Spanish Reteaching Activity 13

Key to Ability Levels

Teaching strategies have been coded for varying learning styles and abilities.

L1 Level 1 activities are **basic** activities that should be within the ability range of all students.

L2 Level 2 activities are **average** activities designed for the ability range of average to above-average students.

L3 Level 3 activities are **challenging** activities designed for the ability range of above-average students.

LEP activities should be within the ability range of **Limited English Proficiency** students.

Performance Assessment

The following chapter project may be assigned at the beginning of the chapter and used for performance assessment. See page T12 for additional Performance Assessment information.

Preparing to Enter Today's Work Force Students can use the material in this chapter to begin preparing for their own entry into the labor force. As they study the chapter, have them write the answers to the following questions. What field or career area interests you? What education and skills are required to enter it? What attitudes, work habits, and other qualities does it take to succeed on the job? What salary can you earn? What will you be willing to do to achieve your short-term job goals? your long-term job goals? What are the costs and benefits of your chosen job? At the end of the chapter, ask students to summarize their findings in a short report.

Additional Resources

Readings for the Student

Fisher, Roger. *Getting to Yes: Negotiating Agreement Without Giving In.* Revised edition. Boston: Houghton Mifflin, 1992.

Heckscher, Charles C. *The New Unionism: Employee Involvement in the Changing Corporation.* New York: Basic Books, Inc., 1988.

Wright, John W., and Dwyer, Edward J. *American Almanac of Jobs and Salaries.* New York: Avon Books, 1992. Published yearly, this is an excellent guide.

Readings for the Teacher

Geoghegan, Thomas. *Which Side Are You On? Trying To Be for Labor When It's Flat on Its Back.* New York: Farrar, Straus, Giroux, 1991. Union since '60s.

Taft, Philip. *Organized Labor in American History.* New York: Harper & Row, 1964.

Multimedia Materials

The Rise of the American Labor Movement: Parts 1 and 2. Two filmstrips and 2 cassettes with guide. Social Studies School Service. 10200 Jefferson Boulevard, P.O. Box 802, Culver City, CA 90232-0802

Salt of the Earth. VHS videocassette. Story of Mexican American miners striking for better conditions. Social Studies School Service. 10200 Jefferson Boulevard, P.O. Box 802, Culver City, CA 90232-0802

Chapter Overview

The American labor force has gone through many changes since the beginning of the Industrial Revolution. Chapter 13 explains or describes: the past and current categories of workers in the labor force; the factors that determine how supply and demand affect wages; the rise of unions; the initial resistance of management and government; the types of shops unions established; and the major issues addressed and the negotiating methods used in collective bargaining.

VIDEODISC

Nightly Business Report

Economics in Action
Use "The American Labor Force" on Disc 2, Side A, Video 18.

Search 2, Play to 6841

CHAPTER

13 THE AMERICAN LABOR FORCE

What skills are required for this job?

Who is likely to seek this kind of employment?

For how many years will these individuals probably do this activity?

Answering Economic Questions

The questions in the above illustration are designed to lead into the main concepts in Chapter 13.

Many students have only a vague idea about what people do on the job and about federal and state laws concerning unskilled workers. They also have little knowledge of the history of the labor movement in the United States. The questions should stimulate students' thinking not only about the type of work being done, but also about the working conditions and regulations for these and other jobs.

Do any government regulations restrict how little these individuals can be paid?

Do any government regulations restrict how long they can work each day or each week?

Who determines how much they are paid?

Your Economics Journal

Keep track of the employed individuals with whom you come in contact over a one-week period. Write down the types of jobs that they do. Next to each type, indicate whether you think their work would be considered low skilled, semiskilled, or highly skilled.

Connecting to Past Learning

Ask students to list jobs they have held in the past, including nonpaying jobs such as volunteer work and doing family chores. Have them include the wage rates and working conditions. After finishing the chapter, ask students what they would change about their previous jobs in light of what they have just learned.

Applying Economics

Tell students to imagine they are interviewing for a job in a fast-food restaurant or convenience store and that they have the freedom to negotiate pay and working conditions. Ask them to consider what they would ask for, what they think the manager would be willing to give them, and how they would go about organizing other workers so that everyone asks for similar pay and conditions.

EXTRA CREDIT PROJECT

Have students investigate and write a report on the labor-management relations in a European, Latin American, or Asian country.

PERFORMANCE ASSESSMENT

Refer to page 304B for "Preparing to Enter Today's Work Force," a Performance Assessment Activity for this chapter.

305

Economic Portfolio

Have students select one of the jobs they recorded in **Your Economics Journal.** Have them interview the person who has this job and ask them how they got it, what skills or knowledge they needed to be hired, what skills or knowledge they needed to acquire on the job, and what they see as the future of their job. Ask students to write a brief report summarizing the information.

Focus

Overview

See the student page for section objectives.

Section 1 explains or describes the different categories of jobs in American industry and the factors of supply and demand that determine the wages for various jobs.

Bellringer

📖 Before presenting the lesson, display Focus Activity Transparency 48 on the overhead projector or copy the material on the chalkboard. Assign the accompanying Focus Activity Sheet.

Motivational Activity

Ask students to list jobs they would like to do to earn extra money. Ask them to also list any skills or knowledge they need to do them.

Preteaching Vocabulary

Have students look up the definitions of the vocabulary terms in the Glossary and use them in a paragraph describing America's labor force.

Visual Instruction

Answer to Figure 13.1 caption question: *Millions of Americans are not in the labor force and are not counted when the unemployment rate is calculated.*

SECTION **1** *Americans at Work*

SECTION 1 FOCUS

Terms to Know civilian labor force, blue-collar, professionals, white-collar, service workers, unskilled workers, semiskilled workers, skilled worker, minimum wage law

Objectives *After reading this section, you should be able to:*
1. List four **categories of workers** depending on skill level and training.
2. Explain how skill, type of job, and location affect **supply and demand in the labor market.**

Wages Depend on Skills, Type of Job, and Location

Everyone from a factory worker to the president of a corporation belongs to the productive resource known as labor. In discussing labor, economists use the term labor force in a specific way. The **civilian labor force** is the total number of people 16 years of age or older who are either employed or actively seeking work. Individuals not able to work, such as disabled people or those in prisons or mental institutions, are not included in the civilian labor force. People in the armed forces or those not looking for a paying job, such as full-time students and homemakers, are excluded as well. Figure 13.1 shows the civilian labor force in comparison to the total working-age population.

**Figure 13.1
Total Work Force**
The percentage of unemployed among those 16 and older is not the same as the nation's unemployment rate. Why? ▼

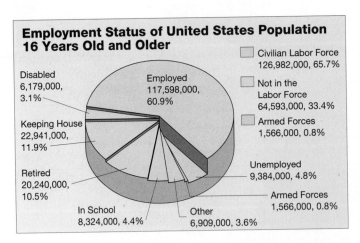

Employment Status of United States Population 16 Years Old and Older

Disabled 6,179,000, 3.1%

Employed 117,598,000, 60.9%

Keeping House 22,941,000, 11.9%

Retired 20,240,000, 10.5%

In School 8,324,000, 4.4%

Other 6,909,000, 3.6%

Armed Forces 1,566,000, 0.8%

Unemployed 9,384,000, 4.8%

- Civilian Labor Force 126,982,000, 65.7%
- Not in the Labor Force 64,593,000, 33.4%
- Armed Forces 1,566,000, 0.8%

Categories of Workers

During the late 1800s, many farm workers moved to cities. This migration occurred in part because of the higher wages paid to workers in the growing industries of the cities. Higher wages also increased the total number of workers by attracting more people to enter the labor force. The migration to cities also occurred because of the increased use of farm machinery. Fewer workers were required. Displaced farm workers found blue-collar jobs. **Blue-collar** jobs include craftworkers, workers in manufacturing, and nonfarm laborers.

306 *Unit 4 Microeconomics : American Business in Action*

Classroom Resources for Section 1

📁 Reproducible Lesson Plan 13.1
💿 *NBR* Video 18 and Video Still 1
📖 Focus Activity Transparency 48
📁 Focus Activity Sheet 48
📁 Guided Reading Activity 13.1
📁 Cooperative Learning Activity 13
📁 Primary and Secondary Source Readings 13

📁 Consumer Application Activities 13 and 19
📁 Section Quiz 13.1
📁 Spanish Section Quiz 13.1
💻 Testmaker
📁 Reinforcing Skills 13

Jobs by Level of Training

Unskilled Workers		groundskeeper, dispatcher, security guard
Semiskilled Workers		bus driver, logger, nurse's aide, word processor, emergency medical technician
Skilled Workers		police officer, computer operator, insurance claims examiner, paralegal, medical records technician
Professionals		architect, optometrist, technical writer, social worker

Figure 13.2
Job Categories
Education and training play a major role in how a particular job is classified. If, to perform a job, virtually no training is needed, the job is classified as unskilled. Professional jobs usually require many years of formal education.

◀

The largest sector of the labor force is white-collar workers. Office workers, salespeople, and **professionals**—highly trained individuals such as doctors, accountants, and engineers, are **white-collar** workers. This sector experienced steady growth throughout the twentieth century.

In recent years, a shift away from farm work and blue-collar jobs to the service sector of the economy has occurred. **Service workers** are those who provide services directly to individuals. Cooks, piano tuners, health-care aides, and barbers are all service workers. The service sector now accounts for many nonfarm jobs.

Classifying jobs as white-collar, blue-collar, service, or farm work is one way of describing the labor force. Another way is to group workers by the level of training or education their jobs require. Figure 13.2 shows examples of these categories. **Unskilled workers** are those whose jobs require no specialized training. Such jobs are considered unskilled, although obviously this work requires skills such as patience and the ability to pace oneself or to work according to a schedule. Such jobs may also demand the ability to work well with people, and so on. **Semiskilled workers** are those whose jobs require some training, often using modern technology. Someone who has learned a trade or craft,

either through a vocational school or as an apprentice to an experienced worker, is considered a **skilled worker**. Professionals are those with college degrees and usually additional education or training.

Although terms such as *semiskilled* are helpful in picturing different areas of the labor force, individuals do not always fall into a single category. A college student, for example, may work at an unskilled job such as cook at a fast-food restaurant while he or she is going to college. Workers may move from one job to another as they gain training and experience. The vice-president of a department store chain, for example, may have begun as a sales clerk. Also, the definitions of technician and professional have become increasingly vague. Some technicians today require considerable training in very difficult and demanding jobs. Moreover, the line between some technicians and scientists, who are professionals, is often very thin.

Supply and Demand in the Labor Market

Supply and demand are factors in the labor market. There, suppliers are the workers who offer their services, while the demand comes from employers who require workers.

Chapter 13 The American Labor Force **307**

Teach

Guided Practice

L2 Analyzing Discuss with students the ways in which the American labor force is changing. Ask them to write a brief description of these changes.

Nightly Business Report
Economics in Action
Use Video Still 1, "Union Membership," on Disc 2, Side A, Video 18.

Search Frame 5969

GLOBAL ECONOMICS

Labor unions in many developed nations argue that immigrants take jobs away from native workers. Actually, immigrants in a free-market economy usually fill jobs no one else wants. They accept low wages and long working hours in exchange for living in a country with more economic opportunity.

◆ ● Meeting Special Needs

Students With Poor Math Skills Both the *mean* and *median* are easily confused by students with poor math skills. Help them by teaching them the following:

1. The median is the middle (both words have a *d* sound, which can be a memory aid). Only by ranking the numbers from

largest to smallest can you find the middle. If there are two "middle numbers" add them and then divide by 2 to find the true middle number, or median.

2. The mean is the average—simply add all the numbers and divide by the number of entries.

Factors That Affect Wages Three major factors affect how supply and demand determine prices or, in this case, wages in the labor market. These factors include: skill, type of job, and location.

The first factor, skill, is the ability a person brings to a job. It may come from talent, initiative, education and/or training, or experience. A brain surgeon and a major-league home-run hitter, for example, may be paid large sums of money, even though their educational backgrounds are quite different. Employers wishing to hire skilled workers must usually pay high wages to bid them away from other potential employers. Another factor in measuring a worker's value is his or her attitude toward work. Some individuals take their jobs seriously and work very hard; others do not. Generally, those who are serious about their work have the "right" attitude—that is, the attitude that will help them succeed in the workplace.

The type of job also affects the amount an employer is willing to pay and a potential employee is willing to accept. Jobs that are unpleasant or dangerous, such as coal mining, often pay high wages compared to other jobs requiring equal levels of skill. In contrast, some jobs are enjoyable or prestigious or desired enough that people are willing to take them even at low wages. Many young people take lower-paying jobs in industries such as filmmaking and publishing for these reasons.

The location of both jobs and workers is the third factor in determining wages. Figure 13.3 shows the differences in wages for three occupations depending on location. If workers are relatively scarce in an area, companies may have to pay high wages to attract workers to move. Alaska, for example, has the highest wages per person in the country. If many unemployed people live in an area and a company needs only a few workers, however, it often can hire enough people even at relatively low wages.

Hourly Wage Difference by Location

Industrial Machinery Repairers	Midwest	$16.17
	West	$14.96
	Northeast	$13.86
	South	$13.22
Insulation Workers	New York City	$39.00
	New Orleans	$18.00
Roustabouts in Oil and Gas	Offshore	$14.00
	Onshore	$12.20

Source: *Occupational Outlook Handbook, 1992-93*

Figure 13.3
Geography and Wages
A skilled machinery repairer will earn much more in the Midwest where blue-collar wages are higher than in the South, which has traditionally had lower wages.

◄

Cooperative Learning

Have the class create a collage of the American labor force. Ask students to bring in magazine, newspaper, and other media pictures of people at work. The jobs can range from manual labor to high-tech, futuristic occupations. Ask the class to create as diverse a collage as possible in terms of range of occupations, types of people doing the work, mix of locations, and unusual images. The collage should help students appreciate the diversity and range of opportunities in the United States economy.

Restrictions on Wages Demand for a product also affects wages. If demand is low, even highly skilled workers may not receive high wages as Figure 13.4 shows.

If the labor market were perfectly competitive, the changing supply and demand for labor would result in constantly shifting wage rates. The labor market, however, is not perfectly competitive. For one thing, the flow of information about jobs is imperfect. Workers cannot know exactly what all other employers will pay for their services. Employers, for their part, do not know what all workers are willing to accept.

In the real world, two other factors affect wages. One is the federal—and sometimes state or city—**minimum wage law**, which sets the lowest legal hourly wage rate that may be paid to certain types of workers. The other is the process of wage negotiations between organized labor and management. Supply and demand have less influence on negotiations than do such things as seniority, or length of time on the job, the company's ability to pay higher wages, and the length of the contract.

Figure 13.4
Demand and Wages
A person may be a highly-skilled electronics worker. His or her wages, however, will probably not be very high if the demand for electronics suddenly drops. ▼

Assess

Meeting Lesson Objectives
Assign Section 1 Review as homework or an in-class activity. Each question in the Review addresses the corresponding numbered objective in the Section Focus.

Evaluate
Assign the Section 1 Quiz in the TCR or use the Testmaker to develop a customized quiz.

Reteach
Organize the class into small groups to discuss the main points under each heading.

Enrich
Invite a local store manager who hires teenage workers to discuss what an employer looks for in a worker.

Close

Have students write a short paragraph explaining how supply and demand can affect wages and other working conditions.

SECTION 1 REVIEW

Understanding Vocabulary
Define civilian labor force, blue-collar, professionals, white-collar, service workers, unskilled workers, semiskilled workers, skilled worker, minimum wage law.

Reviewing Objectives
① What are four categories of workers as determined by skill level and education?
② How do skill, type of job, and location affect supply and demand in the labor market?

Section 1 Review Answers

Understanding Vocabulary
civilian labor force (p. 306), **blue-collar** (p. 306), **professionals** (p. 307), **white-collar** (p. 307), **service workers** (p. 307), **unskilled workers** (p. 307), **semiskilled workers** (p. 307), **skilled worker** (p. 307), **minimum wage law** (p. 309)

Reviewing Objectives
1. unskilled workers, semiskilled workers, skilled workers, and professionals

2. The higher the skill level required for a job, the more dangerous or unpleasant a job, and the scarcer the labor supply in a given location, the higher the wages an employer may pay to attract workers.

Teach

Mean and median are used often in economics to summarize information. They are particularly useful for comparing data over time or among different categories, such as showing an increase or a decrease in average wages in manufacturing over five years.

Make sure students understand the difference between mean and median. Have them go through the calculations several times to be certain they know how to determine both measures.

Additional Practice

Have students complete Reinforcing Skills 13 in the TCR.

LEARNING ECONOMIC SKILLS
Determining Averages: Mean and Median

The most commonly used summary statistic is the average. There are two ways to compute the average: by using the mean or the median. Do you know how to distinguish between these two measures?

Computing the Mean

The *mean* is the average of a series of items. It is found by adding the items and dividing the sum by the number of items in the series. You can find the mean salary of students with part-time jobs by adding the weekly wages and then dividing by the number of students (seven) as shown in Figure A.

Computing the Median

Sometimes using the mean to interpret statistics is misleading. This is especially true if one or two numbers in the series are much larger than the others. A median can be more accurate.

The *median* is the midpoint in any series of numbers arranged in order. For example, in Figure A, $41 is the median weekly wage. In this case, the mean of the series, $60, is much larger than the median, $41. This is because one student earns $175 a week—more than twice as much as any other student.

If an even number of figures are in a series, the median is the mean of the two middle numbers. If you wanted to find the median weekly income of the four students with the highest salaries, you would arrange the incomes in order, add the second and third numbers, and then divide by two as shown in Figure B.

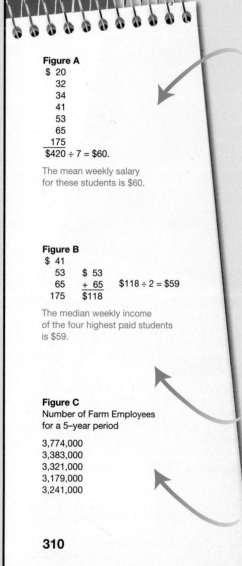

Figure A
```
$ 20
  32
  34
  41
  53
  65
 175
```
$420 ÷ 7 = $60.

The mean weekly salary for these students is $60.

Figure B
```
$ 41
  53     $ 53
  65     + 65     $118 ÷ 2 = $59
 175     $118
```

The median weekly income of the four highest paid students is $59.

Figure C
Number of Farm Employees for a 5–year period

3,774,000
3,383,000
3,321,000
3,179,000
3,241,000

Practicing the Skill

❶ Use Figure C to find the mean number of farm workers employed.

❷ Using Figure C, determine the median number of farm workers employed.

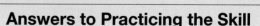

Answers to Practicing the Skill

1. 3,379,600
2. 3,321,000

SECTION **2** *Organized Labor*

S E C T I O N   2   F O C U S

Terms to Know labor union, strike, craft union, industrial union, local union, closed shop, union shop, agency shop, right-to-work laws

Objectives *After reading this section, you should be able to:*
1. Describe the difficulties that labor unions faced when they began to organize in the 1800s.
2. Explain the difference between closed, union, and agency shops as forms of labor organization.

Labor Unions Give Workers Some Control Over Wages and Working Conditions

To have some control over the wages they receive as well as over other working conditions, American workers have formed labor unions. A **labor union** is an association of workers organized to improve wages and working conditions for its members. Unions are based on the idea that workers as a group will have more influence on management than will individual workers acting alone. In discussing labor-management relations, the term *management* refers to those in charge of a company—the executives and managers.

Development of Labor Unions

Working conditions in the 1800s were very different from those of today as **Figure 13.5** shows. The buildings were sometimes poorly lighted and ventilated, and the machinery was sometimes dangerous to operate. When business slumped, factory owners fired employees. When business improved, new employees were hired. No unemployment insurance helped those who were out of work until they found new jobs. Health-care benefits, sick leave, and paid vacations and holidays did not exist. Workers began to form unions to force employers to improve working conditions, shorten the workday, and end child labor.

Figure 13.5 Poor Working Conditions
In the 1800s men, women, and children as young as 5 years old labored from 12 to 14 hours a day, sometimes 6 days a week, often in unsanitary and unsafe factories. ▼

Unionism met strong resistance. In the 1800s, state legislatures, influenced by business interests, passed

Chapter 13 The American Labor Force **311**

Classroom Resources for Section 2

- Reproducible Lesson Plan 13.2
- Focus Activity Transparency 49
- Focus Activity Sheet 49
- Guided Reading Activity 13.2
- Section Quiz 13.2
- Spanish Section Quiz 13.2
- Testmaker

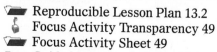

Focus

Overview
See the student page for section objectives.

Section 2 explains or describes: the rise of unions in the American work force; the resistance these groups encountered; and the types of shops they established.

Bellringer
Before presenting the lesson, display Focus Activity Transparency 49 on the overhead projector or copy the material on the chalkboard. Assign the accompanying Focus Activity Sheet.

Motivational Activity
Ask students to imagine working in a factory before unions existed and wanting to make working conditions safer. Discuss how they might get the attention and cooperation of management, and write their suggestions on the chalkboard.

Preteaching Vocabulary
Have students make "union cards." Ask them to write the type of union or shop (or use a symbol) on one side of an index card and the definition on the other side. Encourage pairs of students to flash their cards to each other and ask for definitions.

Teach

Guided Practice

L2 Identifying Have students list some of the reasons unions were needed in the period from the late 1800s to the 1940s. Then have them write a brief paragraph explaining why union membership is declining now. What conditions have changed?

L1 Hypothesizing Ask students what would be some of the benefits and disadvantages of having a free market system with no unions?

DID YOU KNOW

Many working conditions and benefits enjoyed today resulted from hard-won victories gained by organized labor only 60 years ago. These include:

- Laws outlawing labor for children under 16
- Workers' compensation for those injured on the job
- Safer working conditions
- Equal opportunity hiring and promotion practices
- Health benefits
- Five-day workweek and an eight-hour workday
- Paid holidays and vacations
- Grievance procedures for filing complaints

laws against unions, and courts upheld them. Many businesses refused to hire union members or deal with unions. Workers who were found trying to organize unions were fired and blacklisted—kept from being employed. As shown in Figure 13.6, strikes during the late 1800s and early 1900s often resulted in violence between strikers and police. A **strike** is a deliberate work stoppage by workers to force an employer to give in to their demands.

The American Labor Movement The time line in Figure 13.8 (pages 314–315) shows the major dates in the development of the American labor movement. For much of its history, organized labor in the United States has been split into two groups: craft unions and industrial unions. A **craft union** is made up of skilled workers in a specific trade or industry, such as carpentry or printing. For many years, craft unions dominated the labor movement. The first permanent federation, or organization of national labor unions, was the American Federation of Labor (AFL), composed of craft unions.

An **industrial union** is made up of all the workers in an industry regardless of job or level of skill. Attempts to organize industrial unions date back to the late 1800s. The major effort to unionize unskilled and semiskilled workers did not begin until the formation of the Congress of Industrial Organizations (CIO) in 1938. Because they employ large numbers of unskilled and semiskilled work-

ers, the automobile and steel industries were among the first to be organized.

The AFL-CIO During the late 1930s and early 1940s, both the AFL and the CIO launched organizing campaigns that made the lines between industrial and craft unions less clear. AFL unions began recruiting semiskilled and unskilled workers, while the CIO began organizing workers in the skilled trades. The resulting rivalry cost both union federations time and effort. By the mid-1950s, union leaders realized that the labor movement would make greater gains if craft and industrial unions worked together. As a result, the two federations merged in 1955 to form the present AFL-CIO. Today, many unions are affiliated, or joined, with the AFL-CIO. Several independent unions, however, including the National Education Association (NEA), also exist.

**Figure 13.6
Violent Strikes ▶**

Not until the mid-1930s did Congress begin to pass laws to regulate labor-management relations. Before that time, many strikes resulted in violence and injuries.

312   *Unit 4 Microeconomics : American Business in Action*

Students With Limited English Proficiency
Students who have limited English proficiency may have difficulty understanding the types of unions and union shops that have been established. They may find it eas-

ier to learn the material if they outline the chapter, listing the different unions and union shops and their major characteristics in outline form.

Figure 13.7 ▶ Local Union Members
Not all local unions are alike. Membership requirements and the ways in which management relates to union members vary from one kind of shop to another.

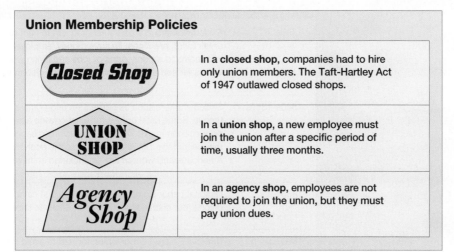

Union Membership Policies

Closed Shop	In a **closed shop**, companies had to hire only union members. The Taft-Hartley Act of 1947 outlawed closed shops.
UNION SHOP	In a **union shop**, a new employee must join the union after a specific period of time, usually three months.
Agency Shop	In an **agency shop**, employees are not required to join the union, but they must pay union dues.

Labor Organization

Today, organized labor operates at three levels: the local union, the national or international union, and the federation. A **local union** consists of the members of a union in a particular factory, company, or geographic area. The local deals with a company by ne-gotiating a contract and making sure the terms of the contract are kept.

The influence that a local has often depends on the type of membership policy it negotiated with management. See **Figure 13.7**.

Supporters of union and agency shops argue that employees in compa-nies that are unionized should be re-quired to pay union dues because they benefit from contracts the union nego-tiates. Opponents believe that a person should not be required to join a union. Since 1947 a number of states have passed **right-to-work laws** that forbid union shops and closed shops. These laws allow workers to continue working in a particular job without joining a union. The employee benefits ne-gotiated by the union must be made available to work-ers who do not join the union. The power of unions in states with right-to-work laws is less than in other states.

Above the locals are the national unions. These orga-nizations are the individual craft or industrial unions that represent locals nationwide.

Chapter 13 The American Labor Force **313**

L1 Research and Writing Have students investigate some of the most famous incidents in union history, such as the Pullman strike, General Motors sit-down strike, or Harlan County, Kentucky, coal miners' strike. Have them write a brief report naming the main issues, events during the strike, and the outcome.

L2 Debating Have students debate the following ques-tion: "Although unions have improved job conditions for workers, have they outlived their usefulness?" Ask vol-unteers to argue the posi-tive and negative positions, citing examples from union history and the present to support their views.

Visual Instruction

Refer students to Figure 13.6 as a starting point for exploring some of the famous protests and strikes in United States labor his-tory such as the Haymarket riot, the General Motors sit-down strike, and the United Mine Workers' strikes of the 1970s. Encour-age examination of the issues involved and any short-term and long-term consequences. Ask students to give oral reports as part of discussion of strikes and benefits to workers generally.

Cooperative Learning

Tell the class to imagine they are histori-ans investigating the roles that women, African Americans, and other groups played in the history of the American labor move-ment. Ask for volunteers or assign different teams to research different groups. Have each team write a brief report on their find-ings. Tell them that the reference librarian can help them locate books, articles, and government publications for their research. Suggest they include illustrations or graph-ics whenever possible.

Independent Practice

L2 Civics Have students choose a federal law regulating organized labor and write a short report about it. Suggest including reasons for enactment, the main points of the law, and any important outcomes for workers and/or the economy. Encourage volunteers to report their findings orally to the class.

DID YOU KNOW

Labor unions in the United States tend to be primarily concerned with collective bargaining and worker rights and benefits. Elsewhere, however, emphasis may be on social and political reform, even to the extent of reorganizing the economic and political systems.

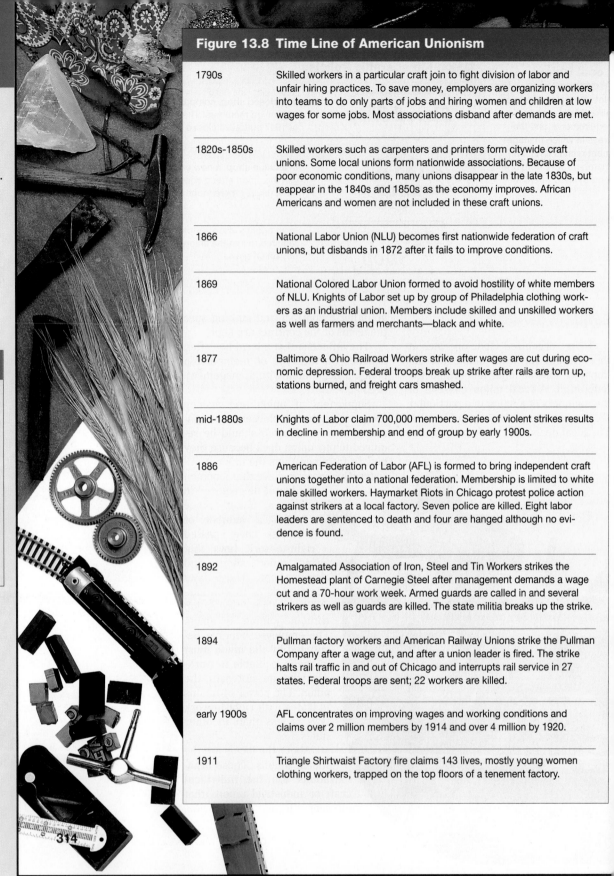

Figure 13.8 Time Line of American Unionism

1790s	Skilled workers in a particular craft join to fight division of labor and unfair hiring practices. To save money, employers are organizing workers into teams to do only parts of jobs and hiring women and children at low wages for some jobs. Most associations disband after demands are met.
1820s-1850s	Skilled workers such as carpenters and printers form citywide craft unions. Some local unions form nationwide associations. Because of poor economic conditions, many unions disappear in the late 1830s, but reappear in the 1840s and 1850s as the economy improves. African Americans and women are not included in these craft unions.
1866	National Labor Union (NLU) becomes first nationwide federation of craft unions, but disbands in 1872 after it fails to improve conditions.
1869	National Colored Labor Union formed to avoid hostility of white members of NLU. Knights of Labor set up by group of Philadelphia clothing workers as an industrial union. Members include skilled and unskilled workers as well as farmers and merchants—black and white.
1877	Baltimore & Ohio Railroad Workers strike after wages are cut during economic depression. Federal troops break up strike after rails are torn up, stations burned, and freight cars smashed.
mid-1880s	Knights of Labor claim 700,000 members. Series of violent strikes results in decline in membership and end of group by early 1900s.
1886	American Federation of Labor (AFL) is formed to bring independent craft unions together into a national federation. Membership is limited to white male skilled workers. Haymarket Riots in Chicago protest police action against strikers at a local factory. Seven police are killed. Eight labor leaders are sentenced to death and four are hanged although no evidence is found.
1892	Amalgamated Association of Iron, Steel and Tin Workers strikes the Homestead plant of Carnegie Steel after management demands a wage cut and a 70-hour work week. Armed guards are called in and several strikers as well as guards are killed. The state militia breaks up the strike.
1894	Pullman factory workers and American Railway Unions strike the Pullman Company after a wage cut, and after a union leader is fired. The strike halts rail traffic in and out of Chicago and interrupts rail service in 27 states. Federal troops are sent; 22 workers are killed.
early 1900s	AFL concentrates on improving wages and working conditions and claims over 2 million members by 1914 and over 4 million by 1920.
1911	Triangle Shirtwaist Factory fire claims 143 lives, mostly young women clothing workers, trapped on the top floors of a tenement factory.

314

Free Enterprise Activity

Encourage students to work in small groups to plan how they would organize a union for workers in an occupation or an industry. Suggest that they develop an outline for an organizing strategy and the goals to be achieved through forming a union. Have a class discussion to compare plans.

Figure 13.8 Time Line of American Unionism

1920s	Opposition by business, unfavorable court rulings, and rising anti-labor and anti-immigration feelings cause decline in union membership.
1929	The Great Depression begins. Sympathy grows among the general public for concerns of organized labor.
1932	Congress passes Norris-LaGuardia Act, the first major pro-labor legislation. Act limits power of the courts to stop picketing and boycotts and makes yellow-dog contracts illegal. This is the practice whereby employers require that employees pledge not to join a union.
1935	National Labor Relations Act (Wagner Act) guarantees labor's right to organize and bargain collectively. Act sets up National Labor Relations Board (NLRB) to oversee the establishment and operation of unions.
1938	To organize unskilled workers in such industries as automobiles and steel, some leaders of the AFL form the Congress of Industrial Organizations (CIO). CIO encourages membership of African Americans and women.
1945-47	Wave of strikes to improve wages and working conditions follows end of World War II and contributes to growing anti-union feelings.
1947	Congress passes Labor-Management Act (Taft-Hartley Act) over strong objections of labor. Act outlaws certain strike tactics, permits states to pass laws making union shops illegal, and allows the President to delay a strike if it will threaten the nation's health and safety.
1955	AFL and CIO unite into a single union, AFL-CIO.
1959	Congress passes Labor Management Reporting and Disclosure Act (Landrum-Griffin Act). Act increases government control over unions and guarantees union members certain rights, such as freedom of speech in union activities and control over union dues.
1962	President Kennedy signs into law an order giving federal employees the right to organize into unions, but not to strike. Union membership among government workers grows during the 1960s and 1970s.
mid-1960s-1970s	Union membership among African Americans, women, Hispanics, and agricultural workers increases.
1981	President Reagan fires 11,400 air traffic controllers for striking illegally. AFL-CIO warns of growing anti-union feelings as economy worsens. Some large unions such as the United Auto Workers negotiate contracts that give back some of their earlier gains.
1982-1994	Union membership decreases to less than 15 percent of the work force.

Chapter 13 The American Labor Force   **315**

Chapter 13, Section 2

Independent Practice

L2 Investigating Ask students to compare and contrast a labor union and a professional association such as the American Bar Association or the American Medical Association with respect to the benefits they try to assure their members. Suggest that they organize their findings in a table or chart. Ask volunteers to give an oral report.

📁 Have students complete Guided Reading Activity 13.2 in the TCR. `LEP`

❓ DID YOU KNOW

The Job Training Partnership Act provides job training and employment services for persons faced with major obstacles to employment. Between October 1983 and the end of the program year in 1991, the program served about 8 million Americans, with a placement rate of nearly 69 percent.

 Cultural Diversity and Economics

Organize students into small groups to research labor unions in two countries of their choice (reserve the right to approve choices to avoid duplication). Have them compare features side by side in a chart or table. Ask a volunteer from each group to report the group's findings. Discuss unions in other countries generally.

Assess

Meeting Lesson Objectives

Assign Section 2 Review as homework or an in-class activity. Each question in the Review addresses the corresponding numbered objective in the Section Focus.

Evaluate

Assign the Section 2 Quiz in the TCR or use the Testmaker to develop a customized quiz.

Reteach

Ask students to write a paragraph on the costs and benefits of belonging to a union.

Enrich

Ask students to write a brief report on a well-known union leader, such as Mary "Mother" Harris Jones, A. Philip Randolph, or Eugene V. Debs.

Close

Discuss with students the contributions and limitations of labor unions.

Figure 13.9 ▶
The AFL-CIO
Representing its member unions, the AFL-CIO lobbies for pro-labor legislation at the state and federal levels. It also offers training and advice to the leadership of member unions and promotes the causes of organized labor.

Those unions that also have members in Canada or Mexico are often called international unions.

To help in negotiating a contract between a local and a particular company, plant, or group of businesses, the nationals make available lawyers, professional negotiators, and other staff members. In certain industries such as steel and mining, the national union negotiates the contract for the entire industry.

Once the majority of union members accepts the contract, all the locals within the industry must work under the contract. National unions also send in organizers to help employees organize campaigns to set up locals.

Some of the largest unions are the International Brotherhood of Teamsters; United Automobile Workers (UAW); United Steelworkers of America (USW); and the American Federation of State, County and Municipal Employees (AFSCME).

At the federation level is the AFL-CIO, which is made up of national and international unions. More than 85 unions with about 14 million members are associated with the AFL-CIO. See Figure 13.9.

SECTION 2 REVIEW

Understanding Vocabulary
Define labor union, strike, craft union, industrial union, local union, closed shop, union shop, agency shop, right-to-work laws.

Reviewing Objectives
1. What obstacles did labor unions face when they began to organize in the 1800s?
2. How do closed shops, union shops, and agency shops differ?

Section 2 Review Answers
Understanding Vocabulary
labor union (p. 311), **strike** (p. 312), **craft union** (p. 312), **industrial union** (p. 312), **local union** (p. 313), **closed shop** (p. 313), **union shop** (p. 313), **agency shop** (p. 313), **right-to-work laws** (p. 313)

Reviewing Objectives
1. State laws outlawed unions; businesses refused to hire union members or to deal with unions and often fired and blacklisted union organizers.
2. In a closed shop, companies must hire only union members. Union shops require new employees to join the union after a specified time on the job, usually three months. In an agency shop, employees are not required to join the union, but they must pay union dues to keep their jobs.

316

Personal Perspective

Thomas Sowell on Discrimination

Profile

- 1930–
- doctorate in economics from the University of Chicago
- senior fellow at the Hoover Institution of War, Revolution and Peace
- taught at leading universities in the United States, Singapore, Israel, Switzerland, and Germany
- published books include *Black Education: Myths and Tragedies* (1972) and *The Economics and Politics of Race* (1983)

In the following excerpt from *The Economics and Politics of Race*, Thomas Sowell discusses racism and discrimination. He is concerned that those who debate these issues understand the meanings of the terms they use.

The question is not about the "right" or "best" definition of the word "racism." Words are servants, not masters. The real problem is to avoid shifting definitions that play havoc with reasoning....

One of the most common concepts encountered in discussions of race and ethnicity is discrimination. Yet it is seldom defined. Various overlapping, and sometimes contradictory, meanings of discrimination are used, sometimes in the same analysis....

The first four definitions can be combined into a single definition of discrimination as the offering of different transaction terms—including no terms at all—to groups who do not differ in the relevant criteria (skill, credit-rating, experience, test scores, etc.)....

To explain its substandard economic position by discrimination is to show that the group as a whole was underpaid or overcharged....

According to Sowell, political discrimina-tion makes economic discrimination more difficult to measure. If the government provides different qualities of schooling to different groups, economic inequalities will develop. People, however, may link such inequalities to a variety of causes other than discrimination.

While discrimination is usually conceived of in economic terms as discrimination against workers, consumers, tenants or credit seekers, there is also political discrimination against all these groups and also against school children, defendants in court, and others who have contact with governmental institutions. Indeed, political discrimination may make it more difficult to measure economic discrimination....

Much direct political discrimination is disguised by phrasing it as a "preference" for one group rather than discrimination against another.

Checking for Understanding

❶ What is the problem to avoid in discussing racism?

❷ How would Sowell define discrimination?

❸ Who may be victims of political discrimination?

Answers to Checking for Understanding

1. shifting definitions: the term *racism* is applied to so many kinds of behavior that arriving at an exact meaning is difficult

2. "the offering of different transaction terms—including no terms at all—to groups who do not differ in the relevant criteria" of qualifications, intelligence, or skills

3. those who have contact with government such as workers, consumers, tenants, or credit seekers; political discrimination, however, may be disguised as "preference" for one group

Background

In addition to teaching at major universities in several countries, Thomas Sowell served on President Reagan's Economic Advisory Panel. Sowell is a leading exponent of the view that the free enterprise system works in the interest of minorities and that government efforts at affirmative action have hindered minority group members rather than helping them.

Teach

Federal laws prohibit discrimination based on sex, race, color, national origin, or creed in hiring workers. Yet definitions of *discrimination* can be confusing and contradictory. Sowell offers a definition based on the effect of a discriminatory practice on a group *as a whole*. Discuss with students the importance of defining the terms they use, particularly those with strong emotional overtones, such as *racism*. Ask students how they can judge when an action or policy against a group is racist or discriminatory.

Focus

Overview

See the student page for section objectives.

Section 3 explains or describes: the basic issues in collective bargaining and the declining importance of collective bargaining as a way for workers to achieve their goals.

Bellringer

Before presenting the lesson, display Focus Activity Transparency 50 on the overhead projector or copy the material on the chalkboard. Assign the accompanying Focus Activity Sheet.

Motivational Activity

Discuss with students why a third party can often succeed in settling an argument when two sides fail to agree.

Preteaching Vocabulary

Have students look up the vocabulary terms in the Glossary. Then ask them to write a paragraph describing how they are related.

SECTION 3 Collective Bargaining

SECTION 3 FOCUS

Terms to Know collective bargaining, mediation, cost-of-living adjustment (COLA), arbitration, picketing, boycott, lockout, injunction

Objectives *After reading this section, you should be able to:*

1. List the six major issues that are involved in **labor-management negotiations**.
2. Describe two workers' actions that can accompany a strike and two **management responses to a strike**.
3. Explain the modern trend in **collective bargaining** in the United States.

A Strike May Occur if Negotiations Break Down

Collective **bargaining** is the process by which unions and employers negotiate the conditions of employment. At the center of the collective bargaining process is compromise. The company wants to keep wages and benefits low to hold its labor costs down and remain competitive in the market. The union wants to increase wages and benefits for its members as much as possible. Obviously, both sides must be prepared to give and take a little.

**Figure 13.10
Labor/Management
Negotiations**

In most cases negotiations are friendly and result in an agreement that satisfies all parties. In the case of a deadlock, however, the two sides may agree to try mediation. ▼

Negotiations

Negotiations take place when labor and management meet to discuss in detail a wide range of contract issues. See **Figure 13.10**. **Figure 13.11** lists a number of the most important issues that labor and management may negotiate. If necessary, labor and management may try mediation. **Mediation** (MEED-ee-AY-shuhn) occurs when a neutral, or disinterested, person steps in and tries to get both sides to reach an agreement. The mediator suggests possible solutions and works to keep the two sides talking with each other.

The federal government, through

318 *Unit 4 Microeconomics : American Business in Action*

Classroom Resources for Section 3

- Reproducible Lesson Plan 13.3
- Focus Activity Transparency 50
- Focus Activity Sheet 50
- Guided Reading Activity 13.3
- Free Enterprise Activity 13
- Economics Laboratory 4
- Economic Simulation 4

- Mathematics Practice for Economics 18
- Performance Assessment Activity 18
- Section Quiz 13.3
- Spanish Section Quiz 13.3
- Chapter 13 Test Forms A and B
- Testmaker

- Enrichment Activity 13
- Economics Vocabulary Activity 13
- Spanish Economics Vocabulary Activity 13
- Audiocassette 13
- Spanish Audiocassette 13
- Reteaching Activity 13

Figure 13.11 Union Contract Issues

Issue	Description
Wages	Most contracts provide for wage increases of a certain percentage for each worker during each year of the contract. Some contracts also provide for an additional increase each year if the general level of prices in the economy rises beyond a certain amount. This provision is known as a **cost-of-living adjustment (COLA)**.
Working hours	The contract establishes the number of hours a day that employees must work. Employees who work longer hours must usually be paid extra wages, called overtime pay.
Fringe benefits	Fringe benefits are payments other than wages made to employees. These can include health and life insurance, a retirement plan, and time off for vacations and holidays.
Working conditions	Contracts often provide for a joint union and management committee to ensure that safe and pleasant working conditions exist. Working conditions are a particularly important issue to employees in industries that deal with poisonous substances or dangerous machinery.
Job security	At issue under job security is protection against layoffs because of technological change or a slowdown in business. Most contracts do not forbid layoffs, but rather set up rules that the employer must follow in laying off workers. For example, those with the least seniority—amount of time spent with the company—are usually laid off first.
Grievance procedures	Grievance procedures are a set of formal rules used to resolve a dispute between union members and management. A grievance, or complaint, may be filed if one side feels that the other is not living up to the terms of the contract. If the union and the company cannot settle the grievance, a third party will often be asked to judge the matter objectively.

the Federal Mediation and Conciliation Service (FMCS), provides a mediator free of charge upon request of either union or management. In a typical year, FMCS mediators are involved in about 20,000 negotiations. In April 1992, for example, FMCS stepped in to help resolve a strike by the United Automobile Workers against Caterpillar, the world's largest builder of earth-moving equipment. A number of state and private mediators also help resolve disputes.

If mediation fails, the negotiation process may go one step further to arbitration. In **arbitration** (AHR-buh-TRAY-shuhn), the two sides submit the issues they cannot agree on to a third party for a final decision. Both sides agree in advance to accept the arbitrator's decision, though one or both sides may not be completely happy with the outcome. The FMCS often helps in these cases by providing labor and management with a list of private arbitrators in their area.

Chapter 13 The American Labor Force **319**

Teach

Guided Practice

L2 Journalism Have students bring in reports on union bargaining from newspaper, magazine, or television accounts. Discuss the issues and the response of management to union demands. Ask students to write a paragraph summarizing the issues.

Visual Instruction

Refer students to the information in Figure 13.11 and have them rank the items in importance, from 1 for most important to 6 for least important. Ask which of the six items they would give up if they had to and why. Tell them that these issues have been the subject of union-management debate for decades.

? DID YOU KNOW

Rapid changes in computerized technology are widening the gap between unskilled and skilled workers. Those without computer skills will fall farther behind in the competition for good jobs and higher pay. In response, many communities offer computer training.

Meeting Special Needs

Abstract Reasoning Deficit Some students may have difficulty understanding how two diametrically opposing viewpoints can ever be resolved in an agreement that both sides accept. Show them the diagram and discuss the process of conflict resolution.

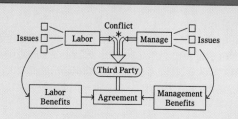

Independent Practice

L2 Interviewing Have students contact the Federal Mediation and Conciliation Service to find a mediator or arbitrator to interview. In the interview, students should ask about the qualifications, training, and employment experience needed to become an arbitrator or mediator.

 Have students complete Guided Reading Activity 13.3 in the TCR. LEP

Visual Instruction

Refer the class to the graph in Figure 13.12. Have students respond to the question in the caption. (*Students might suggest that lower union membership means fewer strikes.*) Have students speculate on the effect of negotiations or union membership in general.

Answer to Figure 13.14 caption: *It increased rapidly, then slowly declined. Answers will vary, but students might suggest that as working conditions improved, fewer workers saw the need to unionize.*

GLOBAL ECONOMICS

In Japan, when contracts expire, unions stage a work stoppage to show their influence with workers. Employees then go back to work, and management and labor leaders meet to discuss a new contract.

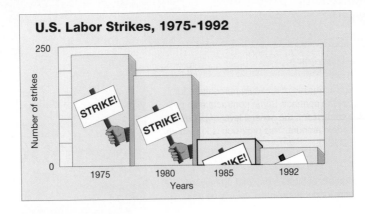

U.S. Labor Strikes, 1975-1992

Figure 13.12 ▲ Striking
Compare the trend in strikes with what is happening in union membership. See **Figure 13.14**. How do you think the two are related?

Figure 13.13 Picketing
Often, members of other unions will not cross a picket line. This may further handicap the business being struck. ▼

Strikes and Management Responses

Most contracts are settled at the bargaining table. Sometimes, though, negotiations break down and a strike results. The number of strikes in the United States has declined sharply since 1975. See **Figure 13.12.**

Strikers usually walk up and down in front of the company carrying picket signs that state their disagreement with the company. **Picketing** is meant to discourage workers from crossing the picket line to work for the employer. It is also aimed at embarrassing the company and building public support for the strike. See **Figure 13.13.**

Striking unions may use a boycott to exert more economic pressure. In a **boycott,** unions urge the public not to purchase goods or services produced by a company. Unions may also ask politicians to push management for a settlement or to support the union's demands publicly.

Strikes can drag on for months and even years. After a long period of time, strikers sometimes become discouraged. Some may decide to go back to work without gaining what they wanted. In most cases, however, strikes are settled as management and labor return to the negotiating table and work out an agreement.

Lockouts When faced with a strike, management has methods of its own to use against strikers. One is the **lockout,** which occurs when management prevents workers from returning to work until they agree to a new contract. Another tactic is to bring in strikebreakers, called *scabs* by strikers. These are people willing to cross a picket line to work for the terms the company offers.

Injunctions Management sometimes requests a court injunction to limit picketing or to prevent a strike from continuing or even occurring. An **injunction** is a legal order of a court preventing some activity. Under the Taft-Hartley Act of 1947, the President of the United States can obtain a court order to delay or halt a strike for up to 80 days if the strike will endanger the nation's safety or health. During this cooling-off period, the two sides must try to reach a settlement.

Collective Bargaining on the Decline

The establishment of the AFL in 1886 is considered the beginning of the modern union era. Since that time, unions have achieved many of their goals. Union supporters list among union accomplishments better wages and working conditions for all employees—union and nonunion. They point out that many workers now enjoy a sense of security and self-respect that helps to maintain some control over their jobs and lives. Union supporters also note that the collective bargaining process has brought more order and fairness to the workplace. It has made clear the rights and responsibilities of both management and labor.

Cooperative Learning

Have the class role-play a labor-management dispute that must be mediated. Choose three students to research conflict resolution procedures used in mediation. Assign six students, three to represent labor and three to represent management, to draw up opposing positions regarding wages, safety on the job, and health benefits. Have the mediators negotiate an agreement between management and labor. The class should critique the session when it is over, evaluating what each side lost and gained.

Because working conditions have improved so dramatically over the years, nonunion workers often see little to gain from joining a union. Moreover, many union members no longer feel the same commitment to organized labor that earlier union members did.

Union Membership, 1935-1992

Source: U.S. Department of Labor, Bureau of Labor Statistics

Critics The labor movement also has its critics. Some opponents charge that unions have grown so large and bureaucratic that they are out of touch with their members' needs. Others claim that increased wages are passed on to consumers in the form of higher prices. Employers often argue that union rules decrease productivity. They point to rules that slow the introduction of new technology or require more employees than necessary to do a job. In addition, corruption among some labor leaders has damaged the reputation of organized labor with the public.

Current Challenges The labor movement today faces many problems. As Figure 13.14 shows, the percentage of union members among the labor force reached a high in the mid-1940s and has been declining since. Today union members in the United States represent only a fraction of the civilian labor force.

One reason for this decline is the changing nature of the economy. More jobs are opening in the white-collar and service sectors, while blue-collar jobs are decreasing due to automation. Many service workers and white-collar employees see themselves as working on their own. They often do not identify with groups of their fellow employees in the same way as an assembly-line worker might. With technology comes the potential loss of manufacturing jobs that may result in a further decline in union membership and a weakening of the role of unions in the future—unless unions find ways to meet these challenges.

Figure 13.14 ▲ Union Membership, 1935-1992
What has happened to union membership during the second half of the twentieth century? What factors are responsible for this trend?

Assess

Meeting Lesson Objectives
Assign Section 3 Review as homework or an in-class activity.

Evaluate
Assign the Section 3 Quiz in the TCR or use the Testmaker to develop a customized quiz.
Assign the Chapter 13 Test Form A or Form B or use the Testmaker to develop a customized test.

Reteach
Have the class outline the section.
Have students complete Reteaching Activity 13 in the TCR.

Enrich
Invite a labor union representative to class to discuss how a union works.
Have students complete Enrichment Activity 13 in the TCR.

Close

Have students write a paragraph on the costs and benefits of collective bargaining.

SECTION 3 REVIEW

Understanding Vocabulary
Define collective bargaining, mediation, cost-of-living adjustment (COLA), arbitration, picketing, boycott, lockout, injunction.

Reviewing Objectives
1. What are the major issues over which union contracts are negotiated?
2. What workers' actions and management responses may accompany a strike?
3. How has collective bargaining in the United States changed in recent years?

Chapter 13 The American Labor Force **321**

Section 3 Review Answers

Understanding Vocabulary
collective bargaining (p. 318), **mediation** (p. 318), **cost-of-living adjustment (COLA)** (p. 319), **arbitration** (p. 319), **picketing** (p. 320), **boycott** (p. 320), **lockout** (p. 320), **injunction** (p. 320)

Reviewing Objectives
1. wages, working hours, fringe benefits, working conditions, job security, and grievance procedures
2. workers: picket lines and boycotts; employers: lockouts, strikebreakers, and injunctions
3. Since the 1950s, union membership overall has declined. This trend appears to have resulted from the changing nature of the economy, including more white-collar and service jobs and increased use of automation and technology.

Readings in Economics

CONGRESSIONAL QUARTERLY   APRIL 12, 1993

Teach

Tell students that until the late 1980s, people entering the work force expected to move upward in job level and financial gains, a situation called upward mobility. "Downward mobility" is a more recent phenomenon. Discuss some reasons for downward mobility and ask students what they would do if they were in Drone's situation.

THE PLAGUE OF DOWNWARD JOB MOBILITY

by Kenneth Jost

James Drone had heard all the stories about corporate downsizing, but the 46-year-old lawyer was unprepared when he became a victim of the trend earlier this year.

Drone was general counsel for a tug and barge business in Houston. The company's fortunes dipped, and Drone, who had worked there for four and a half years, was asked to leave in February. . . .

"I lost quite a bit of sleep, waking up at 3 o'clock in the morning, figuring out what I had done or didn't do," Drone said. "It was strictly economics." Drone, who is married and has four school-age children, is better off than most people who have been sliding down the economic ladder. He got a six-months' severance package and is earning some money practicing law while scouting for another business opportunity.

But even when money is not an issue, the psychological shock of what economists call "downward mobility" can be devastating. "It's an emotional roller-coaster, to say the least," Drone said.

Across the country, the specter of downward mobility has weakened Americans' traditional optimism. A poll taken last year found that more Americans than at any time in the past 20 years felt their personal financial situation was getting worse, not better. And nearly half of those responding to a 1993 poll said they did not think their children would surpass them financially. . . .

Downward mobility poses an array of challenges for workers, employers, and the government—many . . . still only dimly recognized and incompletely understood.

Economic Growth

• THINK ABOUT IT •

1. What is downward mobility?
2. What do economists forecast for the future?

Answers to Think About It

1. Downward mobility describes the situation when workers, because of job layoffs or business failures, find themselves earning less instead of more and taking lower level jobs instead of being promoted to higher level jobs. The effect of moving down the economic ladder may be temporary or permanent.

2. Economists forecast moderate economic growth and slow job growth over the next decade.

13 *Highlights*

Section 1

Americans at Work

Key Terms

civilian labor force (p. 306)
blue-collar (p. 306)
professionals (p. 307)
white-collar (p. 307)
service workers (p. 307)

unskilled workers (p. 307)
semiskilled workers (p. 307)
skilled worker (p. 307)
minimum wage law (p. 309)

Summary

Workers can be divided into categories depending on the type of work. Workers can also be divided into unskilled, semiskilled, skilled, and professional occupations. In the labor market, suppliers are the workers who offer their services, while the demand comes from employers who need workers. Three factors underlie how supply and demand affect wages: skill, type of job, and location.

Section 2

Organized Labor

Key Terms

labor union (p. 311)
strike (p. 312)
craft union (p. 312)
industrial union (p. 312)
local union (p. 313)

closed shop (p. 313)
union shop (p. 313)
agency shop (p. 313)
right-to-work laws (p. 313)

Summary

In the nineteenth century, unions appealed to working people because they seemed to offer a way to force employers to improve working conditions. Unionism, however, met strong resistance for much of the nineteenth century and early twentieth century. Unions succeeded in the twentieth century in establishing closed, union, and agency shops.

Section 3

Collective Bargaining

Key Terms

collective bargaining (p. 318)
mediation (p. 318)
cost-of-living adjustment (COLA) (p. 319)

arbitration (p. 319)
picketing (p. 320)
boycott (p. 320)
lockout (p. 320)
injunction (p. 320)

Summary

The major issues in collective bargaining usually are wages, working hours, fringe benefits, working conditions, job security, and grievance procedures. When collective bargaining, arbitration, or mediation break down, a strike may ensue in which workers picket the struck company. They may organize a boycott to urge the public not to purchase the goods or services produced by the struck company. Management may respond by locking out workers or having a court issue an injunction.

Use the Chapter 13 Highlights to preview, review, condense, or reteach the chapter. A Spanish Chapter Highlights is available in the Spanish Handbook.

Preview/Review

After students read the Chapter 13 Highlights, have them complete Economics Vocabulary Activity 13 in the TCR. Spanish Vocabulary Activities are also available in the Spanish Resource Binder.

Vocabulary Software reinforces the economic terms used in Chapter 13.

Condense

Have students listen to Chapter 13 on the Audiocassettes in the TCR. A 1-page written activity and 1-page test accompany this material. These materials are also available in Spanish.

Reteach

Have students complete Reteaching Activity 13 in the TCR. Spanish Reteaching Activities are also available.

VIDEODISC

Nightly Business Report
Economics in Action
Use "The American Labor Force" on Disc 2, Side A, Video 18.

Search 2, Play to 6841

CHAPTER
13 *Review*

ANSWERS

Identifying Key Terms

1. d
2. a
3. e
4. c
5. g
6. f
7. b
8. semiskilled worker
9. skilled worker
10. professional
11. minimum wage law
12. labor union
13. collective bargaining
14. strike
15. picketing
16. lockout

Recalling Facts and Ideas

Section 1

1. professional
2. Blue-collar workers are employed in manufacturing and trades and usually have a lower level of education. White-collar workers are employed in office and service jobs and generally have college degrees and may also have earned advanced degrees.
3. skill level, type of job, and location

Section 2

4. craft unions and industrial unions
5. the American Federation of Labor and the Congress of Industrial Organizations
6. They protect the right of workers to continue working in a particular job without joining a union.

Section 3

7. working hours, fringe benefits, working conditions, job security, grievance procedures
8. arbitration
9. They stop all work and usually organize a

Identifying Key Terms

Write the letter of the definition in Column B below that correctly defines each term in Column A.

Column A

1. unskilled workers (p. 307)
2. agency shop (p. 313)
3. arbitration (p. 319)
4. injunction (p. 320)
5. right-to-work law (p. 313)
6. closed shop (p. 313)
7. boycott (p. 320)

Column B

a. employees are not required to join a union but must pay union dues
b. refusal to purchase the goods and services of a company
c. court order preventing some activity, often a strike
d. no special training in job-related skills
e. undecided issues between labor and management are given to a third party for a final decision
f. company in which only union members can be hired
g. forbids contracts that require employees to join a union

Use terms from the following list to fill in the blanks in the paragraph below.

minimum wage law (p. 309)
labor union (p. 311)
professional (p. 307)
strike (p. 312)
lockout (p. 320)
semiskilled worker (p. 307)
collective bargaining (p. 318)
skilled worker (p. 307)
picketing (p. 320)

Even though teenagers usually do unskilled work when they are young, most of them eventually become a (8), (9), or (10), particularly if they obtain higher education. In most circumstances, no one can be paid less than the wage rate specified by the (11). Sometimes wages are determined by a (12) through its (13) activities. If union-management negotiations fail, a (14) may ensue and the workers may start (15) the work site. Management may respond by putting a (16) into effect.

Recalling Facts and Ideas

Section 1

1. What is the category of the type of worker who has a higher-education degree and additional training?
2. What is the difference between blue-collar and white-collar workers?
3. What are some factors that determine how much a person is paid for his or her work?

Section 2

4. What are the major kinds of labor unions?
5. In 1955 what two union federations merged?
6. How do right-to-work laws affect workers who do not belong to unions?

Section 3

7. Wages are one of the most important major issues in collective bargaining negotiations. What are other important issues?
8. If management and labor have reached a bargaining deadlock, they may try to engage in mediation. If mediation fails, what is the possible next "friendly" step?
9. What do union workers do when they go on strike?
10. What has been the most recent trend in the importance of labor unions in America?

picket line outside the employer's establishment.
10. Labor unions have been declining in importance.

Critical Thinking

Section 1

Answers will vary, but students should mention that generally employers compete with other

companies for better-educated workers by offering higher wages and better fringe benefits.

Section 2

Answers will vary, but may include improving wages and working conditions, formation of the Congress of Industrial Organizations, encouragement of African Americans and women to join industrial unions, merger of the AFL and

Critical Thinking

Section 1
Determining Cause and Effect Explain why workers with more education and training generally get paid higher wages.

Section 2
Making Generalizations From the time line in Figure 13.8, write five major achievements of labor unions between 1900 and 1962.

Section 3
Predicting Consequences What are the factors that may cause a decline in union membership in the future?

Applying Economic Concepts

Economic Costs and Benefits There are costs and benefits of every activity. Strikes are no exception. Workers clearly believe that the benefits exceed the costs or they would not go on strike. Make a list of the benefits to workers of going on strike. Next to it make a list of the costs of going on strike.

Chapter Projects

1. **Individual Project** Strikes were not always a part of the American labor landscape. Some of the first ones were organized in Lowell, Massachusetts, by female textile workers. Research and write a short report on the conditions that led to the Lowell Female Labor Reform Association.
2. **Cooperative Learning Project** This project uses information from the Career Handbook on pages 560–567 in the reference section of this text. Work in groups based on the following categories: unskilled workers, semi-skilled workers, skilled workers, and professional workers.

Each member of every group should select a particular job from one of the Career Handbook tables. Group members should compile basic information from the tables about salaries, training, job outlook, and working conditions. Each person should research additional information about the job he or she has selected. Then discuss the relationship between education or training and wages. Also discuss other considerations besides wages that may be important in selecting a job or a career.

Reviewing Skills

Determining Averages: Mean and Median

1. **Determining the Mean** Below are data for the number of unemployed persons over a five-year period. Compute the mean number of unemployed.

1988	6,701,000	1991	8,426,000
1989	6,528,000	1992	9,384,000
1990	6,874,000		

2. **Computing the Median** Compute the median unemployment rate for the seven years listed below.

1986	6.9	1990	5.4
1987	6.1	1991	6.6
1988	5.4	1992	7.3
1989	5.2		

Writing About Economics

Persuasive Writing Write a paragraph on the long-term benefits of staying in school and then going on to college or technical school. Indicate the benefits other than higher salaries. Use what you learned about the different types of jobs that you wrote about in Your Economics Journal to strengthen your argument.

325

CIO, and passage of pro-labor legislation such as the Norris-LaGuardia Act and the National Labor Relations Act.

Section 3
Answers will vary, but students should mention the loss of blue-collar jobs; general shift to service industry jobs; improved wages and working conditions; costs of attempting to organize white-collar workers; resistance among today's workers toward being organized; and antiunion bias among the general public.

Applying Economic Concepts

Benefits: greater power of a group to obtain better wages and working conditions; ability to inflict economic losses on management through work stoppage and boycotts; and use of pickets to generate public sympathy for the strike. Costs: loss of wages and other benefits and possible loss of jobs if the strike is not settled; negative publicity from the strike; action from management in the form of lockouts, injunctions, or replacing workers with strikebreakers; and length of time a strike might take.

❓ BONUS QUESTION

The following bonus question may be written on the chalkboard when students take the chapter test.
Q: What is the major difference between mediation and arbitration?
A: In mediation, the decision reached is not binding on the two parties. In arbitration, the decision of the arbitrator binds both parties.

Chapter Projects

1. Make sure that students cite their sources in their report.
2. This exercise can offer students a survey of possible career opportunities or employment position they may not have considered before.

Reviewing Skills

1. 7,582,600
2. 6.1

Writing About Economics

Encourage students to consider these benefits: doing work that interests them, and being able to choose where to live and work.

Measuring Productivity

From the classroom of Jamie G. Daily, Holmes High School, San Antonio, Texas

A Word From the Teacher

This activity is one of the more practical and fun methods I have used to teach the concepts of diminishing returns and productivity. The students discover these concepts by actually becoming actively involved. The activity takes a little over one class period, but I feel it is worth the time involved.

Jamie Daily

Focus

Increases in productivity lower the time and money costs for producers of goods, and therefore may result in lower prices or higher profits, or both. Remind students that increased productivity takes place as a result of increased worker motivation or new and innovative technology. Yet, motivating factors and new technologies have a limited effect. When the law of diminishing returns lowers the rate at which productivity increases, the cost of the increases may be unacceptable.

The purpose of this lab is to determine how the law of diminishing returns affects productivity.

Teach

Measuring Productivity can be extended over several weeks or condensed by holding all production ses-

In Unit 4 you read about financing and producing goods. In this experiment, you will learn about productivity and the law of diminishing returns. (You may want to reread the material on pages 271–275 of the text.)

Productivity is the ability to produce better goods and services faster. In part, it is a measure of the amount of output per worker. An assembly line improves worker productivity up to the point where the law of diminishing returns sets in. In this lab, you will develop an assembly-line process and add workers to the team to determine at what point the law of diminishing returns affects productivity.

Tools

1. Supply of simple pictures to be colored
2. 6-8 boxes of eight crayons
3. Several prototypes of finished product (picture colored with four different colors)
4. A pocket calculator

Procedures

Step A Organize into production teams, with seven students per team. One student on each team will serve as the quality control manager for the team, and the others will be production workers. Arrange desks so that each team is an assembly line. Begin with three production workers on Day

1, expanding as instructed later. Each team needs a box of crayons, a supply of uncolored pictures, and a prototype. Each group must color as many pictures to match the prototype as possible within four minutes. Pictures that do not meet quality standards should be discarded. Record these results for Day 1 on a chart like the following:

Example

Group Name	Total Pictures Colored			
	Day 1	Day 2	Day 3	Day 4

Step B From the students on your team who are not yet working, add one member to the assembly line for Day 2. Work for another four minutes. Record the amount of work produced with teams of four students under Day 2 on your chart.

Step C Repeat this process, adding one student to the assembly line each day, coloring and recording the results until you have six members working on the assembly line (Day 4).

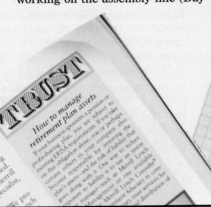

sions in the same week or the same day. Begin the lab by having students complete Step A and prepare the tables in steps A, B, and C. If the lab extends over many weeks, allot time at the end of each week to check students' progress.

When business owners are able to identify the point at which the law of diminishing returns lowers the rate of increased productivity, they may take steps to eliminate costs.

To do this, they may institute managerial changes, eliminate overtime, lay off workers, or set aside their most expensive technologies. The activities in Step B provide a firsthand opportunity to observe changes in productivity as a result of employment and the efforts of individuals. Be sure students added to each team understand that their work will influence the team's productivity.

You may not alter the technology (break the crayons) when the fifth and sixth workers are added.

Step D Prepare a line graph that shows the total number of pictures that were colored each day. Use the graph below as a sample.

Example:

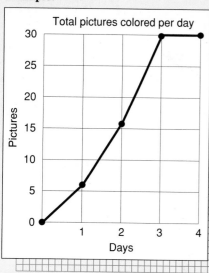

Total pictures colored per day

Then construct a graph that shows productivity per worker during the four days of production. This is accomplished by dividing the total number of pictures colored each day by the total number of assembly line workers. Results should be tabulated on a graph similar to the following "Productivity" graph.

Example:

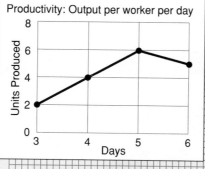

Productivity: Output per worker per day

Lab Report

Step E Use the productivity graphs and your assembly-line experience to answer the questions below.

1. How did your team's productivity compare to that of other teams? What might have accounted for the difference?
2. What were some of the problems in organizing the assembly line?
3. Would a change in technology (more crayons) have helped productivity?

Step F Use the following questions for class discussion

1. Even with additional technology, why would an assembly line eventually reach a point of diminishing returns?
2. Did individual factors, such as personality, influence the team to any extent? How can businesses deal with this type of problem?

327

Assess

Have each student group complete Step D (graphing) and Step E (the report). Have students share their reports and discuss their opinions about the factors influencing productivity. Have the class discuss Step E1.

Close

Discuss Step E2 with students. Encourage them to express their observations about productivity, teamwork, and individuality. After the discussion, have students write a summary of their experiences and findings in their journal.

 DID YOU KNOW

Formulation of the law of diminishing returns with respect to labor as an input in production requires an understanding of maximum output per worker for any given number of workers. Economists evaluate this factor through time and motion studies, a practice advanced by the American engineer, inventor, and efficiency expert Frederick Winslow Taylor in the late 1800s.

Answers to Lab Report
Lab Report E

Student discussions should be based on information in graphs created in Step D. The graphs should show the productivity of each worker and the group as a whole. The session and the identity of workers should appear on the tables.

Unit Goals

After studying this unit, students will be able to:

Explain how to measure economic performance;

Discuss the Federal Reserve system and United States monetary policy;

List methods used to fight unemployment and inflation.

Unit Overview

The five chapters of Unit 5 explain how the nation's economy is managed.

Chapter 14 explains and describes measures of economic performance.

Chapter 15 explains or describes the characteristics of money.

Chapter 16 explains the Federal Reserve.

Chapter 17 explains and describes ways the government spends, collects, and owes money.

Chapter 18 explains how the government fights unemployment and inflation.

Connecting to Past Learning

Discuss how factors and events in the national economy may affect students' communities.

`0:00` OUT OF TIME?

If time does not permit teaching each chapter in this unit, you may use the Chapter Highlights and the Audiocassettes that include a 1-page activity and a 1-page test for each chapter.

328

UNIT 5

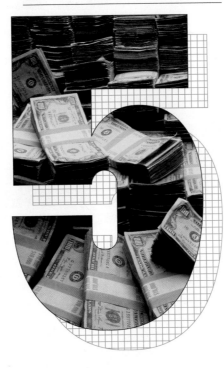

MACROECONOMICS: MANAGING THE NATION'S ECONOMY

Economic Simulation

Stimulating the Economy Ask students to imagine they are part of an economics panel that reports to the President. Recently, the national economy has been in a recession, with unemployment at 7 percent and rising, inflation at 4 percent, investment at an all-time low, and economic growth at 1.9 percent. The President is asking for recommendations to stimulate the economy.

Organize students into task forces to investigate different methods for stimulating economic growth, based on information in the chapters. Have them prepare a written report listing their recommendations.

Beginning the Unit

Refer students to the "Did You Know" questions on page 329. Most students have little idea how events affecting the national economy influence everyone. Discuss with them the implications of each question: What does it mean that "nothing" backs the dollars they hold? Why do people work the equivalent of four months to pay taxes? Why are teenagers more likely to be unemployed than older people? These questions should stimulate their thinking about macroeconomic concepts.

Outcome-Based Project

Writing a Resume and Cover Letter The following unit project is the fifth step in a six-part activity that can be used during the entire economics course. In Unit 5, students learn to prepare resumes and to use job search skills.

Obtain information on preparing cover letters and resumes from a business education teacher or from resume-writing resource books in the local library. Review several resumes of people who have had success in the job search. Have each student write a sample cover letter and a resume for one of the job titles that the class researched in previous units. Students who soon will be entering the job market may write real resumes and letters to potential employers. Have a guest address the class on "The Employment Interview." Students may do mock interviews following this presentation.

? Did You Know

- Nothing "backs" the $1, $5, and other bills that you carry around in your wallet or purse.
- The average American works until about the first week in May to pay for all local, state, and federal taxes.
- Prices rise much less rapidly in the United States than in many countries of the world.
- During national business slowdowns, unemployment among teenagers increases more rapidly than among older people.

In this unit you will be looking at the interrelationships of all sectors of the economy—consumers, businesses, and government. This overall picture is the study of macroeconomics, or the economy as a whole.

 ## Did You Know

Although most people are familiar with $1 and $5 bills, few people can tell you who is pictured on them. In fact, the $1 has George Washington; the $5, Abraham Lincoln; the $10, Alexander Hamilton; the $20, Andrew Jackson; the $50, Ulysses S. Grant; and the $100, Benjamin Franklin. All United States currency bears the nation's official motto, *In God We Trust.*

CHAPTER 14 *MEASURING THE ECONOMY'S PERFORMANCE*

CHAPTER ORGANIZER

Daily Objectives	Special Features	Classroom Resources
Section 1 National Income Accounting • **List** the four categories of GDP in terms of types of goods produced. • **Compare** the three measurements of income—national, personal, and disposable.	**Learning Economic Skills:** Using Index Numbers: Price Indexes, p. 337	Reproducible Lesson Plan 14.1 *NBR* Video 19 and Video Still 2 Focus Activity Transparency 53 Economic Concepts Transparency 10 Guided Reading Activity 14.1 Consumer Application Activity 14 Section Quiz 14.1
Section 2 Correcting Statistics for Inflation • **Describe** the relationship between inflation and the purchasing power of money. • **Make the distinction** between two measures of inflation: the consumer price index (CPI) and the producer price index (PPI).		Reproducible Lesson Plan 14.2 Focus Activity Transparency 54 Focus Activity Sheet 54 Economic Concepts Transparency 13 Guided Reading Activity 14.2 Section Quiz 14.2
Section 3 Aggregate Supply and Demand • **List** two reasons why, when the price level goes down, the aggregate quantity demanded goes up. • **Explain** why, when the price level goes up and wages do not, producers want to supply more to the marketplace and aggregate quantity supplied increases. • **Explain** how the equilibrium price level reflects aggregate demand and aggregate supply.	**Personal Perspective:** John Maynard Keynes on Equilibrium Employment, p. 346	Reproducible Lesson Plan 14.3 Focus Activity Transparency 55 Focus Activity Sheet 55 Economic Concepts Transparencies 14 and 15 Guided Reading Activity 14.3 Section Quiz 14.3 Spanish Section Quiz 14.3 Testmaker
Section 4 Business Fluctuations • **List** the phases of a typical business cycle. • **Describe** three downturns in the United States economy since the 1920s.		Reproducible Lesson Plan 14.4 Focus Activity Transparency 56 Guided Reading Activity 14.4 Section Quiz 14.4
Section 5 Causes and Indicators of Business Fluctuations • **List** the potential causes of business fluctuations. • **List** the broad categories of economic indicators that predict and reflect business fluctuations.	**News Clip:** "McDonald's: 95 Billion Burgers," *Kiplinger's Personal Finance Magazine*, p. 356	Reproducible Lesson Plan 14.5 Focus Activity Transparency 57 Guided Reading Activity 14.5 Free Enterprise Activity 14 Section Quiz 14.5 Testmaker Enrichment Activity 14

 **OUT OF TIME?** If time does not permit teaching this chapter, you may use the Chapter 14 Highlights and the Audiocassettes that include a 1-page activity and a 1-page test.

Chapter 14 Review and Evaluation

Special Features

Chapter 14 Highlights, p. 357
Chapter 14 Review, pp. 358–359

Classroom Resources

- Chapter 14 Test Forms A and B
- Economics Vocabulary Activity 14
- Spanish Economics Vocabulary Activity 14

- Audiocassette 14
- Spanish Audiocassette 14
- Reteaching Activity 14
- Spanish Reteaching Activity 14

Key to Ability Levels

Teaching strategies have been coded for varying learning styles and abilities.

L1 Level 1 activities are **basic** activities that should be within the ability range of all students.

L2 Level 2 activities are **average** activities designed for the ability range of average to above-average students.

L3 Level 3 activities are **challenging** activities designed for the ability range of above-average students.

LEP activities should be within the ability range of **Limited English Proficiency** students.

Performance Assessment

The following chapter project may be assigned at the beginning of the chapter and used for performance assessment. See page T12 for additional Performance Assessment information.

Profiling the Economy Organize the class into five groups and assign each a chapter section (the size of groups may need to be adjusted according to the amount of information in each section). Have the groups develop a current profile of the United States economy, using the most recent economic indicators, indexes, aggregate demand and supply curves, and current stage in the business cycle related to their section.

Have each group compile this information in graphs and charts. Once the data are gathered, ask the groups to work together to summarize the current state of the economy.

Additional Resources

Readings for the Student

Economic Indicators. Periodical providing latest economic statistics, published by the U.S. Department of Commerce, Washington, D.C.

Horton, Carrell P., and Smith, Jessie C., eds. *Statistical Record of Black America.* New York: Gale Research, Inc., 1990.

Statistical Abstract of the United States, 1994. Washington, D.C.: U.S. Department of Commerce, 1994. Updated yearly.

Statistical Yearbook, 1990/91, 38th ed. New York: United Nations, 1993.

Readings for the Teacher

Rukyser, Louis. *Rukyser's Business Almanac.* New York: Simon and Schuster, 1992.

Wattenberg, Ben J. *The First Universal Nation: Leading Indicators and Ideas About the Surge of America in the 1990s.* New York: Macmillan, 1991.

Multimedia Materials

Ups and Downs. Simulation game that introduces students to business fluctuations. Active Learning Consultants, 1992.

What Is a Recession? An Introduction to Economics. VHS videocassette. 19 min. American School Publishers, 1991.

Chapter Overview

Business people, economists, and politicians often need to know how the economy is performing. Chapter 14 explains or describes: key statistics, indicators, indexes, and models used to measure the economy's performance; national income and product accounting; personal and disposable income; how to correct for the effects of inflation; consumer and producer price indexes; aggregate supply and demand; equilibrium price levels; business fluctuations; and the major causes and economic indicators of these cycles.

VIDEODISC

Nightly Business Report
Economics in Action
Use "Measuring the Economy's Performance" on Disc 2, Side A, Video 19.

Search 6928, Play to 15292

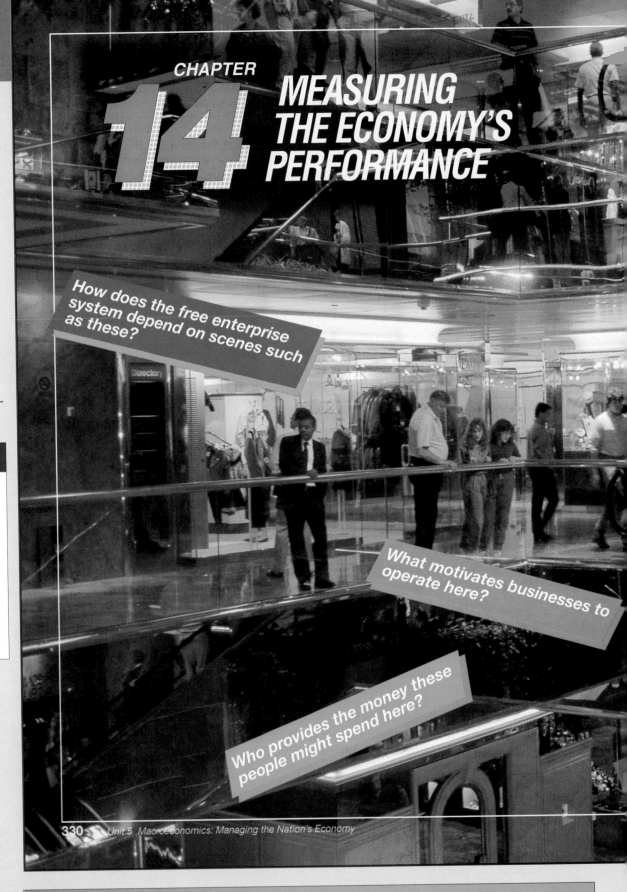

CHAPTER
14 MEASURING THE ECONOMY'S PERFORMANCE

How does the free enterprise system depend on scenes such as these?

What motivates businesses to operate here?

Who provides the money these people might spend here?

Answering Economic Questions

The questions in the above illustration are designed to lead into the main concepts in Chapter 14.

Students may have encountered the phrases "leading economic indicators," "consumer price index," "gross domestic product," and "business cycle" in broadcast news or in the printed media. They probably do not connect such phrases to the economic activity they see around them or to their own individual economic transactions. The questions should stimulate their interest in measures of general economic activity.

What are these people doing?

What choices do these people have as they shop?

Your Economics Journal

For one week, keep track of references in the media to the following: unemployment, consumer spending, manufacturing trends, recession, and prices. After each entry, indicate whether the information was, in your view, positive or negative to the overall economy.

331

Connecting to Past Learning

In Chapter 8, students learned about individual demand and supply curves. Ask them to imagine that they are economic forecasters who must determine the total demand and supply in the economy for a given month. Direct them to the indexes appearing in the Statistical Abstracts of the United States for this information and to think about how they might show the data for these measures.

Applying Economics

Ask students to imagine that a company wishes to sell T-shirts to other nations. The company needs to select countries whose citizens have adequate disposable income to purchase the shirts. Ask students to investigate international economic statistics and recommend four or five suitable countries for overseas sales.

EXTRA CREDIT PROJECT

Interested students may write a short report on how the government calculates unemployment statistics. Ask that reports define unemployment, classify who is and who is not unemployed, and discuss whether official statistics show the true picture of unemployment.

Economic Portfolio

Have students read carefully the references they collected in **Your Economics Journal**. Ask them to write one to two pages summarizing the overall view of economic health and activity presented in the media articles. Have them state whether they themselves are optimistic or pessimistic about the economy and why.

PERFORMANCE ASSESSMENT

Refer to page 330B for "Profiling the Economy," a Performance Assessment Activity for this chapter.

Focus

Overview

See the student page for section objectives.

Section 1 explains or describes how to calculate gross and net domestic product, national income, and personal and disposable personal income, and how these measures are used to evaluate the economy.

Bellringer

Before presenting the lesson, display Focus Activity Transparency 53 on the overhead projector or copy the material on the chalkboard. Assign the accompanying Focus Activity Sheet.

Motivational Activity

Ask students how they would determine a family's total net worth and total income, including all possessions, investments, and salaries or other earned income.

Discuss students' answers and explain that the government also needs to know national income and product figures.

Preteaching Vocabulary

Have students read the Glossary definition of each vocabulary term and then close their books. Call out each term and ask volunteers to try to define the word.

SECTION **1** # National Income Accounting

SECTION 1 FOCUS

Terms to Know national income accounting, gross domestic product (GDP), net exports, depreciation, net domestic product (NDP), national income (NI), personal income (PI), transfer payments, disposable personal income (DI)

Objectives *After reading this section, you should be able to:*

1. List the four categories of GDP in terms of types of goods produced.
2. Compare the three measurements of income—national, personal, and disposable.

A Healthy GDP Equals a Healthy Economy

People can measure how successful they are economically by the size of their incomes and by their overall standard of living, including how much their spendable income will buy. Figure 14.1 shows one example.

The well-being of the overall economy is measured in a similar way. Economists constantly measure and record such factors as the amount of goods and services produced yearly by the nation and the amount of income individuals have to spend.

The measurement of the national economy's performance is called **national income accounting.** This area of economics deals with the overall economy's income and output. It also measures the interaction of consumers, businesses, and governments. The major measurements used for the nation's income and production are gross domestic product, net domestic product, national income, personal income, and disposable personal income. Figure 14.2 shows gross domestic product and its components in descending order of value.

Measuring Gross Domestic Product

The broadest measure of the economy's health is **gross domestic product (GDP).** This is the total dollar value of all *final* goods and services produced in the nation during a single

**Figure 14.1 ▶
Vacations**
People who can afford luxuries such as cruises have a relatively high standard of living.

Classroom Resources for Section 1

- Reproducible Lesson Plan 14.1
- *NBR* Video 19 and Video Still 2
- Focus Activity Transparency 53
- Focus Activity Sheet 53
- Economic Concepts Transparency 10
- Guided Reading Activity 14.1
- Cooperative Learning Activity 14

- Primary and Secondary Source Readings 14
- Consumer Application Activity 14
- Section Quiz 14.1
- Spanish Section Quiz 14.1
- Testmaker
- Reinforcing Skills 14

GDP and Its Components in a Recent Year

Billions of Dollars

Minus: Depreciation

Minus: Indirect Business Tax

Minus: Corporate Taxes, Reinvested Profits, Employer Social Security Contributions

Minus: Personal Taxes

Equals: NDP

Equals: NI

Equals: PI

Equals: DI

Plus: Government and Business Transfer Payments

GDP

6,000 — 5,000 — 4,000 — 3,000 — 2,000 — 0

Gross Domestic Product | Net Domestic Product | National Income | Personal Income | Disposable Personal Income

Source: *Statistical Abstract of the United States, 1992*

year. This figure tells how much American workers have produced in that year that is available for people to purchase. GDP is one way to measure the nation's material standard of living. It also provides a way of comparing what has been produced in one year with what was produced in another year.

Note the word *value* in the definition. Simply adding up the *quantities* of millions of different items produced, such as shoes and cars, would not mean much. How can we measure the strength of the economy, for example, if we know that 3 billion safety pins and 2 space shuttles were produced? What needs to be totaled is the value of the items, using some common measure. Economists use the dollar as this common measure of value. As a result, GDP is always expressed in dollar terms. For example, in 1993, GDP totalled about $6.5 trillion.

The word *final* is also important. To measure the economy's performance accurately, economists add up only the value of final goods and services to avoid *double counting*. To add the price of memory chips to the price of a computer is not realistic. The final price to the buyer already includes the price of the memory chips.

Figure 14.2 ▲ GDP and Its Components
What is the difference in dollars between gross domestic product and disposable personal income?

Teach

Guided Practice

L2 Analyzing Have students write a brief paragraph explaining why GDP and NDP are regarded as measures of economic health.

Visual Instruction

Answer to Figure 14.2 caption question: (*Approximately $1,000 billion, or $1 trillion*).

 VIDEODISC

Nightly Business Report
Economics in Action
Use Video Still 2, "GDP," on Disc 2, Side A, Video 19.

Search Frame 12797

 GLOBAL ECONOMICS

The United Nations uses economic statistics to determine a nation's standard of living. They also show any narrowing or widening of the gap in gross domestic product and personal income between rich and poor nations. Statistics for recent years show the gap is widening.

Meeting Special Needs

Abstract Reasoning Difficulties Some students have difficulty with abstract information. They may grasp more concrete concepts such as individual income but be confused by the use of income statistics.

Go through the calculation of GDP, NDP, NI, PI, and DI statistics with them. Also,

help them understand the effect of community or family economic activity on each individual. Help them see how the total economic activity of the country affects each community, business, and family. Students need to understand that these statistics are relevant to their own lives.

L3 Comparing and Contrasting Have students create a line graph showing the relationship between NDP and DI statistics for the past 20 years. Students can write a brief paragraph or two speculating on the implications for consumer spending when these figures rise and fall.

L2 Decision Making Have students look at current GDP, NDP, PI, and DI statistics with respect to starting a small business of their own choosing and discuss their findings in class.

DID YOU KNOW

Discretionary personal income statistics tell business people how much money consumers have left to spend on items other than food, clothing, shelter, and transportation. Normally, the more disposable income (DI) that consumers have, the more products and services they will purchase. When DI statistics fall, discretionary income falls faster. Companies are likely to reduce both the variety and volume of their products and services, although they may instead cut prices and increase advertising.

Also, only new goods are counted in GDP. The sale of a used car or a secondhand refrigerator is not counted as part of GDP. Such a sale is not due to the production of the nation, but only transfers a product from one person to another. If a new battery is put in an old car, however, that new battery is counted as part of GDP.

GDP Categories In computing GDP, economists measure economic activity in four areas. **Figure 14.3** shows these areas and the percentage of economic activity each represents.

The statistics used in computing GDP are accurate only to a point. Statistics about easily quantifiable things, such as government purchases, are reliable. Some statistics, however, can only be estimated and, therefore, are less reliable. For example, some workers are given food, fuel, or housing in place of or as supplements or additions to wages. An apartment building superintendent, for example, sometimes gets his or her apartment at reduced rent. GDP can include only an estimate of the value of such goods and services. Moreover, GDP omits certain areas of economic activity as **Figure 14.4** shows.

Another Way of Estimating GDP What you have just read is the expenditure approach to measuring GDP. In this method, gross domestic product is measured by what is spent on consumer goods, government goods, business goods, and net exports. Another way to measure GDP is to measure income earned. When gross domestic product is measured this way, four categories of income are measured. **Figure 14.5** shows the income approach.

Net Domestic Product The loss of value because of wear and tear to consumer durables, such as cars, is called **depreciation.** The same concept

Figure 14.3
Economic Activity as Percentage of GDP

In calculating GDP, economists include:

1. consumer goods—goods and services bought by consumers for their direct use;
2. business, or producer, goods—business purchases of tools, machines, buildings, and so on, used to produce other goods; this figure also includes money spent on business inventories;
3. government goods—the goods and services, ranging from paper clips to jet planes, that are bought by federal, state, and local governments;
4. **net exports**—the difference between what the nation sells to other countries (exports) and what it buys from other countries (imports). This figure may be a plus or minus depending on whether the nation sells or buys more. ▶

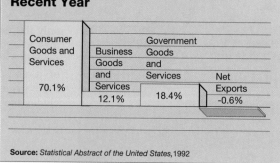

Four Areas of Economic Activity as Percentage of GDP in a Recent Year

Consumer Goods and Services	Business Goods and Services	Government Goods and Services	Net Exports
70.1%	12.1%	18.4%	-0.6%

Source: *Statistical Abstract of the United States,* 1992

Cooperative Learning

The federal government and private groups have compiled statistics on the economic status of some minority groups. Assign a task force from the class to investigate GDP, NDP, NI, PI, and DI statistics for Hispanics and African Americans and to compare them with statistics for the general population. Have them write a brief report on their findings and present it to the class.

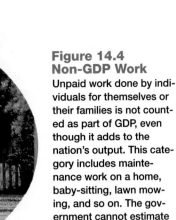

Figure 14.4
Non-GDP Work
Unpaid work done by individuals for themselves or their families is not counted as part of GDP, even though it adds to the nation's output. This category includes maintenance work on a home, baby-sitting, lawn mowing, and so on. The government cannot estimate the value of this work accurately. ◀

Independent Practice
L3 Analyzing Data Have students locate data and prepare a line graph of the United States gross domestic product (GDP) and the net domestic product (NDP) for a recent 10-year period. Ask them to provide a caption indicating which line they think more accurately reflects actual productivity of the economy.

📁 Have students complete Guided Reading Activity 14.1 in the TCR. LEP

applies to producer goods—machines and equipment. GDP disregards this factor. It does not take into account that some output is used merely to keep machines and equipment in working order and to replace them when they wear out.

Net domestic product (NDP) accounts for this loss of value. It measures GDP minus the total loss in value of producer goods through depreciation. In recent years, the amount used by economists to account for depreciation has been a little more than 10 percent of GDP. In 1993, for example, GDP was about $6.5 trillion. Subtracting about $650 billion for depreciation, the NDP was about $5.8 trillion. Because NDP accounts for depreciation, it can be a better measure than GDP of the economy's actual productivity.

Measurements of Income

Measuring income is important because it determines how much money is available to be spent by businesses and individuals.

National Income The total income earned by everyone in the economy is called **national income (NI).** NI includes those who use their own labor to earn an income as well as those who make income through the

DID YOU KNOW

The Supreme Court of the United States exerts an influence on our economy by making decisions related to antitrust legislation, government regulation of business, environmental protection, and relations between labor and management.

Measuring GDP by Income Categories

| Wages | + | Interest | + | Rents | + | Profits | = | GDP |

Wages, including all forms of labor income

Interest received by households

Rent that individuals earn for use of their farms, houses, and stores

Profits that corporations, partnerships, and proprietorships earn

Figure 14.5
Measuring GDP by Income
The income approach to GDP gives about the same figure as the expenditure approach. Using this approach:
Wages + Interest + Rents + Profits = GDP ◀

Chapter 14 Measuring the Economy's Performance **335**

 Free Enterprise Activity

Have students brainstorm developing a for-profit recycling service, perhaps to benefit the school. Possibilities might include collecting recyclable materials for transport to recycling centers and/or using materials to create useful, salable products. Ask students to create an organizational plan. When the proposal is developed, discuss it in class. Encourage those who can to start and participate in the business.

Assess

Meeting Lesson Objectives

Assign Section 1 Review as homework or an in-class activity. Each question in the Review addresses the corresponding numbered objective in the Section Focus.

Evaluate

Assign the Section 1 Quiz in the TCR or use the Testmaker to develop a customized quiz.

Reteach

Organize students into small groups and have them review what each measure discussed in this section represents. At the end, have them explain the roles of taxes, depreciation, and investment in calculating these measures.

Enrich

Ask students to keep track of references to GDP, NDI, PI, and DI in the media. Have them note whether the references were positive or negative and how they were used. Discuss students' observations in class.

Close

Discuss with students the value of measurements and the importance of knowing how they are derived.

---

ownership of the other factors of production. National income is equal to NDP minus indirect business taxes, including items such as sales and property taxes, and license fees.

As GDP is divided into four areas of economic activity, similarly, NI is divided into five types of income. Figure 14.6 shows all of these divisions. NI is equal to the sum of all income resulting from these five different areas of the economy.

Personal Income The total income individuals receive before personal taxes are paid is called **personal income (PI)**. PI can be derived from NI through a two-step process. First, corporate income taxes, profits that businesses put back into their businesses to expand, and Social Security contributions employers make are subtracted from NI. These are subtracted because they represent income that is not available for individuals to spend.

Then, transfer payments are added to NI. **Transfer payments** are welfare payments and other supplementary payments, such as unemployment compensation, Social Security, and Medicaid, that a state or the federal government makes to individuals. These transfer payments add to an individual's income even though they are not in exchange for any current productive activity.

Disposable Personal Income The income that people have left after taxes, including Social Security contributions, is called **disposable personal income (DI)**. It is the income available to an individual for the immediate purchase of goods and services and for savings. DI equals PI minus personal taxes. DI is an important indicator of the economy's health because it measures the actual amount of money income people have available to spend.

Figure 14.6 National Income
National Income (NI) is the total of income from all sources shown here. Wages and salaries, however, make up three-fourths of NI.

Elements of National Income

Wages and salaries paid to employees	Income of self-employed individuals, including farmers and owners of sole proprietorships and partnerships	Rental incomes of property owners	Corporate profits	Interest on savings and investments individuals receive

SECTION 1 REVIEW

Understanding Vocabulary

Define national income accounting, gross domestic product (GDP), net exports, depreciation, net domestic product (NDP), national income (NI), personal income (PI), transfer payments, disposable personal income (DI).

Reviewing Objectives

1. What four categories of economic activity are used to measure GDP?
2. What must be subtracted from national income to determine personal income? What must be added?

Section 1 Review Answers

Understanding Vocabulary

national income accounting (p. 332), **gross domestic product (GDP)** (p. 332), **net exports** (p. 334), **depreciation** (p. 334), **net domestic product (NDP)** (p. 335), **national income (NI)** (p. 335), **personal income (PI)** (p. 336), **transfer payments** (p. 336), **disposable personal income (DI)** (p. 336)

Reviewing Objectives

1. consumer, producer, and government goods and services, purchased and net exports.
2. subtract: corporate income taxes, business income reinvested for expansion, social security contributions; add: transfer payments.

Using Index Numbers: Price Indexes

Most statistics on prices are expressed in terms of price indexes. Do you know what the concept of a price index is and how to use it?

Measuring Inflation

If last year a light bulb cost 50¢ and this year it costs 75¢, there has been a 50 percent price increase. The price is 1.5 times as high. An index number of this price rise is simply 1.5 multiplied by 100; that is, the index number would be 150.

To compare prices, you must decide the base year. A **base year** is the year to which all other years' prices will be compared.

Computing a Price Index

When we deal with many goods, we must pick a representative sample, called the market basket. We compare the cost of the market basket of goods over time. When we do this, we obtain a price index, which is defined as the cost of a market basket of goods today expressed as a percentage of the cost of the market basket of goods in some base year. In the base year, the price index will always be 100.

Calculating a Price Index

Figure A shows two goods in our market basket—corn and computers. The *quantities* in the basket remain the same between the base year, 1983, and the year 1996. Only the price changes.

Practicing the Skill

In the example in Figure A, assume that the price of computers in 1996 was $400. Recompute the price index.

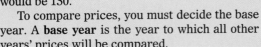

Figure A

Market Basket Quantity

Corn	100 bushels
Computers	2

1983 Unit Price

Corn	$4
Computers	$500

1983 Market Basket Cost

Corn	$400
Computers	$1,000
Total	$1,400

1996 Unit Price

Corn	$8
Computers	$450

1996 Market Basket Cost

Corn	$800
Computers	$900
Total	$1,700

$$\text{Index} = \frac{1996 \text{ cost}}{1983 \text{ cost}} \times 100$$

$$\frac{\$1,700}{\$1,400} \times 100 = \$121.43$$

TEACHING Economic Skills

Teach

Computing price indexes can be confusing to many students. The key concepts are
- A base year for purposes of comparison, set at 100.
- A price index that represents a sample of goods for a particular year.
- A change in the price index for a previous or following year.

With these key ideas in mind, it will be easier for students to learn to calculate price indexes for any year.

 *Additional Practice*

Have students complete Reinforcing Skills 14 in the TCR.

Answers to Practicing the Skill

$1600/$1400 = 1.143 × 100 = 114.30

Focus

Overview

See the student page for section objectives.

Section 2 explains or describes the effect of inflation on purchasing power, and how consumer and producer price indexes and real GDP are used to measure changes in average prices.

Bellringer

Before presenting the lesson, display Focus Activity Transparency 54 on the overhead projector or copy the material on the chalkboard. Assign the accompanying Focus Activity Sheet.

Motivational Activity

Ask students to imagine that each year the cost of CDs rises by $1.00 while their wage/allowance goes up by 50 cents. After two years, CDs cost $2 more, but their earnings have increased only $1. Ask students what is happening to their purchasing power.

Preteaching Vocabulary

Have students create a matrix by writing vocabulary items and definitions in separate columns and color coding the information to help them remember the terms.

SECTION 2 FOCUS

Terms to Know inflation, purchasing power, deflation, consumer price index (CPI), base year, producer price index (PPI), implicit GDP price deflator, real GDP

Objectives *After reading this section, you should be able to:*
1. Describe the relationship between inflation and the purchasing power of money.
2. Make the distinction between two measures of inflation: the consumer price index (CPI) and the producer price index (PPI).

When Is a Dollar Not Worth a Dollar?

Rising or falling prices affect the dollar value of GDP. A prolonged rise in the general price level of goods and services is called **inflation.** For example, last year a hamburger may have cost $2.50. This year it may cost $2.75. The physical output—the hamburger—has not changed, only its money value.

Inflation and the Purchasing Power of Money

American–born author Gertrude Stein once said that a rose is a rose is a rose. A dollar, however, is not always a dollar. As Figure 14.7 shows, the value of a dollar does not stay constant when there is inflation (or deflation). The value of money is usually talked about in terms of its **purchasing power.** A dollar's purchasing power is the real goods and services that it can

**Figure 14.7
The Value of Money**
As economic conditions change, the purchasing power of money changes. ▼

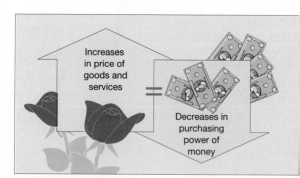

Increases in price of goods and services

Decreases in purchasing power of money

Classroom Resources for Section 2

- Reproducible Lesson Plan 14.2
- Focus Activity Transparency 54
- Focus Activity Sheet 54
- Economic Concepts Transparency 13
- Guided Reading Activity 14.2
- Section Quiz 14.2
- Spanish Section Quiz 14.2
- Testmaker

Consumer Price Index of Selected Categories

	1991	1992	1993
Food 	136.8	138.3	141.1
Clothing	128.7	130.7	131.9
Housing	133.6	135.0	141.5
Medical	177.0	190.1	201.1

1993 = June index
Source: Bureau of Labor Statistics

**Figure 14.8
Selected Consumer
Prices**
Price indexes allow you to compare price levels from year to year.
◄

Guided Practice

L2 Analyzing Refer students to the discussion of PPIs and the implicit GDP price deflator. Discuss with them why it is important to know the real GDP.

Visual Instruction

Refer students to Figures 14.8, 14.9 and 14.10. Show students how the CPI is used to calculate inflation. Discuss with them how increases in CPI means that people may have more money, but it may buy less. Discuss how lower inflation maintains the value of money and can encourage consumer spending answer to Figure 14.9 question: (*1989 and 1990*).

🌐 GLOBAL ECONOMICS

Inflation can have devastating effects on world economic conditions. In the 1920s, for example, Germany suffered *hyperinflation* in which money was devalued so rapidly that it took nearly 19 billion marks to buy a loaf of bread. The economic chaos that resulted helped Adolf Hitler rise to power in the 1930s. Hyperinflation requires stringent government measures to control.

---

buy. If your money income stays the same, but the price of one good that you are buying goes up, your effective purchasing power falls. Therefore, another way of defining inflation is the decline in the purchasing power of money. The faster the rate of inflation, the greater the drop in the purchasing power of money.

The higher GDP figures that result from inflation do not represent any increase in output. To get a true measure of the nation's output in a given year, inflation must be taken into account. **Deflation**, a prolonged decline in the general price level, also affects the dollar value of GDP, but deflation rarely happens.

Measures of Inflation

If all prices rose at the same rate, only one measure of inflation would be needed. Prices in different sectors of the economy, however, rise at different rates. As a result, the government uses several measures of inflation. The three most commonly used are the consumer price index, the producer price index, and the implicit GDP price deflator.

Consumer Price Index (CPI) The government measures the change in price over time of a specific group of goods and services the average household uses. This measurement is the **consumer price index (CPI)**. See Figure 14.8. The group of items, called a market basket, includes about 400 goods and services in the areas of food, housing, transportation, clothing, entertainment, medical care, and personal care. The CPI is the price index that you are probably most familiar with from the news media. Figure 14.9 shows the CPI for several years.

The federal Bureau of Labor Statistics compiles the CPI monthly. In compiling the CPI, the base year is set at the average prices for 1982 to 1984

1985	107.6
1986	109.6
1987	113.6
1988	118.3
1989	124.0
1990	130.7
1991	136.2
1992	140.3
1993*	145.0

*June
Source: Bureau of Labor Statistics

**Figure 14.9
Consumer Price
Index**
When the CPI rises, there is inflation. During which two years shown was inflation the greatest?
◄

Chapter 14 Measuring the Economy's Performance **339**

◆ ◐ Meeting Special Needs

Students With Poor Math Skills Students with poor math ability often have difficulty understanding how inflation affects the purchasing power of money. If wages keep rising, they may reason, then everyone should have more money.

Ask students to imagine they have a rubber dollar that shrinks (buys less) as inflation rises, and expands (buys more) when inflation falls. Tell them that if the dollar shrinks to half its original size (buys half of what it did before), then it will take two shrunken dollars to buy the same amount that one did before.

Independent Practice

L3 Comparing and Contrasting Have students compare the prices of a few market basket items from 40 or 50 years ago with current prices. Then have them compare personal income data for the same periods and determine whether purchasing power today has increased or decreased. Ask students to make a brief report on their findings to the class.

L2 Journalism Have students investigate changes in the various PPI indexes reported in the news media over the past five years. Have them categorize the indexes as those that rose or fell with the overall CPI and those that rose and fell in the opposite direction of the CPI. Have students track these trends on a line chart and explain what the trends indicate about the economy.

Have students complete Guided Reading Activity 14.2 in the TCR. **LEP**

Figure 14.10 ▶ Calculating Inflation
At the end of 1991, the CPI was 136.2. At the end of 1992, it was 140.3, which is a difference of 4.1 (140.3 – 136.2 = 4.1). Now if we use 1991 as the base year, we can find out by what percentage consumer prices on average rose from 1991 to 1992. We do this by dividing 4.1 by 136.2, which gives us 0.0301 (4.1 ÷ 136.2 = 3.01 percent when we multiply by 100 to give the result as a percent).

and is given a value of 100. A **base year** is a year used as a point of comparison for other years in a series of statistics. CPI numbers for later years indicate the percentage that the market basket price has risen since the base year. For example, the 1993 CPI of 145 means the cost of living has risen 45 percent since the period 1982 to 1984 (145 – 100 = 45). The CPI also can be used to calculate inflation from year to year as shown in Figure 14.10.

Producer Price Index Another important measure of inflation the Bureau of Labor Statistics reports monthly is the **producer price index (PPI).** (It used to be called the wholesale price index.) Actually, a number of producer price indexes exist, including one for finished consumer goods such as processed foods; anoth-

er for intermediate materials, supplies, and components; and yet another for crude materials for further processing. Most of the producer prices included are in mining, manufacturing, and agriculture. The PPIs can be considered general-purpose indexes for non-retail markets.

Although in the long run the various PPIs and the CPI generally show the same rate of inflation, that does not work out in the short run. The PPIs usually increase before the CPI because it takes longer for producer price increases to show up in the prices that consumers actually pay for final products. Often, changes in the PPIs are watched as a hint that inflation is going to increase or decrease.

Implicit GDP Price Deflator Government economists issue another mea-

Cooperative Learning

Tell the class that they are responsible for the budget of an average family with two teenaged children. Tell them the total family income is $45,000 and total family expenses are $40,000 per year. The inflation rate is an annual 10 percent, but income is rising only

3 percent yearly. To help the family deal with shrinking purchasing power, ask the class to brainstorm ideas and recommendations for cutting expenses. Tell them that businesses and governments must often make the same kinds of decisions.

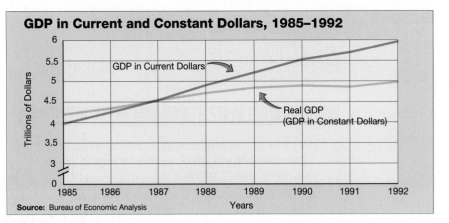

GDP in Current and Constant Dollars, 1985–1992

Source: Bureau of Economic Analysis

**Figure 14.11
GDP in Current
and Constant
Dollars**
Is economic growth in
constant dollars more
or less than growth
measured in current
dollars?

◀

Assess

Meeting Lesson Objectives

Assign Section 2 Review as homework or an in-class activity. Each question in the Review addresses the corresponding numbered objective in the Section Focus.

Evaluate

Assign the Section 2 Quiz in the TCR or use the Testmaker to develop a customized quiz.

Reteach

Have students write a short paragraph explaining the way the government derives CPI, PPIs, and real GDP. Ask them to list ways these indicators are used by the government and others.

Enrich

Ask volunteers to prepare an economic news report concerned with a sharp rise in the CPI and PPI in the past week. Have the students speculate on what this development means to consumers and what it might predict about the economy.

Close

Discuss with students the value of tracking CPI, PPI, and real GDP over time. Ask them to list why these indicators are useful to business, government, and consumers.

---

sure of price changes in GDP called the **implicit GDP price deflator.** This index removes the effects of inflation from GDP so that the overall economy in one year can be compared to another year. When the price deflator is applied to GDP in any year, the new figure is called **real GDP.** See Figure 14.11. The federal government uses 1987 as its base year to measure real GDP. Each year the price deflator is used to adjust GDP in current, or inflated, dollars to GDP in the base year. For example, GDP in current dollars for 1992 was $5,950.7 billion. To find real GDP for 1992, the government divides 1992 GDP by the 1992

price deflator (120.9) and multiplies the result by 100:

$$\$5,950.7 \div 120.9 \times 100 = \$4,922.6$$

Real GDP for 1992 was $4,922.6 billion. This figure may now be compared to 1987 GDP of $4,540.0 billion. This is a more meaningful comparison than comparing 1992 GDP in inflated dollars to 1987 GDP. Figure 14.11 shows both GDP in current dollars and real GDP (in constant dollars) for years 1985 to 1992. Notice that the two curves cross at the year 1987 where GDP in current dollars is equal to real GDP.

SECTION 2 REVIEW

Understanding Vocabulary

Define inflation, purchasing power, deflation, consumer price index (CPI), base year, producer price index (PPI), implicit GDP price deflator, real GDP.

Reviewing Objectives

❶ What is the relationship between the purchasing power of money and the rate of inflation?

❷ What is the difference between what the consumer price index measures and what the producer price index measures?

Chapter 14 Measuring the Economy's Performance **341**

Section 2 Review Answers

Understanding Vocabulary

inflation (p. 338), **purchasing power** (p. 338), **deflation** (p. 339), **consumer price index (CPI)** (p. 339), **base year** (p. 340), **producer price index (PPI)** (p. 340), **implicit GDP price deflator** (p. 340), **real GDP** (p. 341)

Reviewing Objectives

1. The purchasing power of money declines

as inflation increases.

2. CPI: changes in price over time of the market basket purchased by the average household; PPI: changes in price over time of goods and services produced by industries and in the prices of intermediate and crude materials used in further processing

Focus

Overview

See the student page for section objectives.

Section 3 explains or describes an analysis of aggregate demand and supply in the economy, and how to determine the equilibrium price levels.

Bellringer

 Before presenting the lesson, display Focus Activity Transparency 55 on the overhead projector or copy the material on the chalkboard. Assign the accompanying Focus Activity Sheet.

Motivational Activity

Ask students why it might be important to know about changes in total demand and supply in an economy. Write their answers on the chalkboard. Tell them that in Section 3 they will learn how economists determine aggregate supply and demand in relation to price and how they find the equilibrium price level.

Preteaching Vocabulary

Ask students to copy the aggregate demand, aggregate supply, and equilibrium price level diagrams. Have them write the appropriate vocabulary terms on each chart along with the definitions of each term.

SECTION **3** Aggregate Supply and Demand

S E C T I O N   3   F O C U S

Terms to Know aggregates, aggregate demand, aggregate demand curve, aggregate supply, aggregate supply curve

Objectives *After reading this section, you should be able to:*

❶ List two reasons why, when the price level goes down, the aggregate quantity demanded goes up.

❷ Explain why, when the price level goes up and wages do not, producers want to supply more to the marketplace and aggregate quantity supplied increases.

❸ Explain how the equilibrium price level reflects aggregate demand and aggregate supply.

Measuring Supply and Demand in the Whole Economy

The laws of supply and demand can be applied to the economy as a whole, as well as to individual consumer decisions. We would like to know about the demand by all consumers for all goods and services, and the supply by all producers of all goods and services. See Figure 14.12. When we look at the economy as a whole in this way, we are looking at **aggregates**—the summation of all the individual parts in the economy. We call these sums aggregate demand and aggregate supply.

The Aggregate Demand Curve

What is the total, or aggregate, quantity of goods and services in the entire economy that all citizens will demand at any one point in time? To answer this question, we have to relate **aggregate demand** to something

342   *Unit 5 Macroeconomics: Managing the Nation's Economy*

Classroom Resources for Section 3

- Reproducible Lesson Plan 14.3
- Focus Activity Transparency 55
- Focus Activity Sheet 55
- Economic Concepts Transparencies 14 and 15

- Guided Reading Activity 14.3
- Section Quiz 14.3
- Spanish Section Quiz 14.3
- Testmaker

else. The basic law of demand relates the quantity demanded of an individual product to its price. Now we are talking about all products. We cannot talk about all prices because there are millions. We can, however, talk about the *price level*. The relationship we obtain, therefore, is between the aggregate quantity demanded of all goods and services by all people and the average of all prices, which we measure by a price index. If we use the implicit

GDP deflator as our index, our measure of aggregate demand will be based on real domestic output. You can see this relationship in Figure 14.13. It is called the **aggregate demand curve.**

Figure 14.12
Producers and Consumers
These people represent the producers of many of the services available to us. The number of jobs in each of these fields depends on several factors, including demand for specific services. These people also represent all consumers of goods and services. ▼

Aggregate Demand Curve

Price Level

Aggregate
Demand
Curve

AD

Real Domestic Output

Figure 14.13
Aggregate Demand Curve
Although the curve for aggregate demand resembles that for simple demand, it is for the entire economy, not just one good or service.

343

Teach

Guided Practice

L2 Evaluating Lead a class discussion in which students consider the value to businesses and government of knowing a nation's aggregate demand and supply curves, and the equilibrium price level.

? DID YOU KNOW

When government attempts to help the economy, it must walk a fine line between controlling inflation and preventing a rise in unemployment.

🌎 GLOBAL ECONOMICS

The great "commodity rush" of the early 1970s is a good example of aggregate demand outstripping aggregate supply. Nations had lost confidence in the United States dollar as a stable investment and sought commodities such as gold and silver that would hold their value over time. Because there is a limited supply of these metals, aggregate demand drove their prices sharply upward.

◆▶ ⬤ Meeting Special Needs

Interpreting Graphs Students may have trouble grasping the relevance of equilibrium price levels, but study of the graphs in Section 3 should facilitate their understanding. Remind students that because there are literally millions of prices for all the products and services in the nation, economists must consider price levels, or aggregates of prices, for such diverse items as shoes, automobiles, coat hangers, and pharmaceutical products. The same consideration holds true for equilibrium output, or the aggregate of all products and services produced or supplied.

Independent Practice

L3 Research Encourage interested students to research the volume of yearly exports from the United States to Canada from 1982 to 1992. Have them develop an aggregate demand curve using the CPI (Figure 14.9) as the index and showing the demand for American products during that period.

Have students complete Guided Reading Activity 14.3 in the TCR. **LEP**

Visual Instruction

Refer students to Figures 14.13, 14.15, and 14.16 (pp. 343–345). Ask them to explain in a short paragraph why the demand curve slopes downward and the supply curve slopes upward. Ask how consumers are likely to behave as prices fall. Also ask how suppliers are likely to behave as prices rise and wages remain constant.

Figure 14.14
Export Demand
Exports add to the total aggregate demand and quantity demanded in the United States. So as our price level goes down, foreigners buy more of our goods, and a larger quantity of real domestic output is demanded each year.

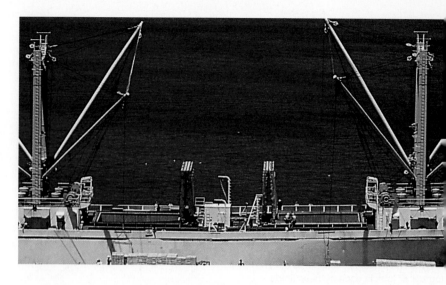

Notice the similarity between the aggregate demand curve labeled *AD* in Figure 14.13 and the individual demand curve you studied in Chapter 8 (pages 182–189). Both of those curves slope downward—they show an inverse relationship. Here as the price level in the nation's economy goes down, a larger quantity of real domestic output is demanded per year. At least two reasons cause this inverse relationship: one has to do with the real purchasing power of your cash, and the other has to do with the relative price of goods and services sold to other countries.

Consider the first reason. Inflation causes the purchasing power of your cash to go down. Deflation causes your purchasing power to go up. Therefore, when the price level goes down, the purchasing power of any cash that you hold will go up. You and everybody else will feel slightly richer because you are able to buy more goods and services.

Also, when the price level goes down in the United States, our goods become relatively better deals for foreigners who want to buy them. Foreigners then demand more of our goods as exports as Figure 14.14 shows.

Demand is only one side of the picture. Let us look at aggregate supply and its curve shown in Figure 14.15.

Figure 14.15 ▶
Aggregate Supply Curve
Similar to the aggregate demand curve, the aggregate supply curve is a macroeconomic measure.

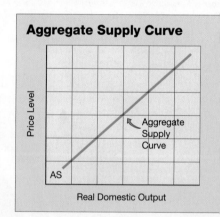

Aggregate Supply Curve

Price Level

Aggregate Supply Curve

AS

Real Domestic Output

 Cooperative Learning

Ask three students to research aggregate demand and supply in the United States over the past five years and make graphs showing demand, supply, and equilibrium price curves. Have three other students research aspects of the general economy for the same period: the level of consumer spending, saving, and investment; business expansion; employment; and rate of inflation.

Have both groups present their findings to the class. Lead a class discussion of whether the aggregate demand and supply curves accurately reflect what was occurring in the economy.

Aggregate Supply and the Aggregate Supply Curve

As the price of a specific product goes up, and if all other prices stay the same, producers of that product find it profitable to produce more. The same is true for all producers in the economy over a short period of time. If the price level goes up and wages do not, overall profits will rise. Producers will want to supply more to the marketplace—they offer more real domestic output as the price level increases. The reverse is true as the price level falls. This is called **aggregate supply.** You can see this positive relationship in Figure 14.15—the **aggregate supply curve.**

Putting Aggregate Demand and Aggregate Supply Together

Just as we are able to compare supply and demand for a given product to find an equilibrium price and quantity, we can compare aggregate demand and aggregate supply here. We do this in Figure 14.16.

The equilibrium price level in our example is determined where the aggregate demand curve crosses the aggregate supply curve, or at an implicit GDP price deflator of 140. The equi-

librium quantity of real GDP demanded and supplied is $7 trillion. As long as nothing changes in this situation, the economy will produce $7 trillion of real domestic output and the price level will remain at 140—there will be neither inflation nor deflation.

**Figure 14.16
The Equilibrium Level of National Output and the Price Level**
The intersection of aggregate demand and supply gives the equilibrium general price level and national output (real domestic output). ▼

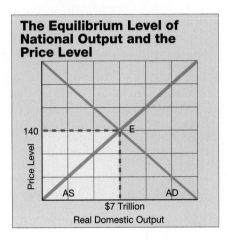

The Equilibrium Level of National Output and the Price Level

(Graph: Price Level on vertical axis, Real Domestic Output on horizontal axis; AS and AD curves intersecting at point E at price level 140 and $7 Trillion)

Assess

Meeting Lesson Objectives

Assign Section 3 Review as homework or an in-class activity. Each question in the Review addresses the corresponding numbered objective in the Section Focus.

Evaluate

Assign the Section 3 Quiz in the TCR or use the Testmaker to develop a customized quiz.

Reteach

Have small groups summarize the meaning of each graph in this section.

Enrich

Have interested students write a brief report on what equilibrium price levels indicate about economic activity.

Close

Discuss with students best ways to measure the overall economic activity of the country.

SECTION 3 REVIEW

Understanding Vocabulary
Define aggregates, aggregate demand, aggregate demand curve, aggregate supply, aggregate supply curve.

Reviewing Objectives
① Why is there an inverse relationship between aggregate quantity demanded and the price level?

② What causes the aggregate supply curve to slope up (rise, going from left to right)?

③ How do you use aggregate demand and supply analysis to determine the equilibrium price level?

Section 3 Review Answers

Understanding Vocabulary
aggregates (p. 342), **aggregate demand** (p. 342), **aggregate demand curve** (p. 343), **aggregate supply** (p. 345), **aggregate supply curve** (p. 345)

Reviewing Objectives
1. As prices fall, consumers demand more goods and services. If prices stay the same, demand remains unchanged. If prices rise, demand will fall as consumers reduce spending.
2. *As prices rise, assuming wages remain the same, suppliers will produce more because they will enjoy greater profits.*
3. overlay aggregate demand and aggregate supply curves—where they intersect represents the equilibrium price level

The stir that Keynes's theories on macroeconomics created is known today as the Keynesian Revolution. In time, Keynes's theories changed the thinking of an entire generation of economists and government economic policy making. In addition, Keynes represented Britain at the Versailles Peace Conference at the conclusion of World War I. There he argued for less harsh reparations be demanded of the Germans, fearing correctly that harsh economic terms imposed on Germany would lead to another world war. He also represented Britain at the Bretton Woods, New Hampshire, meeting of 1944 during which the International Monetary Fund and the World Bank were established.

Teach

The theories of John Maynard Keynes were designed to explain relatively low levels of aggregate demand in industrial societies. Keynes's concepts, however, are not easy to grasp. Help students reason through his argument by breaking it down into steps. Ask them to outline his theory, pointing out the role of supply and demand in his argument.

Personal Perspective

John Maynard Keynes on Equilibrium Employment

Profile

- 1883–1946
- born in Cambridge, England, and educated at Cambridge University
- built a fortune in the stock market
- Keynesian economics named after him
- most influential publication was *The General Theory of Employment, Interest, and Money* (1936)

John Maynard Keynes originated the school of economic thought referred to as Keynesian economics. Keynesian economics supports the liberal use of government spending and taxing to help the economy. This is, in part, because Keynes believed that an economy may reach an equilibrium level of employment that is below full employment. In *The General Theory of Employment, Interest, and Money*, he explained that people buy more when their wages increase, but the total additional consumption is not equal to the total increased wages.

When employment increases, aggregate real income is increased. The psychology of the community is that when aggregate real income is increased aggregate consumption is increased, but not so much as income. . . .

Keynes adds that the equilibrium level of employment depends on the level of investment. If the level of investment is low, full employment cannot be achieved.

Thus, to justify any given amount of employment there must be an amount of current investment sufficient to absorb the excess of output over what the community chooses to consume when employment is at a given level. It follows, that . . . the equilibrium level of employment, [that is] the level at which there is no inducement to employers as a whole either to expand or contract employment, will depend on the amount of current investment.

Keynes believed that his theory explained why large pockets of poverty exist in otherwise rich communities or nations.

. . . This analysis supplies us with an explanation of the paradox of poverty in the midst of plenty.
. . . Moreover the richer the community, the wider will tend to be the gap between its actual and its potential production; and therefore the more obvious and outrageous the defects of the economic system.

Checking for Understanding

❶ According to Keynes, what is the relationship between employment and current investment?

❷ What is the equilibrium level of employment?

❸ According to Keynes, what is one of the defects of the economic system?

Answers to Checking for Understanding

1. The rate of investment in a community or nation determines the rate of employment.

2. The equilibrium level of employment is the level at which employers cannot be induced either to hire more workers or let go of workers.

3. If the propensity to consume and the rate of new investment result in a deficient effective demand, the level of employment will fall below the existing labor supply. This will create large pockets of poverty in the midst of plenty.

S E C T I O N   4   F O C U S

Terms to Know business fluctuations, business cycle, peak, boom, contraction, recession, depression, trough, expansion, recovery

Objectives *After reading this section, you should be able to:*
① List the phases of a typical business cycle.
② Describe three downturns in the United States economy since the 1920s.

Peak and Trough, Boom and Bust

Some years unemployment goes up; some years it goes down. Some years inflation is high; other years it is not. We have fluctuations in virtually all aspects of our economy. The ups and downs in an economy are sometimes called **business fluctuations.** Some people associate these ups and downs in business activity with what has been called the **business cycle**—changes in the level of total output measured by real GDP. The term *business cycle* is somewhat misleading, however. *Cycle* usually refers to a regular series of changes. Changes in business activity in the United States show no such regularity, as you will see. (Consequently, many economists no longer use the term *business cycle*, but prefer to talk about *business fluctuations*.)

Model of the Business Cycle

Figure 14.17 shows an idealized business cycle. According to this model, the phases of a business cycle begin with growth leading to an economic **peak** or **boom**—a period of prosperity. New businesses open, factories are producing at full capacity, and everyone who wants work can find a job.

Eventually, however, real GDP levels off and begins to decline. During this part of the cycle, a **contraction** of the economy occurs. Business activity begins to slow down. If the contraction lasts long enough and is deep

**Figure 14.17
A Model of the Business Cycle**
What does the word *model* indicate about the business cycle shown? ▼

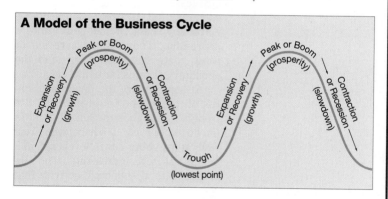

A Model of the Business Cycle

Chapter 14 Measuring the Economy's Performance **347**

Focus

Overview
See the student page for section objectives.
Section 4 explains or describes business fluctuations from peak to trough to recovery; and what happens at each stage and how businesses respond.

Bellringer
Before presenting the lesson, display Focus Activity Transparency 56 on the overhead projector or copy the material on the chalkboard. Assign the accompanying Focus Activity Sheet.

Motivational Activity
Ask students to recall a time of bad weather and good weather. Students should indicate what signs they saw that indicated each cycle of weather was coming and what signaled the end of each cycle.

Tell students Section 4 explains that economies go through similar fluctuations and that these cycles affect everyone.

Preteaching Vocabulary
Have students draw a wavy line (like the one in Figure 14.17) across an 8½-inch × 11-inch sheet of paper. Tell them to write each term in the appropriate place on the line and number it. Then have them write the definition of each term.

Classroom Resources for Section 4

- Reproducible Lesson Plan 14.4
- Focus Activity Transparency 56
- Focus Activity Sheet 56
- Guided Reading Activity 14.4
- Section Quiz 14.4
- Spanish Section Quiz 14.4
- Testmaker

Guided Practice

L2 Hypothesizing Ask students to imagine how a recession-recovery cycle might affect a company that produces T-shirts.

Visual Instruction

Refer students to Figure 14.17. Discuss what takes place at each stage of the fluctuation.

DID YOU KNOW

Business cycles or fluctuations have been occurring almost since the founding of the United States. Severe recessions in the 1820s and in 1873 bankrupted thousands of companies and forced hundreds of banks to close.

GLOBAL ECONOMICS

The economies of nations are so interdependent that a recession in one major nation can produce chain-reaction recessions in other nations. The severe recession of 1981–1982 in the United States, for example, prompted a series of international economic summits throughout the 1980s.

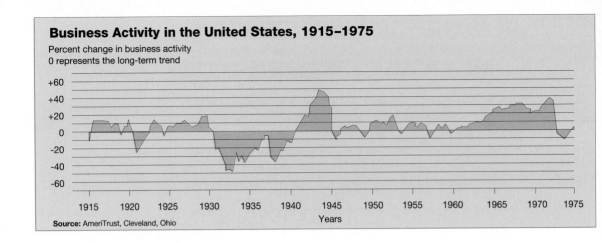

Business Activity in the United States, 1915–1975

Percent change in business activity
0 represents the long-term trend

Source: AmeriTrust, Cleveland, Ohio

Years

Figure 14.18 ▲
Business Activity
American business activity declined more than 40 percent in the Depression, yet bounced back as the nation fought World War II.

enough, the economy can continue downward until it slips into a recession. A **recession** is any period of at least two quarters—six months—during which real GDP does not grow. In a recession, business activity starts to fall at a rapid rate. Factories begin cutting back on production and laying off workers. Consumers, with less income, cut back on purchases. With less money income being spent, factories may reduce production further, laying off even more workers. Faced with a worsening economy, fewer new businesses open and many existing ones may fail. If a recession becomes extremely bad, it deepens into a **depression.** Then millions are out of work, many businesses fail, and the economy operates far below capacity.

At some point, the downward spiral of the economy levels off in a trough. A **trough** is the lowest point in the business cycle. It occurs when real GDP stops going down, levels off, and begins slowly increasing. The increase in total economic activity that

follows is called an **expansion** or a **recovery.** Consumer spending picks up, signaling factories to hire workers and increase production to meet demand. As more people are hired, the public has more income to spend, which further encourages growth. New businesses begin to open, and factory production climbs back toward full capacity. The recovery continues until the economy hits another peak, and a new cycle begins.

Ups and Downs of Business in the United States

What you have just read is a description of the business cycle model. In the real world, as you can see from Figure 14.18, the cycles are not that regular. However, the peaks and troughs are clear. The largest drop that resulted in a depression immediately followed the stock market crash in October 1929. The preceding years had been a time of widespread prosperity as Figure 14.19 shows. By October 1929, heavy speculation had driven stock prices to an all-time peak. Then the stock market began to collapse. Stock prices started to fall in early October and continued to fall. Suddenly,

 Meeting Special Needs

Limited English Proficiency Students who speak English as a second language may have trouble grasping the terminology and concepts of business fluctuations. Help them find resources, such as photo essays or illustrated histories, that show scenes representing each stage of the cycle, such as the Roaring Twenties, Great Depression, and 1970s recession and recovery.

Such images can help them to understand what happens to the economy and to individuals in each stage of the fluctuation.

on October 28, there was a nationwide stampede to unload stocks. In one day the total value of all stocks fell by $14 billion. The next day the economic crisis was even worse.

Not long after the stock market crash, the United States fell into a serious recession. See Figure 14.20 (page 350). Factories shut down, laying off millions of workers. Businesses and banks failed by the thousands. Real GDP fell sharply over the next few years, pushing the nation into the depths of the Great Depression. Then began a recovery, with some short slips downward until about 1936, when another downturn occurred. A gradual upward rise climaxed in the boom period of World War II.

After the war and throughout the 1950s, small ups and downs occurred. Recessions were short and mild, however, and the economy was generally prosperous. From 1960 through 1969, there were no recessionary periods. In the 1970s and the 1980s, the American economy suffered recurring recessions. The 1980s started off with a small recession that developed into the most serious economic downturn by some measurements since World War II. This downturn ended in 1982 and was followed by relative prosperity, except for a severe stock market crash in October 1987. The 1990s began with a mild recession, and then the recovery was relatively slow by historic standards.

Independent Practice

L2 Researching and Reporting Encourage interested students to research times of major economic depression in the United States (1870s, 1890s, 1930s). Ask what caused the depression, how the economy recovered, and how the economy changed afterward (*for example, shifts in population, old industries disappeared, new ones appeared*). Have students report their findings to the class.

L3 Analyzing Assign a group of students to analyze business fluctuations in the economies of other countries. Ask whether they follow the same progression as in the United States, how the countries recover, and what role the governments play. Students can do either a short written or oral report.

Have students complete Guided Reading Activity 14.4 in the TCR. LEP

▼ **Figure 14.19**
Prosperity Before the Crash
The twenties had been a decade in which Americans began buying increasing numbers of radios, stoves, and automobiles. During these years, prices remained stable, and the standard of living rose about 3 percent per year.

349

Cooperative Learning

Assign two teams of four students each to debate the following statement: "In a depression, the best approach is for the government to do nothing because the country will recover on its own." Limit the debate to fifteen minutes for each side. At the end, have the entire class join in the discussion and determine which side offered the better argument in support of their position.

Assess

Meeting Lesson Objectives

Assign Section 4 Review as homework or an in-class activity. Each question in the Review addresses the corresponding numbered objective in the Section Focus.

Evaluate

Assign the Section 4 Quiz in the TCR or use the Testmaker to develop a customized quiz.

Reteach

Ask students what might happen to a small company affected by a typical business "cycle."

Enrich

Invite a stockbroker or stock market analyst to the class to explain how a stock market crash can precipitate or precede a recession or depression.

Close

Have students write a short paragraph describing the different stages of business fluctuations.

▼ Figure 14.20
Recession Conditions
The Great Depression of the 1930s forced millions of Americans out of work. Used to the boom era of the 1920s, Americans during the bust era of the Depression often relied on handouts.

SECTION 4 REVIEW

Understanding Vocabulary

Define business fluctuations, business cycle, peak, boom, contraction, recession, depression, trough, expansion, recovery.

Reviewing Objectives

① What are the phases of a typical business cycle?

② What were the three most severe downturns in the United States economy since the 1920s?

---

350   *Unit 5 Macroeconomics: Managing the Nation's Economy*

Section 4 Review Answers

Understanding Vocabulary
business fluctuations (p. 347), business cycle (p. 347), **peak** or **boom** (p. 347), **contraction** (p. 347), **recession** (p. 348), **depression** (p. 348), **trough** (p. 348), **expansion** or **recovery** (p. 348)

Reviewing Objectives
1. peak or boom, a period of prosperity; contraction or recession, a period of slowdown or stagnation; trough, or the lowest point in the business cycle; expansion or recovery, the period of growth rising to another peak
2. the Great Depression of the 1930s, the recession of 1980–1982, and the stock market crash of 1987

SECTION 5 FOCUS

Terms to Know innovations, economic indicators, leading indicators, coincident indicators, lagging indicators

Objectives *After reading this section, you should be able to:*

❶ List the potential causes of business fluctuations.

❷ List the broad categories of economic indicators that predict and reflect business fluctuations.

Focus

Overview

See the student page for section objectives.

Section 5 explains or describes the possible causes and influences on business fluctuations, and the use of indicators to measure the activity of certain variables in the economy.

Bellringer

Before presenting the lesson, display Focus Activity Transparency 57 on the overhead projector or copy the material on the chalkboard. Assign the accompanying Focus Activity Sheet.

Motivational Activity

Ask students to list some of the good and bad events that have occurred in their lives. Have them underline those they predicted would happen. Discuss with them how easy or hard it may be to predict future events.

Preteaching Vocabulary

Have students look up each vocabulary term in the Glossary and write a paragraph using each one.

Problems in Predicting Economic Changes

For as long as booms and recessions have existed, economists have tried to explain why business fluctuations occur. If they could understand the causes, government could take actions to smooth out business fluctuations. No one theory, however, seems to explain past cycles or to serve as an adequate measure to predict future ones. The difficulty arises because at any one time, several factors are working together to create business fluctuations.

Causes of Business Fluctuations

For many years economists believed that business fluctuations occurred in regular cycles. No one knew why. A nineteenth-century English economist, W. Stanley Jevons, even blamed the cycles on sunspots. See Figure 14.21. Later economists realized that business fluctuations were related to changes in the rate of saving and investing. Today economists link business fluctuations to four main forces: business investment, government activity, external factors, and psychological factors. See Figure 14.22 (pages 352–353).

Business Investment Some economists believe business decisions are the keys to business

Figure 14.21
Crops, Sunspots, and Business?
W. Stanley Jevons believed periodic dark spots that appeared on the surface of the sun about every 11 years caused the weather and crop conditions that affected business.

▼

351

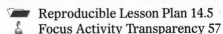

Teach

Guided Practice

L1 Analyzing Information
Refer students to Figure 14.23 (page 354). Discuss the different categories and subgroups of indicators to be sure students understand them. Ask students to pick a subgroup item and explain in a brief paragraph how it might indicate a rise or fall in business activity.

Visual Instruction

Ask students to review Figure 14.22. Have them bring in magazine and newspaper articles concerned with influences affecting the current stage of business fluctuation. Encourage discussion of the impact of each factor on the current economy.

DID YOU KNOW

During peak or boom times, when inflation is likely to be high, the federal government will seek to raise interest rates, making it more costly to borrow money for investment. This action tends to slow down growth and reduce inflation. During times of recession, the government may cut taxes, lower interest rates, and seek foreign investment to aid the economy.

Figure 14.22
Forces That Affect Business Fluctuations
Each of the four forces described here has a major impact on business.

B Government Activity
Government controls the supply of money.

A Business Investment
The computer industry is an example of technology contributing to business growth through innovation.

fluctuations. Suppose a firm believes that prospects for future sales are good. It will most likely increase its capital investment. It will buy new machines, build new factories, expand old ones, and so on. This expansion will create new jobs and more income for consumer spending. After a time, businesses no longer need to expand. When businesses stop purchasing new producer goods, a resulting contraction of the economy may occur.

When businesses anticipate a downturn in the economy, they cut back on their inventories. Producers, in turn, cut back on production to prevent a surplus. Enough inventory cutbacks could lead to a recession. In contrast, if they feel consumer orders are going to rise, businesses will invest in larger inventories. This will stimulate production and increase employment.

Innovations—inventions and new production techniques—can have a similar effect on the economy. When one firm begins to use an innovation, others, to become competitive again, must duplicate the product or production method. All this takes capital. Eventually, however, investment will drop off because no additional capital for the innovation is needed. (This situation is an example of the law of diminishing returns.)

 Meeting Special Needs

Reading Comprehension Disabilities Some students may have problems understanding how certain statistical measures may lag behind others. Give them an example as a commercial greenhouse shipping 20,000 tropical houseplants a week. Sales of the plants begin to fall but production is not affected initially. Thus, sales figures may be a more sensitive indicator of a coming downturn in the economy than production figures. In this case, it takes more time for production figures to reflect market conditions.

◀ C **External Factors**
War, immigration, crop failures, and changing availability of resources are some external factors that affect business cycles.

Independent Practice
L2 Cause and Effect
Encourage interested students to investigate why the oil embargo led to the recession of 1974–1975. Suggest exploring why the action of OPEC had such an impact, how the economy revived, and what action the government took.

 DID YOU KNOW

In 1973, the year of the oil embargo that led to fuel shortages in the United States, our nation was importing just over 6 million barrels of crude oil daily. That figure dropped to about 4.3 million barrels daily in 1982, but it rose to 6.9 million in 1992. Crude oil imports have contributed substantially to an ongoing trade deficit.

Government Activity A number of economists believe that the changing policies of the federal government are a major reason for business cycles. The government affects business activity in two ways: through its policies on taxing and spending and through its control over the supply of money available in the economy.

External Factors Factors outside a nation's economy also influence the business cycle. As you can see from Figure 14.22, wars in particular have an important impact. This impact results from the huge increase in government spending during wartime. The end of wartime spending signals an economic slowdown. Discoveries of new sources of raw materials such as oil may have a favorable effect on the economy by lowering operating costs for certain industries. The sudden loss of raw materials and the resulting higher price, however, can have the opposite effect. The huge increase in oil prices in late 1973 by the Organization of Petroleum Exporting Countries (OPEC) was partially responsible for the recession of 1974–1975. The sharp

decline in world oil prices helped the return of prosperity in the mid-1980s.

Psychological Factors Finally, it is possible that people's psychological reactions to events also cause changes in business activity. The prospects of peace in a troubled area or the discovery of a new oil field can lead to feelings of confidence and optimism. War or the overthrow of the government of an important trading partner can cause pessimism about the future. These psychological factors sometimes

▲ D **Psychological Factors**
Consumer confidence and increased spending may lead to an expansion.

 Cooperative Learning

Tell the class to imagine the President of the United States has asked them to write a report evaluating current economic indicators. Ask for a volunteer team to do the report, or assign a team.

The team's task is to predict, based on their evaluation of the indicators, whether the economy is likely to improve, worsen, or remain the same in the next six months. Ask the team to support their prediction with as much evidence as possible, given that economic forecasting is an inexact activity. Have the team present their report for class discussion.

L3 Applying Knowledge
Have students explain in a short report how a change in psychological factors, such as consumer confidence, can affect some of the leading, coincident, and lagging indicators. Suggest pursuing how business and government leaders attempt to influence psychological factors.

Have students complete Guided Reading Activity 14.5 in the TCR. LEP

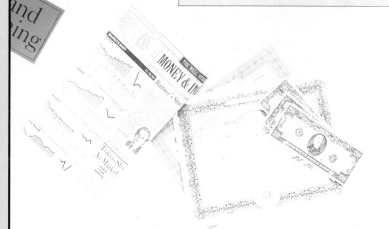

Figure 14.23 Major Economic Indicators

Leading indicators
1. Average workweek for production workers in manufacturing
2. Layoff rate in manufacturing
3. New orders for consumer goods
4. Speed with which companies make deliveries (the busier a company, the longer it will take to fill orders)
5. Number of new businesses formed
6. Number of contracts and orders for plants and equipment
7. Number of building permits issued for private housing units
8. Change in the inventories on hand and on order
9. Change in the PPI for certain nonagricultural raw materials
10. Change in total liquid assets (securities such as Treasury bills and bonds that can easily be turned into currency)
11. Stock prices
12. Supply of money in the economy

Coincident indicators
1. Number of nonagricultural workers who are employed
2. Personal income minus transfer payments
3. Rate of industrial production
4. Sales of manufacturers, wholesalers, and retailers

Lagging indicators
1. Average length of unemployment
2. Size of manufacturing and trade inventories
3. Labor cost per unit of output in manufacturing
4. Average interest rate charged by banks to their best business customers
5. Number of commercial and industrial loans to be repaid
6. Ratio of consumer installment debt to personal income

though these decisions can be based on objective facts, psychological factors such as personal optimism can also influence them.

Economic Indicators

Every day, business and government leaders are faced with the dilemma of trying to predict what will happen to the economy in the coming months and years. Businesspeople base their decisions on such questions as when to build a new plant or what they feel will happen in the future. Government officials also need information about the future in planning taxing and spending policies. To aid these decision makers, government and private economists constantly create and update economic forecasts.

contribute to consumer confidence and increased spending or the lack of confidence and more saving.

Likewise, business executives make decisions based on what they think will happen in the future. Even

Free Enterprise Activity

Encourage students to create a plan for a student employment service. Besides devising organizational structure and operations, they need to consider categories of employment for students, advertising the service, soliciting employers, and developing a bank of employee students. After reviewing their proposal in class, suggest that interested students try to start the business.

These forecasts indicate what is likely to happen in the economy as it moves through the various phases of the business cycle. Although GDP is an important measure of the economy's performance, it is not very helpful in preparing these forecasts. GDP shows what *has* happened in the economy, but it is not a good predictor of what *might* happen. It is also too broad a measure to show detail about activity in the various sectors of the economy.

For these reasons, economists study a number of other economic indicators to learn about the current and possible future state of the economy. See Figure 14.23. **Economic indicators** are statistics that measure variables in the economy, such as stock prices or the dollar amount of loans to be repaid. Each month the Department of Commerce publishes statistics for 300 economic indicators covering all aspects of the state of the economy.

Those statistics that point to what will happen in the economy are called **leading indicators.** Their activity seems to lead to a change in overall business activity—whether it is an upward or a downward trend. Economists can use leading indicators to predict which phase of the business cycle the economy is moving into. Although the Commerce Department keeps track of dozens of leading indicators, those listed in Figure 14.23 are the ones that most concern American economists.

Other economic indicators, whose changes in activity seem to happen at the same time as changes in overall business activity, also help economists. When these **coincident indicators** begin a downswing, they indicate that a contraction in the business cycle has begun. If they begin an upswing, they indicate that the economy is picking up and a recovery is underway.

A third set of indicators seems to lag behind changes in overall business activity. For example, it may be six months after the start of a downturn before businesses begin to reduce their borrowing noticeably. The amount of change in these **lagging indicators,** whether up or down, gives economists clues as to the size and timing of all of the phases of the business cycle.

Although economic indicators are essential in making economic forecasts, they are far from perfect predictors. Often, different indicators within each group move in opposite directions. Another problem is the wide variation in lead or lag time between a change in an indicator and a change in the overall economy.

SECTION 5 REVIEW

Understanding Vocabulary
Define innovations, economic indicators, leading indicators, coincident indicators, lagging indicators.

Reviewing Objectives
1. What are some of the potential causes of business fluctuations?
2. What are the three broad categories of economic indicators?

Assess

Meeting Lesson Objectives
Assign Section 5 Review as homework or an in-class activity. Each question in the Review addresses the corresponding numbered objective in the Section Focus.

Evaluate
Assign the Section 5 Quiz in the TCR or use the Testmaker to develop a customized quiz.

Assign the Chapter 14 Test Form A or Form B or use the Testmaker to develop a customized test.

Reteach
Have students outline Section 5.

Have students complete Reteaching Activity 14 in the TCR.

Enrich
Encourage students to investigate some of the theories developed to explain business cycles.

Have students complete Enrichment Activity 14 in the TCR.

Close
Assign a paragraph on why economic forecasting is so difficult.

Section 5 Review Answers
Understanding Vocabulary
innovations (p. 352), **economic indicators** (p. 354), **leading indicators** (p. 355), **coincident indicators** (p. 355), **lagging indicators** (p. 355)

Reviewing Objectives
1. Some of the potential causes of business fluctuations are changes in business investment, government activity, external factors, and psychological factors.
2. The three broad categories of economic indicators are the leading indicators, coincident indicators, and lagging indicators.

Teach

Discuss with students the idea that sales figures alone do not tell the whole story about a company's health, just as GDP or NI figures do not tell the whole story about an economy's health. A company must also look at its profits, or how much money it is making after paying all expenses. In the case of McDonald's, this figure was flat and the company was not growing. Ask students to point out what the company did to increase growth.

News Clip

Readings in Economics

KIPLINGER'S PERSONAL FINANCE MAGAZINE   JANUARY 1993

McDONALD'S: 95 BILLION BURGERS

by Dan Morea

Just how awesome, how successful, is the restaurant chain that traces its roots to a California eatery started 45 years ago by two brothers named McDonald? Consider this: Sometime in 1993, McDonald's Corp. will have sold enough hamburgers (95 billion—not counting McChickens, Filet-O-Fishes and all the other nonbeef sandwiches) to have fed nearly every human being born since the dawn of time. Or ponder this: In 1993, the hamburgers leaving McDonald's grills (171 per second) would be enough to feed every living person on earth—5.3 billion, give or take a hundred million. Among brand names, only Coke enjoys greater worldwide recognition.

Yes, McDonald's is hugely successful. . . . But scarcely two years ago, the company's juices seemed to have run dry. . . .

So in 1991, McDonald's, a company known for single-minded determination, fired back. In midyear it introduced an "extra-value" menu that knocked 20% off the price of sandwiches and made up the revenue loss with high-markup fries and drinks. For health-conscious eaters, McDonald's replaced its McDLT hamburger with the McLean Deluxe, a burger that is 91% fat-free. . . .

Another ingredient contributes to the recent success of McDonald's: overseas franchises. Truth is, U.S. growth is still nothing to brag about—a few percentage points each year. Right now, the sizzle that McDonald's shareholders hear comes from 4,000 overseas outlets (there are 9,000 in the U.S.). Foreign business now contributes 37% of sales, 40% of profits and most of the growth in franchises.

Those overseas outlets are highly concentrated. Seventy percent are located in just six nations—Australia, Canada, France, Germany, Great Britain and Japan.

• THINK ABOUT IT •

1. *What actions did McDonald's take to overcome its lackluster performance?*

2. *Where is most of McDonald's most profitable growth today?*

Answers to Think About It

1. McDonald's introduced an extra-value menu at 20 percent off, made up resulting losses with high-markup items, added the McLean Deluxe for health-conscious eaters, and expanded its overseas market.

2. overseas outlets, where in late 1992 the revenues were up 16 percent over the previous year

14 *Highlights*

Use the Chapter 14 Highlights to preview, review, condense, or reteach the chapter. A Spanish Chapter Highlights is available in the Spanish Handbook.

National Income Accounting

Key Terms

national income accounting (p. 332)
gross domestic product (GDP) (p. 332)
net exports (p. 334)
depreciation (p. 334)

net domestic product (NDP) (p. 335)
national income (NI) (p. 335)
personal income (PI) (p. 336)
transfer payments (p. 336)
disposable personal income (DI) (p. 336)

Summary
Gross domestic product (GDP) is the total dollar value of all *final* consumer goods, producer goods, government goods, net exports, and services produced in the nation during a single year. Personal income is found by subtracting corporate income taxes, profits, and employer Social Security contributions from national income.

Preview/Review

After students read the Chapter 14 Highlights, have them complete Economics Vocabulary Activity 14 in the TCR. Spanish Vocabulary Activities are also available in the Spanish Resource Binder.

Vocabulary Software reinforces the economic terms used in Chapter 14.

Correcting Statistics for Inflation

Key Terms

inflation (p. 338)
purchasing power (p. 338)
deflation (p. 339)
consumer price index (CPI) (p. 339)

base year (p. 340)
producer price index (PPI) (p. 340)
implicit GDP price deflator (p. 341)
real GDP (p. 341)

Summary
When there is inflation, the purchasing power of money falls. The three ways to measure changes in average prices are by the consumer price index (CPI), producer price index (PPI), and implicit GDP price deflator.

Condense

Have students listen to Chapter 14 on the Audiocassettes in the TCR. A 1-page written activity and 1-page test accompany this material. These materials are also available in Spanish.

Aggregate Supply and Demand

Key Terms

aggregates (p. 342)
aggregate demand (p. 342)

aggregate demand curve (p. 343)
aggregate supply (p. 345)
aggregate supply curve (p. 345)

Summary
Aggregate supply and demand measure the entire economy. The intersection of the aggregate demand and aggregate supply curves determines the equilibrium price level and real GDP (national output).

Reteach

Have students complete Reteaching Activity 14 in the TCR. Spanish Reteaching Activities are also available.

Business Fluctuations

Key Terms

business fluctuations (p. 347)
business cycle (p. 347)

peak (p. 347)
boom (p. 347)
contraction (p. 347)
recession (p. 348)
depression (p. 348)
trough (p. 348)
expansion (p. 348)
recovery (p. 348)

Summary
Business fluctuations are measured from one period of prosperity to another. A typical "cycle" starts with the peak (boom). Then the economy begins to contract, during which a recession (trough) may occur followed by recovery.

VIDEODISC

Nightly Business Report
Economics in Action
Use "Measuring the Economy's Performance" on Disc 2, Side A, Video 19.

Search 6928, Play to 15292

Causes and Indicators of Business Fluctuations

Key Terms

innovations (p. 352)
economic indicators (p. 355)

leading indicators (p. 355)
coincident indicators (p. 355)
lagging indicators (p. 355)

Summary
Economists study many possible causes of business cycles. Economists use leading, coincident, and lagging indicators to measure the activity of certain variables in the economy.

357

ANSWERS

Identifying Key Terms

1. d   4. f
2. a   5. b
3. c   6. e

Recalling Facts and Ideas

Section 1

1. consumer goods, producer goods
2. all wages and forms of labor income and net interest received by households
3. the amount of taxes and Social Security contributions paid

Section 2

4. consumer price index, producer price indexes

5. Inflation refers to a prolonged rise in prices; deflation refers to a prolonged fall in prices.
6. by applying the implicit GDP price deflator to remove the effects of inflation

Section 3

7. as prices fall, a larger quantity of real domestic output is demanded

8. as prices increase, producers will want to supply more to the marketplace, and domestic output increases
9. equilibrium price and quantity of real domestic output demanded and supplied

Section 4

10. peak, contraction, recession, depression, trough, recovery or expansion

11. In a recession, business activity begins to fall at a rapid rate. Industry cuts back, consumers spend less, workers are laid off, fewer new businesses open, and many existing ones fail.

CHAPTER 14 Review

Identifying Key Terms

Write the letter of the definition in Column B below that correctly defines each term in Column A.

Column A
1. base year (p. 340)
2. trough (p. 348)
3. economic indicators (p. 355)
4. expansion (p. 348)
5. real GDP (p. 341)
6. business cycle (p. 347)

Column B
a. economic activity is at its lowest point
b. figures for the nation's total income that have been corrected for inflation
c. measurement of specific aspects of the economy such as stock prices
d. used as a point of comparison for other years in a series of statistics
e. periodic ups and downs in the nation's economic activity
f. business recovery period, when economic activity increases

Recalling Facts and Ideas

Section 1

1. Net exports and government goods are two components of gross domestic product. What are the other two components?
2. Besides profit and rents, what two other categories of income are added in the income approach to estimating GDP?
3. If you were given the statistic on disposable personal income, what other information would you need to derive personal income?

Section 2

4. What are the most commonly used price indexes?
5. What is the difference between inflation and deflation?
6. How would you determine *real* GDP if you knew only GDP?

Section 3

7. Why does the aggregate demand curve slope down?
8. Why does the aggregate supply curve slope up?
9. What is determined at the intersection of the aggregate supply and aggregate demand curves?

Section 4

10. What are the main phases of a business cycle?
11. When the economy enters a recession, what normally happens?
12. When was the most serious downturn in economic activity in the twentieth century in the United States?

Section 5

13. What are two theories of the causes of the ups and downs in overall business activity?
14. How might psychological factors affect the business cycle?
15. What two aspects of government activity affect business cycles?

Critical Thinking

Section 1

Evaluating Information How might knowledge of nationwide economic statistics help you?

---

12. the Great Depression in the 1930s

Section 5

13. (1) changes in the rate of saving and investing; (2) changes in four main activities: business investment, government activity, external factors, and pyschological factors

14. Optimism can lead to increased consumer spending and greater business productivity. Pessimism can make people more cautious,

reducing consumer spending.
15. taxing and spending policies and control of the money supply

Critical Thinking

Section 1

Such knowledge can be useful in determining whether one's wages are keeping current with increases in prices, whether it's a good time to change jobs, who might be the best political

Section 2

Determining Cause and Effect "Inflation just keeps getting worse because the purchasing power of money is going down." Why is this statement meaningless?

Section 3

Making Comparisons What is the difference between the aggregate demand curve and the demand curve in Chapter 8 that discussed the demand for individual goods and services?

Section 4

Analyzing Information Why is it probably better to talk about business fluctuations rather than business cycles?

Section 5

Making Inferences Many theories try to explain why business cycles occur. None of them can be considered "the truth." Why not?

Applying Economic Concepts

Understanding the Business Cycle Try to analyze what you think occurs throughout the economy during a recession. Make a list of some of the things that business owners may do to react to a recession, such as reduce employees' overtime hours.

Chapter Projects

1. **Individual Project** Go to the library and find the latest edition of the *Statistical Abstract of the United States*. Locate the tables in the "Prices" section that give price indexes for consumer goods for selected cities and metropolitan areas. Make a line graph showing the rise in the index for "all items" over the last six years. Draw on the same graph a line indicating the "city average" index for "all items" in a city or area near you during the same period of time.
2. **Cooperative Learning Project** Work in three groups. Each group will choose one of the

following:

- Lagging indicators
- Coincident indicators
- Leading indicators

Each group will do library research to determine the following:

- For each type of indicator, what are the various subgroups?
- How long has the indicator been reported by the United States government?
- Can you find instances when the indicator was wildly inaccurate? For example, what if the leading indicator was still indicating that times were good when, in fact, the economy was already in a serious recession?

Have a class discussion about how useful any of these indicators might be in accurately predicting changes in overall national economic activity.

Reviewing Skills

Using Index Numbers: Price Indexes
Constructing a Price Index Assume the following data on the price of comparable personal computers: 1990 $1,000; 1991 $800; 1992 $700; 1993 $600; 1994 $500; 1995 $250; 1996 $200. Construct a price index for computers using 1990 as the base year.

Writing About Economics

Persuasive Writing Imagine that you are the President. You need to assure the nation that the economy will do better if you are reelected. Write a two-paragraph speech about how you would improve the economic conditions you recorded in Your Economics Journal this week.

359

leader, and where to place one's savings.

Section 2
The decline in purchasing power is the result of inflation and not its cause.

Section 3
The aggregate demand curve refers to the relationship between prices and the demand for all goods and services in an economy. The demand curve refers only to the relationship between prices and demand for individual goods and services.

Section 4
Periodic ups and downs in business activity are more accurately described as fluctuations rather than business cycles. The term *cycle* implies a regular series of changes.

Section 5
None has fully explained the causes that produce business cycles.

Applying Economic Concepts

Students should mention that, in a recession, a downward spiral develops through the economy. Business owners may try to reduce employee hours; control or freeze hiring, raises, and benefits; find cheaper suppliers, distributors; reduce inventory, cut prices, and, in extreme cases, close plants and sell off property.

? BONUS QUESTION

The following bonus question can be written on the chalkboard when students take the chapter test.
Q: Why would you not locate off-road bicycles data on an aggregate demand curve?
A: It does not give data on individual items.

Chapter Projects

1. Graphs will vary according to figures.
2. Students should determine that these indicators generally are more useful in analyzing historical trends than in predicting changes in overall national economic activity.

Reviewing Skills

1996 price ($200) divided by 1990 base year price ($1000) equals .20. Price index is (100 × .20) = 20.

Writing About Economics

Student speeches may touch on expanding employment and productivity, controlling the declining standard of living, tax breaks for the middle class, and reducing the national debt and the trade deficit.

CHAPTER 15 *MONEY AND BANKING*

CHAPTER ORGANIZER

Daily Objectives	Special Features	Classroom Resources

Section 1 The Functions and Characteristics of Money
- **List** the three functions of money.
- **Name** six characteristics that money should have.

Personal Perspective:
John W. Rogers on Money Management, p. 367

- 📁 Reproducible Lesson Plan 15.1
- 💿 *NBR* Video 20
- 🖱 Focus Activity Transparency 58
- 📁 Focus Activity Sheet 58
- 📁 Guided Reading Activity 15.1
- 📁 Cooperative Learning Activity 15
- 📁 Primary and Secondary Source Readings 15
- 📁 Section Quiz 15.1
- 📁 Spanish Section Quiz 15.1
- 📀 Testmaker

Section 2 History of American Money and Banking
- **List** several important events in the history of American money and banking.
- **Describe** six services provided by banks and savings institutions.
- **Discuss** electronic banking and its effects on banking services.

Learning Economic Skills:
Keeping a Checking Account, p. 373
Focus on Free Enterprise:
Case Study, Adams National Bank, pp. 374–375

- 📁 Reproducible Lesson Plan 15.2
- 🖱 Focus Activity Transparency 59
- 📁 Focus Activity Sheet 59
- 📁 Guided Reading Activity 15.2
- 📁 Consumer Application Activity 15
- 📁 Section Quiz 15.2
- 📁 Spanish Section Quiz 15.2
- 📀 Testmaker
- 📁 Reinforcing Skills 15

Section 3 Types of Money in the United States
- **Explain** the difference between money and near moneys.
- **List** the components of the M2 definition of the money supply.

News Clip:
"Had It With Your Bank's Fees?"
Kiplinger's Personal Finance Magazine, p. 380

- 📁 Reproducible Lesson Plan 15.3
- 🖱 Focus Activity Transparency 60
- 📁 Focus Activity Sheet 60
- 📁 Guided Reading Activity 15.3
- 📁 Free Enterprise Activity 15
- 📁 Mathematics Practice for Economics 21
- 📁 Performance Assessment Activity 21
- 📁 Section Quiz 15.3
- 📁 Spanish Section Quiz 15.3
- 📀 Testmaker
- 📁 Enrichment Activity 15

 **OUT OF TIME?** If time does not permit teaching this chapter, you may use the Chapter 15 Highlights and the Audiocassettes that include a 1-page activity and a 1-page test.

Chapter 15 Review and Evaluation

Special Features

Chapter 15 Highlights, p. 381
Chapter 15 Review, pp. 382–383
Point/Counterpoint pp. 384–385

Classroom Resources

- Chapter 15 Test Forms A and B
- Economics Vocabulary Activity 15
- Spanish Economics Vocabulary Activity 15
- Audiocassette 15
- Spanish Audiocassette 15
- Spanish Reteaching Acitivity 15

Key to Ability Levels

Teaching strategies have been coded for varying learning styles and abilities.

L1 Level 1 activities are **basic** activities and should be within the ability range of all students.

L2 Level 2 activities are **average** activities designed for the ability range of average to above-average students.

L3 Level 3 activities are **challenging** activities designed for the ability range of above-average students.

LEP activities should be within the ability range of **Limited English Proficiency** students.

Performance Assessment

The following chapter project may be assigned at the beginning of the chapter and used for performance assessment. See page T12 for additional Performance Assessment information.

Conducting an Interview Organize students into pairs. Have students develop interview questions to determine the methods their adult family members use when paying bills and spending money. The questions should also inquire about the kinds of banking services they use. In addition, students might ask family members the reasons for their choice of methods and services. Students should conduct interviews of their family members and record responses during the time they study Chapter 15. After they complete their interviews, have the students report on the methods their family members use when spending money, the kinds of banking services they use, and any other pertinent information from the interviews. Students might present their information in the form of a chart.

Additional Resources

Readings for the Student

Bruce, Stanley L., and Wentworth, Donald R. *Economic Scenes: Theory in Today's World.* 4th ed. Englewood Cliffs, NJ: Prentice-Hall, 1988.

Klein, John J. *Money in the Economy.* 6th ed. New York: Harcourt Brace Jovanovich, 1988.

Readings for the Teacher

Clark, Simon. *Keynesianism, Monetarism, & the Crisis of the State.* Brookfield, VT.: Gower Publishing Co., 1988.

Mishkin, Frederic S. *The Economics of Money, Banking and Financial Markets.* 3rd ed. New York: Harper Collins, 1992.

Multimedia Materials

The Curious History of Money. Film. Federal Reserve Bank of Boston, Public Services Dept., 600 Atlantic, Boston, MA 02106

Money and Banking. Film. Encyclopaedia Britannica Educational Corporation, 425 N. Michigan Avenue, Chicago, IL 60611

Money: Summing It Up. Film. Federal Reserve Bank of Kansas City, Public Affairs Dept., 925 Grand Avenue, Kansas City, MO 64198

Money Manager. Simulation. Includes teacher's guide and individual student workbooks. Apple IIe. Sterling Swift Company, 7901 South 1H-35, Austin, TX 78744. Students face hypothetical situations of money management.

Chapter Overview

The concept of money, the usage of paper money in the United States, and the amount of money in circulation are probably ideas that students take for granted. Chapter 15 explains or describes: the functions and characteristics of money and modern banking services; the importance of the history of money and banking to the growth of the United States and the types of money used in the United States.

VIDEODISC

Nightly Business Report
Economics In Action
Use "Money and Banking" on Disc 2, Side A, Video 20.

Search 15377, Play to 22824

CHAPTER
15 MONEY AND BANKING

Why are these people waiting in line?

How do you operate an automated teller machine (ATM)?

Why do people need cash?

Answering Economic Questions

The questions in the above illustration are designed to lead into the main concepts in Chapter 15. Students might not be aware that cash is not the only type of money that exists. The questions will help students focus on what money is and the modern banking services that have developed. Have students discuss the questions and use the concepts from their discussion to explain what they think money is.

Besides cash, what other kinds of money exist?

How much money is in circulation?

Why are ATMs so popular?

Your Economics Journal

Keep track of all of the purchases you make during one week. Write down a list of these purchases, the amount of money involved, and how you paid. Indicate after each item whether you purchased it using cash or another form of money.

361

Connecting to Past Learning

Have students recall the types of services offered by banks and savings institutions. List them on the chalkboard. Ask students what other services they think banks and savings institutions provide.

Applying Economics

Have students write a short story about a day without money. Ask them to imagine how they would do everyday activities, such as getting food in the school cafeteria and obtaining gasoline. *(Students might include the idea of barter to pay for these things.)* Call on volunteers to read their stories. Tell students that in Chapter 15 they will learn about the functions and characteristics of money.

EXTRA CREDIT PROJECT

Have students research the trend toward computer banking. If possible, have them visit a bank in their area that offers it. Ask them to gather information on costs, ease of access, possibility of outsider tampering, confidentiality, and number of customer sign-ups over the past year. Have students predict whether computer banking will become commonplace in the future.

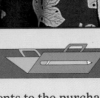
Economic Portfolio

Refer students to the purchases they tracked in **Your Economics Journal.** Suggest that students compile their information in a chart with the following headings: Purchase Made, Cost of Purchase, and Method of Payment. Have students determine the method of payment they used the most. Call on volunteers to share the information in their charts, and discuss with students what factors determined their method of payment for the purchases.

PERFORMANCE ASSESSMENT

Refer to page 360B for "Conducting an Interview," a Performance Assessment Activity for this chapter.

361

Focus

Overview

See the student page for section objectives.

Section 1 explains or describes: the three functions of money; the three types of money; and the six characteristics of money.

Bellringer

Before presenting the lesson, display Focus Activity Transparency 58 on the overhead projector or copy the material on the chalkboard. Assign the accompanying Focus Activity Sheet.

Motivational Activity

Write the word *money* on the chalkboard. Have students make a list of various definitions of the word. Have students compare their definition of *money* with the definition in the text. Tell students that Section 1 discusses the functions and characteristics of money.

Preteaching Vocabulary

Have students find the definitions of the vocabulary terms. Then have students list the words that deal with the function of money (*medium of exchange, unit of accounting, store of value*) and the words that deal with the three types of money (*commodity money, representative money, fiat money*).

SECTION **1** The Functions and Characteristics of Money

SECTION 1 FOCUS

Terms to Know money, medium of exchange, barter, double coincidence of wants, unit of accounting, store of value, commodity money, representative money, fiat money, legal tender

Objectives *After reading this section, you should be able to:*
① List the three **functions of money**.
② Name six **characteristics that money** should have.

It's Only Money

American businesses produce, market, and distribute goods and services. Money makes it possible for businesses to obtain what they need from suppliers and for consumers to obtain goods. **Money** is defined as anything customarily used as a medium of exchange, a unit of accounting, and a store of value. The basis of the market economy is voluntary exchange. In the American economy, the exchange usually involves money in return for a good or service.

The Functions of Money

Most Americans think of money as bills, coins, and checks. Historically, and in other economies, money might be shells, gold, or even goods such as sheep. Economists identify money by the presence or absence of certain functions. Anything that is used as a medium of exchange, a unit of accounting, and a store of value is considered money. **Figure 15.1** shows a partial list of the things that have been used as money. For example, Native Americans used wampum—beads made from shells. Fijians have used whales' teeth.

Medium of Exchange The three functions of money are shown in Figure 15.2 (page 364). To say that money is a **medium of exchange** simply means that a seller will accept it in exchange for a good or service. Most people are paid for their work in money, which they then can use to buy whatever they need or want. Without money people would have to **barter**—exchange goods and services for other goods and services.

Suppose you worked in a grocery

Feathers

Classroom Resources for Section 1

- Reproducible Lesson Plan 15.1
- *NBR* Video 20
- Focus Activity Transparency 58
- Focus Activity Sheet 58
- Guiding Reading Activity 15.1
- Cooperative Learning Activity 15

- Primary and Secondary Source Readings 15
- Section Quiz 15.1
- Spanish Section Quiz 15.1
- Testmaker

store and were paid in groceries because money did not exist. To get whatever else you needed, such as clothes and housing, you would have to find people who have the goods that you want. In addition, those people

Figure 15.1
Selected Items Used as Money
These items are but a sampling of the items that have been used as money.

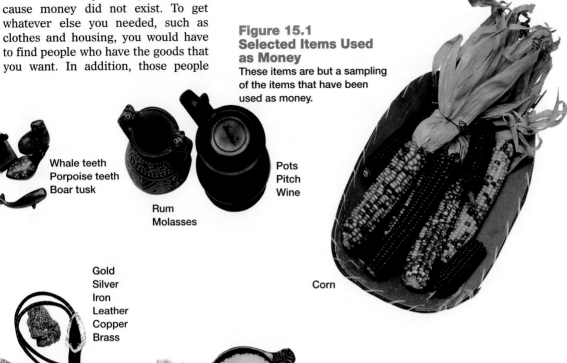

Corn

Whale teeth
Porpoise teeth
Boar tusk

Rum
Molasses

Pots
Pitch
Wine

Gold
Silver
Iron
Leather
Copper
Brass

Rice

Crystal salt

Salt

Tobacco

Round stones with centers
Polished beads (wampum)

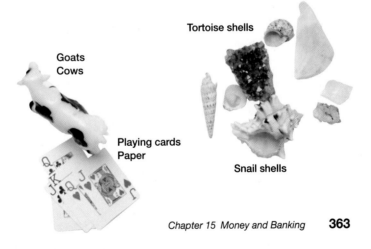

Tortoise shells

Goats
Cows

Playing cards
Paper

Snail shells

Chapter 15 Money and Banking **363**

Guided Practice

L3 Calculating Ask students to bring any foreign money they may have to class. Have them compare the value of the money in relation to the dollar using the exchange rate found in a newspaper. Call on volunteers to list the values on the chalkboard.

DID YOU KNOW

Barter also exists in societies where money is used. More than 300 barter exchanges operate worldwide. These exchanges consist of people who barter services or goods that they believe others may want. Members of the exchanges receive trade credits for the money value of the items or services they offer.

Meeting Special Needs

Learning Disorder Show students with learning disorders the importance of headings and subheadings for understanding the framework of each section. Illustrate the method to students by asking them what they would do if they wanted to know what each section was about. Read the headings for Section 1 aloud. Ask students to rephrase the headings into complete sentences.

GLOBAL ECONOMICS

Many people in economically developing countries of Latin America, Africa, and Asia barter to get many necessities. They produce barely enough food to meet their own needs and, as a result, rarely have any money.

Figure 15.2 ▲ Three Functions of Money

All money serves three functions. The money this woman has is serving as a medium of exchange; the vendor will accept it in exchange for tomatoes. The money is also a unit of accounting—the products in the market are all priced in dollars, so the woman can compare values of different items. Finally, the money serves as a store of value—the woman has stored her purchasing power in the form of dollars.

would have to want the exact goods—in this case, groceries—that you have. Barter requires what economists call a **double coincidence of wants.** Each party to a transaction must want exactly what the other person has to offer. This situation is rare. As a result, people in societies that barter for goods spend great amounts of time and effort making trades with one another. Bartering can work only in small societies with fairly simple economic systems.

Unit of Accounting Money is the yardstick that allows people to compare the values of goods and services in relation to one another. Money that is a measure of value functions in this way as a **unit of accounting.** Each nation uses a basic unit to measure the value of goods, as it uses the foot or meter to measure distance. In the United States, this base unit of value is the dollar. In Japan, it is the yen; in France, the franc. An item for sale is marked with a price that indicates its

value in terms of that unit.

Using money as the single unit of accounting provides a simple and convenient way to compare the values of various items. By using money prices as a factor in comparing goods, people can determine whether one item is a better bargain than another. A single unit of accounting also allows people to keep accurate financial records—records of debts owed, income saved, and so on. Businesspeople can better calculate their profits and losses over the years by using a single money unit of accounting.

Store of Value Money also serves as a **store of value.** You can sell something, such as your labor, and store the purchasing power that results from the sale in the form of money for later use. People usually receive their money income once a week, once every two weeks, or once a month. However, they usually spend their income at different times during a pay period. To be able to buy things be-

Cooperative Learning

Organize the class into small groups. Have each group research the use of bartering and of commodity money by American colonists. Students should write a brief, illustrated report about the problems of conducting business in the colonies without a uniform currency. The report should also include the solutions colonists devised to minimize this problem. Students might focus on a single colony or region. Each group might divide the following tasks among its members: researching the information, writing the report, illustrating the report, and presenting the report to the class.

Figure 15.3 Characteristics of Money

Characteristic	Description
Durable	Money must be able to withstand the wear and tear of being passed from person to person. Paper money lasts on the average of only one year, but old bills can be easily replaced. Coins, in contrast, last for years.
Portable	Money can be carried around easily. Though paper money is not very durable, people can easily carry large sums of paper money.
Divisible	Money must be easily divided into small parts so that purchases of any price can be made. Carrying coins and small bills makes it possible to make purchases of any amount.
Stable in value	Money must be stable in value. Its value cannot change rapidly or its usefulness as a store of value will decrease.
Scarce	Whatever is used as money must be scarce. That is what gives it value.
Accepted	Whatever is used as money must be accepted as a medium of exchange in payment for debts. In the United States, acceptance is based on the knowledge that others will continue to accept paper money, coins, and checks in exchange for desired goods and services.

Independent Practice

L2 Making a Chart Organize students into small groups. Have them review Figure 15.1 on page 363. Then have each group make an illustrated chart of all the things they can find that have been used as money. Ask students to use their completed charts as a bulletin board display.

Have students complete Guided Reading Activity 15.1 in the TCR. LEP

Visual Instruction

Have students review the types and characteristics of money listed in Figure 15.3. On the chalkboard, draw a chart with four columns. Write these heads across the top: Characteristics, Commodity, Representative, and Fiat. Write these heads down the side: Durable, Portable, Divisible, Stable in Value, Scarce, and Accepted. As a class, have students fill in the table. Discuss which money type they think is best suited to the United States economy. Be sure students support their opinions with reasons.

tween paydays, a person can store some of his or her income in cash and some in a checking account. It is important to note that in periods of rapid and unpredictable inflation, money is less able to act as a store of value.

The Types and Characteristics of Money

Anything that people are willing to accept in exchange for goods can serve as money. At various times in history, cattle, salt, animal hides, gems, and tobacco have been used as mediums of exchange. Each of these items has certain characteristics that make it better or worse than others for use as money. Cattle, for example, are difficult to transport, but they are durable. Gems are easy to carry, but they are not easy to split into small pieces to use.

Figure 15.3 lists the major characteristics that to some degree all items used as money must have. Almost any item that meets most of these criteria can be and probably has been used as money. Precious metals, however, particularly gold and silver, are especially well suited as mediums of exchange, and have often been used as such throughout history. It is only in more recent times that paper money has been widely used as a medium of exchange.

Mediums of exchange such as cattle and gems are considered **commodity money.** They have a value as a commodity, or good, aside from their

Chapter 15 Money and Banking **365**

Free Enterprise Activity

Call on volunteers to list on the chalkboard the six characteristics of a pure market economy. *(little or no government control, freedom of enterprise, freedom of choice, private property, profit incentive, and competition)* Ask students how the use of money fits into these characteristics. *(Answers will vary but might include that*

money is the profit that people strive for in running their own businesses.) Then ask what characteristics of a pure market economy would be difficult to achieve in a barter situation. *(Students might indicate that freedom of enterprise, freedom of choice, profit, and competition would be restricted.)*

Assess

Meeting Lesson Objectives

Assign Section 1 Review as homework or an in-class activity.

Evaluate

Assign the Section 1 Quiz in the TCR or use the Testmaker to develop a customized quiz.

Reteach

Have students use the main headings to write an outline of Section 1.

Enrich

Have students research the history of money, including how money developed, what kinds of objects were first used as money, and when and where coins and paper money were first used. Have students draw world maps and indicate each "first" with labels that state the development and give the date and world area.

Close

Have students write a short paragraph that answers the following question: What is money? Discuss students' paragraphs.

value as money. Cattle are used for food and transportation. Gems are used for jewelry.

Representative money is money backed by—exchangeable for—some commodity, such as gold or silver. It is not in itself valuable for nonmoney uses, but it can be exchanged for some valuable item. Like commodity money, the amount of representative money in circulation, or in use by people, is limited because it is linked to some scarce good, such as gold. At one time, the United States government issued representative money in the form of silver and gold certificates. In addition, private banks accepted deposits of gold or silver and issued paper money, called bank notes. These were a promise to convert the paper money into coin or bullion on demand. These banks were supposed to keep enough gold or silver in reserve—on hand—to redeem their bank notes. Often, they did not.

Today all United States money is **fiat** (FEE-uht) **money.** As Figure 15.4 shows, its face value occurs through government fiat, or order. It is in this way declared **legal tender.**

Figure 15.4 ▶
Legal Tender
By law these forms of money must be accepted for payment of public and private debts. In reality, fiat money is accepted because we all have faith that others will accept this money from us when we use it.

SECTION 1 REVIEW

Understanding Vocabulary

Define money, medium of exchange, barter, double coincidence of wants, unit of accounting, store of value, commodity money, representative money, fiat money, legal tender.

Reviewing Objectives

❶ Money must serve as a medium of exchange. What are two other functions that money must also serve?

❷ What are the six major characteristics of money?

Section 1 Review Answers

Understanding Vocabulary

money (p. 362), **medium of exchange** (p. 362), **barter** (p. 362), **double coincidence of wants** (p. 364), **unit of accounting** (p. 364), **store of value** (p. 364), **commodity money** (p. 365), **representative money** (p. 366), **fiat money** (p. 366), **legal tender** (p. 366)

Reviewing Objectives

1. Money must also serve as a unit of accounting and as a store of value.
2. Money must be durable, portable, divisible, stable in value, scarce, and accepted.

Personal Perspective

John W. Rogers on Money Management

Profile

- 1958 –
- attended Princeton University
- founded Ariel Capital Management, a Chicago-based money management firm, at age 24
- led Ariel growth funds to gains of more than 15 percent annually since 1986
- manages about $1.85 billion in assets

John W. Rogers is one of the country's best managers of small-capitalization stocks. Beginning with money from associates and his parents, Rogers built on a successful investment strategy of finding lesser-known companies that were selling for 10 times their earnings or less. Ariel Capital Management grew on a groundswell of rising interest in African American-owned businesses. The following excerpts are taken from the *Chicago Sun-Times*, January 25, 1993 and *Forbes*, September 2, 1991.

In the early '80s, more and more businesses were thinking in terms of minorities. Harold Washington had just been elected mayor of Chicago, and that helped me see there was an opportunity there.... If you trust and have faith in people, they'll trust and have faith in you.

As Ariel Capital Management grew, so much new money began flowing into the firm that Rogers was faced with a dilemma. He could not find enough investment opportunities for all the new money in small company stocks. At first Rogers bought bigger stakes in larger companies. Then, rather than take risks

with more and more capital, he decided to close the larger of two mutual funds to new customers.

We can't take on any more new cash and still preserve our focus.... The emphasis has always been on lesser-known companies. We've got only about 6 stocks overall in the portfolio. I can't handle more money and see consistent results. There are only so many good ideas.

... From now on, it's going to be a very simple story. Our private clients can judge us by just one thing—growth of assets.

Checking for Understanding

❶ What event helped Rogers see a new business opportunity?

❷ What problem resulted from Ariel's success?

❸ How did Rogers try to maintain the company's focus?

Answers to Checking for Understanding

1. The event was the election of Harold Washington, an African American, as mayor of Chicago.

2. So much new money began flowing into the firm that Rogers could not find enough investment opportunities for all the new money in small company stocks.

3. He decided to close the larger of two mutual funds to new customers.

Focus

Overview

See the student page for section objectives.

Section 2 explains or describes: important events in the history of American money and banking; the services provided by banks and savings institutions; and the effects of electronic banking on banking services.

Bellringer

Before presenting the lesson, display Focus Activity Transparency 59 on the overhead projector or copy the material on the chalkboard. Assign the accompanying Focus Activity Sheet.

Motivational Activity

Ask students to list the types of banking services they are familiar with and the costs involved, if any.

Preteaching Vocabulary

Ask students to make up definitions for each vocabulary term on separate slips of paper. Collect the slips and write four of the made-up definitions for each of the words on the chalkboard. Have students vote on which they think are correct and compare the definitions they chose with the actual definitions.

SECTION 2 History of American Money and Banking

SECTION 2 FOCUS

Terms to Know overdraft checking, electronic funds transfer (EFT), monetary standard, automated teller machines (ATMs)

Objectives *After reading this section, you should be able to:*

1. List several important events in the history of American money and banking.
2. Describe six services provided by banks and savings institutions.
3. Discuss electronic banking and its effects on banking services.

Serving the Nation's Financial Needs

During the colonial period, England did not permit the American colonies to print or mint their own money. Bartering was common. Colonists used various goods in place of coins and paper money. In Massachusetts Bay for a time, colonists used Native American wampum as a medium of exchange. In the Virginia Colony, tobacco became commodity money. Though scarce, some European gold and silver coins also circulated in the colonies. The Spanish dolár, later called the *dollar* by colonists, was one of the more common coins.

History of American Banking

The Revolutionary War brought even more confusion to the already haphazard colonial money system. To help pay for the war, the Continental Congress issued bills of credit, called Continentals, that could be used to pay debts. See Figure 15.5. So many of these notes were issued that people often refused to accept them. The money became so worthless that the phrase "not worth a Continental" was

---

Classroom Resources for Section 2

- Reproducible Lesson Plan 15.2
- Focus Activity Transparency 59
- Focus Activity Sheet 59
- Guiding Reading Activity 15.2
- Consumer Application Activity 15

- Section Quiz 15.2
- Spanish Section Quiz 15.2
- Testmaker
- Reinforcing Skills 15

used to describe something of little value.

After the war, establishing a reliable medium of exchange became a major concern of the new nation. The Constitution, ratified in 1788, gave Congress the sole power to mint coins, although private banks were still allowed to print bank notes representing gold and silver on deposit. Because the history of money in the United States is so closely tied to the development of the banking system, the time line in Figure 15.6 (pages 370–371) describes both.

Banking Services

Banks and savings institutions today offer a wide variety of services, including checking accounts, interest on checking, automatic deposit and payment, storage of valuables, transfer of money from one person to another, and overdraft checking. **Overdraft checking** allows a customer to write a check for more money than exists in his or her account. The bank "loans" the needed amount and the customer pays the money back, usually at a relatively high rate of interest.

In general, the types of services are the same across the country. The exact conditions of the services, however, vary from state to state according to each state's banking laws.

In choosing a bank or savings institution for a checking account, you should consider the service charges. Service charges on checking accounts vary from bank to bank and with the type of account. You may be charged from $.25 to $.50 for each check you write. Some institutions offer "free checking"—no per check fee or monthly fee—providing the balance in the account remains above a certain minimum. If it drops below this minimum, a service charge of about $4 to $6 is collected. The minimum balance generally ranges from $100 to $500.

Electronic Banking

One of the most important changes in banking began in the late 1970s with the introduction of the computer. With it came **electronic funds transfer (EFT)**, a system of putting onto computers all the various banking functions that in the past had to be handled on paper.

◄

**Figure 15.5
Continentals**
One of the primary mediums of exchange during the Revolutionary War was the Continental bank note. Continentals, as the notes were called, held little of their original value by the war's end.

Chapter 15 Money and Banking **369**

Teach

Guided Practice

L1 Summarizing Review with students the information about banking services. Then organize the class into small groups. Have each group summarize the information by creating posters advertising the kinds of services available through banks and savings institutions. Display completed posters in the classroom.

Visual Instructions

Refer students to Figure 15.6 on page 370. Ask students to list on the chalkboard examples from the time line that show the positive and negative effects of the banking system on the nation's economic growth.

 GLOBAL ECONOMICS

After the Revolutionary War, the écu, a French coin, was one of the many foreign coins that circulated in the United States. In 1793, legislation made these coins part of the United States monetary system.

◆ ◗ ◯ Meeting Special Needs

Inability to Take Clear Notes Taking notes requires the ability to consolidate and summarize information so that it is sufficiently clear and complete. To help students take good notes, ask them to read the subsection "Banking Services" on page 369 and take notes as they read. Then have student pairs "teach" the subsection information to each other, based only on their notes. Have students compare the effectiveness of their notes in providing essential information. Students should identify unclear or missing information and try to find a pattern of poor notes. They should repeat the reading and note taking, concentrating on places where their first notes were poor.

Independent Practice

L1 Comparing Review with students what electronic funds transfer (EFT) is. Then have students list on the chalkboard the advantages and the disadvantages of EFT compared to checks or cash payments.

L1 Creating a Time Line Have students choose six or seven specific dates in Figure 15.6 and create an illustrated time line. Stress to students that a time line shows events and the order in which they happened. LEP

DID YOU KNOW

Beginning in 1791 United States paper money was backed by both gold and silver. Congress passed the Gold Standard Act in 1900. This legislation officially put the United States on a gold standard. The United States went on and off the gold standard several times before it was abandoned in 1971.

Figure 15.6 Time Line of American Money and Banking

1780s	The new nation has no reliable medium of exchange. National leaders disagree about the type of banking system the nation needs. One group, led by Alexander Hamilton, believes a well-organized banking system is necessary for industrial development. The opposition, led by Thomas Jefferson, argues that only states should have the right to charter banks.
1791	Congress establishes the First Bank of the United States and gives it a 20-year charter. The bank is a private business, though the government supplies one-fifth of its starting capital. It serves as a depository for government funds, makes loans to the government and private individuals and businesses, and regulates the activities of banks with state charters. It also issues bank notes backed by gold.
1792	Congress passes Coinage Act that organizes a mint and establishes the dollar as the basic unit of currency for the nation. The act also places the nation on a bimetallic monetary standard. A **monetary standard** is the manner in which a nation assigns value to its money. The value of the dollar is fixed according to specific quantities of both silver and gold.
1811	Congress refuses to renew the charter of the First Bank because of questions about its legality and fears that it is gaining too much power. Without federal controls, the number of private, state-chartered banks triples in five years. Dozens of banks lend money and issue bank notes freely, many of which are not backed by enough gold or silver reserves.
1816	Congress establishes the Second Bank of the United States after the financial confusion caused by the War of 1812. Like the First Bank, it brings some order to the banking system. It pressures state-chartered banks to limit lending and to keep enough gold and silver in reserve to redeem their bank notes. However, opposition to a strong national bank remains. In 1832 President Andrew Jackson vetoes legislation to extend the Second Bank's charter.
1830s–1860s	The end of the Second Bank brings another rapid rise in state-chartered banks. The amount of money in circulation varies widely. At times banks lend freely and at other times they make few loans. Such shifts in the amount of money available result in major changes in business activity and prices. Many banks issue their own bank notes.
Civil War	To help pay for the war, the United States for the first time since the Revolution issues fiat money. These United States notes, called greenbacks, change in value as confidence in the Union army rises or falls. Difficulties in raising money for the war make clear the need for a better monetary and banking system. In 1863 and 1864, Congress passes the National Bank acts. These acts establish a system of federally chartered private banks, called national banks. The government also sets up a safe, uniform currency by requiring that all national bank notes be fully backed by government bonds. The Comptroller of the Currency is created to grant charters for national banks and to oversee their activities.

Cooperative Learning

Have small groups find out about the various services offered by local banks and savings institutions. Each group should study a different bank or savings institution and present their information in the form of an illustrated chart. Students might divide the following tasks among group members: visiting the chosen bank or savings institution and gathering information about its services, comparing types of services, creating the chart, and presenting the information to the class. When reports are completed, discuss and have students decide which institution is best suited to their personal needs.

Figure 15.6 Time Line of American Money and Banking

Late 1860s–early 1900s	The nation shifts to a gold monetary standard in 1879. Federal government begins redeeming early 1860s greenbacks for gold coins. Despite the new banking system, problems remain. There is no simple way to regulate the amount of national bank notes in circulation, so periodic shortages of money occur. Financial panics occur in 1873, 1884, 1893, and 1907. Many banks with low reserves are forced to close.
1913	To control the amount of money in circulation, Congress establishes the Federal Reserve System. It serves as the nation's central bank with power to regulate reserves in national banks, make loans to member banks, and control the growth of the money supply. In 1914 the system begins issuing fiat money, called Federal Reserve notes. These notes soon become the major form of currency in circulation.
1929	The Great Depression begins. Stocks and other investments owned by banks lose much of their value. Bankrupt businesses and individuals are unable to repay their loans.
1929–1933	A financial panic causes thousands of banks to collapse. When President Franklin Roosevelt takes office, he declares a "bank holiday," closing all banks. Each bank is allowed to reopen only after it proves it is financially sound. Congress passes the Glass-Steagall Banking Act in June, establishing the Federal Deposit Insurance Corporation (FDIC). The new agency helps restore public confidence in banks by insuring funds of individual depositors in case of a bank failure. Nation switches from gold standard to a fiat monetary standard. Government stops converting greenbacks into gold, calls in all gold coins and certificates, and prohibits private ownership of gold.
1930s–1960s	Banking reforms of the 1930s allow banks to enter a period of long-term stability, in which few banks fail.
Late 1960s–1970s	Congress passes a series of laws to protect consumers in dealing with financial institutions. Truth-in-Lending Act of 1968, Equal Credit Opportunity Act of 1974, and Community Reinvestment Act of 1977 make clear the rights and responsibilities of banks and consumers. Banks begin using computers to transfer money electronically and to handle many banking activities. Congress passes Electronic Fund Transfer Act of 1978 to protect consumers using these new services.
1980s–1990s	As part of the general move toward deregulation of business, Congress passes the Depository Institutions Deregulation and Monetary Control Act in 1980. The savings and loan industry faces many bankruptcies. Congress passes the Financial Institutions Reform, Recovery, and Enforcement Act of 1989. The full cost of bailing out the thrifts is $300 billion, or about $4,000 per United States family in future taxes. The FDIC takes over regulation of the thrift institutions industry. Savings and loans and commercial banks continue to fail, but at a slower rate.

Chapter 15 Money and Banking **371**

Independent Practice

L2 Researching Have students research the Second National Bank of the United States. Have them investigate how the Supreme Court decision in *McCulloch v. Maryland* supported the Second National Bank, why President Andrew Jackson opposed the bank, and what action he finally took.

L3 Debating Have teams debate the "free silver" issue in the election of 1896. Have one team investigate the position of the Republican Party and its candidate, William McKinley. Have the other team investigate the position of the Democratic and Populist parties and their candidate, William Jennings Bryan. The rest of the class can act as judges.

Have students complete Guided Reading Activity 15.2 in the TCR. **LEP**

GLOBAL ECONOMICS

The culture and needs of an area help determine the kinds of services banks and savings institutions offer. For example, in 1992 the National Commercial Bank (NCB) of Saudi Arabia opened its first bank for women. The opening of this bank helped provide opportunities for Saudi women who live in a society where their rights are limited to take charge of their own finances.

Free Enterprise Activity

Refer students to the entries for 1929 and 1930s–1960s in Figure 15.6. Remind students that President Hoover was opposed to government programs in dealing with the Depression. He felt that they would destroy personal initiative and would threaten the free enterprise concept. Ask students to pretend they are journalists during this period in history. Have them write an editorial in which they indicate whether they agree or disagree with President Hoover. Be sure students support their editorials logically. Call on volunteers to read their editorials aloud and discuss them with the class.

Assess

Meeting Lesson Objectives

Assign Section 2 Review as homework or an in-class activity.

Evaluate

Assign the Section 2 Quiz in the TCR or use the Testmaker.

Reteach

Ask students to write review questions based on Section 2 subheads.

Enrich

Have groups of three to five students each give a class presentation on American money and banking in one of the eras listed in Figure 15.6.

Close

Ask students to write a paragraph agreeing or disagreeing with the following statement: Modern banking services have improved life for consumers.

One of the most common features of EFT, shown in **Figure 15.7**, is **automated teller machines (ATMs).** These units let consumers do their banking without the help of a teller.

A few banks have authorized customers with home computers to use them for banking transactions. If problems with security can be resolved, many people may one day bank by computer from home.

Figure 15.7 ATMs
ATMs receive deposits, give out funds from checking or savings accounts, transfer funds from one account to another, verify balances, and accept payments. To use an ATM, the customer inserts an encoded plastic card into the machine and enters a personal identification number (PIN) to access his or her account. ▼

EFT Concerns Although EFT can save time, trouble, and costs in making transactions, it does have some drawbacks. The possibility of tampering and lack of privacy are increased because all records are stored in a computer. A person on a computer terminal could call up and read or even alter the account files of a bank customer in any city, if he or she knew how to get around the safeguards built into the system. Another problem for customers—but a benefit for banking institutions—is the loss of "float," or the time between when you write a check and when the sum of the check is deducted from your account.

In response to these and other concerns, the Electronic Fund Transfer Act of 1978 describes the rights and responsibilities of participants in EFT systems. For example, EFT customers are responsible for only $50 in losses when someone illegally uses their card, if they report the card missing within two days. If they wait more than two days, they could be responsible for as much as $500. Users are also protected against computer foul-ups. If the balance appearing on a person's statement or given out by an automatic or human teller is less than the customer believes it should be, the bank must investigate and straighten out the problem within a certain period of time.

SECTION 2 REVIEW

Understanding Vocabulary
Define overdraft checking, electronic funds transfer (EFT), monetary standard, automated teller machines (ATMs).

Reviewing Objectives
❶ What are some of the most important events in the history of American money and banking?

❷ Besides checking accounts, what are some of the other services offered by banks and savings institutions?

❸ How has electronic banking changed banking services?

Section 2 Review Answers
Understanding Vocabulary
overdraft checking (p. 369), **electronic funds transfer (EFT)** (p. 369), **monetary standard** (p. 370), **automated teller machines (ATMs)** (p. 372)

Reviewing Objectives
1. Students' answers should include some entries from Figure 15.6.

2. Students' answers may include interest on checking, automatic deposit and payment, storage of valuables, and overdraft checking.

3. simpler and saves time and costs in making transactions; increased the possibility of tampering and invasion of privacy because records are stored in a computer; has shortened the "float," or the time between writing a check and when the sum is deducted from the account

LEARNING ECONOMIC SKILLS

Keeping a Checking Account

The largest part of the money supply in the United States consists of checkable accounts. Do you know how to write a check and balance a checkbook?

Figure A

Bernadette C. Dabney
12 Vico Lane
Haddonfield, NJ 08033

December 31 19 99

Pay to _cash_ _____ $100.00

One Hundred & 00/xx _____ Dollars

FIRST NATIONAL BANK
OF CHICAGO

Bernadette C. Dabney

Figure B

Number	Date	Description	Payment of Debt	Fee	Deposit of Credit	Balance
						$827 91
						$794 91
132	10/25	Fashion Shop	33 00			332 41
133	11/1	Rent	462 50			270 41
134	11/7	Phone	62 00			220 41
135	11/14	Cash	50 00			210 41
136	11/15	J.W. Little	10 00			189 41
137	11/15	N.Y. Times	21 00			193 41
—	11/22	John's check		4 00		694 02
		Paycheck			500 61	653 86
138	11/23	Walk-A-Bout	40 16			191 36
139	12/1	Rent	462 50			

FIRST NATIONAL BANK OF CHICAGO

123-456-7 ACCOUNT NUMBER

Bernadette C. Dabney
12 Vico Lane
Haddonfield, NJ 08033

1 DEC 1999 STATEMENT DATE

SUMMARY OF ACCOUNTS

ACCOUNT NUMBER	PREVIOUS BALANCE	TOTAL CREDITS	TOTAL DEBITS	TOTAL CHARGES	CURRENT BALANCE
123-456-7	827.91	504.61	628.50	3.00	701.02

PREVIOUS BALANCE	CURRENT BALANCE
827.91	701.02

		CREDITS			BALANCE
DEBITS					794.91
NOV 4	132	33.00			332.41
8	133	462.50			270.41
15	134	62.00			220.41
	135	50.00			199.41
			NOV 22	4.00	203.41
21	137	21.00	23	500.61	704.02
					701.02
SC		3.00			

Writing a Check

Always fill out your checks completely and clearly in ink. See the sample check in **Figure A**.

Balancing Your Checkbook

At the end of each month when you receive your bank statement, balance your checkbook by following these steps:

1 Sort your checks by number. Check each off in your checkbook.

2 Check off your deposit slips.

3 Deduct service charges and bank fees from your checkbook balance.

4 Add to the bank statement balance any deposits that have not cleared.

5 Total the amount of checks that have not cleared. Subtract this total from the amount on your bank statement.

Practicing the Skill

1 Why should you draw a line through the unused space on the dollar amount line on a check?

2 The sample checkbook register in **Figure B** shows that you have a running total of $191.36 in your account. Balance this total against the bank statement in **Figure B** for the month of November.

373

Answers to Practicing the Skill

1. so that others cannot write in additional figures, thus increasing the amount charged to your checking account

2. Step 1: Checks 136, 138, and 139 have not yet cleared. Step 2: Both deposits appear on bank statement. Step 3: $191.36 – 3.00 = $188.36. Step 4: No uncleared deposits. Step 5: $10.00 + $40.16 + $462.50 = $512.66; $701.02 – 512.66 = $188.36. Step 3 agrees with Step 5, so the checkbook register agrees with the bank statement.

Focus

Call on volunteers to read the feature aloud. Have students discuss the reason for the establishment of the Women's National Bank. Discussion should focus on the fact that, during the 1970s, women and minorities had a more difficult time receiving loans and lines of credit than men did.

Teach

L1 Interviewing Organize students into pairs. Ask students to develop a list of questions that they might ask Barbara Blum in an interview. Questions should include inquiries about the reasons for the success and the name change of the Women's National Bank. Call on student pairs to act out their interviews.

L2 Research Have students research the life of Abigail Adams. Students should focus upon her values and actions that made her the namesake for the Adams National Bank. Have students write a brief paragraph in the form of an advertisement that uses this information to announce the name change of the bank.

The Adams National Bank

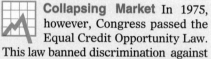

Why Women's Banks? During the 1970s, the idea of banks owned by women, run by women, and catering mostly to women customers gained favor in the banking community. Because women (as well as minorities) seemed to have a harder time receiving bank loans and lines of credit, these banks would specialize in the women's market. A dozen women-owned banks were chartered in the 1970s. Many believed that this marketing niche was here to stay. One of the first of these banks was The Women's National Bank in Washington, D.C. It was actually the first women-owned bank to secure a national charter.

Collapsing Market In 1975, however, Congress passed the Equal Credit Opportunity Law. This law banned discrimination against credit applicants on the grounds of sex or marital status. The perception that women's banks were necessary changed as it became easier for women to receive bank credit. Many of the women's banks had been founded with thin capitalization, and then made loans and extended credit lines for idealistic, rather than sound banking, reasons. Also, many of the women bankers associated with these banks wanted to join the banking mainstream. The banking industry also began to consolidate. Smaller banks merged into larger banks, and the original ownership was diluted. Most of the women's banks chartered in the 1970s either collapsed or were bought out by larger banks.

The Name Change
Very few women-owned banks, however, survived. One survivor was The Women's National Bank. In 1987 The Women's National Bank underwent a name change. According to Barbara Blum, the CEO since 1983, the bank's owners elected to change its name "because a lot of men wouldn't bank here." The new name, according to Blum, was to define the ownership of the bank, and not the customer base. The bank wanted to pursue a broad customer base, rather than the women-only market. The Women's National Bank changed its name to the more generic-sounding The Adams National Bank, but named the holding company that owns the bank the Abigail Adams National Bancorp. By naming the bank for one of the nation's first feminists, the owners were able to keep some of the spirit of the original name.

Since the name change, Barbara Blum has managed to convince her earlier clientele (mainly women's groups and environmental organizations) that the new name did not mean that the bank was abandoning them or turning its back on feminism. The Adams National Bank continues to be successful and is now one of only three women-owned banks in the country (the others being First Women's Bank of Rockville, MD, and Women's Bank of Denver). In 1989, Adams had 3 branches and more than $55 million in assets.

One unique difference between The Adams National Bank and other banks is its support of art and artists. The first floor of the main bank building is actually used as an art gallery. Thus The Adams National Bank keeps its image, both as a solid women-owned bank, and as a supporter of important causes.

Free Enterprise in Action

1. What was the original name of The Adams National Bank?
2. Why did the bank change its name?
3. Why did many women's banks chartered in the 1970s go out of business in the 1980s?

Answers to Free Enterprise in Action

1. Women's National Bank
2. The bank changed its name because it wanted to pursue a broad customer base, rather than the women-only market.
3. There were several reasons, including Congress's passage of the Equal Credit Opportunity Law in 1975, the fact that many women's banks had little capital, and over these banks' frequent preference for making investments out of idealistic rather than profit-oriented motives.

Focus

Overview

See the student page for section objectives.

Section 3 explains or describes the difference between money and near moneys and the components of the M1 and M2 definitions of the money supply.

Bellringer

Before presenting the lesson, display Focus Activity Transparency 60 and assign the accompanying Focus Activity Sheet.

Motivational Activity

Write the following on the chalkboard: Money is more than cash. Ask students what this means. Have them list other things they think constitute money. Tell students that Section 3 describes what constitutes money. Have them compare the items on their list with the information in the section.

Preteaching Vocabulary

Call on students to tell what they think each term means, then check the definitions in the Glossary. LEP

SECTION 3 FOCUS

Terms to Know checking account, demand deposits, checkable deposits, thrift institutions, debit card, near moneys, M1, M2

Objectives *After reading this section, you should be able to:*
1. Explain the difference between money and near moneys.
2. List the components of the **M2** definition of the money supply.

Money Is More Than Cash

When you think of money, you may think only of paper bills and coins. What does it mean to have "money in the bank"?

Money and Near Moneys

Money in use today consists of more than just currency. It also includes deposits in checking and savings accounts in banks and savings institutions, plus certain other investments.

Currency All United States coins in circulation today are token coins. The value of the metal in each coin is less than its exchange value. A quarter, for example, consists of a mixture of copper and nickel. If you melted down a quarter—which is illegal—the value of the resulting metal would be less than 25 cents. The Bureau of the Mint, which is part of the Treasury Department, makes all coins. Of the currency in circulation in the United States today, about 9 percent is in coins.

Most of the nation's currency is in the form of Federal Reserve notes. Federal Reserve banks issue these notes. The Bureau of Printing and Engraving, also part of the Treasury Department, prints all Federal Reserve notes. They are issued in denominations of $1, $5, $10, $20, $50, and $100.

The Treasury Department has also issued United States notes in $100 denominations only. These bills have the words *United States Note* printed across the top and can be distinguished from Federal Reserve notes by a red Treasury seal. United States notes make up less than 1 percent of the paper money in circulation. Both Federal Reserve notes and United States notes are fiat money or legal tender.

Checks A **checking account** is money deposited in a bank that a person can withdraw at any time by writing a

---

Classroom Resources for Section 3

- Reproducible Lesson Plan 15.3
- Focus Activity Transparency 60
- Focus Activity Sheet 60
- Guided Reading Activity 15.3
- Free Enterprise Activity 15
- Mathematics Practice for Economics 21
- Performance Assessment

- Activity 21
- Section Quiz 15.3
- Spanish Section Quiz 15.3
- Chapter 15 Test Forms A and B
- Testmaker
- Enrichment Activity 15
- Economics Vocabulary Activity 15

- Spanish Economics Vocabulary Activity 15
- Audiocassette 15
- Spanish Audiocassette 15
- Reteaching Activity 15
- Spanish Reteaching Activity 15

check. The bank must pay the amount of the check when it is presented for payment, that is, on demand. Such accounts used to be called **demand deposits.** Today we call these **checkable deposits,** and a variety of financial institutions offer them. Commercial banks used to be the only financial institutions that could offer checkable accounts. Today all **thrift institutions**—mutual savings banks, savings and loan associations (S&Ls), and credit unions—offer checkable deposits.

Credit Cards and Debit Cards Even though many people use their credit cards to purchase goods and services, the credit card itself is not money. It does not act as a unit of accounting nor as a store of value. The use of your credit card is really a loan to you by the issuer of the card, whether it is a bank, retail store, gas company, or American Express. See Figure 15.8. Basically, then, credit card "money" represents a future claim on money that you will have later. Credit cards defer rather than complete transactions that ultimately involve the use of money.

As Figure 15.9 illustrates, the **debit card** automatically withdraws money

**Figure 15.9
Using Debit Cards**
If the store in which you are shopping has a direct electronic link to the bank, that transfer may be made instantaneously.

▼

▼ **Figure 15.8
Credit Card Loans**
The proceeds of a credit card loan are paid to the business that sold you something. You must pay back the loan to the issuer of the credit card, either when you get your statement or with interest each month throughout the year if you do not pay off your balance owed.

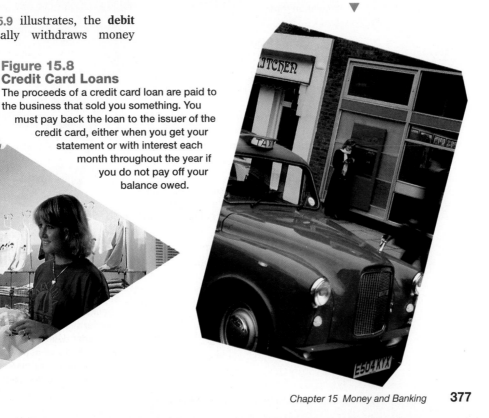

Chapter 15 Money and Banking **377**

Teach

Guided Practice

L1 Differentiating Refer students to Figure 15.11 on page 378. Then write the following headings on the chalkboard: M1 and M2. Call on volunteers to differentiate between the two definitions of money by writing the following items under the correct heading or headings: traveler's checks (*M1 and M2*), Eurodollars (*M2*), money market mutual fund balances (*M2*), checkable deposits (*M1 and M2*), currency (*M1 and M2*). Have students use Figure 15.12 to fill in the remaining moneys under M2. LEP

GLOBAL ECONOMICS

The Eurodollar refers to a transfer of credit in United States dollars from a United States bank to a foreign one. Banks that deal in Eurodollars are sometimes referred to as *Eurobanks.* Most of these banks are in Europe, but some are in New York and Asia.

? DID YOU KNOW

Checks provide an important record of personal expenditures. Checks are often needed in preparing tax returns or resolving disputes over charge accounts.

◆▶⬤ **Meeting Special Needs**

Auditory Disability One type of learning disorder results from inefficient auditory processing. Students with this disability may look as if they are not paying attention when, in reality, these students get "lost" in the confusion of language. To help students with this type of disability listen effectively, cue them with a subtle but consistent gesture when you are coming to an important point.

Independent Practice

L3 Journalism Using interviews or magazine articles, have students find out economists' views on considering credit cards as money. Ask students to find out why some economists favor it and others oppose it. Students might imagine how the addition of credit cards would affect the measurement of the money supply. Have students present their information in the form of an article for the business section of a newspaper.

L2 Creating Graphics Tell students that in 1991, M1 consisted of $897 billion, with currency making up $267 billion, traveler's checks making up $8 billion, demand deposits making up $289 billion, and other checkable deposits making up $333 billion. Have students illustrate this information in a circle graph.

 Have students complete Guided Reading Activity 15.3 in the TCR. LEP

Visual Instruction

Refer students to Figure 15.12. Have them describe how M1 and M2 have changed from 1983 to 1993. (*Both have increased; M1 has more than doubled.*)

Figure 15.10 ▲
Types of Money
Money is not limited just to the bills and coins in circulation today.

from a checkable account. When you use your debit card to purchase something, you are in effect giving an instruction to your bank to transfer money directly from your bank account to the store's bank account. The use of a debit card does not create a loan. Debit card "money" is similar to checkable account money.

Near Moneys Numerous other assets are almost, but not exactly, like money. See Figure 15.10. These assets are called **near moneys.** Their values are stated in terms of money, and they have high liquidity in comparison to other investments, such as stocks. Near moneys can be turned into currency or into a means of payment, such as a check, relatively easily and without the risk of loss of value.

Figure 15.11 ▲
M1 and M2
M1, the narrowest definition of the money supply, consists of moneys that can be spent immediately and against which checks can be written. It includes currency, traveler's checks, and checkable deposits. A broader definition of the money supply, **M2,** includes all of M1, plus such near moneys as money market mutual fund balances and Eurodollars.

Cooperative Learning

Organize the class into small groups. Have students in each group find out how United States money—both coin and paper—is made. Have them include such information as where money is made, what materials are used, what methods are used to prevent counterfeiting, and what happens to worn-out currency. Students should present their information in illustrated reports. Groups might divide the following tasks among their members: researching information, outlining information, writing the report, creating the illustrations, and presenting the report to the class.

For example, if you have a bank savings account, you cannot write a check on it. You can, however, go to the bank and withdraw some or all of your funds. You can then redeposit it in your checking account or take some or all of it in cash.

Time deposits and savings-account balances are near moneys. Both pay interest, and neither can be withdrawn by check. Time deposits require that a depositor notify the financial institution within a certain period of time, often 10 days, before withdrawing money. Savings accounts do not usually require such notification

The Money Supply

How much money is there in the United States today? That question is not so easy to answer. First, the money supply must be defined and agreed upon. Currently, two basic definitions are used, although others exist. The first is called M1 and the second M2. Both definitions include all the paper bills and coins in circulation. Figure 15.11 (page 378) expands on both M1 and M2. Measuring M1 or M2 exactly is difficult. Figure 15.12 shows the growth of M1 and M2 over a 10-year period.

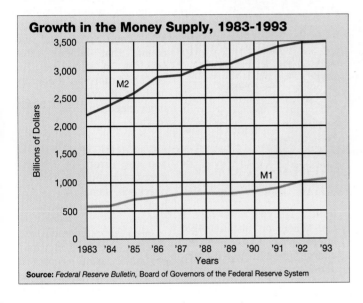

◄

**Figure 15.12
Growth in the Money
Supply, 1983–1993**
With the deregulation of banking services in the early 1980s, the definition of the money supply was enlarged to include the new types of accounts.

Assess

Meeting Lesson Objectives
Assign Section 3 Review as homework or an in-class activity.

Evaluate
Assign the Section 3 Quiz in the TCR or use the Testmaker to develop a customized quiz.
Assign the Chapter 15 Test Form A or Form B or use the Testmaker to develop a customized test.

Reteach
Have students outline Section 3.
Have students complete Reteaching Activity 15 in the TCR.

Enrich
Have students create a poster or mural depicting the origin, structure, and functions of the Treasury Department.
Have students complete Enrichment Activity 15 in the TCR.

Close

Have students in small groups create a poster illustrating the components of United States money.

SECTION 3 REVIEW

Understanding Vocabulary
Define checking account, demand deposits, checkable deposits, thrift institutions, debit card, near moneys, M1, M2.

Reviewing Objectives
❶ What is the difference between money and near moneys?

❷ There are two definitions of money, M1 and M2. What does the M2 definition of money include?

Section 3 Review Answers
Understanding Vocabulary
checking account (p. 376), **demand deposits** (p. 378), **checkable deposits** (p. 378), **thrift institutions** (p. 378), **debit card** (p. 378), **near moneys** (p. 378), **M1** (p.379), **M2** (p. 379)
Reviewing Objectives
1. Money is currency, deposits in checking and savings accounts in banks and savings institutions, plus certain other investments. Near moneys include assets that are almost, but not exactly, money.
2. M2 includes all M1 moneys (currency, traveler's checks, and checkable deposits) and, in addition, such near moneys as money market mutual fund balances and Eurodollars.

Teach

Ask students to list the kinds of banking services that are important to them or their families. Tell students that once they determine the kinds of services that are important to them, they should "shop" for the bank that provides these services at the best price. Tell students that this feature describes the kinds of things people should look for when opening new checking accounts.

Interested students might compare the types of checking accounts offered in local banks, based on the criteria discussed in the feature.

Readings in Economics

KIPLINGER'S PERSONAL FINANCE MAGAZINE   **JANUARY 1993**

HAD IT WITH YOUR BANK'S FEES?

by Kristin Davis

Some banks offer as many as nine different kinds of accounts, says Anne Moore, president of Synergistics, a banking research firm. The key is finding the account that charges least for your banking pattern.

Review recent account statements. How many checks do you write per month? How many ATM transactions do you make? How widely does your balance fluctuate? If you write fewer than ten or so checks, a "basic" account may be cheapest. Fees are usually minimal, but you pay a per-check charge if you go over the limit. . . . If you *never* use a live teller, an account that offers free ATM use but charges a fee for teller transactions may save you money. Wells Fargo and Bank of America offer such accounts.

Compare minimum balances. With interest rates on money-market accounts below 3%, it costs you relatively little in forgone income to keep a minimum balance in a checking account (even a non-interest-bearing one) to avoid checking fees. Keeping the average minimum balance of $500 in a non-interest-bearing account costs you about $15 a year in lost interest—less than the average fee of around $60 a year. . . .

Beware of "special" fees. Some banks charge for things like copies of checks. If you need services such as money orders, cashier's checks or a safe-deposit box, ask about "packaged" accounts that include those services in your fee. But don't pay more for a bundled account if you don't need the extras.

Ask about fee waivers. If you use direct deposit for your paycheck, some banks give you a break. . . .

Skip the middleman when ordering checks. Direct mailers such as Current . . . or Checks in the Mail . . . sell 200 checks for $5 to $7. Banks typically charge twice that.

• THINK ABOUT IT •

1. What four things does Moore think people should look for when opening new accounts?

2. What is the advantage of ordering checks from direct mailers?

Answers to Think About It

1. Moore thinks people should do the following when opening new accounts: review recent account statements (to see how many checks are written per month), compare minimum balances, beware of special fees for services, and ask about fee waivers.

2. Direct mailers usually charge less for checks than banks charge.

Use the Chapter 15 Highlights to preview, review, condense, or reteach the chapter. A Spanish Chapter Highlights is available in the Spanish Handbook.

Preview/Review

After students read the Chapter 15 Highlights, have them complete Economics Vocabulary Activity 15 in the TCR. Spanish Vocabulary Activities are also available in the Spanish Resource Binder.

Vocabulary Software reinforces the economic terms used in Chapter 15.

Condense

Have students listen to Chapter 15 on the Audiocassettes in the TCR. A 1-page written activity and 1-page test accompany this material. These materials are also available in Spanish.

Reteach

Have students complete Reteaching Activity 15 in the TCR. Spanish Reteaching Activities are also available.

Section 1

The Functions and Characteristics of Money

Key Terms

money (p. 362)
medium of exchange (p. 362)
barter (p. 362)
double coincidence of wants (p. 364)
unit of accounting (p. 364)

store of value (p. 364)
commodity money (p. 365)
representative money (p. 366)
fiat money (p. 366)
legal tender (p. 366)

Summary

Anything is considered money that is used as a medium of exchange, a unit of accounting, and a store of value. Today all United States money is fiat money. It is portable, divisible, stable in value, and accepted. Paper currency is not very durable, however.

Section 2

History of American Money and Banking

Key Terms

overdraft checking (p. 369)
electronic funds transfer (EFT) (p. 369)

monetary standard (p. 370)
automated teller machines (ATMs) (p. 372)

Summary

The history of the nation's money and banks has been a process of gradually bringing order to a disordered system. Congress took the first step in this direction in 1792 when it established the dollar as the basic unit of currency and set up the first mint. Modern banking services include many services in addition to checking and savings accounts.

Section 3

Types of Money in the United States

Key Terms

checking account (p. 376)
demand deposits (p. 377)
checkable deposits (p. 377)
thrift institutions (p. 377)

debit card (p. 377)
near moneys (p. 378)
M1 (p. 378)
M2 (p. 378)

Summary

United States money today is in the form of currency, checkable deposits, and near moneys. The M1 definition of the money supply includes currency, traveler's checks, and checkable deposits in commercial banks and thrift institutions. The M2 definition of money includes M1 plus certain near moneys.

Chapter 15 Money and Banking **381**

 VIDEODISC

Nightly Business Report
Economics in Action
Use "Money and Banking" on Disc 2, Side A, Video 20.

Search 15377, Play to 22824

ANSWERS

Identifying Key Terms

1. d
2. c
3. b
4. g
5. f
6. a
7. e
8. representative money

9. store of value
10. checking accounts

Recalling Facts and Ideas

Section 1
1. barter
2. Money should also be portable, stable in value, scarce, and accepted.
3. fiat

Section 2
4. bartering
5. the Great Depression
6. automated teller machines (ATMs)

Section 3
7. $1, $5, $10, $20, $50, and $100
8. Checking accounts used to be called demand deposits because the bank must pay the amount of the check when it is presented for payment on demand.
9. Near moneys are almost, but not exactly, like money. Their values are stated in terms of money, and they can be turned into currency or into a means of payment such as a check relatively easily and without the risk of loss of value.

10. because it does not include near moneys

Critical Thinking

Section 1
Answers will vary but may include: Money is a medium of exchange because a seller will accept it in exchange for a good or serv-

382

Identifying Key Terms

Write the letter of the definition in Column B below that correctly defines each term in Column A.

Column A
1. fiat money (p. 366)
2. checkable deposits (p. 377)
3. M1 (p. 378)
4. commodity money (p. 365)
5. near moneys (p. 378)
6. legal tender (p. 366)
7. electronic funds transfer (EFT) (p. 369)

Column B
a. money that by law must be accepted for payment of debts
b. currency in circulation, traveler's checks, plus checking-type deposits
c. money in a bank that can be withdrawn at any time
d. money that has value because the government has established it as acceptable payment for debts
e. computerized banking functions that previously were handled on paper
f. assets that can be turned into money fairly easily
g. money that has value aside from its value as moneyUse terms from

Use terms from the following list to fill in the blanks in the paragraph below.

store of value (p. 364)
representative money (p. 366)
checking accounts (p. 376)

The United States used to print (8), which consisted of silver and gold certificates. Every money should serve the function of a medium of exchange, a unit of accounting, and a (9). Virtually all banks and thrift institutions offer (10), so that people can withdraw money at any time.

Recalling Facts and Ideas

Section 1
1. What is the alternative to using money?
2. Money should be durable and divisible. What other characteristics should money have?
3. Is the type of money used in the United States commodity, representative, or fiat?

Section 2
4. What type of system did the early colonists use when they bought and sold goods and services?
5. When was the most serious banking panic of the twentieth century?
6. Electronic banking is increasingly common today. What form of this system do most consumers use?

Section 3
7. What are the only denominations of paper currency being issued today by the federal government?
8. Why did checking accounts used to be called demand deposits?
9. What is the distinction between money and near moneys?
10. Why is M1 considered a narrower definition of the money supply than M2?

Critical Thinking

Section 1
Making Comparisons Compare the costs and benefits of engaging in barter to the costs and benefits of using money.

Section 2
Drawing Conclusions Why are pure gold and/or pure silver coins not used as the only money in the United States?

---

ice. Barter requires a double coincidence of wants; that is, each party to a transaction must want exactly what the other person has to offer. This trading usually takes a great deal of time and effort. If a trade is made, however, it saves the effort of exchanging one item for money and using the money to purchase the other. Unlike barter, using money as the single unit of accounting provides a simple and convenient way to com-

pare the values of various items. Money also serves as a store of value. Most money is also easily transportable and durable, whereas some items used in bartering are not.

Section 2
Pure gold and/or pure silver coins are not used as the only money in the United States because these metals are very valuable, their value fluctuates substantially, and they are not as easy to carry as paper money.

Section 3

Making Generalizations Why are debit cards similar to money, whereas credit cards are not?

Applying Economic Concepts

The Functions of Money The three functions of money are medium of exchange, unit of accounting, and store of value. Keep track of any time you use money, see money used, or see dollar values written out somewhere. Try to determine in each instance what function the money is serving. For example, if you see a headline that says "Microsoft Corporation sales increased to $10 billion," you know that money is being used as a unit of accounting.

Chapter Projects

1. Individual Project Do a survey of the ATMs in your area. Some are offered by banks and some are on multiple bank systems. What is the difference? What bank cards, debit cards, and ATM cards can be used in the different machines? What other services do ATMs offer, particularly the ones that are physically connected to a bank?

2. Cooperative Learning Project Between 1929 and 1933, the United States underwent a tragic economic depression. The banking system, prices, incomes, and employment changed dramatically during this period. Work in groups to research a history of the following:

   ■ What happened to incomes and prices?
   ■ What happened to banks and savings accounts?
   ■ What happened to the availability of jobs?

   The members of each group should interview at least one person who lived during that period and who was old enough to be aware of what was happening economically. Each person should take notes on the interviews. Each group will summarize the different interview notes to develop an oral history of what actually happened during the Great Depression.

Reviewing Skills

Keeping a Checking Account
Balancing Your Checkbook Write a paragraph explaining the process you used when you were practicing the skill of balancing a checkbook on page 373.

Writing About Economics

Descriptive Writing During the week, you probably recorded several items in Your Economics Journal that you purchased without using fiat money. Imagine a society in the past or in the future that does not depend on fiat money such as the currency used by the United States. Write a description of how an individual in that society obtains necessities such as food, clothing, and shelter.

383

Reviewing Skills
Students' paragraphs should reflect the steps for balancing a checkbook listed on page 373.

Writing About Economics
Answers will vary. Descriptions may include the use of barter, checking, or electronic funds transfer. Ask volunteers to read their descriptions to the class.

Section 3
Debit cards are considered to be money because the use of a debit card does not create a loan (as the use of a credit card does), and debit card "money" is similar to checkable account money.

Applying Economic Concepts
Answers will vary, but students should indicate the appropriate function of the money used or illustrated.

Chapter Projects
1. Students might present their findings in the form of a chart.
2. Students should develop a detailed list of questions to ask the interviewees. Students might want to make recordings of the oral history they develop.

? BONUS QUESTION

The following bonus question may be written on the chalkboard when students take the chapter test.
Q: Describe a situation in which barter would work as well as exchange of money.
A: Students may suggest trading items of similar value, such as baseball cards or pieces of jewelry.

Focus

The issue of government intervention in economic affairs can be confusing to students. Help students understand that fiscal and monetary policies are developed primarily in response to specific economic problems (such as depression, inflation, and high unemployment). Because the economy is always changing, it is very difficult to devise a policy that works for all similar situations. Thus, economists must look at the overall or long-term effects of government intervention and decide whether it is helpful.

Teach

L2 Research Have students research major government fiscal and monetary actions since 1900. Ask them to write a brief report describing whether their findings support or refute Tobin's views on the beneficial effect of government actions.

L3 Debate Select two teams to debate the topic of government intervention in today's economy. Ask each side to back up its views with statistics, historical evidence, and other supporting data. The class may ask questions and serve as judges for the debate.

ISSUE: Can the Economy Be Fine-Tuned Using Fiscal and Monetary Policies?

For years, economists have debated the question of whether the government should enact activist fiscal and monetary policies to fix economic problems. Not only do economists debate whether these policies should be used, but they also debate whether the policies even work. Traditional Keynesian economics tells us that government should spend more and tax less during bad economic times. Some economists argue that this type of fiscal policy is irresponsible, enlarging the deficit while helping the economy very little.

 In an article in *The New York Times*, Peter Passell presents the traditional Keynesian view. He refers to the Keynesian economists as "they":

As recently as the early 1970s most economists thought they knew how to take the sting out of recessions. A decline in the inclination of businesses and consumers to spend, they said, could leave a gap between the total demand for goods and the economy's capacity to provide them. And while the gap would eventually close without government intervention, eventually could be a very long time indeed. What was needed to offset swings in private demand, they argued, was some combination of tax

cuts and government spending, plus an increase in funds available for bank loans.

In the early 1980s, economist and Nobel Laureate James Tobin offered his view of activist policies to smooth out business cycles:

. . . I don't believe stable government policies necessarily mean the economy will be stabilized. History doesn't suggest the economy will stay on even keel if the government just keeps its hands off or runs things according to some well understood rules. Shocks of nongovernmental origin—from overseas, and in our technology and the tastes of consumers—have created business fluctuations throughout the history of capitalism. What governments have tried to do since 1945 is to offset these shocks.

Sometimes, it is true, government has been the source of shocks. But if you compare pre-World War II history with the recent era, in which governments . . . have pursued activist economic policies, the results of activism have been very good.

Counterpoint

CON Milton Friedman has been one of the major critics of activist fiscal and monetary policies. He writes that, because of time lags involved in fiscal policy, any government action may make the problem even worse. He claims that government intervention policies have intensified business cycles. He also blames the monetary policy of the Federal Reserve for contributing to economic instability, leading to more inflations and contractions than in the pre-Fed years. Friedman has often written in favor of a "monetary rule," whereby the money supply would increase at a fixed rate that does not change to counter business cycles.

In his article in *The New York Times*, Peter Passell writes that today the economics establishment has lost faith in the ability of the government to fine-tune the economy. He quotes economist Gregory Mankiw of Harvard on some of the problems of fiscal policies:

Once the need for fiscal stimulus is recognized, he notes, it may take months to pass the necessary legislation. Hence the full impact may only hit the economy after the recovery is under way and the stimulus is no longer welcome. Even if the stimulus does hit in timely fashion, public fears that it will ignite inflation may push up interest rates and slow business investments.

That should not be a significant problem if the public is convinced that the spending of

tax stimulus is indeed temporary and will evaporate by the time offices and factories are running full tilt. But such convictions do not come easily to a public grown cynical about Washington: "Whenever I hear a politician say 'never again' I don't believe it," Mr. Mankiw, the Harvard economist, said.

Exploring the Issue

Reviewing Facts
1. What does Tobin view as the purpose of fiscal policy?
2. According to Milton Friedman why does fiscal policy harm the economy?

Critical Thinking
3. What do you think a "traditional Keynesian" economist would think of Friedman's idea of a monetary rule?

TEACHING
Point/Counterpoint

L2 Speculating Have students select one serious economic problem (such as the Great Depression, high inflation of late 1970s, recession of 1980–1982) and speculate on what might have happened if the government had not intervened or had intervened. Ask students to suggest alternative actions the government could have taken and what they believe the reults might have been.

Assess

Have students answer the Exploring the Issue questions.

Close

Ask students whether they believe government should use fiscal and monetary policies to intervene in economic affairs. Have them explain their answers.

Answers to Exploring the Issue

Reviewing Facts
1. Tobin believes the purpose of fiscal policy is to offset the shocks the economy receives from various internal and external sources.
2. Friedman believes that because of time lags involved in fiscal policy, any government action will worsen the problem. Also, fiscal policies intensify business cycles and contribute to economic instability, leading to more inflation and contraction.

Critical Thinking
3. Traditional Keynesians would find Friedman's monetary rule much too rigid to respond to the fluctuations in the economy. They would recommend a more flexible use of tax cuts and government spending, and more available credit.

CHAPTER 16 *THE FEDERAL RESERVE SYSTEM AND MONETARY POLICY*

CHAPTER ORGANIZER

Daily Objectives	Special Features	Classroom Resources
Section 1 Money Supply and the Economy • **Contrast** loose money and tight money policies. • **Describe** fractional reserve banking. • **Explain** money expansion in the banking system.	**Personal Perspective:** Milton Friedman on the Federal Reserve, p. 392	📁 Reproducible Lesson Plan 16.1 🔊 *NBR*, Video 21 📊 Focus Activity Transparency 63 📁 Focus Activity Sheet 63 📁 Guided Reading Activity 16.1 📁 Cooperative Learning Activity 16 📁 Primary and Secondary Source Readings 16 📁 Section Quiz 16.1 📁 Spanish Section Quiz 16.1 💿 Testmaker
Section 2 Organization and Functions of the Federal Reserve System • **Describe** the organization of the Federal Reserve System. • **List** the functions of the Federal Reserve System.	**Learning Economic Skills:** Understanding Real and Nominal Values, p. 399	📁 Reproducible Lesson Plan 16.2 📊 Focus Activity Transparency 64 📁 Focus Activity Sheet 64 📁 Guided Reading Activity 16.2 📁 Consumer Application Activity 16 📁 Section Quiz 16.2 📁 Spanish Section Quiz 16.2 💿 Testmaker 📁 Reinforcing Skills 16
Section 3 Regulating the Money Supply • **Describe** the way the Federal Reserve changes the money supply by changing reserve requirements. • **Describe** the way the Federal Reserve changes the money supply by changing the discount rate. • **Identify** how the Fed uses open-market operations. • **List** the difficulties of monetary policy.	**News Clip:** "Central Bank Gripes About a New World," *The New York Times*, p. 406	📁 Reproducible Lesson Plan 16.3 📊 Focus Activity Transparency 65 📁 Focus Activity Sheet 65 📊 Economic Concepts Transparency 18 📁 Guided Reading Activity 16.3 📁 Free Enterprise Activity 16 📁 Mathematics Practice for Economics 22 📁 Performance Assessment Activity 22 📁 Section Quiz 16.3 📁 Spanish Section Quiz 16.3 💿 Testmaker 📁 Enrichment Activity 16

OUT OF TIME? If time does not permit teaching this chapter, you may use the Chapter 16 Highlights and the Audiocassettes that include a 1-page activity and a 1-page test.

Chapter 16 Review and Evaluation

Special Features

Chapter 16 Highlights, p. 407
Chapter 16 Review, pp. 408–409

Classroom Resources

📁 Chapter 16 Test Forms A and B
📁 Economics Vocabulary Activity 16
📁 Spanish Economics Vocabulary
      Activity 16

🎧 Audiocassette 16
🎧 Spanish Audiocassette 16
📁 Reteaching Activity 16
📁 Spanish Reteaching Activity 16

Key to Ability Levels

Teaching strategies have been coded for varying learning styles and abilities.

L1 Level 1 activities are **basic** activities and should be within the ability range of all students.

L2 Level 2 activities are **average** activities designed for the ability range of average to above-average students.

L3 Level 3 activities are **challenging** activities designed for the ability range of above-average students.

LEP activities should be within the ability range of **Limited English Proficiency** students.

Performance Assessment

The following chapter project may be assigned at the beginning of the chapter and used for performance assessment. See page T12 for additional Performance Assessment information.

Researching and Reporting Have students work in small groups to research recent actions taken by the Federal Reserve to regulate the money supply. Encourage students to use newspapers, news magazines, and the *Federal Reserve Bulletin* to locate information. Have students determine what caused the Fed to take action, the results of the action, and reaction to the action from various groups. Each group should present its findings in the form of a newspaper article.

Additional Resources

Readings for the Student

The Federal Reserve System—Purposes and Functions. Board of Governors: Federal Reserve System, 1985.

Historical Beginnings of the Federal Reserve. Boston: Federal Reserve Bank, 1977.

Schiffres, Manuel. "The Federal Reserve Walks Quietly." *Changing Times*, October 1988, p. 16.

Readings for the Teacher

Clark, Simon. *Keynesianism, Monetarism, & the Crisis of the State.* Brookfield, Vt.: Gower Publishing Co., 1988.

Open Market Operations. New York: Federal Reserve Bank, 1985.

Multimedia Materials

The Federal Reserve System. Filmstrips. Social Studies School Service. P.O. Box 802, Culver City, CA 90232-0802

Twenty-four Hours in the Life of a Check. Film. Federal Reserve Bank of St. Louis. Public Information Dept. P.O. Box 442, St. Louis, MO 63166

Macroeconomics. Tutorial/drill/practice. Apple. 10 modules. Intellectual Software, 562 Boston Avenue, Bridgeport, CT 06610

Usecon (Social Studies Volume 3). Simulation. Apple. MECC, 3490 Lexington Avenue, North, St. Paul, MN 55126

Chapter Overview

This chapter explains or describes: how the supply of money in use in the United States today is regulated and why; the differences between tight money and loose money policies and the importance of finding the right balance between the two; fractional reserve banking (the basis of the country's banking system); money creation; the organization and functions of the Federal Reserve System; and the Fed's regulation of the money supply and the problems involved.

VIDEODISC

Nightly Business Report
Economics in Action
Use "Federal Reserve and Monetary Policy" on Disc 2, Side A, Video 21.

Search 22901, Play to 28244

CHAPTER

16 THE FEDERAL RESERVE SYSTEM AND MONETARY POLICY

Who determines how many dollar bills are in circulation?

What happens when dollar bills wear out?

Where will these dollar bills go?

Answering Economic Questions

The questions in the above illustration are designed to lead into the main concepts in Chapter 16. Students might not be aware of the origin of the currency they use. They might not be aware of the agency that determines the amount of dollar bills in circulation. The questions will help students become aware of where currency originates and how it is regulated. Have students discuss the questions. Point out that the currency is printed in Washington, D.C., and is issued from one of the 12 Federal Reserve Banks.

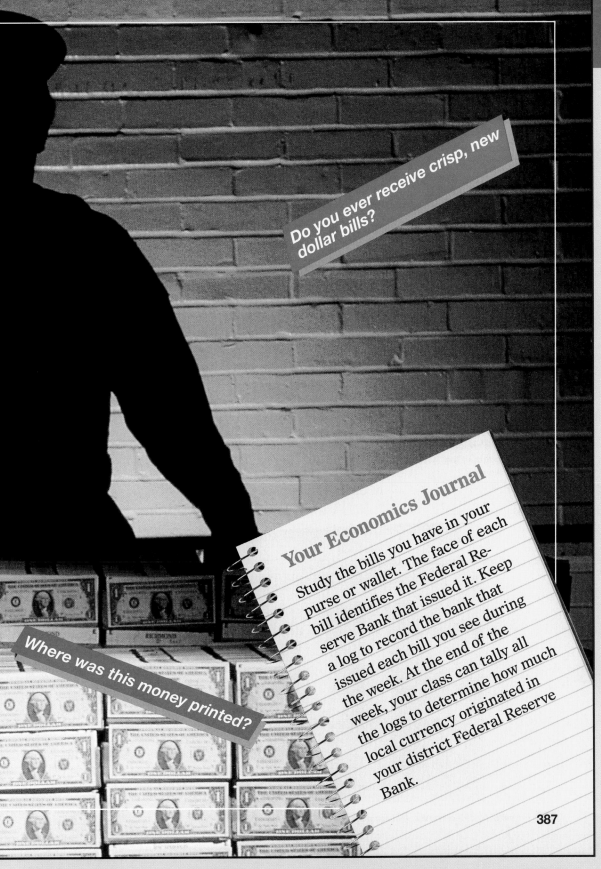

Do you ever receive crisp, new dollar bills?

Where was this money printed?

Your Economics Journal

Study the bills you have in your purse or wallet. The face of each bill identifies the Federal Reserve Bank that issued it. Keep a log to record the bank that issued each bill you see during the week. At the end of the week, your class can tally all the logs to determine how much local currency originated in your district Federal Reserve Bank.

387

Connecting to Past Learning

Ask students to recall and list the types of money that are in use in the United States today. *(currency, deposits in checking and savings accounts in banks and savings institutions, plus certain other investments)* Then ask students to recall what M1 and M2 refer to. *(definitions of the money supply)* Tell students that in Chapter 16 they will learn about the Federal Reserve System and the tools it uses to regulate the nation's money supply.

Applying Economics

Organize the class into small groups to locate current rates of mortgage loans published in the business section of a newspaper. Ask students to compare these rates with the average rates five years earlier and to indicate whether the rates increased or decreased and to speculate on the cause for the change. Have students discuss how the mortgage rates affect consumers.

EXTRA CREDIT PROJECTS

Have students use the *Federal Reserve Bulletin* to report on recent actions suggested by the Federal Open Market Committee in regard to monetary policy.

PERFORMANCE ASSESSMENT

Refer to page 386B for "Researching and Reporting," a Performance Assessment Activity for this chapter.

Economic Portfolio

Refer students to the information in **Your Economics Journal.** Have students use the map on page 395 showing the Federal Reserve districts to determine which district they live in. Have students develop a table in which they list the Federal Reserve Banks from which the bills were issued and to run a tally indicating how many were from each. Then ask students to make a class tally on the chalkboard. Have students determine where most of the bills were issued and to speculate why.

387

Focus

Overview

See the student page for section objectives.

Section 1 explains or describes the difference between loose money and tight money policies and the idea of money expansion in the banking system.

Bellringer

Before presenting the lesson, display Focus Activity Transparency 63 on the overhead projector or copy the material on the chalkboard. Assign the accompanying Focus Activity Sheet.

Motivational Activity

Write the following on the chalkboard: What costs are involved in buying a car? Call on volunteers to list the costs on the chalkboard. *(price, taxes, licenses and other fees, loan interest)* Remind students that, when people borrow money to buy a car, interest on the loan adds to the cost. Tell students that this section discusses factors in making credit available.

Preteaching Vocabulary

Have students read the Glossary definitions of the terms and use them in a paragraph.

SECTION **1** Money Supply and the Economy

S E C T I O N   1   F O C U S

Terms to Know the Fed, monetary policy, loose money policy, tight money policy, fractional reserve banking, reserve requirements

Objectives *After reading this section, you should be able to:*
1. Contrast loose money and tight money policies.
2. Describe fractional reserve banking.
3. Explain money expansion in the banking system.

The Federal Reserve and the Money Supply

Congress created the Federal Reserve System in 1913 as the central banking organization in the United States. Its major purpose was to end the periodic financial panics that had occurred during the 1800s and into the early 1900s. Over the years, many other responsibilities have been added to the Federal Reserve System, or **the Fed**, as it is called. See Figure 16.1. The jobs of the Fed today range from processing checks to serving as the government's banker. Its most important function, however, involves control over the rate of growth of the money supply.

**Figure 16.1
The Fed**
The 12 Federal Reserve banks that serve the nation's banks are distributed throughout the country. Trillions of dollars a year pass through the Fed.

Loose and Tight Money Policies

You may have read a news report in which a business executive or public official complained that money is "too tight." You may have run across a story about an economist warning that money is "too loose." In these cases the terms *tight* and *loose* are referring to the monetary policy of the nation's Federal Reserve System. **Monetary policy** involves changing the rate of growth of the supply of money in circulation to affect the amount of credit and, therefore, business activity in the economy.

Credit, like any good or service,

Classroom Resources for Section 1

- Reproducible Lesson Plan 16.1
- *NBR* Video 21
- Focus Activity Transparency 63
- Focus Activity Sheet 63
- Guided Reading Activity 16.1
- Cooperative Learning Activity 16

- Primary and Secondary Source Readings 16
- Section Quiz 16.1
- Spanish Section Quiz 16.1
- Testmaker

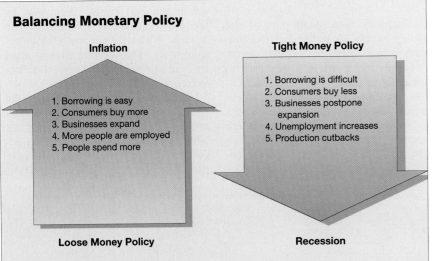

Balancing Monetary Policy

Inflation

Loose Money Policy

1. Borrowing is easy
2. Consumers buy more
3. Businesses expand
4. More people are employed
5. People spend more

Tight Money Policy

1. Borrowing is difficult
2. Consumers buy less
3. Businesses postpone expansion
4. Unemployment increases
5. Production cutbacks

Recession

◀

Figure 16.2 Loose Money Versus Tight Money
Look at the chart and determine the differences between loose money policy and tight money policy. Which of these can lead to a recession? Why is this possible?

Teach

L1 Math Have students sit in a circle. Give the first student 200 fake dollars (in singles) and have the student write number 1 and $200 next to it on a sheet of paper. Tell the first student to keep 10 percent ($20) and pass $180 to the next student. Have this student write 2 on the sheet and $180 next to it. Ask this student to keep $18 and to pass $162 to the third student, who records $162 next to 3. Repeat the process until all have participated. At the chalkboard, add $200 + $180 + $164 to show the expansion at this point equals $542. Tell them the total expansion will be $2,000. Say that students who have studied advanced algebra may recognize that the total money expansion can be found by using the formula for the sum of an infinite geometric series:

$$S = \frac{a_1}{1-r},$$

where a_1 is the amount of the initial deposit ($200) and r is the percent of the excess reserves (.9 or 90 percent).

Visual Instruction

Answer to Figure 16.2 question: *tight money policy; causes businesses to contract.*

Refer students to Figure 16.2 and have them write a paragraph summarizing the characteristics and outcomes of loose money and tight money policies.

---

is subject to the laws of supply and demand. Also, like any good or service, credit has a cost. The cost of credit is the interest that must be paid to obtain it. As the cost of credit increases, the quantity demanded decreases. In contrast, if the cost of borrowing drops, the quantity of credit demanded rises.

Figure 16.2 shows the results of monetary policy decisions. If a country has a **loose money policy,** credit is inexpensive to borrow and abundant. If a country has a **tight money policy,** credit is expensive to borrow and in short supply.

If this is the case, why would any nation want a tight money policy? The answer is to control inflation. See Figure 16.2. If money becomes too plentiful too quickly, prices increase and the purchasing power of the dollar decreases dramatically. This situation occurred during the Revolutionary War. The supply of Continental currency grew so rapidly that notes became almost worthless.

The goal of monetary policy is to strike a balance between tight and loose money. It is the Fed's responsibility to ensure that money and credit are plentiful enough to allow expansion of the economy. The Fed cannot, however, let the money supply become so plentiful that rapid inflation results.

Fractional Reserve Banking

Before you are able to understand how the Fed regulates the nation's money supply, you need to understand the basis of the United States banking system and the way money is created. The banking system is based on what is called **fractional reserve banking.**

Since 1913 the Fed has set specific **reserve requirements** for many banks. They must hold a certain percentage of their total deposits either as cash in their own vaults or as deposits in their district Federal Reserve bank. Currently most financial institutions must keep 10 percent of their checkable deposits in reserves with the Federal Reserve. They do not have to keep any reserves on so-called nonpersonal time deposits.

Independent Practice

L2 Applying Information
Have students make a chart demonstrating how the money supply would increase if the required reserves were 5 percent. Suggest using Figure 16.3 as a reference and demonstrating the multiple expansion for 6 rounds. Ask volunteers to share their charts.

L3 Journalism Have students write a newspaper article telling how fractional reserve banking helps economic growth. Suggest using the information in Section 1. Call on volunteers to read their articles.

Have students complete Guided Reading Activity 16.1 in the TCR. LEP

? DID YOU KNOW

Economists use the following formula to determine the banking system's potential for expanding the money supply:
Expansion Multiple ×
Initial Deposit =
Money Creation
The expansion multiple is

$$\frac{1}{\text{Reserve Requirement}}$$

Money Expansion

Currency is a small part of the money supply. A larger portion consists of bank deposits the public owns. Because banks are not required to keep 100 percent of their deposits in reserve, they can use their deposits to create what is, in effect, new money.

Suppose you sell a government bond to the Fed and receive $1,000. This is $1,000 in "new" money because the Fed simply creates it by writing you a check. You deposit it in a bank. With a 10 percent reserve requirement, $100 of that money must be held in reserve. However, the bank is free to lend the remaining $900.

Suppose another customer asks the same bank for a $900 loan. The bank creates $900 simply by transferring $900 to the customer's checking account. The bank must keep in reserve

Figure 16.3 Expanding the Money Supply
The chart shows how $1,000 expands to $5,000 by simple loans. How does this happen?
▼

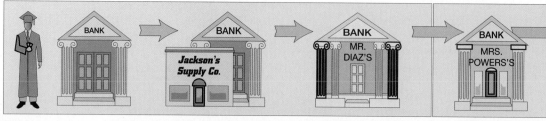

Multiple Expansion of the Money Supply

Round	Deposited by	Amount of Deposit	Required Reserves (20%)	Excess Reserves (80%)	Loaned to	Paid to
1	Student (you) (Bank A)	$1,000	$200.00	$800.00	John Jones	Jackson's Supply Company
2	Jackson's (Bank B)	800	160.00	640.00	Ms. Wang	Mr. Diaz
3	Mr. Diaz (Bank C)	640	128.00	512.00	Mrs. Fontana	Mrs. Powers
4	Mrs. Powers (Bank D)	512	102.40	409.60	Mr. Gibbs	Mr. Santana
5	Mr. F. Santana (Bank E)	409.60	81.92	327.68		
6						
Eventual Totals		$5,000	$1,000			

390

◉◉ Cooperative Learning

Organize the class into small groups. Have each group find out what interest rates local banks are offering for deposits and specific kinds of loans such as new car or home loans. Have students report on the differences in interest rates among the banks and speculate on what these differences indicate about the individual banks. Students might report their findings in a chart. The groups might divide the following tasks among their members: surveying the banks, writing the report, preparing the chart, and reporting findings to the class.

10 percent of this new deposit—$90, but now it can lend the remaining $810. This $810 is in turn treated as a new deposit. Ninety percent of it—$729—can again be lent. The original $1,000 has become $3,439. So it goes; each new deposit gives the bank new funds to continue lending.

Of course, a bank is not likely to continue lending and receiving back the same money. Its customers will most likely withdraw money and spend it or deposit it in another bank; however, this does not stop the creation of money. As the money finds its way into a second and third bank, and so on, each bank can use the nonrequired reserve portion of the money to make more loans.

How the Money Supply Increases

Money expansion may seem confusing. Let's examine step by step the example shown in **Figure 16.3**. **Round 1:** Suppose you have $1,000 that you take to your bank (Bank A) and deposit in your checking account. Assume that the Fed requires your bank to keep 20 percent of its total deposits on re-

serve. Your bank must hold $200 of your deposit on reserve. This leaves the bank with $800 of excess reserves, which is not earning interest.

Round 2: Bank A decides to loan out $800 to earn interest. John Jones applies to the bank for an $800 loan. Bank A finds him creditworthy and credits his account with $800. Mr. Jones borrowed the money to buy a machine for his business from Jackson's Supply Company. He writes a check to Jackson's, and the company deposits it at Bank B, which credits $800 to Jackson's account balance. Bank B's reserves increase by $800. Of this amount, $160 (20 percent of $800) are required reserves, and the remaining $640 are excess reserves.

Round 3: To earn profits, Bank B loans its excess reserves to Ms. Wang, who wants to borrow $640. She, in turn, buys something from Mr. Diaz, who does his banking at Bank C. He deposits the money from Ms. Wang. Bank C now has $640 in new deposits, of which $128 are required reserves. Bank C now loans $512 of excess reserves to Mrs. Fontana, who buys something from Mrs. Powers, and so on. The result is that a deposit of $1,000 in new money that was outside of the banking system has caused the money supply to increase to $5,000. This process is called the multiple expansion of the money supply.

SECTION 1 REVIEW

Understanding Vocabulary

Define the Fed, monetary policy, loose money policy, tight money policy, fractional reserve banking, reserve requirements.

Reviewing Objectives

① What is the difference between loose money and tight money policies?

② What is the purpose of fractional reserve banking?

③ If there is a 10 percent reserve requirement, how much does the money supply expand if the Fed injects $100 of new money?

Assess

Meeting Lesson Objectives

Assign Section 1 Review as homework or an in-class activity.

Evaluate

Assign the Section 1 Quiz in the TCR or use the Testmaker.

Reteach

Ask students to outline the section using headings and details under each.

Enrich

Have students brainstorm questions about present money policy and write to a representative of the Federal Reserve bank in their district, or the closest branch bank in their district, requesting answers.

Close

Have students determine whether a higher or lower reserve requirement is desirable for economic growth.

Section 1 Review Answers

Understanding Vocabulary

the Fed (p. 388), **monetary policy** (p. 388), **loose money policy** (p. 389), **tight money policy** (p. 389), **fractional reserve banking** (p. 389), **reserve requirement** (p. 389)

Reviewing Objectives

1. With a loose money policy, credit is inexpensive and abundant. With a tight money policy, credit is expensive and in short supply.
2. Banks hold a certain percentage of their total deposits in reserve to meet Federal Reserve requirements, thus helping regulate the money supply.
3. The money supply expands by $1,000.

Milton Friedman has been called a modern Adam Smith because he praises free market competition and criticizes government intervention in the economy. He opposes Keynesian economics, which states that government intervention is necessary to keep the economy running smoothly. Friedman claims that bungling by the Fed increased the length and depth of the Great Depression.

Friedman wrote *Capitalism and Freedom* with his wife, Rose, and won the Nobel Prize for his monetary theories. Now retired from the University of Chicago, he and his wife also wrote *Free to Choose*.

Teach

Call on volunteers to read aloud the excerpts from *Capitalism and Freedom*. Ask students to write a summary of the excerpts and then answer the questions in Checking for Understanding.

You might have interested students read other segments of *Capitalism and Freedom* and report on them.

Personal Perspective

Milton Friedman on the Federal Reserve

Profile

- 1912–
- won Nobel Prize for Economics in 1976
- leading supporter of monetarism
- among his many publications are *The Monetary History of the U.S. 1867–1960* with Anna J. Schwartz (1963), *Capitalism and Freedom* (1962), and *Free to Choose* with Rose Friedman (1980)

Milton Friedman has written extensively on the monetary history of the United States. He is often critical of the actions of the Federal Reserve System. In the following excerpt from *Capitalism and Freedom*, Friedman explains why he does not approve of the Federal Reserve and gives a possible replacement solution to regulating the money supply.

The establishment of the Federal Reserve System . . . established a separate official body charged with explicit responsibility for monetary conditions, and supposedly clothed with adequate power to achieve monetary stability or, at least, to prevent pronounced instability. It is therefore instructive to compare experience as a whole before and after its establishment—say, from just after the Civil War to 1914 and from 1914 to date.

. . . The stock of money, prices, and output was decidedly more unstable after the establishment of the Reserve System than before. . . .

The Great Depression in the United States, far from being a sign of the inherent instability of the private enterprise system, is a testament to how much harm can be done by mistakes on the part of a few men when they wield vast power over the monetary system of a country.

. . . Any system which gives so much power and so much discretion to a few men that mistakes—excusable or not—can have such far-reaching effects is a bad system. It is a bad system to believers in freedom just because it gives a few men such power without any effective check by the body politic—this is the key political argument against an "independent" central bank.

. . . My choice at the moment would be . . . instructing the monetary authority to achieve a specified rate of growth in the stock of money. . . . I would specify that the Reserve System shall see to it that the total stock of money so defined rises . . . at an annual rate of X per cent, where X is a number between 3 and 5.

Checking for Understanding

❶ What does Friedman's study reveal about the stability of monetary conditions in the United States after the establishment of the Fed?

❷ What is Friedman's argument against an "independent" central bank?

❸ What rule does Friedman propose to govern decisions of the Federal Reserve System?

Answers to Checking for Understanding

1. The stock of money, prices, and output was more unstable after the establishment of the Reserve System than before.

2. It gives a few people too much power without any kind of check.

3. He proposes a legislated rule instructing the monetary authority to achieve a specified rate of growth in the stock of money.

2 Organization and Functions of the Federal Reserve System

SECTION 2 FOCUS

Terms to Know Federal Open Market Committee (FOMC), check clearing

Objectives *After reading this section, you should be able to:*
1. Describe the organization of the Federal Reserve System.
2. List the functions of the Federal Reserve System.

The Federal Reserve Serves Many Functions

The organization of the Federal Reserve System is shown in Figure 16.5 on page 394. As its name states, the Fed is a system, or network, of banks. Power is not concentrated in a single central bank but is shared by a governing board and 12 district banks.

Organization of the Federal Reserve System

The Federal Reserve System is made up of the Board of Governors assisted by the Federal Advisory Council, the Federal Open Market Committee, 12 Federal Reserve banks, and about 5,000 member banks. This system is responsible for monetary policy in the free enterprise system of the United States.

Board of Governors The Board of Governors directs the operations of the Fed. It establishes policies regarding such things as reserve requirements and discount rates. The board also supervises the 12 district Federal Reserve banks and regulates certain activities of member banks and all other depository institutions.

The seven full-time members of the Board of Governors are appointed by the President of the United States with the approval of the Senate. See Figure 16.4. The President chooses one member as a chairperson. Each member of the board serves for 14 years.

Figure 16.4 The Board
The Board of Governors can raise or lower the discount rate in relation to prevailing market rates.

Chapter 16 The Federal Reserve System and Monetary Policy **393**

Classroom Resources for Section 2

- Reproducible Lesson Plan 16.2
- Focus Activity Transparency 64
- Focus Activity Sheet 64
- Guided Reading Activity 16.2
- Consumer Application Activity 16
- Section Quiz 16.2
- Spanish Section Quiz 16.2
- Testmaker
- Reinforcing Skills 16

Teach

Guided Practice

Researching Have students research the names and affiliations of the board members of their district Federal Reserve bank. Suggest developing a class letter to the board, inquiring about the organization of the board, responsibilities of its members, its main concerns within the System, and the nature of its routine business. Read and discuss any reply from the board.

Visual Instruction

Refer students to Figure 16.5. Ask them to read about and then discuss the organization of the Federal Reserve System, considering the responsibilities of the Board of Governors, the Federal Advisory Council, the Federal Open Market Committee, the Federal Reserve Banks, and the member banks. **LEP**

GLOBAL ECONOMICS

Other nations have central banks with functions comparable to those of the United States Federal Reserve System. They include the Bank of Canada, the Bank of England (Great Britain), the Banque de France, and the Deutsche Bundesbank (Germany).

The terms are arranged so that an opening occurs every two years. Members cannot be reappointed, and their decisions are not subject to the approval of the President or Congress. Their length of term, manner of selection, and independence in working frees members from political pressures. Members do not have to fear that their sometimes-unpopular decisions will cause them to lose their jobs at election time.

The Board of Governors is assisted by the Federal Advisory Council (FAC). It is made up of 12 members elected by the directors of each Federal Reserve bank. The Federal Advisory Council meets at least 4 times each year and reports to the Board of Governors on general business conditions in the nation.

Federal Open Market Committee The **Federal Open Market Committee (FOMC)** meets approximately eight times a year to decide the course of action that the Fed should take to control the money supply.

Federal Reserve Banks Each of the 12 Federal Reserve district banks is set up as a corporation owned by its member banks. A 9-person board of directors made up of bankers and businesspeople supervises each Federal Reserve district bank. The system includes 25 Federal Reserve branch banks as shown on the map in Figure 16.6. These smaller banks act as branch offices and aid the district banks in carrying out their duties.

Member Banks All national banks—those chartered by the federal government—are required to become members of the Federal Reserve System. Banks chartered by the states may join if they choose to do so. Currently, the 5,000 member banks include all of the national banks and some of the state banks. To become a member bank, a national or state bank buys stock in its district's Federal Reserve bank.

Figure 16.5
Organization of the Federal Reserve System
Since the change in banking regulations in the early 1980s, nonmember banks are also subject to some control by the Federal Reserve System.

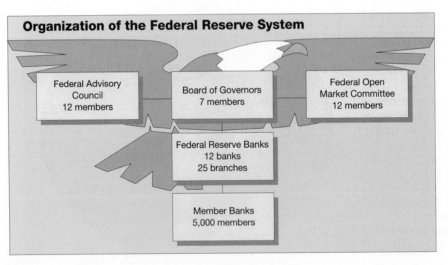

Organization of the Federal Reserve System

Federal Advisory Council
12 members

Board of Governors
7 members

Federal Open Market Committee
12 members

Federal Reserve Banks
12 banks
25 branches

Member Banks
5,000 members

Meeting Special Needs

Attention Deficiency Presenting information in small segments is helpful for students with attention problems. Ask students to read Section 2 and self-monitor their attention to the task. Ask them whether they think it is easier to read through the whole section and then take notes or whether it is better to break the reading into smaller units and vary the activity with writing. Point out that there is not a "correct way." The best approach will be the one that works best for them.

The Twelve Districts of the Federal Reserve System

☆ Board of Governors
○ Federal Reserve Bank Cities
○ Federal Reserve Branch Cities
— Federal Reserve District Boundaries

Seattle
Portland
Helena
⑨
Minneapolis
Cleveland
Buffalo ②
Boston
①
Detroit
Chicago
Pittsburgh ③
New York
⑫
Salt Lake City
Omaha
⑦
④
Cincinnati
Philadelphia
Baltimore
San Francisco
Denver
Kansas City
St Louis
Louisville
Richmond
Washington, D.C.
⑩
Nashville
Charlotte
Los Angeles
Oklahoma City
⑤
⑧
Memphis
Atlanta
El Paso
Dallas
Little Rock
⑥
Birmingham
⑪
Houston
Jacksonville
New Orleans
San Antonio
Miami

Alaska
⑫
Hawaii

Sources: *Federal Reserve Bulletin*, Board of Governors at the Federal Reserve System

In the past, only member banks were required to meet regulations, such as those setting specific reserve requirements. Now all institutions that accept deposits must keep reserves in their district Federal Reserve bank. Federal Reserve services are also available to all depository institutions—member or nonmember—for a fee.

Figure 16.6 ▲
The Federal Reserve System
Look at the map of the Federal Reserve System above. Note that the Fed is headquartered in Washington, D.C., in the building shown on $10 bills. Find and list the 12 Federal Reserve district bank cities.
▼

IN GOD WE TRUST

Guided Practice

L2 Debating Organize volunteers into two teams of two each, with a moderator, to debate the following question: Is the Fed's most important function to regulate the money supply? Have the teams express opposing views before the class, which votes to decide which side makes the more persuasive argument.

Visual Instruction

Answer to Figure 16.6 caption: San Francisco, Kansas City, Minneapolis, Chicago, Dallas, St. Louis, Cleveland, Atlanta, Boston, New York, Philadelphia, Washington, D.C.

? DID YOU KNOW

The idea of government control of the money supply was evident in Egypt during the reign of Ptolemy II. By operating a closed monetary system, the monarchy completely controlled Egypt's money supply. Egypt's sophisticated banking system employed a mixture of private enterprise and direct royal control.

Cooperative Learning

Organize the class into small groups to prepare a television documentary about the Federal Reserve System. The documentary should include "interviews" with members of the Board of Governors and the FOMC and a discussion of the functions of the Federal Reserve. Groups might organize to complete the following tasks: preparing the interviews, creating visuals to present during the documentary, preparing the text for the narration, narrating the documentary, and taping the documentary.

Independent Practice

L2 Creating Graphics Refer students to Figure 16.7 and have them review the functions of the Federal Reserve. Then have students work in pairs to create a poster that illustrates and summarizes these functions. Display completed posters in the classroom.

L3 Linking Past to Present Have students research the First Bank of the United States, which was proposed by Alexander Hamilton in the 1790s. Have students compare the First Bank with the Federal Reserve System today in terms of its makeup and its functions. Students might share their information in a written report.

Figure 16.7 Functions of the Federal Reserve

Responsibility	Description
Clearing checks	**Check clearing** is the method by which a check that has been deposited in one depository institution is transferred to the depository institution on which it was written. Figure 16.9 (page 398) explains this process.
Acting as the federal government's fiscal agent	The federal government collects large sums of money through taxation and spends and distributes even more. It deposits some of this money in the Federal Reserve and distributes the rest among thousands of commercial banks. As the federal government's fiscal, or financial, agent the Fed keeps track of these deposits and holds a checking account for the United States Treasury. Checks for such payments as Social Security, tax refunds, and veterans' benefits are drawn on this account. The Fed also acts as a financial adviser to the federal government.
Supervising member banks	The Fed along with the Comptroller of the Currency and the Federal Deposit Insurance Corporation (FDIC) supervises and regulates member commercial banks. Nonmember commercial and savings banks as well as savings and loan associations and credit unions are regulated by other agencies. Because the comptroller supervises national banks, the Fed oversees state-chartered member banks. Among the Fed's duties are setting limits for loans and investments by member banks, approving bank mergers, and examining the books of member banks.
Holding and setting reserve requirements	All depository institutions are required by law to keep a certain percentage of their deposits in reserve. Each of the 12 Federal Reserve banks holds the reserve requirements of member and nonmember depository institutions in its district. By raising or lowering the percentage required, within the limits set by Congress, the Fed can change the amount of money in circulation.
Supplying paper currency	Since 1914 the Federal Reserve System has been responsible for printing and maintaining much of the nation's paper money. All Federal Reserve notes are printed in Washington, D.C., at the Bureau of Printing and Engraving. Each note, however, has a code number indicating which of the 12 Federal Reserve banks issued it. The money is shipped from the bureau to the appropriate bank to be put into circulation. Much of this money simply replaces old bills; however, each Federal Reserve bank must have on hand a sufficient amount of cash to meet the demands for paper currency during different times of the year. For example, during the Christmas season, commercial banks find that their depositors withdraw large amounts of cash. The banks then must turn to the Federal Reserve banks to replace it. After Christmas, depositors redeposit their money. The banks can then return what they borrowed to their district Federal Reserve bank.
Regulating the money supply	The primary responsibility of the Federal Reserve is determining the amount of money in circulation, which, in turn, affects the amount of credit and business activity in the economy.

396 *Unit 5 Macroeconomics: Managing the Nation's Economy*

 Free Enterprise Activity

Ask students to review the role of government in a pure market economy. *(Students might indicate that in a pure market economy the government has little control over the economy.)* Organize the class into small groups and have each group discuss the answer to the following question: Does the role of the Fed in regulating the nation's money supply oppose the principles of a pure market economy? Then have representatives from each group form a panel to discuss the question. Have the others give their reactions to the discussion.

Figure 16.8 ▶
Federal Reserve Banks
All Federal Reserve banks, like the one in San Francisco, help formulate monetary policy, including regulating the money supply. Before the Fed was established in 1913, the United States had not had a central bank since the Second Bank of the United States in the mid-1800s, and individual banks often printed money.

Independent Practice
L2 Gathering Information
Have students make a Federal Reserve and Related Topics library for the classroom. Have them write to their district Federal Reserve bank for a copy of *Public Information Materials*, a catalog of free materials for use in high schools. Then have them send away for copies of materials that could be used by the class for reference purposes.

Have students complete Guided Reading Activity 16.2 in the TCR. **LEP**

Visual Instruction
Discuss with students whether they have ever heard people say that they have to make sure their check clears. Have students work in pairs and prepare an oral explanation of the steps involved in clearing a check. Students should refer to Figure 16.9 on page 398 to help them with their explanation. Encourage students to be precise and to gear their explanation to a younger student. Call on volunteers to share their explanations with the class.

Today the major advantage of membership is that member banks, as stockholders in their district bank, are able to vote for six of its nine board members. Member banks also receive dividends on their stock in the district bank.

The Functions of the Federal Reserve System

The Federal Reserve has a number of functions as shown in Figure 16.7. Among them are check clearing, acting as the federal government's fiscal agent, supervising member banks, holding and setting reserve requirements, supplying paper currency, and regulating the money supply. The most important function of the Fed is regulating the money supply. See Figure 16.8. Check clearing is also an important and complex function. See Figure 16.9 (page 398).

Consumer Protection The Federal Reserve also sets standards for certain types of consumer legislation, mainly truth-in-lending legislation. By law, sellers of goods and services must make some kinds of information available to people who buy on credit. This information includes the amount of interest and size of the monthly payment to be paid. The Federal Reserve System decides what type of credit information must be supplied to consumers.

Chapter 16 The Federal Reserve System and Monetary Policy **397**

 Cultural Diversity and Economics

Organize students into small groups to research the central bank of another nation and compare and contrast it—perhaps in a table—with the Federal Reserve System. Encourage research to find information about the central banks of European, Asian, African, and South American nations. Have a member of each group present its data and then discuss how the Federal Reserve System might benefit from borrowing practices from other central banks.

Assess

Meeting Lesson Objectives

Assign Section 2 Review as homework or an in-class activity.

Evaluate

Assign the Section 2 Quiz in the TCR or use the Testmaker.

Reteach

Have small groups use Figures 16.5 and 16.7 to write questions about the organization and functions of the Federal Reserve System. Have students take turns answering them.

Enrich

Have students research the findings of the Aldrich Commission that led President Wilson to choose the Federal Reserve Act.

Close

Ask students to rank the functions of the Federal Reserve System in order of importance.

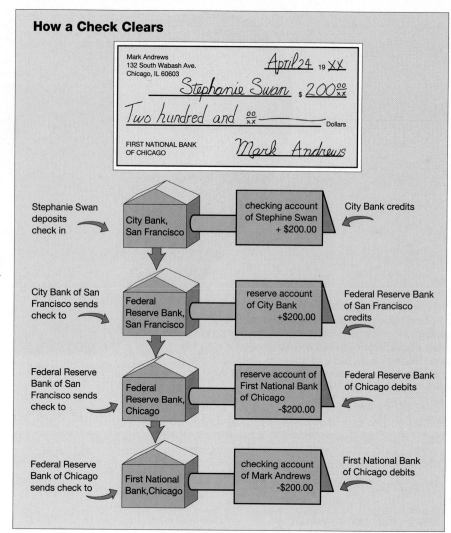

How a Check Clears

Figure 16.9 ▶
Check Clearing
All depository institutions may use the Federal Reserve's check-clearing system. *Reserve account* refers to a bank's account in its Federal Reserve district bank.

SECTION 2 REVIEW

Understanding Vocabulary

Define Federal Open Market Committee (FOMC), check clearing.

Reviewing Objectives

① How is the Federal Reserve System in the United States organized?

② The Federal Reserve clears checks and acts as the government's fiscal agent. What are three other functions of the Federal Reserve?

Section 2 Review Answers

Understanding Vocabulary
Federal Open Market Committee (FOMC) (p. 394), **check clearing** (p. 397)

Reviewing Objectives
1. It consists of the Board of Governors, the Federal Advisory Council, the Federal Open Market Committee, Federal Reserve Banks, and member banks.

2. Answers will vary, but possible answers may include the following: supervising member banks, holding and setting reserve requirements, supplying paper currency, and regulating the money supply.

LEARNING ECONOMIC SKILLS

Understanding Real and Nominal Values

Inflation has been a problem since World War II. This means that to make comparisons between the prices of things in the past and those of today, you have to make the distinction between *nominal*, or *current*, and *real*, or *constant*, values.

The Price of Houses

If a couple told you that they bought their house for $50,000 10 years ago and sold it for $100,000 today, would they have made a "profit" of $50,000? The answer is no, because of inflation. If, for example, the consumer price index (CPI) was 100 when they bought the house and had risen to 200 when they sold their house, the *real* price of their house would not have changed at all, as Figure A shows.

Determining What Happens to Your Income

Sometimes much of the raise a worker receives is eaten away by inflation. To determine the real value of a raise, subtract the rate of inflation. For example, assume you are making $10 an hour (after taxes) this year and next year your boss gives you a 5 percent raise. Are you 5 percent better off? The answer depends on the rate of inflation during that year. If the increase in the CPI was 3 percent, your real salary increase was only 2 percent as Figure B shows.

The government uses an implicit price deflator to compare GDP year by year. See Figure C.

Practicing the Skill

Real GDP in 1987 was $4,539.9 billion. In 1992, nominal GDP was $5,950.7 billion. The implicit GDP price deflator was 120.9. What was real GDP in 1992 expressed in 1987 dollars?

Figure A
Determine Percentage Increase in Nominal Price
Divide amount of increase by original price. Multiply result by 100 to get percent.

$$\frac{50{,}000}{50{,}000} = 1 \times 100 = 100\%$$

Determine Percentage Increase in Consumer Price Index
Divide amount of increase in CPI by original index. Multiply result by 100 to get percent.

$$\frac{100}{100} = 1 \times 100 = 100\%$$

Determine Percentage Increase in Real Price
Subtract percentage increase in CPI from percentage increase in nominal price.

100%	increase in nominal price
−100%	increase in CPI
0%	increase in real price

Figure B
Real salary increase equals increase in nominal salary minus rate of inflation.

5%	nominal raise
− 3%	inflation rate
2%	real raise

Figure C
The real GDP is found by dividing the nominal GDP by the implicit price deflator and multiplying the result by 100.

$$\frac{\text{nominal GDP}}{\text{implicit price deflator}} \times 100 = \text{real GDP}$$

399

Teach

Review with students the meaning of inflation *(the prolonged rise in the general price level of goods and services)*. Ask students to recall various measures of national economic performance and to explain how these measures are corrected for the effects of inflation. *(For example, the GDP measures the total dollar value of goods and services produced in the nation in a single year and the real GDP is the GDP corrected for inflation.)*

Have students read the feature on their own or work through it with them. Then have them complete the activities in Practicing the Skill.

Additional Practice

Have students complete Reinforcing Skills 16 in the TCR.

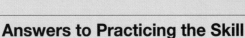

Answers to Practicing the Skill
1. $4,922 billion

Focus

Overview

See the student page for section objectives.

Section 3 explains or describes: the methods the Fed uses to regulate the money supply; changing the reserve requirements; the discount rate; open-market operations; and the difficulties of monetary policy.

Bellringer

Before presenting the lesson, display Focus Activity Transparency 65 and assign the accompanying Focus Activity Sheet.

Motivational Activity

Ask students: How can the amount of money available to you be regulated by the adults in charge of you? Discuss responses.

Preteaching Vocabulary

Using Glossary definitions, have students decide which of the terms refer to ways the Federal Reserve controls the money supply (*discount rate, open-market operations*).

SECTION **3** *Regulating the Money Supply*

SECTION 3 FOCUS

Terms to Know discount rate, prime rate, open-market operations

Objectives *After reading this section, you should be able to:*
1. Describe the way the Federal Reserve changes the money supply by **changing reserve requirements**.
2. Describe the way the Federal Reserve changes the money supply by **changing the discount rate**.
3. Identify how the Fed uses **open-market operations**.
4. List the **difficulties of monetary policy**.

Figure 16.10
The Economy
When a nation's economy is running smoothly with low inflation, people are more inclined to spend income on nonessentials or luxuries. Restaurants enjoy more business during economic booms.

▶

The Fed's Difficult Job

The Federal Reserve has as its goal maintaining enough money to keep the money supply growing steadily and the economy running smoothly without inflation. See **Figure 16.10**. To accomplish this, it has three major tools: reserve requirements, the discount rate, and open-market operations.

Changing Reserve Requirements

The Federal Reserve can choose to control the money supply by changing the reserve requirements of financial institutions. The lower the percentage of deposits that must be kept in reserve, the more dollars are available to loan. The reverse is also true. **Figure 16.11** explains how changes in the reserve requirement affect the nation's money supply.

As **Figure 16.11C** shows, the Fed may raise reserve requirements. To build up its reserves to meet the new requirement, a bank has several possibilities. It can call in some loans, sell off securities or other investments, or borrow from another bank or the Fed-

---

Classroom Resources for Section 3

Raising and Lowering Reserve Requirements

Bank A deposits = $1,000,000
Reserve requirements 10% x $1,000,000 = $100,000
Bank may loan $900,000
Suppose a bank has $1 million in deposits and the reserve requirement is 10 percent. The bank must keep at least $100,000 in reserves.

Bank B deposits = $1,000,000
Fed lowers reserve requirement to 5% x $1,000,000 = $50,000
Bank may loan $950,000
If the Fed wanted to increase the money supply, it could lower the reserve requirement to 5 percent, for example. The bank would then need to keep only $50,000 in reserve. It could lend out the other $950,000. This additional $50,000 would expand the money supply many times over as it was lent and redeposited. This could help pull the economy out of a recession.

Bank C deposits = $1,000,000
Fed raises reserve requirement to 15% x $1,000,000 = $150,000
Bank may loan $850,000
Suppose instead that the Fed wanted to decrease the money supply, or at least slow down its rate of growth. It could do this by increasing the reserve requirement from 10 to 15 percent. The bank in the example above would then need to keep $150,000 on reserve – $50,000 more than before with a 10% reserve requirement.

Teach

Guided Practice

L2 Creating Diagrams Work with students to create a diagram that shows the ways the Fed changes the country's money supply and title it "Ways of Changing the Money Supply." Then call on students to complete the diagram by indicating the ways the Federal Reserve changes the money supply and by providing a brief explanation of each *(decreases or increases the reserve requirement: decreasing it increases the money supply, increasing it decreases the money supply; lowering or raising the discount rate: lowering it increases the money supply, raising it decreases the money supply; using open-market operations: government buys securities and increases the money supply, government sells securities and decreases the money supply)*

---

eral Reserve. Obviously, because all banks would have to increase their reserves, this action would greatly decrease the amount of money in the economy. This could be used to help slow down the economy if it were expanding too rapidly.

Even small changes in the reserve requirement can have major effects on the money supply. As a result, some believe that this tool is not precise enough to make frequent small adjustments to the money supply. In recent years, changing the reserve requirement has not been used often to regulate the money supply.

Changing the Discount Rate

Sometimes a depository institution will find itself without enough reserves to meet its reserve requirement. This situation may occur if customers unexpectedly borrow a great deal of money or if depositors suddenly withdraw large amounts.

The bank must then borrow to meet its reserve requirement, at least temporarily. One of the ways it can do this is to ask its district Federal Reserve bank for a loan. The district bank, like any other bank, will charge interest. The rate of interest the Fed charges is called the **discount rate.**

A bank, like a consumer, follows the law of demand. At higher discount rates, a bank may decide to borrow fewer reserves from the Fed or none at all. It could meet its reserve requirement by borrowing from another bank. This money would then be taken out of circulation and would not be available for lending to individuals or businesses.

If a bank does decide to borrow at a high discount rate, it will need to pass its increased costs on to customers in the form of higher interest rates on loans. For example, it might raise its **prime rate**—the rate it charges its best business customers. High discount rates, by discouraging borrowing, will also keep down the

▲
Figure 16.11 Reserve Requirements
Look at the chart above to see how depository institutions are affected if the Federal Reserve decides to raise or lower the reserve requirement.

◆◐● Meeting Special Needs

Mixed Learners Some students learn best visually. Others are auditory learners. Many are "mixed" learners who use a combination of auditory and visual materials in order to learn. Ask students to look at and then think about the information they get from Figure 16.15. Then ask them to read the paragraphs under the subsection title "The Difficulties of Monetary Policy." Ask students whether the diagram or the paragraphs provide them with more information. Then ask what the difference is between the kind of information they can get from a diagram and from the text.

L1 Classifying Write the following Federal Reserve actions on the chalkboard. Call on volunteers to write next to each action whether the effect will likely create an increase or decrease in the money supply.

a. The Fed lowers the discount rate. *(increase)*

b. The Fed raises the reserve requirement. *(decrease)*

c. The Fed sells Treasury bills. *(decrease)*

d. The Fed buys Treasury bills. *(increase)*

Visual Instruction

Refer students to Figure 16.12 and analyze with them step-by-step what it illustrates. Then, if necessary, to analyze and explain the diagram for you.

---

growth of the money supply. In contrast, if the discount rate is low, even a bank with sufficient reserves might borrow money. The loan will raise the bank's reserves and increase its ability to make loans. Thus, a reduction in the discount rate increases the total money supply.

Open-Market Operations

Buying and selling United States securities, called **open-market operations,** is the tool the Fed most often uses. Open-market operations affect the money supply by changing depository institution reserves, thereby putting money into or taking it out of circulation in the economy.

The term *open market* is used because these securities are traded in the open market through regular securities dealers. An open market is one that is open to private businesses and one that the government does not own or control. When the government buys securities such as Treasury bills, it pumps new reserves into the economy. When the government sells Treasury bills, it takes reserves out of circulation. Figure 16.12 examines this process.

Of course, individuals using cash do not carry out most open-market transactions. Financial institutions and large investors such as mutual

**Figure 16.12
Buying and Selling
Treasury Bills**
Look at this diagram that examines the process of buying and selling Treasury bills. Explain how the government is able to affect the money supply through this process. ▼

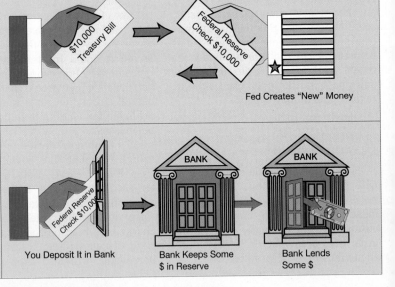

A. Suppose you sell a $10,000 Treasury bill to the Federal Reserve and receive that amount of money in the form of a Federal Reserve check. This is "new" money because the Fed created it simply by writing the check on itself. When you deposit the $10,000 in a bank, that bank will keep part in reserve and lend the rest. *The process of money creation has begun.*

$10,000 Treasury Bill

Federal Reserve Check $10,000

Fed Creates "New" Money

Federal Reserve Check $10,00

BANK BANK

You Deposit It in Bank   Bank Keeps Some $ in Reserve   Bank Lends Some $

Cooperative Learning

Organize students into groups of four students each to investigate and write brief reports explaining how the Fed's policies during World War I, the 1920s, the Great Depression, and World War II affected the economy's overall health. Each student in a group should research and write a brief report about only one period. Have each group combine its reports into books entitled *A History of Federal Reserve Policies.*

funds make most transactions. If a bank purchases Treasury securities from the Fed, the purchase amount will be deducted from the bank's reserve account. The bank then has less money to lend, and the money supply eventually will be smaller. If a bank sells its government securities, the Fed will credit the money to the bank's reserve account. The bank can then make additional loans, and the money supply will grow. In each case, however, the Fed must decide which course is best for the economy in the long-run.

Monetary Policy Decision Making

The Federal Open Market Committee (FOMC) meets periodically to decide how best to control the money supply through open-market operations. At the beginning of each meeting, staff economists present data about what has happened to the money supply in the past, what current credit conditions are like, and what is likely to happen to the economy in the future. Statistics on unemployment, retail sales, gross domestic product, and so on, are presented. The information is discussed, and at the end of the meeting the committee votes on a course of action. The FOMC's decision summarizes current economic conditions and outlines the Fed's long-term goals for its monetary policy. To help meet these goals, the FOMC also sets objectives for the rate of growth of the money supply or the cost of credit for the next month or so.

Independent Practice

L2 Graphing Have students research the average prime interest rates from 1980 to the present and present their information in a bar graph or a line graph. Have students indicate which years would have been best for consumers to obtain loans.

L3 Researching Assign students either big business or labor unions. Have them research the position of each regarding Federal Reserve policy during the recession of the early 1980s. Students should use the information to prepare and present to the class a report on what they think is the best policy for the Fed to pursue in times of high inflation and high unemployment.

GLOBAL ECONOMICS

In recent years, several countries have significantly reduced or even eliminated reserve requirements. Reserve requirements no longer affect bank behavior in Switzerland and the United Kingdom. Canada has begun to eliminate reserve requirements and will do so completely by 1994.

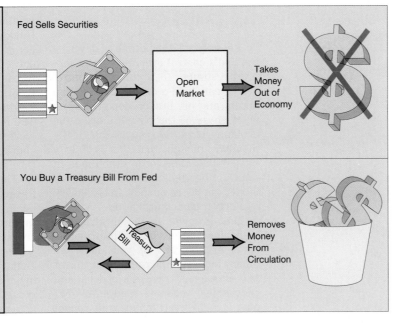

B. When the Fed wants to decrease the money supply, it sells securities on the open market. The sales take money out of the economy. Suppose you decide to buy a Treasury bill and use cash for the transaction. Turning the cash over to the Fed removes the money from circulation.

Fed Sells Securities

Open Market

Takes Money Out of Economy

You Buy a Treasury Bill From Fed

Treasury Bill

Removes Money From Circulation

Chapter 16 The Federal Reserve System and Monetary Policy **403**

Free Enterprise Activity

One way the Fed regulates the nation's money supply is through the purchase and sales of securities, such as Treasury bills (T-bills). Have students research Treasury bills. Have them find out the minimum value, maturity rates, and interest rates of these securities. Finally, have students examine the advantages and disadvantages of buying T-bills. Ask students to use their information to determine whether T-bills would be an investment they would be interested in.

Figure 16.13 ▶ Changing the Money Supply
The brake/accelerator model is one way to remember how the Fed can regulate the money supply. Explain how the model works.

Changing the Money Supply

To increase the money supply: accelerate
1. Reduce reserve requirements
2. Reduce discount rate for borrowing reserves
3. Buy government securities in the open market

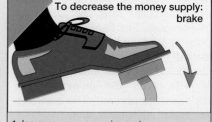

To decrease the money supply: brake
1. Increase reserve requirements
2. Raise discount rate for borrowing reserves
3. Sell government securities in the open market

Figure 16.14 Independence of the Fed
The Fed is free of executive branch control. For example, when President Clinton, a Democrat, took office, Alan Greenspan, whom President Reagan, a Republican, had appointed to chair the Fed, continued his term.

The Difficulties of Monetary Policy

Economists sometimes describe the Fed's control over the money supply as similar to a driver's control over a car. Like a driver, the Fed can accelerate or brake, depending on what phase of the business cycle the economy is in. See Figure 16.13. Remember, though, that this is only a model and, therefore, simplified. In reality, the Fed cannot control the money supply as quickly and as surely as a driver can control a car.

One problem is the difficulty in gathering and evaluating information about M1 and M2. As you know, the money supply is measured in terms of M1—currency, traveler's checks, and checkable accounts—and M2—M1 plus certain near moneys. In recent years, new savings and investment opportunities have appeared. Keeping track of the growth of M1 and M2 becomes more difficult as money is shifted from savings accounts into interest-paying checkable accounts or from checkable accounts into money market deposit accounts (MMDAs). The increased use of credit cards and electronic funds transfer has also changed the way money circulates through the economy.

Throughout its history, the Federal Reserve's monetary policies have been criticized. In instances of rising inflation, the Federal Reserve increased the amount of money in circulation, thereby worsening inflation. During other periods when the economy was slowing down and going into recession, the Federal Reserve decreased the money supply. This action

 Cultural Diversity and Economics

In recent years the Federal Reserve System has cooperated with financial institutions, businesses, and community groups to create programs that help finance affordable housing and minority businesses. For example, the Federal Reserve Banks of New York and Boston cosponsored a meeting that addressed credit problems faced by Native Americans. Ask students whether they think it is important for the Federal Reserve System to deal with issues facing minorities and people in low-income areas. Ask them to give reasons for their opinions.

made the recession worse. To prevent such misjudgments, some critics of the Federal Reserve have requested that the money supply simply be increased at the same rate every year. They recommend that the Fed *not* engage in monetary policy.

The Fed's Board of Governors is protected from direct political pressure. See Figure 16.14. It nonetheless still receives conflicting advice from many directions as shown in Figure 16.15. The President could suggest one course of action—lower interest rates, for example—while members of Congress may be urging a different course. Private business may call for one policy, while organized labor asks for the opposite. Finally, the Fed is not the only force working to affect the economy. The spending and taxing policies of the federal government are also at work. The Federal Reserve's task is to consider all these factors as it plots a course for the growth of the economy.

Meeting Lesson Objectives

Assign Section 3 Review as homework or an in-class activity.

Evaluate

Assign the Section 3 Quiz in the TCR or use the Testmaker.

Assign the Chapter 16 Test Form A or Form B or use the Testmaker.

Reteach

Have students write responses to the directive in each section objective.

Have students complete Reteaching Activity 16 in the TCR.

Enrich

Have students research and write a brief biography of the current or a past Fed chairperson.

Have students complete Enrichment Activity 16 in the TCR.

Close

Have students review the ways the Fed controls the money supply.

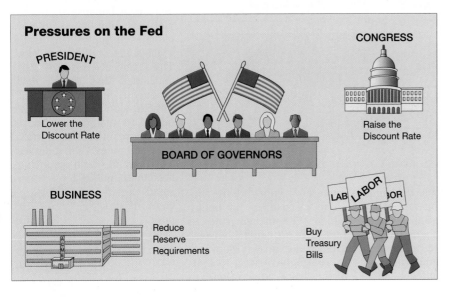

Pressures on the Fed

PRESIDENT — Lower the Discount Rate

CONGRESS — Raise the Discount Rate

BOARD OF GOVERNORS

BUSINESS — Reduce Reserve Requirements

LABOR — Buy Treasury Bills

Figure 16.15 Pressures
Examine the chart and explain how the Federal Reserve could be influenced by outside pressures.

SECTION 3 REVIEW

Understanding Vocabulary
Define discount rate, prime rate, open-market operations.

Reviewing Objectives
1. How can the Federal Reserve System use reserve requirements to alter the money supply?
2. How does the discount rate affect the money supply?
3. How does the Fed use open-market operations?
4. What are some of the difficulties of carrying out monetary policy?

Section 3 Review Answers
Understanding Vocabulary
discount rate (p. 401), prime rate (p. 401), open-market operations (p. 402)
Reviewing Objectives
1. To decrease the money supply, the Fed raises the reserve requirement; to increase the money supply, the Fed lowers the reserve requirement.
2. A reduction in the discount rate increases the money supply, and an increase in the discount rate decreases the money supply.
3. When the government buys securities on the open market, it increases the money supply; when it sells securities, it decreases the money supply.
4. It is difficult to gather and evaluate information about M1 and M2; the Fed is not the only force working to affect the economy.

News Clip

Readings in Economics

THE NEW YORK TIMES   **AUGUST 23, 1993**

CENTRAL BANK GRIPES ABOUT A NEW WORLD

by Steven Greenhouse

To most people the analogy would be farfetched, but at a conference of central bankers . . . , the bankers often compared themselves to generals waging war.

The reason offered is that those who forge monetary policy, like those who wage war, have to grapple with an unending torrent of chance and change. . . .

Benjamin M. Friedman, a Harvard University economist, said, "It may be true that war is the human activity most vitally subject to chance and happenstance, but monetary policy runs a close second. . . ."

As a result of the rapid changes in capital markets, many central banks have discovered that their tried-and-true rules for carrying out monetary policy have become as useless as buggy whips. Without neat rules to lean back on, central bankers often feel exposed. Many are increasingly turning to seat-of-the-pants discretion to guide policy—a development that caused heated debate here. . . .

Probably the strongest lament among the central bankers was that the tool they used most to guide monetary policy—growth in the money supply—had become unreliable.

For most of the 1970's and 1980's, the Federal Reserve and many other countries' central banks sought to create a certain level of growth in the money supply. Those targets would more or less steer their economies toward a desired level of inflation and economic growth. Briefly put, X amount of monetary growth produced Y amount of economic growth.

That relationship has broken down because of financial deregulation and major changes in the way that individuals invest their savings. The Federal Reserve has concluded that it can now produce a certain amount of growth with less growth in one of its major money-supply indexes, the M-2, a measure of money that includes cash, savings and checking accounts, and small certificates of deposit.

• THINK ABOUT IT •

1. What is the chief role of central banks?

2. Why has the relationship between monetary growth and economic growth broken down?

Answers to Think About It

1. guiding monetary policy
2. because of financial deregulation and major changes in the way that individuals invest their savings

16 *Highlights*

Use the Chapter 16 Highlights to preview, review, condense, or reteach the chapter. A Spanish Chapter Highlights is available in the Spanish Handbook.

Preview/Review

After students read the Chapter 16 Highlights, have them complete Economics Vocabulary Activity 16 in the TCR. Spanish Vocabulary Activities are also available in the Spanish Resource Binder.

Vocabulary Software reinforces the economic terms used in Chapter 16.

Condense

Have students listen to Chapter 16 on the Audiocassettes in the TCR. A 1-page written activity and 1-page test accompany this material. These materials are also available in Spanish.

Reteach

Have students complete Reteaching Activity 16 in the TCR. Spanish Reteaching Activities are also available.

Section 1

Money Supply and the Economy

Key Terms
the Fed (p. 388)
monetary policy (p. 388)
loose money policy (p. 389)
tight money policy (p. 389)

fractional reserve banking (p. 389)
reserve requirements (p. 389)

Summary
A loose money policy means that the growth of the money supply is increased and money is abundant and inexpensive to borrow. With a tight money policy, the opposite occurs. With the system of fractional reserve banking, only a fraction of the deposits in a bank are kept on hand. The rest are lent to borrowers or otherwise invested. Because of the fractional reserve banking system, for any given change in new money in circulation, a multiple change will occur in the money supply.

Section 2

Organization and Functions of the Federal Reserve System

Key Terms
Federal Open Market Committee (FOMC) (p. 394)
check clearing (p. 396)

Summary
The Board of Governors of the Federal Reserve System directs the operations of the Federal Reserve System and establishes policies regarding such things as reserve requirements and discount rates. The Federal Reserve System serves many functions in addition to clearing checks for banks and regulating the money supply.

Section 3

Regulating the Money Supply

Key Terms
discount rate (p. 401)
prime rate (p. 401)
open-market operations (p. 402)

Summary
To regulate the money supply, the Fed uses changes in reserve requirements, the discount rate, and open-market operations. Monetary policy is sometimes difficult because the government may not always have accurate information on M1 and M2. Also, the Fed is not the only force working to affect the economy.

 VIDEODISC

Nightly Business Report
Economics in Action
Use "Federal Reserve and Monetary Policy" on Disc 2, Side A, Video 21.

Search 22901, Play to 28244

CHAPTER

16 Review

ANSWERS

Identifying Key Terms

1. a
2. e
3. d
4. f
5. b
6. c
7. loose money policy
8. fractional reserve banking
9. check clearing
10. discount rate

Recalling Facts and Ideas

Section 1

1. loose money policy and tight money policy
2. A fraction of the money is kept in reserve and the rest is free to be loaned.
3. because the Fed has set specific reserve requirements for banks

Section 2

4. It directs the operations of the Federal Reserve System.
5. 12 Federal Reserve banks and 25 branches

6. the Federal Reserve System

Section 3

7. changing the discount rate and using open-market operations
8. raise reserve requirements, increase the discount rate, sell securities on the open market
9. because money is shifted among savings accounts, interest-paying checkable accounts, and money market deposit accounts, and because of the increased use of credit cards and electronic transfers
10. because sometimes its actions have worsened inflation or recession

Identifying Key Terms

Write the letter of the definition in Column B below that correctly defines each term in Column A.

Column A

1. the Fed (p. 388)
2. prime rate (p. 401)
3. tight money policy (p. 389)
4. reserve requirements (p. 389)
5. monetary policy (p. 388)
6. open-market operations (p. 402)

Column B

a. the central banking system in the United States
b. means of changing the growth rate of supply of money in the economy
c. purchases and sales of United States securities by the Federal Reserve System
d. situation in which credit is expensive to borrow and in short supply
e. interest rate that the Federal Reserve charges banks for loans
f. require banks to keep a certain percentage of their deposits as cash on account with the Federal Reserve

Use terms from the following list to fill in the blanks in the paragraph below.

fractional reserve banking (p. 389)
discount rate (p. 401)
loose money policy (p. 389)
check clearing (p. 396)

When credit is inexpensive to borrow, we can be pretty sure that the Fed has engaged in (7) . Because banks do not have to keep 100 percent of their deposits on reserve, we have a (8) system. One of the functions in the Federal Reserve is to handle (9) , which is the method by which a check deposited in one bank is transferred to another bank. Sometimes banks need to borrow from a Federal Reserve district bank. The rate that they pay is called the (10) .

Recalling Facts and Ideas

Section 1

1. What are the two basic types of monetary policies?
2. In a fractional reserve banking system, what happens to the money supply when the Fed injects $100 of new money into the American economy?
3. Why do banks have to keep money in reserve accounts?

Section 2

4. What does the Board of Governors do within the Federal Reserve System?
5. How many Federal Reserve banks and branches are there?
6. Which agency of the federal government supplies paper currency to the economy?

Section 3

7. The Fed can change the money supply in circulation by changing reserve requirements. What are two other methods that it can use to do this?
8. If the Fed wants to decrease the money supply, what can it do?
9. Why is it difficult for the Fed to gather and evaluate information about M1 and M2?
10. Why do some of the Fed's critics think the Fed should not engage in monetary policy?

Critical Thinking

Section 1

Format may vary, but steps should resemble those in Figure 16.3.

Section 2

Member banks, as stockholders in their district bank, are able to vote for six of its nine board members and receive dividends on their stock in the district banks. In the past only member banks were required to meet regulations, such as those setting specific reserve requirements.

Section 3

Answers will vary but should suggest that it would be more affected by policies called for by the administration and, in general, more affected by shifting political trends.

Critical Thinking

Section 1
Expressing Problems Clearly Draw a flowchart to show how a bank creates money.

Section 2
Making Comparisons What is the advantage to Federal Reserve membership today? How does this differ from the past?

Section 3
Analyzing Information How do you think the Fed would operate differently if it were under the control of the executive branch?

Applying Economic Concepts

Monetary Policy Imagine that you are a member of the Federal Open Market Committee. Eight times a year, you meet with the other members of the FOMC. The research staff presents information on the state of the economy. Write a list of the different types of information you think the members of the FOMC receive during their meetings.

Chapter Projects

1. **Individual Project** In a library, check the most recent issue of the *Federal Reserve Bulletin* for the current reserve requirements and discount rate. Check the same month's issue for the last four years to see how often they have changed and how much. Track these data on a chart.
2. **Cooperative Learning Project** Work in three groups. Each group will study one potential tool of monetary policy:

   - changing reserve requirements
   - changing the discount rate
   - changing the money supply via open-market operations

   The task of each group is to develop a con-

vincing argument in favor of its monetary tool over the use of the other two monetary tools. Members of each group can contribute separate arguments. Appoint one member to summarize the arguments and present that summary in a short speech to the class using an outline.

Reviewing Skills

Understanding Real and Nominal Values
The Real Cost of College Below are some hypothetical numbers that show a price index each year and the nominal dollar price of attending one academic year in a private university.

Private University

Year	Price Index	Tuition
1980	68.4	$10,040
1985	96.0	$12,343
1990	104.0	$16,420
1995	119.0	$21,200

What was the real cost for each academic year in a private university?

Writing About Economics

Informative Writing Write a letter to someone who has never seen American money. Include a paragraph about the currency you have seen this week and a summary from Your Economics Journal record that tracked where the money was issued.

409

Applying Economic Concepts

Answers will vary but might include such items as change in monetary policy, discount rate, reserve requirement, and treasury securities issues and trading.

Chapter Projects

1. Format of chart may vary among students but the values presented should be identical.

2. Encourage students to use an outline that is as fully developed as possible in presenting their arguments.

Reviewing Skills

The real cost went up.

Writing About Economics

Letters should describe currency and identify the issuing Federal Reserve Banks.

? BONUS QUESTION

The following bonus question may be written on the chalkboard when students take the chapter test.
Q: When the Federal Reserve requirement is 5 percent, how much of a $100 deposit may a bank lend?
A: $95

CHAPTER 17 GOVERNMENT SPENDS, COLLECTS, AND OWES

CHAPTER ORGANIZER

Daily Objectives	Special Features	Classroom Resources
Section 1 Growth in the Size of Government • **Describe** two measurements of government growth. • **Explain** why government has grown rapidly.		📁 Reproducible Lesson Plan 17.1 💿 *NBR* Video 23 and Video Still 4 🔦 Focus Activity Transparency 67 📁 Guided Reading Activity 17.1 📁 Cooperative Learning Activity 17 📁 Primary and Secondary Source Readings 17 📁 Consumer Application Activity 5 📁 Section Quiz 17.1
Section 2 The Functions of Government • **List** four examples of public goods. • **Describe** the two main areas through which government redistributes income. • **List** four ways government regulates economic activity. • **Name** two ways government promotes economic stability.	**Personal Perspective:** Robert Reich on Government, p. 420	📁 Reproducible Lesson Plan 17.2 🔦 Focus Activity Transparency 68 📁 Focus Activity Sheet 68 📁 Guided Reading Activity 17.2 📁 Consumer Application Activity 17 📁 Section Quiz 17.2 📁 Spanish Section Quiz 17.2 💻 Testmaker
Section 3 The Federal Budget and the National Debt • **List** the steps in the federal budget-making process. • **Explain** how deficit spending increases the nation's public debt. • **Discuss** various attempts at deficit reduction.	**Learning Economic Skills:** Understanding Federal Income Tax Withholding, p. 427	📁 Reproducible Lesson Plan 17.3 💿 *NBR* Video 15 🔦 Focus Activity Transparency 70 📁 Focus Activity Sheet 70 📁 Guided Reading Activity 17.3 📁 Free Enterprise Activity 17 📁 Consumer Application Activity 18 📁 Section Quiz 17.3 📁 Reinforcing Skills 17
Section 4 Taxation • **Give an example** of a tax levied according to each of the two principles of taxation. • **List** the three forms of taxation according to their effect on taxpayers. • **Explain** how taxes are used to direct economic activity.	**News Clip:** "Summer Festivals: The High Price of Having Fun," *Governing*, p. 432	📁 Reproducible Lesson Plan 17.4 💿 *NBR* Video 13 and Video Still 8 🔦 Focus Activity Transparency 71 📁 Guided Reading Activity 17.4 📁 Performance Assessment Activity 23 📁 Section Quiz 17.4 📁 Enrichment Activity 17

`0:00` OUT OF TIME? If time does not permit teaching this chapter, you may use the Chapter 17 Highlights and the Audiocassettes that include a 1-page activity and a 1-page test.

Chapter 17 Review and Evaluation

Special Features	Classroom Resources

Chapter 17 Highlights, p. 433
Chapter 17 Review, pp. 434–435

- Chapter 17 Test Forms A and B
- Economics Vocabulary Activity 17
- Spanish Economics Vocabulary Activity 17

- Audiocassette 17
- Spanish Audiocassette 17
- Reteaching Activity 17
- Spanish Reteaching Activity 17

Key to Ability Levels

Teaching strategies have been coded for varying learning styles and abilities.

L1 Level 1 activities are **basic** activities and should be within the ability range of all students.

L2 Level 2 activities are **average** activities designed for the ability range of average to above-average students.

L3 Level 3 activities are **challenging** activities designed for the ability range of above-average students.

LEP activities should be within the ability range of **Limited English Proficiency** students.

Performance Assessment

The following chapter project may be assigned at the beginning of the chapter and used for performance assessment. See page T12 for additional Performance Assessment information.

Filling Out Tax Forms After students complete the Skill Lesson on student page 429, assign each a job and income and ask them to work in pairs to complete a tax return for someone employed in that occupation. Ask students to discuss possible expenses and deductions and to decide together on other variables, such as home ownership and/or part-time self-employment. After the teams complete the tax forms, have a team member report on the ease or difficulty they had in filling out tax forms. Students might report their findings in a proposal about simplifying the tax return process.

Additional Resources

Readings for the Student

Riemer, D. R. *The Prisoners of Welfare.* New York: Praeger Publications, 1988.

Swedberg, Richard. *Economics and Sociology.* Princeton, N.J.: Princeton University Press, 1990.

Readings for the Teacher

Schick, A. *The Capacity to Budget.* Washington, D.C.: Urban Institute Press, 1990.

Weaver, Carolyn L., ed. *Social Security's Looming Surpluses.* Washington, D.C.: AEI Press, 1990.

Multimedia Materials

Changing Taxes—Public Goods and Services. Videotape. 15 min. From the Give and Take Series. Agency for Instructional Technology, Box A, Bloomington, IN 47402

Taxation and Public Policy. From the Personal Finance Series. Videotape. 30 min. Great Plains Instructional Television Library. University of Nebraska, P.O. Box 80669, Lincoln, NE 68501

Chapter Overview

Except at tax time and when we break the law, government is largely an invisible force in our lives, supporting many of the services we take for granted and fostering many of the economic advantages we seek. Many Americans think of government as something outside their daily lives. This chapter introduces students to the evidence of government's role in our everyday lives. Chapter 17 explains or describes: the growth of government over the course of this century to include public works projects and health and other benefits for citizens; the ways in which government contributes to the public good; the budget-making process; the national debt; and the principles of taxation.

VIDEODISC

Nightly Business Report
Economics in Action
Use "How Government Spends, Collects, and Owes" on Disc 2, Side A, Video 23.

Search 34436, Play to 41063

CHAPTER

17 GOVERNMENT SPENDS, COLLECTS, AND OWES

Who decides what paintings and sculptures to put in museums?

Who usually owns big museums?

410   Unit 5 Macroeconomics: Managing the Nation's Economy

Answering Economic Questions

The questions in the above illustration are designed to lead into the main concepts in Chapter 17. Students might not be aware of the many different ways in which government affects the quality of life in the United States. They might be surprised, for example, to learn of the government's role in our nation's cultural life. These questions will increase their awareness of the impact of government on our everyday lives.

Have students discuss the questions and explain their reasons for thinking as they do.

Why are there not more museums?

How expensive is it to operate a museum?

Why do people go to museums?

Your Economics Journal

Keep track of what you do during a one-day period. List each activity. Indicate what role the government might have in that activity. For example, when you drive, it is usually on a government-provided public road.

411

Connecting to Past Learning

Ask students to discuss which goods and services they buy with their own money, which things require help from their parents, and which involve help from the government.

Applying Economics

Tell students to imagine they have graduated from a public high school and a state university and now work as fact-checkers for a magazine, earning $1,500 monthly, with health insurance paid. After they pay for necessities and set aside a little for savings, not much is left, so they read library books and swim and play sports in the parks. They use public transportation but plan to buy a car. Have students tell which of their activities are at least somewhat dependent on government.

 EXTRA CREDIT PROJECT

Have interested students learn how corporations and small business use deficit financing. Ask students to present models of how deficit financing is used by creating flow charts or spending maps and adding captions, which they can read to the class.

 PERFORMANCE ASSESSMENT

Refer to page 410B for "Filling Out Tax Forms," a Performance Assessment Activity for this chapter.

Economic Portfolio

Have students make a list of things they like to do and examine how government may support, regulate, or tax them. Discuss this list of items and write on the chalkboard the ways in which government is part of the students' lives. Then have students identify things they do without any government involvement. List those things on the chalkboard. Ask students to write a paragraph about the pros and cons of government involvement in their lives.

Overview

See the student page for section objectives.

Section 1 explains or describes: the measurements of government growth; why government has grown rapidly since the Great Depression; and government spending relative to gross national product.

Bellringer

Before presenting the lesson, display Focus Activity Transparency 67 and assign the accompanying Focus Activity Sheet.

Motivational Activity

Write the following statement for students to complete: Some people think government should be bigger. Some think it should be smaller. I think _____.

Call on volunteers to read and give reasons for their answers.

Preteaching Vocabulary

Ask students working in pairs to write the title Public Works Projects on a sheet of paper and to develop proposals for projects that would provide jobs and much-needed goods or services today.

SECTION **1** Growth in the Size of Government

Terms to Know public-works projects, Medicare

Objectives *After reading this section, you should be able to:*

① Describe two measurements of government growth.

② Explain why government has grown rapidly.

Is More Government Better Government?

In the United States, the forces of supply and demand operating in the marketplace affect many of the decisions that answer the basic economic questions you learned about in Chapter 2. The United States is not a pure market economy, however. In addition to market forces, other forces affect the distribution of resources throughout the economy. One of the most important of these forces is government on all levels—local, state, and federal. Government at every level is involved in almost every aspect of the United States economy.

Government Growth

Government has grown considerably in the last 50 or so years. In 1929, just before the Great Depression began, government at all levels employed slightly more than 3 million civilian workers. During the Depression, however, there was a need for more government services, as Figure 17.1 illustrates. Today slightly fewer than 3 million people work for the federal government alone. If you add local and state employees, government employs about 18.7 million civilian workers. This figure represents more than a sixfold increase during a period in which the population only doubled.

As the functions of government have grown, so has government spending. Figure 17.2 shows one way of looking at government activities.

412 *Unit 5 Macroeconomics: Managing the Nation's Economy*

Classroom Resources for Section 1

- Reproducible Lesson Plan 17.1
- *NBR* Video 23 and Video Still 4
- Focus Activity Transparency 67
- Focus Activity Sheet 67
- Guided Reading Activity 17.1
- Cooperative Learning Activity 17

- Primary and Secondary Source Readings 17
- Consumer Application Activity 5
- Section Quiz 17.1
- Spanish Section Quiz 17.1
- Testmaker

Government in the Economy

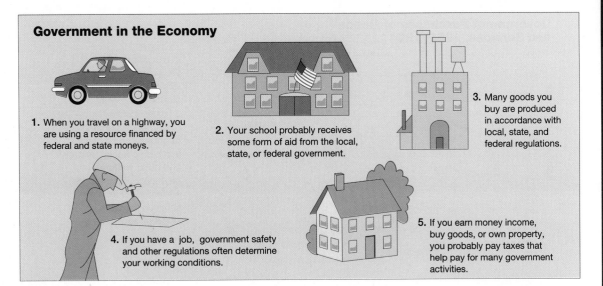

1. When you travel on a highway, you are using a resource financed by federal and state moneys.

2. Your school probably receives some form of aid from the local, state, or federal government.

3. Many goods you buy are produced in accordance with local, state, and federal regulations.

4. If you have a job, government safety and other regulations often determine your working conditions.

5. If you earn money income, buy goods, or own property, you probably pay taxes that help pay for many government activities.

Figure 17.1
Government Growth

As more people lost their jobs during the Great Depression, local government services, such as soup kitchens, proved inadequate. New government services and a larger government labor force resulted.

▼

Figure 17.3 (page 414) shows another.

As you can see from Figure 17.3, the different levels of government have grown at different rates. During the early 1960s, state and local governments spent less than the federal government. The federal government paid for national defense, **public-works projects,** and the salaries of members of Congress, federal judges, and the employees of executive departments such as the State Department. This situation continued until the mid-1960s. Then, state and local government spending for such items as sewers, roads, and schools increased rapidly.

Why Has Government Grown?

Economists have often tried to explain the huge growth in government spending since the Great Depression. One theory is that as the nation became richer, especially in the late 1960s and early 1970s, people demanded more government services to even out certain income inequities. This goal relates to the economic

Figure 17.2 ▲
Government in the Economy

Government plays a major role in most aspects of our lives. Some individuals argue that government should be even larger. Others believe that government has grown too large and that the private sector should provide goods and services without government intervention.

Chapter 17 Government Spends, Collects, and Owes **413**

Teach

Guided Practice

L2 Analyzing Have students work in small groups to identify laws and regulations that touch their lives, including those that protect and those that restrict. Ask students to suggest revisions to these laws to make them more effective.

L3 Creating Tables Have students create tables showing goods and services produced by the government, the private sector, and both, today and in the 1920s. Have them highlight things that have not changed.

 VIDEODISC

Nightly Business Report
Economics in Action
Use Video Still 4, "Federal Spending/Deficit," on Disc 2, Side A, Video 23.

Search Frame 35529

◆▶◯ Meeting Special Needs

Reading Disability Students with various reading and organizational difficulties may have problems reading the graphs that contain multiple lines of information. Before reading the text in Section 1, ask students to look at the tables and interpret each line of information. Encourage students to write down the information on a sheet of paper or on the chalkboard. Then have them read Section 1 and discuss how the graphs illustrate the information in the section.

Independent Practice

L2 Interviewing Have students interview senior citizens in the community about the effect of government growth on their lives. Suggest that students devise questions that will encourage interviewees to discuss the advantages and disadvantages of government growth.

Have students complete Guided Reading Activity 17.1 in the TCR. LEP

Visual Instruction

Ask students to copy or trace the graph in Figure 17.3 on a sheet of paper and extend each line to show where they think spending will be in the years 2010 and 2050.

🌍 GLOBAL ECONOMICS

Many nations, such as China, Cuba, Great Britain, France, and Italy, have a unitary system of government in which power and responsibility rest mainly with the central government. The United States, Argentina, Australia, Austria, Brazil, Burma, India, Mexico, and Switzerland have a federal system, in which power is shared between states or provinces and the central government.

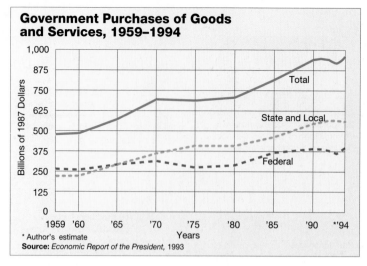

Government Purchases of Goods and Services, 1959–1994

Total
State and Local
Federal

Billions of 1987 Dollars

1959 '60 '65 '70 '75 '80 '85 '90 *'94
Years
* Author's estimate
Source: *Economic Report of the President,* 1993

◀ **Figure 17.3
Government Purchases of Goods and Services, 1959–1994**

Government purchases of goods and services (excluding Social Security and other welfare payments and interest) corrected for inflation show an increase in all levels of government.

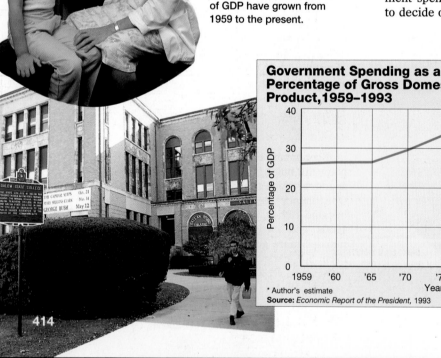

▼ **Figure 17.4
Government Spending as a Percentage of Gross Domestic Product, 1959–1993**

Total government expenditures, including Social Security and other welfare payments, as well as interest payments, expressed as a percentage of GDP have grown from 1959 to the present.

Government Spending as a Percentage of Gross Domestic Product, 1959–1993

Percentage of GDP

1959 '60 '65 '70 '75 '80 '85 '90 *'93
Years
* Author's estimate
Source: *Economic Report of the President,* 1993

414

---

question of who should share in what is produced.

In the late 1970s and early 1980s, however, the economy suffered a series of recessions. Americans began to feel that maintaining all the programs they wanted was too costly. At some point, Americans—voters and politicians alike—had lost sight of the economic principle of scarcity. To remedy the situation, politicians began to think of ways to cut government spending. In doing so, they had to decide on the trade-offs Americans

---

Cooperative Learning

Organize students into groups of five or six to research and develop a plan for a community public works project that would result in a new or improved facility or provide a welcome benefit. Suggest considering matters of cost, local government approval, funding, labor pool, job skills training, and so forth. Have a member of each group present its plan for class review and discussion. If a plan emerges that the students themselves could implement, encourage volunteers to follow through, and likewise to approach the local government for implementation if that would be required.

would be willing to accept: fewer services and less money for research, education, public assistance, and health care, for example.

Today total government *purchases* represent about 20 percent of GDP. This figure, however, does not include such items as interest payments on the national debt and transfer payments such as welfare programs. Total government *outlays* exceed one-third of GDP. See Figure 17.4. Moreover, the size of government cannot be measured only by the cost of government spending. Any discussion of government's size must include where government spends this money.

The True Size of Government
When the government taxes you to provide you with a particular service, such as **Medicare** (health care for the aged), this cost of government is included in government spending. What if the government legislates a requirement that your employer provide that same service? Is there any difference? State governments are doing just that. In Massachusetts, for example, employers with five or more employees must provide medical insurance for each employee. On one hand, government taxes employees to pay for government-provided health insurance and, on the other hand, it requires that employers provide health insurance directly. The true size of government may be even greater than government estimates show.

Can We Say That the Growth of Government Is Good or Bad?
Everyone knows that government in the United States has grown in the 1900s—particularly during the Depression and during the 1960s and 1970s. See Figure 17.5. Can we say whether this is good or bad for society?

Is there an answer to such a debate? Not really, because the side that one takes depends on one's values. No right or wrong answer exists when values are at stake.

Figure 17.5 ▶
1960s and 1970s Government Growth
More aid was demanded for education, medical care, welfare, and so on. The economy was booming, and many believed that taxpayers could afford higher government spending.

SECTION 1 REVIEW

Understanding Vocabulary
Define public-works projects, Medicare.

Reviewing Objectives
1. How rapidly has government grown since 1929?
2. What do some economists believe caused the rapid growth of government?

Chapter 17 Government Spends, Collects, and Owes **415**

Section 1 Review Answers
Understanding Vocabulary
public-works projects (p. 413), **Medicare** (p. 415)
Reviewing Objectives
1. During a period when population doubled, government employment increased sixfold.
2. Some economists believe government grew during a period of increasing wealth in the 1960s and 1970s because people demanded increased government service.

Focus

Overview

See the student page for section objectives.

Section 2 explains or describes: four examples of public goods; social insurance and public assistance in the United States; four ways government regulates the economy; and two ways government promotes economic stability.

Bellringer

Before presenting the lesson, display Focus Activity Transparency 68 and assign the accompanying Focus Activity Sheet.

Motivational Activity

Have students list what they expect government should do for citizens. Call on volunteers to read and discuss their lists. Tell students that Section 2 will consider functions of government in the United States and identify programs and regulations that help it fulfill its role.

Preteaching Vocabulary

Assign each student to create a scenario based on one of the 14 vocabulary terms. Then organize the class into two teams. Have students from each team take turns telling their scenario. The listening team must then identify the term involved.

---

2 The Functions of Government

SECTION 2 FOCUS

Terms to Know public goods, merit good, Social Security, workers' compensation, Supplemental Security Income, Aid to Families With Dependent Children, Medicaid, demerit goods, income redistribution, social insurance programs, public-assistance programs, welfare

Objectives *After reading this section, you should be able to:*

1. List four examples of **public goods**.
2. Describe the two main areas through which government **redistributes income**.
3. List four ways government **regulates economic activity**.
4. Name two ways government **promotes economic stability**.

What Government Does for You

Government in the United States serves four important functions: (1) providing public goods, (2) redistributing income and providing for the public well-being, (3) regulating economic activity, and (4) ensuring economic stability. Federal, state, and local governments share responsibilities for the first three functions. The fourth responsibility, ensuring economic stability, is handled almost entirely by the federal government.

Providing Public Goods

Public goods are goods or services that government sometimes supplies to its citizens. Many individuals can use these goods at the same time, without reducing the benefit each person receives. Public goods include national defense and certain types of health care.

National defense is one of the few public goods only the federal government provides. Usually different levels of government share responsibilities. For example, the legal system, which is a type of public good, involves all three levels. Federal, state, and local governments maintain separate systems of courts, correctional institutions, and law-enforcement agencies.

Merit Goods In any society, certain goods and services are considered to have special merit. A **merit good** is defined as any good that the government has deemed socially desirable. Examples of merit goods in our society are museums, ballets, and virtually

---

Classroom Resources for Section 2

- Reproducible Lesson Plan 17.2
- Focus Activity Transparency 68
- Focus Activity Sheet 68
- Guided Reading Activity 17.2
- Consumer Application Activity 17
- Section Quiz 17.2
- Spanish Section Quiz 17.2
- Testmaker

Social Insurance and Public-Assistance Programs

Social Insurance Programs

Social Security

Social Security, a federal program, provides monthly payments to people who are retired or unable to work.

Workers' Compensation

Workers' Compensation, a state program, extends payments for medical care to workers injured on the job. Also, people who have lost jobs can receive payments through unemployment insurance.

Medicare

Medicare, a federal program, provides low-cost health care for the aged and disabled.

Both programs also pay benefits to dependents of workers who have died.

Public–Assistance Programs

Supplemental Security Income

Supplemental Security Income covers federal programs including food stamps, veterans' benefits, and payments to the aged, blind, and disabled.

Aid to Families With Dependent Children

Aid to Families With Dependent Children is a state-run program that provides money to needy single parents raising young children.

Medicaid

Medicaid, a state and federal program, provides free health care for low-income and disabled persons.

---

all plays and classical music concerts. The government provides these merit goods to the people in society who would not otherwise purchase them at a full market price. Governments, therefore, often subsidize classical music concerts, ballets, museums, and plays.

Demerit Goods At the opposite end of the socially desirable spectrum are **demerit goods,** goods that the government has deemed socially undesirable. Gambling and injurious drugs such as heroin are examples. The government exercises its role in the area of demerit goods by taxing, regulating, or prohibiting the manufacture, sale, and use of such goods. For example, governments justify very high

taxes on alcohol and tobacco products by declaring them demerit goods. The government prohibits many other drugs and strictly regulates prescription medicines.

Redistributing Income

Another function of government is to provide for the public well-being by assisting specific groups such as the aged, the ill, and the poor. Through their elected representatives, Americans have chosen to see that almost everyone in the nation is provided with a certain minimum level of income. See Figure 17.6. This task is accomplished primarily through **income redistribution,** using tax receipts to help citizens in need.

Figure 17.6 ▲
Social Insurance and Public Assistance
Government programs that redistribute income taken from some people through taxation and given to others fall into two areas: social insurance and public assistance.

Teach

Guided Practice

L1 Organizing Have students make a list of all the functions of government described in this section and organize them into a table under the categories federal government, state government, and both.

Visual Instruction

Have students refer to Figure 17.8 on page 419 as a starting point to research federal regulations regarding application of fertilizers, insecticides, and disease-control agents in agriculture, forestry, and landscaping. Organize students into small groups to prepare a report on each product type in each industry for class presentation and discussion.

GLOBAL ECONOMICS

In nations with command economies, government not only regulates, but may also own, most production and distribution systems. State ownership can sometimes discourage opposition to a variety of practices, including those that threaten health and safety.

◆◗◯ Meeting Special Needs

Hearing Disability Students whose hearing is impaired may have problems contributing to role-playing and discussion activities. In assigning such activities, direct students to

include letters and memos that can be shared with the class as part of any spoken presentation.

Independent Practice

L3 Applying Information
Ask students to study the major functions of government regulations in Figure 17.7. Tell students that different interest groups such as corporations, labor organizations, environmental groups, health and safety organizations, and consumer organizations strive to influence government regulation with respect to industry. Ask students to identify a good or service and describe how different groups would press for government regulation of the production, distribution, or consumption of that good or service.

 Have students complete Guided Reading Activity 17.2 in the TCR. **LEP**

DID YOU KNOW

The United States was one of the last industrialized nations to implement a form of social security.

Figure 17.7 Major Functions of Government Regulations

1	Protecting Consumers
2	Promoting Competition
3	Supervising Labor and Management Relations
4	Regulating Negative By-products of the Production Process

Figure 17.7 ▶ Government Regulations
Government under the American free enterprise system regulates certain aspects of the economy. For example, industrial processes, such as the spray painting process shown on page 419, are regulated.

Social insurance programs pay benefits to retired and disabled workers, their families, and the unemployed. Benefits are financed by taxes that workers and employers have paid into the programs. **Public-assistance programs,** often called **welfare,** make payments based on need, regardless of whether an individual or his or her employer has paid taxes.

Regulating Economic Activity

Figure 17.7 illustrates the four major ways in which the government regulates economic activity. One of the most important regulatory functions concerns the production process and emitting pollutants into the atmosphere as Figure 17.8 shows. When a steel mill produces steel, for example, the resulting pollution from the smokestacks may cause health problems in the surrounding area. The steel mill does not have to correct these negative by-products in the absence of a law. Therefore, the federal government has often stepped in to require plants to install equipment that will reduce pollution. Local and state governments also have pollution laws. These include everything from city laws against littering to state laws regulating the dumping of toxic wastes in rivers.

Promoting Economic Stability

Encouraging and promoting economic stability means smoothing the ups and downs in the nation's overall business activity. Such intervention helps shield citizens from the effects of business fluctuations.

This function is the responsibility of only the federal government. The high unemployment rates during the Great Depression of the 1930s, and new theories about possible ways in which government could reduce unemployment, led to a landmark piece of legislation at the end of World War II. The Employment Act of 1946 specifies clearly the federal government's responsibility for economy-wide stabilization:

The Congress hereby declares that it is the continuing policy and responsibility of the Federal Government to use all practicable means consistent with its needs and obligations and other essential considerations of national policy, with assistance and cooperation of industry, agriculture, labor and State and local governments, to coordinate and utilize all its plans, functions, and resources for the purpose of creating and maintaining, in a manner calculated to foster and promote free

418 *Unit 5 Macroeconomics: Managing the Nation's Economy*

 Cooperative Learning

Have students work in small groups to develop a budget plan for a school club or a business they might start. Recommend researching as much information as possible on the income and expenses of similar organizations. Have students develop graphics such as a pie chart to illustrate their plans. Encourage them to consult with other groups for ideas on income or expenses they might have missed.

◄
**Figure 17.8
Protecting Citizens**
Government, through the
Environmental Protection
Agency, regulates industri-
al emissions of pollutants.
For example, industrial
processes, such as high-
pressure spray painting,
must comply with emis-
sions regulations.

competitive enterprise and the general welfare, conditions under
which there will be afforded useful
employment opportunities, including
self-employment, for those able,
willing, and seeking to work and to
promote maximum employment,
production, and purchasing power.

One way that the federal government
attempts to stabilize the overall national economy is through monetary
policy. The federal government also
can use fiscal policy, which is the
government's set of financial policies
on taxation and spending, to even out
the business cycle.

SECTION 2 REVIEW

Understanding Vocabulary

Define public goods, merit good,
Social Security, workers'
compensation, Supplemental
Security Income, Aid to Families
With Dependent Children,
Medicaid, demerit goods, income
redistribution, social insurance
programs, public-assistance
programs, welfare.

Reviewing Objectives

1 What are public goods?
2 How does government
redistribute income?
3 How does government
regulate economic activity?
4 What two tools does the
government use to promote
economic stability?

Chapter 17 Government Spends, Collects, and Owes   **419**

Section 2 Review Answers

Understanding Vocabulary
public goods (p. 416), **merit good**
(p. 416), **Social Security** (p. 417),
workers' compensation (p. 417), **Supplemental Security Income** (p. 417),
**Aid to Families With Dependent Chil-
dren** (p. 417), **Medicaid** (p. 417),
demerit goods (p. 417), **income redis-**
tribution (p. 417), **social insurance
programs** (p. 418), **public-assistance
programs** (p. 418), **welfare** (p. 418)
Reviewing Objectives
1. Public goods are goods and services supplied to all citizens
2. largely through social insurance
and public assistance

3. by passing laws to protect consumers, promote competition,
supervise labor-management relations, and regulate negative by-
products of production
4. through monetary policy and fiscal
policy

President Bill Clinton appointed Robert Reich as his Secretary of Labor. A lawyer as well as a political economist, Reich believes social programs have potential as investments in the future.

Teach

Have volunteers read aloud the excerpts from Reich's *Tale of a New America.* Then have others paraphrase each excerpt to ensure everyone's understanding of Reich's ideas. Finally, have students answer the questions in Checking for Understanding.

You might have interested students create model programs to reflect Reich's perspective on public assistance. Encourage students to create detailed plans and to show how each aspect of the plan forms an investment in the future by creating training or increasing a recipient's chances for long-term employment.

Personal Perspective

Robert Reich on Government

Profile

- 1946–
- lawyer and political economist
- head of the Department of Labor under President Clinton
- previously a lecturer at Harvard University's Kennedy School of Government
- authored a number of books including *Minding America's Business* with Ira C. Magaziner (1982) and *Tales of a New America* (1987)

In the following excerpts from *Tales of a New America*, Robert Reich talks about the social program known as "workfare," and then goes on to talk about the problem of cutting all social programs as a way of decreasing consumption and increasing investment.

Programs [workfare] *that simply require able-bodied recipients to take any job offered or assigned to them, regardless of the skills it conveys or the salary it pays, are not so much a screen to sort the willing from the shiftless as they are a simple penalty on requiring aid. The purpose of such programs . . . is to deter misrepresentation by making welfare less attractive to all recipients. To the extent that beneficiaries are capable of work but aspire to a life of leisure, such requirements might indeed enforce responsibility. But they do nothing to increase people's capacity to take active responsibility for their fate.*

Reich discusses the need for "workfare" to help people on a long-term basis.

Assistance is conditioned upon the recipients taking steps to improve their prospects by, for example, finishing high school or obtaining vocational training. Along the way they might be counseled in how to find a job and perform reliably in it, and assisted with day care for

their small children and with transportation to and from work. Regardless of the specific features of the program, the basic logic is to impose requirements that improve recipients' odds for a more self-sufficient future. . . .

Consider the implications of redefining investment to include not just bricks, mortar, and machines, but also spending on the health and education (both technical and moral) of our nation's children. First, cutting taxes solely to increase the pool of savings available for investment is a dubious strategy in a world of global capital markets. . . . Second, reducing government spending on the capacity of the next generation to produce wealth means cutting a crucial investment. . . . Far from constituting luxuries to be traded off against growth and productivity, investments in human capital ought to be viewed as a central means of achieving prosperity.

Checking for Understanding

❶ What is "workfare"?
❷ How can "workfare" be more productive?
❸ Why should the government be careful in cutting social programs in order to devote more resources to investment?

Answers to Checking for Understanding

1. a set of programs requiring ablebodied recipients to take any job offered, regardless of skills conveyed or salary paid
2. by requiring recipients to take steps to improve their job prospects, such as finishing high school or pursuing vocational training
3. Additional savings may not mean productive national investments given global capital markets; cutting programs equals lack of investment in the future; and social programs improving prospects for recipients need to be seen as investment rather than consumption.

The Federal Budget and the National Debt

SECTION 3 FOCUS

Terms to Know fiscal year, deficit financing, national debt, balanced-budget amendment

Objectives *After reading this section, you should be able to:*

① List the steps in the federal **budget-making process**.
② Explain how **deficit spending increases the nation's public debt**.
③ Discuss various **attempts at deficit reduction**.

Budget Deficits Add to the National Debt

To carry out all of its functions, government must spend large sums of money. As a result, the federal budget is huge and has numerous categories. Figure 17.9 shows the major areas of spending.

Considerable debate and compromise are necessary in preparing an annual budget. Because all resources are scarce, an increase in spending in one area will cause a decrease in spending in some other area. Every spending action by the government has its own opportunity cost, and trade-offs between types of spending, even for the government, always exist. This fact was overlooked in some years when the economy was booming and government was collecting large revenues. In the 1990s all levels of government became more aware of the dangers of overspending because of the massive federal debt.

The Budget-Making Process

A complicated budget-making process goes on throughout every year, not only in Washington, D.C., but in every state and local government unit.

Figure 17.9 Federal Spending

The federal budget is based on a fiscal, rather than a calendar, year. Spending is calculated from the beginning of the budget year on October 1 of one year to September 30 of the next year, which is the federal government's **fiscal year**. ▼

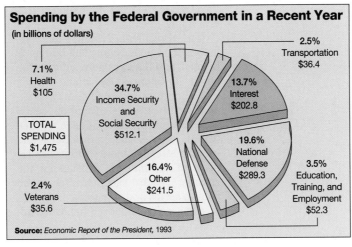

Spending by the Federal Government in a Recent Year
(in billions of dollars)

- 7.1% Health $105
- 34.7% Income Security and Social Security $512.1
- TOTAL SPENDING $1,475
- 2.4% Veterans $35.6
- 16.4% Other $241.5
- 2.5% Transportation $36.4
- 13.7% Interest $202.8
- 19.6% National Defense $289.3
- 3.5% Education, Training, and Employment $52.3

Source: *Economic Report of the President,* 1993

Focus

Overview

See the student page for section objectives.

Section 3 explains or describes: the steps in the federal budget-making process; how deficit spending increases the nation's public debt; various attempts at deficit reduction; and pie charts of federal spending and state and local spending in a recent year.

 VIDEODISC

Nightly Business Report
Economics in Action
Use "Government Spending" on Disc 1, Side B, Video 15.

Search 35044, Play to 40416

Bellringer

🔖 Before presenting the lesson, display Focus Activity Transparency 70 and assign the accompanying Focus Activity Sheet.

Motivational Activity

Have students discuss how they finance goods and services they cannot afford in one lump sum.

Preteaching Vocabulary

Ask students to plan a budget meeting using the section terms.

Classroom Resources for Section 3

- 📁 Reproducible Lesson Plan 17.3
- ⊙ *NBR* Video 15
- 🔖 Focus Activity Transparency 70
- 📁 Focus Activity Sheet 70
- 📁 Guided Reading Activity 17.3
- 📁 Free Enterprise Activity 17
- 📁 Consumer Application Activity 18
- 📁 Section Quiz 17.3
- 📁 Spanish Section Quiz 17.3
- 🖥 Testmaker
- 📁 Reinforcing Skills 17

Teach

Guided Practice

L1 Panel Discussion Organize students into groups to conduct panel discussions on issues related to the federal budget. Discussion topics might include how spending should be allocated between human resources (social needs) and national defense, whether a balanced budget is desirable or even possible, and how to control deficit spending.

Visual Instruction

Have students combine the information in Figures 17.9 on page 421 and 17.12 to create a bar graph of all government spending. Ask students to differentiate federal spending from state and local spending by position in the graph or by color.

GLOBAL ECONOMICS

Our nation's net budget outlay for fiscal 1992 was more than $1.3 trillion. About 1 percent of this amount, or around $14.7 billion, went to foreign aid, with less than half earmarked for economic development and slightly more for military assistance.

The Federal Budget-Making Process

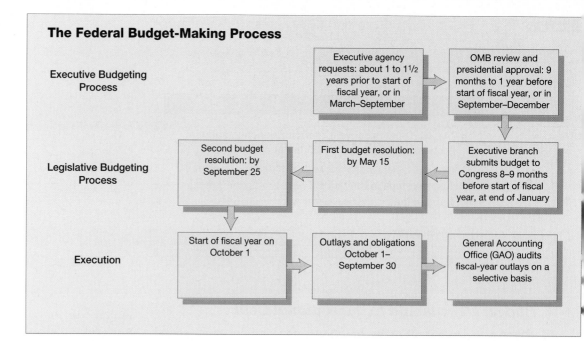

Figure 17.10 ▲
The Federal Budget-Making Process
The Office of Management and Budget (OMB) starts the budget process, with the advice of the Council of Economic Advisers (CEA) and the Treasury Department.

The Federal Budget About eighteen months before the fiscal year begins on October 1, the executive branch of the government begins to prepare a budget as Figure 17.10 shows. Working with the President, the Office of Management and Budget (OMB) makes an outline of a tentative budget for the next fiscal year. The various departments and agencies receive this outline and usually start bargaining with the OMB for a larger allocation of federal funds. See Figure 17.11.

The President reviews and approves the budget plan. The budget is printed, and the President submits the budget to Congress by January. Then its committees and subcommittees examine the budget's proposals, while the Congressional Budget Office (CBO) advises the committees and subcommittees about different aspects of the budget. Throughout the summer each subcommittee then holds a series of discussions.

Congress is supposed to pass a second budget resolution setting binding limits on spending and taxes for the upcoming fiscal year. In practice, however, the required budget resolutions often do not get passed on time. Moreover, when they are passed, the resolutions are not always treated as binding. As a result, the fiscal year sometimes starts without a budget, and the agencies must operate on the basis of a continuing congressional resolution. They can continue spending as they spent the year before until the new resolution is passed.

State and Local Budgets Figure 17.12 shows how state and local governments spend the revenues they collect. By far the largest single category in state and local expenditures is education because state and local funds provide most elementary and secondary education, as well as a considerable portion of higher education. Other large expenses are for public assistance (welfare), hospitals, health

 Meeting Special Needs

Organizing Disability Some students might have trouble differentiating the steps in the budget process. Have these students read statements in Section 3 and then restate them by numbering them in order or by drawing graphics on the chalkboard.

WELL, I'M OPEN TO SUGGESTIONS...

BUDGET

POINT A

POINT B

**Figure 17.11
The Budget
Challenge**
Point B represents the
final budget. How does
the cartoonist capture
the complexity of the
budget-making
process?

Independent Practice

L3 Speech Writing Ask students to write a campaign platform speech telling how they think the federal budget should be reshaped and how the deficit should be treated. Suggest that they treat their speeches as persuasive essays, but caution them to defend their ideas with facts and figures and to account for opposing points of view.

 DID YOU KNOW

Federal budget figures dramatize the tremendous growth over the past 20 years. In 1993, the government's receipts totaled about $1,408 billion. Its deficit totaled more than $254.7 billion, an amount greater than the federal government's total receipts of $207.3 billion for 1973.

maintenance, and highways. The "other" general expenditure also is large. It includes expenditures for state parks. See Figure 17.13 (page 424).

Deficit Spending and the Nation's Public Debt

In spite of the budget process outlined above, federal government revenues have not been equal to government expenditures. For years, the federal government has spent more than it has received. When government spends more than it collects through taxation, it must raise the extra money through borrowing. This borrowing is similar to an individual overspending his or her income and using credit. The government's spending more money than it takes in is called **deficit financing.** From 1940 through 1995, the federal government

**Figure 17.12
Government
Spending**
State and local government
expenditures increased in
recent years, as these
governments shouldered the
rising costs of social welfare
programs.

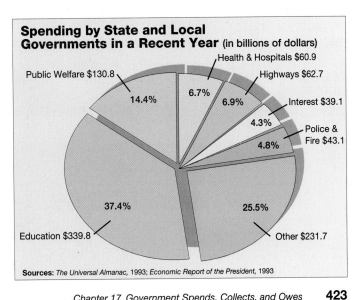

**Spending by State and Local
Governments in a Recent Year** (in billions of dollars)

- Public Welfare $130.8 — 14.4%
- Health & Hospitals $60.9 — 6.7%
- Highways $62.7 — 6.9%
- Interest $39.1 — 4.3%
- Police & Fire $43.1 — 4.8%
- Education $339.8 — 37.4%
- Other $231.7 — 25.5%

Sources: *The Universal Almanac*, 1993; *Economic Report of the President*, 1993

Chapter 17 Government Spends, Collects, and Owes **423**

Cooperative Learning

Ask students to divide the task of researching deficit financing in various levels of government throughout the United States. Suggest creating a chart or graph comparing the deficit of various cities and states. Accompanying text should note the level at which deficit spending becomes crippling and identify which groups of Americans are more affected by regional or local deficit spending.

Independent Practice

L3 Analyzing Data Ask small groups to research publications such as *Barron's* and the *Wall Street Journal* to trace the pattern and volume of investment in United States government securities during the last 20 years. Have each group examine a five-year period and combine their data in a table. Ask students to discuss what they think these data may suggest about the economic future of the United States.

GLOBAL ECONOMICS

Foreign investors buy United States Government treasury notes and bills. As of September 1993, these investors held $591.9 billion of U.S. government securities. Ranked in order of investment holdings, the primary investors were from the United Kingdom, Japan, Germany, Spain, Switzerland, and Taiwan.

had a deficit in 49 out of the 56 years. Federal government spending averaged 23 percent of GDP through the early 1990s. Federal government revenues, however, were roughly 19 percent of GDP. The difference had to be made up by borrowing.

Government Borrowing Government borrows by selling securities to individuals and businesses. Federal securities include Treasury bonds, notes, and bills. When you buy United States savings bonds, you are also lending money to the federal government. In

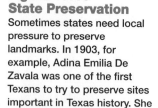
**Figure 17.13
State Preservation**
Sometimes states need local pressure to preserve landmarks. In 1903, for example, Adina Emilia De Zavala was one of the first Texans to try to preserve sites important in Texas history. She barricaded herself inside the Alamo to prevent it from being torn down. Today the Alamo is a state park and the state's number one tourist attraction.

Free Enterprise Activity

Have the class brainstorm creating a board game called Free Enterprise. Encourage students to research real board games to use as models and to include market economy elements of competition, profit, supply and demand, and so forth, as well as government regulation. Suggest that they create a mock-up and test and perfect it through actual play. If students succeed in developing a game that is fun to play, have them consider making it available to other classes for cost of materials.

United States Gross National Debt, 1986–1993

Billions of Dollars

| | 1986 | 1987 | 1988 | 1989 | 1990 | 1991 | 1992 | 1993 |

$4,500
$4,000
$3,500
$3,000
$2,500
$2,000
$1,500
$1,000

Year

Source: *Economic Report of the President*, 1993

Figure 17.14 ▲
Gross National Debt
The national debt of the United States more than doubled between 1986 and 1993. Many feared that such a rise would mortgage young Americans' futures.

Independent Practice

L2 Making a Table Have students make a table comparing the pros and cons of lowering spending to balance the federal budget and the pros and cons of raising taxes to balance the budget.

Have students complete Guided Reading Activity 17.3 in the TCR. LEP

 DID YOU KNOW

In 1992 the United States had a negative balance of trade with many of its trading partners. There were a few exceptions, however. They included nations of eastern Europe and the former Soviet republics, as well as Central and South America and the Middle East.

addition, individual agencies of the federal government, such as the Tennessee Valley Authority, are authorized to sell bonds. State and local governments can borrow by selling municipal bonds to finance some of their activities.

Each year the federal government creates new debt by issuing new securities. At the same time, it retires old debt by paying off bonds, notes, and bills as they come due. The total amount of debt outstanding for the federal government is called the **national debt** or public debt. As you can see from Figure 17.14, in recent years the dollar amount of the national debt has been growing at a steep rate. This increase concerns many public officials and private citizens who think the government is living too far beyond its means. Others, however, have pointed out that the national debt expressed as a percentage of GDP has actually decreased steadily

 ## Cultural Diversity and Economics

Organize students into small groups to research the principal imports of American products in countries of Africa, Asia, Latin America, and Europe. Ask them not only to identify the kind and volume of our exports but also to speculate on any cultural impact these exports may have. Ask students to assemble trade data in tables and any cultural notes in a paragraph accompanying their figures. Have a class discussion of their findings.

Assess

Meeting Lesson Objectives

Assign Section 3 Review as homework or an in-class activity.

Evaluate

Assign the Section 3 Quiz in the TCR or use the Testmaker.

Reteach

Ask students to create a circle graph of personal spending and to develop a balanced budget for the next school year. Remind students to take into account any outstanding debts at the start of the new budget year.

Enrich

Have students research and write a report on the terms of the Gramm-Rudman-Hollings Act of 1985. Ask interested students to also investigate budget resolutions or amendments since 1985.

Close

Discuss with students the effect of issuing government bonds for deficit financing. Encourage consideration of the effect of debt, the investment opportunities for citizens, and possible alternatives to deficit financing.

**Figure 17.15
Cutting Government Programs to Reduce the Deficit**
The Budget Reconciliation Act of 1993 proposed spending cuts in many programs. Among the programs slated for reduced funding were student loans. The act proposed cutting student loans by $3.6 billion by 1998.
▶

since World War II until the last few years. They believe that federal borrowing, if controlled, is not necessarily a reason for alarm.

Attempts at Deficit Reduction

Some argue that congressional legislation should limit the deficit. See Figure 17.15. Others think the only way to reduce federal government budget deficits is by a **balanced-budget amendment** to the Constitution. Two-thirds of the state legislatures can petition Congress for a constitutional convention to address this issue. To date, the required number of legislative petitions has not been filed.

As an alternative, Congress has the option of passing such a constitutional amendment, which it would then submit to the states for ratification. Several amendment bills have been proposed. As of 1994, however, Congress had passed no such amendment. Congress did pass the Gramm-Rudman-Hollings Act, also known as the Balanced Budget Act, in December 1985. Its goal was to reach a balanced budget by fiscal year 1991. After Congress failed for two years to comply with the act's target deficit reductions, Congress revised it. Congress again failed to meet the required deficit reductions for the first four years of the revised act. Yet another revision was passed in 1990, only to be virtually eliminated by the Budget Enforcement Act of 1990.

SECTION 3 REVIEW

Understanding Vocabulary
Define fiscal year, deficit financing, national debt, balanced-budget amendment.

Reviewing Objectives
1. What are the steps in the federal budget-making process?

2. In what type of activity does the federal government engage when it spends more than it receives?

3. What attempts have been made to reduce the federal deficit?

Section 3 Review Answers

Understanding Vocabulary
fiscal year (p. 421), deficit financing (p. 423), national debt (p. 425), balanced-budget amendment (p. 426)

Reviewing Objectives
1. The OMB prepares an outline; the various departments bargain; the President submits the budget to Congress; committees and subcommittees examine it and pass a second budget resolution.
2. The government engages in deficit financing.
3. The Senate has voted on a balanced budget amendment, and Congress passed the Gramm-Rudman-Hollings Act (Balanced Budget Act).

LEARNING ECONOMIC SKILLS

Understanding Federal Income Tax Withholding

Each year employers withhold a portion of the federal income tax so that employees do not have to make one large payment at the end of the year. Have you ever filled out a Form W-4 for withholding?

The Personal Allowances Worksheet

How much should your employer withhold? Your employer provides Form W-4, which includes a Personal Allowances Worksheet to help determine your "allowances." The more "allowances" you claim, the less the employer will withhold for income tax purposes. See Figure A.

Employee's Withholding Allowance Certificate

Attached to the worksheet is a certificate that the employee files with his or her employer. The employer may then determine how much tax to withhold each pay period. The certificate asks for the employee's name, address, Social Security number, and marital status. Then it provides a box for the employee to fill in his or her allowances from line G. Employees may have an additional amount withheld, or they may claim an exemption from withholding, providing they can show that they had no tax liability in the last tax year and will have none for the coming tax year.

Figure A

Personal Allowances Worksheet

A. Enter "1" for **yourself** if no one else can claim you as a dependent. ____

B. Enter "1" if
You are single and have only one job;

You are married, have only one job,

and your spouse does not work; or

Your wages from a second job or your spouse's wages (or the total of both) are $1,000 or less. ____

C. Enter "1" for your **spouse**. ____

D. Enter the number of dependents whom you will claim. ____

E. Enter "1" if you will file as **head of household** on your tax return. ____

F. Enter "1" if you have at least $1,500 of **child or dependent care expenses** for which you plan to claim a credit. ____

G. Add lines A through F and enter the total . ____

Practicing the Skill

❶ Assume that you are a working single parent and a head of household. You have one child and child care expenses of $2,300 per year. How many allowances should you claim?

❷ Under what conditions would an employee file for an exemption from withholding?

TEACHING
Economic Skills

Teach

Use the following activity to guide students through the steps in calculating federal income tax withholding. Organize students in groups and assign each group certain conditions. For example, one group might represent a single person with no dependents *(1)*, another might represent a working married couple with an infant *(3)*, and a third might represent a single person who supports a younger sibling *(2)*. A fourth group might represent a working couple with one child in school and one adult employed child *(3)*. Have the groups determine their tax withholding and encourage them to identify conditions under which they might claim an exemption from withholding.

Additional Practice

Have students complete Reinforcing Skills 17 in the TCR.

Answers to Practicing the Skill

1. five
2. Answers will vary but should indicate that a person might file for exemption from withholding by showing no tax liability for the past year and the coming tax year.

Focus

Overview

See the student page for section objectives.

Section 4 explains or describes: principles of taxation; forms of taxation; and how taxes are used.

VIDEODISC

Nightly Business Report
Economics in Action
Use "The American Tax System" on Disc 1, Side B, Video 13.

Search 22368, Play to 29590

Bellringer

Before presenting the lesson, display Focus Activity Transparency 71.

Motivational Activity

Ask students to compile a list of the taxes they pay as individuals.

Preteaching Vocabulary

Have students identify the taxes they pay as progressive, regressive, or proportional.

SECTION **4** Taxation

SECTION 4 FOCUS

Terms to Know benefits-received principle, ability-to-pay principle, progressive tax, regressive tax, proportional tax

Objectives *After reading this section, you should be able to:*
1. Give an example of a tax levied according to each of the two principles of taxation.
2. List the three forms of taxation according to their effect on taxpayers.
3. Explain how taxes are used to direct economic activity.

Taxes Distribute the Cost of Government Among Taxpayers

You, the American taxpayer, are the source of most of the money the government spends. About 85 percent of federal, state, and local government revenue comes from taxation. Figure 17.16 lists the major taxes that the various levels of government use to raise revenue.

Principles of Taxation

Taxes can be justified according to one of two major principles. Under the **benefits-received principle,** those who use a particular government service support it with taxes in proportion to the benefit they receive. Those who do not use a service do not pay taxes for it. For example, a gasoline tax to pay for highway construction and repair is based on the benefits-received principle. Those who use the highways often buy more gasoline and, therefore, pay more in gasoline taxes.

A tax based on the benefits-received principle is useful in raising money to pay for a service only certain individuals use. Many government services, however—national defense, for example—benefit everyone equally. Also, those who most need services, such as the aged and poor, are the individuals least able to pay taxes.

Under the **ability-to-pay principle,** those with higher incomes pay more taxes than those with lower incomes, regardless of the number of government services they use. For example, in most cities all property owners, even those without school-aged children, must pay property taxes to support the local school system.

Forms of Taxation

Actual taxes are classified according to the effect they have on those who are taxed as shown in Figure 17.17 (page 430). In the United States today, these classifications include progressive taxes, regressive taxes, and proportional taxes. Congress

---

Classroom Resources for Section 4

- Reproducible Lesson Plan 17.4
- *NBR* Video 13 and Video Still 8
- Focus Activity Transparency 71
- Focus Activity Sheet 71
- Guided Reading Activity 17.4
- Mathematics Practice for Economics 23

- Performance Assessment Activity 23
- Section Quiz 17.4
- Spanish Section Quiz 17.4
- Chapter 17 Test Forms A and B
- Testmaker
- Enrichment Activity 17

- Economics Vocabulary Activity 17
- Spanish Economics Vocabulary Activity 17
- Audiocassette 17
- Spanish Audiocassette 17
- Reteaching Activity 17
- Spanish Reteaching Activity 17

Figure 17.16 Major Taxes

Tax	Description	Type
Personal income	Tax is a percentage of income and a major source of federal revenue; many states and local governments also levy	Progressive at the federal level, but is sometimes proportional at the state level
Social insurance	Taxes covered by the Federal Insurance Contributions Act (FICA); second largest source of federal revenue	Proportional up to $60,600 in 1994, regressive above that
Corporate income	Federal tax as a percentage of corporate profits; some states also levy	At the federal level, progressive up to $100,000, proportional above that
Excise	Tax paid by the consumer on the manufacture, use, and consumption of certain goods; major federal taxes are on alcohol, tobacco, and gasoline; some states also levy	Regressive if people with higher incomes spend a lower proportion of income on taxed items
Estate	Federal tax on the property of someone who has died; some states also levy	Progressive; percentage increases with the value of the estate
Inheritance	Tax paid by those who inherit property; state tax only	Varies by state
Gift	Tax paid by the person who gives a gift; federal tax only	Progressive; percentage increases with the value of the gift
Sales	Tax paid on purchases; almost all states as well as many local governments levy; rate varies from state to state and within states; items taxed also vary	Regressive if people with higher incomes spend a lower proportion of income on taxed items
Property	State and local taxation of the value of property; both real property, such as buildings and land, and personal property, such as stocks, bonds, and home furnishings, may be taxed	Proportional; percentage is set by state and local governments
Customs duties	Tax on imports; paid by the importer	Proportional

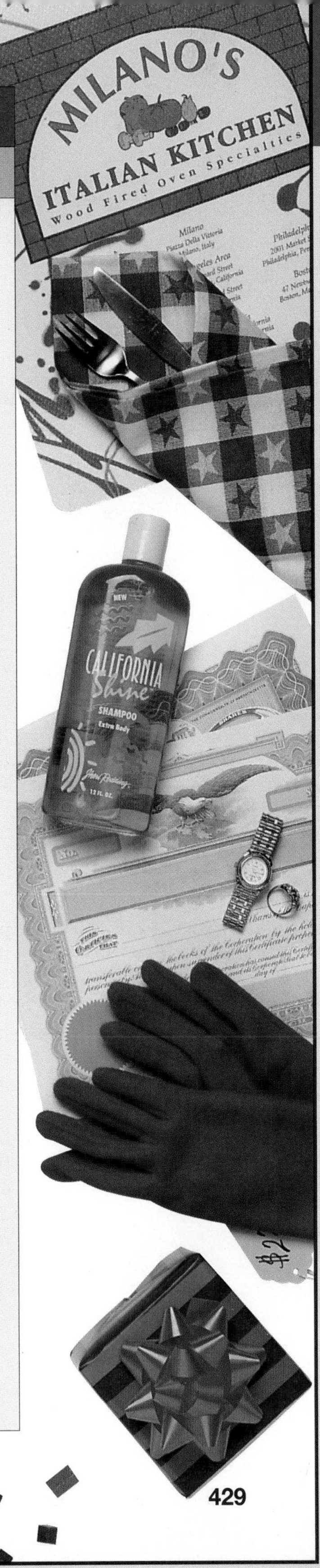

429

Teach

Guided Practice

L2 Making Judgments Have students identify benefits-received taxes they have paid. Then ask individuals to nominate other goods and services for the benefits-received category. Ask students to justify their nomination by describing the advantages of placing a good or service in this category.

GLOBAL ECONOMICS

Although the United States still collects tariffs on imported goods, the purpose is not to raise revenue. It is to protect certain domestic industries from foreign competition.

VIDEODISC

Nightly Business Report
Economics in Action
Use Video Still 8, "Value-Added Tax," on Disc 1, Side B, Video 13.

Search Frame 28629

Meeting Special Needs

Language Comprehension Disability You might want to have students who have difficulty with comprehension or who have limited English proficiency read statements in Section 4 and then restate them in their own words. Listen carefully to make sure that students are not simply repeating phrases directly from the book. Encourage students to test their understanding further by giving an example of each kind of tax discussed in the section.

L1 Tax Proposal Have students use their knowledge of kinds of taxes to propose a fair tax to raise money to benefit the community in some way.

 Have students complete Guided Reading Activity 17.4 in the TCR. LEP

Visual Instruction

Refer students to Figure 17.18. Ask them to make a list of federal and state homeowners' tax deductions. Also, have students suggest some expense or home improvement cost they think should be deductible and tell why. Ask volunteers to read their list and suggestions and discuss.

? DID YOU KNOW

The United States attempted to levy an income tax in 1894, but the Supreme Court ruled it unconstitutional. After the Sixteenth Amendment authorized Congress to enact taxes on personal incomes, the Revenue Act of 1913 was passed. Most citizens were untouched by this tax, and the tax had little impact on government finances.

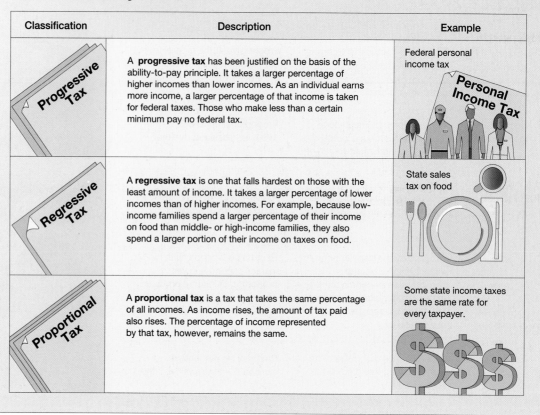

Taxes Classified by Their Effects

Classification	Description	Example
Progressive Tax	A **progressive tax** has been justified on the basis of the ability-to-pay principle. It takes a larger percentage of higher incomes than lower incomes. As an individual earns more income, a larger percentage of that income is taken for federal taxes. Those who make less than a certain minimum pay no federal tax.	Federal personal income tax
Regressive Tax	A **regressive tax** is one that falls hardest on those with the least amount of income. It takes a larger percentage of lower incomes than of higher incomes. For example, because low-income families spend a larger percentage of their income on food than middle- or high-income families, they also spend a larger portion of their income on taxes on food.	State sales tax on food
Proportional Tax	A **proportional tax** is a tax that takes the same percentage of all incomes. As income rises, the amount of tax paid also rises. The percentage of income represented by that tax, however, remains the same.	Some state income taxes are the same rate for every taxpayer.

Figure 17.17 ▲ Taxes Classified by Their Effects Do you think that higher taxes for the wealthy are fair? Why or why not?

passed a tax law in 1986 to make the tax code more fair. It eliminated many of the deductions and tax shelters that had seemed to favor the wealthy. The new tax code lowered the top tax rates for individuals gradually from 50 percent to 28 percent. It also shifted some of the tax burden from individuals by raising corporate taxes. Tax legislation in 1993 increased the top tax rates for high-income earning individuals. Corporate taxes were also increased.

Taxes as a Way of Directing Economic Activity

Taxation is more than a way for government to raise money. It is also a way in which government can direct the use of resources by businesses and individuals and a way to regulate economic activity.

Encouraging Business Taxes are commonly used to encourage certain activities by businesses and individuals. Often cities and states will temporarily reduce or exempt taxes for a company as a way of persuading it to locate in a particular area. Governments at all levels encourage investment in their bonds by offering tax-free interest. Taxes are also used to direct resources toward investments that are desirable but costly. See Figure 17.18.

Discouraging Activities Taxes can also be used to discourage certain activities. Excise taxes, for example, are

 ## Cooperative Learning

Ask students to think of themselves as the House of Representatives. Have them select members to form a Tax Change Committee to research and then organize a restructuring of the corporate income tax. The aim is to ensure equalized distribution of tax burden and tax payment by all corporations. Members of the committee should present their plan to the House, which will examine the merits of the proposal, modify it as deemed necessary, and vote on the measure.

supposed to discourage the use of such items as cigarettes and gasoline. These taxes are sometimes known as "sin taxes." Customs duties are supposed to reduce sales of imported goods. Other taxes are used as penalties for certain actions. For example, a person withdrawing money from an Individual Retirement Account (IRA) before age 59½ must pay 10 percent of it as a federal tax penalty.

Controlling Economic Activity

Taxes also can be used to control the nature and growth of economic activity. Government does this by adjusting tax rates and the distribution of taxes—who pays which taxes. Government officials, however, must keep in mind that individuals and businesses may react to these changes. For example, raising taxes for a state or city can actually decrease revenues if businesses and homeowners move away to escape high taxes. A city can also find itself short of funds if it grants too many tax reductions to try to attract business.

Figure 17.18 ▲
Tax Deductions
Many states encourage homeowners to insulate their homes by allowing the cost to be deducted from their income before computing their state income taxes.

S E C T I O N 4 R E V I E W

Understanding Vocabulary
Define benefits-received principle, ability-to-pay principle, progressive tax, regressive tax, proportional tax.

Reviewing Objectives
① Gasoline taxes and property taxes are examples of what principles of taxation?

② What are the three forms of taxation, according to their effect on taxpayers?

③ How does government use taxes to encourage or discourage certain activities?

Assess

Meeting Lesson Objectives
Assign Section 4 Review as homework or an in-class activity.

Evaluate
📁 Assign the Section 4 Quiz in the TCR or use the Testmaker.
📁 Assign the Chapter 17 Test Form A or Form B or use the Testmaker.

Reteach
Organize the class into small groups to list the taxes they pay during an average day. Point out that lists may vary slightly because of differing activities pursued. Ask students to create a table from their information for presentation to the class.
📁 Have students complete Reteaching Activity 17 in the TCR.

Enrich
Have students research tax proposals made by presidential and congressional candidates in recent elections.
📁 Have students complete Enrichment Activity 17 in the TCR.

Close
Discuss with students the support that different taxes might enjoy among different groups of people.

Section 4 Review Answers

Understanding Vocabulary
benefits-received principle (p. 428), **ability-to-pay principle** (p. 428), **progressive tax** (p. 430), **regressive tax** (p. 430), **proportional tax** (p. 430)

Reviewing Objectives
1. gasoline taxes—benefits-received principle, property taxes—ability-to-pay principle

2. progressive, regressive, and proportional

3. Answers should mention that government reduces taxes to encourage companies to locate in an area or to encourage investors to buy bonds. It raises taxes to discourage use of some items, purchase of imported goods, or certain actions.

News Clip

Readings in Economics

GOVERNING   AUGUST 1993

Teach

Point out to students that this article about protecting rights comes from a trade journal called *Governing*. Explain that political readers have special economic concerns because of their responsibility to promote the public good. *Governing* offers analysis of such issues.

Have students use the information in the feature to write guidelines for community leaders who plan to hold neighborhood festivals. Suggest that their guidelines identify the problems and the benefits of festivals and their opinions about maximizing safety and income while minimizing physical and financial risk. As they continue the course, students might collect additional clips about successful festivals.

SUMMER FESTIVALS: THE HIGH PRICE OF HAVING FUN
by Charles Mahtesian

In 1990, after six years of existence, Washington, D.C.'s annual Riverfest celebration drowned in a current of red ink. No one questioned its popularity—in fact, local residents complained that it attracted too many spectators—but city officials deemed it too expensive to operate.

... By pulling the plug on Riverfest, Washington joined a growing number of cash-strapped cities that have been reconsidering the pros and cons of the summer festival, one of the showcase economic development and promotion schemes for local government in the 1980s. In recent years there has been a major change in urban festival psychology.

... It is no longer possible for cities to ignore the fact that any large-scale festival requires significant police overtime and sanitation services. And in the case of smaller charity events, more than a few cities have calculated that it would be cheaper to cancel the event and make a direct charitable contribution from the treasury than to assign city cops and garbage collectors. So what most cities are now doing is telling the festivals if they want city services, it will cost them.

The truth, however, is that only a handful of special events draw huge crowds and make big money. There is a misguided perception, says Carolyn Pendergast, vice president of the International Festivals Association, that festivals are cash cows. "A lot of times festivals are perceived as large events that draw large numbers of people," she says, "but in reality, most festivals are at around the break-even point."

• THINK ABOUT IT •

1. Why are many cities across the United States canceling summer festivals?
2. What necessary city services contribute to the large costs of holding a festival?

Answers to Think About It

1. because the cities are short on cash and the festivals are expensive.
2. Police protection and city sanitation services contribute to the large costs of a festival.

CHAPTER 17 *Highlights*

Using Chapter 17 HIGHLIGHTS

Use the Chapter 17 Highlights to preview, review, condense, or reteach the chapter. A Spanish Chapter Highlights is available in the Spanish Handbook.

Preview/Review

After students read the Chapter 17 Highlights, have them complete Economics Vocabulary Activity 17 in the TCR. Spanish Vocabulary Activities are also available in the Spanish Resource Binder.

Vocabulary Software reinforces the economic terms used in Chapter 17.

Condense

Have students listen to Chapter 17 on the Audiocassettes in the TCR. A 1-page written activity and 1-page test accompany this material. These materials are also available in Spanish.

Reteach

Have students complete Reteaching Activity 17 in the TCR. Spanish Reteaching Activities are also available.

Section 1

Growth in the Size of Government

Key Terms

public-works projects (p. 413)

Medicare (p. 415)

Summary

Government in the United States has grown from about 3 million employees in 1929 to about 19 million today. Several factors are responsible for this spurt in government growth.

Section 2

The Functions of Government

Key Terms

public goods (p. 416)
merit good (p. 416)
Social Security (p. 417)
workers' compensation (p. 417)
Supplemental Security Income (p. 417)
Aid to Families With Dependent Children (p. 417)
Medicaid (p. 417)

demerit goods (p. 417)
income redistribution (p. 417)
social insurance programs (p. 418)
public-assistance programs (p. 418)
welfare (p. 418)

Summary

Four important functions of government are: (1) providing public goods, (2) redistributing income and providing for the public well-being, (3) regulating economic activity, and (4) ensuring economic stability. The government provides public goods to all citizens. Government uses social insurance programs and public assistance programs to redistribute income. At the same time, government works to promote economic stability.

Section 3

The Federal Budget and the National Debt

Key Terms

fiscal year (p. 421)
deficit financing (p. 423)
national debt (p. 425)

balanced-budget amendment (p. 426)

Summary

The federal budget-making process includes several steps involving the executive and legislative branches. Even with safeguards and attempts at deficit reduction, the national debt is growing at a rapid rate.

Section 4

Taxation

Key Terms

benefits-received principle (p. 428)
ability-to-pay principle (p. 428)

progressive tax (p. 430)
regressive tax (p. 430)
proportional tax (p. 430)

Summary

Two principles of taxation are the benefits-received principle and the ability-to-pay principle. Taxes are classified according to how they spread the tax burden among taxpayers, while some taxes are levied to affect economic activity.

Chapter 17 Government Spends, Collects, and Owes **433**

 VIDEODISC

Nightly Business Report
Economics in Action
Use "The American Tax System" on Disc 1, Side B, Video 13.

Search 22368, Play to 29590

 VIDEODISC

Nightly Business Report
Economics in Action
Use "How Government Spends, Collects, and Owes" on Disc 2, Side A, Video 23.

Search 34436, Play to 41063

Use "Government Spending" on Disc 1, Side B, Video 15.

Search 35044, Play to 40416

ANSWERS

Identifying Key Terms

1. c
2. d
3. b
4. a
5. e

Note: Answers 6, 7, 8 and answers 10 and 11 may be in any order.
6. Medicare
7. social security
8. workers' compensation

9. welfare
10. Medicaid
11. Supplemental Security Income

Recalling Facts and Ideas

Section 1
1. The government has grown as an employer and in spending and taxation.
2. 35 percent

Section 2
3. The main functions of government are to provide public goods, redistribute income, and provide for the public well-being; regulate economic activity; and ensure economic stability.
4. Answers may vary but might include such public goods as schools, parks, and highways.
5. The government encourages the use or purchase of merit goods.

Section 3
6. The OMB prepares an outline for the budget; the various departments bargain; the President submits the budget to Congress; committees and subcommittees examine it and pass a second budget resolution.
7. 49 out of 56 years

8. spending that exceeds income

Section 4
9. personal income tax, social insurance, corporate income tax, excise taxes, estate tax, inheritance tax, gift tax, sales tax, property tax, and customs duties
10. proportional
11. Government also uses taxes to direct economic activity.

Identifying Key Terms

Write the letter of the definition in Column B below that correctly defines each term in Column A.

Column A
1. benefits-received principle (p. 428)
2. public goods (p. 416)
3. ability-to-pay principle (p. 428)
4. income redistribution (p. 417)
5. national debt (p. 425)

Column B
a. the taking of money from some to give to others
b. system by which those with higher incomes pay higher taxes
c. payment for a particular government service by those who use the services
d. goods and services whose use by one person does not reduce use by another
e. amount of money the government owes

Use terms from the following list to fill in the blanks in the paragraph below.

Medicare (p. 415)
Supplemental Security Income (p. 417)
workers' compensation (p. 417)
Social Security (p. 417)
Medicaid (p. 417)
welfare (p. 418)

Major income redistribution programs are in place in the United States. Social insurance programs pay benefits to people in the form of (6), (7), and (8). Many public assistance programs are often called (9). They include Aid to Families With Dependent Children as well as (10) and (11).

Recalling Facts and Ideas

Section 1
1. In what ways has the government grown since the Great Depression?
2. What percent of GDP is accounted for by total government purchases of goods and services?

Section 2
3. What are the main functions of government?
4. Give some examples of public goods (but do not confuse them with all government-provided goods).
5. If the government designates a particular good or service as a merit good, what does the government normally do?

Section 3
6. What are the main steps in the federal government budget-making process?
7. How frequently has the federal government used deficit financing since World War II?
8. What causes the nation's public debt?

Section 4
9. What are the principal taxes that exist in the United States today?
10. If all income were taxed at exactly the same rate, what type of tax would be in existence?
11. Besides raising revenue, what other uses does government have for taxes?

Critical Thinking

Section 1
Synthesizing Information Look at Figure 17.3 on page 414. When were the two periods of rapid growth in government purchases? Why?

Critical Thinking
Section 1
Rapid growth occurred from about 1960 to 1970 because, as the nation became richer, people demanded more government services to even out certain income inequities. High demand for services, and possibly goods, continued from 1980 to 1992.

Section 2
Making Comparisons What is the difference between Medicare and Medicaid?

Section 3
Determining Cause and Effect Why is it impossible for the government to spend more than it receives without increasing the national debt?

Section 4
Drawing Conclusions What is the process by which taxes can direct economic activity?

Applying Economic Concepts

Theories of Taxation You learned about two theories of taxation, one of which was the benefits-received theory. Assume that you want to use this theory to justify a progressive income tax system. Write a list of the reasons explaining why, as a person's income goes up, that person receives more benefits from the government and therefore should be taxed progressively.

Chapter Projects

1. **Individual Project** A number of states have laws that require a balanced state budget. Check your state constitution to see if your state has such a requirement. Research and write a brief report explaining why and when the amendment was passed, and whether it makes the budget process more difficult.

2. **Cooperative Learning Project** Work in groups representing each of at least three regions of the United States. Each member of each group should pick one or more states to research. The information needed will be:

   ■ Highest tax rate applied to personal income
   ■ Highest tax rate applied to corporate income
   ■ Sales tax rate

   Each group should determine which states have the highest tax rate.

Reviewing Skills

Understanding Federal Income Tax Withholding

1. **Determining Allowances** How many allowances should you claim on Form W-4 if you are a single person with only one job and your parents claim you as a dependent on their federal income tax return? Use the worksheet below as your guide.

   Personal Allowances Worksheet

   A. Enter "1" for **yourself** if no one else can claim you as a dependent. ——

   B. Enter "1" if
   You are single and have only one job;
   You are married, have only one job, and your spouse does not work; or
   Your wages from a second job or your spouse's wages (or the total of both) are $1,000 or less. ——

   C. Enter "1" for your **spouse**. ——

   D. Enter the number of dependents whom you will claim. ——

   E. Enter "1" if you will file as **head of household** on your tax return. ——

   F. Enter "1" if you have at least $1,500 of **child or dependent care expenses** for which you plan to claim a credit. ——

   G. Add lines A through F and enter the total. ——

2. **Understanding Withholding** Why do employers withhold taxes from each paycheck?

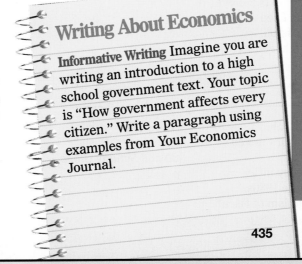

Writing About Economics

Informative Writing Imagine you are writing an introduction to a high school government text. Your topic is "How government affects every citizen." Write a paragraph using examples from Your Economics Journal.

435

Section 2
Medicare is part of federal social insurance. It is offered to retired and disabled citizens and financed by the citizen's employer contributions. Medicaid is part of public assistance and is available to needy citizens regardless of employer contributions. Medicaid funding is partly federal and partly state.

Section 3
Spending more than it receives requires the government to borrow money by issuing bonds. This borrowing increases the national debt.

Section 4
By reducing taxes, government can encourage companies to locate in a certain area or encourage investors to buy bonds. By raising taxes, government can discourage the use of items, the sale of imported goods, or actions such as the early use of retirement funds.

Applying Economic Concepts

Answers will vary, but student lists should reflect an understanding of progressive taxation and benefits-received theory.

? BONUS QUESTION

The following bonus question may be written on the chalkboard when students take the chapter test.
Q: Why is it the responsibility of everyone who can to pay taxes?
A: because everyone receives benefits from government

Chapter Projects
1. Review with students the information in their reports and the logic behind the opinions they expressed.
2. Students might present their information in a chart or table.

Reviewing Skills
1. one

2. Employers withhold taxes by law, to make sure that income tax is paid.

Writing About Economics
Have students describe the government's influence as a provider of public goods, and social insurance and public assistance programs; as a force for redistributing income; and as a promoter of economic stability.

CHAPTER 18 *CONTROLLING UNEMPLOYMENT AND INFLATION*

CHAPTER ORGANIZER

Daily Objectives	Special Features	Classroom Resources
Section 1 Unemployment and Inflation • **List** two problems that economists face in measuring unemployment. • **Distinguish** between the causes of demand-pull inflation and cost-push inflation.	**Personal Perspective:** Paul Samuelson on Unemployment and Inflation, p. 442	📁 Reproducible Lesson Plan 18.1 💿 *NBR* Videos 22 and 25 🔍 Focus Activity Transparency 76 📁 Focus Activity Sheet 76 🔍 Economic Concepts Transparencies 16 and 17 📁 Guided Reading Activity 18.1 📁 Cooperative Learning Activity 18 📁 Primary and Secondary Source Readings 18 📁 Free Enterprise Activity 18 📁 Section Quiz 18.1 📁 Spanish Section Quiz 18.1 💻 Testmaker
Section 2 The Fiscal Policy Approach to Stabilization • **Explain** a simple model of how income flows between businesses and consumers. • **Explain** how Keynesian economists believe fiscal policy should have been used at the beginning of the Great Depression. • **Indicate** how fiscal policy might reduce inflation.	**Learning Economic Skills:** Using the Consumer Price Index, p. 447	📁 Reproducible Lesson Plan 18.2 💿 *NBR* Video 24 🔍 Focus Activity Transparency 77 📁 Focus Activity Sheet 77 🔍 Economic Concepts Transparency 19 📁 Guided Reading Activity 18.2 📁 Section Quiz 18.2 📁 Spanish Section Quiz 18.2 💻 Testmaker 📁 Reinforcing Skills 18
Section 3 Monetarism and the Economy • **Explain** the monetarists' view of the Fed's role in the Great Depression. • **Describe** how monetarist theory influenced government policy in the 1980s. • **Explain** the monetarists' criticism of fiscal policy.	**News Clip:** "Teenagers' Cash," *Boston Sunday Globe,* p. 452	📁 Reproducible Lesson Plan 18.3 🔍 Focus Activity Transparency 85 📁 Focus Activity Sheet 85 📁 Guided Reading Activity 18.3 📁 Economics Laboratory 5 📁 Economics Simulation 5 📁 Mathematics Practice for Economics 24 📁 Performance Assessment Activity 24 📁 Section Quiz 18.3 📁 Spanish Section Quiz 18.3 💻 Testmaker 📁 Enrichment Activity 18

 OUT OF TIME? If time does not permit teaching this chapter, you may use the Chapter 18 Highlights and the Audiocassettes that include a 1-page activity and a 1-page test.

Chapter 18 Review and Evaluation

Special Features

Chapter 18 Highlights, p. 453
Chapter 18 Review, pp. 454–455
Economics Lab, pp. 456–457

Classroom Resources

- Chapter 18 Test Forms A and B
- Economics Vocabulary Activity 18
- Spanish Economics Vocabulary Activity 18
- Audiocassette 18
- Spanish Audiocassette 18
- Reteaching Activity 18
- Spanish Reteaching Activity 18

Key to Ability Levels

Teaching strategies have been coded for varying learning styles and abilities.

L1 Level 1 activities are **basic** activities and should be within the ability range of all students.

L2 Level 2 activities are **average** activities designed for the ability range of average to above-average students.

L3 Level 3 activities are **challenging** activities designed for the ability range of above-average students.

LEP activities should be within the ability range of **Limited English Proficiency** students.

Performance Assessment

The following chapter project may be assigned at the beginning of the chapter and used for performance assessment. See page T12 for additional Performance Assessment information.

Researching Prices Have students work in pairs to survey prices of an item in several local retail outlets. Encourage them to choose a staple, such as bread or butter, or an item that has been on the market for at least 30 years. Students can read old advertisements in newspapers or magazines to see how prices have changed over the years. If possible, also have students repeat their retail surveys after several months go by. After they complete their research, have the student pairs report on inflation as it applies to the item they researched. Have students illustrate their findings in a graph.

Additional Resources

Readings for the Student

Bauman, J. F. *In the Eye of the Great Depression.* DeKalb, Ill.: Northern Illinois University Press, 1988.

Rostow, W. W. *Theorists of Economic Growth from David Hume to the Present.* Oxford, England: Oxford University Press, 1990.

Readings for the Teacher

Dimand, Robert W. *The Origins of the Keynesian Revolution.* Stanford, Calif.: Stanford University Press, 1988. A historical look at Keynesian theory.

Wilbur, Charles K. *Beyond Reagonomics.* Notre Dame, Ind.: University of Notre Dame Press, 1990.

Multimedia Materials

Economics USA Series. Videotapes. 30 min. Annenberg CPB Collection, 1213 Wilmette Avenue, Wilmette, IL 60091. Videotapes cover topics including economic growth, fiscal policy, inflation, Keynesian theory, monetary policy, stabilization policy, and stagflation.

Money and Inflation. From Milton Friedman Speaking—A Series. Videotape. 81 min. Harcourt Brace Jovanovich, Inc., 757 Third Avenue, New York, NY 10017. Friedman discusses his views on money availability and inflation.

Chapter Overview

Far from being remote economic concepts, inflation and unemployment are important issues for most Americans. Chapter 18 explains or describes: the demand-pull and cost-push theories about inflation's causes; stabilization policies used by the government; the causes and effects of unemployment; the difficulty of gathering accurate unemployment statistics; the flow of income between businesses and consumers; and the ways in which fiscal policy might reduce inflation.

VIDEODISC

Nightly Business Report
Economics in Action
Use "Economic Growth and Stability" on Disc 2, Side A, Video 22, and "Fighting Unemployment and Inflation" on Disc 2, Side B, Video 25.

Search 41152, Play to 48096

Search 1, Play to 6420

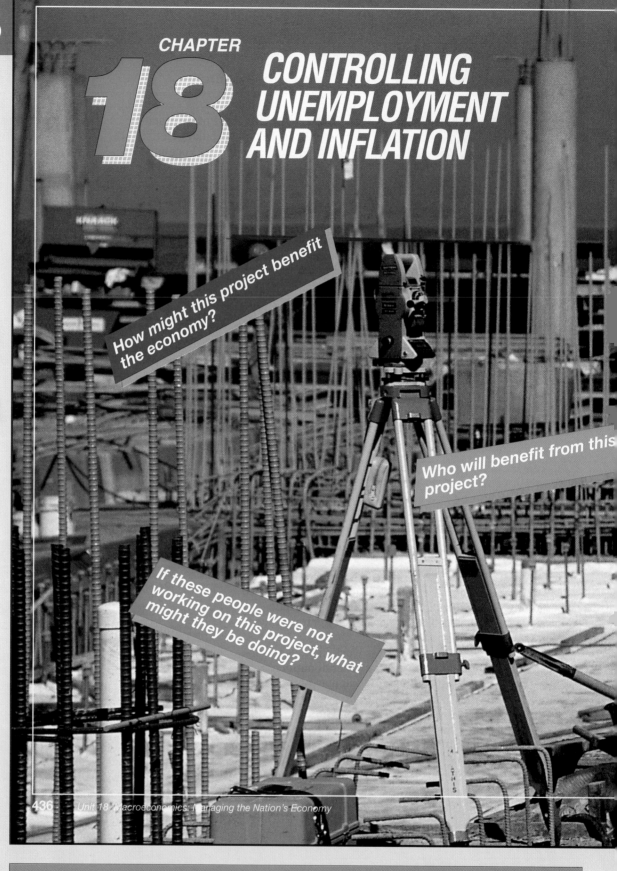

CHAPTER

18 CONTROLLING UNEMPLOYMENT AND INFLATION

How might this project benefit the economy?

Who will benefit from this project?

If these people were not working on this project, what might they be doing?

Answering Economic Questions

The questions in the above illustration are designed to lead into the main concepts in Chapter 18. Students might be interested to learn that many projects of enduring value are funded by federal programs. They also might be surprised to learn that federal work programs are often a viable alternative to public assistance.

Have students discuss the questions and explain their reasons for their answers.

436

Who pays for federally funded projects?

How does federal spending affect employment?

Your Economics Journal

Keep track of the number of times that you read about or hear about the topics of unemployment and inflation. Write down the source from which you heard or read this information. After each entry, indicate whether the economic news was good.

437

Connecting to Past Learning

Ask volunteers to recall for the class their own adventures in hunting for a job. Then have students list jobs that are plentiful and easy to get, jobs that are plentiful but require special skills, and jobs that are scarce and therefore hard to get. Finally, encourage students to brainstorm about the causes of unemployment.

Applying Economics

Tell students to imagine they have a take-home monthly paycheck of $1,200. Tell students they have a car payment of $200 per month, car insurance of $150 per month, and a food budget of $200 per month. Tell them that their rent is currently $500 per month and that this amount includes utilities and water. Ask students to calculate how much discretionary income they have *($150.00)*, and write the amount on the chalkboard. Now have students discuss how they would make ends meet if their rent rose by $50.00 and their grocery bill rose by $40.00 each month for three months.

EXTRA CREDIT PROJECT

Have students research and report on economic theories that build upon the ground-breaking theories of Keynes and Friedman.

PERFORMANCE ASSESSMENT

Refer to page 436B for "Researching Prices," a Performance Assessment Activity for this chapter.

Economic Portfolio

Have students list any jobs they hold and jobs held by family members and friends. Have students categorize the jobs according to the type of function they perform. For example, selling shoes is a retail job. Waiting tables is a service industry job. Ask students to identify the types of jobs found in their community and name the conditions that might put these jobs in danger. Have students compare this information with their Economics Journal. Have them observe whether any of these conditions have occurred and, if so, whether there is any correlation with unemployment and/or inflation in their community.

Focus

Overview

See the student page for section objectives.

Section 1 explains or describes: measures of unemployment; two problems that economists face in developing unemployment statistics; the demand-pull and cost-push theories about the causes of inflation; the concept of stagflation; why stagflation is harmful to the economy; and the difference between anticipated and unanticipated inflation.

Bellringer

Before presenting the lesson, display Focus Transparency 76 on the overhead projector or copy the material on the chalkboard. Assign the accompanying Focus Activity Sheet.

Motivational Activity

Ask students what price increases they notice most easily and encourage them to discuss how price increases affect them as consumers.

Preteaching Vocabulary

Ask students to write scenarios describing each of the vocabulary terms. Encourage volunteers to read their scenarios and have students identify the vocabulary terms that apply.

SECTION 1 # Unemployment and Inflation

SECTION 1 FOCUS

Terms to Know stabilization policies, unemployment rate, full employment, underground economy, demand-pull inflation, stagflation, cost-push inflation

Objectives *After reading this section, you should be able to:*
1. List two problems that economists face in **measuring unemployment**.
2. Distinguish between the causes of demand-pull inflation and cost-push **inflation**.

**Figure 18.1
Trying to Track
the Economy**
In the 1830s President Jackson and his successor had little insight into economic problems. Today, knowledgeable economists advise Presidents, but they often disagree about the causes and cures of the economic problems that periodically face the nation. ▼

Two Problems That Destabilize the Economy

The American economy experiences ups and downs in its overall business activity—booms, recessions, and even depressions. To keep the economy healthy and to make the future more predictable for planning, saving, and investing, the federal government uses monetary and fiscal policies. Together these are called **stabilization** (STAY-buh-luh-ZAY-shuhn) **policies**. Unfortunately, neither policy is always successful in solving the complex problems of the economy, as Figure 18.1 explains. Two of the biggest threats to the nation's economic stability are high unemployment and too much inflation.

Measuring Unemployment

The **unemployment rate** is the percentage of the civilian labor force that is without jobs but that is actively looking for work. High unemployment is usually a sign that all is not well with the economy. Moreover, the waste of human resources that unemployment causes is an extremely serious problem. Unemployment can reduce living standards, disrupt families, and take from an individual his or her feeling of self-respect. As a result, maintaining a low unemployment rate is one of the major goals in stabilizing the economy.

438

Classroom Resources for Section 1

Reproducible Lesson Plan 18.1
NBR Videos 22 and 25
Focus Activity Transparency 76
Focus Activity Sheet 76
Economics Concepts Transparencies 16 and 17
Guided Reading Activity 18.1

Cooperative Learning Activity 18
Primary and Secondary Source Readings 18
Free Enterprise Activity 18
Section Quiz 18.1
Spanish Section Quiz 18.1
Testmaker

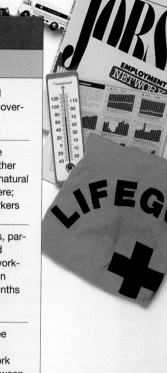

Figure 18.2 Types of Unemployment

Type	Definition	Characteristics
Cyclical	Unemployment associated with fluctuations up or down in the business cycle	Rises during recessions and depressions; falls during recoveries and booms
Structural	Unemployment caused by changes in the economy such as technological advances or discoveries of natural resources	Can result when workers are replaced by computers or other machines or when cheaper natural resources are found elsewhere; often affects less skilled workers
Seasonal	Unemployment caused by changes in the seasons or weather	Affects construction workers, particularly in the Northeast and Midwest; also affects farm workers who are needed in certain areas only during certain months of the growing season
Frictional	Temporary unemployment between jobs because of firings, layoffs, voluntary searches for new jobs, or retraining	Always exists to some degree because of the time needed between jobs to find new work and the imperfect match between openings and applicants

Types of Unemployment Many types of unemployment exist. Figure 18.2 describes these kinds of unemployment. Some people work in seasonal jobs or jobs that are sensitive to technological advances or changes in the marketplace. As a result, not all unemployment can be eliminated. Moreover, economists disagree over what the level of full employment should be.

In the 1960s, some economists thought the unemployment rate should not exceed 4 percent. This figure was raised to 5 to 6 percent in the 1970s. After much careful study, economists now generally have come to consider the economy at **full employment** when the unemployment rate is less than 6.5 percent. It is important to remember that the unemployment rate is only an estimate. The unemployment rate does not include people who are out of

work and have stopped looking for work. Nor does it include people who work in family businesses without receiving pay.

Economists classify unemployment into four broad categories: cyclical, structural, seasonal, and frictional. Most of the people who are in these unemployment categories are out of work because of forces beyond their control.

Unemployment is difficult to measure accurately because government statisticians cannot possibly interview every person in and out of the labor force. Survey results are also imperfect because of the existence of the underground economy. The **underground economy** consists of people who do not follow federal and state laws with respect to reporting earnings as Figure 18.3 (page 440) shows.

Chapter 18 Controlling Unemployment and Inflation **439**

Teach

Guided Practice

L3 Problem Solving Have small groups develop lists of jobs that make people prone to cyclical, structural, seasonal, and frictional unemployment. Encourage students to brainstorm ways to eliminate or soften the conditions that cause unemployment in each category. Ask volunteers to share their ideas with the class and discuss.

VIDEODISC

Nightly Business Report
Economics in Action
Use Video Still 3, "Civilian Unemployment," on Disc 2, Side A, Video 22.

Search Frame 28939

◆▶○ Meeting Special Needs

Reading and Organizational Disabilities Students with reading or organizational disabilities may have problems interpreting circular graphics. Before reading the text in Section 1, ask students to look at Figure 18.5. Have students work as a group to tell what information the graphic conveys. Students

should first read the information from the graphic. Then students should rephrase the text in order to show comprehension. If students have difficulty, they may work together to comprehend what the graphic is saying.

L1 Calculating Have students use the information on measuring unemployment to calculate the raw number of Americans unemployed at the rate currently recommended by economists. Remind students that the population of the United States is approximately 260 million people. Ask students to calculate the approximate raw number of unemployed of their community, township, or county, based on national unemployment. Ask students if they think these calculations are accurate and have them explain their answers.

Have students complete Guided Reading Activity 18.1 in the TCR. **LEP**

Visual Instruction

Encourage students to study Figure 18.5 carefully and then use it as a model for drawing a similar graphic explaining the demand-pull theory of inflation. Some students might wish to personalize their graphics by including illustrations of each event in the graphic.

The Underground Economy

Illegal Activities		
1. Tax Avoiders These people work for cash payments without reporting their earnings to the Internal Revenue Service.	2. Gamblers and Drug Traffickers These people may be working, but will deny they are when interviewed by government officials.	3. People Working "Off The Books" These people are officially unemployed and are receiving unemployment benefits, but are really working.

Figure 18.3 ▲ The Underground Economy
How do illegal activities make measuring the true unemployment rate difficult?

Figure 18.4 Higher Inflation, Lower Living Standards
If you earn $300 per week and inflation averaged 5 percent this year, how much per week would you have to earn next year to maintain your purchasing power?

▼

Higher Inflation, Lower Living Standards

Your Raise	Inflation Rate	Purchasing Power
5%	1%	4%
5%	8%	–3%

Inflation

A second major problem that faces the nation is inflation. The economy can usually adapt to gradually rising prices. Unpredictable inflation, however, has a destabilizing effect on the economy. Consumers and businesses act differently than they would if the economy were growing at a stable rate. For example, during periods of unanticipated high inflation, consumers may borrow and spend more. They realize that the dollars they use to make loan payments will be worth less and less as inflation rises. As a result, creditors eventually raise interest rates to maintain the level of profit they had before inflation began to rise rapidly. This, in turn, tends to have a slowing effect on the economy's growth. In the long run in a time of anticipated high inflation, consumers and businesses often borrow less because of the high interest rates.

Inflation may also affect consumers' living standards. Suppose you receive a 5 percent raise in a year in which inflation has risen 8 percent. As Figure 18.4 shows, you have actually lost purchasing power. Inflation is a particularly serious problem for people who live on *fixed* incomes, such as those who are retired. Each year a little of the purchasing power of that income is eaten away.

Unfortunately, no single answer explains why inflation occurs. Two competing ideas have developed, however: the demand-pull theory and the cost-push theory.

Demand-Pull Theory of Inflation According to the theory of **demand-pull inflation,** prices rise as the result of excessive business and consumer demand. If demand increases faster than total supply, the resulting shortage will lead to the bidding up of prices.

Demand-pull inflation can occur for several reasons. Inflation can occur if the Federal Reserve causes the money supply to grow too rapidly. Individuals, in their attempt to spend the additional dollars, will compete for the limited supply of goods and services. This increased demand will cause prices to rise. Increases in government spending and in business investments for expansion can also increase overall demand. It can also increase if taxes are reduced or consumers begin saving less. Either results in more money income being spent.

Cooperative Learning

Have students work in teams to develop a chart that records price changes in their community over time. Have each team choose a class of consumer goods such as bread or butter. Have them measure the highest, lowest, and average price for each of five to ten goods in that category. Then have students record their information on an overall chart. Encourage the teams to update the chart every week, watching for price increases and reductions.

Cost-Push Theory of Inflation The demand-pull theory indicates that inflation usually happens only when there is full employment in the economy. Before full employment is reached, increased demand will increase output and reduce unemployment. Experience, however, has shown that rising prices and unemployment can occur at the same time. This combination of inflation and low economic activity is sometimes called **stagflation.** The United States experienced this type of inflation for the first time during the 1969-1970 recession. It remained a problem through much of the 1970s; it appeared again in 1982; and, to a lesser extent, it was evident in 1990-1991.

According to some economists, stagflation is a result of cost-push inflation at work in the economy. The theory of **cost-push inflation** states that the wage demands of labor unions and the excessive profit motive of large corporations push up prices as shown in Figure 18.5.

According to this theory, large unions have the power to demand and receive wage increases that are not necessarily justified by the productivity of workers. When businesses have to pay higher wages, their costs increase. To maintain their profit level, businesses must raise prices. Each time this happens, it causes the cost of living to go up. Workers then demand higher wages to balance the decline in their purchasing power.

During periods of cost-push inflation, unemployment can remain high. Prices are being adjusted for higher wages and profits and not because of increased aggregate demand—total demand for goods and services. Without additional aggregate demand, producers have no reason to increase output by hiring new workers. As a result, unemployment continues.

Figure 18.5 Cost-Push Inflation

Cost-push inflation may also result from increasing costs of natural resources. Where on the circle would you place the costs of resources?
▼

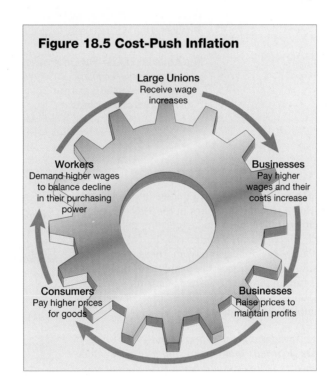

Figure 18.5 Cost-Push Inflation

Large Unions
Receive wage increases

Businesses
Pay higher wages and their costs increase

Businesses
Raise prices to maintain profits

Consumers
Pay higher prices for goods

Workers
Demand higher wages to balance decline in their purchasing power

---

SECTION 1 REVIEW

Understanding Vocabulary
Define stabilization policies, unemployment rate, full employment, underground economy, demand-pull inflation, stagflation, cost-push inflation.

Reviewing Objectives
1. What are two problems the government faces in measuring unemployment?
2. If prices are going up because too many consumer dollars are competing for goods and services, what type of inflation is occurring?

Section 1 Review Answers

Understanding Vocabulary
stabilization policies (p. 438), **unemployment rate** (p. 438), **full employment** (p. 439), **underground economy** (p. 439), **demand-pull inflation** (p. 440), **stagflation** (p. 441), **cost-push inflation** (p. 441)

Reviewing Objectives
1. the inability of statisticians to interview every person in and out of the labor force, and the existence of an underground economy.
2. Demand-pull inflation occurs when "too many dollars are chasing too few goods."

Assess

Meeting Lesson Objectives
Assign Section 1 Review as homework or an in-class activity. Each question in the Review addresses the corresponding numbered objective in the Section Focus.

Evaluate
Assign the Section 1 Quiz in the TCR or use the Testmaker.

Reteach
Ask students to draw a circular graphic showing how high inflation affects consumer spending and the economy as a whole.

Enrich
Have students research information on wage and price controls instituted in the early 1970s. Encourage students to discuss the reasoning behind these controls and the extent to which these controls did or did not help the economy.

Close

Have students list on the chalkboard some of the ways in which high unemployment affects the economy. Then help students consider ways in which these economic forces might affect the overall quality of life. Do the same with the issue of inflation.

Background

Paul Samuelson is considered a pioneer in mathematical economics because he studied the theories of Keynes and other economists and moved beyond them to try to explain current conditions.

Teach

Have volunteers read aloud the quoted excerpts from Samuelson's *Full Employment, Guideposts and Economic Stability*. Students should paraphrase each excerpt to gain a better understanding of Samuelson's ideas. Then have students create a time line of thoughts about inflation and economics. Remind students to include pure Keynesian theory on the time line. Finally, have students answer the questions in Checking for Understanding.

Interested students might read chapters from any of Samuelson's published works in order to understand the philosophical basis of his work in economics. Have these students report on the ways in which Samuelson's ideas go beyond Keynesian economic theory.

Personal Perspective

Paul Samuelson on Unemployment and Inflation

Profile

- 1915–
- graduate school at Harvard University
- taught at the Massachusetts Institute of Technology
- publications include *Full Employment, Guideposts and Economic Stability* with Arthur F. Burns (1967) and numerous editions of *Principles of Economics*

Paul Samuelson participated in a series of Rational Debate Seminars in the 1966–67 academic year. The following excerpt is taken from *Full Employment, Guideposts and Economic Stability*, a publication from these seminars. Samuelson addresses the problem of maintaining full employment without causing rapid inflation. He says we have moved beyond "simple Keynesianism."

*D*uring the great slump of the 1930s economists learned that expansionary fiscal and monetary policies could bring a depressed economic system toward full employment. You might call these the days of happy and simple Keynesianism.

However, by the end of World War II when full employment had long been a reality, the honeymoon was over.

. . . Perhaps even with government intervention, we cannot long enjoy both high employment and reasonable price stability. That is the basic issue we face. . . .

Samuelson believed that government could produce steady growth by establishing wage-price guideposts along with fiscal and monetary policies.

I cannot stress too strongly that wage-price guideposts are not substitutes for proper macro-economic fiscal and monetary policies. Economists have always known that excessively easy monetary policy and/or enlarged expenditures coupled with small tax receipts can produce demand-pull inflation. The only cure for that situation is tighter money and/or more restrictive fiscal policy.

Samuelson concludes that some unemployment might be necessary in order to keep price increases under control.

. . . *E*xperience suggests that in the short run there is a trade-off between the intensity of unemployment of men [and women] and capital and the intensity of price increase.

Checking for Understanding

❶ What basic issue did economists face after World War II?

❷ What did Samuelson believe to be the cure for demand-pull inflation?

❸ What trade-off seemed to be likely?

Answers to Checking for Understanding

1. After World War II, economists faced price instability (inflation) at full employment.

2. Samuelson believed that the only cure for demand-pull inflation was tighter money and/or more restrictive fiscal policy.

3. A trade-off between the intensity of unemployment of people and capital, and the intensity of price increase (some unemployment might be necessary in order to keep price increases under control) seemed to be likely.

SECTION 2 The Fiscal Policy Approach to Stabilization

SECTION 2 FOCUS

Terms to Know fiscal policy, circular flow of income

Objectives *After reading this section, you should be able to:*

① Explain a simple model of **how income flows** between businesses and consumers.

② Explain how Keynesian economists believe **fiscal policy** should have been used at the beginning of the Great Depression.

③ Indicate how **fiscal policy** might reduce **inflation**.

Government Policies of Taxing and Spending

Most economists fall into one of two groups on the question of economic stabilization. Both groups share some ideas, but they take different approaches toward controlling unemployment and inflation. One group emphasizes the role of monetary policy and of the Federal Reserve in stabilizing the economy. The other group concentrates more on the use of fiscal policy. **Fiscal policy** is the federal government's use of taxation and spending policies to affect overall business activity. John Maynard Keynes, shown in Figure 18.6, developed fiscal policy theories during the Great Depression. Keynes believed that the forces of supply and demand operated too slowly in a serious recession and that government should step in to stimulate aggregate demand.

The Circular Flow of Income

Many economists use what is known as the **circular flow of income** in explaining their theories. This model pictures income as flowing continually between businesses and consumers. Income flows from businesses to households as wages, rent, interest, and profits. These are payments for the use of the factors of production households control—their

**Figure 18.6
John Maynard Keynes**
Keynes and his followers believed that fiscal policy could help reduce unemployment. ◀

Chapter 18 Controlling Unemployment and Inflation **443**

Classroom Resources for Section 2

- Reproducible Lesson Plan 18.2
- *NBR* Video 24
- Focus Activity Transparency 77
- Focus Activity Sheet 77
- Guided Reading Activity 18.2

- Section Quiz 18.2
- Spanish Section Quiz 18.2
- Testmaker
- Reinforcing Skills 18

LESSON PLAN
Chapter 18, Section 2

Focus

Overview

See the student page for section objectives.

Section 2 explains or describes: a simple model of how income flows between businesses and consumers; how Keynesian economists believe fiscal policy should have been used at the beginning of the Great Depression; and how fiscal policy might reduce inflation.

 VIDEODISC

Nightly Business Report
Economics in Action
Use "Economic Growth and Stability" on Disc 2, Side A, Video 24.

Search 41152, Play to 48096

Bellringer

Before presenting the lesson, display Focus Transparency 77 and assign the accompanying Focus Activity Sheet.

Motivational Activity

Have students list reasons why the following statement might be true: What is good for business is good for the consumer.

Preteaching Vocabulary

Ask students to develop stories or skits that illustrate the term *circular flow of income.*

443

Teach

Guided Practice

L2 Extrapolating Have students work in groups to create diagrams expressing the Keynesian view of the slide into the Great Depression. Then have students modify their diagrams, adding labels and arrows that show how Keynesians think the Great Depression could have been avoided. Ask volunteers to explain their diagrams.

Visual Instruction

Ask students to look at Figure 18.7 and study the diagram. Then point out to students that larger purchases often require some savings, which are later placed into the circular flow of income. Ask them to identify savings that begin as leakages in the circular flow of income but later become a part of that circular flow.

VIDEODISC

Nightly Business Report
Economics in Action
Use Video Stills 5 and 6, "The Laffer Curve" and "Money Supply," on Disc 2, Side A, Video 24.

Search Frame 45643

Search Frame 47502

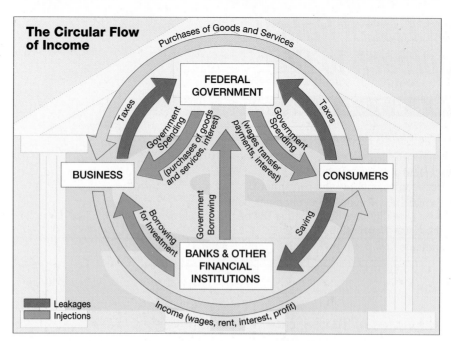

The Circular Flow of Income

Purchases of Goods and Services

FEDERAL GOVERNMENT

Taxes — Government Spending (purchases of goods and services, interest) — Government Spending (wages transfer payments, interest) — Taxes

BUSINESS — Government Borrowing — CONSUMERS

Borrowing for Investment — Saving

BANKS & OTHER FINANCIAL INSTITUTIONS

Income (wages, rent, interest, profit)

Leakages
Injections

**Figure 18.7
The Circular
Flow of Income**
Government occupies a central position in the circular flow of income. By using fiscal policy, the federal government partially controls the levels of leakages and injections. This, in turn, may control the overall level of economic activity.

---

labor, land, capital, and entrepreneurship. Income flows from households to businesses as payments for consumer goods and services.

Not all income, however, follows this circular flow. Some of it is removed from the economy through consumer saving and government taxation. Economists use the term *leakage* to refer to this removal of money income. Figure 18.7 shows these leakages.

Offsetting these leakages are injections of income into the economy. Injections occur through business investment and government spending. The term *investment*, in this sense, means the purchase of new plants and equipment and increases in inventories. Much of the income for investment comes from saving—a part of the leakage from circular flow. Government spending benefits both businesses and consumers. Businesses sell goods and services to government agencies, while consumers receive wages and transfer payments. Interest payments on government borrowing flow to both sectors.

In Keynesian theory, both leakages and injections of income have an effect on aggregate demand, as Figure 18.7 shows. Leakages reduce aggregate demand by removing income from the economy. This is income that households could have used to purchase goods and services or that businesses could have used. Injections increase aggregate demand by placing more dollars in the hands of households and businesses. Ideally, leakages and injections balance each other. In this state of equilibrium, the income that households save is reinjected through business investment. Income taken out through taxes is returned through government spending.

What happens if leakages of income are greater than injections? If saving and taxes are greater than business investment and government spending, economic activity will decrease. Aggregate demand will drop, and because businesses will not be able to sell all of their goods, they will lay off workers. Unemployment will increase.

 Meeting Special Needs

Hearing and Speech Disabilities Students with hearing or speech difficulties may be concerned about explaining diagrams or making other oral presentations to the class. Encourage these students to use posters, charts, writing on the chalkboard, and other visuals to supplement their presentations and create confidence in their ability to explain what they know.

In contrast, if more income is injected than leaked, the economy may eventually expand too rapidly and cause inflation. This view supports the demand-pull theory of inflation. If business invests heavily and/or government spends large amounts of money, more income will be injected into the economy. The same will happen if households reduce saving or the government cuts taxes. In all these cases, aggregate demand increases.

Fiscal Policy and Unemployment

Keynesian economists believe the Great Depression resulted from a serious imbalance in leakages and injections. They point out that during the 1920s, the public engaged in a higher level of saving than usual. As long as businesses continued to invest, injections balanced leakages. In the months following the stock market crash of 1929, however, the desire and ability of businesses to invest also collapsed. Capital investment fell steeply, reducing output and causing a high rate of unemployment. As you can see from Figure 18.8, unemployment eventually reached about 25 percent.

According to Keynesian theory, at the beginning of the Depression, government should have filled the gap created when businesses began limiting their investments. The government could have increased injections of government spending or cut taxes to reduce its own leakages. Either would have given businesses and consumers more spendable income. Either would have brought leakages and injections back into equilibrium.

During the 1930s, the federal government did create a number of jobs programs to hire unemployed workers. See Figure 18.9 (page 446). These new jobs reduced some unemployment and injected more wages into the economy. These were not enough, though, to make up for the large drop in consumer demand. It was not until World War II that the nation moved

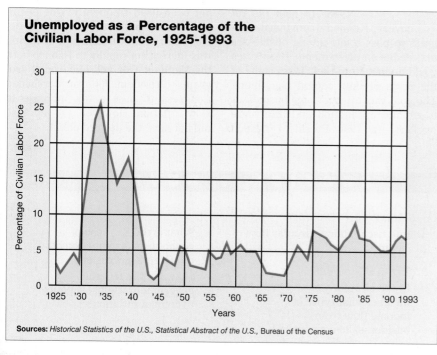

Unemployed as a Percentage of the Civilian Labor Force, 1925–1993

Percentage of Civilian Labor Force

Years

Sources: *Historical Statistics of the U.S., Statistical Abstract of the U.S.,* Bureau of the Census

Figure 18.8
Unemployed as a Percentage of the Civilian Labor Force, 1925-1993
During which year after the Great Depression did unemployment peak?

Chapter 18 Controlling Unemployment and Inflation **445**

Independent Practice

L3 Comparing and Contrasting Point out to students that the Keynesian view supports the demand-pull theory described in Section 1. Ask students to write an essay comparing and contrasting Keynesian economics and the cost-push theory of inflation.

Have students complete Guided Reading Activity 18.2 in the TCR. **LEP**

GLOBAL ECONOMICS

The Great Depression struck the entire developed world, and may have been one of the catalysts to begin World War II. Because so many people were dissatisfied with government during the Depression years, it was easier for a dictator like Adolf Hitler to come to power.

DID YOU KNOW

Employment concerns are not limited to Western, or even modern, economies. For example, archaeologists have found symbols connected with job placement in the ruins of ancient Babylon.

Cooperative Learning

Organize the class into groups to design and make a board game called Keynesian Balance. Ask students to model the game after Monopoly, Life, Risk, or some other game they know well. Suggest that players represent individual nations or economies and that they begin their game design by determining the objective of the game, the positive and negative events that could occur, and the way in which players will try to maintain economic balance. Students may wish to divide tasks such as drawing artwork, writing the rules, and designing and making game pieces among themselves. Have groups share their games with the class or with other classes.

Assess

Meeting Lesson Objectives

Assign Section 2 Review as homework or an in-class activity.

Evaluate

Assign the Section 2 Quiz in the TCR or use the Testmaker.

Reteach

Lead students in a discussion of specific means the government might have taken, according to Keynesians, to ease or reverse the Great Depression. Have students explain how these actions would, in theory, have helped the economy.

Enrich

Have interested students research and report on the events that accompanied the peaks and valleys of unemployment from 1926 to the present.

Close

Have students discuss how they think supporters of Keynesian economics and fiscal policy would view additional government intervention in today's economy. Have students give reasons to support their opinions.

**Figure 18.9
Jobs Programs, 1930s**
Posters such as this one announced employment opportunities created by the government during the Great Depression.

out of the Great Depression. After the war, the government cut back its spending. The economy was strong enough by then to continue operating without the extra government aid.

Since the Great Depression, many public officials and labor leaders have suggested starting jobs programs to reduce unemployment and stimulate the economy. Several suggestions for forming new government-sponsored jobs programs to bring down unemployment rates were made in the early 1980s and again in 1992 and 1993.

Cuts in federal taxes are another way in which fiscal policy has been used in an attempt to speed up economic activity and fight unemployment. For example, when President John F. Kennedy took office in 1961, the nation was slowly pulling itself out of a recession that had started in 1958. To help the recovery, Kennedy convinced Congress to pass a law giving businesses tax credits on investments. Businesses could deduct from their taxes some of the costs of new capital equipment. The goal was to encourage businesses to expand production and hire more workers. In 1964 President Lyndon

Johnson signed into law a tax cut of about $11 billion. Keynesian economists believe that as a result, unemployment fell from 5.2 percent in 1964 to 4.5 percent in 1965. This stimulated investment and consumer spending.

Fiscal Policy and Inflation

Fiscal-policy supporters also believe that inflation can be reduced by increasing taxes and/or reducing government spending. They argue that such actions will reduce the aggregate demand for goods and services.

Tax Increase Because people are paying higher taxes, they are taking home less spendable income. They will, therefore, have to cut back on their purchases. As purchases decline, businesses will cut back on production. This reduction in demand will cause businesses to reconsider raising prices. Often, as inflation falls, unemployment rises slightly because of less business activity.

When Policy Failed Fiscal policy as a means of reducing inflation has not been used frequently. One example of its application, however, occurred in 1968. Government spending was increasing rapidly to finance both the Vietnam War and new social programs. President Johnson persuaded Congress to pass a tax increase to slow inflation. However, the increase did not have the desired effect.

SECTION 2 REVIEW

Understanding Vocabulary
Define fiscal policy, circular flow of income.

Reviewing Objectives
1. In the circular flow of income, what types of income flow from businesses to consumers?

2. What is the Keynesian economists' explanation of the Great Depression?
3. How can the federal government use fiscal policy to combat inflation?

Section 2 Review Answers
Understanding Vocabulary
fiscal policy (p. 443), **circular flow of income** (p. 443)

Reviewing Objectives
1. types of income such as wages, rent, interest, and profits flow from businesses to consumers in the circular flow of income.
2. Keynesian economists believe the desire

of business to invest collapsed with the stock market crash. The leakage of capital investment caused unemployment.

3. to combat inflation by increasing taxes and/or reducing government spending in order to reduce the aggregate demand for goods and services.

LEARNING ECONOMIC SKILLS
Using the Consumer Price Index

The most often reported price index in America is the consumer price index, or CPI. Changes in the CPI show changes in the cost of a market basket of goods based on quantities in the base year. Do you know how to interpret the CPI?

The Monthly Survey

Every month the Bureau of Labor Statistics samples stores and other retail outlets. It obtains more than 600,000 food prices per year, 350,000 other prices, and 700,000 estimates of rent charges. Every month the *Monthly Labor Review* lists the consumer price indexes for many goods and services.

Figure A

CPI for Selected Consumer Groups*			
Year	Food	Clothes	Medical Care
1983	99.4	100.2	100.6
1984	103.2	102.1	106.8
1985	105.6	105.0	113.5
1986	109.0	105.9	122.0
1987	113.5	110.6	130.1
1988	118.2	115.4	138.6
1989	125.1	118.6	149.3
1990	132.4	124.1	162.8
1991	136.3	128.7	177.0
1992	137.9	131.9	190.1

*1982-84 =100

Consumer Price Indexes for Selected Consumer Groups

Every month the consumer price index for groups of consumer expenditures is compiled. At the end of each year, the yearly change in the prices is reflected in a summary of statistics. Figure A shows the consumer price indexes for selected consumer groups for a 10-year period (base years 1982-84 = 100).

Inflation is the percent change in prices from year to year. To determine the inflation rate for an item, divide the CPI increase by the previous price and multiply by 100. As Figure B shows, the CPI for clothes increased 4.8 from 1987 to 1988. The rate of inflation for clothes was 4.3%.

Figure B

CPI for Clothes

1988   115.4
1987   −110.6
CPI increase = 4.8

$\frac{4.8}{110.6} = .043 \times 100 = 4.3\%$ rate of inflation

Practicing the Skill

❶ What was the rate of inflation for food between 1990 and 1991?

❷ For which group listed did the consumer price index go up the most between 1991 and 1992?

447

Use the following activity to guide students through the mathematics for inflation rates for various classes of goods. Ask students to note the CPI for medical care in 1985 and 1990. Have them subtract the figure for 1985 from the figure for 1990 to get the CPI increase. Have a volunteer write the subtraction problem and answer on the chalkboard. (*49.3*) Have students divide this number by the 1985 CPI to find out the percentage by which prices in medical care have risen. (*43.4 percent*) Ask interested students to calculate the inflation for food and clothing prices over the same period.

Additional Practice

Have students complete Reinforcing Skills 18 in the TCR.

Answers to Practicing the Skill

1. 3.9 percent
2. Between 1991 and 1992, the consumer price index for medical care increased the most.

Focus

Overview

See the student page for section objectives.

Section 3 explains or describes: the theory of monetarism; the monetarists' views of the Fed's role in the Great Depression; how monetarist theory influenced government policy in the 1980s; and the monetarists' major criticisms of fiscal policy.

Bellringer

Before presenting the lesson, display Focus Transparency 85 and assign the accompanying Focus Activity Sheet.

Motivational Activity

Ask students to complete the following statements: When money is more available to me, I _____.

Preteaching Vocabulary

Ask students to use the four vocabulary terms in an imaginary news story about the economy.

Figure 18.10 Money Supply and Aggregate Demand
Monetarists believe that an increase in the rate of growth of the money supply increases aggregate demand for goods and services. If the economy is operating below capacity, this extra demand will lead to a rise in output. To produce more, businesses will have to hire more workers, and unemployment will decrease. If there is already full employment, this increased demand will lead to a rise in prices—inflation.
▼

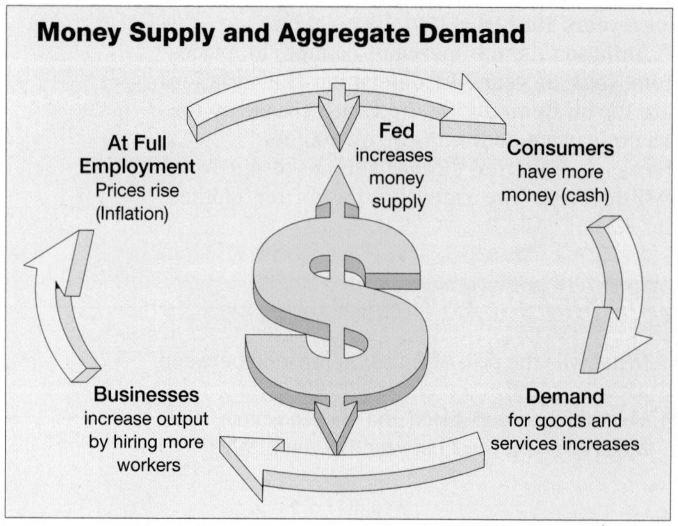

SECTION 3 Monetarism and the Economy

SECTION 3 FOCUS

Terms to Know monetarism, monetarists, monetary rule, time lags

Objectives After reading this section, you should be able to:
❶ Explain the monetarists' view of the Fed's role in the Great Depression.
❷ Describe how monetarist theory influenced government policy in the 1980s.
❸ Explain the monetarists' criticism of fiscal policy.

The Theory of Monetarism

Monetarism is the theory that deals with the relation between the amount of money the Federal Reserve places in circulation and the level of activity in the economy. The supporters of this theory are called **monetarists**. Monetarism is often linked with Milton Friedman. Operating under the monetarist theory, the Fed can use reserve requirements, the discount rate, and open-market operations to change the growth of the money supply. Friedman and his supporters believe that when the amount of money in circulation expands, people spend more. See Figure 18.10.

Money Supply and Aggregate Demand

At Full Employment
Prices rise (Inflation)

Fed increases money supply

Consumers have more money (cash)

Demand for goods and services increases

Businesses increase output by hiring more workers

Monetarist View of the Great Depression

Friedman views much of what happened during the Great Depression differently from the supporters of Keynes. Monetarists do not deny the importance of decisions made by businesses about investments in the early 1930s. Friedman, however, places more emphasis on the drop in the amount of money in circulation as a cause for the drop in aggregate demand. See Figure 18.11. This, in turn, caused businesses to reduce their investment. Despite the Fed's stated goal of stimulating the economy, the

---

Classroom Resources for Section 3

- Reproducible Lesson Plan 18.3
- Focus Activity Transparency 85
- Focus Activity Sheet 85
- Guided Reading Activity 18.3
- Economics Laboratory 5
- Economic Simulation 5
- Mathematics Practice for Economics 24

- Performance Assessment Activity 24
- Section Quiz 18.3
- Spanish Section Quiz 18.3
- Chapter 18 Test Forms A and B
- Testmaker
- Enrichment Activity 18

- Economics Vocabulary Activity 18
- Spanish Economics Vocabulary Activity 18
- Audiocassette 18
- Spanish Audiocassette 18
- Reteaching Activity 18
- Spanish Reteaching Activity 18

**Figure 18.11
Decrease in Money
in Circulation,
1929-1933**

To monetarists, the reduction
in the amount of money in circulation could mean only one
thing—a reduction in aggregate demand. With less
demand, fewer workers were
needed and unemployment
increased. ▶

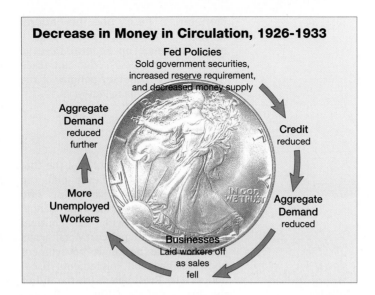

Decrease in Money in Circulation, 1926-1933

Fed Policies
Sold government securities,
increased reserve requirement,
and decreased money supply

Aggregate
Demand
reduced
further

Credit
reduced

Aggregate
Demand
reduced

More
Unemployed
Workers

Businesses
Laid workers off
as sales
fell

Teach

Guided Practice

L3 Debating Organize the
class into an even number
of groups. Assign half the
groups to take the Keynesian point of view and half to
take the monetarist point of
view. Assign the groups to
prepare for a debate on one
of the issues that Keynesians and monetarists view
differently.

**GLOBAL
ECONOMICS**

The differences between
industrialized economies
and developing
economies sometimes
makes it very hard for
developing economies to
experience growth. Infla-
tion in industrialized
countries, for example,
causes many Africans to
pay more for the goods
they receive than they
get for the raw materials
they export.

money supply decreased by one-third
from the start of the recession in 1929
to the depths of the Great Depression
in 1933 and 1934.

The monetarists claim that what
would have been just another recession became the Great Depression because of the Fed's actions. During the
period, the Fed claimed it wanted
banks to loosen their credit. At the
same time, the Fed continued to sell
government securities. This reduced
the money supply. The monetarists
believe that the Fed should have increased greatly the amount of money
in circulation. As a result, people
would have started spending more,
and businesses would have been able
to invest more.

Government Policy According to Monetarists

Friedman and his monetarist followers believe the economy is so complex and so little understood that
government does more harm than
good in trying to second-guess businesspeople and consumers. As a result, monetarists generally oppose

using fiscal policy to stimulate or slow
the economy. For example, they do
not believe the government should operate with budget deficits each year in
an attempt to stimulate the economy.
Instead, monetarists believe that the
government should balance the federal budget. This action would keep government from competing with private
business to borrow money in the credit market. It would also reduce the
amount of interest that the government must pay each year.

The Fed, according to monetarists,
should also stop trying to smooth
the ups and downs in the economy.
Rather, the Fed should allow the
money supply to grow at a rate of perhaps 3 to 5 percent per year. This policy is called a **monetary rule.**

Monetarists believe that a steady
growth in the money supply within
strict guidelines (or targets, as they
are called) is the best way to provide
businesses and consumers with more
certainty about the future. According
to monetarism, this policy would result in a controlled expansion of the
economy without rapid inflation or
high unemployment.

Chapter 18 Controlling Unemployment and Inflation **449**

◆◯ Meeting Special Needs

Hearing Disability Students with hearing
disabilities may have trouble following all
the points in a debate. This will make it difficult for the students to develop a coherent
rebuttal. In this situation, direct all debating

students to create and display graphics to
accompany the points they wish to make.
This will also make the debates more interesting for the entire class.

Independent Practice

L3 Writing Have students add from 5 to 15 percent to the GDP to account for the underground economy. Ask them to write a paragraph suggesting how, if the government could collect all money owed to it, this might affect government spending, taxation, and debt.

 Have students complete Guided Reading Activity 18.3 in the TCR. **LEP**

Visual Instruction

Tell students to study Figure 18.12. Ask them to discuss the relation between changes in inflation and unemployment, and ask them why one usually goes up while the other goes down. Point out, however, that during two years of the period covered in the figure, this was not the case. Ask students why there can be exceptions to the general rule, why the Fed adopted a looser money policy in 1983, and what effect this seems to have had.

? DID YOU KNOW

The total amount of money in circulation in the United States has grown during every decade since 1930. For the 60-year period from 1930 to 1990, this total increased from $4.522 billion to $257.664 billion. This represented a per capita increase from $36.74 to $1,028.71.

450

Monetarist Theory and the Federal Reserve Monetarist theory had a major influence on Federal Reserve policies in the 1980s. You can trace the changing monetary policies of the Fed from the 1970s in Figure 18.12.

Monetarists' Criticism of Fiscal Policy

Monetarists point out that the theory of fiscal policy never ends up being the reality of fiscal policy. Two reasons account for this discrepancy. One has to do with the political process of fiscal policy. Monetarists point out that no single government body designs and implements fiscal policy. The President, with the aid of the director of the Office of Management and Budget (OMB), the secretary of the Treasury, and the Council of Economic Advisers, designs, but only *recommends*, the desired mix of taxes and government expenditures. Congress, with the aid of many committees (the House Ways and Means Committee, the Senate Finance Committee, and the Senate Budget Committee, to name a few), actually enacts fiscal policy. One built-in organizational problem is that the power to enact fiscal policy does not rest with one government institution. Disagreement as to the proper fiscal policy emerges among members of Congress and between Congress and the President.

Monetarists also point out that even if fiscal policy could be enacted when the President wanted, there are various **time lags** between when it is enacted and when it becomes effective. It takes many months if not years

Figure 18.12 Changing Fed Policies
What happened to the unemployment rate when Fed policies began to lower inflation in 1980-1982? ▼

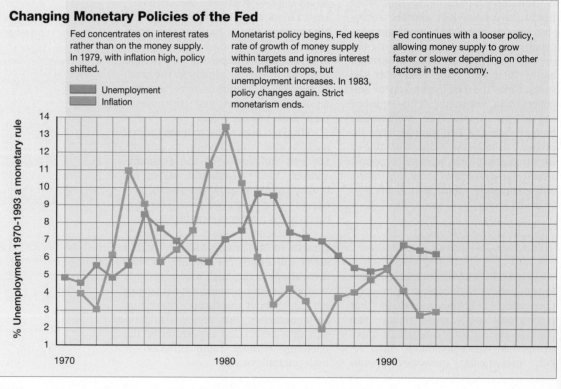

Changing Monetary Policies of the Fed

Fed concentrates on interest rates rather than on the money supply. In 1979, with inflation high, policy shifted.

Monetarist policy begins, Fed keeps rate of growth of money supply within targets and ignores interest rates. Inflation drops, but unemployment increases. In 1983, policy changes again. Strict monetarism ends.

Fed continues with a looser policy, allowing money supply to grow faster or slower depending on other factors in the economy.

Unemployment
Inflation

 Cooperative Learning

Encourage students to show how difficult it can be to get a policy enacted by telling the class to imagine it is a legislative body convening to pass a law regarding gun control. Organize the class into groups and assign each group its own agenda. Have groups meet and work out a compromise within a given time span. When the class has developed its gun control law, ask each group how close it came to enacting its original agenda.

for fiscal policy stimulus to cause employment to rise in the economy. Consequently, a fiscal policy designed to combat a recession might not produce results until the economy is already experiencing inflation. In this event, the fiscal policy worsens the situation.

Monetarists also point out that many fiscal policy actions have been enacted after the end of the recessions, as shown in Figure 18.13.

Just because the monetarists point out the failures of fiscal policy does not mean that they favor stabilizing the economy through monetary policy. Remember from our previous discussion that they favor a monetary rule, which means, in effect, no monetary policy either.

Figure 18.13
Faulty Timing
If you were a member of Congress, how would your knowledge of time lags affect your decisions on economic issues?

◀

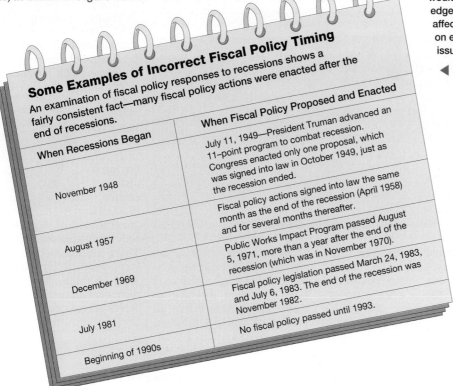

Some Examples of Incorrect Fiscal Policy Timing

An examination of fiscal policy responses to recessions shows a fairly consistent fact—many fiscal policy actions were enacted after the end of recessions.

When Recessions Began	When Fiscal Policy Proposed and Enacted
November 1948	July 11, 1949—President Truman advanced an 11–point program to combat recession. Congress enacted only one proposal, which was signed into law in October 1949, just as the recession ended.
August 1957	Fiscal policy actions signed into law the same month as the end of the recession (April 1958) and for several months thereafter.
December 1969	Public Works Impact Program passed August 5, 1971, more than a year after the end of the recession (which was in November 1970).
July 1981	Fiscal policy legislation passed March 24, 1983, and July 6, 1983. The end of the recession was November 1982.
Beginning of 1990s	No fiscal policy passed until 1993.

SECTION 3 REVIEW

Understanding Vocabulary
Define monetarism, monetarists, monetary rule, time lags.

Reviewing Objectives
1. How would a monetarist explain the effect of the Fed's role in the Great Depression?

2. What type of monetary policy would monetarists prefer that the Federal Reserve System follow?
3. Why do monetarists criticize fiscal policy?

Assess

Meeting Lesson Objectives
Assign Section 3 Review as homework or an in-class activity.

Evaluate
Assign the Section 3 Quiz in the TCR or use the Testmaker.

Assign the Chapter 18 Test Forms A or B or use the Testmaker.

Reteach
Help the class develop a graph expressing the effects of fiscal and monetary policy in a hypothetical situation.

Have students complete Reteaching Activity 18 in the TCR.

Enrich
Have students research and create a timeline showing the typical time lags that occur between the writing of a bill or policy, the discussion of the matter in committees, its passage through the legislature, its enactment, and its effective date.

Have students complete Enrichment Activity 18 in the TCR.

Close
Have students discuss how the saying "Not to decide is to decide" applies to various economic theories.

Section 3 Review Answers
Understanding Vocabulary
monetarism (p. 448), monetarists (p. 448), monetary rule (p. 449), time lags (p. 450)
Reviewing Objectives
1. the Fed's reduction of the amount of money in circulation caused a reduction in credit and aggregate demand and thus increased unemployment
2. a monetary rule; that is, not try to smooth the ups and downs in the economy
3. because the economy is too complex for fiscal measures to successfully adjust investment or spending

Point out to students that this article about the power of teenagers as consumers comes from the *Boston Sunday Globe*, which is a general-interest newspaper that reports on local and national news and trends.

Have students use the information in the feature to develop spending guidelines that might benefit teenagers as a group. For example, students might urge teenagers to shop at stores that carry goods they like, that support local events they think are valuable, or that contribute money or time to causes they think are important. Interested students might wish to promote these suggestions in a buying guide for teenagers in their community.

News Clip

Readings in Economics

BOSTON SUNDAY GLOBE   **AUGUST 15, 1993**

TEENAGERS' CASH
by Joanne Ball Artis

Armed with her first paycheck last month from her camp counseling job—$180 a week after deductions—Katie Burns, 13, headed straight for the mall.

Once at South Shore Plaza in Braintree [Massachusetts], Burns began supplementing her summer wardrobe: shorts and Jordache jeans from Cummings, totaling $48; a $10.50 shirt from The Gap; another shirt from JW for $20; an outfit from Jordan Marsh for "$40 something. . . ."

Burns, of Dorchester, counts herself part of a fast-growing, moneyed class of consumers: teenagers.

Their economic clout is unequaled by any previous generation of teenagers and so is the advertising directed at them. US teenagers had an income of nearly $70 billion last year—more than $90 billion by some estimates. According to national surveys, teen-agers also influence the spending of more than $140 billion of their parents' money. . . .

Merchants who once saw trouble in teenagers congregating in front of their stores now see dollar signs, as teen-agers have emerged as an economic force behind everything from fashion to entertainment equipment to hair care. . . .

Today's teenagers are markedly different from their predecessors, said Joanna Jacobson, senior vice president of marketing at Converse, head- quartered in North Reading. "These kids started making their own buying decisions earlier than other generations. At 4 years old they're picking out footwear. These are decisions that before were solely held by mom. By the time they're teenagers they're incredibly sophisticated consumers."

• THINK ABOUT IT •

1. According to this article, how much money do teenagers have available to them?

2. Why do many merchants now welcome the sight of teenagers congregating outside their stores?

Answers to Think About It

1. Teenagers in the United States have between $70 billion and $90 billion a year available to them.

2. Many merchants now welcome teenagers outside their stores because they hope they will spend money inside their stores.

CHAPTER 18 *Highlights*

Section 1

Unemployment and Inflation

Key Terms
stabilization policies (p. 438)
unemployment rate (p. 438)
full employment (p. 439)
underground economy (p. 439)
demand-pull inflation (p. 440)
stagflation (p. 441)
cost-push inflation (p. 441)

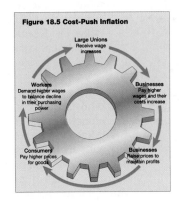

Figure 18.5 Cost-Push Inflation

Large Unions
Receive wage increases

Businesses
Pay higher wages and their costs increase

Businesses
Raise prices to maintain profits

Consumers
Pay higher prices for goods

Workers
Demand higher wages to balance decline in their purchasing power

Summary
Defining full employment is difficult because economists do not agree about what the level of full employment should be. The underground economy makes surveys of unemployment inaccurate. Demand-pull inflation generally happens during times of full employment. Cost-push inflation most often occurs when inflation and unemployment are both high.

Section 2

The Fiscal Policy Approach to Stabilization

Key Terms
fiscal policy (p. 443)
circular flow of income (p. 443)

Summary
Economists use a model to explain the circular flow of income. Keynesian economists believe that fiscal policy—government taxation and spending—should be used to regulate the overall level of economic activity. They want the government to use fiscal policy to reduce inflation.

Section 3

Monetarism and the Economy

Key Terms
monetarism (p. 448)
monetarists (p. 448)
monetary rule (p. 449)
time lags (p. 450)

Summary
Monetarists believe that the Federal Reserve System made errors that deepened the Great Depression. Their theories influenced government policies beginning in the 1980s. Monetarists are critical of the ability of fiscal policy to address the problems of inflation and unemployment.

Chapter 18 Controlling Unemployment and Inflation **453**

 VIDEODISC

Nightly Business Report
Economics in Action
Use "Fighting Unemployment and Inflation" on Disc 2, Side B, Video 25.

Search 1, Play to 6420

Using Chapter 18 *HIGHLIGHTS*

Use the Chapter 18 Highlights to preview, review, condense, or reteach the chapter. A Spanish Chapter Highlights is available in the Spanish Handbook.

Preview/Review
After students read the Chapter 18 Highlights, have them complete Economics Vocabulary Activity 18 in the TCR. Spanish Vocabulary Activities are also available in the Spanish Resource Binder.
Vocabulary Software reinforces the economic terms used in Chapter 18.

Condense
Have students listen to Chapter 18 on the Audiocassettes in the TCR. A 1-page written activity and 1-page test accompany this material. These materials are also available in Spanish.

Reteach
Have students complete Reteaching Activity 18 in the TCR. Spanish Reteaching Activities are also available.

 **VIDEODISC**

Nightly Business Report
Economics in Action
Use "Unemployment and Inflation" on Disc 2, Side A, Video 22.

Search 28325, Play to 34352

Use "Economic Growth and Stability" on Disc 2, Side A, Video 24.

Search 41152, Play to 48096

453

CHAPTER **18** Review

ANSWERS

Identifying Key Terms
Explanations will vary but should demonstrate an understanding of the terms.
1. monetarism
2. monetary rule
3. time lags

Recalling Facts and Ideas
Section 1
1. the underground economy
2. Excessive business and consumer demand causes demand-pull inflation.
3. The wage demands of labor unions and the excessive profit motive of large corporations cause cost-push inflation.

Section 2
4. Leakages out of the circular flow of income include consumer saving and government taxation.
5. Injections of income into the circular flow of income are business investment and government spending.
6. Keynesians think the federal government should have increased injections of government spending or cut taxes to reduce its own leakages.

Section 3
7. Milton Friedman
8. the drop in the amount of money in circulation

9. Monetarists believe the Fed should allow the money supply to grow at a rate of perhaps 3 to 5 percent per year.
10. Answers may vary but should include examples from Figure 18.13, such as passage of President Truman's program in 1949, the law signed

Identifying Key Terms

Write a one-sentence explanation of the following terms.

unemployment rate (p. 438)	demand-pull inflation (p. 440)
full employment (p. 439)	stagflation (p. 441)
underground economy (p. 439)	cost-push inflation (p. 441)

Use terms from the following list to fill in the blanks in the paragraph below.

monetarism (p. 448)   time lags (p. 450)
monetary rule (p. 449)

Keynesian economists believe that the Great Depression was caused by reduced capital investment in the economy. Those who believe in __(1)__ disagree. They think that the Great Depression was caused by a significant reduction by the Federal Reserve System in the money supply. Monetarists argue in favor of a __(2)__. They also think that __(3)__ are so severe that fiscal policy never can be effective.

Recalling Facts and Ideas

Section 1
1. Many individuals are not included in the government statisticians' monthly estimates of those who are working. In which part of the economy are these unreported workers?
2. What causes demand-pull inflation?
3. What causes cost-push inflation?

Section 2
4. What are the leakages out of the circular flow of income?

5. What are the injections of income into the circular flow of income?
6. What do Keynesian economists think the government should have done during the Great Depression?

Section 3
7. Who is the economist most often linked to monetarism?
8. What one factor do monetarists associate with having caused the Great Depression?
9. What do monetarists believe the Fed should do in terms of monetary policy?
10. What are some examples of incorrect fiscal policy timing?

Critical Thinking

Section 1
Analyzing Information Why can full employment never be defined as zero unemployment?

Section 2
Understanding Cause and Effect Why might the unemployment rate rise if fiscal policy were used to combat inflation?

Section 3
Identifying Alternatives According to the monetarists, what is the alternative to using fiscal policy to combat unemployment or inflation?

Applying Economic Concepts

Unanticipated Versus Anticipated Inflation Unanticipated inflation may affect you in many ways. For example, when inflation is high, banks

in 1958, the Public Works Impact Program passed in 1971, and the fiscal policies passed in 1983 and 1993.

Critical Thinking
Section 1
Unemployment will always occur as people lose jobs, quit jobs and look for new ones, or leave work to get additional education and

training. Also, unemployment will always occur because of seasonal jobs or jobs that are sensitive to technological advances or changes in the marketplace.

Section 2
If fiscal policy were used to combat inflation, government would raise taxes and/or reduce spending. This would reduce the aggregate demand for goods and services. Consumers

charge higher interest rates to compensate for inflation. If you borrowed money at the high interest rates and then the rate of inflation fell, you would be worse off. You would be paying too much interest on that borrowed money. Make a list of other problems that you might encounter if there were a change in the rate of inflation that you did not anticipate.

Chapter Projects

1. **Individual Project** Numerous government publications give the unemployment rates for various groups of workers according to the following:
   - age
   - occupation
   - race
   - gender

   Two of these publications are *The Statistical Abstract of the United States* and *The Economic Report of the President*. Using either of these sources, draw a graph that shows the unemployment rates for the past five years for various groups of workers according to the classifications given above.

2. **Cooperative Learning Project** Organize into four groups. The first three groups will each track one of the following: government fiscal policies, monetary policies, and major economic indicators. The last group will create visuals from the information that is collected.

   Using the front page of at least 10 consecutive issues of the *Wall Street Journal*, 3 groups will record a summary of news in each of their categories. Fiscal policy includes taxes and government spending. Monetary policy includes central bank interest rates, money supply, open-market operations, and reserve requirements. Economic indicators include such measurements as the CPI, industrial production, producer prices, sales, stocks and bonds, and unemployment. Each item should include the category, the date of the news, and a brief summary of the news.

As the information is being gathered, the last group should begin creating headlines that place the events in chronological order on a bulletin board. Discuss the state of the economy as reflected in the headlines to conclude the project.

Reviewing Skills

Using the Consumer Price Index

1. **Calculating the Consumer Price Index** The figures below show the percent change per year of the consumer price index for several years. Assume that the base year for this price index is 1987 (when the price index is equal to 100). Calculate what the price index is at the end of 1992.

   1988—4.4%   1989—4.6%   1990—6.1%
   1991—3.1%   1992—2.9%

2. **Specific Price Indexes** Look at the data below showing renters' versus homeowners' costs of shelter. (a) Which price index increased more from 1983 to 1988? (b) Which price index increased more during the entire time span? (c) By how much more did the faster-rising price index increase than the slower-rising price index?

Years	Renters	Homeowners
1983	103.0	102.5
1988	133.6	131.1
1992	160.9	155.3

Writing About Economics

Expository Writing Using information gathered in Your Economics Journal, write a letter to the editor about unemployment or inflation. Explain how the government should deal with the problem, either through fiscal or monetary policy.

455

would take home less spendable income. Therefore, they would cut back on spending, causing businesses to cut back on production. The slow-down in production would probably cause unemployment.

Section 3
Monetarists believe the alternative to using fiscal policy to combat unemployment or inflation is to use a monetary rule.

Applying Economic Concepts
Answers will vary, but should demonstrate an understanding of the way different rates of inflation affect the value of money.

Chapter Projects
1. Review with students the information covered in these publications. Discuss possible ways the information can be displayed in their graphs.

2. After discussing the state of the economy, students might extrapolate any implications of the news items for the future of the economy.

? BONUS QUESTION

The following bonus question may be written on the chalkboard when students take the chapter test.
Q: How are business purchases of industrial equipment part of the flow of money to the consumer?
A: Industrial equipment must be made by workers. Workers earn wages from the sale of what they produce. Workers become consumers when they spend their wages.

Reviewing Skills
1. 122.9
2. a. Renters
   b. Renters
   c. 4.7 percent

Writing About Economics
In their editorials about unemployment or inflation, students should explain the reasons why the policies they recommend can be expected to work.

A Word From the Teacher

Assign the students to pick up a 1040 EZ at the Post Office or library and fill it out while completing this exercise.

Phil Peters

Focus

Government in the United States provides public goods, promotes public well-being, regulates economic activity, redistributes income, and works to ensure economic stability. Remind students that to perform these functions, government needs income, which it obtains largely through taxation.

The purpose of this lab is to provide practice at filling out tax forms and determining withholding for various income levels.

Teach

Filing a Tax Return can begin by having students complete steps A and B. They next determine their taxable income in Step C and their refund or additional tax in Step D.

Every tax form begins with a determination of filing status and exemptions to adjust gross income and determine taxable income. Filing a 1040 EZ form is a useful introduction to preparing any 1040 tax form. Encourage students to obtain and fill out a more complex 1040 form.

Filing a Tax Return

From the classroom of Phil Peters, Gahanna Lincoln High School, Gahanna, Ohio

In Unit 5 you studied the federal government's role in the nation's economy. In this experiment, you will learn more about the federal income tax and your responsibilities as a taxpayer. (You may want to reread the material on pages 428–431 of the text.)

Regardless of whether you file income tax form 1040, 1040A, or 1040EZ, the Internal Revenue Service has divided your reporting into five main steps. The simplest federal income tax form is 1040EZ for single and married filers with no dependents. The steps below relate to this form.

Tools

1. Calculator
2. Tax table (sample provided)

Procedures

Step A In part, the amount of your income tax depends on your filing status. Whether you were single or married on December 31 determines your status for the entire year. Copy the table below and fill in your status.

Example

1 Filing Status	☐ Single	☐ Married filing joint return (even if only had one income)

Step B In this step you add together all the sources of your income. It includes wages, salaries, tips, interest, and other earnings. For example, assume you had a part-time job. Your employer reports on your withholding statement (W-2 form) that you earned $8,500 last year. In addition, the bank reports that it paid you $38 in interest on your passbook savings account last year. Finally, you earned $560 in tips as a waiter at a local restaurant. Calculate your total income on a table like this one.

Example

2	Total wages, salaries, and tips. This should be shown in box 1 of your W-2 form(s). Attach your W-2 form(s).	_____
3	Taxable interest income of $400 or less. If the total is over $400, you cannot use Form 1040EZ.	_____
4	Add lines 2 and 3. This is your **adjusted gross income**.	_____

Step C Your status and exemption(s) help determine how much of your adjusted gross income is taxable. If you are single, and no one else may claim you as a dependent on another tax return, you may deduct $6,050.

456

Determine your taxable income on a table like this one.

Example

4	Adjusted gross income	_____
5	Minus	$6,050.00
6	**Taxable income**	_____

Step D Your employer withheld part of your wages and paid it to the Internal Revenue Service (IRS). Your employer reports this to you in Box 9 of your W-2 form. *Assume that your employer reports withholding $390.*

Now you can determine the tax you owe by using the tax table that is in your tax booklet. Find your tax from this segment of the table:

Example

If Form 1040EZ, line 6, is—		And you are—	
At least	But less than	Single	Married filing jointly
			Your tax is—
3,000			
3,000	3,050	454	454
3,050	3,100	461	461
3,100	3,150	469	469
3,150	3,200	476	476
3,200	3,250	484	484
3,250	3,300	491	491
3,300	3,350	499	499
3,350	3,400	506	506

Step E Next, determine whether enough taxes have been withheld from your income or whether you owe the government an additional amount. If more was withheld than you owe, the government will refund part of your money. If less was withheld

than you owe, you must pay the IRS the balance by check or money order.

Example

7	Enter your Federal income tax withheld from box 2 of your W-2 form(s).	_____
8	**Tax** (from tax tables)	_____
9	If line 7 is larger than line 8, subtract line 8 from line 7. This is your **refund**.	_____
10	If line 8 is larger than line 7, subtract line 7 from line 8. This is the **amount you owe**.	_____

Lab Report

Step F Use what you have learned about filing an income tax return to answer the following questions.

1. Did you owe additional taxes to the IRS? If so, how much? If not, how much was your refund?
2. Why might an employer have failed to withhold enough taxes?
3. What is one advantage and one disadvantage of having more taxes withheld than what you owe?
4. What was the percentage in taxes you paid on your adjusted gross income?
5. What was the percentage in taxes you paid on your taxable income?

Assess

Have each student complete Step D (tax table) and Step E (determining tax). Encourage students to share E-4 of their reports and discuss why they prefer to withhold more or less than they need to withhold.

Close

Discuss with students tax withholding and its possible influence upon individual spending and saving.

 DID YOU KNOW

Self-employed persons who receive fees for their services are obligated to pay an estimated federal income tax quarterly. These quarterly payments compare with the withholding taxes paid by employers for employees. Self-employed persons are entitled to a tax refund if they overpay, but some choose to apply any overpayment to their estimated tax for the following year. Failure to pay quarterly taxes makes the self-employed taxpayer liable to pay a penalty.

457

Answers to Lab Report
Lab Report F

Students' answers should take into account their filing status. This should be the only variable in their returns.

Unit Goals

After studying this unit, students will be able to:

Explain imports and exports;

Describe how other nations' economies are becoming more like ours;

Describe economic growth in developing nations;

Explain the trend toward a global economy.

Unit Overview

Unit 6 introduces the global economy and the United States' place in it.

Chapter 19 explains: the benefits of world trade; its financing; and limits on it.

Chapter 20 describes: capitalism and socialism; the mixed economy of the People's Republic of China; economic change in Russia, Sweden, and Latin America.

Chapter 21 describes: characteristics of developing nations; economic development; obstacles to growth; and industrialization and the future.

Chapter 22 describes: global economy; global integration; direct foreign investment in the United States; multinational businesses; and the need for tolerance.

`0:00` OUT OF TIME?

If time does not permit teaching each chapter in this unit, you may use the Chapter Highlights and the Audiocassettes that include a 1-page activity and a 1-page test for each chapter.

458

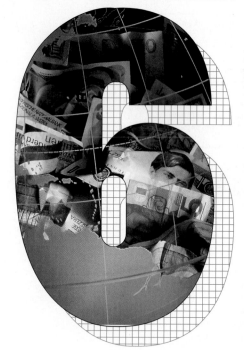

U N I T 6

THE INTERNATIONAL SCENE

Economic Simulation

Trade-offs Have the class assume the role of a legislative committee reviewing the North American Free Trade Agreement (NAFTA) or the General Agreement on Tariffs and Trade (GATT). Encourage students to organize themselve into subcommittees to research potential domestic benefits and costs, potential extra-national benefits and costs, citizen objections and concerns, and international opinion. Have a speaker from each subcommittee summarize subcommittee findings and outline the most important issue related to that subcommittee topic.

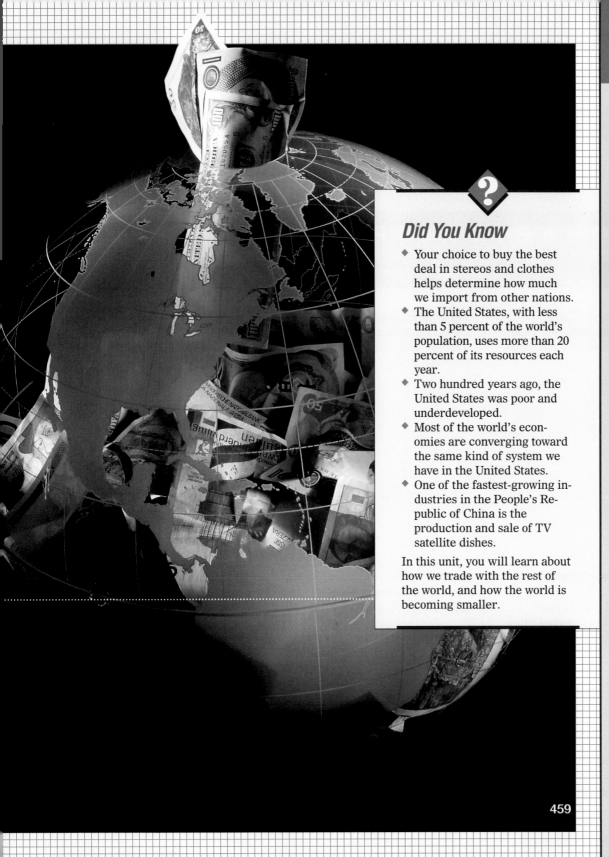

Connecting to Past Learning

Have students discuss movies, literature, styles, and foods from other countries that have enriched their lives. Ask them to think about the ways in which these goods or ideas may have come to them.

Beginning the Unit

Refer students to the "Did You Know" questions on page 459. Ask them how knowing the relevant facts might help them take informed positions on international trade agreements among developed nations and aid packages to developing nations.

Outcome-Based Project

Building a Strategy This unit project is the final step in a six-part activity that can be used during the entire course. In Unit 6 students build a strategy for living in the global economy.

Have students describe a specific career from the jobs they listed in the first five units, or from the Career Handbook in their textbook. Based on the beginning salary in that career, each student should build a budget that includes housing, utilities, transportation, food, clothing, medical and dental expenses, travel, entertainment, savings, taxes, insurance, charitable giving, and personal expenses. Newspaper ads may help students estimate expenses.

Did You Know

- Your choice to buy the best deal in stereos and clothes helps determine how much we import from other nations.
- The United States, with less than 5 percent of the world's population, uses more than 20 percent of its resources each year.
- Two hundred years ago, the United States was poor and underdeveloped.
- Most of the world's economies are converging toward the same kind of system we have in the United States.
- One of the fastest-growing industries in the People's Republic of China is the production and sale of TV satellite dishes.

In this unit, you will learn about how we trade with the rest of the world, and how the world is becoming smaller.

459

Did You Know

The following are facts about the United States economy.
- Major agricultural products include corn, wheat, barley, oats, sugar, potatoes, soybeans, fruits, beef, veal, and pork.
- Major industrial products include petroleum products, fertilizers, cement, pig iron and steel, plastics and resins, newsprint, motor vehicles, machinery, natural gas, and electricity.
- Major natural resources include coal, oil, copper, gold, silver, minerals, and timber.
- Major exports include machinery, chemicals, aircraft, military equipment, cereals, motor vehicles, and grains.
- Major imports include crude and partly refined petroleum, machinery, and cars.

CHAPTER 19 TRADING WITH OTHER NATIONS

CHAPTER ORGANIZER

Daily Objectives	Special Features	Classroom Resources
Section 1 The Benefits of World Trade • **Explain** the benefits of international trade. • **Contrast** absolute advantage with comparative advantage.	**Personal Perspective:** David Ricardo on Trading With Other Nations, p. 466	Reproducible Lesson Plan 19.1 *NBR* Video 27 and Video Stills 1 and 2 Focus Activity Transparency 86 Focus Activity Sheet 86 Economic Concepts Transparency 20 Guided Reading Activity 19.1 Cooperative Learning Activity 19 Primary and Secondary Source Readings 19 Consumer Application Activity 20 Section Quiz 19.1 Spanish Section Quiz 19.1 Testmaker
Section 2 Financing World Trade • **Explain** the need for exchange rates in foreign currencies. • **Explain** how the forces of supply and demand determine flexible exchange rates. • **Describe** what has happened to America's balance of trade over the last two decades.	**Learning Economic Skills:** Exchanging Foreign Currency, p. 471	Reproducible Lesson Plan 19.2 Focus Activity Transparency 87 Focus Activity Sheet 87 Economic Concepts Transparency 21 Guided Reading Activity 19.2 Section Quiz 19.2 Spanish Section Quiz 19.2 Testmaker Reinforcing Skills 19
Section 3 Restrictions on World Trade • **List** three ways that imports can be restricted. • **Explain** the main arguments for and against free trade. • **List** one worldwide trade agreement and three regional trade agreements.	**News Clip:** "Taking Sides," *USA Today*, p. 476	Reproducible Lesson Plan 19.3 Focus Activity Transparency 88 Focus Activity Sheet 88 Guided Reading Activity 19.3 Free Enterprise Activities 19 and 20 Mathematics Practice for Economics 25 Performance Assessment Activity 25 Section Quiz 19.3 Spanish Section Quiz 19.3 Testmaker Enrichment Activity 19

 OUT OF TIME? If time does not permit teaching this chapter, you may use the Chapter 19 Highlights and the Audiocassettes that include a 1-page activity and a 1-page test.

Chapter 19 Review and Evaluation

Special Features

Chapter 19 Highlights, p. 477
Chapter 19 Review, pp. 478–479

Classroom Resources

- Chapter 19 Test Forms A and B
- Economics Vocabulary Activity 19
- Spanish Economics Vocabulary Activity 19
- Audiocassette 19
- Spanish Audiocassette 19
- Reteaching Activity 19
- Spanish Reteaching Activity 19

Key to Ability Levels

Teaching strategies have been coded for varying learning styles and abilities.

L1 Level 1 activities are **basic** activities and should be within the ability range of all students.

L2 Level 2 activities are **average** activities designed for the ability range of average to above-average students.

L3 Level 3 activities are **challenging** activities designed for the ability range of above-average students.

LEP activities should be within the ability range of **Limited English Proficiency** students.

Performance Assessment

The following chapter project may be assigned at the beginning of the chapter and used for performance assessment. See page T12 for additional Performance Assessment information.

Conducting a Survey Have students work in pairs to conduct a survey of merchant, consumer, and worker opinions regarding the General Agreement on Tariffs and Trade (GATT) and the North American Free Trade Agreement (NAFTA). Survey forms should identify the economic role of the respondents and ask questions that allow a range of responses. Because few respondents know the details of these trade agreements, the survey should include statements that describe principles of the agreements. Questions related to these principles should allow a range of responses, such as "strongly agree," "moderately agree," "moderately disagree," and "strongly disagree." Have students organize their results in a bar graph.

Additional Resources

Readings for the Student

Hackett, Clifford. *Cautious Revolution.* Westport, Conn.: Greenwood Press, 1990. An introduction to and history of the European Community.

Tracy, James D., ed. *Rise of the Merchant Empires.* Cambridge, England: Cambridge University Press, 1990.

Readings for the Teacher

Krieger, Andrew J. *The Money Bazaar.* New York: Times Books, 1992. Traces the development and workings of the foreign exchange market.

Wallace, Helen, ed. *The Wider Western Europe.* New York: St. Martin's Press, 1991. Explores economic and political relations between European Community nations.

Multimedia Materials

Foreign Trade—Challenge of a Changing World. 16 mm film, 19 min. Modern Learning Division of Wards Natural Science, P.O. Box 1712, Rochester, NY 14603. Discusses incentives to foreign trade and the importance of trade balance in the world economy.

Resources and World Trade. Videotape or 16mm film, 14 min. Phoenix/BFA Films and Video Inc., 470 Park Avenue South, New York, NY 10016

Chapter Overview

International trade involves huge corporations and major governmental bodies but affects the everyday lives of workers and consumers. Chapter 19 explains or describes: how corporations and major governmental bodies affect the everyday lives of workers; the absolute and comparative benefits of international trade; the need for international rates of exchange and their relationship to America's changing balance of trade; and the major arguments for and against free trade.

VIDEODISC

Nightly Business Report
Economics in Action Use "International Trade" on Disc 2, Side B, Video 27.

Search 12796, Play to 19102

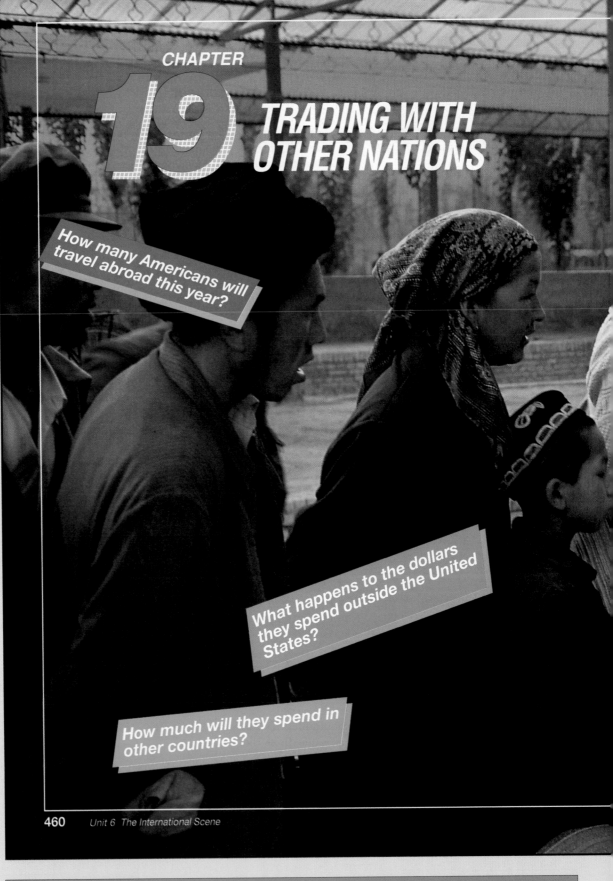

CHAPTER

19 TRADING WITH OTHER NATIONS

How many Americans will travel abroad this year?

What happens to the dollars they spend outside the United States?

How much will they spend in other countries?

Answering Economic Questions

The information in the above illustration is designed to lead into the main concepts in Chapter 19. Students might be unaware that many foreign-made parts are used to manufacture domestic products. They also might be surprised to learn that there are many items that would be impossible for Americans to acquire if it were not for international trade.

Have students discuss the information and think about ways in which international trade touches their lives.

460

What percent of goods in American stores are foreign-made?

Connecting to Past Learning

Ask students to share with the class the brand names of goods they own or admire. Ask students to discuss the reputation of the brand and of the country associated with the brand of each item. Tell students that in Chapter 19 they will explore the impact of international trade upon quality of life, the economy of the United States, and the economies of developing nations.

Applying Economics

Tell students to imagine they have an opportunity to increase sales of a product by exporting it. Ask them to list the laws, customs, consumer preferences, and miscellaneous information they would need to research concerning the country receiving the product.

Your Economics Journal

Keep track of what you wear during one week. Examine the clothing labels to find out where each was produced and put this information next to the name of each product. If it was not produced in the United States, write why you think you or your family bought this imported item.

Do any government restrictions affect what Americans can buy from abroad?

461

EXTRA CREDIT PROJECT

Have students read articles about current views on free trade in North America, South America, Europe, Asia, or Africa from at least three different newspapers or journals. Have them write a summary of their findings, comparing and contrasting the ideas and opinions expressed.

PERFORMANCE ASSESSMENT

Refer to page 460B for "Conducting a Survey," a Performance Assessment Activity for this chapter.

Economic Portfolio

Have students build on the activity they did in **Your Economics Journal** by listing by country of origin the imported goods (other than clothing) they own or use, as well as those of family members. For example, a product may be categorized as Japanese even if the manufacturer has a plant in the United States, because the company is Japanese owned. Have students note whether the countries best known for exports are those most commonly named (they may or may not be the same countries).

Focus

Overview

See the student page for section objectives.

Section 1 explains or describes: the benefits of international trade; the differences between absolute advantage and comparative advantage and how to calculate both; and a comparison of United States exports and imports in a recent year.

Bellringer

Before presenting the lesson, display Focus Activity Transparency 86 on the overhead projector or copy the material on the chalkboard. Assign the accompanying Focus Activity Sheet.

Motivational Activity

Write the following statement for students to complete: "Made in America" means ____. Call on volunteers to read their statements and tell how they would identify an item made in the United States.

Preteaching Vocabulary

Ask students to write sentences using the four vocabulary terms in this section. They next should rewrite the sentences, leaving blanks for the vocabulary words. Have students trade papers and then complete one another's sentences.

SECTION **1** *The Benefits of World Trade*

SECTION 1 FOCUS

Terms to Know imports, exports, absolute advantage, specialization, comparative advantage

Objectives *After reading this section, you should be able to:*
1. Explain the **benefits of international trade**.
2. Contrast **absolute advantage with comparative advantage**.

Exports Pay for Imports

What would happen if the United States could no longer buy goods from other countries or sell goods in return? Before you answer, you should be aware that the value of **imports**—goods bought from other countries for domestic use—is about 10 percent of GDP in the United States. That figure seems small. Many inconveniences would result, however, without imports. For example, we would have no coffee, chocolate, or pepper. Consider also that more than 60 percent of the radios, television sets, and motorcycles sold in the United States are imported. Many raw materials also come from foreign sources. More than 90 percent of the bauxite, from which aluminum is made, is imported.

Benefits of Trade

Imports tell only half the story. Many American workers are employed in industries that export their products overseas. **Exports** are goods sold to other countries. For example, more than 11 percent of the nation's trucks and buses and 40 percent of its engineering and scientific instruments are sold overseas. In addition, about one-third of the corn, half of the cotton, and almost two-thirds of the wheat produced in the United States are shipped abroad.

Made in the U.S.A.? Sometimes it is hard to distinguish between goods made in America and those purchased abroad. Consider the Boeing 777.

Classroom Resources for Section 1

- Reproducible Lesson Plan 19.1
- NBR Video 27 and Video Stills 1 and 2
- Focus Activity Transparency 86
- Focus Activity Sheet 86
- Economic Concepts Transparency 20
- Guided Reading Activity 19.1
- Cooperative Learning Activity 19

- Primary and Secondary Source Readings 19
- Consumer Application Activity 20
- Section Quiz 19.1
- Spanish Section Quiz 19.1
- Testmaker

This new plane is hardly "made in America." International suppliers provide rudders, elevators, outboard flaps, wing-tip assemblies, engines, nose-landing gears, nose-landing gear doors, and main-landing gears. Japanese suppliers, in particular, provide cargo doors, fuselage panels, and passenger doors. The complicated Boeing 777 jet aircraft is a jigsaw puzzle in which the pieces come from all over the world. The same is true for both American and foreign cars, as shown in Figure 19.1.

If you buy an American-made IBM computer, many of its parts are made abroad. If you drink American-brand orange juice, such as Minute Maid or Tropicana, you will find in tiny print on the label that it is made from concentrate from not only the United States but from Mexico and Brazil as well. In short, international trade affects you whether you like it or not. We have truly entered an age of a global economy, so learning about international trade is simply learning about everyday life.

Why does trade occur among nations? A voluntary exchange is a transaction that benefits both parties.

Differences Among Nations Nations benefit through world trade because each differs in the type and amount of the factors of production it has avail-

able for use. The availability of natural resources is considered one of the most important of these differences. See Figure 19.2 (page 464).

The type and amount of labor and capital available to a nation are equally important. For example, much of the economy of the United States is based on high-technology production. A highly skilled labor force and large amounts of capital—in the form of advanced equipment and machinery—make this possible. Another nation having the same natural resources but without the same labor and capital resources as the United States could have a very different economy.

Absolute and Comparative Advantage

The amount of importing and exporting a nation does is affected by the specific combination of all its resources. Depending on this combination, a nation has either an absolute or a comparative advantage in production.

Figure 19.1
Who Made the Parts?
The Ford Crown Victoria has shock absorbers from Japan, front-end spindles from England, electronic engine controls from Spain, electronic anti-lock brake system controls from Germany, and seats, windshields, instrument panels, and fuel tanks from Mexico.

Teach

Guided Practice
L2 Creating a Game Have small groups develop an international trade version of Go Fish. Ask students to devise cards for different items that are traded internationally and to create a wild card based on comparative and absolute advantage.

GLOBAL ECONOMICS

In 1990 the United States and West Germany led the world in imports, with $473.4 billion and $269.8 billion, respectively. They also led in exports, with $363.8 billion and $341.4 billion.

VIDEODISC

Nightly Business Report
Economics in Action
Use Video Stills 1 and 2, "Balance of Trade/Trade Suplus" and "Balance of Trade/Trade Deficit," on Disc 2, Side B, Video 27.

Search Frame 15264

Search Frame 15413

  Meeting Special Needs

Organizational Disability Students with organizational difficulties may have problems translating one kind of graphic to another. Before reading the text in Section 1, ask stu

dents to look at Figure 19.3 and work as a group to tell what information the graphic conveys. Encourage students to write notes on the information in sentence form.

464

Independent Practice

L3 Ranking Have students rank the personal and national benefits of trade discussed in this section. Have students discuss and explain their value judgments.

L3 Writing Have students write a story or a news article about a real or imaginary community anywhere in the world that uses only what it produces. Tell students that this fact may be incidental or central to the story, but it must be made clear through the descriptions of the land, the work people do, and the goods they produce and use.

Have students complete Guided Reading Activity 19.1 in the TCR. **LEP**

Visual Instruction

Ask students to study the data on United States imports and exports in Figure 19.3 and use the information to create a circle graph of United States imports.

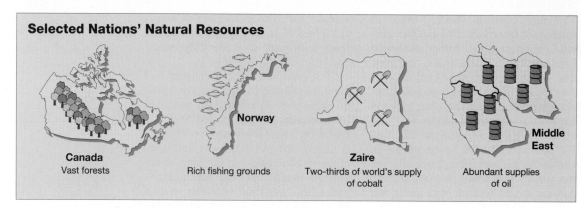

Selected Nations' Natural Resources

Canada
Vast forests

Norway
Rich fishing grounds

Zaire
Two-thirds of world's supply of cobalt

Middle East
Abundant supplies of oil

Figure 19.2 ▲
Selected Nations' Natural Resources
The chart shows how certain nations have abundant supplies of one natural resource. In the Middle East, for example, oil is not only the most important resource, it is one of the few. In Canada, in contrast, vast forests are one of many resources.

Absolute Advantage The particular distribution of resources in a nation often gives it an absolute advantage over another nation in the production of one or more products. Brazil's tropical climate and inexpensive labor make it ideally suited for growing bananas. Even using the same amount of land, labor, capital, and entrepreneurship, a country with a moderate climate, such as France, would produce far fewer bananas. Brazil, therefore, has an absolute advantage in banana production over France. **Absolute advantage** is the ability of one country, using the same amount of resources as another country, to produce a particular product at less cost.

A nation often finds it profitable to produce and export a limited assortment of goods for which it is particularly suited. This concept is usually known as **specialization** (SPESH-uh-luh-ZAY-shuhn). Specialization helps determine the goods the United States imports and exports, as shown in Figure 19.3. For example, it is because of specialization that many people associate Japan with consumer electronics.

Comparative Advantage A nation may not need to have an absolute advantage in the production of a certain good to find it profitable to specialize

and then to trade with other countries. For example, consider two imaginary nations, Country X and Country Y. Assume that each country produces only soybeans and corn.

When producing only soybeans, Country X produces 10 million bushels, while Country Y produces only 8 million. The next year, suppose the two countries decide to grow only corn. Country X produces 50 million bushels, while Country Y produces 25 million. According to this example, Country X has an absolute advantage in the production of both soybeans and corn. That is, with the same amount of inputs, Country X can produce more of either crop than Country Y.

Does this mean that Country X will produce both crops and, therefore, have no reason to trade with Country Y? No. Country X can produce slightly more soybeans than Country Y, however, it can produce a great deal more corn. It would make little sense for Country X to take land, labor, and capital resources away from the efficient production of corn and use them for the less efficient production of soybeans. Country X's opportunity cost—what it gives up to get something else—would be less if it invested all its resources in the production of corn. It could export its surplus corn and use the money it receives to import soybeans from Country Y.

Cooperative Learning

Have students work in teams to represent various countries around the globe and to simulate trading among them. Point out to students that they will need to research the imports and exports of their particular country. They will also need to know about the nation's transportation, currency, and political situation. Ask students to report on the difficulties and benefits they experience in their attempts to participate in international trade. Call on volunteers to make suggestions regarding agreements and conventions that might make trading take place more smoothly.

Country X has a comparative advantage in corn production. **Comparative advantage** is the ability of a country to produce a product at a *lower opportunity cost* than another country. Country Y has a comparative advantage in soybean production. Country Y can produce about the same amount of soybeans as Country X, but only half as much corn. By using its resources to grow soybeans only, Country Y is only giving up the relatively inefficient production of corn. Country Y, then, has a lower opportunity cost for soybean production than does Country X. Country Y should produce the maximum amount of soybeans, export soybeans to Country X, and import corn. Both countries benefit when each country concentrates on that production for which it is relatively most efficient.

The Relationship Between Imports and Exports You should consider international trade as an economic activity just like any other. It is subject to the same economic principles. International trade can be looked at as a kind of production process that transforms exports into imports. For you and everyone else in the United States, the purpose of international trade is to obtain imports, not to export. What we gain as a country from international trade is the ability to import the things that we want. We have to export other things in order to pay for those imports. A fundamental proposition in international trade is:

In the long run, exports pay for imports.

The reason that exports ultimately pay for imports is that people in other countries want something in exchange for goods that are shipped to the United States. For the most part, they want goods made in the United States.

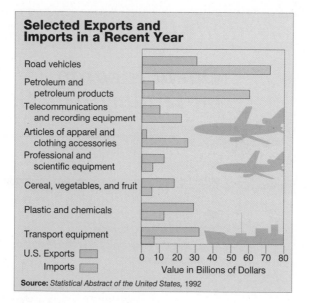

Selected Exports and Imports in a Recent Year

Road vehicles

Petroleum and petroleum products

Telecommunications and recording equipment

Articles of apparel and clothing accessories

Professional and scientific equipment

Cereal, vegetables, and fruit

Plastic and chemicals

Transport equipment

U.S. Exports
Imports

Value in Billions of Dollars

Source: *Statistical Abstract of the United States, 1992*

Figure 19.3 ▲
Exports and Imports of the U.S.
Look at the graph above to see what products the United States imports and exports. Name the products that the United States exports more than it imports.

SECTION 1 REVIEW

Understanding Vocabulary
Define imports, exports, absolute advantage, specialization, comparative advantage.

Reviewing Objectives
1. How important is international trade to the total United States economy?
2. What is the difference between absolute advantage and comparative advantage?

Assess

Meeting Lesson Objectives
Assign Section 1 Review as homework or an in-class activity.

Evaluate
Assign the Section 1 Quiz in the TCR or use the Testmaker.

Reteach
Engage students in a discussion of ways in which the United States would be poorer without the benefit of international trade.

Enrich
Ask interested students to find out the primary imports and exports of the region or state where they live. Have them identify the factors of production that give the exports an absolute or comparative advantage.

Close

Ask students to comment on the impact of a negative trade balance in light of the principle that exports pay for imports.

Section 1 Review Answers

Understanding Vocabulary
imports (p. 462), exports (p. 462), absolute advantage (p. 464), specialization (p. 464), comparative advantage (p. 465)

Reviewing Objectives
1. Imports account for 10 percent of the GDP. Exports include 11 percent of our trucks and buses, 40 percent of our engineering and scientific instruments.
2. absolute advantage: result of production costs lower than those of other countries; comparative advantage: result of opportunity costs lower than those of other countries

Personal Perspective

David Ricardo on Trading With Other Nations

Profile

- 1772–1823
- made a fortune as a stockbroker in London
- member of House of Commons for five years
- introduced the principle of comparative advantage to international trade
- published the *Principles of Political Economy and Taxation* in 1817

In the following excerpt from the *Principles of Political Economy and Taxation*, David Ricardo stresses the importance of trade and the gains that can be had from international trade.

No extension of foreign trade will immediately increase the amount of value in a country, although it will very powerfully contribute to increase the mass of commodities, and therefore the sum of enjoyments. . . .

It is quite as important to the happiness of mankind that our enjoyments should be increased by the better distribution of labour, by each country producing those commodities for which by its situation, its climate, and its other natural or artificial advantages it is adapted, and by their exchanging them for the commodities of other countries as that they should be augmented by a rise in the rate of profit.

Foreign trade, then, [is] highly beneficial to a country as it increases the amount and variety of the objects on which revenue may be expended, and affords, by the abundance and cheapness of commodities, incentives to saving, and to its accumulation of capital. . . .

Under a system of perfectly free commerce, each country naturally devotes its capital and labour to such employments as are most beneficial to each. This pursuit of individual advantage is admirably connected with the universal good of the whole. By stimulating industry, by rewarding ingenuity, and by using most efficaciously [effectively] the peculiar powers bestowed by nature, it distributes labour most effectively and most economically: while, by increasing the general mass of productions, it diffuses general benefit, and binds together, by one common tie of interest and intercourse, the universal society of nations throughout the civilised world. It is this principle which determines that wine shall be made in France and Portugal, that corn shall be grown in America and Poland, and that hardware and other goods shall be manufactured in England.

Checking for Understanding

❶ How does trade help increase the "sum of enjoyments" in a specific country?
❷ Why is trade good for a country?
❸ Why is trade good for the world?

Answers to Checking for Understanding

1. Foreign trade allows individual countries to concentrate on producing goods for which they are suited. It creates abundance, incentives to saving, and the accumulation of capital.
2. because it makes more goods available at lower prices and stimulates saving
3. Foreign trade benefits the world by distributing labor effectively and diffusing the benefits of each country's labor. It also binds together the nations of the world by their common interests.

SECTION 2 FOCUS

Terms to Know foreign exchange markets, fixed rate of exchange, International Monetary Fund (IMF), devaluation, flexible exchange rates, depreciation, balance of trade

Objectives *After reading this section, you should be able to:*

① Explain the need for exchange rates in foreign currencies.

② Explain how the forces of supply and demand determine flexible exchange rates.

③ Describe what has happened to America's balance of trade over the last two decades.

Focus

Overview

See the student page for section objectives.

Section 2 explains or describes: the transition from a fixed rate of exchange to the current flexible rate of exchange among international currencies; how the forces of supply and demand determine the flexible exchange rate; and changes in America's balance of trade over the last two decades.

Bellringer

Before presenting the lesson, display Focus Activity Transparency 87 and assign the accompanying Focus Activity Sheet.

Motivational Activity

Have students list on a sheet of paper reasons certain of their possessions, such as a CD, might cost a different amount at different times. Call on volunteers to read their lists. Tell students that Section 2 will discuss the flexible value of currency.

Preteaching Vocabulary

Have students write terms on separate index cards and the definition on the other side of the card. Students may refer to the cards as they study the section.

Trading Currencies in Foreign Exchange Markets

The United States uses the dollar as its medium of exchange; France uses francs; Great Britain, pounds; and Japan, yen. Figure 19.4 shows some of the variety of world currencies. To engage in world trade, countries must have a way of exchanging one type of currency for another. A Japanese videodisc player manufacturer who exports players to the United States probably does not want American dollars in payment. The firm needs Japanese currency to pay its workers and suppliers. Fortunately, international trade is organized so that individuals and businesses can easily and quickly convert one currency to another. **Foreign exchange markets** allow for these conversions. Foreign exchange markets deal in buying and selling foreign currency for businesses that want to import goods from other countries. Some of the currency trading takes place through banks.

Fixed Exchange Rates

From 1944 to the early 1970s, the foreign exchange market operated with a **fixed rate of exchange.** Under this system, a national government sets the value of its currency in relation to a single standard. Then, a government can establish equivalents between its currency and that of other countries. The **International Monetary Fund (IMF)** monitored a fixed exchange rate system. Member

**Figure 19.4
World Currencies**
Some national currencies have the same name. Canada, Australia, and the United States, for example, all call their currencies dollars. Other countries, such as Portugal with its escudos, have currencies with unique names. Most can be exchanged for other currencies, thus making international trade easier.
▼

467

Classroom Resources for Section 2

- Reproducible Lesson Plan 19.2
- Focus Activity Transparency 87
- Focus Activity Sheet 87
- Economic Concepts Transparency 21
- Guided Reading Activity 19.2

- Section Quiz 19.2
- Spanish Section Quiz 19.2
- Testmaker
- Reinforcing Skills 19

Guided Practice

L2 Making Connections Discuss with students the United States balance of trade and the change from a fixed to a flexible exchange rate. Have the class consider connections between exchange rates and balance of trade. (*Students should point out that when a currency depreciates, more currency is required to purchase the same amount of goods as before.*)

L2 Developing a Rationale Have small groups list economic reasons for promoting political stability. Suggest applying these reasons to international affairs by bringing in news of coups, revolutions, and dictatorships. Ask students how political conditions in these countries might affect their trading status.

Visual Instruction

Ask students to study Figure 19.5. Lead a discussion in which they speculate on the merits of a weak versus a strong American dollar in relation to the persistent United States trade deficit.

governments of the International Monetary Fund (including the United States, of course) were obligated to keep their foreign exchange rates more or less fixed.

A fixed rate of exchange had some advantages for world trade. Importers and exporters knew exactly how much of a foreign currency they could purchase with their own nation's money. Also, the system allowed central banks to affect the level of exports and imports in their country by devaluing the currency. **Devaluation** means lowering a currency's value in relation to other currencies by government order.

Take a Japanese VCR as an example. Figure 19.5 shows how the cost of a Japanese VCR would decrease after Japan devalues its yen by one-half.

This system of fixed exchange rates eventually proved impractical. The basic problem was the difficulty of fixing exchange rates in an international economic climate that was constantly changing. Suppose one nation such as the United States suffered from high inflation and a trading partner such as Japan did not. Then American goods would become very costly for the Japanese to buy. Because the

price of Japanese goods would not be rising, Americans could use their inflated, or "cheaper," dollars to buy more Japanese products. The United States would be importing huge quantities of goods but exporting little to Japan.

Flexible Exchange Rates

Most of the world's nations arrived at the solution of the **flexible exchange rates.** Under this arrangement, the forces of supply and demand are allowed to set the price of various currencies. With flexible exchange rates, a currency's price may change, or float, up or down a little each day. For example, Japanese currency might be trading at 112.6 yen to the dollar on one day and 117.8 yen to the dollar on the next. On August 15, 1971, President Richard Nixon officially announced what would become the end of fixed American exchange rates. The International Monetary Fund slowly lost its importance in the world as fewer and fewer countries attempted to fix their exchange rates.

The forces actually determining exchange rates are the supply and demand of goods and services that can

Figure 19.5 ▶
Effect of Devaluation
These charts show how devaluation of the Japanese yen affects consumers in the United States. Do you think an American consumer would prefer to buy a VCR before or after devaluation? Why?

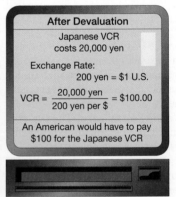

Effects of Official Devaluation of Japanese Yen

Before Devaluation	After Devaluation
Japanese VCR costs 20,000 yen	Japanese VCR costs 20,000 yen
Exchange Rate: 100 yen = $1 U.S.	Exchange Rate: 200 yen = $1 U.S.
$VCR = \dfrac{20,000 \text{ yen}}{100 \text{ yen per } \$} = \$200.00$	$VCR = \dfrac{20,000 \text{ yen}}{200 \text{ yen per } \$} = \$100.00$
An American would have to pay $200 for the Japanese VCR	An American would have to pay $100 for the Japanese VCR

Meeting Special Needs

Language Comprehension Difficulty Students who have difficulty with comprehension or who have limited English proficiency may need help to understand sentences presented in the vocabulary activity. Have these students work together with proficient speakers to create and decode the sentences.

Depreciation Affects Cost

Before Depreciation	After Depreciation
$10 in U.S.A. Exchange Rate: $1.00 = 5 francs	$10 in U.S.A. Exchange Rate: $1.00 = 4 francs
50 francs in France	40 francs in France

Depreciation of U.S. dollar lowers cost of jeans to a French citizen.

◀ **Figure 19.6**
Depreciation Affects Cost
In the example of depreciation given in the chart, how does the French consumer benefit? How does the American manufacturer of jeans benefit? Do you think the American consumer ever benefits from depreciation? ▼

be bought with a particular currency. For example, suppose the amount of dollars wanted by Japanese exporters is greater than the quantity of dollars supplied by Americans who want to buy Japanese goods. Because the quantity demanded exceeds that supplied, the American dollar will become more expensive in relation to the yen. It will take more yen to equal $1. If the quantity of dollars American importers supplied is more than the quantity demanded by Japanese exporters, the price of a dollar will become cheaper in relation to the yen. Fewer yen will equal $1.

When the price of a currency falls through the action of supply and demand, it is termed **depreciation.** As with devaluation, depreciation of a country's currency improves its competitive edge in trade. **Figure 19.6** uses the price of jeans as an example of the effect of depreciation.

Besides import-export transactions, political or economic instability within a country may encourage people to exchange their currency for a more stable currency, often the United States dollar. In that case, the value of the dollar would rise in relation to the other nation's currency. A country that is experiencing rapid inflation will find its

currency falling in value in relation to other currencies. Such depreciation happened to Brazil's and Mexico's money during the 1980s.

Exchange Rates and the Balance of Trade

The rate at which a currency is being exchanged can have an important effect on a nation's balance of trade. The **balance of trade** is the difference between the value of a nation's exports and its imports. If a nation's currency depreciates, the nation will likely export more goods because its products will become cheaper to other nations. If a nation's currency increases in value, or price, the amount of its exports will drop.

Chapter 19 Trading With Other Nations **469**

Independent Practice

L3 Writing Have students brainstorm possible reasons for the change in the United States balance of trade. Then have them write a short essay telling how the United States might create a more equal or positive balance of trade.

L3 Comparing and Contrasting Ask students to imagine that they are running a duty-free shop or another type of international store. Have them develop a chart for their customers, telling the cost of various items in three or more different currencies.

📁 Have students complete Guided Reading Activity 19.2 in the TCR. **LEP**

❓ DID YOU KNOW

The United States exports about $25 billion worth of food and live animals in a year. It exports more than six times that amount in machinery and transport equipment.

Cooperative Learning

Ask students to imagine that currency is somehow unavailable or that they live in a barter economy. Have them work together to develop an international rate of exchange involving goods rather than currency. Have students make sure their item-based rate of exchange reflects the values of currency in given countries. Remind students that they will need to find out the purchasing power of the currencies of several countries before they can figure out the relative value of items in each country.

Assess

Meeting Lesson Objectives

Assign Section 2 Review as homework or an in-class activity. Each question in the Review addresses the corresponding numbered objective in the Section Focus.

Evaluate

Assign the Section 2 Quiz in the TCR or use the Testmaker to develop a customized quiz.

Reteach

Lead students in an imaginary shopping trip to a country of their choice. Begin with a given amount of currency and help students decide what they want to buy. Have students note whether the item is a "good deal" in American dollars, unavailable in America, or simply higher priced in America because of import costs.

Enrich

Have students write a brief history of the rise and decline of the International Monetary Fund.

Close

Discuss with students how the foreign value of a country's currency is related to its domestic economy. Have students discuss how currency value affects imports, exports, and buying power.

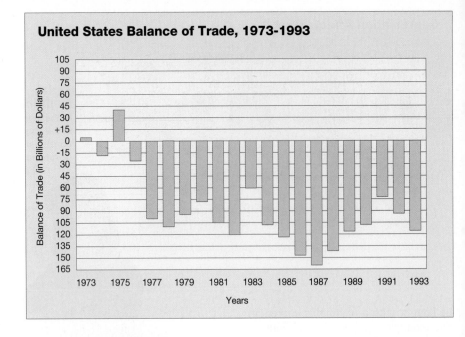

United States Balance of Trade, 1973-1993

Figure 19.7 ▲
Balance of Trade
This graph shows how the United States has basically had a negative balance of trade since the early 1970s.
Since 1977, in what year was the United States balance of trade most unfavorable? Least unfavorable?

When the value of goods leaving a nation exceeds the value of those coming in, a positive balance of trade is said to exist. In this case, the nation is bringing in more money as payments for goods than it is paying out. A negative balance of trade exists when the value of goods coming into a country is greater than the value of those going out. This situation is called a trade deficit. As you can see from Figure 19.7, the United States has had a negative balance of trade for many years beginning in the 1970s.

SECTION 2 REVIEW

Understanding Vocabulary

Define foreign exchange markets, fixed rate of exchange, International Monetary Fund (IMF), devaluation, flexible exchange rates, depreciation, balance of trade.

Reviewing Objectives

1. Why do nations need a system of currency exchange rates?
2. How do the forces of supply and demand determine flexible exchange rates?
3. What has been the normal state of America's balance of trade in recent years?

Section 2 Review Answers

Understanding Vocabulary
foreign exchange markets (p. 467), fixed rate of exchange (p. 467), International Monetary Fund (IMF) (p. 467), devaluation (p. 468), flexible exchange rates (p. 468), depreciation (p. 469), balance of trade (p. 469)

Reviewing Objectives
1. to engage in world trade
2. The currency of a nation whose goods are more in demand has a greater value than the currency of a nation whose goods are less in demand.
3. America has had a negative balance of trade.

LEARNING ECONOMIC SKILLS
Exchanging Foreign Currency

Many Americans at one time or another will travel to another country where they will have to exchange United States money for the local currency. Do you know how to exchange foreign currency?

The Dollar Value of Foreign Currency

Prices of foreign currencies are posted at places where you can buy foreign money, such as foreign-exchange counters in airports and banks throughout the world. Prices are also listed in major newspapers.

When you exchange your dollars for another currency, you will be "paid" the exchange rate as shown in Figure A.

If you were in France on this particular day, exchanging $1, you would get back approximately 5.8 francs. If you exchange $1,000, you would get back 5,773 francs.

Figure A

National Currencies	Unit of Other Currencies per Dollar
Belgian franc	34.935
British pound	.6636
Hong Kong dollar	7.7565
French franc	5.7733
German mark	1.7112
Japanese yen	108.10
Swiss franc	1.507
Thai baht	25.24

Units of Currency Per Dollar

Exchange rates can all be expressed in their mirror image. If, for example, one United States dollar buys 100 Japanese yen, then one Japanese yen is equal to one cent. Figure B expresses units of other currencies per dollar.

Suppose you want to buy a piece of crystal in France. It costs 4,827 francs. To find out how much it is in American dollars, you multiply that number times the dollar value of one franc, or $4,827 \times .1732 = \$836.03$.

Figure B

National Currencies	Dollars per Unit of Foreign Currencies
Belgian franc	.0286
British pound	1.507
Hong Kong dollar	.1289
French franc	.1732
German mark	.5844
Japanese yen	.0093
Swiss franc	.6636
Thai baht	.0396

Practicing the Skill

Study Figure B. Someone offers you 10,000 Belgian francs for a valuable painting. How much less would you be paid in Belgian francs than in Swiss francs in terms of dollars?

471

Answers to Practicing the Skill
$6,350.00

Focus

Overview

See the student page for section objectives.

Section 3 explains or describes: how imports can be restricted by tariffs, quotas, and embargoes; the main arguments for and against free trade; the worldwide trade agreement known as GATT; and the regional agreements of the EU, NAFTA, and the United States-Canadian Free Trade Agreement (FTA).

Bellringer

Before presenting the lesson, display Focus Activity Transparency 88 and assign the accompanying Focus Activity Sheet.

Motivational Activity

Have students discuss ways in which an inability to borrow would affect their personal budget and their lives.

Preteaching Vocabulary

Assign students countries and have them take turns explaining how each term might affect their country's relationship with other countries.

SECTION 3 **Restrictions on World Trade**

SECTION 3 FOCUS

Terms to Know tariff, revenue tariff, protective tariff, import quota, embargo, protectionists, General Agreement on Tariffs and Trade (GATT), U.S.-Canadian Free Trade Agreement, North American Free Trade Agreement (NAFTA)

Objectives *After reading this section, you should be able to:*
1. List three ways that imports can be restricted.
2. Explain the main arguments for and against free trade.
3. List one worldwide trade agreement and three regional trade agreements.

To Trade or Not to Trade?

The difficulties different currencies cause are only one problem of world trade. There are also natural barriers, which include the differences in languages and cultures between various trading partners. In addition, nations may set restrictions to discourage or limit trade. Three major barriers to world trade are tariffs, quotas, and embargoes.

Three Ways to Restrict Imports

The most commonly used barrier to free trade is the **tariff,** a tax on imports. A **revenue tariff** is one used primarily to raise income without restricting imports. Although tariffs today account for less than 2 percent of the federal government's income, they were the major source of federal funding until the early 1900s.

A **protective tariff** is one designed to raise the cost of imported goods and thereby protect domestic producers, as Figure 19.8 shows. As Figure 19.9 shows, tariff rates have been as high as 62 percent of the value of the imported goods. Tariffs are much lower today but are still used to pro-

**Figure 19.8
Domestic Goods**
As you learned from the law of demand, the quantity demanded of an item falls as the price rises. Higher prices for foreign goods because of tariffs mean that Americans will buy more domestic goods and fewer goods from abroad. ▼

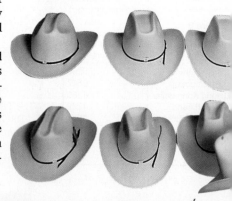

Classroom Resources for Section 3

- Reproducible Lesson Plan 19.3
- Focus Activity Transparency 88
- Focus Activity Sheet 88
- Guided Reading Activity 19.3
- Free Enterprise Activities 19 and 20

- Section Quiz 19.3
- Spanish Section Quiz 19.3
- Chapter 19 Test Forms A and B
- Testmaker
- Enrichment Activity 19
- Economics Vocabulary Activity 19

- Spanish Economics Vocabulary Activity 19
- Audiocassette 19
- Spanish Audiocassette 19
- Reteaching Activity 19
- Spanish Reteaching Activity 19

Tariff Rates in the United States, 1820-1990

Duties Collected as a Percentage of Dutiable Imports

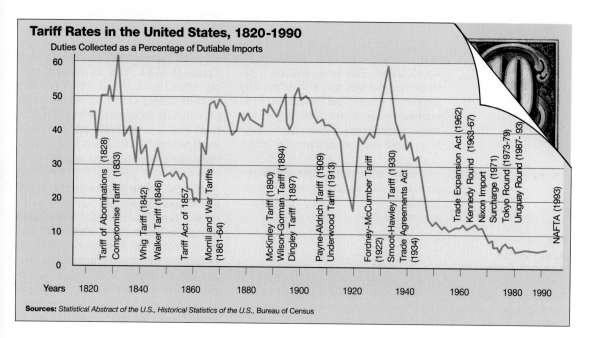

Years

Sources: *Statistical Abstract of the U.S.*, *Historical Statistics of the U.S.*, Bureau of Census

tect such industries as textiles from foreign competition.

An alternative method for restricting imports is the quota system. An **import quota** is a restriction imposed on the value of or the number of units of a particular good that can be brought into the country. The United States has placed quotas on imports of sugar, shoes, shirts, and cloth.

An **embargo** is a complete restriction on the import or export of a particular good. Often embargoes are enacted for political reasons. For example, in 1980 President Jimmy Carter ordered a halt of all grain sales to the Soviet Union. This was in response to Soviet intervention in Afghanistan. President Ronald Reagan lifted the grain embargo in 1981, however, he placed new restrictions on the sale to the Soviets of certain high-technology equipment such as computers. The United States has also ordered embargoes on goods from certain countries. In 1986, Congress passed an embargo on trade with South Africa. It ended in 1993.

Figure 19.9 ▲
Tariff Rates

As you can see on the graph, United States tariff rates have fluctuated greatly over the last 180 years. What seems to be the trend in tariff rates now? Why do you think this is the case?

Chapter 19 Trading With Other Nations **473**

Teach

Guided Practice

L2 Creating Profiles Have students talk with three adults about the arguments for and against free trade and create a profile for each one that includes opinions about free-trade issues. Have students make the profiles as complete as possible, including the age, gender, and occupation of the people interviewed.

🌐 GLOBAL ECONOMICS

Many countries around the world set aside free trade zones or foreign trade zones to encourage international trade. In these zones, goods can be imported, stored, assembled, exhibited, or processed without import taxes. Taxes are paid only to the importing country, not to the country where the trade is occurring. The United States has about 185 foreign trade zones, administered by the U.S. Department of Commerce.

◆ ● Meeting Special Needs

Hearing Disability Students with hearing difficulties may have trouble following all the arguments for and against free trade unless the point of view is well established each time an opinion is described. You may want to write on the chalkboard headings

stating "For" and "Against." Ask students to write summaries of arguments for and against free trade under the proper heading whenever they present information to the class.

Independent Practice

L2 Creating a Table Ask students to use information in this section to create a table showing how GATT, NAFTA, the EU, and the United States-Canadian FTA are similar and how they are different. Have students write an accompanying paragraph summarizing the information in the table.

Have students complete Guided Reading Activity 19.3 in the TCR. **LEP**

Visual Instruction

Ask students to use the reasons given in Figures 19.10 and 19.11 to create a chart showing arguments for and against free trade side by side.

Assess

Meeting Lesson Objectives

Assign Section 3 Review as homework or an in-class activity.

Arguments For and Against Free Trade

Since World War II, the trend has been toward relaxing barriers to world trade. The pros and cons of trade restrictions are still often the subject of intense public debate. **Protectionists** are those who argue for trade restrictions. Figure 19.10 outlines three main arguments for trade protection.

Those who favor free or unrestricted trade usually point to three benefits. Figure 19.11 examines these arguments.

Figure 19.10 Arguments Against Free Trade
Protectionists object to free trade based on the three areas shown below.

Trade Agreements

For much of the 1900s, nations have worked to lower trade restrictions. Recent agreements have followed this pattern.

A **Job security is threatened.** Opponents of relaxing trade restrictions argue that many domestic workers will be unemployed if foreign competitors sell goods at lower prices than American firms. In the 1980s, American steel mills laid off many workers due to foreign competition. ▼

B **Protection of the nation's economic security is needed.** Certain industries, such as oil, should be protected against foreign competition. Protectionists argue that these industries are crucial to the economy of the United States. ▼

C **Protection of infant industries is needed.** Tariffs and quotas are needed as temporary protection for new, infant industries. If foreign competition is restricted for a time, a young industry such as video camera manufacturing may become strong enough to compete in the world market. ▼

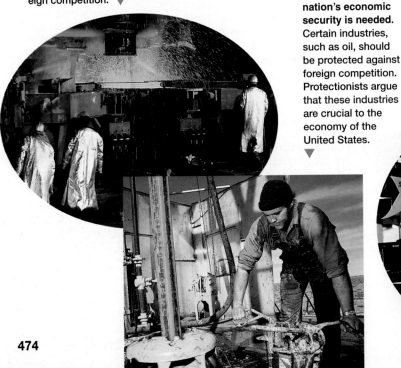

474

The General Agreement on Tariffs and Trade (GATT) After World War II, numerous bilateral trade agreements were brought together in the **General Agreement on Tariffs and Trade (GATT)**. The agreement was signed in 1947 and took effect January 1, 1948. Under GATT, countries meet periodically to negotiate tariff reductions that are mutually advantageous to all members. The latest GATT tariff reductions were reached in 1993.

Regional Trade Agreements Three of the most important agreements to reduce tariff barriers are the unified European Union (EU), which was formerly called the European Community and the European common market, the **U.S.-Canadian Free Trade Agreement**, and the **North American Free Trade Agreement (NAFTA)**. The European Union currently consists of 12

Cooperative Learning

Point out to students that immigrant communities throughout the United States often have unique imports for sale. Organize students into groups to research and develop lists of the interesting and/or unusual specialty items imported by more recent immigrant groups such as Chinese, Middle Easterners, Southeast Asians, Indians, Pakistanis, Hispanics, Haitians, and others. Students might include natural and prepared foods and various manufactured items such as saris and chadors. Have an "international bazaar" in which a member of each group tells about the wares discovered.

Figure 19.11
Arguments For
Free Trade

People who want free trade base their support on the three areas shown below.

A **Competition means improved products.** Foreign competition encourages United States firms to improve technology and production methods.

B **Trade restrictions damage export industries, putting Americans out of work.** The fewer goods the United States imports, the less American money there is available outside the United States to buy American exports.

$11.95

C **Specialization and comparative advantage lowers prices.** The consumer benefits because comparative advantage in production brings more goods at lower prices.

Evaluate

Assign the Section 3 Quiz in the TCR or use the Testmaker.

Assign the Chapter 19 Test Form A or Form B or use the Testmaker.

Reteach

Discuss with students how free trade would affect tariffs as well as imports and exports of various goods.

Have students complete Reteaching Activity 19 in the TCR.

Enrich

Have students research any embargoes the United States government is currently enacting.

Have students complete Enrichment Activity 19 in the TCR.

Close

Have students locate the nations in GATT and the countries in the European Union on a world political map.

member nations—France, Germany, Britain, Denmark, Italy, Spain, Greece, Portugal, Luxembourg, Belgium, Holland, and Ireland. Starting on January 1, 1993, the EU eliminated most of its restrictions on trade among its member states. Also, both labor and capital are supposed to be freely mobile within those 12 nations.

On January 1, 1989, a historic free trade agreement (FTA) between the United States and Canada took effect. The goal is to eliminate high tariffs on furniture, textiles, appliances, petrochemicals, plastics, metal, paper, and fish products. The U.S.-Canadian FTA guarantees that both countries have access to each other's petroleum, gas, coal, and electricity at prices paid by nationals under comparable commercial circumstances.

The North American Free Trade Agreement (NAFTA) is designed to extend the U.S.-Canadian FTA to include Mexico. The United States Congress approved NAFTA in 1993. NAFTA will likely benefit some industries and hurt others. Mexico will probably import more industrial machinery and grain from the United States. It will also import more United States banking services. Industries in the United States that will be hardest hit by increased competition from Mexico will be footwear, steel, and clothes. Citrus growers, too, particularly in California and Florida, may face increased competition from lower-priced Mexican fruit growers.

SECTION 3 REVIEW

Understanding Vocabulary
Define tariff, revenue tariff, protective tariff, import quota, embargo, protectionists, General Agreement on Tariffs and Trade (GATT), U.S.-Canadian Free Trade Agreement, North American Free Trade Agreement (NAFTA).

Reviewing Objectives
1. How can a nation restrict imports?
2. What are three arguments for and three arguments against free trade?
3. What are one international and three regional trade agreements?

Chapter 19 Trading With Other Nations **475**

Section 3 Review Answers

Understanding Vocabulary
tariff (p. 472), **revenue tariff** (p. 472), **protective tariff** (p. 472), **import quota** (p. 473), **embargo** (p. 473), **protectionists** (p. 474), **General Agreement on Tariffs and Trade (GATT)** (p. 474), **U.S.-Canadian Free Trade Agreement** (p. 474), **North American**

Free Trade Agreement (NAFTA) (p. 474)

Reviewing Objectives
1. through tariffs, quotas, and embargoes
2. arguments for: improved quality through competition, comparative advantage from specialization,

health of export industry; arguments against: loss of job security, need to protect infant industries, need to protect economic security

3. GATT, U.S.-Canadian FTA, European Union, NAFTA

Teach

Point out to students that this article about the NAFTA debate comes from *USA Today*, a general interest newspaper that focuses on issues of national concern.

Have students use the information in the feature to develop a dramatic sketch or short play about two brothers, one in Mexico or Canada, and one in the United States, who discuss how they think NAFTA will affect their lives. Have students think about changes in job opportunities, spending habits, and the local economy. Ask students to rehearse and perform their play for the class.

News Clip

Readings in Economics

USA TODAY	SEPTEMBER 15, 1993

TAKING SIDES
by Juan J. Walte

Raul and Roberto Quinones run a thriving business from four stores here [Ciudad Juarez, Mexico], selling Mexican-made ceramic tiles to Americans who cross the Rio Grande to buy at low prices.

But the brothers spend much of their free time debating the merits of the North American Free Trade Agreement. . . .

The Quinones brothers' debate is taking place on both sides of the border, with both Mexicans and Americans arguing both sides of the issue. . . .

But the debate is especially intense here and in El Paso across the border, where people say their whole future is meshed with the fate of the proposed NAFTA agreement. . . .

"Look around you and you'll see we are already very much under the influence of the 'American way of life'."

True, Mexicans cross the international bridges to spend their money at El Paso malls and dozens of stores near the border.

Even on the Mexican side of the border they can shop at Wal-Mart and K Mart and eat at McDonald's, Burger King and Church's Chicken.

Many of the Mexicans visiting those U.S. franchises earn their money at U.S.-owned businesses that set up in free-trade zones along the border.

About 2,100 such plants—called *maquiladoras* (Spanish for "twin plants"— referring to the connections within a plant in the USA) — have opened here, employing 500,000, primarily in low-skill, low-paying jobs. . . .

Most are assembly plants where workers piece together parts made in the USA or Japan. The final product is exported; it cannot be sold here.

The fate of these businesses remains open to question.

• THINK ABOUT IT •

1. What is the subject being debated?

2. What are maquiladoras?

Answers to Think About It

1. the passage of NAFTA
2. *Maquiladoras* are "twin plants"— plants with connections in the United States—that have opened in Mexico recently.

19 Highlights

Use the Chapter 19 highlights to preview, review, condense, or reteach the chapter. A Spanish Chapter Highlights is available in the Spanish Handbook.

Preview/Review

After students read the Chapter 19 Highlights, have them complete Economics Vocabulary Activity 19 in the TCR. Spanish Vocabulary Activities are also available in the Spanish Resource Binder.

Vocabulary Software reinforces the economic terms used in Chapter 19.

Condense

Have students listen to Chapter 19 on the Audiocassettes in the TCR. A 1-page written activity and 1-page test accompany this material. These materials are also available in Spanish.

Reteach

Have students complete Reteaching Activity 19 in the TCR. Spanish Reteaching Activities are also available.

Section 1

The Benefits of World Trade

Key Terms
imports (p. 462)
exports (p. 462)
absolute advantage
(p. 464)
specialization (p. 464)
comparative advantage
(p. 465)

Summary

Nations benefit from world trade because each nation differs in the type and amount of the factors of production it has available for use. Absolute advantage is the ability of a country, using the same amount of resources as another country, to produce more of a particular good than the other country. If a country has a comparative advantage in at least one product, it will be advantageous for that country to specialize in the production of that good. The country can then trade with other countries to obtain other goods it desires.

Section 2

Financing World Trade

Key Terms
foreign exchange markets
(p. 467)
fixed rate of exchange
(p. 467)
International Monetary
Fund (IMF) (p. 467)

devaluation (p. 468)
flexible exchange rates
(p. 468)
depreciation (p. 469)
balance of trade (p. 469)

Summary

With a fixed rate of exchange, national governments set the value of their currencies in relation to a single standard. With flexible exchange rates, the forces of supply and demand set the prices of currencies. When the value of our exports exceeds the value of our imports, we are running a surplus in our balance of trade.

Section 3

Restrictions on World Trade

Key Terms
tariff (p. 472)
revenue tariff (p. 472)
protective tariff (p. 472)
import quota (p. 473)
embargo (p. 473)
protectionists (p. 474)

General Agreement on
Tariffs and Trade
(GATT) (p. 474)
U.S.-Canadian Free Trade
Agreement (p. 474)
North American Free
Trade Agreement
(NAFTA) (p. 474)

Summary

Legal restrictions on world trade are attempts to protect a nation's industries and workers. The pros and cons of trade restrictions are often intensely debated. GATT and several regional trade agreements govern most of the world's trade.

Chapter 19 Trading With Other Nations **477**

 VIDEODISC

Nightly Business Report
Economics in Action
Use "International Trade" on Disc 2, Side B, Video 27.

Search 12796, Play to 19102

CHAPTER
19 Review

ANSWERS

Identifying Key Terms

1. f
2. a
3. e
4. b
5. g
6. c
7. d

Paragraphs will vary but should demonstrate an understanding of the key terms.

Recalling Facts and Ideas

Section 1

1. by determining its own opportunity costs and those of other countries for the same goods
2. improved products, strengthened export industries, lower prices
3. absolute advantage

Section 2

4. International Monetary Fund (IMF)
5. Differing rates of inflation can unbalance the cost of goods among various countries.

Section 3

6. A revenue tariff raises income. A protective tariff restricts trade to protect domestic industry.

7. loss of job security for United States workers, need to protect infant industries, need to protect the nation's economic security
8. exports
9. France, Germany, Britain, Denmark, Italy, Spain, Greece, Portugal, Luxembourg, Belgium, Holland, and Ireland

---

Identifying Key Terms

Write the letter of the definition in Column B below that correctly defines each term in Column A.

Column A	Column B
1. absolute advantage (p. 464)	a. lowering of currency's value in relation to other currencies
2. devaluation (p. 468)	b. complete restriction on the import or export of a particular good
3. depreciation (p. 469)	c. difference between the value of a nation's exports and its imports
4. embargo (p. 473)	d. ability of a nation to produce a product at a lower opportunity cost
5. protectionists (p. 474)	e. drop of the price of a currency in response to supply and demand
6. balance of trade (p. 469)	f. ability of a country to use the same amount of resources as another to produce a product at less cost
7. comparative advantage (p. 465)	g. those who oppose the relaxation of trade restrictions

Write a paragraph on tariffs and international and regional agreements to reduce tariffs using the following words:

revenue tariff (p. 472)
protective tariff (p. 472)
import quota (p. 473)

General Agreement on Tariffs and Trade (GATT) (p. 474)
U.S.-Canadian Free Trade Agreement (p. 474).
North American Free Trade Agreement (NAFTA) (p. 474)

Recalling Facts and Ideas

Section 1

1. How does a country determine whether it has a comparative advantage in the production of certain goods?
2. What does the United States gain as a country from international trade?
3. "America can produce more compact discs per labor hour than can any other country in the world." Is this an example of an absolute or a comparative advantage?

Section 2

4. What international organization monitored the world's fixed exchange rate system?
5. Why is it difficult to maintain a system of fixed rates of exchange?

Section 3

6. What is the difference between a revenue tariff and a protective tariff?
7. What are three arguments against free trade?
8. What is also affected when restrictions are put on imports?
9. What are the 12 member nations of the European Union (EU)?

Critical Thinking

Section 1

Drawing Conclusions Some people worry that highly competitive nations will end up producing everything. How do absolute and comparative advantage relate to this conclusion?

Section 2

Making Predictions If the value of the dollar fell in relation to other currencies, what would you expect to happen to American exports?

Critical Thinking

Section 1

Answers should demonstrate understanding of specialization and comparative advantage.

Section 2

Answers should include an expectation that American exports would increase because our goods would be inexpensive—if other nations did not impose protective tariffs.

Section 3

A tariff can account for a high percentage of the price of a good, so tariff protection of infant industries promotes buying, allowing industries to recoup costs before the industries must compete with those of other nations.

Section 3
Determining Cause and Effect How does protection of infant industries allow them to grow?

Applying Economic Concepts

The Benefits of International Trade Even though international trade accounts for only about 10 percent of the American economy, it affects all Americans. To understand how international trade affects you, try to describe what your world would be like if international trade were outlawed. You can do this by writing a list of all the products you would *not* be able to purchase or whose price would go up dramatically without international trade. Some examples that quickly come to mind are rice and coffee. What are some others?

Chapter Projects

1. **Individual Project** There are virtually no restrictions on trade within the 50 states, mainly because the Constitution forbids it. First find the section or sections in the Constitution that prohibit at least one restriction on international trade and write them down. Next write out a list of the problems that might arise if the Constitution had been silent on trade among the several states.
2. **Cooperative Learning Project** Working in groups of four, concentrate on one or more countries taken from the following list:
   - Mexico
   - Canada
   - Japan
   - Zaire
   - Morocco

   Each member of the group will research one of the following items:
   - The size of the international sector within each country (i.e., the percentage of GDP accounted for by imports or exports)
   - The natural resource base of the nation
   - The top three items that are exported
   - The top three items that are imported

Each group will decide what the relationship is between the natural resource base and what is exported and what is imported. Each group will try to determine whether any relationship exists between what is imported and what is exported. Finally, each group will write a summary of how life in each country would be different if international trade were prohibited.

Reviewing Skills

Exchanging Foreign Currency
Using the Right Currency Look at the set of exchange rates with the U.S. dollar below.

Currency	Units per Dollar
Argentine peso	0.9901
Australian dollar	1.4995
Irish pound	0.6971
New Zealand dollar	1.846
Philippine peso	27.33
Singapore dollar	1.6245
Taiwan dollar	26.34

You are selling a valuable ring to a foreigner who offers you 1,000 pesos. You think she is referring to Argentinean pesos, but in fact she is referring to Philippine pesos. What is the difference in the dollar price?

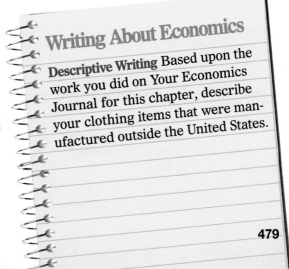

Writing About Economics

Descriptive Writing Based upon the work you did on Your Economics Journal for this chapter, describe your clothing items that were manufactured outside the United States.

Applying Economic Concepts
Review students' lists of products with them.

Chapter Projects
1. Review with students their lists of problems that might arise if there were no free trade between the states.
2. Have students work together to encode their information on a world map complete with a table for comparing the international sector of each country. Suggest that students combine their paragraphs in a booklet to accompany the map. Students might title their booklets "International Trade."

Reviewing Skills
$953.51

Writing About Economics
Students' descriptions should include clothing with labels signifying that it was made elsewhere. Students should also try to include domestic items for which components were imported.

? BONUS QUESTION

The following bonus question may be written on the chalkboard when students take the chapter test.
Q. How might a high exchange rate for the dollar affect your vacation in a foreign country?
A. If more units of foreign currency were available for each dollar, it would make travel cheaper there.

CHAPTER 20

CONVERGING ECONOMIC SYSTEMS

CHAPTER ORGANIZER

Daily Objectives	Special Features	Classroom Resources
Section 1 Comparing Capitalism and Socialism • **List** five characteristics of pure market capitalism. • **List** six characteristics of pure socialism. • **Describe** the development of socialism. • **Compare** planning under socialism and under capitalism. • **Explain** the benefits of capitalism.	**Learning Economic Skills:** Understanding Economic News, p. 486	Reproducible Lesson Plan 20.1 *NBR* Video 26 Focus Activity Transparency 89 Focus Activity Sheet 89 Guided Reading Activity 20.1 Cooperative Learning Activity 20 Primary and Secondary Source Readings 20 Section Quiz 20.1 Spanish Section Quiz 20.1 Testmaker Reinforcing Skills 20
Section 2 Changing Authoritarian Socialism—The Case of China • **Explain** how the Chinese economic system developed following World War II. • **Describe** the benefits of special economic zones in the People's Republic of China.	**Personal Perspective:** Karl Marx on Communism, p. 491	Reproducible Lesson Plan 20.2 Focus Activity Transparency 90 Focus Activity Sheet 90 Guided Reading Activity 20.2 Free Enterprise Activity 21 Section Quiz 20.2 Spanish Section Quiz 20.2 Testmaker
Section 3 Nations Move Toward the Market System • **Explain** what has been happening in terms of ownership of business in Russia since privatization. • **Describe** four changes in Sweden's economy in the 1990s. • **Indicate** some of the changes in Latin American economic systems. • **Discuss** how the supply and demand model helps analyze converging economic systems.	**News Clip:** "Why China Does It Better," *Newsweek*, p. 496	Reproducible Lesson Plan 20.3 Focus Activity Transparency 91 Focus Activity Sheet 91 Guided Reading Activity 20.3 Consumer Application Activity 21 Mathematics Practice for Economics 26 Performance Assessment Activity 26 Section Quiz 20.3 Spanish Section Quiz 20.3 Testmaker Enrichment Activity 20

0:00 OUT OF TIME? If time does not permit teaching this chapter, you may use Chapter 20 Highlights and the Audiocassettes that include a 1-page activity and a 1-page test.

Chapter 20 Review and Evaluation

Special Features

Chapter 20 Highlights, p. 497
Chapter 20 Review, pp. 498–499
Point/Counterpoint, pp. 500–501

Classroom Resources

- Chapter 20 Test Forms A and B
- Economics Vocabulary Activity 20
- Spanish Economics Vocabulary Activity 20

- Audiocassette 20
- Spanish Audiocassette
- Reteaching Activity 20
- Spanish Reteaching Activity 20

Key to Ability Levels

Teaching strategies have been coded for varying learning styles and abilities.

L1 Level 1 activities are **basic** activities and should be within the ability range of all students.

L2 Level 2 activities are **average** activities designed for the ability of the average to above-average students.

L3 Level 3 activities are **challenging** activities designed for the ability range of above-average students.

LEP activities should be within the ability range of **Limited English Proficiency** students.

Performance Assessment

The following chapter project may be assigned at the beginning of the chapter and used for performance assessment. See page T12 for additional Performance Assessment information.

Researching Economic History Have students work in small groups, each group taking responsibility for a particular continent or region of the world, and research which countries have had socialist economies at some time in the twentieth century. Have students do written reports on their findings. Students should include in their reports their understanding of why many of these countries have turned toward capitalism today.

Additional Resources

Readings for the Student

Adler, Mortimer J. *Haves Without Have-nots*. New York: Macmillan, 1991.

Blackburn, Robin, ed. *After the Fall*. London: Verso Editions, 1992.

Readings for the Teacher

Cornwall, John. *Theory of Economic Breakdown*. Oxford, England: Blackwell, 1990.

Marglin, Stephen A., ed. *The Golden Age of Capitalism*. Oxford, England: Oxford University Press, 1990.

Ulam, Adam B. *The Communists*. New York: Charles Scribner's Sons, 1992.

Multimedia Materials

Capitalism, Socialism, Communism—A Series. 35 mm film or videotape. 24–27 min. each. National Geographic Society, 17th and M Streets NW, Washington, DC 20036.

China Commune. 35 mm film. 35 min. Westinghouse Learning Corporation. 2400 Ardmore Boulevard, Pittsburgh, PA 15221.

China Looks West. Videotape. 25 min. Journal Films, Inc., 930 Pittner, Evanston, IL 60202.

Scholastic World Geography, Cultures, and Economics Data Bases for pfs: FILE. Apple. Scholastic Software, Division of Scholastic, Inc., 730 Broadway, New York, NY 10003. Second disk drive recommended.

Chapter Overview

Chapter 20 explains or describes: the movement from socialist to capitalist economies worldwide; the advantages of decentralized capitalism with respect to efficiency, economic freedom, and profit motivation; the growth of a market economy in the People's Republic of China and the creation of special economic zones; and trends in other nations toward blending capitalism and socialism.

VIDEODISC

Nightly Business Report
Economics in Action
Use "Comparative Economic Systems" on Disc 2, Side B, Video 26.

Search 6509, Play to 12721

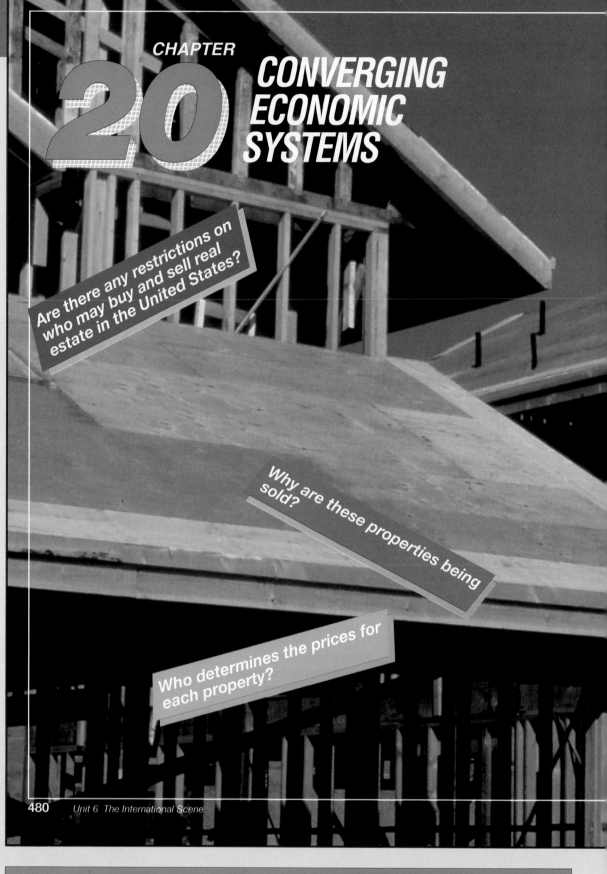

CHAPTER

20 CONVERGING ECONOMIC SYSTEMS

Are there any restrictions on who may buy and sell real estate in the United States?

Why are these properties being sold?

Who determines the prices for each property?

Answering Economic Questions

The information in the above illustration is designed to lead into the main concepts in Chapter 20. Students might never have thought about the freedom conveyed by property ownership and the ability to buy and sell in response to personal goals. They may not have considered the benefits and costs of restrictions on business. Have students discuss the questions and think about ways in which they exercise economic freedom each day.

Who owns these houses?

Who has put these houses up for sale?

Who is permitted to buy these houses?

Your Economics Journal

Keep track of the products and services you buy during the week. For each, try to find out whether the price was determined by supply and demand or by an agency of government. For example, cable TV rates are regulated by the federal government.

481

Connecting to Past Learning

Ask students to share with the class the economic choices they have made freely, in response to their own goals or needs. Have students examine how they would have been hampered economically if they were not allowed to make the choice they made. Point out to students that socialist economic systems require extensive planning that necessarily reaches into the personal lives of citizens.

Applying Economics

Tell students that property ownership is a basic right in capitalism. Ask them to imagine they have property they want to sell. Have them find out about federal and local government regulations such as EPA requirements that affect zoning laws and transfers of property.

This chapter will examine the considerations that have led many nations to move toward market capitalism.

EXTRA CREDIT PROJECT

Have interested students report on state laws or local ordinances limiting the free market. Encourage students to discuss the reasons for these laws and resulting trade-offs.

Economic Portfolio

Have students identify the countries that are ruled by communist parties or have been in the past. Ask them to share their impressions of the economic conditions in those countries. Have students scan the newspapers for news about changes occurring in socialist or formerly socialist nations. Ask them to cut out and keep clippings to refer to and share throughout the remainder of the course.

PERFORMANCE ASSESSMENT

Refer to page 480B for "Researching Economic History," a Performance Assessment Activity for this chapter.

Focus

Overview

See the student page for section objectives.

Section 1 explains or describes: the characteristics of pure market capitalism and pure socialism; economic planning under capitalist and socialist systems; and the benefits of capitalism.

Bellringer

Before presenting the lesson, display Focus Activity Transparency 89 on the overhead projector or copy the material on the chalkboard. Assign the accompanying Focus Activity Sheet.

Motivational Activity

Ask students to complete the following sentence: The place where I plan to live is _____, and I plan to work as a _____. Then ask them to share their responses with the class. Tell students that this section will discuss the freedom of the capitalist economic system and compare it with socialist economic systems.

Preteaching Vocabulary

Have students write sentences using each vocabulary term once. Ask volunteers to read the sentences aloud except for the vocabulary terms. Have the class identify the missing term in each sentence that is read.

482

SECTION 1 Comparing Capitalism and Socialism

SECTION 1 FOCUS

Terms to Know three *P*'s, private property rights, price system, communism, proletariat, democratic socialism, authoritarian socialism

Objectives *After reading this section, you should be able to:*
1. List five characteristics of **pure market capitalism.**
2. List six characteristics of **pure socialism.**
3. Describe **the development of socialism.**
4. Compare **planning under socialism and under capitalism.**
5. Explain the **benefits of capitalism.**

Figure 20.1 Characteristics of Pure Capitalism
Market capitalism operates on the basis of the **three *P*'s:**
- Prices
- Profits
- Private property

Under pure capitalism government is limited to providing such public goods as defense and police protection. ▼

Characteristics of Pure Capitalism

1. **Private property rights** exist, are legal, and are enforced by the government.

2. Pure capitalism is a **price system.** Prices are allowed to seek their own level as determined by the forces of supply and demand.

3. Resources, including labor, are free to move in and out of industries in competing geographic locations. The movement of resources follows the lure of profits — higher expected profits create an incentive for more resources to go where those profits are expected to occur.

4. Those who take risks may be rewarded by higher profits. When those risks turn out to be bad business decisions, the risk takers lose money.

5. The four basic economic questions are all decided in a decentralized way by individuals. What and how much should be produced, who should produce what, how it should be produced, and for whom it should be produced are all left to the market.

482 *Unit 6 The International Scene*

Who Should Control Pricing and Production?

When you buy a sweater, change jobs, or invest in a savings bond, you are affecting the nation's economy. Some government intervention occurs in the American economy, but it is largely the marketplace that answers the four basic economic questions. See Chapter 2. In command economies, government, not the market, answers these four basic questions.

In this chapter you will study different economic systems. You must remember, though, that all principles of economics apply to all economic systems. No matter what the system, the fundamental economic problem of scarcity must be solved.

The system that we know best in the United States is market capitalism. At the other extreme is pure command socialism.

Pure Market Capitalism

In its purest theoretical form, market capitalism, or pure capitalism, has distinct characteristics and components. **Figures 20.1** and **20.2** show these.

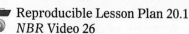

Classroom Resources for Section 1

- Reproducible Lesson Plan 20.1
- *NBR* Video 26
- Focus Activity Transparency 89
- Focus Activity Sheet 89
- Guided Reading Activity 20.1
- Cooperative Learning Activity 20

- Primary and Secondary Source Readings 20
- Section Quiz 20.1
- Spanish Section Quiz 20.1
- Testmaker
- Reinforcing Skills 20

Pure Socialism

Pure socialism is an economic system in which there is virtually no private property and the state owns virtually all the factors of production. Figure 20.3 lists the characteristics of pure socialism.

A **Price System** ▲

B **Decentralization**
▶

**Figure 20.2
The Components
of Pure
Capitalism**
Pure capitalism has five characteristics, as shown in this illustration.

C
Resources
▼

D
**Private
Property**
▼

Characteristics of Pure Socialism

1. Most prices are set by the state, rather than by forces of supply and demand.

2. Most of the major factors of production are owned by the state. Private property rights are strictly limited to small tools that an individual needs for an occupation.

3. Economic decisions about what and how much, how, and for whom to produce, are all made by the state through its central planning agencies and other administrative units.

4. The movement of resources, particularly labor, is strictly controlled. The central planning authority makes all the decisions.

5. Individual risk taking is not allowed. The state takes all of the risk when it decides which new companies shall be formed. All citizens pay for unsuccessful risk taking.

6. Taxation is often used to redistribute income.

Figure 20.3 ▲
Characteristics of Pure Socialism
Few examples of pure command socialism exist today. Perhaps the most extensively centralized controlled command social system is in North Korea. There has also been a command system in Cuba under dictator Fidel Castro.

E **Profit/Loss** ▼

Teach

Guided Practice

L2 Applying Information
Have small groups develop a one- or two-minute scene showing how each characteristic of pure market capitalism or pure socialism operates. Ask the groups to perform their scenes.

Visual Instruction

Ask the class to look over Figure 20.2 and discuss how socialism and capitalism address the four basic questions and the problem of scarcity. Encourage students to make a visual comparison by writing information on a two-column table headed Pure Capitalism and Pure Socialism.

🌐 GLOBAL ECONOMICS

Theorists of several European nations have influenced the directions of economic thought. For example, in the 1770s, Scottish economist Adam Smith showed how to implement a laissez-faire approach to economic policies. German philosopher Karl Marx influenced the development of socialism in the 1800s. In the 1930s, British economist John Maynard Keynes urged increased government involvement in capitalist economies.

◆▶◯ Meeting Special Needs

Hearing Disability Students with hearing difficulties may have problems performing scenes if they are not allowed to see the speaker with whom they are performing. Encourage these students to focus on their partners rather than the audience while performing. If necessary, have students perform their scenes at a table with two chairs that face each other.

Independent Practice

L2 Organizing Information Have students create a visual explanation of the characteristics of market capitalism. Ask students to organize and color code the characteristics according to their application to the three *P*s.

L3 Comparing and Contrasting Ask students to create a pair of charts comparing the benefits of capitalism and socialism and the drawbacks of each.

Have students complete Guided Reading Activity 20.1 in the TCR. LEP

DID YOU KNOW

The Soviet Union became the first socialist country, following a revolution in 1917, led by V. I. Lenin and the Bolshevik (Communist) Party. The revolution gained support through programs opposing poverty and inequality, prevalent under Russian czars. Russia's military defeats in World War I and resulting economic deprivation also hastened the revolution.

The Change From Capitalism to Socialism According to Marx

Step 1	Step 2
Capitaism would suffer extreme recessions and depressions that would harm workers. A few rich capitalists would have all industrial power.	The wide gap between the rich and the poor would cause workers to unite and overthrow capitalism.
Step 3	**Step 4**
The victorious workers would establish a new socialist system. Workers, through the state, would own and control the means of production.	The system would evolve into pure **communism**—an ideal system with no need for a government. Workers would contribute to society to their full abilities and, in return, take only what they needed.

Figure 20.4 ▲ The End of Capitalism Clearly Marx did not accurately predict what would happen in capitalist nations.

The Development of Socialism

Socialism as a modern economic system grew out of protests against the problems caused by the Industrial Revolution of the 1800s.

The Marxian View of Socialism Karl Marx viewed history as a continual struggle between various groups, or classes, in society. He saw this struggle in his own day as going on between capitalists—owners of the land, machines, and factories—and the **proletariat** (PROH-luh-TER-ee-uht), or workers. Marx believed capitalists exploited the proletariat, or used them unfairly. According to Marx, the value of goods depends only on how much labor is used in producing them. When capitalists sold a good and kept the profit, they were taking money that rightly belonged to the proletariat.

Despite capitalism's dominance in the nineteenth century, Marx believed it was doomed to fail. Marx outlined the collapse of capitalism and predicted the evolution of socialism into communism as Figure 20.4 shows.

Socialism Since Marx In the twentieth century, socialism has split into two major trends: democratic socialism and authoritarian socialism. **Democratic socialism** is a type of socialist system that works within the constitutional framework of a nation to elect socialists to office. In democratic socialist nations, government usually controls only some areas of the economy.

Authoritarian socialism, in contrast, follows the lead of Marx. Its supporters advocate revolution as the means to overthrow capitalism and bring about socialist goals. In authori-

Figure 20.5 ▶ Planning in Market and Command Economies Planning is unavoidable, no matter what the economic system. The United States has a highly planned economy. The difference between economic planning in the United States and in command economies is who does the planning.

Planning in Market and Command Economies

The Market System: Decentralized	The Command System: Centralized
In the United States market system, planning is undertaken by private firms, individuals, and elected government representatives. In the private sector in the United States, all plans are built around relative prices. It is changing relative prices in our market economy that communicates scarcity and priorities. The market system coordinates "the plan."	In pure socialist systems, central planners undertake the planning on behalf of everyone. The signals given to central planners in socialist economies have proved to be weak, inaccurate, or nonexistent, however. The result generally has been low rates of growth and low standards of living in centrally planned socialist economies.

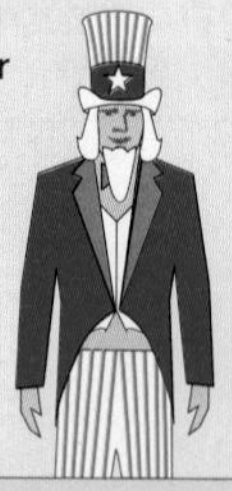

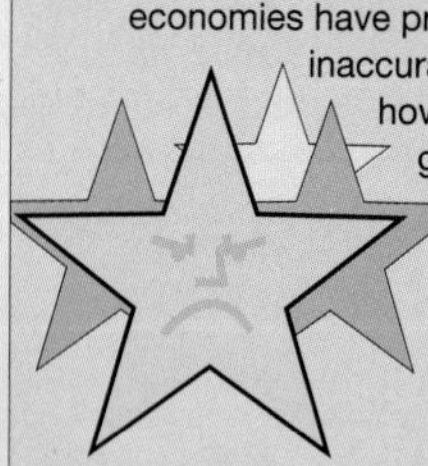

Cooperative Learning

Have students discuss the reasons why Marx's predictions about the end of capitalism have not come true. Ask them to write the reasons on the chalkboard. Then have students brainstorm an alternative view of the future of capitalism. Remind them to base their predictions on logical reasons, based in fact.

tarian socialist nations, a central government controls the entire economy. *Communism,* the term Marx applied to his ideal society, has come to mean any authoritarian socialist system.

Planning Under Capitalism and Socialism

It is often said that pure socialism requires centralized economic planning, and pure capitalism does not. The reality is that all economies are planned in one way or another. See Figure 20.5.

The Benefits of Capitalism

Many economists like to compare the advantages and disadvantages of capitalism and socialism. Often such comparisons are based on individual values. Those who place a high value on personal freedom, initiative, and individuality prefer capitalism. Such critics of socialism point out that socialism brings with it immense government intervention in all parts of the economy and, by necessity, in people's personal lives. By definition, a socialist system is one in which government controls numerous production and pricing decisions throughout the nation.

The supporters of capitalism point out that capitalism allows for more efficiency in the marketplace and for greater rates of economic growth. Moreover, considerable evidence shows that unregulated economic systems—those that are closer to pure capitalism—have higher rates of economic growth.

Of course, capitalism as it exists in the world has some problems. Critics point out that income is unequally distributed throughout the economy. They also say that although capitalist nations have enough government-provided goods such as highways, they do not have enough schools and museums for the general public. Such critics clearly value the political goals of socialism. They overlook the fact that despite their shortcomings, capitalist countries are economically healthier. Comparison of historical economic statistics—such as GDP, food consumption, and ownership of goods such as automobiles, for example—tells us that capitalist nations have had higher living standards, more economic freedom, and higher rates of growth. In addition, a look at emigration figures and patterns tells us that more people have moved from socialist nations to live in capitalist nations than the reverse.

Assess

Meeting Lesson Objectives

Assign Section 1 Review as homework or an in-class activity.

Evaluate

Assign the Section 1 Quiz in the TCR or use the Testmaker to develop a customized quiz.

Reteach

List countries or areas of economic activity and ask volunteers to explain how business might operate in each.

Enrich

Have students list the economic growth rates of 20 to 50 countries and compare lists.

Close

Discuss the benefits and drawbacks of socialism and capitaism. Ask students to explain the appeal of each model to some people.

SECTION 1 REVIEW

Understanding Vocabulary

Define three *P*'s, private property rights, price system, communism, proletariat, democratic socialism, authoritarian socialism.

Reviewing Objectives

1. What are the key characteristics of pure market capitalism?

2. What are the key characteristics of pure socialism?

3. What were the major steps in the development of socialism?

4. How does planning under socialism differ from planning under capitalism?

5. What are the benefits of capitalism?

Section 1 Review Answers

Understanding Vocabulary
three *Ps* (p. 482), **private property rights** (p. 482), **price system** (p. 482), **communism** (p. 484), **proletariat** (p. 484), **democratic socialism** (p. 484), **authoritarian socialism** (p. 484)

Reviewing Objectives
1. private property; price system;
   free movement of resources; rewards/losses to risk takers; decentralized decision making
2. prices, economic decisions set by state; state-owned production factors controlled movement of resources; no individual risk taking; taxation to redistribute income
3. grew out of protests against Industrial Revolution; split: democratic favoring democracy; authoritarian advocating revolution
4. centralized under socialism, decentralizd under capitalsm
5. personal freedom, rewards, market efficiency

Teach

Point out to students that an ability to understand economic news, including an ability to interpret information and editorials, can help them understand world events and make judgments about the economies of countries worldwide. Then use this activity to guide students through the characteristics of news articles and editorials.

Ask students to study the two paragraphs, identify the facts and opinions, and explain how they identified them. Then ask students to identify the background information from Chapter 20 that would help them understand the article.

Additional Practice

Have students complete Reinforcing Skills 20 in the TCR.

LEARNING ECONOMIC SKILLS
Understanding Economic News

Newspapers and magazines are good sources of economic news. Understanding economic news requires the ability to interpret information. You can do this if you know the background of the news and look for the five *W*'s and one *H* of news articles.

Knowing the Background or Context of Economic News

Economic news can be better understood when the reader knows some of the background to the news. Sometimes the news article gives the reader this background. Other times the writer assumes that the reader knows the context. Look at the news article in **Figure A**. Knowing something about China's changing economy would help you understand the article.

Note that there are two types of economic news articles: strictly news and editorials. While a news story should be factual or descriptive and simply inform, an editorial is meant to persuade the reader about a point of view.

The Five *W*'s and One *H* of News Articles

The most important information in a news article is usually at the beginning. Look for the who, what, where, and when in the opening paragraphs. The rest of the article often describes the why and how.

Practicing the Skill

Study the headlines from 1989 in **Figure B**. What background should the reader know to best understand the news articles that would accompany these headlines?

Figure A

China: The Next Great Economy?

If current trends continue, China may be the world's next great economy. This is the conclusion of a new report from the International Institute for Management Development.

China's economic growth leaped ahead in the 1980s, when some parts of the country became the fastest-growing regions of the world.

Figure B

Soviet '88 Economic Report Gloomy

Sweden to Allow More Foreign Investment

Soviets to Receive U.S.-Subsidized Wheat

Communists Lose 19 of 23 Cabinet Posts in Poland

Hungarian Communist Party Renounces Marxism

Berlin Wall Opens

Poland Announces Privatization Plans

486

Answers to Practicing the Skill

Student answers may vary but should suggest the need to know political and economic situations behind events.

SECTION 2 Changing Authoritarian Socialism—The Case of China

SECTION 2 FOCUS

Terms to Know five-year plans, special economic zones

Objectives *After reading this section, you should be able to:*

1. Explain how the Chinese economic system developed following World War II.
2. Describe the benefits of special economic zones in the People's Republic of China.

Economic Change in the People's Republic

The People's Republic of China remains the largest nation that has some form of command socialism. A growing geographic area of modern-day China, however, has an economic system that is much closer to that of the United States. See Figure 20.6.

Development of China's Economic System

The communists won China's civil war following World War II. The new government started an economic system based on so-called **five-year plans.** The first such five-year plan, implemented in 1953, failed to fully meet expectations. Starting in the mid-1950s, the Chinese began to alter their strict centralized planning. In 1958 they reformed their system to allow decision-making powers for local governments rather than only from the central government. The national planning system was transformed into a regional planning system. The 1958 reforms did not transform the Chinese economy, however, because it was still not governed by capitalism's three *P*'s—prices, profits, and private property. Economic conditions worsened after 1958.

**Figure 20.6
The Shift to a Free Market**

China—after the failure of command economies throughout the world—began to allow limited free enterprise. ▼

Chapter 20 Converging Economic Systems **487**

Focus

Overview

See the student page for section objectives.

Section 2 explains or describes: how the Chinese economic system developed after World War II; the Chinese five-year plans implemented in the 1950s; the creation of special economic zones in China; and why those zones thrive.

Bellringer

Before presenting the lesson, display Focus Activity Transparency 90 or copy the material on the chalkboard and assign the Focus Activity Sheet.

Motivational Activity

Have students write on a sheet of paper the benefits and differences between owning something and using it. Then explain that this section will examine how the benefits of personal responsibility have led China to establish special economic zones where capitalism flourishes.

Preteaching Vocabulary

List for students events in China that this section describes. Ask them to identify these events as related to a five-year plan, special economic zones, or both.

Classroom Resources for Section 2

- Reproducible Lesson Plan 20.2
- Focus Activity Transparency 90
- Focus Activity Sheet 90
- Free Enterprise Activity 21
- Guided Reading Activity 20.2
- Section Quiz 20.2
- Spanish Section Quiz 20.2
- Testmaker

Guided Practice

L2 Role Playing Organize the class into two groups and assign one half the role of state-run facility manager and the other half the role of private firm manager. Have students brainstorm the pros and cons of their positions. Then have them take turns interviewing one another in order to write articles on the work life of each type of manager.

Visual Instruction

Have students study Figure 20.7 and also a political map of China. Ask them to pinpoint possible locations for additional special economic zones and explain why the locations they chose might be successful.

GLOBAL ECONOMICS

China ranks among the top 10 world producers of goods and services, yet its per capita production is lower than that of most countries around the world. For this reason, economists consider China a developing economy.

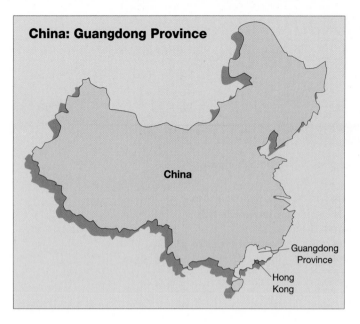
China: Guangdong Province

China

Guangdong Province

Hong Kong

Figure 20.7 ▲ The Return of Capitalism
Guangdong Province in southern China was the site of the rebirth of free enterprise in the nation. In 1997 the capitalist enclave of Hong Kong will rejoin the nation of China.

In 1978 Chinese leaders designed a reform to motivate individuals to work harder. Private individuals were permitted to rent land for up to 15 years. Each peasant household became responsible for its own plot of land. Whatever it produced in excess of a minimum amount the state required remained the property of the household. The results were impressive. Between 1979 and 1984, overall farm productivity increased dramatically.

Another set of reforms and a restructuring of the economy occurred in the mid-1980s. These reforms are continuing today. Managers in state-owned businesses are allowed much more decision-making power than before. They can set production according to market demand after they fulfill state production requirements. They also are allowed to sell part of their output to whomever they choose at market prices.

The problem with state-run factories is that managers have little incentive to make them run efficiently. Rather, these managers maximize the income and benefits for their workers. After all, their workers are politically important. Now, the government is shedding itself of many firms. In the early 1980s, state-run companies accounted for 70 percent of industrial production. Today it is less than 50 percent and is declining steadily.

Special Economic Zones

Beginning in 1979, the Chinese party designated certain geographic areas in the People's Republic of China as **special economic zones.** One of them is Guangdong Province, which you can see on the map in Figure 20.7.

Figure 20.8 Capitalist Investors
Signs of free enterprise abound in today's China. ▼

Meeting Special Needs

Language Comprehension Difficulty Students who have difficulty with comprehension or who have limited English proficiency may need extra time interviewing others and working quotes into their articles. Encourage these students to use a tape recorder to help them capture information they might want to use in their interviews.

◀ **Figure 20.9 Rising Living Standard**

A On a per-person basis, China's living standard is relatively low compared to that in the United States and Japan. Nonetheless, it is much higher than it was before China started on its road to capitalism in 1979.

Independent Practice

L1 Making a Time Line Have students use the information in this section to make a time line of important economic events in China.

L2 Graphing Have students graph information regarding China's economic growth, including for the years from 1949 to 1978. Ask students to trace the decreasing number of state-run companies from the early 1980s through the early 1990s and projected into the early 2000s. Have them speculate on the future population of cities in which companies are privatized.

Have students complete Guided Reading Activity 20.2 in the TCR. **LEP**

Move Toward Capitalism For the last decade and a half, this formerly command socialist region of the country has been moving toward unrestricted decentralized capitalism. Not surprisingly, the economy of the region has grown faster every year than any other place in the world.

A foreigner dropping into the city of Shenzhen, which is not far from Hong Kong, would have difficulty knowing he or she was in the People's Republic of China. There are McDonald's restaurants, business executives with portable phones and pagers, advertisements for Levi's, Seven UP, Heinz, and Head & Shoulders shampoo everywhere. See Figure 20.8.

There is a stock market and an active property market. The population of Shenzhen has grown from 50,000 in 1980 to more than 200,000 today. All these changes have affected the Chinese people. See Figure 20.9.

Spread of Capitalism Outside Guangdong Province, China is moving more slowly toward a market economy. In the summer of 1992, for example, the government announced that it would no longer use state-controlled pricing of raw materials. At the beginning of the 1990s, the government had al-

ready started phasing out its below-market prices for electricity, coal, iron, steel, oil, and telecommunications. Further, the government has continued to sell parts of its state-owned firms to private individuals.

Since 1979 when special economic zones were started, China's annual rate of economic growth—the increase in total national output per year—has averaged between 9 and 10 percent each year as shown in **Figure 20.10** (page 490).

B Workers at a modern plant earn much higher wages than they did a few years ago. ▼

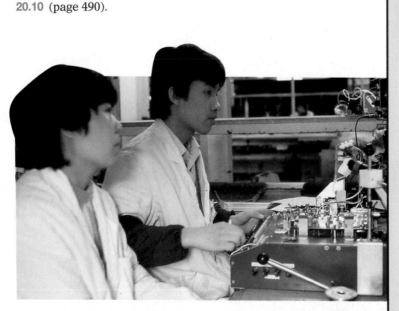

DID YOU KNOW

The birthplace of Mao Zedong, the leader of the Chinese revolution, once received up to 60,000 visitors a day. Today large numbers of Chinese travel there to commemorate the egalitarian values of Chinese socialism when Mao lived.

Chapter 20 Converging Economic Systems **489**

Cooperative Learning

Have students work in small groups to develop plans for a new business in China. Have them describe the business, tell why it might be successful there, and outline ways in which they would adapt their production and marketing plans to fit into Chinese cul-

ture. Remind students that their plans would have to be accepted by the Chinese government. Have them, therefore, include in their plans an explanation of ways in which the new business would help the Chinese people or economy.

Assess

Meeting Lesson Objectives

Assign Section 2 Review as homework or an in-class activity. Each question in the Review addresses the corresponding numbered objective in the Section Focus.

Evaluate

Assign the Section 2 Quiz in the TCR or use the Testmaker to develop a customized quiz.

Reteach

Have students work together to develop a list of products and services in China that are now subject to market prices. Ask students to speculate on the kinds of production that might be privatized next.

Enrich

Have interested students research and report on social and political events that led to the adoption of a socialist system in China.

Close

Discuss with students how the special economic zones created in China would affect the economy of the entire country and the world at large.

**Figure 20.10
Growth of People's Republic of China's Economy, 1979–1992**
Since opening special economic zones in 1979, China's economic growth rate has generally been impressive. ▶

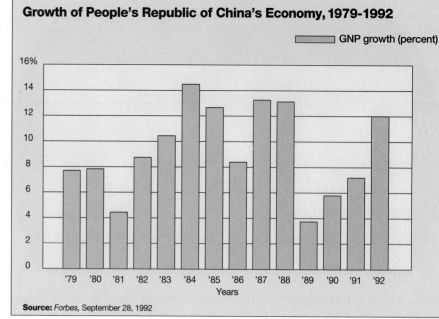

Growth of People's Republic of China's Economy, 1979-1992

Source: *Forbes,* September 28, 1992

Prospects for the Future Not surprisingly, most of China's economic growth has been in the non-state sector, which includes private enterprises and foreign-invested businesses. Government leaders now believe that the state-run sector of manufacturing will account for only 25 percent of business volume in the year 2000—down from its current 50 percent today. The future in China looks much brighter than it does in other former socialist countries, such as Russia and countries of eastern Europe.

SECTION 2 REVIEW

Understanding Vocabulary
Define five-year plans, special economic zones.

Reviewing Objectives
1. The communist Chinese based their economic system on what concepts immediately following World War II?

2. What has been the economic growth rate in special economic zones in the People's Republic of China?

Section 2 Review Answers

Understanding Vocabulary
five-year plans (p. 487), **special economic zones** (p. 488)

Reviewing Objectives
1. The communist Chinese based their system on the concepts of centralized planning.

2. The economic growth rate in China since special economic zones were created has averaged between 9 and 10 percent per year.

Personal Perspective

Karl Marx on Communism

- 1818–1883
- born in Germany and educated in Bonn and Berlin
- deeply influenced by philosopher George Hegel
- published *The Communist Manifesto* with Friedrich Engels (1848) and *Das Kapital* (1867)

In the following excerpt from *The Communist Manifesto*, Karl Marx answers some questions most frequently asked of Communists: "Who are the Communists and what is their basic theory?"

The Communists do not form a separate party opposed to other working-class parties.

They have no interests separate and apart from those of the proletariat as a whole.

They do not set up any sectarian principles of their own, by which to shape and mold the proletarian movement.

. . . The immediate aim of the Communists is the same as that of all the other proletarian parties: formation of the proletariat into a class, overthrow of the bourgeois supremacy, conquest of political power by the proletariat.

. . . In this sense, the theory of the Communists may be summed up in the single phrase: Abolition of private property. . . .

Property, in its present form, is based on the antagonism of capital and wage labor.

. . . It has been objected that upon the abolition of private property all work will cease, and universal laziness will overtake us.

According to this, bourgeois society ought long ago to have gone to the dogs through sheer idleness; for those of its members who work, acquire nothing, and those who acquire anything, do not work. The whole of this objection is but another expression of the tautology [needless repetition of an idea]: *that there can no longer be any wage labor when there is no longer any capital.*

. . . The workingmen have no country. We cannot take from them what they have not got. Since the proletariat must first of all acquire political supremacy, must rise to be the leading class of the nation, must constitute itself the nation, it is, so far, itself national, though not in the bourgeois sense of the word.

National differences and antagonisms between peoples are daily vanishing, owing to the development of the bourgeoisie, to freedom of commerce, to the world market, to uniformity in the mode of production and in the conditions of life corresponding thereto.

The supremacy of the proletariat will cause them to vanish still faster.

Checking for Understanding

1. What single phrase sums up communist theory?
2. Why was incentive to work an issue Marx had to address?
3. What did Marx mean when he wrote "The workingmen have no country"?

Answers to Checking for Understanding

1. abolition of private property
2. Marx had to address the issue of incentive to work because some believed that when private property was abolished "all work would cease and universal laziness will overtake us."
3. He meant that working people have little or no political power. They do not control the countries in which they live.

Background

Karl Marx was a social philosopher as well as a thinker on economic issues. He was critical of capitalist employers for their emphasis on profit and developed a plan for a classless society, which he called communism.

Teach

Have volunteers read aloud the quoted excerpts from *The Communist Manifesto*. Ask students to paraphrase each excerpt to gain a better understanding of Marx's ideas. Then have them answer the questions in Checking for Understanding.

You might have interested students read portions of *Das Kapital* in order to delve further into Marx's economic theories.

Focus

Overview

See the student page for section objectives.

Section 3 explains or describes: privatization of Russian and eastern European economies; economic change in Sweden and Latin America; and the effect of incentive structures on economies worldwide.

Bellringer

Before presenting the lesson, display Focus Activity Transparency 91 on the overhead projector or copy the material on the chalkboard. Assign the accompanying Focus Activity Sheet.

Motivational Activity

Ask students to complete the statement: Privatization tends to reduce government bureaucracies because ____. Have volunteers read and explain their sentence.

Preteaching Vocabulary

Ask students to write a sentence for each term, using it correctly.

SECTION **3** Nations Move Toward the Market System

SECTION 3 FOCUS

Terms to Know privatization, secondary market, welfare state

Objectives *After reading this section, you should be able to:*
1. Explain what has been happening in terms of ownership of business in Russia since privatization.
2. Describe four changes in Sweden's economy in the 1990s.
3. Indicate some of the changes in Latin American economic systems.
4. Discuss how the supply and demand model helps analyze converging economic systems.

Figure 20.11 Russian Economic Changes
Russia and the other republics within formerly centrally planned economies are now all moving at different rates toward market capitalism. One of the ways they are moving toward market capitalism is by privatizing former state industries. ▼

492

Recipe for Economic Growth—a Little More Market

Economics textbooks written 10 or 15 years ago included sections on the Soviet Union and its satellite countries in Eastern Europe. The centralized command economy lasted for 74 years in the Soviet Union, and more than 40 years in Eastern Europe. In the Soviet Union, from the revolution in 1917 until the economic and political system collapsed on Christmas Day in 1991, it consisted of five-year plans, central-planning commissions, and hundreds of other types of commissions. Today all of that is fading history, as Figure 20.11 shows.

Privatization in Russia

Privatization simply means the change from state ownership of business, land, and buildings to private ownership. The private owners can be partnerships, domestic or foreign corporations, or individuals. Sometimes workers even buy the companies in which they are working, and foreign companies have purchased formerly state-owned companies in Russia and elsewhere. Volkswagen of Germany, for example, bought the state-owned

---

Classroom Resources for Section 3

autoworks in Czechoslovakia before that nation split in two in 1993.

Resistance to Privatization When a state enterprise is sold to a private interest, disruptions can occur. In particular, workers may find themselves out of a job. One of the problems with state-owned firms is that they are inefficiently run. When private owners take over, they often modernize the equipment and streamline the production processes. Consequently they sometimes require fewer workers. Because of the possibility of increased unemployment, many sectors of the population have resisted privatization.

Some workers even demanded that old-style centralized planning be brought back to Russia. They held demonstrations against the market-capitalist reforms that Russian President Boris Yeltsin had supported. Frustrations with continued economic problems contributed to the coup, or revolt, that attempted to oust Yeltsin in the fall of 1993.

Privatization by Voucher By 1993 the Russian government had started to make good on its promise of mass privatization. At the end of 1992, each Russian citizen had received a privatization voucher with a face value of 10,000 rubles (worth about $25 then, but probably less than $10 at exchange

rates in the fall of 1993). Voucher owners could either sell them for cash to other investors, the way securities are sold in a **secondary market,** or they could use them to buy shares in the privatization of 6,000 companies scheduled to occur in 1993.

Value of Vouchers What would these vouchers buy you in terms of factories and capital? *The Economist,* a British publication, calculated that if you purchased every voucher on the secondary market in May 1993, you would have to pay $730 million. In principle, this was the price tag for obtaining ownership of roughly half of Russia's manufacturing industry!

For $730 million the most you could buy in the United States was one company like Cray Research, which builds super computers, or in Great Britain, the engineering company, Vickers. So, it would seem that for the same price, buying half of Russia's manufacturing industry would be a good deal.

Not everyone was convinced, however. Tremendous problems remain in this former Soviet republic. See Figure 20.12.

Certainly a change in the incentive structure can alter factory managers' behavior, but these changes will not necessarily happen overnight. In addition, even if a factory manages to

Figure 20.12 ▲
Challenges Facing Russian Manufacturing
In many factories, production lines work only three to four days a week. Many factories have plenty of physical capital, but it is so outdated and poorly maintained that its market value is effectively zero. In addition, a cadre of managers who have never been forced to look at "the bottom line" (profits) still run many factories.

Chapter 20 Converging Economic Systems **493**

Guided Practice

L2 Comparing and Contrasting Display two political maps of the Eastern Hemisphere, one from 1991 or earlier with the U.S.S.R. intact and a current map. Ask students to study both maps and choose two countries from the current map. Have each student develop a paragraph describing political and economic conditions in each country in 1989 and today.

L2 Debating Organize the class into two groups and ask each to research aspects of Sweden's economy that are socialist and aspects that are capitalist. Then assign a point of view to each group and have them debate whether the economy of Sweden is predominantly capitalist or socialist.

GLOBAL ECONOMICS

Socialist parties are strong or dominant in Argentina, Australia, Belgium, Canada, Denmark, France, Germany, Great Britain, Greece, India, Israel, Italy, New Zealand, Norway, Portugal, and Spain. They are also powerful in former Soviet nations and in many nations of Africa, the Middle East, and Southeast Asia.

Meeting Special Needs

Visual Disability Students with visual or spatial difficulties may have trouble interpreting political maps without help. Encourage these students to work in pairs or small groups to locate individual countries and list them on their papers. Then have students write down the economic system of the countries they listed.

Independent Practice

L3 Writing Ask students to list the benefits and drawbacks of investing in Russian privatization.

 Have students complete Guided Reading Activity 20.3 in the TCR. `LEP`

Visual Instruction

Ask students to examine the graph in Figure 20.13. Encourage them to research the principal sources of tax revenue for both nations, as well as per capita spending for education, health care, and welfare and unemployment benefits. Have volunteers report orally. Discuss their findings.

? DID YOU KNOW

Most socialists oppose communism and wish to work within the framework of various governments.

Figure 20.13 ▶ Tax Levels in Sweden and the United States, 1960–1990

Tax levels in Sweden in 1960 were about equal to those in the United States, but rose to more than 20 percentage points higher. Despite these high taxes, the Swedes enjoyed a high standard of living. ▼

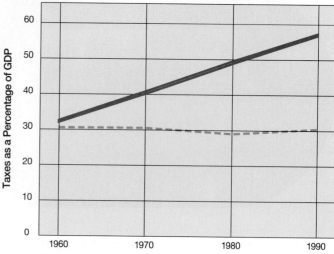

Tax Levels in Sweden and the United States, 1960-1990

Taxes as a Percentage of GDP

Sources: *Statistical Abstract of The United States, 1982, 1992* — Sweden - - - U.S.A.

produce a marketable product, sometimes the distribution system in Russia is so poor that the product cannot get to the right geographical location in the market in order to be sold. Finally, there continues to be a deep-seated suspicion of for-profit activities. Privatization will probably not lead to immediate increases in Russian output.

Changes in Sweden

Sweden has been labeled a **welfare state**—a blend of capitalism and socialism. It combines private ownership of the means of production and competitive allocation of resources with the goal of social equality for its citizens. The so-called Swedish model helped transform what was an underdeveloped country in 1870 into a modern nation with one of the highest per-capita incomes in the world a century later.

Government Expenditures and Taxes Currently government expenditures (and taxes) account for almost 60 percent of Sweden's annual economic activity. As recently as 1960, this figure was little more than 30 percent. See Figure 20.13

Swedish Welfare The Swedish government passed an employment security bill in the 1970s that almost guarantees lifelong employment. It also passed a law requiring labor union participation in company decision making. Full employment has existed for a number of years because the government took over many large industries and firms, such as steelworks. The government sector's share of employment was 20 percent in 1970, but today it is close to 35 percent.

Move Toward Free Enterprise Now Sweden has initiated changes in the model of combining capitalism with welfare socialism. In the 1990s, the government started to cut taxes and eliminate some public jobs. It also eased business regulation and approved foreign ownership of certain companies. The government ended the monopoly in both taxicabs and airlines and has plans to move further toward a market system in the future.

494 *Unit 6 The International Scene*

Cooperative Learning

Point out to students that management and labor issues differ in different countries. Have them work together in small groups to find out how the process of privatization differs in Russia, China, and Latin America. Ask students to research the labor traditions of each region and explain which traditions make privatization easy or difficult. Then have them report on the prospects for privatization in each country.

Changes in Latin America

Many nations in Latin America—especially Mexico, Venezuela, Chile, Brazil, and Argentina—have experienced high rates of growth since the mid-1980s. Though virtually all Latin American countries have economic systems that operate under market capitalism, most have had large government sectors. Since 1985, however, many government enterprises have been privatized.

Mexico is a good example as Figure 20.14 shows. Other countries in Latin America are trying to follow the Mexican model, but because of multiparty infighting, they are not having an easy time. (One party has dominated Mexico for many years.) Nonetheless, Chile has privatized its airlines, phones, utilities, and pension funds. The Argentinean government has sold state-run oil fields, waterworks, petrochemical plants, and even army housing.

Converging Economic Systems

Many of the consequences of the changes in economic systems throughout the world can be analyzed by using the method of economic analysis that you have already learned in this text. The supply and demand model helps to predict what will happen when property is privatized, markets are freed, and the lure of profits becomes legal. Remember that the differences across countries are less related to cultures, religions, creeds, and ethnic characteristics and more related to how the structure and use of incentives are changing. The model that you can use most successfully always asks the question, How will people react to changed incentives?

**Figure 20.14
Privatizing in Mexico**
In 1989 Mexico made a wholesale move to free markets. The government started to sell off its vast holdings of companies and at the same time reduced the size of the government bureaucracy. Private companies in Mexico are building toll roads and phone systems.

SECTION 3 REVIEW

Understanding Vocabulary
Define privatization, secondary market, welfare state.

Reviewing Objectives
1. What has been happening to state-owned property in Russia and in eastern Europe?
2. How has the Swedish economy been changing?
3. How have Latin American economies been changing in recent years?
4. What economic model helps predict what will happen as economies shift from command to market systems?

Assess

Meeting Lesson Objectives
Assign Section 3 Review as homework or an in-class activity. Each question in the Review addresses the corresponding numbered objective in the Section Focus.

Evaluate
Assign the Section 3 Quiz in the TCR or use the Testmaker to develop a customized quiz.
Assign the Chapter 20 Test Form A or Form B or use the Testmaker to develop a customized test.

Reteach
Have students discuss the shift in values that privatization brings.
Have students complete Reteaching Activity 20 in the TCR.

Enrich
Have students report on movements toward market capitalism in a former Soviet republic.
Have students complete Enrichment Activity 20 in the TCR.

Close

Discuss with students how economic systems are moving together.

Section 3 Review Answers
Understanding Vocabulary
privatization (p. 492), **secondary market** (p. 493), **welfare state** (p. 494)
Reviewing Objectives
1. State-owned property in Russia and eastern Europe is being privatized.
2. The Swedish economy has been reducing taxes, eliminating some public jobs, easing regulation, approving foreign ownership of companies, ending transport monopolies, and planning moves toward market economy.
3. Latin American economies have been privatizing in recent years and experiencing higher rates of growth.
4. the supply and demand model

Teach

Explain to students that general interest news magazines such as *Newsweek* often examine international news and economic trends that are important for the people of the United States.

Have students use the information in the feature to predict economic and social changes that might occur in China and Russia over the next 10 years. Ask them to write descriptions of a major city in Russia and a major city in China about 10 years from now.

Readings in Economics

NEWSWEEK   APRIL 12, 1993

WHY CHINA DOES IT BETTER

by Joe Klein

As Russia unravels, China booms....

What have the Chinese done right that the Russians have done wrong?

... It might be argued that there have been three major factors in China's economic surge, two of which the Russians can't replicate. Obviously, Deng Xiaoping's [Chinese leader's] transition model was more sophisticated than anything the Russians have tried. Deng gradually liberated the economy, and prices—first encouraging farmers to grow for profit, then inviting foreign investment in rudimentary light industries (toys, shoes, clothing), which created the explosive growth in provinces like Guangdong that is now spreading inland....

But even if Boris Yeltsin [Russian leader] had followed Deng's model, there are two other factors that he couldn't have matched. For one thing, the Chinese seem to have an entrepreneurial edge. Their farmers welcomed the chance to make a profit. Their emerging middle class rushed to buy stocks when the Shenzhen exchange opened (they even rioted last year trying to gain access). Most Russians, by contrast, have reacted to liberalization with their distinctive mixture of skepticism and pessimism....

In much of Southeast Asia, ethnic Chinese already run the show—and that is the third, and perhaps most significant, factor at work here: the power and pride of the Chinese diaspora [people scattered outside their homelands]. There are an estimated 55 million Chinese living outside the People's Republic. They include a disproportionate number of successful businessmen who have now decided that it's safe to invest on the mainland.... The diasporans are ... returning home to sweep their ancestors' graves. They are the entrepreneurial heart of a Greater China that seems destined to become an economic, cultural—and perhaps military—superpower in the next century.

• THINK ABOUT IT •

1. What two economies, moving toward market systems, are contrasted in this article?

2. What three factors account for China's relative success in beginning to develop a market system?

Answers to Think About It

1. the economies of Russia and China

2. gradual liberation of the economy, beginning with farmers; the desire of the Chinese to make a profit; and the 55 million Chinese outside China, including business people willing to invest there

20 Highlights

Use the Chapter 20 Highlights to preview, review, condense, or reteach the chapter. A Spanish Chapter Highlights is available in the Spanish Handbook.

Section 1

Comparing Capitalism and Socialism

Key Terms
three *P*'s (p. 482)
private property rights
(p. 482)
price system (p. 482)
communism (p. 484)
proletariat (p. 484)
democratic socialism
(p. 484)
authoritarian socialism
(p. 484)

Summary
Pure market capitalism can be described on the basis of the three *P*'s—prices, profits, and private property. Private property rights exist and are legal; prices are allowed to seek their own level as determined by supply and demand; resources move to where the highest profits are made. In pure socialism, most prices are set by the state, the major factors of production are owned by the state, economic decisions are made by the state through central-planning agencies, and the movement of resources is strictly controlled. Planning under capitalism is decentralized. Capitalism offers personal freedom and rewards individual initiative.

Preview/Review

After students read the Chapter 20 Highlights, have them complete Economics Vocabulary Activity 20 in the TCR. Spanish Vocabulary Activities are also available in the Spanish Resource Binder.

Vocabulary Software reinforces the economic terms used in Chapter 20.

Section 2

Changing Authoritarian Socialism–The Case of China

Key Terms
five-year plans (p. 487)
special economic zones
(p. 488)

Summary
After World War II, the Chinese instituted a series of five-year plans, none of which worked very well. Starting in 1979, special economic zones were designated. The rates of economic growth in these special economic zones have been extremely high.

Condense

Have students listen to Chapter 20 on the Audiocassettes in the TCR. A 1-page written activity and 1-page test accompany this material. These materials are also available in Spanish.

Reteach

Have students complete Reteaching Activity 20 in the TCR. Spanish Reteaching Activities are also available.

Section 3

Nations Move Toward the Market System

Key Terms
privatization (p. 492)
secondary market (p. 493)
welfare state (p. 494)

Summary
The trend in Russia, in the other former Soviet republics, and in eastern Europe, is toward increased privatization. Sweden, a welfare state for many years, has also moved recently toward privatization and less welfare. Led by Mexico's changes in the mid-1980s, an increasingly large number of countries in Latin America are privatizing government-owned companies.

Chapter 20 Converging Economic Systems **497**

 VIDEODISC

Nightly Business Report
Economics in Action
Use "Comparative Economic Systems" on Disc 2, Side B, Video 26.

Search 6509, Play to 12721

Chapter 20
REVIEW

ANSWERS

Identifying Key Terms
1. private property rights

2. price system
3. five-year plans
4. privatization
5. secondary market
Students' paragraphs will
vary but should use each of
the given vocabulary terms
in a meaningful way.

Recalling Facts and Ideas
Section 1
1. Supply and demand
   determine prices.
2. because prices are
   allowed to seek their own
   level in response to supply and demand
3. No, the state takes the
   risks, and the citizens
   pay collectively for risks
   that fail.
4. communism

Section 2
5. They have created
   extraordinary economic
   growth and large centers
   of population and ac-
   quainted parts of China
   with Western goods and
   services.
6. The economy of China as
   a whole has grown by 9 to
   10 percent each year
   since the start of economic reforms in 1979.

Section 3
7. Russia and the countries
   of eastern Europe are
   privatizing many industries and adopting capitalism.
8. because it combines private ownership of the
   means of production with
   competitive allocation of
   resources to meet a goal
   of social equality for its
   citizens
9. Many nations are aban-
   doning socialism and
   moving toward capital-
   ism.

498

Identifying Key Terms

Use terms from the following list to fill in the
blanks in the paragraph below.

private property   five-year plans (p. 487)
  rights (p. 482)   privatization (p. 492)
price system (p. 482)   secondary market (p. 493)

In pure market capitalism, __(1)__ are guaranteed by the government. Pure market capitalism
can be described as a __(2)__ because supply and
demand determine prices. After World War II,
the Chinese government instituted several __(3)__.
In the former Soviet Union and in eastern Europe (as well as in parts of China), __(4)__ is occurring at a rapid pace. There is even a __(5)__ for
the buying and selling of shares of newly privatized companies.

Write a paragraph on different types of socialism using the following words:

communism (p. 484)
proletariat (p. 484)
democratic socialism (p. 484)
authoritarian socialism (p. 484)
welfare state (p. 494)

Recalling Facts and Ideas

Section 1
1. What is the role of supply and demand in
   pure market capitalism?
2. Why do we call pure capitalism a price
   system?
3. Can individuals take business risks under
   pure socialism? Explain.
4. What term did Karl Marx apply to his ideal
   society?

Section 2
5. How have special economic zones changed
   parts of the People's Republic of China?
6. In what way can you tell that capitalism has
   benefited the People's Republic of China?

Section 3
7. Describe the main economic change that is
   occurring in the former Soviet Union and in
   eastern Europe.
8. Why has Sweden been labeled a welfare
   state?
9. In what way have the world's economic systems converged?

Critical Thinking

Section 1
Making Comparisons Compare the type of planning used in a decentralized capitalist system
with the type of planning used in a centralized
command socialist system.

Section 2
Determining Cause and Effect Why do you
think Guangdong Province has had such a high
economic rate of growth compared to the rest of
the People's Republic of China?

Section 3
Making Inferences What is the relationship between privatization and decentralization of an
economy?

Applying Economic Concepts

The Importance of Profits In many economies
through the years, profits have been given "bad

Critical Thinking
Section 1
In a decentralized capitalist system, private
firms, individuals, and elected government representatives undertake planning, which is built
around relative prices. The market system
coordinates "the plan." In a socialist command
system, central planners plan on behalf of
everyone, using criteria not fully expressed by
prices.
Section 2
Answers will vary but may note the population
density, proximity to the market economy of
Hong Kong, and the concentration of foreign
investments in this area.
Section 3
Decentralization is an automatic consequence
of privatization.

press." Specifically, journalists and politicians as well as laypersons have often decried profits as "evil." Yet economic theory tells us that profits are necessary as a type of signal in our economic system. Make a list of what profits signal in our economy and the results of those signals. Then list some of the things that might happen if profits were outlawed, or at least restricted severely.

- How fast it is being privatized
- The benefits of privatization
- The problems associated with privatization

Your group should present a conclusion about privatization in its part of the world. Are the problems of privatization more than outweighed by the benefits?

Chapter Projects

1. **Individual Project** Today the United States is not a pure market capitalist economy. There are many elements of government planning and control. Write down as complete a list as you can of those parts of our American economic system that do *not* follow the five key attributes of pure market capitalism listed on page 482. For example, in the United States not just anyone could start a new electric utility company and offer electricity for sale. The government regulates who can offer electricity and, indeed, maintains a monopoly for the one electric utility company in each area.
2. **Cooperative Learning Project** In much of the world, government is selling off government-owned businesses and property. The speed of privatization in each country is different, though. Working in groups of four, look at privatization in different parts of the world. These areas should include:
   - Russia
   - The other republics of the former Soviet Union
   - Eastern Europe
   - The European Community (Union)
   - Latin America
   - People's Republic of China

   The members of each group should look for magazine and newspaper articles on privatization in their designated area of the world. Each person should attempt to find out at least the following:
   - How much of the country's government-owned businesses and property is being privatized

Reviewing Skills

Understanding Economic News
The Five *W*'s and one *H* Look at the following economic news article. List four of the five *W*'s.

> President Clinton signed his hard-won budget-reconciliation bill ... into law at a White House ceremony Aug. 10, just four days after it squeaked through the Senate with the tiebreaking vote of Vice President Al Gore. But back on Capitol Hill, members were already girding for another round of budget fights, and there was talk of undoing some of what Clinton had just signed.
>
> —*Congressional Quarterly*, August 14, 1993

Writing About Economics
Comparative Writing Write a letter to a pen pal in Sweden. Using information about prices from Your Economics Journal, explain how the economic system in the United States is primarily a free-market system, but not entirely so.

499

Applying Economic Concepts
Answers will vary but should demonstrate an awareness that profits signal business efficiency and how incentives spur productivity. Responses may differ about who should control profits and their use.

Chapter Projects
1. Review students' lists and have them organize items by type of good or service and the missing characteristics of pure market capitalism.
2. Have students develop a book with chapters on the countries they have researched. Chapters should include photos, drawings, graphs or charts, and written summary.

Reviewing Skills
Who: President Clinton; what: signed budget-reconciliation bill; when: August 10, 1993; where: White House

Writing About Economics
Students' letters should include prices and explain how supply and demand influence them. Students should also explain how government planning and regulation combine with market capitalism.

BONUS QUESTION
The following bonus question may be written on the chalkboard when students take the chapter test.
Q: How might the growth of market capitalism affect the world economy?
A: It should stimulate economic growth.

Focus

The North American Free Trade Agreement (NAFTA) became a major topic of debate in Congress and in numerous public forums in late 1993. Point out to students that while this was the most recent round of public discussion of free trade in the United States, the underlying issues of free trade and protectionism have inspired strong controversies on several occasions in the last 200 years. Have students read the arguments for and against free trade.

Teach

L1 Cartoons Have each student draw a cartoon that supports or opposes some aspects of free trade as presented in the Point/Counterpoint.

L2 Journalism Ask students to write a national magazine editorial that supports either a free-trade or a protectionist position with regard to a particular industry such as automobile manufacturing or consumer electronics. The editorials should address the issues of what effect the policy advocated will have on the domestic industry they select.

Issue: Does Free Trade Help or Hurt Americans?

Although most economists favor free trade, the popular wisdom today is that free trade steals American jobs and helps other countries at the expense of the United States. In particular, many people feel that we import too much from Japan, while Japan restricts American imports. They feel that only through protectionism (more tariffs and quotas) or managed trade (asking that a minimum percentage of Japans's industrial needs will be purchased from American suppliers) can the United States lower its trade deficit and Japanese trade surplus. Those in favor of free trade feel just as firmly that more protectionism or managed trade will hurt the United States as much as any other country.

PRO Marc Levinson writes in *Newsweek* that, even though some jobs disappear as a result of free trade, this is simply a result of economic change. More new jobs will be created to replace the old ones, and imports from free trade lead to greater efficiency and actually keep down the inflation rate. He says industries sheltered from foreign competition have the greatest price rises.

Economist Alan Binder agrees that protectionism only leads to "job swapping" — protecting jobs in some industries while destroying jobs in others. He argues that the cost of saving jobs is extremely high and that it is doubtful that any jobs are actually saved in the long run. Finally, Martin B. Zuckerman writes in *U.S. News and World Report* that protecting American jobs is actually putting the United States last, not first:

America-first protectionists never work through to the logical end of their policies; if they did, America would come last. Yes, some jobs may be saved by keeping out a cheaper foreign product. But it does not end there. Take steel. Some 17,000 jobs have been saved through restrictions on imports. But stop cheering. According to the Center for the Study of American Business, the more expensive domestic steel has cost an extra $150,000 for every single job saved. That higher cost has been paid by steel users not simply in cash but also in work lost. In fact, 54,200 jobs were lost in other industries to save the 17,000 in steel. Another example is textiles and apparel. Tariffs are adding about $20 billion annually to consumer bills, leaving less to spend on the output of other workers.

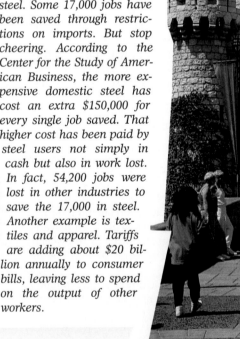

Counterpoint

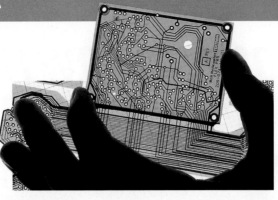

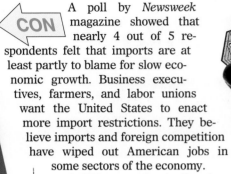

CON A poll by *Newsweek* magazine showed that nearly 4 out of 5 respondents felt that imports are at least partly to blame for slow economic growth. Business executives, farmers, and labor unions want the United States to enact more import restrictions. They believe imports and foreign competition have wiped out American jobs in some sectors of the economy.

A 1992 survey by the *Los Angeles Times* found that 70 percent of respondents would support protectionist measures against Japan, and 41 percent selected "tightening restrictions on trade with Japan" as the best way to stimulate the U.S. economy. In presenting the results of this poll, staff writer Karl Schoenberger presents a typical view of those against free trade:

Another respondent . . . said it's not the fault of the Japanese that they have prospered while America's economy declined. The blame, he said, should be placed on the U.S. Government, which "is responsible for the trade agreements we make with foreign governments and should make sure we get treated fairly.

"I don't believe we have a fair deal in our trade with Japan, because we're open to their products and they're closed to ours." . . . "I believe in an eye for an eye, and it's not Japan's fault that the American government doesn't protect our interests."

Katherine Newman writes in *Newsweek* about the future and places the blame on United States trade policies:

The international economy is less an opportunity than a threat. It's not just that imports have put their jobs at risk. Their unhappiness is broader . . . and the blame is pinned squarely on what is perceived to be America's diminished position in the world economy.

Here, voices rise in criticism of our international competitors, and our politicians. International competition means endless worries about future living standards.

Exploring the Issue

Reviewing Facts
❶ Why does it seem that economists and non-economists disagree over the free trade issue?

Critical Thinking
Analyzing Information
❷ If free trade means that some jobs are lost, while others are created, why should anyone be unhappy?

L3 **Researching and Analyzing** Organize students into groups to investigate the major positions in the debate on NAFTA. Each group should take responsibility for exploring a set of positions, such as those of the political parties, big businesses, smaller businesses, organized labor, the major media, and environmental organizations. In addition, each group should use its research to suggest reasons for the particular positions taken. Have students present their findings orally and discuss the similarities and differences among the positions.

Assess

Have students answer the Exploring the Issues questions.

Close

Have students discuss how they think the passage of NAFTA might affect them. Make sure they address matters such as the availability of consumer goods, the job market, and any other issues about which they may be concerned (for example, relations with Canada or conditions in Mexico). The students should cite facts to back up their opinions.

Answers to Exploring the Issues
Reviewing Facts
1. Most economists believe that free trade results in an overall increase in jobs, greater efficiency, and decreased inflation. Most other people, in contrast, hold that free trade, at least with some countries, can slow economic growth and increase unemployment.

Critical Thinking
2. At the least, those who lose their jobs, whose wages decline, or whose businesses fail as a result of increased competition from abroad may not be happy.

CHAPTER 21
ECONOMIC GROWTH IN DEVELOPING NATIONS

CHAPTER ORGANIZER

Daily Objectives	Special Features	Classroom Resources

Section 1 Characteristics of Developing Nations
- **Indicate** about how many developed and developing nations exist in the world.
- **List** five characteristics of developing nations
- **List** the Four Tigers.

Focus on Free Enterprise:
Case Study, The Chicago Pizza Pie Factory, p. 508

- Reproducible Lesson Plan 21.1
- *NBR* Video 28 and Video Still 3
- Focus Activity Transparency 92
- Guided Reading Activity 21.1
- Cooperative Learning Activity 21
- Primary and Secondary Source Readings 21
- Section Quiz 21.1
- Testmaker

Section 2 The Process of Economic Development
- **Describe** two major outside sources for financing economic development.
- **Identify** five nations that supply foreign aid and two agencies through which aid is given.
- **List** four reasons for giving foreign aid.

Learning Economic Skills:
Recognizing Trends, p. 516

- Reproducible Lesson Plan 21.2
- Focus Activity Transparency 93
- Focus Activity Sheet 93
- Guided Reading Activity 21.2
- Free Enterprise Activity 21
- Consumer Application Activity 21
- Section Quiz 21.2
- Reinforcing Skills 21

Section 3 Obstacles to Growth in Developing Nations
- **List** some of the obstacles to economic growth in developing nations.
- **Explain** why Indonesia failed to experience rapid economic growth.

Personal Perspective:
Thomas Malthus on Overpopulation, p. 521

- Reproducible Lesson Plan 21.3
- Focus Activity Transparency 94
- Focus Activity Sheet 94
- Guided Reading Activity 21.3
- Section Quiz 21.3
- Spanish Section Quiz 21.3

Section 4 Industrialization and the Future
- **Explain** four problems associated with rapid industrialization in developing nations.
- **Explain** the importance of property rights for economic development.
- **List** three factors besides poverty that influence economic development.
- **Describe** the relationship between information flows and economic cooperation.

News Clip:
"Is Singapore a Model for the West?" *Time*, p. 526

- Reproducible Lesson Plan 21.4
- *NBR* Video 30
- Focus Activity Transparency 95
- Focus Activity Sheet 95
- Guided Reading Activity 21.4
- Mathematics Practice for Economics 27
- Performance Assessment Activity 27
- Section Quiz 21.4
- Spanish Section Quiz 21.4
- Enrichment Activity

 OUT OF TIME? If time does not permit teaching this chapter, you may use the Chapter 21 Highlights and the Audiocassettes that include a 1-page activity and a 1-page test.

Chapter 21 Review and Evaluation

Special Features

Chapter 21 Highlights, p. 527
Chapter 21 Review, pp. 528–529

Classroom Resources

- Chapter 21 Test Forms A and B
- Economics Vocabulary Activity 21
- Spanish Economics Vocabulary Activity 21

- Audiocassette 21
- Spanish Audiocassette 21
- Reteaching Activity 21
- Spanish Reteaching Activity 21

Key to Ability Levels

Teaching strategies have been coded for varying learning styles and abilities.

L1 Level 1 activities are **basic** activities and should be within the ability range of all students.

L2 Level 2 activities are **average** activities designed for the ability range of average to above-average students.

L3 Level 3 activities are **challenging** activities designed for the ability range of above-average students.

LEP activities should be within the ability range of **Limited English Proficiency** students.

Performance Assessment

The following chapter project may be assigned at the beginning of the chapter and used for performance assessment. See page T12 for additional Performance Assessment information.

Researching Foreign Policies Have students clip news articles about current United States foreign aid from newspapers and newsmagazines. Have students assemble their clippings on a bulletin board divided into three categories: economic assistance, technical assistance, and military assistance. Ask students to use the information on the bulletin board to write a report explaining United States foreign aid policies. Students might include charts, graphs, and photos to accompany their reports.

Additional Resources

Readings for the Student

Rostow, Walter. *Rich Countries and Poor Countries: Reflections from the Past—Lessons for the Future.* Boulder, Col.: Westview, 1987.

Todaro, Michael P. *Economic Development in the Third World.* White Plains, N.Y.: Longman, 1989.

Readings for the Teacher

Dell, Sidney. *International Development Policies: Perspectives for Industrial Countries.* Durham, N.C.: Duke University Press, 1991.

Sorensen, George. *Democracy, Dictatorship, and Development.* New York: St. Martin's Press, 1991.

Williams, Marc. *Third World Cooperation.* New York: St. Martin's Press, 1991.

Multimedia Materials

The Giant and the Dwarf: India's Green Revolution. Filmstrip. Social Studies School Service. P.O. Box 802, Culver City, CA 90232-0802

Limits (Social Studies Volume 1). Computer software. Simulation. Apple. MECC, 3490 Lexington Avenue, North, St. Paul, MN 55126. Students can alter present trends in world economy.

Rice Farming. Computer software. Simulation. Apple. Social Studies School Service. P.O. Box 802, Culver City, CA 90232-0802

Chapter Overview

The problems Americans face are those associated with being relatively rich—unemployment and pollution. Developing nations, however, struggle with life-threatening problems such as widespread poverty and hunger. In many cases, developing nations must deal with keeping their people alive. Chapter 21 explains or describes: the criteria used to define a nation as *developing;* the choices these nations have available for financing their economic development; the obstacles these nations face and their need for balanced growth; and the possible future for developing nations.

 VIDEODISC

Nightly Business Report

Economics in Action
Use "Economic Growth in Developing Nations" on Disc 2, Side B, Video 28.

Search 19182, Play to 26079

CHAPTER

21 ECONOMIC GROWTH IN DEVELOPING NATIONS

What will be the benefits of building this dam in Brazil?

How much does a project like this cost?

Who is paying for this construction project?

Answering Economic Questions

The questions in the above illustration are designed to lead into the main concepts in Chapter 21. The questions will help students focus on how construction and other types of projects are financed in developing nations. The questions will also help students think about the concept of foreign aid and their feelings about it. Have students discuss the questions and explain whether they think foreign aid is beneficial or detrimental both for the nation giving it and the one receiving it.

Should the United States increase foreign aid for projects like this?

Who is employed on this project?

Your Economics Journal

Keep track of all the foreign countries that you read about or hear mentioned on the radio or on TV. Collect clippings and make a list of these countries. After the name of each country, indicate whether you think it is a developing country.

503

Connecting to Past Learning

Review with students the kinds of economic systems (*capitalism, socialism, traditional, mixed*). Remind them that socialism plays an important role in economically developing countries. Tell them Chapter 21 discusses obstacles facing developing economies and explains how governments can affect development.

Applying Economics

Ask students whether they favor giving aid to foreign nations. Then have them discuss criteria nations should meet to qualify for aid, the kind of aid they favor giving, and why. Tell students that Chapter 21 discusses the major kinds of foreign aid.

EXTRA CREDIT PROJECT

Have students research organizations such as the Ford Foundation, International Finance Corporation (IFC), and agencies of the United Nations that offer loans or grants to economically developing nations. Have students do short reports with graphs of trends in the assistance offered. Students might combine their work into a pamphlet entitled *International Organizations and Economic Development*.

PERFORMANCE ASSESSMENT

Refer to page 502 for "Researching Foreign Policies," a Performance Assessment Activity for this chapter.

Economic Portfolio

Refer students to the information in **Your Economics Journal**. Ask students to record their countries in a two-column table labeled Developed Economies and Developing Economies. Ask students to indicate what factors they used to decide whether a country had a developed economy or a developing economy.

Focus

Overview

See the student page for section objectives.

Section 1 explains or describes developed and developing nations and the factors economists use to measure a nation's prosperity.

Bellringer

Before presenting the lesson, display Focus Activity Transparency 92 on the overhead projector or copy the material on the chalkboard. Assign the accompanying Focus Activity Sheet.

Motivational Activity

Write Germany, United States, and Great Britain in one column and India, Brazil, and Sudan in a second column. Have students discuss possible differences between the countries in the two columns. *(Answers will vary but might include the idea that the nations in the second column are less industrialized and economically developed.)* Tell students that Section 1 discusses the characteristics of developed and developing nations.

Preteaching Vocabulary

Have students find the definitions of the vocabulary terms in Section 1 or in the Glossary. Then have students use all three words in a sentence.

SECTION **1** *Characteristics of Developing Nations*

S E C T I O N 1 F O C U S

Terms to Know developed nations, developing nations, subsistence agriculture, infant mortality

Objectives *After reading this section, you should be able to:*

1. Indicate about how many developed and developing nations exist in the world.
2. List five characteristics of developing nations.
3. List the Four Tigers.

How the Other Three-Fourths of the World Lives

Many Americans may not realize it, but even the poorest families in the United States usually have an income far above the average income in much of the rest of the world. More than one-half of the world's population lives at or close to subsistence, with just enough to survive.

Developed and Developing Nations

Of the more than 175 nations in the world, only about 30 are considered **developed nations**. See Figure 21.1. These nations include the United States, Canada, most European countries, plus Japan, Australia, and New Zealand.

The remaining three-fourths of the world's population live in **developing nations.** These are nations with less industrial development and a relatively low standard of living. Within this general definition, however, nations differ in many ways. Figure 21.2 compares two developing nations, Madagascar and Mexico. The average income per person in Mexico is only one-fifth that of the United States. In contrast, Mexico is much more developed and prosperous than almost all other devel-

Figure 21.1
Life in Developed Nations
Many people in developed nations with industrial economies live comfortably. These nations with about 25 percent of the world's population account for almost 80 percent of world GDP. ▼

Classroom Resources for Section 1

- Reproducible Lesson Plan 21.1
- *NBR* Video 28 and Video Still 3
- Focus Activity Transparency 92
- Focus Activity Sheet 92
- Guided Reading Activity 21.1
- Cooperative Learning Activity 21

- Primary and Secondary Source Readings 21
- Section Quiz 21.1
- Spanish Section Quiz 21.1
- Testmaker

oping nations. In Madagascar, average per capita income is very much less than average per capita income in the United States.

Besides differences in the standard of living among developing nations, great differences often exist within a nation. For example, about 26 percent of India's population lives and works in urban areas, many of which are like those in developed nations. In rural India, however, the majority of the population may not have enough to eat. The average family lives three to a room, often in mud houses. Only a fraction of these homes have running water and electricity.

Economic Characteristics

Economists often use per-person GDP as a rough measure of a nation's prosperity. While source estimates of world economic data vary, the United States and other developed nations have per capita GDP that ranges between $12,000 per year and about $27,000 per year.

Low GDP Per capita GDP in developing nations, in contrast, is considerably less, and in the world's poorest nations it is extremely low. Look at Figure 21.3 (page 506), which shows per capita GDP for a number of developing countries and for a number of developed countries. While developing nations may have many natural and human resources, they lack the equipment, financing, and knowledge necessary to put those resources to use.

An Agricultural Economy Agriculture is central to developing nations' economies. Much of the population exists through **subsistence agriculture.**

Teach

Guided Practice

L2 Creating a Plan Review with students the reasons for low literacy rates in developing nations. Then tell them to imagine they have been asked to recommend educational programs in a developing nation. Have small groups discuss the types of programs they think would be most beneficial and share their recommendations.

Visual Instruction

Refer students to Figure 21.2 and ask what the number of telephones per 100 people indicates about a nation. (*A level of communication technology available to most people*) Answer to figure 21.2 question: Per capita GDP of Mexico is ten times greater.

Figure 21.2 ▶
Two Developing Nations
Among developing nations there is a wide variance in standards of living. How does the per capita GDP of Madagascar compare to that of Mexico?
▼

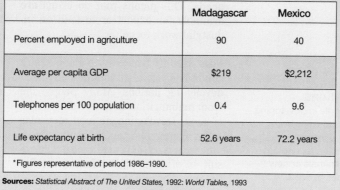

Two Developing Nations*

	Madagascar	Mexico
Percent employed in agriculture	90	40
Average per capita GDP	$219	$2,212
Telephones per 100 population	0.4	9.6
Life expectancy at birth	52.6 years	72.2 years

*Figures representative of period 1986–1990.

Sources: *Statistical Abstract of The United States, 1992; World Tables, 1993*

505

 VIDEODISC

Nightly Business Report
Economics in Action
Use Video Still 3, "GDP Per Capita," on Disc 2, Side B, Video 28.

Search Frame 20433

◆▶◼ Meeting Special Needs

Reading Disability Students with various reading and organizational difficulties may have problems relating graphics and the main text. Before reading the text in Section 1, ask students to look at the graphics. Have them tell what the graphics illustrate. Then have them read Section 1, restate what the graphics illustrate, and explain why they were included in the section.

Independent Practice

L2 Creating Maps Have students refer to the *Statistical Abstract of the United States* to prepare a list of developed and developing nations. Then have them draw a map of the world (leaving a margin for a short paragraph), label the countries, and color code the map to distinguish the two categories. Have students write a generalization in the margin stating by hemisphere and continent where developed and developing nations are likely to be found.

 Have students complete Guided Reading Activity 21.1 in the TCR. LEP

Visual Instruction

Figure 21.3 compares developed nations with the highest GDP per capita to several developing nations with low per capita GDP. (Estimates of GDP in China vary widely. Per capita GDP may be more than $1,000.) Answer to Figure 21.3 question: *Answers may vary but should point out that most people in developing countries can only afford basic necessities.*

Answer to Figure 21.5 question: *Inverse.*

GLOBAL ECONOMICS

As of 1992, South Korea had 10 companies that ranked in the Forbes International 500. To qualify, sales had to be at least $3.4 billion.

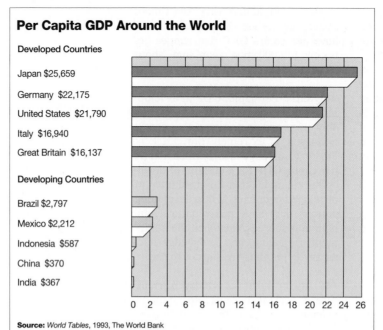

Per Capita GDP Around the World

Developed Countries

Japan $25,659
Germany $22,175
United States $21,790
Italy $16,940
Great Britain $16,137

Developing Countries

Brazil $2,797
Mexico $2,212
Indonesia $587
China $370
India $367

0 2 4 6 8 10 12 14 16 18 20 22 24 26

Source: *World Tables*, 1993, The World Bank

**Figure 21.3
Measuring GDP**
What do you think the huge difference in per capita GDP between developing and developed countries means in terms of everyday life?

**Figure 21.4
Agriculture
in Developing
Nations**
People in developing nations may not have modern farming technology or animals or new types of seed.

506 *Unit 6 The International Scene*

See Figure 21.4. Each family grows just enough to take care of its own needs. This means that no crops are available for export or to feed an industrial work force.

Poor Health Conditions Poor health conditions are also common in many developing nations. Many people die from malnutrition or illness due to lack of food. Developing nations may also suffer from a shortage of modern doctors, hospitals, and medicines. The result is often a high **infant mortality** (infants who die during the first year of life) rate and a low life expectancy among adults.

Low Literacy Rate A fourth characteristic of developing nations is a low adult literacy rate—the percentage of people who are able to read and write. Governments have few resources to build and maintain schools. Many children miss school to help their families with farming. The lack of a large pool of educated workers makes it difficult to train the population for needed technical and engineering jobs.

Rapid Population Growth A fifth characteristic of developing nations—rapid population growth—is often the source of many other problems in developing nations, such as lack of food and housing. For example, the population in the United States grows at less than 1 percent a year. The growth rate in many developing nations in Africa and Latin America is three and sometimes four times this rate. This means a nation such as Ghana, with a growth rate of 3.2 percent, will double its population in 22 years.

Figure 21.5 lists several economic and social statistics for a number of nations. As you can see, the differences between developing and developed nations are often large. In Afghanistan, the infant mortality rate is more than 17 times higher than in the United States.

Cooperative Learning

Point out to students that population growth in some countries is such a serious problem that the governments of these countries have established programs to curb the problem. Organize the class into small groups. Have each group find out what has been done in China and in India to curb population growth. Groups might divide the following tasks among their members: researching the information, writing the report, illustrating the report, and presenting the findings to the class.

Figure 21.5 ▶ Comparing Nations

What relationship between literacy rates and infant mortality rates is apparent from the chart?

Economic and Social Statistics for Selected Nations in a Recent Year

Life Expectancy at Birth	Infant Mortality: Deaths Per 1,000 Live Births	Country	Literacy (%)	Per Capita Daily Caloric Supply Available
76	10	United States	99*	3,702
79	4	Japan	99	2,700
75	10	Australia	98	3,810
74	13	Israel	88	3,140
73	12	Italy	94	3,004
68	31	China	32	2,620
64	52	Mexico	81	2,580
59	110	Pakistan	27	2,220
54	94	India	44	2,121
50	135	Mozambique	29	1,642
48	107	Bangladesh	34	1,840
38	172	Afghanistan	7	1,690

* True functional literacy is much lower in the United States.
Source: United Nations, *World Development Report*, 1993

The Four Tigers

Developing countries vary greatly in their ability to experience economic growth. One group has achieved annual economic growth rates that are two to three times that of the United States. Three newly industrialized countries—Singapore, Taiwan, and South Korea—and the British crown colony (until 1997) of Hong Kong are the so-called Four Tigers. From 1960 to 1990, per capita GDP in these countries grew more than fivefold.

In contrast during the same period, some sub-Saharan African nations saw a fall in per capita GDP. For many parts of the world, the income gap between nations has increased rather than decreased recently.

SECTION 1 REVIEW

Understanding Vocabulary
Define developed nations, developing nations, subsistence agriculture, infant mortality.

Reviewing Objectives
1. About how many nations in the world are considered developed?

2. What are five economic characteristics of developing nations?

3. What are the Four Tigers?

Assign Section 1 Review as homework or an in-class activity. Each question in the Review addresses the corresponding numbered objective in the Section Focus.

Evaluate
Assign the Section 1 Quiz in the TCR or use the Testmaker to develop a customized quiz.

Reteach
Have students use the headings in Section 1 and write a main idea sentence for each heading. Have volunteers write their sentences on the chalkboard.

Enrich
Have students research traditional and commercial agricultural practice in developing and some developed nations. They should compare how a crop is grown in each case. Students might consider preparing the land; the kinds of fertilizers used; disease, weed, and pest control; cultivation; and harvesting.

Close

Have students work in small groups and, using Section 1, compare their life with that of a person in a developing nation. Call on volunteers to share comparisons.

Section 1 Review Answers

Understanding Vocabulary
developed nations (p. 504), **developing nations** (p. 504), **subsistence agriculture** (p. 505), **infant mortality** (p. 506)

Reviewing Objectives
1. About 30 nations are considered developed.
2. The five characteristics of most developing countries are an agricultural economy, poor health conditions, low GDP, low literacy rate, and rapid population growth.
3. The Four Tigers are the newly industrialized countries of Singapore, Hong Kong, Taiwan, and South Korea.

Focus on Free Enterprise

The Chicago Pizza Pie Factory

Focus

The focus of this feature considers how one man's taste for an unavailable food (Chicago-style pizza) inspired him to create a chain of successful theme restaurants in the British Isles and Europe.

Teach

L2 Summarizing Information After students read the feature, ask them to develop the main ingredients in Robert Payton's recipe for creating a successful restaurant chain. (*Suggested answer: Identify a dining preference that is not being satisfied. Prepare the food with authentic ingredients. Serve the food in an atmosphere that adds to the enjoyment of eating it.*)

L3 Developing a Concept Ask students to use the Chicago Pizza Pie Factory as a model for a theme restaurant they would like to set up and operate. Have them write a list of all the elements that they think would help make the restaurant a success. Suggest naming the type of food served, the restaurant theme, a location, type of atmosphere, entertainment, and prices. Encourage volunteers to tell about their theme restaurants.

Missing Chicago-Style Pizza The Chicago Pizza Pie Factory is a very successful chain of pizza restaurants in Europe. They are even recommended in Frommer's travel guides for both London and the United Kingdom. The idea behind the Chicago Pizza Pie Factory is for Americans and Europeans alike to discover a little piece of Chicago in Europe.

The Factory was founded by an American, Robert Payton, and still operates under his ownership. Payton, a former Chicago advertising executive, was transferred to London in the early 1970s. Although he liked London, he missed certain amenities from home. One of the main things he missed was the pizza—in particular, deep-dish Chicago-style pizza.

Payton felt that in London there was a market for pizza ready to be tapped. He quit his advertising job, sold other investors on his idea, and formed a company called My Kinda Town, Ltd. Payton invested all his savings into the company's first venture—a pizza restaurant in the heart of London.

The European-Style Chicago Pizza One of Payton's start-up problems was trying to make authentic, Chicago-style pizza using European ingredients. He used wedding cake pans to get the right deep-dish look and texture, and he found a Danish cheese that resembled the cheese used in Chicago. Unable to find the "right" cooking oil, he obtained the recipe from a Chicago oil supplier and began to make his own oil.

508

Bears, Bulls, and Cubs The theme of The Chicago Pizza Pie Factory is centered around the city of Chicago, not just its pizza. Chicago street signs and memorabilia, as well as Chicago Bears, Bulls, and Cubs posters and banners, decorate the walls. The television replays videos of Chicago's teams. A Chicago radio station also sends tapes each week to provide background music and Chicago news and weather.

Expanding Through Europe The taste of Chicago-style pizza served in a Chicago-like atmosphere proved to be so popular among London natives and visiting Americans that Payton's company moved to expand. A Chicago Pizza Pie Factory opened up in Barcelona and another in Paris. My Kinda Town, Ltd. also started up different restaurants following the same winning formula. The Chicago Rib Shack, Chicago Meatpackers, Tacos, The Criterion, Salsa!, and Henry J Bean's But His Friends All Call Him Hank Bar and Grill all proved to be quite successful. Currently, there are more than 20 restaurants across Europe that are modeled after the first Chicago Pizza Pie Factory. These restaurants are located in Germany, Spain, France, Belgium, and Ireland. A Chicago Pizza Pie Factory has even

opened up in Israel. Some of the restaurants are owned directly by Payton, while others are franchises. Overall, the Chicago Pizza Pie Factory has proved to be a successful idea that has continued to grow throughout Europe. It is now possible to travel around Europe without ever being too far from the tastes and sounds of Chicago or Chicago-style pizza.

Free Enterprise in Action

1 Why did Robert Payton choose to start a pizza business in London?

2 Why was it difficult to find the tools and ingredients for Chicago-style pizza?

3 How was a Chicago atmosphere created in the European restaurants?

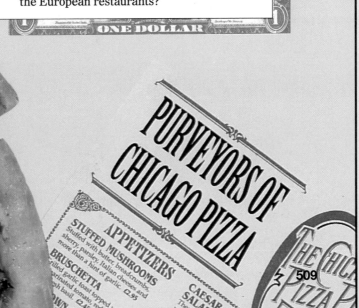

509

Answers to Free Enterprise in Action

1. He missed the deep-dish Chicago-style pizza he enjoyed at home.
2. because they were not available in Europe
3. Chicago street signs, sports posters, and banners decorate the walls. The television replays Chicago teams' videos, and tapes provide Chicago news and weather.

L1 Interpreting Information Tell students that a spin-off is a new product or concept based on a proven successful product or concept. Explain that spin-offs occur with some frequency in developing new television programs and in filming sequels to movies. Ask students to identify the spin-offs of the first Chicago Pizza Pie Factory.

Assess

Ask students to develop a 30-second radio commercial for the London Chicago Pizza Pie Factory. Tell them it can be spoken, sung, or both spoken and sung. Have volunteers perform their commercial.

Close

Ask students to discuss what they think it takes for a business that serves the public to succeed.

Focus

Overview

See the student page for section objectives.

Section 2 explains or describes: ways of financing economic development; the major sources of foreign aid; and the reasons for giving foreign aid.

Bellringer

Before presenting the lesson, display Focus Activity Transparency 93 on the overhead projector or copy the material on the chalkboard. Assign the accompanying Focus Activity Sheet.

Motivational Activity

Have students, working alone or in small groups, act as finance ministers of developing countries who must each prepare a list of ways to raise money to develop their economies. Discuss the lists and tell students that Section 2 explains financing economic development. Have them compare their lists with information in the section.

Preteaching Vocabulary

Ask students to find the meaning of the vocabulary terms in the Glossary and tell how the terms are related.

SECTION **2** The Process of Economic Development

SECTION 2 FOCUS

Terms to Know foreign aid, economic assistance, technical assistance, military assistance

Objectives *After reading this section, you should be able to:*
1. Describe two major outside sources for financing economic development.
2. Identify five nations that supply foreign aid and two international agencies through which aid is given.
3. List four reasons for giving foreign aid.

Most nations pass through three stages of economic development. The first is the agricultural stage, when most of the population has jobs in farming. The second is the manufacturing stage, when much of the population has jobs in industry. In the third stage, many workers shift into the service sector—sales, food service, repair work, and so on. In its economic development, the United States has followed these stages. It began as an agricultural nation in the late eighteenth century and passed into an industrial economy in the late nineteenth century. The mid-twentieth century saw the beginning of rapid growth of the service sector.

**Figure 21.6
The Agricultural Stage**
What are two basic needs of nations in the agricultural stage?

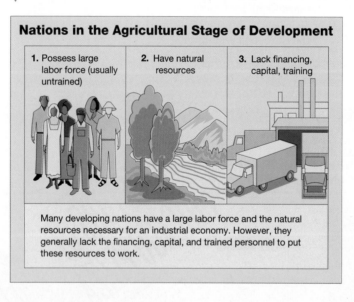

Nations in the Agricultural Stage of Development

1. Possess large labor force (usually untrained)
2. Have natural resources
3. Lack financing, capital, training

Many developing nations have a large labor force and the natural resources necessary for an industrial economy. However, they generally lack the financing, capital, and trained personnel to put these resources to work.

Financing Economic Development

Most developing nations are still in the agricultural stage. As Figure 21.6 shows, three factors are evident in this stage. A basic problem for many developing nations is how to finance the equipment and training necessary to improve their standard of living.

One source of money capital is domestic savings. Many people believe that people in developing nations cannot save because they are barely subsisting. In fact, even very poor people do save something for their future. However, it may not be in a form that

---

Classroom Resources for Section 2

- Reproducible Lesson Plan 21.2
- Focus Activity Transparency 93
- Focus Activity Sheet 93
- Guided Reading Activity 21.2
- Free Enterprise Activity 22

- Consumer Application Activity 22
- Section Quiz 21.2
- Spanish Section Quiz 21.2
- Testmaker
- Reinforcing Skills 21

Attractions and Risks to Foreign Investors

Attractions:

1. Low wage rates
2. Few regulations
3. Abundant raw materials

Risks:

1. Political instability - uncertainty
2. Threat of losing investment if government takes over private firms

◀ **Figure 21.7** ▲
Attractions and Risks to Foreign Investors
Why would it be in a developing nation's best interest to discourage terrorism within its borders?

is useful for capital investment. For example, in a traditional economy, saving may involve storing grain that can later be traded for other goods. While this is saving, it does not provide a pool of money capital from which businesses can borrow for investment. Although they have some money capital available from domestic savings, many developing nations must look to outside sources for investment capital.

Foreign Investment: Attractions and Problems The two major outside sources of capital are investment by foreign businesses and foreign aid from developed nations. Developing nations often have attractions for investors and also some problems, as shown in Figure 21.7. Investment may include a corporation's setting up

branch offices, fully owned companies, or buying into companies in developing nations.

Developing Nations: Problems With Foreign Investment Problems exist from the developing nation's viewpoint as well. In nations with heavy foreign investment, citizens often resent the economic control these foreign companies have over their resources. For example, the Gulf and Western Corporation (now Paramount) has been accused of operating a "state within a state" in the Dominican Republic. During the late 1970s, Gulf and Western owned 264,000 acres, or 8 percent, of the nation's arable land. It produced one-third of the nation's sugar and had investments in livestock, tobacco, and fruit and vegetable production as well. The

Chapter 21 Economic Growth in Developing Nations **511**

Chapter 21, Section 2

Teach

Guided Practice

L1 Making Inferences Refer students to Figure 21.6. Ask them to use the information to write a paragraph explaining why economic development would be difficult in a nation in the agricultural stage of development.

L1 Classifying Draw a table on the chalkboard. Across the top write three column headings: Source of Money Capital, Impact on Economic Growth, and Potential Problems. Make three rows down the left side and number them 1 to 3. Have students fill in the table during a class discussion of ways in which developing nations might raise money capital.

Visual Instruction

Answer to Figure 21.6 question: *Money Capital and Education.* Answer to Figure 21.7 question: *Terrorism discourages foreign investment.*

 Meeting Special Needs

Study Strategy Although thinking about reading is often helpful for students with reading comprehension difficulties, a more precise measure of understanding is whether they can write a summary of what they have read. In Section 2, have each student read a subsection and summarize the information by writing two or three sentences. Then ask partners to compare their summaries and which sentences were more accurate and why.

511

Independent Practice

L2 Writing Ask students to work in small groups to assume the role of the leadership of a developed country who must decide on the amount, type, and distribution of foreign aid to developing countries. Each group should write a paper naming the recipients, type of aid, and reasons for giving it. Call on volunteers from each group to read its paper to the class.

L3 Debating Review with students the reasons developed nations give foreign aid to developing nations. Then organize the class into two groups. Have one group brainstorm reasons the United States should reduce its foreign aid. Have the other group brainstorm reasons the United States should continue it. Then ask volunteers from each group to debate the following: Resolved, that the United States should reduce its foreign aid.

DID YOU KNOW

The United States began the Marshall Plan in 1948. The plan, considered a major contributing factor in the rapid economic recovery of Western Europe after World War II, gave the countries about $13 billion for rebuilding.

**Figure 21.8 ▲
Corporate Control
Over Foreign Resources**

Local and international groups accused Gulf and Western of, among other things, contributing to a food shortage in the Dominican Republic. Supposedly the corporation did this by converting farmland from growing food for local consumption to the more profitable production of sugar cane. In its defense, Gulf and Western maintained that its investments had improved the nation's standard of living. The company increased fruit and vegetable production and sold some land to its employees.

company owned resort hotels, shipping facilities, part of the nation's railway system, and more than 80 other businesses. Figure 21.8 explains some of the problems that arose.

Assistance From Other Nations Foreign aid is a second type of financing available to nations. It has played an increasingly important role in economic development.

Foreign aid is the money, goods, and services given by governments and private organizations to help other nations and their citizens. There are several kinds of foreign aid as shown in Figure 21.9.

Emergency shipments of food, clothing, and medical supplies to victims of drought, earthquakes, floods, and so on, are also considered foreign aid. Governments, many private organizations, and several agencies of the United Nations provide such assistance. This type of foreign aid, however, is not directed toward economic development.

Who Supplies Foreign Aid?

Many of the developed nations of the world offer some type of foreign aid to developing nations. Although the dollar amount of American foreign aid has been increasing in recent years, the amount of aid after correcting for inflation has actually fallen. Expressed in constant dollars—dollars adjusted for inflation—the United States gives only about one-fourth of what it gave in the years immediately following World War II. At that time, the United States devoted most of its foreign assistance to help rebuild

 Cooperative Learning

Ask students to work in small groups to report on the founding of the Peace Corps proposed by President John Kennedy and the history of its efforts in economically developing nations. Have students use their findings to make a wall poster showing the

countries and Peace Corps program achievements. Groups might divide the following tasks among their members: research, report writing, creating the poster, and oral presentation to the class.

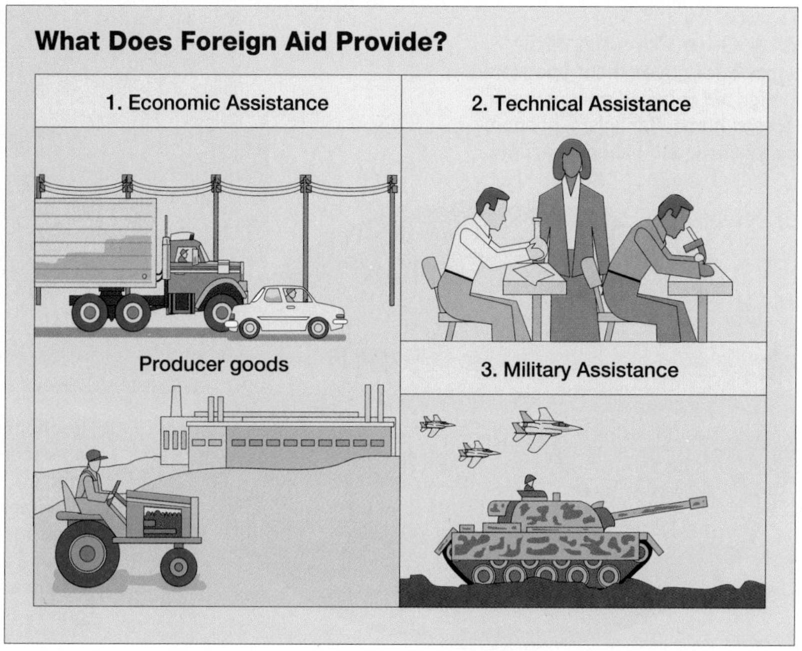

What Does Foreign Aid Provide?

1. Economic Assistance

Producer goods

2. Technical Assistance

3. Military Assistance

Figure 21.9 ►
Kinds of Foreign Aid
Foreign aid may be in the form of economic, technical, or military assistance.

1 **Economic assistance** consists of loans and outright grants of money or equipment to other nations. One use of such aid is to help build transportation and communications systems. Roads, bridges, and airports, for example, must be built to link isolated regions to the overall economy. A second use for economic assistance is to purchase basic producer goods. These include machinery that will increase a nation's productivity.

2 **Technical assistance** includes providing professionals such as engineers, teachers, technicians, and so on, to teach skills. Such training is designed to strengthen a nation's human resources in the same way economic assistance increases a nation's capital resources.

3 **Military assistance** involves giving either economic or technical assistance to a nation's armed forces. For example, a country may lend a developing nation the money to purchase airplanes or tanks, or it might make a gift of such goods.

Europe's war-torn economy through the Marshall Plan.

A New Focus In the 1950s, after European nations had regained much of their economic strength, the United States shifted the focus of its foreign-aid program to developing nations. Today most American foreign aid is sent to developing nations in the Middle East and Southeast Asia. Nations in Africa receive about 11 percent, in Latin America, 7 percent, and in East Asia and the Pacific, 5 percent. Figure 21.10 shows one example of American foreign aid.

Comparing Aid Many other major industrial nations also give foreign aid. France and Great Britain, for example, have concentrated most of their aid programs on their former colonies in Africa and Asia. Germany and

Figure 21.10 ▲
American Foreign Aid
The goal of technical assistance is to make people self-sufficient.

L2 Writing a Journal Entry
Ask students to imagine they are living in a developing nation that is currently the recipient of heavy foreign investment. Have them write a journal entry explaining how this investment has been used in their country and how they personally feel about it. Call on volunteers to read their journal entries to the class and discuss.

Visual Instruction
Refer students to Figures 21.9 and 21.10. Ask them to research the amount the United States spent annually on foreign aid during a recent five-year period. Suggest a further breakdown into allocations for economic, technological, and military assistance. Ask volunteers to report their findings.

? DID YOU KNOW

A United States government program that makes farm products available to developing countries is Food for Peace. This program donates agricultural products to countries in Asia, Latin America, and Africa. The program gives higher priority to countries that try to solve their own problems of economic growth.

Free Enterprise Activity

Tell students that foreign investments help finance economic development in developing nations. Organize the class into small groups to consult the *Readers' Guide to Periodical Literature* to help them research either a company's investments abroad or at home. Students should investigate the amount of money invested, the uses to which it has been put, and the consequences for the company and/or nation. Suggest that students use their information for a panel discussion on the pros and cons of investing from the viewpoint of companies and countries.

Independent Practice

L3 Geography Have students research major recipients of American foreign aid and locate them on a map. Have them find out the total dollars each country receives. Then ask students to write a report that explains why the United States supports the countries it does.

L2 Journalism Have students write newspaper editorials explaining the type of foreign aid they think is most beneficial to the recipient nation. Ask students to include reasons for their opinion. Call on volunteers to read their editorials to the class.

Have students complete Guided Reading Activity 21.2 in the TCR. LEP

GLOBAL ECONOMICS

Japan gives much of its economic aid to Asian nations such as Vietnam and China. It provides technical assistance to Pacific islands such as Western Samoa and Fiji. Much of the foreign aid given by France, Belgium, Italy, Great Britain, and Germany is in technical assistance.

Figure 21.11
Why Give Foreign Aid?

Support for government-sponsored foreign aid is based on four major factors: humanitarianism, economics, politics, and national security.

B Economics ▲
American foreign aid often widens the markets for American exports and provides new opportunities for private investment. This is, in part, because nations are often required to spend American foreign aid on American-made goods and services.

▲
A Humanitarianism
Many rich nations, including the United States, have decided that they have a responsibility to help end world hunger and disease.

Japan both began giving aid to developing nations after their economies had recovered from World War II. Today several nations devote a greater percentage of their GDP to foreign aid than does the United States. Norway's foreign aid, for example, is about 0.8 percent of that nation's GDP. By comparison, foreign aid given by the United States is less than 0.2 percent of its GDP.

Channels of Aid The United States channels much of its foreign aid to other nations through the Agency for International Development (AID). Some nations channel their foreign aid through a number of United Nations agencies, including the International Bank for Reconstruction and Development—usually called the World Bank. The World Bank was set up in 1945 to make loans to developing nations at low interest rates. Two affiliates of the bank are the International Development Association (IDA) and the International Finance Corporation (IFC). The IDA lends money to nations that are the least able to obtain financing from other sources. The IFC encourages private investment in developing nations. In the 1980s, foreign aid agencies grew increasingly alarmed as many developing nations found themselves unable to repay their foreign debts. The World Bank, for example, had to reschedule payments for several nations. Growing foreign debt has been the focus of several international meetings.

Reasons for Giving Foreign Aid

Humanitarianism is the basis of some foreign aid. The relief of human suffering is a major goal in particular of many private aid organizations.

At least three other reasons can be given for providing support for government-sponsored foreign aid. See Figure 21.11. The first involves economics. It is usually in the best interests of developed nations to encourage international trade.

Politics is also a reason for giving foreign aid. During the cold war, an important objective of American for-

Cultural Diversity and Economics

Point out to students that investors in foreign countries often have to deal with cultural differences. For example, a potential investor may need a letter of approval from the nation's chief executive, which might take several months. Permits, sometimes involving payoffs to government officials and workers, may also be needed. Have students imagine they are investors in a developing nation and prepare a list of the things they might need to know about the culture and ways of doing business there. Lead a class discussion to consider the importance for investors to understand the culture of the nation in which they are investing.

C Politics
Foreign aid has been given to make developing nations more prosperous and stable and enhance the appeal of democracy. The United States also has used foreign aid to build political friends that will support it in such international bodies as the United Nations.

◀

▲ **D National Security**
Through alliances, or partnerships with other nations, the United States has gained overseas military bases and observation posts that it can use to gather information about other nations.

eign aid and that of other major capitalist nations was to prevent Communists from coming to power.

A fourth reason for giving foreign aid is to help protect a nation's own security. Economic aid is often, in effect, a down payment on a military alliance with a developing nation. However, this type of plan can backfire if a friendly government loses power. In such a situation, the military equipment given that nation would fall into the hands of the new government, one that may be hostile to the nation that supplied the military equipment.

SECTION 2 REVIEW

Understanding Vocabulary
Define foreign aid, economic assistance, technical assistance, military assistance.

Reviewing Objectives
❶ From where do developing countries obtain outside sources of financing for economic development?

❷ What agencies channel aid from major industrial nations to developing nations?

❸ Why do nations give foreign aid?

Assess

Meeting Lesson Objectives
Assign Section 2 Review as homework or an in-class activity. Each question in the Review addresses the corresponding numbered objective in the Section Focus.

Evaluate
Assign the Section 2 Quiz in the TCR or use the Testmaker to develop a customized quiz.

Reteach
Have students use these main entries in an outline: Ways of Financing Economic Development, Types of Foreign Aid, and Reasons for Foreign Aid. Then have them use Section 2 to fill in the subentries of the outline. Discuss student outlines with the class.

Enrich
Ask students to choose a developing nation that has received considerable foreign aid and investment. Have them write a report on how that aid has been used. Have volunteers share their reports.

Close
Have students conduct a panel discussion on whether the United States should provide foreign aid prior to eliminating hunger and poverty here. Have students provide specific reasons for their opinions.

Section 2 Review Answers
Understanding Vocabulary
foreign aid (p. 512), **economic assistance** (p. 513), **technical assistance** (p. 513), **military assistance** (p. 513)

Reviewing Objectives
1. through investments by foreign businesses and foreign aid from developed nations

2. The Agency for International Development (AID) and the World Bank and its affiliates, the International Development Association (IDA) and the International Finance Corporation (IFC)

3. Nations give foreign aid for humanitarian, economic, political, and national security reasons.

515

Copy on the chalkboard the graph showing GDP in Current and Constant Dollars, 1985–1992 on page 341, but show only Current Dollars. Ask students to interpret a trend from this graph. Then insert the rest of the data. Discuss why the measure of current dollars was inadequate to understand the trend.

Have students read the feature and then ask them why being able to read trends is an important skill for consumers, officials, savers, investors, and businesspeople. Ask students to name at least one type of trend that would be important to each. Be sure through questioning that students understand the effect that inflation and population changes can have on determining the reliability of a trend.

Additional Practice

Have students complete Reinforcing Skills 21 in the TCR.

LEARNING ECONOMIC SKILLS
Recognizing Trends

To predict what will happen in the future, you have to recognize trends and what has happened in the past. Can you recognize a trend?

What is a Trend?

A trend is the general movement of change over a period of time. Businesspeople and government officials must often make decisions about the future based on their reading of trends. For example, clearly there is a trend in the labor force in the United States as shown in **Figure A**. The labor force is continually increasing. Trends can be downward also; for example, the percentage of the population in America that smokes cigarettes is going down.

Establishing a trend requires a long enough period of time to be able to recognize a general pattern. Otherwise, what you thought was a trend may only be a temporary change.

Real versus Nominal Trends

Of key importance in recognizing trends in prices, production, or income is to make sure that you correct for inflation (or deflation). **Figure B** shows per capita disposable personal income in uncorrected nominal dollars. It appears that the trend in the average, per capita, disposable personal income is upward. In inflation–corrected, or real, dollars, however, there is no trend at all from 1988 to 1992.

Practicing the Skill

Figure C shows data on the average duration of unemployment expressed in number of weeks. Is there a trend in the average number of weeks of unemployment? Why or why not?

Figure A Labor Force (including resident armed forces, in millions)

1986	119,540
1988	123,379
1990	126,424
1992	128,548

Figure B Per Capita Disposable Personal Income

Dollars (in thousands)

— nominal dollars
— real dollars

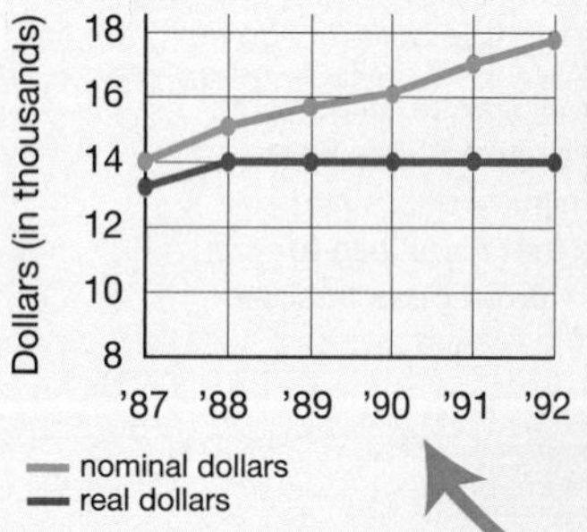

Figure C

1986	15
1987	14.5
1988	13.5
1989	11.9
1990	12.1
1991	13.8
1992	17.9

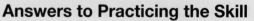

Answers to Practicing the Skill

Yes, the figure shown decreased from 1986 to 1989, and then it increased from 1989 to 1992.

SECTION **3** Obstacles to Growth in Developing Nations

SECTION 3 FOCUS

Terms to Know bureaucracies, nationalization

Objectives *After reading this section, you should be able to:*

❶ List some of the **obstacles to economic growth** in developing nations.

❷ Explain why **Indonesia** failed to experience rapid economic growth.

The successful rebuilding of the European economy following World War II convinced many economists that injections, or additions, of money capital into a nation could achieve rapid economic growth. See Figure 21.12. As a result, billions of dollars flowed into developing nations during the 1950s and 1960s. However, aid to many of these nations failed to produce the same growth as it did in Europe.

Critics of foreign aid pointed out that Europe's rapid recovery following the war was a special case. In 1945 Europe already had skilled labor forces, advanced organizations such as corporations and trade groups, and experienced government **bureaucracies,** or offices and agencies. It lacked only the money capital to rebuild the physical machinery of what had been well-functioning economies. Economists today are using much the same arguments to explain the rapid economic growth of Singapore, South Korea, Taiwan, and Hong Kong.

Four Obstacles to Growth

Many developing nations, however, face a number of obstacles to growth that are not immediately solved by injections of money capital. See Figure 21.13 (page 518). Attitudes and beliefs are usually slow to change. In many developing nations, people live and work much as their ancestors did hundreds of years before. Innovation of any sort is often viewed with suspicion. A high

Figure 21.12 Rebuilding Europe
Through the Marshall Plan, the United States provided billions of dollars to rebuild Europe.

▼

517

Focus

Overview
See the student page for section objectives.

Section 3 explains or describes obstacles to economic growth in developing nations and the reasons Indonesia failed to experience economic growth.

Bellringer
Before presenting the lesson, display Focus Activity Transparency 94 on the overhead projector or copy the material on the chalkboard. Assign the accompanying Focus Activity Sheet.

Motivational Activity
Ask students to locate Indonesia on a world map. Have them list on the chalkboard what they know about the standard of living and the economy there. Tell students that in Section 3 they will learn why Indonesia did not experience economic growth for many years after it became independent in 1949.

Preteaching Vocabulary
Have students read the definitions of *bureaucracies* and *nationalize* in Section 3. Then, as they read the section, have them indicate how these words are related to economic growth in Europe after World War II and to obstacles to economic growth in Indonesia.

Classroom Resources for Section 3

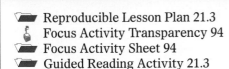

- Reproducible Lesson Plan 21.3
- Focus Activity Transparency 94
- Focus Activity Sheet 94
- Guided Reading Activity 21.3

- Section Quiz 21.3
- Spanish Section Quiz 21.3
- Testmaker

Teach

Guided Practice

L1 Comparing and Contrasting Refer students to Figure 21.14 and discuss with them what it illustrates. Have them write a paragraph in which they contrast the approaches of Sukarno and Suharto in trying to structure economic development.

L2 Creating a Poster Ask students to choose one example from the case study about Indonesia to illustrate each of the four obstacles to economic development. Have students present their information in a poster.

Figure 21.13 ▶ Analyzing the Obstacles Some of the obstacles to growth are more difficult to remove than others. Rank the obstacles from most to least difficult and give reasons for your ranking.

Obstacles to Economic Growth

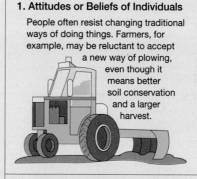

1. Attitudes or Beliefs of Individuals
People often resist changing traditional ways of doing things. Farmers, for example, may be reluctant to accept a new way of plowing, even though it means better soil conservation and a larger harvest.

2. Continued Rapid Population Growth
Population growing at more rapid rate than per capita GDP = Lower Standard of Living

3. Misuse of Resources
- Aid to military should have been used for needed agricultural development.
- Training for people in political science should have been in more needed field of engineering.
- People in power sometimes use foreign aid to increase their own wealth rather than to improve the lives of all the people.

4. Trade Restrictions
Quotas and tariffs prevent the purchase of cheaper foreign substitutes (imports).

TARIFF
TARIFF
QUOTA FILLED

population growth rate may reduce the rate of growth of a nation's standard of living. Even if a nation's economy is growing, per capita GDP will decrease if its population is growing at a faster rate.

Nations have been held back from more rapid development through the misuse of natural or human resources. For example, defense spending as a percentage of GDP is more than 8 percent in Ethiopia, almost 8 percent in Egypt, and more than 12 percent in Libya. All of these percentages are higher than in the United States—a very developed country.

Trade restrictions on imports are a fourth obstacle to growth. To develop domestic industries, many developing nations have used import restrictions such as quotas and tariffs.

Case Study: Indonesia

When Indonesia won independence from the Netherlands in 1949, it seemed well equipped for economic growth. With a population of about 76 million, it was the world's sixth most populous nation. It was rich in minerals such as nickel, tin, bauxite, and copper, and had vast oil reserves as well as valuable farmland and rain forests. During his regime, President Achmed Sukarno (soo-KAHR-noh) obtained foreign aid totaling more than $2 billion from both capitalist and communist nations. Yet at the end of this time, Indonesia's economy was a disaster.

The reasons behind this failure reveal some of the problems of trying to bring rapid growth to developing

 Meeting Special Needs

Reading Disability Sometimes, reading comprehension is greatly influenced by a student's weak decoding skills. The effort needed to comprehend is overshadowed by the energy expended in decoding. By the time this student finishes a paragraph, he or she may have forgotten the beginning. For students with very poor reading skills, have a good reader tape-record the material so that the student can listen while following the text. Remind students to look at all the visuals in the section.

Figure 21.14 Indonesia's Economy under Sukarno and Suharto

President Sukarno's Regime (1949–1965)

1. Loss of foreign aid from the United States due to strong opposition to capitalism.
2. Foreign aid from former Soviet Union and others was often wasted on projects for the rich such as sports stadiums and department stores. Mineral resources were not developed and decaying roads and rail lines went without repairs.
3. **Nationalization** of businesses placed them under government ownership, discouraging foreign investment.
4. Heavy regulation of business, a huge government bureaucracy, and widespread corruption hurt the economy.
5. Inflation soared out of control. The nation's price index rose from 100 in 1953 to 3,000 only 10 years later. By the mid-1960s, the national debt was $2.5 billion.

General Suharto's Regime (1965–)

1. Control of the money supply was tightened and confidence in government increased. Corruption was reduced and bureaucracy decreased.
2. Alliances with some Western nations were made.
3. Foreign aid and investment increased and resources were focused on improving agricultural output and oil production.
4. Industry was developed. More money could be spent on industry because less was needed to import food.

nations. One problem involved attitudes. Indonesians lacked a sense of national identity. Indonesia had been formed from several former Dutch colonies, and its people were divided by nationality, religion, and politics. These differences sometimes resulted in violent clashes. The major blame for economic failure, however, can be placed on Sukarno's economic policies. Later improvement in Indonesia's economy is credited to General Suharto (soo-HAR-toh) who replaced Sukarno in 1965. See Figure 21.14 for a comparison of economic policy under two regimes in Indonesia.

Due chiefly to Suharto's economic policies, Indonesia was one of the fastest-growing economies among developing nations by the end of the 1970s. This was in part due to growth in industry. Mostly, however, it was the result of increases in food output and oil production. Unfortunately, Indonesia, like many developing nations recently, has found that reliance on a few products can be dangerous. In the early 1980s, the world "oil glut" and falling prices for farm products cut deeply into the nation's trade income. Despite Indonesia's promising growth, this change, along with its rapidly growing population, make the future uncertain.

Chapter 21 Economic Growth in Developing Nations **519**

Independent Practice

L2 Researching Ask students to choose a developing nation with a large base of natural resources such as Brazil or Saudi Arabia. Have them research its economic development and explain in an illustrated report why development has been slow. Call on volunteers to read their reports to the class.

Have students complete Guided Reading Activity 21.3 in the TCR. **LEP**

Visual Instruction

Refer students to Figure 21.15 on page 520 as a starting point for reporting on the economy of Indonesia, using the most recent data. Ask volunteers to present their findings orally and discuss prospects for the Indonesian economy.

GLOBAL ECONOMICS

Suharto has cultivated good relations with the United States. In 1990 Indonesia received approximately $48 million in economic aid and approximately $2 million in military aid from the United States. In the past three years, more than $18 billion in investment capital has been poured into Indonesia, much of it into the garment, textile, and export-oriented manufacturing sectors.

Cooperative Learning

Organize the class into small groups to research and report on the standard of living in Indonesia today. Considerations might include infant mortality rate, life expectancy, literacy rate, urbanization rate, and per capita income. Encourage use of graphics to illustrate reports. Groups may assign the following tasks among their members: researching the information, writing the report, creating a chart, and presenting the information to the class.

Assess

Meeting Lesson Objectives

Assign Section 3 Review as homework or an in-class activity. Each question in the Review addresses the corresponding numbered objective in the Section Focus.

Evaluate

Assign the Section 3 Quiz in the TCR or use the Testmaker to develop a customized quiz.

Reteach

Have students list the obstacles to growth in developing nations and give an example of each.

Enrich

Have students research the current economic situation in a developing nation and explore how the four obstacles to growth have affected development there. Have them write a case study similar to the one in the text, addressing historical factors, obstacles to growth, and future prospects.

Close

Have students write a short paragraph on this topic: How to overcome obstacles to economic growth in developing nations. Have them examine each obstacle discussed in Section 3.

Figure 21.15 ▶
Contrasts
The influence of foreign investment on showcases like Jakarta may not change the lives of people in rural areas.

▼

Indonesia's value as a case study lies in the variety of lessons it teaches about foreign aid. On the one hand, it illustrates that simply pouring money capital into a developing nation will not guarantee economic growth. See Figure 21.15. On the other hand, Indonesia also shows that growth can occur if government restrictions on economic activity are reduced. For- eign aid must be used wisely in combination with domestic savings, foreign investment, and government policies that ensure economic stability. Finally, the case study points out that growth of a developing nation's economy may prove temporary if it depends on only one or two products. Changes in world market conditions have a major impact on nations with such narrowly based economies. Developed nations with broad, diverse, or varied economies are not as affected by ups and downs in the prices of specific goods.

SECTION 3 REVIEW

Understanding Vocabulary
Define bureaucracies, nationalization.

Reviewing Objectives
❶ What are the main obstacles to economic growth in developing nations?

❷ Why did Indonesia fail to experience rapid economic growth?

Section 3 Review Answers

Understanding Vocabulary
bureaucracies (p. 517), **nationalization** (p. 519)

Reviewing Objectives
1. The main obstacles to economic growth in developing nations are attitudes, rapid population growth, misuse of resources, and trade restrictions.

2. Indonesia failed to experience rapid economic growth because Indonesians lacked a sense of national identity. In addition, the policies of President Sukarno with regard to nationalization and regulation of businesses, together with a large bureaucracy and widespread corruption, burdened the economy.

Personal Perspective

Thomas Malthus on Overpopulation

Profile

- 1766–1834
- English minister
- theorized that the world population was growing much faster than world food production
- published *An Essay on the Principle of Population: or, a View of Its Past and Present Effects on Human Happiness* in 1798 and a revised second edition in 1803

Thomas Malthus foresaw future world problems caused by a world population that was growing faster than food production. In the following excerpts from the *Essay*, Malthus concludes that population will always outpace the supply of food.

... *I say, that the power of population is indefinitely greater than the power in the earth to produce subsistence for man.*

Population, when unchecked, increases in a geometrical ratio. Subsistence increases only in an arithmetical ratio. A slight acquaintance with numbers will show the immensity of the first power in comparison of the second.

By that law of our nature which makes food necessary to the life of man, the effects of these two unequal powers must be kept equal.

Malthus says that people will always struggle to survive, and no social system can improve this condition.

... *This natural inequality of the two powers of population and of production in the earth and that great law of our nature which must constantly keep their effects equal form the great difficulty that to me appears insurmountable in the way to the perfectibility of society. All other arguments are of slight and subordinate consideration in comparison of this. I see no way by which man can escape from the weight of this law which pervades all animated nature. No fancied equality, no agrarian regulations in their utmost extent, could remove the pressure of it even for a single century. And it appears, therefore, to be decisive against the possible existence of a society, all the members of which should live in ease, happiness, and comparative leisure; and feel no anxiety about providing the means of subsistence for themselves and families.*

Checking for Understanding

1. What is Malthus's principle, simply stated?
2. How fast does he say population increases?
3. Why can there be no happy, worry-free, ideal society according to Malthus?

Background

Thomas Malthus's essay summarizes his observations made while traveling in other countries. In the second edition of his essay, Malthus claimed that humanity was doomed to poverty unless the rate of population growth was slowed. In this century some nations have suffered and continue to suffer from overpopulation and food shortages. Nevertheless, the Malthusian theory is inaccurate for industrialized nations such as the United States. First, Malthus assumed a fixed, or unchanging, level of technology. However, improved farming technology and practices have greatly increased the supply of food. Second, the population of industrialized areas has not grown at the rate predicted by Malthus, even though people live longer.

Teach

Have volunteers read the excerpts from Malthus's essay and summarize them in their own words. Interested students might research the green revolution and discuss how such technological advances as this invalidated Malthus's theories. Then have students answer the questions in Checking for Understanding.

Answers to Checking for Understanding

1. World population is growing faster than food production.
2. at a geometrical rate
3. because the inequality in population growth and food production as a law of nature cannot be overcome

Focus

Overview

See the student page for section objectives.

Section 4 explains the problems associated with rapid industrialization in developing nations and the factors that determine the various routes to economic development.

VIDEODISC

Nightly Business Report
Economics in Action
Use "Technological and Social Change" on Disc 2, Side B, Video 30.

Search 32546, Play to 41061

Bellringer

Before presenting the lesson, display Focus Activity Transparency 95 and assign the accompanying Focus Activity Sheet.

Motivational Activity

Have students discuss what developing nations need most for their economic future. Have students compare their suggestions with the information in the section.

Preteaching Vocabulary

Ask volunteers to tell what they think each vocabulary term means. Have them compare their definitions to the Glossary.

SECTION 4 Industrialization and the Future

SECTION 4 FOCUS

Terms to Know property rights, vicious cycle of poverty

Objectives *After reading this section, you should be able to:*

1. Explain four problems associated with rapid industrialization in developing nations.
2. Explain the importance of property rights for economic development.
3. List three factors besides poverty that influence economic development.
4. Describe the relationship between information flows and economic cooperation.

Toward Global Industrialization

The high standard of living of any developed nation is most often a result of its high level of industrialization. As you read earlier in this chapter, industrialization is the second stage of economic development. As a result, many developing nations have tried to improve their standard of living by shifting their resources away from agriculture to industry. Attempts at rapid industrialization, however, can prove a wasteful use of scarce resources.

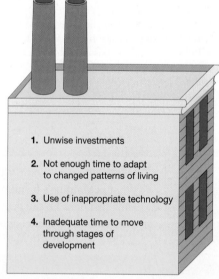

Problems of Rapid Industrialization

Figure 21.16 ▶ Industrialization in Developing Nations
Historically, economists have emphasized the benefits of rapid industrialization. Today, however, they are aware that this process may cause problems.

1. Unwise investments

2. Not enough time to adapt to changed patterns of living

3. Use of inappropriate technology

4. Inadequate time to move through stages of development

Problems of Rapid Industrialization

There are four problems of rapid industrialization, as shown in Figure 21.16. For example, some developing nations have invested in steel factories and automobile plants. However, these nations do not necessarily have a comparative advantage in producing steel or automobiles. As a result, the people in these nations are worse off. Citizens receive less economic value from their resources than they would have received from other investments. In India, for instance, steel mills produce steel at two to three times what it would cost if it were imported.

522 *Unit 6 The International Scene*

Classroom Resources for Section 4

- Reproducible Lesson Plan 21.4
- *NBR* Video 30
- Focus Activity Transparency 95
- Focus Activity Sheet 95
- Guided Reading Activity 21.4
- Mathematics Practice for Economics 27
- Performance Assessment Activity 27
- Section Quiz 21.4

- Spanish Section Quiz 21.4
- Chapter 21 Test Forms A and B
- Testmaker
- Enrichment Activity 21
- Economics Vocabulary Activity 21
- Audiocassette 21
- Spanish Audiocassette 21
- Reteaching Activity 21

Adapting to Change Rapid economic change also can be harmful if a nation's population does not have time to adapt to new patterns of living and working. Suppose much of a nation is converted from subsistence farming to growing one crop for export. This may displace large numbers of people who are no longer needed for farming. Unable to find work in the countryside, many will migrate to already overcrowded cities.

Using Appropriate Technology Another aspect of industrialization and balanced growth is the need to use technology that is appropriate, or suitable, to a culture. For example, instead of buying tractors, it may be better for a nation using wooden plows to first replace them with ones made of steel. See Figure 21.17. The benefits of modernization can be distributed more widely because plows are cheaper than tractors.

Allowing Adequate Time for Change Many economists believe industrialization is generally more beneficial if it comes about naturally. Time allows nations to adapt successfully to one stage of development before moving on to the next. Gradually, the developing nation increases its income and savings and its number of skilled and educated workers. Economic conditions reach the point where businesspeople freely decide to build factories instead of increasing farm output. This is exactly what has happened in many nations in Southeast Asia.

The Importance of Property Rights for Economic Development

If you were in a country in which bank accounts and businesses were periodically taken over by the government, how willing would you be to leave your money capital in a savings

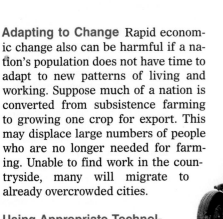

Figure 21.17 ▲
Which Technology? Many farmers in developing nations may be unable to use modern equipment such as the tractor. In addition, along with the tractors come the problems of supplying fuel, spare parts, maintenance, and so on.

account or to invest in a local business? In the United States and in other developed countries, the government may not legally take private property without paying a fair market value. This protection of private property is known as **property rights.** Private property may not be secure in numerous developing countries, however. Private property was nationalized in Cuba in the 1960s and, for a time in the 1970s, in Chile.

The more certain private property rights are, the more investment there will be. When people have property rights that are supported and enforced by the government, they feel confident about making investments. In fact, some historians have attempted to show that it was the development of well-defined property rights that allowed western Europe to increase its growth rate after many centuries of stagnation during the Middle Ages. The degree of certainty of reaping the gains from investing determines the extent to which businesspersons in other countries will invest money capital in developing countries.

Teach

Guided Practice

L1 Writing Have students write a paragraph in which they answer the following question: What role should industrialization have in developing nations? Students should use the information in Section 4 in writing their paragraphs.

Visual Instruction

Refer students to Figure 21.18 on page 524 and discuss with them the factors that influence economic development. Organize students into small groups and have them determine which factor they consider most important in influencing economic development. Discuss the groups' choices.

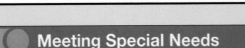

Meeting Special Needs

Learning Disability Students with learning disabilities in reading or with other reading comprehension problems often do not practice or use good self-appraisal and self-management skills while they read. Encourage these skills by making students aware of the need for these unconscious activities. As stu-dents read Section 4, tell them to be aware of processes they use to help them understand the material. Have them note the number of times they reread phrases or sentences. Explain that rereading is important for understanding.

Independent Practice

L3 Debating Have two groups of students research and debate whether foreign aid is harmful or helpful to developing nations. Students should be specific about the types of foreign aid they are discussing. The side opposing foreign aid should present alternatives to foreign aid. The rest of the class should critique the debate.

 Have students complete Guided Reading Activity 21.4 in the TCR. LEP

GLOBAL ECONOMICS

In recent years corporations have found economic opportunities in developing nations. General Electric has established a joint venture in India to produce low-cost ovens, opened a jet-engine repair facility in Indonesia, established a joint venture plastics business in Mexico, and invested in medical systems in China and India.

**Figure 21.18
Factors Influencing
Economic Development**
Three major factors affect the development of nations economically.

A Trade With the Outside World ▲
The more a country trades with the outside world, in general the faster it will grow. Therefore, developing nations can develop more quickly if they stop restricting trade.

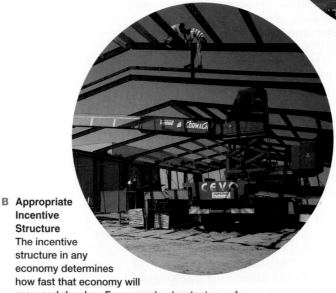

**B Appropriate
Incentive
Structure**
The incentive structure in any economy determines how fast that economy will grow and develop. For example, developing countries need reasonable tax rates that are not too high and a legal system that protects private property rights. ▲

C A Supportive Political Structure
Typically, in countries in which government-owned business accounts for a small percentage of GDP, more economic development can be found. If, however, the political system supports and enforces any types of price controls, there will be less incentive for entrepreneurs to enter businesses for which goods produced are in relatively scarce supply. ▼

Factors That Influence Economic Development

Several major factors influence economic development as Figure 21.18 shows. Natural resources such as trees and minerals and reduced population growth are almost always mentioned as important factors as well. The lack of one of these factors, however, does not necessarily put a less-developed country into the trap of underdevelopment or into the **vicious cycle of poverty.** Presumably developing nations are poor because they cannot save and invest, but they cannot save and invest because they are poor as Figure 21.19 shows.

Cooperative Learning

Point out to students that people in most parts of the world are aware of goods such as automobiles, televisions, radios, and canned foods. Organize the class into small groups and ask them to imagine being members of an economic planning commission in a developing nation with little industry. They must find ways to get citizens to save money and delay buying automobiles and televisions, decide what parts of the economy should be developed first, and determine where to obtain aid. Groups should discuss solutions to each concern, have a member record them, and have another present them to the class.

Remember that every developed country today was at one time a developing country. In 1800 the British Crown colony of Hong Kong was a barren rock. A hundred years later it was a substantial port. Not too many hundreds of years ago, the United States was completely underdeveloped. Today it is a sophisticated economic superpower. Clearly we must look to factors beyond poverty to determine the various routes to development.

Economic development normally depends on individuals who are able to perceive opportunities and then take advantage of those opportunities. Entrepreneurship is one of the four factors of production. It is entrepreneurs who are willing to take risks and who will, in fact, take advantage of economic opportunities when they arise. Risk taking, however, will not occur if the risk takers cannot expect a reward. The political system must be such that risk takers are rewarded. That requires well-established property rights and no fear of government nationalization of business.

Increased Information Leads to Cooperation

Because of the media, information about the higher living standards of developed countries is known even in the most remote villages of developing nations today.

One effect of this increased flow of information has been to convince developing nations of the benefits of working together. These nations have come to realize that, compared to large developed nations such as the United States, each developing nation has little influence over world trade. Together, however, the developing nations can and do have power in the international economic community.

A second trend in recent years has been toward more cooperation between developed and developing nations. Since 1981 leaders of developing nations and leaders of developed nations have met many times. A major purpose of those meetings is to establish global negotiations aimed at a more equal distribution of the world's wealth and resources. Some suggestions to achieve this goal included low tariffs for developing nations, an "income tax" on developed nations to pay for international assistance programs, and the use of profits from seafloor mining to finance development in poor nations.

The Cycle of Poverty

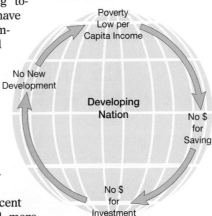

▲
**Figure 21.19
The Poverty Cycle**
This diagram represents the theory that low per capita incomes prevent the amount of saving and investing needed to achieve acceptable rates of economic growth.

SECTION 4 REVIEW

Understanding Vocabulary
Define property rights, vicious cycle of poverty.

Reviewing Objectives
1. What are four problems of rapid industrialization in developing nations?
2. Why are property rights important for economic development?
3. In addition to poverty, what factors influence economic development?
4. What is the relationship between increased information flows and international economic cooperation?

Section 4 Review Answers
Understanding Vocabulary
property rights (p. 523), **vicious cycle of poverty** (p. 524)
Reviewing Objectives
1. unwise investments, insufficient time to adapt to changed living patterns, inappropriate technology, and inadequate time for all development stages
2. because, when supported and enforced, they promote investor confidence
3. trade with the outside world, human attitudes and aptitudes, and a nation's political structure
4. Increased information flow encourages developing nations to work together to achieve economic power.

Assess

Meeting Lesson Objectives
Assign Section 4 Review as homework or an in-class activity. Each question in the Review addresses the corresponding numbered objective in the Section Focus.

Evaluate
Assign the Section 4 Quiz in the TCR or use the Testmaker to develop a customized quiz.

Assign the Chapter 21 Test Form A or Form B or use the Testmaker to develop a customized test.

Reteach
Ask students to write several paragraphs summarizing Section 4. Then tell them to reread the section, add any details they missed and correct any errors in their paragraphs.

Have students complete Reteaching Activity 21 in the TCR.

Enrich
Have students research the World Bank or the International Monetary Fund and write a brief report on its makeup and functions.

Have students complete Enrichment Activity 21 in the TCR.

Close

Ask students to write editorials predicting the economic future of developing nations.

Teach

Ask students to find Singapore on a map of the world. Point out that Singapore is one of the world's few true city-states and the only one having an air force and army. It is a center for world trade, and its per capita income and standard of living are among the highest in Asia. Singapore achieved its success in only 25 years despite having few natural resources and only a bit of land.

Ask volunteers to read the feature and identify advantages and disadvantages to living in Singapore. Then have students answer the questions in Think About It.

DID YOU KNOW

English common law formed the foundation of American private property rights. After the American Revolution, the states carried out land-law reforms, dismantling much of the feudal past. In the early 1800s, private property rights reinforced the goals of American public policy—economic growth, an expanding population, and a healthy middle class.

News Clip

Readings in Economics

TIME   JANUARY 18, 1993

IS SINGAPORE A MODEL FOR THE WEST?

by Jay Branegan

Singapore, long an object of curiosity for its unique blend of open economics, authoritarian politics and social engineering, is attracting attention as a model modern society.

. . . But what makes Singapore work would hardly succeed in the individualist West. There are hefty penalties, vigorously enforced, on human foibles: littering ($625), failing to flush a public toilet ($94) or eating on the subway ($312). The sale of chewing gum was banned last year, and 514 people were convicted of illegally smoking in public.

. . . With low pollution, lush tropical greenery, a mix of modern skyscrapers and colonial-era buildings, the city resembles a clean and efficient theme park; even the subway stations are as spotless and shiny as Disney World.

. . . The industrial policy debate here was settled long ago: the government coldly ushers fading industries like textiles offstage, and targets promising new ones like biotechnology with investment, grants and retraining workers.

Oddly in such a capitalist nirvana, the government owns scores of firms, from the telephone, electricity and airline companies to banks, supermarkets and taxis, but they all run on a competitive, profit-making basis. Says a Western analyst: "Fortune 500 executives love it here because the government runs the country the way AT&T would."

Most citizens would agree with Goh, [a] small businessman: "We have plenty of freedom here, except political freedom."

• THINK ABOUT IT •

1. *What laws illustrate the strict political control of Singapore's government?*

2. *How would you classify Singapore's economic system?*

526

Answers to Think About It

1. laws against littering, failing to flush a public toilet, eating on the subway

2. mixed

21 *Highlights*

Using Chapter 21
HIGHLIGHTS

Use the Chapter 21 Highlights to preview, review, condense, or reteach the chapter. A Spanish Chapter Highlights is available in the Spanish Handbook.

Preview/Review

After students read the Chapter 21 Highlights, have them complete Economics Vocabulary Activity 21 in the TCR. Spanish Vocabulary Activities are also available in the Spanish Resource Binder.

Vocabulary Software reinforces the economic terms used in Chapter 21.

Condense

Have students listen to Chapter 21 on the Audiocassettes in the TCR. A 1-page written activity and 1-page test accompany this material. These materials are also available in Spanish.

Reteach

Have students complete Reteaching Activity 21 in the TCR. Spanish Reteaching Activities are also available.

Section 1

Characteristics of Developing Nations

Key Terms

developed nations (p. 504)
developing nations (p. 504)

subsistence agriculture (p. 505)
infant mortality (p. 506)

Summary

Three of every four people in the world live in developing nations. Economists consider several factors when they measure the development of a nation. Several Asian nations have shown steady and rapid growth in recent years.

Section 2

The Process of Economic Development

Key Terms

foreign aid (p. 512)
economic assistance (p. 513)
technical assistance (p. 513)

military assistance (p. 513)

Summary

The economic development of a nation may be financed through a combination of domestic savings and foreign investment and aid. Foreign aid consists of economic, technical, and military assistance. Many industrial nations supply foreign aid because of humanitarian goals, economic and political goals, and national security objectives.

Section 3

Obstacles to Growth in Developing Nations

Key Terms

bureaucracies (p. 517)
nationalization (p. 519)

Summary

Developing nations face several obstacles to growth. Indonesia's lack of economic growth teaches us that simply pouring money into a developing nation will not guarantee economic growth. Foreign aid must be used wisely along with domestic savings, foreign investment, and government policies that ensure economic stability.

Section 4

Industrialization and the Future

Key Terms

property rights (p. 523)
vicious cycle of poverty (p. 524)

Summary

Rapid industrialization may not be the answer for developing nations that do not have a comparative advantage in producing some good that they decide to manufacture. The more certain private property rights are, the more investment, both domestic and from abroad, there will be.

VIDEODISC

Nightly Business Report
Economics in Action
Use "Economic Growth in Developing Nations" on Disc 2, Side B, Video 28.

Search 19182, Play to 26079

VIDEODISC

Nightly Business Report
Economics in Action
Use "Technological and Social Change" on Disc 2, Side B, Video 30.

Search 32546, Play to 41061

Identifying Key Terms

Write the letter of the definition in Column B below that correctly defines each term in Column A.

Column A
1. foreign aid (p. 512)
2. subsistence agriculture (p. 505)
3. developing nations (p. 504)
4. technical assistance (p. 513)

Column B
a. raising food sufficient for one's own or one's family's needs only
b. nonindustrialized countries
c. money, goods, and services given by one nation to another nation
d. aid in the form of professional expertise from engineers, doctors, teachers, and other specialists

Write a paragraph on different types of development problems, using the following words.

developed nations (p. 504)
bureaucracies (p. 517)
nationalization (p. 519)
property rights (p. 523)
vicious cycle of poverty (p. 524)

Recalling Facts and Ideas

Section 1

1. The per capita income in countries such as the United States, Japan, and Germany is approximately how many thousands of dollars?
2. What characteristics identify most developing nations?

3. What area of the world has seen rapid economic growth in recent years?

Section 2

4. List two affiliates of the World Bank.
5. What is the difference between military assistance and technical assistance?
6. In what stage of development are most developing nations?
7. What are some reasons for giving foreign aid?

Section 3

8. How does defense spending expressed as a percentage of GDP compare in many developing countries with the same variable in the United States?
9. How is rapid population growth an obstacle to economic development?
10. How do international trade restrictions hinder economic growth of developing nations?

Section 4

11. What is true about the early history of every developed country in the world today?
12. Why are property rights a factor in economic development?
13. How can a developing nation's government influence foreign investment?

Critical Thinking

Section 1

Making Inferences Some developed countries in the world today, such as the United States, have large natural resource bases. Does this necessarily mean that many natural resources are required in order for a country to have economic growth and development?

such as a nation's trade with the outside world, its infrastructure, and its political structure contribute to its economic growth and development.

Section 2

Answers will vary but should include the following: The level of development and education that existed in Europe's war-torn economy at the end of World War II was higher than the levels in today's developing nations. To

Section 2

Making Comparisons What is the difference between the level of development and education that existed in Europe's war-torn economy at the end of World War II and the level of development and education that exists in today's developing nations? How does your answer impact on the potential use of foreign aid in today's developing nations?

Section 3

Drawing Conclusions Why do restrictions on international trade represent an obstacle to economic growth for a developing nation?

Section 4

Determining Cause and Effect What is the relationship between well-defined and government-enforced private property rights and the incentive structure for investment in a nation?

Applying Economic Concepts

Foreign Aid Many republics of the former Soviet Union are extremely poor. Even the largest and one of the richest republics, Russia, has a per capita income that is a small percentage of that in the United States. The developed countries have been giving foreign aid to Russia during the 1990s. Use the information you have obtained in this chapter about the problems facing developing countries and the difficulty of using foreign aid correctly. Make a list of the obstacles that Russia faces in properly putting to good use the foreign aid that it is receiving.

Chapter Projects

1. **Individual Project** Select a developing nation and write a research report about the economic and social conditions of that nation by collecting facts on housing, food production, transportation, medical care, and the role of the government. The most reliable sources are the International Monetary Fund Reports, United Nations reports, and government statistical bulletins.

2. **Cooperative Learning Project** Organize into at least five groups. Each group will study one part of the world, such as: northern Africa, Central Africa, Southeast Asia, Central America, or western Europe.

    The goal of each group is to determine the percentage of the economy devoted to agriculture and the percentage devoted to industry. Each member of each group will obtain the relevant information for one or more countries in his or her chosen region. Compare the information obtained, selecting one person to prepare summary statistics for your group's region.

Reviewing Skills

Recognizing Trends

Spotting Real Trends Below are the data for the United States government's expenditures on international aid in various years. What can you say about the trend in spending on international aid?

1989	$9.6 billion
1990	$13.8 billion
1991	$15.9 billion
1992	$16.1 billion
1993	$18.7 billion

Writing About Economics

Comparative Writing Choose two of the countries about which you have collected similar information in Your Economics Journal. Write a brief radio news story that compares economic conditions in these two countries. Remember that news answers the who, what, when, where, and sometimes the why and how of events.

529

improve the levels, foreign aid to today's developing countries might be most beneficial in the form of technical assistance.

Section 3
Restrictions such as quotas and tariffs sometimes prevent the purchase of cheaper foreign substitutes for inefficiently produced domestic goods, so the developing economy suffers.

Section 4
Well-defined and government-enforced private property rights increase the incentive for investment.

Applying Economic Concepts
Answers will vary, but students' lists should include the obstacles discussed in the chapter.

? BONUS QUESTION

The following bonus question may be written on the chalkboard when students take the chapter test.
Q: How would you explain reduced per capita calorie consumption in a country with a population explosion?
A: The country cannot grow or buy enough food to feed its people.

Chapter Projects
1. Students might summarize their information in a chart or table.
2. Encourage students to use circle graphs to illustrate the percentages.

Reviewing Skills
The trend appears to be increased government expenditure.

Writing About Economics
Encourage students to answer the who, what, when, where, why, and how questions in describing the events.

529

CHAPTER 22 *THE GLOBAL ECONOMY*

CHAPTER ORGANIZER

Daily Objectives	Special Features	Classroom Resources

Section 1 Reasons for and Results of Global Integration

- **Explain** how improved telecommunications have caused increased global integration.
- **Name** three kinds of financial instruments now traded in global markets.
- **Identify** a major problem with the worldwide stock market.

Critical Thinking Skills:
Making Inferences
From Statistics, p. 536

- Reproducible Lesson Plan 22.1
- *NBR* Video 29
- Focus Activity Transparency 96
- Focus Activity Sheet 96
- Guided Reading Activity 22.1
- Cooperative Learning Activity 22
- Primary and Secondary Source Readings 22
- Section Quiz 22.1
- Spanish Section Quiz 22.1
- Testmaker
- Reinforcing Skills 22

Section 2 Direct Foreign Investment— Should We Be Worried?

- **Explain** the history of foreign investment in the United States.
- **Indicate** how important Japanese foreign investment is in the United States.
- **Describe** concerns that nations may have about direct foreign investment.

Personal Perspective:
Laura Tyson on the
Global Economy, p. 542

- Reproducible Lesson Plan 22.2
- Focus Activity Transparency 97
- Focus Activity Sheet 97
- Guided Reading Activity 22.2
- Section Quiz 22.2
- Spanish Section Quiz 22.2
- Testmaker

Section 3 Multinationals and Economic Competition

- **Indicate** the number of multinationals in the world today.
- **Identify** important cross-border investments.
- **Describe** the advantages of corporate alliances.
- **Explain** why South Korea has lost foreign investment dollars.
- **Discuss** how recent immigration patterns have increased the need for tolerance in the United States.

News Clip:
"The Invasion of the
American Way," *NRC
Handelsblad*, p. 548

- Reproducible Lesson Plan 22.3
- Focus Activity Transparency 98
- Focus Activity Sheet 98
- Economic Concepts Transparency 22
- Guided Reading Activity 22.3
- Economics Laboratory 6
- Economic Simulation 6
- Mathematics Practice for Economics 28
- Performance Assessment Activity 28
- Section Quiz 22.3
- Spanish Section Quiz 22.3
- Testmaker

0:00 OUT OF TIME? If time does not permit teaching this chapter, you may use the Chapter 22 Highlights and the Audiocassettes that include a 1-page activity and a 1-page test.

Chapter 22 Review and Evaluation

Special Features

Chapter 22 Highlights, p. 549
Chapter 22 Review, pp. 550–551
Economics Lab, pp. 552–553

Classroom Resources

Chapter 22 Test Forms A and B
Economics Vocabulary Activity 22
Spanish Economics Vocabulary
Activity 22

Audiocassette 22
Spanish Audiocassette 22
Reteaching Activity 22
Spanish Reteaching Activity 22

Key to Ability Levels

Teaching strategies have been coded for varying learning styles and abilities.

L1 Level 1 activities are **basic** activities and should be within the ability range of all students.

L2 Level 2 activities are **average** activities designed for the ability range of average to above-average students.

L3 Level 3 activities are **challenging** activities designed for the ability range of above-average students.

LEP activities should be within the ability range of **Limited English Proficiency** students.

Performance Assessment

The following chapter project may be assigned at the beginning of the chapter and used for performance assessment. See page T12 for additional Performance Assessment information.

Taking Samples Have students work in pairs to choose sample retail outlets and list 25 goods of different types sold by each outlet. Goods should be listed by type and selling price. Then have students note whether each good comes from the United States or another country. Encourage students to find out the origin of raw materials used in making some of the goods.

Additional Resources

Readings for the Student

SIRS Global Perspectives. Boca Raton, Fla.: Social Issues Resources Service, 1991.

Sklair, Leslie. *Sociology of the Global System.* Baltimore, Md: Johns Hopkins University Press, 1991.

Readings for the Teacher

Estell, Kenneth, ed. *World Trade Resources Guide.* Detroit: Gale Research Company, 1992.

Rugman, Alan M. *Multinationals and Canada-U.S. Free Trade.* Columbia, S.C.: University of South Carolina Press, 1990.

Thurow, Lester C. *Head to Head.* New York: Morrow, 1992.

Multimedia Materials

Challenge of Business on an International Scale. From the Business File Series. Videotape. 29 min. PBS Video. 475 L'Enfant Plaza SW, Washington, DC 20024

Global Agenda. Videotape. 30 min. Intercollegiate Video Clearinghouse. P.O. Drawer 33000R, Miami, FL 33133

Globe Master II. Apple. Versa Computing, Inc. 8870 Conestoga Circle, Newbury Park, CA 91320

World Trade and U.S. Jobs. Videotape. 30 min. Intercollegiate Video Clearinghouse. P.O. Drawer 33000R, Miami, FL 33133

Chapter Overview

As telecommunications and travel speed news from one corner of the earth to another, society is becoming increasingly global. Chapter 22 explains or describes: the role of telecommunications in increasing global integration; financial instruments traded in global markets; the problem of the worldwide stock market; the history of foreign investments in the United States; the importance of Japanese investments here; concerns of nations about direct foreign investment; world multinationals today; important cross-border investments; advantages of corporate alliances; loss of foreign investments in South Korea; and recent immigration patterns and the growing need for tolerance in the United States.

 VIDEODISC

Nightly Business Report
Economics in Action
Use "Global Economic Challenges" on Disc 2, Side B, Video 29.

Search 26164, Play to 32470

CHAPTER
22
THE GLOBAL ECONOMY

How does the state of Japan's economy affect our economy?

How would a person in Tokyo find out a day's closing figures on the New York Stock Exchange?

How have improved methods of worldwide communications impacted economic fluctuations?

Does the United States have many investments in foreign markets?

530   Unit 22 The International Scene

Answering Economic Questions

The questions in the above illustration are designed to lead into the main concepts in Chapter 22. Students might be unaware that innovations in the United States affect the economic growth of our trading partners. They also might be surprised to consider that telephones were a rather new technology at the beginning of the twentieth century. Have students discuss the questions and think about ways in which forms of global communication have changed their lives.

崇敬会
商店会

How are world economies connected?

How would a drastic change in the stock market in the United States affect people in Tokyo?

Your Economics Journal

Write a list of all the businesses with which you have contact during a one-week period. After each name, indicate whether you believe the ownership of that business is local; that is, is the business owned by someone who lives in your community?

531

Focus

Overview

See the student page for section objectives.

Section 1 explains or describes: how improved telecommunications have increased global integration; the kinds of financial instruments now traded in global markets; and problems with links among worldwide stock markets.

Bellringer

Before presenting the lesson, display Focus Activity Transparency 96 on the overhead projector or copy the material on the chalkboard. Assign the accompanying Focus Activity Sheet.

Motivational Activity

Have students estimate how often and how long they talked on the telephone over the last week. Then have them estimate the number of letters or notes they wrote and the time they spent writing. Ask students to tell when each mode of communication is preferable and why, for many people, telephoning has all but replaced letter and note writing. Tell students that Section 1 will discuss the impact of telecommunications upon the world economy.

Preteaching Vocabulary

Ask students to study the definitions of the Glossary terms.

SECTION 1 FOCUS

Terms to Know global integration, telecommunications

Objectives *After reading this section, you should be able to:*

❶ Explain how improved telecommunications have caused increased global integration.

❷ Name three kinds of financial instruments now traded in global markets.

❸ Identify a major problem with the worldwide stock market.

Global Trade Affects All of Us

In the United States it would not be unusual to ride on a bus that was made in Germany or in a Japanese-made car. Suppose you eat lunch at a local restaurant. You may not know it, but a Canadian owns the restaurant. Some of the restaurant's food has been imported from Mexico, France, and Spain. While reading the newspaper at lunch, you read about interest rates falling because political upheavals in other countries have caused businesses there to invest their money capital in politically stable America.

We now live not just as Americans, but as part of the global economy. **Global integration** has increased dramatically over the past several decades. Many reasons explain this increase. One has to do with improved **telecommunications,** or long-distance electronic communications.

Improved Telecommunications

The first transatlantic telegraph cable was completed in 1867. Before then it took two weeks to find out the price of the dollar in London. The telegraph cable reduced that time to two minutes. With the invention of the semiconductor—the computer chip—

Figure 22.1 Decreasing Costs

The price per million units of computing power (expressed in millions of instructions per second) from 1978 to 1995 has fallen dramatically. ▼

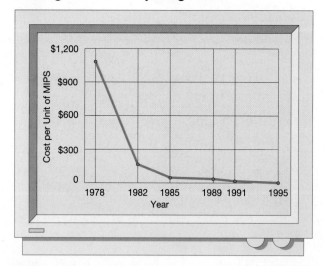

Falling Cost of Computing Power

Classroom Resources for Section 1

- Reproducible Lesson Plan 22.1
- *NBR* Video 29
- Focus Activity Transparency 96
- Focus Activity Sheet 96
- Guided Reading Activity 22.1
- Cooperative Learning Activity 22

- Primary and Secondary Source Readings 22
- Section Quiz 22.1
- Spanish Section Quiz 22.1
- Testmaker
- Reinforcing Skills 22

**Figure 22.2
Satellite
Communications**
Even in the People's
Republic of China—
where the government
has much control—
satellite dishes are a
growth industry. More
Chinese are seeing
how the rest of the
world looks, thinks, and
operates. ◀

Teach

Guided Practice

L2 Panel Discussion
Have small groups develop
a panel discussion on a topic
such as geography and
accessibility of communication, bilingual education,
speed of financial transactions, and cultural conflict.
Remind students to focus on
the effect of telecommunications on their topic.

L3 Writing Have students
choose a country with a different culture than that in
the United States. Ask students to brainstorm about
how people from this country might respond to view-
ing American culture via
television. Have students
write a cause-and-effect
essay about how this expo-
sure to American culture
might affect the people's
cultural, economic, and
political life.

🌐 GLOBAL ECONOMICS

Communications satel-
lites worldwide give peo-
ple access to computer
data and telecommunica-
tions. The United States
has more than 20 satel-
lites for domestic use.
Canada also has several.
Eulelsat and *Arabsat*
serve European and Arab
nations. *INTELSAT*, a
network of 18 satellites,
reaches more than 600
earth stations.

telecommunications really took off.
Look at how much the price of computing power has fallen just in the last
few years in Figure 22.1.

Several other inventions and factors have influenced the rapid improvement in worldwide telecommunications. Communications satellites
circle the earth day and night. Radio
and television waves, beamed up to
them, are reflected down to other
parts of the earth. On the earth itself,
fiber-optic cables are being placed
throughout much of North America
and already exist in parts of Europe.
Cellular telephones are another important aspect of this worldwide communications system.

Consider some of the ways cheap
and readily available satellite television has transformed the information
received in the Eastern Hemisphere.

Before the 1990s virtually all of the
television (and radio) available in the
Eastern Hemisphere was state-run
and state-controlled. Viewers saw few
programs and advertisements from
other parts of the world. Today, people in Asia receive sports, music, soap
operas, news, and advertisements free
of government control via satellite.
See Figure 22.2.

How does this increase in communications affect the rest of the world,
particularly Asia? Viewers in other
parts of the world are changing their
habits. In India they go so far as to
buy copies of outfits worn by popular
music television personalities. In addition, because most popular programs
are transmitted in English throughout
the world, more of the world's people
want to learn English as a second
language.

Chapter 22 The Global Economy **533**

 Meeting Special Needs

Visual Disability Students with visual difficulties may have problems reading and
creating bar graphs quickly. Encourage students to work on bar graphs in small groups,
discussing the information that is presented
or that will be presented on the graph. Stu-

dents who have difficulty reading small type
may need written information reprinted in a
larger size. Students may also wish to present bar graphs using dark-lined, large-scale
grid paper.

Independent Practice

L2 Comparing and Contrasting Have students list across the top of a page the different methods of communication used by people worldwide. Then ask students to create a chart showing the advantages and disadvantages of each form of communication. After they have entered all the information in their charts, encourage students to color code each entry so the number of advantages and disadvantages can be seen at a glance.

Have students complete Guided Reading Activity 22.1 in the TCR. LEP

Visual Instruction

Answer to Figure 22.3 question: *Australia; Italy.*

Have students study Figure 22.3 to note the extent to which the 1987 stock market crash in the United States affected foreign stock markets. Organize a discussion of the ways in which global telecommunications can trigger a crisis in stock markets in different countries.

**Figure 22.3
Global Crash**

Examine the graph to see how the stock market crash of 1987 affected certain nations of the world. Which nation shown experienced the greatest change as a result of the 1987 stock market crash? Which nation shown was least affected? ▶

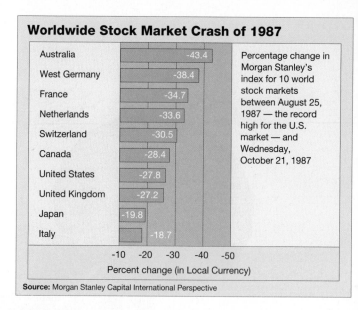

Worldwide Stock Market Crash of 1987

Australia	-43.4
West Germany	-38.4
France	-34.7
Netherlands	-33.6
Switzerland	-30.5
Canada	-28.4
United States	-27.8
United Kingdom	-27.2
Japan	-19.8
Italy	-18.7

Percent change (in Local Currency)

Percentage change in Morgan Stanley's index for 10 world stock markets between August 25, 1987 — the record high for the U.S. market — and Wednesday, October 21, 1987

Source: Morgan Stanley Capital International Perspective

The Globalization of Financial Markets

Because of the speed and power of computers and the affordability of telecommunications, the world has become one financial market. This globalization started in the 1960s and 1970s, when United States banks developed worldwide branch networks for loans and foreign exchange trading. Today money and financial capital markets are truly global, and many instruments are traded on them.

Markets for United States government securities (bonds the United States government sells), foreign exchange, and shares of stocks are now trading continuously, in vast quantities, around the world. For example, trading in United States government securities is the world's fastest growing 24-hour market. Foreign exchange—the buying and selling of foreign currencies—became a 24-hour worldwide market in the 1970s. Worldwide markets exist in commodities such as grains, gold and silver, and stocks. The worldwide stock market, started in about the mid-1970s, however, has some problems.

Problems With the Worldwide Stock Market

When each country's stock market is linked worldwide, problems can arise. One such problem occurred during the biggest one-day stock market crash that the United States has ever faced. Historians emphasize the Great Depression that started when the stock market crashed on October 28, 1929. Another huge stock market crash occurred on October 19, 1987, almost 60 years later. The Dow Jones Industrial Average fell 501 points, the largest one-day loss in United States history. In less than seven hours, more than $500 billion of corporate value disappeared. The stock markets in Sydney, London, and Hong Kong soon followed. Two years later the United States stock market finally regained its previous level, but several other world markets took even longer to recover.

The important lesson of the crash of 1987 was that a globalized financial market, through its electronic information system, now causes everybody everywhere to feel the effects of a financial panic. In Figure 22.3 you see

Cooperative Learning

Have students work in teams to design an ideal form of telecommunications that improves current cellular phone communications. Have teams brainstorm about the advantages and disadvantages of cellular phones, the obstacles that keep them from universal use, and the form of communication they think would be ideal. Then ask teams to draw an annotated picture of their ideal form of telecommunications, along with a short explanation of how it would work.

that many other countries experienced even more severe drops in their stock market index than the United States did in the crash of 1987.

Many managers of investment companies looked worldwide to sell their shares on October 19, 1987. They did not think they could sell their shares in the United States at very attractive prices because of the declining stock market. Investment managers in other countries did the same thing. The United States crash led to stock sales in foreign markets, which caused their stock markets to crash, too. Foreigners sold in the United States market in response. This vicious cycle continued for several days. Figure 22.4 gives some idea of the worldwide impact.

Figure 22.4 ▲
Impact of the '87 Crash

The collapse of the stock market affects most of the world's people in one way or another. It is, therefore, major news. The newspapers shown here devoted their front pages to the story and news magazines ran feature stories in their next issues.

SECTION 1 REVIEW

Understanding Vocabulary
Define global integration, telecommunications.

Reviewing Objectives
① How have improved telecommunications affected global integration?

② What kinds of financial instruments are traded in global markets?

③ What major problem affected the worldwide stock market in 1987?

Chapter 22 The Global Economy **535**

Meeting Lesson Objectives
Assign Section 1 Review as homework or an in-class activity. Each question in the Review addresses the corresponding numbered objective in the Section Focus.

Evaluate
Assign the Section 1 Quiz in the TCR or use the Testmaker to develop a customized quiz.

Reteach
Ask students to identify cultural and economic differences among nations and elements of global integration that bridge these differences.

Enrich
Have students analyze the stock market crash of 1987 by creating a time line for the years 1983 to 1992. Suggest including significant events that contributed to or resulted from the crash.

Close
Ask students to discuss ways in which telecommunications can bridge and widen differences between cultures and economies. Encourage speculation about the future of nations as individual entities.

Section 1 Review Answers

Understanding Vocabulary
global integration (p. 532), telecommunications (p. 532)

Reviewing Objectives
1. By increasing the speed of communications and the number of people who receive information, improved telecommunications have led people throughout the world to change many of their habits.

2. United States government securities, foreign currency, stocks, and commodities such as grains and gold and silver

3. the United States stock market crash

Teach

Point out to students that the ability to make inferences allows us to understand the probable effects of news events and therefore to make predictions. Have them study the table in Figure A showing United States military aid. Ask students to identify trends they can infer from the figure. *(Answers will vary but may suggest continuing or future conflicts in Latin America and parts of Asia, and present and future reduced threat in Europe and Africa.)*

Additional Practice

Have students complete Reinforcing Skills 22 in the TCR.

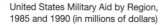

Critical Thinking Skills

Making Inferences From Statistics

To infer means to evaluate information and arrive at a conclusion. For example, a person may infer that an item is not selling well because prices for that item are declining. To imply is to express or to suggest something indirectly. Generally, a speaker or writer implies, and a reader infers. Making inferences is an important study skill and a vital economics skill.

Analyzing Statistics

Often a graph or a table contains more information than a reader may see at first glance. For example, **Figure A** shows changes in United States military aid by region between 1985 and 1990. To make inferences from this, follow these steps:

❶ Read the labels on the table to understand exactly what is being reported.

❷ Compare the statistical information to determine trends or changes.

❸ Ask yourself why the changes may have occurred.

❹ Apply related information that you may already know to make inferences from the table.

For example, based on decreased military aid to Africa, you might infer that the region had fewer conflicts in 1990 than it did in 1985.

Figure A

United States Military Aid by Region, 1985 and 1990 (in millions of dollars)

Region	1985	1990
Europe	$ 531	$ 89
Near East and South Asia	4,248	4,241
Africa	279	114
Latin America	269	234

Figure B

Direct Foreign Investment (millions of dollars)

Region	1981	1990
New England	$ 5,686	$ 19,402
Middle Atlantic	20,216	71,136
West South Central	34,651	82,951
Mountain	12,353	33,077
Pacific	34,409	120,164

Practicing the Skill

Study the statistics in **Figure B** about direct foreign investment in various regions of the country. From the data, what can you infer about the relationship between geography and foreign investment? Why does this relationship exist?

Answers to Practicing the Skill

Answers may vary but may include: foreign investments increased most in areas where they were already greatest in 1981; continued rapid growth in the Pacific may reflect large Japanese investment in the United States.

Direct Foreign Investment—Should We Be Worried?

SECTION 2 FOCUS

Terms to Know direct foreign investment (DFI)

Objectives *After reading this section, you should be able to:*

1. Explain the history of foreign investment in the United States.
2. Indicate how important Japanese foreign investment is in the United States.
3. Describe concerns that nations may have about direct foreign investment.

Who Owns Whom?

Nothing seems more American than Burger King or the Pillsbury Dough Boy, right? Not quite, for those companies are now owned by the British. In addition, the Japanese own about 40 percent of the office space in downtown Los Angeles. An Indonesian firm owns Chicken of the Sea Tuna, and a German company owns A&P Supermarkets. A group from East Asia owns the Algonquin Hotel in New York—a famous gathering place of American writers and artists. Mitsubishi, a Japanese company, owns half of Rockefeller Center in the middle of Manhattan. Foreign investment in the United States, however, is not new. See Figure 22.5.

Foreign Investment, Then and Now

Direct foreign investment (DFI) in the United States has increased to the point where some Americans want to restrict it. Direct foreign investment is evidence of the global integration of the American economy. In any one year, foreigners purchase billions of dollars of American real estate and businesses. Any time political upheaval strikes any other part of the world, foreign investment in the United

**Figure 22.5
Foreign Investment**
Foreign investment in the United States is not new. In the late 1800s, for example, the British helped finance the expansion of the railroads. ▼

537

Teach

Guided Practice

L2 Evaluating Current Events Have students in small groups look through recent newspapers and magazines for international news and discuss which events they think may affect direct foreign investment in the United States. Remind them that destabilizing events in a foreign country may increase the value of investments here.

L3 Presenting a News Program Have small groups of students imagine a situation in which the United States Federal Reserve might try to reduce the real value of debt owed by foreigners by creating runaway inflation. Ask students to analyze the effects of this action. Then have each group present a news program telling about the events that led to and followed the Fed's action.

GLOBAL ECONOMICS

The World Bank is a key organization in helping developing countries attract direct foreign investment. In addition to offering low-interest loans, the World Bank has an affiliate, The International Finance Corporation, which invests directly in enterprises in developing countries.

**Figure 22.6
Foreign Investment in the United States**
Foreigners own much of downtown Los Angeles as well as many formerly American-owned companies. S.A.Q. of Switzerland now owns the Carnation Company. The Japanese company Bridgestone owns Firestone Tire and Rubber. Carnation and Firestone were both formerly American owned. ▶

States increases because we remain a politically stable country.

Foreigners Have Always Invested in the United States The United States has a long history of foreign investment. For example, Great Britain was the biggest foreign investor in American railroads in the late 1800s and early 1900s. At the beginning of World War I, the United States owed more money to foreign lenders than any other country in the world.

Foreign Control of American Companies Many people argue against foreign ownership of American companies because they are worried about foreign control. Is foreign control important? See Figure 22.6. Presumably, foreign investors purchase American assets in order to maximize profits. Foreigners' interest in running a corporation would seem to be identical to the interest of any domestic investor who owned the same corporation. The profit-making behavior of a corporation presumably does not depend on the nationality of that corporation. If the British took over a hotel on Miami

Beach, would the service necessarily be any different in the long run? Economists do not think so.

What about the foreign investors' influence over the United States government? Foreigners own about 14 percent of all United States government securities that now exist. Can they use this to control United States foreign policy? Probably not. Foreigners purchase United States government securities when they think the rate of return is higher than they can get elsewhere. Remember that whenever foreigners buy United States government securities or private corporate securities, they free up United States financial capital for other productive uses.

It is actually the United States government that has more control over foreigners. Because they own about 14 percent of the United States public debt, as you can see in Figure 22.7, foreign investors are subject to United States government policy. For example, the federal government could, through its Federal Reserve System, create tremendous inflation. In so doing, it would wipe out the real value of the United States government debt

Meeting Special Needs

Language Disability Students who have difficulty with the English language may need help interpreting economic and political terminology, especially when these terms appear within news programs or articles.

Encourage students to paraphrase news items that contain difficult economic or political terminology. After clarifying any misconceptions, have students give a concrete interpretation of the news they convey.

that foreigners own.

Finally, in a larger sense, because foreign corporations do invest in the United States, they may indirectly influence our government. Our government cannot make the business climate in America too difficult for these corporations or they will take their investments elsewhere.

Japanese Investment

In recent years the Japanese have invested heavily in the United States, as Figure 22.8 (page 540) shows. Some social, political, and economic commentators have raised the question of whether they are "buying up America." A few years ago an American historian, Theodore White, wrote, "The Japanese are on the move again in one of history's most brilliant commercial offenses as they go about dismantling American industry." Mr. White suggested that the Japanese economic invasion of the United States during the 1980s was equivalent to its military attack on Pearl Harbor in 1941. Is this true?

Europe's Share of the United States Today, western European investors own about 50 percent of all foreign-owned assets in the United States.

Japan's share of total foreign holdings in the United States is less than 15 percent. Japan owns a little more than 1 percent of an estimated $16 trillion in American capital. Compared to western European ownership of American assets, Japan's does not look so imposing.

Why does Japanese investment in the United States seem like such a threat today? The answer probably lies with the more visible direct investments that Japan has made. Conspicuous Japanese investment in the United States also reminds Americans of the special relationship that exists between Japan and the United States: Japan relies almost exclusively on the United States for its national defense. In effect, the American taxpayer provides Japan's national defense system. This special relationship has allowed Japan to concentrate on economic growth while the United States has presumably borne a disproportionate share of defense costs.

Direct Foreign Investment

Despite the concern some have about foreigners owning the United States, the total share of foreign ownership of American industries is about 6 percent.

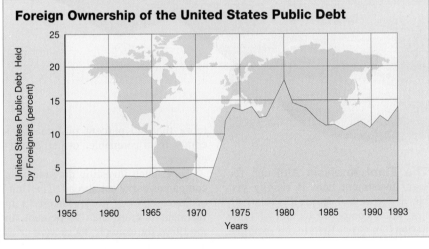

Foreign Ownership of the United States Public Debt

United States Public Debt Held by Foreigners (percent)

25 — 20 — 15 — 10 — 5 — 0

1955 1960 1965 1970 1975 1980 1985 1990 1993

Years

Figure 22.7 Foreign Ownership
Examine this graph carefully to see how foreign ownership of the United States public debt has changed. When did foreigners own their largest percentage? What has been the most recent trend? How do you explain this?

◀

Chapter 22 The Global Economy **539**

Independent Practice

L2 Making Cartoons Ask students to create two sets of cartoons. Each set should consist of two cartoons—the first showing a fear concerning the effects of foreign ownership of domestic businesses and the second showing the reality of this situation.

L1 Comparing and Contrasting Have students compare and contrast Japan's and western Europe's holdings in the United States by making a simple bar chart of foreign investments.

Visual Instruction

Answer to Figure 22.7 question: *1980; a slight increase in the 1990s; answers will vary but might include a reference to a stable economy in the United States.*

DID YOU KNOW

Foreign aid is a form of investment because economic development in a country leads to increased demand for goods and services. Thus, through foreign aid, economically developed countries like the United States, Japan, France, and Saudi Arabia, make significant contributions to stimulating demand worldwide.

Cooperative Learning

Organize students into small groups representing mutual fund investment companies. Give each group $100,000 for foreign investments. Tell students to use travel guides and world stock market listings to select investments. Groups should make choices based on past performance of the property or holding, its monetary or prestige value, and their ideas about the future of the country and the holding. Have each group give a presentation to the class, pretending the class is a group of stockholders to whom the group must justify the foreign investments.

Independent Practice

L2 Analyzing Ask students to write a short essay discussing possible reasons why government and business in the United States may find it acceptable for foreign interests to hold a certain percentage of the country's public debt.

Have students complete Guided Reading Activity 22.2 in the TCR. LEP

Visual Instruction

Refer students to Figure 22.8. Have them investigate possible economic, political, and military factors contributing to the trend indicated by the graph. Ask volunteers to report orally.

Figure 22.8 ▶
Direct Investment Positions, United States and Japan
Clearly, Japan has invested much more heavily in the United States than this country has in Japan. When the Japanese purchased 51 percent of an American landmark—Rockefeller Center in New York City —it generated a great deal of publicity. ▼

Direct Investment Positions, United States and Japan

● ● ● ● Japanese Investment in the United States
★ ★ ★ ★ United States Investment in Japan

The Final Analysis Although foreign investment here is readily visible, as Figure 22.9 shows, it is relatively low when compared to that of other nations. In Great Britain, for example, more than 20 percent of total sales comes from companies owned by foreigners.

How much investing do American companies carry out abroad? The United States' share of worldwide direct investment is more than 40 percent. In the 1970s, for example, there were cries

 Free Enterprise Activity

Have students develop a directory of foreign-produced consumer goods available in their area that they think interest their age group. Students may work in groups to research products such as clothing, electronics, or sports equipment. Students should then compile price and other product information in a directory that could be shared with other students. The cost of production could be recovered by selling low-cost advertisements to the businesses whose consumer goods are featured in the directory.

Assess

Meeting Lesson Objectives

Assign Section 2 Review as homework or an in-class activity. Each question in the Review addresses the corresponding numbered objective in the Section Focus.

Evaluate

Assign the Section 2 Quiz in the TCR or use the Testmaker to develop a customized quiz.

Reteach

Have students create a chart on the chalkboard that shows the pros and cons of direct investment, using the point of view of both the host nation and the investors.

Enrich

Have interested students research direct foreign investments that originates in various countries. Tell them to organize their information in a circle graph.

Close

Discuss with students whether they think the United States will increase investments in Japan in the future, and whether Japan's investments in the United States will increase. Encourage students to use Figures 22.7 on page 539 and 22.8 on page 540 for reference.

in Europe, especially France, that the United States was going to dominate its society. Indeed, throughout the world many people fear that United States culture has taken over everybody else's culture. Some people have called this *economic imperialism.*

Here is another way to view investment: If a Texas company purchases a business in Omaha, Nebraska, not many people worry. Nebraska will not likely try to pass legislation to prevent Texans—or other Americans, for that matter—from owning any kinds of businesses there. No one doubts that the reason the Texas firm purchased the Nebraska firm was to make a profit.

Most purchasers of goods and services anywhere in the world have little knowledge about who ultimately owns the company that provided the good or service—and they do not really care.

Some even argue that we should *encourage* direct investment and debt purchases by foreigners. Why? Foreigners then would have an increased incentive for the American economy to remain strong, for real estate prices *not* to collapse, for the legal structure to stay on a stable course, and for United States businesses to compete effectively by providing goods and services that consumers want.

Figure 22.9 ▲ Visible Foreign Investment
Unlike Burger King or Firestone or some other companies that are not obviously owned by foreigners, there are some companies that are clearly visible as being foreign-owned. Mazda and Toyota are only two of these.

SECTION 2 REVIEW

Understanding Vocabulary
Define direct foreign investment (DFI).

Reviewing Objectives
① Give a brief history of foreign investment in the United States.

② Explain the significance of Japan's economic investment in the United States.

③ Why are there national concerns about direct foreign investment?

Section 2 Review Answers
Understanding Vocabulary
direct foreign investment (DFI) (p. 537)
Reviewing Objectives
1. It expanded rapidly in the 1800s and early 1900s and has continued to grow in recent decades. Japanese investment has been especially strong since the mid-1980s.

2. Although Japanese investments are less than 15 percent of foreign holdings in the United States, they are higher in the western states and in certain industries, and often are particularly conspicuous.

3. because of worries about foreign control of key sectors of the American economy and government policy

Background

Laura Tyson has studied and taught at institutions of higher education across the continent. She believes free trade must be moderated because of the protectionist policies of foreign competitors.

Teach

Have volunteers read aloud the quoted excerpts from the article in *Fortune*. Then have students paraphrase each excerpt to gain a better understanding of Tyson's ideas. Finally, have them answer the questions in Checking for Understanding.

You might have interested students read the entire interview in *Fortune* or find other interviews to supplement their reading here.

Personal Perspective

Laura Tyson on the Global Economy

Profile

- 1948–
- Ph.D. from Massachusetts Institute of Technology
- taught at the University of California at Berkeley
- Chairperson of President Clinton's Council of Economic Advisers
- advocate of economic and trade policies to spur United States competitiveness abroad

In this article from *Fortune* magazine, Laura Tyson talks about free trade in the real world. She believes free trade may not be a real choice for policy-makers in a world where protectionist policies create unfair advantages for foreign competitors.

Trade isn't always free. And the choice of policy-makers is often not between free trade and protectionism. It is somewhere in the middle, between one kind of manipulated trade and another.

In an ideal world, our competitive industries would not be meeting subsidized or protected industries abroad. But that is not the world we face.... Do we want to be in the business of influencing market outcomes? It's a very hard call, and it is not one that I think any of us take lightly. We would much rather start with an effort to try to reduce the subsidy or protectionist activity abroad.

...There is no social or global justification for certain types of subsidies. Production subsidies... are simply market grabbing. But research and development subsidies may have the defense of at least possibly creating innovations.

Laura Tyson describes how the United States can improve its trade balance with Japan. She hints that the United States might limit imports through "quantitative market-share indicators."

The trade imbalance between the U.S. and Japan is primarily a macroeconomic phenomenon, the result of big U.S. budget deficits and big Japanese surpluses. The U.S. is now on an appropriate course, and it's time for the Japanese to get on one as well, by stimulating their economy.

When you have negotiated and been unable to address the problem of structural barriers, and there is evidence that competitive opportunities in an industry are not being accorded to competitive producers, then moving to a set of quantitative market-share indicators for foreign imports may be defensible. This should be a last step.

Checking for Understanding

❶ What is the choice that policy-makers often face?

❷ What measures would be the United States' first effort to make trade fair?

❸ What would be the United States' last resort?

Answers to Checking for Understanding

1. The choice is often not between free trade and protectionism but between one kind of manipulated trade and another.
2. The first measure the United States should use to make trade fair would be to try to reduce subsidies and general protectionist activity abroad.
3. The last resort the United States should use to make trade fair would be to move to a set of quantitative market-share indicators for foreign imports.

542

LESSON PLAN
Chapter 22, Section 3

SECTION 3 FOCUS

Terms to Know multinationals, allegiances, foreign affiliates, alliances, tolerance

Objectives *After reading this section, you should be able to:*

❶ Indicate the number of multinationals in the world today.

❷ Identify important cross-border investments.

❸ Describe the advantages of corporate alliances.

❹ Explain why South Korea has lost foreign investment dollars.

❺ Discuss how recent immigration patterns have increased the need for tolerance in the United States.

Focus

Overview

See the student page for section objectives.

Section 3 explains or describes: the size and number of multinationals: the concepts of regional investment clusters and alliances; and, why countries may choose to treat foreign businesses well.

Bellringer

⚑ Before presenting the lesson, display Focus Activity Transparency 98 and assign the accompanying Focus Activity Sheet.

Motivational Activity

Lead students in a discussion of allegiances to family friends and classmates. Say that Section 3 will explain the operations of multinationals, discuss their various allegiances, and explain their impact on the trend toward global integration.

Preteaching Vocabulary

Have groups present short scenarios for each vocabulary term. Have the class identify the terms.

Cross-Border Investing by Multinationals

For the last few years, international investing has grown faster than world output and faster than world trade. Much cross-border investing is undertaken by **multinationals.** See Figure 22.10. In the past, critics argued that because these firms are so large, they may dominate the world economy. Such firms were seen as ruthless companies that would exploit the poor and manipulate governments. Few people agree with such sentiments today. Multinationals bring modern technology and management skills to developing countries.

The Size and Number of Multinationals

In the 1970s, many people predicted that a few hundred multinationals would control 80 percent of the world's production by the mid-1980s. By the mid-1990s, there were an estimated 35,000 multinationals with 170,000 **foreign affiliates,** or branches of their firms. The largest 100 multinationals (excluding those in banking and finance) account for more than $3 trillion of worldwide assets. Figure 22.11 (page 544) lists the top 25 multinationals.

Figure 22.10 Multinationals
A multinational firm is simply one that does business in many countries and has offices and factories in many countries around the world. In a sense, a multinational firm has many national **allegiances,** or loyalties, not necessarily just to the country in which it has its main or principal office. ▼

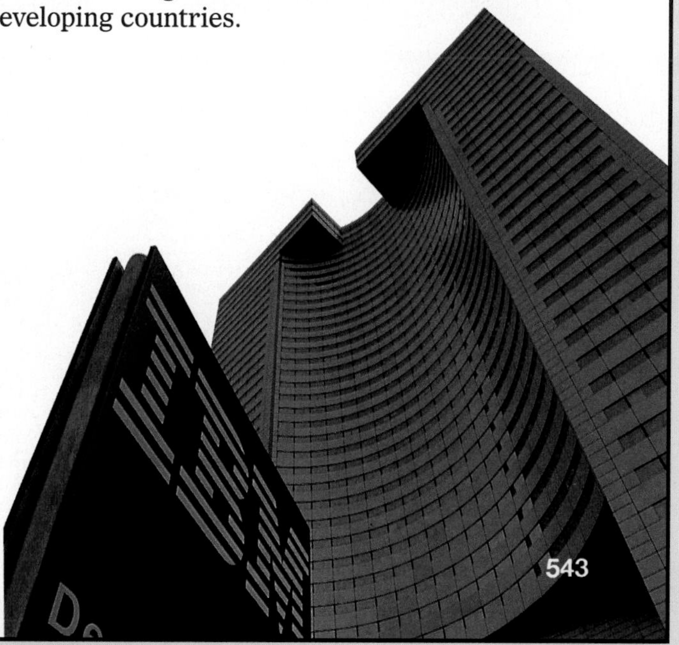

543

Classroom Resources for Section 3

- Reproducible Lesson Plan 22.3
- Focus Activity Transparency 98
- Focus Activity Sheet 98
- Economics Concepts Transparency 22
- Guided Reading Activity 22.3
- Economics Laboratory 6
- Economic Simulation 6

- Mathematics Practice for Economics 28
- Performance Assessment Activity 28
- Section Quiz 22.3
- Spanish Section Quiz 22.3
- Chapter 22 Test Forms A and B
- Testmaker

- Enrichment Activity 22
- Economics Vocabulary Activity 22
- Spanish Economics Vocabulary Activity 22
- Audiocassette 22
- Spanish Audiocassette 22
- Reteaching Activity 22

Teach

Guided Practice

L2 Applying Information
Have students in small groups propose alliances between firms that they think might benefit both the firms and consumers. Encourage students to suggest the kinds of new development that might grow out of alliances between the firms they name.

Visual Instruction

Ask students to examine Figure 22.11 and identify the multinationals that have a larger percentage of foreign sales than domestic. Have them identify the multinational with the largest percentage of foreign sales.

Answer to Figure 22.11 question: *Answers will vary. Students might suggest that countries with the strongest economies appear the most often.*

GLOBAL ECONOMICS

The profit motivation of multinationals becomes clear when one examines the reasons that a firm goes multinational. Most firms develop into multinational corporations to take advantage of lower production and labor costs and taxes in foreign countries, to gain control over the raw materials they need, and to avoid international tariffs.

Figure 22.11 The Largest Multinationals in the World

Largest Nonfinancial Multinationals, 1990, Ranked by Foreign Assets

Rank		Industry	Country	Foreign assets $bn	Total assets $bn	Foreign sales $bn	% of total sales
1	Royal Dutch/Shell	Oil	Britain/Holland	n.a.	106.3	56.0	49
2	Ford Motor Co.	Cars and trucks	United States	55.2	173.7	47.3	48
3	General Motors	Cars and trucks	United States	52.6	180.2	37.3	31
4	Exxon	Oil	United States	51.6	87.7	90.5	86
5	IBM	Computers	United States	45.7	87.6	41.9	61
6	British Petroleum	Oil	Britain	39.7	59.3	46.6	79
7	Nestlé	Food	Switzerland	n.a.	27.9	33.0	98
8	Unilever	Food	Britain/Holland	n.a.	24.8	16.7	42
9	Asea Brown Boveri	Electrical	Switzerland/Sweden	n.a.	30.2	22.7	85
10	Philips Electronics	Electronics	Holland	n.a.	30.6	28.6	93
11	Alcatel Alsthom	Telecoms	France	n.a.	38.2	17.7	67
12	Mobil	Oil	United States	22.3	41.7	44.3	77
13	Fiat	Cars and trucks	Italy	19.5	66.3	15.8	33
14	Siemens	Electrical	Germany	n.a.	50.1	15.1	40
15	Hanson	Diversified	Britain	n.a.	27.7	5.6	46
16	Volkswagen	Cars and trucks	Germany	n.a.	41.9	27.5	65
17	Elf Aquitaine	Oil	France	17.0	42.6	12.2	38
18	Mitsubishi	Trading	Japan	16.7	73.8	41.2	32
19	General Electric	Diversified	United States	16.5	153.9	8.3	14
20	Mitsui	Trading	Japan	15.0	60.8	43.6	32
21	Matsushita Electric Industrial	Electronics	Japan	n.a.	59.1	16.6	40
22	News Corp.	Publishing	Australia	14.6	20.7	5.3	78
23	Ferruzzi/Montedison	Diversified	Italy	13.5	30.8	9.1	59
24	Bayer	Chemicals	Germany	n.a.	25.4	21.8	84
25	Roche Holding	Drugs	Switzerland	n.a.	17.9	6.8	96

Sources: United Nations and *The Economist*, March 27, 1993

Figure 22.11 ▲
The Largest Multinationals in the World
Examine the chart above. Notice that certain nations and certain industries appear several times on the list of the world's largest multinationals. Why do you think this is the case?

Meeting Special Needs

Hearing Disability Students with hearing difficulties may have trouble following other students' presentations in class. Encourage presenting students to supplement verbal information with visual cues such as writing on the chalkboard or handing out key information so that all students can follow the presentations.

Worldwide Ownership The top 100 multinationals are very important, accounting for probably about 45 percent of all cross-border assets. This means nothing, however, without comparing these assets to the worldwide total. No one knows the value of the world's assets today, but a best guess is about $20 to $25 trillion. If this is true, the top 100 multinationals account for only about 15 percent of the world's productive assets—hardly a dominant share.

It is also true today that the United States and Great Britain no longer dominate multinationals. In 1970, for example, of the 7,000 multinationals identified by the United Nations, the Americans and the British owned more than 50 percent. Today, Americans, Japanese, Germans, and the Swiss own about half of the 35,000 multinationals. Numerous multinationals are based in the industrializing Asian countries such as Taiwan and South Korea.

The Regional Flavor of Cross-Border Investments

While it may be true that many of the biggest multinationals invest everywhere in the world, most do not. Most invest in regions that are closest to home. For example, the European Union (EU) plus Scandinavia and Switzerland engage in more foreign direct investment in western Europe itself than anywhere else.

In a world in which borders matter less, the line separating sales at home and those abroad becomes less important. The most appropriate way to look at patterns of direct investment is to include direct domestic sales as a part of regional sales. European firms principally invest in western Europe. American firms principally invest in the United States, Canada, Mexico, and South America. Japanese firms principally invest in Japan, South Korea, Greater China, and Southeast

Asia. Figure 22.12, for example, shows Japanese investment in Tokyo. Some obvious exceptions to this rule of regional investing by multinationals do exist. For historical reasons, the British as part of the EU invest heavily in India, once a colony of Great Britain.

Beyond Multinationals— Alliances

In addition to multinational direct investments in other countries, firms in different countries are forming **alliances.** These may be joint ventures. Indeed, many foreign governments have insisted that multinationals enter their markets through joint ventures with local firms in the hope that locals will capture some of the profits. Companies also make licensing deals. For example, an American jogging shoe company licensed its design to a company in South Korea.

Most alliances have been between firms from industrialized countries. Alliances are even popular within nations like the United States. For example, International Business Machines (IBM) developed its personal computer in alliance with Microsoft (for the software), Intel (for the central processing unit), and Lotus. In the late 1980s, IBM entered into an alliance with Siemens of Germany to work on memory chips. In the 1990s, IBM

**Figure 22.12
Japan's Major
Investment**

Japan, like most countries, invests most heavily in its own nation. Downtown Tokyo shows evidence of how heavily Japanese companies dominate the nation's capital. ▼

545

Independent Practice
L3 Analyzing Economic
Interests and Foreign Policy Ask small groups to research the economic interests of countries such as the United States, Great Britain, France, Germany, and Japan in the Persian Gulf region. Each group should study a particular country and such factors as its volume of trade; the size, profitability, and character of its investments in the Gulf region; the economic or strategic importance of the region's raw materials; and the extent of its dependence on the Gulf nations as sources of these raw materials. Student oral reports should consider possible connections between the countries' economic interests and policy positions during the Persian Gulf War.

Cooperative Learning

Point out to students that in the past several years, developing nations have begun making demands of multinationals regarding environmental protection, hiring, and labor. As a result, multinationals must negotiate to fulfill plans for expansion. Organize small groups of students to choose a multinational that plans to expand in a foreign country. Ask groups to explain the main points of the multinational's plan and the government's demands for controls. Groups may wish to divide among themselves responsibilities such as doing research, making visuals, and organizing key information.

Independent Practice

L2 Creating a Graphic
Remind students that the top 100 multinationals (excluding those in banking and finance) account for more than $3 trillion of the world's assets. Ask students to make a bar graph showing the foreign sales and domestic sales of the top 10 multinationals. Have students represent each of the top 10 multinationals with a bar. The bar should represent that multinational's total sales. Students should divide the bar into foreign sales and domestic sales and distinguish the two by using color or a pattern.

Have students complete Guided Reading Activity 22.3 in the TCR. **LEP**

Visual Instruction

Answer to Figure 22.13 question: *It would probably discourage other investment.*

Refer students to Figure 22.13 and the text following the Subhead: A Case Study in South Korea. Have them research the current status of foreign investment in South Korea and report orally.

Assess

Meeting Lesson Objectives

Assign Section 3 Review as homework or an in-class activity. Each question in the Review addresses the corresponding numbered objective in the Section Focus.

**Figure 22.13
Investing in
South Korea**
Many multinationals pulled out of South Korea in the early 1990s. How might this affect other potential foreign investors' decisions? ▶

entered into an alliance with Apple Computers, once its archrival.

Alliances can be seen as each firm's acceptance of its own limitations, whether they be financial, technological, or geographical. Alliances can be used to help a firm leapfrog its competitors or catch up with them. Such a strategy is particularly effective in an industry that has seen rapid changes such as computer memory chips and software.

A Case Study in South Korea

Multinationals, by their very nature, can move money capital from one part of the world to another. One reason they move money capital is if they think they can make a higher long-run average rate of return on their investment elsewhere. When one country starts offering better "deals" to multinational firms, they will take them. When one country makes life difficult for multinationals or foreign investors in general, money capital will flow out of that country.

This capital flow is exactly what has happened to South Korea. See **Figure 22.13**. In the early 1990s, foreign investors withdrew large amounts of money capital from South Korea. As reasons they cited complex govern-

ment regulations and a lack of incentive to remain in the country. In 1992 new foreign investment dropped more than 35 percent from the previous year. The value of the joint ventures South Korea lost in 1992 was more than five times the value of the previous year's losses. In the early 1990s, General Motors Corporation, Goodyear Tire and Rubber Company, and DuPont Company abandoned their plans to build sophisticated production facilities in South Korea.

ALCOA Consider one specific example. The Aluminum Company of America (ALCOA) created a joint venture with South Korea's Samsun Industrial Company. The American company wanted skilled labor to manufacture aircraft parts for export to Asia. The South Korean company wanted technology that it did not yet have. The plan was for ALCOA to take over and retool one of Samsun's aluminum plants. The total investment by both companies was to be about $40 million, but the deal went sour. ALCOA wanted to build defense-related component parts as well as commercial ones. South Korea's military establishment was worried. The government therefore issued guidelines to give other companies a better chance at obtaining defense industry business. ALCOA pulled out.

Free Enterprise Activity

Have students imagine that they own a multinational corporation and want to increase its investments in Central America. Ask them to consider how much weight to put on different factors. They should address the cost of raw materials and labor; the potential for expanding markets; the

development of roads, ports, and communications; and the stability of the country's political system. Have the class discuss the proposed investments. Point out to students that their views may depend on their values and their corporation's products.

Other companies have found that it takes years before their request to build factories is approved. Cargill Corporation had to wait four years after its application to build a $21 million soybean processing plant.

Investing in the People's Republic
Where are many foreign investors taking their money? Amazingly, many of them are going to the People's Republic of China. See Figure 22.14. Much of the money being invested in China is being taken out of South Korea. In a world of mobile financial capital, governments cannot treat foreign businesses poorly and expect them to continue investing.

The Global Village and Tolerance

One of the results of the globalization of our world is increased immigration. America has become a truly multicultural society because of such immigration. In many cities the combined numbers of African Americans, Hispanics, Asians, and other minorities now constitute a majority of the population. In the 1980s, for example, the Asian population in America increased more than 100 percent and the Hispanic population more than 50 percent. Public schools are more diverse than ever. This diversity means that the need for

tolerance and open-mindedness is more important today than it ever has been. **Tolerance** can be defined as a fair, objective, and permissive attitude toward the opinions, practices, religions, races, and nationalities of others that differ from one's own. It also includes an interest in and concern for the ideas, opinions, and practices that are foreign to one's own. For Americans this includes learning one or more foreign languages and maintaining friendships with those of different ethnic/cultural/national/religious backgrounds.

Nothing in our Constitution or in our laws requires us to be open-minded and tolerant. These qualities are part of our heritage. Those who acquire and use them will benefit, as will the nation as a whole.

**Figure 22.14
The China
Business Boom**
China used to be known as an impossible place to do business. It was not attractive to foreign investors. Today foreign investors are investing at the rate of $50 to $75 million a day in the People's Republic of China. ▼

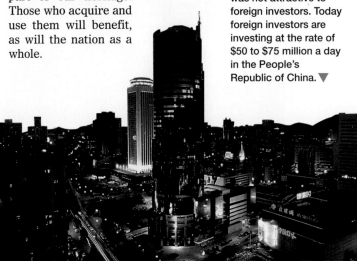

SECTION 3 REVIEW

Understanding Vocabulary
Define multinationals, allegiances, foreign affiliates, alliances, tolerance.

Reviewing Objectives
❶ Approximately how many multinationals are there in the world today?
❷ Give an example of a cross-border investment.
❸ What are the advantages of corporate alliances?
❹ What caused many foreign investors to reduce their investments in South Korea?
❺ How have recent patterns of immigration to the United States increased the need for tolerance?

Evaluate
▱ Assign the Section 3 Quiz in the TCR or use the Testmaker to develop a customized quiz.

◉ Assign the Chapter 22 Test Form A or Form B or use the Testmaker to develop a customized test.

Reteach
Identify for students several multinationals, their main products, and their origins. Then ask students to predict where each multinational is likely to invest in the future.

▱ Have students complete Reteaching Activity 22 in the TCR.

Enrich
Have students research and report on alliances between businesses such as the Body Shop or Pueblo to People and indigenous cultures that wish to undergo development but keep their cultures intact.

▱ Have students complete Enrichment Activity 22 in the TCR.

Close

Have students suggest ways in which host countries might encourage tolerance among their citizens for the cultural values of recent immigrants.

Section 3 Review Answers
Understanding Vocabulary
multinationals (p. 543), **allegiances** (p. 543), **foreign affiliates** (p. 543), **alliances** (p. 545), **tolerance** (p. 547)
Reviewing Objectives
1. about 35,000, with 170,000 foreign affiliates
2. United States investment in Canada, Mexico, and South America
3. They let firms accept their limitations and help them leapfrog or catch up with competitors.
4. government regulations and lack of incentive to remain
5. Increased cultural diversity has called for increased tolerance.

Readings in Economics

NRC HANDELSBLAD   NOVEMBER 1992

Teach

Point out to students that this article about the dominance of American culture comes from *NRC Handelsblad,* a European paper with interest in international business.

Have students use the information in the feature as a springboard to visualize and draw the image of Americans and American life from an Asian, African, or European perspective. Encourage students to include in their drawings both a male and a female, distinct clothing styles, and hot consumer items in the United States.

THE INVASION OF THE AMERICAN WAY

by Maarten Huygen

The American way of life is on its way—via videocassettes, movies, and shopping habits—toward overrunning the world. And American culture, computers, and the English language are not content to conquer a single continent; they are on their way toward making the "American Era" a planetary phenomenon.

The fruits of the harvest are sweet. If a "European" culture ever emerges, it will be an adaptation to or a copy of American culture, the only one powerful enough to overpower every other culture. Every Euro-citizen can now watch Oprah Winfrey on his own national channel, dubbed or subtitled in his own language. There are no local equivalents, in spite of the limits that Europe imposed in 1991 on the import of American programs. . . .

The most popular band in Vietnam sings Bruce Springsteen numbers. In Eastern Europe, since the Berlin Wall fell, the thin strains of Voice of America, and the few films and tapes that circulated officially and unofficially, have been replaced by a deluge of American images, sounds, and words.

For many Europeans, when we made our first trip to the United States, we found everything familiar, since we had seen it all on TV. . . .

But it is not just the powerful communications apparatus that makes American culture so prominent. There is also the very openness of America itself. Many new developments come out of the American subcultures. It was only in an American form that African rhythms reached a world audience, first through jazz and the blues and now through rap. Country music, the favorite of the now-graying baby boomers, began among the fiddle-playing Scottish immigrants in the Ozark mountains of Arkansas. Only America can cultivate so many diverse elements in every last corner of its continent.

• THINK ABOUT IT •

1. What has made the spread of American culture possible?
2. How have subcultures played a role in the spread of American culture?

Answers to Think About It

1. Communications and the openness of American subcultures have made the spread of American culture possible.
2. New developments in American culture come out of American subcultures.

22 Highlights

Section 1

Reasons for and Results of Global Integration

Key Terms
global integration (p. 532)
telecommunications (p. 532)

Summary
One of the most important reasons for increased global integration has been improved telecommunications due to the dramatically reduced cost of computer chips. Today many financial instruments are traded on world markets. Events in one national market impact other markets around the world.

Section 2

Direct Foreign Investment— Should We Be Worried?

Key Terms
direct foreign investment
(DFI) (p. 537)

Summary
Foreigners have always invested in the United States and continue to do so today. Foreign direct investment is a relatively small part of our total economy, however. The ultimate reason for direct foreign investment on the part of nations like Japan is to maximize profits.

Section 3

Multinationals and Economic Competition

Key Terms
multinationals (p. 543)
allegiances (p. 543)
foreign affiliates (p. 543)
alliances (p. 545)
tolerance (p. 547)

Summary
Cross-border investing is undertaken by 35,000 multinationals throughout the world. Most multinationals invest in regions that are close to home; for example, United States companies invest primarily in the United States, Canada, Mexico, and South America. Corporations may form alliances with former competitors for many reasons. World competition for foreign investment funds means that when government bureaucratic hassles and high taxes become a problem in one country, foreigners take their investments to other countries where the climate is more favorable for business investment.

Chapter 22 The Global Economy **549**

Using Chapter 22 HIGHLIGHTS

Use the Chapter 22 Highlights to preview, review, condense, or reteach the chapter. A Spanish Chapter Highlights is available in the Spanish Handbook.

Preview/Review

After students read the Chapter 22 Highlights, have them complete Economics Vocabulary Activity 22 in the TCR. Spanish Vocabulary Activities are also available in the Spanish Resource Binder.

Vocabulary Software reinforces the economic terms used in Chapter 22.

Condense

Have students listen to Chapter 22 on the Audiocassettes in the TCR. A 1-page written activity and 1-page test accompany this material. These materials are also available in Spanish.

Reteach

Have students complete Reteaching Activity 22 in the TCR. Spanish Reteaching Activities are also available.

 VIDEODISC

Nightly Business Report
Economics in Action
Use "Global Economic Challenges" on Disc 2, Side B, Video 29.

Search 26164, Play to 32470

ANSWERS

Identifying Key Terms

1. global integration
2. telecommunications
3. direct foreign investment

4. multinationals
5. allegiance
6. foreign affiliates
7. tolerance

Recalling Facts and Ideas

Section 1

1. Improved telecommunications have increased the speed with which news from one part of the world reaches another. They have also enabled companies to communicate over long distances in order to establish global business links.
2. Many other countries also experienced severe drops in their stock market indexes.
3. English is the leading second language in the world because most popular television programs are transmitted in English throughout the world.

Section 2

4. Japan's
5. United States government securities are safe investments for foreigners because the United States is a politically stable country.
6. No; it relies almost exclusively on the United States for its national defense.
7. more than 40 percent

Section 3

8. by bringing modern technology and management skills to these countries
9. the United States, Japan, Germany, and Switzerland

Identifying Key Terms

Use terms from the following list to fill in the blanks in the paragraph below.

global integration (p. 532)
telecommunications (p. 532)
direct foreign investment (p. 537)
foreign affiliates (p. 543)
multinationals (p. 543)
allegiances (p. 543)
tolerance (p. 547)

   (1)   has increased over the past several decades, in part due to the rapid spread of cheap   (2) . There has been   (3)   in the United States and elsewhere for hundreds of years. Much of this has been undertaken by   (4) , which are companies that do business and have offices and factories in many countries. Such large businesses apparently do not have any single national   (5) . They do have almost 200,000   (6) . When dealing with other people with different cultures, the watchword is   (7) .

Recalling Facts and Ideas

Section 1

1. Why have improved telecommunications led to increased global integration?
2. What happened elsewhere when the stock market crashed in the United States in 1987?
3. What language is the leading second language in the world and why?

Section 2

4. What foreign nation's investors own half of the office space in downtown Los Angeles?
5. Why do foreigners purchase United States government securities?

6. Has Japan had to spend very much money on its national defense since World War II? Explain your answer.
7. What is the United States share of worldwide direct investment?

Section 3

8. How can multinationals help developing countries throughout the world?
9. What four countries own about half of the 35,000 multinationals that exist today?
10. In geographic terms, where do most companies invest?
11. Why do firms in different countries form alliances with one another?

Critical Thinking

Section 1

Making Generalizations While cheap telecommunications are widespread in the United States, they are not so widespread in Africa, Asia, and South America. What will happen to global integration as the rest of the world catches up with the United States?

Section 2

Drawing Conclusions The Japanese government does not spend much money on defense. Explain how this would affect foreign investment.

Section 3

Evaluating Information "Because multinational firms have no allegiance to any one country's government, they are dangerous to every country's stability." What is your opinion of this statement?

10. regions that are closest to them
11. Corporate alliances allow firms in different countries to accept their financial, technological, or geographical limitations and help them leapfrog their competitors or catch up with them.

Critical Thinking

Section 1
Global integration will probably increase.

Section 2
The Japanese government has spent little on national defense since World War II, allowing it to concentrate on stimulating Japan's economic growth. This has contributed to a rapid increase in Japanese corporations' and banks' foreign investments.

Applying Economic Concepts

Investment Incentives While the popular press may refer to "foreigners" as if they were different types of people when they invest in the United States, just about everybody makes each investment for one reason—to earn the highest rate of return possible on that investment. Consequently, Americans should not be afraid of the British, the French, the Germans, the Japanese, the Dutch, or anybody else owning "too much" of America. Make a list of the reasons that people sometimes give for why they are afraid of direct foreign investment in this country. For each reason, present a one-sentence counter argument.

Chapter Projects

1. **Individual Project** Choose a country other than the United States and investigate how much direct foreign investment occurs there each year. Try to establish the dollar volume of such direct foreign investment, what percentage of total investment this represents, and the major foreign countries that do the investing. Write a summary of your results. (United Nations and World Bank publications are useful sources.)
2. **Cooperative Learning Project** Working in groups of four, study the following innovations:
   - the fax machine
   - overnight delivery service (e.g., Federal Express and Airborne)
   - plain-paper copy machines
   - high-speed computer modems
   - satellite television
   - portable cellular phones
   - microcomputers

   Each team member will be responsible for one or more of the following:
   - Explaining what the innovation involves
   - Information on when it was first used and how much it cost then
   - How the innovation changed the way business is done
   - The future of the innovation

Reviewing Skills

Making Inferences

1. **Understanding Symbols** What can you infer from the content of the cartoon?
2. **Recognizing Point of View** Examine the cartoon and determine the cartoonist's point of view.

3. **Analyzing Information** In Jamaica about 3,500 people work in offices connected to the United States by satellite signals. They make airline reservations, process tickets, and handle credit card applications for Americans. Skilled workers in Jamaica earn far less than their counterparts in the United States. Based on this, what inference can you draw about the global workforce?

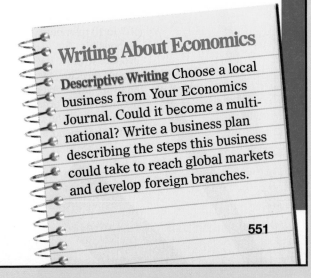

Writing About Economics

Descriptive Writing Choose a local business from Your Economics Journal. Could it become a multinational? Write a business plan describing the steps this business could take to reach global markets and develop foreign branches.

551

A Word From the Teacher

This lesson gives students a learning opportunity they will remember and talk about for a long time. Excitement grows as the students begin compiling information and deciding what news is actually newsworthy. To get maximum motivation, mention the activity early and encourage students to begin collecting information.

Cliff Booth

Focus

The global economy affects us as consumers and businesspeople. To judge soundly how international economic events affect our economy, students need to understand the role of telecommunications in the worldwide link-up of economic and political cause and effect.

This lab provides students with a sense of the resources available and the information they can offer.

Teach

Economic News Report can be extended over several weeks or condensed into one session by providing recent newspapers, videotapes of news programs, and transcripts. Begin the lab by organizing students into teams and having each team complete steps A, B, and C and pre-

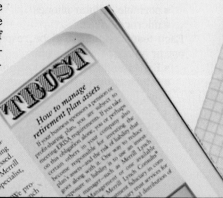

Economic News Report

From the classroom of Cliff Booth, Tuscaloosa County High School, Northport, Alabama

In Unit 6 you read about international economics. In this experiment, you will learn how economic events in distant parts of the world affect you. (You may want to reread the material on pages 532–547 of the text.)

Today Americans have nearly instant access to international economic events that affect governments and consumers. To become more responsible citizens and wiser consumers, students must associate what is taught in the classroom with what is going on in the real world. In this lab, you will research international economic news, design a news presentation, and simulate a broadcast called Economic News Report (ENR).

Tools

1. Copies of newspapers and magazines
2. Radio and television news reports
3. Cassette tape recorder or videotape camera; tapes
4. Props for a television set

Procedures

Step A The class will form teams of 7 to 10 members. Each group will be responsible for a segment of news broadcast time. Each group will select a news director, two news anchors, one analyst, and several reporters. The news director organizes the order of the news and the format of the broadcast. The anchors share responsibili-

ties for the main news stories. The analyst prepares an editorial comment on one or more events. The reporters prepare additional news stories.

Step B Reporters and anchors should scan magazines, newspapers, and television and radio news reports, collecting a wide variety of international economic news stories. Clippings and notes should be brought to class where the news team, led by the director, will choose the stories that will make up the newscast. The analyst should read all the news stories and begin to prepare an editorial comment. The following table will help the team organize the newscast. Stories should be no longer than one minute and should be placed in a logical order with smooth transitions from one to another.

Example

Title of event and summary	Reporter or anchor	Time in seconds	Order

pare the appropriate tables. If the lab extends over several weeks, allot time at the end of each week to check students' progress.

When putting together a news program, producers may create an in-depth report on a single subject or a general report on recent news. In either case, producers, writers, and

directors attempt to provide a variety of reports in order to cover many angles and speak to many interests. The sample newscast in Step C includes a variety of topics. Student teams should also choose several topics or angles of a topic.

Step C After reporters, anchors, and the analyst have rewritten and edited their stories for length, the director should prepare a preliminary newscast format.

Example

Economic News Report Format Date:			
Story	Read by	Length in sec.	Program time
Eurodollar	J. Wright anchor	40	:40
European markets	B. Engle reporter	35	1:15
Wall Street affected	R. Sanchez anchor	45	2:00
China's GDP	S. Smalz reporter	30	2:30
China's growth	J. Wright anchor	60	3:30
Commercial break		60	4:30
Developing nations' debt	R. Sanchez anchor	60	5:30
Bad weather in Brazil	V. Paine reporter	40	6:10
Brazil (wrap to commentary)	J. Wright anchor	20	6:30
Growth, slow or fast	T. Soong analyst	60	7:30
Tomorrow's feature	R. Sanchez anchor	20	7:50
Close	Sanchez and Wright	10	8:00

If the teams plan to videotape the news, the class should create a set with charts, pictures, or other props. After the set is ready, news teams should rehearse.

For example, anchors will introduce stories by reporters. For videotape, reporters may tape at remote locations, and the tape may be edited to insert these reports. For audiotaping to simulate a radio report, teams should rehearse using a recorder. After all the technical issues have been resolved, each team's director should prepare a final news format for the team. Each team should present the newscast to the class live or by tape.

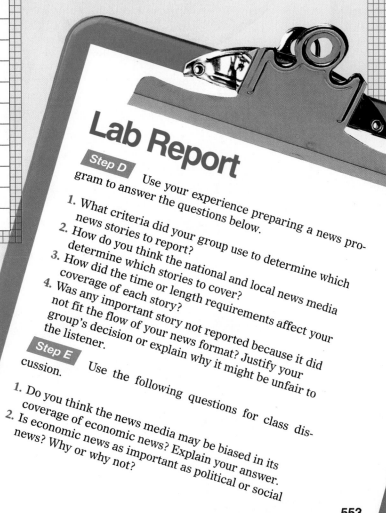

Lab Report

Step D Use your experience preparing a news program to answer the questions below.

1. What criteria did your group use to determine which news stories to report?
2. How do you think the national and local news media determine which stories to cover?
3. How did the time or length requirements affect your coverage of each story?
4. Was any important story not reported because it did not fit the flow of your news format? Justify your group's decision or explain why it might be unfair to the listener.

Step E Use the following questions for class discussion.

1. Do you think the news media may be biased in its coverage of economic news? Explain your answer.
2. Is economic news as important as political or social news? Why or why not?

553

Assess

Have each student complete Step D (the report). Organize the class into small groups containing a member or two from each news team. Have each group compare information gathered and presented by different students and answer Step D2 together.

Close

Discuss with students the ways in which individuals affect how news is presented. Encourage students to express their opinions about bias in the news media and about the importance of economic news. After the discussion, have students write summaries of their findings in their journals.

DID YOU KNOW

Many books, encyclopedias, news magazines, and other sources of information are now being entered on databases available to online subscribers. This breakthrough in telecommunications means a greatly increased readership for many media.

Answers to Lab Report

Lab Report D
Students' answers will be opinions but should be supported by facts or careful judgments. Students should be able to recount the decision-making process that resulted in inclusion of some news stories and not others.

554

APPENDIX

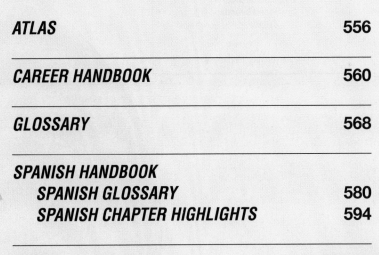

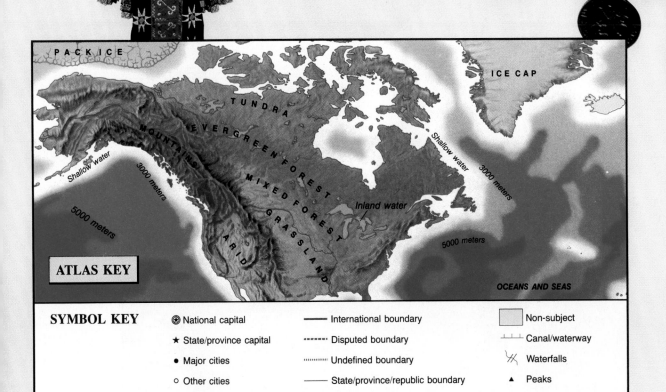

PACK ICE

ICE CAP

TUNDRA

EVERGREEN FOREST

MOUNTAINS

MIXED FOREST

Shallow water

Shallow water

3000 meters

3000 meters

Inland water

GRASSLAND

5000 meters

ARID

5000 meters

OCEANS AND SEAS

ATLAS KEY

SYMBOL KEY		
⊛ National capital	—— International boundary	� Non-subject
★ State/province capital	---- Disputed boundary	┼┼┼ Canal/waterway
● Major cities	········· Undefined boundary	✕ Waterfalls
○ Other cities	—— State/province/republic boundary	▲ Peaks

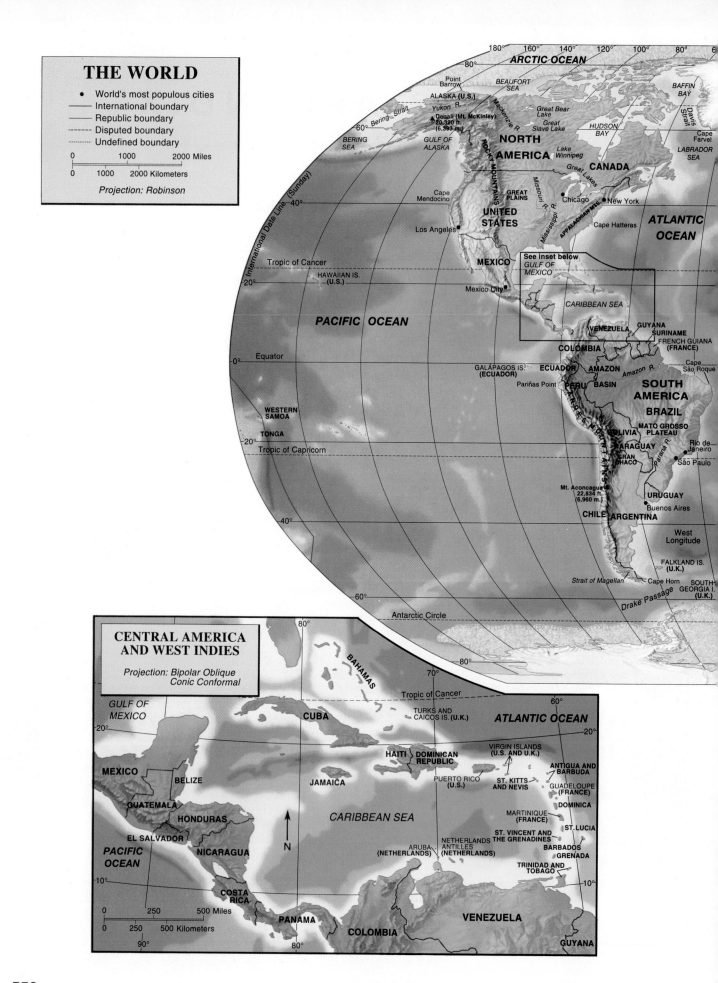

THE WORLD

- World's most populous cities
— International boundary
— Republic boundary
--- Disputed boundary
···· Undefined boundary

0   1000   2000 Miles

0   1000   2000 Kilometers

Projection: Robinson

ARCTIC OCEAN

Point Barrow

BEAUFORT SEA

BAFFIN BAY

ALASKA (U.S.)

Yukon R.

Bering Strait

Denali (Mt. McKinley) 20,320 ft. (6,193 m.)

Mackenzie R.

Great Bear Lake

Great Slave Lake

HUDSON BAY

Davis Strait

Cape Farvel

BERING SEA

GULF OF ALASKA

NORTH AMERICA

ROCKY MOUNTAINS

Lake Winnipeg

Great Lakes

CANADA

LABRADOR SEA

Cape Mendocino

GREAT PLAINS

Missouri R.

Chicago

New York

ATLANTIC OCEAN

Los Angeles

UNITED STATES

Mississippi R.

APPALACHIAN Mts.

Cape Hatteras

International Date Line (Sunday)

Tropic of Cancer

MEXICO

See inset below GULF OF MEXICO

HAWAIIAN IS. (U.S.)

Mexico City

CARIBBEAN SEA

PACIFIC OCEAN

Equator

GALÁPAGOS IS. (ECUADOR)

ECUADOR

VENEZUELA

COLOMBIA

GUYANA

SURINAME

FRENCH GUIANA (FRANCE)

AMAZON

Amazon R.

Cape São Roque

Pariñas Point

PERU

BASIN

SOUTH AMERICA

BRAZIL

WESTERN SAMOA

ANDES MTS.

MATO GROSSO PLATEAU

TONGA

BOLIVIA

Tropic of Capricorn

PARAGUAY

GRAN CHACO

Paraná R.

Rio de Janeiro

São Paulo

Mt. Aconcagua 22,834 ft. (6,960 m.)

URUGUAY

Buenos Aires

CHILE

ARGENTINA

West Longitude

FALKLAND IS. (U.K.)

Strait of Magellan

Cape Horn

SOUTH GEORGIA I. (U.K.)

Drake Passage

Antarctic Circle

CENTRAL AMERICA AND WEST INDIES

Projection: Bipolar Oblique Conic Conformal

GULF OF MEXICO

BAHAMAS

CUBA

TURKS AND CAICOS IS. (U.K.)

ATLANTIC OCEAN

Tropic of Cancer

MEXICO

BELIZE

HAITI

DOMINICAN REPUBLIC

VIRGIN ISLANDS (U.S. AND U.K.)

ANTIGUA AND BARBUDA

JAMAICA

PUERTO RICO (U.S.)

ST. KITTS AND NEVIS

GUADELOUPE (FRANCE)

GUATEMALA

DOMINICA

HONDURAS

CARIBBEAN SEA

MARTINIQUE (FRANCE)

ST. LUCIA

EL SALVADOR

N

ST. VINCENT AND THE GRENADINES

PACIFIC OCEAN

NICARAGUA

ARUBA (NETHERLANDS)

NETHERLANDS ANTILLES (NETHERLANDS)

BARBADOS

GRENADA

TRINIDAD AND TOBAGO

0   250   500 Miles

0   250   500 Kilometers

COSTA RICA

PANAMA

COLOMBIA

VENEZUELA

GUYANA

556

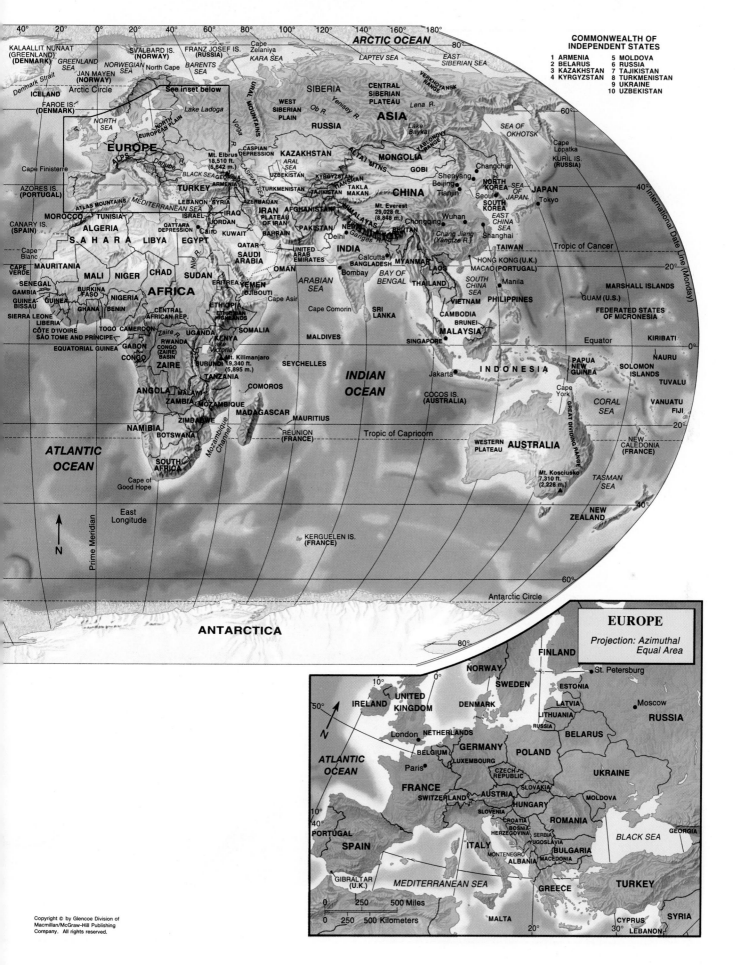

ARCTIC OCEAN

40° 20° 0° 20° 40° 60° 80° 100° 120° 140° 160° 180°

KALAALLIT NUNAAT (GREENLAND) (DENMARK)
GREENLAND SEA
SVALBARD IS. (NORWAY)
FRANZ JOSEF IS. (RUSSIA)
Cape Zelaniya
LAPTEV SEA
EAST SIBERIAN SEA
80°

JAN MAYEN (NORWAY)
NORWEGIAN SEA
North Cape
BARENTS SEA
KARA SEA

Denmark Strait
ICELAND
Arctic Circle
See inset below
URAL MOUNTAINS
SIBERIA
VERKHOYANSK RANGE

FAROE IS. (DENMARK)
NORTH SEA
NORTH EUROPEAN PLAIN
Lake Ladoga
WEST SIBERIAN PLAIN
Ob R.
Yenisey R.
CENTRAL SIBERIAN PLATEAU
Lena R.
60°

EUROPE
ALPS
Danube R.
Volga R.
RUSSIA
Lake Baykal
SEA OF OKHOTSK
Cape Lopatka
KURIL IS. (RUSSIA)

Cape Finisterre
Mt. Elbrus 18,510 ft. (5,642 m.)
CASPIAN DEPRESSION
KAZAKHSTAN
ALTAI MTNS
MONGOLIA
YABLONOVY RANGE

AZORES IS. (PORTUGAL)
TURKEY
GEORGIA
ARMENIA
ARAL SEA
UZBEKISTAN
KYRGYZSTAN
TIANSHAN
TAKLA MAKAN
GOBI
Changchun
Shenyang
NORTH KOREA
SEA OF JAPAN
JAPAN
40°

BLACK SEA
CASPIAN SEA
TURKMENISTAN
TAJIKISTAN
CHINA
Beijing
Tianjin
Seoul
SOUTH KOREA
Tokyo

MOROCCO
TUNISIA
LEBANON
SYRIA
IRAQ
IRAN
AFGHANISTAN
HIMALAYAS
Mt. Everest 29,028 ft. (8,848 m.)
Chongqing
Wuhan
EAST CHINA SEA

ATLAS MOUNTAINS
MEDITERRANEAN SEA
ISRAEL
JORDAN
PLATEAU OF IRAN
KUWAIT
PAKISTAN
NEPAL
BHUTAN
Chang Jiang (Yangtze R.)
Shanghai

CANARY IS. (SPAIN)
ALGERIA
LIBYA
EGYPT
Cairo
QATTARA DEPRESSION
BAHRAIN
Delhi
Ganges R.
TAIWAN
Tropic of Cancer
20°

Cape Blanc
SAHARA
Nile R.
QATAR
SAUDI ARABIA
UNITED ARAB EMIRATES
INDIA
Calcutta
HONG KONG (U.K.)
MACAO (PORTUGAL)

CAPE VERDE
MAURITANIA
MALI
NIGER
CHAD
SUDAN
ERITREA
YEMEN
OMAN
BANGLADESH
MYANMAR
LAOS
THAILAND
SOUTH CHINA SEA
Manila
MARSHALL ISLANDS

SENEGAL
GAMBIA
BURKINA FASO
NIGERIA
BENIN
AFRICA
ERITREA
DJIBOUTI
ARABIAN SEA
Bombay
BAY OF BENGAL
VIETNAM
CAMBODIA
PHILIPPINES
GUAM (U.S.)
FEDERATED STATES OF MICRONESIA

GUINEA-BISSAU
GUINEA
GHANA
CENTRAL AFRICAN REP.
ETHIOPIA
ETHIOPIAN HIGHLANDS
Cape Asir
Cape Comorin
SRI LANKA
BRUNEI
MALAYSIA

SIERRA LEONE
LIBERIA
CÔTE D'IVOIRE
TOGO
CAMEROON
UGANDA
SOMALIA
MALDIVES
SINGAPORE
KIRIBATI

EQUATORIAL GUINEA
GABON
ZAIRE
Zaire R.
RWANDA
CONGO (ZAIRE) BASIN
KENYA
Lake Victoria
Equator
NAURU
0°

SÃO TOMÉ AND PRÍNCIPE
CONGO
BURUNDI
Mt. Kilimanjaro 19,340 ft. (5,895 m.)
TANZANIA
SEYCHELLES
INDIAN OCEAN
INDONESIA
PAPUA NEW GUINEA
SOLOMON ISLANDS
TUVALU

ANGOLA
MALAWI
ZAMBIA
MOZAMBIQUE
COMOROS
Jakarta
Cape York
CORAL SEA
VANUATU
FIJI

ATLANTIC OCEAN
NAMIBIA
ZIMBABWE
BOTSWANA
MADAGASCAR
MAURITIUS
RÉUNION (FRANCE)
Tropic of Capricorn
GREAT DIVIDING RANGE
NEW CALEDONIA (FRANCE)
20°

SOUTH AFRICA
Mozambique Channel
WESTERN PLATEAU
AUSTRALIA

Cape of Good Hope
Mt. Kosciusko 7,310 ft. (2,228 m.)
TASMAN SEA
40°

East Longitude
KERGUELEN IS. (FRANCE)
NEW ZEALAND

N
Prime Meridian
Antarctic Circle
60°

ANTARCTICA

COMMONWEALTH OF INDEPENDENT STATES
1 ARMENIA   5 MOLDOVA
2 BELARUS   6 RUSSIA
3 KAZAKHSTAN 7 TAJIKISTAN
4 KYRGYZSTAN 8 TURKMENISTAN
              9 UKRAINE
             10 UZBEKISTAN

International Date Line (Monday)

EUROPE

Projection: Azimuthal Equal Area

FINLAND
NORWAY
SWEDEN
St. Petersburg
50°
10°
IRELAND
UNITED KINGDOM
DENMARK
ESTONIA
LATVIA
LITHUANIA
Moscow
RUSSIA

N
London
NETHERLANDS
RUSSIA
BELARUS

ATLANTIC OCEAN
Belgium
GERMANY
POLAND
UKRAINE

Paris
LUXEMBOURG
CZECH REPUBLIC
SLOVAKIA

FRANCE
SWITZERLAND
AUSTRIA
HUNGARY
MOLDOVA

10°
SLOVENIA
CROATIA
ROMANIA
40°
PORTUGAL
BOSNIA HERZEGOVINA
SERBIA
BLACK SEA
GEORGIA

SPAIN
ITALY
MONTENEGRO
YUGOSLAVIA
BULGARIA
MACEDONIA
ALBANIA

GIBRALTAR (U.K.)
MEDITERRANEAN SEA
GREECE
TURKEY

0   250   500 Miles
0   250   500 Kilometers

MALTA
CYPRUS
SYRIA
LEBANON
20°
30°

557

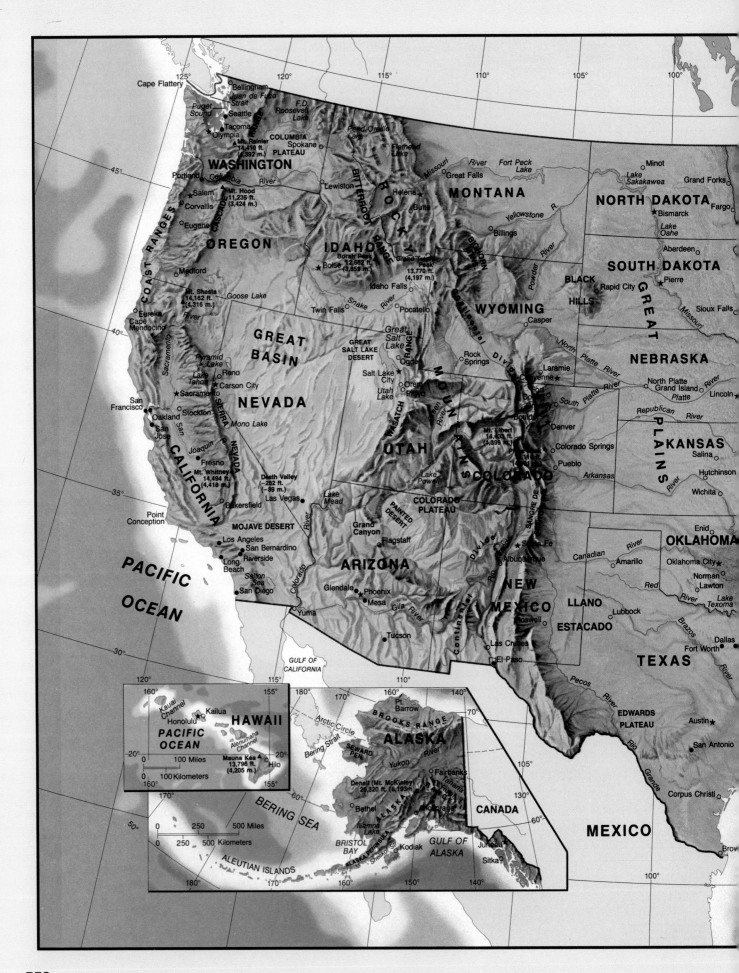

Cape Flattery
125°
120°
115°
110°
105°
100°

Bellingham
Juan de Fuca Strait
Puget Sound
Seattle
Tacoma
Olympia
▲ Mt. Rainier 14,410 ft. (4,392 m.)
COLUMBIA PLATEAU
F.D. Roosevelt Lake
Spokane
Pend Oreille Lake
Flathead Lake
45°
Missouri River
Fort Peck Lake
Great Falls
Minot
Lake Sakakawea
Grand Forks

WASHINGTON
Portland
Columbia River
Lewiston
ROCKY
Helena
Butte
MONTANA
Yellowstone R.
Billings
NORTH DAKOTA
★ Bismarck
Fargo
Lake Oahe

Salem
Mt. Hood 11,235 ft. (3,424 m.)
Corvallis
CASCADE
OREGON
BITTERROOT RANGE
IDAHO
Borah Peak 12,662 ft. (3,859 m.)
★ Boise
Grand Teton Peak 13,770 ft. (4,197 m.)
BIG HORN
Powder River
WYOMING
Casper
Aberdeen
SOUTH DAKOTA
★ Pierre

Eugene
Medford
Mt. Shasta 14,162 ft. (4,316 m.)
Goose Lake
Idaho Falls
BLACK HILLS
Rapid City
Sioux Falls

COAST RANGES
Eureka
Cape Mendocino
River
40°
Twin Falls
Snake River
Pocatello
Continental Divide
Rock Springs
North Platte River
Laramie
Cheyenne
GREAT
PLAINS
NEBRASKA
North Platte
Grand Island
Platte
Lincoln

GREAT BASIN
Sacramento
Pyramid Lake
Reno
Lake Tahoe
Carson City
★ Sacramento
NEVADA
GREAT SALT LAKE DESERT
Great Salt Lake
Salt Lake City ★
Ogden
Orem Provo
WASATCH RANGE
MOUNTAINS
Green River
Boulder
Denver
Colorado Springs
Pueblo
Republican River
KANSAS
Salina
Hutchinson
Wichita

San Francisco
Oakland
San Jose
Stockton
Mono Lake
Joaquin
Fresno
SIERRA NEVADA
Mt. Whitney 14,494 ft. (4,418 m.)
Death Valley -282 ft. (-89 m.)
Utah Lake
UTAH
Lake Powell
Mt. Elbert 14,433 ft. (4,399 m.)
COLORADO
Arkansas River
35°

CALIFORNIA
Bakersfield
Las Vegas
Lake Mead
COLORADO PLATEAU
PAINTED DESERT
Enid
OKLAHOMA

Point Conception
MOJAVE DESERT
Los Angeles
San Bernardino
Riverside
Long Beach
Salton Sea
San Diego
River
Colorado
Grand Canyon
ARIZONA
Flagstaff
Sante Fe ★
Albuquerque
Canadian River
Amarillo
Oklahoma City ★
Norman
Lawton
Red River
Lake Texoma

PACIFIC
OCEAN
Yuma
Glendale
Phoenix
Mesa
Gila River
Tucson
NEW MEXICO
Roswell
Continental Divide
LLANO ESTACADO
Lubbock
Brazos River
Dallas
Fort Worth

30°
GULF OF CALIFORNIA
SANGRE DE
Rio
Las Cruces
El Paso
Pecos River
EDWARDS PLATEAU
Austin ★
San Antonio

120°
160°
155°
Kauai Channel
Kailua
Honolulu
HAWAII
PACIFIC OCEAN
Alenuihaha Channel
20°
Mauna Kea 13,796 ft. (4,205 m.)
Hilo
160°
155°
180°
170°
160°
Pt. Barrow
BROOKS RANGE
70°
ALASKA
Seward Pen.
Yukon River
60°
Tanana River
Fairbanks
CANADA
60°
Rio Grande
Corpus Christi
MEXICO

0 100 Miles
0 100 Kilometers
20°
Arctic Circle
Bering Strait
BERING SEA
60°
Denali (Mt. McKinley) 20,320 ft. (6,193m.)
Bethel
Iliamna Lake
ALASKA
Anchorage
105°
Juneau
130°
Sitka
130°

170°
0 250 500 Miles
0 250 500 Kilometers
BRISTOL BAY
ALASKA PENINSULA
Kodiak
Shelikof Str.
GULF OF ALASKA
140°
100°
Brow

ALEUTIAN ISLANDS
50°
180°
170°
160°
150°

UNITED STATES

- ◎ National capital
- ★ State capital
- ● Major city
- ○ Other city
- ▬▬ International boundary
- ▬ State boundary

0   100   200 Miles
0   100   200 Kilometers

Projection: Albers Equal Area

CANADA

MAINE
Moosehead Lake
Bangor
Mt. Washington
6,288 ft.
(1,905 m.) ★ Augusta
Lewiston
N.H.
Portland
Montpelier
VT.
Concord
Manchester
Burlington
Lake
Champlain
Hudson
ADIRONDACK MTNS.
Lake Ontario
Utica
Albany
Worcester
MASS.
Boston
Cape Cod
Rochester
Syracuse
Springfield
Niagara Falls
Buffalo
NEW YORK
Hartford
Providence
R.I.
CONN.
Binghamton
New Haven
Erie
Susquehanna River
Yonkers
Newark
New York
N.J.
Cleveland
Allentown
Trenton
Youngstown
PENNSYLVANIA
Philadelphia
Akron
Camden
Canton
Harrisburg
Wilmington
Pittsburgh
Dover
Wheeling
DEL.
OHIO
Baltimore
MD.
Columbus
DELAWARE BAY
WEST
Annapolis
ATLANTIC
Parkersburg
Arlington
Washington
OCEAN
Dayton
VIRGINIA
D.C.
Cincinnati
Charleston
Newport
Huntington
Richmond
News
Roanoke
CHESAPEAKE
VIRGINIA
BAY
Roanoke River
Norfolk
Greensboro
Durham
Cape Hatteras
Winston-Salem
Raleigh
Mt. Mitchell
NORTH
6,684 ft.
(2,037 m.)
CAROLINA
Charlotte
Spartanburg
Greenville
Columbia
SOUTH
CAROLINA
Augusta
Charleston
Atlanta
Savannah
GEORGIA
Macon
Columbus
Albany

Lake Superior

MINNESOTA
Duluth
Red Lake

Lake
of the
Woods

MICHIGAN
Lake Huron
St. Lawrence River
River

WISCONSIN
Green Bay
Appleton
Lake Michigan

Minneapolis
St. Paul
Mississippi River
Rochester

Milwaukee
Madison
Racine
Grand Rapids
Flint
Lansing
Detroit

Sioux City
Dubuque
Cedar Rapids
Davenport
Rockford
Chicago
South Bend
Toledo
Ann Arbor
Fort Wayne

IOWA
Des Moines
Aurora
Gary
Joliet
Hammond

CENTRAL
Omaha
Council Bluffs
Peoria
LOWLAND
ILLINOIS
Springfield
Decatur
Muncie
Indianapolis
INDIANA

Topeka
Kansas
City
Independence
Lawrence
Kansas City
Jefferson City
St. Louis
East St. Louis
Evansville

Harry S. Truman Res.
MISSOURI
Springfield

Wabash R.
Ohio River
Louisville
Frankfort
Lexington
KENTUCKY
Owensboro

Tulsa
OZARK PLATEAU
Cumberland River
Knoxville
R.S. Kerr Res.
ARKANSAS
Nashville
Chattanooga
PLATEAU
APPALACHIAN
MOUNTAINS

Lake
Eufaula
Fort Smith
North Little Rock
Memphis
Huntsville
Little Rock
Hot Springs
Pine Bluff
Tennessee River
TENNESSEE

Greenville
Birmingham
Tuscaloosa
CUMBERLAND

Shreveport
Meridian
Jackson
ALABAMA
Montgomery
Columbus

LOUISIANA
Hattiesburg
Alabama R.
Chattahoochee
COASTAL

Sam Rayburn
Reservoir
Toledo
Bend
Res.
MISSISSIPPI
PLAIN

Houston
Baton Rouge
Lake
Pontchartrain
Biloxi
Mobile
Pensacola
Lake Charles
Lafayette
New Orleans
Tallahassee

Jacksonville

FLORIDA

GULF OF MEXICO

Orlando
Cape
Canaveral
Tampa
St. Petersburg

N

Lake
Okeechobee
Palm Beach
Miami
Miami Beach

Cape Sable

Key West
Strait of Florida

THE
BAHAMAS

CUBA

General Outlook

Trends in the Labor Force The American civilian labor force is expected to surpass 140 million in the year 2000, increasing a little more than one percent per year. This figure represents a slower rate of growth than in the recent past, mainly because the rate of population growth has slowed.

Labor is an increasingly diverse group as the United States approaches the twenty-first century. Women and minority group members make up a growing share of workers. African Americans, Hispanics, Asians, and other groups will soon account for about one-third of labor force entrants. By 2000, it is estimated 4 out of 5 women between the ages of 25 and 54 will be in the labor force, and women will account for nearly one-half of the total workers.

Trends in Occupations The new jobs that will be added to the United States economy by 2000 will not be evenly distributed across occupations. The shift from goods-producing to service-producing jobs will continue. By 2000 nearly 4 out of 5 new jobs, however, will be in industries that provide services. Job creation will be fastest in such fields as health care, business services, and retail trade. Education, government, transportation, and communications industries will also account for significant job growth. Among goods-producing industries, only construction employment is expected to increase significantly. Manufacturing, mining, and agricultural jobs will either remain steady or decline slightly.

Occupational Profiles How do various occupations compare in earnings, job requirements, opportunities, and working conditions? The following tables and profiles provide a sampling of information about a broad range of careers. In the tables, most salaries represent approximate yearly averages for beginning and top levels, unless designated otherwise. In some cases, only the median range is available. The "Training" column uses symbols for levels and kinds of training normally required:

HS = high school, **Tr** = some specialized training, **TS** = technical school, **AD** = 2-year associate degree, **CD** = 4-year college degree, **ACD** = advanced college degree, **L** = license (usually by testing), **Exam** = examination.

"Job Outlook" and "Working Conditions" categories give very brief descriptions of general conditions. You should seek out more specific information about job opportunities and the nature of the work before making a career decision. The *Occupational Outlook Handbook,* a Department of Labor publication, provides details about hundreds of careers.

Executive, Administrative, and Managerial

Occupation	Salaries	Training	Job Outlook	Working Conditions
Certified Public Accountant	$25,000-$45,000	ACD,L	favorable	office, some travel
College Registrar	$46,000 median	ACD	average	office, some travel
Financial Manager	$18,300-$68,000	CD or ACD	favorable	office, regular hours
Hospital Administrator (CEO)	$70,000-$203,000	ACD	very favorable	long hours, some travel
Hotel Manager	$25,000-$80,000	TS or CD	favorable	some stress, weekends
Industrial Production Manager	$68,000 median	CD and Tr	average	long, irregular hours
Insurance Underwriter	$24,000-$54,000	CD	favorable	office, 30-40 hour week
Marketing Manager	$20,000-$79,000	CD or ACD	favorable	long hours, travel
Personnel Manager	$19,000-$65,000	TS or CD	favorable	office, some travel
Property, Real Estate Manager	$10,300-$47,300	CD	favorable	travel, long hours
Purchasing Agent	$16,100-$45,300	CD	average	35-40 hour week
Restaurant Manager	$18,200-$48,000	AD, CD, or Tr	favorable	evenings, stress
Underwriter	$23,900-$54,100	CD	average	office, some travel
Wholesale Buyer	$13,500-$46,700	CD and Tr	average	long hours, travel

Career Handbook

Professional Specialty

Occupation	Salaries	Training	Job Outlook	Working Conditions
Architect	$18,000-$66,000	ACD, L	favorable	office, deadlines
Actuary	$28,300-$62,000	CD, L	favorable	office, some travel
Biological Scientist	$13,000-$55,600	CD, ACD	favorable	laboratory, vary
Chemical Engineer	$32,000-$94,000	CD, L	favorable	40 hour week, some stress
Computer Systems Analyst	$23,000-$63,000	CD or TS	very favorable	40+ hour week, office
Economist	$19,000-$68,000	CD, ACD	average	deadlines, some travel
Lawyer	$25,000-$120,000	ACD, L	favorable	long hours, some travel
Meteorologist	$17,0000-$45,000	CD	favorable	irregular hours
Psychologist	$25,000-$67,000	ACD, L	very favorable	vary with type of practice
Social Worker	$23,000-$36,000	CD, L	favorable	some stress
Statistician	$38,600-$54,700	CD, ACD	favorable	office, regular hours
Surveyor	$17,400-$43,700	CD or Tr, L	average	office and field work
Teacher, Secondary School	$33,700 average	CD, ACD	favorable	long hours, some stress
Technical Writer	$20,000-$45,000	CD	favorable	deadlines

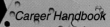

Medical Professional

Occupation	Salaries	Training	Job Outlook	Working Conditions
Chiropractor	$24,000-$180,000	ACD, L	favorable	average workweek
Dentist	$85,000 average	ACD, L	average	vary, some weekends
Optometrist	$75,000 average	ACD, L	average	office
Physician Assistant	$40,000 average	CD, L	very favorable	vary greatly
Recreational Therapist	$15,000-$30,000	CD	favorable	physically demanding
Veterinarian	$27,000-$100,000	ACD, L	favorable	vary, long hours

Medical Technical

Occupation	Salaries	Training	Job Outlook	Working Conditions
Dental Hygienist	$15-$20 per hour	CD or TS, L	favorable	some part time
Dispensing Optician	$18,000-$35,000	Tr or AD	favorable	standing
Emergency Medical Technician	$30,000 average	Tr, L	average	physically demanding
Licensed Practical Nurse	$10-$15 per hour	Tr, L	very favorable	irregular hours, stress
Medical Records Technician	$23,000 average	Ad, L	very favorable	office, some stress
Radiologic Technologist	$12 to $20 per hour	Tr, AD	very favorable	emotional stress

Technical

Occupation	Salaries	Training	Job Outlook	Working Conditions
Broadcast Technician	$13,000-$48,000	CD	below average	irregular schedule
Computer Programmer	$19,000-$52,000	Tr or CD	favorable	long hours at times
Drafter	$15,000-$42,000	AD	below average	some eyestrain
Engineering Technician	$20,000-$39,000	Tr or AD	favorable	40 hour week
Paralegal	$20,000-$28,000	AD	favorable	some overtime
Pilot, airline	$40,000-$165,000	Flight Tr, L	favorable	irregular schedule

Marketing and Sales

Occupation	Salaries	Training	Job Outlook	Working Conditions
Advertising Sales	$27,000 median	HS or CD	very favorable	competitive, stress
Insurance Agent	$15,000-$59,000	HS or CD, L	average	long hours, travel
Manufacturing Sales Representative	$16,000-$60,000	Tr or CD	average	travel
Real Estate Agent	$19,000 median (varies widely)	Tr, L	average	long hours, travel
Securities Agent	$28,000-$79,000	CD, L	favorable	vary
Travel Agent	$12,000-$22,000	Tr	favorable	office

Clerical and Administrative Support

Occupation	Salaries	Training	Job Outlook	Working Conditions
Bank Teller	$10,000-$21,500	HS	below average	some part time
Computer Operator	$13,000-$34,000	Tr or CD	below average	hours vary
Dispatcher	$10,000-$34,000	HS	below average	stress, sitting long hours
Insurance Claims Examiner	$30,000 median	CD or Tr	average	office, some travel
Mail Carrier	$24,000-$30,000	HS, exam	below average	early hours
Word Processor	$20,000 median	HS, Tr	below average	stress, some part time

Services

Occupation	Salaries	Training	Job Outlook	Working Conditions
Barber	$7-$14 per hour	Tr, L	average	standing, long hours
Chef	$12,000-$40,000	HS, Tr	favorable	vary
Flight Attendant	$13,000-$35,000	HS, Tr	very favorable	nights, weekends
Groundskeeper	$7.50 per hour median	HS	favorable	weather, some part time
Nurse's Aide	$10,000-$22,000	Tr	favorable	hours vary
Police Officer	$19,000-$37,000	HS, Tr, Exam	average	hazardous, irregular hours
Security Guard	$5-$12 per hour	Tr	favorable	night and irregular hours

Construction Trades, Repair, Mechanic

Occupation	Salaries	Training	Job Outlook	Working Conditions
Automotive Body Repairer	$6-$19 per hour	Tr	average	strenuous
Carpenter	$240-$740 per week	3-4 yr. Tr	average	outdoors
Diesel Mechanic	$15 per hour	Tr/AD	average	physically demanding
Electrician	$300-$840 per week	4-5 yr. Tr	favorable	strenuous, dangerous
Heating, Air Conditioning Technician	$270-$780 per week	Tr/AD	average	vary, some outdoors
Plumber	$290-$680 per week	4-5 yr. Tr	average	strenuous
Roustabout	$12 per hour average	Tr/AD	below average	strenuous, outdoors

Agriculture, Forestry, Transportation

Occupation	Salaries	Training	Job Outlook	Working Conditions
Bus Driver	$200-$600 per week	Tr, L	favorable	stress, varying hours
Farm Manager	$15,000-$32,000`	Tr/CD	below average	vary from long hours to part time
Ship captain, Mate	$280-$1000 per week	Tr, L	below average	irregular hours, travel
Timber Cutter, Logger	$16,000 average	Tr	below average	dangerous
Truck Driver	$8-$14 per hour	Tr, L	average	long hours, stress

ability-to-pay principle: principle of taxation in which those with higher incomes pay more taxes than those with lower incomes, regardless of the number of government services they use (p. 428).

absolute advantage: ability of one country, using the same quantity of resources as another country, to produce a particular product at less cost (p. 464).

accounts receivable: money owed to a business by its customers (p. 266).

agency shop: company in which employees are not required to join the union, but must pay union dues (p. 313).

aggregate (A-grih-guht) demand: total quantity of goods and services in the entire economy that all citizens will demand at any one time (p. 342).

aggregate demand curve: a graphed line showing the relationship between the aggregate quantity demanded of all goods and services by all people and the average of all prices, measured by the implicit GDP deflator (p. 343).

aggregates: summation of all the individual parts in the economy (p. 342).

aggregate supply: real domestic output of producers based on the rise and fall of prices (p. 345).

aggregate supply curve: a graphed line showing the microeconomic measure of aggregate demand based on real domestic output using the implicit GDP deflator as the price index (p. 345).

Aid to Families with Dependent Children: state-run public-assistance program that provides money to needy parents raising young children (p. 417).

allegiances: loyalties to countries, people, or causes (p. 543).

alliances: joint ventures formed by firms in different countries; often between firms from industrialized countries (p. 545).

annual percentage rate (APR): cost of credit expressed as a yearly percentage (p. 93).

antitrust legislation: laws passed by federal and state governments to prevent new monopolies from forming and to break up those that already exist (p. 244).

arbitration (AHR-buh-TRAY-shuhn): stage of negotiation process in which union and management submit the issues they cannot agree on to a third party for a final decision. Both sides agree in advance to accept the arbitrator's decision (p. 319).

articles of incorporation: document filed with the state establishing a corporation within a state; these articles include basic information about the corporation, the board of directors, and the stock being issued (p. 221).

assembly line: production system in which the good being produced moves on a conveyor belt past workers who perform individual tasks in assembling it (p. 275).

assets: items of value such as houses, cars, jewelry, and so on (p. 214).

authoritarian socialism: system that supports revolution as the means to overthrow capitalism and bring about socialist goals; the entire economy is controlled by a central government; also called communism (p. 484).

automated teller machines (ATMs): units that allow consumers to do their banking without the help of a teller (p. 372).

automation: production process in which machines do the work and people oversee them (p. 275).

bait and switch: deceptive advertising practice in which a store attracts consumers with an ad offering a product at a low price, then tries to sell a similar product but at a higher price (p. 65).

balanced-budget amendment: proposal to reduce the federal government budget deficits by amending the Constitution (p. 426).

balance of trade: difference between the value of a nation's exports and its imports (p. 469).

bankruptcy: the inability to pay debts based on the income received; a condition in which debtors give up most of what they own for distribution to creditors (p. 100).

barriers to entry: obstacles to competition that prevent others from entering a market (p. 238).

barter: exchange of goods and services for other goods and services (p. 362).

base year: year used as a point of comparison for other years in a series of statistics (p. 340).

benefits-received principle: system of taxation in which those who use a particular government service support it with taxes in proportion to the benefit they receive; those who do not use a service do not pay taxes for it (p. 428).

blue-collar: category of workers employed in crafts, manufacturing, and nonfarm labor (p. 306).

bond: certificate issued by a company or the government in exchange for borrowed money; a bond promises to pay a stated rate of interest over a stated period of time and to repay the borrowed amount in full at the end of that time (p. 155).

boom: period of prosperity in a business cycle in which economic activity is at its highest point; also called peak (p. 347).

boycott: economic pressure exerted by unions urging the public not to purchase the goods or services produced by a company (p. 320).

brand name: word, picture, or logo on a product that helps consumers distinguish it from similar products (p. 66).

broker: person who acts as a go-between for buyers and sellers of stocks and bonds (p. 157).

bureaucracies: offices and agencies of the government that deal with a specific area (p. 517).

business cycle: irregular changes in the level of total output measured by real GDP (p. 347).

business fluctuations: ups and downs in an economy (p. 347).

capital: all property—machines, buildings, tools, and money—used in the production of other goods and services (p. 10).

capital gain: increase in value of stock or bond from the time it was bought to the time it was sold (p. 157).

capitalism: economic system in which private individuals own the factors of production and decide how to use them within the limits of the law (p. 37); also called market economic system (p. 33), free enterprise system (p. 38).

capital loss: decrease in value of a stock or bond from the time it was bought to the time it was sold (p. 158).

cartel: arrangement among groups of industrial businesses, often in different countries, to reduce international competition by controlling the price, production, and distribution of goods; international form of monopoly (p. 239).

certificates of deposit (CDs): time deposits that state the amount of the deposit, maturity, and rate of interest being paid; CDs earn more interest than savings accounts, but there is a penalty for early withdrawal; also called savings certificates (p. 148).

channels of distribution: routes by which goods are moved from producers to consumers (p. 293).

charge account: credit extended to a consumer allowing the consumer to buy goods or services from a particular company and to pay for them later (p. 89). *See also* installment charge account; regular charge account; revolving charge account.

checkable deposits: money deposited in a bank that can be withdrawn at any time by presenting a check; formerly called demand deposits (p. 377).

check clearing: method by which a check that has been deposited in one depository institution is transferred to the depository institution on which it was written (p. 396).

checking account: account in which deposited money can be withdrawn at any time by writing a check (p. 376).

circular flow of income: economic model that pictures income as flowing continuously between businesses and consumers; income flows from businesses to households as wages, rent, interest, and profits; income flows from households to businesses as payments for consumer goods and services (p. 443).

civilian labor force: total number of people 16 years or older who are either employed or actively seeking work (p. 306).

closed shop: company in which only union members may be hired; outlawed in 1947 (p. 313).

closing costs: fees involved in arranging for a mortgage or in transferring ownership of property; can include fees for title search, legal costs, loan application, credit report, house inspections, and taxes (p. 129).

coincident indicators: economic indicators whose changes in activity seem to happen at the same time as changes in overall business activity (p. 355)

collateral (kuh-LA-tuh-ruhl): something of value that a borrower lets the lender claim if a loan is not repaid (p. 95).

collective bargaining: process by which unions and employers negotiate the conditions of employment (p. 318).

command economic system: system in which the government controls the factors of production and makes all decisions about their use; also called controlled economy (p. 33).

commercial bank: bank offering wide range of services; main functions are to accept deposits, lend money, and transfer funds among banks, individuals, and businesses (p. 86).

commodity money: mediums of exchange such as cattle and gems that have value as a commodity, or a good, aside from their value as money (p. 365).

communism: term used by Karl Marx for his ideal society in which no government is necessary; has come to mean any authoritarian socialist system that supports revolution as a means to overthrow capitalism and bring about socialist goals; a central government controls the entire economy (p. 484).

comparative advantage: ability of a country to produce a product at a lower opportunity cost than another country (p. 465).

comparison shopping: getting information on the types and prices of products available from different stores and companies (p. 66).

competition: rivalry among producers or sellers of similar goods to win more business by offering the lowest prices or better quality (p. 39).

competitive advertising: advertising that attempts to persuade consumers that a product is different from and superior to any other (p. 64).

complementary good: one product often used with another product; as the price of the second product decreases, the demand for the first product will increase; as the price of the second product increases, the demand for the first product will decrease (p. 188).

condominium: separately owned single unit in an apartment building or a series of townhouses; common areas such as hallways and the land on which the building is built are owned in common (p. 126).

conglomerate merger: buying out of unrelated businesses (p. 245).

conglomerates: large corporations made up of smaller corporations dealing in unrelated activities (p. 245).

consumer: any person or group that buys or uses goods and services to satisfy personal needs and wants (p. 58).

consumer durables: manufactured items that people use for long periods of time before replacement (p. 80).

consumer finance company: company that makes loans directly to consumers at high rates of interest (p. 88).

consumer goods: goods produced for individuals and sold directly to the public to be used as they are (p. 271).

consumerism: movement to educate buyers about the purchases they make and to demand better and safer products from manufacturers (p. 68).

consumer price index (CPI): government measure of the change in price over time of a specific group of goods and services used by the average household (p. 339).

contraction: part of the business cycle during which economic activity is slowing down; also called a trough (p. 347).

convenience stores: stores open from 16 to 24 hours a day, carrying a limited selection of items generally at higher prices than supermarkets or warehouse stores (p. 109).

cooperative (co-op): apartment whose owner owns equal shares in the company that owns the building and the land on which the building stands; the owner does not own his or her own apartment but rather holds a lease on it (p. 126).

corporate charter: license to operate granted to a corporation by the state where it is established (p. 221).

corporation: organization owned by many people but treated by the law as though it were a person; it can own property, pay taxes, make contracts, and sue and be sued (p. 219).

cosigner: person who signs a loan contract along with the borrower and promises to repay the loan if the borrower does not (p. 96).

cost-benefit analysis: a financial process in which a business estimates the cost of action and compares it with the benefits of that action (p. 258).

cost-of-living adjustment (COLA): union contract or other provision providing for an additional wage increase each year if the general level of prices in the economy rises beyond a certain level (p. 319).

cost-push inflation: theory that the wage demands of labor unions and the excessive profit motive of large corporations push up prices resulting in stagflation (p. 441).

craft union: union made up of skilled workers in a specific trade or industry (p. 312).

credit: receipt of money either directly or indirectly to buy goods and services in the present with the promise to pay for them in the future (p. 80).

credit bureau: private business that investigates a person's income, current debts, personal life, and past history of borrowing and repaying debts to determine the risk involved in lending money to that person (p. 94).

credit card: credit device that allows a person to make purchases at many kinds of stores, restaurants, hotels, and other businesses without paying cash (p. 90).

credit check: investigation of a person's income, current debts, personal life, and past history of borrowing and repaying debts (p. 94).

credit limit: maximum amount of goods or services a person or business can buy on the promise to pay in the future (p. 89).

credit rating: rating of the risk involved in lending money to a specific person or business (p. 94).

credit union: depository institution owned and operated by its members to provide savings accounts and low-interest loans to its members only (p. 87).

D

debit card: credit device used to make cashless purchases of goods and services; money is electronically withdrawn from the consumer's checkable account and transferred directly to the store's bank account (pp. 91, 377).

debt financing: raising money for a business through borrowing (p. 265). *See also* intermediate-term financing; long-term financing; short-term financing.

deficit financing: spending by the government that exceeds the money it takes in through taxation (p. 423).

deflation: prolonged decline in the general price level (p. 339).

demand curve: line plotted on a graph showing the quantity demanded of a good or service at each possible price (p. 183).

demand deposits: money deposited in a bank that can be withdrawn at any time; now called checkable deposits (p. 377).

demand-pull inflation: theory that prices rise as the result of excessive business and consumer demand; demand increases faster than total supply resulting in shortages leading to higher prices (p. 440).

demerit goods: goods such as gambling and injurious drugs that the government has deemed socially undesirable; use is discouraged through taxation, regulation, or prohibition of the manufacture, sale, and use of such goods (p. 417).

democratic socialism: system that works within the constitutional framework of a nation to elect socialists to office; the government usually controls only some areas of the economy (p. 484).

depreciate (di-PREE-shee-AYT): decline in value over time; occurs as an item wears out or becomes outdated (p. 126).

depreciation (goods): loss of value because of wear and tear to consumer durables, such as cars: also applies to producer goods—machines and equipment (p. 334).

depreciation (monetary): fall in price of a currency through the action of supply and demand; often improves a country's competitive edge in trade (p. 469).

depression: major slowdown of economic activity during which millions are out of work, many businesses fail, and the economy operates at far below capacity (p. 348).

deregulation: gradual reduction of government regulation and control over business activity (p. 246).

devaluation: lowering a currency's value in relation to other currencies by government order (p. 468).

developed nations: nations with relatively high standards of living and economies based more on industry than on agriculture (p. 504).

developing nations: nations with little industrial development and low standards of living (p. 504).

direct foreign investment (DFI): purchase by foreigners of real estate and businesses in another country (p. 537).

direct-mail advertising: type of promotion using a mailer that usually includes a letter describing the product or service and an order blank or application form (p. 291).

discount rate: interest rate the Fed charges on loans to banks (p. 401).

discretionary (dis-KREH-shuh-NEHR-ee) income: money income a person has left to spend on extras after necessities have been bought (p. 58).

disposable income: income remaining for people to spend or save after all taxes have been paid (p. 58).

disposable personal income (DI): income remaining for people to spend or save after all taxes have been paid (p. 336). *See* disposable income.

distribution of income: money payment for work, the amount of health care, education, food, and so on, that each person receives; distribution of goods and services among all members of an economic system (p. 31).

diversification: spreading of investments in several different types of accounts to lower overall risk (p. 164).

dividends: money return a stockholder receives on the amount he or she originally invested in the company by purchasing stock (p. 155).

division of labor: breaking down of a job into small tasks; each task may be performed by a different worker (p. 275).

double coincidence of wants: situation resulting when each party to a transaction wants exactly what the other person has to offer, allowing a direct exchange of goods; this is a requirement for bartering (p. 364).

durability: ability of an item to last a long time (p. 115).

E

economic assistance: loans and outright grants of money or equipment to other nations to add to their capital resources (p. 513).

economic efficiency: wise use of available resources so that people will be confortable given the amount and their need of available resources (p. 45).

economic growth: expansion of the economy to produce more goods, jobs, and wealth (p. 45).

economic indicators: statistics that measure variables in the economy (p. 355).

economic model: simplified representation of the real world which shows people's reactions to changes in the economy; theory (p. 18).

economics: study of how individuals and nations make choices about ways to use scarce resources to fulfill their needs and wants (p. 8).

economic system: way in which a nation uses its resources to satisfy its people's needs and wants (p. 30).

economy: all activity in a nation that affects the production, distribution, and use of goods and services (p. 18).

elastic demand: situation in which the rise or fall in price of a product greatly affects the amount of that product which people are willing to buy; if the prices of certain products rise, consumers will buy cheaper substitutes (p. 185).

elasticity: economic concept dealing with consumers' responsiveness to an increase or decrease in prices; price responsiveness (p. 185).

electronic funds transfer (EFT): system of putting onto computers all the various banking functions that in the past were handled on paper (p. 369).

embargo: complete restriction on the import or export of a particular good (p. 473).

entrepreneur: person who starts a business to gain profits and is willing to take the risks involved (p. 208).

entrepreneurship (AHN-truh-pruh-NUHR-SHIP): ability to start new businesses, to introduce new products and techniques, and to improve management techniques (p. 11).

equilibrium price: price of a product or service at which the amount producers are willing to supply is equal to the amount consumers are willing to buy. On a graph, the equilibrium price is where the supply curve and the demand curve intersect (p. 197).

equity (E-kwuh-tee): amount of money invested in a property minus the debt, such as the mortgage payments that are still owed (p. 130).

equity (value): that which is fair and just (p. 45).

equity financing: raising money for a company by selling stock in the company (p. 267).

ethical behavior: acting in accordance with moral and ethical convictions about right and wrong (p. 71).

excise (EK-syz) tax: tax on the manufacture, sale, or use within the country of specific products, such as liquor, gasoline, and automobiles (p. 136).

expansion: portion of the business cycle in which economic activity slowly increases; also called a recovery (p. 348).

exports: goods sold to other countries (p. 462).

factors of production: resources of land, labor, capital, and entrepreneurship used to produce goods and services (p. 11).

Fed, the: Federal Reserve System created by Congress in

571

1913 as the nation's central banking organization; functions include processing checks, serving as the government's banker, and controlling the rate of growth of the money supply (p. 388).

Federal Open Market Committee (FOMC): 12-member committee in the Federal Reserve System which meets approximately eight times a year to decide the course of action that the Fed should take to control the money supply (p. 394).

fiat (FEE-uht) money: money that has value because a government fiat, or order, has established it as acceptable for payment of debts (p. 366).

finance charge: cost of credit expressed in dollars and cents (p. 91).

finance company: company that takes over contracts for installment debts from stores and adds a fee for collecting the debt; also make loans directly to consumers (p. 87).

fiscal policy: federal government's use of taxation and spending policies to affect overall business activity (p. 443).

fiscal year: year by which accounts are kept; for the federal government, October 1 to September 30 of the next year (p. 421).

five-year plans: centralized planning system that was the basis for China's economic system; eventually was transformed to a regional planning system leading to limited free enterprise (p. 487).

fixed rate of exchange: system under which a national government sets the value of its currency in relation to a single standard then it establishes equivalents between its currency and that of other countries (p. 467).

flexible exchange rates: arrangement in which the forces of supply and demand are allowed to set the price of various currencies (p. 468).

foreign affiliates: branches of multinational firms (p. 543).

foreign aid: money, goods, and services given by governments and private organizations to help other nations and their citizens (p. 512).

foreign exchange markets: markets dealing in buying and selling foreign currency for businesses that want to import goods from other countries; some currency trading takes place through banks (p. 467).

form utility: the conversion of raw materials to finished goods to satisfy consumer wants (p. 284).

fractional reserve banking: system in which only a fraction of the deposits in a bank is kept on hand, or in reserve; the remainder is available to lend to borrowers or is otherwise invested (p. 389).

franchise: contract in which one business (the franchiser) sells to another business (the franchisee) the right to use the franchiser's name and sell its products (p. 222).

free enterprise system: system in which individuals own the factors of production and decide how to use them within legal limits. Also called capitalism (p. 38).

full employment: condition of the economy when the un-

employment rate is lower than a certain number established by economists' studies (p. 439).

General Agreement on Tariffs and Trade (GATT): trade agreement under which countries meet periodically to negotiate tariff reductions that are mutually advantageous to all members; in effect since January 1, 1948 (p. 474).

generalization (JEN-ruh-luh-ZAY-shuhn): statement that pulls together common ideas among facts and is true in most cases (p. 21).

generic (juh-NER-ihk) brands: general name for a product rather than a specific brand name given by the manufacturer (p. 66).

geographic monopolies: market situations occurring when an individual seller has control over a market because of the location (p. 239).

global integration: interdependency among the countries of the world, especially within financial markets and telecommunications (p. 532).

goods and services: end results of factors of production; goods are the things people buy; services are the activities done for others for a fee (p. 11).

government monopolies: market situations created by the government and protected by legal barriers to entry; activity exclusive to government (p. 239).

gross domestic product (GDP): total dollar value of all *final* goods and services produced in the nation in a single year (p. 332).

horizontal merger: buy-out of a company by one in the same business (p. 245).

hypotheses: educated guesses or predictions, used as starting points for investigations (p. 19).

imperfect competition: market situation in which individual or group buys or sells a good or service in amounts large enough to affect price; includes monopoly, oligopoly, and monopolistic competition (p. 237).

implicit GDP price deflator: price index that removes the effect of inflation from GDP so that the overall economy in one year can be compared to another year (p. 341).

import quota: restriction imposed on the value of or on the number of units of a particular good that can be brought into the country (p. 473).

imports: goods bought from other countries for domestic use (p. 462).

income redistribution: government activity that takes income from some people through taxation and uses it to help citizens in need (p. 417).

Individual Retirement Account (IRA): private retirement plan that allows individuals or married couples to save a certain amount of their earnings per year, dependent on total income; also depending on income, the contribution is not taxed and the interest is tax deferred (p. 162).

industrial union: union made up of all the workers in an industry regardless of job or skill level (p. 312).

inelastic demand: situation in which a price change of a product has little impact on the quantity demanded by consumers (p. 186).

infant mortality: death rate of infants who die during first year of life (p. 506).

inflation: prolonged rise in the general price level of goods and services (p. 338).

informative advertising: advertising that benefits consumers by giving information about a product (p. 64).

injunction: court order preventing some activity (p. 320).

innovations: inventions and new production techniques (p. 352).

inside information: information available to a broker that no one else has; it is illegal for a broker to give out this information and illegal for a client to profit from it (p. 159).

installment charge account: credit extended to a consumer allowing the consumer to buy major items such as furniture, televisions, and refrigerators from a particular store and to pay for them in equal payments, or installments, spread over a period of time (p. 90).

installment debt: type of loan repaid with equal payments, or installments, over a specific period of time (p. 80).

interest: amount of money the borrower must pay for the use of someone else's money (p. 80). Payment people receive when they lend money, allowing someone to use their money (p. 146).

interlocking directorate: situation occurring when the majority of members of the boards of directors of competing corporations are the same; in effect, having one group of people manage both companies (p. 244).

intermediate-term financing: borrowing money by a business for 1 to 10 years (p. 265).

International Monetary Fund (IMF): agency whose member governments are obligated to keep their foreign exchange rates more or less fixed (p. 467).

inventory: supply of whatever items are used in a business, such as raw materials or goods for sale (p. 210).

invisible hand: term used by Adam Smith to describe the effect of competition in guiding individuals toward working for their own self-interest, thereby achieving the maximum good for society (p. 37).

joint venture: temporary partnership set up between individuals or companies for a specific purpose and for a short period of time (p. 217).

Keogh (KEE-oh) Plan: retirement plan that allows self-employed individuals to save a maximum of 15 percent of their income up to a specified amount each year and to deduct that amount from their yearly taxable income (p. 161).

labor: work people do; often called a human resource (p. 10).

labor union: association of workers organized to improve wages and working conditions for its members (p. 311).

lagging indicators: indicators that seem to lag behind changes in overall business activity (p. 355)

land: in economics, term used to refer to natural resources and surface land; all things found in nature, on or in the water and earth. Economically, the most important are surface land and mineral deposits (p. 10).

law of demand: economic rule which states that the quantity demanded and price move in opposite directions; as price goes up, quantity demanded goes down; as price goes down, quantity demanded goes up. There is an inverse, or opposite, relationship between demand and price (p. 177).

law of diminishing marginal utility: economic rule stating that the additional satisfaction a consumer gets from purchasing one more unit of a product will lessen with each additional unit purchased (p. 177).

law of diminishing returns: economic rule stating that after some point, adding units of a factor of production (such as labor) to all the other factors of production (such as equipment) increases total output for a time; after a certain point, the extra output for each additional unit will begin to decrease (p. 192).

law of supply: economic rule stating that as the price rises for a good, the quantity supplied rises. As the price falls, the quantity supplied also falls (p. 191).

leading indicators: statistics that point to what will happen in the economy (p. 355)

lease: long-term agreement describing the terms under which property is rented (p. 126).

leasing: renting rather than buying such items as equipment, housing, and cars (p. 266).

legal tender: money that must by law be accepted for payment of public and private debts (p. 366).

liability insurance: insurance that pays for bodily injury and property damage; required by many states before licensing an automobile (p. 139).

limited liability: situation in which an owner's responsibility for a company's debts is limited to the size of the owner's investment in the firm (p. 220).

limited partnership: special form of partnership in which the partners are not equal; the general partner(s) assumes responsibility for all management duties and debts; the other partner(s) contributes money or property and has no voice in management (p. 217).

line of credit: maximum amount of money a company can borrow from a bank during a period of time, usually one year, without having to reapply for a loan (p. 266).

local union: members of a union in a particular factory, company, or geographic area; the local deals with a company by negotiating a contract and making sure contract terms are kept (p. 313).

lockout: situation which occurs when management prevents workers from returning to work until they agree to a new contract (p. 320).

long-term financing: money borrowed by a business for a period of more than 10 years (p. 265).

loose money policy: monetary policy that makes credit inexpensive and abundant, possibly leading to inflation (p. 389).

M1: narrowest definition of the money supply; consists of moneys that can be spent immediately and against which checks can be written; includes all the paper bills and coins in circulation including currency, travelers checks, and checkable deposits (p. 378).

M2: broader definition of the money supply; includes all of M1, plus such near moneys as money market mutual fund balances and Eurodollars; includes all paper bills and coins in circulation (p. 378).

market: freely chosen activity between buyers and sellers of goods and services in which business is done with those who best satisfy the needs and wants of those involved (p. 33).

market economic system: system in which individuals own the factors of production and make economic decisions through free interaction while looking out for their own best interests; the government does not intervene; capitalism (p. 33).

marketing: all the activities needed to move goods and services from the producer to the consumer; includes market research, advertising and promotion, and distribution (p. 282).

market research: gathering, recording, and analyzing data about the types of goods and services that people want (p. 284).

market survey: survey in which researchers gather information about possible users of a product based on such characteristics as age, sex, income, education, and location; written questionnaires and personal interviews are often used (p. 284).

maturity: period of time at which time deposits will pay a stated rate of interest (p. 148).

mechanization: combined labor of people and machines; originally, machines were combined with unskilled workers to replace skilled handwork (p. 274).

mediation (MEE-dee-AY-shuhn): stage in contract negotiations between union and management, in which a neutral person steps in and tries to get both sides to reach an agreement (p. 318).

Medicaid: state and federal public-assistance program that provides free health care for low-income and disabled persons (p. 417).

Medicare: government program that provides health care for the aged (p. 415).

medium of exchange: use of money in exchange for goods or services (p. 362).

merger: situation occurring when one corporation buys more than half the stock of another corporation (p. 245). *See also* conglomerate merger; horizontal merger; vertical merger.

merit good: any good or service that the government has deemed socially desirable such as museums, ballets, and classical music concerts; often subsidized by government so that all people may enjoy it (p. 416).

military assistance: either economic or technical assistance to a nation's armed forces (p. 513).

minimum wage law: federal, state, or city law which sets the lowest legal hourly wage rate that may be paid to certain types of workers (p. 309).

mixed economy: system combining characteristics of more than one type of economy with others so that the mix varies and the economic system created leans more toward one pure type than another (p. 34).

monetarism (MAH-nuh-te-RIH-zuhm): theory that deals with the relationship between the amount of money the Federal Reserve places in circulation and the level of activity in the economy (p. 448).

monetarists: supporters of the theory of monetarism, often linked with Milton Friedman (p. 448).

monetary policy: policy that involves changing the rate of growth of the supply of money in circulation to affect the amount of credit and, therefore, business activity in the economy (p. 388).

monetary rule: monetarists' policy that the Fed should allow the money supply to grow at a specified rate (perhaps 3 to 5 percent) per year and not use fiscal policy to stimulate or slow the economy (p. 449).

monetary standard: manner in which a nation assigns value to its money (p. 370).

money: anything customarily used as a medium of exchange, a unit of accounting, and a store of value (p. 362).

money market deposit account (MMDA): account that pays relatively high rates of interest, requires a minimum balance, and allows immediate access to money (p. 148).

money market fund: type of mutual fund that uses investors' money to make short-term loans to businesses and banks; most allow investors to write checks against their investments in the fund (p. 158).

monopolistic competition: market situation in which a large number of sellers offer similar but slightly different products and each has some control over price (p. 240).

mortgage: installment debt owed on real property—houses, buildings, or land (p. 81).

multinationals: firms that do business and have offices or factories in many countries (p. 543).

mutual fund: investment company that pools the money of many individuals to buy stocks, bonds, or other investments (p. 158).

national debt: total amount of debt outstanding for the federal government; public debt (p. 425).

national income (NI): total income earned by everyone in the economy (p. 335).

national income accounting: measurement of the national economy's performance, dealing with the overall economy's income and output as well as the interaction of consumers, businesses, and governments (p. 332).

nationalization: placement of railroads, businesses, and so on, under government ownership (p. 519).

natural monopolies: market situations resulting when one company forces its competitors out of business by producing goods or services at the lowest cost; usually found in industries that need large investments to get started and when it is more efficient to have one company rather than several (p. 239).

near moneys: assets, such as savings accounts, that can be turned into money or into a means of payment relatively easily and without the risk of loss of value (p. 378).

net domestic product (NDP): value of nation's total output (GDP) minus total value lost through wear and tear on machines and equipment (p. 335).

net exports: difference between what the nation sells to other countries (exports) and what it buys from other countries (imports). (p. 334).

North American Free Trade Agreement (NAFTA): trade agreement designed to reduce tariff barriers among Mexico, Canada, and the United States; approved in 1993 (p. 474). *See also* U.S.-Canadian Free Trade Agreement.

oligopoly (AH-luh-GAH-puh-lee): industry dominated by a few suppliers that exercise some control over price (p. 240).

open-market operations: buying and selling of United States securities by the Fed to affect the money supply by changing depository institution reserves or by putting money into or taking it out of circulation in the economy (p. 402).

opportunity cost: value of the next best alternative given up for the alternative that was chosen (p. 14).

over-the-counter market: purchase and sale of stocks and bonds, often of smaller, lesser-known companies, which takes place outside the organized stock exchanges; most over-the-counter stocks are quoted in the National Association of Securities Dealers Automated Quotations (NASDAQ) listings (p. 157).

overdraft checking: checking account that allows a customer to write a check for more money than exists in his or her account (p. 369).

ownership utility: utility created by assuring orderly transfer of ownership of desired goods (p. 284).

partnership: business that two or more individuals own and operate (p. 217).

passbook savings account: account for which a depositor receives a booklet in which deposits, withdrawals, and interest are recorded; also called a regular savings account (p. 147).

past-due notices: reminders sent by businesses and lending institutions that debt payments are overdue (p. 96).

patent: right granted by the government to exclusively manufacture an invention for a specified number of years (p. 239).

peak: period of prosperity in a business cycle in which economic activity is at its highest point; also called a boom (p. 347).

penetration pricing: selling a new product at a low price to attract customers away from an established product (p. 290).

pension plans: company plans that provide for retirement income (p. 161).

perfect competition: market situation in which there are numerous buyers and sellers, and no one buyer or seller can affect price (p. 232).

personal income (PI): total income individuals receive before personal taxes are paid (p. 336).

picketing: activity in which striking workers walk up and down in front of a workplace carrying signs that state their disagreement with the company (p. 320).

place utility: utility created by having a good available where a consumer wants to buy it (p. 284).

points: fee paid to a lender and computed as percentage points of a loan (p. 129).

price elasticity of demand: economic concept that deals with how much demand varies according to changes in price (p. 185).

price leadership: practice of setting prices close to those charged by other companies selling similar products; found especially in oligopolies (p. 289).

price system: system of pure capitalism that allows prices to seek their own level as determined by the forces of supply and demand (p. 482).

prime rate: rate of interest banks charge on loans to their best business customers (p. 401).

principal: amount of money originally borrowed in a loan (p. 80).

private-labeled products: store-brand products carried by some supermarket chains and club wholesale chains as a lower cost alternative to national brands (p. 110).

private property: whatever is owned by individuals or groups rather than the federal, state, or local governments (p. 38).

private property rights: rights of individuals or groups to own goods; these rights are enforced by the government (p. 482).

privatization: change from state ownership of business, land, and buildings to private ownership (p. 492).

producer goods: goods produced for businesses to use in making other goods (p. 271).

producer price index (PPI): measure of the change in price over time of a specific group of goods used by businesses; formerly wholesale price index (p. 340).

product differentiation: manufacturers' use of minor differences in quality and features to try to differentiate between similar goods and services (p. 240).

production: process of changing resources into goods that satisfy the needs and wants of individuals and businesses (p. 271).

production possibilities: all the combinations of goods and services that can be produced from a fixed amount of resources in a given period of time (p. 15).

productivity: ability to produce greater quantities of goods and services in better and faster ways (p. 10).

product life cycle: series of stages that a product goes through from first introduction to complete withdrawal from the market; a cycle has no fixed number of months or years (p. 291).

professionals: highly educated individuals with college degrees and usually additional education or training (p. 307).

profit: money left after all the costs of production—wages, rent, interest, and taxes have been paid (p. 39).

profit incentive: desire to make money that motivates people to produce and sell goods and services that others want to buy (p. 39).

progressive tax: tax that takes a larger percentage of higher incomes than lower incomes; justified on the basis of the ability-to-pay principle (p. 430).

proletariat (PROH-luh-TER-ee-uht): term used by Karl Marx to mean workers (p. 484).

promissory (prah-muh-SOHR-ee) note: written agreement to repay a loan by a specified time and with a specified rate of interest (p. 266).

promotion: use of advertising and other methods to inform consumers that a new or improved product or service is available and to persuade them to purchase it (p. 290).

property rights: protection of private property; the govern-ment may not legally take private property without paying fair market value (p. 523).

proportional tax: tax that takes the same percentage of all incomes; as income rises, the amount of tax paid also rises (p. 430).

proprietor: owner of a business; from the Latin word *proprietas*, meaning "property" (p. 213).

protectionists: people who argue for trade restrictions (p. 474).

protective tariff: tax on imports used to raise the cost of imported goods and thereby protect domestic producers (p. 472).

public-assistance programs: government programs that make payments based on need; also called welfare (p. 418).

public goods: goods or services that government sometimes supplies to its citizens; can be used by many individuals at the same time without reducing the benefit each person receives (p. 416).

public-works projects: publicly-used facilities such as schools and highways, built by federal, state, or local governments with public money (p. 413).

purchasing power: the real goods and services that money can buy; determines the value of the money (p. 338).

pure monopoly: most extreme market form of imperfect competition in which a single seller controls the supply of a good or service and thus has control over price (p. 237). *See also* geographic monopolies; government monopolies;natural monopolies; technological monopoly.

rational choice: involves choosing the alternative that has the greatest value from among comparable quality products (p. 61).

real estate taxes: taxes paid on land and buildings (p. 125).

real GDP: figure resulting when the GDP is adjusted for inflation by applying the price deflator (p. 341).

real income effect: economic rule stating that individuals cannot keep buying the same quantity of a product if its price rises while their income stays the same; this works in reverse direction also—if the price of a product decreases and income remains the same, purchasing power is increased and the amount of product purchased will likely be increased (p. 179).

recession: portion of the business cycle in which the nation's output, the real GDP, does not grow for at least two quarters (six months) (p. 348).

recovery: portion of the business cycle in which economic activity increases; also called an expansion (p. 348).

registration fee: licensing fee, usually annual, paid to a state for the right to use a car (p. 137).

regressive tax: tax that takes a larger percentage of lower incomes than higher incomes (p. 430).

regular charge account: credit extended to a consumer

allowing the consumer to buy goods or services from a particular store and to pay for them later. Interest is charged on that part of the account not paid within a certain period of time. Also known as a 30-day charge (p. 89).

representative money: money not valuable in itself for nonmoney uses which can be exchanged for some valuable commodity such as gold or silver (p. 366).

reregulation: federal government regulation and control over business activity of formerly heavily-regulated industries (p. 246).

reserve requirements: regulations set by the Fed, requiring banks to keep a certain percentage of their deposits as cash in their own vaults or as deposits in their district Federal Reserve Bank (p. 389).

resource: anything that people can use to make or obtain what they need or want (p. 8).

retailers: businesses that sell consumer goods directly to the public (p. 294).

revenue tariff: tax on imports used primarily to raise income without restricting imports (p. 472).

revolving charge account: credit extended to a consumer allowing the consumer to buy goods or services from a particular store and to pay for them later. Usually a certain portion of the balance must be paid each month; interest is charged on the amount not paid (p. 89).

right-to-work laws: state laws forbidding union shops and closed shops; workers are allowed to continue working in a particular job without joining a union (p. 313).

robotics: sophisticated computer-controlled machinery that operates an assembly line (p. 275).

S

saving: nonuse of income for a period of time so that it can be used later (p. 146).

savings and loan association (S&L): depository institution that, like a commercial bank, accepts deposits and lends money. Originally established to lend money for home building, federal laws in the 1980s permitted S&Ls to provide some of the same services as banks (p. 86).

savings banks: depository institutions originally set up to serve small savers overlooked by commercial banks; most of their business comes from savings accounts and home loans (p. 86).

savings bonds: bonds issued by the federal government as a way of borrowing money; bonds are purchased at half the face value and then increase in value every six months until full face value is reached (p. 155).

scarcity: state in which people do not and cannot have enough income, time, or other resources to satisfy their every desire (p. 9).

secondary market: process through which owners of securities sell the securities to other investors for cash (p. 493)

secured loan: loan that is backed up by collateral (p. 95).

security deposit: money a renter lets an owner hold; if the rent is not paid or an apartment is damaged, the owners may keep all or part of the deposit (p. 130).

semiskilled workers: people whose jobs require some training, in job-related skills, often using modern technology (p. 307).

service flow: amount of use a person gets from an item over time and the value a person places on this use (p. 115).

service workers: people who provide services directly to individuals (p. 307).

shortages: situations occurring when, at the going price, the quantity demanded is greater than the quantity supplied (p. 198).

short-term financing: money borrowed by a business for any period of time less than a year (p. 265).

skilled worker: person who has learned a trade or craft either through a vocational school or as an apprentice to an experienced worker (p. 307).

small business incubator: a business that helps small businesses develop by providing such forms of assistance as a low-rent building, management advice, and computers; often operated with state and federal funds (p. 215).

social insurance programs: government programs that pay benefits to retired and disabled workers, their families, and the unemployed; financed by taxes paid into programs by workers and employers (p. 418).

Social Security: federal program that provides monthly payments to people who are retired or unable to work (p. 417).

sole proprietorship: business owned by one person; most basic type of business organization (p. 213).

special economic zones: designated geographic areas in the People's Republic of China which, since 1979, have been moving toward restricted decentralized capitalism (p. 488).

specialization (SPE-shuh-luh-ZAY-shuhn): concept that it is profitable for a nation to produce and export a limited assortment of goods for which it is particularly suited (p. 464).

stabilization (STAY-buh-lih-ZAY-shuhn) policies: attempt by the federal government to keep the economy healthy and to make the future more predictable for planning, saving, and investing; includes monetary and fiscal policies (p. 438).

stagflation: combination of inflation and low economic activity (p. 441).

standard of living: material well-being of an individual, group, or nation measured by the average value of goods and services used by the average citizen during a given period of time (p. 45).

startups: newly-established businesses; business advice and assistance are available from the federal and state governments, colleges, and universities (p. 214)

statement savings account: account similar to a passbook savings account except that instead of a passbook, the depositor receives a monthly statement showing all transactions (p. 147).

stock: share of ownership in the corporation issuing the stock; entitles the buyer to a certain part of the future profits and assets of the corporation (p. 154).

stockholders: people who have invested in a corporation and own stock; stockholders hold a claim against a certain part of the profits (p. 155).

store of value: use of money to store purchasing power for later use (p. 364).

strike: deliberate work stoppage by workers to force an employer to give in to their demands (p. 312).

subsistence agriculture: raising of just enough food by a family to take care of its own needs; no crops are available for export or to feed an industrial work force (p. 505).

substitution effect: economic principle stating that if two items satisfy the same need and the price of one rises, people will buy the other (p. 179).

Supplemental Security Income: federal programs that include food stamps, veterans' benefits, and payments to the aged, blind, and disabled (p. 417).

supply curve: line plotted on a graph that shows the quantities supplied of a good or service at each possible price (p. 194).

surplus: situation occurring when supply is greater than demand (p. 198).

tariff: tax on imports; most commonly used barrier to free trade (p. 472). *See also* protective tariff; revenue tariff

tax-exempt bonds: bonds sold by local and state governments; interest paid on the bond is not taxed by the federal government (p. 155).

technical assistance: aid, in the form of professionals such as engineers, teachers, and technicians, supplied by nations to teach skills to individuals in other nations; strengthens a nation's human resources (p. 513).

technological monopoly: market situation resulting when a seller develops a product or production process for which it obtains a patent; company holds exclusive rights to the new invention for a specified number of years (p. 239).

technology: any use of land, labor, and capital that produces goods and services more efficiently. Today, generally means the use of science to develop new products and new methods for producing and distributing goods and services (pp. 11, 197).

telecommunications: long-distance communications, usually electronic, using communications satellites, and fiber-optic cables (p. 532).

test marketing: offering a product for sale in a small area for a limited period of time to see how well it sells before offering it nationally (p. 285).

three P's: prices, profits, and private property—the basis

of market capitalism (p. 482).

thrift institutions: mutual savings banks, savings and loan associations (S&Ls), and credit unions that offer many of the same services as commercial banks (p. 377).

tight money policy: monetary policy which makes credit expensive and in short supply in an effort to slow the economy (p. 389).

time deposits: savings plans that require savers to leave their money on deposit for certain periods of time (p. 148).

time lags: periods between the time fiscal policy is enacted and the time it becomes effective (p. 450).

time utility: utility created by having a good available when a consumer wants to buy it (p. 284).

tolerance: fair, objective, and permissive attitude toward the opinions, and practices of other religions, races, and nationalities (p. 547).

trade-off: exchanging one thing for the use of another; often making unavoidable choices because of the problem of scarcity (p. 13).

trade credit: credit extended by a seller to a business buying goods; allows a buyer to take immediate possession of goods to pay for them at some future date (p. 266).

traditional economic system: system in which economic decisions are based on customs, beliefs, and ways of doing things that have been handed down from generation to generation (p. 32).

transfer payments: welfare and other supplementary payments, such as unemployment compensation, Social Security, and Medicaid, that a state or the federal government makes to individuals, adding to an individual's income even though the payments are not in exchange for any current productive activity (p. 336).

Treasury bills: certificates issued by the U.S. Treasury in exchange for borrowed money in minimum amounts of $10,000 and maturing during a period ranging from three months to one year (p. 156).

Treasury bonds: certificates issued by the U.S. Treasury in exchange for borrowed money in minimum amounts of $1,000 or $5,000 and maturing in 10 or more years (p. 156).

Treasury notes: certificates issued by the U.S. Treasury in exchange for borrowed money with minimum amounts of $1,000 or $5,000 and maturing in 2 to 10 years (p. 156).

trough: lowest portion of the business cycle in which the downward spiral of the economy levels off (p. 348).

underground economy: transactions by people who do not follow federal and state laws with respect to reporting earnings; includes tax avoiders, gamblers and drug traffickers, and those illegally receiving unemployment benefits (p. 439).

unemployment rate: percentage of the civilian labor force that is without jobs but that is actively looking for work (p. 438).

union shop: company that requires that new company employees to join a union after a specific period of time, usually three months (p. 313).

unit of accounting: use of money as a yardstick for comparing the values of goods and services in relation to one another (p. 364).

unlimited liability: requirement that an owner is personally and fully responsible for all losses and debts of a business (p. 214).

unsecured loan: loan guaranteed only by a promise to repay it (p. 95).

unskilled workers: people whose jobs require no specialized training (p. 307).

U.S.-Canadian Free Trade Agreement: trade agreement between the United States and Canada designed to eliminate high tariffs on such things as furniture, textiles, and paper; guarantees that both countries have access to each others' petroleum, gas, coal, and electricity at prices paid by nationals under comparable commercial circumstances (p. 474).

usury law: law restricting the amount of interest that can be charged for credit (p. 99).

utility: ability of any good or service to satisfy consumer wants (pp. 177, 282). *See also* form utility; ownership utility; place utility; time utility.

values: beliefs or characteristics that an individual or group considers important, such as religious freedom, and equal opportunity (p. 20).

vertical merger: a merger in which a business that is buying from or selling to another business merges with that business (p. 245).

vicious cycle of poverty: trap in which a less-developed country with low per-capital incomes cannot save and invest enough to achieve acceptable rates of economic growth (p. 524).

voluntary exchange: principle that is the basis of activity in a market economy; a buyer and a seller exercise their economic freedoms by working out their own terms of, exchange (p. 176).

wants: economists' term for everything people desire beyond basic goods and services that meet their needs (p. 9).

warehouse food store: store that carries a limited number of brands and items; less expensive than supermarkets; goods are often available only in large quantities (p. 109).

warranty: promise made by a manufacturer or a seller to repair or replace a product within a certain period of time if it is found to be faulty (p. 60).

welfare: public-assistance programs that make payments based on need; includes Supplemental Security Income, Aid to Families with Dependent Children, and Medicaid (p. 418).

welfare state: country that is a blend of capitalism and socialism, combining private ownership of the means of production and competitive allocation of resources with the goal of social equality for its citizens (p. 494).

white-collar: category of workers employed in offices, sales, or professional positions (p. 307).

wholesalers: businesses that purchase large quantities of goods from producers for resale to other businesses (p. 293).

Workers' Compensation: government program that extends payments for medical care to workers injured on the job; people who have lost jobs can receive payments through unemployment insurance (p. 417).

ability-to-pay principle/capacidad de pago, principio de la principio de tributación el cual prescribe que aquellos que tengan ingresos más altos paguen más impuestos que aquellos que tengan ingresos más bajos, irrespectivamente del número de servicios gubernamentales que usen (p. 428).

absolute advantage/ventaja absoluta capacidad de un país, que use la misma cantidad de recursos que otro, para producir un determinado producto a menos costo. (p. 464).

accounts receivable/cuentas por cobrar dineros que le deben los clientes a un negocio (p. 266).

agency shop/empresa con cotización sindical obligatoria compañía en la cual no se les exige a los empleados pertenecer al sindicato, pero que aun así deben pagarle cuotas a éste (p. 313).

aggregate demand/demanda total cantidad total de bienes y servicios en la totalidad de la economía que todos los ciudadanos demandan en un momento dado (p. 342).

aggregate demand curve/demanda total, curva de línea gráfica que demuestra la relación entre la cantidad total que demandan todos los ciudadanos, y el promedio de todos los precios, medidos mediante el índice implícito de deflación del PNB (p. 343).

aggregates/agregados suma de todas las partes que individualmente componen la economía (p. 342).

aggregate supply/oferta total producción nacional real basada en la subida y caída de los precios (p. 345).

aggregate supply curve/oferta total, curva de línea gráfica que demuestra la relación entre la demanda total cuando ésta se mide basándola en la producción nacional real y usando el índice implícito de deflación del PNB como índice de precios (p. 345).

Aid to Families with Dependent Children/Ayuda a Familias con Hijos Dependientes programa de asistencia pública en los Estados Unidos que administran los estados, el cual proporciona dinero a padres necesitados de hijos pequeños (p. 417).

allegiances/lealtades fidelidad a causas, países y personas (p.543).

alliances/alianzas negocios en conjunto formados por firmas en distintos países; a menudo entre firmas de países industrializados (p. 545).

annual percentage rate (APR)/índice de porcentaje anual costo del crédito expresado en términos de porcentaje anual (p. 93).

antitrust legislation/leyes antimonopolistas leyes promulgadas por el gobierno federal y estatal para impedir la formación de nuevos monopolios y para romper los que ya existan (p. 244).

arbitration/arbitraje etapa en un proceso de negociación en la cual el sindicato y la gerencia plantean a un tercero los asuntos sobre los cuales no se pueden poner de acuerdo para que éste dé una decisión final. Ambas partes aceptan por adelantado la decisión del árbitro (p. 319).

articles of incorporation/escritura de constitución documento que establece en un estado una sociedad; dicho documento abarca cierta información básica sobre la sociedad, la junta directiva y las acciones que se emiten (p. 221).

assembly line/cadena de montaje sistema de producción en la cual al artículo que se fabrica lo lleva una banda transportadora a los trabajadores que a su vez lo ensamblan (p. 275).

authoritarian socialism/socialismo autoritario sistema que respalda la revolución como medio para derribar al capitalismo y lograr metas socialistas; un gobierno central controla toda la economía; también llamado comunismo (p. 484).

automated teller machines/cajeros automáticos unidades que les permiten a los clientes realizar sus transacciones bancarias sin la ayuda de un cajero (p. 372).

automation/automatización proceso de producción en el cual las máquinas realizan el trabajo y el personal humano lo fiscaliza (p. 275).

bait and switch/publicidad con cebo práctica publicitaria engañosa mediante la cual una tienda atrae a los consumidores con un anuncio de un producto a bajo precio, y entonces trata de venderles un producto similar a precio superior (p. 65).

balanced budget amendment/enmienda del presupuesto equilibrado propuesta para reducir los déficits del gobierno federal mediante enmiendas a la Constitución (p. 426).

balance of trade/balanza comercial diferencia entre el valor de las exportaciones y las importaciones de una nación (p. 469).

bankruptcy/bancarrota incapacidad de pagar deudas con los ingresos percibidos; condición en la cual los deudores renuncian a la mayor parte de sus propiedades para distribuir éstas a sus acreedores (p. 100).

barriers to entry/barreras para entrar en un mercado obstáculos a la competencia para impedir que otros tengan acceso al mercado (p. 238).

barter/trueque intercambio de bienes y servicios por otros bienes y servicios (p. 362).

base year/año base año utilizado como punto de comparación para los demás años en una serie estadística (p. 340).

benefits-received principle/beneficios recibidos, principio de sistema tributario en el cual los que hacen uso de un cierto servicio que preste el gobierno mantienen al mismo con impuestos en proporción a los beneficios que reciban; los que no usen dicho servicio no pagan impuestos por el mismo (p. 428).

blue-collar/obreros categoría de trabajadores que se desempeñan en artesanías, fábricas y trabajo no agrícola (p. 306).

bond/bono certificado emitido por una compañía o el gobierno a cambio de un préstamo de dinero; el bono promete pagar un cierto tipo de interés durante un cierto plazo de tiempo y devolver la suma prestada en su totalidad al final de dicho plazo (p. 155).

boom/auge, período de período de prosperidad en un ciclo comercial en el cual la actividad económica está en su más elevado punto; llamado también máximo o cumbre (p. 347).

boycott/boicot presión económica ejercida por los sindicatos que le urgen al público que no adquieran los bienes y servicios que produzca una compañía (p. 320).

brand name/marca de fábrica palabra, imagen o logotipo en un producto que ayuda a los consumidores a distinguirlo de otros productos similares (p. 66).

broker/corredor persona que actúa como intermediario entre los compradores y vendedores de bonos y acciones (p. 157).

bureaucracies/burocracias oficinas y agencias del gobierno que se desempeñan en su propio y específico campo en la administración del gobierno (p.517).

business cycle/ciclo económico cambios irregulares en el nivel de la producción total medida por el PNB real (p. 347).

business fluctuations/fluctuaciones económicas sube-y-bajas en la economía (p. 347).

capital/capital todas las propiedades: máquinas, edificios, herramientas y dinero—que se usen en la producción de otros bienes y servicios (p. 10).

capital gains/ganacias de capital aumento en el valor de acciones o bonos desde el momento en que se compran hasta el momento en que se vendan (p. 157).

capitalism/capitalismo sistema económico en el cual personas particulares son dueñas de los factores de producción y deciden cómo utilizarlos dentro del margen de la ley; también llamado sistema de mercado; sistema de libre empresa (p. 37).

capital loss/capital, pérdidas de disminución en el valor de acciones o bonos desde el momento en que se compran hasta el momento en que se vendan (p. 158).

cartel/cartel convenio entre grupos de negocios industriales, a menudo en distintos países, de reducir la competencia internacional controlando el precio, producción y distribución de bienes; una forma internacional de monopolio (p. 239).

certificates of deposit/certificados de depósito depósitos a plazo que declaran la cantidad del depósito, el vencimiento y el tipo de interés que paga; los CD ganan más interés que las cuentas de ahorro, pero tienen penalidad por retirar fondos antes de tiempo; se les llama también certificados de ahorro (p. 148).

channels of distribution/canales de distribución rutas mediante las cuales se distribuyen los bienes de los productores a los consumidores (p. 293).

charge account/cuenta de crédito crédito extendido a un con-

sumidor que le permite a éste comprarle bienes y servicios a cierta compañía y pagarlos luego. (p. 89). *Vea también* cuenta de crédito a plazos (installment charge account); cuenta de crédito regular (regular charge account); cuenta de crédito rotativa (revolving charge account).

checkable deposits/depósitos verificables dinero depositado en un banco que se puede extraer en cualquier momento presentando un cheque; anteriormente llamados *demand deposits* (depósitos disponibles o extraíbles a la vista) (p. 377).

check clearing/compensación de[r] cheques bancarios método mediante el cual un cheque que ha sido depositado en una institución depositaria se transfiere a la institución depositaria en la que fue hecho (p. 396).

checking account/cuenta corriente bancaria cuenta en la cual el dinero depositado se puede extraer en cualquier momento haciendo un cheque (p. 376).

circular flow of income/flujo circular de ingresos modelo económico que representa a los ingresos como si fluyeran contínuamente entre los negocios y los consumidores; los ingresos fluyen de los negocios a los domicilios como sueldos, alquileres, intereses y ganancias; los ingresos fluyen de los domicilios a los negocios como pagos por los bienes y los servicios de consumo (p. 443).

civilian labor force/fuerza laboral civil número total de personas de 16 años o más que estén bien empleadas o procurando activamente trabajo (p. 306).

closed shop/empresa con sindicación obligatoria compañía en la cual sólo pueden trabajar los que pertenezcan al sindicato; prohibido en 1947 (p. 313).

closing costs/costos de cierre costos en que se incurre al tramitar una hipoteca o transferir el título de una propiedad; puede incluir gastos por concepto de investigación del título, costos jurídicos, solicitud del préstamo, informe de crédito, inspecciones de la casa e impuestos (p. 129).

collateral/garantía algo de valor que el prestatario permite que el prestamista reclame para sí si no se devuelve el préstamo (p. 95).

collective bargaining/convenio colectivo proceso mediante el cual los sindicatos y los empleadores o patronos negocian las condiciones de empleo (p. 318).

command economic system/sistema de economía dirigida sistema en el cual el gobierno controla los factores de producción y toma todas las decisiones con respecto a su uso; también llamado de economía controlada (p. 33).

commercial bank/banco comercial banco que ofrece una amplia gama de servicios; sus principales funciones son aceptar depósitos, prestar dinero y transferir fondos entre bancos, individuos y negocios (p. 86).

commodity money/dinero mercancía medios de intercambio tales como ganado o joyas que tienen valor como artículo o bien comerciable, fuera de su valor como dinero (p. 365).

communism/comunismo término usado por Carlos Marx para describir su sociedad ideal en la cual no hace falta gobierno; ha venido a significar cualquier tipo de sistema social-ista autoritario que respalda la revolución como medio para derrocar al capitalismo y lograr metas socialistas; un gob-ierno central controla toda la economía (p. 484).

comparative advantage/ventaja comparativa capacidad de un país de producir un producto a un costo de oportunidad menor que otro país (p. 465).

comparison shopping/comparación de las condiciones de venta obtener información sobre los tipos y precios de los productos que hay en distintos comercios y compañías (p. 66).

competition/competencia rivalidad entre los productores o vendedores de artículos similares para conseguirse más ne-gocio ofreciendo los precios más bajos o de mejor calidad (p. 39).

competitive advertising/publicidad competidora publicidad que intenta persuadir a los consumidores de que un produc-to es distinto y superior a cualquier otro (p. 64).

complementary good/bien competitiva producto que a menudo se utiliza con otro; al disminuir el precio del segun-do producto, la demanda por el primero aumenta; al aumen-tar el precio del segundo producto, la demanda por el primero disminuye (p. 188).

condominium/condominio unidades, cada cual con su dueño por separado, en un edificio de apartamentos o en una serie de *townhouses;* las áreas comunes tales como los pasillos y el terreno en el cual está construido el edificio son propiedad en común de todos (p. 126).

conglomerate merger/fusión de conglomerados adquisición de negocios que no están relacionados entre sí (p. 245).

conglomerates/conglomerados grandes compañías compues-tas de compañías más pequeñas que se desempeñan en ac-tividades que no están relacionadas entre sí (p. 245).

consumer/consumidor cualquier persona o grupo que compre o utilice bienes y servicios para satisfacer necesidades o deseos personales (p. 58).

consumer durables/bienes duraderos de consumo artículos fabricados que usan las personas durante largo tiempo antes de reemplazarlos (p. 80).

consumer finance company/compañía financiera para el con-sumidor compañía que le hace préstamos directamente al consumidor a altas tasas de interés (p. 88).

consumer goods/bienes de consumo hienés producidos para personas y vendidos directamente al público para que los usen tal como están (p. 271).

consumerism/consumismo movimiento pára educar a los compradores acerca de la compras que hacen y demandar productos mejores y más seguros a los fabricantes (p. 68).

consumer price index/índice de precios al consumidor medida usada por el gobierno del cambio en precios durante cierto tiempo de un grupo específico de bienes y servicios que uti-liza el domicilio promedio (p. 339).

contraction/contracción parte del ciclo comercial durante el cual la actividad económica está más lenta; llamada tam-bién punto bajo ("trough") (p. 347).

convenience stores/tiendas de artículos de consumo frequente tiendas que abren de 16 a 24 horas al día, y que tienen una selección limitada de artículos, por lo general a un precio más elevado que los supermercados o las tiendas al-macenes (p. 109).

cooperative/cooperativas apartamento cuyo dueño tiene in-tereses por partes iguales en la compañía que es propi-etaria del edificio y del terreno sobre el cual está éste; el dueño no es propietario exclusivo del apartamento en sí sino más bien que tiene un arrendamiento por el mismo (p. 126).

corporate charter/escritura de constitución licencia para fun-cionar que le concede a la sociedad el estado en el cual se ha establecido ésta (p. 221).

corporation/corporación organización propiedad de muchas personas la cual, sin embargo, la ley la trata como si fuera una persona; puede tener propiedad, pagar impuestos, hacer contratos y demandar y ser demandada (p. 219).

cosigner/consignatario persona que firma un contrato de préstamo junto con el prestatario y promete devolver el préstamo si este último no lo hace (p. 96).

cost-benefit analysis/análisis de costo-beneficio proceso fi-nanciero mediante el cual un negocio calcula el costo de una acción y la compara con los beneficios de ésta (p. 258).

cost-of-living adjustment (COLA)/ajuste por costo de vida contrato sindical o disposición de algún otro tipo que pre-scribe un aumento adicional en los salarios si el nivel gener-al de los precios en la economía sube más allá de cierto nivel (p. 319).

cost-push inflation/inflación con estancamiento teoría que las demandas salariales de los sindicatos laborales y el excesi-vo afán de lucro de las grandes compañías empujan hacia arriba los precios, lo cual resulta en "estanca-flación" (p. 441).

craft union/gremio sindicato compuesto por obreros califica-dos en un oficio o industria específico (p. 312).

credit/crédito lo que permite a una persona recibir dinero di-rectamente o indirectamente para comprar bienes y servi-cios en el presente con la promesa de pagarlos en el futuro (p. 80).

credit bureau/crédito, agencia de informes de negocio partic-ular que investiga los ingresos, deudas actuales, vida per-sonal e historial de préstamos y pago de deudas de una persona para determinar el riesgo en prestarle dinero a dicha persona (p. 94).

credit card/crédito, tarjeta de dispositivo de crédito que le permita a una persona hacer compras en muchos tipos de tiendas, restaurantes, hoteles y demás negocios sin pagar en efectivo (p. 90).

credit check/crédito, investigación del investigación de los in-gresos, deudas actuales, vida personal e historial de présta-mos y pago de deudas de una persona (p. 94).

credit limit/crédito, límite del máxima cantidad de bienes y servicios que una persona o negocio puede adquirir bajo promesa de pagarlos en el futuro (p. 89).

credit rating/crédito, evaluación de evaluación del riesgo en prestarle dinero a un cierto negocio o persona (p. 94).

credit union/crédito, unión de institución depositaria que es propiedad de y está administrada por sus miembros para proporcionarles exclusivamente a éstos cuentas de ahorro y préstamos de bajos intereses (p. 87).

debit card/débito, tarjeta de dispositivo de crédito que se utiliza para hacer compra de bienes y servicios sin usar efectivo; el dinero se extrae electrónicamente de la cuenta corriente del consumidor y se transfiere directamente a la cuenta bancaria de la tienda (pp. 91, 377).

debt financing/financiamiento mediante créditos a la emisión de obligaciones recaudación de dinero para un negocio con préstamos (p. 265). *Vea también* financiamiento a mediano plazo; a largo plazo; y a corto plazo.

deficit financing/financiamiento del déficit gastos del gobierno que exceden lo que éste recauda a través de impuestos (p. 423).

deflation/deflación declinación prolongada en el nivel general de precios (p. 339).

demand curve/demanda, curva de línea gráfica que demuestra la cantidad que se demanda de un bien o servicio a cada precio posible (p. 183).

demand deposits/depósitos a la vista dinero depositado en banco que se puede extraer en cualquier momento; llamados ahora depósitos extraíbles por cheque (checkable deposits) (p. 377).

demand-pull inflation/inflación de demanda teoría que dice que los precios suben como resultado de demanda excesiva por parte de los negocios y el consumidor; la demanda aumenta más rápido que la oferta total lo cual resulta en insuficiencias de oferta que causan precios más elevados (p. 440).

demerit goods/bienes de demerito bienes tales como juegos al azar y drogas peligrosas que el gobierno considera son socialmente indeseables; se desalienta su uso mediante impuestos, regulaciones o prohibición de la fabricación, venta y uso de dichos bienes (p. 417).

democratic socialism/socialismo democrático sistema que funciona dentro del contexto constitucional de una nación para elegir socialistas a cargos públicos; el gobierno usualmente controla solamente algunas áreas de la economía (p. 484).

depreciate/depreciar declinar en valor con el pasar del tiempo; ocurre al irse gastando un artículo o al quedarse obsoleto (p. 126).

depreciation (goods)/sobregiro pérdida de valor a causa de desgaste y deterioro de bienes duraderos de consumo, tales como automóviles; también se aplica a los bienes de producción, tales como maquinaria y equipos (p. 369).

depreciation (monetary)/depreciación (monetaria) caída del precio de una divisa a causa de la acción de la oferta y la demanda (p. 469).

depression/depresión declinación de importancia en la actividad económica durante la cual millones de personas se quedan sin trabajo, fracasan numerosos negocios y la economía funciona muy por debajo de su capacidad (p. 348).

deregulation/desregulación reducción gradual en la regulación y control gubernamentales de las actividades comerciales (p. 246).

devaluation/devaluación baja del valor de una moneda en relación con otras por orden del gobierno (p. 468).

developed nations/naciones desarrolladas naciones con niveles relativamente altos de vida basados más en la industria que en la agricultura (p. 504).

developing nations/naciones en vías de desarrollo naciones de poco desarrollo industrial y bajos niveles de vida (p. 504).

direct foreign investment (DFI)/inversión extranjera directa compra por parte de extranjeros de cosas tales como bienes raíces y negocios en otro país (p. 537).

direct-mail advertising/publicidad directa por correo tipo de promoción que utiliza un anuncio postal, el cual por lo general contiene una carta que describe el producto o servicio y un pedido o solicitud en blanco (p. 291).

discount rate/tasa de descuento tasa de interés que la Reserva Federal carga sobre los préstamos a los bancos (p. 401).

discretionary income/ingreso discrecional ingreso monetario que queda para gastarlo en cosas adicionales después de haber adquirido lo necesario (p. 58).

disposable income/ingreso disponible ingreso que queda para gastarlo o ahorrarlo después de haber pagado todos los impuestos (p. 58).

disposable personal income/ingreso disponible personal ingreso que queda para gastarlo o ahorrarlo después de haber pagado todos los impuestos (p. 336).

distribution of income/distribución de ingresos pago monetario por el trabajo, para cuidados a la salud, para la educación, para alimentos, etc., que cada persona recibe; distribución de bienes y servicios a través de todos los miembros de una economía (p. 31).

diversification/diversificación distribución de las inversiones a varios diferentes tipos de cuentas para reducir el riesgo general (p. 164).

dividends/dividendos réditos monetarios que el accionista recibe sobre la suma que invirtiera en la compañía al comprar las acciones (p. 155).

division of labor/división de trabajo reparto de una labor en varias tareas más pequeñas; cada una la puede realizar un obrero distinto (p. 275).

double coincidence of wants/doble coincidencia de necesidades situación que resulta cuando cada participante en una transacción desea exactamente lo que la otra parte tiene que ofrecer, permitiendo así un intercambio directo de bienes; es un requisito para los trueques (p. 364).

durability/durabilidad capacidad de un artículo de durar largo tiempo (p. 115).

economic assistance/asistencia económica préstamos y francas donaciones de dinero o equipos a otras naciones para aumentar sus recursos de capital (p. 513).

economic efficiency/eficiencia económica uso sabio de los recursos disponibles para que el pueblo salga bien económicamente (p. 45).

economic growth/crecimiento económico expansión de la economía para producir más bienes, empleos y riqueza (p. 45).

economic model/modelo económico representación simplificada del mundo real que demuestra las reacciones de las personas a cambios en la economía; teoría (p. 18).

economics/economía (disciplina) estudio de cómo los individuos y las naciones toman decisiones en cuanto a las maneras de utilizar los escasos recursos para satisfacer sus deseos y necesidades (p. 8).

economic system/sistema económico manera en la cual una nación utiliza sus recursos para satisfacer los deseos y necesidades de su pueblo (p. 30).

economy/economía la suma de las actividades de una nación que afectan la producción, distribución y uso de los bienes y servicios (p. 18).

elastic demand/demanda elástica situación en la cual la subida o caída en el precio de un producto afecta grandemente la cantidad de ese producto que el público está dispuesto a comprar; si los precios de ciertos productos aumentan, los consumidores compran sustitutos más baratos (p. 185).

elasticity/elasticidad concepto económico que tiene que ver con la respuesta del consumidor a los aumentos o disminuciones en precios; sensibilidad a los precios (p. 185).

electronic funds transfer (EFT)/transferencia electrónica de fondos sistema para realizar en computadoras todas las diversas funciones bancarias que en el pasado se hacían con papel (p. 369).

embargo/embargo restricción total sobre la exportación o importación de determinado artículo (p. 473).

entrepreneur/empresario[r] persona que comienza un negocio para obtener ganancias y está dispuesta a afrontar los riesgos que esto implica (p. 208).

entrepreneurship/espíritu empresarial[r] la facultad de empezar nuevos negocios, introducir nuevos productos y técnicas y mejorar las técnicas de administración (p. 11).

equilibrium price/precio de equilibrio precio de un producto o servicio al cual la cantidad del mismo que los productores están dispuestos a suministrar es igual a la cantidad que los consumidores están dispuestos a adquirir. En una gráfica, el precio de equilibrio queda donde la curva de la oferta y la de la demanda se intersectan (p. 197).

equity (financial)/equidad cantidad de dinero que se invierte en una propiedad menos las deudas, tales como pagos de hipoteca, que se deban (p. 130).

equity (value)/equidad lo que es equitativo y justo (p. 45).

equity financing/financiamiento por venta de participación recaudación de dinero para una compañía vendiendo acciones de ésta (p. 267).

ethical behavior/comportamiento ético conducta de acuerdo con convicciones éticas y morales acerca del bien y del mal (p. 71).

excise tax/impuesto interno sobre el consumo impuesto sobre la fabricación, venta o uso dentro del país de determinados productos, tales como licores, gasolina y automóviles (p. 136).

expansion/expansión porción del ciclo comercial durante el cual la actividad económica lentamente aumenta; se le llama también recuperación (p. 348).

exports/exportaciones artículos que se venden a otros países (p. 462).

factors of production/factores de producción recursos de tierras, mano de obra, capital y capacidad emprendedora para producir bienes y servicios (p. 11).

"Fed, the"/El "Fed" sistema creado por el Congreso en 1913 como la organización central bancaria de la nación; entre sus funciones se encuentran el procesamiento de cheques, servir como banquero del gobierno, y control de la tasa de crecimiento del suministro de dinero (p. 388).

Federal Open Market Committee (FOMC)/Comisión Federal de Mercado Abierto comité de doce miembros del Sistema de laReserva Federal que se reúne aproximadamente ocho veces al año para decidir el curso de acción que la Reserva debe seguir para controlar el suministro del dinero en circulación (p. 394).

fiat money/moneda de curso legal dinero que tiene valor a causa de orden o decreto del gobierno que establece que es aceptable para el pago de deudas. También *moneda fiduciaria* (p. 366).

finance charge/gasto financiero costo del crédito expresado en dólares y centavos (p. 91).

finance company/compañía financiera compañía que asume los contratos de las ventas a plazos de las tiendas y les añade un honorario por cobrar la deuda; también hace préstamos directamente a los consumidores (p. 87).

fiscal policy/política fiscal uso de los impuestos y de las políticas de gastos por parte del gobierno federal para afectar la actividad general del comercio (p. 443).

fiscal year/año fiscal año durante el cual se llevan las cuentas; para el gobierno federal, desde el 1 de octubre al 30 de septiembre del año entrante (p. 421).

five-year plans/planes quinquenales sistema de planificación central que formó la base para el sistema económico chino; finalmente terminó por transformarse en un sistema de planificación regional que condujo a un sistema limitado de libre empresa (p. 487).

fixed rate of exchange/tipo de cambio fijo sistema bajo elcual un gobierno nacional fija el valor de su moneda en relación a una norma exclusiva; el gobierno establece los equivalentes entre su moneda y las de otros países (p. 467).

flexible exchange rates/tipos de cambio flexibles situación en la cual se permite que las fuerzas de la oferta y la demanda impongan los precios de las distintas monedas (p. 468).

foreign affiliates/filiales extranjeras sucursales de firmas multinacionales (p. 543).

foreign aid/ayuda exterior dinero, bienes y servicios que dan los gobiernos e instituciones particulares para ayudar a otras naciones y los ciudadanos de éstas (p. 512).

foreign exchange markets/los mercados de divisas bolsas que negocian con la compra y venta de divisas extranjeras para los negocios que quieran importar productos de otros países; algún cambio de monedas tiene lugar a través de los bancos (p. 467).

form utility/utilidad de forma la conversión de materia prima en productos terminados para satisfacer los deseos de los consumidores (p. 284).

fractional reserve banking/reserva parcial bancaria sistema en el cual sólo una fracción de los depósitos de un banco se mantiene a mano, o en reserva; el resto está disponible para prestárselo a los prestatarios o para invertirlo en otra cosa (p. 389).

franchise/franquicia contrato en el cual un negocio (el otorgante) le vende a otro negocio (el concesionario) el derecho a usar el nombre del otorgante y vender sus productos (p. 222).

free enterprise system/sistema de libre empresa sistema en el cual los particulares son dueños de los factores de producción y deciden cómo usarlos dentro de los márgenes de la ley; llamado también capitalismo (p. 38).

full employment/pleno empleo condición de la economía cuando la tasa de desempleo está por debajo de cierto número establecidos por estudios de los economistas (p. 439).

General Agreement on Tariffs and Trade (GATT)/Acuerdo General sobre Aranceles Aduaneros y Comercio acuerdo de comercio de acuerdo con el cual los distintos países se reúnen periódicamente para negociar reducciones arancelarias que convienen mutuamente a todos los miembros; en efecto desde el 1 de enero de 1948 (p. 474).

generalization/generalización frase que unifica ideas comunes entre los distintos datos y que es acertada en la mayoría de los casos (p. 21).

generic brands/nombres genéricos nombres generales para productos en vez de para nombres específicos de marca dado por los fabricantes (p. 66).

geographic monopolies/monopolios geográficos situaciones de mercado que ocurren cuando un vendedor controla individualmente un mercado a causa de la ubicación del vendedor (p. 239).

global integration/integración mundial interdependencia entre los países del mundo, especialmente en los mercados financieros y las telecomunicaciones (p. 532).

goods and services/productos y servicios resultados finales de los factores de producción; los bienes son lo que el público compra; los servicios son las actividades que se hacen por los demás a cambio de honorarios (p. 11).

government monopolies/monopolios estatales situaciones de mercado creadas por el gobierno y protegidas por barreras legales al acceso; actividad exclusiva al gobierno (p. 239).

gross domestic product (GDP)/producto nacional bruto (PNB) valor total en dólares de todos los productos y servicios finales en la nación durante un solo año (p. 332).

horizontal merger/fusión horizontal compra total de una compañía por otra en el mismo giro (p. 245).

hypotheses/hipótesis opiniones o predicciones basadas en información, que se utilizan como puntos de partida para iniciar investigaciones (p. 19).

imperfect competition/competencia imperfecta situación de mercado en la cual un particular o grupo compra o vende un bien o un servicio en cantidades lo suficientemente grandes como para afectar el precio; abarca monopolio, oligopolio y la competencia monopolística (p. 237).

implicit GDP price deflator/índice implícito de deflación precios del PNB índice de precios que le quita el efecto de la inflación al PNB para que la economía general de un año se pueda comparar con la de otro (p. 341).

import quota/cuota de importación restricción impuesta al valor o al número de unidades de un artículo en particular que se pueda traer al país (p. 473).

imports/importaciones artículos que se traen de otros países para uso nacional (p. 462).

income redistribution/redistribución del ingreso actividad gubernamental que toman los ingresos de ciertas personas mediante los impuestos y los usan para ayudar a los ciudadanos necesitados (p. 417).

Individual Retirement Account (IRA)/Cuenta de Retiro Individualo (IRA) plan privado de retiro que les permite a individuos o a parejas casadas ahorrar cierta cantidad de sus ingresos al año, dependiendo del total de los ingresos; dependiendo también de los ingresos, no se le gravan impuestos a esta cantidad y se difiere el impuesto sobre los intereses (p. 162).

industrial union/sindicato industrial sindicato compuesto por todos los trabajadores en una industria irrespectivamente del puesto o del nivel de capacitación (p. 312).

inelastic demand/demanda inelástica situación en la cual la subida o caída de precios de un producto tiene poco impacto en la cantidad que demandan los consumidores (p. 186).

infant mortality/mortalidad infantil índice de mortalidad de lactantes que mueren durante el primer año de vida (p. 506).

inflation/inflación aumento prolongado en el nivel general de precios de los bienes y servicios (p. 338).

informative advertising/publicidad de información publicidad que beneficia a los consumidores al darles información sobre un producto (p. 64).

injunction/interdicción laboral orden judicial que prohíbe cierta actividad (p. 320).

inside information/información interior de un empresa información disponible a un corredor de bolsa pero que no posee nadie más; es ilegal que un corredor dé esta información a alguien de afuera y que un cliente se beneficie de ésta (p. 159).

installment charge account/cuenta de crédito a plazos crédito que se extiende al consumidor permitiéndole a éste comprar artículos de cierto valor, tales como sofás, televisores y refrigeradores a una tienda y pagarlos en pagos, o plazos, iguales que se distribuyen a lo largo de cierto período de tiempo (p. 90).

installment debt/préstamo a plazos tipo de préstamo que se devuelve con pagos iguales, o plazos, que se distribuyen a lo largo de cierto período de tiempo (p. 80).

interest/interés cantidad de dinero que el prestatario debe pagar por el uso del dinero ajeno (p. 80). Pago que se percibe cuando se presta dinero, permitiendo a otra persona hacer uso de éste (p. 146).

interlocking directorate/consejo de administración coincidente situación que ocurre cuando la mayoría de los miembros de juntas directivas de compañías competidoras son los mismos en efecto haciendo que un solo grupo de personas administre ambas compañías (p. 244).

intermediate-term financing/financiamiento a medio plazo préstamo a un negocio durante de uno a diez años (p. 265).

International Monetary Fund (IMF)/Fondo Monetario Internacional (FMI) agencia cuyos gobiernos miembros están obligados a mantener sus tasas de cambio más o menos fijas (p. 467).

inventory/inventario suministro de cualquier tipo de artículos que se usan en un negocio, tales como materias primas o mercancías a la venta (p. 210).

invisible hand/mano invisible término usado por Adam Smith para describir el efecto de la competencia en guiar a los individuos a trabajar para su propio interés, y por ese medio lograr el máximo bien de la sociedad (p. 37).

joint venture/sociedad de personas asociación temporal que se establece entre individuos o compañías con un fin específico y durante un breve período de tiempo (p. 217).

Keogh Plan/Plan Keogh, plan de retiro que le permite al que trabaja por su cuenta ahorrar cada año un máximo del 15 por ciento de sus ingresos hasta llegar a cierta cantidad específica y descontarle esa cantidad a sus ingresos anuales gravables (p. 161).

labor/trabajo tareas que la gente realiza; a menudo llamado un recurso humano. También llamado *mano de obra* (p. 10).

labor union/sindicato asociación de trabajadores que se organizan para mejorar los sueldos y condiciones de trabajo para sus miembros (p. 311).

land/tierra en economía, término que se usa para referirse a los recursos naturales y los terrenos superficiales; todas las cosas que se encuentran en la naturaleza, en las aguas y en la tierra. Económicamente, lo más importante son los terrenos de la superficie y los depósitos minerales (p. 10).

law of demand/ley de la demanda regla económica que declara que la cantidad que se demanda y el precio se mueven en direcciones opuestas; al subir el precio, la cantidad demandada baja; al bajar el precio, la cantidad demandada sube. Existe una relación inversa, u opuesta, entre el precio y la demanda (p. 177).

law of diminishing marginal utility/ley de la utilidad marginal decreciente regla económica que declara que la satisfacción adicional que deriva un consumidor de comprar una unidad más de un producto irá disminuyendo con cada unidad adicional que éste adquiera (p. 177).

law of diminishing returns/ley de rendimientos decrecientes regla económica que declara que después de cierto punto, el añadir una unidad de un factor de producción (tal como la mano de obra) a todos los demás factores de producción (tales como equipos) aumenta el rendimiento total por cierto tiempo; después de cierto punto, el rendimiento adicional por cada unidad añadida empieza a decrecer (p. 192).

law of supply/ley de la oferta regla económica que declara que al subir el precio de un producto, la cantidad que se ofrece del mismo aumenta; al caer el precio, la oferta del producto también disminuye (p. 191).

lease/arrendamiento contrato a largo plazo que describe los términos y condiciones bajo los cuales una propiedad se arrienda (p. 126).

leasing/arrendar alquilar en vez de comprar ciertos artículos como equipos, viviendas y automóviles (p. 266).

legal tender/moneda de curso legal moneda que por ley se tiene que aceptar como pago de deudas públicas y privadas (p. 366).

liability insurance/seguro de responsabilidad civil seguro que paga lesiones corporales y daños a la propiedad; lo exigen muchos estados antes de otorgar la matrícula para automóviles (p. 139).

limited partnership/sociedad de personas con responsabilidad limitada forma especial de sociedad en la cual no todos los socios son iguales; los socios generales asumen responsabilidad de todas las deudas y tareas administrativas; los demás socios contribuyen dinero o propiedades y no tienen voz en la gerencia (p. 217).

line of credit/línea de crédito máxima cantidad de dinero que una compañía puede pedirle prestado a un banco durante un período de tiempo, por lo general un año, sin tener que solicitar de nuevo un préstamo (p. 266).

local union/sindicato local miembros de un sindicato en una cierta fábrica, compañía o zona geográfica; el sindicato local tiene tratos con la compañía para negociar contratos y asegurarse de que los términos y condiciones de éste se cumplan (p. 313).

lockout/cierre patronal situación que ocurre cuando la gerencia les impide a los trabajadores volver a su trabajo sino hasta que éstos hayan aceptado un nuevo contrato (p. 320).

long-term financing/financiamiento a largo plazo dinero que se le presta a un negocio durante un período de más de diez años (p. 265).

loose money policy/política de dinero disponible política monetaria que da crédito abundante y barato, y que posiblemente conduce a la inflación (p. 389).

M1: definición más estricta del suministro de dinero; consisten en dineros que se pueden gastar inmediatamente y contra los cuales se pueden hacer cheques; abarca todas las demás letras o documentos en papel y monedas en circulación incluyendo moneda, cheques de viajero y depósitos extraíbles por cheque (p. 378).

M2: definición más amplia del suministro de dinero; abarca a toda la M1, más aquellos bienes convertibles en dinero tales como los mercados monetarios, saldos de fondos mutualistas y Eurodólares; abarca todas las letras y documentos en papel y monedas en circulación (p. 378).

market/mercado actividad libremente escogida entre compradores y vendedores de bienes y servicios en la cual se hacen negocios con aquéllos que puedan satisfacer mejor las necesidades y deseos de los participantes (p. 33).

market economic system/sistema de economía de mercado sistema en el cual los particulares son dueños de los factores de producción y toman las decisiones económicas a través de la libre interacción mientras que al mismo tiempo protegen sus propios intereses; el gobierno no interviene; capitalismo (p. 33).

marketing/mercadeo todas las actividades necesarias para trasladar bienes y servicios del productor al consumidor; abarca la investigación de mercados, publicidad y promoción, y la distribución (p. 282).

market research/investigación de mercado recolección, registro y análisis de datos acerca de los tipos de bienes y servicios que desea el público (p. 284).

market survey/encuesta de mercado encuesta en la cual los investigadores reúnen datos acerca de posibles usuarios de un producto basado en tales características como la edad, el sexo, ingresos, educación y ubicación; a menudo se usan cuestionarios escritos y entrevistas personales (p. 284).

maturity/vencimiento período de tiempo durante el cual los depósitos pagan una determinada tasa de interés (p. 148).

mechanization/mecanización trabajo combinado de personas y máquinas; originalmente, se combinan las máquinas con obreros no calificados para reemplazar a los calificados (p. 274).

mediation/mediación etapa en las negociaciones de contratos entre el sindicato y la gerencia, en la cual una persona neutral intercede y trata que las dos partes lleguen a un acuerdo (p. 318).

Medicaid/Medicaid programa de asistencia pública estatal y federal que les proporciona a personas incapacitadas o de bajos ingresos cuidados gratis a la salud (p. 417).

Medicare/Medicare programa gubernamental que proporciona cuidados a la salud a personas de edad avanzada (p. 415).

medium of exchange/medios de cambio uso del dinero a cambio de bienes o servicios (p. 362).

merger/fusión situación que ocurre cuando una sociedad compra más de la mitad de las acciones de otra (p. 245). *Vea también* fusión de conglomerados (conglomerate merger), fusión horizontal (horizontal merger), fusión vertical (vertical merger).

merit good/bien preferente cualquier bien o servicio que el gobierno haya considerablemente socialmente deseable, tales como museos, el ballet y conciertos de música clásica; a menudo subvencionados por el gobierno para que el público general pueda disfrutarlos (p. 416).

military assistance/asistencia militar asistencia económica o técnica a las fuerzas armadas de una nación (p. 513).

minimum wage law/ley de salario mínimo ley federal, estatal o municipal que fija el salario legal más bajo por hora que se le puede pagar a ciertos tipos de trabajadores (p. 309).

mixed economy/economía mixta sistema que combina las características de más de un tipo de economía variando la mezcla para que el sistema se incline más hace un tipo puro que al otro (p. 34).

monetarism/monetarismo teoría que trata la relación entre la cantidad de dinero que la Reserva Federal pone en circulación y el nivel de actividad en la economía (p. 448).

monetarists/los monetaristas personas que apoyan la teoría del monetarismo, a menudo vinculados con Milton Friedman (p. 448).

monetary policy/política monetaria política que trata de cambiar la tasa de crecimiento del dinero en circulación para afectar la cantidad de crédito y, por lo tanto, la actividad comercial en la economía (p. 388).

monetary rule/principio monetario política monetarista que insiste que la Reserva Federal debe permitir el suministro del dinero en circulación crecer a una tasa especificada (quizá del 3 al 5 por ciento) al año y no usar la política fiscal para estimular ni desacelerar la economía (p. 449).

monetary standard/patrón monetario manera en que una nación asigna valor a su moneda (p. 370).

money/dinero toda cosa de uso general como medio de intercambio, unidad contable y acopio de valor (p. 362).

money market deposit account (MMDA)/cuenta de depósito en el mercado monetario cuenta que paga tasas relativamente altas de interés, requiere un saldo mínimo y permite extraer fondos en persona en cualquier momento (p. 148).

money market fund/fondos mutuos tipo de fondo mutualista que use el dinero de los inversionistas para hacer préstamos a corto plazo a negocios y bancos; la mayor parte les permite a los inversionistas hacer cheques contra sus inversiones en el fondo (p. 158).

monopolistic competition/competencia monopolista situación de mercado en la cual un gran número de vendedores ofrecen productos similares pero ligeramente diferentes y cada uno tiene cierto control sobre los precios (p. 240).

mortgage/hipoteca préstamo a plazos que se debe sobre bienes raíces: casas, edificios o terreno (p. 81).

multinationals/empresas transnacionales firmas que hacen negocios y tienen oficinas o fábricas en muchos países (p. 543).

mutual fund/fondo mutuo compañía inversionista que reúne los dineros de muchos individuos para comprar acciones, bonos u otras inversiones (p. 158).

national debt/deuda pública cantidad total de la deuda pendiente del gobierno federal; deuda pública (p. 425).

national income/renta nacional total de rentas o ingresos que ganará todo el mundo en la economía (p. 335).

national income accounting/contabilidad de la renta nacional medición del rendimiento de la economía nacional, que trata sobre los ingresos y producción de la economía en general así como la interacción entre los consumidores, los negocios y los gobiernos (p. 332).

nationalization/nacionalización colocación de los ferrocarriles, los negocios, etc., bajo propiedad del estado (p. 519).

natural monopolies/monopolios naturales situaciones de mercado que resultan cuando una compañía lleva a sus competidores a la quiebra produciendo bienes y servicios en costo más bajo; por lo general se encuentra en industrias que necesitan grandes inversiones para empezar, y cuando es más eficiente tener una sola compañía que varias (p. 239).

near moneys/cuasidinero activo tal como cuentas de ahorro, que se puede convertir en dinero o medio de pago con relativa facilidad y sin el riesgo de perder valor (p. 378).

net domestic product (NDP)/producto neto nacional (PNN) valor total del producto nacional (PNB) menos el valor total perdido a causa de desgaste y deterioro de la maquinaria y equipos (p. 335).

net exports/exportaciones netas diferencia entre lo que la nación le vende a otros países (exportaciones) y lo que le compra a éstos (importaciones) (p. 334).

North American Free Trade Agreement (NAFTA)/Tratado de Libre Comercio para América del Norte acuerdo comercial diseñado para reducir las barreras arancelarias entre México, Canadá y los Estados Unidos; aprobado en 1993 (p. 474). *Vea también* Acuerdo de Libre Comercio E.E.U.U.-Canadá (U.S.-Canada Free Trade Agreement).

oligopoly/oligopolio industria dominada por unos pocos suministradores que ejercen cierto control sobre los precios (p. 240).

open-market operations/operaciones de mercado abierto compra y venta por parte de la Reserva Federal de obligaciones del gobierno de los Estados Unidos para afectar el suministro de dinero cambiando las reservas institucionales de depósito o colocando o sacando dinero de la circulación en la economía (p. 402).

opportunity cost/costo de oportunidad valor de la segunda mejor alternativa después de haber renunciado a la que se escogiera (p. 14).

over-the-counter market/mercado de valores no oficial compra y venta de acciones y bonos, con frecuencia de compañías más pequeñas y menos conocidas, que tiene lugar fuera de las bolsas de valores organizadas; la mayor parte de los valores "no vendidos en la Bolsa" se cotizan en los listados de la National Association of Securities Dealers Automated Quotations (NASDAQ) (p. 157).

overdraft checking/sobrigiro cuenta corriente que permite a un cliente hacer un cheque por más dinero de lo que existe en ésta (p. 369).

ownership utility/utilidad de la transferibilidad del título utilidad creada al asegurar la transferencia ordenada del título de los bienes deseados (p. 284).

partnership/sociedad de personas con responsabilidad limitada negocio propiedad de dos o más individuos que lo hacen funcionar (p. 217).

passbook savings account/cuenta de ahorro con libreta cuenta para la cual el depositante recibe una libreta en la cual se llevan los depósitos, extracciones e intereses; también llamada cuenta de ahorro regular (p. 147).

past-due notices/notificaciones de vencimiento recordatorios que envían los negocios e instituciones de préstamo que los pagos están ya sobrevencidos y morosos (p. 96).

patent/patente derecho otorgado por el gobierno para fabricar con exclusividad un invento durante un número específico de años (p. 239).

peak/cumbre período de prosperidad en un ciclo comercial en el cual la actividad económica está en su más elevado punto; llamado también de auge (boom) (p.347).

penetration pricing/precios de penetración vender un nuevo producto a un precio bajo para sustraerle clientes a un producto establecido (p. 290).

pension plans/planes de pensiones planes de compañía que hacen provisiones para tener ingresos en la jubilación o retiro (p. 161).

perfect competition/competencia perfecta situación de mercado en la que existen numerosos compradores y vendedores, y ningún comprador ni vendedor puede afectar el precio (p. 232).

personal income (PI)/renta personal total de rentas o ingresos que reciben los individuos antes de pagar sus impuestos personales (p. 336).

picketing/piquetes laborales actividad en la cual los huelguistas marchan de un lado a otro en frente al centro de trabajo portando letreros que declaran su desacuerdo con la compañía (p. 320).

place utility/utilidad de lugar utilidad creada al hacer que un artículo esté disponible donde el consumidor desea adquirirlo (p. 284).

points/puntos porcentuales honorario que se paga a un prestamista y se computa como puntos de porcentaje de un préstamo (p. 129).

price elasticity of demand/elasticidad de precios de la demanda concepto económico que versa sobre cuánto varía la demanda dependiendo de los cambios en el precio (p. 185).

price leadership/liderazgo en precios práctica de fijar precios muy cercanos a los de las demás compañías que vendan productos similares; se encuentra especialmente en los oligopolios (p. 289).

price system/sistema de precios sistema de capitalismo puro que permite que los precios encuentren su propio nivel, tal como lo determinen las fuerzas de la oferta y la demanda (p. 482).

prime rate/tasa mínima de interés tipo o tasa de interés que los bancos cobran sobre los préstamos a sus mejores clientes comerciales (p. 401).

principal/principal suma de dinero que se pidiera prestado originalmente en un préstamo (p. 80).

private-labeled products/productos con etiquetas de la casa productos con la marca de la tienda que tienen algunas cadenas de supermercados y de asociaciones de mayoristas como alternativas de bajo costo a las marcas nacionales (p. 110).

private property/propiedad privada bienes de los que son propietarios individuos o grupos en vez de los gobiernos federales, estatales o locales (p. 38).

private property rights/derechos de propiedad privada los derechos de individuos o grupos a ser propietarios de bienes; el gobierno pone en vigor y hace valer estos derechos (p. 482).

privatization/privatización cambio de la propiedad estatal de los negocios, terrenos y edificios a la propiedad privada (p. 492).

producer goods/bienes de producción bienes producidos para que los negocios los usen en producir otros artículos (p. 271).

producer price index (PPI)/índice de precio de producción medida del cambio en precio al pasar el tiempo de un grupo específico de productos utilizados por negocios; anteriormente llamado índice de precios mayoristas (p. 340).

product differentiation/diferenciación de productos uso por parte del fabricante de pequeñas diferencias en características y calidad para intentar diferenciar entre bienes y servicios que son similares (p. 240).

production/producción proceso de convertir los recursos en bienes que satisfagan los deseos y necesidades de comercios e individuos (p. 271).

production possibilities/posibilidades de producción todas las combinaciones de bienes y servicios que se puedan producir con una cierta cantidad fija de recursos en un determinado período de tiempo (p. 15).

productivity/productividad capacidad de producir mayores cantidades de bienes y servicios mejor y más rápidamente (p. 10).

product life cycle/ciclo de vida de un producto serie de etapas por las que atraviesa un producto desde su primera introducción hasta su completo retiro del mercado; el ciclo no tiene un número fijo de meses ni años (p. 291).

professionals/profesionales individuos altamente educados con títulos universitarios y usualmente educación o capacitación adicional (p. 307).

profit/utilidades dinero que queda después que se hayan pagado todos los costos de producción: salarios, alquiler, intereses e impuestos (p. 39). También llamado *ganacia* y *lucro*.

profit incentive/incentivos para obtener utilidades deseo de hacer dinero que motiva a las personas a producir y vender bienes y servicios que los demás quieran comprar (p. 39).

progressive tax/impuesto progresivo impuesto que grava un porcentaje superior de los ingresos más altos en comparación con los más bajos; se le justifica en base al principio de la capacidad económica (p. 430).

proletariat/el proletariado término usado por Carlos Marx para denominar a los trabajadores (p. 484).

promissory note/pagaré convenio escrito para la devolución de un préstamo en determinado momento y a una tasa específica de interés (p. 266).

promotion/promoción uso de la publicidad y demás métodos para informar a los consumidores que un nuevo o mejorado producto o servicio está a su disposición y persuadirlos a que lo compren (p. 290).

property rights/derechos de propiedad privada protección de la propiedad privada; el gobierno no puede legalmente tomar propiedad privada sin pagar por ella el justo valor en el mercado (p. 523).

proportional tax/impuesto proporcional impuesto que toma el mismo porcentaje de todos los ingresos; al aumentar los ingresos, la cantidad de impuesto que se paga también aumenta (p. 430).

proprietor/propietario dueño de un negocio; de la palabra en latín proprietas, que significa "propiedad" (p. 213).

protectionists/proteccionistas aquellos que abogan a favor de restricciones comerciales (p. 474).

protective tariff/arancel proteccionista impuesto sobre las importaciones que se utiliza para aumentar los costos de los bienes importados y de esa manera proteger los productores nacionales (p. 472).

public assistance programs/programas de asistencia pública programas gubernamentales que hacen pagos basados en la necesidad; llamados también de bienestar social (p. 418).

public goods/bienes públicos bienes y servicios que el gobierno a veces suministra a sus ciudadanos; los pueden utilizar muchos individuos al mismo tiempo sin reducir el beneficio que recibe cada cual (p. 416).

public works projects/proyectos de obras públicas instalaciones de uso público tales como escuelas y carreteras, construidas por los gobiernos federales, estatales o locales con dineros públicos (p. 413).

purchasing power/poder adquisitivo los bienes y servicios que el dinero puede realmente comprar; determina el valor que tiene el dinero (p. 338).

pure monopoly/monopolio puro la forma más extrema de competencia imperfecta en la cual un solo vendedor controla la oferta de un bien o servicio y de esa manera controla el precio (p. 237). *Vea también* monopolios geográficos; monopolios gubernamentales; monopolios naturales; monopolio tecnológico.

rational choice/selección racional la selección de la alternativa que tenga el mayor valor de entre productos que tienen una calidad comparable (p. 61).

real estate taxes/impuestos sobre bienes inmuebles impuestos que se pagan por concepto de terrenos y edificios (p. 125).

real GDP/PNB real cifra que resulta cuando se compensa la inflación en el Producto Nacional Bruto aplicando el índice de deflación de precios (p. 341).

real income effect/efecto de ingreso real regla económica que declara que el público no puede seguir comprando la misma cantidad de un producto si el precio de éste sube mientras que sus ingresos se mantienen igual; esto tiene efecto en la dirección opuesta también: si el precio de un producto disminuye y los ingresos permanecen igual, el poder adquisitivo aumenta y la cantidad del producto que se compra probablemente aumentará también (p. 179).

recession/recesión porción del ciclo comercial en la cual la producción nacional, el PNB real, no crece durante al menos dos trimestres (seis meses) (p. 348).

recovery/recuperación porción del ciclo comercial en la cual la actividad económica aumenta; llamada también expansión (p. 348).

registration fee/derecho de registro derecho o cargo de matriculación que cobra el estado, por lo general anualmente, por el derecho de usar un auto (p. 137).

regressive tax/impuesto regresivo impuesto que toma un porcentaje mayor de los ingresos más bajos que de los más altos (p. 430).

regular charge account/cuenta de crédito regular crédito que se le extiende a un consumidor y que le permite comprar bienes y servicios a cierta tienda y pagarlos luego. El interés se cobra por la porción de la cuenta que quede sin pagar en el plazo de cierto período de tiempo. Conocido también como el cargo de 30 días (p. 89).

representative money/dinero en cuenta dinero sin valor de por sí para usos no monetarios que se puede intercambiar por algún artículo comerciable valioso tal como el oro o la plata (p. 366).

reregulation/nueva regulación regulación y control del gobierno federal sobre la actividad comercial de las antiguamente fuertemente reguladas industrias (p. 246).

reserve requirements/reserva obligatoria regulaciones impuestas por la Reserva Federal, que exigen a los bancos que mantengan en efectivo en sus cajas fuertes un cierto porcentaje de sus depósitos o que lo depositen en el Banco de la Reserva Federal de su distrito (p. 389).

resource/recurso cualquier cosa que las personas puedan usar para hacer u obtener lo que deseen o necesiten (p. 8).

retailers/detallistas negocios que le venden bienes de consumo directamente al público (p. 294).

revenue tariff/arancel financiero impuesto sobre las importaciones usado principalmente para recaudar rentas sin restringir las importaciones (p. 472).

revolving charge account/cuenta de crédito rotativa crédito que se le extiende a un consumidor y que le permite comprar bienes y servicios a cierta tienda y pagarlos luego. Por lo general cierta porción del saldo se tiene que pagar cada mes; el interés se cobra sobre la cantidad no pagada (p. 89).

right-to-work laws/ley sobre libertad laboral leyes estatales que prohíben los talleres donde los obreros tienen que pertenecer al sindicato y los talleres cerrados; a los trabajadores se les permite seguir trabajando en cierto puesto sin tener que hacerse miembros del sindicato (p. 313).

robotics/robótica maquinaria con control por computadora altamente sofisticado que funciona en las líneas de montaje (p. 275).

saving/ahorro el no usar los ingresos durante cierto tiempo para poder usarlos después (p. 146).

savings and loan association (S&L)/asociación de ahorro y préstamo institución depositaria que, como un banco comercial, acepta depósitos y presta dinero. Originalmente se establecieron para hacer préstamos para construir casas, pero las leyes federales de la década de 1980 les permitieron prestar algunos de los mismos servicios que los bancos (p. 86).

savings banks/bancos de ahorro instituciones depositarias originalmente establecidas para servir a los pequeños ahorradores dejados al margen por los bancos comerciales; la mayor parte del negocio de estas instituciones proviene de cuentas de ahorro y préstamos para casas (p. 86).

savings bonds/bonos de ahorro bonos emitidos por el gobierno federal a manera de pedir dinero prestado; los bonos se compran a mitad de su valor nominal y aumentan entonces de valor cada seis meses hasta llegar a su pleno valor nominal (p. 155).

scarcity/escasez condición en la cual el público no tiene ni puede tener suficientes ingresos, tiempo y demás recursos para satisfacer todas sus necesidades (p. 9).

secondary market/mercado secundario proceso a través del cual los dueños de valores las venden a otros inversionistas a cambio de efectivo (p. 493).

secured loan/préstamo garantizado préstamo que está respaldado por una garantía (collateral) (p. 95).

security deposit/depósito de garantía dinero que el inquilino que alquila deposita con el dueño; si el alquiler no se paga o el apartamento queda dañado, el dueño puede quedarse con todo o parte del depósito (p. 130).

semiskilled workers/obreros semicualificados personas cuyos trabajos requieren algún entrenamiento en técnicas relacionadas con el trabajo, a menudo utilizando tecnología moderna (p. 307).

service flow/flujo de servicio cantidad de uso que una persona le saca a un artículo durante cierto tiempo y el valor que dicha persona le da a ese uso (p. 115).

service workers/trabajadores en el área de servicios personas que le proporcionan servicios directamente a los demás (p. 307).

shortages/falta situaciones que ocurren cuando, al precio existente, la cantidad que se demanda es mayor que la oferta disponible (p. 198).

short-term financing/financiamiento a corto plazo dinero que pide prestado un negocio por cualquier período de tiempo que sea menos de un año (p. 265).

skilled worker/profesionales persona que ha aprendido una ocupación u oficio bien a través de una escuela de capacitación o como aprendiz de un obrero con experiencia (p. 307).

small business incubator/incubador de pequeños negocios negocio que ayuda a negocios pequeños a desarrollarse proporcionándoles tales formas de ayuda como edificios de bajo alquiler, asesoría administrativa y computadoras; frecuentemente funcionan con fondos estatales y federales (p. 215).

social insurance programs/programas de seguro social programas gubernamentales que pagan beneficios a los trabajadores retirados e incapacidados, a sus familias y los desempleados; financiados con impuestos que pagan a estos programas los trabajadores y los patronos (p. 418).

Social Security/Seguro Social programa federal que proporciona pagos mensuales a personas que están retiradas o que no pueden trabajar (p. 417).

sole proprietorship/empresada propietario único negocio propiedad de una sola persona; el tipo más básico de organización de negocios (p. 213).

special economic zones/zonas económicas especiales zonas geográficas designadas en la República Popular China las cuales, a partir de 1979, se han estado moviendo hacia un capitalismo descentralizado restringido (p. 488).

specialization/especialización concepto según el cual le es beneficioso a una nación producir y exportar un surtido limitado de bienes para los cuales está particularmente bien dotada (p. 464).

stabilization policies/políticas de estabilización intento por parte del gobierno federal de mantener la economía saludable y hacer que el futuro sea más predecible para la planificación, el ahorro y las inversiones; abarca las políticas monetarias y fiscales (p. 438).

stagflation/inflación con estancamiento combinación de inflación y estancamiento económico (p. 441).

standard of living/nivel de vida bienestar material de un individuo, grupo o nación medido por el valor promedio de los bienes y servicios que usa el ciudadano promedio durante un cierto período de tiempo (p. 45).

startups/negocios recién establecidos nuevos negocios; hay asesoría y ayuda disponibles de parte de los gobiernos estatales y federal, así como de las universidades y facultades (p. 214).

statement savings account/cuenta de ahorros con estado de cuenta cuenta similar a la cuenta de ahorro de libreta, excepto que en vez de la libreta, el depositante recibe un estado de cuenta mensual donde se ven todas las transacciones (p. 147).

stock/acciones participación propietaria en la sociedad que emite las acciones; éstas le dan el derecho al comprador a cierta parte de las futuras ganancias y bienes de la sociedad (p. 154).

stockholders/accionistas personas que han invertido en una sociedad y poseen acciones; los accionistas pueden reclamar cierta parte de las ganancias (p. 155).

store of value/reserva de valor uso del dinero para guardarlo y así hacer acopio de poder adquisitivo para usarlo más adelante (p. 364).

strike/huelga paro deliberado de los trabajadores para forzar a un patrono a ceder a sus demandas (p. 312).

subsistence agriculture /agricultura de subsistencia cultivar para una familia sólo suficiente comida para satisfacer sus propias necesidades; no hay cultivos para la exportación ni para alimentar a una fuerza laboral industrial (p. 506).

substitution effect/efecto de sustitución principio económico que dice que si dos artículos satisfacen la misma necesidad y el precio de uno aumenta, el público comprará el otro (p. 179).

Supplemental Security Income/Ingreso de Seguridad Suplementario programas federales que abarcan los cupones de alimentos, los beneficios a los veteranos y los pagos a las personas ciegas, de edad o incapacitadas (p. 417).

supply curve/curva de oferta línea trazada en una gráfica que demuestra las cantidades ofrecidas de un bien o un servicio a cada precio posible (p. 194).

surplus/superávit situación que ocurre cuando la oferta es mayor que la demanda (p. 198). También llamado *excedente*.

tariff/arancel impuesto sobre las importaciones; la barrera más comúnmente usada para liberar el comercio (p. 472). *Vea también* arancel protector; arancel para rentas

tax-exempt bonds/bonos exentos de impuesto bonos vendidos por gobiernos locales y estatales; el gobierno federal no grava el interés que pagan los bonos (p. 155).

technical assistance/asistencia técnica ayuda, en la forma de profesionales tales como ingenieros, maestros y técnicos que suministran naciones para enseñar conocimientos y técnicas a individuos en otras naciones; fortalece los recursos humanos de una nación (p. 513).

technological monopoly/monopolio tecnológico situación de mercado que resulta cuando un vendedor desarrolla un producto o proceso de producción para el cual obtiene una patente; la compañía posee los derechos exclusivos a la nueva invención por un cierto número de años (p. 239).

technology/tecnología todo uso de terrenos, mano de obra o capital que produzca bienes y servicios con más eficiencia. Hoy, por lo general, significa el uso de la ciencia para desarrollar nuevos productos y métodos para producir y distribuir bienes y servicios (pp. 11, 197).

telecommunications/telecomunicaciones comunicaciones a larga distancia, por lo general electrónicas, que usan satélites de comunicación y cable de fibra óptica (p. 532).

test marketing/mercadeo de prueba ofrecer un producto a la venta en una zona pequeña por un período limitado de tiempo para ver qué tal se vende antes de ofrecerlo nacionalmente (p. 285).

three P's/las tres "P's" del inglés "prices, profits and private property", o sea, precios, ganancias o lucro y propiedad privada, las tres bases del capitalismo de mercado (p. 482).

thrift institutions/instituciones de ahorro bancos de ahorro mutualistas, asociaciones de ahorro y préstamo ("S&L's") y uniones de crédito que ofrecen muchos de los mismos servicios que ofrecen los bancos comerciales (p. 377).

tight money policy/política de dinero escaso política monetaria que hace que haya poco suministro de crédito y que éste sea caro es un esfuerzo por desacelerar la economía (p. 389).

time deposits/depósitos a plazo planes de ahorros que requieren que los ahorradores dejen sus dineros en depósito por cierto tiempo (p. 148).

time lags/desface cronológico períodos entre el momento que la política fiscal se promulga y el momento en que entra en efecto (p. 450).

time utility/utilidad de tiempo utilidad creada al poner un artículo a la disposición del consumidor cuando éste quiere adquirirlo (p. 284).

tolerance/tolerancia actitud justa, objetiva y permisiva con las opiniones y prácticas de otras religiones, razas y nacionalidades (p. 547).

trade-off/compensación de factores alternativos cambiar una cosa por el uso de otra, a menudo tomando decisiones inevitables y difíciles a causa del problema de la escasez (p. 13).

trade credit/crédito comercial crédito que extiende un vendedor a un negocio que le compra artículos; le permite al comprador tomar posesión inmediata de éstos y pagarlos en algún momento en el futuro (p. 266).

traditional economic system/sistema económico tradicional sistema en el cual las decisiones económicas se basan en las costumbres, creencias y maneras de hacer las cosas que se han pasado de generación en generación (p. 32).

transfer payments/pagos de transferencia pagos de bienestar social y demás pagos suplementarios, tales como compensación por desempleo, *Social Security* y *Medicaid*, que el gobierno federal o estatal les hacen a individuos, lo cual aumenta el ingreso del individuo aunque los pagos no se hagan a cambio de ninguna actividad productiva actualmente (p. 336).

Treasury bills/pagarés del Tesoro certificados emitidos por la Tesorería Federal de los Estados Unidos en cantidades mínimas de $10,000 a cambio de dinero prestado y que vencen durante un período que abarca desde tres meses hasta un año (p. 156).

Treasury bonds/bonos del Tesoro a largo plazo certificados emitidos por la Tesorería Federal de los Estados Unidos en cantidades mínimas de $1,000 ó $5,000 a cambio de dinero prestado y que vencen en diez o más años (p. 156).

Treasury notes/bonos del Tesor a corto plazo certificados emitidos por la Tesorería Federal de los Estados Unidos en cantidades mínimas de $1,000 o $5,000 a cambio de dinero prestado y que vencen en el plazo de dos a diez años (p. 156).

trough/punto bajo porción más baja del ciclo comercial en el cual la caída en espiral de la economía empieza a nivelarse (p. 348).

underground economy/economía sumergida transacciones que hace la gente que no obedecen las leyes federales y estatales con respecto a declarar sus ingresos; abarca a los que evitan pagar impuestos, los jugadores y los narcotraficantes y aquéllos que ilegalmente reciben beneficios de desempleo (p. 439).

unemployment rate/índice de desempleo porcentaje de la fuerza laboral civil que está sin trabajo pero que está activamente buscando empleo (p. 438).

union shop/empresa con sindicación eventual obligatoria compañía en la que se exige que los nuevos empleados se hagan miembros del sindicato después de cierto tiempo, por lo general tres meses (p. 313).

unit of accounting/unidad de contabilidad uso del dinero como punto de comparación de los valores que tienen los bienes y servicios entre sí (p. 364).

unsecured loan/préstamo no garantizado préstamo garantizado solamente por la promesa de devolverlo (p. 95).

unskilled workers/obruros no cualificados personas cuyos empleos no exigen capacitación especializada (p. 307).

U.S.-Canadian Free Trade Agreement/Acuerdo de Libre Comercio entre los E.E.U.U. y Canadá convenio comercial entre los Estados Unidos y Canadá para eliminar ciertos aranceles alto sobre cosas tales como muebles, textiles y papel; garantiza que cada país tendrá acceso al petróleo, gas, carbón piedra y electricidad del otro, a precios que pagan los ciudadanos de la otra nación en circunstancias comerciales comparables (p. 474).

usury law/ley antiusura ley que restringe la cantidad de interés que se le puede cargar al crédito (p. 99).

utility/utilidad capacidad de cualquier bien o servicio de satisfacer los deseos del consumidor (pp. 177, 282). *Vea también* utilidad de la forma (form utility); utilidad de la transferibilidad de título (ownership utility); utilidad de lugar (place utility); utilidad de tiempo (time utility).

values/valores (morales) creencias o características que un individuo o grupo considera importante, tales como la libertad religiosa y la oportunidad igualitaria (p. 20).

vertical merger/fusión vertical fusión en la que un negocio que le compra o vende a otro negocio se fusiona con éste (p. 245).

vicious cycle of poverty/ciclo vicioso de la pobreza trampa en la que cae un país menos desarrollado con bajos ingresos *per cápita* y que no puede ahorrar e invertir lo suficiente como para lograr tasas aceptables de crecimiento económico (p. 524).

voluntary exchange/intercambio voluntario principio que forma la base de la actividad en una economía de mercado; el comprador y el vendedor ejercen sus libertades económicas resolviendo sus propios términos y condiciones de intercambio (p. 176).

wants/necesidades término de los economistas para todo lo que el público desea que va más allá de los bienes y servicios básicos que satisfacen sus necesidades (p. 9).

warehouse food store/almacén para compra de alimentos tienda que dispone de un número limitado de marcas y artículos; menos cara que los supermercados; los artículos frecuentemente están disponibles sólo en grandes cantidades (p. 109).

warranty/garantía promesa que hace un fabricante o vendedor que reparará o reemplazará un producto dentro de un cierto período de tiempo si se determina que tiene fallas (p. 60).

welfare/bienestar social programas de asistencia pública que hacen pagos basados en la necesidad; abarca el *Ingreso Suplementario de Seguridad* (Supplemental Security Income), *Ayuda a Familias con Hijos Dependientes* (Aid to Families with Dependent Children), y *Medicaid* (p. 418).

welfare state/estado de bienestar país que es una mezcla de capitalismo y socialismo, que combina la propiedad privada de los medios de producción y la asignación competitiva de los recursos con la meta de lograr la igualdad social de sus ciudadanos (p. 494).

white-collar/empleados de oficina categoría de empleados que trabajan en oficinas, ventas o cargos profesionales (p. 307).

wholesalers/mayoristas negocios que compran grandes cantidades de artículos a los productores para revenderlos a otros negocios (p. 293).

workers' compensation/indemnización por accidente de trabajo programa gubernamental que hace pagos para el cuidado médico de obreros lesionados en el trabajo; las personas que han perdido sus empleos pueden recibir pagos a través del seguro contra desempleo (p. 417).

Los problemas básicos en Economía

Términos claves:

economía (p. 8)
recursos (p. 8)
escasez (p. 9)
necesidades (p. 9)
tierra (p. 10)
trabajo (p. 10)
capital (p. 10)
productividad (p. 10)

espíritu empresarial (p. 11)
factores de producción
  (p. 11)
productos y servicios (p. 11)
tecnología (p. 11)

Resumen

La escasez es el problema básico en economía. La economía es el estudio de cómo los individuos y las naciones deciden utilizar los recursos escasos para satisfacer sus necesidades. La tierra, el trabajo, el capital y la iniciativa son factores de producción. Algunos economistas incluyen la tecnología.

Compensación de factores alternativos ("Trade-Offs")

Términos claves

compensación de factores
  alternativos (p. 13)
costo de oportunidad (p. 14)
posibilidades de producción
  (p. 15)

Resumen

Cuando un bien o actividad debe ser abandonado para ser sustituido por otro, ha ocurrido una compensación de factores alternativos. Lo que debe ser sustituido es el coste de oportunidad (o de sustitución) de una acción. Una curva de posibilidades de producción muestra la máxima cantidad de bienes que pueden ser producidos con los recursos de la nación en un período determinado. Cuando una nación opera de acuerdo con la curva de posibilidades de producción, está produciendo de una manera eficiente.

¿Qué hacen los economistas?

Términos claves

economía (p. 18)
modelo económico (p. 18)
hipótesis (p. 19)
valores (p. 20)
generalización (p. 21)

Resumen

Los economistas observan la información proveniente del mundo real para probar los modelos económicos que ellos han formulado sobre el comportamiento de los individuos y las empresas. Los modelos económicos son representaciones de la realidad que sólo toman en consideración los factores más importantes que pueden influir en un problema. Los modelos económicos y los economistas no dicen si determinadas políticas son buenas o malas, debido a que tales juicios dependen de los valores de cada individuo.

CAPITULO

2 Puntos destacados

Sección 1

Sistemas económicos

Términos claves

sistema económico (p. 30)
distribución de ingresos (p. 31)
sistema económico tradicional (p. 32)
sistema de economía dirigida (p. 33)

sistema de economía de mercado (p. 33)
mercado (p. 33)
economía mixta (p. 34)

Resumen

Todos los sistemas económicos responden a cuatro preguntas básicas que determinan el uso de los recursos. En un sistema tradicional las decisiones económicas son dictadas por lo que se hizo en el pasado. El gobierno controla los factores de producción en un sistema de economía dirigida. En un sistema de mercado, los individuos de acuerdo con sus propios intereses deciden las respuestas a las cuatro preguntas básicas. Una economía dirigida contiene elementos de los sistemas de economía dirigida y de mercado.

Sección 2

Características de la Economía de los Estados Unidos

Términos claves

mano invisible (p. 37)
capitalismo (p. 37)
sistema de libre empresa (p. 38)
propiedad privada (p. 38)

utilidades (p. 39)
incentivos para obtener utilidades (p. 39)
competencia (p. 39)

Resumen

La decisión de los consumidores es la clave del uso de los recursos en un sistema de libre empresa. Libre empresa significa que los individuos privados son dueños de las empresas, compiten en mercados libres y obtienen utilidades. El papel del estado en una economía de mercado es objeto de debates públicos.

Sección 3

Los objetivos de la nación

Términos claves

eficiencia económica (p. 45)
crecimiento económico (p. 45)
equidad (p. 45)
nivel de vida (p. 45)

Resumen

Una nación fija sus objetivos económicos en base a su sistema de valores. Algunos objetivos del sistema económico de los Estados Unidos son la eficiencia, el crecimiento, la seguridad, la equidad, la estabilidad y la libertad individual. La libertad personal, la diversidad en los estilos de vida y un alto nivel de vida son beneficios de un sistema de libre empresa.

CAPITULO

3 Puntos destacados

Resumen

Parte del ingreso disponible es discrecional y no tiene que ser gastado en necesidades básicas. Un consumidor inteligente considera varios factores antes de hacer una compra.

Resumen

El valor del tiempo y los esfuerzos de un consumidor para obtener información no deben exceder el valor obtenido al haber hecho la mejor decisión con respecto a un producto. Cierta publicidad tiene fines de información, otra es esencialmente competitiva. Antes de comprar los consumidores deben comparar las condiciones de venta de un producto.

Resumen

Los consumidores tienen importantes derechos y fuentes de ayuda. Agencias privadas y estatales ofrecen información y ayuda al consumidor. Los consumidores tienen también varias responsabilidades incluyendo la responsabilidad de comportarse con ética.

4 *Puntos destacados*

Los estadounidenses y el crédito

Términos claves
crédito (p. 80)
capital de un préstamo
(p. 80)

interés (p. 80)
deuda a plazos (p. 80)
bienes de consumo
duraderos (p. 80)
hipoteca (p. 81)

Resumen
El pago de una deuda a largo plazo brinda algunas ventajas al prestatario. Las personas compran al crédito por varias razones. No obstante, los consumidores deben siempre decidir con cuidado si han de tomar dinero a préstamo y el monto del mismo.

Fuentes de préstamos y créditos

Términos claves
banco comercial (p. 86)
institución de ahorro y
préstamo (p. 86)
banco de ahorro (p. 86)
cooperativa de crédito
(p. 87)
compañía financiera (p. 87)
compañía de créditos
personales (p. 88)
cuenta de crédito (p. 89)
cuenta crédito regular
(p. 89)

límite de crédito (p. 89)
cuenta corriente rotativa
(p. 89)
cuenta corriente a plazo
(p. 90)
tarjeta de crédito (p. 90)
tarjeta de débito (p. 91)
cargo de financiamiento
(p. 91)
tasa de porcentaje anual
(p. 93)

Resumen
Los consumidores que desean tomar dinero a préstamo pueden escoger entre seis tipos de instituciones financieras. Los consumidores que quieren abrir una cuenta corriente pueden seleccionar entre una cuenta regular, una cuenta rotativa o una cuenta a plazo. En todos los casos, los consumidores deben tener en cuenta que la tasa de porcentaje anual no es igual al cargo de financiamiento convenido.

Solicitud de crédito

Términos claves
agencia de crédito (p. 94)
cheque de crédito (p. 94)
clasificación crediticia
(p. 94)

garantía (colateral) (p. 95)
préstamo con garantía
(p. 95)
préstamo sin garantía (p. 95)
cosignatario (p. 96)
notificaciones de
vencimiento (p. 96)

Resumen
Varios factores se toman en cuenta cuando las instituciones financieras evalúan la solvencia de una persona. Una vez que a una persona se le otorga un crédito, tiene la responsabilidad de usarlo con inteligencia.

Regulación del crédito por el gobierno

Términos claves
leyes sobre usura (p. 99)
quiebra (p. 100)

Resumen
La Ley de Iguales Oportunidades de Crédito ("Equal Credit Opportunity Act") prohíbe la discriminación en el otorgamiento de préstamos en base a varios factores. Muchos estados tienen leyes sobre la usura que también protegen a los prestatarios. Los prestatarios que agotan su capacidad de crédito pueden declararse en quiebra.

CAPITULO

5 Puntos destacados

Sección 1

Comprando alimentos

Términos claves
almacén para compra de
   alimentos (p. 109)
tiendas de artículos de
   consumo frecuente (p. 109)
productos con etiquetas de
   la casa (p. 110)

Resumen
Los consumidores deben conocer las muchas sugerencias útiles que se obtienen comparando las condiciones de venta de un bien o producto antes de hacer una compra. Existen tres clases importantes de tiendas de comestibles; cada una ofrece sus ventajas.

Sección 2

Selección de ropa

Términos claves
durabilidad (p. 115)
flujo de servicio (p. 115)

Resumen
Los valores de cada persona influyen en su elección de ropa. El valor de la ropa es determinado por el estilo, la durabilidad y el costo de mantenimiento. Reconocer el momento oportuno es un factor importante en la venta de ropa.

CAPÍTULO

6 Puntos destacados

Necesidades y preferencias de vivienda

Términos claves

impuestos sobre bienes
  inmuebles (p. 125)
condominios (p. 126)
cooperativas (p. 126)
arrendamiento (p. 126)
depreciar (p. 126)

Resumen

Existen cinco tipos diferentes de viviendas disponibles a los consumidores. Los arrendatarios deben tomar en cuenta los pros y los contras de compartir un apartamiento o una casa antes de firmar un contrato de arrendamiento.

Arrendar o comprar

Términos claves

costos de cierre (p. 129)
puntos porcentuales (p. 129)
equidad (p. 130)
depósito de garantía (p. 130)

Resumen

Al tomar una decisión sobre su vivienda, se debe considerar las ventajas y desventajas de arrendar y comprar una casa. Existen normas que determinan cuánto se debe gastar en una casa. Tanto el arrendatario como el arrendador tienen derechos y responsabilidades.

Compra y manejo de un automóvil

Resumen

La compra de un automóvil implica varios gastos. El dueño de un auto debe también hacer gastos relacionados con el manejo y el mantenimiento del mismo.

Términos claves

impuesto interno sobre el
  consumo (p. 136)
derecho de registro (p. 137)
seguro de responsabilidad
  civil (p. 139)

7 Puntos destacados

¿Para qué ahorrar?

Términos claves

ahorro (p. 146)
interés (p. 146)
cuenta de ahorro con libreta
  (p. 147)
cuenta de ahorro con estado
  de cuenta (p. 147)
cuenta de depósito en el
  mercado monetario
  (p. 148)

depósito a plazo (p. 148)
vencimiento (p. 148)
certificados de depósito
  (p. 148)

Resumen

Toda persona debe decidir el momento más oportuno para ahorrar e invertir. Los inversionistas principiantes deben comparar las cuentas de ahorro con libreta, con estado de cuenta y en el mercado monetario. Las cuentas de depósito a plazo brindan asimismo algunas ventajas.

Las inversiones: corriendo riesgos con sus ahorros

Términos claves

acciones (p. 154)
accionistas (p. 155)
dividendos (p. 155)
bonos (p. 155)
bonos exentos de impuesto
  (p. 155)
bonos de ahorro (p. 155)
bonos del Tesoro a corto
  plazo (p. 156)
pagarés del Tesoro (p. 156)
bonos del Tesoro a largo
  plazo (p. 156)

mercado de valores no
  oficial (p. 157)
ganancias de capital
  (plusvalía) (p. 157)
corredor (p. 157)
pérdidas de capital
  (minusvalía) (p. 158)
fondos mutuos (p. 158)
fondo de inversión a corto
  plazo en el mercado
  de dinero (p. 158)
información interior de una
  empresa (p. 159)

Resumen

Las acciones y los bonos ofrecen al inversionista opciones con ventajas distintas. Algunos fondos de inversión disponibles en los mercados de acciones y bonos implican menos riesgos que las acciones y los bonos individuales. Los consejos especulativos no ayudan a los inversionistas a hacerse ricos de la noche a la mañana en el mercado de valores.

Planes especiales de ahorro y objetivos

Términos claves

planes de pensiones (p. 161)
Plan Keogh (p. 161)
Cuenta de Retiro Individual
  o IRA (p. 162)
diversificación (p. 164)

Resumen

Los planes de pensiones patrocinados por individuos o empresas ayudan a las personas a ahorrar para el momento de su jubilación. Los intereses y el riesgo deben tomarse en cuenta antes de decidir la cantidad que se debe ahorrar e invertir.

8 Puntos destacados

Resumen
En una economía de mercado, el principio de intercambio voluntario ayuda a determinar el precio que los consumidores están dispuestos a pagar por un producto o servicio determinado. La ley de la demanda, según es afectada por la utilidad marginal decreciente, el efecto de ingreso real y el efecto de sustitución, explica cómo reaccionan los consumidores ante las variaciones de precios.

Resumen
Los economistas con frecuencia dibujan la curva de demanda para entender mejor la dinámica de los precios. La elasticidad de precios de la demanda influye en las variaciones del precio de un producto. Además de esta elasticidad, otros factores determinan la demanda en una economía de mercado.

Resumen
En el sistema de mercado libre, el incentivo de obtener mayores ganancias afecta la cantidad de productos que los fabricantes están dispuestos y en capacidad de ofrecer. Igual que la curva de demanda, la curva de oferta muestra la relación entre el nivel de la oferta y los precios.

Resumen
Cuatro factores determinan la oferta en una economía de mercado. Un cambio en la oferta puede, con frecuencia, producir cambios significativos en los precios. Tanto la falta como el superávit afectan el precio en una economía de mercado. Algunas veces este cambio adopta la forma de un cambio en el precio de equilibrio. Aunque la oferta y la demanda influyen conjuntamente en los precios, las fuerzas que se ocultan detrás de la oferta y la demanda pueden asimismo alterar el precio de un producto o servicio.

9 Puntos destacados

Resumen
Poner en marcha un negocio requiere dos etapas. Una vez que las etapas esten completadas, los empresarios deben considerar detenidamente los cuatro elementos claves de todo negocio.

Resumen
La forma de organización empresarial más común en los Estados Unidos es la de propietario único, que tiene sus ventajas y desventajas. Las sociedades de dos o más personas tienen también sus ventajas y desventajas. Las sociedades de personas con responsabilidad limitada tienen que seguir directrices específicas.

Resumen
Muchas personas comparten la propiedad de las corporaciones, lo que tiene ventajas y desventajas diferentes de las de otras formas de organización empresarial. Las franquicias, por medio de las cuales el franquiciador vende a otro negocio el derecho de usar su nombre y vender sus productos, son comunes en algunas industrias.

10 Puntos destacados

Competencia perfecta

Término clave

competencia perfecta
(p. 232)

Resumen

La competencia perfecta tiene cuatro condiciones que conducen a que las empresas no tengan control de los precios. En los Estados Unidos la agricultura es la rama que se acerca más a cumplir con estas condiciones. Aunque ideal de sí, la competencia perfecta casi no existe en el mundo real.

Monopolio, oligopolio y la competencia monopolista

Términos claves

competencia imperfecta
(p. 237)
monopolio puro (p. 237)
barreras para entrar en un
mercado (p. 238)
monopolios naturales
(p. 239)
monopolios geográficos
(p. 239)
monopolio tecnológico
(p. 239)

patente (p. 239)
monopolios estatales (p. 239)
cartele (p. 239)
oligopolio (p. 240)
diferenciación de productos
(p. 240)
competencia monopolista
(p. 240)

Resumen

Tres condiciones conducen a que un negocio llegue a tener control casi total de los precios en el mercado (monopolio puro). Las cuatro condiciones que producen un oligopolio dan a los vendedores control limitado sobre los precios. La competencia monopolista es el tipo de estructura de mercado más común en los Estados Unidos.

Políticas gubernamentales de haia la competencia

Términos claves

leyes antimonopolistas
(p. 244)
consejo de administración
coincidente (p. 244)
fusión (p. 245)
fusión horizontal (p. 245)

fusión vertical (p. 245)
conglomerados (p. 245)
fusión de conglomerados
(p. 245)
desregulación (p. 246)
nueva regulación (p. 246)

Resumen

Las leyes federales prohíben los consejos de administración coincidentes, pero permiten las fusiones de empresas siempre que no signifiquen la formación de un monopolio. Para promover la competencia y proteger a los consumidores el gobierno ha creado muchas agencias federales regulativas. Muchos de los reglamentos emitidos por estas agencias han sido eliminados, pero algunas personas están a favor de una nueva regulación.

CAPITULO
11 *Puntos destacados*

Resumen

Las personas y las empresas invierten sus ahorros en muchos lugares incluyendo diferentes bancos, fondos mutuos y planes de pensiones. Financiando sus inversiones, las personas esperan ganar interés. Las empresas recurren a estas inversiones para financiar la expansión. Este financiamiento de la expansión es una forma de determinar la asignación de recursos en un sistema de mercado libre.

Resumen

Cuando las empresas toman dinero prestado, el plazo para pagar la deuda es un factor importante que debe ser tomado en cuenta. Las empresas que toman dinero prestado consideran la tasa de interés, las condiciones del mercado y su capacidad para hacer frente a la carga de la deuda. Algunas veces las empresas consiguen capital financiero vendiendo acciones o bonos.

Resumen

El proceso de producción implica diseño del producto, planificación, compra, control de calidad y control de existencias. La tecnología ha aumentado la productividad. La mecanización, la cadena de montaje, la división del trabajo, la automatización y la robótica se han combinado para hacer más eficiente la producción.

12 Puntos destacados

El papel cambiante de la mercadotecnia ("marketing")

Términos claves

mercadotecnia (p. 282)
utilidad (p. 282)
utilidad por la forma (p. 284)
utilidad de tiempo (p. 284)
utilidad de emplazamiento (p. 284)
utilidad de la posesión (p. 284)

investigación de mercado (p. 284)
informe de mercado (p. 284)
comercialización de prueba (p. 285)

Resumen

El desarrollo de la mercadotecnia en los Estados Unidos ha tenido cuatro etapas, que han conducido a la soberanía del consumidor. Mediante una serie de preguntas elaboradas de antemano, los estudios de mercados tratan de descubrir la calidad, las características y los estilos que los consumidores desean en un producto, el tipo de embalaje que atraerá a los consumidores y el precio que los moverá a comprar.

Los componentes básicos de la mercadotecnia

Términos claves

liderazgo en la fijación de precios (p. 289)
fijación de precios de penetración (p. 290)
publicidad (p. 290)

publicidad directa por correo (p. 291)
ciclo de vida del producto (p. 291)

Resumen

Los cuatro componentes básicos de mercadotecnia son el producto, el precio, el lugar y la publicidad. Al fijar el precio de un producto, una empresa debe tomar en cuenta los costes de producción, publicidad, venta y distribución, así como las utilidades que desea obtener y el precio que los competidores están cobrando por el mismo producto. El precio es usado también en las estrategias de mercadotecnia. El lugar donde se vende el producto y el tipo de publicidad usada ayudan a determinar el éxito de ese producto.

Canales de distribución

Términos claves

canales de distribución (p. 293)
mayoristas (p. 293)
vendedores al por menor (p. 294)

Resumen

Los mayoristas compran grandes cantidades de productos de los fabricantes para venderlos a otros negocios. Los vendedores al por menor venden bienes de consumo directamente al público. Como parte del proceso de distribución, las mercancías pueden ser almacenadas por el fabricante, el mayorista o el vendedores al por menor para su futura venta. Los aumentos más significativos en la distribución de productos se han logrado por medio de los club-almacenes ("club-warehouses") y la publicidad directa por correo.

CAPITULO

13 Puntos destacados

Sección 1

La fuerza laboral en los Estados Unidos

Términos claves

fuerza laboral civil (p. 306)
obreros (p. 306)
profesionales (p. 307)
empleados de oficina (p. 307)
trabajadores en el área de
   servicios (p. 307)

obreros no cualificados
   (p. 307)
obreros semicualificados
   (p. 307)
obreros cualificados (p. 307)
ley del salario mínimo
   (p. 309)

Resumen

Los trabajadores pueden ser clasificados por categorías según el tipo de trabajo. Los trabajadores también pueden ser clasificados como no cualificados, semicualificados, cualificados y profesionales. En el mercado de trabajo, la oferta viene de los trabajadores que ofrecen sus servicios y la demanda de los empleadores que necesitan trabajadores. Tres factores determinan cómo la oferta y la demanda afectan los salarios: la capacidad, el tipo de trabajo y el lugar.

Sección 2

Trabajo organizado

Términos claves

sindicato (p. 311)
huelga (p. 312)
gremio (p. 312)
sindicato industrial
   (p. 312)
sindicato local (p. 313)
empresa con sindicación
   obligatoria ("closed shop")
   (p. 313)

empresa con sindicación
   eventual obligatoria
   ("union shop") (p. 313)
empresa con cotización
   sindical obligatoria
   ("agency shop") (p. 313)
ley sobre libertad laboral
   (p. 313)

Resumen

En el siglo XIX, los sindicatos atraían a los trabajadores porque parecían ofrecer un medio para obligar a los empleadores a mejorar las condiciones de trabajo. No obstante, el sindicalismo encontró mucha resistencia durante la mayor parte del siglo XIX y principios del XX. Los sindicatos lograron en el siglo XX establecer empresas donde los trabajadores tienen que estar sindicados, sindicarse transcurrido cierto tiempo o cotizar al sindicato.

Sección 3

Convenio colectivo

Términos claves

convenio colectivo (p. 318)
mediación (p. 318)
ajuste por coste de vida
   (p. 319)
arbitraje (p. 319)

piquetes laborales (p. 320)
boicot (p. 320)
cierre patronal ("lockout")
   (p. 320)
interdicción laboral (p. 320)

Resumen

Los asuntos más importantes tratados usualmente en las negociaciones colectivas de trabajo son los salarios, las horas de trabajo, los beneficios complementarios, las condiciones de trabajo, la seguridad en el trabajo y los procedimientos de presentación de agravios. Cuando se rompen las negociaciones colectivas, el arbitraje o la mediación, puede surgir una huelga en la que piquetes de huelguistas pueden hacer guardia alrededor de las instalaciones de la empresa y organizar un boicot exhortando al público a no comprar los productos o servicios fabricados por dicha empresa. La administración puede responder declarando un cierre patronal u obteniendo una interdicción judicial contra los trabajadores.

14 Puntos destacados

Sección 1

Contabilidad del ingreso nacional

Términos claves
contabilidad del ingreso nacional (p. 332)
producto interior bruto (PIB) (p. 332)
exportaciones netas (p. 334)

depreciación (p. 334)
producto interior neto (PIN) (p. 335)
ingreso nacional (p. 335)
ingreso personal (p. 336)
pagos de transferencia (p. 336)
ingreso personal disponible (p. 336)

Resumen
El producto interior bruto (PIB) es el valor total en dólares de todos los bienes finales de consumo, de producción y estatales, las exportaciones netas y los servicios producidos en la nación durante un año. El ingreso personal se encuentra restando del ingreso nacional los impuestos sobre la renta de las corporaciones, las utilidades y las contribuciones de los empleadores al Seguro Social.

Sección 2

Corrigiendo las estadísticas para la inflación

Términos claves
inflación (p. 338)
poder adquisitivo (p. 338)
deflación (p. 339)
índice de precios de consumo (IPC) (p. 339)

año base (p. 340)
índice de precios al productor (IPP) (p. 340)
deflactor (corrector) de precios del PIB implícito (p. 341)
PIB real (p. 341)

Resumen
Cuando hay inflación, el dinero pierde su poder adquisitivo. Las tres formas de medir los cambios en los precios promedios son el índice de precios al consumidor (IPC), el índice de precios al productor (IPP) y el deflactor de precios del PIB implícito.

Sección 3

Suma total de la oferta y la demanda

Términos claves
suma total (p. 342)
demanda global (p. 342)

curva de demanda global (p. 343)
oferta total (p. 345)
curva de oferta total (p. 345)

Resumen
La suma total de la oferta y la demanda de bienes y servicios representa el total de la economía. La intersección de las curvas de demanda global y de oferta total determina el nivel de precios de equilibrio y el PIB real (producción nacional).

Sección 4

Fluctuaciones económicas

Términos claves
fluctuaciones económicas (p. 347)
ciclos económicos (p. 347)

punto máximo (p. 347)
apogeo ("boom") (p. 347)
contracción (p. 347)
recesión (p. 348)
depresión (p. 348)
punto mínimo (p. 348)
expansión (p. 348)
recuperación (p. 348)

Resumen
Las fluctuaciones económicas se miden de un período de prosperidad a otro. Un "ciclo" típico comienza con el punto máximo (auge); luego la economía comienza a contraerse, período durante el cual puede darse una recesión (punto mínimo) seguida de una recuperación.

Sección 5

Causas e indicadores de las fluctuaciones económicas

Términos claves
innovaciones (p. 352)
indicadores económicos (p. 355)

indicadores anticipados (p. 355)
indicadores coincidentes (p. 355)
indicadores de retardo (p. 355)

Resumen
La economía estudia muchas posibles causas de los ciclos económicos. Los economistas usan indicadores anticipados, coincidentes y de retardo para medir la actividad de algunas variables en la economía.

15 Puntos destacados

Resumen

Se considera dinero todo lo que es usado como medio de cambio, unidad de contabilidad y reserva de valor. Actualmente, todo el dinero de los Estados Unidos es papel moneda. Es portátil, divisible, de valor estable y aceptado. No obstante, el papel moneda no es muy duradero.

Resumen

La historia del dinero y la banca del país ha sido un proceso de ordenamiento gradual de un sistema desordenado. El Congreso dio el primer paso en esta dirección en 1792 cuando estableció el dólar como la unidad básica de cambio y estableció la primera casa de la moneda. Los servicios bancarios modernos incluyen muchos servicios además de las cuentas de cheques y ahorro.

Resumen

Actualmente la oferta monetaria de los Estados Unidos se compone de dinero en circulación, depósitos verificables y cuasidinero. La definición M1 de la oferta monetaria incluye el dinero en circulación, los cheques viajeros y los depósitos verificables en los bancos comerciales y las instituciones de ahorro. La definición de dinero M2 incluye la definición M1 más algunos activos fácilmente convertibles en dinero (cuasidinero).

---

16 *Puntos destacados*

La oferta monetaria y la economía

Términos claves

El "Fed" (p. 388)
política monetaria (p. 388)
política de dinero disponible
(p. 389)
política de dinero escaso
(p. 389)
reserva parcial bancaria
(p. 389)
reserva obligatoria (p. 389)

Resumen

Una política de dinero disponible significa que el crecimiento de la oferta monetaria ha aumentado y hay dinero en abundancia y es barato de tomar prestado. Con una política de dinero escaso ocurre lo contrario. Con el sistema de reserva parcial bancaria, sólo una fracción de los depósitos en un banco se mantiene disponible. El resto es dado en préstamo o invertido. Debido al sistema de reserva parcial bancaria, cualquier cambio en el dinero nuevo en circulación producirá un cambio múltiple en la oferta monetaria.

Organización y funciones del Sistema de la Reserva Federal

Términos claves

Comisión Federal de
Mercado Abierto (FOMC)
(p. 394)
compensación de cheques
bancarios (p. 396)

Resumen

La Junta Directiva del Sistema de la Reserva Federal dirige las operaciones del Sistema de la Reserva Federal y establece políticas con respecto a asuntos como la reserva obligatoria y las tasas de descuento. El Sistema de la Reserva Federal ejerce muchas funciones además de compensar cheques para los bancos y reglamentar la oferta monetaria.

Regulación de la oferta monetaria

Términos claves

tasa de descuento (p. 401)
tasa mínima de interés
(p. 401)
operaciones de mercado
abierto (p. 402)

Resumen

Para regular la oferta monetaria, el Fed emplea cambios en la reserva obligatoria, la tasa de descuento y las operaciones de mercado abierto. Algunas veces resulta difícil diseñar políticas monetarias porque el gobierno no tiene siempre información correcta sobre las definiciones M1 y M2. Además, el Fed no es la única fuerza que afecta la economía.

CAPITULO

17 *Puntos destacados*

---

18 Puntos destacados

Sección 1

Desempleo e inflación

Términos claves

políticas de estabilización (p. 438)
índice de desempleo (p. 438)
pleno empleo (p. 439)
economía sumergida (p. 439)
inflación de demanda (p. 440)
inflación con estancamiento (p. 441)
inflación de costes (p. 441)

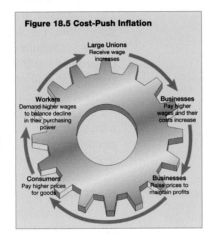

Figure 18.5 Cost-Push Inflation

Large Unions
Receive wage increases

Businesses
Pay higher wages and their costs increase

Businesses
Raise prices to maintain profits

Consumers
Pay higher prices for goods

Workers
Demand higher wages to balance decline in their purchasing power

Resumen

Medir el desempleo es difícil porque los economistas no están de acuerdo sobre el nivel de pleno empleo. Las investigaciones sobre desempleo son inexactas debido a la economía sumergida. La inflación de demanda ocurre generalmente en tiempos de pleno empleo. La inflación de costes ocurre con frecuencia cuando los índices de inflación y desempleo son altos.

Sección 2

Política fiscal y estabilización

Términos claves

política fiscal (p. 443)
flujo circular de ingresos (p. 443)

Resumen

Los economistas usan un modelo para explicar el flujo circular de ingresos. Los economistas keynesianos creen que la política fiscal (los impuestos y los gastos del gobierno) debe ser usada para regular el nivel global de la actividad económica. Quieren que el gobierno use la política fiscal para reducir la inflación.

Sección 3

El monetarismo y la economía

Términos claves

monetarismo (p. 448)
los monetaristas (p. 448)
principio monetario (p. 449)
desface cronológico (p. 450)

Resumen

Los monetaristas creen que el Sistema de la Reserva Federal cometió errores que profundizaron la Gran Depresión. Sus teorías influyeron en las políticas gubernamentales a partir de la década de los 1980. Los monetaristas cuestionan la capacidad de la política fiscal para resolver los problemas de la inflación y el desempleo.

19 Puntos destacados

Resumen

Las naciones se benefician del comercio mundial porque los factores de producción disponibles en cada nación son diferentes. La ventaja absoluta es la capacidad de un país de producir más cantidad de un producto determinado que otra nación, usando la misma cantidad de recursos. Si un país tiene al menos una ventaja comparativa con respecto a un producto, es ventajoso para ese país especializarse en la producción de dicho producto. Puede entonces establecer relaciones de intercambio con otros países para obtener los productos que desea.

Resumen

Con un tipo de cambio fijo, el gobierno nacional fija el valor de su moneda con relación a un solo patrón. Con un tipo de cambio flexible, las fuerzas de la oferta y la demanda de bienes determinan los precios de las monedas. Cuando el valor de nuestras exportaciones excede el valor de nuestras importaciones, tenemos un superávit en nuestra balanza comercial.

Resumen

Las restricciones legales al comercio mundial tratan de proteger a las industrias y a los trabajadores del país. Los pros y los contras de las restricciones al comercio son con frecuencia objeto de intensos debates. La mayor parte del comercio mundial se rige por el GATT y varios tratados comerciales regionales.

20 Puntos destacados

Comparación entre el capitalismo y el socialismo

Términos claves

Las tres "P" (p. 482)
derechos de propiedad privada (p. 482)
sistema de precios (p. 482)
comunismo (p. 484)
el proletariado (p. 484)
socialismo democrático (p. 484)
socialismo autoritario (p. 484)

Resumen

El capitalismo de mercado puro puede ser descrito en base a las llamadas tres "P": precios ("prices"), utilidades ("profits") y propiedad privada ("private property"). Los derechos de propiedad privada existen y son legales; se permite a los precios alcanzar sus propios niveles de acuerdo con la oferta y la demanda; los recursos son dirigidos a las áreas que producen mayores utilidades. En el socialismo puro, el estado fija la mayoría de los precios, el estado es dueño de los principales factores de producción, las decisiones económicas son tomadas por el estado por medio de sus agencias de planificación centralizada y el movimiento de los recursos está estrictamente controlado. La planificación en el capitalismo está descentralizada. El capitalismo ofrece libertad personal y premia la iniciativa individual.

Cambios en el socialismo autoritario: el caso de China

Términos claves

planes quinquenales (p. 487)
zonas económicas especiales (p. 488)

Resumen

Después de la Segunda Guerra mundial, los chinos establecieron una serie de planes quinquenales, ninguno de los cuales dio los resultados esperados. A partir de 1979, se designaron zonas económicas especiales. El índice de crecimiento en estas zonas económicas especiales ha sido muy alto.

Las naciones se dirigen al sistema de mercado

Términos claves

privatización (p. 492)
mercado secundario (p. 493)
estado de bienestar (p. 494)

Resumen

La tendencia en Rusia, en las otras repúblicas de la antigua Unión Soviética y en la Europa oriental es hacia una privatización cada vez mayor. Suecia, que ha sido un estado de bienestar durante muchos años, ha avanzado recientemente hacia la privatización y a una menor participación del estado en la satisfacción de las necesidades básicas del individuo. Empezando con los cambios en México a mediados de la década de los 1980, un número cada vez mayor de países en América Latina están privatizando las compañías pertenecientes al estado.

Características de las naciones en vías de desarrollo

Términos claves

naciones desarrolladas (p. 504)

naciones en vías de desarrollo (p. 504)

agricultura de subsistencia (p. 505)

mortalidad infantil (p. 506)

Resumen

Tres de cada cuatro personas en el mundo viven en naciones en vías de desarrollo. Cuando los economistas miden el desarrollo de una nación consideran varios factores. Varias naciones asiáticas han demostrado un crecimiento rápido y estable en años recientes.

El proceso de desarrollo económico

Términos claves

ayuda exterior (p. 512)

asistencia económica (p. 513)

asistencia técnica (p. 513)

asistencia militar (p. 513)

Resumen

El desarrollo económico de una nación puede ser financiado por medio de una combinación de ahorros domésticos e inversiones y ayuda exterior. La ayuda exterior se compone de asistencia económica, técnica y militar. Muchas naciones industriales brindan ayuda exterior por razones humanitarias, económicas y políticas y de seguridad nacional.

Obstáculos al crecimiento en las naciones en vías de desarrollo

Términos claves

burocracias (p. 517)

nacionalización (p. 519)

Resumen

Las naciones en vías de desarrollo tienen que hacer frente a varios obstáculos que dificultan su crecimiento. La falta de desarrollo económico de Indonesia nos enseña que el solo hecho de proporcionar dinero a una nación en desarrollo no garantiza el crecimiento económico. La ayuda exterior debe ser usada con sabidurían, junto con los ahorros domésticos, la inversión extranjera y políticas gubernamentales que aseguren la estabilidad económica.

La industrialización y el futuro

Términos claves

derechos de propiedad privada (p. 523)

ciclo vicioso de la pobreza (p. 524)

Resumen

La rápida industrialización no es necesariamente la solución para las naciones en vías de desarrollo que no tienen una ventaja comparativa en la producción de determinados bienes que deciden fabricar. Mientras más seguridad existe con respecto a los derechos de propiedad privada, mayor será la inversión tanto doméstica como extranjera.

CAPITULO

22 Puntos destacados

Sección 1

Causas y resultados de la integración mundial

Términos claves

integración mundial (p. 532)
telecomunicaciones (p. 532)

Resumen

Una de las razones más importantes de la mayor integración mundial ha sido las mejoras en las telecomunicaciones debidas a las reducciones considerables de los costos de los "chips" (plaquetas) de computadoras. En la actualidad, mucho instrumentos financieros se venden en los mercados internacionales. Los acontecimientos en un mercado nacional repercuten en otros mercados por todo el mundo.

Sección 2

¿Debe preocuparnos la inversión extranjera directa?

Términos clave

inversión extranjera directa (p. 537)

Resumen

Los extranjeros han invertido siempre en los Estados Unidos y lo siguen haciendo actualmente. Pero la inversión extranjera directa es una parte relativamente pequeña de nuestra economía considerada en su totalidad. No obstante, el objetivo último de la inversión extranjera directa por parte de naciones como el Japón es aumentar al máximo las utilidades.

Sección 3

Las empresas transnacionales y la competencia económica

Términos claves

empresas transnacionales (p. 543)
lealtades (p. 543)
filiales extranjeras (p. 543)
alianzas (p. 545)
tolerancia (p. 547)

Resumen

La inversión fuera de las fronteras nacionales corre a cargo de 35.000 empresas transnacionales por todo el mundo. La mayoría de las transnacionales invierten en regiones que están cerca de casa. Por ejemplo, las compañías de los Estados Unidos invierten principalmente en los Estados Unidos, Canadá, México y América del Sur. Las corporaciones pueden formar alianzas con antiguos competidores por muchas razones. La competencia internacional por los fondos de inversión extranjera significa que cuando las complicaciones de las burocracias estatales y los altos impuestos se vuelven un problema en un determinado país, los extranjeros invierten en otros países con un clima más favorable para la inversión.

TEXT DESIGN: Martucci Studio

COVER DESIGN: Martucci Studio, PHOTOS (l) Suzanne and Nick Geary/Tony Stone/Worldwide (r) Martucci Studio.

ILLUSTRATION: Martucci Studio/Jerry D. Malone

PHOTO RESEARCH: Susan Van Etten

PHOTO CREDITS: i, (l) Susan and Nick Geary/Tony Stone, Worldwide, (r) Martucci Studio. iv, (b) Pictor/Uniphoto v, ©Martucci Studio vi, ©Martucci Studio (bl) Courtesy, Ramsey & Muspratt Collections vii, (t) Courtesy, Charles B. Wang/Computer Associates (m) The Granger Collection (b) ©Martucci Studio viii, (tl&br) The Granger Collection (tr&bl) ©Martucci Studio ix, (tr) ©Martucci Studio (m) Vince Streano/Tony Stone Images/Chicago Inc. (br) David Austen/Stock Boston (bm) Barrie Rokeach/The Image Bank (bl) ©Susan Van Etten x, (t) David Hiser/Tony Stone Images/Chicago Inc. (m) © Martucci Studio (b) Uniphoto xi, (tl) ©Martucci Studio (l) ©Moore & Associates (m) Wide World (b) ©Martucci Studio 4–5, Jake Rais/The Image Bank 6–7, ©Martucci Studio 8, ©Martucci Studio 9, (t) Arnold J. Kaplan/The Picture Cube (b) Wide World 10, Gary Cralle/The Image Bank 11, (l) Guido Alberto Rossi/The Image Bank (r) Don Carroll/The Image Bank 13, (1) Duggal/The Image Bank (r) Arthur Tilley/FPG 14, D.D. Morrison/The Picture Cube 14–15, Chris Hackett/The Image Bank 16, ©Paul Conklin 17, Courtesy, New School for Social Research 18, Jeff Greenburg/The Picture Cube 19, ©Martucci Studio 20, Jay Freis/The Image Bank 20–21, ©Martucci Studio 22, Courtesy, Hyde Athletic Industries, Inc. 23, (t) Gary Cralle/The Image Bank (ml) D.D. Morrison/The Picture Cube (mr) Chris Hackett/The Image Bank (b) Jay Freis/The Image Bank 24, ©Martucci Studio 26, Bob Daemmrich/Stock Boston 26–27, Jim Karageorge 27, Bob Daemmrich/Stock Boston 28–29, Tom McCarthy/The Picture Cube 31, (tr) Alvis Upitis/The Image Bank (l) Pete Turner/The Image Bank 30–31, Pictor/Uniphoto 32, Irven DeVore/Anthrophoto 33, ©Susan Van Etten 34, ©Martucci Studio 35, (t) Pamela Zully/The Image Bank (b) Owen Franken/Stock Boston 37, ©Martucci Studio 38, (l) Bob Daemmrich/Stock Boston (r) Tony Freeman/Photo Edit 39, (r) ©Susan Van Etten (b) ©Paul Conklin 41, The Granger Collection 42–43, ©Martucci Studio 45, (tr) Larry Lawfer/The Picture Cube (tl) Richard Ustinich/The Image Bank (mr) Fotographia, Inc. Stock Boston (br) Eddie Hironaka/The Image Bank 44–45, Bob Daemmrich/Stock Boston 46, (t) ©Susan Van Etten (m) ©Susan Van Etten (b) Steve Dunwell/The Image Bank 48, (l) ©Martucci Studio (t&m) Courtesy, Southwest Airlines/Pam Francis 49, (t) ©Martucci Studio (b) Richard Ustinich/The Image Bank 50, Tom McCarthy/The Picture Cube 54–55, ©Mark Thayer 56–57, Mike Kagan/Monkmeyer Press Photos 59, ©Susan Van Etten 60, 61, ©Martucci Studio 62, Courtesy, Leadership Memphis 63, ©Susan Van Etten 64, ©Martucci Studio 65, ©Susan Van Etten 66, 68, ©Martucci Studio 69, (r) Michael Newman/Photo Edit (l) ©Martucci Studio 70–71, 72, ©Martucci Studio 73, (t) ©Susan Van Etten (b) ©Martucci Studio 74, Mike Kagan/Monkmeyer Press Photos 76, Steve Dunwell/The Image Bank 76–77, Ross H. Horowitz/Stockphotos 77, ©Susan Van Etten 78–79, ©Martucci Studios 81, Gerard Champlong/The Image Bank 82, (l) ©Susan Van Etten (r) ©Martucci Studio 83, ©Martucci Studio 84, Courtesy, Ronal Homer/Boston Bank of Commerce 86, (l) Rob

Crandall/Stock Boston (b) Karl Gehring/Gamma-Liaison 87, (l) David Young-Wolff/Photo Edit (tr) ©Susan Van Etten 88, ©Benson, Arizona Republic, 8/89, Reprinted by permission of Tribune Media Services. 89, Jeff Smith/The Image Bank 90–91, 92, ©Martucci Studio 94, Tony Freeman/Photo Edit 94–95, ©Susan Van Etten 95, Costa Manos/Magnum 96, David Young-Wolff/Photo Edit 98, Robert V. Eckert, Jr./Stock Boston 99, Vera Kelly/FPG 101, ©Martucci Studio 102, (l) ©Susan Van Etten (c) Jane Art/The Image Bank (b) ©Susan Van Etten 103, Jeff Smith/The Image Bank 104–105, ©Martucci Studio 106–107, Gary Gladstone/The Image Bank 108–109, ©Martucci Studio 108–109, Stephen McBrady/Photo Edit 109, (m) Mark Richards/Photo Edit (r) ©Susan Van Etten 110–111, ©Martucci Studio 112, The Bettmann Archive 114, (l) Kevin Forest/The Image Bank (c) Nancy Brown/The Image Bank (r) Mel DiGiacomo/The Image Bank 115, (l) David Browell/The Image Bank (c) Nancy Brown/The Image Bank (r) Eric Wheater/The Image Bank 116, (t) ©Susan Van Etten (b) ©Martucci Studio 118, (t) Williamson/Edwards Concept/The Image Bank (b) ©Martucci Studio 119, (t) ©Stephen McBrady/Photo Edit (br) Mark Richards/Photo Edit 120, Gary Gladstone/The Image Bank 121, Nancy Brown/The Image Bank 112–123, ©Susan Van Etten 125, (t) Frank Siteman/Monkmeyer Press Photos (b) Marc Romanelli/The Image Bank 126, (t) ©Susan Van Etten (b) Tony Freeman/Photo Edit 127, (r) Amy Etra/Photo Edit (l) ©Susan Van Etten 128, The Bettmann Archive 130–133, ©Martucci Studio 135, Stephen Frisch/Stock Boston 136, ©Martucci Studio 137, Lisa J. Goodman/The Image Bank 138, ©Susan Van Etten 139, ©Martucci Studio 140, (t) Reggie Parker/FPG (b) Elizabeth Zuckerman/Photo Edit 141, (t) ©Martucci Studio (m) Frank Siteman/Monkmeyer Press Photos (b) Stephen Frisch/Stock Boston 142, ©Susan Van Etten 144–145, George Ombremski/The Image Bank 146–147, 148, ©Martucci Studio 148, (b) Murray Alcosser/The Image Bank 151, Wide World 152–153, 154, 155, 156, ©Martucci Studio 157, David Jeffery/The Image Bank 160, ©Susan Van Etten 161, Larry Pierce/The Image Bank 164, ©Martucci Studio 166, (t) Steve Niedorf/The Image Bank (bl) ©Susan Van Etten (r) Brett Fromer/The Image Bank 167, (t) ©Susan Van Etten (l) ©Martucci Studio 169, George Ombremski/The Image Bank 172–173, Jook Leung/FPG 174–175, ©Martucci Studio 176, Michael Newman/Photo Edit 177, Bob Daemmrich/Stock Boston 178, 180–181, 184–185, 186, 188, ©Martucci Studio 190, The Granger Collection 191, ©Martucci Studio 192, Steve Allen/The Image Bank 193, 196, ©Martucci Studio 198–199, Bill Varie/The Image Bank 200, Dorothy Littell/Stock Boston 201, ©Martucci Studio 202, Courtesy, Goody's Department Store 203, (t) Michael Newman/Photo Edit (b) Bill Varie/The Image Bank 204, ©Martucci Studio 206–207, Don Swetzer/Tony Stone Images/Chicago, Inc. 209, Peter M. Miller/The Image Bank 211, Lawrence Migdale/Stock Boston 212, Wide World 213, ©Susan Van Etten 214, 215, 216, ©Martucci Studio 217, Lawrence Migdale/Stock Boston 220, ©Martucci Studio 223, David Young-Wolff/Photo Edit 224, ©Joe Moore & Associates 225, (t) Lawrence Migdale/Stock Boston (b) David Young-Wolff/Photo Edit 226, Don Swetzer/Tony Stone Images/Chicago, Inc. 228, Benn Mitchell/The Image Bank 228–229, Pete Turner/The Image Bank 229,

Spencer Grant/Stock Boston 230–231, George Goodwin/Monkmeyer Press Photos 232–233, ©Susan Van Etten 234, Grafton Smith/The Image Bank 235, (l) Steve Proehl/The Image Bank (r) James Carmichael/The Image Bank 237, ©Susan Van Etten 239, (tr) ©Martucci Studio (lr) Tennessee Valley Authority (tl&bl) ©Susan Van Etten 240, ©Susan Van Etten 242, ©Martucci Studio 243, Courtesy, Ramsey & Muspratt Collection 244, The Granger Collection 246, Michael R. Schneps/The Image Bank 248, (l) Terje Rakke/The Image Bank (r) Romilly Lockyer/The Image Bank 249, Grafton Smith/The Image Bank 250, George Goodwin/Monkmeyer Press Photos 254–255, FPG 256–257, Stacy Pick/Stock Boston 260, David Young-Wolff/Photo Edit 261, ©Susan Van Etten 262, Gabriel Covian/The Image Bank 263, David Hamilton/The Image Bank 265, 266, 267, ©Martucci Studio 269, Greg Pease/Tony Stone Images/Chicago, Inc. 270, Courtesy, Dabney & Resnick 271, Erik Leigh Simmons/The Image Bank 272, (l) Les Wollam (r) Jaime Villaseca/The Image Bank 273, Schneps/The Image Bank 274, (t) Michael Melford/The Image Bank (b) The Bettmann Archive 275, (bl) The Bettmann Archive (tl) Ellis Herwig/The Picture Cube (tr) Steve Dunwell/The Image Bank 276, (bl) ©Susan Van Etten (t) Keith Philpott/The Image Bank (bl) Courtesy, Howard Wright 277, Greg Pease/Tony Stone Images/Chicago, Inc. 278, Stacy Pick/Stock Boston 279, Michael Melford/The Image Bank 280–281, ©Martucci Studio 283, (l) The Granger Collection (r) U. of Louisville Photo Archives, Caufield & Shook Collection/Susan Van Etten Historical Files (ll&lr) The Granger Collection 284, (l) Steve Dunwell/The Image Bank (r) Lincoln Russell/Stock Boston (m) Christopher Johnson/Stock Boston (ll) ©Susan Van Etten 288–289, ©Martucci Studio 292, Courtesy, Charles B. Wang/Computer Associates 293, ©Susan Van Etten 294–295, Mark Richards/Photo Edit 295, (ll) © Martucci Studio (lr) ©Susan Van Etten 296–297, ©Martucci Studio 298, (ll) ©Martucci Studio (l) Marc Solomon/The Image Bank (r) ©Susan Van Etten 299, The Granger Collection 300, ©Martucci Studio 302, Lou Jones/The Image Bank 302–303, Lawrence Fried/The Image Bank 303, Alvis Upitis/The Image Bank 304–305, David Young-Wolff/Photo Edit 309, Larry Keenan Associates/The Image Bank 311, 312–313, The Granger Collection 314–315, ©Martucci Studio 316, (l) Bob Daemmrich/Stock Boston (r) ©Susan Van Etten 317, 318, Wide World 319, ©Martucci Studio 320, Rick Browne/Stock Boston 322, (t) ©Susan Van Etten (b) Rob Crandall/Stock Boston 323, ©Susan Van Etten 324, David Young-Wolff/Photo Edit 328–329, Hunter/Freeman Studio, San Francisco 330–331, Hans Wolf/The Image Bank 332–333, ©Susan Van Etten 335, David Brownell/The Image Bank 340, ©Martucci Studio 342–343, ©Jim Pickerell/FPG 344, Louis Padilla/The Image Bank 346, UPI/The Bettmann Archive 349, The Granger Collection 350, Library of Congress/Susan Van Etten Historical Files 351, Bryan F. Peterson/The Stock Market 352, (l) Alvis Upitis/Stock Boston (r) Steve Gottlieb/FPG 353, (t) Susan Van Etten Historical Files (b) Mark Richards/Photo Edit 354, ©Martucci Studio 356, (t) ©Susan Van Etten (l) Donald Dietz/Stock Boston (b) ©Martucci Studio 357, David Brownell/The Image Bank 358, Hans Wolf/The Image Bank 360–361, 362–363, ©Martucci Studio 364, Frank Siteman/Stock Boston 365–366, ©Martucci

627

Studio 367, Courtesy, Ariel Capital Management 368, The Granger Collection 370–371, ©Martucci Studio 372, R. Rathe/FPG 374, 375, ©Martucci Studio 377, (l) Andy Caulfield/The Image Bank (t) Gerald French/FPG (b) Jay Freis/The Image Bank 378, (r) ©Susan Van Etten (l) ©Martucci Studio 380, (l&r) ©Susan Van Etten (b) ©Martucci Studio 381, ©Susan Van Etten 382, R. Rathe/FPG 383, ©Martucci Studio 384, ©Susan Van Etten 384–385, John Lei/Stock Boston 385, Bernard Roussel/The Image Bank 386–387, Al Satterwhite/The Image Bank 388, ©Susan Van Etten 390, ©Martucci Studio 392, Wide World 393, ©Paul Conklin 395–396, ©Martucci Studio 397, ©Susan Van Etten 400, Richard Pasley/Stock Boston 404, (l) White House Press Office (r) L. Chryslin/The Image Bank 406, (l) Comstock (r) Murray Alcosser/The Image Bank 407, (t) Richard Pasley/Stock Boston (m) ©Paul Conklin (b) L. Chryslin/The Image Bank 408, Al Satterwhite/The Image Bank 410–411, Lawrence Migdale/Stock Boston 412–413, The Granger Collection 414, (t) Bob Daemmrich/Stock Boston (b) David Hamilton/The Image Bank 415, David Young-Wolff/Photo Edit 419, R. Schoen 420, ©Paul Conklin 423, ©McNelly/Reprinted by Permission of Tribune Media Services 424–425, ©Susan Van Etten 426, (l) David Hamilton/The Image Bank (r) Ellis Herwig/Stock Boston 428–429, ©Martucci Studio 432, (l) Bob Daemmrich/Stock Boston (r) J. Ramey/The Image Bank (b) ©Susan Van Etten 433, ©Susan Van Etten 434, Lawrence Migdale/Stock Boston 436–437, ©Susan Van Etten 438, G&V

Chapman/The Image Bank 439, ©Martucci Studio 442, Wide World 443, UPI/The Bettmann Archive 446, The Granger Collection 449, 452, ©Martucci Studio 453, G&V Chapman/The Image Bank 454, ©Susan Van Etten 458–459, Uniphoto 460–461, 463, ©Susan Van Etten 466, The Granger Collection 467, 469, ©Martucci Studio 472–473, Barrie Rokeach/The Image Bank 474, (l) Mahaux/The Image Bank (b) Bill Gillette/Stock Boston (r) ©Susan Van Etten 475, (t) ©Susan Van Etten (l) Kim Steele/The Image Bank (br) ©Martucci Studio 476, (t&m) Phil Borden/Photo Edit (b) ©Susan Van Etten 477, ©Martucci Studio 478, ©Susan Van Etten 480–481, Miguel/The Image Bank 483, (t) ©Martucci Studio (m) Gary Gladstone/The Image Bank (bm) Pat Lacroix/The Image Bank (ll) ©Susan Van Etten (lr) Hans Wolf/The Image Bank 487, ©Susan Van Etten 488, Don Klumpp/The Image Bank 491, The Granger Collection 492, Vince Streano/Tony Stone Images/Chicago, Inc. 493, Valdimir Pcholkin/FPG 494, Travelpix/FPG 495, 496, (t) ©Susan Van Etten 496, (b) ©Paul Conklin 497, Vince Streano/Tony Stone Images/Chicago, Inc. 498, Miguel/The Image Bank 500, Steve Dunwell/The Image Bank 502–503, ©Paul Conklin 504, Eastcott/Momatuk/Woodfin Camp & Associates 505, (l) David Hiser/Tony Stone Images/Chicago, Inc. (r) David R. Austen/Stock Boston 506, ©Susan Van Etten 508–509, ©Martucci Studio 511, Xavier Richer/Tony Stone Images/Chicago, Inc. 512, Carol Lee/Tony Stone Images/Chicago, Inc. 513, ©Susan Van Etten 514, (l) Dorothy Littell/Stock Boston (r) John McDermott/Tony Stone Images/Chicago,

Inc. 515, (l) Blanche/Gamma-Liaison (r) D. H. Hassell/Stock Boston 517, (t) David M. Doody/FPG (b) FPG 519, Wide World 520, (l) Dallas & John Heaton/Stock Boston (r) David Austen/Stock Boston 521, The Granger Collection 523, (l) ©Susan Van Etten (r) Cary Wolinsky/Stock Boston 524, (t) Jay Freis/The Image Bank (b) Mahaux Photo/The Image Bank (m) Harold Sund/The Image Bank 526, (t) David Ball/The Picture Cube (b) Dave Bartruff/Stock Boston (m) Guido Rossi/The Image Bank 527, Eascott/Momatuk/Woodfin Camp & Associates 528, ©Paul Conklin 530–531, Charles Gupton/Stock Boston 533, Forest Anderson/Gamma-Liaison 535, ©Susan Van Etten 537, Library of Congress/Susan Van Etten Historical Files 538, David Frazier/Tony Stone Images/Chicago, Inc. 540, Telegraph Colour Library/FPG 541, ©Susan Van Etten 542, ©Paul Conklin 543, Thomas Craig/FPG 544, ©Martucci Studio 545, David Ball/The Picture Cube 546, P&G Bowater/The Image Bank 547, Alistair Berg/Gamma-Liaison 548, (t) Jeff Greenberg/Photo Edit (b) Andy Caulfield/The Image Bank (l) Alan Oddie/Photo Edit 549, (t) David Frazier/Tony Stone Images/Chicago, Inc. (b) Alistair Berg/Gamma-Liaison 550, Charles Gupton/Stock Boston 551, ©1993 Ohman/Oregonian 554, (t) ©Martucci Studio, (tl), (ml), (ll), The Granger Collection, (m) Frank Siteman/Stock Boston, (lr) Nancy Brown/Image Bank. 555, (tl) Kevin Forest/Image Bank, (r) ©Martucci Studio. 560, ©Donald Dietz/Stock Boston. 561–567, Martucci Studio.